HOW TO SAVE THOUSANDS OF DOLLARS ON YOUR MORTGAGE

A COMPLETE GUIDE TO ACCELERATED-PAYMENT PLANS

Michael Sherman, Ph.D.

CONTEMPORARY
BOOKS, INC.
CHICAGO ■ NEW YORK

Great care has been taken to ensure exact figures in the production of these tables, but there is no guarantee of accuracy assumed by the author or publisher of this book.

CONTENTS

INTRODUCTION

The purpose of this book is to show borrowers and lenders alike how the more rapid payment of their mortgages will result in a savings of interest paid through the mortgage term. You need no advanced mathematical skills to understand the tables. Just read the instructions and follow the directions as described in the examples.

At least one of two attributes are required for an accelerated payment mortgage plan. Either the borrower must make larger payments or he must make payments more frequently. There are four popular plans used in real estate finance to accelerate the payoff of mortgages. Each of these loan plans is described in a separate tabular section. The loan plans are: Short-Term Amortizing Mortgages, Biweekly Mortgages, Growing Equity Mortgages, and Augmented Payment Mortgages.

The traditional mortgage most commonly used in real estate finance is a 30-year, fully amortized mortgage. The mortgage payment is based upon the amount of money loaned, the simple interest rate on the mortgage, and the mortgage term. The 30-year, fully amortized mortgage requires 360 equal monthly payments to pay off the loan. Throughout the tables, the monthly payment entries for the 30-year mortgage are rounded up to the next highest cent to ensure complete amortization of the loan. We use this 30-year mortgage as the benchmark against which we compare each accelerated payment plan. All interest savings calculations are compared with the 30-year mortgage. The total-interest figures and the interest-saved figures are rounded to the nearest dollar amount.

At the beginning of each tabular section, we describe in detail the nature of each accelerated payment plan and provide an example to demonstrate how to use the table. Once you know which accelerated payment plan suits your particular needs, turn to the appropriate section and follow through the example shown. Remember that when loan amounts aren't exactly equal to the entries displayed in the left-hand column of each page, simply combine the entries shown to achieve the applicable loan amount. To obtain a high degree of accuracy, combine as few entries as possible when you solve a problem.

1

SHORT-TERM AMORTIZING MORTGAGES

If you shorten the term of payments through which you want to pay off your loan, you must pay more each month. The most popular shorter term amortization periods are 15 years, 20 years, and 25 years. In this section we compare the widely used 30-year mortgage with these three shorter term plans. Each page of this section contains these four mortgage plans, identified by their amortization periods at the top of the columns.

Here is how to use this table. First find the page with the interest rate for the desired loan. Look down the first column to find your loan amount. Then read across the page and find the columns which represent the 30-year plan and the desired alternative shorter term plan. The first group of columns represents the 30-year loan plan. Within this group, you find both the monthly payment and the total interest paid through the life of the loan. Each shorter term plan's group of columns shows the monthly payment, the total interest paid, and the all-important third column, the interest saved. This third column is the difference between the interest paid on the 30-year loan and the desired shorter term loan.

EXAMPLE

How much interest will you save on a $75,750 mortgage at 12.75% interest if you choose to pay off the mortgage in 15 years rather than 30 years? How much is the difference in the payments between the two plans?

First, find the 12.75% interest rate on page 27. Move down the loan amount column until you find a row entry for $75,750. Since there is no row entry for exactly this loan amount, you must combine the three row entries from $50, $700, and $75,000 to get the interest saved. The interest-saved entries for the 15-year loan are $85, $1,165, and $124,814; and their sum is $126,064.

The corresponding payment entries for the 30-year mortgage are $0.55, $7.61, and $815.02; and their sum is $823.18. The corresponding payment entries for the 15-year mortgage are $0.63, $8.75 and $936.63; and their sum is $946.01. Therefore the difference in the payments for the two mortgage plans is $946.01 less $823.18, or $122.83.

SHORT-TERM AMORTIZING MORTGAGES

AMOUNT OF LOAN	30 YEARS		25 YEARS			20 YEARS			15 YEARS		
	MONTHLY PAYMENT	TOTAL INTRST	MONTHLY PAYMENT	TOTAL INTRST	INTRST SAVED	MONTHLY PAYMENT	TOTAL INTRST	INTRST SAVED	MONTHLY PAYMENT	TOTAL INTRST	INTRST SAVED
$ 50	0.34	72	0.36	58	14	0.39	44	28	0.45	31	41
100	0.67	141	0.71	113	28	0.78	87	54	0.90	62	79
200	1.34	282	1.42	226	56	1.56	174	108	1.80	124	158
300	2.00	420	2.13	339	81	2.33	259	161	2.70	186	234
400	2.67	561	2.83	449	112	3.11	346	215	3.60	248	313
500	3.33	699	3.54	562	137	3.88	431	268	4.50	310	389
600	4.00	840	4.25	675	165	4.66	518	322	5.40	372	468
700	4.66	978	4.95	785	193	5.43	603	375	6.30	434	544
800	5.33	1,119	5.66	898	221	6.21	690	429	7.20	496	623
900	5.99	1,256	6.37	1,011	245	6.98	775	481	8.09	556	700
1,000	6.66	1,398	7.07	1,121	277	7.76	862	536	8.99	618	780
2,000	13.31	2,792	14.14	2,242	550	15.51	1,722	1,070	17.98	1,236	1,556
3,000	19.96	4,186	21.21	3,363	823	23.26	2,582	1,604	26.97	1,855	2,331
4,000	26.62	5,583	28.28	4,484	1,099	31.02	3,445	2,138	35.96	2,473	3,110
5,000	33.27	6,977	35.34	5,602	1,375	38.77	4,305	2,672	44.95	3,091	3,886
6,000	39.92	8,371	42.41	6,723	1,648	46.52	5,165	3,206	53.93	3,707	4,664
7,000	46.58	9,769	49.48	7,844	1,925	54.28	6,027	3,742	62.92	4,326	5,443
8,000	53.23	11,163	56.55	8,965	2,198	62.03	6,887	4,276	71.91	4,944	6,219
9,000	59.88	12,557	63.62	10,086	2,471	69.78	7,747	4,810	80.90	5,562	6,995
10,000	66.54	13,954	70.68	11,204	2,750	77.53	8,607	5,347	89.89	6,180	7,774
11,000	73.19	15,348	77.75	12,325	3,023	85.29	9,470	5,878	98.88	6,798	8,550
12,000	79.84	16,742	84.82	13,446	3,296	93.04	10,330	6,412	107.86	7,415	9,327
13,000	86.49	18,136	91.89	14,567	3,569	100.79	11,190	6,946	116.85	8,033	10,103
14,000	93.15	19,534	98.95	15,685	3,849	108.55	12,052	7,482	125.84	8,651	10,883
15,000	99.80	20,928	106.02	16,806	4,122	116.30	12,912	8,016	134.83	9,269	11,659
16,000	106.45	22,322	113.09	17,927	4,395	124.05	13,772	8,550	143.82	9,888	12,434
17,000	113.11	23,720	120.16	19,048	4,672	131.81	14,634	9,086	152.81	10,506	13,214
18,000	119.76	25,114	127.23	20,169	4,945	139.56	15,494	9,620	161.79	11,122	13,992
19,000	126.41	26,508	134.29	21,287	5,221	147.31	16,354	10,154	170.78	11,740	14,768
20,000	133.07	27,905	141.36	22,408	5,497	155.06	17,214	10,691	179.77	12,359	15,546
21,000	139.72	29,299	148.43	23,529	5,770	162.82	18,077	11,222	188.76	12,977	16,322
22,000	146.37	30,693	155.50	24,650	6,043	170.57	18,937	11,756	197.75	13,595	17,098
23,000	153.02	32,087	162.56	25,768	6,319	178.32	19,797	12,290	206.74	14,213	17,874
24,000	159.68	33,485	169.63	26,889	6,596	186.08	20,659	12,826	215.72	14,830	18,655
25,000	166.33	34,879	176.70	28,010	6,869	193.83	21,519	13,360	224.71	15,448	19,431
26,000	172.98	36,273	183.77	29,131	7,142	201.58	22,379	13,894	233.70	16,066	20,207
27,000	179.64	37,670	190.84	30,252	7,418	209.34	23,242	14,428	242.69	16,684	20,986
28,000	186.29	39,064	197.90	31,370	7,694	217.09	24,102	14,962	251.68	17,302	21,762
29,000	192.94	40,458	204.97	32,491	7,967	224.84	24,962	15,496	260.67	17,921	22,537
30,000	199.60	41,856	212.04	33,612	8,244	232.59	25,822	16,034	269.65	18,537	23,319
32,500	216.23	45,343	229.71	36,413	8,930	251.98	27,975	17,368	292.12	20,082	25,261
35,000	232.86	48,830	247.38	39,214	9,616	271.36	30,126	18,704	314.59	21,626	27,204
40,000	266.13	55,807	282.72	44,816	10,991	310.12	34,429	21,378	359.54	24,717	31,090
45,000	299.39	62,780	318.06	50,418	12,362	348.89	38,734	24,046	404.48	27,806	34,974
50,000	332.66	69,758	353.39	56,017	13,741	387.65	43,036	26,722	449.42	30,896	38,862
55,000	365.92	76,731	388.73	61,619	15,112	426.42	47,341	29,390	494.36	33,985	42,746
60,000	399.19	83,708	424.07	67,221	16,487	465.18	51,643	32,065	539.30	37,074	46,634
65,000	432.45	90,682	459.41	72,823	17,859	503.95	55,948	34,734	584.24	40,163	50,519
70,000	465.72	97,659	494.75	78,425	19,234	542.71	60,250	37,409	629.18	43,252	54,407
75,000	498.98	104,633	530.09	84,027	20,606	581.48	64,555	40,078	674.13	46,343	58,290
80,000	532.25	111,610	565.43	89,629	21,981	620.24	68,858	42,752	719.07	49,433	62,177
85,000	565.51	118,584	600.77	95,231	23,353	659.01	73,162	45,422	764.01	52,522	66,062
90,000	598.78	125,561	636.11	100,833	24,728	697.77	77,465	48,096	808.95	55,611	69,950
95,000	632.04	132,534	671.45	106,435	26,099	736.54	81,770	50,764	853.89	58,700	73,834
100,000	665.31	139,512	706.78	112,034	27,478	775.30	86,072	53,440	898.83	61,789	77,723
105,000	698.57	146,485	742.12	117,636	28,849	814.07	90,377	56,108	943.77	64,879	81,606
110,000	731.84	153,462	777.46	123,238	30,224	852.83	94,679	58,783	988.72	67,970	85,492
115,000	765.10	160,436	812.80	128,840	31,596	891.60	98,984	61,452	1,033.66	71,059	89,377
120,000	798.37	167,413	848.14	134,442	32,971	930.36	103,286	64,127	1,078.60	74,148	93,265
125,000	831.63	174,387	883.48	140,044	34,343	969.13	107,591	66,796	1,123.54	77,237	97,150
130,000	864.90	181,364	918.82	145,646	35,718	1,007.89	111,894	69,470	1,168.48	80,326	101,038
135,000	898.16	188,338	954.16	151,248	37,090	1,046.66	116,198	72,140	1,213.42	83,416	104,922
140,000	931.43	195,315	989.50	156,850	38,465	1,085.42	120,501	74,814	1,258.36	86,505	108,810
145,000	964.69	202,288	1,024.83	162,449	39,839	1,124.19	124,806	77,482	1,303.31	89,596	112,692
150,000	997.96	209,266	1,060.17	168,051	41,215	1,162.95	129,108	80,158	1,348.25	92,685	116,581
155,000	1,031.22	216,239	1,095.51	173,653	42,586	1,201.72	133,413	82,826	1,393.19	95,774	120,465
160,000	1,064.49	223,216	1,130.85	179,255	43,961	1,240.48	137,715	85,501	1,438.13	98,863	124,353
165,000	1,097.75	230,190	1,166.19	184,857	45,333	1,279.25	142,020	88,170	1,483.07	101,953	128,237
170,000	1,131.02	237,167	1,201.53	190,459	46,708	1,318.01	146,322	90,845	1,528.01	105,042	132,125
175,000	1,164.28	244,141	1,236.87	196,061	48,080	1,356.78	150,627	93,514	1,572.95	108,131	136,010
180,000	1,197.55	251,118	1,272.21	201,663	49,455	1,395.54	154,930	96,188	1,617.90	111,222	139,896
185,000	1,230.81	258,092	1,307.55	207,265	50,827	1,434.31	159,234	98,858	1,662.84	114,311	143,781
190,000	1,264.08	265,069	1,342.89	212,867	52,202	1,473.07	163,537	101,532	1,707.78	117,400	147,669
195,000	1,297.34	272,042	1,378.22	218,466	53,576	1,511.84	167,842	104,200	1,752.72	120,490	151,552
200,000	1,330.61	279,020	1,413.56	224,068	54,952	1,550.60	172,144	106,876	1,797.66	123,579	155,441

SHORT-TERM AMORTIZING MORTGAGES 7.25%

AMOUNT OF LOAN	30 YEARS		25 YEARS			20 YEARS			15 YEARS		
	MONTHLY PAYMENT	TOTAL INTRST	MONTHLY PAYMENT	TOTAL INTRST	INTRST SAVED	MONTHLY PAYMENT	TOTAL INTRST	INTRST SAVED	MONTHLY PAYMENT	TOTAL INTRST	INTRST SAVED
$ 50	0.35	76	0.37	61	15	0.40	46	30	0.46	33	43
100	0.69	148	0.73	119	29	0.80	92	56	0.92	66	82
200	1.37	293	1.45	235	58	1.59	182	111	1.83	129	164
300	2.05	438	2.17	351	87	2.38	271	167	2.74	193	245
400	2.73	583	2.90	470	113	3.17	361	222	3.66	259	324
500	3.42	731	3.62	586	145	3.96	450	281	4.57	323	408
600	4.10	876	4.34	702	174	4.75	540	336	5.48	386	490
700	4.78	1,021	5.06	818	203	5.54	630	391	6.40	452	569
800	5.46	1,166	5.79	937	229	6.33	719	447	7.31	516	650
900	6.14	1,310	6.51	1,053	257	7.12	809	501	8.22	580	730
1,000	6.83	1,459	7.23	1,169	290	7.91	898	561	9.13	643	816
2,000	13.65	2,914	14.46	2,338	576	15.81	1,794	1,120	18.26	1,287	1,627
3,000	20.47	4,369	21.69	3,507	862	23.72	2,693	1,676	27.39	1,930	2,439
4,000	27.29	5,824	28.92	4,676	1,148	31.62	3,589	2,235	36.52	2,574	3,250
5,000	34.11	7,280	36.15	5,845	1,435	39.52	4,485	2,795	45.65	3,217	4,063
6,000	40.94	8,738	43.37	7,011	1,727	47.43	5,383	3,355	54.78	3,860	4,878
7,000	47.76	10,194	50.60	8,180	2,014	55.33	6,279	3,915	63.91	4,504	5,690
8,000	54.58	11,649	57.83	9,349	2,300	63.24	7,178	4,471	73.03	5,145	6,504
9,000	61.40	13,104	65.06	10,518	2,586	71.14	8,074	5,030	82.16	5,789	7,315
10,000	68.22	14,559	72.29	11,687	2,872	79.04	8,970	5,589	91.29	6,432	8,127
11,000	75.04	16,014	79.51	12,853	3,161	86.95	9,868	6,146	100.42	7,076	8,938
12,000	81.87	17,473	86.74	14,022	3,451	94.85	10,764	6,709	109.55	7,719	9,754
13,000	88.69	18,928	93.97	15,191	3,737	102.75	11,660	7,268	118.68	8,362	10,566
14,000	95.51	20,384	101.20	16,360	4,024	110.66	12,558	7,826	127.81	9,006	11,378
15,000	102.33	21,839	108.43	17,529	4,310	118.56	13,454	8,385	136.93	9,647	12,192
16,000	109.15	23,294	115.65	18,695	4,599	126.47	14,353	8,941	146.06	10,291	13,003
17,000	115.97	24,749	122.88	19,864	4,885	134.37	15,249	9,500	155.19	10,934	13,815
18,000	122.80	26,208	130.11	21,033	5,175	142.27	16,145	10,063	164.32	11,578	14,630
19,000	129.62	27,663	137.34	22,202	5,461	150.18	17,043	10,620	173.45	12,221	15,442
20,000	136.44	29,118	144.57	23,371	5,747	158.08	17,939	11,179	182.58	12,864	16,254
21,000	143.26	30,574	151.79	24,537	6,037	165.98	18,835	11,739	191.71	13,508	17,066
22,000	150.08	32,029	159.02	25,706	6,323	173.89	19,734	12,295	200.83	14,149	17,880
23,000	156.91	33,488	166.25	26,875	6,613	181.79	20,630	12,858	209.96	14,793	18,695
24,000	163.73	34,943	173.48	28,044	6,899	189.70	21,528	13,415	219.09	15,436	19,507
25,000	170.55	36,398	180.71	29,213	7,185	197.60	22,424	13,974	228.22	16,080	20,318
26,000	177.37	37,853	187.93	30,379	7,474	205.50	23,320	14,533	237.35	16,723	21,130
27,000	184.19	39,308	195.16	31,548	7,760	213.41	24,218	15,090	246.48	17,366	21,942
28,000	191.01	40,764	202.39	32,717	8,047	221.31	25,114	15,650	255.61	18,010	22,754
29,000	197.84	42,222	209.62	33,886	8,336	229.21	26,010	16,212	264.74	18,653	23,569
30,000	204.66	43,678	216.85	35,055	8,623	237.12	26,909	16,769	273.86	19,295	24,383
32,500	221.71	47,316	234.92	37,976	9,340	256.88	29,151	18,165	296.69	20,904	26,412
35,000	238.77	50,957	252.99	40,897	10,060	276.64	31,394	19,563	319.51	22,512	28,445
40,000	272.88	58,237	289.13	46,739	11,498	316.16	35,878	22,359	365.15	25,727	32,510
45,000	306.98	65,513	325.27	52,581	12,932	355.67	40,361	25,152	410.79	28,942	36,571
50,000	341.09	72,792	361.41	58,423	14,369	395.19	44,846	27,946	456.44	32,159	40,633
55,000	375.20	80,072	397.55	64,265	15,807	434.71	49,330	30,742	502.08	35,374	44,698
60,000	409.31	87,352	433.69	70,107	17,245	474.23	53,815	33,537	547.72	38,590	48,762
65,000	443.42	94,631	469.83	75,949	18,682	513.75	58,300	36,331	593.37	41,807	52,824
70,000	477.53	101,911	505.97	81,791	20,120	553.27	62,785	39,126	639.01	45,022	56,889
75,000	511.64	109,190	542.11	87,633	21,557	592.79	67,270	41,920	684.65	48,237	60,953
80,000	545.75	116,470	578.25	93,475	22,995	632.31	71,754	44,716	730.30	51,454	65,016
85,000	579.85	123,746	614.39	99,317	24,429	671.82	76,237	47,509	775.94	54,669	69,077
90,000	613.96	131,026	650.53	105,159	25,867	711.34	80,722	50,304	821.58	57,884	73,142
95,000	648.07	138,305	686.67	111,001	27,304	750.86	85,206	53,099	867.22	61,100	77,205
100,000	682.18	145,585	722.81	116,843	28,742	790.38	89,691	55,894	912.87	64,317	81,268
105,000	716.29	152,864	758.95	122,685	30,179	829.90	94,176	58,688	958.51	67,532	85,332
110,000	750.40	160,144	795.09	128,527	31,617	869.42	98,661	61,483	1,004.15	70,747	89,397
115,000	784.51	167,424	831.23	134,369	33,055	908.94	103,146	64,278	1,049.80	73,964	93,460
120,000	818.62	174,703	867.37	140,211	34,492	948.46	107,630	67,073	1,095.44	77,179	97,524
125,000	852.73	181,983	903.51	146,053	35,930	987.97	112,113	69,870	1,141.08	80,394	101,589
130,000	886.83	189,259	939.65	151,895	37,364	1,027.49	116,598	72,661	1,186.73	83,611	105,648
135,000	920.94	196,538	975.79	157,737	38,801	1,067.01	121,082	75,456	1,232.37	86,827	109,711
140,000	955.05	203,818	1,011.93	163,579	40,239	1,106.53	125,567	78,251	1,278.01	90,042	113,776
145,000	989.16	211,098	1,048.07	169,421	41,677	1,146.05	130,052	81,046	1,323.66	93,259	117,839
150,000	1,023.27	218,377	1,084.22	175,266	43,111	1,185.57	134,537	83,840	1,369.30	96,474	121,903
155,000	1,057.38	225,657	1,120.36	181,108	44,549	1,225.09	139,022	86,635	1,414.94	99,689	125,968
160,000	1,091.49	232,936	1,156.50	186,950	45,986	1,264.61	143,506	89,430	1,460.59	102,906	130,030
165,000	1,125.60	240,216	1,192.64	192,792	47,424	1,304.13	147,991	92,225	1,506.23	106,121	134,095
170,000	1,159.70	247,492	1,228.78	198,634	48,858	1,343.64	152,474	95,018	1,551.87	109,337	138,155
175,000	1,193.81	254,772	1,264.92	204,476	50,296	1,383.16	156,958	97,814	1,597.52	112,554	142,218
180,000	1,227.92	262,051	1,301.06	210,318	51,733	1,422.68	161,443	100,608	1,643.16	115,769	146,282
185,000	1,262.03	269,331	1,337.20	216,160	53,171	1,462.20	165,928	103,403	1,688.80	118,984	150,347
190,000	1,296.14	276,610	1,373.34	222,002	54,608	1,501.72	170,413	106,197	1,734.44	122,199	154,411
195,000	1,330.25	283,890	1,409.48	227,844	56,046	1,541.24	174,898	108,992	1,780.09	125,416	158,474
200,000	1,364.36	291,170	1,445.62	233,686	57,484	1,580.76	179,382	111,788	1,825.73	128,631	162,539

SHORT-TERM AMORTIZING MORTGAGES

AMOUNT OF LOAN	30 YEARS		25 YEARS			20 YEARS			15 YEARS		
	MONTHLY PAYMENT	TOTAL INTRST	MONTHLY PAYMENT	TOTAL INTRST	INTRST SAVED	MONTHLY PAYMENT	TOTAL INTRST	INTRST SAVED	MONTHLY PAYMENT	TOTAL INTRST	INTRST SAVED
$ 50	0.35	76	0.37	61	15	0.41	48	28	0.47	35	41
100	0.70	152	0.74	122	30	0.81	94	58	0.93	67	85
200	1.40	304	1.48	244	60	1.62	189	115	1.86	135	169
300	2.10	456	2.22	366	90	2.42	281	175	2.79	202	254
400	2.80	608	2.96	488	120	3.23	375	233	3.71	268	340
500	3.50	760	3.70	610	150	4.03	467	293	4.64	335	425
600	4.20	912	4.44	732	180	4.84	562	350	5.57	403	509
700	4.90	1,064	5.18	854	210	5.64	654	410	6.49	468	596
800	5.60	1,216	5.92	976	240	6.45	748	468	7.42	536	680
900	6.30	1,368	6.66	1,098	270	7.26	842	526	8.35	603	765
1,000	7.00	1,520	7.39	1,217	303	8.06	934	586	9.28	670	850
2,000	13.99	3,036	14.78	2,434	602	16.12	1,869	1,167	18.55	1,339	1,697
3,000	20.98	4,553	22.17	3,651	902	24.17	2,801	1,752	27.82	2,008	2,545
4,000	27.97	6,069	29.56	4,868	1,201	32.23	3,735	2,334	37.09	2,676	3,393
5,000	34.97	7,589	36.95	6,085	1,504	40.28	4,667	2,922	46.36	3,345	4,244
6,000	41.96	9,106	44.34	7,302	1,804	48.34	5,602	3,504	55.63	4,013	5,093
7,000	48.95	10,622	51.73	8,519	2,103	56.40	6,536	4,086	64.90	4,682	5,940
8,000	55.94	12,138	59.12	9,736	2,402	64.45	7,468	4,670	74.17	5,351	6,787
9,000	62.93	13,655	66.51	10,953	2,702	72.51	8,402	5,253	83.44	6,019	7,636
10,000	69.93	15,175	73.90	12,170	3,005	80.56	9,334	5,841	92.71	6,688	8,487
11,000	76.92	16,691	81.29	13,387	3,304	88.62	10,269	6,422	101.98	7,356	9,335
12,000	83.91	18,208	88.68	14,604	3,604	96.68	11,203	7,005	111.25	8,025	10,183
13,000	90.90	19,724	96.07	15,821	3,903	104.73	12,135	7,589	120.52	8,694	11,030
14,000	97.90	21,244	103.46	17,038	4,206	112.79	13,070	8,174	129.79	9,362	11,882
15,000	104.89	22,760	110.85	18,255	4,505	120.84	14,002	8,758	139.06	10,031	12,729
16,000	111.88	24,277	118.24	19,472	4,805	128.90	14,936	9,341	148.33	10,699	13,578
17,000	118.87	25,793	125.63	20,689	5,104	136.96	15,870	9,923	157.60	11,368	14,425
18,000	125.86	27,310	133.02	21,906	5,404	145.01	16,802	10,508	166.87	12,037	15,273
19,000	132.86	28,830	140.41	23,123	5,707	153.07	17,737	11,093	176.14	12,705	16,125
20,000	139.85	30,346	147.80	24,340	6,006	161.12	18,669	11,677	185.41	13,374	16,972
21,000	146.84	31,862	155.19	25,557	6,305	169.18	19,603	12,259	194.68	14,042	17,820
22,000	153.83	33,379	162.58	26,774	6,605	177.24	20,538	12,841	203.95	14,711	18,668
23,000	160.82	34,895	169.97	27,991	6,904	185.29	21,470	13,425	213.22	15,380	19,515
24,000	167.82	36,415	177.36	29,208	7,207	193.35	22,404	14,011	222.49	16,048	20,367
25,000	174.81	37,932	184.75	30,425	7,507	201.40	23,336	14,596	231.76	16,717	21,215
26,000	181.80	39,448	192.14	31,642	7,806	209.46	24,270	15,178	241.03	17,385	22,063
27,000	188.79	40,964	199.53	32,859	8,105	217.52	25,205	15,759	250.30	18,054	22,910
28,000	195.79	42,484	206.92	34,076	8,408	225.57	26,137	16,347	259.57	18,723	23,761
29,000	202.78	44,001	214.31	35,293	8,708	233.63	27,071	16,930	268.84	19,391	24,610
30,000	209.77	45,517	221.70	36,510	9,007	241.68	28,003	17,514	278.11	20,060	25,457
32,500	227.25	49,310	240.18	39,554	9,756	261.82	30,337	18,973	301.28	21,730	27,580
35,000	244.73	53,103	258.65	42,595	10,508	281.96	32,670	20,433	324.46	23,403	29,700
40,000	279.69	60,688	295.60	48,680	12,008	322.24	37,338	23,350	370.81	26,746	33,942
45,000	314.65	68,274	332.55	54,765	13,509	362.52	42,005	26,269	417.16	30,089	38,185
50,000	349.61	75,860	369.50	60,850	15,010	402.80	46,672	29,188	463.51	33,432	42,428
55,000	384.57	83,445	406.45	66,935	16,510	443.08	51,339	32,106	509.86	36,775	46,670
60,000	419.53	91,031	443.40	73,020	18,011	483.36	56,006	35,025	556.21	40,118	50,913
65,000	454.49	98,616	480.35	79,105	19,511	523.64	60,674	37,942	602.56	43,461	55,155
70,000	489.46	106,206	517.30	85,190	21,016	563.92	65,341	40,865	648.91	46,804	59,402
75,000	524.42	113,791	554.25	91,275	22,516	604.20	70,008	43,783	695.26	50,147	63,644
80,000	559.38	121,377	591.20	97,360	24,017	644.48	74,675	46,702	741.61	53,490	67,887
85,000	594.34	128,962	628.15	103,445	25,517	684.76	79,342	49,620	787.97	56,835	72,127
90,000	629.30	136,548	665.10	109,530	27,018	725.04	84,010	52,538	834.32	60,178	76,370
95,000	664.26	144,134	702.05	115,615	28,519	765.32	88,677	55,457	880.67	63,521	80,613
100,000	699.22	151,719	739.00	121,700	30,019	805.60	93,344	58,375	927.02	66,864	84,855
105,000	734.18	159,305	775.95	127,785	31,520	845.88	98,011	61,294	973.37	70,207	89,098
110,000	769.14	166,890	812.90	133,870	33,020	886.16	102,678	64,212	1,019.72	73,550	93,340
115,000	804.10	174,476	849.84	139,952	34,524	926.44	107,346	67,130	1,066.07	76,893	97,583
120,000	839.06	182,062	886.79	146,037	36,025	966.72	112,013	70,049	1,112.42	80,236	101,826
125,000	874.02	189,647	923.74	152,122	37,525	1,007.00	116,680	72,967	1,158.77	83,579	106,068
130,000	908.98	197,233	960.69	158,207	39,026	1,047.28	121,347	75,886	1,205.12	86,922	110,311
135,000	943.94	204,818	997.64	164,292	40,526	1,087.56	126,014	78,804	1,251.47	90,265	114,553
140,000	978.91	212,408	1,034.59	170,377	42,031	1,127.84	130,682	81,726	1,297.82	93,608	118,800
145,000	1,013.87	219,993	1,071.54	176,462	43,531	1,168.12	135,349	84,644	1,344.17	96,951	123,042
150,000	1,048.83	227,579	1,108.49	182,547	45,032	1,208.39	140,014	87,565	1,390.52	100,294	127,285
155,000	1,083.79	235,164	1,145.44	188,632	46,532	1,248.67	144,681	90,483	1,436.87	103,637	131,527
160,000	1,118.75	242,750	1,182.39	194,717	48,033	1,288.95	149,348	93,402	1,483.22	106,980	135,770
165,000	1,153.71	250,336	1,219.34	200,802	49,534	1,329.23	154,016	96,320	1,529.58	110,324	140,012
170,000	1,188.67	257,921	1,256.29	206,887	51,034	1,369.51	158,682	99,239	1,575.93	113,667	144,254
175,000	1,223.63	265,507	1,293.24	212,972	52,535	1,409.79	163,350	102,157	1,622.28	117,010	148,497
180,000	1,258.59	273,092	1,330.19	219,057	54,035	1,450.07	168,017	105,075	1,668.63	120,353	152,739
185,000	1,293.55	280,678	1,367.14	225,142	55,536	1,490.35	172,684	107,994	1,714.98	123,696	156,982
190,000	1,328.51	288,264	1,404.09	231,227	57,037	1,530.63	177,351	110,913	1,761.33	127,039	161,225
195,000	1,363.47	295,849	1,441.04	237,312	58,537	1,570.91	182,018	113,831	1,807.68	130,382	165,467
200,000	1,398.43	303,435	1,477.99	243,397	60,038	1,611.19	186,686	116,749	1,854.03	133,725	169,710

AMOUNT OF LOAN	30 YEARS		25 YEARS			20 YEARS			15 YEARS		
	MONTHLY PAYMENT	TOTAL INTRST	MONTHLY PAYMENT	TOTAL INTRST	INTRST SAVED	MONTHLY PAYMENT	TOTAL INTRST	INTRST SAVED	MONTHLY PAYMENT	TOTAL INTRST	INTRST SAVED
$ 50	0.36	80	0.38	64	16	0.42	51	29	0.48	36	44
100	0.72	159	0.76	128	31	0.83	99	60	0.95	71	88
200	1.44	318	1.52	256	62	1.65	196	122	1.89	140	178
300	2.15	474	2.27	381	93	2.47	293	181	2.83	209	265
400	2.87	633	3.03	509	124	3.29	390	243	3.77	279	354
500	3.59	792	3.78	634	158	4.11	486	306	4.71	348	444
600	4.30	948	4.54	762	186	4.93	583	365	5.65	417	531
700	5.02	1,107	5.29	887	220	5.75	680	427	6.59	486	621
800	5.74	1,266	6.05	1,015	251	6.57	777	489	7.54	557	709
900	6.45	1,422	6.80	1,140	282	7.39	874	548	8.48	626	796
1,000	7.17	1,581	7.56	1,268	313	8.21	970	611	9.42	696	885
2,000	14.33	3,159	15.11	2,533	626	16.42	1,941	1,218	18.83	1,389	1,770
3,000	21.50	4,740	22.66	3,798	942	24.63	2,911	1,829	28.24	2,083	2,657
4,000	28.66	6,318	30.22	5,066	1,252	32.84	3,882	2,436	37.66	2,779	3,539
5,000	35.83	7,899	37.77	6,331	1,568	41.05	4,852	3,047	47.07	3,473	4,426
6,000	42.99	9,476	45.32	7,596	1,880	49.26	5,822	3,654	56.48	4,166	5,310
7,000	50.15	11,054	52.88	8,864	2,190	57.47	6,793	4,261	65.89	4,860	6,194
8,000	57.32	12,635	60.43	10,129	2,506	65.68	7,763	4,872	75.31	5,556	7,079
9,000	64.48	14,213	67.98	11,394	2,819	73.89	8,734	5,479	84.72	6,250	7,963
10,000	71.65	15,794	75.54	12,662	3,132	82.10	9,704	6,090	94.13	6,943	8,851
11,000	78.81	17,372	83.09	13,927	3,445	90.31	10,674	6,698	103.55	7,639	9,733
12,000	85.97	18,949	90.64	15,192	3,757	98.52	11,645	7,304	112.96	8,333	10,616
13,000	93.14	20,530	98.20	16,460	4,070	106.73	12,615	7,915	122.37	9,027	11,503
14,000	100.30	22,108	105.75	17,725	4,383	114.94	13,586	8,522	131.78	9,720	12,388
15,000	107.47	23,689	113.30	18,990	4,699	123.15	14,556	9,133	141.20	10,416	13,273
16,000	114.63	25,267	120.86	20,258	5,009	131.36	15,526	9,741	150.61	11,110	14,157
17,000	121.80	26,848	128.41	21,523	5,325	139.57	16,497	10,351	160.02	11,804	15,044
18,000	128.96	28,426	135.96	22,788	5,638	147.78	17,467	10,959	169.43	12,497	15,929
19,000	136.12	30,003	143.52	24,056	5,947	155.99	18,438	11,565	178.85	13,193	16,810
20,000	143.29	31,584	151.07	25,321	6,263	164.19	19,406	12,178	188.26	13,887	17,697
21,000	150.45	33,162	158.62	26,586	6,576	172.40	20,376	12,786	197.67	14,581	18,581
22,000	157.62	34,743	166.18	27,854	6,889	180.61	21,346	13,397	207.09	15,276	19,467
23,000	164.78	36,321	173.73	29,119	7,202	188.82	22,317	14,004	216.50	15,970	20,351
24,000	171.94	37,898	181.28	30,384	7,514	197.03	23,287	14,611	225.91	16,664	21,234
25,000	179.11	39,480	188.84	31,652	7,828	205.24	24,258	15,222	235.32	17,358	22,122
26,000	186.27	41,057	196.39	32,917	8,140	213.45	25,228	15,829	244.74	18,053	23,004
27,000	193.44	42,638	203.94	34,182	8,456	221.66	26,198	16,440	254.15	18,747	23,891
28,000	200.60	44,216	211.50	35,450	8,766	229.87	27,169	17,047	263.56	19,441	24,775
29,000	207.76	45,794	219.05	36,715	9,079	238.08	28,139	17,655	272.97	20,135	25,659
30,000	214.93	47,375	226.60	37,980	9,395	246.29	29,110	18,265	282.39	20,830	26,545
32,500	232.84	51,322	245.49	41,147	10,175	266.81	31,534	19,788	305.92	22,566	28,756
35,000	250.75	55,270	264.37	44,311	10,959	287.34	33,962	21,308	329.45	24,301	30,969
40,000	286.57	63,165	302.14	50,642	12,523	328.38	38,811	24,354	376.52	27,774	35,391
45,000	322.39	71,060	339.90	56,970	14,090	369.43	43,663	27,397	423.58	31,244	39,816
50,000	358.21	78,956	377.67	63,301	15,655	410.48	48,515	30,441	470.64	34,715	44,241
55,000	394.03	86,851	415.44	69,632	17,219	451.53	53,367	33,484	517.71	38,188	48,663
60,000	429.85	94,746	453.20	75,960	18,786	492.57	58,217	36,529	564.77	41,659	53,087
65,000	465.67	102,641	490.97	82,291	20,350	533.62	63,069	39,572	611.83	45,129	57,512
70,000	501.49	110,536	528.74	88,622	21,914	574.67	67,921	42,615	658.90	48,602	61,934
75,000	537.31	118,432	566.50	94,950	23,482	615.72	72,773	45,659	705.96	52,073	66,359
80,000	573.13	126,327	604.27	101,281	25,046	656.76	77,622	48,705	753.03	55,545	70,782
85,000	608.96	134,226	642.03	107,609	26,617	697.81	82,474	51,752	800.09	59,016	75,210
90,000	644.78	142,121	679.80	113,940	28,181	738.86	87,326	54,795	847.15	62,487	79,634
95,000	680.60	150,016	717.57	120,271	29,745	779.91	92,178	57,838	894.22	65,960	84,056
100,000	716.42	157,911	755.33	126,599	31,312	820.95	97,028	60,883	941.28	69,430	88,481
105,000	752.24	165,806	793.10	132,930	32,876	862.00	101,880	63,926	988.34	72,901	92,905
110,000	788.06	173,702	830.87	139,261	34,441	903.05	106,732	66,970	1,035.41	76,374	97,328
115,000	823.88	181,597	868.63	145,589	36,008	944.10	111,584	70,013	1,082.47	79,845	101,752
120,000	859.70	189,492	906.40	151,920	37,572	985.14	116,434	73,058	1,129.54	83,317	106,175
125,000	895.52	197,387	944.17	158,251	39,136	1,026.19	121,286	76,101	1,176.60	86,788	110,599
130,000	931.34	205,282	981.93	164,579	40,703	1,067.24	126,138	79,144	1,223.66	90,259	115,023
135,000	967.16	213,178	1,019.70	170,910	42,268	1,108.29	130,990	82,188	1,270.73	93,731	119,447
140,000	1,002.98	221,073	1,057.47	177,241	43,832	1,149.33	135,839	85,234	1,317.79	97,202	123,871
145,000	1,038.80	228,968	1,095.23	183,569	45,399	1,190.38	140,691	88,277	1,364.85	100,673	128,295
150,000	1,074.62	236,863	1,133.00	189,900	46,963	1,231.43	145,543	91,320	1,411.92	104,146	132,717
155,000	1,110.44	244,758	1,170.76	196,228	48,530	1,272.48	150,395	94,363	1,458.98	107,616	137,142
160,000	1,146.26	252,654	1,208.53	202,559	50,095	1,313.52	155,245	97,409	1,506.05	111,089	141,565
165,000	1,182.09	260,552	1,246.30	208,890	51,662	1,354.57	160,097	100,455	1,553.11	114,560	145,992
170,000	1,217.91	268,448	1,284.06	215,218	53,230	1,395.62	164,949	103,499	1,600.17	118,031	150,417
175,000	1,253.73	276,343	1,321.83	221,549	54,794	1,436.66	169,798	106,545	1,647.24	121,503	154,840
180,000	1,289.55	284,238	1,359.60	227,880	56,358	1,477.71	174,650	109,588	1,694.30	124,974	159,264
185,000	1,325.37	292,133	1,397.36	234,208	57,925	1,518.76	179,502	112,631	1,741.37	128,447	163,686
190,000	1,361.19	300,028	1,435.13	240,539	59,489	1,559.81	184,354	115,674	1,788.43	131,917	168,111
195,000	1,397.01	307,924	1,472.90	246,870	61,054	1,600.85	189,204	118,720	1,835.49	135,388	172,536
200,000	1,432.83	315,819	1,510.66	253,198	62,621	1,641.90	194,056	121,763	1,882.56	138,861	176,958

SHORT-TERM AMORTIZING MORTGAGES

AMOUNT OF LOAN	30 YEARS		25 YEARS			20 YEARS			15 YEARS		
	MONTHLY PAYMENT	TOTAL INTRST	MONTHLY PAYMENT	TOTAL INTRST	INTRST SAVED	MONTHLY PAYMENT	TOTAL INTRST	INTRST SAVED	MONTHLY PAYMENT	TOTAL INTRST	INTRST SAVED
$ 50	0.37	83	0.39	67	16	0.42	51	32	0.48	36	47
100	0.74	166	0.78	134	32	0.84	102	64	0.96	73	93
200	1.47	329	1.55	265	64	1.68	203	126	1.92	146	183
300	2.21	496	2.32	396	100	2.51	302	194	2.87	217	279
400	2.94	658	3.09	527	131	3.35	404	254	3.83	289	369
500	3.67	821	3.86	658	163	4.19	506	315	4.78	360	461
600	4.41	988	4.64	792	196	5.02	605	383	5.74	433	555
700	5.14	1,150	5.41	923	227	5.86	706	444	6.69	504	646
800	5.88	1,317	6.18	1,054	263	6.70	808	509	7.65	577	740
900	6.61	1,480	6.95	1,185	295	7.53	907	573	8.61	650	830
1,000	7.34	1,642	7.72	1,316	326	8.37	1,009	633	9.56	721	921
2,000	14.68	3,285	15.44	2,632	653	16.73	2,015	1,270	19.12	1,442	1,843
3,000	22.02	4,927	23.16	3,948	979	25.10	3,024	1,903	28.67	2,161	2,766
4,000	29.36	6,570	30.88	5,264	1,306	33.46	4,030	2,540	38.23	2,881	3,689
5,000	36.69	8,208	38.60	6,580	1,628	41.83	5,039	3,169	47.79	3,602	4,606
6,000	44.03	9,851	46.31	7,893	1,958	50.19	6,046	3,805	57.34	4,321	5,530
7,000	51.37	11,493	54.03	9,209	2,284	58.56	7,054	4,439	66.90	5,042	6,451
8,000	58.71	13,136	61.75	10,525	2,611	66.92	8,061	5,075	76.46	5,763	7,373
9,000	66.04	14,774	69.47	11,841	2,933	75.28	9,067	5,707	86.01	6,482	8,292
10,000	73.38	16,417	77.19	13,157	3,260	83.65	10,076	6,341	95.57	7,203	9,214
11,000	80.72	18,059	84.90	14,470	3,589	92.01	11,082	6,977	105.13	7,923	10,136
12,000	88.06	19,702	92.62	15,786	3,916	100.38	12,091	7,611	114.68	8,642	11,060
13,000	95.39	21,340	100.34	17,102	4,238	108.74	13,098	8,242	124.24	9,363	11,977
14,000	102.73	22,983	108.06	18,418	4,565	117.11	14,106	8,877	133.80	10,084	12,899
15,000	110.07	24,625	115.78	19,734	4,891	125.47	15,113	9,512	143.35	10,803	13,822
16,000	117.41	26,268	123.50	21,050	5,218	133.84	16,122	10,146	152.91	11,524	14,744
17,000	124.74	27,906	131.21	22,363	5,543	142.20	17,128	10,778	162.47	12,245	15,661
18,000	132.08	29,549	138.93	23,679	5,870	150.56	18,134	11,415	172.02	12,964	16,585
19,000	139.42	31,191	146.65	24,995	6,196	158.93	19,143	12,048	181.58	13,684	17,507
20,000	146.76	32,834	154.37	26,311	6,523	167.29	20,150	12,684	191.14	14,405	18,429
21,000	154.10	34,476	162.09	27,627	6,849	175.66	21,158	13,318	200.69	15,124	19,352
22,000	161.43	36,115	169.80	28,940	7,175	184.02	22,165	13,950	210.25	15,845	20,270
23,000	168.77	37,757	177.52	30,256	7,501	192.39	23,174	14,583	219.80	16,564	21,193
24,000	176.11	39,400	185.24	31,572	7,828	200.75	24,180	15,220	229.36	17,285	22,115
25,000	183.45	41,042	192.96	32,888	8,154	209.12	25,189	15,853	238.92	18,006	23,036
26,000	190.78	42,681	200.68	34,204	8,477	217.48	26,195	16,486	248.47	18,725	23,956
27,000	198.12	44,323	208.40	35,520	8,803	225.84	27,202	17,121	258.03	19,445	24,878
28,000	205.46	45,966	216.11	36,833	9,133	234.21	28,210	17,756	267.59	20,166	25,800
29,000	212.80	47,608	223.83	38,149	9,459	242.57	29,217	18,391	277.14	20,885	26,723
30,000	220.13	49,247	231.55	39,465	9,782	250.94	30,226	19,021	286.70	21,606	27,641
32,500	238.48	53,353	250.85	42,755	10,598	271.85	32,744	20,609	310.59	23,406	29,947
35,000	256.82	57,455	270.14	46,042	11,413	292.76	35,262	22,193	334.48	25,206	32,249
40,000	293.51	65,664	308.73	52,619	13,045	334.58	40,299	25,365	382.27	28,809	36,855
45,000	330.20	73,872	347.32	59,196	14,676	376.40	45,336	28,538	430.05	32,409	41,463
50,000	366.89	82,080	385.91	65,773	16,307	418.23	50,375	31,705	477.83	36,009	46,071
55,000	403.58	90,289	424.50	72,350	17,939	460.05	55,412	34,877	525.61	39,610	50,679
60,000	440.26	98,494	463.09	78,927	19,567	501.87	60,449	38,045	573.40	43,212	55,282
65,000	476.95	106,702	501.69	85,507	21,195	543.69	65,486	41,216	621.18	46,812	59,890
70,000	513.64	114,910	540.28	92,084	22,826	585.51	70,522	44,388	668.96	50,413	64,497
75,000	550.33	123,119	578.87	98,661	24,458	627.34	75,562	47,557	716.74	54,013	69,106
80,000	587.02	131,327	617.46	105,238	26,089	669.16	80,598	50,729	764.53	57,615	73,712
85,000	623.70	139,532	656.05	111,815	27,717	710.98	85,635	53,897	812.31	61,216	78,316
90,000	660.39	147,740	694.64	118,392	29,348	752.80	90,672	57,068	860.09	64,816	82,924
95,000	697.08	155,949	733.23	124,969	30,980	794.62	95,709	60,240	907.87	68,417	87,532
100,000	733.77	164,157	771.82	131,546	32,611	836.45	100,748	63,409	955.66	72,019	92,138
105,000	770.46	172,366	810.41	138,123	34,243	878.27	105,785	66,581	1,003.44	75,619	96,747
110,000	807.15	180,574	849.00	144,700	35,874	920.09	110,822	69,752	1,051.22	79,220	101,354
115,000	843.83	188,779	887.59	151,277	37,502	961.91	115,858	72,921	1,099.00	82,820	105,959
120,000	880.52	196,987	926.18	157,854	39,133	1,003.73	120,895	76,092	1,146.79	86,422	110,565
125,000	917.21	205,196	964.78	164,434	40,762	1,045.56	125,934	79,262	1,194.57	90,023	115,173
130,000	953.90	213,404	1,003.37	171,011	42,393	1,087.38	130,971	82,433	1,242.35	93,623	119,781
135,000	990.59	221,612	1,041.96	177,588	44,024	1,129.20	136,008	85,604	1,290.14	97,225	124,387
140,000	1,027.28	229,821	1,080.55	184,165	45,656	1,171.02	141,045	88,776	1,337.92	100,826	128,995
145,000	1,063.96	238,026	1,119.14	190,742	47,284	1,212.84	146,082	91,944	1,385.70	104,426	133,600
150,000	1,100.65	246,234	1,157.73	197,319	48,915	1,254.67	151,121	95,113	1,433.48	108,028	138,208
155,000	1,137.34	254,442	1,196.32	203,896	50,546	1,296.49	156,158	98,284	1,481.27	111,629	142,813
160,000	1,174.03	262,651	1,234.91	210,473	52,178	1,338.31	161,194	101,457	1,529.05	115,229	147,422
165,000	1,210.72	270,859	1,273.50	217,050	53,809	1,380.13	166,231	104,628	1,576.83	118,830	152,030
170,000	1,247.40	279,064	1,312.09	223,627	55,437	1,421.95	171,268	107,796	1,624.61	122,430	156,634
175,000	1,284.09	287,272	1,350.68	230,204	57,068	1,463.78	176,307	110,965	1,672.40	126,032	161,240
180,000	1,320.78	295,481	1,389.27	236,781	58,700	1,505.60	181,344	114,137	1,720.18	129,632	165,849
185,000	1,357.47	303,689	1,427.87	243,361	60,328	1,547.42	186,381	117,308	1,767.96	133,233	170,456
190,000	1,394.16	311,898	1,466.46	249,938	61,960	1,589.24	191,418	120,480	1,815.74	136,833	175,065
195,000	1,430.85	320,106	1,505.05	256,515	63,591	1,631.06	196,454	123,652	1,863.53	140,435	179,671
200,000	1,467.53	328,311	1,543.64	263,092	65,219	1,672.89	201,494	126,817	1,911.31	144,036	184,275

AMOUNT OF LOAN	30 YEARS		25 YEARS			20 YEARS			15 YEARS		
	MONTHLY PAYMENT	TOTAL INTRST	MONTHLY PAYMENT	TOTAL INTRST	INTRST SAVED	MONTHLY PAYMENT	TOTAL INTRST	INTRST SAVED	MONTHLY PAYMENT	TOTAL INTRST	INTRST SAVED
$ 50	0.38	87	0.40	70	17	0.43	53	34	0.49	38	49
100	0.76	174	0.79	137	37	0.86	106	68	0.98	76	98
200	1.51	344	1.58	274	70	1.71	210	134	1.95	151	193
300	2.26	514	2.37	411	103	2.56	314	200	2.92	226	288
400	3.01	684	3.16	548	136	3.41	418	266	3.89	300	384
500	3.76	854	3.95	685	169	4.27	525	329	4.86	375	479
600	4.51	1,024	4.74	822	202	5.12	629	395	5.83	449	575
700	5.26	1,194	5.52	956	238	5.97	733	461	6.80	524	670
800	6.02	1,367	6.31	1,093	274	6.82	837	530	7.77	599	768
900	6.77	1,537	7.10	1,230	307	7.67	941	596	8.74	673	864
1,000	7.52	1,707	7.89	1,367	340	8.53	1,047	660	9.71	748	959
2,000	15.03	3,411	15.77	2,731	680	17.05	2,092	1,319	19.41	1,494	1,917
3,000	22.54	5,114	23.66	4,098	1,016	25.57	3,137	1,977	29.11	2,240	2,874
4,000	30.06	6,822	31.54	5,462	1,360	34.09	4,182	2,640	38.81	2,986	3,836
5,000	37.57	8,525	39.43	6,829	1,696	42.61	5,226	3,299	48.51	3,732	4,793
6,000	45.08	10,229	47.31	8,193	2,036	51.13	6,271	3,958	58.21	4,478	5,751
7,000	52.59	11,932	55.20	9,560	2,372	59.65	7,316	4,616	67.91	5,224	6,708
8,000	60.11	13,640	63.08	10,924	2,716	68.17	8,361	5,279	77.62	5,972	7,668
9,000	67.62	15,343	70.97	12,291	3,052	76.69	9,406	5,937	87.32	6,718	8,625
10,000	75.13	17,047	78.85	13,655	3,392	85.21	10,450	6,597	97.02	7,464	9,583
11,000	82.64	18,750	86.73	15,019	3,731	93.73	11,495	7,255	106.72	8,210	10,540
12,000	90.16	20,458	94.62	16,386	4,072	102.25	12,540	7,918	116.42	8,956	11,502
13,000	97.67	22,161	102.50	17,750	4,411	110.77	13,585	8,576	126.12	9,702	12,459
14,000	105.18	23,865	110.39	19,117	4,748	119.29	14,630	9,235	135.82	10,448	13,417
15,000	112.69	25,568	118.27	20,481	5,087	127.81	15,674	9,894	145.53	11,195	14,373
16,000	120.21	27,276	126.16	21,848	5,428	136.34	16,722	10,554	155.23	11,941	15,335
17,000	127.72	28,979	134.04	23,212	5,767	144.86	17,766	11,213	164.93	12,687	16,292
18,000	135.23	30,683	141.93	24,579	6,104	153.38	18,811	11,872	174.63	13,433	17,250
19,000	142.75	32,390	149.81	25,943	6,447	161.90	19,856	12,534	184.33	14,179	18,211
20,000	150.26	34,094	157.70	27,310	6,784	170.42	20,901	13,193	194.03	14,925	19,169
21,000	157.77	35,797	165.58	28,674	7,123	178.94	21,946	13,851	203.73	15,671	20,126
22,000	165.28	37,501	173.46	30,038	7,463	187.46	22,990	14,511	213.44	16,419	21,082
23,000	172.80	39,208	181.35	31,405	7,803	195.98	24,035	15,173	223.14	17,165	22,043
24,000	180.31	40,912	189.23	32,769	8,143	204.50	25,080	15,832	232.84	17,911	23,001
25,000	187.82	42,615	197.12	34,136	8,479	213.02	26,125	16,490	242.54	18,657	23,958
26,000	195.33	44,319	205.00	35,500	8,819	221.54	27,170	17,149	252.24	19,403	24,916
27,000	202.85	46,026	212.89	36,867	9,159	230.06	28,214	17,812	261.94	20,149	25,877
28,000	210.36	47,730	220.77	38,231	9,499	238.58	29,259	18,471	271.64	20,895	26,835
29,000	217.87	49,433	228.66	39,598	9,835	247.10	30,304	19,129	281.35	21,643	27,790
30,000	225.38	51,137	236.54	40,962	10,175	255.62	31,349	19,788	291.05	22,389	28,748
32,500	244.17	55,401	256.25	44,375	11,026	276.93	33,963	21,438	315.30	24,254	31,147
35,000	262.95	59,662	275.96	47,788	11,874	298.23	36,575	23,087	339.55	26,119	33,543
40,000	300.51	68,184	315.39	54,617	13,567	340.83	41,799	26,385	388.06	29,851	38,333
45,000	338.07	76,705	354.81	61,443	15,262	383.43	47,023	29,682	436.57	33,583	43,122
50,000	375.64	85,230	394.23	68,269	16,961	426.04	52,250	32,980	485.08	37,314	47,916
55,000	413.20	93,752	433.65	75,095	18,657	468.64	57,474	36,278	533.58	41,044	52,708
60,000	450.76	102,274	473.08	81,924	20,350	511.24	62,698	39,576	582.09	44,776	57,498
65,000	488.33	110,799	512.50	88,750	22,049	553.85	67,924	42,875	630.60	48,508	62,291
70,000	525.89	119,320	551.92	95,576	23,744	596.45	73,148	46,172	679.10	52,238	67,082
75,000	563.45	127,842	591.34	102,402	25,440	639.05	78,372	49,470	727.61	55,970	71,872
80,000	601.02	136,367	630.77	109,231	27,136	681.66	83,598	52,769	776.12	59,702	76,665
85,000	638.58	144,889	670.19	116,057	28,832	724.26	88,822	56,067	824.62	63,432	81,457
90,000	676.14	153,410	709.61	122,883	30,527	766.86	94,046	59,364	873.13	67,163	86,247
95,000	713.71	161,936	749.03	129,709	32,227	809.47	99,273	62,663	921.64	70,895	91,041
100,000	751.27	170,457	788.46	136,538	33,919	852.07	104,497	65,960	970.15	74,627	95,830
105,000	788.83	178,979	827.88	143,364	35,615	894.67	109,721	69,258	1,018.65	78,357	100,622
110,000	826.40	187,504	867.30	150,190	37,314	937.28	114,947	72,557	1,067.16	82,089	105,415
115,000	863.96	196,026	906.72	157,016	39,010	979.88	120,171	75,855	1,115.67	85,821	110,205
120,000	901.52	204,547	946.15	163,845	40,702	1,022.48	125,395	79,152	1,164.17	89,551	114,996
125,000	939.09	213,072	985.57	170,671	42,401	1,065.09	130,622	82,450	1,212.68	93,282	119,790
130,000	976.65	221,594	1,024.99	177,497	44,097	1,107.69	135,846	85,748	1,261.19	97,014	124,580
135,000	1,014.21	230,116	1,064.41	184,323	45,793	1,150.29	141,070	89,046	1,309.69	100,744	129,372
140,000	1,051.78	238,641	1,103.84	191,152	47,489	1,192.90	146,296	92,345	1,358.20	104,476	134,165
145,000	1,089.34	247,162	1,143.26	197,978	49,184	1,235.50	151,520	95,642	1,406.71	108,208	138,954
150,000	1,126.90	255,684	1,182.68	204,804	50,880	1,278.10	156,744	98,940	1,455.22	111,940	143,744
155,000	1,164.47	264,209	1,222.10	211,630	52,579	1,320.71	161,970	102,239	1,503.72	115,670	148,539
160,000	1,202.03	272,731	1,261.53	218,459	54,272	1,363.31	167,194	105,537	1,552.23	119,401	153,330
165,000	1,239.59	281,252	1,300.95	225,285	55,967	1,405.91	172,418	108,834	1,600.74	123,133	158,119
170,000	1,277.16	289,778	1,340.37	232,111	57,667	1,448.52	177,645	112,133	1,649.24	126,863	162,915
175,000	1,314.72	298,299	1,379.79	238,937	59,362	1,491.12	182,869	115,430	1,697.75	130,595	167,704
180,000	1,352.28	306,821	1,419.22	245,766	61,055	1,533.72	188,093	118,728	1,746.26	134,327	172,494
185,000	1,389.85	315,346	1,458.64	252,592	62,754	1,576.33	193,319	122,027	1,794.76	138,057	177,289
190,000	1,427.41	323,868	1,498.06	259,418	64,450	1,618.93	198,543	125,325	1,843.27	141,789	182,079
195,000	1,464.97	332,389	1,537.48	266,244	66,145	1,661.53	203,767	128,622	1,891.78	145,520	186,869
200,000	1,502.54	340,914	1,576.91	273,073	67,841	1,704.14	208,994	131,920	1,940.29	149,252	191,662

AMOUNT OF LOAN	30 YEARS		25 YEARS			20 YEARS			15 YEARS		
	MONTHLY PAYMENT	TOTAL INTRST	MONTHLY PAYMENT	TOTAL INTRST	INTRST SAVED	MONTHLY PAYMENT	TOTAL INTRST	INTRST SAVED	MONTHLY PAYMENT	TOTAL INTRST	INTRST SAVED
$ 50	0.39	90	0.41	73	17	0.44	56	34	0.50	40	50
100	0.77	177	0.81	143	34	0.87	109	68	0.99	78	99
200	1.54	354	1.62	286	68	1.74	218	136	1.97	155	199
300	2.31	532	2.42	426	106	2.61	326	206	2.96	233	299
400	3.08	709	3.23	569	140	3.48	435	274	3.94	309	400
500	3.85	886	4.03	709	177	4.34	542	344	4.93	387	499
600	4.62	1,063	4.84	852	211	5.21	650	413	5.91	464	599
700	5.39	1,240	5.64	992	248	6.08	759	481	6.90	542	698
800	6.16	1,418	6.45	1,135	283	6.95	868	550	7.88	618	800
900	6.93	1,595	7.25	1,275	320	7.82	977	618	8.87	697	898
1,000	7.69	1,768	8.06	1,418	350	8.68	1,083	685	9.85	773	995
2,000	15.38	3,537	16.11	2,833	704	17.36	2,166	1,371	19.70	1,546	1,991
3,000	23.07	5,305	24.16	4,248	1,057	26.04	3,250	2,055	29.55	2,319	2,986
4,000	30.76	7,074	32.21	5,663	1,411	34.72	4,333	2,741	39.39	3,090	3,984
5,000	38.45	8,842	40.27	7,081	1,761	43.40	5,416	3,426	49.24	3,863	4,979
6,000	46.14	10,610	48.32	8,496	2,114	52.07	6,497	4,113	59.09	4,636	5,974
7,000	53.83	12,379	56.37	9,911	2,468	60.75	7,580	4,799	68.94	5,409	6,970
8,000	61.52	14,147	64.42	11,326	2,821	69.43	8,663	5,484	78.78	6,180	7,967
9,000	69.21	15,916	72.48	12,744	3,172	78.11	9,746	6,170	88.63	6,953	8,963
10,000	76.90	17,684	80.53	14,159	3,525	86.79	10,830	6,854	98.48	7,726	9,958
11,000	84.59	19,452	88.58	15,574	3,878	95.47	11,913	7,539	108.33	8,499	10,953
12,000	92.27	21,217	96.63	16,989	4,228	104.14	12,994	8,223	118.17	9,271	11,946
13,000	99.96	22,986	104.68	18,404	4,582	112.82	14,077	8,909	128.02	10,044	12,942
14,000	107.65	24,754	112.74	19,822	4,932	121.50	15,160	9,594	137.87	10,817	13,937
15,000	115.34	26,522	120.79	21,237	5,285	130.18	16,243	10,279	147.72	11,590	14,932
16,000	123.03	28,291	128.84	22,652	5,639	138.86	17,326	10,965	157.56	12,361	15,930
17,000	130.72	30,059	136.89	24,067	5,992	147.53	18,407	11,652	167.41	13,134	16,925
18,000	138.41	31,828	144.95	25,485	6,343	156.21	19,490	12,338	177.26	13,907	17,921
19,000	146.10	33,596	153.00	26,900	6,696	164.89	20,574	13,022	187.11	14,680	18,916
20,000	153.79	35,364	161.05	28,315	7,049	173.57	21,657	13,707	196.95	15,451	19,913
21,000	161.48	37,133	169.10	29,730	7,403	182.25	22,740	14,393	206.80	16,224	20,909
22,000	169.17	38,901	177.15	31,145	7,756	190.93	23,823	15,078	216.65	16,997	21,904
23,000	176.86	40,670	185.21	32,563	8,107	199.60	24,904	15,766	226.50	17,770	22,900
24,000	184.54	42,434	193.26	33,978	8,456	208.28	25,987	16,447	236.34	18,541	23,893
25,000	192.23	44,203	201.31	35,393	8,810	216.96	27,070	17,133	246.19	19,314	24,889
26,000	199.92	45,971	209.36	36,808	9,163	225.64	28,154	17,817	256.04	20,087	25,884
27,000	207.61	47,740	217.42	38,226	9,514	234.32	29,237	18,503	265.88	20,858	26,882
28,000	215.30	49,508	225.47	39,641	9,867	243.00	30,320	19,188	275.73	21,631	27,877
29,000	222.99	51,276	233.52	41,056	10,220	251.67	31,401	19,875	285.58	22,404	28,872
30,000	230.68	53,045	241.57	42,471	10,574	260.35	32,484	20,561	295.43	23,177	29,868
32,500	249.90	57,464	261.70	46,010	11,454	282.05	35,192	22,272	320.05	25,109	32,355
35,000	269.12	61,883	281.83	49,549	12,334	303.74	37,898	23,985	344.66	27,039	34,844
40,000	307.57	70,722	322.10	56,630	14,095	347.13	43,311	27,414	393.90	30,902	39,823
45,000	346.02	79,567	362.36	63,708	15,859	390.53	48,727	30,840	443.14	34,766	44,802
50,000	384.46	88,406	402.62	70,786	17,620	433.92	54,141	34,265	492.37	38,627	49,779
55,000	422.91	97,248	442.88	77,864	19,384	477.31	59,554	37,694	541.61	42,490	54,758
60,000	461.35	106,086	483.14	84,942	21,144	520.70	64,968	41,118	590.85	46,353	59,733
65,000	499.80	114,928	523.40	92,020	22,908	564.09	70,382	44,546	640.09	50,216	64,712
70,000	538.24	123,766	563.66	99,098	24,668	607.48	75,795	47,971	689.32	54,079	69,688
75,000	576.69	132,608	603.93	106,179	26,429	650.87	81,209	51,399	738.56	57,941	74,667
80,000	615.14	141,450	644.19	113,257	28,193	694.26	86,622	54,828	787.80	61,804	79,646
85,000	653.58	150,289	684.45	120,335	29,954	737.65	92,036	58,253	837.03	65,665	84,624
90,000	692.03	159,131	724.71	127,413	31,718	781.05	97,452	61,679	886.27	69,529	89,602
95,000	730.47	167,969	764.97	134,491	33,478	824.44	102,866	65,103	935.51	73,392	94,577
100,000	768.92	176,811	805.23	141,569	35,242	867.83	108,279	68,532	984.74	77,253	99,558
105,000	807.36	185,650	845.49	148,647	37,003	911.22	113,693	71,957	1,033.98	81,116	104,534
110,000	845.81	194,492	885.75	155,725	38,767	954.61	119,106	75,386	1,083.22	84,980	109,512
115,000	884.26	203,334	926.02	162,806	40,528	998.00	124,520	78,814	1,132.46	88,843	114,491
120,000	922.70	212,172	966.28	169,884	42,288	1,041.39	129,934	82,238	1,181.69	92,704	119,468
125,000	961.15	221,014	1,006.54	176,962	44,052	1,084.78	135,347	85,667	1,230.93	96,567	124,447
130,000	999.59	229,852	1,046.80	184,040	45,812	1,128.18	140,763	89,089	1,280.17	100,431	129,421
135,000	1,038.04	238,694	1,087.06	191,118	47,576	1,171.57	146,177	92,517	1,329.40	104,292	134,402
140,000	1,076.48	247,533	1,127.32	198,196	49,337	1,214.96	151,590	95,943	1,378.64	108,155	139,378
145,000	1,114.93	256,375	1,167.58	205,274	51,101	1,258.35	157,004	99,371	1,427.88	112,018	144,357
150,000	1,153.38	265,217	1,207.85	212,355	52,862	1,301.74	162,418	102,799	1,477.11	115,880	149,337
155,000	1,191.82	274,055	1,248.11	219,433	54,622	1,345.13	167,831	106,224	1,526.35	119,743	154,312
160,000	1,230.27	282,897	1,288.37	226,511	56,386	1,388.52	173,245	109,652	1,575.59	123,606	159,291
165,000	1,268.71	291,736	1,328.63	233,589	58,147	1,431.91	178,658	113,078	1,624.83	127,469	164,267
170,000	1,307.16	300,578	1,368.89	240,667	59,911	1,475.30	184,072	116,506	1,674.06	131,331	169,247
175,000	1,345.60	309,416	1,409.15	247,745	61,671	1,518.70	189,488	119,928	1,723.30	135,194	174,222
180,000	1,384.05	318,298	1,449.41	254,823	63,435	1,562.09	194,902	123,356	1,772.54	139,057	179,201
185,000	1,422.49	327,096	1,489.68	261,904	65,192	1,605.48	200,315	126,781	1,821.77	142,919	184,177
190,000	1,460.94	335,938	1,529.94	268,982	66,956	1,648.87	205,729	130,209	1,871.01	146,782	189,156
195,000	1,499.39	344,780	1,570.20	276,060	68,720	1,692.26	211,142	133,638	1,920.25	150,645	194,135
200,000	1,537.83	353,619	1,610.46	283,138	70,481	1,735.65	216,556	137,063	1,969.48	154,506	199,113

SHORT-TERM AMORTIZING MORTGAGES 8.75%

AMOUNT OF LOAN	30 YEARS		25 YEARS			20 YEARS			15 YEARS		
	MONTHLY PAYMENT	TOTAL INTRST	MONTHLY PAYMENT	TOTAL INTRST	INTRST SAVED	MONTHLY PAYMENT	TOTAL INTRST	INTRST SAVED	MONTHLY PAYMENT	TOTAL INTRST	INTRST SAVED
$ 50	0.40	94	0.42	76	18	0.45	58	36	0.50	40	54
100	0.79	184	0.83	149	35	0.89	114	70	1.00	80	104
200	1.58	369	1.65	295	74	1.77	225	144	2.00	160	209
300	2.37	553	2.47	441	112	2.66	338	215	3.00	240	313
400	3.15	734	3.29	587	147	3.54	450	284	4.00	320	414
500	3.94	918	4.12	736	182	4.42	561	357	5.00	400	518
600	4.73	1,103	4.94	882	221	5.31	674	429	6.00	480	623
700	5.51	1,284	5.76	1,028	256	6.19	786	498	7.00	560	724
800	6.30	1,468	6.58	1,174	294	7.07	897	571	8.00	640	828
900	7.09	1,652	7.40	1,320	332	7.96	1,010	642	9.00	720	932
1,000	7.87	1,833	8.23	1,469	364	8.84	1,122	711	10.00	800	1,033
2,000	15.74	3,666	16.45	2,935	731	17.68	2,243	1,423	19.99	1,598	2,068
3,000	23.61	5,500	24.67	4,401	1,099	26.52	3,365	2,135	29.99	2,398	3,102
4,000	31.47	7,329	32.89	5,867	1,462	35.35	4,484	2,845	39.98	3,196	4,133
5,000	39.34	9,162	41.11	7,333	1,829	44.19	5,606	3,556	49.98	3,996	5,166
6,000	47.21	10,996	49.33	8,799	2,197	53.03	6,727	4,269	59.97	4,795	6,201
7,000	55.07	12,825	57.56	10,268	2,557	61.86	7,846	4,979	69.97	5,595	7,230
8,000	62.94	14,658	65.78	11,734	2,924	70.70	8,968	5,690	79.96	6,393	8,265
9,000	70.81	16,492	74.00	13,200	3,292	79.54	10,090	6,402	89.96	7,193	9,299
10,000	78.68	18,325	82.22	14,666	3,659	88.38	11,211	7,114	99.95	7,991	10,334
11,000	86.54	20,154	90.44	16,132	4,022	97.21	12,330	7,824	109.94	8,789	11,365
12,000	94.41	21,988	98.66	17,598	4,390	106.05	13,452	8,536	119.94	9,589	12,399
13,000	102.28	23,821	106.88	19,064	4,757	114.89	14,574	9,247	129.93	10,387	13,434
14,000	110.14	25,650	115.11	20,533	5,117	123.72	15,693	9,957	139.93	11,187	14,463
15,000	118.01	27,484	123.33	21,999	5,485	132.56	16,814	10,670	149.92	11,986	15,498
16,000	125.88	29,317	131.55	23,465	5,852	141.40	17,936	11,381	159.92	12,786	16,531
17,000	133.74	31,146	139.77	24,931	6,215	150.24	19,058	12,088	169.91	13,584	17,562
18,000	141.61	32,980	147.99	26,397	6,583	159.07	20,177	12,803	179.91	14,384	18,596
19,000	149.48	34,813	156.21	27,863	6,950	167.91	21,298	13,515	189.90	15,182	19,631
20,000	157.35	36,646	164.43	29,329	7,317	176.75	22,420	14,226	199.89	15,980	20,666
21,000	165.21	38,476	172.66	30,798	7,678	185.58	23,539	14,937	209.89	16,780	21,696
22,000	173.08	40,309	180.88	32,264	8,045	194.42	24,661	15,648	219.88	17,578	22,731
23,000	180.95	42,142	189.10	33,730	8,412	203.26	25,782	16,360	229.88	18,378	23,764
24,000	188.81	43,972	197.32	35,196	8,776	212.10	26,904	17,068	239.87	19,177	24,795
25,000	196.68	45,805	205.54	36,662	9,143	220.93	28,023	17,782	249.87	19,977	25,828
26,000	204.55	47,638	213.76	38,128	9,510	229.77	29,145	18,493	259.86	20,775	26,863
27,000	212.41	49,468	221.98	39,594	9,874	238.61	30,266	19,202	269.86	21,575	27,893
28,000	220.28	51,301	230.21	41,063	10,238	247.44	31,386	19,915	279.85	22,373	28,928
29,000	228.15	53,134	238.43	42,529	10,605	256.28	32,507	20,627	289.85	23,173	29,961
30,000	236.02	54,967	246.65	43,995	10,972	265.12	33,629	21,338	299.84	23,971	30,996
32,500	255.68	59,545	267.20	47,660	11,885	287.21	36,430	23,115	324.83	25,969	33,576
35,000	275.35	64,126	287.76	51,328	12,798	309.30	39,232	24,894	349.81	27,966	36,160
40,000	314.69	73,288	328.86	58,658	14,630	353.49	44,838	28,450	399.78	31,960	41,328
45,000	354.02	82,447	369.97	65,991	16,456	397.67	50,441	32,006	449.76	35,957	46,490
50,000	393.36	91,610	411.08	73,324	18,286	441.86	56,046	35,564	499.73	39,951	51,659
55,000	432.69	100,768	452.18	80,654	20,114	486.05	61,652	39,116	549.70	43,946	56,822
60,000	472.03	109,931	493.29	87,987	21,944	530.23	67,255	42,676	599.67	47,941	61,990
65,000	511.36	119,090	534.40	95,320	23,770	574.42	72,861	46,229	649.65	51,937	67,153
70,000	550.70	128,252	575.51	102,653	25,599	618.60	78,464	49,788	699.62	55,932	72,320
75,000	590.03	137,411	616.61	109,983	27,428	662.79	84,070	53,341	749.59	59,926	77,485
80,000	629.37	146,573	657.72	117,316	29,257	706.97	89,673	56,900	799.56	63,921	82,652
85,000	668.70	155,732	698.83	124,649	31,083	751.16	95,278	60,454	849.54	67,917	87,815
90,000	708.04	164,894	739.93	131,979	32,915	795.34	100,882	64,012	899.51	71,912	92,982
95,000	747.37	174,053	781.04	139,312	34,741	839.53	106,487	67,566	949.48	75,906	98,147
100,000	786.71	183,216	822.15	146,645	36,571	883.72	112,093	71,123	999.45	79,901	103,315
105,000	826.04	192,374	863.26	153,978	38,396	927.90	117,696	74,678	1,049.43	83,897	108,477
110,000	865.38	201,537	904.36	161,308	40,229	972.09	123,302	78,235	1,099.40	87,892	113,645
115,000	904.71	210,696	945.47	168,641	42,055	1,016.27	128,905	81,791	1,149.37	91,887	118,809
120,000	944.05	219,858	986.58	175,974	43,884	1,060.46	134,510	85,348	1,199.34	95,881	123,977
125,000	983.38	229,017	1,027.68	183,304	45,713	1,104.64	140,114	88,903	1,249.32	99,878	129,139
130,000	1,022.72	238,179	1,068.79	190,637	47,542	1,148.83	145,719	92,460	1,299.29	103,872	134,307
135,000	1,062.05	247,338	1,109.90	197,970	49,368	1,193.01	151,322	96,016	1,349.26	107,867	139,471
140,000	1,101.39	256,500	1,151.01	205,303	51,197	1,237.20	156,928	99,572	1,399.23	111,861	144,639
145,000	1,140.72	265,659	1,192.11	212,633	53,026	1,281.39	162,534	103,125	1,449.21	115,858	149,801
150,000	1,180.06	274,822	1,233.22	219,966	54,856	1,325.57	168,137	106,685	1,499.18	119,852	154,970
155,000	1,219.39	283,980	1,274.33	227,299	56,681	1,369.76	173,742	110,238	1,549.15	123,847	160,133
160,000	1,258.73	293,143	1,315.43	234,629	58,514	1,413.94	179,345	113,797	1,599.12	127,842	165,301
165,000	1,298.06	302,302	1,356.54	241,962	60,340	1,458.13	184,951	117,351	1,649.10	131,838	170,464
170,000	1,337.40	311,464	1,397.65	249,295	62,169	1,502.31	190,554	120,910	1,699.07	135,833	175,631
175,000	1,376.73	320,623	1,438.76	256,628	63,995	1,546.50	196,160	124,463	1,749.04	139,827	180,796
180,000	1,416.07	329,785	1,479.86	263,958	65,827	1,590.68	201,763	128,022	1,799.01	143,822	185,963
185,000	1,455.40	338,944	1,520.97	271,291	67,653	1,634.87	207,369	131,575	1,848.99	147,818	191,126
190,000	1,494.74	348,106	1,562.08	278,624	69,482	1,679.06	212,974	135,132	1,898.96	151,813	196,293
195,000	1,534.07	357,265	1,603.19	285,957	71,308	1,723.24	218,578	138,687	1,948.93	155,807	201,458
200,000	1,573.41	366,428	1,644.29	293,287	73,141	1,767.43	224,183	142,245	1,998.90	159,802	206,626

11

SHORT-TERM AMORTIZING MORTGAGES

AMOUNT OF LOAN	30 YEARS		25 YEARS			20 YEARS			15 YEARS		
	MONTHLY PAYMENT	TOTAL INTRST	MONTHLY PAYMENT	TOTAL INTRST	INTRST SAVED	MONTHLY PAYMENT	TOTAL INTRST	INTRST SAVED	MONTHLY PAYMENT	TOTAL INTRST	INTRST SAVED
$ 50	0.41	98	0.42	76	22	0.45	58	40	0.51	42	56
100	0.81	192	0.84	152	40	0.90	116	76	1.02	84	108
200	1.61	380	1.68	304	76	1.80	232	148	2.03	165	215
300	2.42	571	2.52	456	115	2.70	348	223	3.05	249	322
400	3.22	759	3.36	608	151	3.60	464	295	4.06	331	428
500	4.03	951	4.20	760	191	4.50	580	371	5.08	414	537
600	4.83	1,139	5.04	912	227	5.40	696	443	6.09	496	643
700	5.64	1,330	5.88	1,064	266	6.30	812	518	7.10	578	752
800	6.44	1,518	6.72	1,216	302	7.20	928	590	8.12	662	856
900	7.25	1,710	7.56	1,368	342	8.10	1,044	666	9.13	743	967
1,000	8.05	1,898	8.40	1,520	378	9.00	1,160	738	10.15	827	1,071
2,000	16.10	3,796	16.79	3,037	759	18.00	2,320	1,476	20.29	1,652	2,144
3,000	24.14	5,690	25.18	4,554	1,136	27.00	3,480	2,210	30.43	2,477	3,213
4,000	32.19	7,588	33.57	6,071	1,517	35.99	4,638	2,950	40.58	3,304	4,284
5,000	40.24	9,486	41.96	7,588	1,898	44.99	5,798	3,688	50.72	4,130	5,356
6,000	48.28	11,381	50.36	9,108	2,273	53.99	6,958	4,423	60.86	4,955	6,426
7,000	56.33	13,279	58.75	10,625	2,654	62.99	8,118	5,161	71.00	5,780	7,499
8,000	64.37	15,173	67.14	12,142	3,031	71.98	9,275	5,898	81.15	6,607	8,566
9,000	72.42	17,071	75.53	13,659	3,412	80.98	10,435	6,636	91.29	7,432	9,639
10,000	80.47	18,969	83.92	15,176	3,793	89.98	11,595	7,374	101.43	8,257	10,712
11,000	88.51	20,864	92.32	16,696	4,168	98.97	12,753	8,111	111.57	9,083	11,781
12,000	96.56	22,762	100.71	18,213	4,549	107.97	13,913	8,849	121.72	9,910	12,852
13,000	104.61	24,660	109.10	19,730	4,930	116.97	15,073	9,587	131.86	10,735	13,925
14,000	112.65	26,554	117.49	21,247	5,307	125.97	16,233	10,321	142.00	11,560	14,994
15,000	120.70	28,452	125.88	22,764	5,688	134.96	17,390	11,062	152.14	12,385	16,067
16,000	128.74	30,346	134.28	24,284	6,062	143.96	18,550	11,796	162.29	13,212	17,134
17,000	136.79	32,244	142.67	25,801	6,443	152.96	19,710	12,534	172.43	14,037	18,207
18,000	144.84	34,142	151.06	27,318	6,824	161.96	20,870	13,272	182.57	14,863	19,279
19,000	152.88	36,037	159.45	28,835	7,202	170.95	22,028	14,009	192.72	15,690	20,347
20,000	160.93	37,935	167.84	30,352	7,583	179.95	23,188	14,747	202.86	16,515	21,420
21,000	168.98	39,833	176.24	31,872	7,961	188.95	24,348	15,485	213.00	17,340	22,493
22,000	177.02	41,727	184.63	33,389	8,338	197.94	25,506	16,221	223.14	18,165	23,562
23,000	185.07	43,625	193.02	34,906	8,719	206.94	26,666	16,959	233.29	18,992	24,633
24,000	193.11	45,520	201.41	36,423	9,097	215.94	27,826	17,694	243.43	19,817	25,703
25,000	201.16	47,418	209.80	37,940	9,478	224.94	28,986	18,432	253.57	20,643	26,775
26,000	209.21	49,316	218.20	39,460	9,856	233.93	30,143	19,173	263.71	21,468	27,848
27,000	217.25	51,210	226.59	40,977	10,233	242.93	31,303	19,907	273.86	22,295	28,915
28,000	225.30	53,108	234.98	42,494	10,614	251.93	32,463	20,645	284.00	23,120	29,988
29,000	233.35	55,006	243.37	44,011	10,995	260.93	33,623	21,383	294.14	23,945	31,061
30,000	241.39	56,900	251.76	45,528	11,372	269.92	34,781	22,119	304.28	24,770	32,130
32,500	261.51	61,644	272.74	49,322	12,322	292.42	37,681	23,963	329.64	26,835	34,809
35,000	281.62	66,383	293.72	53,116	13,267	314.91	40,578	25,805	355.00	28,900	37,483
40,000	321.85	75,866	335.68	60,704	15,162	359.90	46,376	29,490	405.71	33,028	42,838
45,000	362.09	85,352	377.64	68,292	17,060	404.88	52,171	33,181	456.42	37,156	48,196
50,000	402.32	94,835	419.60	75,880	18,955	449.87	57,969	36,866	507.14	41,285	53,550
55,000	442.55	104,318	461.56	83,468	20,850	494.85	63,764	40,554	557.85	45,413	58,905
60,000	482.78	113,801	503.52	91,056	22,745	539.84	69,562	44,239	608.56	49,541	64,260
65,000	523.01	123,284	545.48	98,644	24,640	584.83	75,359	47,925	659.28	53,670	69,614
70,000	563.24	132,766	587.44	106,232	26,534	629.81	81,154	51,612	709.99	57,798	74,968
75,000	603.47	142,249	629.40	113,820	28,429	674.80	86,952	55,297	760.70	61,926	80,323
80,000	643.70	151,732	671.36	121,408	30,324	719.79	92,750	58,982	811.42	66,056	85,676
85,000	683.93	161,215	713.32	128,996	32,219	764.77	98,545	62,670	862.13	70,183	91,032
90,000	724.17	170,701	755.28	136,584	34,117	809.76	104,342	66,359	912.84	74,311	96,390
95,000	764.40	180,184	797.24	144,172	36,012	854.74	110,138	70,046	963.56	78,441	101,743
100,000	804.63	189,667	839.20	151,760	37,907	899.73	115,935	73,732	1,014.27	82,569	107,098
105,000	844.86	199,150	881.16	159,348	39,802	944.72	121,733	77,417	1,064.98	86,696	112,454
110,000	885.09	208,632	923.12	166,936	41,696	989.70	127,528	81,104	1,115.70	90,826	117,806
115,000	925.32	218,115	965.08	174,524	43,591	1,034.69	133,326	84,789	1,166.41	94,954	123,161
120,000	965.55	227,598	1,007.04	182,112	45,486	1,079.68	139,123	88,475	1,217.12	99,082	128,516
125,000	1,005.78	237,081	1,049.00	189,700	47,381	1,124.66	144,918	92,163	1,267.84	103,211	133,870
130,000	1,046.01	246,564	1,090.96	197,288	49,276	1,169.65	150,716	95,848	1,318.55	107,339	139,225
135,000	1,086.25	256,050	1,132.92	204,876	51,174	1,214.64	156,514	99,536	1,369.26	111,467	144,583
140,000	1,126.48	265,533	1,174.88	212,464	53,069	1,259.62	162,309	103,224	1,419.98	115,596	149,937
145,000	1,166.71	275,016	1,216.84	220,052	54,964	1,304.61	168,106	106,910	1,470.69	119,724	155,292
150,000	1,206.94	284,498	1,258.80	227,640	56,858	1,349.59	173,902	110,596	1,521.40	123,852	160,646
155,000	1,247.17	293,981	1,300.76	235,228	58,753	1,394.58	179,699	114,282	1,572.12	127,982	165,999
160,000	1,287.40	303,464	1,342.72	242,816	60,648	1,439.57	185,497	117,967	1,622.83	132,109	171,355
165,000	1,327.63	312,947	1,384.68	250,404	62,543	1,484.55	191,292	121,655	1,673.54	136,237	176,710
170,000	1,367.86	322,430	1,426.64	257,992	64,438	1,529.54	197,090	125,340	1,724.26	140,367	182,063
175,000	1,408.09	331,912	1,468.60	265,580	66,332	1,574.53	202,887	129,025	1,774.97	144,495	187,417
180,000	1,448.33	341,399	1,510.56	273,168	68,231	1,619.51	208,682	132,717	1,825.68	148,622	192,777
185,000	1,488.56	350,882	1,552.52	280,756	70,126	1,664.50	214,480	136,402	1,876.40	152,752	198,130
190,000	1,528.79	360,364	1,594.48	288,344	72,020	1,709.48	220,275	140,089	1,927.11	156,880	203,484
195,000	1,569.02	369,847	1,636.44	295,932	73,915	1,754.47	226,073	143,774	1,977.82	161,008	208,839
200,000	1,609.25	379,330	1,678.40	303,520	75,810	1,799.46	231,870	147,460	2,028.54	165,137	214,193

SHORT-TERM AMORTIZING MORTGAGES 9.25%

AMOUNT OF LOAN	30 YEARS		25 YEARS			20 YEARS			15 YEARS		
	MONTHLY PAYMENT	TOTAL INTRST	MONTHLY PAYMENT	TOTAL INTRST	INTRST SAVED	MONTHLY PAYMENT	TOTAL INTRST	INTRST SAVED	MONTHLY PAYMENT	TOTAL INTRST	INTRST SAVED
$ 50	0.42	101	0.43	79	22	0.46	60	41	0.52	44	57
100	0.83	199	0.86	158	41	0.92	121	78	1.03	85	114
200	1.65	394	1.72	316	78	1.84	242	152	2.06	171	223
300	2.47	589	2.57	471	118	2.75	360	229	3.09	256	333
400	3.30	788	3.43	629	159	3.67	481	307	4.12	342	446
500	4.12	983	4.29	787	196	4.58	599	384	5.15	427	556
600	4.94	1,178	5.14	942	236	5.50	720	458	6.18	512	666
700	5.76	1,374	6.00	1,100	274	6.42	841	533	7.21	598	776
800	6.59	1,572	6.86	1,258	314	7.33	959	613	8.24	683	889
900	7.41	1,768	7.71	1,413	355	8.25	1,080	688	9.27	769	999
1,000	8.23	1,963	8.57	1,571	392	9.16	1,198	765	10.30	854	1,109
2,000	16.46	3,926	17.13	3,139	787	18.32	2,397	1,529	20.59	1,706	2,220
3,000	24.69	5,888	25.70	4,710	1,178	27.48	3,595	2,293	30.88	2,558	3,330
4,000	32.91	7,848	34.26	6,278	1,570	36.64	4,794	3,054	41.17	3,411	4,437
5,000	41.14	9,810	42.82	7,846	1,964	45.80	5,992	3,818	51.46	4,263	5,547
6,000	49.37	11,773	51.39	9,417	2,356	54.96	7,190	4,583	61.76	5,117	6,656
7,000	57.59	13,732	59.95	10,985	2,747	64.12	8,389	5,343	72.05	5,969	7,763
8,000	65.82	15,695	68.52	12,556	3,139	73.27	9,585	6,110	82.34	6,821	8,874
9,000	74.05	17,658	77.08	14,124	3,534	82.43	10,783	6,875	92.63	7,673	9,985
10,000	82.27	19,617	85.64	15,692	3,925	91.59	11,982	7,635	102.92	8,526	11,091
11,000	90.50	21,580	94.21	17,263	4,317	100.75	13,180	8,400	113.22	9,380	12,200
12,000	98.73	23,543	102.77	18,831	4,712	109.91	14,378	9,165	123.51	10,232	13,311
13,000	106.95	25,502	111.33	20,399	5,103	119.07	15,577	9,925	133.80	11,084	14,418
14,000	115.18	27,465	119.90	21,970	5,495	128.23	16,775	10,690	144.09	11,936	15,529
15,000	123.41	29,428	128.46	23,538	5,890	137.39	17,974	11,454	154.38	12,788	16,640
16,000	131.63	31,387	137.03	25,109	6,278	146.54	19,170	12,217	164.68	13,642	17,745
17,000	139.86	33,350	145.59	26,677	6,673	155.70	20,368	12,982	174.97	14,495	18,855
18,000	148.09	35,312	154.15	28,245	7,067	164.86	21,566	13,746	185.26	15,347	19,965
19,000	156.31	37,272	162.72	29,816	7,456	174.02	22,765	14,507	195.55	16,199	21,073
20,000	164.54	39,234	171.28	31,384	7,850	183.18	23,963	15,271	205.84	17,051	22,183
21,000	172.77	41,197	179.85	32,955	8,242	192.34	25,162	16,035	216.14	17,905	23,292
22,000	180.99	43,156	188.41	34,523	8,633	201.50	26,360	16,796	226.43	18,757	24,399
23,000	189.22	45,119	196.97	36,091	9,028	210.65	27,556	17,563	236.72	19,610	25,509
24,000	197.45	47,082	205.54	37,662	9,420	219.81	28,754	18,328	247.01	20,462	26,620
25,000	205.67	49,041	214.10	39,230	9,811	228.97	29,953	19,088	257.30	21,314	27,727
26,000	213.90	51,004	222.66	40,798	10,206	238.13	31,151	19,853	267.59	22,166	28,838
27,000	222.13	52,967	231.23	42,369	10,598	247.29	32,350	20,617	277.89	23,020	29,947
28,000	230.35	54,926	239.79	43,937	10,989	256.45	33,548	21,378	288.18	23,872	31,054
29,000	238.58	56,889	248.36	45,508	11,381	265.61	34,746	22,143	298.47	24,725	32,164
30,000	246.81	58,852	256.92	47,076	11,776	274.77	35,945	22,907	308.76	25,577	33,275
32,500	267.37	63,753	278.33	50,999	12,754	297.66	38,938	24,815	334.49	27,708	36,045
35,000	287.94	68,658	299.74	54,922	13,736	320.56	41,934	26,724	360.22	29,840	38,818
40,000	329.08	78,469	342.56	62,768	15,701	366.35	47,924	30,545	411.68	34,102	44,367
45,000	370.21	88,276	385.38	70,614	17,662	412.15	53,916	34,360	463.14	38,365	49,911
50,000	411.34	98,082	428.20	78,460	19,622	457.94	59,906	38,176	514.60	42,628	55,454
55,000	452.48	107,893	471.02	86,306	21,587	503.73	65,895	41,998	566.06	46,891	61,002
60,000	493.61	117,700	513.83	94,149	23,551	549.53	71,887	45,813	617.52	51,154	66,546
65,000	534.74	127,506	556.65	101,995	25,511	595.32	77,877	49,629	668.98	55,416	72,090
70,000	575.88	137,317	599.47	109,841	27,476	641.11	83,866	53,451	720.44	59,679	77,638
75,000	617.01	147,124	642.29	117,687	29,437	686.91	89,858	57,266	771.90	63,942	83,182
80,000	658.15	156,934	685.11	125,533	31,401	732.70	95,848	61,086	823.36	68,205	88,729
85,000	699.28	166,741	727.93	133,379	33,362	778.49	101,838	64,903	874.82	72,468	94,273
90,000	740.41	176,548	770.75	141,225	35,323	824.29	107,830	68,718	926.28	76,730	99,818
95,000	781.55	186,358	813.57	149,071	37,287	870.08	113,819	72,539	977.74	80,993	105,365
100,000	822.68	196,165	856.39	156,917	39,248	915.87	119,809	76,356	1,029.20	85,256	110,909
105,000	863.81	205,972	899.21	164,763	41,209	961.67	125,801	80,171	1,080.66	89,519	116,453
110,000	904.95	215,782	942.03	172,609	43,173	1,007.46	131,790	83,992	1,132.12	93,782	122,000
115,000	946.08	225,589	984.84	180,452	45,137	1,053.25	137,780	87,809	1,183.58	98,044	127,545
120,000	987.22	235,399	1,027.66	188,298	47,101	1,099.05	143,772	91,627	1,235.04	102,307	133,092
125,000	1,028.35	245,206	1,070.48	196,144	49,062	1,144.84	149,762	95,444	1,286.50	106,570	138,636
130,000	1,069.48	255,013	1,113.30	203,990	51,023	1,190.63	155,751	99,262	1,337.95	110,831	144,182
135,000	1,110.62	264,823	1,156.12	211,836	52,987	1,236.43	161,743	103,080	1,389.41	115,094	149,729
140,000	1,151.75	274,630	1,198.94	219,682	54,948	1,282.22	167,733	106,897	1,440.87	119,357	155,273
145,000	1,192.88	284,437	1,241.76	227,528	56,909	1,328.01	173,722	110,715	1,492.33	123,619	160,818
150,000	1,234.02	294,247	1,284.58	235,374	58,873	1,373.81	179,714	114,533	1,543.79	127,882	166,365
155,000	1,275.15	304,054	1,327.40	243,220	60,834	1,419.60	185,704	118,350	1,595.25	132,145	171,909
160,000	1,316.29	313,864	1,370.22	251,066	62,798	1,465.39	191,694	122,170	1,646.71	136,408	177,456
165,000	1,357.42	323,671	1,413.04	258,912	64,759	1,511.19	197,686	125,985	1,698.17	140,671	183,000
170,000	1,398.55	333,478	1,455.85	266,755	66,723	1,556.98	203,675	129,803	1,749.63	144,933	188,545
175,000	1,439.69	343,288	1,498.67	274,601	68,687	1,602.77	209,665	133,623	1,801.09	149,196	194,092
180,000	1,480.82	353,095	1,541.49	282,447	70,648	1,648.57	215,657	137,438	1,852.55	153,459	199,636
185,000	1,521.95	362,902	1,584.31	290,293	72,609	1,694.36	221,646	141,256	1,904.01	157,722	205,180
190,000	1,563.09	372,712	1,627.13	298,139	74,573	1,740.15	227,636	145,076	1,955.47	161,985	210,727
195,000	1,604.22	382,519	1,669.95	305,985	76,534	1,785.95	233,628	148,891	2,006.93	166,247	216,272
200,000	1,645.36	392,330	1,712.77	313,831	78,499	1,831.74	239,618	152,712	2,058.39	170,510	221,820

13

SHORT-TERM AMORTIZING MORTGAGES

AMOUNT OF LOAN	30 YEARS MONTHLY PAYMENT	30 YEARS TOTAL INTRST	25 YEARS MONTHLY PAYMENT	25 YEARS TOTAL INTRST	25 YEARS INTRST SAVED	20 YEARS MONTHLY PAYMENT	20 YEARS TOTAL INTRST	20 YEARS INTRST SAVED	15 YEARS MONTHLY PAYMENT	15 YEARS TOTAL INTRST	15 YEARS INTRST SAVED
$ 50	0.43	105	0.44	82	23	0.47	63	42	0.53	45	60
100	0.85	206	0.88	164	42	0.94	126	80	1.05	89	117
200	1.69	408	1.75	325	83	1.87	249	159	2.09	176	232
300	2.53	611	2.63	489	122	2.80	372	239	3.14	265	346
400	3.37	813	3.50	650	163	3.73	495	318	4.18	352	461
500	4.21	1,016	4.37	811	205	4.67	621	395	5.23	441	575
600	5.05	1,218	5.25	975	243	5.60	744	474	6.27	529	689
700	5.89	1,420	6.12	1,136	284	6.53	867	553	7.31	616	804
800	6.73	1,623	6.99	1,297	326	7.46	990	633	8.36	705	918
900	7.57	1,825	7.87	1,461	364	8.39	1,114	711	9.40	792	1,033
1,000	8.41	2,028	8.74	1,622	406	9.33	1,239	789	10.45	881	1,147
2,000	16.82	4,055	17.48	3,244	811	18.65	2,476	1,579	20.89	1,760	2,295
3,000	25.23	6,083	26.22	4,866	1,217	27.97	3,713	2,370	31.33	2,639	3,444
4,000	33.64	8,110	34.95	6,485	1,625	37.29	4,950	3,160	41.77	3,519	4,591
5,000	42.05	10,138	43.69	8,107	2,031	46.61	6,186	3,952	52.22	4,400	5,738
6,000	50.46	12,166	52.43	9,729	2,437	55.93	7,423	4,743	62.66	5,279	6,887
7,000	58.86	14,190	61.16	11,348	2,842	65.25	8,660	5,530	73.10	6,158	8,032
8,000	67.27	16,217	69.90	12,970	3,247	74.58	9,899	6,318	83.54	7,037	9,180
9,000	75.68	18,245	78.64	14,592	3,653	83.90	11,136	7,109	93.99	7,918	10,327
10,000	84.09	20,272	87.37	16,211	4,061	93.22	12,373	7,899	104.43	8,797	11,475
11,000	92.50	22,300	96.11	17,833	4,467	102.54	13,610	8,690	114.87	9,677	12,623
12,000	100.91	24,328	104.85	19,455	4,873	111.86	14,846	9,482	125.31	10,556	13,772
13,000	109.32	26,355	113.59	21,077	5,278	121.18	16,083	10,272	135.75	11,435	14,920
14,000	117.72	28,379	122.32	22,696	5,683	130.50	17,320	11,059	146.20	12,316	16,063
15,000	126.13	30,407	131.06	24,318	6,089	139.82	18,557	11,850	156.64	13,195	17,212
16,000	134.54	32,434	139.80	25,940	6,494	149.15	19,796	12,638	167.08	14,074	18,360
17,000	142.95	34,462	148.53	27,559	6,903	158.47	21,033	13,429	177.52	14,954	19,508
18,000	151.36	36,490	157.27	29,181	7,309	167.79	22,270	14,220	187.97	15,835	20,655
19,000	159.77	38,517	166.01	30,803	7,714	177.11	23,506	15,011	198.41	16,714	21,803
20,000	168.18	40,545	174.74	32,422	8,123	186.43	24,743	15,802	208.85	17,593	22,952
21,000	176.58	42,569	183.48	34,044	8,525	195.75	25,980	16,589	219.29	18,472	24,097
22,000	184.99	44,596	192.22	35,666	8,930	205.07	27,217	17,379	229.73	19,351	25,245
23,000	193.40	46,624	200.96	37,288	9,336	214.40	28,456	18,168	240.18	20,232	26,392
24,000	201.81	48,652	209.69	38,907	9,745	223.72	29,693	18,959	250.62	21,112	27,540
25,000	210.22	50,679	218.43	40,529	10,150	233.04	30,930	19,749	261.06	21,991	28,688
26,000	218.63	52,707	227.17	42,151	10,556	242.36	32,166	20,541	271.50	22,870	29,837
27,000	227.04	54,734	235.90	43,770	10,964	251.68	33,403	21,331	281.95	23,751	30,983
28,000	235.44	56,758	244.64	45,392	11,366	261.00	34,640	22,118	292.39	24,630	32,128
29,000	243.85	58,786	253.38	47,014	11,772	270.32	35,877	22,909	302.83	25,509	33,277
30,000	252.26	60,814	262.11	48,633	12,181	279.64	37,114	23,700	313.27	26,389	34,425
32,500	273.28	65,881	283.96	52,688	13,193	302.95	40,208	25,673	339.38	28,588	37,293
35,000	294.30	70,948	305.80	56,740	14,208	326.25	43,300	27,648	365.48	30,786	40,162
40,000	336.35	81,086	349.48	64,844	16,242	372.86	49,486	31,600	417.69	35,184	45,902
45,000	378.39	91,220	393.17	72,951	18,269	419.46	55,670	35,550	469.91	39,584	51,636
50,000	420.43	101,355	436.85	81,055	20,300	466.07	61,857	39,498	522.12	43,982	57,373
55,000	462.47	111,489	480.54	89,162	22,327	512.68	68,043	43,446	574.33	48,379	63,110
60,000	504.52	121,627	524.22	97,266	24,361	559.28	74,227	47,400	626.54	52,777	68,850
65,000	546.56	131,762	567.91	105,373	26,389	605.89	80,414	51,348	678.75	57,175	74,587
70,000	588.60	141,896	611.59	113,477	28,419	652.50	86,600	55,296	730.96	61,573	80,323
75,000	630.65	152,034	655.28	121,584	30,450	699.10	92,784	59,250	783.17	65,971	86,063
80,000	672.69	162,168	698.96	129,688	32,480	745.71	98,970	63,198	835.38	70,368	91,800
85,000	714.73	172,303	742.65	137,795	34,508	792.32	105,157	67,146	887.60	74,768	97,535
90,000	756.77	182,437	786.33	145,899	36,538	838.92	111,341	71,096	939.81	79,166	103,271
95,000	798.82	192,575	830.02	154,006	38,569	885.53	117,527	75,048	992.02	83,564	109,011
100,000	840.86	202,710	873.70	162,110	40,600	932.14	123,714	78,996	1,044.23	87,961	114,749
105,000	882.90	212,844	917.39	170,217	42,627	978.74	129,898	82,946	1,096.44	92,359	120,485
110,000	924.94	222,978	961.07	178,321	44,657	1,025.35	136,084	86,894	1,148.65	96,757	126,221
115,000	966.99	233,116	1,004.76	186,428	46,688	1,071.96	142,270	90,846	1,200.86	101,155	131,961
120,000	1,009.03	243,251	1,048.44	194,532	48,719	1,118.56	148,454	94,797	1,253.07	105,553	137,698
125,000	1,051.07	253,385	1,092.13	202,639	50,746	1,165.17	154,641	98,744	1,305.29	109,952	143,433
130,000	1,093.12	263,523	1,135.81	210,743	52,780	1,211.78	160,827	102,696	1,357.50	114,350	149,173
135,000	1,135.16	273,658	1,179.50	218,850	54,808	1,258.38	167,011	106,647	1,409.71	118,748	154,910
140,000	1,177.20	283,792	1,223.18	226,954	56,838	1,304.99	173,198	110,594	1,461.92	123,146	160,646
145,000	1,219.24	293,926	1,266.87	235,061	58,865	1,351.60	179,384	114,542	1,514.13	127,543	166,383
150,000	1,261.29	304,064	1,310.55	243,165	60,899	1,398.20	185,568	118,496	1,566.34	131,941	172,123
155,000	1,303.33	314,199	1,354.23	251,269	62,930	1,444.81	191,754	122,445	1,618.55	136,339	177,860
160,000	1,345.37	324,333	1,397.92	259,376	64,957	1,491.41	197,938	126,395	1,670.76	140,737	183,596
165,000	1,387.41	334,468	1,441.60	267,480	66,988	1,538.02	204,125	130,343	1,722.98	145,136	189,332
170,000	1,429.46	344,606	1,485.29	275,587	69,019	1,584.63	210,311	134,295	1,775.19	149,534	195,072
175,000	1,471.50	354,740	1,528.97	283,691	71,049	1,631.23	216,495	138,245	1,827.40	153,932	200,808
180,000	1,513.54	364,874	1,572.66	291,798	73,076	1,677.84	222,682	142,192	1,879.61	158,330	206,544
185,000	1,555.59	375,012	1,616.34	299,902	75,110	1,724.45	228,868	146,144	1,931.82	162,728	212,284
190,000	1,597.63	385,147	1,660.03	308,009	77,138	1,771.05	235,052	150,095	1,984.03	167,125	218,022
195,000	1,639.67	395,281	1,703.71	316,113	79,168	1,817.66	241,238	154,043	2,036.24	171,523	223,758
200,000	1,681.71	405,416	1,747.40	324,220	81,196	1,864.27	247,425	157,991	2,088.45	175,921	229,495

SHORT-TERM AMORTIZING MORTGAGES 9.75%

AMOUNT OF LOAN	30 YEARS		25 YEARS			20 YEARS			15 YEARS		
	MONTHLY PAYMENT	TOTAL INTRST	MONTHLY PAYMENT	TOTAL INTRST	INTRST SAVED	MONTHLY PAYMENT	TOTAL INTRST	INTRST SAVED	MONTHLY PAYMENT	TOTAL INTRST	INTRST SAVED
$ 50	0.43	105	0.45	85	20	0.48	65	40	0.53	45	60
100	0.86	210	0.90	170	40	0.95	128	82	1.06	91	119
200	1.72	419	1.79	337	82	1.90	256	163	2.12	182	237
300	2.58	629	2.68	504	125	2.85	384	245	3.18	272	357
400	3.44	838	3.57	671	167	3.80	512	326	4.24	363	475
500	4.30	1,048	4.46	838	210	4.75	640	408	5.30	454	594
600	5.16	1,258	5.35	1,005	253	5.70	768	490	6.36	545	713
700	6.02	1,467	6.24	1,172	295	6.64	894	573	7.42	636	831
800	6.88	1,677	7.13	1,339	338	7.59	1,022	655	8.48	726	951
900	7.74	1,886	8.03	1,509	377	8.54	1,150	736	9.54	817	1,069
1,000	8.60	2,096	8.92	1,676	420	9.49	1,278	818	10.60	908	1,188
2,000	17.19	4,188	17.83	3,349	839	18.98	2,555	1,633	21.19	1,814	2,374
3,000	25.78	6,281	26.74	5,022	1,259	28.46	3,830	2,451	31.79	2,722	3,559
4,000	34.37	8,373	35.65	6,695	1,678	37.95	5,108	3,265	42.38	3,628	4,745
5,000	42.96	10,466	44.56	8,368	2,098	47.43	6,383	4,083	52.97	4,535	5,931
6,000	51.55	12,558	53.47	10,041	2,517	56.92	7,661	4,897	63.57	5,443	7,115
7,000	60.15	14,654	62.38	11,714	2,940	66.40	8,936	5,718	74.16	6,349	8,305
8,000	68.74	16,746	71.30	13,390	3,356	75.89	10,214	6,532	84.75	7,255	9,491
9,000	77.33	18,839	80.21	15,063	3,776	85.37	11,489	7,350	95.35	8,163	10,676
10,000	85.92	20,931	89.12	16,736	4,195	94.86	12,766	8,165	105.94	9,069	11,862
11,000	94.51	23,024	98.03	18,409	4,615	104.34	14,042	8,982	116.53	9,975	13,049
12,000	103.10	25,116	106.94	20,082	5,034	113.83	15,319	9,797	127.13	10,883	14,233
13,000	111.70	27,212	115.85	21,755	5,457	123.31	16,594	10,618	137.72	11,790	15,422
14,000	120.29	29,304	124.76	23,428	5,876	132.80	17,872	11,432	148.32	12,698	16,606
15,000	128.88	31,397	133.68	25,104	6,293	142.28	19,147	12,250	158.91	13,604	17,793
16,000	137.47	33,489	142.59	26,777	6,712	151.77	20,425	13,064	169.50	14,510	18,979
17,000	146.06	35,582	151.50	28,450	7,132	161.25	21,700	13,882	180.10	15,418	20,164
18,000	154.65	37,674	160.41	30,123	7,551	170.74	22,978	14,696	190.69	16,324	21,350
19,000	163.24	39,766	169.32	31,796	7,970	180.22	24,253	15,513	201.28	17,230	22,536
20,000	171.84	41,862	178.23	33,469	8,393	189.71	25,530	16,332	211.88	18,138	23,724
21,000	180.43	43,955	187.14	35,142	8,813	199.19	26,806	17,149	222.47	19,045	24,910
22,000	189.02	46,047	196.06	36,818	9,229	208.68	28,083	17,964	233.06	19,951	26,096
23,000	197.61	48,140	204.97	38,491	9,649	218.16	29,358	18,782	243.66	20,859	27,281
24,000	206.20	50,232	213.88	40,164	10,068	227.65	30,636	19,596	254.25	21,765	28,467
25,000	214.79	52,324	222.79	41,837	10,487	237.13	31,911	20,413	264.85	22,673	29,651
26,000	223.39	54,420	231.70	43,510	10,910	246.62	33,189	21,231	275.44	23,579	30,841
27,000	231.98	56,513	240.61	45,183	11,330	256.10	34,464	22,049	286.03	24,485	32,028
28,000	240.57	58,605	249.52	46,856	11,749	265.59	35,742	22,863	296.63	25,393	33,212
29,000	249.16	60,698	258.43	48,529	12,169	275.07	37,017	23,681	307.22	26,300	34,398
30,000	257.75	62,790	267.35	50,205	12,585	284.56	38,294	24,496	317.81	27,206	35,584
32,500	279.23	68,023	289.62	54,386	13,637	308.27	41,485	26,538	344.30	29,474	38,549
35,000	300.71	73,256	311.90	58,570	14,686	331.99	44,678	28,578	370.78	31,740	41,516
40,000	343.67	83,721	356.46	66,938	16,783	379.41	51,058	32,663	423.75	36,275	47,446
45,000	386.62	94,183	401.02	75,306	18,877	426.84	57,442	36,741	476.72	40,810	53,373
50,000	429.58	104,649	445.57	83,671	20,978	474.26	63,822	40,827	529.69	45,344	59,305
55,000	472.54	115,114	490.13	92,039	23,075	521.69	70,206	44,908	582.65	49,877	65,237
60,000	515.50	125,580	534.69	100,407	25,173	569.12	76,589	48,991	635.62	54,412	71,168
65,000	558.46	136,046	579.24	108,772	27,274	616.54	82,970	53,076	688.59	58,946	77,100
70,000	601.41	146,508	623.80	117,140	29,368	663.97	89,353	57,155	741.56	63,481	83,027
75,000	644.37	156,973	668.36	125,508	31,465	711.39	95,734	61,239	794.53	68,015	88,958
80,000	687.33	167,439	712.91	133,873	33,566	758.82	102,117	65,322	847.50	72,550	94,889
85,000	730.29	177,904	757.47	142,241	35,663	806.24	108,498	69,406	900.46	77,083	100,821
90,000	773.24	188,366	802.03	150,609	37,757	853.67	114,881	73,485	953.43	81,617	106,749
95,000	816.20	198,832	846.59	158,977	39,855	901.10	121,264	77,568	1,006.40	86,152	112,680
100,000	859.16	209,298	891.14	167,342	41,956	948.52	127,645	81,653	1,059.37	90,687	118,611
105,000	902.12	219,763	935.70	175,710	44,053	995.95	134,028	85,735	1,112.34	95,221	124,542
110,000	945.07	230,225	980.26	184,078	46,147	1,043.37	140,409	89,816	1,165.30	99,754	130,471
115,000	988.03	240,691	1,024.81	192,443	48,248	1,090.80	146,792	93,899	1,218.27	104,289	136,402
120,000	1,030.99	251,156	1,069.37	200,811	50,345	1,138.23	153,175	97,981	1,271.24	108,823	142,333
125,000	1,073.95	261,622	1,113.93	209,179	52,443	1,185.65	159,556	102,066	1,324.21	113,358	148,264
130,000	1,116.91	272,088	1,158.48	217,544	54,544	1,233.08	165,939	106,149	1,377.18	117,892	154,196
135,000	1,159.86	282,550	1,203.04	225,912	56,638	1,280.50	172,320	110,230	1,430.14	122,425	160,125
140,000	1,202.82	293,015	1,247.60	234,280	58,735	1,327.93	178,703	114,312	1,483.11	126,960	166,055
145,000	1,245.78	303,481	1,292.15	242,645	60,836	1,375.35	185,084	118,397	1,536.08	131,494	171,987
150,000	1,288.74	313,946	1,336.71	251,013	62,933	1,422.78	191,467	122,479	1,589.05	136,029	177,917
155,000	1,331.69	324,408	1,381.27	259,381	65,027	1,470.21	197,850	126,558	1,642.02	140,564	183,844
160,000	1,374.65	334,874	1,425.82	267,746	67,128	1,517.63	204,231	130,643	1,694.99	145,098	189,776
165,000	1,417.61	345,340	1,470.38	276,114	69,226	1,565.06	210,614	134,726	1,747.95	149,631	195,709
170,000	1,460.57	355,805	1,514.94	284,482	71,323	1,612.48	216,995	138,810	1,800.92	154,166	201,639
175,000	1,503.53	366,271	1,559.50	292,850	73,421	1,659.91	223,378	142,893	1,853.89	158,700	207,571
180,000	1,546.48	376,733	1,604.05	301,215	75,518	1,707.34	229,762	146,971	1,906.86	163,235	213,498
185,000	1,589.44	387,198	1,648.61	309,583	77,615	1,754.76	236,142	151,056	1,959.83	167,769	219,429
190,000	1,632.40	397,664	1,693.17	317,951	79,713	1,802.19	242,526	155,138	2,012.79	172,302	225,362
195,000	1,675.36	408,130	1,737.72	326,316	81,814	1,849.61	248,906	159,224	2,065.76	176,837	231,293
200,000	1,718.31	418,592	1,782.28	334,684	83,908	1,897.04	255,290	163,302	2,118.73	181,371	237,221

15

SHORT-TERM AMORTIZING MORTGAGES

AMOUNT OF LOAN	30 YEARS		25 YEARS			20 YEARS			15 YEARS		
	MONTHLY PAYMENT	TOTAL INTRST	MONTHLY PAYMENT	TOTAL INTRST	INTRST SAVED	MONTHLY PAYMENT	TOTAL INTRST	INTRST SAVED	MONTHLY PAYMENT	TOTAL INTRST	INTRST SAVED
$ 50	0.44	108	0.46	88	20	0.49	68	40	0.54	47	61
100	0.88	217	0.91	173	44	0.97	133	84	1.08	94	123
200	1.76	434	1.82	346	88	1.94	266	168	2.15	187	247
300	2.64	650	2.73	519	131	2.90	396	254	3.23	281	369
400	3.52	867	3.64	692	175	3.87	529	338	4.30	374	493
500	4.39	1,080	4.55	865	215	4.83	659	421	5.38	468	612
600	5.27	1,297	5.46	1,038	259	5.80	792	505	6.45	561	736
700	6.15	1,514	6.37	1,211	303	6.76	922	592	7.53	655	859
800	7.03	1,731	7.27	1,381	350	7.73	1,055	676	8.60	748	983
900	7.90	1,944	8.18	1,554	390	8.69	1,186	758	9.68	842	1,102
1,000	8.78	2,161	9.09	1,727	434	9.66	1,318	843	10.75	935	1,226
2,000	17.56	4,322	18.18	3,454	868	19.31	2,634	1,688	21.50	1,870	2,452
3,000	26.33	6,479	27.27	5,181	1,298	28.96	3,950	2,529	32.24	2,803	3,676
4,000	35.11	8,640	36.35	6,905	1,735	38.61	5,266	3,374	42.99	3,738	4,902
5,000	43.88	10,797	45.44	8,632	2,165	48.26	6,582	4,215	53.74	4,673	6,124
6,000	52.66	12,958	54.53	10,359	2,599	57.91	7,898	5,060	64.48	5,606	7,352
7,000	61.44	15,118	63.61	12,083	3,035	67.56	9,214	5,904	75.23	6,541	8,577
8,000	70.21	17,276	72.70	13,810	3,466	77.21	10,530	6,746	85.97	7,475	9,801
9,000	78.99	19,436	81.79	15,537	3,899	86.86	11,846	7,590	96.72	8,410	11,026
10,000	87.76	21,594	90.88	17,264	4,330	96.51	13,162	8,432	107.47	9,345	12,249
11,000	96.54	23,754	99.96	18,988	4,766	106.16	14,478	9,276	118.21	10,278	13,476
12,000	105.31	25,912	109.05	20,715	5,197	115.81	15,794	10,118	128.96	11,213	14,699
13,000	114.09	28,072	118.14	22,442	5,630	125.46	17,110	10,962	139.70	12,146	15,926
14,000	122.87	30,233	127.22	24,166	6,067	135.11	18,426	11,807	150.45	13,081	17,152
15,000	131.64	32,390	136.31	25,893	6,497	144.76	19,742	12,648	161.20	14,016	18,374
16,000	140.42	34,551	145.40	27,620	6,931	154.41	21,058	13,493	171.94	14,949	19,602
17,000	149.19	36,708	154.48	29,344	7,364	164.06	22,374	14,334	182.69	15,884	20,824
18,000	157.97	38,869	163.57	31,071	7,798	173.71	23,690	15,179	193.43	16,817	22,052
19,000	166.74	41,026	172.66	32,798	8,228	183.36	25,006	16,020	204.18	17,752	23,274
20,000	175.52	43,187	181.75	34,525	8,662	193.01	26,322	16,865	214.93	18,687	24,500
21,000	184.30	45,348	190.83	36,249	9,099	202.66	27,638	17,710	225.67	19,621	25,727
22,000	193.07	47,505	199.92	37,976	9,529	212.31	28,954	18,551	236.42	20,556	26,949
23,000	201.85	49,666	209.01	39,703	9,963	221.96	30,270	19,396	247.16	21,489	28,177
24,000	210.62	51,823	218.09	41,427	10,396	231.61	31,586	20,237	257.91	22,424	29,399
25,000	219.40	53,984	227.18	43,154	10,830	241.26	32,902	21,082	268.66	23,359	30,625
26,000	228.17	56,141	236.27	44,881	11,260	250.91	34,218	21,923	279.40	24,292	31,849
27,000	236.95	58,302	245.35	46,605	11,697	260.56	35,534	22,768	290.15	25,227	33,075
28,000	245.73	60,463	254.44	48,332	12,131	270.21	36,850	23,613	300.89	26,160	34,303
29,000	254.50	62,620	263.53	50,059	12,561	279.86	38,166	24,454	311.64	27,095	35,525
30,000	263.28	64,781	272.62	51,786	12,995	289.51	39,482	25,299	322.39	28,030	36,751
32,500	285.22	70,179	295.33	56,099	14,080	313.64	42,774	27,405	349.25	30,365	39,814
35,000	307.16	75,578	318.05	60,415	15,163	337.76	46,062	29,516	376.12	32,702	42,876
40,000	351.03	86,371	363.49	69,047	17,324	386.01	52,642	33,729	429.85	37,373	48,998
45,000	394.91	97,168	408.92	77,676	19,492	434.26	59,222	37,946	483.58	42,044	55,124
50,000	438.79	107,964	454.36	86,308	21,656	482.52	65,805	42,159	537.31	46,716	61,248
55,000	482.67	118,761	499.79	94,937	23,824	530.77	72,385	46,376	591.04	51,387	67,374
60,000	526.55	129,558	545.23	103,569	25,989	579.02	78,965	50,593	644.77	56,059	73,499
65,000	570.43	140,355	590.66	112,198	28,157	627.27	85,545	54,810	698.50	60,730	79,625
70,000	614.31	151,152	636.10	120,830	30,322	675.52	92,125	59,027	752.23	65,401	85,751
75,000	658.18	161,945	681.53	129,459	32,486	723.77	98,705	63,240	805.96	70,073	91,872
80,000	702.06	172,742	726.97	138,091	34,651	772.02	105,285	67,457	859.69	74,744	97,998
85,000	745.94	183,538	772.40	146,720	36,818	820.27	111,865	71,673	913.42	79,416	104,122
90,000	789.82	194,335	817.84	155,352	38,983	868.52	118,445	75,890	967.15	84,087	110,248
95,000	833.70	205,132	863.27	163,981	41,151	916.78	125,027	80,105	1,020.88	88,758	116,374
100,000	877.58	215,929	908.71	172,613	43,316	965.03	131,607	84,322	1,074.61	93,430	122,499
105,000	921.46	226,726	954.14	181,242	45,484	1,013.28	138,187	88,539	1,128.34	98,101	128,625
110,000	965.33	237,519	999.58	189,874	47,645	1,061.53	144,767	92,752	1,182.07	102,773	134,746
115,000	1,009.21	248,316	1,045.01	198,503	49,813	1,109.78	151,347	96,969	1,235.80	107,444	140,872
120,000	1,053.09	259,112	1,090.45	207,173	51,977	1,158.03	157,927	101,185	1,289.53	112,115	146,997
125,000	1,096.97	269,909	1,135.88	215,764	54,145	1,206.28	164,507	105,402	1,343.26	116,787	153,122
130,000	1,140.85	280,706	1,181.32	224,396	56,310	1,254.53	171,087	109,619	1,396.99	121,458	159,248
135,000	1,184.73	291,503	1,226.75	233,025	58,478	1,302.78	177,667	113,836	1,450.72	126,130	165,373
140,000	1,228.61	302,300	1,272.19	241,657	60,643	1,351.04	184,250	118,050	1,504.45	130,801	171,499
145,000	1,272.48	313,093	1,317.62	250,287	62,807	1,399.29	190,830	122,263	1,558.18	135,472	177,621
150,000	1,316.36	323,890	1,363.06	258,918	64,972	1,447.54	197,410	126,480	1,611.91	140,144	183,746
155,000	1,360.24	334,686	1,408.49	267,547	67,139	1,495.79	203,990	130,696	1,665.64	144,815	189,871
160,000	1,404.12	345,483	1,453.93	276,179	69,304	1,544.04	210,570	134,913	1,719.37	149,487	195,996
165,000	1,448.00	356,280	1,499.36	284,808	71,472	1,592.29	217,150	139,130	1,773.10	154,158	202,122
170,000	1,491.88	367,077	1,544.80	293,440	73,637	1,640.54	223,730	143,347	1,826.83	158,829	208,248
175,000	1,535.76	377,874	1,590.23	302,069	75,805	1,688.79	230,310	147,564	1,880.56	163,501	214,373
180,000	1,579.63	388,667	1,635.67	310,701	77,966	1,737.04	236,890	151,777	1,934.29	168,172	220,495
185,000	1,623.51	399,464	1,681.10	319,330	80,134	1,785.30	243,472	155,992	1,988.02	172,844	226,620
190,000	1,667.39	410,260	1,726.54	327,962	82,298	1,833.55	250,052	160,208	2,041.75	177,515	232,745
195,000	1,711.27	421,057	1,771.97	336,591	84,466	1,881.80	256,632	164,425	2,095.48	182,186	238,871
200,000	1,755.15	431,854	1,817.41	345,223	86,631	1,930.05	263,212	168,642	2,149.22	186,860	244,994

AMOUNT OF LOAN	30 YEARS MONTHLY PAYMENT	30 YEARS TOTAL INTRST	25 YEARS MONTHLY PAYMENT	25 YEARS TOTAL INTRST	25 YEARS INTRST SAVED	20 YEARS MONTHLY PAYMENT	20 YEARS TOTAL INTRST	20 YEARS INTRST SAVED	15 YEARS MONTHLY PAYMENT	15 YEARS TOTAL INTRST	15 YEARS INTRST SAVED
$ 50	0.45	112	0.47	91	21	0.50	70	42	0.55	49	63
100	0.90	224	0.93	179	45	0.99	138	86	1.09	96	128
200	1.80	448	1.86	358	90	1.97	273	175	2.18	192	256
300	2.69	668	2.78	534	134	2.95	408	260	3.27	289	379
400	3.59	892	3.71	713	179	3.93	543	349	4.36	385	507
500	4.49	1,116	4.64	892	224	4.91	678	438	5.45	481	635
600	5.38	1,337	5.56	1,068	269	5.89	814	523	6.54	577	760
700	6.28	1,561	6.49	1,247	314	6.88	951	610	7.63	673	888
800	7.17	1,781	7.42	1,426	355	7.86	1,086	695	8.72	770	1,011
900	8.07	2,005	8.34	1,602	403	8.84	1,222	783	9.81	866	1,139
1,000	8.97	2,229	9.27	1,781	448	9.82	1,357	872	10.90	962	1,267
2,000	17.93	4,455	18.53	3,559	896	19.64	2,714	1,741	21.80	1,924	2,531
3,000	26.89	6,680	27.80	5,340	1,340	29.45	4,068	2,612	32.70	2,886	3,794
4,000	35.85	8,906	37.06	7,118	1,788	39.27	5,425	3,481	43.60	3,848	5,058
5,000	44.81	11,132	46.32	8,896	2,236	49.09	6,782	4,350	54.50	4,810	6,322
6,000	53.77	13,357	55.59	10,677	2,680	58.90	8,136	5,221	65.40	5,772	7,585
7,000	62.73	15,583	64.85	12,455	3,128	68.72	9,493	6,090	76.30	6,734	8,849
8,000	71.69	17,808	74.12	14,236	3,572	78.54	10,850	6,958	87.20	7,696	10,112
9,000	80.65	20,034	83.38	16,014	4,020	88.35	12,204	7,830	98.10	8,658	11,376
10,000	89.62	22,263	92.64	17,792	4,471	98.17	13,561	8,702	109.00	9,620	12,643
11,000	98.58	24,489	101.91	19,573	4,916	107.99	14,918	9,571	119.90	10,582	13,907
12,000	107.54	26,714	111.17	21,351	5,363	117.80	16,272	10,442	130.80	11,544	15,170
13,000	116.50	28,940	120.43	23,129	5,811	127.62	17,629	11,311	141.70	12,506	16,434
14,000	125.46	31,166	129.70	24,910	6,256	137.44	18,986	12,180	152.60	13,468	17,698
15,000	134.42	33,391	138.96	26,688	6,703	147.25	20,340	13,051	163.50	14,430	18,961
16,000	143.38	35,617	148.23	28,469	7,148	157.07	21,697	13,920	174.40	15,392	20,225
17,000	152.34	37,842	157.49	30,247	7,595	166.88	23,051	14,791	185.30	16,354	21,488
18,000	161.30	40,068	166.75	32,025	8,043	176.70	24,408	15,660	196.20	17,316	22,752
19,000	170.26	42,294	176.02	33,806	8,488	186.52	25,765	16,529	207.10	18,278	24,016
20,000	179.23	44,523	185.28	35,584	8,939	196.33	27,119	17,404	218.00	19,240	25,283
21,000	188.19	46,748	194.55	37,365	9,383	206.15	28,476	18,272	228.89	20,200	26,548
22,000	197.15	48,974	203.81	39,143	9,831	215.97	29,833	19,141	239.79	21,162	27,812
23,000	206.11	51,200	213.07	40,921	10,279	225.78	31,187	20,013	250.69	22,124	29,076
24,000	215.07	53,425	222.34	42,702	10,723	235.60	32,544	20,881	261.59	23,086	30,339
25,000	224.03	55,651	231.60	44,480	11,171	245.42	33,901	21,750	272.49	24,048	31,603
26,000	232.99	57,876	240.86	46,258	11,618	255.23	35,255	22,621	283.39	25,010	32,866
27,000	241.95	60,102	250.13	48,039	12,063	265.05	36,612	23,490	294.29	25,972	34,130
28,000	250.91	62,328	259.39	49,817	12,511	274.87	37,969	24,359	305.19	26,934	35,394
29,000	259.87	64,553	268.66	51,598	12,955	284.68	39,323	25,230	316.09	27,896	36,657
30,000	268.84	66,782	277.92	53,376	13,406	294.50	40,680	26,102	326.99	28,858	37,924
32,500	291.24	72,346	301.08	57,824	14,522	319.04	44,070	28,276	354.24	31,263	41,083
35,000	313.64	77,910	324.24	62,272	15,638	343.58	47,459	30,451	381.49	33,668	44,242
40,000	358.45	89,042	370.56	71,168	17,874	392.66	54,238	34,804	435.99	38,478	50,564
45,000	403.25	100,170	416.88	80,064	20,106	441.74	61,018	39,152	490.48	43,286	56,884
50,000	448.06	111,302	463.20	88,960	22,342	490.83	67,799	43,503	544.98	48,096	63,206
55,000	492.86	122,430	509.52	97,856	24,574	539.91	74,578	47,852	599.48	52,906	69,524
60,000	537.67	133,561	555.33	106,749	26,812	588.99	81,358	52,203	653.98	57,716	75,845
65,000	582.47	144,689	602.15	115,645	29,044	638.07	88,137	56,552	708.47	62,525	82,164
70,000	627.28	155,821	648.47	124,541	31,280	687.16	94,918	60,903	762.97	67,335	88,486
75,000	672.08	166,949	694.79	133,437	33,512	736.24	101,698	65,251	817.47	72,145	94,804
80,000	716.89	178,080	741.11	142,333	35,747	785.32	108,477	69,603	871.97	76,955	101,125
85,000	761.69	189,208	787.43	151,229	37,979	834.40	115,256	73,952	926.46	81,763	107,445
90,000	806.50	200,340	833.75	160,125	40,215	883.48	122,035	78,305	980.96	86,573	113,767
95,000	851.30	211,468	880.07	169,021	42,447	932.57	128,817	82,651	1,035.46	91,383	120,085
100,000	896.11	222,600	926.39	177,917	44,683	981.65	135,596	87,004	1,089.96	96,193	126,407
105,000	940.91	233,728	972.71	186,813	46,915	1,030.73	142,375	91,353	1,144.45	101,001	132,727
110,000	985.72	244,859	1,019.03	195,709	49,150	1,079.81	149,154	95,705	1,198.95	105,811	139,048
115,000	1,030.52	255,987	1,065.35	204,605	51,382	1,128.89	155,934	100,053	1,253.45	110,621	145,366
120,000	1,075.33	267,119	1,111.66	213,498	53,621	1,177.98	162,715	104,404	1,307.95	115,431	151,688
125,000	1,120.13	278,247	1,157.98	222,394	55,853	1,227.06	169,494	108,753	1,362.44	120,239	158,008
130,000	1,164.94	289,378	1,204.30	231,290	58,088	1,276.14	176,274	113,104	1,416.94	125,049	164,329
135,000	1,209.74	300,506	1,250.62	240,186	60,320	1,325.22	183,053	117,453	1,471.44	129,859	170,647
140,000	1,254.55	311,638	1,296.94	249,082	62,556	1,374.31	189,834	121,804	1,525.94	134,669	176,969
145,000	1,299.35	322,766	1,343.26	257,978	64,788	1,423.39	196,614	126,152	1,580.43	139,477	183,289
150,000	1,344.16	333,898	1,389.58	266,874	67,024	1,472.47	203,393	130,505	1,634.93	144,287	189,611
155,000	1,388.96	345,026	1,435.90	275,770	69,256	1,521.55	210,172	134,854	1,689.43	149,097	195,929
160,000	1,433.77	356,157	1,482.22	284,666	71,491	1,570.63	216,951	139,206	1,743.93	153,907	202,250
165,000	1,478.57	367,285	1,528.54	293,562	73,723	1,619.72	223,733	143,552	1,798.42	158,716	208,569
170,000	1,523.38	378,417	1,574.86	302,458	75,959	1,668.80	230,512	147,905	1,852.92	163,526	214,891
175,000	1,568.18	389,545	1,621.18	311,354	78,191	1,717.88	237,291	152,254	1,907.42	168,336	221,209
180,000	1,612.99	400,676	1,667.49	320,247	80,429	1,766.96	244,070	156,606	1,961.92	173,146	227,530
185,000	1,657.79	411,804	1,713.81	329,143	82,661	1,816.05	250,852	160,952	2,016.41	177,954	233,850
190,000	1,702.60	422,936	1,760.13	338,039	84,897	1,865.13	257,631	165,305	2,070.91	182,764	240,172
195,000	1,747.40	434,064	1,806.45	346,935	87,129	1,914.21	264,410	169,654	2,125.41	187,574	246,490
200,000	1,792.21	445,196	1,852.77	355,831	89,365	1,963.29	271,190	174,006	2,179.91	192,384	252,812

AMOUNT OF LOAN	30 YEARS		25 YEARS			20 YEARS			15 YEARS		
	MONTHLY PAYMENT	TOTAL INTRST	MONTHLY PAYMENT	TOTAL INTRST	INTRST SAVED	MONTHLY PAYMENT	TOTAL INTRST	INTRST SAVED	MONTHLY PAYMENT	TOTAL INTRST	INTRST SAVED
$ 50	0.46	116	0.48	94	22	0.50	70	46	0.56	51	65
100	0.92	231	0.95	185	46	1.00	140	91	1.11	100	131
200	1.83	459	1.89	367	92	2.00	280	179	2.22	200	259
300	2.75	690	2.84	552	138	3.00	420	270	3.32	298	392
400	3.66	918	3.78	734	184	4.00	560	358	4.43	397	521
500	4.58	1,149	4.73	919	230	5.00	700	449	5.53	495	654
600	5.49	1,376	5.67	1,101	275	6.00	840	536	6.64	595	781
700	6.41	1,608	6.61	1,283	325	6.99	978	630	7.74	693	915
800	7.32	1,835	7.56	1,468	367	7.99	1,118	717	8.85	793	1,042
900	8.24	2,066	8.50	1,650	416	8.99	1,258	808	9.95	891	1,175
1,000	9.15	2,294	9.45	1,835	459	9.99	1,398	896	11.06	991	1,303
2,000	18.30	4,588	18.89	3,667	921	19.97	2,793	1,795	22.11	1,980	2,608
3,000	27.45	6,882	28.33	5,499	1,383	29.96	4,190	2,692	33.17	2,971	3,911
4,000	36.59	9,172	37.77	7,331	1,841	39.94	5,586	3,586	44.22	3,960	5,212
5,000	45.74	11,466	47.21	9,163	2,303	49.92	6,981	4,485	55.27	4,949	6,517
6,000	54.89	13,760	56.66	10,998	2,762	59.91	8,378	5,382	66.33	5,939	7,821
7,000	64.04	16,054	66.10	12,830	3,224	69.89	9,774	6,280	77.38	6,928	9,126
8,000	73.18	18,345	75.54	14,662	3,683	79.88	11,171	7,174	88.44	7,919	10,426
9,000	82.33	20,639	84.98	16,494	4,145	89.86	12,566	8,073	99.49	8,908	11,731
10,000	91.48	22,933	94.42	18,326	4,607	99.84	13,962	8,971	110.54	9,897	13,036
11,000	100.63	25,227	103.86	20,158	5,069	109.83	15,359	9,868	121.60	10,888	14,339
12,000	109.77	27,517	113.31	21,993	5,524	119.81	16,754	10,763	132.65	11,877	15,640
13,000	118.92	29,811	122.75	23,825	5,986	129.79	18,150	11,661	143.71	12,868	16,943
14,000	128.07	32,105	132.19	25,657	6,448	139.78	19,547	12,558	154.76	13,857	18,248
15,000	137.22	34,399	141.63	27,489	6,910	149.76	20,942	13,457	165.81	14,846	19,553
16,000	146.36	36,690	151.07	29,321	7,369	159.75	22,340	14,350	176.87	15,837	20,853
17,000	155.51	38,984	160.52	31,156	7,828	169.73	23,735	15,249	187.92	16,826	22,158
18,000	164.66	41,278	169.96	32,988	8,290	179.71	25,130	16,148	198.98	17,816	23,462
19,000	173.81	43,572	179.40	34,820	8,752	189.70	26,528	17,044	210.03	18,805	24,767
20,000	182.95	45,862	188.84	36,652	9,210	199.68	27,923	17,939	221.08	19,794	26,068
21,000	192.10	48,156	198.28	38,484	9,672	209.66	29,318	18,838	232.14	20,785	27,371
22,000	201.25	50,450	207.72	40,316	10,134	219.65	30,716	19,734	243.19	21,774	28,676
23,000	210.40	52,744	217.17	42,151	10,593	229.63	32,111	20,633	254.25	22,765	29,979
24,000	219.54	55,034	226.61	43,983	11,051	239.62	33,509	21,525	265.30	23,754	31,280
25,000	228.69	57,328	236.05	45,815	11,513	249.60	34,904	22,424	276.35	24,743	32,585
26,000	237.84	59,622	245.49	47,647	11,975	259.58	36,299	23,323	287.41	25,734	33,888
27,000	246.98	61,913	254.93	49,479	12,434	269.57	37,697	24,216	298.46	26,723	35,190
28,000	256.13	64,207	264.38	51,314	12,893	279.55	39,092	25,115	309.52	27,714	36,493
29,000	265.28	66,501	273.82	53,146	13,355	289.54	40,490	26,011	320.57	28,703	37,798
30,000	274.43	68,795	283.26	54,978	13,817	299.52	41,885	26,910	331.62	29,692	39,103
32,500	297.30	74,528	306.86	59,558	14,970	324.48	45,375	29,153	359.26	32,167	42,361
35,000	320.16	80,258	330.47	64,141	16,117	349.44	48,866	31,392	386.89	34,640	45,618
40,000	365.90	91,724	377.68	73,304	18,420	399.36	55,846	35,878	442.16	39,589	52,135
45,000	411.64	103,190	424.89	82,467	20,723	449.28	62,827	40,363	497.43	44,537	58,653
50,000	457.37	114,653	472.10	91,630	23,023	499.19	69,806	44,847	552.70	49,486	65,167
55,000	503.11	126,120	519.30	100,790	25,330	549.11	76,786	49,334	607.97	54,435	71,685
60,000	548.85	137,586	566.51	109,953	27,633	599.03	83,819	53,819	663.24	59,383	78,203
65,000	594.59	149,052	613.72	119,116	29,936	648.95	90,748	58,304	718.51	64,332	84,720
70,000	640.32	160,515	660.93	128,279	32,236	698.87	97,729	62,786	773.78	69,280	91,235
75,000	686.06	171,982	708.14	137,442	34,540	748.79	104,710	67,272	829.05	74,229	97,753
80,000	731.80	183,448	755.35	146,605	36,843	798.71	111,690	71,758	884.32	79,178	104,270
85,000	777.53	194,911	802.56	155,768	39,143	848.63	118,671	76,240	939.59	84,126	110,785
90,000	823.27	206,377	849.77	164,931	41,446	898.55	125,652	80,725	994.86	89,075	117,302
95,000	869.01	217,844	896.98	174,094	43,750	948.47	132,633	85,211	1,050.13	94,023	123,821
100,000	914.74	229,306	944.19	183,257	46,049	998.38	139,611	89,695	1,105.40	98,972	130,334
105,000	960.48	240,773	991.40	192,420	48,353	1,048.30	146,592	94,181	1,160.67	103,921	136,852
110,000	1,006.22	252,239	1,038.60	201,580	50,659	1,098.22	153,573	98,666	1,215.94	108,869	143,370
115,000	1,051.96	263,706	1,085.81	210,743	52,963	1,148.14	160,554	103,152	1,271.21	113,818	149,888
120,000	1,097.69	275,168	1,133.02	219,906	55,262	1,198.06	167,534	107,634	1,326.48	118,766	156,402
125,000	1,143.43	286,635	1,180.23	229,069	57,566	1,247.98	174,515	112,120	1,381.75	123,715	162,920
130,000	1,189.17	298,101	1,227.44	238,232	59,869	1,297.90	181,496	116,605	1,437.02	128,664	169,437
135,000	1,234.90	309,564	1,274.65	247,395	62,169	1,347.82	188,477	121,087	1,492.29	133,612	175,952
140,000	1,280.64	321,030	1,321.86	256,558	64,472	1,397.74	195,458	125,572	1,547.56	138,561	182,469
145,000	1,326.38	332,497	1,369.07	265,721	66,776	1,447.66	202,438	130,059	1,602.83	143,509	188,988
150,000	1,372.11	343,960	1,416.28	274,884	69,076	1,497.57	209,417	134,543	1,658.10	148,458	195,502
155,000	1,417.85	355,426	1,463.49	284,047	71,379	1,547.49	216,398	139,028	1,713.37	153,407	202,019
160,000	1,463.59	366,892	1,510.70	293,210	73,682	1,597.41	223,378	143,514	1,768.64	158,355	208,537
165,000	1,509.32	378,355	1,557.90	302,370	75,985	1,647.33	230,359	147,996	1,823.91	163,304	215,051
170,000	1,555.06	389,822	1,605.11	311,533	78,289	1,697.25	237,340	152,482	1,879.18	168,252	221,570
175,000	1,600.80	401,288	1,652.32	320,696	80,592	1,747.17	244,321	156,967	1,934.45	173,201	228,087
180,000	1,646.54	412,754	1,699.53	329,859	82,895	1,797.09	251,302	161,452	1,989.72	178,150	234,604
185,000	1,692.27	424,217	1,746.74	339,022	85,195	1,847.01	258,282	165,935	2,044.99	183,098	241,119
190,000	1,738.01	435,684	1,793.95	348,185	87,499	1,896.93	265,263	170,421	2,100.26	188,047	247,637
195,000	1,783.75	447,150	1,841.16	357,348	89,802	1,946.85	272,244	174,906	2,155.53	192,995	254,155
200,000	1,829.48	458,613	1,888.37	366,511	92,102	1,996.76	279,222	179,391	2,210.80	197,944	260,669

AMOUNT OF LOAN	30 YEARS		25 YEARS			20 YEARS			15 YEARS		
	MONTHLY PAYMENT	TOTAL INTRST	MONTHLY PAYMENT	TOTAL INTRST	INTRST SAVED	MONTHLY PAYMENT	TOTAL INTRST	INTRST SAVED	MONTHLY PAYMENT	TOTAL INTRST	INTRST SAVED
$ 50	0.47	119	0.49	97	22	0.51	72	47	0.57	53	66
100	0.94	238	0.97	191	47	1.02	145	93	1.13	103	135
200	1.87	473	1.93	379	94	2.04	290	183	2.25	205	268
300	2.81	712	2.89	567	145	3.05	432	280	3.37	307	405
400	3.74	946	3.85	755	191	4.07	577	369	4.49	408	538
500	4.67	1,181	4.82	946	235	5.08	719	462	5.61	510	671
600	5.61	1,420	5.78	1,134	286	6.10	864	556	6.73	611	809
700	6.54	1,654	6.74	1,322	332	7.11	1,006	648	7.85	713	941
800	7.47	1,889	7.70	1,510	379	8.13	1,151	738	8.97	815	1,074
900	8.41	2,128	8.66	1,698	430	9.14	1,294	834	10.09	916	1,212
1,000	9.34	2,362	9.63	1,889	473	10.16	1,438	924	11.21	1,018	1,344
2,000	18.67	4,721	19.25	3,775	946	20.31	2,874	1,847	22.42	2,036	2,685
3,000	28.01	7,084	28.87	5,661	1,423	30.46	4,310	2,774	33.63	3,053	4,031
4,000	37.34	9,442	38.49	7,547	1,895	40.61	5,746	3,696	44.84	4,071	5,371
5,000	46.68	11,805	48.11	9,433	2,372	50.77	7,185	4,620	56.05	5,089	6,716
6,000	56.01	14,164	57.73	11,319	2,845	60.92	8,621	5,543	67.26	6,107	8,057
7,000	65.35	16,526	67.35	13,205	3,321	71.07	10,057	6,469	78.47	7,125	9,401
8,000	74.68	18,885	76.97	15,091	3,794	81.22	11,493	7,392	89.68	8,142	10,743
9,000	84.02	21,247	86.59	16,977	4,270	91.38	12,931	8,316	100.89	9,160	12,087
10,000	93.35	23,606	96.21	18,863	4,743	101.53	14,367	9,239	112.10	10,178	13,428
11,000	102.69	25,968	105.84	20,752	5,216	111.68	15,803	10,165	123.31	11,196	14,772
12,000	112.02	28,327	115.46	22,638	5,689	121.83	17,239	11,088	134.52	12,214	16,113
13,000	121.36	30,690	125.08	24,524	6,166	131.98	18,675	12,015	145.73	13,231	17,459
14,000	130.69	33,048	134.70	26,410	6,638	142.14	20,114	12,934	156.94	14,249	18,799
15,000	140.03	35,411	144.32	28,296	7,115	152.29	21,550	13,861	168.15	15,267	20,144
16,000	149.36	37,770	153.94	30,182	7,588	162.44	22,986	14,784	179.36	16,285	21,485
17,000	158.70	40,132	163.56	32,068	8,064	172.59	24,422	15,710	190.57	17,303	22,829
18,000	168.03	42,491	173.18	33,954	8,537	182.75	25,860	16,631	201.78	18,320	24,171
19,000	177.37	44,853	182.80	35,840	9,013	192.90	27,296	17,557	212.99	19,338	25,515
20,000	186.70	47,212	192.42	37,726	9,486	203.05	28,732	18,480	224.19	20,354	26,858
21,000	196.04	49,574	202.04	39,612	9,962	213.20	30,168	19,406	235.40	21,372	28,202
22,000	205.37	51,933	211.67	41,501	10,432	223.36	31,606	20,327	246.61	22,390	29,543
23,000	214.71	54,296	221.29	43,387	10,909	233.51	33,042	21,254	257.82	23,408	30,888
24,000	224.04	56,654	230.91	45,273	11,381	243.66	34,478	22,176	269.03	24,425	32,229
25,000	233.38	59,017	240.53	47,159	11,858	253.81	35,914	23,103	280.24	25,443	33,574
26,000	242.71	61,376	250.15	49,045	12,331	263.96	37,350	24,026	291.45	26,461	34,915
27,000	252.04	63,734	259.77	50,931	12,803	274.12	38,789	24,945	302.66	27,479	36,255
28,000	261.38	66,097	269.39	52,817	13,280	284.27	40,225	25,872	313.87	28,497	37,600
29,000	270.71	68,456	279.01	54,703	13,753	294.42	41,661	26,795	325.08	29,514	38,942
30,000	280.05	70,818	288.63	56,589	14,229	304.57	43,097	27,721	336.29	30,532	40,286
32,500	303.39	76,720	312.69	61,307	15,413	329.95	46,688	30,032	364.31	33,076	43,644
35,000	326.72	82,619	336.74	66,022	16,597	355.34	50,282	32,337	392.34	35,621	46,998
40,000	373.40	94,424	384.84	75,452	18,972	406.10	57,464	36,960	448.38	40,708	53,716
45,000	420.07	106,225	432.95	84,885	21,340	456.86	64,646	41,579	504.43	45,797	60,428
50,000	466.75	118,030	481.05	94,315	23,715	507.62	71,829	46,201	560.48	50,886	67,144
55,000	513.42	129,831	529.16	103,748	26,083	558.38	79,011	50,820	616.53	55,975	73,856
60,000	560.09	141,632	577.26	113,178	28,454	609.14	86,194	55,438	672.57	61,063	80,569
65,000	606.77	153,437	625.37	122,611	30,826	659.90	93,376	60,061	728.62	66,152	87,285
70,000	653.44	165,238	673.47	132,041	33,197	710.67	100,561	64,677	784.67	71,241	93,997
75,000	700.12	177,043	721.57	141,471	35,572	761.43	107,743	69,300	840.72	76,330	100,713
80,000	746.79	188,844	769.68	150,904	37,940	812.19	114,926	73,918	896.76	81,417	107,427
85,000	793.46	200,646	817.78	160,334	40,312	862.95	122,108	78,538	952.81	86,506	114,140
90,000	840.14	212,450	865.89	169,767	42,683	913.71	129,290	83,160	1,008.86	91,595	120,855
95,000	886.81	224,252	913.99	179,197	45,055	964.47	136,473	87,779	1,064.91	96,684	127,568
100,000	933.49	236,056	962.10	188,630	47,426	1,015.23	143,655	92,401	1,120.95	101,771	134,285
105,000	980.16	247,858	1,010.20	198,060	49,798	1,066.00	150,840	97,018	1,177.00	106,860	140,998
110,000	1,026.83	259,659	1,058.31	207,493	52,166	1,116.76	158,022	101,637	1,233.05	111,949	147,710
115,000	1,073.51	271,464	1,106.41	216,923	54,541	1,167.52	165,205	106,259	1,289.10	117,038	154,426
120,000	1,120.18	283,265	1,154.52	226,354	56,909	1,218.28	172,387	110,878	1,345.14	122,125	161,140
125,000	1,166.86	295,070	1,202.62	235,786	59,284	1,269.04	179,570	115,500	1,401.19	127,214	167,856
130,000	1,213.53	306,871	1,250.73	245,219	61,652	1,319.80	186,752	120,119	1,457.24	132,303	174,568
135,000	1,260.20	318,672	1,298.83	254,649	64,023	1,370.56	193,934	124,738	1,513.28	137,390	181,282
140,000	1,306.88	330,477	1,346.93	264,079	66,398	1,421.33	201,119	129,358	1,569.33	142,479	187,998
145,000	1,353.55	342,278	1,395.04	273,512	68,766	1,472.09	208,302	133,976	1,625.38	147,568	194,710
150,000	1,400.23	354,083	1,443.14	282,942	71,141	1,522.85	215,484	138,599	1,681.43	152,657	201,426
155,000	1,446.90	365,884	1,491.25	292,375	73,509	1,573.61	222,666	143,218	1,737.47	157,745	208,139
160,000	1,493.58	377,689	1,539.35	301,805	75,884	1,624.37	229,849	147,840	1,793.52	162,834	214,855
165,000	1,540.25	389,490	1,587.46	311,238	78,252	1,675.13	237,031	152,459	1,849.57	167,923	221,567
170,000	1,586.92	401,291	1,635.56	320,668	80,623	1,725.89	244,214	157,077	1,905.62	173,012	228,279
175,000	1,633.60	413,096	1,683.67	330,101	82,995	1,776.66	251,398	161,698	1,961.66	178,099	234,997
180,000	1,680.27	424,897	1,731.77	339,531	85,366	1,827.42	258,581	166,316	2,017.71	183,188	241,709
185,000	1,726.95	436,702	1,779.88	348,964	87,738	1,878.18	265,763	170,939	2,073.76	188,277	248,425
190,000	1,773.62	448,503	1,827.98	358,394	90,109	1,928.94	272,946	175,557	2,129.81	193,366	255,137
195,000	1,820.29	460,304	1,876.09	367,827	92,477	1,979.70	280,128	180,176	2,185.85	198,453	261,851
200,000	1,866.97	472,109	1,924.19	377,257	94,852	2,030.46	287,310	184,799	2,241.90	203,542	268,567

19

11.00% SHORT-TERM AMORTIZING MORTGAGES

AMOUNT OF LOAN	30 YEARS MONTHLY PAYMENT	30 YEARS TOTAL INTRST	25 YEARS MONTHLY PAYMENT	25 YEARS TOTAL INTRST	25 YEARS INTRST SAVED	20 YEARS MONTHLY PAYMENT	20 YEARS TOTAL INTRST	20 YEARS INTRST SAVED	15 YEARS MONTHLY PAYMENT	15 YEARS TOTAL INTRST	15 YEARS INTRST SAVED
$ 50	0.48	123	0.50	100	23	0.52	75	48	0.57	53	70
100	0.96	246	0.99	197	49	1.04	150	96	1.14	105	141
200	1.91	488	1.97	391	97	2.07	297	191	2.28	210	278
300	2.86	730	2.95	585	145	3.10	444	286	3.41	314	416
400	3.81	972	3.93	779	193	4.13	591	381	4.55	419	553
500	4.77	1,217	4.91	973	244	5.17	741	476	5.69	524	693
600	5.72	1,459	5.89	1,167	292	6.20	888	571	6.82	628	831
700	6.67	1,701	6.87	1,361	340	7.23	1,035	666	7.96	733	968
800	7.62	1,943	7.85	1,555	388	8.26	1,182	761	9.10	838	1,105
900	8.58	2,189	8.83	1,749	440	9.29	1,330	859	10.23	941	1,248
1,000	9.53	2,431	9.81	1,943	488	10.33	1,479	952	11.37	1,047	1,384
2,000	19.05	4,858	19.61	3,883	975	20.65	2,956	1,902	22.74	2,093	2,765
3,000	28.57	7,285	29.41	5,823	1,462	30.97	4,433	2,852	34.10	3,138	4,147
4,000	38.10	9,716	39.21	7,763	1,953	41.29	5,910	3,806	45.47	4,185	5,531
5,000	47.62	12,143	49.01	9,703	2,440	51.61	7,386	4,757	56.83	5,229	6,914
6,000	57.14	14,570	58.81	11,643	2,927	61.94	8,866	5,704	68.20	6,276	8,294
7,000	66.67	17,001	68.61	13,583	3,418	72.26	10,342	6,659	79.57	7,323	9,678
8,000	76.19	19,428	78.41	15,523	3,905	82.58	11,819	7,609	90.93	8,367	11,061
9,000	85.71	21,856	88.22	17,466	4,390	92.90	13,296	8,560	102.30	9,414	12,442
10,000	95.24	24,286	98.02	19,406	4,880	103.22	14,773	9,513	113.66	10,459	13,827
11,000	104.76	26,714	107.82	21,346	5,368	113.55	16,252	10,462	125.03	11,505	15,209
12,000	114.28	29,141	117.62	23,286	5,855	123.87	17,729	11,412	136.40	12,552	16,589
13,000	123.81	31,572	127.42	25,226	6,346	134.19	19,206	12,366	147.76	13,597	17,975
14,000	133.33	33,999	137.22	27,166	6,833	144.51	20,682	13,317	159.13	14,643	19,356
15,000	142.85	36,426	147.02	29,106	7,320	154.83	22,159	14,267	170.49	15,688	20,738
16,000	152.38	38,857	156.82	31,046	7,811	165.16	23,638	15,219	181.86	16,735	22,122
17,000	161.90	41,284	166.62	32,986	8,298	175.48	25,115	16,169	193.23	17,781	23,503
18,000	171.42	43,711	176.43	34,929	8,782	185.80	26,592	17,119	204.59	18,826	24,885
19,000	180.95	46,142	186.23	36,869	9,273	196.12	28,069	18,073	215.96	19,873	26,269
20,000	190.47	48,569	196.03	38,809	9,760	206.44	29,546	19,023	227.32	20,918	27,651
21,000	199.99	50,996	205.83	40,749	10,247	216.76	31,022	19,974	238.69	21,964	29,032
22,000	209.52	53,427	215.63	42,689	10,738	227.09	32,502	20,925	250.06	23,011	30,416
23,000	219.04	55,854	225.43	44,629	11,225	237.41	33,978	21,876	261.42	24,056	31,798
24,000	228.56	58,282	235.23	46,569	11,713	247.73	35,455	22,827	272.79	25,102	33,180
25,000	238.09	60,712	245.03	48,509	12,203	258.05	36,932	23,780	284.15	26,147	34,565
26,000	247.61	63,140	254.83	50,449	12,691	268.37	38,409	24,731	295.52	27,194	35,946
27,000	257.13	65,567	264.64	52,392	13,175	278.70	39,888	25,679	306.89	28,240	37,327
28,000	266.66	67,998	274.44	54,332	13,666	289.02	41,365	26,633	318.25	29,285	38,713
29,000	276.18	70,425	284.24	56,272	14,153	299.34	42,842	27,583	329.62	30,332	40,093
30,000	285.70	72,852	294.04	58,212	14,640	309.66	44,318	28,534	340.98	31,376	41,476
32,500	309.51	78,924	318.54	63,062	15,862	335.47	48,013	30,911	369.40	33,992	44,932
35,000	333.32	84,995	343.04	67,912	17,083	361.27	51,705	33,290	397.81	36,606	48,389
40,000	380.93	97,135	392.05	77,615	19,520	412.88	59,091	38,044	454.64	41,835	55,300
45,000	428.55	109,278	441.06	87,318	21,960	464.49	66,478	42,800	511.47	47,065	62,213
50,000	476.17	121,401	490.06	97,018	24,403	516.10	73,864	47,557	568.30	52,294	69,127
55,000	523.78	133,561	539.07	106,721	26,840	567.71	81,250	52,311	625.13	57,523	76,038
60,000	571.40	145,704	588.07	116,421	29,283	619.32	88,637	57,067	681.96	62,752	82,951
65,000	619.02	157,847	637.08	126,124	31,723	670.93	96,023	61,824	738.79	67,982	89,865
70,000	666.63	169,987	686.08	135,824	34,163	722.54	103,410	66,577	795.62	73,212	96,775
75,000	714.25	182,130	735.09	145,527	36,603	774.15	110,796	71,334	852.45	78,441	103,689
80,000	761.86	194,270	784.10	155,230	39,040	825.76	118,182	76,088	909.28	83,670	110,600
85,000	809.48	206,413	833.10	164,930	41,483	877.37	125,569	80,844	966.11	88,900	117,513
90,000	857.10	218,556	882.11	174,633	43,923	928.97	132,953	85,603	1,022.94	94,129	124,427
95,000	904.71	230,696	931.11	184,333	46,363	980.58	140,339	90,357	1,079.77	99,359	131,337
100,000	952.33	242,839	980.12	194,036	48,803	1,032.19	147,726	95,113	1,136.60	104,588	138,251
105,000	999.94	254,978	1,029.12	203,736	51,242	1,083.80	155,112	99,866	1,193.43	109,817	145,161
110,000	1,047.56	267,122	1,078.13	213,439	53,683	1,135.41	162,498	104,624	1,250.26	115,047	152,075
115,000	1,095.18	279,265	1,127.14	223,142	56,123	1,187.02	169,885	109,380	1,307.09	120,276	158,989
120,000	1,142.79	291,404	1,176.14	232,842	58,562	1,238.63	177,271	114,133	1,363.92	125,506	165,898
125,000	1,190.41	303,548	1,225.15	242,545	61,003	1,290.24	184,658	118,890	1,420.75	130,735	172,813
130,000	1,238.03	315,691	1,274.15	252,245	63,446	1,341.85	192,044	123,647	1,477.58	135,964	179,727
135,000	1,285.64	327,830	1,323.16	261,948	65,882	1,393.46	199,430	128,400	1,534.41	141,194	186,636
140,000	1,333.26	339,974	1,372.16	271,648	68,326	1,445.07	206,817	133,157	1,591.24	146,423	193,551
145,000	1,380.87	352,113	1,421.17	281,351	70,762	1,496.68	214,203	137,910	1,648.07	151,653	200,460
150,000	1,428.49	364,256	1,470.17	291,051	73,205	1,548.29	221,590	142,666	1,704.90	156,882	207,374
155,000	1,476.11	376,400	1,519.18	300,754	75,646	1,599.90	228,976	147,424	1,761.73	162,111	214,289
160,000	1,523.72	388,539	1,568.19	310,457	78,082	1,651.51	236,362	152,177	1,818.56	167,341	221,198
165,000	1,571.34	400,682	1,617.19	320,157	80,525	1,703.12	243,749	156,933	1,875.39	172,570	228,112
170,000	1,618.95	412,822	1,666.20	329,860	82,962	1,754.73	251,135	161,687	1,932.22	177,800	235,022
175,000	1,666.57	424,965	1,715.20	339,560	85,405	1,806.33	258,519	166,446	1,989.05	183,029	241,936
180,000	1,714.19	437,108	1,764.21	349,263	87,845	1,857.94	265,906	171,202	2,045.88	188,258	248,850
185,000	1,761.80	449,248	1,813.21	358,963	90,285	1,909.55	273,292	175,956	2,102.71	193,488	255,760
190,000	1,809.42	461,391	1,862.22	368,666	92,725	1,961.16	280,680	180,713	2,159.54	198,717	262,674
195,000	1,857.04	473,534	1,911.23	378,369	95,165	2,012.77	288,065	185,469	2,216.37	203,947	269,587
200,000	1,904.65	485,674	1,960.23	388,069	97,605	2,064.38	295,451	190,223	2,273.20	209,176	276,498

20

AMOUNT OF LOAN	30 YEARS		25 YEARS			20 YEARS			15 YEARS		
	MONTHLY PAYMENT	TOTAL INTRST	MONTHLY PAYMENT	TOTAL INTRST	INTRST SAVED	MONTHLY PAYMENT	TOTAL INTRST	INTRST SAVED	MONTHLY PAYMENT	TOTAL INTRST	INTRST SAVED
$ 50	0.49	126	0.50	100	26	0.53	77	49	0.58	54	72
100	0.98	253	1.00	200	53	1.05	152	101	1.16	109	144
200	1.95	502	2.00	400	102	2.10	304	198	2.31	216	286
300	2.92	751	3.00	600	151	3.15	456	295	3.46	323	428
400	3.89	1,000	4.00	800	200	4.20	608	392	4.61	430	570
500	4.86	1,250	5.00	1,000	250	5.25	760	490	5.77	539	711
600	5.83	1,499	5.99	1,197	302	6.30	912	587	6.92	646	853
700	6.80	1,748	6.99	1,397	351	7.35	1,064	684	8.07	753	995
800	7.78	2,001	7.99	1,597	404	8.40	1,216	785	9.22	860	1,141
900	8.75	2,250	8.99	1,797	453	9.45	1,368	882	10.38	968	1,282
1,000	9.72	2,499	9.99	1,997	502	10.50	1,520	979	11.53	1,075	1,424
2,000	19.43	4,995	19.97	3,991	1,004	20.99	3,038	1,957	23.05	2,149	2,846
3,000	29.14	7,490	29.95	5,985	1,505	31.48	4,555	2,935	34.58	3,224	4,266
4,000	38.86	9,990	39.93	7,979	2,011	41.98	6,075	3,915	46.10	4,298	5,692
5,000	48.57	12,485	49.92	9,976	2,509	52.47	7,593	4,892	57.62	5,372	7,113
6,000	58.28	14,981	59.90	11,970	3,011	62.96	9,110	5,871	69.15	6,447	8,534
7,000	67.99	17,476	69.88	13,964	3,512	73.45	10,628	6,848	80.67	7,521	9,955
8,000	77.71	19,976	79.86	15,958	4,018	83.95	12,148	7,828	92.19	8,594	11,382
9,000	87.42	22,471	89.85	17,955	4,516	94.44	13,666	8,805	103.72	9,670	12,801
10,000	97.13	24,967	99.83	19,949	5,018	104.93	15,183	9,784	115.24	10,743	14,224
11,000	106.84	27,462	109.81	21,943	5,519	115.42	16,701	10,761	126.76	11,817	15,645
12,000	116.56	29,962	119.79	23,937	6,025	125.92	18,221	11,741	138.29	12,892	17,070
13,000	126.27	32,457	129.78	25,934	6,523	136.41	19,738	12,719	149.81	13,966	18,491
14,000	135.98	34,953	139.76	27,928	7,025	146.90	21,256	13,697	161.33	15,039	19,914
15,000	145.69	37,448	149.74	29,922	7,526	157.39	22,774	14,674	172.86	16,115	21,333
16,000	155.41	39,948	159.72	31,916	8,032	167.89	24,294	15,654	184.38	17,188	22,760
17,000	165.12	42,443	169.71	33,913	8,530	178.38	25,811	16,632	195.90	18,262	24,181
18,000	174.83	44,939	179.69	35,907	9,032	188.87	27,329	17,610	207.43	19,337	25,602
19,000	184.54	47,434	189.67	37,901	9,533	199.36	28,846	18,588	218.95	20,411	27,023
20,000	194.26	49,934	199.65	39,895	10,039	209.86	30,366	19,568	230.47	21,485	28,449
21,000	203.97	52,429	209.64	41,892	10,537	220.35	31,884	20,545	242.00	22,560	29,869
22,000	213.68	54,925	219.62	43,886	11,039	230.84	33,402	21,523	253.52	23,634	31,291
23,000	223.40	57,424	229.60	45,880	11,544	241.33	34,919	22,505	265.04	24,707	32,717
24,000	233.11	59,920	239.58	47,874	12,046	251.83	36,439	23,481	276.57	25,783	34,137
25,000	242.82	62,415	249.56	49,868	12,547	262.32	37,957	24,458	288.09	26,856	35,559
26,000	252.53	64,911	259.55	51,865	13,046	272.81	39,474	25,437	299.61	27,930	36,981
27,000	262.25	67,410	269.53	53,859	13,551	283.30	40,992	26,418	311.14	29,005	38,405
28,000	271.96	69,906	279.51	55,853	14,053	293.80	42,512	27,394	322.66	30,079	39,827
29,000	281.67	72,401	289.49	57,847	14,554	304.29	44,030	28,371	334.18	31,152	41,249
30,000	291.38	74,897	299.48	59,844	15,053	314.78	45,547	29,350	345.71	32,228	42,669
32,500	315.66	81,138	324.43	64,829	16,309	341.01	49,342	31,796	374.52	34,914	46,224
35,000	339.95	87,382	349.39	69,817	17,565	367.24	53,138	34,244	403.38	37,599	49,783
40,000	388.51	99,864	399.30	79,790	20,074	419.71	60,730	39,134	460.94	42,969	56,895
45,000	437.07	112,345	449.21	89,763	22,582	472.17	68,321	44,024	518.56	48,341	64,004
50,000	485.64	124,830	499.12	99,736	25,094	524.63	75,911	48,919	576.18	53,712	71,118
55,000	534.20	137,312	549.04	109,712	27,600	577.10	83,504	53,808	633.79	59,082	78,230
60,000	582.76	149,794	598.95	119,685	30,109	629.56	91,094	58,700	691.41	64,454	85,340
65,000	631.32	162,275	648.86	129,658	32,617	682.02	98,685	63,590	749.03	69,825	92,450
70,000	679.89	174,760	698.77	139,631	35,129	734.48	106,275	68,485	806.65	75,197	99,563
75,000	728.45	187,242	748.68	149,604	37,638	786.95	113,868	73,374	864.26	80,567	106,675
80,000	777.01	199,724	798.60	159,580	40,144	839.41	121,458	78,266	921.88	85,938	113,786
85,000	825.58	212,209	848.51	169,553	42,656	891.87	129,049	83,160	979.50	91,310	120,899
90,000	874.14	224,690	898.42	179,526	45,164	944.34	136,642	88,048	1,037.12	96,682	128,008
95,000	922.70	237,172	948.33	189,499	47,673	996.80	144,232	92,940	1,094.73	102,051	135,121
100,000	971.27	249,657	998.24	199,472	50,185	1,049.26	151,822	97,835	1,152.35	107,423	142,234
105,000	1,019.83	262,139	1,048.16	209,448	52,691	1,101.72	159,413	102,726	1,209.97	112,795	149,344
110,000	1,068.39	274,620	1,098.07	219,421	55,199	1,154.19	167,006	107,614	1,267.58	118,164	156,456
115,000	1,116.96	287,106	1,147.98	229,394	57,712	1,206.65	174,596	112,510	1,325.20	123,536	163,570
120,000	1,165.52	299,587	1,197.89	239,367	60,220	1,259.11	182,186	117,401	1,382.82	128,908	170,679
125,000	1,214.08	312,069	1,247.80	249,340	62,729	1,311.58	189,779	122,290	1,440.44	134,279	177,790
130,000	1,262.64	324,550	1,297.72	259,316	65,234	1,364.04	197,370	127,180	1,498.05	139,649	184,901
135,000	1,311.21	337,036	1,347.63	269,289	67,747	1,416.50	204,960	132,076	1,555.67	145,021	192,015
140,000	1,359.77	349,517	1,397.54	279,262	70,255	1,468.96	212,550	136,967	1,613.29	150,392	199,125
145,000	1,408.33	361,999	1,447.45	289,235	72,764	1,521.43	220,143	141,856	1,670.90	155,762	206,237
150,000	1,456.90	374,484	1,497.36	299,208	75,276	1,573.89	227,734	146,750	1,728.52	161,134	213,350
155,000	1,505.46	386,966	1,547.28	309,184	77,782	1,626.35	235,324	151,642	1,786.14	166,505	220,461
160,000	1,554.02	399,447	1,597.19	319,157	80,290	1,678.81	242,914	156,533	1,843.76	171,877	227,570
165,000	1,602.59	411,932	1,647.10	329,130	82,802	1,731.28	250,507	161,425	1,901.37	177,247	234,685
170,000	1,651.15	424,414	1,697.01	339,103	85,311	1,783.74	258,098	166,316	1,958.99	182,618	241,796
175,000	1,699.71	436,896	1,746.92	349,076	87,820	1,836.20	265,688	171,208	2,016.61	187,990	248,906
180,000	1,748.28	449,381	1,796.84	359,052	90,329	1,888.67	273,281	176,100	2,074.23	193,361	256,020
185,000	1,796.84	461,862	1,846.75	369,025	92,837	1,941.13	280,871	180,991	2,131.84	198,731	263,131
190,000	1,845.40	474,344	1,896.66	378,998	95,346	1,993.59	288,462	185,882	2,189.46	204,103	270,241
195,000	1,893.96	486,826	1,946.57	388,971	97,855	2,046.05	296,052	190,774	2,247.08	209,474	277,352
200,000	1,942.53	499,311	1,996.48	398,944	100,367	2,098.52	303,645	195,666	2,304.69	214,844	284,467

SHORT-TERM AMORTIZING MORTGAGES

AMOUNT OF LOAN	30 YEARS		25 YEARS			20 YEARS			15 YEARS		
	MONTHLY PAYMENT	TOTAL INTRST	MONTHLY PAYMENT	TOTAL INTRST	INTRST SAVED	MONTHLY PAYMENT	TOTAL INTRST	INTRST SAVED	MONTHLY PAYMENT	TOTAL INTRST	INTRST SAVED
$ 50	0.50	130	0.51	103	27	0.54	80	50	0.59	56	74
100	1.00	260	1.02	206	54	1.07	157	103	1.17	111	149
200	1.99	516	2.04	412	104	2.14	314	202	2.34	221	295
300	2.98	773	3.05	615	158	3.20	468	305	3.51	332	441
400	3.97	1,029	4.07	821	208	4.27	625	404	4.68	442	587
500	4.96	1,286	5.09	1,027	259	5.34	782	504	5.85	553	733
600	5.95	1,542	6.10	1,230	312	6.40	936	606	7.01	662	880
700	6.94	1,798	7.12	1,436	362	7.47	1,093	705	8.18	772	1,026
800	7.93	2,055	8.14	1,642	413	8.54	1,250	805	9.35	883	1,172
900	8.92	2,311	9.15	1,845	466	9.60	1,404	907	10.52	994	1,317
1,000	9.91	2,568	10.17	2,051	517	10.67	1,561	1,007	11.69	1,104	1,464
2,000	19.81	5,132	20.33	4,099	1,033	21.33	3,119	2,013	23.37	2,207	2,925
3,000	29.71	7,696	30.50	6,150	1,546	32.00	4,680	3,016	35.05	3,309	4,387
4,000	39.62	10,263	40.66	8,198	2,065	42.66	6,238	4,025	46.73	4,411	5,852
5,000	49.52	12,827	50.83	10,249	2,578	53.33	7,799	5,028	58.41	5,514	7,313
6,000	59.42	15,391	60.99	12,297	3,094	63.99	9,358	6,033	70.10	6,618	8,773
7,000	69.33	17,959	71.16	14,348	3,611	74.66	10,918	7,041	81.78	7,720	10,239
8,000	79.23	20,523	81.32	16,396	4,127	85.32	12,477	8,046	93.46	8,823	11,700
9,000	89.13	23,087	91.49	18,447	4,640	95.98	14,035	9,052	105.14	9,925	13,162
10,000	99.03	25,651	101.65	20,495	5,156	106.65	15,596	10,055	116.82	11,028	14,623
11,000	108.94	28,218	111.82	22,546	5,672	117.31	17,154	11,064	128.51	12,132	16,086
12,000	118.84	30,782	121.98	24,594	6,188	127.98	18,715	12,067	140.19	13,234	17,548
13,000	128.74	33,346	132.15	26,645	6,701	138.64	20,274	13,072	151.87	14,337	19,009
14,000	138.65	35,914	142.31	28,693	7,221	149.31	21,834	14,080	163.55	15,439	20,475
15,000	148.55	38,478	152.48	30,744	7,734	159.97	23,393	15,085	175.23	16,541	21,937
16,000	158.45	41,042	162.64	32,792	8,250	170.63	24,951	16,091	186.92	17,646	23,396
17,000	168.35	43,606	172.80	34,840	8,766	181.30	26,512	17,094	198.60	18,748	24,858
18,000	178.26	46,174	182.97	36,891	9,283	191.96	28,070	18,104	210.28	19,850	26,324
19,000	188.16	48,738	193.13	38,939	9,799	202.63	29,631	19,107	221.96	20,953	27,785
20,000	198.06	51,302	203.30	40,990	10,312	213.29	31,190	20,112	233.64	22,055	29,247
21,000	207.97	53,869	213.46	43,038	10,831	223.96	32,750	21,119	245.32	23,158	30,711
22,000	217.87	56,433	223.63	45,089	11,344	234.62	34,309	22,124	257.01	24,262	32,171
23,000	227.77	58,997	233.79	47,137	11,860	245.28	35,867	23,130	268.69	25,364	33,633
24,000	237.67	61,561	243.96	49,188	12,373	255.95	37,428	24,133	280.37	26,467	35,094
25,000	247.58	64,129	254.12	51,236	12,893	266.61	38,986	25,143	292.05	27,569	36,560
26,000	257.48	66,693	264.29	53,287	13,406	277.28	40,547	26,146	303.73	28,671	38,022
27,000	267.38	69,257	274.45	55,335	13,922	287.94	42,106	27,151	315.42	29,776	39,481
28,000	277.29	71,824	284.62	57,386	14,438	298.61	43,666	28,158	327.10	30,878	40,946
29,000	287.19	74,388	294.78	59,434	14,954	309.27	45,225	29,163	338.78	31,980	42,408
30,000	297.09	76,952	304.95	61,485	15,467	319.93	46,783	30,169	350.46	33,083	43,869
32,500	321.85	83,366	330.36	66,608	16,758	346.59	50,682	32,684	379.67	35,841	47,525
35,000	346.61	89,780	355.77	71,731	18,049	373.26	54,582	35,198	408.87	38,597	51,183
40,000	396.12	102,603	406.59	81,977	20,626	426.58	62,379	40,224	467.28	44,110	58,493
45,000	445.64	115,430	457.42	92,226	23,204	479.90	70,176	45,254	525.69	49,624	65,806
50,000	495.15	128,254	508.24	102,472	25,782	533.22	77,973	50,281	584.10	55,138	73,116
55,000	544.67	141,081	559.06	112,718	28,363	586.54	85,770	55,311	642.51	60,652	80,429
60,000	594.18	153,905	609.89	122,967	30,938	639.86	93,566	60,339	700.92	66,166	87,739
65,000	643.69	166,728	660.71	133,213	33,515	693.18	101,363	65,365	759.33	71,679	95,049
70,000	693.21	179,556	711.53	143,459	36,097	746.51	109,162	70,394	817.74	77,193	102,363
75,000	742.72	192,379	762.36	153,708	38,671	799.83	116,959	75,420	876.15	82,707	109,672
80,000	792.24	205,206	813.18	163,954	41,252	853.15	124,756	80,450	934.56	88,221	116,985
85,000	841.75	218,030	864.00	174,200	43,830	906.47	132,553	85,477	992.97	93,735	124,295
90,000	891.27	230,857	914.83	184,449	46,408	959.79	140,350	90,507	1,051.38	99,248	131,609
95,000	940.78	243,681	965.65	194,695	48,986	1,013.11	148,146	95,535	1,109.79	104,762	138,919
100,000	990.30	256,508	1,016.47	204,941	51,567	1,066.43	155,943	100,565	1,168.19	110,274	146,234
105,000	1,039.81	269,332	1,067.30	215,190	54,142	1,119.76	163,742	105,590	1,226.60	115,788	153,544
110,000	1,089.33	282,159	1,118.12	225,436	56,723	1,173.08	171,539	110,620	1,285.01	121,302	160,857
115,000	1,138.84	294,982	1,168.94	235,682	59,300	1,226.40	179,336	115,646	1,343.42	126,816	168,166
120,000	1,188.35	307,806	1,219.77	245,931	61,875	1,279.72	187,133	120,673	1,401.83	132,329	175,477
125,000	1,237.87	320,633	1,270.59	256,177	64,456	1,333.04	194,930	125,703	1,460.24	137,843	182,790
130,000	1,287.38	333,457	1,321.41	266,423	67,034	1,386.36	202,726	130,731	1,518.65	143,357	190,100
135,000	1,336.90	346,284	1,372.24	276,672	69,612	1,439.69	210,526	135,758	1,577.06	148,871	197,413
140,000	1,386.41	359,108	1,423.06	286,918	72,190	1,493.01	218,322	140,786	1,635.47	154,385	204,723
145,000	1,435.93	371,935	1,473.88	297,164	74,771	1,546.33	226,119	145,816	1,693.88	159,898	212,037
150,000	1,485.44	384,758	1,524.71	307,413	77,345	1,599.65	233,916	150,842	1,752.29	165,412	219,346
155,000	1,534.96	397,586	1,575.53	317,659	79,927	1,652.97	241,713	155,873	1,810.70	170,926	226,660
160,000	1,584.47	410,409	1,626.36	327,908	82,501	1,706.29	249,510	160,899	1,869.11	176,440	233,969
165,000	1,633.99	423,236	1,677.18	338,154	85,082	1,759.61	257,306	165,930	1,927.52	181,954	241,282
170,000	1,683.50	436,060	1,728.00	348,400	87,660	1,812.94	265,106	170,954	1,985.93	187,467	248,593
175,000	1,733.02	448,887	1,778.83	358,649	90,238	1,866.26	272,902	175,985	2,044.34	192,981	255,906
180,000	1,782.53	461,711	1,829.65	368,895	92,816	1,919.58	280,699	181,012	2,102.75	198,495	263,216
185,000	1,832.04	474,534	1,880.47	379,141	95,393	1,972.90	288,496	186,038	2,161.16	204,009	270,525
190,000	1,881.56	487,362	1,931.30	389,390	97,972	2,026.22	296,293	191,069	2,219.57	209,523	277,839
195,000	1,931.07	500,185	1,982.12	399,636	100,549	2,079.54	304,090	196,095	2,277.98	215,036	285,149
200,000	1,980.59	513,012	2,032.94	409,882	103,130	2,132.86	311,886	201,126	2,336.38	220,548	292,464

SHORT-TERM AMORTIZING MORTGAGES 11.75%

AMOUNT OF LOAN	30 YEARS MONTHLY PAYMENT	30 YEARS TOTAL INTRST	25 YEARS MONTHLY PAYMENT	25 YEARS TOTAL INTRST	25 YEARS INTRST SAVED	20 YEARS MONTHLY PAYMENT	20 YEARS TOTAL INTRST	20 YEARS INTRST SAVED	15 YEARS MONTHLY PAYMENT	15 YEARS TOTAL INTRST	15 YEARS INTRST SAVED
$ 50	0.51	134	0.52	106	28	0.55	82	52	0.60	58	76
100	1.01	264	1.04	212	52	1.09	162	102	1.19	114	150
200	2.02	527	2.07	421	106	2.17	321	206	2.37	227	300
300	3.03	791	3.11	633	158	3.26	482	309	3.56	341	450
400	4.04	1,054	4.14	842	212	4.34	642	412	4.74	453	601
500	5.05	1,318	5.18	1,054	264	5.42	801	517	5.93	567	751
600	6.06	1,582	6.21	1,263	319	6.51	962	620	7.11	680	902
700	7.07	1,845	7.25	1,475	370	7.59	1,122	723	8.29	792	1,053
800	8.08	2,109	8.28	1,684	425	8.67	1,281	828	9.48	906	1,203
900	9.09	2,372	9.32	1,896	476	9.76	1,442	930	10.66	1,019	1,353
1,000	10.10	2,636	10.35	2,105	531	10.84	1,602	1,034	11.85	1,133	1,503
2,000	20.19	5,268	20.70	4,210	1,058	21.68	3,203	2,065	23.69	2,264	3,004
3,000	30.29	7,904	31.05	6,315	1,589	32.52	4,805	3,099	35.53	3,395	4,509
4,000	40.38	10,537	41.40	8,420	2,117	43.35	6,404	4,133	47.37	4,527	6,010
5,000	50.48	13,173	51.74	10,522	2,651	54.19	8,006	5,167	59.21	5,658	7,515
6,000	60.57	15,805	62.09	12,627	3,178	65.03	9,607	6,198	71.05	6,789	9,016
7,000	70.66	18,438	72.44	14,732	3,706	75.86	11,206	7,232	82.89	7,920	10,518
8,000	80.76	21,074	82.79	16,837	4,237	86.70	12,808	8,266	94.74	9,053	12,021
9,000	90.85	23,706	93.14	18,942	4,764	97.54	14,410	9,296	106.58	10,184	13,522
10,000	100.95	26,342	103.48	21,044	5,298	108.38	16,011	10,331	118.42	11,316	15,026
11,000	111.04	28,974	113.83	23,149	5,825	119.21	17,610	11,364	130.26	12,447	16,527
12,000	121.13	31,607	124.18	25,254	6,353	130.05	19,212	12,395	142.10	13,578	18,029
13,000	131.23	34,243	134.53	27,359	6,884	140.89	20,814	13,429	153.94	14,709	19,534
14,000	141.32	36,875	144.88	29,464	7,411	151.72	22,413	14,462	165.78	15,840	21,035
15,000	151.42	39,511	155.22	31,566	7,945	162.56	24,014	15,497	177.62	16,972	22,539
16,000	161.51	42,144	165.57	33,671	8,473	173.40	25,616	16,528	189.47	18,105	24,039
17,000	171.60	44,776	175.92	35,776	9,000	184.24	27,218	17,558	201.31	19,236	25,540
18,000	181.70	47,412	186.27	37,881	9,531	195.07	28,817	18,595	213.15	20,367	27,045
19,000	191.79	50,044	196.62	39,986	10,058	205.91	30,418	19,626	224.99	21,498	28,546
20,000	201.89	52,680	206.96	42,088	10,592	216.75	32,020	20,660	236.83	22,629	30,051
21,000	211.98	55,313	217.31	44,193	11,120	227.58	33,619	21,694	248.67	23,761	31,552
22,000	222.08	57,949	227.66	46,298	11,651	238.42	35,221	22,728	260.51	24,892	33,057
23,000	232.17	60,581	238.01	48,403	12,178	249.26	36,822	23,759	272.36	26,025	34,556
24,000	242.26	63,214	248.36	50,508	12,706	260.09	38,422	24,792	284.20	27,156	36,058
25,000	252.36	65,850	258.70	52,610	13,240	270.93	40,023	25,827	296.04	28,287	37,563
26,000	262.45	68,482	269.05	54,715	13,767	281.77	41,625	26,857	307.88	29,418	39,064
27,000	272.55	71,118	279.40	56,820	14,298	292.61	43,226	27,892	319.72	30,550	40,568
28,000	282.64	73,750	289.75	58,925	14,825	303.44	44,826	28,924	331.56	31,681	42,069
29,000	292.73	76,383	300.10	61,030	15,353	314.28	46,427	29,956	343.40	32,812	43,571
30,000	302.83	79,019	310.44	63,132	15,887	325.12	48,029	30,990	355.24	33,943	45,076
32,500	328.06	85,602	336.31	68,393	17,209	352.21	52,030	33,572	384.85	36,773	48,829
35,000	353.30	92,188	362.18	73,654	18,534	379.30	56,032	36,156	414.45	39,601	52,587
40,000	403.77	105,357	413.92	84,176	21,181	433.49	64,038	41,319	473.66	45,259	60,098
45,000	454.24	118,526	465.66	94,698	23,828	487.67	72,041	46,485	532.86	50,915	67,611
50,000	504.71	131,696	517.40	105,220	26,476	541.86	80,046	51,650	592.07	56,573	75,123
55,000	555.18	144,865	569.14	115,742	29,123	596.04	88,050	56,815	651.28	62,230	82,635
60,000	605.65	158,034	620.88	126,264	31,770	650.23	96,055	61,979	710.48	67,886	90,148
65,000	656.12	171,203	672.62	136,786	34,417	704.41	104,058	67,145	769.69	73,544	97,659
70,000	706.59	184,372	724.36	147,308	37,064	758.60	112,064	72,308	828.90	79,202	105,170
75,000	757.06	197,542	776.10	157,830	39,712	812.79	120,070	77,472	888.10	84,858	112,684
80,000	807.53	210,711	827.84	168,352	42,359	866.97	128,073	82,638	947.31	90,516	120,195
85,000	858.00	223,880	879.58	178,874	45,006	921.16	136,078	87,802	1,006.52	96,174	127,706
90,000	908.47	237,049	931.32	189,396	47,653	975.34	144,082	92,967	1,065.72	101,830	135,219
95,000	958.94	250,218	983.06	199,918	50,300	1,029.53	152,087	98,131	1,124.93	107,487	142,731
100,000	1,009.41	263,388	1,034.80	210,440	52,948	1,083.71	160,090	103,298	1,184.14	113,145	150,243
105,000	1,059.89	276,560	1,086.54	220,962	55,598	1,137.90	168,096	108,464	1,243.34	118,801	157,759
110,000	1,110.36	289,730	1,138.28	231,484	58,246	1,192.08	176,099	113,631	1,302.55	124,459	165,271
115,000	1,160.83	302,899	1,190.02	242,006	60,893	1,246.27	184,105	118,794	1,361.76	130,117	172,782
120,000	1,211.30	316,068	1,241.76	252,528	63,540	1,300.45	192,108	123,960	1,420.96	135,773	180,295
125,000	1,261.77	329,237	1,293.50	263,050	66,187	1,354.64	200,114	129,123	1,480.17	141,431	187,806
130,000	1,312.24	342,406	1,345.24	273,572	68,834	1,408.82	208,117	134,289	1,539.38	147,088	195,318
135,000	1,362.71	355,576	1,396.98	284,094	71,482	1,463.01	216,122	139,454	1,598.58	152,744	202,832
140,000	1,413.18	368,745	1,448.72	294,616	74,129	1,517.19	224,126	144,619	1,657.79	158,402	210,343
145,000	1,463.65	381,914	1,500.46	305,138	76,776	1,571.38	232,131	149,783	1,717.00	164,060	217,854
150,000	1,514.12	395,083	1,552.20	315,660	79,423	1,625.57	240,137	154,946	1,776.20	169,716	225,367
155,000	1,564.59	408,252	1,603.94	326,182	82,070	1,679.75	248,140	160,112	1,835.41	175,374	232,878
160,000	1,615.06	421,422	1,655.68	336,704	84,718	1,733.94	256,146	165,276	1,894.62	181,032	240,390
165,000	1,665.53	434,591	1,707.42	347,226	87,365	1,788.12	264,149	170,442	1,953.82	186,688	247,903
170,000	1,716.00	447,760	1,759.16	357,748	90,012	1,842.31	272,154	175,606	2,013.03	192,345	255,415
175,000	1,766.47	460,929	1,810.90	368,270	92,659	1,896.49	280,158	180,771	2,072.23	198,001	262,928
180,000	1,816.94	474,098	1,862.64	378,792	95,306	1,950.68	288,163	185,935	2,131.44	203,659	270,439
185,000	1,867.41	487,268	1,914.38	389,314	97,954	2,004.86	296,166	191,102	2,190.65	209,317	277,951
190,000	1,917.88	500,437	1,966.12	399,836	100,601	2,059.05	304,172	196,265	2,249.85	214,973	285,464
195,000	1,968.35	513,606	2,017.86	410,358	103,248	2,113.23	312,175	201,431	2,309.06	220,631	292,975
200,000	2,018.82	526,775	2,069.60	420,880	105,895	2,167.42	320,181	206,594	2,368.27	226,289	300,486

23

12.00%   SHORT-TERM AMORTIZING MORTGAGES

AMOUNT OF LOAN	30 YEARS		25 YEARS			20 YEARS			15 YEARS		
	MONTHLY PAYMENT	TOTAL INTRST	MONTHLY PAYMENT	TOTAL INTRST	INTRST SAVED	MONTHLY PAYMENT	TOTAL INTRST	INTRST SAVED	MONTHLY PAYMENT	TOTAL INTRST	INTRST SAVED
$ 50	0.52	137	0.53	109	28	0.56	84	53	0.61	60	77
100	1.03	271	1.06	218	53	1.11	166	105	1.21	118	153
200	2.06	542	2.11	433	109	2.21	330	212	2.41	234	308
300	3.09	812	3.16	648	164	3.31	494	318	3.61	350	462
400	4.12	1,083	4.22	866	217	4.41	658	425	4.81	466	617
500	5.15	1,354	5.27	1,081	273	5.51	822	532	6.01	582	772
600	6.18	1,625	6.32	1,296	329	6.61	986	639	7.21	698	927
700	7.21	1,896	7.38	1,514	382	7.71	1,150	746	8.41	814	1,082
800	8.23	2,163	8.43	1,729	434	8.81	1,314	849	9.61	930	1,233
900	9.26	2,434	9.48	1,944	490	9.91	1,478	956	10.81	1,046	1,388
1,000	10.29	2,704	10.54	2,162	542	11.02	1,645	1,059	12.01	1,162	1,542
2,000	20.58	5,409	21.07	4,321	1,088	22.03	3,287	2,122	24.01	2,322	3,087
3,000	30.86	8,110	31.60	6,480	1,630	33.04	4,930	3,180	36.01	3,482	4,628
4,000	41.15	10,814	42.13	8,639	2,175	44.05	6,572	4,242	48.01	4,642	6,172
5,000	51.44	13,518	52.67	10,801	2,717	55.06	8,214	5,304	60.01	5,802	7,716
6,000	61.72	16,219	63.20	12,960	3,259	66.07	9,857	6,362	72.02	6,964	9,255
7,000	72.01	18,924	73.73	15,119	3,805	77.08	11,499	7,425	84.02	8,124	10,800
8,000	82.29	21,624	84.26	17,278	4,346	88.09	13,142	8,482	96.02	9,284	12,340
9,000	92.58	24,329	94.80	19,440	4,889	99.10	14,784	9,545	108.02	10,444	13,885
10,000	102.87	27,033	105.33	21,599	5,434	110.11	16,426	10,607	120.02	11,604	15,429
11,000	113.15	29,734	115.86	23,758	5,976	121.12	18,069	11,665	132.02	12,764	16,970
12,000	123.44	32,438	126.39	25,917	6,521	132.14	19,714	12,724	144.03	13,925	18,513
13,000	133.72	35,139	136.92	28,076	7,063	143.15	21,356	13,783	156.03	15,085	20,054
14,000	144.01	37,844	147.46	30,238	7,606	154.16	22,998	14,846	168.03	16,245	21,599
15,000	154.30	40,548	157.99	32,397	8,151	165.17	24,641	15,907	180.03	17,405	23,143
16,000	164.58	43,249	168.52	34,556	8,693	176.18	26,283	16,966	192.03	18,565	24,684
17,000	174.87	45,953	179.05	36,715	9,238	187.19	27,926	18,027	204.03	19,725	26,228
18,000	185.16	48,658	189.59	38,877	9,781	198.20	29,568	19,090	216.04	20,887	27,771
19,000	195.44	51,358	200.12	41,036	10,322	209.21	31,210	20,148	228.04	22,047	29,311
20,000	205.73	54,063	210.65	43,195	10,868	220.22	32,853	21,210	240.04	23,207	30,856
21,000	216.01	56,764	221.18	45,354	11,410	231.23	34,495	22,269	252.04	24,367	32,397
22,000	226.30	59,468	231.71	47,513	11,955	242.24	36,138	23,330	264.04	25,527	33,941
23,000	236.59	62,172	242.25	49,675	12,497	253.25	37,780	24,392	276.04	26,687	35,485
24,000	246.87	64,873	252.78	51,834	13,039	264.27	39,425	25,448	288.05	27,849	37,024
25,000	257.16	67,578	263.31	53,993	13,585	275.28	41,067	26,511	300.05	29,009	38,569
26,000	267.44	70,278	273.84	56,152	14,126	286.29	42,710	27,568	312.05	30,169	40,109
27,000	277.73	72,983	284.38	58,314	14,669	297.30	44,352	28,631	324.05	31,329	41,654
28,000	288.02	75,687	294.91	60,473	15,214	308.31	45,994	29,693	336.05	32,489	43,198
29,000	298.30	78,388	305.44	62,632	15,756	319.32	47,637	30,751	348.05	33,649	44,739
30,000	308.59	81,092	315.97	64,791	16,301	330.33	49,279	31,813	360.06	34,811	46,281
32,500	334.30	87,848	342.30	70,190	17,658	357.86	53,386	34,462	390.06	37,711	50,137
35,000	360.02	94,607	368.63	75,589	19,018	385.39	57,494	37,113	420.06	40,611	53,996
40,000	411.45	108,122	421.29	86,387	21,735	440.44	65,706	42,416	480.07	46,413	61,709
45,000	462.88	121,637	473.96	97,188	24,449	495.49	73,918	47,719	540.08	52,214	69,423
50,000	514.31	135,152	526.62	107,986	27,166	550.55	82,132	53,020	600.09	58,016	77,136
55,000	565.74	148,666	579.28	118,784	29,882	605.60	90,344	58,322	660.10	63,818	84,848
60,000	617.17	162,181	631.94	129,582	32,599	660.66	98,558	63,623	720.11	69,620	92,561
65,000	668.60	175,696	684.60	140,380	35,316	715.71	106,770	68,926	780.11	75,420	100,276
70,000	720.03	189,211	737.26	151,178	38,033	770.77	114,985	74,226	840.12	81,222	107,989
75,000	771.46	202,726	789.92	161,976	40,750	825.82	123,197	79,529	900.13	87,023	115,703
80,000	822.90	216,244	842.58	172,774	43,470	880.87	131,409	84,835	960.14	92,825	123,419
85,000	874.33	229,759	895.25	183,575	46,184	935.93	139,623	90,136	1,020.15	98,627	131,132
90,000	925.76	243,274	947.91	194,373	48,901	990.98	147,835	95,439	1,080.16	104,429	138,845
95,000	977.19	256,788	1,000.57	205,171	51,617	1,046.04	156,050	100,738	1,140.16	110,229	146,559
100,000	1,028.62	270,303	1,053.23	215,969	54,334	1,101.09	164,262	106,041	1,200.17	116,031	154,272
105,000	1,080.05	283,818	1,105.89	226,767	57,051	1,156.15	172,476	111,342	1,260.18	121,832	161,986
110,000	1,131.48	297,333	1,158.55	237,565	59,768	1,211.20	180,688	116,645	1,320.19	127,634	169,699
115,000	1,182.91	310,848	1,211.21	248,363	62,485	1,266.25	188,900	121,948	1,380.20	133,436	177,412
120,000	1,234.34	324,362	1,263.87	259,161	65,201	1,321.31	197,114	127,248	1,440.21	139,238	185,124
125,000	1,285.77	337,877	1,316.54	269,962	67,915	1,376.36	205,326	132,551	1,500.22	145,040	192,837
130,000	1,337.20	351,392	1,369.20	280,760	70,632	1,431.42	213,541	137,851	1,560.22	150,840	200,552
135,000	1,388.63	364,907	1,421.86	291,558	73,349	1,486.47	221,753	143,154	1,620.23	156,641	208,266
140,000	1,440.06	378,422	1,474.52	302,356	76,066	1,541.53	229,967	148,455	1,680.24	162,443	215,979
145,000	1,491.49	391,936	1,527.18	313,154	78,782	1,596.58	238,179	153,757	1,740.25	168,245	223,691
150,000	1,542.92	405,451	1,579.84	323,952	81,499	1,651.63	246,391	159,060	1,800.26	174,047	231,404
155,000	1,594.35	418,966	1,632.50	334,750	84,216	1,706.69	254,606	164,360	1,860.27	179,849	239,117
160,000	1,645.79	432,484	1,685.16	345,548	86,936	1,761.74	262,818	169,666	1,920.27	185,649	246,835
165,000	1,697.22	445,999	1,737.82	356,346	89,653	1,816.80	271,032	174,967	1,980.28	191,450	254,549
170,000	1,748.65	459,514	1,790.49	367,147	92,367	1,871.85	279,244	180,270	2,040.29	197,252	262,262
175,000	1,800.08	473,029	1,843.15	377,945	95,084	1,926.91	287,458	185,571	2,100.30	203,054	269,975
180,000	1,851.51	486,544	1,895.81	388,743	97,801	1,981.96	295,670	190,874	2,160.31	208,856	277,688
185,000	1,902.94	500,058	1,948.47	399,541	100,517	2,037.01	303,882	196,176	2,220.32	214,658	285,400
190,000	1,954.37	513,573	2,001.13	410,339	103,234	2,092.07	312,097	201,476	2,280.32	220,458	293,115
195,000	2,005.80	527,088	2,053.79	421,137	105,951	2,147.12	320,309	206,779	2,340.33	226,259	300,829
200,000	2,057.23	540,603	2,106.45	431,935	108,668	2,202.18	328,523	212,080	2,400.34	232,061	308,542

SHORT-TERM AMORTIZING MORTGAGES 12.25%

AMOUNT OF LOAN	30 YEARS MONTHLY PAYMENT	30 YEARS TOTAL INTRST	25 YEARS MONTHLY PAYMENT	25 YEARS TOTAL INTRST	25 YEARS INTRST SAVED	20 YEARS MONTHLY PAYMENT	20 YEARS TOTAL INTRST	20 YEARS INTRST SAVED	15 YEARS MONTHLY PAYMENT	15 YEARS TOTAL INTRST	15 YEARS INTRST SAVED
$ 50	0.53	141	0.54	112	29	0.56	84	57	0.61	60	81
100	1.05	278	1.08	224	54	1.12	169	109	1.22	120	158
200	2.10	556	2.15	445	111	2.24	338	218	2.44	239	317
300	3.15	834	3.22	666	168	3.36	506	328	3.65	357	477
400	4.20	1,112	4.29	887	225	4.48	675	437	4.87	477	635
500	5.24	1,386	5.36	1,108	278	5.60	844	542	6.09	596	790
600	6.29	1,664	6.44	1,332	332	6.72	1,013	651	7.30	714	950
700	7.34	1,942	7.51	1,553	389	7.83	1,179	763	8.52	834	1,108
800	8.39	2,220	8.58	1,774	446	8.95	1,348	872	9.74	953	1,267
900	9.44	2,498	9.65	1,995	503	10.07	1,517	981	10.95	1,071	1,427
1,000	10.48	2,773	10.72	2,216	557	11.19	1,686	1,087	12.17	1,191	1,582
2,000	20.96	5,546	21.44	4,432	1,114	22.38	3,371	2,175	24.33	2,379	3,167
3,000	31.44	8,318	32.16	6,648	1,670	33.56	5,054	3,264	36.49	3,568	4,750
4,000	41.92	11,091	42.87	8,861	2,230	44.75	6,740	4,351	48.66	4,759	6,332
5,000	52.40	13,864	53.59	11,077	2,787	55.93	8,423	5,441	60.82	5,948	7,916
6,000	62.88	16,637	64.31	13,293	3,344	67.12	10,109	6,528	72.98	7,136	9,501
7,000	73.36	19,410	75.03	15,509	3,901	78.30	11,792	7,618	85.15	8,327	11,083
8,000	83.84	22,182	85.74	17,722	4,460	89.49	13,478	8,704	97.31	9,516	12,666
9,000	94.32	24,955	96.46	19,938	5,017	100.68	15,163	9,792	109.47	10,705	14,250
10,000	104.79	27,724	107.18	22,154	5,570	111.86	16,846	10,878	121.63	11,893	15,831
11,000	115.27	30,497	117.90	24,370	6,127	123.05	18,532	11,965	133.80	13,084	17,413
12,000	125.75	33,270	128.61	26,583	6,687	134.23	20,215	13,055	145.96	14,273	18,997
13,000	136.23	36,043	139.33	28,799	7,244	145.42	21,901	14,142	158.12	15,462	20,581
14,000	146.71	38,816	150.05	31,015	7,801	156.60	23,584	15,232	170.29	16,652	22,164
15,000	157.19	41,588	160.77	33,231	8,357	167.79	25,270	16,318	182.45	17,841	23,747
16,000	167.67	44,361	171.48	35,444	8,917	178.98	26,955	17,406	194.61	19,030	25,331
17,000	178.15	47,134	182.20	37,660	9,474	190.16	28,638	18,496	206.78	20,220	26,914
18,000	188.63	49,907	192.92	39,876	10,031	201.35	30,324	19,583	218.94	21,409	28,498
19,000	199.11	52,680	203.64	42,092	10,588	212.53	32,007	20,673	231.10	22,598	30,082
20,000	209.58	55,449	214.35	44,305	11,144	223.72	33,693	21,756	243.26	23,787	31,662
21,000	220.06	58,222	225.07	46,521	11,701	234.90	35,376	22,846	255.43	24,977	33,245
22,000	230.54	60,994	235.79	48,737	12,257	246.09	37,062	23,932	267.59	26,166	34,828
23,000	241.02	63,767	246.51	50,953	12,814	257.27	38,745	25,022	279.75	27,355	36,412
24,000	251.50	66,540	257.22	53,166	13,374	268.46	40,430	26,110	291.92	28,546	37,994
25,000	261.98	69,313	267.94	55,382	13,931	279.65	42,116	27,197	304.08	29,734	39,579
26,000	272.46	72,086	278.66	57,598	14,488	290.83	43,799	28,287	316.24	30,923	41,163
27,000	282.94	74,858	289.38	59,814	15,044	302.02	45,485	29,373	328.41	32,114	42,744
28,000	293.42	77,631	300.09	62,027	15,604	313.20	47,168	30,463	340.57	33,303	44,328
29,000	303.89	80,400	310.81	64,243	16,157	324.39	48,854	31,546	352.73	34,491	45,909
30,000	314.37	83,173	321.53	66,459	16,714	335.57	50,537	32,636	364.89	35,680	47,493
32,500	340.57	90,105	348.32	71,996	18,109	363.54	54,750	35,355	395.30	38,654	51,451
35,000	366.77	97,037	375.12	77,536	19,501	391.50	58,960	38,077	425.71	41,628	55,409
40,000	419.16	110,898	428.70	88,610	22,288	447.43	67,383	43,515	486.52	47,574	63,324
45,000	471.56	124,762	482.29	99,687	25,075	503.36	75,806	48,956	547.34	53,521	71,241
50,000	523.95	138,622	535.88	110,764	27,858	559.29	84,230	54,392	608.15	59,467	79,155
55,000	576.35	152,486	589.46	121,838	30,648	615.22	92,653	59,833	668.97	65,415	87,071
60,000	628.74	166,346	643.05	132,915	33,431	671.14	101,074	65,272	729.78	71,360	94,986
65,000	681.14	180,210	696.64	143,992	36,218	727.07	109,497	70,713	790.60	77,308	102,902
70,000	733.53	194,071	750.23	155,069	39,002	783.00	117,920	76,151	851.41	83,254	110,817
75,000	785.93	207,935	803.81	166,143	41,792	838.93	126,343	81,592	912.23	89,201	118,734
80,000	838.32	221,795	857.40	177,220	44,575	894.86	134,766	87,029	973.04	95,147	126,648
85,000	890.72	235,659	910.99	188,297	47,362	950.78	143,187	92,472	1,033.86	101,095	134,564
90,000	943.11	249,520	964.57	199,371	50,149	1,006.71	151,610	97,910	1,094.67	107,041	142,479
95,000	995.51	263,384	1,018.16	210,448	52,936	1,062.64	160,034	103,350	1,155.49	112,988	150,396
100,000	1,047.90	277,244	1,071.75	221,525	55,719	1,118.57	168,457	108,787	1,216.30	118,934	158,310
105,000	1,100.30	291,108	1,125.34	232,602	58,506	1,174.50	176,880	114,228	1,277.12	124,882	166,226
110,000	1,152.69	304,968	1,178.92	243,676	61,292	1,230.43	185,303	119,665	1,337.93	130,827	174,141
115,000	1,205.09	318,832	1,232.51	254,753	64,079	1,286.35	193,724	125,108	1,398.75	136,775	182,057
120,000	1,257.48	332,693	1,286.10	265,830	66,863	1,342.28	202,147	130,546	1,459.56	142,721	189,972
125,000	1,309.88	346,557	1,339.68	276,904	69,653	1,398.21	210,570	135,987	1,520.38	148,668	197,889
130,000	1,362.27	360,417	1,393.27	287,981	72,436	1,454.14	218,994	141,423	1,581.19	154,614	205,803
135,000	1,414.67	374,281	1,446.86	299,058	75,223	1,510.07	227,417	146,864	1,642.01	160,562	213,719
140,000	1,467.06	388,142	1,500.45	310,135	78,007	1,566.00	235,840	152,302	1,702.82	166,508	221,634
145,000	1,519.45	402,002	1,554.03	321,208	80,793	1,621.92	244,261	157,741	1,763.64	172,455	229,547
150,000	1,571.85	415,866	1,607.62	332,286	83,580	1,677.85	252,684	163,182	1,824.45	178,401	237,465
155,000	1,624.24	429,726	1,661.21	343,363	86,363	1,733.78	261,107	168,619	1,885.27	184,349	245,377
160,000	1,676.64	443,590	1,714.80	354,440	89,150	1,789.71	269,530	174,060	1,946.08	190,294	253,296
165,000	1,729.03	457,451	1,768.38	365,514	91,937	1,845.64	277,954	179,497	2,006.90	196,242	261,209
170,000	1,781.43	471,315	1,821.97	376,591	94,724	1,901.56	286,374	184,941	2,067.71	202,188	269,127
175,000	1,833.82	485,175	1,875.56	387,668	97,507	1,957.49	294,798	190,377	2,128.53	208,135	277,040
180,000	1,886.22	499,039	1,929.14	398,742	100,297	2,013.42	303,221	195,818	2,189.34	214,081	284,958
185,000	1,938.61	512,900	1,982.73	409,819	103,081	2,069.35	311,644	201,256	2,250.16	220,029	292,871
190,000	1,991.01	526,764	2,036.32	420,896	105,868	2,125.28	320,067	206,697	2,310.97	225,975	300,789
195,000	2,043.40	540,624	2,089.91	431,973	108,651	2,181.21	328,490	212,134	2,371.79	231,922	308,702
200,000	2,095.80	554,488	2,143.49	443,047	111,441	2,237.13	336,911	217,577	2,432.60	237,868	316,620

12.50% SHORT-TERM AMORTIZING MORTGAGES

AMOUNT OF LOAN	30 YEARS		25 YEARS			20 YEARS			15 YEARS		
	MONTHLY PAYMENT	TOTAL INTRST	MONTHLY PAYMENT	TOTAL INTRST	INTRST SAVED	MONTHLY PAYMENT	TOTAL INTRST	INTRST SAVED	MONTHLY PAYMENT	TOTAL INTRST	INTRST SAVED
$ 50	0.54	144	0.55	115	29	0.57	87	57	0.62	62	82
100	1.07	285	1.10	230	55	1.14	174	111	1.24	123	162
200	2.14	570	2.19	457	113	2.28	347	223	2.47	245	325
300	3.21	856	3.28	684	172	3.41	518	338	3.70	366	490
400	4.27	1,137	4.37	911	226	4.55	692	445	4.94	489	648
500	5.34	1,422	5.46	1,138	284	5.69	866	556	6.17	611	811
600	6.41	1,708	6.55	1,365	343	6.82	1,037	671	7.40	732	976
700	7.48	1,993	7.64	1,592	401	7.96	1,210	783	8.63	853	1,140
800	8.54	2,274	8.73	1,819	455	9.09	1,382	892	9.87	977	1,297
900	9.61	2,560	9.82	2,046	514	10.23	1,555	1,005	11.10	1,098	1,462
1,000	10.68	2,845	10.91	2,273	572	11.37	1,729	1,116	12.33	1,219	1,626
2,000	21.35	5,686	21.81	4,543	1,143	22.73	3,455	2,231	24.66	2,439	3,247
3,000	32.02	8,527	32.72	6,816	1,711	34.09	5,182	3,345	36.98	3,656	4,871
4,000	42.70	11,372	43.62	9,086	2,286	45.45	6,908	4,464	49.31	4,876	6,496
5,000	53.37	14,213	54.52	11,356	2,857	56.81	8,634	5,579	61.63	6,093	8,120
6,000	64.04	17,054	65.43	13,629	3,425	68.17	10,361	6,693	73.96	7,313	9,741
7,000	74.71	19,896	76.33	15,899	3,997	79.53	12,087	7,809	86.28	8,530	11,366
8,000	85.39	22,740	87.23	18,169	4,571	90.90	13,816	8,924	98.61	9,750	12,990
9,000	96.06	25,582	98.14	20,442	5,140	102.26	15,542	10,040	110.93	10,967	14,615
10,000	106.73	28,423	109.04	22,712	5,711	113.62	17,269	11,154	123.26	12,187	16,236
11,000	117.40	31,264	119.94	24,982	6,282	124.98	18,995	12,269	135.58	13,404	17,860
12,000	128.08	34,109	130.85	27,255	6,854	136.34	20,722	13,387	147.91	14,624	19,485
13,000	138.75	36,950	141.75	29,525	7,425	147.70	22,448	14,502	160.23	15,841	21,109
14,000	149.42	39,791	152.65	31,795	7,996	159.06	24,174	15,617	172.55	17,061	22,730
15,000	160.09	42,632	163.56	34,068	8,564	170.43	25,903	16,729	184.88	18,278	24,354
16,000	170.77	45,477	174.46	36,338	9,139	181.79	27,630	17,847	197.21	19,498	25,979
17,000	181.44	48,318	185.37	38,611	9,707	193.15	29,356	18,962	209.53	20,715	27,603
18,000	192.11	51,160	196.27	40,881	10,279	204.51	31,082	20,078	221.86	21,935	29,225
19,000	202.78	54,001	207.17	43,151	10,850	215.87	32,809	21,192	234.18	23,152	30,849
20,000	213.46	56,846	218.08	45,424	11,422	227.23	34,535	22,311	246.51	24,372	32,474
21,000	224.13	59,687	228.98	47,694	11,993	238.59	36,262	23,425	258.83	25,589	34,098
22,000	234.80	62,528	239.88	49,964	12,564	249.96	37,990	24,538	271.16	26,809	35,719
23,000	245.47	65,369	250.79	52,237	13,132	261.32	39,717	25,652	283.49	28,028	37,341
24,000	256.15	68,214	261.69	54,507	13,707	272.68	41,443	26,771	295.81	29,246	38,968
25,000	266.82	71,055	272.59	56,777	14,278	284.04	43,170	27,885	308.14	30,465	40,590
26,000	277.49	73,896	283.50	59,050	14,846	295.40	44,896	29,000	320.46	31,683	42,213
27,000	288.16	76,738	294.40	61,320	15,418	306.76	46,622	30,116	332.79	32,902	43,836
28,000	298.84	79,582	305.30	63,590	15,992	318.12	48,349	31,233	345.11	34,120	45,462
29,000	309.51	82,424	316.21	65,863	16,561	329.49	50,078	32,346	357.44	35,339	47,085
30,000	320.18	85,265	327.11	68,133	17,132	340.85	51,804	33,461	369.76	36,557	48,708
32,500	346.86	92,370	354.37	73,811	18,559	369.25	56,120	36,250	400.57	39,603	52,767
35,000	373.55	99,478	381.63	79,489	19,989	397.65	60,436	39,042	431.39	42,650	56,828
40,000	426.91	113,688	436.15	90,845	22,843	454.46	69,070	44,618	493.01	48,742	64,946
45,000	480.27	127,897	490.66	102,198	25,699	511.27	77,705	50,192	554.64	54,835	73,052
50,000	533.63	142,107	545.18	113,554	28,553	568.08	86,339	55,768	616.27	60,929	81,178
55,000	587.00	156,320	599.70	124,910	31,410	624.88	94,971	61,349	677.89	67,020	89,300
60,000	640.36	170,530	654.22	136,266	34,264	681.69	103,606	66,924	739.52	73,114	97,416
65,000	693.72	184,739	708.74	147,622	37,117	738.50	112,240	72,499	801.14	79,205	105,534
70,000	747.09	198,952	763.25	158,975	39,977	795.30	120,872	78,080	862.77	85,299	113,653
75,000	800.45	213,162	817.77	170,331	42,831	852.11	129,506	83,656	924.40	91,392	121,770
80,000	853.81	227,372	872.29	181,687	45,685	908.92	138,141	89,231	986.02	97,484	129,888
85,000	907.17	241,581	926.81	193,043	48,538	965.72	146,773	94,808	1,047.65	103,577	138,004
90,000	960.54	255,794	981.32	204,396	51,398	1,022.53	155,407	100,387	1,109.27	109,669	146,125
95,000	1,013.90	270,004	1,035.84	215,752	54,252	1,079.34	164,042	105,962	1,170.90	115,762	154,242
100,000	1,067.26	284,214	1,090.36	227,108	57,106	1,136.15	172,676	111,538	1,232.53	121,855	162,359
105,000	1,120.63	298,427	1,144.88	238,464	59,963	1,192.95	181,308	117,119	1,294.15	127,947	170,480
110,000	1,173.99	312,636	1,199.39	249,817	62,819	1,249.76	189,942	122,694	1,355.78	134,040	178,596
115,000	1,227.35	326,846	1,253.91	261,173	65,673	1,306.57	198,577	128,269	1,417.41	140,134	186,712
120,000	1,280.71	341,056	1,308.43	272,529	68,527	1,363.37	207,209	133,847	1,479.03	146,225	194,831
125,000	1,334.08	355,269	1,362.95	283,885	71,384	1,420.18	215,843	139,426	1,540.66	152,319	202,950
130,000	1,387.44	369,478	1,417.47	295,241	74,237	1,476.99	224,478	145,000	1,602.28	158,410	211,068
135,000	1,440.80	383,688	1,471.98	306,594	77,094	1,533.79	233,110	150,578	1,663.91	164,504	219,184
140,000	1,494.17	397,901	1,526.50	317,950	79,951	1,590.60	241,744	156,157	1,725.54	170,597	227,304
145,000	1,547.53	412,111	1,581.02	329,306	82,805	1,647.41	250,378	161,733	1,787.16	176,689	235,422
150,000	1,600.89	426,320	1,635.54	340,662	85,658	1,704.22	259,013	167,307	1,848.79	182,782	243,538
155,000	1,654.25	440,530	1,690.05	352,015	88,515	1,761.02	267,645	172,885	1,910.41	188,874	251,656
160,000	1,707.62	454,743	1,744.57	363,371	91,372	1,817.83	276,279	178,464	1,972.04	194,967	259,776
165,000	1,760.98	468,953	1,799.09	374,727	94,226	1,874.64	284,914	184,039	2,033.67	201,061	267,892
170,000	1,814.34	483,162	1,853.61	386,083	97,079	1,931.44	293,546	189,616	2,095.29	207,152	276,010
175,000	1,867.71	497,376	1,908.12	397,436	99,940	1,988.25	302,180	195,196	2,156.92	213,246	284,130
180,000	1,921.07	511,585	1,962.64	408,792	102,793	2,045.06	310,814	200,771	2,218.54	219,337	292,248
185,000	1,974.43	525,795	2,017.16	420,148	105,647	2,101.87	319,449	206,346	2,280.17	225,431	300,364
190,000	2,027.79	540,004	2,071.68	431,504	108,500	2,158.67	328,081	211,923	2,341.80	231,524	308,480
195,000	2,081.16	554,218	2,126.20	442,860	111,358	2,215.48	336,715	217,503	2,403.42	237,616	316,602
200,000	2,134.52	568,427	2,180.71	454,213	114,214	2,272.29	345,350	223,077	2,465.05	243,709	324,718

SHORT-TERM AMORTIZING MORTGAGES 12.75%

AMOUNT OF LOAN	30 YEARS MONTHLY PAYMENT	30 YEARS TOTAL INTRST	25 YEARS MONTHLY PAYMENT	25 YEARS TOTAL INTRST	25 YEARS INTRST SAVED	20 YEARS MONTHLY PAYMENT	20 YEARS TOTAL INTRST	20 YEARS INTRST SAVED	15 YEARS MONTHLY PAYMENT	15 YEARS TOTAL INTRST	15 YEARS INTRST SAVED
$ 50	0.55	148	0.56	118	30	0.58	89	59	0.63	63	85
100	1.09	292	1.11	233	59	1.16	178	114	1.25	125	167
200	2.18	585	2.22	466	119	2.31	354	231	2.50	250	335
300	3.27	877	3.33	699	178	3.47	533	344	3.75	375	502
400	4.35	1,166	4.44	932	234	4.62	709	457	5.00	500	666
500	5.44	1,458	5.55	1,165	293	5.77	885	573	6.25	625	833
600	6.53	1,751	6.66	1,398	353	6.93	1,063	688	7.50	750	1,001
700	7.61	2,040	7.77	1,631	409	8.08	1,239	801	8.75	875	1,165
800	8.70	2,332	8.88	1,864	468	9.24	1,418	914	10.00	1,000	1,332
900	9.79	2,624	9.99	2,097	527	10.39	1,594	1,030	11.24	1,123	1,501
1,000	10.87	2,913	11.10	2,330	583	11.54	1,770	1,143	12.49	1,248	1,665
2,000	21.74	5,826	22.19	4,657	1,169	23.08	3,539	2,287	24.98	2,496	3,330
3,000	32.61	8,740	33.28	6,984	1,756	34.62	5,309	3,431	37.47	3,745	4,995
4,000	43.47	11,649	44.37	9,311	2,338	46.16	7,078	4,571	49.96	4,993	6,656
5,000	54.34	14,562	55.46	11,638	2,924	57.70	8,848	5,714	62.45	6,241	8,321
6,000	65.21	17,476	66.55	13,965	3,511	69.23	10,615	6,861	74.94	7,489	9,987
7,000	76.07	20,385	77.64	16,292	4,093	80.77	12,385	8,000	87.42	8,736	11,649
8,000	86.94	23,298	88.73	18,619	4,679	92.31	14,154	9,144	99.91	9,984	13,314
9,000	97.81	26,212	99.82	20,946	5,266	103.85	15,924	10,288	112.40	11,232	14,980
10,000	108.67	29,121	110.91	23,273	5,848	115.39	17,694	11,427	124.89	12,480	16,641
11,000	119.54	32,034	122.00	25,600	6,434	126.92	19,461	12,573	137.38	13,728	18,306
12,000	130.41	34,948	133.09	27,927	7,021	138.46	21,230	13,718	149.87	14,977	19,971
13,000	141.28	37,861	144.18	30,254	7,607	150.00	23,000	14,861	162.35	16,223	21,638
14,000	152.14	40,770	155.27	32,581	8,189	161.54	24,770	16,000	174.84	17,471	23,299
15,000	163.01	43,684	166.36	34,908	8,776	173.08	26,539	17,145	187.33	18,719	24,965
16,000	173.88	46,597	177.45	37,235	9,362	184.61	28,306	18,291	199.82	19,968	26,629
17,000	184.74	49,506	188.54	39,562	9,944	196.15	30,076	19,430	212.31	21,216	28,290
18,000	195.61	52,420	199.63	41,889	10,531	207.69	31,846	20,574	224.80	22,464	29,956
19,000	206.48	55,333	210.72	44,216	11,117	219.23	33,615	21,718	237.28	23,710	31,623
20,000	217.34	58,242	221.82	46,546	11,696	230.77	35,385	22,857	249.77	24,959	33,283
21,000	228.21	61,156	232.91	48,873	12,283	242.31	37,154	24,002	262.26	26,207	34,949
22,000	239.08	64,069	244.00	51,200	12,869	253.84	38,922	25,147	274.75	27,455	36,614
23,000	249.94	66,978	255.09	53,527	13,451	265.38	40,691	26,287	287.24	28,703	38,275
24,000	260.81	69,892	266.18	55,854	14,038	276.92	42,461	27,431	299.73	29,951	39,941
25,000	271.68	72,805	277.27	58,181	14,624	288.46	44,230	28,575	312.21	31,198	41,607
26,000	282.55	75,718	288.36	60,508	15,210	300.00	46,000	29,718	324.70	32,446	43,272
27,000	293.41	78,628	299.45	62,835	15,793	311.53	47,767	30,861	337.19	33,694	44,934
28,000	304.28	81,541	310.54	65,162	16,379	323.07	49,537	32,004	349.68	34,942	46,599
29,000	315.15	84,454	321.63	67,489	16,965	334.61	51,306	33,148	362.17	36,191	48,263
30,000	326.01	87,364	332.72	69,816	17,548	346.15	53,076	34,288	374.66	37,439	49,925
32,500	353.18	94,645	360.45	75,635	19,010	374.99	57,498	37,147	405.88	40,558	54,087
35,000	380.35	101,926	388.17	81,451	20,475	403.84	61,922	40,004	437.10	43,678	58,248
40,000	434.68	116,485	443.63	93,089	23,396	461.53	70,767	45,718	499.54	49,917	66,568
45,000	489.02	131,047	499.08	104,724	26,323	519.22	79,613	51,434	561.98	56,156	74,891
50,000	543.35	145,606	554.53	116,359	29,247	576.91	88,458	57,148	624.42	62,396	83,210
55,000	597.69	160,168	609.98	127,994	32,174	634.60	97,304	62,864	686.87	68,637	91,531
60,000	652.02	174,727	665.44	139,632	35,095	692.29	106,150	68,577	749.31	74,876	99,851
65,000	706.36	189,290	720.89	151,267	38,023	749.98	114,995	74,295	811.75	81,115	108,175
70,000	760.69	203,848	776.34	162,902	40,946	807.67	123,841	80,007	874.19	87,354	116,494
75,000	815.02	218,407	831.79	174,537	43,870	865.36	132,686	85,721	936.63	93,593	124,814
80,000	869.36	232,970	887.25	186,175	46,795	923.05	141,532	91,438	999.07	99,833	133,137
85,000	923.69	247,528	942.70	197,810	49,718	980.74	150,378	97,150	1,061.52	106,074	141,454
90,000	978.03	262,091	998.15	209,445	52,646	1,038.44	159,226	102,865	1,123.96	112,313	149,778
95,000	1,032.36	276,650	1,053.60	221,080	55,570	1,096.13	168,071	108,579	1,186.40	118,552	158,098
100,000	1,086.70	291,212	1,109.06	232,718	58,494	1,153.82	176,917	114,295	1,248.84	124,791	166,421
105,000	1,141.03	305,771	1,164.51	244,353	61,418	1,211.51	185,762	120,009	1,311.28	131,030	174,741
110,000	1,195.37	320,333	1,219.96	255,988	64,345	1,269.20	194,608	125,725	1,373.73	137,271	183,062
115,000	1,249.70	334,892	1,275.42	267,626	67,266	1,326.89	203,454	131,438	1,436.17	143,511	191,381
120,000	1,304.04	349,454	1,330.87	279,261	70,193	1,384.58	212,299	137,155	1,498.61	149,750	199,704
125,000	1,358.37	364,013	1,386.32	290,896	73,117	1,442.27	221,145	142,868	1,561.05	155,989	208,024
130,000	1,412.71	378,576	1,441.77	302,531	76,045	1,499.96	229,990	148,586	1,623.49	162,228	216,348
135,000	1,467.04	393,134	1,497.23	314,169	78,965	1,557.65	238,836	154,298	1,685.93	168,467	224,667
140,000	1,521.38	407,697	1,552.68	325,804	81,893	1,615.34	247,682	160,015	1,748.38	174,708	232,989
145,000	1,575.71	422,256	1,608.13	337,439	84,817	1,673.03	256,527	165,729	1,810.82	180,948	241,308
150,000	1,630.04	436,814	1,663.58	349,074	87,740	1,730.72	265,373	171,441	1,873.26	187,187	249,627
155,000	1,684.38	451,377	1,719.04	360,712	90,665	1,788.41	274,218	177,159	1,935.70	193,426	257,951
160,000	1,738.71	465,936	1,774.49	372,347	93,589	1,846.10	283,064	182,872	1,998.14	199,665	266,271
165,000	1,793.05	480,498	1,829.94	383,982	96,516	1,903.79	291,910	188,588	2,060.59	205,906	274,592
170,000	1,847.38	495,057	1,885.39	395,617	99,440	1,961.48	300,755	194,302	2,123.03	212,145	282,912
175,000	1,901.72	509,619	1,940.85	407,255	102,364	2,019.18	309,603	200,016	2,185.47	218,385	291,234
180,000	1,956.05	524,178	1,996.30	418,890	105,288	2,076.87	318,449	205,729	2,247.91	224,624	299,554
185,000	2,010.39	538,740	2,051.75	430,525	108,215	2,134.56	327,294	211,446	2,310.35	230,863	307,877
190,000	2,064.72	553,299	2,107.20	442,160	111,139	2,192.25	336,140	217,159	2,372.80	237,104	316,195
195,000	2,119.06	567,862	2,162.66	453,798	114,064	2,249.94	344,986	222,876	2,435.24	243,343	324,519
200,000	2,173.39	582,420	2,218.11	465,433	116,987	2,307.63	353,831	228,589	2,497.68	249,582	332,838

27

AMOUNT OF LOAN	30 YEARS		25 YEARS			20 YEARS			15 YEARS		
	MONTHLY PAYMENT	TOTAL INTRST	MONTHLY PAYMENT	TOTAL INTRST	INTRST SAVED	MONTHLY PAYMENT	TOTAL INTRST	INTRST SAVED	MONTHLY PAYMENT	TOTAL INTRST	INTRST SAVED
$ 50	0.56	152	0.57	121	31	0.59	92	60	0.64	65	87
100	1.11	300	1.13	239	61	1.18	183	117	1.27	129	171
200	2.22	599	2.26	478	121	2.35	364	235	2.54	257	342
300	3.32	895	3.39	717	178	3.52	545	350	3.80	384	511
400	4.43	1,195	4.52	956	239	4.69	726	469	5.07	513	682
500	5.54	1,494	5.64	1,192	302	5.86	906	588	6.33	639	855
600	6.64	1,790	6.77	1,431	359	7.03	1,087	703	7.60	768	1,022
700	7.75	2,090	7.90	1,670	420	8.21	1,270	820	8.86	895	1,195
800	8.85	2,386	9.03	1,909	477	9.38	1,451	935	10.13	1,023	1,363
900	9.96	2,686	10.16	2,148	538	10.55	1,632	1,054	11.39	1,150	1,536
1,000	11.07	2,985	11.28	2,384	601	11.72	1,813	1,172	12.66	1,279	1,706
2,000	22.13	5,967	22.56	4,768	1,199	23.44	3,626	2,341	25.31	2,556	3,411
3,000	33.19	8,948	33.84	7,152	1,796	35.15	5,436	3,512	37.96	3,833	5,115
4,000	44.25	11,930	45.12	9,536	2,394	46.87	7,249	4,681	50.61	5,110	6,820
5,000	55.31	14,912	56.40	11,920	2,992	58.58	9,059	5,853	63.27	6,389	8,523
6,000	66.38	17,897	67.68	14,304	3,593	70.30	10,872	7,025	75.92	7,666	10,231
7,000	77.44	20,878	78.95	16,685	4,193	82.02	12,685	8,193	88.57	8,943	11,935
8,000	88.50	23,860	90.23	19,069	4,791	93.73	14,495	9,365	101.22	10,220	13,640
9,000	99.56	26,842	101.51	21,453	5,389	105.45	16,308	10,534	113.88	11,498	15,344
10,000	110.62	29,823	112.79	23,837	5,986	117.16	18,118	11,705	126.53	12,775	17,048
11,000	121.69	32,808	124.07	26,221	6,587	128.88	19,931	12,877	139.18	14,052	18,756
12,000	132.75	35,790	135.35	28,605	7,185	140.59	21,742	14,048	151.83	15,329	20,461
13,000	143.81	38,772	146.62	30,986	7,786	152.31	23,554	15,218	164.49	16,608	22,164
14,000	154.87	41,753	157.90	33,370	8,383	164.03	25,367	16,386	177.14	17,885	23,868
15,000	165.93	44,735	169.18	35,754	8,981	175.74	27,178	17,557	189.79	19,162	25,573
16,000	177.00	47,720	180.46	38,138	9,582	187.46	28,990	18,730	202.44	20,439	27,281
17,000	188.06	50,702	191.74	40,522	10,180	199.17	30,801	19,901	215.10	21,718	28,984
18,000	199.12	53,683	203.02	42,906	10,777	210.89	32,614	21,069	227.75	22,995	30,688
19,000	210.18	56,665	214.29	45,287	11,378	222.60	34,424	22,241	240.40	24,272	32,393
20,000	221.24	59,646	225.57	47,671	11,975	234.32	36,237	23,409	253.05	25,549	34,097
21,000	232.31	62,632	236.85	50,055	12,577	246.04	38,050	24,582	265.71	26,828	35,804
22,000	243.37	65,613	248.13	52,439	13,174	257.75	39,860	25,753	278.36	28,105	37,508
23,000	254.43	68,595	259.41	54,823	13,772	269.47	41,673	26,922	291.01	29,382	39,213
24,000	265.49	71,576	270.69	57,207	14,369	281.18	43,483	28,093	303.66	30,659	40,917
25,000	276.55	74,558	281.96	59,588	14,970	292.90	45,296	29,262	316.32	31,938	42,620
26,000	287.62	77,543	293.24	61,972	15,571	304.61	47,106	30,437	328.97	33,215	44,328
27,000	298.68	80,525	304.52	64,356	16,169	316.33	48,919	31,606	341.62	34,492	46,033
28,000	309.74	83,506	315.80	66,740	16,766	328.05	50,732	32,774	354.27	35,769	47,737
29,000	320.80	86,488	327.08	69,124	17,364	339.76	52,542	33,946	366.93	37,047	49,441
30,000	331.86	89,470	338.36	71,508	17,962	351.48	54,355	35,115	379.58	38,324	51,146
32,500	359.52	96,927	366.55	77,465	19,462	380.77	58,885	38,042	411.21	41,518	55,409
35,000	387.17	104,381	394.75	83,425	20,956	410.06	63,414	40,967	442.84	44,711	59,670
40,000	442.48	119,293	451.14	95,342	23,951	468.64	72,474	46,819	506.10	51,098	68,195
45,000	497.79	134,204	507.53	107,259	26,945	527.21	81,530	52,674	569.36	57,485	76,719
50,000	553.10	149,116	563.92	119,176	29,940	585.79	90,590	58,526	632.63	63,873	85,243
55,000	608.41	164,028	620.31	131,093	32,935	644.37	99,649	64,379	695.89	70,260	93,768
60,000	663.72	178,939	676.71	143,013	35,926	702.95	108,708	70,231	759.15	76,647	102,292
65,000	719.03	193,851	733.10	154,930	38,921	761.53	117,767	76,084	822.41	83,034	110,817
70,000	774.34	208,762	789.49	166,847	41,915	820.11	126,826	81,936	885.67	89,421	119,341
75,000	829.65	223,674	845.88	178,764	44,910	878.69	135,886	87,788	948.94	95,809	127,865
80,000	884.96	238,586	902.27	190,681	47,905	937.27	144,945	93,641	1,012.20	102,196	136,390
85,000	940.27	253,497	958.67	202,601	50,896	995.84	154,002	99,495	1,075.46	108,583	144,914
90,000	995.58	268,409	1,015.06	214,518	53,891	1,054.42	163,061	105,348	1,138.72	114,970	153,439
95,000	1,050.89	283,320	1,071.45	226,435	56,885	1,113.00	172,120	111,200	1,201.99	121,358	161,962
100,000	1,106.20	298,232	1,127.84	238,352	59,880	1,171.58	181,179	117,053	1,265.25	127,745	170,487
105,000	1,161.51	313,144	1,184.23	250,269	62,875	1,230.16	190,238	122,906	1,328.51	134,132	179,012
110,000	1,216.82	328,055	1,240.62	262,186	65,869	1,288.74	199,298	128,757	1,391.77	140,519	187,536
115,000	1,272.13	342,967	1,297.02	274,106	68,861	1,347.32	208,357	134,610	1,455.03	146,905	196,062
120,000	1,327.44	357,878	1,353.41	286,023	71,855	1,405.90	217,416	140,462	1,518.30	153,294	204,584
125,000	1,382.75	372,790	1,409.80	297,940	74,850	1,464.47	226,473	146,317	1,581.56	159,681	213,109
130,000	1,438.06	387,702	1,466.19	309,857	77,845	1,523.05	235,532	152,170	1,644.82	166,068	221,634
135,000	1,493.37	402,613	1,522.58	321,774	80,839	1,581.63	244,591	158,022	1,708.08	172,454	230,159
140,000	1,548.68	417,525	1,578.97	333,691	83,834	1,640.21	253,650	163,875	1,771.34	178,841	238,684
145,000	1,603.99	432,436	1,635.37	345,611	86,825	1,698.79	262,710	169,726	1,834.61	185,230	247,206
150,000	1,659.30	447,348	1,691.76	357,528	89,820	1,757.37	271,769	175,579	1,897.87	191,617	255,731
155,000	1,714.61	462,260	1,748.15	369,445	92,815	1,815.95	280,828	181,432	1,961.13	198,003	264,257
160,000	1,769.92	477,171	1,804.54	381,362	95,809	1,874.53	289,887	187,284	2,024.39	204,390	272,781
165,000	1,825.23	492,083	1,860.93	393,279	98,804	1,933.10	298,944	193,139	2,087.65	210,777	281,306
170,000	1,880.54	506,994	1,917.33	405,199	101,795	1,991.68	308,003	198,991	2,150.92	217,166	289,828
175,000	1,935.85	521,906	1,973.72	417,116	104,790	2,050.26	317,063	204,843	2,214.18	223,552	298,354
180,000	1,991.16	536,818	2,030.11	429,033	107,785	2,108.84	326,122	210,696	2,277.44	229,939	306,879
185,000	2,046.47	551,729	2,086.50	440,950	110,779	2,167.42	335,181	216,548	2,340.70	236,326	315,403
190,000	2,101.78	566,641	2,142.89	452,867	113,774	2,226.00	344,240	222,401	2,403.97	242,715	323,926
195,000	2,157.09	581,552	2,199.28	464,784	116,768	2,284.58	353,299	228,253	2,467.23	249,101	332,451
200,000	2,212.40	596,464	2,255.68	476,704	119,760	2,343.16	362,358	234,106	2,530.49	255,488	340,976

AMOUNT OF LOAN	30 YEARS MONTHLY PAYMENT	30 YEARS TOTAL INTRST	25 YEARS MONTHLY PAYMENT	25 YEARS TOTAL INTRST	25 YEARS INTRST SAVED	20 YEARS MONTHLY PAYMENT	20 YEARS TOTAL INTRST	20 YEARS INTRST SAVED	15 YEARS MONTHLY PAYMENT	15 YEARS TOTAL INTRST	15 YEARS INTRST SAVED
$ 50	0.57	155	0.58	124	31	0.60	94	61	0.65	67	88
100	1.13	307	1.15	245	62	1.19	186	121	1.29	132	175
200	2.26	614	2.30	490	124	2.38	371	243	2.57	263	351
300	3.38	917	3.45	735	182	3.57	557	360	3.85	393	524
400	4.51	1,224	4.59	977	247	4.76	742	482	5.13	523	701
500	5.63	1,527	5.74	1,222	305	5.95	928	599	6.41	654	873
600	6.76	1,834	6.89	1,467	367	7.14	1,114	720	7.70	786	1,048
700	7.89	2,140	8.03	1,709	431	8.33	1,299	841	8.98	916	1,224
800	9.01	2,444	9.18	1,954	490	9.52	1,485	959	10.26	1,047	1,397
900	10.14	2,750	10.33	2,199	551	10.71	1,670	1,080	11.54	1,177	1,573
1,000	11.26	3,054	11.47	2,441	613	11.90	1,856	1,198	12.82	1,308	1,746
2,000	22.52	6,107	22.94	4,882	1,225	23.79	3,710	2,397	25.64	2,615	3,492
3,000	33.78	9,161	34.41	7,323	1,838	35.69	5,566	3,595	38.46	3,923	5,238
4,000	45.04	12,214	45.87	9,761	2,453	47.58	7,419	4,795	51.27	5,229	6,985
5,000	56.29	15,264	57.34	12,202	3,062	59.48	9,275	5,989	64.09	6,536	8,728
6,000	67.55	18,318	68.81	14,643	3,675	71.37	11,129	7,189	76.91	7,844	10,474
7,000	78.81	21,372	80.27	17,081	4,291	83.27	12,985	8,387	89.73	9,151	12,221
8,000	90.07	24,425	91.74	19,522	4,903	95.16	14,838	9,587	102.54	10,457	13,968
9,000	101.32	27,475	103.21	21,963	5,512	107.05	16,692	10,783	115.36	11,765	15,710
10,000	112.58	30,529	114.68	24,404	6,125	118.95	18,548	11,981	128.18	13,072	17,457
11,000	123.84	33,582	126.14	26,842	6,740	130.84	20,402	13,180	141.00	14,380	19,202
12,000	135.10	36,636	137.61	29,283	7,353	142.74	22,258	14,378	153.81	15,686	20,950
13,000	146.36	39,690	149.08	31,724	7,966	154.63	24,111	15,579	166.63	16,993	22,697
14,000	157.61	42,740	160.54	34,162	8,578	166.53	25,967	16,773	179.45	18,301	24,439
15,000	168.87	45,793	172.01	36,603	9,190	178.42	27,821	17,972	192.27	19,609	26,184
16,000	180.13	48,847	183.48	39,044	9,803	190.31	29,674	19,173	205.08	20,914	27,933
17,000	191.39	51,900	194.94	41,482	10,418	202.21	31,530	20,370	217.90	22,222	29,678
18,000	202.64	54,950	206.41	43,923	11,027	214.10	33,384	21,566	230.72	23,528	31,420
19,000	213.90	58,004	217.88	46,364	11,640	226.00	35,240	22,764	243.53	24,835	33,169
20,000	225.16	61,058	229.35	48,805	12,253	237.89	37,094	23,964	256.35	26,143	34,915
21,000	236.42	64,111	240.81	51,243	12,868	249.79	38,950	25,161	269.17	27,451	36,660
22,000	247.68	67,165	252.28	53,684	13,481	261.68	40,803	26,362	281.99	28,758	38,407
23,000	258.93	70,215	263.75	56,125	14,090	273.57	42,657	27,558	294.80	30,064	40,151
24,000	270.19	73,268	275.21	58,563	14,705	285.47	44,513	28,755	307.62	31,372	41,896
25,000	281.45	76,322	286.68	61,004	15,318	297.36	46,366	29,956	320.44	32,679	43,643
26,000	292.71	79,376	298.15	63,445	15,931	309.26	48,222	31,154	333.26	33,987	45,389
27,000	303.96	82,426	309.61	65,883	16,543	321.15	50,076	32,350	346.07	35,293	47,133
28,000	315.22	85,479	321.08	68,324	17,155	333.05	51,932	33,547	358.89	36,600	48,879
29,000	326.48	88,533	332.55	70,765	17,768	344.94	53,786	34,747	371.71	37,908	50,625
30,000	337.74	91,586	344.02	73,206	18,380	356.83	55,639	35,947	384.53	39,215	52,371
32,500	365.88	99,217	372.68	79,304	19,913	386.57	60,277	38,940	416.57	42,483	56,734
35,000	394.03	106,851	401.35	85,405	21,446	416.31	64,914	41,937	448.61	45,750	61,101
40,000	450.31	122,112	458.69	97,607	24,505	475.78	74,187	47,925	512.70	52,286	69,826
45,000	506.60	137,376	516.02	109,806	27,570	535.25	83,460	53,916	576.79	58,822	78,554
50,000	562.89	152,640	573.36	122,008	30,632	594.72	92,733	59,907	640.87	65,357	87,283
55,000	619.18	167,905	630.69	134,207	33,698	654.19	102,006	65,899	704.96	71,893	96,012
60,000	675.47	183,169	688.03	146,409	36,760	713.66	111,279	71,891	769.05	78,429	104,740
65,000	731.76	198,434	745.36	158,608	39,826	773.13	120,551	77,883	833.13	84,963	113,471
70,000	788.05	213,698	802.70	170,810	42,888	832.61	129,826	83,872	897.22	91,500	122,198
75,000	844.34	228,962	860.03	183,009	45,953	892.08	139,099	89,863	961.31	98,036	130,926
80,000	900.62	244,223	917.37	195,211	49,012	951.55	148,372	95,851	1,025.39	104,570	139,653
85,000	956.91	259,488	974.70	207,410	52,078	1,011.02	157,645	101,843	1,089.48	111,106	148,382
90,000	1,013.20	274,752	1,032.04	219,612	55,140	1,070.49	166,918	107,834	1,153.57	117,643	157,109
95,000	1,069.49	290,016	1,089.37	231,811	58,205	1,129.96	176,190	113,826	1,217.65	124,177	165,839
100,000	1,125.78	305,281	1,146.71	244,013	61,268	1,189.44	185,466	119,815	1,281.74	130,713	174,568
105,000	1,182.07	320,545	1,204.04	256,212	64,333	1,248.91	194,738	125,807	1,345.83	137,249	183,296
110,000	1,238.36	335,810	1,261.38	268,414	67,396	1,308.38	204,011	131,799	1,409.92	143,786	192,024
115,000	1,294.64	351,070	1,318.71	280,613	70,457	1,367.85	213,284	137,786	1,474.00	150,320	200,750
120,000	1,350.93	366,335	1,376.05	292,815	73,520	1,427.32	222,557	143,778	1,538.09	156,856	209,479
125,000	1,407.22	381,599	1,433.38	305,014	76,585	1,486.79	231,830	149,769	1,602.18	163,392	218,207
130,000	1,463.51	396,864	1,490.72	317,216	79,648	1,546.26	241,102	155,762	1,666.26	169,927	226,937
135,000	1,519.80	412,128	1,548.05	329,415	82,713	1,605.74	250,378	161,750	1,730.35	176,463	235,665
140,000	1,576.09	427,392	1,605.39	341,617	85,775	1,665.21	259,650	167,742	1,794.44	182,999	244,393
145,000	1,632.38	442,657	1,662.72	353,816	88,841	1,724.68	268,923	173,734	1,858.52	189,534	253,123
150,000	1,688.67	457,921	1,720.06	366,018	91,903	1,784.15	278,196	179,725	1,922.61	196,070	261,851
155,000	1,744.95	473,182	1,777.39	378,217	94,965	1,843.62	287,469	185,713	1,986.70	202,606	270,576
160,000	1,801.24	488,446	1,834.73	390,419	98,027	1,903.09	296,742	191,704	2,050.78	209,140	279,306
165,000	1,857.53	503,711	1,892.06	402,618	101,093	1,962.57	306,017	197,694	2,114.87	215,677	288,034
170,000	1,913.82	518,975	1,949.40	414,820	104,155	2,022.04	315,290	203,685	2,178.96	222,213	296,762
175,000	1,970.11	534,240	2,006.73	427,019	107,221	2,081.51	324,562	209,678	2,243.04	228,747	305,493
180,000	2,026.40	549,504	2,064.07	439,221	110,283	2,140.98	333,835	215,669	2,307.13	235,283	314,221
185,000	2,082.69	564,768	2,121.40	451,420	113,348	2,200.45	343,108	221,660	2,371.22	241,820	322,948
190,000	2,138.97	580,029	2,178.74	463,622	116,407	2,259.92	352,381	227,648	2,435.30	248,354	331,675
195,000	2,195.26	595,294	2,236.07	475,821	119,473	2,319.39	361,654	233,640	2,499.39	254,890	340,404
200,000	2,251.55	610,558	2,293.41	488,023	122,535	2,378.87	370,929	239,629	2,563.48	261,426	349,132

13.50%   SHORT-TERM AMORTIZING MORTGAGES

AMOUNT OF LOAN	30 YEARS		25 YEARS			20 YEARS			15 YEARS		
	MONTHLY PAYMENT	TOTAL INTRST	MONTHLY PAYMENT	TOTAL INTRST	INTRST SAVED	MONTHLY PAYMENT	TOTAL INTRST	INTRST SAVED	MONTHLY PAYMENT	TOTAL INTRST	INTRST SAVED
$ 50	0.58	159	0.59	127	32	0.61	96	63	0.65	67	92
100	1.15	314	1.17	251	63	1.21	190	124	1.30	134	180
200	2.30	628	2.34	502	126	2.42	381	247	2.60	268	360
300	3.44	938	3.50	750	188	3.63	571	367	3.90	402	536
400	4.59	1,252	4.67	1,001	251	4.83	759	493	5.20	536	716
500	5.73	1,563	5.83	1,249	314	6.04	950	613	6.50	670	893
600	6.88	1,877	7.00	1,500	377	7.25	1,140	737	7.79	802	1,075
700	8.02	2,187	8.16	1,748	439	8.46	1,330	857	9.09	936	1,251
800	9.17	2,501	9.33	1,999	502	9.66	1,518	983	10.39	1,070	1,431
900	10.31	2,812	10.50	2,250	562	10.87	1,709	1,103	11.69	1,204	1,608
1,000	11.46	3,126	11.66	2,498	628	12.08	1,899	1,227	12.99	1,338	1,788
2,000	22.91	6,248	23.32	4,996	1,252	24.15	3,796	2,452	25.97	2,675	3,573
3,000	34.37	9,373	34.97	7,491	1,882	36.23	5,695	3,678	38.95	4,011	5,362
4,000	45.82	12,495	46.63	9,989	2,506	48.30	7,592	4,903	51.94	5,349	7,146
5,000	57.28	15,621	58.29	12,487	3,134	60.37	9,489	6,132	64.92	6,686	8,935
6,000	68.73	18,743	69.94	14,982	3,761	72.45	11,388	7,355	77.90	8,022	10,721
7,000	80.18	21,865	81.60	17,480	4,385	84.52	13,285	8,580	90.89	9,360	12,505
8,000	91.64	24,990	93.26	19,978	5,012	96.59	15,182	9,808	103.87	10,697	14,293
9,000	103.09	28,112	104.91	22,473	5,639	108.67	17,081	11,031	116.85	12,033	16,079
10,000	114.55	31,238	116.57	24,971	6,267	120.74	18,978	12,260	129.84	13,371	17,867
11,000	126.00	34,360	128.23	27,469	6,891	132.82	20,877	13,483	142.82	14,708	19,652
12,000	137.45	37,482	139.88	29,964	7,518	144.89	22,774	14,708	155.80	16,044	21,438
13,000	148.91	40,608	151.54	32,462	8,146	156.96	24,670	15,936	168.79	17,382	23,226
14,000	160.36	43,730	163.20	34,960	8,770	169.04	26,570	17,160	181.77	18,719	25,011
15,000	171.82	46,855	174.85	37,455	9,400	181.11	28,466	18,389	194.75	20,055	26,800
16,000	183.27	49,977	186.51	39,953	10,024	193.18	30,363	19,614	207.74	21,393	28,584
17,000	194.73	53,103	198.16	42,448	10,655	205.26	32,262	20,841	220.72	22,730	30,373
18,000	206.18	56,225	209.82	44,946	11,279	217.33	34,159	22,066	233.70	24,066	32,159
19,000	217.63	59,347	221.48	47,444	11,903	229.41	36,058	23,289	246.69	25,404	33,943
20,000	229.09	62,472	233.13	49,939	12,533	241.48	37,955	24,517	259.67	26,741	35,731
21,000	240.54	65,594	244.79	52,437	13,157	253.55	39,852	25,742	272.65	28,077	37,517
22,000	252.00	68,720	256.45	54,935	13,785	265.63	41,751	26,969	285.64	29,415	39,305
23,000	263.45	71,842	268.10	57,430	14,412	277.70	43,648	28,194	298.62	30,752	41,090
24,000	274.90	74,964	279.76	59,928	15,036	289.77	45,545	29,419	311.60	32,088	42,876
25,000	286.36	78,090	291.42	62,426	15,664	301.85	47,444	30,646	324.58	33,424	44,666
26,000	297.81	81,212	303.07	64,921	16,291	313.92	49,341	31,871	337.57	34,763	46,449
27,000	309.27	84,337	314.73	67,419	16,918	326.00	51,240	33,097	350.55	36,099	48,238
28,000	320.72	87,459	326.39	69,917	17,542	338.07	53,137	34,322	363.53	37,435	50,024
29,000	332.17	90,581	338.04	72,412	18,169	350.14	55,034	35,547	376.52	38,774	51,807
30,000	343.63	93,707	349.70	74,910	18,797	362.22	56,933	36,774	389.50	40,110	53,597
32,500	372.26	101,514	378.84	81,152	20,362	392.40	61,676	39,838	421.96	43,453	58,061
35,000	400.90	109,324	407.98	87,394	21,930	422.59	66,422	42,902	454.42	46,796	62,528
40,000	458.17	124,941	466.26	99,878	25,063	482.95	75,908	49,033	519.33	53,479	71,462
45,000	515.44	140,558	524.55	112,365	28,193	543.32	85,397	55,161	584.25	60,165	80,393
50,000	572.71	156,176	582.83	124,849	31,327	603.69	94,886	61,290	649.16	66,849	89,327
55,000	629.98	171,793	641.11	137,333	34,460	664.06	104,374	67,419	714.08	73,534	98,259
60,000	687.25	187,410	699.39	149,817	37,593	724.43	113,863	73,547	779.00	80,220	107,190
65,000	744.52	203,027	757.67	162,301	40,726	784.80	123,352	79,675	843.91	86,904	116,123
70,000	801.79	218,644	815.96	174,788	43,856	845.17	132,841	85,803	908.83	93,589	125,055
75,000	859.06	234,262	874.24	187,272	46,990	905.54	142,330	91,932	973.74	100,273	133,989
80,000	916.33	249,879	932.52	199,756	50,123	965.90	151,816	98,063	1,038.66	106,959	142,920
85,000	973.61	265,500	990.80	212,240	53,260	1,026.27	161,305	104,195	1,103.58	113,644	151,856
90,000	1,030.88	281,117	1,049.09	224,727	56,390	1,086.64	170,794	110,323	1,168.49	120,328	160,789
95,000	1,088.15	296,734	1,107.37	237,211	59,523	1,147.01	180,282	116,452	1,233.41	127,014	169,720
100,000	1,145.42	312,351	1,165.65	249,695	62,656	1,207.38	189,771	122,580	1,298.32	133,698	178,653
105,000	1,202.69	327,968	1,223.93	262,179	65,789	1,267.75	199,260	128,708	1,363.24	140,383	187,585
110,000	1,259.96	343,586	1,282.21	274,663	68,923	1,328.12	208,749	134,837	1,428.16	147,069	196,517
115,000	1,317.23	359,203	1,340.50	287,150	72,053	1,388.49	218,238	140,965	1,493.07	153,753	205,450
120,000	1,374.50	374,820	1,398.78	299,634	75,186	1,448.85	227,724	147,096	1,557.99	160,438	214,382
125,000	1,431.77	390,437	1,457.06	312,118	78,319	1,509.22	237,213	153,224	1,622.90	167,122	223,315
130,000	1,489.04	406,054	1,515.34	324,602	81,452	1,569.59	246,702	159,352	1,687.82	173,808	232,246
135,000	1,546.31	421,672	1,573.63	337,089	84,583	1,629.96	256,190	165,482	1,752.74	180,493	241,179
140,000	1,603.58	437,289	1,631.91	349,573	87,716	1,690.33	265,679	171,610	1,817.65	187,177	250,112
145,000	1,660.85	452,906	1,690.19	362,057	90,849	1,750.70	275,168	177,738	1,882.57	193,863	259,043
150,000	1,718.12	468,523	1,748.47	374,541	93,982	1,811.07	284,657	183,866	1,947.48	200,546	267,977
155,000	1,775.39	484,140	1,806.75	387,025	97,115	1,871.44	294,146	189,994	2,012.40	207,232	276,908
160,000	1,832.66	499,758	1,865.04	399,512	100,246	1,931.80	303,632	196,126	2,077.31	213,916	285,842
165,000	1,889.94	515,378	1,923.32	411,999	103,382	1,992.17	313,121	202,257	2,142.23	220,601	294,777
170,000	1,947.21	530,996	1,981.60	424,480	106,516	2,052.54	322,610	208,386	2,207.15	227,287	303,709
175,000	2,004.48	546,613	2,039.88	436,964	109,649	2,112.91	332,098	214,515	2,272.06	233,971	312,642
180,000	2,061.75	562,230	2,098.17	449,451	112,779	2,173.28	341,587	220,643	2,336.98	240,656	321,574
185,000	2,119.02	577,847	2,156.45	461,935	115,912	2,233.65	351,076	226,771	2,401.89	247,340	330,507
190,000	2,176.29	593,464	2,214.73	474,419	119,045	2,294.02	360,565	232,899	2,466.81	254,026	339,438
195,000	2,233.56	609,082	2,273.01	486,903	122,179	2,354.39	370,054	239,028	2,531.73	260,711	348,371
200,000	2,290.83	624,699	2,331.29	499,387	125,312	2,414.75	379,540	245,159	2,596.64	267,395	357,304

AMOUNT OF LOAN	30 YEARS		25 YEARS			20 YEARS			15 YEARS		
	MONTHLY PAYMENT	TOTAL INTRST	MONTHLY PAYMENT	TOTAL INTRST	INTRST SAVED	MONTHLY PAYMENT	TOTAL INTRST	INTRST SAVED	MONTHLY PAYMENT	TOTAL INTRST	INTRST SAVED
$ 50	0.59	162	0.60	130	32	0.62	99	63	0.66	69	93
100	1.17	321	1.19	257	64	1.23	195	126	1.32	138	183
200	2.34	642	2.37	511	131	2.46	390	252	2.63	273	369
300	3.50	960	3.56	768	192	3.68	583	377	3.95	411	549
400	4.67	1,281	4.74	1,022	259	4.91	778	503	5.26	547	734
500	5.83	1,599	5.93	1,279	320	6.13	971	628	6.58	684	915
600	7.00	1,920	7.11	1,533	387	7.36	1,166	754	7.89	820	1,100
700	8.16	2,238	8.30	1,790	448	8.58	1,359	879	9.21	958	1,280
800	9.33	2,559	9.48	2,044	515	9.81	1,554	1,005	10.52	1,094	1,465
900	10.49	2,876	10.67	2,301	575	11.03	1,747	1,129	11.84	1,231	1,645
1,000	11.66	3,198	11.85	2,555	643	12.26	1,942	1,256	13.15	1,367	1,831
2,000	23.31	6,392	23.70	5,110	1,282	24.51	3,882	2,510	26.30	2,734	3,658
3,000	34.96	9,586	35.54	7,662	1,924	36.77	5,825	3,761	39.45	4,101	5,485
4,000	46.61	12,780	47.39	10,217	2,563	49.02	7,765	5,015	52.60	5,468	7,312
5,000	58.26	15,974	59.24	12,772	3,202	61.28	9,707	6,267	65.75	6,835	9,139
6,000	69.91	19,168	71.08	15,324	3,844	73.53	11,647	7,521	78.90	8,202	10,966
7,000	81.56	22,362	82.93	17,879	4,483	85.78	13,587	8,775	92.05	9,569	12,793
8,000	93.21	25,556	94.78	20,434	5,122	98.04	15,530	10,026	105.20	10,936	14,620
9,000	104.87	28,753	106.62	22,986	5,767	110.29	17,470	11,283	118.35	12,303	16,450
10,000	116.52	31,947	118.47	25,541	6,406	122.55	19,412	12,535	131.50	13,670	18,277
11,000	128.17	35,141	130.32	28,096	7,045	134.80	21,352	13,789	144.65	15,037	20,104
12,000	139.82	38,335	142.16	30,648	7,687	147.05	23,292	15,043	157.80	16,404	21,931
13,000	151.47	41,529	154.01	33,203	8,326	159.31	25,234	16,295	170.95	17,771	23,758
14,000	163.12	44,723	165.86	35,758	8,965	171.56	27,174	17,549	184.10	19,138	25,585
15,000	174.77	47,917	177.70	38,310	9,607	183.82	29,117	18,800	197.25	20,505	27,412
16,000	186.42	51,111	189.55	40,865	10,246	196.07	31,057	20,054	210.40	21,872	29,239
17,000	198.07	54,305	201.40	43,420	10,885	208.32	32,997	21,308	223.55	23,239	31,066
18,000	209.73	57,503	213.24	45,972	11,531	220.58	34,939	22,564	236.70	24,606	32,897
19,000	221.38	60,697	225.09	48,527	12,170	232.83	36,879	23,818	249.85	25,973	34,724
20,000	233.03	63,891	236.94	51,082	12,809	245.09	38,822	25,069	263.00	27,340	36,551
21,000	244.68	67,085	248.78	53,634	13,451	257.34	40,762	26,323	276.15	28,707	38,378
22,000	256.33	70,279	260.63	56,189	14,090	269.59	42,702	27,577	289.30	30,074	40,205
23,000	267.98	73,473	272.48	58,744	14,729	281.85	44,644	28,829	302.45	31,441	42,032
24,000	279.63	76,667	284.32	61,296	15,371	294.10	46,584	30,083	315.60	32,808	43,859
25,000	291.28	79,861	296.17	63,851	16,010	306.36	48,526	31,335	328.75	34,175	45,686
26,000	302.93	83,055	308.02	66,406	16,649	318.61	50,466	32,589	341.90	35,542	47,513
27,000	314.59	86,252	319.86	68,958	17,294	330.86	52,406	33,846	355.05	36,909	49,343
28,000	326.24	89,446	331.71	71,513	17,933	343.12	54,349	35,097	368.20	38,276	51,170
29,000	337.89	92,640	343.56	74,068	18,572	355.37	56,289	36,351	381.35	39,643	52,997
30,000	349.54	95,834	355.40	76,620	19,214	367.63	58,231	37,603	394.50	41,010	54,824
32,500	378.67	103,821	385.02	83,006	20,815	398.26	63,082	40,739	427.38	44,428	59,393
35,000	407.79	111,804	414.64	89,392	22,412	428.90	67,936	43,868	460.25	47,845	63,959
40,000	466.05	127,778	473.87	102,161	25,617	490.17	77,641	50,137	526.00	54,680	73,098
45,000	524.31	143,752	533.10	114,930	28,822	551.44	87,346	56,406	591.75	61,515	82,237
50,000	582.56	159,722	592.34	127,702	32,020	612.71	97,050	62,672	657.50	68,350	91,372
55,000	640.82	175,695	651.57	140,471	35,224	673.98	106,755	68,940	723.25	75,185	100,510
60,000	699.07	191,665	710.80	153,240	38,425	735.25	116,460	75,205	789.00	82,020	109,645
65,000	757.33	207,639	770.04	166,012	41,627	796.52	126,165	81,474	854.75	88,855	118,784
70,000	815.58	223,609	829.27	178,781	44,828	857.79	135,870	87,739	920.50	95,690	127,919
75,000	873.84	239,582	888.50	191,550	48,032	919.06	145,574	94,008	986.25	102,525	137,057
80,000	932.10	255,556	947.74	204,322	51,234	980.33	155,279	100,277	1,051.99	109,358	146,198
85,000	990.35	271,526	1,006.97	217,091	54,435	1,041.60	164,984	106,542	1,117.74	116,193	155,333
90,000	1,048.61	287,500	1,066.20	229,860	57,640	1,102.87	174,689	112,811	1,183.49	123,028	164,472
95,000	1,106.86	303,470	1,125.44	242,632	60,838	1,164.14	184,394	119,076	1,249.24	129,863	173,607
100,000	1,165.12	319,443	1,184.67	255,401	64,042	1,225.41	194,098	125,345	1,314.99	136,698	182,745
105,000	1,223.37	335,413	1,243.90	268,170	67,243	1,286.68	203,803	131,610	1,380.74	143,533	191,880
110,000	1,281.63	351,387	1,303.14	280,942	70,445	1,347.95	213,508	137,879	1,446.49	150,368	201,019
115,000	1,339.88	367,357	1,362.37	293,711	73,646	1,409.22	223,213	144,144	1,512.24	157,203	210,154
120,000	1,398.14	383,330	1,421.60	306,480	76,850	1,470.49	232,918	150,412	1,577.99	164,038	219,292
125,000	1,456.40	399,304	1,480.84	319,252	80,052	1,531.76	242,622	156,682	1,643.74	170,873	228,431
130,000	1,514.65	415,274	1,540.07	332,021	83,253	1,593.03	252,327	162,947	1,709.49	177,708	237,566
135,000	1,572.91	431,248	1,599.30	344,790	86,458	1,654.30	262,032	169,216	1,775.24	184,543	246,705
140,000	1,631.16	447,218	1,658.54	357,562	89,656	1,715.57	271,737	175,481	1,840.99	191,378	255,840
145,000	1,689.42	463,191	1,717.77	370,331	92,860	1,776.84	281,442	181,749	1,906.74	198,213	264,978
150,000	1,747.67	479,161	1,777.00	383,100	96,061	1,838.11	291,146	188,015	1,972.49	205,048	274,113
155,000	1,805.93	495,135	1,836.24	395,872	99,263	1,899.38	300,851	194,284	2,038.24	211,883	283,252
160,000	1,864.19	511,108	1,895.47	408,641	102,467	1,960.65	310,556	200,552	2,103.98	218,716	292,392
165,000	1,922.44	527,078	1,954.70	421,410	105,668	2,021.92	320,261	206,817	2,169.73	225,551	301,527
170,000	1,980.70	543,052	2,013.94	434,182	108,870	2,083.19	329,966	213,086	2,235.48	232,386	310,666
175,000	2,038.95	559,022	2,073.17	446,951	112,071	2,144.46	339,670	219,352	2,301.23	239,221	319,801
180,000	2,097.21	574,996	2,132.40	459,720	115,276	2,205.73	349,375	225,621	2,366.98	246,056	328,940
185,000	2,155.46	590,966	2,191.64	472,492	118,474	2,267.00	359,080	231,886	2,432.73	252,891	338,075
190,000	2,213.72	606,939	2,250.87	485,261	121,678	2,328.28	368,787	238,152	2,498.48	259,726	347,213
195,000	2,271.97	622,909	2,310.10	498,030	124,879	2,389.55	378,492	244,417	2,564.23	266,561	356,348
200,000	2,330.23	638,883	2,369.34	510,802	128,081	2,450.82	388,197	250,686	2,629.98	273,396	365,487

31

SHORT-TERM AMORTIZING MORTGAGES

AMOUNT OF LOAN	30 YEARS		25 YEARS			20 YEARS			15 YEARS		
	MONTHLY PAYMENT	TOTAL INTRST	MONTHLY PAYMENT	TOTAL INTRST	INTRST SAVED	MONTHLY PAYMENT	TOTAL INTRST	INTRST SAVED	MONTHLY PAYMENT	TOTAL INTRST	INTRST SAVED
$ 50	0.60	166	0.61	133	33	0.63	101	65	0.67	71	95
100	1.19	328	1.21	263	65	1.25	200	128	1.34	141	187
200	2.37	653	2.41	523	130	2.49	398	255	2.67	281	372
300	3.56	982	3.62	786	196	3.74	598	384	4.00	420	562
400	4.74	1,306	4.82	1,046	260	4.98	795	511	5.33	559	747
500	5.93	1,635	6.02	1,306	329	6.22	993	642	6.66	699	936
600	7.11	1,960	7.23	1,569	391	7.47	1,193	767	8.00	840	1,120
700	8.30	2,288	8.43	1,829	459	8.71	1,390	898	9.33	979	1,309
800	9.48	2,613	9.64	2,092	521	9.95	1,588	1,025	10.66	1,119	1,494
900	10.67	2,941	10.84	2,352	589	11.20	1,788	1,153	11.99	1,258	1,683
1,000	11.85	3,266	12.04	2,612	654	12.44	1,986	1,280	13.32	1,398	1,868
2,000	23.70	6,532	24.08	5,224	1,308	24.88	3,971	2,561	26.64	2,795	3,737
3,000	35.55	9,798	36.12	7,836	1,962	37.31	5,954	3,844	39.96	4,193	5,605
4,000	47.40	13,064	48.16	10,448	2,616	49.75	7,940	5,124	53.27	5,589	7,475
5,000	59.25	16,330	60.19	13,057	3,273	62.18	9,923	6,407	66.59	6,986	9,344
6,000	71.10	19,596	72.23	15,669	3,927	74.62	11,909	7,687	79.91	8,384	11,212
7,000	82.95	22,862	84.27	18,281	4,581	87.05	13,892	8,970	93.23	9,781	13,081
8,000	94.79	26,124	96.31	20,893	5,231	99.49	15,878	10,246	106.54	11,177	14,947
9,000	106.64	29,390	108.34	23,502	5,888	111.92	17,861	11,529	119.86	12,575	16,815
10,000	118.49	32,656	120.38	26,114	6,542	124.36	19,846	12,810	133.18	13,972	18,684
11,000	130.34	35,922	132.42	28,726	7,196	136.79	21,830	14,092	146.50	15,370	20,552
12,000	142.19	39,188	144.46	31,338	7,850	149.23	23,815	15,373	159.81	16,766	22,422
13,000	154.04	42,454	156.49	33,947	8,507	161.66	25,798	16,656	173.13	18,163	24,291
14,000	165.89	45,720	168.53	36,559	9,161	174.10	27,784	17,936	186.45	19,561	26,159
15,000	177.74	48,986	180.57	39,171	9,815	186.53	29,767	19,219	199.77	20,959	28,027
16,000	189.58	52,249	192.61	41,783	10,466	198.97	31,753	20,496	213.08	22,354	29,895
17,000	201.43	55,515	204.64	44,392	11,123	211.40	33,736	21,779	226.40	23,752	31,763
18,000	213.28	58,781	216.68	47,004	11,777	223.84	35,722	23,059	239.72	25,150	33,631
19,000	225.13	62,047	228.72	49,616	12,431	236.27	37,705	24,342	253.04	26,547	35,500
20,000	236.98	65,313	240.76	52,228	13,085	248.71	39,690	25,623	266.35	27,943	37,370
21,000	248.83	68,579	252.79	54,837	13,742	261.14	41,674	26,905	279.67	29,341	39,238
22,000	260.68	71,845	264.83	57,449	14,396	273.58	43,659	28,186	292.99	30,738	41,107
23,000	272.53	75,111	276.87	60,061	15,050	286.01	45,642	29,469	306.31	32,136	42,975
24,000	284.37	78,373	288.91	62,673	15,700	298.45	47,628	30,745	319.62	33,532	44,841
25,000	296.22	81,639	300.95	65,285	16,354	310.89	49,614	32,025	332.94	34,929	46,710
26,000	308.07	84,905	312.98	67,894	17,011	323.32	51,597	33,308	346.26	36,327	48,578
27,000	319.92	88,171	325.02	70,506	17,665	335.76	53,582	34,589	359.58	37,724	50,447
28,000	331.77	91,437	337.06	73,118	18,319	348.19	55,566	35,871	372.89	39,120	52,317
29,000	343.62	94,703	349.10	75,730	18,973	360.63	57,551	37,152	386.21	40,518	54,185
30,000	355.47	97,969	361.13	78,339	19,630	373.06	59,534	38,435	399.53	41,915	56,054
32,500	385.09	106,132	391.23	84,869	21,263	404.15	64,496	41,636	432.82	45,408	60,724
35,000	414.71	114,296	421.32	91,396	22,900	435.24	69,458	44,838	466.11	48,900	65,394
40,000	473.95	130,622	481.51	104,453	26,169	497.41	79,378	51,244	532.70	55,886	74,736
45,000	533.20	146,952	541.70	117,510	29,442	559.59	89,302	57,650	599.29	62,872	84,080
50,000	592.44	163,278	601.89	130,567	32,711	621.77	99,225	64,053	665.88	69,858	93,420
55,000	651.68	179,605	662.07	143,621	35,984	683.94	109,146	70,459	732.46	76,843	102,762
60,000	710.93	195,935	722.26	156,678	39,257	746.12	119,069	76,866	799.05	83,829	112,106
65,000	770.17	212,261	782.45	169,735	42,526	808.29	128,990	83,271	865.64	90,815	121,446
70,000	829.42	228,591	842.64	182,792	45,799	870.47	138,913	89,678	932.22	97,800	130,791
75,000	888.66	244,918	902.83	195,849	49,069	932.65	148,836	96,082	998.81	104,786	140,132
80,000	947.90	261,244	963.01	208,903	52,341	994.82	158,757	102,487	1,065.40	111,772	149,472
85,000	1,007.15	277,574	1,023.20	221,960	55,614	1,057.00	168,680	108,894	1,131.99	118,758	158,816
90,000	1,066.39	293,900	1,083.39	235,017	58,883	1,119.17	178,601	115,299	1,198.57	125,743	168,157
95,000	1,125.63	310,227	1,143.58	248,074	62,153	1,181.35	188,524	121,703	1,265.16	132,729	177,498
100,000	1,184.88	326,557	1,203.77	261,131	65,426	1,243.53	198,447	128,110	1,331.75	139,715	186,842
105,000	1,244.12	342,883	1,263.95	274,185	68,698	1,305.70	208,368	134,515	1,398.33	146,699	196,184
110,000	1,303.36	359,210	1,324.14	287,242	71,968	1,367.88	218,291	140,919	1,464.92	153,686	205,524
115,000	1,362.61	375,540	1,384.33	300,299	75,241	1,430.05	228,212	147,328	1,531.51	160,672	214,868
120,000	1,421.85	391,866	1,444.52	313,356	78,510	1,492.23	238,135	153,731	1,598.09	167,656	224,210
125,000	1,481.09	408,192	1,504.71	326,413	81,779	1,554.41	248,058	160,134	1,664.68	174,642	233,550
130,000	1,540.34	424,522	1,564.89	339,467	85,055	1,616.58	257,979	166,543	1,731.27	181,629	242,893
135,000	1,599.58	440,849	1,625.08	352,524	88,325	1,678.76	267,902	172,947	1,797.86	188,615	252,234
140,000	1,658.83	457,179	1,685.27	365,581	91,598	1,740.93	277,823	179,356	1,864.44	195,599	261,580
145,000	1,718.07	473,505	1,745.46	378,638	94,867	1,803.11	287,746	185,759	1,931.03	202,585	270,920
150,000	1,777.31	489,832	1,805.65	391,695	98,137	1,865.29	297,670	192,162	1,997.62	209,572	280,260
155,000	1,836.56	506,162	1,865.83	404,749	101,413	1,927.46	307,590	198,572	2,064.20	216,556	289,606
160,000	1,895.80	522,488	1,926.02	417,806	104,682	1,989.64	317,514	204,974	2,130.79	223,542	298,946
165,000	1,955.04	538,814	1,986.21	430,863	107,951	2,051.81	327,434	211,380	2,197.38	230,528	308,286
170,000	2,014.29	555,144	2,046.40	443,920	111,224	2,113.99	337,358	217,786	2,263.97	237,515	317,629
175,000	2,073.53	571,471	2,106.59	456,977	114,494	2,176.17	347,281	224,190	2,330.55	244,499	326,972
180,000	2,132.77	587,797	2,166.77	470,031	117,766	2,238.34	357,202	230,595	2,397.14	251,485	336,312
185,000	2,192.02	604,127	2,226.96	483,088	121,039	2,300.52	367,125	237,002	2,463.73	258,471	345,656
190,000	2,251.26	620,454	2,287.15	496,145	124,309	2,362.69	377,046	243,408	2,530.31	265,456	354,998
195,000	2,310.50	636,780	2,347.34	509,202	127,578	2,424.87	386,969	249,811	2,596.90	272,442	364,338
200,000	2,369.75	653,110	2,407.53	522,259	130,851	2,487.05	396,892	256,218	2,663.49	279,428	373,682

SHORT-TERM AMORTIZING MORTGAGES 14.25%

AMOUNT OF LOAN	30 YEARS MONTHLY PAYMENT	30 YEARS TOTAL INTRST	25 YEARS MONTHLY PAYMENT	25 YEARS TOTAL INTRST	25 YEARS INTRST SAVED	20 YEARS MONTHLY PAYMENT	20 YEARS TOTAL INTRST	20 YEARS INTRST SAVED	15 YEARS MONTHLY PAYMENT	15 YEARS TOTAL INTRST	15 YEARS INTRST SAVED
$ 50	0.61	170	0.62	136	34	0.64	104	66	0.68	72	98
100	1.21	336	1.23	269	67	1.27	205	131	1.35	143	193
200	2.41	668	2.45	535	133	2.53	407	261	2.70	286	382
300	3.62	1,003	3.67	801	202	3.79	610	393	4.05	429	574
400	4.82	1,335	4.90	1,070	265	5.05	812	523	5.40	572	763
500	6.03	1,671	6.12	1,336	335	6.31	1,014	657	6.75	715	956
600	7.23	2,003	7.34	1,602	401	7.58	1,219	784	8.10	858	1,145
700	8.44	2,338	8.57	1,871	467	8.84	1,422	916	9.45	1,001	1,337
800	9.64	2,670	9.79	2,137	533	10.10	1,624	1,046	10.79	1,142	1,528
900	10.85	3,006	11.01	2,403	603	11.36	1,826	1,180	12.14	1,285	1,721
1,000	12.05	3,338	12.23	2,669	669	12.62	2,029	1,309	13.49	1,428	1,910
2,000	24.10	6,676	24.46	5,338	1,338	25.24	4,058	2,618	26.98	2,856	3,820
3,000	36.15	10,014	36.69	8,007	2,007	37.86	6,086	3,928	40.46	4,283	5,731
4,000	48.19	13,348	48.92	10,676	2,672	50.47	8,113	5,235	53.95	5,711	7,637
5,000	60.24	16,686	61.15	13,345	3,341	63.09	10,142	6,544	67.43	7,137	9,549
6,000	72.29	20,024	73.38	16,014	4,010	75.71	12,170	7,854	80.92	8,566	11,458
7,000	84.33	23,359	85.61	18,683	4,676	88.33	14,199	9,160	94.41	9,994	13,365
8,000	96.38	26,697	97.84	21,352	5,345	100.94	16,226	10,471	107.89	11,420	15,277
9,000	108.43	30,035	110.07	24,021	6,014	113.56	18,254	11,781	121.38	12,848	17,187
10,000	120.47	33,369	122.30	26,690	6,679	126.18	20,283	13,086	134.86	14,275	19,094
11,000	132.52	36,707	134.53	29,359	7,348	138.79	22,310	14,397	148.35	15,703	21,004
12,000	144.57	40,045	146.76	32,028	8,017	151.41	24,338	15,707	161.83	17,129	22,916
13,000	156.61	43,380	158.99	34,697	8,683	164.03	26,367	17,013	175.32	18,558	24,822
14,000	168.66	46,718	171.21	37,363	9,355	176.65	28,396	18,322	188.81	19,986	26,732
15,000	180.71	50,056	183.44	40,032	10,024	189.26	30,422	19,634	202.29	21,412	28,644
16,000	192.75	53,390	195.67	42,701	10,689	201.88	32,451	20,939	215.78	22,840	30,550
17,000	204.80	56,728	207.90	45,370	11,358	214.50	34,480	22,248	229.26	24,267	32,461
18,000	216.85	60,066	220.13	48,039	12,027	227.11	36,506	23,560	242.75	25,695	34,371
19,000	228.90	63,404	232.36	50,708	12,696	239.73	38,535	24,869	256.24	27,123	36,281
20,000	240.94	66,738	244.59	53,377	13,361	252.35	40,564	26,174	269.72	28,550	38,188
21,000	252.99	70,076	256.82	56,046	14,030	264.97	42,593	27,483	283.21	29,978	40,098
22,000	265.04	73,414	269.05	58,715	14,699	277.58	44,619	28,795	296.69	31,404	42,010
23,000	277.08	76,749	281.28	61,384	15,365	290.20	46,648	30,101	310.18	32,832	43,917
24,000	289.13	80,087	293.51	64,053	16,034	302.82	48,677	31,410	323.66	34,259	45,828
25,000	301.18	83,425	305.74	66,722	16,703	315.43	50,703	32,722	337.15	35,687	47,738
26,000	313.22	86,759	317.97	69,391	17,368	328.05	52,732	34,027	350.64	37,115	49,644
27,000	325.27	90,097	330.20	72,060	18,037	340.67	54,761	35,336	364.12	38,542	51,555
28,000	337.32	93,435	342.42	74,726	18,709	353.29	56,790	36,645	377.61	39,970	53,465
29,000	349.36	96,770	354.65	77,395	19,375	365.90	58,816	37,954	391.09	41,396	55,374
30,000	361.41	100,108	366.88	80,064	20,044	378.52	60,845	39,263	404.58	42,824	57,284
32,500	391.53	108,451	397.46	86,738	21,713	410.06	65,914	42,537	438.29	46,392	62,059
35,000	421.65	116,794	428.03	93,409	23,385	441.61	70,986	45,808	472.01	49,962	66,832
40,000	481.88	133,477	489.18	106,754	26,723	504.69	81,126	52,351	539.44	57,099	76,378
45,000	542.11	150,160	550.32	120,096	30,064	567.78	91,267	58,893	606.87	64,237	85,923
50,000	602.35	166,846	611.47	133,441	33,405	630.86	101,406	65,440	674.29	71,372	95,474
55,000	662.58	183,529	672.62	146,786	36,743	693.95	111,548	71,981	741.72	78,510	105,019
60,000	722.82	200,215	733.76	160,128	40,087	757.04	121,690	78,525	809.15	85,647	114,568
65,000	783.05	216,898	794.91	173,473	43,425	820.12	131,829	85,069	876.58	92,784	124,114
70,000	843.29	233,584	856.05	186,815	46,769	883.21	141,970	91,614	944.01	99,922	133,662
75,000	903.52	250,267	917.20	200,160	50,107	946.29	152,110	98,157	1,011.44	107,059	143,208
80,000	963.75	266,950	978.35	213,505	53,445	1,009.38	162,251	104,699	1,078.87	114,197	152,753
85,000	1,023.99	283,636	1,039.49	226,847	56,789	1,072.47	172,393	111,243	1,146.30	121,334	162,302
90,000	1,084.22	300,319	1,100.64	240,192	60,127	1,135.55	182,532	117,787	1,213.73	128,471	171,848
95,000	1,144.46	317,006	1,161.79	253,537	63,469	1,198.64	192,674	124,332	1,281.16	135,609	181,397
100,000	1,204.69	333,688	1,222.93	266,879	66,809	1,261.72	202,813	130,875	1,348.58	142,744	190,944
105,000	1,264.93	350,375	1,284.08	280,224	70,151	1,324.81	212,954	137,421	1,416.01	149,882	200,493
110,000	1,325.16	367,058	1,345.23	293,569	73,489	1,387.90	223,096	143,962	1,483.44	157,019	210,039
115,000	1,385.40	383,744	1,406.37	306,911	76,833	1,450.98	233,235	150,509	1,550.87	164,157	219,587
120,000	1,445.63	400,427	1,467.52	320,256	80,171	1,514.07	243,377	157,050	1,618.30	171,294	229,133
125,000	1,505.86	417,110	1,528.66	333,598	83,512	1,577.15	253,516	163,594	1,685.73	178,431	238,679
130,000	1,566.10	433,796	1,589.81	346,943	86,853	1,640.24	263,658	170,138	1,753.16	185,569	248,227
135,000	1,626.33	450,479	1,650.96	360,288	90,191	1,703.33	273,799	176,680	1,820.59	192,706	257,773
140,000	1,686.57	467,165	1,712.10	373,630	93,535	1,766.41	283,938	183,227	1,888.02	199,844	267,321
145,000	1,746.80	483,848	1,773.25	386,975	96,873	1,829.50	294,080	189,768	1,955.45	206,981	276,867
150,000	1,807.04	500,534	1,834.40	400,320	100,214	1,892.58	304,219	196,315	2,022.87	214,117	286,417
155,000	1,867.27	517,217	1,895.54	413,662	103,555	1,955.67	314,361	202,856	2,090.30	221,254	295,963
160,000	1,927.50	533,900	1,956.69	427,007	106,893	2,018.76	324,502	209,398	2,157.73	228,391	305,509
165,000	1,987.74	550,586	2,017.84	440,352	110,234	2,081.84	334,642	215,944	2,225.16	235,529	315,057
170,000	2,047.97	567,269	2,078.98	453,694	113,575	2,144.93	344,783	222,486	2,292.59	242,666	324,603
175,000	2,108.21	583,956	2,140.13	467,039	116,917	2,208.01	354,922	229,034	2,360.02	249,804	334,152
180,000	2,168.44	600,638	2,201.27	480,381	120,257	2,271.10	365,064	235,574	2,427.45	256,941	343,697
185,000	2,228.68	617,325	2,262.42	493,726	123,599	2,334.19	375,206	242,119	2,494.88	264,078	353,247
190,000	2,288.91	634,008	2,323.57	507,071	126,937	2,397.27	385,305	248,663	2,562.31	271,216	362,792
195,000	2,349.14	650,690	2,384.71	520,413	130,277	2,460.36	395,486	255,204	2,629.74	278,353	372,337
200,000	2,409.38	667,377	2,445.86	533,758	133,619	2,523.44	405,626	261,751	2,697.16	285,489	381,888

33

14.50%   SHORT-TERM AMORTIZING MORTGAGES

AMOUNT OF LOAN	30 YEARS		25 YEARS			20 YEARS			15 YEARS		
	MONTHLY PAYMENT	TOTAL INTRST	MONTHLY PAYMENT	TOTAL INTRST	INTRST SAVED	MONTHLY PAYMENT	TOTAL INTRST	INTRST SAVED	MONTHLY PAYMENT	TOTAL INTRST	INTRST SAVED
$ 50	0.62	173	0.63	139	34	0.64	104	69	0.69	74	99
100	1.23	343	1.25	275	68	1.28	207	136	1.37	147	196
200	2.45	682	2.49	547	135	2.56	414	268	2.74	293	389
300	3.68	1,025	3.73	819	206	3.84	622	403	4.10	438	587
400	4.90	1,364	4.97	1,091	273	5.12	829	535	5.47	585	779
500	6.13	1,707	6.22	1,366	341	6.40	1,036	671	6.83	729	978
600	7.35	2,046	7.46	1,638	408	7.68	1,243	803	8.20	876	1,170
700	8.58	2,389	8.70	1,910	479	8.96	1,450	939	9.56	1,021	1,368
800	9.80	2,728	9.94	2,182	546	10.24	1,658	1,070	10.93	1,167	1,561
900	11.03	3,071	11.18	2,454	617	11.52	1,865	1,206	12.29	1,312	1,759
1,000	12.25	3,410	12.43	2,729	681	12.80	2,072	1,338	13.66	1,459	1,951
2,000	24.50	6,820	24.85	5,455	1,365	25.60	4,144	2,676	27.32	2,918	3,902
3,000	36.74	10,226	37.27	8,181	2,045	38.40	6,216	4,010	40.97	4,375	5,851
4,000	48.99	13,636	49.69	10,907	2,729	51.20	8,288	5,348	54.63	5,833	7,803
5,000	61.23	17,043	62.11	13,633	3,410	64.00	10,360	6,683	68.28	7,290	9,753
6,000	73.48	20,453	74.53	16,359	4,094	76.80	12,432	8,021	81.94	8,749	11,704
7,000	85.72	23,859	86.96	19,088	4,771	89.60	14,504	9,355	95.59	10,206	13,653
8,000	97.97	27,269	99.38	21,814	5,455	102.40	16,576	10,693	109.25	11,665	15,604
9,000	110.22	30,679	111.80	24,540	6,139	115.20	18,648	12,031	122.90	13,122	17,557
10,000	122.46	34,086	124.22	27,266	6,820	128.00	20,720	13,366	136.56	14,581	19,505
11,000	134.71	37,496	136.64	29,992	7,504	140.80	22,792	14,704	150.21	16,038	21,458
12,000	146.95	40,902	149.06	32,718	8,184	153.60	24,864	16,038	163.87	17,497	23,405
13,000	159.20	44,312	161.49	35,447	8,865	166.40	26,936	17,376	177.52	18,954	25,358
14,000	171.44	47,718	173.91	38,173	9,545	179.20	29,008	18,710	191.18	20,412	27,306
15,000	183.69	51,128	186.33	40,899	10,229	192.00	31,080	20,048	204.83	21,869	29,259
16,000	195.93	54,535	198.75	43,625	10,910	204.80	33,152	21,383	218.49	23,328	31,207
17,000	208.18	57,945	211.17	46,351	11,594	217.60	35,224	22,721	232.14	24,785	33,160
18,000	220.43	61,355	223.59	49,077	12,278	230.40	37,296	24,059	245.80	26,244	35,111
19,000	232.67	64,761	236.02	51,806	12,955	243.20	39,368	25,393	259.45	27,701	37,060
20,000	244.92	68,171	248.44	54,532	13,639	256.00	41,440	26,731	273.11	29,160	39,011
21,000	257.16	71,578	260.86	57,258	14,320	268.80	43,512	28,066	286.76	30,617	40,961
22,000	269.41	74,988	273.28	59,984	15,004	281.60	45,584	29,404	300.42	32,076	42,912
23,000	281.65	78,394	285.70	62,710	15,684	294.40	47,656	30,738	314.07	33,533	44,861
24,000	293.90	81,804	298.12	65,436	16,368	307.20	49,728	32,076	327.73	34,991	46,813
25,000	306.14	85,210	310.55	68,165	17,045	320.00	51,800	33,410	341.38	36,448	48,762
26,000	318.39	88,620	322.97	70,891	17,729	332.80	53,872	34,748	355.04	37,907	50,713
27,000	330.64	92,030	335.39	73,617	18,413	345.60	55,944	36,086	368.69	39,364	52,666
28,000	342.88	95,437	347.81	76,343	19,094	358.40	58,016	37,421	382.35	40,823	54,614
29,000	355.13	98,847	360.23	79,069	19,778	371.20	60,088	38,759	396.00	42,282	56,567
30,000	367.37	102,253	372.65	81,795	20,458	384.00	62,160	40,093	409.66	43,739	58,514
32,500	397.99	110,776	403.71	88,613	22,163	416.00	67,340	43,436	443.79	47,382	63,394
35,000	428.60	119,296	434.76	95,428	23,868	448.00	72,520	46,776	477.93	51,027	68,269
40,000	489.83	136,339	496.87	109,061	27,278	512.00	82,880	53,459	546.21	58,318	78,021
45,000	551.06	153,382	558.98	122,694	30,688	576.00	93,240	60,142	614.48	65,606	87,776
50,000	612.28	170,421	621.09	136,327	34,094	640.00	103,600	66,821	682.76	72,897	97,524
55,000	673.51	187,464	683.19	149,957	37,507	704.00	113,960	73,504	751.03	80,185	107,279
60,000	734.74	204,506	745.30	163,590	40,916	768.00	124,320	80,186	819.31	87,476	117,030
65,000	795.97	221,549	807.41	177,223	44,326	832.00	134,680	86,869	887.58	94,764	126,785
70,000	857.19	238,588	869.52	190,856	47,732	896.00	145,040	93,548	955.86	102,055	136,533
75,000	918.42	255,631	931.63	204,489	51,142	960.00	155,400	100,231	1,024.13	109,343	146,288
80,000	979.65	272,674	993.74	218,122	54,552	1,024.00	165,760	106,914	1,092.41	116,634	156,040
85,000	1,040.88	289,717	1,055.84	231,752	57,965	1,088.00	176,120	113,597	1,160.68	123,922	165,795
90,000	1,102.11	306,760	1,117.95	245,385	61,375	1,152.00	186,480	120,280	1,228.96	131,213	175,547
95,000	1,163.33	323,799	1,180.06	259,018	64,781	1,216.00	196,840	126,959	1,297.23	138,501	185,298
100,000	1,224.56	340,842	1,242.17	272,651	68,191	1,280.00	207,200	133,642	1,365.51	145,792	195,050
105,000	1,285.79	357,884	1,304.28	286,284	71,600	1,344.00	217,560	140,324	1,433.78	153,080	204,804
110,000	1,347.02	374,927	1,366.38	299,914	75,013	1,408.00	227,920	147,007	1,502.06	160,371	214,556
115,000	1,408.24	391,968	1,428.49	313,547	78,419	1,472.00	238,280	153,686	1,570.33	167,659	224,307
120,000	1,469.47	409,009	1,490.60	327,180	81,829	1,536.00	248,640	160,369	1,638.61	174,950	234,059
125,000	1,530.70	426,052	1,552.71	340,813	85,239	1,600.00	259,000	167,052	1,706.88	182,238	243,814
130,000	1,591.93	443,095	1,614.82	354,446	88,649	1,664.00	269,360	173,735	1,775.16	189,529	253,566
135,000	1,653.16	460,138	1,676.92	368,076	92,062	1,728.00	279,720	180,418	1,843.43	196,817	263,321
140,000	1,714.38	477,177	1,739.03	381,709	95,468	1,792.00	290,080	187,097	1,911.71	204,108	273,069
145,000	1,775.61	494,220	1,801.14	395,342	98,878	1,856.00	300,440	193,780	1,979.98	211,396	282,824
150,000	1,836.84	511,262	1,863.25	408,975	102,287	1,920.00	310,800	200,462	2,048.26	218,687	292,575
155,000	1,898.07	528,305	1,925.36	422,608	105,697	1,984.00	321,160	207,145	2,116.53	225,975	302,330
160,000	1,959.29	545,344	1,987.47	436,241	109,103	2,048.00	331,520	213,824	2,184.81	233,266	312,078
165,000	2,020.52	562,387	2,049.57	449,871	112,516	2,112.00	341,880	220,507	2,253.08	240,544	321,833
170,000	2,081.75	579,430	2,111.68	463,504	115,926	2,176.00	352,240	227,190	2,321.36	247,845	331,585
175,000	2,142.98	596,473	2,173.79	477,137	119,336	2,240.00	362,600	233,873	2,389.63	255,133	341,340
180,000	2,204.21	613,516	2,235.90	490,770	122,746	2,304.00	372,960	240,556	2,457.91	262,424	351,092
185,000	2,265.43	630,555	2,298.01	504,403	126,152	2,368.00	383,320	247,235	2,526.18	269,712	360,843
190,000	2,326.66	647,598	2,360.11	518,033	129,565	2,432.00	393,680	253,918	2,594.46	277,003	370,595
195,000	2,387.89	664,640	2,422.22	531,666	132,974	2,496.00	404,040	260,600	2,662.73	284,291	380,349
200,000	2,449.12	681,683	2,484.33	545,299	136,384	2,560.00	414,400	267,283	2,731.01	291,582	390,101

AMOUNT OF LOAN	30 YEARS		25 YEARS			20 YEARS			15 YEARS		
	MONTHLY PAYMENT	TOTAL INTRST	MONTHLY PAYMENT	TOTAL INTRST	INTRST SAVED	MONTHLY PAYMENT	TOTAL INTRST	INTRST SAVED	MONTHLY PAYMENT	TOTAL INTRST	INTRST SAVED
$ 50	0.63	177	0.64	142	35	0.65	106	71	0.70	76	101
100	1.25	350	1.27	281	69	1.30	212	138	1.39	150	200
200	2.49	696	2.53	559	137	2.60	424	272	2.77	299	397
300	3.74	1,046	3.79	837	209	3.90	636	410	4.15	447	599
400	4.98	1,393	5.05	1,115	278	5.20	848	545	5.54	597	796
500	6.23	1,743	6.31	1,393	350	6.50	1,060	683	6.92	746	997
600	7.47	2,089	7.57	1,671	418	7.80	1,272	817	8.30	894	1,195
700	8.72	2,439	8.84	1,952	487	9.09	1,482	957	9.68	1,042	1,397
800	9.96	2,786	10.10	2,230	556	10.39	1,694	1,092	11.07	1,193	1,593
900	11.21	3,136	11.36	2,508	628	11.69	1,906	1,230	12.45	1,341	1,795
1,000	12.45	3,482	12.62	2,786	696	12.99	2,118	1,364	13.83	1,489	1,993
2,000	24.89	6,960	25.23	5,569	1,391	25.97	4,233	2,727	27.66	2,979	3,981
3,000	37.34	10,442	37.85	8,355	2,087	38.96	6,350	4,092	41.48	4,466	5,976
4,000	49.78	13,921	50.46	11,138	2,783	51.94	8,466	5,455	55.31	5,956	7,965
5,000	62.23	17,403	63.08	13,924	3,479	64.92	10,581	6,822	69.13	7,443	9,960
6,000	74.67	20,881	75.69	16,707	4,174	77.91	12,698	8,183	82.96	8,933	11,948
7,000	87.12	24,363	88.31	19,493	4,870	90.89	14,814	9,549	96.78	10,420	13,943
8,000	99.56	27,842	100.92	22,276	5,566	103.87	16,929	10,913	110.61	11,910	15,932
9,000	112.01	31,324	113.54	25,062	6,262	116.86	19,046	12,278	124.43	13,397	17,927
10,000	124.45	34,802	126.15	27,845	6,957	129.84	21,162	13,640	138.26	14,887	19,915
11,000	136.90	38,284	138.77	30,631	7,653	142.82	23,277	15,007	152.08	16,374	21,910
12,000	149.34	41,762	151.38	33,414	8,348	155.81	25,394	16,368	165.91	17,864	23,898
13,000	161.79	45,244	164.00	36,200	9,044	168.79	27,510	17,734	179.73	19,351	25,893
14,000	174.23	48,723	176.61	38,983	9,740	181.77	29,625	19,098	193.56	20,841	27,882
15,000	186.68	52,205	189.22	41,766	10,439	194.76	31,742	20,463	207.38	22,328	29,877
16,000	199.12	55,683	201.84	44,552	11,131	207.74	33,858	21,825	221.21	23,818	31,865
17,000	211.57	59,165	214.45	47,335	11,830	220.73	35,975	23,190	235.03	25,305	33,860
18,000	224.01	62,644	227.07	50,121	12,523	233.71	38,090	24,554	248.86	26,795	35,849
19,000	236.46	66,126	239.68	52,904	13,222	246.69	40,206	25,920	262.68	28,282	37,844
20,000	248.90	69,604	252.30	55,690	13,914	259.68	42,323	27,281	276.51	29,772	39,832
21,000	261.34	73,082	264.91	58,473	14,609	272.66	44,438	28,644	290.33	31,259	41,823
22,000	273.79	76,564	277.53	61,259	15,305	285.64	46,554	30,010	304.16	32,749	43,815
23,000	286.23	80,043	290.14	64,042	16,001	298.63	48,671	31,372	317.98	34,236	45,807
24,000	298.68	83,525	302.76	66,828	16,697	311.61	50,786	32,739	331.81	35,726	47,799
25,000	311.12	87,003	315.37	69,611	17,392	324.59	52,902	34,101	345.63	37,213	49,790
26,000	323.57	90,485	327.99	72,397	18,088	337.58	55,019	35,466	359.46	38,703	51,782
27,000	336.01	93,964	340.60	75,180	18,784	350.56	57,134	36,830	373.28	40,190	53,774
28,000	348.46	97,446	353.22	77,966	19,480	363.54	59,250	38,196	387.11	41,680	55,766
29,000	360.90	100,924	365.83	80,749	20,175	376.53	61,367	39,557	400.93	43,167	57,757
30,000	373.35	104,406	378.44	83,532	20,874	389.51	63,482	40,924	414.76	44,657	59,749
32,500	404.46	113,106	409.98	90,494	22,612	421.97	68,773	44,333	449.32	48,378	64,728
35,000	435.57	121,805	441.52	97,456	24,349	454.43	74,063	47,742	483.88	52,098	69,707
40,000	497.80	139,208	504.59	111,377	27,831	519.35	84,644	54,564	553.01	59,542	79,666
45,000	560.02	156,607	567.66	125,298	31,309	584.26	95,222	61,385	622.13	66,983	89,624
50,000	622.24	174,006	630.74	139,222	34,784	649.18	105,803	68,203	691.26	74,427	99,579
55,000	684.47	191,409	693.81	153,143	38,266	714.10	116,384	75,025	760.38	81,868	109,541
60,000	746.69	208,808	756.88	167,064	41,744	779.02	126,965	81,843	829.51	89,312	119,496
65,000	808.91	226,208	819.96	180,988	45,220	843.94	137,546	88,662	898.63	96,753	129,455
70,000	871.14	243,610	883.03	194,909	48,701	908.85	148,124	95,486	967.76	104,197	139,413
75,000	933.36	261,010	946.10	208,830	52,180	973.77	158,705	102,305	1,036.88	111,638	149,372
80,000	995.59	278,412	1,009.18	222,754	55,658	1,038.69	169,286	109,126	1,106.01	119,082	159,330
85,000	1,057.81	295,812	1,072.25	236,675	59,137	1,103.61	179,866	115,946	1,175.13	126,523	169,289
90,000	1,120.03	313,211	1,135.32	250,596	62,615	1,168.52	190,445	122,766	1,244.26	133,967	179,244
95,000	1,182.26	330,614	1,198.40	264,520	66,094	1,233.44	201,026	129,588	1,313.38	141,408	189,206
100,000	1,244.48	348,013	1,261.47	278,441	69,572	1,298.36	211,606	136,407	1,382.51	148,852	199,161
105,000	1,306.70	365,412	1,324.54	292,362	73,050	1,363.28	222,187	143,225	1,451.63	156,293	209,119
110,000	1,368.93	382,815	1,387.62	306,286	76,529	1,428.20	232,768	150,047	1,520.76	163,737	219,078
115,000	1,431.15	400,214	1,450.69	320,207	80,007	1,493.11	243,346	156,868	1,589.88	171,178	229,036
120,000	1,493.38	417,617	1,513.76	334,128	83,489	1,558.03	253,927	163,690	1,659.01	178,622	238,995
125,000	1,555.60	435,016	1,576.84	348,052	86,964	1,622.95	264,508	170,508	1,728.13	186,063	248,953
130,000	1,617.82	452,415	1,639.91	361,973	90,442	1,687.87	275,089	177,326	1,797.26	193,507	258,908
135,000	1,680.05	469,818	1,702.98	375,894	93,924	1,752.78	285,667	184,151	1,866.39	200,950	268,868
140,000	1,742.27	487,217	1,766.06	389,818	97,399	1,817.70	296,248	190,969	1,935.51	208,392	278,825
145,000	1,804.49	504,616	1,829.13	403,739	100,877	1,882.62	306,829	197,787	2,004.64	215,835	288,781
150,000	1,866.72	522,019	1,892.20	417,660	104,359	1,947.54	317,410	204,609	2,073.76	223,277	298,742
155,000	1,928.94	539,418	1,955.28	431,584	107,834	2,012.46	327,990	211,428	2,142.89	230,720	308,698
160,000	1,991.17	556,821	2,018.35	445,505	111,316	2,077.37	338,569	218,252	2,212.01	238,162	318,659
165,000	2,053.39	574,220	2,081.42	459,426	114,794	2,142.29	349,150	225,070	2,281.14	245,605	328,615
170,000	2,115.61	591,620	2,144.50	473,350	118,270	2,207.21	359,730	231,890	2,350.26	253,047	338,573
175,000	2,177.84	609,022	2,207.57	487,271	121,751	2,272.13	370,311	238,711	2,419.39	260,490	348,532
180,000	2,240.06	626,422	2,270.64	501,192	125,230	2,337.04	380,890	245,532	2,488.51	267,932	358,490
185,000	2,302.29	643,824	2,333.71	515,113	128,711	2,401.96	391,470	252,354	2,557.64	275,375	368,449
190,000	2,364.51	661,224	2,396.79	529,037	132,187	2,466.88	402,051	259,173	2,626.76	282,817	378,407
195,000	2,426.73	678,623	2,459.86	542,958	135,665	2,531.80	412,632	265,991	2,695.89	290,260	388,363
200,000	2,488.96	696,026	2,522.93	556,879	139,147	2,596.72	423,213	272,813	2,765.01	297,702	398,324

35

SHORT-TERM AMORTIZING MORTGAGES

AMOUNT OF LOAN	30 YEARS		25 YEARS			20 YEARS			15 YEARS		
	MONTHLY PAYMENT	TOTAL INTRST	MONTHLY PAYMENT	TOTAL INTRST	INTRST SAVED	MONTHLY PAYMENT	TOTAL INTRST	INTRST SAVED	MONTHLY PAYMENT	TOTAL INTRST	INTRST SAVED
$ 50	0.64	180	0.65	145	35	0.66	108	72	0.70	76	104
100	1.27	357	1.29	287	70	1.32	217	140	1.40	152	205
200	2.53	711	2.57	571	140	2.64	434	277	2.80	304	407
300	3.80	1,068	3.85	855	213	3.96	650	418	4.20	456	612
400	5.06	1,422	5.13	1,139	283	5.27	865	557	5.60	608	814
500	6.33	1,779	6.41	1,423	356	6.59	1,082	697	7.00	760	1,019
600	7.59	2,132	7.69	1,707	425	7.91	1,298	834	8.40	912	1,220
700	8.86	2,490	8.97	1,991	499	9.22	1,513	977	9.80	1,064	1,426
800	10.12	2,843	10.25	2,275	568	10.54	1,730	1,113	11.20	1,216	1,627
900	11.38	3,197	11.53	2,559	638	11.86	1,946	1,251	12.60	1,368	1,829
1,000	12.65	3,554	12.81	2,843	711	13.17	2,161	1,393	14.00	1,520	2,034
2,000	25.29	7,104	25.62	5,686	1,418	26.34	4,322	2,782	28.00	3,040	4,064
3,000	37.94	10,658	38.43	8,529	2,129	39.51	6,482	4,176	41.99	4,558	6,100
4,000	50.58	14,209	51.24	11,372	2,837	52.68	8,643	5,566	55.99	6,078	8,131
5,000	63.23	17,763	64.05	14,215	3,548	65.84	10,802	6,961	69.98	7,596	10,167
6,000	75.87	21,313	76.85	17,055	4,258	79.01	12,962	8,351	83.98	9,116	12,197
7,000	88.52	24,867	89.66	19,898	4,969	92.18	15,123	9,744	97.98	10,636	14,231
8,000	101.16	28,418	102.47	22,741	5,677	105.35	17,284	11,134	111.97	12,155	16,263
9,000	113.80	31,968	115.28	25,584	6,384	118.52	19,445	12,523	125.97	13,675	18,293
10,000	126.45	35,522	128.09	28,427	7,095	131.68	21,603	13,919	139.96	15,193	20,329
11,000	139.09	39,072	140.90	31,270	7,802	144.85	23,764	15,308	153.96	16,713	22,359
12,000	151.74	42,626	153.70	34,110	8,516	158.02	25,925	16,701	167.96	18,233	24,393
13,000	164.38	46,177	166.51	36,953	9,224	171.19	28,086	18,091	181.95	19,751	26,426
14,000	177.03	49,731	179.32	39,796	9,935	184.36	30,246	19,485	195.95	21,271	28,460
15,000	189.67	53,281	192.13	42,639	10,642	197.52	32,405	20,876	209.94	22,789	30,492
16,000	202.32	56,835	204.94	45,482	11,353	210.69	34,566	22,269	223.94	24,309	32,526
17,000	214.96	60,386	217.75	48,325	12,061	223.86	36,726	23,660	237.93	25,827	34,559
18,000	227.60	63,936	230.55	51,165	12,771	237.03	38,887	25,049	251.93	27,347	36,589
19,000	240.25	67,490	243.36	54,008	13,482	250.20	41,048	26,442	265.93	28,867	38,623
20,000	252.89	71,040	256.17	56,851	14,189	263.36	43,206	27,834	279.92	30,386	40,654
21,000	265.54	74,594	268.98	59,694	14,900	276.53	45,367	29,227	293.92	31,906	42,688
22,000	278.18	78,145	281.79	62,537	15,608	289.70	47,528	30,617	307.91	33,424	44,721
23,000	290.83	81,699	294.60	65,380	16,319	302.87	49,689	32,010	321.91	34,944	46,755
24,000	303.47	85,249	307.40	68,220	17,029	316.03	51,847	33,402	335.91	36,464	48,785
25,000	316.12	88,803	320.21	71,063	17,740	329.20	54,008	34,795	349.90	37,982	50,821
26,000	328.76	92,354	333.02	73,906	18,448	342.37	56,169	36,185	363.90	39,502	52,852
27,000	341.40	95,904	345.83	76,749	19,155	355.54	58,330	37,574	377.89	41,020	54,884
28,000	354.05	99,458	358.64	79,592	19,866	368.71	60,490	38,968	391.89	42,540	56,918
29,000	366.69	103,008	371.45	82,435	20,573	381.87	62,649	40,359	405.89	44,060	58,948
30,000	379.34	106,562	384.25	85,275	21,287	395.04	64,810	41,752	419.88	45,578	60,984
32,500	410.95	115,442	416.27	92,381	23,061	427.96	70,210	45,232	454.87	49,377	66,065
35,000	442.56	124,322	448.30	99,490	24,832	460.88	75,611	48,711	489.86	53,175	71,147
40,000	505.78	142,081	512.34	113,702	28,379	526.72	86,413	55,668	559.84	60,771	81,310
45,000	569.00	159,840	576.38	127,914	31,926	592.56	97,214	62,626	629.82	68,368	91,472
50,000	632.23	177,603	640.42	142,126	35,477	658.40	108,016	69,587	699.80	75,964	101,639
55,000	695.45	195,362	704.46	156,338	39,024	724.24	118,818	76,544	769.78	83,560	111,802
60,000	758.67	213,121	768.50	170,550	42,571	790.08	129,619	83,502	839.76	91,157	121,964
65,000	821.89	230,880	832.54	184,762	46,118	855.92	140,421	90,459	909.74	98,753	132,127
70,000	885.12	248,643	896.59	198,977	49,666	921.76	151,222	97,421	979.72	106,350	142,293
75,000	948.34	266,402	960.63	213,189	53,213	987.60	162,024	104,378	1,049.70	113,946	152,456
80,000	1,011.56	284,162	1,024.67	227,401	56,761	1,053.44	172,826	111,336	1,119.67	121,541	162,621
85,000	1,074.78	301,921	1,088.71	241,613	60,308	1,119.28	183,627	118,294	1,189.65	129,137	172,784
90,000	1,138.00	319,680	1,152.75	255,825	63,855	1,185.12	194,429	125,251	1,259.63	136,733	182,947
95,000	1,201.23	337,443	1,216.79	270,037	67,406	1,250.96	205,230	132,213	1,329.61	144,330	193,113
100,000	1,264.45	355,202	1,280.84	284,252	70,950	1,316.79	216,030	139,172	1,399.59	151,926	203,276
105,000	1,327.67	372,961	1,344.88	298,464	74,497	1,382.63	226,831	146,130	1,469.57	159,523	213,438
110,000	1,390.89	390,720	1,408.92	312,676	78,044	1,448.47	237,633	153,087	1,539.55	167,119	223,601
115,000	1,454.12	408,483	1,472.96	326,888	81,595	1,514.31	248,434	160,049	1,609.53	174,715	233,768
120,000	1,517.34	426,242	1,537.00	341,100	85,142	1,580.15	259,236	167,006	1,679.51	182,312	243,930
125,000	1,580.56	444,002	1,601.04	355,312	88,690	1,645.99	270,038	173,964	1,749.49	189,908	254,094
130,000	1,643.78	461,761	1,665.08	369,524	92,237	1,711.83	280,839	180,922	1,819.47	197,505	264,256
135,000	1,707.00	479,520	1,729.13	383,739	95,781	1,777.67	291,641	187,879	1,889.45	205,101	274,419
140,000	1,770.23	497,283	1,793.17	397,951	99,332	1,843.51	302,442	194,841	1,959.43	212,697	284,586
145,000	1,833.45	515,042	1,857.21	412,163	102,879	1,909.35	313,244	201,798	2,029.41	220,294	294,748
150,000	1,896.67	532,801	1,921.25	426,375	106,426	1,975.19	324,046	208,755	2,099.39	227,890	304,911
155,000	1,959.89	550,560	1,985.29	440,587	109,973	2,041.03	334,847	215,713	2,169.37	235,487	315,073
160,000	2,023.12	568,323	2,049.33	454,799	113,524	2,106.87	345,649	222,674	2,239.34	243,081	325,242
165,000	2,086.34	586,082	2,113.38	469,014	117,068	2,172.71	356,450	229,632	2,309.32	250,678	335,404
170,000	2,149.56	603,842	2,177.42	483,226	120,616	2,238.55	367,252	236,590	2,379.30	258,274	345,568
175,000	2,212.78	621,601	2,241.46	497,438	124,163	2,304.39	378,054	243,547	2,449.28	265,870	355,731
180,000	2,276.00	639,360	2,305.50	511,650	127,710	2,370.23	388,855	250,505	2,519.26	273,467	365,893
185,000	2,339.23	657,123	2,369.54	525,862	131,261	2,436.07	399,657	257,466	2,589.24	281,063	376,060
190,000	2,402.45	674,882	2,433.58	540,074	134,808	2,501.91	410,458	264,424	2,659.22	288,660	386,222
195,000	2,465.67	692,641	2,497.62	554,286	138,355	2,567.74	421,258	271,383	2,729.20	296,256	396,385
200,000	2,528.89	710,400	2,561.67	568,501	141,899	2,633.58	432,059	278,341	2,799.18	303,852	406,548

SHORT-TERM AMORTIZING MORTGAGES 15.25%

AMOUNT OF LOAN	30 YEARS MONTHLY PAYMENT	TOTAL INTRST	25 YEARS MONTHLY PAYMENT	TOTAL INTRST	INTRST SAVED	20 YEARS MONTHLY PAYMENT	TOTAL INTRST	INTRST SAVED	15 YEARS MONTHLY PAYMENT	TOTAL INTRST	INTRST SAVED
$ 50	0.65	184	0.66	148	36	0.67	111	73	0.71	78	106
100	1.29	364	1.31	293	71	1.34	222	142	1.42	156	208
200	2.57	725	2.61	583	142	2.68	443	282	2.84	311	414
300	3.86	1,090	3.91	873	217	4.01	662	428	4.26	467	623
400	5.14	1,450	5.21	1,163	287	5.35	884	566	5.67	621	829
500	6.43	1,815	6.51	1,453	362	6.68	1,103	712	7.09	776	1,039
600	7.71	2,176	7.81	1,743	433	8.02	1,325	851	8.51	932	1,244
700	9.00	2,540	9.11	2,033	507	9.35	1,544	996	9.92	1,086	1,454
800	10.28	2,901	10.41	2,323	578	10.69	1,766	1,135	11.34	1,241	1,660
900	11.57	3,265	11.71	2,613	652	12.02	1,985	1,280	12.76	1,397	1,868
1,000	12.85	3,626	13.01	2,903	723	13.36	2,206	1,420	14.17	1,551	2,075
2,000	25.69	7,248	26.01	5,803	1,445	26.71	4,410	2,838	28.34	3,101	4,147
3,000	38.54	10,874	39.01	8,703	2,171	40.06	6,614	4,260	42.51	4,652	6,222
4,000	51.38	14,497	52.02	11,606	2,891	53.42	8,821	5,676	56.67	6,201	8,296
5,000	64.23	18,123	65.02	14,506	3,617	66.77	11,025	7,098	70.84	7,751	10,372
6,000	77.07	21,745	78.02	17,406	4,339	80.12	13,229	8,516	85.01	9,302	12,443
7,000	89.92	25,371	91.02	20,306	5,065	93.48	15,435	9,936	99.18	10,852	14,519
8,000	102.76	28,994	104.03	23,209	5,785	106.83	17,639	11,355	113.34	12,401	16,593
9,000	115.61	32,620	117.03	26,109	6,511	120.18	19,843	12,777	127.51	13,952	18,668
10,000	128.45	36,242	130.03	29,009	7,233	133.53	22,047	14,195	141.68	15,502	20,740
11,000	141.30	39,868	143.03	31,909	7,959	146.89	24,254	15,614	155.85	17,053	22,815
12,000	154.14	43,490	156.04	34,812	8,678	160.24	26,458	17,032	170.01	18,602	24,888
13,000	166.98	47,113	169.04	37,712	9,401	173.59	28,662	18,451	184.18	20,152	26,961
14,000	179.83	50,739	182.04	40,612	10,127	186.95	30,868	19,871	198.35	21,703	29,036
15,000	192.67	54,361	195.04	43,512	10,849	200.30	33,072	21,289	212.52	23,254	31,107
16,000	205.52	57,987	208.05	46,415	11,572	213.65	35,276	22,711	226.68	24,802	33,185
17,000	218.36	61,610	221.05	49,315	12,295	227.01	37,482	24,128	240.85	26,353	35,257
18,000	231.21	65,236	234.05	52,215	13,021	240.36	39,686	25,550	255.02	27,904	37,332
19,000	244.05	68,858	247.05	55,115	13,743	253.71	41,890	26,968	269.19	29,454	39,404
20,000	256.90	72,484	260.06	58,018	14,466	267.06	44,094	28,390	283.35	31,003	41,481
21,000	269.74	76,106	273.06	60,918	15,188	280.42	46,301	29,805	297.52	32,554	43,552
22,000	282.59	79,732	286.06	63,818	15,914	293.77	48,505	31,227	311.69	34,104	45,628
23,000	295.43	83,355	299.06	66,718	16,637	307.12	50,709	32,646	325.86	35,655	47,700
24,000	308.28	86,981	312.07	69,621	17,360	320.48	52,915	34,066	340.02	37,204	49,777
25,000	321.12	90,603	325.07	72,521	18,082	333.83	55,119	35,484	354.19	38,754	51,849
26,000	333.96	94,226	338.07	75,421	18,805	347.18	57,323	36,903	368.36	40,305	53,921
27,000	346.81	97,852	351.07	78,321	19,531	360.54	59,530	38,322	382.53	41,855	55,997
28,000	359.65	101,474	364.08	81,224	20,250	373.89	61,734	39,740	396.69	43,404	58,070
29,000	372.50	105,100	377.08	84,124	20,976	387.24	63,938	41,162	410.86	44,955	60,145
30,000	385.34	108,722	390.08	87,024	21,698	400.59	66,142	42,580	425.03	46,505	62,217
32,500	417.45	117,782	422.59	94,277	23,505	433.98	71,655	46,127	460.45	50,381	67,401
35,000	449.57	126,845	455.10	101,530	25,315	467.36	77,166	49,679	495.87	54,257	72,588
40,000	513.79	144,964	520.11	116,033	28,931	534.12	88,189	56,775	566.70	62,006	82,958
45,000	578.01	163,084	585.12	130,536	32,548	600.89	99,214	63,870	637.54	69,757	93,327
50,000	642.23	181,203	650.13	145,039	36,164	667.65	110,236	70,967	708.38	77,508	103,695
55,000	706.46	199,326	715.15	159,545	39,781	734.42	121,261	78,065	779.22	85,260	114,066
60,000	770.68	217,445	780.16	174,048	43,397	801.18	132,283	85,162	850.05	93,009	124,436
65,000	834.90	235,564	845.17	188,551	47,013	867.95	143,308	92,256	920.89	100,760	134,804
70,000	899.13	253,687	910.19	203,057	50,630	934.71	154,330	99,357	991.73	108,511	145,176
75,000	963.35	271,806	975.20	217,560	54,246	1,001.48	165,355	106,451	1,062.57	116,263	155,543
80,000	1,027.57	289,925	1,040.21	232,063	57,862	1,068.24	176,378	113,547	1,133.40	124,012	165,913
85,000	1,091.79	308,044	1,105.22	246,566	61,478	1,135.01	187,402	120,642	1,204.24	131,763	176,281
90,000	1,156.02	326,167	1,170.24	261,072	65,095	1,201.77	198,425	127,742	1,275.08	139,514	186,653
95,000	1,220.24	344,286	1,235.25	275,575	68,711	1,268.54	209,450	134,836	1,345.92	147,266	197,020
100,000	1,284.46	362,406	1,300.26	290,078	72,328	1,335.30	220,472	141,934	1,416.75	155,015	207,391
105,000	1,348.69	380,528	1,365.28	304,584	75,944	1,402.07	231,497	149,031	1,487.59	162,766	217,762
110,000	1,412.91	398,648	1,430.29	319,087	79,561	1,468.83	242,519	156,129	1,558.43	170,517	228,131
115,000	1,477.13	416,767	1,495.30	333,590	83,177	1,535.60	253,544	163,223	1,629.27	178,269	238,498
120,000	1,541.36	434,890	1,560.31	348,093	86,797	1,602.36	264,566	170,324	1,700.10	186,018	248,872
125,000	1,605.58	453,009	1,625.33	362,599	90,410	1,669.13	275,591	177,418	1,770.94	193,769	259,240
130,000	1,669.80	471,128	1,690.34	377,102	94,026	1,735.89	286,614	184,514	1,841.78	201,520	269,608
135,000	1,734.02	489,247	1,755.35	391,605	97,642	1,802.66	297,638	191,609	1,912.62	209,272	279,975
140,000	1,798.25	507,370	1,820.37	406,111	101,259	1,869.42	308,661	198,709	1,983.45	217,021	290,349
145,000	1,862.47	525,489	1,885.38	420,614	104,875	1,936.19	319,686	205,803	2,054.29	224,772	300,717
150,000	1,926.69	543,608	1,950.39	435,117	108,491	2,002.95	330,708	212,900	2,125.13	232,523	311,085
155,000	1,990.92	561,731	2,015.41	449,623	112,108	2,069.72	341,733	219,998	2,195.97	240,275	321,456
160,000	2,055.14	579,850	2,080.42	464,126	115,724	2,136.48	352,755	227,095	2,266.80	248,024	331,826
165,000	2,119.36	597,970	2,145.43	478,629	119,341	2,203.25	363,780	234,190	2,337.64	255,775	342,195
170,000	2,183.58	616,089	2,210.44	493,132	122,957	2,270.01	374,802	241,287	2,408.48	263,526	352,563
175,000	2,247.81	634,212	2,275.46	507,638	126,574	2,336.78	385,827	248,385	2,479.32	271,278	362,934
180,000	2,312.03	652,331	2,340.47	522,141	130,190	2,403.54	396,850	255,481	2,550.15	279,027	373,304
185,000	2,376.25	670,450	2,405.48	536,644	133,806	2,470.31	407,874	262,576	2,620.99	286,778	383,672
190,000	2,440.48	688,573	2,470.50	551,150	137,423	2,537.07	418,897	269,676	2,691.83	294,529	394,044
195,000	2,504.70	706,692	2,535.51	565,653	141,039	2,603.84	429,922	276,770	2,762.67	302,281	404,411
200,000	2,568.92	724,811	2,600.52	580,156	144,655	2,670.60	440,944	283,867	2,833.50	310,030	414,781

15.50% SHORT-TERM AMORTIZING MORTGAGES

AMOUNT OF LOAN	30 YEARS		25 YEARS			20 YEARS			15 YEARS		
	MONTHLY PAYMENT	TOTAL INTRST	MONTHLY PAYMENT	TOTAL INTRST	INTRST SAVED	MONTHLY PAYMENT	TOTAL INTRST	INTRST SAVED	MONTHLY PAYMENT	TOTAL INTRST	INTRST SAVED
$ 50	0.66	188	0.66	148	40	0.68	113	75	0.72	80	108
100	1.31	372	1.32	296	76	1.36	226	146	1.44	159	213
200	2.61	740	2.64	592	148	2.71	450	290	2.87	317	423
300	3.92	1,111	3.96	888	223	4.07	677	434	4.31	476	635
400	5.22	1,479	5.28	1,184	295	5.42	901	578	5.74	633	846
500	6.53	1,851	6.60	1,480	371	6.77	1,125	726	7.17	791	1,060
600	7.83	2,219	7.92	1,776	443	8.13	1,351	868	8.61	950	1,269
700	9.14	2,590	9.24	2,072	518	9.48	1,575	1,015	10.04	1,107	1,483
800	10.44	2,958	10.56	2,368	590	10.84	1,802	1,156	11.48	1,266	1,692
900	11.75	3,330	11.88	2,664	666	12.19	2,026	1,304	12.91	1,424	1,906
1,000	13.05	3,698	13.20	2,960	738	13.54	2,250	1,448	14.34	1,581	2,117
2,000	26.10	7,396	26.40	5,920	1,476	27.08	4,499	2,897	28.68	3,162	4,234
3,000	39.14	11,090	39.60	8,880	2,210	40.62	6,749	4,341	43.02	4,744	6,346
4,000	52.19	14,788	52.79	11,837	2,951	54.16	8,998	5,790	57.36	6,325	8,463
5,000	65.23	18,483	65.99	14,797	3,686	67.70	11,248	7,235	71.70	7,906	10,577
6,000	78.28	22,181	79.19	17,757	4,424	81.24	13,498	8,683	86.04	9,487	12,694
7,000	91.32	25,875	92.39	20,717	5,158	94.78	15,747	10,128	100.38	11,068	14,807
8,000	104.37	29,573	105.58	23,674	5,899	108.32	17,997	11,576	114.72	12,650	16,923
9,000	117.41	33,268	118.78	26,634	6,634	121.85	20,247	13,024	129.06	14,231	19,037
10,000	130.46	36,966	131.98	29,594	7,372	135.39	22,494	14,472	143.40	15,812	21,154
11,000	143.50	40,660	145.18	32,554	8,106	148.93	24,743	15,917	157.74	17,393	23,267
12,000	156.55	44,358	158.37	35,511	8,847	162.47	26,993	17,365	172.08	18,974	25,384
13,000	169.59	48,052	171.57	38,471	9,581	176.01	29,242	18,810	186.42	20,556	27,496
14,000	182.64	51,750	184.77	41,431	10,319	189.55	31,492	20,258	200.76	22,137	29,613
15,000	195.68	55,445	197.97	44,391	11,054	203.09	33,742	21,703	215.10	23,718	31,727
16,000	208.73	59,143	211.16	47,348	11,795	216.63	35,991	23,152	229.44	25,299	33,844
17,000	221.77	62,837	224.36	50,308	12,529	230.16	38,238	24,599	243.78	26,880	35,957
18,000	234.82	66,535	237.56	53,268	13,267	243.70	40,488	26,047	258.12	28,462	38,073
19,000	247.86	70,230	250.76	56,228	14,002	257.24	42,738	27,492	272.46	30,043	40,187
20,000	260.91	73,928	263.95	59,185	14,743	270.78	44,987	28,941	286.80	31,624	42,304
21,000	273.95	77,622	277.15	62,145	15,477	284.32	47,237	30,385	301.14	33,205	44,417
22,000	287.00	81,320	290.35	65,105	16,215	297.86	49,486	31,834	315.48	34,786	46,534
23,000	300.04	85,014	303.55	68,065	16,949	311.40	51,736	33,278	329.82	36,368	48,646
24,000	313.09	88,712	316.74	71,022	17,690	324.94	53,986	34,726	344.16	37,949	50,763
25,000	326.13	92,407	329.94	73,982	18,425	338.48	56,235	36,172	358.50	39,530	52,877
26,000	339.18	96,105	343.14	76,942	19,163	352.01	58,482	37,623	372.84	41,111	54,994
27,000	352.22	99,799	356.34	79,902	19,897	365.55	60,732	39,067	387.18	42,692	57,107
28,000	365.27	103,497	369.53	82,859	20,638	379.09	62,982	40,515	401.52	44,274	59,223
29,000	378.31	107,192	382.73	85,819	21,373	392.63	65,231	41,961	415.86	45,855	61,337
30,000	391.36	110,890	395.93	88,779	22,111	406.17	67,481	43,409	430.20	47,436	63,454
32,500	423.97	120,129	428.92	96,176	23,953	440.02	73,105	47,024	466.05	51,389	68,740
35,000	456.59	129,372	461.92	103,576	25,796	473.86	78,726	50,646	501.90	55,342	74,030
40,000	521.81	147,852	527.90	118,370	29,482	541.56	89,974	57,878	573.60	63,248	84,604
45,000	587.04	166,334	593.89	133,167	33,167	609.25	101,220	65,114	645.30	71,154	95,180
50,000	652.26	184,814	659.88	147,964	36,850	676.95	112,468	72,346	717.00	79,060	105,754
55,000	717.49	203,296	725.86	162,758	40,538	744.64	123,714	79,582	788.70	86,966	116,330
60,000	782.72	221,779	791.85	177,555	44,224	812.33	134,959	86,820	860.40	94,872	126,907
65,000	847.94	240,258	857.84	192,352	47,906	880.03	146,207	94,051	932.10	102,778	137,483
70,000	913.17	258,741	923.83	207,149	51,592	947.72	157,453	101,288	1,003.80	110,684	148,057
75,000	978.39	277,220	989.81	221,943	55,277	1,015.42	168,701	108,519	1,075.50	118,590	158,630
80,000	1,043.62	295,703	1,055.80	236,740	58,963	1,083.11	179,946	115,757	1,147.20	126,496	169,207
85,000	1,108.84	314,182	1,121.79	251,537	62,645	1,150.80	191,192	122,990	1,218.90	134,402	179,780
90,000	1,174.07	332,665	1,187.78	266,334	66,331	1,218.50	202,440	130,225	1,290.60	142,308	190,357
95,000	1,239.30	351,148	1,253.76	281,128	70,020	1,286.19	213,686	137,462	1,362.30	150,214	200,934
100,000	1,304.52	369,627	1,319.75	295,925	73,702	1,353.89	224,934	144,693	1,434.00	158,120	211,507
105,000	1,369.75	388,110	1,385.74	310,722	77,388	1,421.58	236,179	151,931	1,505.69	166,024	222,086
110,000	1,434.97	406,589	1,451.72	325,516	81,073	1,489.27	247,425	159,164	1,577.39	173,930	232,659
115,000	1,500.20	425,072	1,517.71	340,313	84,759	1,556.97	258,673	166,399	1,649.09	181,836	243,236
120,000	1,565.43	443,555	1,583.70	355,110	88,445	1,624.66	269,918	173,637	1,720.79	189,742	253,813
125,000	1,630.65	462,034	1,649.69	369,907	92,127	1,692.36	281,166	180,868	1,792.49	197,648	264,386
130,000	1,695.88	480,517	1,715.67	384,701	95,816	1,760.05	292,412	188,105	1,864.19	205,554	274,963
135,000	1,761.10	498,996	1,781.66	399,498	99,498	1,827.74	303,658	195,338	1,935.89	213,460	285,536
140,000	1,826.33	517,479	1,847.65	414,295	103,184	1,895.44	314,906	202,573	2,007.59	221,366	296,113
145,000	1,891.55	535,958	1,913.64	429,092	106,866	1,963.13	326,151	209,807	2,079.29	229,272	306,686
150,000	1,956.78	554,441	1,979.62	443,886	110,555	2,030.83	337,399	217,042	2,150.99	237,178	317,263
155,000	2,022.01	572,924	2,045.61	458,683	114,241	2,098.52	348,645	224,279	2,222.69	245,084	327,840
160,000	2,087.23	591,403	2,111.60	473,480	117,923	2,166.21	359,890	231,513	2,294.39	252,990	338,413
165,000	2,152.46	609,886	2,177.58	488,274	121,612	2,233.91	371,138	238,748	2,366.09	260,896	348,990
170,000	2,217.68	628,365	2,243.57	503,071	125,294	2,301.60	382,384	245,981	2,437.79	268,802	359,563
175,000	2,282.91	646,848	2,309.56	517,868	128,980	2,369.30	393,632	253,216	2,509.49	276,708	370,140
180,000	2,348.14	665,330	2,375.55	532,665	132,665	2,436.99	404,878	260,452	2,581.19	284,614	380,716
185,000	2,413.36	683,810	2,441.53	547,459	136,351	2,504.68	416,123	267,687	2,652.89	292,520	391,293
190,000	2,478.59	702,292	2,507.52	562,256	140,036	2,572.38	427,371	274,921	2,724.59	300,426	401,866
195,000	2,543.81	720,772	2,573.51	577,053	143,719	2,640.07	438,617	282,155	2,796.29	308,332	412,440
200,000	2,609.04	739,254	2,639.50	591,850	147,404	2,707.77	449,865	289,389	2,867.99	316,238	423,016

SHORT-TERM AMORTIZING MORTGAGES 15.75%

AMOUNT OF LOAN	30 YEARS MONTHLY PAYMENT	30 YEARS TOTAL INTRST	25 YEARS MONTHLY PAYMENT	25 YEARS TOTAL INTRST	25 YEARS INTRST SAVED	20 YEARS MONTHLY PAYMENT	20 YEARS TOTAL INTRST	20 YEARS INTRST SAVED	15 YEARS MONTHLY PAYMENT	15 YEARS TOTAL INTRST	15 YEARS INTRST SAVED
$ 50	0.67	191	0.67	151	40	0.69	116	75	0.73	81	110
100	1.33	379	1.34	302	77	1.38	231	148	1.46	163	216
200	2.65	754	2.68	604	150	2.75	460	294	2.91	324	430
300	3.98	1,133	4.02	906	227	4.12	689	444	4.36	485	648
400	5.30	1,508	5.36	1,208	300	5.50	920	588	5.81	646	862
500	6.63	1,887	6.70	1,510	377	6.87	1,149	738	7.26	807	1,080
600	7.95	2,262	8.04	1,812	450	8.24	1,378	884	8.71	968	1,294
700	9.28	2,641	9.38	2,114	527	9.61	1,606	1,035	10.16	1,129	1,512
800	10.60	3,016	10.72	2,416	600	10.99	1,838	1,178	11.62	1,292	1,724
900	11.93	3,395	12.06	2,718	677	12.36	2,066	1,329	13.07	1,453	1,942
1,000	13.25	3,770	13.40	3,020	750	13.73	2,295	1,475	14.52	1,614	2,156
2,000	26.50	7,540	26.79	6,037	1,503	27.46	4,590	2,950	29.03	3,225	4,315
3,000	39.74	11,306	40.18	9,054	2,252	41.18	6,883	4,423	43.54	4,837	6,469
4,000	52.99	15,076	53.58	12,074	3,002	54.91	9,178	5,898	58.06	6,451	8,625
5,000	66.24	18,846	66.97	15,091	3,755	68.63	11,471	7,375	72.57	8,063	10,783
6,000	79.48	22,613	80.36	18,108	4,505	82.36	13,766	8,847	87.08	9,674	12,939
7,000	92.73	26,383	93.76	21,128	5,255	96.08	16,059	10,324	101.60	11,288	15,095
8,000	105.97	30,149	107.15	24,145	6,004	109.81	18,354	11,795	116.11	12,900	17,249
9,000	119.22	33,919	120.54	27,162	6,757	123.53	20,647	13,272	130.62	14,512	19,407
10,000	132.47	37,689	133.93	30,179	7,510	137.26	22,942	14,747	145.14	16,125	21,564
11,000	145.71	41,456	147.33	33,199	8,257	150.98	25,235	16,221	159.65	17,737	23,719
12,000	158.96	45,226	160.72	36,216	9,010	164.71	27,530	17,696	174.16	19,349	25,877
13,000	172.21	48,996	174.11	39,233	9,763	178.43	29,823	19,173	188.68	20,962	28,034
14,000	185.45	52,762	187.51	42,253	10,509	192.16	32,118	20,644	203.19	22,574	30,188
15,000	198.70	56,532	200.90	45,270	11,262	205.89	34,414	22,118	217.70	24,186	32,346
16,000	211.94	60,298	214.29	48,287	12,011	219.61	36,706	23,592	232.21	25,798	34,500
17,000	225.19	64,068	227.68	51,304	12,764	233.34	39,002	25,066	246.73	27,411	36,657
18,000	238.44	67,838	241.08	54,324	13,514	247.06	41,294	26,544	261.24	29,023	38,815
19,000	251.68	71,605	254.47	57,341	14,264	260.79	43,590	28,015	275.75	30,635	40,970
20,000	264.93	75,375	267.86	60,358	15,017	274.51	45,882	29,493	290.27	32,249	43,126
21,000	278.17	79,141	281.26	63,378	15,763	288.24	48,178	30,963	304.78	33,860	45,281
22,000	291.42	82,911	294.65	66,395	16,516	301.96	50,470	32,441	319.29	35,472	47,439
23,000	304.67	86,681	308.04	69,412	17,269	315.69	52,766	33,915	333.81	37,086	49,595
24,000	317.91	90,448	321.43	72,429	18,019	329.41	55,058	35,390	348.32	38,698	51,750
25,000	331.16	94,218	334.83	75,449	18,769	343.14	57,354	36,864	362.83	40,309	53,909
26,000	344.41	97,988	348.22	78,466	19,522	356.86	59,646	38,342	377.35	41,923	56,065
27,000	357.65	101,754	361.61	81,483	20,271	370.59	61,942	39,812	391.86	43,535	58,219
28,000	370.90	105,524	375.01	84,503	21,021	384.31	64,234	41,290	406.37	45,147	60,377
29,000	384.14	109,290	388.40	87,520	21,770	398.04	66,530	42,760	420.88	46,758	62,532
30,000	397.39	113,060	401.79	90,537	22,523	411.77	68,825	44,235	435.40	48,372	64,688
32,500	430.51	122,484	435.27	98,081	24,403	446.08	74,559	47,925	471.68	52,402	70,082
35,000	463.62	131,903	468.76	105,628	26,275	480.39	80,294	51,609	507.96	56,433	75,470
40,000	529.85	150,746	535.72	120,716	30,030	549.02	91,765	58,981	580.53	64,495	86,251
45,000	596.08	169,589	602.69	135,807	33,782	617.65	103,236	66,353	653.09	72,556	97,033
50,000	662.31	188,432	669.65	150,895	37,537	686.27	114,705	73,727	725.66	80,619	107,813
55,000	728.54	207,274	736.61	165,983	41,291	754.90	126,176	81,098	798.22	88,680	118,594
60,000	794.78	226,121	803.58	181,074	45,047	823.53	137,647	88,474	870.79	96,742	129,379
65,000	861.01	244,964	870.54	196,162	48,802	892.15	149,116	95,848	943.36	104,805	140,159
70,000	927.24	263,806	937.51	211,253	52,553	960.78	160,587	103,219	1,015.92	112,866	150,940
75,000	993.47	282,649	1,004.47	226,341	56,308	1,029.41	172,058	110,591	1,088.49	120,928	161,721
80,000	1,059.70	301,492	1,071.44	241,432	60,060	1,098.03	183,527	117,965	1,161.05	128,989	172,503
85,000	1,125.93	320,335	1,138.40	256,520	63,815	1,166.66	194,998	125,337	1,233.62	137,052	183,283
90,000	1,192.16	339,178	1,205.37	271,611	67,567	1,235.29	206,470	132,708	1,306.18	145,112	194,066
95,000	1,258.39	358,020	1,272.33	286,699	71,321	1,303.91	217,938	140,082	1,378.75	153,175	204,845
100,000	1,324.62	376,863	1,339.29	301,787	75,076	1,372.54	229,410	147,453	1,451.31	161,236	215,627
105,000	1,390.85	395,706	1,406.26	316,878	78,828	1,441.17	240,881	154,825	1,523.88	169,298	226,408
110,000	1,457.08	414,549	1,473.22	331,966	82,583	1,509.79	252,350	162,199	1,596.44	177,359	237,190
115,000	1,523.31	433,392	1,540.19	347,057	86,335	1,578.42	263,821	169,571	1,669.01	185,422	247,970
120,000	1,589.55	452,238	1,607.15	362,145	90,093	1,647.05	275,292	176,946	1,741.57	193,483	258,755
125,000	1,655.78	471,081	1,674.12	377,236	93,845	1,715.67	286,761	184,320	1,814.14	201,545	269,536
130,000	1,722.01	489,924	1,741.08	392,324	97,600	1,784.30	298,232	191,692	1,886.71	209,608	280,316
135,000	1,788.24	508,766	1,808.05	407,415	101,351	1,852.93	309,703	199,063	1,959.27	217,669	291,097
140,000	1,854.47	527,609	1,875.01	422,503	105,106	1,921.55	321,172	206,437	2,031.84	225,731	301,878
145,000	1,920.70	546,452	1,941.97	437,591	108,861	1,990.18	332,643	213,809	2,104.40	233,792	312,660
150,000	1,986.93	565,295	2,008.94	452,682	112,613	2,058.81	344,114	221,181	2,176.97	241,855	323,440
155,000	2,053.16	584,138	2,075.90	467,770	116,368	2,127.43	355,583	228,555	2,249.53	249,915	334,223
160,000	2,119.39	602,980	2,142.87	482,861	120,119	2,196.06	367,054	235,926	2,322.10	257,978	345,002
165,000	2,185.62	621,823	2,209.83	497,949	123,874	2,264.69	378,526	243,297	2,394.66	266,039	355,784
170,000	2,251.85	640,666	2,276.80	513,040	127,626	2,333.31	389,994	250,672	2,467.23	274,101	366,565
175,000	2,318.08	659,509	2,343.76	528,128	131,381	2,401.94	401,466	258,043	2,539.79	282,162	377,347
180,000	2,384.32	678,355	2,410.73	543,219	135,136	2,470.57	412,937	265,418	2,612.36	290,225	388,130
185,000	2,450.55	697,198	2,477.69	558,307	138,891	2,539.19	424,406	272,792	2,684.92	298,286	398,912
190,000	2,516.78	716,041	2,544.66	573,398	142,643	2,607.82	435,877	280,164	2,757.49	306,348	409,693
195,000	2,583.01	734,884	2,611.62	588,486	146,398	2,676.45	447,348	287,536	2,830.06	314,411	420,473
200,000	2,649.24	753,726	2,678.58	603,574	150,152	2,745.07	458,817	294,909	2,902.62	322,472	431,254

39

AMOUNT OF LOAN	30 YEARS MONTHLY PAYMENT	30 YEARS TOTAL INTRST	25 YEARS MONTHLY PAYMENT	25 YEARS TOTAL INTRST	25 YEARS INTRST SAVED	20 YEARS MONTHLY PAYMENT	20 YEARS TOTAL INTRST	20 YEARS INTRST SAVED	15 YEARS MONTHLY PAYMENT	15 YEARS TOTAL INTRST	15 YEARS INTRST SAVED
$ 50	0.68	195	0.68	154	41	0.70	118	77	0.74	83	112
100	1.35	386	1.36	308	78	1.40	236	150	1.47	165	221
200	2.69	768	2.72	616	152	2.79	470	298	2.94	329	439
300	4.04	1,154	4.08	924	230	4.18	703	451	4.41	494	660
400	5.38	1,537	5.44	1,232	305	5.57	937	600	5.88	658	879
500	6.73	1,923	6.80	1,540	383	6.96	1,170	753	7.35	823	1,100
600	8.07	2,305	8.16	1,848	457	8.35	1,404	901	8.82	988	1,317
700	9.42	2,691	9.52	2,156	535	9.74	1,638	1,053	10.29	1,152	1,539
800	10.76	3,074	10.88	2,464	610	11.14	1,874	1,200	11.75	1,315	1,759
900	12.11	3,460	12.23	2,769	691	12.53	2,107	1,353	13.22	1,480	1,980
1,000	13.45	3,842	13.59	3,077	765	13.92	2,341	1,501	14.69	1,644	2,198
2,000	26.90	7,684	27.18	6,154	1,530	27.83	4,679	3,005	29.38	3,288	4,396
3,000	40.35	11,526	40.77	9,231	2,295	41.74	7,018	4,508	44.07	4,933	6,593
4,000	53.80	15,368	54.36	12,308	3,060	55.66	9,358	6,010	58.75	6,575	8,793
5,000	67.24	19,206	67.95	15,385	3,821	69.57	11,697	7,509	73.44	8,219	10,987
6,000	80.69	23,048	81.54	18,462	4,586	83.48	14,035	9,013	88.13	9,863	13,185
7,000	94.14	26,890	95.13	21,539	5,351	97.39	16,374	10,516	102.81	11,506	15,384
8,000	107.59	30,732	108.72	24,616	6,116	111.31	18,714	12,018	117.50	13,150	17,582
9,000	121.03	34,571	122.30	27,690	6,881	125.22	21,053	13,518	132.19	14,794	19,777
10,000	134.48	38,413	135.89	30,767	7,646	139.13	23,391	15,022	146.88	16,438	21,975
11,000	147.93	42,255	149.48	33,844	8,411	153.04	25,730	16,525	161.56	18,081	24,174
12,000	161.38	46,097	163.07	36,921	9,176	166.96	28,070	18,027	176.25	19,725	26,372
13,000	174.82	49,935	176.66	39,998	9,937	180.87	30,409	19,526	190.94	21,369	28,566
14,000	188.27	53,777	190.25	43,075	10,702	194.78	32,747	21,030	205.62	23,012	30,765
15,000	201.72	57,619	203.84	46,152	11,467	208.69	35,086	22,533	220.31	24,656	32,963
16,000	215.17	61,461	217.43	49,229	12,232	222.61	37,426	24,035	235.00	26,300	35,161
17,000	228.61	65,300	231.02	52,306	12,994	236.52	39,765	25,535	249.68	27,942	37,358
18,000	242.06	69,142	244.60	55,380	13,762	250.43	42,103	27,039	264.37	29,587	39,555
19,000	255.51	72,984	258.19	58,457	14,527	264.34	44,442	28,542	279.06	31,231	41,753
20,000	268.96	76,826	271.78	61,534	15,292	278.26	46,782	30,044	293.75	32,875	43,951
21,000	282.40	80,664	285.37	64,611	16,053	292.17	49,121	31,543	308.43	34,517	46,147
22,000	295.85	84,506	298.96	67,688	16,818	306.08	51,459	33,047	323.12	36,162	48,344
23,000	309.30	88,348	312.55	70,765	17,583	319.99	53,799	34,550	337.81	37,806	50,542
24,000	322.75	92,190	326.14	73,842	18,348	333.91	56,138	36,052	352.49	39,448	52,742
25,000	336.19	96,028	339.73	76,919	19,109	347.82	58,477	37,551	367.18	41,092	54,936
26,000	349.64	99,870	353.32	79,996	19,874	361.73	60,815	39,055	381.87	42,737	57,133
27,000	363.09	103,712	366.90	83,070	20,642	375.64	63,154	40,558	396.55	44,379	59,333
28,000	376.54	107,554	380.49	86,147	21,407	389.56	65,494	42,060	411.24	46,023	61,531
29,000	389.98	111,393	394.08	89,224	22,169	403.47	67,833	43,560	425.93	47,667	63,726
30,000	403.43	115,235	407.67	92,301	22,934	417.38	70,171	45,064	440.62	49,312	65,923
32,500	437.05	124,838	441.64	99,992	24,846	452.16	76,018	48,820	477.33	53,419	71,419
35,000	470.67	134,441	475.62	107,686	26,755	486.94	81,866	52,575	514.05	57,529	76,912
40,000	537.91	153,648	543.56	123,068	30,580	556.51	93,562	60,086	587.49	65,748	87,900
45,000	605.15	172,854	611.50	138,450	34,404	626.07	105,257	67,597	660.92	73,966	98,888
50,000	672.38	192,057	679.45	153,835	38,222	695.63	116,951	75,106	734.36	82,185	109,872
55,000	739.62	211,263	747.39	169,217	42,046	765.20	128,648	82,615	807.79	90,402	120,861
60,000	806.86	230,470	815.34	184,602	45,868	834.76	140,342	90,128	881.23	98,621	131,849
65,000	874.10	249,676	883.28	199,984	49,692	904.32	152,037	97,639	954.66	106,839	142,837
70,000	941.33	268,879	951.23	215,369	53,510	973.88	163,731	105,148	1,028.10	115,058	153,821
75,000	1,008.57	288,085	1,019.17	230,751	57,334	1,043.45	175,428	112,657	1,101.53	123,275	164,810
80,000	1,075.81	307,292	1,087.12	246,136	61,156	1,113.01	187,122	120,170	1,174.97	131,495	175,797
85,000	1,143.05	326,498	1,155.06	261,518	64,980	1,182.57	198,817	127,681	1,248.40	139,712	186,786
90,000	1,210.29	345,704	1,223.00	276,900	68,804	1,252.14	210,514	135,190	1,321.84	147,931	197,773
95,000	1,277.52	364,907	1,290.95	292,285	72,622	1,321.70	222,208	142,699	1,395.27	156,149	208,758
100,000	1,344.76	384,114	1,358.89	307,667	76,447	1,391.26	233,902	150,212	1,468.71	164,368	219,746
105,000	1,412.00	403,320	1,426.84	323,052	80,268	1,460.82	245,597	157,723	1,542.14	172,585	230,735
110,000	1,479.24	422,526	1,494.78	338,434	84,092	1,530.39	257,294	165,232	1,615.58	180,804	241,722
115,000	1,546.48	441,733	1,562.73	353,819	87,914	1,599.95	268,988	172,745	1,689.01	189,022	252,711
120,000	1,613.71	460,936	1,630.67	369,201	91,735	1,669.51	280,682	180,254	1,762.45	197,241	263,695
125,000	1,680.95	480,142	1,698.62	384,586	95,556	1,739.07	292,377	187,765	1,835.88	205,458	274,684
130,000	1,748.19	499,348	1,766.56	399,968	99,380	1,808.64	304,074	195,274	1,909.32	213,678	285,670
135,000	1,815.43	518,555	1,834.50	415,350	103,205	1,878.20	315,768	202,787	1,982.75	221,895	296,660
140,000	1,882.66	537,758	1,902.45	430,735	107,023	1,947.76	327,462	210,296	2,056.19	230,114	307,644
145,000	1,949.90	556,964	1,970.39	446,141	110,847	2,017.33	339,159	217,805	2,129.62	238,332	318,632
150,000	2,017.14	576,170	2,038.34	461,502	114,668	2,086.89	350,854	225,316	2,203.06	246,551	329,619
155,000	2,084.38	595,377	2,106.28	476,884	118,493	2,156.45	362,548	232,829	2,276.49	254,768	340,609
160,000	2,151.62	614,583	2,174.23	492,269	122,314	2,226.01	374,242	240,341	2,349.93	262,987	351,596
165,000	2,218.85	633,786	2,242.17	507,651	126,135	2,295.58	385,939	247,847	2,423.36	271,205	362,581
170,000	2,286.09	652,992	2,310.12	523,036	129,956	2,365.14	397,634	255,358	2,496.80	279,424	373,568
175,000	2,353.33	672,199	2,378.06	538,418	133,781	2,434.70	409,328	262,871	2,570.23	287,641	384,558
180,000	2,420.57	691,405	2,446.00	553,800	137,605	2,504.27	421,025	270,380	2,643.67	295,861	395,544
185,000	2,487.81	710,612	2,513.95	569,185	141,427	2,573.83	432,719	277,893	2,717.10	304,078	406,534
190,000	2,555.04	729,814	2,581.89	584,567	145,247	2,643.39	444,414	285,400	2,790.54	312,297	417,517
195,000	2,622.28	749,021	2,649.84	599,952	149,069	2,712.95	456,108	292,913	2,863.97	320,515	428,506
200,000	2,689.52	768,227	2,717.78	615,334	152,893	2,782.52	467,805	300,422	2,937.41	328,734	439,493

AMOUNT OF LOAN	30 YEARS		25 YEARS			20 YEARS			15 YEARS		
	MONTHLY PAYMENT	TOTAL INTRST	MONTHLY PAYMENT	TOTAL INTRST	INTRST SAVED	MONTHLY PAYMENT	TOTAL INTRST	INTRST SAVED	MONTHLY PAYMENT	TOTAL INTRST	INTRST SAVED
$ 50	0.69	198	0.69	157	41	0.71	120	78	0.75	85	113
100	1.37	393	1.38	314	79	1.42	241	152	1.49	168	225
200	2.73	783	2.76	628	155	2.83	479	304	2.98	336	447
300	4.10	1,176	4.14	942	234	4.24	718	458	4.46	503	673
400	5.46	1,566	5.52	1,256	310	5.65	956	610	5.95	671	895
500	6.83	1,959	6.90	1,570	389	7.06	1,194	765	7.44	839	1,120
600	8.19	2,348	8.28	1,884	464	8.47	1,433	915	8.92	1,006	1,342
700	9.56	2,742	9.65	2,195	547	9.88	1,671	1,071	10.41	1,174	1,568
800	10.92	3,131	11.03	2,509	622	11.29	1,910	1,221	11.89	1,340	1,791
900	12.29	3,524	12.41	2,823	701	12.70	2,148	1,376	13.38	1,508	2,016
1,000	13.65	3,914	13.79	3,137	777	14.11	2,386	1,528	14.87	1,677	2,237
2,000	27.30	7,828	27.58	6,274	1,554	28.21	4,770	3,058	29.73	3,351	4,477
3,000	40.95	11,742	41.36	9,408	2,334	42.31	7,154	4,588	44.59	5,026	6,716
4,000	54.60	15,656	55.15	12,545	3,111	56.41	9,538	6,118	59.45	6,701	8,955
5,000	68.25	19,570	68.93	15,679	3,891	70.51	11,922	7,648	74.31	8,376	11,194
6,000	81.90	23,484	82.72	18,816	4,668	84.61	14,306	9,178	89.18	10,052	13,432
7,000	95.55	27,398	96.50	21,950	5,448	98.71	16,690	10,708	104.04	11,727	15,671
8,000	109.20	31,312	110.29	25,087	6,225	112.81	19,074	12,238	118.90	13,402	17,910
9,000	122.85	35,226	124.07	28,221	7,005	126.91	21,458	13,768	133.76	15,077	20,149
10,000	136.50	39,140	137.86	31,358	7,782	141.01	23,842	15,298	148.62	16,752	22,388
11,000	150.15	43,054	151.64	34,492	8,562	155.11	26,226	16,828	163.48	18,426	24,628
12,000	163.80	46,968	165.43	37,629	9,339	169.21	28,610	18,358	178.35	20,103	26,865
13,000	177.45	50,882	179.22	40,766	10,116	183.31	30,994	19,888	193.21	21,778	29,104
14,000	191.10	54,796	193.00	43,900	10,896	197.41	33,378	21,418	208.07	23,453	31,343
15,000	204.75	58,710	206.79	47,037	11,673	211.51	35,762	22,948	222.93	25,127	33,583
16,000	218.39	62,620	220.57	50,171	12,449	225.61	38,146	24,474	237.79	26,802	35,818
17,000	232.04	66,534	234.36	53,308	13,226	239.71	40,530	26,004	252.65	28,477	38,057
18,000	245.69	70,448	248.14	56,442	14,006	253.81	42,914	27,534	267.52	30,154	40,294
19,000	259.34	74,362	261.93	59,579	14,783	267.91	45,298	29,064	282.38	31,828	42,534
20,000	272.99	78,276	275.71	62,713	15,563	282.01	47,682	30,594	297.24	33,503	44,773
21,000	286.64	82,190	289.50	65,850	16,340	296.11	50,066	32,124	312.10	35,178	47,012
22,000	300.29	86,104	303.28	68,984	17,120	310.22	52,453	33,651	326.96	36,853	49,251
23,000	313.94	90,018	317.07	72,121	17,897	324.32	54,837	35,181	341.82	38,528	51,490
24,000	327.59	93,932	330.85	75,255	18,677	338.42	57,221	36,711	356.69	40,204	53,728
25,000	341.24	97,846	344.64	78,392	19,454	352.52	59,605	38,241	371.55	41,879	55,967
26,000	354.89	101,760	358.43	81,529	20,231	366.62	61,989	39,771	386.41	43,554	58,206
27,000	368.54	105,674	372.21	84,663	21,011	380.72	64,373	41,301	401.27	45,229	60,445
28,000	382.19	109,588	386.00	87,800	21,788	394.82	66,757	42,831	416.13	46,903	62,685
29,000	395.84	113,502	399.78	90,934	22,568	408.92	69,141	44,361	430.99	48,578	64,924
30,000	409.49	117,416	413.57	94,071	23,345	423.02	71,525	45,891	445.86	50,255	67,161
32,500	443.61	127,200	448.03	101,909	25,291	458.27	77,485	49,715	483.01	54,442	72,758
35,000	477.73	136,983	482.49	109,747	27,236	493.52	83,445	53,538	520.16	58,629	78,354
40,000	545.98	156,553	551.42	125,426	31,127	564.02	95,365	61,188	594.47	67,005	89,548
45,000	614.23	176,123	620.35	141,105	35,018	634.53	107,287	68,836	668.78	75,380	100,743
50,000	682.47	195,689	689.28	156,784	38,905	705.03	119,207	76,482	743.09	83,756	111,933
55,000	750.72	215,259	758.20	172,460	42,799	775.53	131,127	84,132	817.40	92,132	123,127
60,000	818.97	234,829	827.13	188,139	46,690	846.03	143,047	91,782	891.71	100,508	134,321
65,000	887.21	254,396	896.06	203,818	50,578	916.53	154,967	99,429	966.01	108,882	145,514
70,000	955.46	273,966	964.98	219,494	54,472	987.04	166,890	107,076	1,040.32	117,258	156,708
75,000	1,023.71	293,536	1,033.91	235,173	58,363	1,057.54	178,810	114,726	1,114.63	125,633	167,903
80,000	1,091.95	313,102	1,102.84	250,852	62,250	1,128.04	190,730	122,372	1,188.94	134,009	179,093
85,000	1,160.20	332,672	1,171.77	266,531	66,141	1,198.54	202,650	130,022	1,263.25	142,385	190,287
90,000	1,228.45	352,242	1,240.69	282,207	70,035	1,269.05	214,572	137,670	1,337.56	150,761	201,481
95,000	1,296.69	371,808	1,309.62	297,886	73,922	1,339.55	226,492	145,316	1,411.86	159,135	212,673
100,000	1,364.94	391,378	1,378.55	313,565	77,813	1,410.05	238,412	152,966	1,486.17	167,511	223,867
105,000	1,433.19	410,948	1,447.47	329,241	81,707	1,480.55	250,332	160,616	1,560.48	175,886	235,062
110,000	1,501.43	430,515	1,516.40	344,920	85,595	1,551.06	262,254	168,261	1,634.79	184,262	246,253
115,000	1,569.68	450,085	1,585.33	360,599	89,486	1,621.56	274,174	175,911	1,709.10	192,638	257,447
120,000	1,637.93	469,655	1,654.25	376,275	93,380	1,692.06	286,094	183,561	1,783.41	201,014	268,641
125,000	1,706.17	489,221	1,723.18	391,954	97,267	1,762.56	298,014	191,207	1,857.72	209,390	279,831
130,000	1,774.42	508,791	1,792.11	407,633	101,158	1,833.06	309,934	198,857	1,932.02	217,764	291,027
135,000	1,842.67	528,361	1,861.04	423,312	105,049	1,903.57	321,857	206,504	2,006.33	226,139	302,222
140,000	1,910.91	547,928	1,929.96	438,988	108,940	1,974.07	333,777	214,151	2,080.64	234,515	313,413
145,000	1,979.16	567,498	1,998.89	454,667	112,831	2,044.57	345,697	221,801	2,154.95	242,891	324,607
150,000	2,047.41	587,068	2,067.82	470,346	116,722	2,115.07	357,617	229,451	2,229.26	251,267	335,801
155,000	2,115.65	606,634	2,136.74	486,022	120,612	2,185.58	369,539	237,095	2,303.57	259,643	346,991
160,000	2,183.90	626,204	2,205.67	501,701	124,503	2,256.08	381,459	244,745	2,377.87	268,017	358,187
165,000	2,252.15	645,774	2,274.60	517,380	128,394	2,326.58	393,379	252,395	2,452.18	276,392	369,382
170,000	2,320.39	665,340	2,343.53	533,059	132,281	2,397.08	405,299	260,041	2,526.49	284,768	380,572
175,000	2,388.64	684,910	2,412.45	548,735	136,175	2,467.58	417,219	267,691	2,600.80	293,144	391,766
180,000	2,456.89	704,480	2,481.38	564,414	140,066	2,538.09	429,142	275,338	2,675.11	301,520	402,960
185,000	2,525.13	724,047	2,550.31	580,093	143,954	2,608.59	441,062	282,985	2,749.42	309,896	414,151
190,000	2,593.38	743,617	2,619.23	595,769	147,848	2,679.09	452,982	290,635	2,823.72	318,270	425,347
195,000	2,661.63	763,187	2,688.16	611,448	151,739	2,749.59	464,902	298,285	2,898.03	326,645	436,542
200,000	2,729.87	782,753	2,757.09	627,127	155,626	2,820.10	476,824	305,929	2,972.34	335,021	447,732

16.50% SHORT-TERM AMORTIZING MORTGAGES

AMOUNT OF LOAN	30 YEARS MONTHLY PAYMENT	30 YEARS TOTAL INTRST	25 YEARS MONTHLY PAYMENT	25 YEARS TOTAL INTRST	25 YEARS INTRST SAVED	20 YEARS MONTHLY PAYMENT	20 YEARS TOTAL INTRST	20 YEARS INTRST SAVED	15 YEARS MONTHLY PAYMENT	15 YEARS TOTAL INTRST	15 YEARS INTRST SAVED
$ 50	0.70	202	0.70	160	42	0.72	123	79	0.76	87	115
100	1.39	400	1.40	320	80	1.43	243	157	1.51	172	228
200	2.78	801	2.80	640	161	2.86	486	315	3.01	342	459
300	4.16	1,198	4.20	960	238	4.29	730	468	4.52	514	684
400	5.55	1,598	5.60	1,280	318	5.72	973	625	6.02	684	914
500	6.93	1,995	7.00	1,600	395	7.15	1,216	779	7.52	854	1,141
600	8.32	2,395	8.39	1,917	478	8.58	1,459	936	9.03	1,025	1,370
700	9.70	2,792	9.79	2,237	555	10.01	1,702	1,090	10.53	1,195	1,597
800	11.09	3,192	11.19	2,557	635	11.44	1,946	1,246	12.03	1,365	1,827
900	12.47	3,589	12.59	2,877	712	12.87	2,189	1,400	13.54	1,537	2,052
1,000	13.86	3,990	13.99	3,197	793	14.29	2,430	1,560	15.04	1,707	2,283
2,000	27.71	7,976	27.97	6,391	1,585	28.58	4,859	3,117	30.08	3,414	4,562
3,000	41.56	11,962	41.95	9,585	2,377	42.87	7,289	4,673	45.12	5,122	6,840
4,000	55.41	15,948	55.93	12,779	3,169	57.16	9,718	6,230	60.15	6,827	9,121
5,000	69.26	19,934	69.92	15,976	3,958	71.45	12,148	7,786	75.19	8,534	11,400
6,000	83.11	23,920	83.90	19,170	4,750	85.74	14,578	9,342	90.23	10,241	13,679
7,000	96.97	27,909	97.88	22,364	5,545	100.03	17,007	10,902	105.26	11,947	15,962
8,000	110.82	31,895	111.86	25,558	6,337	114.32	19,437	12,458	120.30	13,654	18,241
9,000	124.67	35,881	125.85	28,755	7,126	128.61	21,866	14,015	135.34	15,361	20,520
10,000	138.52	39,867	139.83	31,949	7,918	142.90	24,296	15,571	150.38	17,068	22,799
11,000	152.37	43,853	153.81	35,143	8,710	157.18	26,723	17,130	165.41	18,774	25,079
12,000	166.22	47,839	167.79	38,337	9,502	171.47	29,153	18,686	180.45	20,481	27,358
13,000	180.07	51,825	181.78	41,534	10,291	185.76	31,582	20,243	195.49	22,188	29,637
14,000	193.93	55,815	195.76	44,728	11,087	200.05	34,012	21,803	210.52	23,894	31,921
15,000	207.78	59,801	209.74	47,922	11,879	214.34	36,442	23,359	225.56	25,601	34,200
16,000	221.63	63,787	223.72	51,116	12,671	228.63	38,871	24,916	240.60	27,308	36,479
17,000	235.48	67,773	237.71	54,313	13,460	242.92	41,301	26,472	255.64	29,015	38,758
18,000	249.33	71,759	251.69	57,507	14,252	257.21	43,730	28,029	270.67	30,721	41,038
19,000	263.18	75,745	265.67	60,701	15,044	271.50	46,160	29,585	285.71	32,428	43,317
20,000	277.03	79,731	279.65	63,895	15,836	285.79	48,590	31,141	300.75	34,135	45,596
21,000	290.89	83,720	293.64	67,092	16,628	300.07	51,017	32,703	315.78	35,840	47,880
22,000	304.74	87,706	307.62	70,286	17,420	314.36	53,446	34,260	330.82	37,548	50,158
23,000	318.59	91,692	321.60	73,480	18,212	328.65	55,876	35,816	345.86	39,255	52,437
24,000	332.44	95,678	335.58	76,674	19,004	342.94	58,306	37,372	360.90	40,962	54,716
25,000	346.29	99,664	349.57	79,871	19,793	357.23	60,735	38,929	375.93	42,667	56,997
26,000	360.14	103,650	363.55	83,065	20,585	371.52	63,165	40,485	390.97	44,375	59,275
27,000	373.99	107,636	377.53	86,259	21,377	385.81	65,594	42,042	406.01	46,082	61,554
28,000	387.85	111,626	391.51	89,453	22,173	400.10	68,024	43,602	421.04	47,787	63,839
29,000	401.70	115,612	405.50	92,650	22,962	414.39	70,454	45,158	436.08	49,494	66,118
30,000	415.55	119,598	419.48	95,844	23,754	428.68	72,883	46,715	451.12	51,202	68,396
32,500	450.18	129,565	454.43	103,829	25,736	464.40	78,956	50,609	488.71	55,468	74,097
35,000	484.81	139,532	489.39	111,817	27,715	500.12	85,029	54,503	526.30	59,734	79,798
40,000	554.06	159,462	559.30	127,790	31,672	571.57	97,177	62,285	601.49	68,268	91,194
45,000	623.32	179,395	629.22	143,766	35,629	643.01	109,322	70,073	676.67	76,801	102,594
50,000	692.58	199,329	699.13	159,739	39,590	714.46	121,470	77,859	751.86	85,335	113,994
55,000	761.84	219,262	769.04	175,712	43,550	785.90	133,616	85,646	827.04	93,867	125,395
60,000	831.09	239,192	838.95	191,685	47,507	857.35	145,764	93,428	902.23	102,401	136,791
65,000	900.35	259,126	908.86	207,658	51,468	928.79	157,910	101,216	977.42	110,936	148,190
70,000	969.61	279,060	978.78	223,634	55,426	1,000.24	170,058	109,002	1,052.60	119,468	159,592
75,000	1,038.87	298,993	1,048.69	239,607	59,386	1,071.68	182,203	116,790	1,127.79	128,002	170,991
80,000	1,108.12	318,923	1,118.60	255,580	63,343	1,143.13	194,351	124,572	1,202.97	136,535	182,388
85,000	1,177.38	338,857	1,188.51	271,553	67,304	1,214.57	206,497	132,360	1,278.16	145,069	193,788
90,000	1,246.64	358,790	1,258.43	287,529	71,261	1,286.02	218,645	140,145	1,353.34	153,601	205,189
95,000	1,315.90	378,724	1,328.34	303,502	75,222	1,357.46	230,790	147,934	1,428.53	162,135	216,589
100,000	1,385.15	398,654	1,398.25	319,475	79,179	1,428.91	242,938	155,716	1,503.71	170,668	227,986
105,000	1,454.41	418,588	1,468.16	335,448	83,140	1,500.35	255,084	163,504	1,578.90	179,202	239,386
110,000	1,523.67	438,521	1,538.07	351,421	87,100	1,571.80	267,232	171,289	1,654.08	187,734	250,787
115,000	1,592.93	458,455	1,607.99	367,397	91,058	1,643.24	279,378	179,077	1,729.27	196,269	262,186
120,000	1,662.18	478,385	1,677.90	383,370	95,015	1,714.69	291,526	186,859	1,804.46	204,803	273,582
125,000	1,731.44	498,318	1,747.81	399,343	98,975	1,786.13	303,671	194,647	1,879.64	213,335	284,983
130,000	1,800.70	518,252	1,817.72	415,316	102,936	1,857.58	315,819	202,433	1,954.83	221,869	296,383
135,000	1,869.95	538,182	1,887.64	431,292	106,890	1,929.02	327,965	210,217	2,030.01	230,402	307,780
140,000	1,939.21	558,116	1,957.55	447,265	110,851	2,000.47	340,113	218,003	2,105.20	238,936	319,180
145,000	2,008.47	578,049	2,027.46	463,238	114,811	2,071.91	352,258	225,791	2,180.38	247,468	330,581
150,000	2,077.73	597,983	2,097.37	479,211	118,772	2,143.36	364,406	233,577	2,255.57	256,003	341,980
155,000	2,146.98	617,913	2,167.28	495,184	122,729	2,214.80	376,552	241,361	2,330.75	264,535	353,378
160,000	2,216.24	637,846	2,237.20	511,160	126,686	2,286.25	388,700	249,146	2,405.94	273,069	364,777
165,000	2,285.50	657,780	2,307.11	527,133	130,647	2,357.69	400,846	256,934	2,481.12	281,602	376,178
170,000	2,354.76	677,714	2,377.02	543,106	134,608	2,429.14	412,994	264,720	2,556.31	290,136	387,578
175,000	2,424.01	697,644	2,446.93	559,079	138,565	2,500.58	425,139	272,505	2,631.50	298,670	398,974
180,000	2,493.27	717,577	2,516.85	575,055	142,522	2,572.03	437,287	280,290	2,706.68	307,202	410,375
185,000	2,562.53	737,511	2,586.76	591,028	146,483	2,643.47	449,433	288,078	2,781.87	315,737	421,774
190,000	2,631.79	757,444	2,656.67	607,001	150,443	2,714.92	461,581	295,863	2,857.05	324,269	433,175
195,000	2,701.04	777,374	2,726.58	622,974	154,400	2,786.36	473,726	303,648	2,932.24	332,803	444,571
200,000	2,770.30	797,308	2,796.49	638,947	158,361	2,857.81	485,874	311,434	3,007.42	341,336	455,972

AMOUNT OF LOAN	30 YEARS		25 YEARS			20 YEARS			15 YEARS		
	MONTHLY PAYMENT	TOTAL INTRST	MONTHLY PAYMENT	TOTAL INTRST	INTRST SAVED	MONTHLY PAYMENT	TOTAL INTRST	INTRST SAVED	MONTHLY PAYMENT	TOTAL INTRST	INTRST SAVED
$ 50	0.71	206	0.71	163	43	0.73	125	81	0.77	89	117
100	1.41	408	1.42	326	82	1.45	248	160	1.53	175	233
200	2.82	815	2.84	652	163	2.90	496	319	3.05	349	466
300	4.22	1,219	4.26	978	241	4.35	744	475	4.57	523	696
400	5.63	1,627	5.68	1,304	323	5.80	992	635	6.09	696	931
500	7.03	2,031	7.09	1,627	404	7.24	1,238	793	7.61	870	1,161
600	8.44	2,438	8.51	1,953	485	8.69	1,486	952	9.13	1,043	1,395
700	9.84	2,842	9.93	2,279	563	10.14	1,734	1,108	10.65	1,217	1,625
800	11.25	3,250	11.35	2,605	645	11.59	1,982	1,268	12.18	1,392	1,858
900	12.65	3,654	12.77	2,931	723	13.04	2,230	1,424	13.70	1,566	2,088
1,000	14.06	4,062	14.18	3,254	808	14.48	2,475	1,587	15.22	1,740	2,322
2,000	28.11	8,120	28.36	6,508	1,612	28.96	4,950	3,170	30.43	3,477	4,643
3,000	42.17	12,181	42.54	9,762	2,419	43.44	7,426	4,755	45.64	5,215	6,966
4,000	56.22	16,239	56.72	13,016	3,223	57.92	9,901	6,338	60.86	6,955	9,284
5,000	70.27	20,297	70.90	16,270	4,027	72.40	12,376	7,921	76.07	8,693	11,604
6,000	84.33	24,359	85.08	19,524	4,835	86.87	14,849	9,510	91.28	10,430	13,929
7,000	98.38	28,417	99.26	22,778	5,639	101.35	17,324	11,093	106.50	12,170	16,247
8,000	112.44	32,478	113.44	26,032	6,446	115.83	19,799	12,679	121.71	13,908	18,570
9,000	126.49	36,536	127.62	29,286	7,250	130.31	22,274	14,262	136.92	15,646	20,890
10,000	140.54	40,594	141.80	32,540	8,054	144.79	24,750	15,844	152.14	17,385	23,209
11,000	154.60	44,656	155.98	35,794	8,862	159.27	27,225	17,431	167.35	19,123	25,533
12,000	168.65	48,714	170.16	39,048	9,666	173.74	29,698	19,016	182.56	20,861	27,853
13,000	182.71	52,776	184.34	42,302	10,474	188.22	32,173	20,603	197.78	22,600	30,176
14,000	196.76	56,834	198.52	45,556	11,278	202.70	34,648	22,186	212.99	24,338	32,496
15,000	210.81	60,892	212.70	48,810	12,082	217.18	37,123	23,769	228.20	26,076	34,816
16,000	224.87	64,953	226.88	52,064	12,889	231.66	39,598	25,355	243.42	27,816	37,137
17,000	238.92	69,011	241.06	55,318	13,693	246.13	42,071	26,940	258.63	29,553	39,458
18,000	252.98	73,073	255.24	58,572	14,501	260.61	44,546	28,527	273.84	31,291	41,782
19,000	267.03	77,131	269.42	61,826	15,305	275.09	47,022	30,109	289.06	33,031	44,100
20,000	281.08	81,189	283.60	65,080	16,109	289.57	49,497	31,692	304.27	34,769	46,420
21,000	295.14	85,250	297.78	68,334	16,916	304.05	51,972	33,278	319.48	36,506	48,744
22,000	309.19	89,308	311.96	71,588	17,720	318.53	54,447	34,861	334.70	38,246	51,062
23,000	323.25	93,370	326.14	74,842	18,528	333.00	56,920	36,450	349.91	39,984	53,386
24,000	337.30	97,428	340.32	78,096	19,332	347.48	59,395	38,033	365.12	41,722	55,706
25,000	351.35	101,486	354.50	81,350	20,136	361.96	61,870	39,616	380.34	43,461	58,025
26,000	365.41	105,548	368.68	84,604	20,944	376.44	64,346	41,202	395.55	45,199	60,349
27,000	379.46	109,606	382.86	87,858	21,748	390.92	66,821	42,785	410.76	46,937	62,669
28,000	393.52	113,667	397.04	91,112	22,555	405.39	69,294	44,373	425.97	48,675	64,992
29,000	407.57	117,725	411.22	94,366	23,359	419.87	71,769	45,956	441.19	50,414	67,311
30,000	421.62	121,783	425.40	97,620	24,163	434.35	74,244	47,539	456.40	52,152	69,631
32,500	456.76	131,934	460.85	105,755	26,179	470.55	80,432	51,502	494.43	56,497	75,437
35,000	491.89	142,080	496.30	113,890	28,190	506.74	86,618	55,462	532.47	60,845	81,235
40,000	562.16	162,378	567.20	130,160	32,218	579.13	98,991	63,387	608.53	69,535	92,843
45,000	632.43	182,675	638.10	146,430	36,245	651.52	111,365	71,310	684.60	78,228	104,447
50,000	702.70	202,972	709.00	162,700	40,272	723.91	123,738	79,234	760.67	86,921	116,051
55,000	772.97	223,269	779.90	178,970	44,299	796.31	136,114	87,155	836.73	95,611	127,658
60,000	843.24	243,566	850.80	195,240	48,326	868.70	148,488	95,078	912.80	104,304	139,262
65,000	913.51	263,864	921.70	211,510	52,354	941.09	160,862	103,000	988.86	112,995	150,869
70,000	983.78	284,161	992.60	227,780	56,381	1,013.48	173,235	110,926	1,064.93	121,687	162,477
75,000	1,054.05	304,458	1,063.50	244,050	60,408	1,085.87	185,609	118,849	1,141.00	130,380	174,078
80,000	1,124.32	324,755	1,134.40	260,320	64,435	1,158.26	197,982	126,773	1,217.06	139,071	185,684
85,000	1,194.59	345,052	1,205.30	276,590	68,462	1,230.65	210,356	134,696	1,293.13	147,763	197,289
90,000	1,264.86	365,350	1,276.20	292,860	72,490	1,303.04	222,730	142,620	1,369.19	156,454	208,896
95,000	1,335.13	385,647	1,347.10	309,130	76,517	1,375.43	235,103	150,544	1,445.26	165,147	220,500
100,000	1,405.40	405,944	1,418.00	325,400	80,544	1,447.82	247,477	158,467	1,521.33	173,839	232,105
105,000	1,475.67	426,241	1,488.90	341,670	84,571	1,520.22	259,853	166,388	1,597.39	182,530	243,711
110,000	1,545.94	446,538	1,559.80	357,940	88,598	1,592.61	272,226	174,312	1,673.46	191,223	255,315
115,000	1,616.21	466,836	1,630.70	374,210	92,626	1,665.00	284,600	182,236	1,749.52	199,914	266,922
120,000	1,686.48	487,133	1,701.60	390,480	96,653	1,737.39	296,974	190,159	1,825.59	208,606	278,527
125,000	1,756.75	507,430	1,772.50	406,750	100,680	1,809.78	309,347	198,083	1,901.66	217,299	290,131
130,000	1,827.02	527,727	1,843.40	423,020	104,707	1,882.17	321,721	206,006	1,977.72	225,990	301,737
135,000	1,897.29	548,024	1,914.30	439,290	108,734	1,954.56	334,094	213,930	2,053.79	234,682	313,342
140,000	1,967.56	568,322	1,985.20	455,560	112,762	2,026.95	346,468	221,854	2,129.85	243,373	324,949
145,000	2,037.83	588,619	2,056.10	471,830	116,789	2,099.34	358,842	229,777	2,205.92	252,066	336,553
150,000	2,108.10	608,916	2,127.00	488,100	120,816	2,171.73	371,215	237,701	2,281.99	260,758	348,158
155,000	2,178.37	629,213	2,197.90	504,370	124,843	2,244.13	383,591	245,622	2,358.05	269,449	359,764
160,000	2,248.64	649,510	2,268.80	520,640	128,870	2,316.52	395,965	253,545	2,434.12	278,142	371,368
165,000	2,318.91	669,808	2,339.70	536,910	132,898	2,388.91	408,338	261,470	2,510.18	286,832	382,976
170,000	2,389.18	690,105	2,410.60	553,180	136,925	2,461.30	420,712	269,393	2,586.25	295,525	394,580
175,000	2,459.45	710,402	2,481.50	569,450	140,952	2,533.69	433,086	277,316	2,662.32	304,218	406,184
180,000	2,529.72	730,699	2,552.40	585,720	144,979	2,606.08	445,459	285,240	2,738.38	312,908	417,791
185,000	2,599.99	750,996	2,623.30	601,990	149,006	2,678.47	457,833	293,163	2,814.45	321,601	429,395
190,000	2,670.26	771,294	2,694.20	618,260	153,034	2,750.86	470,206	301,088	2,890.52	330,294	441,000
195,000	2,740.53	791,591	2,765.10	634,530	157,061	2,823.25	482,580	309,011	2,966.58	338,984	452,607
200,000	2,810.80	811,888	2,836.00	650,800	161,088	2,895.64	494,954	316,934	3,042.65	347,677	464,211

43

17.00%   SHORT-TERM AMORTIZING MORTGAGES

AMOUNT OF LOAN	30 YEARS		25 YEARS			20 YEARS			15 YEARS		
	MONTHLY PAYMENT	TOTAL INTRST	MONTHLY PAYMENT	TOTAL INTRST	INTRST SAVED	MONTHLY PAYMENT	TOTAL INTRST	INTRST SAVED	MONTHLY PAYMENT	TOTAL INTRST	INTRST SAVED
$ 50	0.72	209	0.72	166	43	0.74	128	81	0.77	89	120
100	1.43	415	1.44	332	83	1.47	253	162	1.54	177	238
200	2.86	830	2.88	664	166	2.94	506	324	3.08	354	476
300	4.28	1,241	4.32	996	245	4.41	758	483	4.62	532	709
400	5.71	1,656	5.76	1,328	328	5.87	1,009	647	6.16	709	947
500	7.13	2,067	7.19	1,657	410	7.34	1,262	805	7.70	886	1,181
600	8.56	2,482	8.63	1,989	493	8.81	1,514	968	9.24	1,063	1,419
700	9.98	2,893	10.07	2,321	572	10.27	1,765	1,128	10.78	1,240	1,653
800	11.41	3,308	11.51	2,653	655	11.74	2,018	1,290	12.32	1,418	1,890
900	12.84	3,722	12.95	2,985	737	13.21	2,270	1,452	13.86	1,595	2,127
1,000	14.26	4,134	14.38	3,314	820	14.67	2,521	1,613	15.40	1,772	2,362
2,000	28.52	8,267	28.76	6,628	1,639	29.34	5,042	3,225	30.79	3,542	4,725
3,000	42.78	12,401	43.14	9,942	2,459	44.01	7,562	4,839	46.18	5,312	7,089
4,000	57.03	16,531	57.52	13,256	3,275	58.68	10,083	6,448	61.57	7,083	9,448
5,000	71.29	20,664	71.89	16,567	4,097	73.35	12,604	8,060	76.96	8,853	11,811
6,000	85.55	24,798	86.27	19,881	4,917	88.01	15,122	9,676	92.35	10,623	14,175
7,000	99.80	28,928	100.65	23,195	5,733	102.68	17,643	11,285	107.74	12,393	16,535
8,000	114.06	33,062	115.03	26,509	6,553	117.35	20,164	12,898	123.13	14,163	18,899
9,000	128.32	37,195	129.41	29,823	7,372	132.02	22,685	14,510	138.52	15,934	21,261
10,000	142.57	41,325	143.78	33,134	8,191	146.69	25,206	16,119	153.91	17,704	23,621
11,000	156.83	45,459	158.16	36,448	9,011	161.35	27,724	17,735	169.30	19,474	25,985
12,000	171.09	49,592	172.54	39,762	9,830	176.02	30,245	19,347	184.69	21,244	28,348
13,000	185.34	53,722	186.92	43,076	10,646	190.69	32,766	20,956	200.08	23,014	30,708
14,000	199.60	57,856	201.30	46,390	11,466	205.36	35,286	22,570	215.47	24,785	33,071
15,000	213.86	61,990	215.67	49,701	12,289	220.03	37,807	24,183	230.86	26,555	35,435
16,000	228.11	66,120	230.05	53,015	13,105	234.69	40,326	25,794	246.25	28,325	37,795
17,000	242.37	70,253	244.43	56,329	13,924	249.36	42,846	27,407	261.64	30,095	40,158
18,000	256.63	74,387	258.81	59,643	14,744	264.03	45,367	29,020	277.03	31,865	42,522
19,000	270.88	78,517	273.19	62,957	15,560	278.70	47,888	30,629	292.42	33,636	44,881
20,000	285.14	82,650	287.56	66,268	16,382	293.37	50,409	32,241	307.81	35,406	47,244
21,000	299.40	86,784	301.94	69,582	17,202	308.03	52,927	33,857	323.20	37,176	49,608
22,000	313.65	90,914	316.32	72,896	18,018	322.70	55,448	35,466	338.59	38,946	51,968
23,000	327.91	95,048	330.70	76,210	18,838	337.37	57,969	37,079	353.98	40,716	54,332
24,000	342.17	99,181	345.08	79,524	19,657	352.04	60,490	38,691	369.37	42,487	56,694
25,000	356.42	103,311	359.45	82,835	20,476	366.71	63,010	40,301	384.76	44,257	59,054
26,000	370.68	107,445	373.83	86,149	21,296	381.37	65,529	41,916	400.15	46,027	61,418
27,000	384.94	111,578	388.21	89,463	22,115	396.04	68,050	43,528	415.54	47,797	63,781
28,000	399.19	115,708	402.59	92,777	22,931	410.71	70,570	45,138	430.93	49,567	66,141
29,000	413.45	119,842	416.97	96,091	23,751	425.38	73,091	46,751	446.32	51,338	68,504
30,000	427.71	123,976	431.34	99,402	24,574	440.05	75,612	48,364	461.71	53,108	70,868
32,500	463.35	134,306	467.29	107,687	26,619	476.72	81,913	52,393	500.18	57,532	76,774
35,000	498.99	144,636	503.23	115,969	28,667	513.39	88,214	56,422	538.66	61,959	82,677
40,000	570.28	165,301	575.12	132,536	32,765	586.73	100,815	64,486	615.61	70,810	94,491
45,000	641.56	185,962	647.01	149,103	36,859	660.07	113,417	72,545	692.56	79,661	106,301
50,000	712.84	206,622	718.90	165,670	40,952	733.41	126,018	80,604	769.51	88,512	118,110
55,000	784.13	227,287	790.79	182,237	45,050	806.75	138,620	88,667	846.46	97,363	129,924
60,000	855.41	247,948	862.68	198,804	49,144	880.09	151,222	96,726	923.41	106,214	141,734
65,000	926.69	268,608	934.57	215,371	53,237	953.43	163,823	104,785	1,000.36	115,065	153,543
70,000	997.98	289,273	1,006.46	231,938	57,335	1,026.77	176,425	112,848	1,077.31	123,916	165,357
75,000	1,069.26	309,934	1,078.35	248,505	61,429	1,100.11	189,026	120,908	1,154.26	132,767	177,167
80,000	1,140.55	330,598	1,150.24	265,072	65,526	1,173.45	201,628	128,970	1,231.21	141,618	188,980
85,000	1,211.83	351,259	1,222.13	281,639	69,620	1,246.79	214,230	137,029	1,308.16	150,469	200,790
90,000	1,283.11	371,920	1,294.02	298,206	73,714	1,320.13	226,831	145,089	1,385.11	159,320	212,600
95,000	1,354.40	392,584	1,365.91	314,773	77,811	1,393.47	239,433	153,151	1,462.06	168,171	224,413
100,000	1,425.68	413,245	1,437.80	331,340	81,905	1,466.81	252,034	161,211	1,539.01	177,022	236,223
105,000	1,496.96	433,906	1,509.69	347,907	85,999	1,540.15	264,636	169,270	1,615.96	185,873	248,033
110,000	1,568.25	454,570	1,581.58	364,474	90,096	1,613.49	277,238	177,332	1,692.91	194,724	259,846
115,000	1,639.53	475,231	1,653.47	381,041	94,190	1,686.83	289,839	185,392	1,769.86	203,575	271,656
120,000	1,710.82	495,895	1,725.36	397,608	98,287	1,760.17	302,441	193,454	1,846.81	212,426	283,469
125,000	1,782.10	516,556	1,797.25	414,175	102,381	1,833.51	315,042	201,514	1,923.76	221,277	295,279
130,000	1,853.38	537,217	1,869.14	430,742	106,475	1,906.85	327,644	209,573	2,000.71	230,128	307,089
135,000	1,924.67	557,881	1,941.03	447,309	110,572	1,980.19	340,246	217,635	2,077.66	238,979	318,902
140,000	1,995.95	578,542	2,012.92	463,876	114,666	2,053.53	352,847	225,695	2,154.61	247,830	330,712
145,000	2,067.23	599,203	2,084.81	480,443	118,760	2,126.87	365,449	233,754	2,231.56	256,681	342,522
150,000	2,138.52	619,867	2,156.70	497,010	122,857	2,200.21	378,050	241,817	2,308.51	265,532	354,333
155,000	2,209.80	640,528	2,228.59	513,577	126,951	2,273.55	390,652	249,876	2,385.46	274,383	366,145
160,000	2,281.09	661,192	2,300.48	530,144	131,048	2,346.89	403,254	257,938	2,462.41	283,234	377,958
165,000	2,352.37	681,853	2,372.37	546,711	135,142	2,420.23	415,855	265,998	2,539.36	292,085	389,768
170,000	2,423.65	702,514	2,444.26	563,278	139,236	2,493.57	428,457	274,057	2,616.31	300,936	401,578
175,000	2,494.94	723,178	2,516.15	579,845	143,333	2,566.91	441,058	282,120	2,693.26	309,787	413,391
180,000	2,566.22	743,839	2,588.04	596,412	147,427	2,640.25	453,660	290,179	2,770.21	318,638	425,201
185,000	2,637.50	764,500	2,659.93	612,979	151,521	2,713.59	466,262	298,238	2,847.16	327,489	437,011
190,000	2,708.79	785,164	2,731.82	629,546	155,618	2,786.93	478,863	306,301	2,924.11	336,340	448,824
195,000	2,780.07	805,825	2,803.71	646,113	159,712	2,860.27	491,465	314,360	3,001.06	345,191	460,634
200,000	2,851.36	826,490	2,875.60	662,680	163,810	2,933.61	504,066	322,424	3,078.01	354,042	472,448

44

AMOUNT OF LOAN	30 YEARS		25 YEARS			20 YEARS			15 YEARS		
	MONTHLY PAYMENT	TOTAL INTRST	MONTHLY PAYMENT	TOTAL INTRST	INTRST SAVED	MONTHLY PAYMENT	TOTAL INTRST	INTRST SAVED	MONTHLY PAYMENT	TOTAL INTRST	INTRST SAVED
$ 50	0.73	213	0.73	169	44	0.75	130	83	0.78	90	123
100	1.45	422	1.46	338	84	1.49	258	164	1.56	181	241
200	2.90	844	2.92	676	168	2.98	515	329	3.12	362	482
300	4.34	1,262	4.38	1,014	248	4.46	770	492	4.68	542	720
400	5.79	1,684	5.84	1,352	332	5.95	1,028	656	6.23	721	963
500	7.23	2,103	7.29	1,687	416	7.43	1,283	820	7.79	902	1,201
600	8.68	2,525	8.75	2,025	500	8.92	1,541	984	9.35	1,083	1,442
700	10.13	2,947	10.21	2,363	584	10.41	1,798	1,149	10.90	1,262	1,685
800	11.57	3,365	11.67	2,701	664	11.89	2,054	1,311	12.46	1,443	1,922
900	13.02	3,787	13.12	3,036	751	13.38	2,311	1,476	14.02	1,624	2,163
1,000	14.46	4,206	14.58	3,374	832	14.86	2,566	1,640	15.57	1,803	2,403
2,000	28.92	8,411	29.16	6,748	1,663	29.72	5,133	3,278	31.14	3,605	4,806
3,000	43.38	12,617	43.73	10,119	2,498	44.58	7,699	4,918	46.71	5,408	7,209
4,000	57.84	16,822	58.31	13,493	3,329	59.44	10,266	6,556	62.28	7,210	9,612
5,000	72.30	21,028	72.89	16,867	4,161	74.30	12,832	8,196	77.84	9,011	12,017
6,000	86.76	25,234	87.46	20,238	4,996	89.16	15,398	9,836	93.41	10,814	14,420
7,000	101.22	29,439	102.04	23,612	5,827	104.01	17,962	11,477	108.98	12,616	16,823
8,000	115.68	33,645	116.62	26,986	6,659	118.87	20,529	13,116	124.55	14,419	19,226
9,000	130.14	37,850	131.19	30,357	7,493	133.73	23,095	14,755	140.11	16,220	21,630
10,000	144.60	42,056	145.77	33,731	8,325	148.59	25,662	16,394	155.68	18,022	24,034
11,000	159.06	46,262	160.35	37,105	9,157	163.45	28,228	18,034	171.25	19,825	26,437
12,000	173.52	50,467	174.92	40,476	9,991	178.31	30,794	19,673	186.82	21,628	28,839
13,000	187.98	54,673	189.50	43,850	10,823	193.16	33,358	21,315	202.38	23,428	31,245
14,000	202.44	58,878	204.07	47,221	11,657	208.02	35,925	22,953	217.95	25,231	33,647
15,000	216.90	63,084	218.65	50,595	12,489	222.88	38,491	24,593	233.52	27,034	36,050
16,000	231.36	67,290	233.23	53,969	13,321	237.74	41,058	26,232	249.09	28,836	38,454
17,000	245.82	71,495	247.80	57,340	14,155	252.60	43,624	27,871	264.65	30,637	40,858
18,000	260.28	75,701	262.38	60,714	14,987	267.46	46,190	29,511	280.22	32,440	43,261
19,000	274.74	79,906	276.96	64,088	15,818	282.31	48,754	31,152	295.79	34,242	45,664
20,000	289.20	84,112	291.53	67,459	16,653	297.17	51,321	32,791	311.36	36,045	48,067
21,000	303.66	88,318	306.11	70,833	17,485	312.03	53,887	34,431	326.92	37,846	50,472
22,000	318.12	92,523	320.69	74,207	18,316	326.89	56,454	36,069	342.49	39,648	52,875
23,000	332.58	96,729	335.26	77,578	19,151	341.75	59,020	37,709	358.06	41,451	55,278
24,000	347.04	100,934	349.84	80,952	19,982	356.61	61,586	39,348	373.63	43,253	57,681
25,000	361.50	105,140	364.42	84,326	20,814	371.47	64,153	40,987	389.19	45,054	60,086
26,000	375.96	109,346	378.99	87,697	21,649	386.32	66,717	42,629	404.76	46,857	62,489
27,000	390.42	113,551	393.57	91,071	22,480	401.18	69,283	44,268	420.33	48,659	64,892
28,000	404.88	117,757	408.14	94,442	23,315	416.04	71,850	45,907	435.90	50,462	67,295
29,000	419.34	121,962	422.72	97,816	24,146	430.90	74,416	47,546	451.46	52,263	69,699
30,000	433.80	126,168	437.30	101,190	24,978	445.76	76,982	49,186	467.03	54,065	72,103
32,500	469.95	136,682	473.74	109,622	27,060	482.90	83,396	53,286	505.95	58,571	78,111
35,000	506.10	147,196	510.18	118,054	29,142	520.05	89,812	57,384	544.87	63,077	84,119
40,000	578.40	168,224	583.06	134,918	33,306	594.34	102,642	65,582	622.71	72,088	96,136
45,000	650.70	189,252	655.94	151,782	37,470	668.63	115,471	73,781	700.55	81,099	108,153
50,000	723.00	210,280	728.83	168,649	41,631	742.93	128,303	81,977	778.38	90,108	120,172
55,000	795.30	231,308	801.71	185,513	45,795	817.22	141,133	90,175	856.22	99,120	132,188
60,000	867.60	252,336	874.59	202,377	49,959	891.51	153,962	98,374	934.06	108,131	144,205
65,000	939.90	273,364	947.47	219,241	54,123	965.80	166,792	106,572	1,011.90	117,142	156,222
70,000	1,012.20	294,392	1,020.35	236,105	58,287	1,040.09	179,622	114,770	1,089.73	126,151	168,241
75,000	1,084.49	315,416	1,093.24	252,972	62,444	1,114.39	192,454	122,962	1,167.57	135,163	180,253
80,000	1,156.79	336,444	1,166.12	269,836	66,608	1,188.68	205,283	131,161	1,245.41	144,174	192,270
85,000	1,229.09	357,472	1,239.00	286,700	70,772	1,262.97	218,113	139,359	1,323.25	153,185	204,287
90,000	1,301.39	378,500	1,311.88	303,564	74,936	1,337.26	230,942	147,558	1,401.09	162,196	216,304
95,000	1,373.69	399,528	1,384.76	320,428	79,100	1,411.55	243,772	155,756	1,478.92	171,206	228,322
100,000	1,445.99	420,556	1,457.65	337,295	83,261	1,485.85	256,604	163,952	1,556.76	180,217	240,339
105,000	1,518.29	441,584	1,530.53	354,159	87,425	1,560.14	269,434	172,150	1,634.60	189,228	252,356
110,000	1,590.59	462,612	1,603.41	371,023	91,589	1,634.43	282,263	180,349	1,712.44	198,239	264,373
115,000	1,662.89	483,640	1,676.29	387,887	95,753	1,708.72	295,093	188,547	1,790.28	207,250	276,390
120,000	1,735.19	504,668	1,749.17	404,751	99,917	1,783.02	307,925	196,743	1,868.11	216,260	288,408
125,000	1,807.49	525,696	1,822.06	421,618	104,078	1,857.31	320,754	204,942	1,945.95	225,271	300,425
130,000	1,879.79	546,724	1,894.94	438,482	108,242	1,931.60	333,584	213,140	2,023.79	234,282	312,442
135,000	1,952.09	567,752	1,967.82	455,346	112,406	2,005.89	346,414	221,338	2,101.63	243,293	324,459
140,000	2,024.39	588,780	2,040.70	472,210	116,570	2,080.18	359,243	229,537	2,179.46	252,303	336,477
145,000	2,096.68	609,805	2,113.59	489,077	120,728	2,154.48	372,075	237,730	2,257.30	261,314	348,491
150,000	2,168.98	630,833	2,186.47	505,941	124,892	2,228.77	384,905	245,928	2,335.14	270,325	360,508
155,000	2,241.28	651,861	2,259.35	522,805	129,056	2,303.06	397,734	254,127	2,412.98	279,336	372,525
160,000	2,313.58	672,889	2,332.23	539,669	133,220	2,377.35	410,564	262,325	2,490.82	288,348	384,541
165,000	2,385.88	693,917	2,405.11	556,533	137,384	2,451.64	423,394	270,523	2,568.65	297,357	396,560
170,000	2,458.18	714,945	2,478.00	573,400	141,545	2,525.94	436,226	278,719	2,646.49	306,368	408,577
175,000	2,530.48	735,973	2,550.88	590,264	145,709	2,600.23	449,055	286,918	2,724.33	315,379	420,594
180,000	2,602.78	757,001	2,623.76	607,128	149,873	2,674.52	461,885	295,116	2,802.17	324,391	432,610
185,000	2,675.08	778,029	2,696.64	623,992	154,037	2,748.81	474,714	303,315	2,880.01	333,402	444,627
190,000	2,747.38	799,057	2,769.52	640,856	158,201	2,823.10	487,544	311,513	2,957.84	342,411	456,646
195,000	2,819.68	820,085	2,842.41	657,723	162,362	2,897.40	500,376	319,709	3,035.68	351,422	468,663
200,000	2,891.98	841,113	2,915.29	674,587	166,526	2,971.69	513,206	327,907	3,113.52	360,434	480,679

SHORT-TERM AMORTIZING MORTGAGES

AMOUNT OF LOAN	30 YEARS		25 YEARS			20 YEARS			15 YEARS		
	MONTHLY PAYMENT	TOTAL INTRST	MONTHLY PAYMENT	TOTAL INTRST	INTRST SAVED	MONTHLY PAYMENT	TOTAL INTRST	INTRST SAVED	MONTHLY PAYMENT	TOTAL INTRST	INTRST SAVED
$ 50	0.74	216	0.74	172	44	0.76	132	84	0.79	92	124
100	1.47	429	1.48	344	85	1.51	262	167	1.58	184	245
200	2.94	858	2.96	688	170	3.01	522	336	3.15	367	491
300	4.40	1,284	4.44	1,032	252	4.52	785	499	4.73	551	733
400	5.87	1,713	5.92	1,376	337	6.02	1,045	668	6.30	734	979
500	7.34	2,142	7.39	1,717	425	7.53	1,307	835	7.88	918	1,224
600	8.80	2,568	8.87	2,061	507	9.03	1,567	1,001	9.45	1,101	1,467
700	10.27	2,997	10.35	2,405	592	10.54	1,830	1,167	11.03	1,285	1,712
800	11.74	3,426	11.83	2,749	677	12.04	2,090	1,336	12.60	1,468	1,958
900	13.20	3,852	13.30	3,090	762	13.55	2,352	1,500	14.18	1,652	2,200
1,000	14.67	4,281	14.78	3,434	847	15.05	2,612	1,669	15.75	1,835	2,446
2,000	29.33	8,559	29.56	6,868	1,691	30.10	5,224	3,335	31.50	3,670	4,889
3,000	43.99	12,836	44.33	10,299	2,537	45.15	7,836	5,000	47.24	5,503	7,333
4,000	58.66	17,118	59.11	13,733	3,385	60.20	10,448	6,670	62.99	7,338	9,780
5,000	73.32	21,395	73.88	17,164	4,231	75.25	13,060	8,335	78.73	9,171	12,224
6,000	87.98	25,673	88.66	20,598	5,075	90.30	15,672	10,001	94.48	11,006	14,667
7,000	102.65	29,954	103.43	24,029	5,925	105.35	18,284	11,670	110.23	12,841	17,113
8,000	117.31	34,232	118.21	27,463	6,769	120.40	20,896	13,336	125.97	14,675	19,557
9,000	131.97	38,509	132.98	30,894	7,615	135.45	23,508	15,001	141.72	16,510	21,999
10,000	146.64	42,790	147.76	34,328	8,462	150.50	26,120	16,670	157.46	18,343	24,447
11,000	161.30	47,068	162.53	37,759	9,309	165.55	28,732	18,336	173.21	20,178	26,890
12,000	175.96	51,346	177.31	41,193	10,153	180.60	31,344	20,002	188.95	22,011	29,335
13,000	190.63	55,627	192.08	44,624	11,003	195.65	33,956	21,671	204.70	23,846	31,781
14,000	205.29	59,904	206.86	48,058	11,846	210.70	36,568	23,336	220.45	25,681	34,223
15,000	219.95	64,182	221.63	51,489	12,693	225.75	39,180	25,002	236.19	27,514	36,668
16,000	234.62	68,463	236.41	54,923	13,540	240.80	41,792	26,671	251.94	29,349	39,114
17,000	249.28	72,741	251.19	58,357	14,384	255.85	44,404	28,337	267.68	31,182	41,559
18,000	263.94	77,018	265.96	61,788	15,230	270.89	47,014	30,004	283.43	33,017	44,001
19,000	278.61	81,300	280.74	65,222	16,078	285.94	49,626	31,674	299.17	34,851	46,449
20,000	293.27	85,577	295.51	68,653	16,924	300.99	52,238	33,339	314.92	36,686	48,891
21,000	307.93	89,855	310.29	72,087	17,768	316.04	54,850	35,005	330.67	38,521	51,334
22,000	322.60	94,136	325.06	75,518	18,618	331.09	57,462	36,674	346.41	40,354	53,782
23,000	337.26	98,414	339.84	78,952	19,462	346.14	60,074	38,340	362.16	42,189	56,225
24,000	351.92	102,691	354.61	82,383	20,308	361.19	62,686	40,005	377.90	44,022	58,669
25,000	366.59	106,972	369.39	85,817	21,155	376.24	65,298	41,674	393.65	45,857	61,115
26,000	381.25	111,250	384.16	89,248	22,002	391.29	67,910	43,340	409.40	47,692	63,558
27,000	395.91	115,528	398.94	92,682	22,846	406.34	70,522	45,006	425.14	49,525	66,003
28,000	410.58	119,809	413.71	96,113	23,696	421.39	73,134	46,675	440.89	51,360	68,449
29,000	425.24	124,086	428.49	99,547	24,539	436.44	75,746	48,340	456.63	53,193	70,893
30,000	439.90	128,364	443.26	102,978	25,386	451.49	78,358	50,006	472.38	55,028	73,336
32,500	476.56	139,062	480.20	111,560	27,502	489.11	84,886	54,176	511.74	59,613	79,449
35,000	513.22	149,759	517.14	120,142	29,617	526.73	91,415	58,344	551.11	64,200	85,559
40,000	586.54	171,154	591.02	137,306	33,848	601.98	104,475	66,679	629.84	73,371	97,783
45,000	659.85	192,546	664.89	154,467	38,079	677.23	117,535	75,011	708.57	82,543	110,003
50,000	733.17	213,941	738.77	171,631	42,310	752.48	130,595	83,346	787.29	91,712	122,229
55,000	806.48	235,333	812.65	188,795	46,538	827.72	143,653	91,680	866.02	100,884	134,449
60,000	879.80	256,728	886.52	205,956	50,772	902.97	156,712	100,015	944.75	110,055	146,673
65,000	953.12	278,123	960.40	223,120	55,003	978.22	169,773	108,350	1,023.48	119,226	158,897
70,000	1,026.43	299,515	1,034.28	240,284	59,231	1,053.46	182,830	116,685	1,102.21	128,398	171,117
75,000	1,099.75	320,910	1,108.15	257,445	63,465	1,128.71	195,890	125,020	1,180.94	137,569	183,341
80,000	1,173.07	342,305	1,182.03	274,609	67,696	1,203.96	208,950	133,355	1,259.67	146,741	195,564
85,000	1,246.38	363,697	1,255.91	291,773	71,924	1,279.21	222,010	141,687	1,338.40	155,912	207,785
90,000	1,319.70	385,092	1,329.78	308,934	76,158	1,354.45	235,068	150,024	1,417.13	165,083	220,009
95,000	1,393.01	406,484	1,403.66	326,098	80,386	1,429.70	248,128	158,356	1,495.85	174,253	232,231
100,000	1,466.33	427,879	1,477.53	343,259	84,620	1,504.95	261,188	166,691	1,574.58	183,424	244,455
105,000	1,539.65	449,274	1,551.41	360,423	88,851	1,580.19	274,246	175,028	1,653.31	192,596	256,678
110,000	1,612.96	470,666	1,625.29	377,587	93,079	1,655.44	287,306	183,360	1,732.04	201,767	268,899
115,000	1,686.28	492,061	1,699.16	394,748	97,313	1,730.69	300,366	191,695	1,810.77	210,939	281,122
120,000	1,759.60	513,456	1,773.04	411,912	101,544	1,805.94	313,426	200,030	1,889.50	220,110	293,346
125,000	1,832.91	534,848	1,846.92	429,076	105,772	1,881.18	326,483	208,365	1,968.23	229,281	305,567
130,000	1,906.23	556,243	1,920.79	446,237	110,006	1,956.43	339,543	216,700	2,046.96	238,453	317,790
135,000	1,979.54	577,634	1,994.67	463,401	114,233	2,031.68	352,603	225,031	2,125.69	247,624	330,010
140,000	2,052.86	599,030	2,068.55	480,565	118,465	2,106.92	365,661	233,369	2,204.41	256,794	342,236
145,000	2,126.18	620,425	2,142.42	497,726	122,699	2,182.17	378,721	241,704	2,283.14	265,965	354,460
150,000	2,199.49	641,816	2,216.30	514,890	126,926	2,257.42	391,781	250,035	2,361.87	275,137	366,679
155,000	2,272.81	663,212	2,290.18	532,054	131,158	2,332.66	404,838	258,374	2,440.60	284,308	378,904
160,000	2,346.13	684,607	2,364.05	549,215	135,392	2,407.91	417,898	266,709	2,519.33	293,479	391,128
165,000	2,419.44	705,998	2,437.93	566,379	139,619	2,483.16	430,958	275,040	2,598.06	302,651	403,347
170,000	2,492.76	727,394	2,511.81	583,543	143,851	2,558.41	444,018	283,376	2,676.79	311,822	415,572
175,000	2,566.07	748,785	2,585.68	600,704	148,081	2,633.65	457,076	291,709	2,755.52	320,994	427,791
180,000	2,639.39	770,180	2,659.56	617,868	152,312	2,708.90	470,136	300,044	2,834.25	330,165	440,015
185,000	2,712.71	791,576	2,733.43	635,029	156,547	2,784.15	483,196	308,380	2,912.97	339,335	452,241
190,000	2,786.02	812,967	2,807.31	652,193	160,774	2,859.39	496,254	316,713	2,991.70	348,506	464,461
195,000	2,859.34	834,362	2,881.19	669,357	165,005	2,934.64	509,314	325,048	3,070.43	357,677	476,685
200,000	2,932.66	855,758	2,955.06	686,518	169,240	3,009.89	522,374	333,384	3,149.16	366,849	488,909

SHORT-TERM AMORTIZING MORTGAGES 17.75%

AMOUNT OF LOAN	30 YEARS MONTHLY PAYMENT	30 YEARS TOTAL INTRST	25 YEARS MONTHLY PAYMENT	25 YEARS TOTAL INTRST	25 YEARS INTRST SAVED	20 YEARS MONTHLY PAYMENT	20 YEARS TOTAL INTRST	20 YEARS INTRST SAVED	15 YEARS MONTHLY PAYMENT	15 YEARS TOTAL INTRST	15 YEARS INTRST SAVED
$ 50	0.75	220	0.75	175	45	0.77	135	85	0.80	94	126
100	1.49	436	1.50	350	86	1.53	267	169	1.60	188	248
200	2.98	873	3.00	700	173	3.05	532	341	3.19	374	499
300	4.47	1,309	4.50	1,050	259	4.58	799	510	4.78	560	749
400	5.95	1,742	5.99	1,397	345	6.10	1,064	678	6.37	747	995
500	7.44	2,178	7.49	1,747	431	7.63	1,331	847	7.97	935	1,243
600	8.93	2,615	8.99	2,097	518	9.15	1,596	1,019	9.56	1,121	1,494
700	10.41	3,048	10.49	2,447	601	10.67	1,861	1,187	11.15	1,307	1,741
800	11.90	3,484	11.98	2,794	690	12.20	2,128	1,356	12.74	1,493	1,991
900	13.39	3,920	13.48	3,144	776	13.72	2,393	1,527	14.34	1,681	2,239
1,000	14.87	4,353	14.98	3,494	859	15.25	2,660	1,693	15.93	1,867	2,486
2,000	29.74	8,706	29.95	6,985	1,721	30.49	5,318	3,388	31.85	3,733	4,973
3,000	44.61	13,060	44.93	10,479	2,581	45.73	7,975	5,085	47.78	5,600	7,460
4,000	59.47	17,409	59.90	13,970	3,439	60.97	10,633	6,776	63.70	7,466	9,943
5,000	74.34	21,762	74.88	17,464	4,298	76.21	13,290	8,472	79.63	9,333	12,429
6,000	89.21	26,116	89.85	20,955	5,161	91.45	15,948	10,168	95.55	11,199	14,917
7,000	104.07	30,465	104.83	24,449	6,016	106.69	18,606	11,859	111.48	13,066	17,399
8,000	118.94	34,818	119.80	27,940	6,878	121.93	21,263	13,555	127.40	14,932	19,886
9,000	133.81	39,172	134.78	31,434	7,738	137.17	23,921	15,251	143.33	16,799	22,373
10,000	148.67	43,521	149.75	34,925	8,596	152.41	26,578	16,943	159.25	18,665	24,856
11,000	163.54	47,874	164.73	38,419	9,455	167.66	29,238	18,636	175.18	20,532	27,342
12,000	178.41	52,228	179.70	41,910	10,318	182.90	31,896	20,332	191.10	22,398	29,830
13,000	193.27	56,577	194.67	45,401	11,176	198.14	34,554	22,023	207.03	24,265	32,312
14,000	208.14	60,930	209.65	48,895	12,035	213.38	37,211	23,719	222.95	26,131	34,799
15,000	223.01	65,284	224.62	52,386	12,898	228.62	39,869	25,415	238.87	27,997	37,287
16,000	237.88	69,637	239.60	55,880	13,757	243.86	42,526	27,111	254.80	29,864	39,773
17,000	252.74	73,986	254.57	59,371	14,615	259.10	45,184	28,802	270.72	31,730	42,256
18,000	267.61	78,340	269.55	62,865	15,475	274.34	47,842	30,498	286.65	33,597	44,743
19,000	282.48	82,693	284.52	66,356	16,337	289.58	50,499	32,194	302.57	35,463	47,230
20,000	297.34	87,042	299.50	69,850	17,192	304.82	53,157	33,885	318.50	37,330	49,712
21,000	312.21	91,396	314.47	73,341	18,055	320.07	55,817	35,579	334.42	39,196	52,200
22,000	327.08	95,749	329.45	76,835	18,914	335.31	58,474	37,275	350.35	41,063	54,686
23,000	341.94	100,098	344.42	80,326	19,772	350.55	61,132	38,966	366.27	42,929	57,169
24,000	356.81	104,452	359.40	83,820	20,632	365.79	63,790	40,662	382.20	44,796	59,656
25,000	371.68	108,805	374.37	87,311	21,494	381.03	66,447	42,358	398.12	46,662	62,143
26,000	386.54	113,154	389.34	90,802	22,352	396.27	69,105	44,049	414.05	48,529	64,625
27,000	401.41	117,508	404.32	94,296	23,212	411.51	71,762	45,746	429.97	50,395	67,113
28,000	416.28	121,861	419.29	97,787	24,074	426.75	74,420	47,441	445.90	52,262	69,599
29,000	431.15	126,214	434.27	101,281	24,933	441.99	77,078	49,136	461.82	54,128	72,086
30,000	446.01	130,564	449.24	104,772	25,792	457.23	79,735	50,829	477.74	55,993	74,571
32,500	483.18	141,445	486.68	113,504	27,941	495.34	86,382	55,063	517.56	60,661	80,784
35,000	520.35	152,326	524.12	122,236	30,090	533.44	93,026	59,300	557.37	65,327	86,999
40,000	594.68	174,085	598.99	139,697	34,388	609.64	106,314	67,771	636.99	74,658	99,427
45,000	669.02	195,847	673.86	157,158	38,689	685.85	119,604	76,243	716.61	83,990	111,857
50,000	743.35	217,606	748.73	174,619	42,987	762.05	132,892	84,714	796.24	93,323	124,283
55,000	817.69	239,368	823.61	192,083	47,285	838.26	146,182	93,186	875.86	102,655	136,713
60,000	892.02	261,127	898.48	209,544	51,583	914.46	159,470	101,657	955.48	111,986	149,141
65,000	966.35	282,886	973.35	227,005	55,881	990.67	172,761	110,125	1,035.11	121,320	161,566
70,000	1,040.69	304,648	1,048.23	244,469	60,179	1,066.87	186,049	118,599	1,114.73	130,651	173,997
75,000	1,115.02	326,407	1,123.10	261,930	64,477	1,143.08	199,339	127,068	1,194.35	139,983	186,424
80,000	1,189.36	348,170	1,197.97	279,391	68,779	1,219.28	212,627	135,543	1,273.98	149,316	198,854
85,000	1,263.69	369,928	1,272.85	296,855	73,073	1,295.49	225,918	144,010	1,353.60	158,648	211,280
90,000	1,338.03	391,691	1,347.72	314,316	77,375	1,371.69	239,206	152,485	1,433.22	167,980	223,711
95,000	1,412.36	413,450	1,422.59	331,777	81,673	1,447.90	252,496	160,954	1,512.85	177,313	236,137
100,000	1,486.70	435,212	1,497.46	349,238	85,974	1,524.10	265,784	169,428	1,592.47	186,645	248,567
105,000	1,561.03	456,971	1,572.34	366,702	90,269	1,600.31	279,074	177,897	1,672.09	195,976	260,995
110,000	1,635.37	478,733	1,647.21	384,163	94,570	1,676.51	292,362	186,371	1,751.72	205,310	273,423
115,000	1,709.70	500,492	1,722.08	401,624	98,868	1,752.72	305,653	194,839	1,831.34	214,641	285,851
120,000	1,784.04	522,254	1,796.96	419,088	103,166	1,828.92	318,941	203,313	1,910.96	223,973	298,281
125,000	1,858.37	544,013	1,871.83	436,549	107,464	1,905.13	332,231	211,782	1,990.59	233,306	310,707
130,000	1,932.70	565,772	1,946.70	454,010	111,762	1,981.33	345,519	220,253	2,070.21	242,638	323,134
135,000	2,007.04	587,534	2,021.58	471,474	116,060	2,057.54	358,810	228,724	2,149.83	251,969	335,565
140,000	2,081.37	609,293	2,096.45	488,935	120,358	2,133.74	372,098	237,195	2,229.46	261,303	347,990
145,000	2,155.71	631,056	2,171.32	506,396	124,660	2,209.95	385,388	245,668	2,309.08	270,634	360,422
150,000	2,230.04	652,814	2,246.19	523,857	128,957	2,286.15	398,676	254,138	2,388.70	279,966	372,848
155,000	2,304.38	674,577	2,321.07	541,321	133,256	2,362.36	411,966	262,611	2,468.33	289,299	385,278
160,000	2,378.71	696,336	2,395.94	558,782	137,554	2,438.56	425,254	271,082	2,547.95	298,631	397,705
165,000	2,453.05	718,098	2,470.81	576,243	141,855	2,514.77	438,545	279,553	2,627.57	307,963	410,135
170,000	2,527.38	739,857	2,545.69	593,707	146,150	2,590.97	451,833	288,024	2,707.20	317,296	422,561
175,000	2,601.72	761,619	2,620.56	611,168	150,451	2,667.18	465,123	296,496	2,786.82	326,628	434,991
180,000	2,676.05	783,378	2,695.43	628,629	154,749	2,743.38	478,411	304,967	2,866.44	335,959	447,419
185,000	2,750.39	805,140	2,770.31	646,093	159,047	2,819.59	491,702	313,438	2,946.07	345,293	459,847
190,000	2,824.72	826,899	2,845.18	663,554	163,345	2,895.79	504,990	321,909	3,025.69	354,624	472,275
195,000	2,899.05	848,658	2,920.05	681,015	167,643	2,972.00	518,280	330,378	3,105.31	363,956	484,702
200,000	2,973.39	870,420	2,994.92	698,476	171,944	3,048.20	531,568	338,852	3,184.94	373,289	497,131

47

18.00% SHORT-TERM AMORTIZING MORTGAGES

AMOUNT OF LOAN	30 YEARS		25 YEARS			20 YEARS			15 YEARS		
	MONTHLY PAYMENT	TOTAL INTRST	MONTHLY PAYMENT	TOTAL INTRST	INTRST SAVED	MONTHLY PAYMENT	TOTAL INTRST	INTRST SAVED	MONTHLY PAYMENT	TOTAL INTRST	INTRST SAVED
$ 50	0.76	224	0.76	178	46	0.78	137	87	0.81	96	128
100	1.51	444	1.52	356	88	1.55	272	172	1.62	192	252
200	3.02	887	3.04	712	175	3.09	542	345	3.23	381	506
300	4.53	1,331	4.56	1,068	263	4.63	811	520	4.84	571	760
400	6.03	1,771	6.07	1,421	350	6.18	1,083	688	6.45	761	1,010
500	7.54	2,214	7.59	1,777	437	7.72	1,353	861	8.06	951	1,263
600	9.05	2,658	9.11	2,133	525	9.26	1,622	1,036	9.67	1,141	1,517
700	10.55	3,098	10.63	2,489	609	10.81	1,894	1,204	11.28	1,330	1,768
800	12.06	3,542	12.14	2,842	700	12.35	2,164	1,378	12.89	1,520	2,022
900	13.57	3,985	13.66	3,198	787	13.89	2,434	1,551	14.50	1,710	2,275
1,000	15.08	4,429	15.18	3,554	875	15.44	2,706	1,723	16.11	1,900	2,529
2,000	30.15	8,854	30.35	7,105	1,749	30.87	5,409	3,445	32.21	3,798	5,056
3,000	45.22	13,279	45.53	10,659	2,620	46.30	8,112	5,167	48.32	5,698	7,581
4,000	60.29	17,704	60.70	14,210	3,494	61.74	10,818	6,886	64.42	7,596	10,108
5,000	75.36	22,130	75.88	17,764	4,366	77.17	13,521	8,609	80.53	9,495	12,635
6,000	90.43	26,555	91.05	21,315	5,240	92.60	16,224	10,331	96.63	11,393	15,162
7,000	105.50	30,980	106.23	24,869	6,111	108.04	18,930	12,050	112.73	13,291	17,689
8,000	120.57	35,405	121.40	28,420	6,985	123.47	21,633	13,772	128.84	15,191	20,214
9,000	135.64	39,830	136.57	31,971	7,859	138.90	24,338	15,494	144.94	17,089	22,741
10,000	150.71	44,256	151.75	35,525	8,731	154.34	27,042	17,214	161.05	18,989	25,267
11,000	165.78	48,681	166.92	39,076	9,605	169.77	29,745	18,936	177.15	20,887	27,794
12,000	180.86	53,110	182.10	42,630	10,480	185.20	32,448	20,662	193.26	22,787	30,323
13,000	195.93	57,535	197.27	46,181	11,354	200.64	35,154	22,381	209.36	24,685	32,850
14,000	211.00	61,960	212.45	49,735	12,225	216.07	37,857	24,103	225.46	26,583	35,377
15,000	226.07	66,385	227.62	53,286	13,099	231.50	40,560	25,825	241.57	28,483	37,902
16,000	241.14	70,810	242.79	56,837	13,973	246.93	43,263	27,547	257.67	30,381	40,429
17,000	256.21	75,236	257.97	60,391	14,845	262.37	45,969	29,267	273.78	32,280	42,956
18,000	271.28	79,661	273.14	63,942	15,719	277.80	48,672	30,989	289.88	34,178	45,483
19,000	286.35	84,086	288.32	67,496	16,590	293.23	51,375	32,711	305.98	36,076	48,010
20,000	301.42	88,511	303.49	71,047	17,464	308.67	54,081	34,430	322.09	37,976	50,535
21,000	316.49	92,936	318.67	74,601	18,335	324.10	56,784	36,152	338.19	39,874	53,062
22,000	331.56	97,362	333.84	78,152	19,210	339.53	59,487	37,875	354.30	41,774	55,588
23,000	346.63	101,787	349.01	81,703	20,084	354.97	62,193	39,594	370.40	43,672	58,115
24,000	361.71	106,216	364.19	85,257	20,959	370.40	64,896	41,320	386.51	45,572	60,644
25,000	376.78	110,641	379.36	88,808	21,833	385.83	67,599	43,042	402.61	47,470	63,171
26,000	391.85	115,066	394.54	92,362	22,704	401.27	70,305	44,761	418.71	49,368	65,698
27,000	406.92	119,491	409.71	95,913	23,578	416.70	73,008	46,483	434.82	51,268	68,223
28,000	421.99	123,916	424.89	99,467	24,449	432.13	75,711	48,205	450.92	53,166	70,750
29,000	437.06	128,342	440.06	103,018	25,324	447.57	78,417	49,925	467.03	55,065	73,277
30,000	452.13	132,767	455.23	106,569	26,198	463.00	81,120	51,647	483.13	56,963	75,804
32,500	489.81	143,832	493.17	115,451	28,381	501.58	87,879	55,953	523.39	61,710	82,122
35,000	527.48	154,893	531.11	124,333	30,560	540.16	94,638	60,255	563.65	66,457	88,436
40,000	602.84	177,022	606.98	142,094	34,928	617.33	108,159	68,863	644.17	75,951	101,071
45,000	678.19	199,148	682.85	159,855	39,293	694.50	121,680	77,468	724.69	85,444	113,704
50,000	753.55	221,278	758.72	177,616	43,662	771.66	135,198	86,080	805.22	94,940	126,338
55,000	828.90	243,404	834.59	195,377	48,027	848.83	148,719	94,685	885.74	104,433	138,971
60,000	904.26	265,534	910.46	213,138	52,396	925.99	162,238	103,296	966.26	113,927	151,607
65,000	979.61	287,660	986.33	230,899	56,761	1,003.16	175,758	111,902	1,046.78	123,420	164,240
70,000	1,054.96	309,786	1,062.21	248,663	61,123	1,080.32	189,277	120,509	1,127.30	132,914	176,872
75,000	1,130.32	331,915	1,138.08	266,424	65,491	1,157.49	202,798	129,117	1,207.82	142,408	189,507
80,000	1,205.67	354,041	1,213.95	284,185	69,856	1,234.65	216,316	137,725	1,288.34	151,901	202,140
85,000	1,281.03	376,171	1,289.82	301,946	74,225	1,311.82	229,837	146,334	1,368.86	161,395	214,776
90,000	1,356.38	398,297	1,365.69	319,707	78,590	1,388.99	243,358	154,939	1,449.38	170,888	227,409
95,000	1,431.74	420,426	1,441.56	337,468	82,958	1,466.15	256,876	163,550	1,529.90	180,382	240,044
100,000	1,507.09	442,552	1,517.43	355,229	87,323	1,543.32	270,397	172,155	1,610.43	189,877	252,675
105,000	1,582.44	464,678	1,593.31	372,993	91,685	1,620.48	283,915	180,763	1,690.95	199,371	265,307
110,000	1,657.80	486,808	1,669.18	390,739	96,054	1,697.65	297,436	189,372	1,771.47	208,865	277,943
115,000	1,733.15	508,934	1,745.05	408,515	100,419	1,774.81	310,954	197,980	1,851.99	218,358	290,576
120,000	1,808.51	531,064	1,820.92	426,276	104,788	1,851.98	324,475	206,589	1,932.51	227,852	303,212
125,000	1,883.86	553,190	1,896.79	444,037	109,153	1,929.14	337,994	215,196	2,013.03	237,345	315,845
130,000	1,959.22	575,319	1,972.66	461,798	113,521	2,006.31	351,514	223,805	2,093.55	246,839	328,480
135,000	2,034.57	597,445	2,048.54	479,562	117,883	2,083.48	365,035	232,410	2,174.07	256,333	341,112
140,000	2,109.92	619,571	2,124.41	497,323	122,248	2,160.64	378,554	241,017	2,254.59	265,826	353,745
145,000	2,185.28	641,701	2,200.28	515,084	126,617	2,237.81	392,074	249,627	2,335.12	275,322	366,379
150,000	2,260.63	663,827	2,276.15	532,845	130,982	2,314.97	405,593	258,234	2,415.64	284,815	379,012
155,000	2,335.99	685,956	2,352.02	550,606	135,350	2,392.14	419,114	266,842	2,496.16	294,309	391,647
160,000	2,411.34	708,082	2,427.89	568,367	139,715	2,469.30	432,632	275,450	2,576.68	303,802	404,280
165,000	2,486.70	730,212	2,503.76	586,128	144,084	2,546.47	446,153	284,059	2,657.20	313,296	416,916
170,000	2,562.05	752,338	2,579.64	603,892	148,446	2,623.63	459,671	292,667	2,737.72	322,790	429,548
175,000	2,637.40	774,464	2,655.51	621,653	152,811	2,700.80	473,192	301,272	2,818.24	332,283	442,181
180,000	2,712.76	796,594	2,731.38	639,414	157,180	2,777.97	486,713	309,881	2,898.76	341,777	454,817
185,000	2,788.11	818,720	2,807.25	657,175	161,545	2,855.13	500,231	318,489	2,979.28	351,270	467,450
190,000	2,863.47	840,849	2,883.12	674,936	165,913	2,932.30	513,752	327,097	3,059.80	360,764	480,085
195,000	2,938.82	862,975	2,958.99	692,697	170,278	3,009.46	527,270	335,705	3,140.33	370,259	492,716
200,000	3,014.18	885,105	3,034.86	710,458	174,647	3,086.63	540,791	344,314	3,220.85	379,753	505,352

BIWEEKLY MORTGAGES

A very popular method of accelerating the payments on your 30-year mortgage is to make one-half of the 30-year payment every two weeks. Since you will make 26 payments every two weeks in each year, you make the equivalent of one extra monthly payment each year. This extra payment results in the shortening of your mortgage term.

Each lender has its own particular "daily basis" method for computing accrued interest on their biweekly mortgages. Lenders take the annual simple interest rate and divide by their daily basis to get the daily interest factor. Lenders will normally use either 360, 364, or 365 for the daily basis. Lenders who use a 365-day basis earn slightly less interest than lenders who use a 360-day basis, and thus their mortgage terms are shorter.

There are four mortgage plans on each page; the benchmark 30-year monthly payment mortgage and the three most popular alternative biweekly mortgage plans, each distinguished by the "daily basis" shown at the top of the plan's group of columns. Immediately below the daily basis for each alternative plan, you find the term (number of payments) of the biweekly mortgage. The number of payments includes a fractional last payment. The last biweekly payment needed to pay off this mortgage is somewhat less than the other regular biweekly payments.

Here is how to use this table. First, find the page with the interest rate for the desired loan. Look down the first column to find your loan amount. Then read across the page and find the columns which represent the 30-year plan and the desired alternative biweekly plan. The first group of columns represents the 30-year loan plan. Within this group, you find both the monthly payment and the total interest paid through the life of the loan. Each biweekly plan's group of columns shows the biweekly payment, the total interest paid, and the all-important third column, the interest saved. This third column is the difference between the interest paid on the 30-year loan and the desired biweekly payment loan.

EXAMPLE

How much interest will you save on a $56,500 mortgage at 13.00% interest if your lender offers a biweekly mortgage calculated on a 365-day basis? How much will your biweekly payment be? How long will it take to pay off this biweekly mortgage?

First find the 13.00% interest rate on page 76. Move down the loan amount column until you find a row entry for $56,500. Since there is no row entry for exactly this loan amount, you must combine the three entries from $500, $6,000, and $50,000 to get the interest saved. The interest-saved entries for the 365-day basis biweekly mortgage are $703, $8,430, and $70,241; and their sum is $79,374. The corresponding payment entries for the 30-year mortgage are $5.54, $66.38, and $553.10; and their sum is $625.02. The corresponding payment entries for the 365-day basis biweekly mortgage are $2.77, $33.19, and $276.55; and their sum is $312.51. At the top of the page, under the 365-day basis, you find that 466.011 biweekly payments are needed to pay off the mortgage. Multipy the fraction 0.011 times $312.51 to get $3.44, the very last payment. Therefore you will make 466 biweekly payments of $312.51 and one final payment of $3.44 to pay off this mortgage. The biweekly mortgage payment is exactly one-half the monthly mortgage payment. But since the borrower is making more frequent payments, the loan pays off in slightly less than 18 years.

7.00%   BIWEEKLY MORTGAGES

AMOUNT OF LOAN	30 YEARS		360 DAY BASIS 627.409 PAYMENTS			364 DAY BASIS 616.400 PAYMENTS			365 DAY BASIS 613.779 PAYMENTS		
	MONTHLY PAYMENT	TOTAL INTRST	BWEEKLY PAYMENT	TOTAL INTRST	INTRST SAVED	BWEEKLY PAYMENT	TOTAL INTRST	INTRST SAVED	BWEEKLY PAYMENT	TOTAL INTRST	INTRST SAVED
$ 50	0.34	72	0.17	57	15	0.17	55	17	0.17	54	18
100	0.67	141	0.34	113	28	0.34	110	31	0.34	109	32
200	1.34	282	0.67	220	62	0.67	213	69	0.67	211	71
300	2.00	420	1.00	327	93	1.00	316	104	1.00	314	106
400	2.67	561	1.34	441	120	1.34	426	135	1.34	422	139
500	3.33	699	1.67	548	151	1.67	529	170	1.67	525	174
600	4.00	840	2.00	655	185	2.00	633	207	2.00	628	212
700	4.66	978	2.33	762	216	2.33	736	242	2.33	730	248
800	5.33	1,119	2.67	875	244	2.67	846	273	2.67	839	280
900	5.99	1,256	3.00	982	274	3.00	949	307	3.00	941	315
1,000	6.66	1,398	3.33	1,089	309	3.33	1,053	345	3.33	1,044	354
2,000	13.31	2,792	6.66	2,179	613	6.66	2,105	687	6.66	2,088	704
3,000	19.96	4,186	9.98	3,262	924	9.98	3,152	1,034	9.98	3,126	1,060
4,000	26.62	5,583	13.31	4,351	1,232	13.31	4,204	1,379	13.31	4,169	1,414
5,000	33.27	6,977	16.64	5,440	1,537	16.64	5,257	1,720	16.64	5,213	1,764
6,000	39.92	8,371	19.96	6,523	1,848	19.96	6,303	2,068	19.96	6,251	2,120
7,000	46.58	9,769	23.29	7,612	2,157	23.29	7,356	2,413	23.29	7,295	2,474
8,000	53.23	11,163	26.62	8,702	2,461	26.62	8,409	2,754	26.62	8,339	2,824
9,000	59.88	12,557	29.94	9,785	2,772	29.94	9,462	3,102	29.94	9,377	3,180
10,000	66.54	13,954	33.27	10,874	3,080	33.27	10,508	3,446	33.27	10,420	3,534
11,000	73.19	15,348	36.60	11,963	3,385	36.60	11,560	3,788	36.60	11,464	3,884
12,000	79.84	16,742	39.92	13,046	3,696	39.92	12,607	4,135	39.92	12,502	4,240
13,000	86.49	18,136	43.25	14,135	4,001	43.25	13,659	4,477	43.25	13,546	4,590
14,000	93.15	19,534	46.58	15,225	4,309	46.58	14,712	4,822	46.58	14,590	4,944
15,000	99.80	20,928	49.90	16,308	4,620	49.90	15,758	5,170	49.90	15,628	5,300
16,000	106.45	22,322	53.23	17,397	4,925	53.23	16,811	5,511	53.23	16,671	5,651
17,000	113.11	23,720	56.56	18,486	5,234	56.56	17,864	5,856	56.56	17,715	6,005
18,000	119.76	25,114	59.88	19,569	5,545	59.88	18,910	6,204	59.88	18,753	6,361
19,000	126.41	26,508	63.21	20,659	5,849	63.21	19,963	6,545	63.21	19,797	6,711
20,000	133.07	27,905	66.54	21,748	6,157	66.54	21,015	6,890	66.54	20,841	7,064
21,000	139.72	29,299	69.86	22,831	6,468	69.86	22,062	7,237	69.86	21,879	7,420
22,000	146.37	30,693	73.19	23,920	6,773	73.19	23,114	7,579	73.19	22,922	7,771
23,000	153.02	32,087	76.51	25,003	7,084	76.51	24,161	7,926	76.51	23,960	8,127
24,000	159.68	33,485	79.84	26,092	7,393	79.84	25,213	8,272	79.84	25,004	8,481
25,000	166.33	34,879	83.17	27,182	7,697	83.17	26,266	8,613	83.17	26,048	8,831
26,000	172.98	36,273	86.49	28,265	8,008	86.49	27,312	8,961	86.49	27,086	9,187
27,000	179.64	37,670	89.82	29,354	8,316	89.82	28,365	9,305	89.82	28,130	9,540
28,000	186.29	39,064	93.15	30,443	8,621	93.15	29,418	9,646	93.15	29,174	9,890
29,000	192.94	40,458	96.47	31,526	8,932	96.47	30,464	9,994	96.47	30,211	10,247
30,000	199.60	41,856	99.80	32,615	9,241	99.80	31,517	10,339	99.80	31,255	10,601
32,500	216.23	45,343	108.12	35,335	10,008	108.12	34,145	11,198	108.12	33,862	11,481
35,000	232.86	48,830	116.43	38,049	10,781	116.43	36,767	12,063	116.43	36,462	12,368
40,000	266.13	55,807	133.07	43,489	12,318	133.07	42,024	13,783	133.07	41,676	14,131
45,000	299.39	62,780	149.70	48,923	13,857	149.70	47,275	15,505	149.70	46,883	15,897
50,000	332.66	69,758	166.33	54,357	15,401	166.33	52,526	17,232	166.33	52,090	17,668
55,000	365.92	76,731	182.96	59,791	16,940	182.96	57,777	18,954	182.96	57,297	19,434
60,000	399.19	83,708	199.60	65,231	18,477	199.60	63,033	20,675	199.60	62,510	21,198
65,000	432.45	90,682	216.23	70,663	20,017	216.23	68,284	22,398	216.23	67,717	22,965
70,000	465.72	97,659	232.86	76,098	21,561	232.86	73,535	24,124	232.86	72,925	24,734
75,000	498.98	104,633	249.49	81,532	23,101	249.49	78,786	25,847	249.49	78,132	26,501
80,000	532.25	111,610	266.13	86,972	24,638	266.13	84,043	27,567	266.13	83,345	28,265
85,000	565.51	118,584	282.76	92,406	26,178	282.76	89,293	29,291	282.76	88,552	30,032
90,000	598.78	125,561	299.39	97,840	27,721	299.39	94,544	31,017	299.39	93,759	31,802
95,000	632.04	132,534	316.02	103,274	29,260	316.02	99,795	32,739	316.02	98,966	33,568
100,000	665.31	139,512	332.66	108,714	30,798	332.66	105,052	34,460	332.66	104,180	35,332
105,000	698.57	146,485	349.29	114,148	32,337	349.29	110,302	36,183	349.29	109,387	37,098
110,000	731.84	153,462	365.92	119,582	33,880	365.92	115,553	37,909	365.92	114,594	38,868
115,000	765.10	160,436	382.55	125,015	35,421	382.55	120,804	39,632	382.55	119,801	40,635
120,000	798.37	167,413	399.19	130,455	36,958	399.19	126,061	41,352	399.19	125,014	42,399
125,000	831.63	174,387	415.82	135,889	38,498	415.82	131,311	43,076	415.82	130,222	44,165
130,000	864.90	181,364	432.45	141,323	40,041	432.45	136,562	44,802	432.45	135,429	45,935
135,000	898.16	188,338	449.08	146,757	41,581	449.08	141,813	46,525	449.08	140,636	47,702
140,000	931.43	195,315	465.72	152,197	43,118	465.72	147,070	48,245	465.72	145,849	49,466
145,000	964.69	202,288	482.35	157,631	44,657	482.35	152,321	49,967	482.35	151,056	51,232
150,000	997.96	209,266	498.98	163,065	46,201	498.98	157,571	51,695	498.98	156,263	53,003
155,000	1,031.22	216,239	515.61	168,498	47,741	515.61	162,822	53,417	515.61	161,471	54,768
160,000	1,064.49	223,216	532.25	173,938	49,278	532.25	168,079	55,137	532.25	166,684	56,532
165,000	1,097.75	230,190	548.88	179,372	50,818	548.88	173,330	56,860	548.88	171,891	58,299
170,000	1,131.02	237,167	565.51	184,806	52,361	565.51	178,580	58,587	565.51	177,098	60,069
175,000	1,164.28	244,141	582.14	190,240	53,901	582.14	183,831	60,310	582.14	182,305	61,836
180,000	1,197.55	251,118	598.78	195,680	55,438	598.78	189,088	62,030	598.78	187,519	63,599
185,000	1,230.81	258,092	615.41	201,114	56,978	615.41	194,339	63,753	615.41	192,726	65,366
190,000	1,264.08	265,069	632.04	206,548	58,521	632.04	199,589	65,480	632.04	197,933	67,136
195,000	1,297.34	272,042	648.67	211,981	60,061	648.67	204,840	67,202	648.67	203,140	68,902
200,000	1,330.61	279,020	665.31	217,421	61,599	665.31	210,097	68,923	665.31	208,353	70,667

AMOUNT OF LOAN	30 YEARS		360 DAY BASIS 622.336 PAYMENTS			364 DAY BASIS 610.904 PAYMENTS			365 DAY BASIS 608.187 PAYMENTS		
	MONTHLY PAYMENT	TOTAL INTRST	BWEEKLY PAYMENT	TOTAL INTRST	INTRST SAVED	BWEEKLY PAYMENT	TOTAL INTRST	INTRST SAVED	BWEEKLY PAYMENT	TOTAL INTRST	INTRST SAVED
$ 50	0.35	76	0.18	62	14	0.18	60	16	0.18	59	17
100	0.69	148	0.35	118	30	0.35	114	34	0.35	113	35
200	1.37	293	0.69	229	64	0.69	222	71	0.69	220	73
300	2.05	438	1.03	341	97	1.03	329	109	1.03	326	112
400	2.73	583	1.37	453	130	1.37	437	146	1.37	433	150
500	3.42	731	1.71	564	167	1.71	545	186	1.71	540	191
600	4.10	876	2.05	676	200	2.05	652	224	2.05	647	229
700	4.78	1,021	2.39	787	234	2.39	760	261	2.39	754	267
800	5.46	1,166	2.73	899	267	2.73	868	298	2.73	860	306
900	6.14	1,310	3.07	1,011	299	3.07	975	335	3.07	967	343
1,000	6.83	1,459	3.42	1,128	331	3.42	1,089	370	3.42	1,080	379
2,000	13.65	2,914	6.83	2,251	663	6.83	2,172	742	6.83	2,154	760
3,000	20.47	4,369	10.24	3,373	996	10.24	3,256	1,113	10.24	3,228	1,141
4,000	27.29	5,824	13.65	4,495	1,329	13.65	4,339	1,485	13.65	4,302	1,522
5,000	34.11	7,280	17.06	5,617	1,663	17.06	5,422	1,858	17.06	5,376	1,904
6,000	40.94	8,738	20.47	6,739	1,999	20.47	6,505	2,233	20.47	6,450	2,288
7,000	47.76	10,194	23.88	7,861	2,333	23.88	7,588	2,606	23.88	7,524	2,670
8,000	54.58	11,649	27.29	8,984	2,665	27.29	8,672	2,977	27.29	8,597	3,052
9,000	61.40	13,104	30.70	10,106	2,998	30.70	9,755	3,349	30.70	9,671	3,433
10,000	68.22	14,559	34.11	11,228	3,331	34.11	10,838	3,721	34.11	10,745	3,814
11,000	75.04	16,014	37.52	12,350	3,664	37.52	11,921	4,093	37.52	11,819	4,195
12,000	81.87	17,473	40.94	13,478	3,995	40.94	13,010	4,463	40.94	12,899	4,574
13,000	88.69	18,928	44.35	14,601	4,327	44.35	14,094	4,834	44.35	13,973	4,955
14,000	95.51	20,384	47.76	15,723	4,661	47.76	15,177	5,207	47.76	15,047	5,337
15,000	102.33	21,839	51.17	16,845	4,994	51.17	16,260	5,579	51.17	16,121	5,718
16,000	109.15	23,294	54.58	17,967	5,327	54.58	17,343	5,951	54.58	17,195	6,099
17,000	115.97	24,749	57.99	19,089	5,660	57.99	18,426	6,323	57.99	18,269	6,480
18,000	122.80	26,208	61.40	20,211	5,997	61.40	19,510	6,698	61.40	19,343	6,865
19,000	129.62	27,663	64.81	21,334	6,329	64.81	20,593	7,070	64.81	20,417	7,246
20,000	136.44	29,118	68.22	22,456	6,662	68.22	21,676	7,442	68.22	21,491	7,627
21,000	143.26	30,574	71.63	23,578	6,996	71.63	22,759	7,815	71.63	22,564	8,010
22,000	150.08	32,029	75.04	24,700	7,329	75.04	23,842	8,187	75.04	23,638	8,391
23,000	156.91	33,488	78.46	25,828	7,660	78.46	24,932	8,556	78.46	24,718	8,770
24,000	163.73	34,943	81.87	26,951	7,992	81.87	26,015	8,928	81.87	25,792	9,151
25,000	170.55	36,398	85.28	28,073	8,325	85.28	27,098	9,300	85.28	26,866	9,532
26,000	177.37	37,853	88.69	29,195	8,658	88.69	28,181	9,672	88.69	27,940	9,913
27,000	184.19	39,308	92.10	30,317	8,991	92.10	29,264	10,044	92.10	29,014	10,294
28,000	191.01	40,764	95.51	31,439	9,325	95.51	30,347	10,417	95.51	30,088	10,676
29,000	197.84	42,222	98.92	32,561	9,661	98.92	31,431	10,791	98.92	31,162	11,060
30,000	204.66	43,678	102.33	33,684	9,994	102.33	32,514	11,164	102.33	32,236	11,442
32,500	221.71	47,316	110.86	36,492	10,824	110.86	35,225	12,091	110.86	34,924	12,392
35,000	238.77	50,957	119.39	39,301	11,656	119.39	37,936	13,021	119.39	37,611	13,346
40,000	272.88	58,237	136.44	44,912	13,325	136.44	43,352	14,885	136.44	42,981	15,256
45,000	306.98	65,513	153.49	50,522	14,991	153.49	48,768	16,745	153.49	48,351	17,162
50,000	341.09	72,792	170.55	56,139	16,653	170.55	54,190	18,602	170.55	53,726	19,066
55,000	375.20	80,072	187.60	61,750	18,322	187.60	59,606	20,466	187.60	59,096	20,976
60,000	409.31	87,352	204.66	67,367	19,985	204.66	65,028	22,324	204.66	64,472	22,880
65,000	443.42	94,631	221.71	72,978	21,653	221.71	70,444	24,187	221.71	69,841	24,790
70,000	477.53	101,911	238.77	78,595	23,316	238.77	75,866	26,045	238.77	75,217	26,694
75,000	511.64	109,190	255.82	84,206	24,984	255.82	81,281	27,909	255.82	80,586	28,604
80,000	545.75	116,470	272.88	89,823	26,647	272.88	86,703	29,767	272.88	85,962	30,508
85,000	579.85	123,746	289.93	95,434	28,312	289.93	92,119	31,627	289.93	91,332	32,414
90,000	613.96	131,026	306.98	101,045	29,981	306.98	97,535	33,491	306.98	96,701	34,325
95,000	648.07	138,305	324.04	106,662	31,643	324.04	102,977	35,348	324.04	102,077	36,228
100,000	682.18	145,585	341.09	112,273	33,312	341.09	108,373	37,212	341.09	107,447	38,138
105,000	716.29	152,864	358.15	117,890	34,974	358.15	113,795	39,069	358.15	112,822	40,042
110,000	750.40	160,144	375.20	123,500	36,644	375.20	119,211	40,933	375.20	118,192	41,952
115,000	784.51	167,424	392.26	129,118	38,306	392.26	124,633	42,791	392.26	123,567	43,857
120,000	818.62	174,703	409.31	134,728	39,975	409.31	130,049	44,654	409.31	128,937	45,766
125,000	852.73	181,983	426.37	140,345	41,638	426.37	135,471	46,512	426.37	134,313	47,670
130,000	886.83	189,259	443.42	145,956	43,303	443.42	140,887	48,372	443.42	139,682	49,577
135,000	920.94	196,538	460.47	151,567	44,971	460.47	146,303	50,235	460.47	145,052	51,486
140,000	955.05	203,818	477.53	157,184	46,634	477.53	151,725	52,093	477.53	150,428	53,390
145,000	989.16	211,098	494.58	162,795	48,303	494.58	157,141	53,957	494.58	155,797	55,301
150,000	1,023.27	218,377	511.64	168,412	49,965	511.64	162,563	55,814	511.64	161,173	57,204
155,000	1,057.38	225,657	528.69	174,023	51,634	528.69	167,979	57,678	528.69	166,542	59,115
160,000	1,091.49	232,936	545.75	179,640	53,296	545.75	173,401	59,535	545.75	171,918	61,018
165,000	1,125.60	240,216	562.80	185,251	54,965	562.80	178,817	61,399	562.80	177,288	62,928
170,000	1,159.70	247,492	579.85	190,862	56,630	579.85	184,233	63,259	579.85	182,657	64,835
175,000	1,193.81	254,772	596.91	196,479	58,293	596.91	189,655	65,117	596.91	188,032	66,739
180,000	1,227.92	262,051	613.96	202,089	59,962	613.96	195,071	66,980	613.96	193,402	68,649
185,000	1,262.03	269,331	631.02	207,706	61,625	631.02	200,493	68,838	631.02	198,778	70,553
190,000	1,296.14	276,610	648.07	213,317	63,293	648.07	205,909	70,701	648.07	204,148	72,462
195,000	1,330.25	283,890	665.13	218,934	64,956	665.13	211,331	72,559	665.13	209,523	74,367
200,000	1,364.36	291,170	682.18	224,545	66,625	682.18	216,746	74,424	682.18	214,893	76,277

7.50% BIWEEKLY MORTGAGES

AMOUNT OF LOAN	30 YEARS		360 DAY BASIS 617.147 PAYMENTS			364 DAY BASIS 605.303 PAYMENTS			365 DAY BASIS 602.493 PAYMENTS		
	MONTHLY PAYMENT	TOTAL INTRST	BWEEKLY PAYMENT	TOTAL INTRST	INTRST SAVED	BWEEKLY PAYMENT	TOTAL INTRST	INTRST SAVED	BWEEKLY PAYMENT	TOTAL INTRST	INTRST SAVED
$ 50	0.35	76	0.18	61	15	0.18	59	17	0.18	58	18
100	0.70	152	0.35	116	36	0.35	112	40	0.35	111	41
200	1.40	304	0.70	232	72	0.70	224	80	0.70	222	82
300	2.10	456	1.05	348	108	1.05	336	120	1.05	333	123
400	2.80	608	1.40	464	144	1.40	447	161	1.40	443	165
500	3.50	760	1.75	580	180	1.75	559	201	1.75	554	206
600	4.20	912	2.10	696	216	2.10	671	241	2.10	665	247
700	4.90	1,064	2.45	812	252	2.45	783	281	2.45	776	288
800	5.60	1,216	2.80	928	288	2.80	895	321	2.80	887	329
900	6.30	1,368	3.15	1,044	324	3.15	1,007	361	3.15	998	370
1,000	7.00	1,520	3.50	1,160	360	3.50	1,119	401	3.50	1,109	411
2,000	13.99	3,036	7.00	2,320	716	7.00	2,237	799	7.00	2,217	819
3,000	20.98	4,553	10.49	3,474	1,079	10.49	3,350	1,203	10.49	3,320	1,233
4,000	27.97	6,069	13.99	4,634	1,435	13.99	4,468	1,601	13.99	4,429	1,640
5,000	34.97	7,589	17.49	5,794	1,795	17.49	5,587	2,002	17.49	5,538	2,051
6,000	41.96	9,106	20.98	6,948	2,158	20.98	6,699	2,407	20.98	6,640	2,466
7,000	48.95	10,622	24.48	8,108	2,514	24.48	7,818	2,804	24.48	7,749	2,873
8,000	55.94	12,138	27.97	9,262	2,876	27.97	8,930	3,208	27.97	8,852	3,286
9,000	62.93	13,655	31.47	10,422	3,233	31.47	10,049	3,606	31.47	9,960	3,695
10,000	69.93	15,175	34.97	11,582	3,593	34.97	11,167	4,008	34.97	11,069	4,106
11,000	76.92	16,691	38.46	12,735	3,956	38.46	12,280	4,411	38.46	12,172	4,519
12,000	83.91	18,208	41.96	13,895	4,313	41.96	13,399	4,809	41.96	13,281	4,927
13,000	90.90	19,724	45.45	15,049	4,675	45.45	14,511	5,213	45.45	14,383	5,341
14,000	97.90	21,244	48.95	16,209	5,035	48.95	15,630	5,614	48.95	15,492	5,752
15,000	104.89	22,760	52.45	17,369	5,391	52.45	16,748	6,012	52.45	16,601	6,159
16,000	111.88	24,277	55.94	18,523	5,754	55.94	17,861	6,416	55.94	17,703	6,574
17,000	118.87	25,793	59.44	19,683	6,110	59.44	18,979	6,814	59.44	18,812	6,981
18,000	125.86	27,310	62.93	20,837	6,473	62.93	20,092	7,218	62.93	19,915	7,395
19,000	132.86	28,830	66.43	21,997	6,833	66.43	21,210	7,620	66.43	21,024	7,806
20,000	139.85	30,346	69.93	23,157	7,189	69.93	22,329	8,017	69.93	22,132	8,214
21,000	146.84	31,862	73.42	24,311	7,551	73.42	23,441	8,421	73.42	23,235	8,627
22,000	153.83	33,379	76.92	25,471	7,908	76.92	24,560	8,819	76.92	24,344	9,035
23,000	160.82	34,895	80.41	26,625	8,270	80.41	25,672	9,223	80.41	25,446	9,449
24,000	167.82	36,415	83.91	27,785	8,630	83.91	26,791	9,624	83.91	26,555	9,860
25,000	174.81	37,932	87.41	28,945	8,987	87.41	27,910	10,022	87.41	27,664	10,268
26,000	181.80	39,448	90.90	30,099	9,349	90.90	29,022	10,426	90.90	28,767	10,681
27,000	188.79	40,964	94.40	31,259	9,705	94.40	30,141	10,823	94.40	29,875	11,089
28,000	195.79	42,484	97.90	32,419	10,065	97.90	31,259	11,225	97.90	30,984	11,500
29,000	202.78	44,001	101.39	33,573	10,428	101.39	32,372	11,629	101.39	32,087	11,914
30,000	209.77	45,517	104.89	34,733	10,784	104.89	33,490	12,027	104.89	33,195	12,322
32,500	227.25	49,310	113.63	37,626	11,684	113.63	36,281	13,029	113.63	35,961	13,349
35,000	244.73	53,103	122.37	40,520	12,583	122.37	39,071	14,032	122.37	38,727	14,376
40,000	279.69	60,688	139.85	46,308	14,380	139.85	44,652	16,036	139.85	44,259	16,429
45,000	314.65	68,274	157.33	52,096	16,178	157.33	50,232	18,042	157.33	49,790	18,484
50,000	349.61	75,860	174.81	57,883	17,977	174.81	55,813	20,047	174.81	55,322	20,538
55,000	384.57	83,445	192.29	63,671	19,774	192.29	61,394	22,051	192.29	60,853	22,592
60,000	419.53	91,031	209.77	69,459	21,572	209.77	66,974	24,057	209.77	66,385	24,646
65,000	454.49	98,616	227.25	75,247	23,369	227.25	72,555	26,061	227.25	71,917	26,699
70,000	489.46	106,206	244.73	81,034	25,172	244.73	78,136	28,070	244.73	77,448	28,758
75,000	524.42	113,791	262.21	86,822	26,969	262.21	83,716	30,075	262.21	82,980	30,811
80,000	559.38	121,377	279.69	92,610	28,767	279.69	89,297	32,080	279.69	88,511	32,866
85,000	594.34	128,962	297.17	98,398	30,564	297.17	94,878	34,084	297.17	94,043	34,919
90,000	629.30	136,548	314.65	104,185	32,363	314.65	100,459	36,089	314.65	99,574	36,974
95,000	664.26	144,134	332.13	109,973	34,161	332.13	106,039	38,095	332.13	105,106	39,028
100,000	699.22	151,719	349.61	115,761	35,958	349.61	111,620	40,099	349.61	110,638	41,081
105,000	734.18	159,305	367.09	121,548	37,757	367.09	117,201	42,104	367.09	116,169	43,136
110,000	769.14	166,890	384.57	127,336	39,554	384.57	122,781	44,109	384.57	121,701	45,189
115,000	804.10	174,476	402.05	133,124	41,352	402.05	128,362	46,114	402.05	127,232	47,244
120,000	839.06	182,062	419.53	138,912	43,150	419.53	133,943	48,119	419.53	132,764	49,298
125,000	874.02	189,647	437.01	144,699	44,948	437.01	139,523	50,124	437.01	138,295	51,352
130,000	908.98	197,233	454.49	150,487	46,746	454.49	145,104	52,129	454.49	143,827	53,406
135,000	943.94	204,818	471.97	156,275	48,543	471.97	150,685	54,133	471.97	149,359	55,459
140,000	978.91	212,408	489.46	162,069	50,339	489.46	156,272	56,136	489.46	154,896	57,512
145,000	1,013.87	219,993	506.94	167,857	52,136	506.94	161,852	58,141	506.94	160,428	59,565
150,000	1,048.83	227,579	524.42	173,644	53,935	524.42	167,433	60,146	524.42	165,959	61,620
155,000	1,083.79	235,164	541.90	179,432	55,732	541.90	173,014	62,150	541.90	171,491	63,673
160,000	1,118.75	242,750	559.38	185,220	57,530	559.38	178,594	64,156	559.38	177,023	65,727
165,000	1,153.71	250,336	576.86	191,007	59,329	576.86	184,175	66,161	576.86	182,554	67,782
170,000	1,188.67	257,921	594.34	196,795	61,126	594.34	189,756	68,165	594.34	188,086	69,835
175,000	1,223.63	265,507	611.82	202,583	62,924	611.82	195,336	70,171	611.82	193,617	71,890
180,000	1,258.59	273,092	629.30	208,371	64,721	629.30	200,917	72,175	629.30	199,149	73,943
185,000	1,293.55	280,678	646.78	214,158	66,520	646.78	206,498	74,180	646.78	204,680	75,998
190,000	1,328.51	288,264	664.26	219,946	68,318	664.26	212,079	76,185	664.26	210,212	78,052
195,000	1,363.47	295,849	681.74	225,734	70,115	681.74	217,659	78,190	681.74	215,744	80,105
200,000	1,398.43	303,435	699.22	231,522	71,913	699.22	223,240	80,195	699.22	221,275	82,160

54

AMOUNT OF LOAN	30 YEARS		360 DAY BASIS 611.848 PAYMENTS			364 DAY BASIS 599.601 PAYMENTS			365 DAY BASIS 596.701 PAYMENTS		
	MONTHLY PAYMENT	TOTAL INTRST	BWEEKLY PAYMENT	TOTAL INTRST	INTRST SAVED	BWEEKLY PAYMENT	TOTAL INTRST	INTRST SAVED	BWEEKLY PAYMENT	TOTAL INTRST	INTRST SAVED
$ 50	0.36	80	0.18	60	20	0.18	58	22	0.18	57	23
100	0.72	159	0.36	120	39	0.36	116	43	0.36	115	44
200	1.44	318	0.72	241	77	0.72	232	86	0.72	230	88
300	2.15	474	1.08	361	113	1.08	348	126	1.08	344	130
400	2.87	633	1.44	481	152	1.44	463	170	1.44	459	174
500	3.59	792	1.80	601	191	1.80	579	213	1.80	574	218
600	4.30	948	2.15	715	233	2.15	689	259	2.15	683	265
700	5.02	1,107	2.51	836	271	2.51	805	302	2.51	798	309
800	5.74	1,266	2.87	956	310	2.87	921	345	2.87	913	353
900	6.45	1,422	3.23	1,076	346	3.23	1,037	385	3.23	1,027	395
1,000	7.17	1,581	3.59	1,197	384	3.59	1,153	428	3.59	1,142	439
2,000	14.33	3,159	7.17	2,387	772	7.17	2,299	860	7.17	2,278	881
3,000	21.50	4,740	10.75	3,577	1,163	10.75	3,446	1,294	10.75	3,415	1,325
4,000	28.66	6,318	14.33	4,768	1,550	14.33	4,592	1,726	14.33	4,551	1,767
5,000	35.83	7,899	17.92	5,964	1,935	17.92	5,745	2,154	17.92	5,693	2,206
6,000	42.99	9,476	21.50	7,155	2,321	21.50	6,891	2,585	21.50	6,829	2,647
7,000	50.15	11,054	25.08	8,345	2,709	25.08	8,038	3,016	25.08	7,965	3,089
8,000	57.32	12,635	28.66	9,536	3,099	28.66	9,185	3,450	28.66	9,101	3,534
9,000	64.48	14,213	32.24	10,726	3,487	32.24	10,331	3,882	32.24	10,238	3,975
10,000	71.65	15,794	35.83	11,923	3,871	35.83	11,484	4,310	35.83	11,380	4,414
11,000	78.81	17,372	39.41	13,113	4,259	39.41	12,630	4,742	39.41	12,516	4,856
12,000	85.97	18,949	42.99	14,303	4,646	42.99	13,777	5,172	42.99	13,652	5,297
13,000	93.14	20,530	46.57	15,494	5,036	46.57	14,923	5,607	46.57	14,788	5,742
14,000	100.30	22,108	50.15	16,684	5,424	50.15	16,070	6,038	50.15	15,925	6,183
15,000	107.47	23,689	53.74	17,881	5,808	53.74	17,223	6,466	53.74	17,067	6,622
16,000	114.63	25,267	57.32	19,071	6,196	57.32	18,369	6,898	57.32	18,203	7,064
17,000	121.80	26,848	60.90	20,262	6,586	60.90	19,516	7,332	60.90	19,339	7,509
18,000	128.96	28,426	64.48	21,452	6,974	64.48	20,662	7,764	64.48	20,475	7,951
19,000	136.12	30,003	68.06	22,642	7,361	68.06	21,809	8,194	68.06	21,611	8,392
20,000	143.29	31,584	71.65	23,839	7,745	71.65	22,961	8,623	71.65	22,754	8,830
21,000	150.45	33,162	75.23	25,029	8,133	75.23	24,108	9,054	75.23	23,890	9,272
22,000	157.62	34,743	78.81	26,220	8,523	78.81	25,255	9,488	78.81	25,026	9,717
23,000	164.78	36,321	82.39	27,410	8,911	82.39	26,401	9,920	82.39	26,162	10,159
24,000	171.94	37,898	85.97	28,601	9,297	85.97	27,548	10,350	85.97	27,298	10,600
25,000	179.11	39,480	89.56	29,797	9,683	89.56	28,700	10,780	89.56	28,441	11,039
26,000	186.27	41,057	93.14	30,988	10,069	93.14	29,847	11,210	93.14	29,577	11,480
27,000	193.44	42,638	96.72	32,178	10,460	96.72	30,993	11,645	96.72	30,713	11,925
28,000	200.60	44,216	100.30	33,368	10,848	100.30	32,140	12,076	100.30	31,849	12,367
29,000	207.76	45,794	103.88	34,559	11,235	103.88	33,287	12,507	103.88	32,985	12,809
30,000	214.93	47,375	107.47	35,755	11,620	107.47	34,439	12,936	107.47	34,127	13,248
32,500	232.84	51,322	116.42	38,731	12,591	116.42	37,306	14,016	116.42	36,968	14,354
35,000	250.75	55,270	125.38	41,714	13,556	125.38	40,178	15,092	125.38	39,814	15,456
40,000	286.57	63,165	143.29	47,672	15,493	143.29	45,917	17,248	143.29	45,501	17,664
45,000	322.39	71,060	161.20	53,630	17,430	161.20	51,656	19,404	161.20	51,188	19,872
50,000	358.21	78,956	179.11	59,588	19,368	179.11	57,395	21,561	179.11	56,875	22,081
55,000	394.03	86,851	197.02	65,546	21,305	197.02	63,133	23,718	197.02	62,562	24,289
60,000	429.85	94,746	214.93	71,504	23,242	214.93	68,872	25,874	214.93	68,249	26,497
65,000	465.67	102,641	232.84	77,463	25,178	232.84	74,611	28,030	232.84	73,936	28,705
70,000	501.49	110,536	250.75	83,421	27,115	250.75	80,186	30,186	250.75	79,623	30,913
75,000	537.31	118,432	268.66	89,379	29,053	268.66	86,089	32,343	268.66	85,310	33,122
80,000	573.13	126,327	286.57	95,337	30,990	286.57	91,828	34,499	286.57	90,997	35,330
85,000	608.96	134,226	304.48	101,295	32,931	304.48	97,567	36,659	304.48	96,684	37,542
90,000	644.78	142,121	322.39	107,254	34,867	322.39	103,305	38,816	322.39	102,370	39,751
95,000	680.60	150,016	340.30	113,212	36,804	340.30	109,044	40,972	340.30	108,057	41,959
100,000	716.42	157,911	358.21	119,170	38,741	358.21	114,783	43,128	358.21	113,744	44,167
105,000	752.24	165,806	376.12	125,128	40,678	376.12	120,522	45,284	376.12	119,431	46,375
110,000	788.06	173,702	394.03	131,086	42,616	394.03	126,261	47,441	394.03	125,118	48,584
115,000	823.88	181,597	411.94	137,045	44,552	411.94	132,000	49,597	411.94	130,805	50,792
120,000	859.70	189,492	429.85	143,003	46,489	429.85	137,738	51,754	429.85	136,492	53,000
125,000	895.52	197,387	447.76	148,961	48,426	447.76	143,477	53,910	447.76	142,179	55,208
130,000	931.34	205,282	465.67	154,919	50,363	465.67	149,216	56,066	465.67	147,866	57,416
135,000	967.16	213,178	483.58	160,877	52,301	483.58	154,955	58,223	483.58	153,553	59,625
140,000	1,002.98	221,073	501.49	166,836	54,237	501.49	160,694	60,379	501.49	159,240	61,833
145,000	1,038.80	228,968	519.40	172,794	56,174	519.40	166,433	62,535	519.40	164,926	64,042
150,000	1,074.62	236,863	537.31	178,752	58,111	537.31	172,172	64,691	537.31	170,613	66,250
155,000	1,110.44	244,758	555.22	184,710	60,048	555.22	177,910	66,848	555.22	176,300	68,458
160,000	1,146.26	252,654	573.13	190,668	61,986	573.13	183,649	69,005	573.13	181,987	70,667
165,000	1,182.09	260,552	591.05	196,633	63,919	591.05	189,394	71,158	591.05	187,680	72,872
170,000	1,217.91	268,448	608.96	202,591	65,857	608.96	195,133	73,315	608.96	193,367	75,081
175,000	1,253.73	276,343	626.87	208,549	67,794	626.87	200,872	75,471	626.87	199,054	77,289
180,000	1,289.55	284,238	644.78	214,507	69,731	644.78	206,611	77,627	644.78	204,741	79,497
185,000	1,325.37	292,133	662.69	220,466	71,667	662.69	212,350	79,783	662.69	210,428	81,705
190,000	1,361.19	300,028	680.60	226,424	73,604	680.60	218,088	81,940	680.60	216,115	83,913
195,000	1,397.01	307,924	698.51	232,382	75,542	698.51	223,827	84,097	698.51	221,802	86,122
200,000	1,432.83	315,819	716.42	238,340	77,479	716.42	229,566	86,253	716.42	227,489	88,330

55

AMOUNT OF LOAN	30 YEARS		360 DAY BASIS 606.444 PAYMENTS			364 DAY BASIS 593.806 PAYMENTS			365 DAY BASIS 590.819 PAYMENTS		
	MONTHLY PAYMENT	TOTAL INTRST	BWEEKLY PAYMENT	TOTAL INTRST	INTRST SAVED	BWEEKLY PAYMENT	TOTAL INTRST	INTRST SAVED	BWEEKLY PAYMENT	TOTAL INTRST	INTRST SAVED
$ 50	0.37	83	0.19	65	18	0.19	63	20	0.19	62	21
100	0.74	166	0.37	124	42	0.37	120	46	0.37	119	47
200	1.47	329	0.74	249	80	0.74	239	90	0.74	237	92
300	2.21	496	1.11	373	123	1.11	359	137	1.11	356	140
400	2.94	658	1.47	491	167	1.47	473	185	1.47	469	189
500	3.67	821	1.84	616	205	1.84	593	228	1.84	587	234
600	4.41	988	2.21	740	248	2.21	712	276	2.21	706	282
700	5.14	1,150	2.57	859	291	2.57	826	324	2.57	818	332
800	5.88	1,317	2.94	983	334	2.94	946	371	2.94	937	380
900	6.61	1,480	3.31	1,107	373	3.31	1,065	415	3.31	1,056	424
1,000	7.34	1,642	3.67	1,226	416	3.67	1,179	463	3.67	1,168	474
2,000	14.68	3,285	7.34	2,451	834	7.34	2,359	926	7.34	2,337	948
3,000	22.02	4,927	11.01	3,677	1,250	11.01	3,538	1,389	11.01	3,505	1,422
4,000	29.36	6,570	14.68	4,903	1,667	14.68	4,717	1,853	14.68	4,673	1,897
5,000	36.69	8,208	18.35	6,128	2,080	18.35	5,896	2,312	18.35	5,842	2,366
6,000	44.03	9,851	22.02	7,354	2,497	22.02	7,076	2,775	22.02	7,010	2,841
7,000	51.37	11,493	25.69	8,580	2,913	25.69	8,255	3,238	25.69	8,178	3,315
8,000	58.71	13,136	29.36	9,805	3,331	29.36	9,434	3,702	29.36	9,346	3,790
9,000	66.04	14,774	33.02	11,025	3,749	33.02	10,607	4,167	33.02	10,509	4,265
10,000	73.38	16,417	36.69	12,250	4,167	36.69	11,787	4,630	36.69	11,677	4,740
11,000	80.72	18,059	40.36	13,476	4,583	40.36	12,966	5,093	40.36	12,845	5,214
12,000	88.06	19,702	44.03	14,702	5,000	44.03	14,145	5,557	44.03	14,014	5,688
13,000	95.39	21,340	47.70	15,927	5,413	47.70	15,325	6,015	47.70	15,182	6,158
14,000	102.73	22,983	51.37	17,153	5,830	51.37	16,504	6,479	51.37	16,350	6,633
15,000	110.07	24,625	55.04	18,379	6,246	55.04	17,683	6,942	55.04	17,519	7,106
16,000	117.41	26,268	58.71	19,604	6,664	58.71	18,862	7,406	58.71	18,687	7,581
17,000	124.74	27,906	62.37	20,824	7,082	62.37	20,036	7,870	62.37	19,849	8,057
18,000	132.08	29,549	66.04	22,050	7,499	66.04	21,215	8,334	66.04	21,018	8,531
19,000	139.42	31,191	69.71	23,275	7,916	69.71	22,394	8,797	69.71	22,186	9,005
20,000	146.76	32,834	73.38	24,501	8,333	73.38	23,573	9,261	73.38	23,354	9,480
21,000	154.10	34,476	77.05	25,727	8,749	77.05	24,753	9,723	77.05	24,523	9,953
22,000	161.43	36,115	80.72	26,952	9,163	80.72	25,932	10,183	80.72	25,691	10,424
23,000	168.77	37,757	84.39	28,178	9,579	84.39	27,111	10,646	84.39	26,859	10,898
24,000	176.11	39,400	88.06	29,403	9,997	88.06	28,291	11,109	88.06	28,028	11,372
25,000	183.45	41,042	91.73	30,629	10,413	91.73	29,470	11,572	91.73	29,196	11,846
26,000	190.78	42,681	95.39	31,849	10,832	95.39	30,643	12,038	95.39	30,358	12,323
27,000	198.12	44,323	99.06	33,074	11,249	99.06	31,822	12,501	99.06	31,527	12,796
28,000	205.46	45,966	102.73	34,300	11,666	102.73	33,002	12,964	102.73	32,695	13,271
29,000	212.80	47,608	106.40	35,526	12,082	106.40	34,181	13,427	106.40	33,863	13,745
30,000	220.13	49,247	110.07	36,751	12,496	110.07	35,360	13,887	110.07	35,031	14,216
32,500	238.48	53,353	119.24	39,812	13,541	119.24	38,305	15,048	119.24	37,949	15,404
35,000	256.82	57,455	128.41	42,873	14,582	128.41	41,251	16,204	128.41	40,867	16,588
40,000	293.51	65,664	146.76	49,002	16,662	146.76	47,147	18,517	146.76	46,709	18,955
45,000	330.20	73,872	165.10	55,124	18,748	165.10	53,037	20,835	165.10	52,544	21,328
50,000	366.89	82,080	183.45	61,252	20,828	183.45	58,934	23,146	183.45	58,386	23,694
55,000	403.58	90,289	201.79	67,374	22,915	201.79	64,824	25,465	201.79	64,221	26,068
60,000	440.26	98,494	220.13	73,497	24,997	220.13	70,715	27,779	220.13	70,057	28,437
65,000	476.95	106,702	238.48	79,625	27,077	238.48	76,611	30,091	238.48	75,899	30,803
70,000	513.64	114,910	256.82	85,747	29,163	256.82	82,501	32,409	256.82	81,734	33,176
75,000	550.33	123,119	275.17	91,875	31,244	275.17	88,398	34,721	275.17	87,576	35,543
80,000	587.02	131,327	293.51	97,997	33,330	293.51	94,288	37,039	293.51	93,411	37,916
85,000	623.70	139,532	311.85	104,120	35,412	311.85	100,178	39,354	311.85	99,247	40,285
90,000	660.39	147,740	330.20	110,248	37,492	330.20	106,075	41,665	330.20	105,088	42,652
95,000	697.08	155,949	348.54	116,370	39,579	348.54	111,965	43,984	348.54	110,924	45,025
100,000	733.77	164,157	366.89	122,498	41,659	366.89	117,861	46,296	366.89	116,766	47,391
105,000	770.46	172,366	385.23	128,620	43,746	385.23	123,752	48,614	385.23	122,601	49,765
110,000	807.15	180,572	403.58	134,749	45,823	403.58	129,648	50,926	403.58	128,443	52,131
115,000	843.83	188,779	421.92	140,871	47,908	421.92	135,539	53,240	421.92	134,278	54,501
120,000	880.52	196,987	440.26	146,993	49,994	440.26	141,429	55,558	440.26	140,114	56,873
125,000	917.21	205,196	458.61	153,121	52,075	458.61	147,325	57,871	458.61	145,956	59,240
130,000	953.90	213,404	476.95	159,243	54,161	476.95	153,216	60,188	476.95	151,791	61,613
135,000	990.59	221,612	495.30	165,372	56,240	495.30	159,112	62,500	495.30	157,633	63,979
140,000	1,027.28	229,821	513.64	171,494	58,327	513.64	165,003	64,818	513.64	163,468	66,353
145,000	1,063.96	238,026	531.98	177,616	60,410	531.98	170,893	67,133	531.98	169,304	68,722
150,000	1,100.65	246,234	550.33	183,744	62,490	550.33	176,789	69,445	550.33	175,145	71,089
155,000	1,137.34	254,442	568.67	189,867	64,575	568.67	182,680	71,762	568.67	180,981	73,461
160,000	1,174.03	262,651	587.02	195,995	66,656	587.02	188,576	74,075	587.02	186,823	75,828
165,000	1,210.72	270,859	605.36	202,117	68,742	605.36	194,466	76,393	605.36	192,658	78,201
170,000	1,247.40	279,064	623.70	208,239	70,825	623.70	200,357	78,707	623.70	198,494	80,570
175,000	1,284.09	287,272	642.05	214,367	72,905	642.05	206,253	81,019	642.05	204,335	82,937
180,000	1,320.78	295,481	660.39	220,490	74,991	660.39	212,144	83,337	660.39	210,171	85,310
185,000	1,357.47	303,689	678.74	226,618	77,071	678.74	218,040	85,649	678.74	216,012	87,677
190,000	1,394.16	311,898	697.08	232,740	79,158	697.08	223,930	87,968	697.08	221,848	90,050
195,000	1,430.85	320,106	715.43	238,868	81,238	715.43	229,827	90,279	715.43	227,690	92,416
200,000	1,467.53	328,311	733.77	244,990	83,321	733.77	235,717	92,594	733.77	233,525	94,786

56

BIWEEKLY MORTGAGES   8.25%

AMOUNT OF LOAN	30 YEARS MONTHLY PAYMENT	30 YEARS TOTAL INTRST	360 DAY BASIS 600.938 PAYMENTS BWEEKLY PAYMENT	TOTAL INTRST	INTRST SAVED	364 DAY BASIS 587.923 PAYMENTS BWEEKLY PAYMENT	TOTAL INTRST	INTRST SAVED	365 DAY BASIS 584.853 PAYMENTS BWEEKLY PAYMENT	TOTAL INTRST	INTRST SAVED
$ 50	0.38	87	0.19	64	23	0.19	62	25	0.19	61	26
100	0.76	174	0.38	128	46	0.38	123	51	0.38	122	52
200	1.51	344	0.76	257	87	0.76	247	97	0.76	244	100
300	2.26	514	1.13	379	135	1.13	364	150	1.13	361	153
400	3.01	684	1.51	507	177	1.51	488	196	1.51	483	201
500	3.76	854	1.88	630	224	1.88	605	249	1.88	600	254
600	4.51	1,024	2.26	758	266	2.26	729	295	2.26	722	302
700	5.26	1,194	2.63	880	314	2.63	846	348	2.63	838	356
800	6.02	1,367	3.01	1,009	358	3.01	970	397	3.01	960	407
900	6.77	1,537	3.39	1,137	400	3.39	1,093	444	3.39	1,083	454
1,000	7.52	1,707	3.76	1,260	447	3.76	1,211	496	3.76	1,199	508
2,000	15.03	3,411	7.52	2,519	892	7.52	2,421	990	7.52	2,398	1,013
3,000	22.54	5,114	11.27	3,773	1,341	11.27	3,626	1,488	11.27	3,591	1,523
4,000	30.06	6,822	15.03	5,032	1,790	15.03	4,836	1,986	15.03	4,790	2,032
5,000	37.57	8,525	18.79	6,292	2,233	18.79	6,047	2,478	18.79	5,989	2,536
6,000	45.08	10,229	22.54	7,545	2,684	22.54	7,252	2,977	22.54	7,183	3,046
7,000	52.59	11,932	26.30	8,805	3,127	26.30	8,462	3,470	26.30	8,382	3,550
8,000	60.11	13,640	30.06	10,064	3,576	30.06	9,673	3,967	30.06	9,581	4,059
9,000	67.62	15,343	33.81	11,318	4,025	33.81	10,878	4,465	33.81	10,774	4,569
10,000	75.13	17,047	37.57	12,577	4,470	37.57	12,088	4,959	37.57	11,973	5,074
11,000	82.64	18,750	41.32	13,831	4,919	41.32	13,293	5,457	41.32	13,166	5,584
12,000	90.16	20,458	45.08	15,090	5,368	45.08	14,504	5,954	45.08	14,365	6,093
13,000	97.67	22,161	48.84	16,350	5,811	48.84	15,714	6,447	48.84	15,564	6,597
14,000	105.18	23,865	52.59	17,603	6,262	52.59	16,919	6,946	52.59	16,757	7,108
15,000	112.69	25,568	56.35	18,863	6,705	56.35	18,129	7,439	56.35	17,956	7,612
16,000	120.21	27,276	60.11	20,122	7,154	60.11	19,340	7,936	60.11	19,156	8,120
17,000	127.72	28,979	63.86	21,376	7,603	63.86	20,545	8,434	63.86	20,349	8,630
18,000	135.23	30,683	67.62	22,635	8,048	67.62	21,755	8,928	67.62	21,548	9,135
19,000	142.75	32,390	71.38	23,895	8,495	71.38	22,966	9,424	71.38	22,747	9,643
20,000	150.26	34,094	75.13	25,148	8,946	75.13	24,171	9,923	75.13	23,940	10,154
21,000	157.77	35,797	78.89	26,408	9,389	78.89	25,381	10,416	78.89	25,139	10,658
22,000	165.28	37,501	82.64	27,662	9,839	82.64	26,586	10,915	82.64	26,332	11,169
23,000	172.80	39,208	86.40	28,921	10,287	86.40	27,797	11,411	86.40	27,531	11,677
24,000	180.31	40,912	90.16	30,181	10,731	90.16	29,007	11,905	90.16	28,730	12,182
25,000	187.82	42,615	93.91	31,434	11,181	93.91	30,212	12,403	93.91	29,924	12,691
26,000	195.33	44,319	97.67	32,694	11,625	97.67	31,422	12,897	97.67	31,123	13,196
27,000	202.85	46,026	101.43	33,953	12,073	101.43	32,633	13,393	101.43	32,322	13,704
28,000	210.36	47,730	105.18	35,207	12,523	105.18	33,838	13,892	105.18	33,515	14,215
29,000	217.87	49,433	108.94	36,466	12,967	108.94	35,048	14,385	108.94	34,714	14,719
30,000	225.38	51,137	112.69	37,720	13,417	112.69	36,253	14,884	112.69	35,907	15,230
32,500	244.17	55,401	122.09	40,869	14,532	122.09	39,280	16,121	122.09	38,905	16,496
35,000	262.95	59,662	131.48	44,011	15,651	131.48	42,300	17,362	131.48	41,896	17,766
40,000	300.51	68,184	150.26	50,297	17,887	150.26	48,341	19,843	150.26	47,880	20,304
45,000	338.07	76,705	169.04	56,583	20,122	169.04	54,383	22,322	169.04	53,864	22,841
50,000	375.64	85,230	187.82	62,868	22,362	187.82	60,424	24,806	187.82	59,847	25,383
55,000	413.20	93,752	206.60	69,154	24,598	206.60	66,465	27,287	206.60	65,831	27,921
60,000	450.76	102,274	225.38	75,439	26,835	225.38	72,506	29,768	225.38	71,814	30,460
65,000	488.33	110,799	244.17	81,731	29,068	244.17	78,553	32,246	244.17	77,804	32,995
70,000	525.89	119,320	262.95	88,017	31,303	262.95	84,594	34,726	262.95	83,787	35,533
75,000	563.45	127,842	281.73	94,302	33,540	281.73	90,636	37,206	281.73	89,771	38,071
80,000	601.02	136,367	300.51	100,588	35,779	300.51	96,677	39,690	300.51	95,754	40,613
85,000	638.58	144,889	319.29	106,873	38,016	319.29	102,718	42,171	319.29	101,738	43,151
90,000	676.14	153,410	338.07	113,159	40,251	338.07	108,759	44,651	338.07	107,721	45,689
95,000	713.71	161,936	356.86	119,451	42,485	356.86	114,806	47,130	356.86	113,711	48,225
100,000	751.27	170,457	375.64	125,736	44,721	375.64	120,847	49,610	375.64	119,694	50,763
105,000	788.83	178,979	394.42	132,022	46,957	394.42	126,889	52,090	394.42	125,678	53,301
110,000	826.40	187,504	413.20	138,308	49,196	413.20	132,930	54,574	413.20	131,661	55,843
115,000	863.96	196,026	431.98	144,593	51,433	431.98	138,971	57,055	431.98	137,645	58,381
120,000	901.52	204,547	450.76	150,879	53,668	450.76	145,012	59,535	450.76	143,628	60,919
125,000	939.09	213,072	469.55	157,170	55,902	469.55	151,059	62,013	469.55	149,618	63,454
130,000	976.65	221,594	488.33	163,456	58,138	488.33	157,100	64,494	488.33	155,601	65,993
135,000	1,014.21	230,116	507.11	169,742	60,373	507.11	163,142	66,974	507.11	161,585	68,531
140,000	1,051.78	238,641	525.89	176,027	62,614	525.89	169,183	69,458	525.89	167,568	71,073
145,000	1,089.34	247,162	544.67	182,313	64,849	544.67	175,224	71,938	544.67	173,552	73,610
150,000	1,126.90	255,682	563.45	188,599	67,085	563.45	181,265	74,419	563.45	179,535	76,149
155,000	1,164.47	264,209	582.24	194,890	69,319	582.24	187,312	76,897	582.24	185,525	78,684
160,000	1,202.03	272,731	601.02	201,176	71,555	601.02	193,353	79,378	601.02	191,508	81,223
165,000	1,239.59	281,252	619.80	207,461	73,791	619.80	199,395	81,857	619.80	197,492	83,760
170,000	1,277.16	289,778	638.58	213,747	76,031	638.58	205,436	84,342	638.58	203,475	86,303
175,000	1,314.72	298,299	657.36	220,033	78,266	657.36	211,477	86,822	657.36	209,459	88,840
180,000	1,352.28	306,821	676.14	226,318	80,503	676.14	217,518	89,303	676.14	215,443	91,378
185,000	1,389.85	315,346	694.93	232,610	82,736	694.93	223,560	91,786	694.93	221,432	93,914
190,000	1,427.41	323,868	713.71	238,895	84,973	713.71	229,607	94,261	713.71	227,415	96,453
195,000	1,464.97	332,389	732.49	245,181	87,208	732.49	235,648	96,741	732.49	233,399	98,990
200,000	1,502.54	340,914	751.27	251,467	89,447	751.27	241,689	99,225	751.27	239,383	101,531

57

8.50% BIWEEKLY MORTGAGES

AMOUNT OF LOAN	30 YEARS		360 DAY BASIS 595.339 PAYMENTS			364 DAY BASIS 581.961 PAYMENTS			365 DAY BASIS 578.811 PAYMENTS		
	MONTHLY PAYMENT	TOTAL INTRST	BWEEKLY PAYMENT	TOTAL INTRST	INTRST SAVED	BWEEKLY PAYMENT	TOTAL INTRST	INTRST SAVED	BWEEKLY PAYMENT	TOTAL INTRST	INTRST SAVED
$ 50	0.39	90	0.20	69	21	0.20	66	24	0.20	66	24
100	0.77	177	0.39	132	45	0.39	127	50	0.39	126	51
200	1.54	354	0.77	258	96	0.77	248	106	0.77	246	108
300	2.31	532	1.16	391	141	1.16	375	157	1.16	371	161
400	3.08	709	1.54	517	192	1.54	496	213	1.54	491	218
500	3.85	886	1.93	649	237	1.93	623	263	1.93	617	269
600	4.62	1,063	2.31	775	288	2.31	744	319	2.31	737	326
700	5.39	1,240	2.70	907	333	2.70	871	369	2.70	863	377
800	6.16	1,418	3.08	1,034	384	3.08	992	426	3.08	983	435
900	6.93	1,595	3.47	1,166	429	3.47	1,119	476	3.47	1,108	487
1,000	7.69	1,768	3.85	1,292	476	3.85	1,241	527	3.85	1,228	540
2,000	15.38	3,537	7.69	2,578	959	7.69	2,475	1,062	7.69	2,451	1,086
3,000	23.07	5,305	11.54	3,870	1,435	11.54	3,716	1,589	11.54	3,679	1,626
4,000	30.76	7,074	15.38	5,156	1,918	15.38	4,951	2,123	15.38	4,902	2,172
5,000	38.45	8,842	19.23	6,448	2,394	19.23	6,191	2,651	19.23	6,131	2,711
6,000	46.14	10,610	23.07	7,734	2,876	23.07	7,426	3,184	23.07	7,353	3,257
7,000	53.83	12,379	26.92	9,027	3,352	26.92	8,666	3,713	26.92	8,582	3,797
8,000	61.52	14,147	30.76	10,313	3,834	30.76	9,901	4,246	30.76	9,804	4,343
9,000	69.21	15,916	34.61	11,605	4,311	34.61	11,142	4,774	34.61	11,033	4,883
10,000	76.90	17,684	38.45	12,891	4,793	38.45	12,376	5,308	38.45	12,255	5,429
11,000	84.59	19,452	42.30	14,183	5,269	42.30	13,617	5,835	42.30	13,484	5,968
12,000	92.27	21,217	46.14	15,469	5,748	46.14	14,852	6,365	46.14	14,706	6,511
13,000	99.96	22,986	49.98	16,755	6,231	49.98	16,086	6,900	49.98	15,929	7,057
14,000	107.65	24,754	53.83	18,047	6,707	53.83	17,327	7,427	53.83	17,157	7,597
15,000	115.34	26,522	57.67	19,333	7,189	57.67	18,562	7,960	57.67	18,380	8,142
16,000	123.03	28,291	61.52	20,625	7,666	61.52	19,802	8,489	61.52	19,608	8,683
17,000	130.72	30,059	65.36	21,911	8,148	65.36	21,037	9,022	65.36	20,831	9,228
18,000	138.41	31,828	69.21	23,203	8,625	69.21	22,278	9,550	69.21	22,060	9,768
19,000	146.10	33,596	73.05	24,490	9,106	73.05	23,512	10,084	73.05	23,282	10,314
20,000	153.79	35,364	76.90	25,782	9,582	76.90	24,753	10,611	76.90	24,511	10,853
21,000	161.48	37,133	80.74	27,068	10,065	80.74	25,988	11,145	80.74	25,733	11,400
22,000	169.17	38,901	84.59	28,360	10,541	84.59	27,228	11,673	84.59	26,962	11,939
23,000	176.86	40,670	88.43	29,646	11,024	88.43	28,463	12,207	88.43	28,184	12,486
24,000	184.54	42,434	92.27	30,932	11,502	92.27	29,698	12,736	92.27	29,407	13,027
25,000	192.23	44,203	96.12	32,224	11,979	96.12	30,938	13,265	96.12	30,635	13,568
26,000	199.92	45,971	99.96	33,510	12,461	99.96	32,173	13,798	99.96	31,858	14,113
27,000	207.61	47,740	103.81	34,802	12,938	103.81	33,413	14,327	103.81	33,086	14,654
28,000	215.30	49,508	107.65	36,088	13,420	107.65	34,648	14,860	107.65	34,309	15,199
29,000	222.99	51,276	111.50	37,380	13,896	111.50	35,889	15,387	111.50	35,537	15,739
30,000	230.68	53,045	115.34	38,666	14,379	115.34	37,123	15,922	115.34	36,760	16,285
32,500	249.90	57,464	124.95	41,888	15,576	124.95	40,216	17,248	124.95	39,822	17,642
35,000	269.12	61,883	134.56	45,109	16,774	134.56	43,309	18,574	134.56	42,885	18,998
40,000	307.57	70,725	153.79	51,557	19,168	153.79	49,500	21,225	153.79	49,015	21,710
45,000	346.02	79,567	173.01	58,000	21,567	173.01	55,685	23,882	173.01	55,140	24,427
50,000	384.46	88,406	192.23	64,442	23,964	192.23	61,870	26,536	192.23	61,265	27,141
55,000	422.91	97,248	211.46	70,890	26,358	211.46	68,061	29,187	211.46	67,395	29,853
60,000	461.35	106,086	230.68	77,333	28,753	230.68	74,247	31,839	230.68	73,520	32,566
65,000	499.80	114,928	249.90	83,775	31,153	249.90	80,432	34,496	249.90	79,645	35,283
70,000	538.24	123,766	269.12	90,218	33,548	269.12	86,617	37,149	269.12	85,770	37,996
75,000	576.69	132,608	288.35	96,666	35,942	288.35	92,808	39,800	288.35	91,900	40,708
80,000	615.14	141,450	307.57	103,108	38,342	307.57	98,994	42,456	307.57	98,025	43,425
85,000	653.58	150,289	326.79	109,551	40,738	326.79	105,179	45,110	326.79	104,150	46,139
90,000	692.03	159,131	346.02	115,999	43,132	346.02	111,370	47,761	346.02	110,280	48,851
95,000	730.47	167,969	365.24	122,442	45,527	365.24	117,551	50,414	365.24	116,405	51,564
100,000	768.92	176,811	384.46	128,884	47,927	384.46	123,741	53,070	384.46	122,530	54,281
105,000	807.36	185,650	403.68	135,326	50,324	403.68	129,926	55,724	403.68	128,654	56,996
110,000	845.81	194,492	422.91	141,775	52,717	422.91	136,117	58,375	422.91	134,785	59,707
115,000	884.26	203,334	442.13	148,217	55,117	442.13	142,302	61,032	442.13	140,910	62,424
120,000	922.70	212,172	461.35	154,660	57,512	461.35	148,488	63,684	461.35	147,034	65,138
125,000	961.15	221,014	480.58	161,108	59,906	480.58	154,679	66,335	480.58	153,165	67,849
130,000	999.59	229,852	499.80	167,550	62,302	499.80	160,864	68,988	499.80	159,290	70,562
135,000	1,038.04	238,694	519.02	173,993	64,701	519.02	167,049	71,645	519.02	165,414	73,280
140,000	1,076.48	247,533	538.24	180,435	67,098	538.24	173,235	74,298	538.24	171,539	75,994
145,000	1,114.93	256,375	557.47	186,884	69,491	557.47	179,426	76,949	557.47	177,670	78,705
150,000	1,153.38	265,217	576.69	193,326	71,891	576.69	185,611	79,606	576.69	183,795	81,422
155,000	1,191.82	274,055	595.91	199,768	74,287	595.91	191,796	82,259	595.91	189,919	84,136
160,000	1,230.27	282,897	615.14	206,217	76,680	615.14	197,987	84,910	615.14	196,050	86,847
165,000	1,268.71	291,736	634.36	212,659	79,077	634.36	204,173	87,563	634.36	202,175	89,561
170,000	1,307.16	300,578	653.58	219,102	81,476	653.58	210,358	90,220	653.58	208,299	92,279
175,000	1,345.60	309,416	672.80	225,544	83,872	672.80	216,543	92,873	672.80	214,424	94,992
180,000	1,384.05	318,258	692.03	231,992	86,266	692.03	222,734	95,524	692.03	220,555	97,703
185,000	1,422.49	327,096	711.25	238,435	88,661	711.25	228,920	98,176	711.25	226,679	100,417
190,000	1,460.94	335,938	730.47	244,877	91,061	730.47	235,105	100,833	730.47	232,804	103,134
195,000	1,499.39	344,780	749.70	251,326	93,454	749.70	241,296	103,484	749.70	238,935	105,845
200,000	1,537.83	353,619	768.92	257,768	95,851	768.92	247,481	106,138	768.92	245,059	108,560

58

AMOUNT OF LOAN	30 YEARS		360 DAY BASIS 589.651 PAYMENTS			364 DAY BASIS 575.926 PAYMENTS			365 DAY BASIS 572.701 PAYMENTS		
	MONTHLY PAYMENT	TOTAL INTRST	BWEEKLY PAYMENT	TOTAL INTRST	INTRST SAVED	BWEEKLY PAYMENT	TOTAL INTRST	INTRST SAVED	BWEEKLY PAYMENT	TOTAL INTRST	INTRST SAVED
$ 50	0.40	94	0.20	68	26	0.20	65	29	0.20	65	29
100	0.79	184	0.40	136	48	0.40	130	54	0.40	129	55
200	1.58	369	0.79	266	103	0.79	255	114	0.79	252	117
300	2.37	553	1.19	402	151	1.19	385	168	1.19	382	171
400	3.15	734	1.58	532	202	1.58	510	224	1.58	505	229
500	3.94	918	1.97	662	256	1.97	635	283	1.97	628	290
600	4.73	1,103	2.37	797	306	2.37	765	338	2.37	757	346
700	5.51	1,284	2.76	927	357	2.76	890	394	2.76	881	403
800	6.30	1,468	3.15	1,057	411	3.15	1,014	454	3.15	1,004	464
900	7.09	1,652	3.55	1,193	459	3.55	1,145	507	3.55	1,133	519
1,000	7.87	1,833	3.94	1,323	510	3.94	1,269	564	3.94	1,256	577
2,000	15.74	3,666	7.87	2,641	1,025	7.87	2,533	1,133	7.87	2,507	1,159
3,000	23.61	5,500	11.81	3,964	1,536	11.81	3,802	1,698	11.81	3,764	1,736
4,000	31.47	7,329	15.74	5,281	2,048	15.74	5,065	2,264	15.74	5,014	2,315
5,000	39.34	9,162	19.67	6,598	2,564	19.67	6,328	2,834	19.67	6,265	2,897
6,000	47.21	10,996	23.61	7,922	3,074	23.61	7,598	3,398	23.61	7,521	3,475
7,000	55.07	12,825	27.54	9,239	3,586	27.54	8,861	3,964	27.54	8,772	4,053
8,000	62.94	14,658	31.47	10,556	4,102	31.47	10,124	4,534	31.47	10,023	4,635
9,000	70.81	16,492	35.41	11,880	4,612	35.41	11,394	5,098	35.41	11,279	5,213
10,000	78.68	18,325	39.34	13,197	5,128	39.34	12,657	5,668	39.34	12,530	5,795
11,000	86.54	20,154	43.27	14,514	5,640	43.27	13,920	6,234	43.27	13,781	6,373
12,000	94.41	21,988	47.21	15,837	6,151	47.21	15,189	6,799	47.21	15,037	6,951
13,000	102.28	23,821	51.14	17,155	6,666	51.14	16,453	7,368	51.14	16,288	7,533
14,000	110.14	25,650	55.07	18,472	7,178	55.07	17,716	7,934	55.07	17,539	8,111
15,000	118.01	27,484	59.01	19,795	7,689	59.01	18,985	8,499	59.01	18,795	8,689
16,000	125.88	29,317	62.94	21,113	8,204	62.94	20,249	9,068	62.94	20,046	9,271
17,000	133.74	31,146	66.87	22,430	8,716	66.87	21,512	9,634	66.87	21,297	9,849
18,000	141.61	32,980	70.81	23,753	9,227	70.81	22,781	10,199	70.81	22,553	10,427
19,000	149.48	34,813	74.74	25,071	9,742	74.74	24,045	10,768	74.74	23,804	11,009
20,000	157.35	36,646	78.68	26,394	10,252	78.68	25,314	11,332	78.68	25,060	11,586
21,000	165.21	38,476	82.61	27,711	10,765	82.61	26,577	11,899	82.61	26,311	12,165
22,000	173.08	40,309	86.54	29,028	11,281	86.54	27,841	12,468	86.54	27,562	12,747
23,000	180.95	42,142	90.48	30,352	11,790	90.48	29,110	13,032	90.48	28,818	13,324
24,000	188.81	43,972	94.41	31,669	12,303	94.41	30,373	13,599	94.41	30,069	13,903
25,000	196.68	45,805	98.34	32,986	12,819	98.34	31,637	14,168	98.34	31,319	14,486
26,000	204.55	47,638	102.28	34,310	13,328	102.28	32,906	14,732	102.28	32,576	15,062
27,000	212.41	49,468	106.21	35,627	13,841	106.21	34,169	15,299	106.21	33,827	15,641
28,000	220.28	51,301	110.14	36,944	14,357	110.14	35,432	15,869	110.14	35,077	16,224
29,000	228.15	53,134	114.08	38,267	14,867	114.08	36,702	16,432	114.08	36,334	16,800
30,000	236.02	54,967	118.01	39,585	15,382	118.01	37,965	17,002	118.01	37,584	17,383
32,500	255.68	59,545	127.84	42,881	16,664	127.84	41,126	18,419	127.84	40,714	18,831
35,000	275.35	64,126	137.68	46,183	17,943	137.68	44,293	19,833	137.68	43,849	20,277
40,000	314.69	73,288	157.35	52,782	20,506	157.35	50,622	22,666	157.35	50,115	23,173
45,000	354.02	82,447	177.01	59,374	23,073	177.01	56,945	25,502	177.01	56,374	26,073
50,000	393.36	91,610	196.68	65,973	25,637	196.68	63,273	28,337	196.68	62,639	28,971
55,000	432.69	100,768	216.35	72,571	28,197	216.35	69,602	31,166	216.35	68,904	31,864
60,000	472.03	109,931	236.02	79,169	30,762	236.02	75,930	34,001	236.02	75,169	34,762
65,000	511.36	119,090	255.68	85,762	33,328	255.68	82,253	36,837	255.68	81,428	37,662
70,000	550.70	128,252	275.35	92,360	35,892	275.35	88,581	39,671	275.35	87,693	40,559
75,000	590.03	137,411	295.02	98,959	38,452	295.02	94,910	42,501	295.02	93,958	43,453
80,000	629.37	146,573	314.69	105,557	41,016	314.69	101,238	45,335	314.69	100,223	46,350
85,000	668.70	155,732	334.35	112,150	43,582	334.35	107,561	48,171	334.35	106,483	49,249
90,000	708.04	164,894	354.02	118,748	46,146	354.02	113,869	51,005	354.02	112,748	52,146
95,000	747.37	174,053	373.69	125,347	48,706	373.69	120,218	53,835	373.69	119,013	55,040
100,000	786.71	183,216	393.36	131,945	51,271	393.36	126,546	56,670	393.36	125,278	57,938
105,000	826.04	192,374	413.02	138,538	53,836	413.02	132,869	59,505	413.02	131,537	60,837
110,000	865.38	201,537	432.69	145,136	56,401	432.69	139,197	62,340	432.69	137,802	63,735
115,000	904.71	210,696	452.36	151,735	58,961	452.36	145,526	65,170	452.36	144,067	66,629
120,000	944.05	219,858	472.03	158,333	61,525	472.03	151,854	68,004	472.03	150,332	69,526
125,000	983.38	229,017	491.69	164,926	64,091	491.69	158,177	70,840	491.69	156,591	72,426
130,000	1,022.72	238,179	511.36	171,524	66,655	511.36	164,506	73,673	511.36	162,856	75,323
135,000	1,062.05	247,338	531.03	178,122	69,216	531.03	170,834	76,504	531.03	169,121	78,217
140,000	1,101.39	256,500	550.70	184,721	71,779	550.70	177,162	79,338	550.70	175,386	81,114
145,000	1,140.72	265,659	570.36	191,313	74,346	570.36	183,485	82,174	570.36	181,646	84,013
150,000	1,180.06	274,822	590.03	197,912	76,910	590.03	189,814	85,008	590.03	187,911	86,911
155,000	1,219.39	283,980	609.70	204,510	79,470	609.70	196,142	87,838	609.70	194,176	89,804
160,000	1,258.73	293,143	629.37	211,109	82,034	629.37	202,471	90,672	629.37	200,441	92,702
165,000	1,298.06	302,302	649.03	217,701	84,601	649.03	208,793	93,509	649.03	206,700	95,602
170,000	1,337.40	311,464	668.70	224,300	87,164	668.70	215,122	96,342	668.70	212,965	98,499
175,000	1,376.73	320,623	688.37	230,898	89,725	688.37	221,450	99,173	688.37	219,230	101,393
180,000	1,416.07	329,785	708.04	237,496	92,289	708.04	227,779	102,006	708.04	225,495	104,290
185,000	1,455.40	338,944	727.70	244,089	94,855	727.70	234,101	104,843	727.70	231,755	107,189
190,000	1,494.74	348,106	747.37	250,687	97,419	747.37	240,430	107,676	747.37	238,020	110,086
195,000	1,534.07	357,265	767.04	257,286	99,979	767.04	246,758	110,507	767.04	244,285	112,980
200,000	1,573.41	366,428	786.71	263,884	102,544	786.71	253,087	113,341	786.71	250,550	115,878

9.00% BIWEEKLY MORTGAGES

AMOUNT OF LOAN	30 YEARS MONTHLY PAYMENT	30 YEARS TOTAL INTRST	360 DAY BASIS 583.881 PAYMENTS BWEEKLY PAYMENT	TOTAL INTRST	INTRST SAVED	364 DAY BASIS 569.826 PAYMENTS BWEEKLY PAYMENT	TOTAL INTRST	INTRST SAVED	365 DAY BASIS 566.529 PAYMENTS BWEEKLY PAYMENT	TOTAL INTRST	INTRST SAVED
$ 50	0.41	98	0.21	73	25	0.21	70	28	0.21	69	29
100	0.81	192	0.41	139	53	0.41	134	58	0.41	132	60
200	1.61	380	0.81	273	107	0.81	262	118	0.81	259	121
300	2.42	571	1.21	406	165	1.21	389	182	1.21	386	185
400	3.22	759	1.61	540	219	1.61	517	242	1.61	512	247
500	4.03	951	2.02	679	272	2.02	651	300	2.02	644	307
600	4.83	1,139	2.42	813	326	2.42	779	360	2.42	771	368
700	5.64	1,330	2.82	947	383	2.82	907	423	2.82	898	432
800	6.44	1,518	3.22	1,080	438	3.22	1,035	483	3.22	1,024	494
900	7.25	1,710	3.63	1,219	491	3.63	1,168	542	3.63	1,157	553
1,000	8.05	1,898	4.03	1,353	545	4.03	1,296	602	4.03	1,283	615
2,000	16.10	3,796	8.05	2,700	1,096	8.05	2,587	1,209	8.05	2,561	1,235
3,000	24.14	5,690	12.07	4,047	1,643	12.07	3,878	1,812	12.07	3,838	1,852
4,000	32.19	7,588	16.10	5,400	2,188	16.10	5,174	2,414	16.10	5,121	2,467
5,000	40.24	9,486	20.12	6,748	2,738	20.12	6,465	3,021	20.12	6,399	3,087
6,000	48.28	11,381	24.14	8,095	3,286	24.14	7,756	3,625	24.14	7,676	3,705
7,000	56.33	13,279	28.17	9,448	3,831	28.17	9,052	4,227	28.17	8,959	4,320
8,000	64.37	15,173	32.19	10,795	4,378	32.19	10,343	4,830	32.19	10,237	4,936
9,000	72.42	17,071	36.21	12,142	4,929	36.21	11,633	5,438	36.21	11,514	5,557
10,000	80.47	18,969	40.24	13,495	5,474	40.24	12,930	6,039	40.24	12,797	6,172
11,000	88.51	20,864	44.26	14,843	6,021	44.26	14,220	6,644	44.26	14,075	6,789
12,000	96.56	22,762	48.28	16,190	6,572	48.28	15,511	7,251	48.28	15,352	7,410
13,000	104.61	24,660	52.31	17,543	7,117	52.31	16,808	7,852	52.31	16,635	8,025
14,000	112.65	26,554	56.33	18,890	7,664	56.33	18,098	8,456	56.33	17,913	8,641
15,000	120.70	28,452	60.35	20,237	8,215	60.35	19,389	9,063	60.35	19,190	9,262
16,000	128.74	30,346	64.37	21,584	8,762	64.37	20,680	9,666	64.37	20,467	9,879
17,000	136.79	32,244	68.40	22,937	9,307	68.40	21,976	10,268	68.40	21,751	10,493
18,000	144.84	34,142	72.42	24,285	9,857	72.42	23,267	10,875	72.42	23,028	11,114
19,000	152.88	36,037	76.44	25,632	10,405	76.44	24,557	11,480	76.44	24,305	11,732
20,000	160.93	37,935	80.47	26,985	10,950	80.47	25,854	12,081	80.47	25,589	12,346
21,000	168.98	39,833	84.49	28,332	11,501	84.49	27,145	12,688	84.49	26,866	12,967
22,000	177.02	41,727	88.51	29,679	12,048	88.51	28,435	13,292	88.51	28,143	13,584
23,000	185.07	43,625	92.54	31,032	12,593	92.54	29,732	13,893	92.54	29,427	14,198
24,000	193.11	45,520	96.56	32,380	13,140	96.56	31,022	14,498	96.56	30,704	14,816
25,000	201.16	47,418	100.58	33,727	13,691	100.58	32,313	15,105	100.58	31,981	15,437
26,000	209.21	49,316	104.61	35,074	14,236	104.61	33,609	15,707	104.61	33,265	16,051
27,000	217.25	51,210	108.63	36,427	14,783	108.63	34,900	16,310	108.63	34,542	16,668
28,000	225.30	53,108	112.65	37,774	15,334	112.65	36,191	16,917	112.65	35,819	17,289
29,000	233.35	55,006	116.68	39,127	15,879	116.68	37,487	17,519	116.68	37,103	17,903
30,000	241.39	56,900	120.70	40,474	16,426	120.70	38,778	18,122	120.70	38,380	18,520
32,500	261.51	61,644	130.76	43,848	17,796	130.76	42,010	19,634	130.76	41,579	20,065
35,000	281.62	66,383	140.81	47,216	19,167	140.81	45,237	21,146	140.81	44,773	21,610
40,000	321.85	75,866	160.93	53,964	21,902	160.93	51,702	24,164	160.93	51,172	24,694
45,000	362.09	85,352	181.05	60,712	24,640	181.05	58,167	27,185	181.05	57,570	27,782
50,000	402.32	94,835	201.16	67,454	27,381	201.16	64,626	30,209	201.16	63,963	30,872
55,000	442.55	104,318	221.28	74,201	30,117	221.28	71,091	33,227	221.28	70,362	33,956
60,000	482.78	113,801	241.39	80,943	32,858	241.39	77,550	36,251	241.39	76,754	37,047
65,000	523.01	123,284	261.51	87,691	35,593	261.51	84,015	39,269	261.51	83,153	40,131
70,000	563.24	132,766	281.62	94,433	38,333	281.62	90,474	42,292	281.62	89,546	43,220
75,000	603.47	142,249	301.74	101,180	41,069	301.74	96,939	45,310	301.74	95,944	46,305
80,000	643.70	151,732	321.85	107,922	43,810	321.85	103,398	48,334	321.85	102,337	49,395
85,000	683.93	161,215	341.97	114,670	46,545	341.97	109,863	51,352	341.97	108,736	52,479
90,000	724.17	170,701	362.09	121,417	49,284	362.09	116,328	54,373	362.09	115,134	55,567
95,000	764.40	180,184	382.20	128,159	52,025	382.20	122,787	57,397	382.20	121,527	58,657
100,000	804.63	189,667	402.32	134,907	54,760	402.32	129,252	60,415	402.32	127,926	61,741
105,000	844.86	199,150	422.43	141,649	57,501	422.43	135,712	63,438	422.43	134,319	64,831
110,000	885.09	208,632	442.55	148,397	60,235	442.55	142,176	66,456	442.55	140,717	67,915
115,000	925.32	218,115	462.66	155,138	62,977	462.66	148,636	69,479	462.66	147,110	71,005
120,000	965.55	227,598	482.78	161,886	65,712	482.78	155,101	72,497	482.78	153,509	74,089
125,000	1,005.78	237,081	502.89	168,628	68,453	502.89	161,560	75,521	502.89	159,902	77,179
130,000	1,046.01	246,564	523.01	175,376	71,188	523.01	168,025	78,539	523.01	166,300	80,264
135,000	1,086.25	256,050	543.13	182,124	73,927	543.13	174,490	81,560	543.13	172,699	83,351
140,000	1,126.48	265,533	563.24	188,865	76,668	563.24	180,949	84,584	563.24	179,092	86,441
145,000	1,166.71	275,016	583.36	195,613	79,403	583.36	187,414	87,602	583.36	185,490	89,526
150,000	1,206.94	284,498	603.47	202,355	82,143	603.47	193,873	90,625	603.47	191,883	92,615
155,000	1,247.17	293,981	623.59	209,102	84,879	623.59	200,338	93,643	623.59	198,282	95,699
160,000	1,287.40	303,464	643.70	215,844	87,620	643.70	206,797	96,667	643.70	204,675	98,789
165,000	1,327.63	312,947	663.82	222,592	90,355	663.82	213,262	99,685	663.82	211,073	101,874
170,000	1,367.86	322,430	683.93	229,334	93,096	683.93	219,721	102,709	683.93	217,466	104,964
175,000	1,408.09	331,912	704.05	236,081	95,831	704.05	226,186	105,726	704.05	223,865	108,047
180,000	1,448.33	341,399	724.17	242,829	98,570	724.17	232,651	108,748	724.17	230,263	111,136
185,000	1,488.56	350,882	744.28	249,571	101,311	744.28	239,116	111,772	744.28	236,656	114,226
190,000	1,528.79	360,364	764.40	256,319	104,045	764.40	245,575	114,789	764.40	243,055	117,309
195,000	1,569.02	369,847	784.51	263,060	106,787	784.51	252,034	117,813	784.51	249,448	120,399
200,000	1,609.25	379,330	804.63	269,808	109,522	804.63	258,499	120,831	804.63	255,846	123,484

BIWEEKLY MORTGAGES 9.25%

AMOUNT OF LOAN	30 YEARS		360 DAY BASIS 578.036 PAYMENTS			364 DAY BASIS 563.668 PAYMENTS			365 DAY BASIS 560.304 PAYMENTS		
	MONTHLY PAYMENT	TOTAL INTRST	BWEEKLY PAYMENT	TOTAL INTRST	INTRST SAVED	BWEEKLY PAYMENT	TOTAL INTRST	INTRST SAVED	BWEEKLY PAYMENT	TOTAL INTRST	INTRST SAVED
$ 50	0.42	101	0.21	71	30	0.21	68	33	0.21	68	33
100	0.83	199	0.42	143	56	0.42	137	62	0.42	135	64
200	1.65	394	0.83	280	114	0.83	268	126	0.83	265	129
300	2.47	589	1.24	417	172	1.24	399	190	1.24	395	194
400	3.30	788	1.65	554	234	1.65	530	258	1.65	525	263
500	4.12	983	2.06	691	292	2.06	661	322	2.06	654	329
600	4.94	1,178	2.47	828	350	2.47	792	386	2.47	784	394
700	5.76	1,374	2.88	965	409	2.88	923	451	2.88	914	460
800	6.59	1,572	3.30	1,108	464	3.30	1,060	512	3.30	1,049	523
900	7.41	1,768	3.71	1,245	523	3.71	1,191	577	3.71	1,179	589
1,000	8.23	1,963	4.12	1,382	581	4.12	1,322	641	4.12	1,308	655
2,000	16.46	3,926	8.23	2,757	1,169	8.23	2,639	1,287	8.23	2,611	1,315
3,000	24.69	5,888	12.35	4,139	1,749	12.35	3,961	1,927	12.35	3,920	1,968
4,000	32.91	7,848	16.46	5,514	2,334	16.46	5,278	2,570	16.46	5,223	2,625
5,000	41.14	9,810	20.57	6,890	2,920	20.57	6,595	3,215	20.57	6,525	3,285
6,000	49.37	11,773	24.69	8,272	3,501	24.69	7,917	3,856	24.69	7,834	3,939
7,000	57.59	13,732	28.80	9,647	4,085	28.80	9,234	4,498	28.80	9,137	4,595
8,000	65.82	15,695	32.91	11,023	4,672	32.91	10,550	5,145	32.91	10,440	5,255
9,000	74.05	17,658	37.03	12,405	5,253	37.03	11,873	5,785	37.03	11,748	5,910
10,000	82.27	19,617	41.14	13,780	5,837	41.14	13,189	6,428	41.14	13,051	6,566
11,000	90.50	21,580	45.25	15,156	6,424	45.25	14,506	7,074	45.25	14,354	7,226
12,000	98.73	23,543	49.37	16,538	7,005	49.37	15,828	7,715	49.37	15,662	7,881
13,000	106.95	25,502	53.48	17,913	7,589	53.48	17,145	8,357	53.48	16,965	8,537
14,000	115.18	27,465	57.59	19,289	8,176	57.59	18,462	9,003	57.59	18,268	9,197
15,000	123.41	29,428	61.71	20,671	8,757	61.71	19,784	9,644	61.71	19,576	9,852
16,000	131.63	31,387	65.82	22,046	9,341	65.82	21,101	10,286	65.82	20,879	10,508
17,000	139.86	33,350	69.93	23,422	9,928	69.93	22,417	10,933	69.93	22,182	11,168
18,000	148.09	35,312	74.05	24,804	10,508	74.05	23,740	11,572	74.05	23,491	11,821
19,000	156.31	37,272	78.16	26,179	11,093	78.16	25,056	12,216	78.16	24,793	12,479
20,000	164.54	39,234	82.27	27,555	11,679	82.27	26,373	12,861	82.27	26,096	13,138
21,000	172.77	41,197	86.39	28,937	12,260	86.39	27,695	13,502	86.39	27,405	13,792
22,000	180.99	43,156	90.50	30,312	12,844	90.50	29,012	14,144	90.50	28,708	14,448
23,000	189.22	45,119	94.61	31,688	13,431	94.61	30,329	14,790	94.61	30,010	15,109
24,000	197.45	47,082	98.73	33,069	14,013	98.73	31,651	15,431	98.73	31,319	15,763
25,000	205.67	49,041	102.84	34,445	14,596	102.84	32,968	16,073	102.84	32,622	16,419
26,000	213.90	51,004	106.95	35,821	15,183	106.95	34,284	16,720	106.95	33,925	17,079
27,000	222.13	52,967	111.07	37,202	15,765	111.07	35,607	17,360	111.07	35,233	17,734
28,000	230.35	54,926	115.18	38,578	16,348	115.18	36,931	18,003	115.18	36,536	18,390
29,000	238.58	56,889	119.29	39,954	16,935	119.29	38,240	18,649	119.29	37,839	19,050
30,000	246.81	58,852	123.41	41,335	17,517	123.41	39,562	19,290	123.41	39,147	19,705
32,500	267.37	63,753	133.69	44,778	18,975	133.69	42,857	20,896	133.69	42,407	21,346
35,000	287.94	68,658	143.97	48,220	20,438	143.97	46,151	22,507	143.97	45,667	22,991
40,000	329.08	78,469	164.54	55,110	23,359	164.54	52,746	25,723	164.54	52,192	26,277
45,000	370.21	88,276	185.11	62,000	26,276	185.11	59,341	28,935	185.11	58,718	29,558
50,000	411.34	98,082	205.67	68,885	29,197	205.67	65,930	32,152	205.67	65,238	32,844
55,000	452.48	107,893	226.24	75,777	32,118	226.24	72,524	35,369	226.24	71,763	36,130
60,000	493.61	117,700	246.81	82,665	35,035	246.81	79,119	38,581	246.81	78,289	39,411
65,000	534.74	127,506	267.37	89,549	37,957	267.37	85,708	41,798	267.37	84,808	42,698
70,000	575.88	137,317	287.94	96,440	40,877	287.94	92,303	45,014	287.94	91,334	45,983
75,000	617.01	147,124	308.51	103,330	43,794	308.51	98,897	48,227	308.51	97,859	49,265
80,000	658.15	156,934	329.08	110,220	46,714	329.08	105,492	51,442	329.08	104,385	52,549
85,000	699.28	166,741	349.64	117,105	49,636	349.64	112,081	54,660	349.64	110,905	55,836
90,000	740.41	176,548	370.21	123,995	52,553	370.21	118,676	57,872	370.21	117,430	59,118
95,000	781.55	186,358	390.78	130,885	55,473	390.78	125,270	61,088	390.78	123,956	62,402
100,000	822.68	196,165	411.34	137,769	58,396	411.34	131,859	64,306	411.34	130,475	65,690
105,000	863.81	205,972	431.91	144,660	61,312	431.91	138,454	67,518	431.91	137,001	68,971
110,000	904.95	215,782	452.48	151,550	64,232	452.48	145,048	70,734	452.48	143,526	72,256
115,000	946.08	225,589	473.04	158,434	67,155	473.04	151,638	73,951	473.04	150,046	75,543
120,000	987.22	235,399	493.61	165,324	70,075	493.61	158,232	77,167	493.61	156,572	78,827
125,000	1,028.35	245,206	514.18	172,215	72,991	514.18	164,827	80,379	514.18	163,097	82,109
130,000	1,069.48	255,013	534.74	179,099	75,914	534.74	171,416	83,597	534.74	169,617	85,396
135,000	1,110.62	264,823	555.31	185,989	78,834	555.31	178,010	86,813	555.31	176,142	88,681
140,000	1,151.75	274,630	575.88	192,879	81,751	575.88	184,605	90,025	575.88	182,668	91,962
145,000	1,192.88	284,437	596.44	199,764	84,673	596.44	191,194	93,243	596.44	189,188	95,249
150,000	1,234.02	294,247	617.01	206,654	87,593	617.01	197,789	96,458	617.01	195,713	98,534
155,000	1,275.15	304,054	637.58	213,544	90,510	637.58	204,383	99,671	637.58	202,239	101,815
160,000	1,316.29	313,864	658.15	220,434	93,430	658.15	210,978	102,886	658.15	208,764	105,100
165,000	1,357.42	323,671	678.71	227,319	96,352	678.71	217,567	106,104	678.71	215,284	108,387
170,000	1,398.55	333,478	699.28	234,209	99,269	699.28	224,162	109,316	699.28	221,809	111,669
175,000	1,439.69	343,288	719.85	241,099	102,189	719.85	230,756	112,532	719.85	228,335	114,953
180,000	1,480.82	353,095	740.41	247,984	105,111	740.41	237,345	115,750	740.41	234,855	118,240
185,000	1,521.95	362,902	760.98	254,874	108,028	760.98	243,940	118,962	760.98	241,380	121,522
190,000	1,563.09	372,712	781.55	261,764	110,948	781.55	250,535	122,177	781.55	247,906	124,806
195,000	1,604.22	382,519	802.11	268,648	113,871	802.11	257,124	125,395	802.11	254,425	128,094
200,000	1,645.36	392,330	822.68	275,539	116,791	822.68	263,718	128,612	822.68	260,951	131,379

61

9.50% BIWEEKLY MORTGAGES

AMOUNT OF LOAN	30 YEARS		360 DAY BASIS 572.124 PAYMENTS			364 DAY BASIS 557.462 PAYMENTS			365 DAY BASIS 554.035 PAYMENTS		
	MONTHLY PAYMENT	TOTAL INTRST	BWEEKLY PAYMENT	TOTAL INTRST	INTRST SAVED	BWEEKLY PAYMENT	TOTAL INTRST	INTRST SAVED	BWEEKLY PAYMENT	TOTAL INTRST	INTRST SAVED
$ 50	0.43	105	0.22	76	29	0.22	73	32	0.22	72	33
100	0.85	206	0.43	146	60	0.43	140	66	0.43	138	68
200	1.69	408	0.85	286	122	0.85	274	134	0.85	271	137
300	2.53	611	1.27	427	184	1.27	408	203	1.27	404	207
400	3.37	813	1.69	567	246	1.69	542	271	1.69	536	277
500	4.21	1,016	2.11	707	309	2.11	676	340	2.11	669	347
600	5.05	1,218	2.53	847	371	2.53	810	408	2.53	802	416
700	5.89	1,420	2.95	988	432	2.95	945	475	2.95	934	486
800	6.73	1,623	3.37	1,128	495	3.37	1,079	544	3.37	1,067	556
900	7.57	1,825	3.79	1,268	557	3.79	1,213	612	3.79	1,200	625
1,000	8.41	2,028	4.21	1,409	619	4.21	1,347	681	4.21	1,332	696
2,000	16.82	4,055	8.41	2,812	1,243	8.41	2,688	1,367	8.41	2,659	1,396
3,000	25.23	6,083	12.62	4,220	1,863	12.62	4,035	2,048	12.62	3,992	2,091
4,000	33.64	8,110	16.82	5,623	2,487	16.82	5,377	2,733	16.82	5,319	2,791
5,000	42.05	10,138	21.03	7,032	3,106	21.03	6,723	3,415	21.03	6,651	3,487
6,000	50.46	12,166	25.23	8,435	3,731	25.23	8,065	4,101	25.23	7,978	4,188
7,000	58.86	14,190	29.43	9,838	4,352	29.43	9,406	4,784	29.43	9,305	4,885
8,000	67.27	16,217	33.64	11,246	4,971	33.64	10,753	5,464	33.64	10,638	5,579
9,000	75.68	18,245	37.84	12,649	5,596	37.84	12,094	6,151	37.84	11,965	6,280
10,000	84.09	20,272	42.05	14,058	6,214	42.05	13,441	6,831	42.05	13,297	6,975
11,000	92.50	22,300	46.25	15,461	6,839	46.25	14,783	7,517	46.25	14,624	7,676
12,000	100.91	24,328	50.46	16,869	7,459	50.46	16,130	8,198	50.46	15,957	8,371
13,000	109.32	26,355	54.66	18,272	8,083	54.66	17,471	8,884	54.66	17,284	9,071
14,000	117.72	28,379	58.86	19,675	8,704	58.86	18,812	9,567	58.86	18,611	9,768
15,000	126.13	30,407	63.07	21,084	9,323	63.07	20,159	10,248	63.07	19,943	10,464
16,000	134.54	32,434	67.27	22,487	9,947	67.27	21,500	10,934	67.27	21,270	11,164
17,000	142.95	34,462	71.48	23,895	10,567	71.48	22,847	11,615	71.48	22,602	11,860
18,000	151.36	36,490	75.68	25,298	11,192	75.68	24,189	12,301	75.68	23,929	12,561
19,000	159.77	38,517	79.89	26,707	11,810	79.89	25,536	12,981	79.89	25,262	13,255
20,000	168.18	40,545	84.09	28,110	12,435	84.09	26,877	13,668	84.09	26,589	13,956
21,000	176.58	42,569	88.29	29,513	13,056	88.29	28,218	14,351	88.29	27,916	14,653
22,000	184.99	44,596	92.50	30,921	13,675	92.50	29,565	15,031	92.50	29,248	15,348
23,000	193.40	46,624	96.70	32,324	14,300	96.70	30,907	15,717	96.70	30,575	16,049
24,000	201.81	48,652	100.91	33,733	14,919	100.91	32,253	16,399	100.91	31,908	16,744
25,000	210.22	50,679	105.11	35,136	15,543	105.11	33,595	17,084	105.11	33,235	17,444
26,000	218.63	52,707	109.32	36,545	16,162	109.32	34,942	17,765	109.32	34,567	18,140
27,000	227.04	54,734	113.52	37,948	16,786	113.52	36,283	18,451	113.52	35,894	18,840
28,000	235.44	56,758	117.72	39,350	17,408	117.72	37,624	19,134	117.72	37,221	19,537
29,000	243.85	58,786	121.93	40,759	18,027	121.93	38,971	19,815	121.93	38,553	20,233
30,000	252.26	60,814	126.13	42,162	18,652	126.13	40,313	20,501	126.13	39,880	20,934
32,500	273.28	65,881	136.64	45,675	20,206	136.64	43,672	22,209	136.64	43,203	22,678
35,000	294.30	70,948	147.15	49,188	21,760	147.15	47,031	23,917	147.15	46,526	24,422
40,000	336.35	81,086	168.18	56,220	24,866	168.18	53,754	27,332	168.18	53,178	27,908
45,000	378.39	91,220	189.20	63,246	27,974	189.20	60,472	30,748	189.20	59,823	31,397
50,000	420.43	101,355	210.22	70,272	31,083	210.22	67,190	34,165	210.22	66,469	34,886
55,000	462.47	111,489	231.24	77,298	34,191	231.24	73,908	37,581	231.24	73,115	38,374
60,000	504.52	121,627	252.26	84,324	37,303	252.26	80,625	41,002	252.26	79,761	41,866
65,000	546.56	131,762	273.28	91,350	40,412	273.28	87,343	44,419	273.28	86,407	45,355
70,000	588.60	141,896	294.30	98,376	43,520	294.30	94,061	47,835	294.30	93,053	48,843
75,000	630.65	152,034	315.33	105,408	46,626	315.33	100,784	51,250	315.33	99,704	52,330
80,000	672.69	162,168	336.35	112,434	49,734	336.35	107,502	54,666	336.35	106,350	55,818
85,000	714.73	172,303	357.37	119,460	52,843	357.37	114,220	58,083	357.37	112,995	59,308
90,000	756.77	182,437	378.39	126,486	55,951	378.39	120,938	61,499	378.39	119,641	62,796
95,000	798.82	192,575	399.41	133,512	59,063	399.41	127,656	64,919	399.41	126,287	66,288
100,000	840.86	202,710	420.43	140,538	62,172	420.43	134,374	68,336	420.43	132,933	69,777
105,000	882.90	212,844	441.45	147,564	65,280	441.45	141,092	71,752	441.45	139,579	73,265
110,000	924.94	222,978	462.47	154,590	68,388	462.47	147,809	75,169	462.47	146,225	76,753
115,000	966.99	233,116	483.50	161,622	71,494	483.50	154,533	78,583	483.50	152,876	80,240
120,000	1,009.03	243,251	504.52	168,648	74,603	504.52	161,251	82,000	504.52	159,522	83,729
125,000	1,051.07	253,385	525.54	175,674	77,711	525.54	167,969	85,416	525.54	166,168	87,217
130,000	1,093.12	263,523	546.56	182,700	80,823	546.56	174,686	88,837	546.56	172,813	90,710
135,000	1,135.16	273,658	567.58	189,726	83,932	567.58	181,404	92,254	567.58	179,459	94,199
140,000	1,177.20	283,792	588.60	196,752	87,040	588.60	188,122	95,670	588.60	186,105	97,687
145,000	1,219.24	293,926	609.62	203,778	90,148	609.62	194,840	99,086	609.62	192,751	101,175
150,000	1,261.29	304,064	630.65	210,810	93,254	630.65	201,563	102,501	630.65	199,402	104,662
155,000	1,303.33	314,199	651.67	217,836	96,363	651.67	208,281	105,918	651.67	206,048	108,151
160,000	1,345.37	324,333	672.69	224,862	99,471	672.69	214,999	109,334	672.69	212,694	111,639
165,000	1,387.41	334,468	693.71	231,888	102,580	693.71	221,717	112,751	693.71	219,340	115,128
170,000	1,429.46	344,606	714.73	238,914	105,692	714.73	228,435	116,171	714.73	225,985	118,621
175,000	1,471.50	354,740	735.75	245,940	108,800	735.75	235,153	119,587	735.75	232,631	122,109
180,000	1,513.54	364,874	756.77	252,966	111,908	756.77	241,871	123,003	756.77	239,277	125,597
185,000	1,555.59	375,012	777.80	259,998	115,014	777.80	248,594	126,418	777.80	245,928	129,084
190,000	1,597.63	385,147	798.82	267,024	118,123	798.82	255,312	129,835	798.82	252,574	132,573
195,000	1,639.67	395,281	819.84	274,050	121,231	819.84	262,030	133,251	819.84	259,220	136,061
200,000	1,681.71	405,416	840.86	281,076	124,340	840.86	268,747	136,669	840.86	265,866	139,550

BIWEEKLY MORTGAGES 9.75%

AMOUNT OF LOAN	30 YEARS MONTHLY PAYMENT	TOTAL INTRST	360 DAY BASIS 566.153 PAYMENTS BWEEKLY PAYMENT	TOTAL INTRST	INTRST SAVED	364 DAY BASIS 551.214 PAYMENTS BWEEKLY PAYMENT	TOTAL INTRST	INTRST SAVED	365 DAY BASIS 547.729 PAYMENTS BWEEKLY PAYMENT	TOTAL INTRST	INTRST SAVED
$ 50	0.43	105	0.22	75	30	0.22	71	34	0.22	71	34
100	0.86	210	0.43	143	67	0.43	137	73	0.43	136	74
200	1.72	419	0.86	287	132	0.86	274	145	0.86	271	148
300	2.58	629	1.29	430	199	1.29	411	218	1.29	407	222
400	3.44	838	1.72	574	264	1.72	548	290	1.72	542	296
500	4.30	1,048	2.15	717	331	2.15	685	363	2.15	678	370
600	5.16	1,258	2.58	861	397	2.58	822	436	2.58	813	445
700	6.02	1,467	3.01	1,004	463	3.01	959	508	3.01	949	518
800	6.88	1,677	3.44	1,148	529	3.44	1,096	581	3.44	1,084	593
900	7.74	1,886	3.87	1,291	595	3.87	1,233	653	3.87	1,220	666
1,000	8.60	2,096	4.30	1,434	662	4.30	1,370	726	4.30	1,355	741
2,000	17.19	4,188	8.60	2,869	1,319	8.60	2,740	1,448	8.60	2,710	1,478
3,000	25.78	6,281	12.89	4,298	1,983	12.89	4,105	2,176	12.89	4,060	2,221
4,000	34.37	8,373	17.19	5,732	2,641	17.19	5,475	2,898	17.19	5,415	2,958
5,000	42.96	10,466	21.48	7,161	3,305	21.48	6,840	3,626	21.48	6,765	3,701
6,000	51.55	12,558	25.78	8,595	3,963	25.78	8,210	4,348	25.78	8,120	4,438
7,000	60.15	14,654	30.08	10,030	4,624	30.08	9,581	5,073	30.08	9,476	5,178
8,000	68.74	16,746	34.37	11,459	5,287	34.37	10,945	5,801	34.37	10,825	5,921
9,000	77.33	18,839	38.67	12,893	5,946	38.67	12,315	6,524	38.67	12,181	6,658
10,000	85.92	20,931	42.96	14,322	6,609	42.96	13,680	7,251	42.96	13,530	7,401
11,000	94.51	23,024	47.26	15,756	7,268	47.26	15,050	7,974	47.26	14,886	8,138
12,000	103.10	25,116	51.55	17,185	7,931	51.55	16,415	8,701	51.55	16,235	8,881
13,000	111.70	27,212	55.85	18,620	8,592	55.85	17,785	9,427	55.85	17,591	9,621
14,000	120.29	29,304	60.15	20,054	9,250	60.15	19,156	10,148	60.15	18,946	10,358
15,000	128.88	31,397	64.44	21,483	9,914	64.44	20,520	10,877	64.44	20,296	11,101
16,000	137.47	33,489	68.74	22,917	10,572	68.74	21,890	11,599	68.74	21,651	11,838
17,000	146.06	35,582	73.03	24,346	11,236	73.03	23,255	12,327	73.03	23,001	12,581
18,000	154.65	37,674	77.33	25,781	11,893	77.33	24,625	13,049	77.33	24,356	13,318
19,000	163.24	39,766	81.62	27,209	12,557	81.62	25,990	13,776	81.62	25,706	14,060
20,000	171.84	41,862	85.92	28,644	13,218	85.92	27,360	14,502	85.92	27,061	14,801
21,000	180.43	43,955	90.22	30,078	13,877	90.22	28,731	15,224	90.22	28,416	15,539
22,000	189.02	46,047	94.51	31,507	14,540	94.51	30,095	15,952	94.51	29,766	16,281
23,000	197.61	48,140	98.81	32,942	15,198	98.81	31,465	16,675	98.81	31,121	17,019
24,000	206.20	50,232	103.10	34,370	15,862	103.10	32,830	17,402	103.10	32,471	17,761
25,000	214.79	52,324	107.40	35,805	16,519	107.40	34,200	18,124	107.40	33,826	18,498
26,000	223.39	54,420	111.70	37,239	17,181	111.70	35,571	18,849	111.70	35,181	19,239
27,000	231.98	56,513	115.99	38,668	17,845	115.99	36,935	19,578	115.99	36,531	19,982
28,000	240.57	58,605	120.29	40,103	18,502	120.29	38,306	20,299	120.29	37,886	20,719
29,000	249.16	60,698	124.58	41,531	19,167	124.58	39,670	21,028	124.58	39,236	21,462
30,000	257.75	62,790	128.88	42,966	19,824	128.88	41,040	21,750	128.88	40,591	22,199
32,500	279.23	68,023	139.62	46,546	21,477	139.62	44,460	23,563	139.62	43,974	24,049
35,000	300.71	73,256	150.36	50,127	23,129	150.36	47,881	25,375	150.36	47,357	25,899
40,000	343.67	83,721	171.84	57,288	26,433	171.84	54,721	29,000	171.84	54,122	29,599
45,000	386.62	94,183	193.31	64,443	29,740	193.31	61,555	32,628	193.31	60,881	33,302
50,000	429.58	104,649	214.79	71,604	33,045	214.79	68,395	36,254	214.79	67,647	37,002
55,000	472.54	115,114	236.27	78,765	36,349	236.27	75,235	39,879	236.27	74,412	40,702
60,000	515.50	125,580	257.75	85,926	39,654	257.75	82,075	43,505	257.75	81,177	44,403
65,000	558.46	136,046	279.23	93,087	42,959	279.23	88,915	47,131	279.23	87,942	48,104
70,000	601.41	146,508	300.71	100,248	46,260	300.71	95,756	50,752	300.71	94,708	51,800
75,000	644.37	156,973	322.19	107,409	49,564	322.19	102,596	54,377	322.19	101,473	55,500
80,000	687.33	167,439	343.67	114,570	52,869	343.67	109,436	58,003	343.67	108,238	59,201
85,000	730.29	177,904	365.15	121,731	56,173	365.15	116,276	61,628	365.15	115,003	62,901
90,000	773.24	188,366	386.62	128,886	59,480	386.62	123,110	65,256	386.62	121,763	66,603
95,000	816.20	198,832	408.10	136,047	62,785	408.10	129,950	68,882	408.10	128,528	70,304
100,000	859.16	209,298	429.58	143,208	66,090	429.58	136,791	72,507	429.58	135,293	74,005
105,000	902.12	219,763	451.06	150,369	69,394	451.06	143,631	76,132	451.06	142,059	77,704
110,000	945.07	230,225	472.54	157,530	72,695	472.54	150,471	79,754	472.54	148,824	81,401
115,000	988.03	240,691	494.02	164,691	76,000	494.02	157,311	83,380	494.02	155,589	85,102
120,000	1,030.99	251,156	515.50	171,852	79,304	515.50	164,151	87,005	515.50	162,354	88,802
125,000	1,073.95	261,622	536.98	179,013	82,609	536.98	170,991	90,631	536.98	169,120	92,502
130,000	1,116.91	272,088	558.46	186,174	85,914	558.46	177,831	94,257	558.46	175,885	96,203
135,000	1,159.86	282,550	579.93	193,329	89,221	579.93	184,666	97,884	579.93	182,644	99,906
140,000	1,202.82	293,015	601.41	200,490	92,525	601.41	191,506	101,509	601.41	189,410	103,605
145,000	1,245.78	303,481	622.89	207,651	95,830	622.89	198,346	105,135	622.89	196,175	107,306
150,000	1,288.74	313,946	644.37	214,812	99,134	644.37	205,186	108,760	644.37	202,940	111,006
155,000	1,331.69	324,408	665.85	221,973	102,435	665.85	212,026	112,382	665.85	209,705	114,703
160,000	1,374.65	334,874	687.33	229,134	105,740	687.33	218,866	116,008	687.33	216,471	118,403
165,000	1,417.61	345,340	708.81	236,295	109,045	708.81	225,706	119,634	708.81	223,236	122,104
170,000	1,460.57	355,805	730.29	243,456	112,349	730.29	232,546	123,259	730.29	230,001	125,804
175,000	1,503.53	366,271	751.77	250,617	115,654	751.77	239,386	126,885	751.77	236,766	129,505
180,000	1,546.48	376,733	773.24	257,772	118,961	773.24	246,221	130,512	773.24	243,526	133,207
185,000	1,589.44	387,198	794.72	264,933	122,265	794.72	253,061	134,137	794.72	250,291	136,907
190,000	1,632.40	397,664	816.20	272,094	125,570	816.20	259,901	137,763	816.20	257,056	140,608
195,000	1,675.36	408,130	837.68	279,255	128,875	837.68	266,741	141,389	837.68	263,822	144,308
200,000	1,718.31	418,592	859.16	286,416	132,176	859.16	273,581	145,011	859.16	270,587	148,005

63

10.00% BIWEEKLY MORTGAGES

AMOUNT OF LOAN	30 YEARS		360 DAY BASIS 560.129 PAYMENTS			364 DAY BASIS 544.933 PAYMENTS			365 DAY BASIS 541.395 PAYMENTS		
	MONTHLY PAYMENT	TOTAL INTRST	BWEEKLY PAYMENT	TOTAL INTRST	INTRST SAVED	BWEEKLY PAYMENT	TOTAL INTRST	INTRST SAVED	BWEEKLY PAYMENT	TOTAL INTRST	INTRST SAVED
$ 50	0.44	108	0.22	73	35	0.22	70	38	0.22	69	39
100	0.88	217	0.44	146	71	0.44	140	77	0.44	138	79
200	1.76	434	0.88	293	141	0.88	280	154	0.88	276	158
300	2.64	650	1.32	439	211	1.32	419	231	1.32	415	235
400	3.52	867	1.76	586	281	1.76	559	308	1.76	553	314
500	4.39	1,080	2.20	732	348	2.20	699	381	2.20	691	389
600	5.27	1,297	2.64	879	418	2.64	839	458	2.64	829	468
700	6.15	1,514	3.08	1,025	489	3.08	978	536	3.08	967	547
800	7.03	1,731	3.52	1,172	559	3.52	1,118	613	3.52	1,106	625
900	7.90	1,944	3.95	1,313	631	3.95	1,252	692	3.95	1,239	705
1,000	8.78	2,161	4.39	1,459	702	4.39	1,392	769	4.39	1,377	784
2,000	17.56	4,322	8.78	2,918	1,404	8.78	2,785	1,537	8.78	2,753	1,569
3,000	26.33	6,479	13.17	4,377	2,102	13.17	4,177	2,302	13.17	4,130	2,349
4,000	35.11	8,640	17.56	5,836	2,804	17.56	5,569	3,071	17.56	5,507	3,133
5,000	43.88	10,797	21.94	7,289	3,508	21.94	6,956	3,841	21.94	6,878	3,919
6,000	52.66	12,958	26.33	8,748	4,210	26.33	8,348	4,610	26.33	8,255	4,703
7,000	61.44	15,118	30.72	10,207	4,911	30.72	9,740	5,378	30.72	9,632	5,486
8,000	70.21	17,276	35.11	11,666	5,610	35.11	11,133	6,143	35.11	11,008	6,268
9,000	78.99	19,436	39.50	13,125	6,311	39.50	12,525	6,911	39.50	12,385	7,051
10,000	87.76	21,594	43.88	14,578	7,016	43.88	13,912	7,682	43.88	13,756	7,838
11,000	96.54	23,754	48.27	16,037	7,717	48.27	15,304	8,450	48.27	15,133	8,621
12,000	105.31	25,912	52.66	17,496	8,416	52.66	16,696	9,216	52.66	16,510	9,402
13,000	114.09	28,072	57.05	18,955	9,117	57.05	18,088	9,984	57.05	17,887	10,185
14,000	122.87	30,233	61.44	20,414	9,819	61.44	19,481	10,752	61.44	19,263	10,970
15,000	131.64	32,390	65.82	21,868	10,522	65.82	20,867	11,523	65.82	20,635	11,755
16,000	140.42	34,551	70.21	23,327	11,224	70.21	22,260	12,291	70.21	22,011	12,540
17,000	149.19	36,708	74.60	24,786	11,922	74.60	23,652	13,056	74.60	23,388	13,320
18,000	157.97	38,869	78.99	26,245	12,624	78.99	25,044	13,825	78.99	24,765	14,104
19,000	166.74	41,026	83.37	27,698	13,328	83.37	26,431	14,595	83.37	26,136	14,890
20,000	175.52	43,187	87.76	29,157	14,030	87.76	27,823	15,364	87.76	27,513	15,674
21,000	184.30	45,348	92.15	30,616	14,732	92.15	29,216	16,132	92.15	28,890	16,458
22,000	193.07	47,505	96.54	32,075	15,430	96.54	30,608	16,897	96.54	30,266	17,239
23,000	201.85	49,666	100.93	33,534	16,132	100.93	32,000	17,666	100.93	31,643	18,023
24,000	210.62	51,823	105.31	34,987	16,836	105.31	33,387	18,436	105.31	33,014	18,809
25,000	219.40	53,984	109.70	36,446	17,538	109.70	34,779	19,205	109.70	34,391	19,593
26,000	228.17	56,141	114.09	37,905	18,236	114.09	36,171	19,970	114.09	35,768	20,373
27,000	236.95	58,302	118.48	39,364	18,938	118.48	37,564	20,738	118.48	37,144	21,158
28,000	245.73	60,463	122.87	40,823	19,640	122.87	38,956	21,507	122.87	38,521	21,942
29,000	254.50	62,620	127.25	42,276	20,344	127.25	40,343	22,277	127.25	39,893	22,727
30,000	263.28	64,781	131.64	43,735	21,046	131.64	41,735	23,046	131.64	41,269	23,512
32,500	285.22	70,179	142.61	47,380	22,799	142.61	45,213	24,966	142.61	44,708	25,471
35,000	307.16	75,578	153.58	51,025	24,553	153.58	48,691	26,887	153.58	48,147	27,431
40,000	351.03	86,371	175.52	58,314	28,057	175.52	55,647	30,724	175.52	55,026	31,345
45,000	394.91	97,168	197.46	65,603	31,565	197.46	62,602	34,566	197.46	61,904	35,264
50,000	438.79	107,964	219.40	72,892	35,072	219.40	69,558	38,406	219.40	68,782	39,182
55,000	482.67	118,761	241.34	80,182	38,579	241.34	76,514	42,247	241.34	75,660	43,101
60,000	526.55	129,558	263.28	87,471	42,087	263.28	83,470	46,088	263.28	82,538	47,020
65,000	570.43	140,355	285.22	94,760	45,595	285.22	90,426	49,929	285.22	89,417	50,938
70,000	614.31	151,152	307.16	102,049	49,103	307.16	97,382	53,770	307.16	96,295	54,857
75,000	658.18	161,945	329.09	109,333	52,612	329.09	104,332	57,613	329.09	103,168	58,777
80,000	702.06	172,742	351.03	116,622	56,120	351.03	111,288	61,454	351.03	110,046	62,696
85,000	745.94	183,538	372.97	123,911	59,627	372.97	118,244	65,294	372.97	116,924	66,614
90,000	789.82	194,335	394.91	131,201	63,134	394.91	125,199	69,136	394.91	123,802	70,533
95,000	833.70	205,132	416.85	138,490	66,642	416.85	132,155	72,977	416.85	130,681	74,451
100,000	877.58	215,929	438.79	145,779	70,150	438.79	139,111	76,818	438.79	137,559	78,370
105,000	921.46	226,726	460.73	153,068	73,658	460.73	146,067	80,659	460.73	144,437	82,289
110,000	965.33	237,519	482.67	160,357	77,162	482.67	153,023	84,496	482.67	151,315	86,204
115,000	1,009.21	248,316	504.61	167,647	80,669	504.61	159,979	88,337	504.61	158,193	90,123
120,000	1,053.09	259,112	526.55	174,936	84,176	526.55	166,934	92,178	526.55	165,072	94,040
125,000	1,096.97	269,909	548.49	182,225	87,684	548.49	173,890	96,019	548.49	171,950	97,959
130,000	1,140.85	280,706	570.43	189,514	91,192	570.43	180,846	99,860	570.43	178,828	101,878
135,000	1,184.73	291,503	592.37	196,804	94,699	592.37	187,802	103,701	592.37	185,706	105,797
140,000	1,228.61	302,300	614.31	204,093	98,207	614.31	194,758	107,542	614.31	192,584	109,716
145,000	1,272.48	313,093	636.24	211,376	101,717	636.24	201,708	111,385	636.24	199,457	113,636
150,000	1,316.36	323,890	658.18	218,666	105,224	658.18	208,664	115,226	658.18	206,335	117,555
155,000	1,360.24	334,686	680.12	225,955	108,731	680.12	215,620	119,066	680.12	213,214	121,472
160,000	1,404.12	345,483	702.06	233,244	112,239	702.06	222,576	122,907	702.06	220,092	125,391
165,000	1,448.00	356,280	724.00	240,533	115,747	724.00	229,531	126,749	724.00	226,970	129,310
170,000	1,491.88	367,077	745.94	247,823	119,254	745.94	236,487	130,590	745.94	233,848	133,229
175,000	1,535.76	377,874	767.88	255,112	122,762	767.88	243,443	134,431	767.88	240,726	137,148
180,000	1,579.63	388,667	789.82	262,401	126,266	789.82	250,399	138,268	789.82	247,605	141,062
185,000	1,623.51	399,464	811.76	269,690	129,774	811.76	257,355	142,109	811.76	254,483	144,981
190,000	1,667.39	410,260	833.70	276,980	133,280	833.70	264,311	145,949	833.70	261,361	148,899
195,000	1,711.27	421,057	855.64	284,269	136,788	855.64	271,266	149,791	855.64	268,239	152,818
200,000	1,755.15	431,854	877.58	291,558	140,296	877.58	278,222	153,632	877.58	275,117	156,737

AMOUNT OF LOAN	30 YEARS		360 DAY BASIS 554.060 PAYMENTS			364 DAY BASIS 538.629 PAYMENTS			365 DAY BASIS 535.041 PAYMENTS		
	MONTHLY PAYMENT	TOTAL INTRST	BWEEKLY PAYMENT	TOTAL INTRST	INTRST SAVED	BWEEKLY PAYMENT	TOTAL INTRST	INTRST SAVED	BWEEKLY PAYMENT	TOTAL INTRST	INTRST SAVED
$ 50	0.45	112	0.23	77	35	0.23	74	38	0.23	73	39
100	0.90	224	0.45	149	75	0.45	142	82	0.45	141	83
200	1.80	448	0.90	299	149	0.90	285	163	0.90	282	166
300	2.69	668	1.35	448	220	1.35	427	241	1.35	422	246
400	3.59	892	1.80	597	295	1.80	570	322	1.80	563	329
500	4.49	1,116	2.25	747	369	2.25	712	404	2.25	704	412
600	5.38	1,337	2.69	890	447	2.69	849	488	2.69	839	498
700	6.28	1,561	3.14	1,040	521	3.14	991	570	3.14	980	581
800	7.17	1,781	3.59	1,189	592	3.59	1,134	647	3.59	1,121	660
900	8.07	2,005	4.04	1,338	667	4.04	1,276	729	4.04	1,262	743
1,000	8.97	2,229	4.49	1,488	741	4.49	1,418	811	4.49	1,402	827
2,000	17.93	4,455	8.97	2,970	1,485	8.97	2,832	1,623	8.97	2,799	1,656
3,000	26.89	6,680	13.45	4,452	2,228	13.45	4,245	2,435	13.45	4,196	2,484
4,000	35.85	8,906	17.93	5,934	2,972	17.93	5,658	3,248	17.93	5,593	3,313
5,000	44.81	11,132	22.41	7,416	3,716	22.41	7,071	4,061	22.41	6,990	4,142
6,000	53.77	13,357	26.89	8,899	4,458	26.89	8,484	4,873	26.89	8,387	4,970
7,000	62.73	15,583	31.37	10,381	5,202	31.37	9,897	5,686	31.37	9,784	5,799
8,000	71.69	17,808	35.85	11,863	5,945	35.85	11,310	6,498	35.85	11,181	6,627
9,000	80.65	20,034	40.33	13,345	6,689	40.33	12,723	7,311	40.33	12,578	7,456
10,000	89.62	22,263	44.81	14,827	7,436	44.81	14,136	8,127	44.81	13,975	8,288
11,000	98.58	24,489	49.29	16,310	8,179	49.29	15,549	8,940	49.29	15,372	9,117
12,000	107.54	26,714	53.77	17,792	8,922	53.77	16,962	9,752	53.77	16,769	9,945
13,000	116.50	28,940	58.25	19,274	9,666	58.25	18,375	10,565	58.25	18,166	10,774
14,000	125.46	31,166	62.73	20,756	10,410	62.73	19,788	11,378	62.73	19,563	11,603
15,000	134.42	33,391	67.21	22,238	11,153	67.21	21,201	12,190	67.21	20,960	12,431
16,000	143.38	35,617	71.69	23,721	11,896	71.69	22,614	13,003	71.69	22,357	13,260
17,000	152.34	37,842	76.17	25,203	12,639	76.17	24,027	13,815	76.17	23,754	14,088
18,000	161.30	40,068	80.65	26,685	13,383	80.65	25,440	14,628	80.65	25,151	14,917
19,000	170.26	42,294	85.13	28,167	14,127	85.13	26,853	15,441	85.13	26,548	15,746
20,000	179.23	44,523	89.62	29,655	14,868	89.62	28,272	16,251	89.62	27,950	16,573
21,000	188.19	46,748	94.10	31,137	15,611	94.10	29,685	17,063	94.10	29,347	17,401
22,000	197.15	48,974	98.58	32,619	16,355	98.58	31,098	17,876	98.58	30,744	18,230
23,000	206.11	51,200	103.06	34,101	17,099	103.06	32,511	18,689	103.06	32,141	19,059
24,000	215.07	53,425	107.54	35,584	17,841	107.54	33,924	19,501	107.54	33,538	19,887
25,000	224.03	55,651	112.02	37,066	18,585	112.02	35,337	20,314	112.02	34,935	20,716
26,000	232.99	57,876	116.50	38,548	19,328	116.50	36,750	21,126	116.50	36,332	21,544
27,000	241.95	60,102	120.98	40,030	20,072	120.98	38,163	21,939	120.98	37,729	22,373
28,000	250.91	62,328	125.46	41,512	20,816	125.46	39,576	22,752	125.46	39,126	23,202
29,000	259.87	64,553	129.94	42,995	21,558	129.94	40,989	23,564	129.94	40,523	24,030
30,000	268.84	66,782	134.42	44,477	22,305	134.42	42,403	24,379	134.42	41,920	24,862
32,500	291.24	72,346	145.62	48,182	24,164	145.62	45,935	26,411	145.62	45,413	26,933
35,000	313.64	77,910	156.82	51,888	26,022	156.82	49,468	28,442	156.82	48,905	29,005
40,000	358.45	89,042	179.23	59,304	29,738	179.23	56,538	32,504	179.23	55,895	33,147
45,000	403.25	100,170	201.63	66,715	33,455	201.63	63,604	36,566	201.63	62,880	37,290
50,000	448.06	111,302	224.03	74,126	37,176	224.03	70,669	40,633	224.03	69,865	41,437
55,000	492.86	122,430	246.43	81,537	40,893	246.43	77,734	44,696	246.43	76,850	45,580
60,000	537.67	133,561	268.84	88,953	44,608	268.84	84,805	48,756	268.84	83,840	49,721
65,000	582.47	144,689	291.24	96,364	48,325	291.24	91,870	52,819	291.24	90,825	53,864
70,000	627.28	155,821	313.64	103,775	52,046	313.64	98,936	56,885	313.64	97,810	58,011
75,000	672.08	166,949	336.04	111,186	55,763	336.04	106,001	60,948	336.04	104,795	62,154
80,000	716.89	178,080	358.45	118,603	59,477	358.45	113,072	65,008	358.45	111,785	66,295
85,000	761.69	189,208	380.85	126,014	63,194	380.85	120,137	69,071	380.85	118,770	70,438
90,000	806.50	200,340	403.25	133,425	66,915	403.25	127,202	73,138	403.25	125,755	74,585
95,000	851.30	211,468	425.65	140,836	70,632	425.65	134,267	77,201	425.65	132,740	78,728
100,000	896.11	222,600	448.06	148,252	74,348	448.06	141,338	81,262	448.06	139,730	82,870
105,000	940.91	233,728	470.46	155,663	78,065	470.46	148,403	85,325	470.46	146,715	87,013
110,000	985.72	244,859	492.86	163,074	81,785	492.86	155,469	89,390	492.86	153,700	91,159
115,000	1,030.52	255,987	515.26	170,485	85,502	515.26	162,534	93,453	515.26	160,685	95,302
120,000	1,075.33	267,119	537.67	177,901	89,218	537.67	169,605	97,514	537.67	167,675	99,444
125,000	1,120.13	278,247	560.07	185,312	92,935	560.07	176,670	101,577	560.07	174,660	103,587
130,000	1,164.94	289,378	582.47	192,723	96,655	582.47	183,735	105,643	582.47	181,645	107,733
135,000	1,209.74	300,506	604.87	200,134	100,372	604.87	190,801	109,705	604.87	188,630	111,876
140,000	1,254.55	311,638	627.28	207,551	104,087	627.28	197,871	113,767	627.28	195,621	116,017
145,000	1,299.35	322,766	649.68	214,962	107,804	649.68	204,936	117,830	649.68	202,605	120,161
150,000	1,344.16	333,898	672.08	222,373	111,525	672.08	212,002	121,896	672.08	209,590	124,308
155,000	1,388.96	345,026	694.48	229,784	115,242	694.48	219,067	125,959	694.48	216,575	128,451
160,000	1,433.77	356,157	716.89	237,200	118,957	716.89	226,138	130,019	716.89	223,566	132,591
165,000	1,478.57	367,285	739.29	244,611	122,674	739.29	233,203	134,082	739.29	230,550	136,735
170,000	1,523.38	378,417	761.69	252,022	126,395	761.69	240,268	138,149	761.69	237,535	140,882
175,000	1,568.18	389,545	784.09	259,433	130,112	784.09	247,334	142,211	784.09	244,520	145,025
180,000	1,612.99	400,676	806.50	266,849	133,827	806.50	254,404	146,272	806.50	251,511	149,165
185,000	1,657.79	411,804	828.90	274,260	137,544	828.90	261,470	150,334	828.90	258,495	153,309
190,000	1,702.60	422,936	851.30	281,671	141,265	851.30	268,535	154,401	851.30	265,480	157,456
195,000	1,747.40	434,064	873.70	289,082	144,982	873.70	275,600	158,464	873.70	272,465	161,599
200,000	1,792.21	445,196	896.11	296,499	148,697	896.11	282,671	162,525	896.11	279,456	165,740

65

AMOUNT OF LOAN	30 YEARS		360 DAY BASIS 547.956 PAYMENTS			364 DAY BASIS 532.307 PAYMENTS			365 DAY BASIS 528.676 PAYMENTS		
	MONTHLY PAYMENT	TOTAL INTRST	BWEEKLY PAYMENT	TOTAL INTRST	INTRST SAVED	BWEEKLY PAYMENT	TOTAL INTRST	INTRST SAVED	BWEEKLY PAYMENT	TOTAL INTRST	INTRST SAVED
$ 50	0.46	116	0.23	76	40	0.23	72	44	0.23	72	44
100	0.92	231	0.46	152	79	0.46	145	86	0.46	143	88
200	1.83	459	0.92	304	155	0.92	290	169	0.92	286	173
300	2.75	690	1.38	456	234	1.38	435	255	1.38	430	260
400	3.66	918	1.83	603	315	1.83	574	344	1.83	567	351
500	4.58	1,149	2.29	755	394	2.29	719	430	2.29	711	438
600	5.49	1,376	2.75	907	469	2.75	864	512	2.75	854	522
700	6.41	1,608	3.21	1,059	549	3.21	1,009	599	3.21	997	611
800	7.32	1,835	3.66	1,206	629	3.66	1,148	687	3.66	1,135	700
900	8.24	2,066	4.12	1,358	708	4.12	1,293	773	4.12	1,278	788
1,000	9.15	2,294	4.58	1,510	784	4.58	1,438	856	4.58	1,421	873
2,000	18.30	4,588	9.15	3,014	1,574	9.15	2,871	1,717	9.15	2,837	1,751
3,000	27.45	6,882	13.73	4,523	2,359	13.73	4,309	2,573	13.73	4,259	2,623
4,000	36.59	9,172	18.30	6,028	3,144	18.30	5,741	3,431	18.30	5,675	3,497
5,000	45.74	11,466	22.87	7,532	3,934	22.87	7,174	4,292	22.87	7,091	4,375
6,000	54.89	13,760	27.45	9,041	4,719	27.45	8,612	5,148	27.45	8,512	5,248
7,000	64.04	16,054	32.02	10,546	5,508	32.02	10,044	6,010	32.02	9,928	6,126
8,000	73.18	18,345	36.59	12,050	6,295	36.59	11,477	6,868	36.59	11,344	7,001
9,000	82.33	20,639	41.17	13,559	7,080	41.17	12,915	7,724	41.17	12,766	7,873
10,000	91.48	22,933	45.74	15,064	7,869	45.74	14,348	8,585	45.74	14,182	8,751
11,000	100.63	25,227	50.32	16,573	8,654	50.32	15,786	9,441	50.32	15,603	9,624
12,000	109.77	27,517	54.89	18,077	9,440	54.89	17,218	10,299	54.89	17,019	10,498
13,000	118.92	29,811	59.46	19,581	10,230	59.46	18,651	11,160	59.46	18,435	11,376
14,000	128.07	32,105	64.04	21,091	11,014	64.04	20,089	12,016	64.04	19,856	12,249
15,000	137.22	34,399	68.61	22,595	11,804	68.61	21,522	12,877	68.61	21,272	13,127
16,000	146.36	36,690	73.18	24,099	12,591	73.18	22,954	13,736	73.18	22,689	14,001
17,000	155.51	38,984	77.76	25,609	13,375	77.76	24,392	14,592	77.76	24,110	14,874
18,000	164.66	41,278	82.33	27,113	14,165	82.33	25,825	15,453	82.33	25,526	15,752
19,000	173.81	43,572	86.91	28,623	14,949	86.91	27,263	16,309	86.91	26,947	16,625
20,000	182.95	45,862	91.48	30,127	15,735	91.48	28,695	17,167	91.48	28,363	17,499
21,000	192.10	48,156	96.05	31,631	16,525	96.05	30,128	18,028	96.05	29,779	18,377
22,000	201.25	50,450	100.63	33,141	17,309	100.63	31,566	18,884	100.63	31,201	19,249
23,000	210.40	52,744	105.20	34,645	18,099	105.20	32,999	19,745	105.20	32,617	20,127
24,000	219.54	55,034	109.77	36,149	18,885	109.77	34,431	20,603	109.77	34,033	21,001
25,000	228.69	57,328	114.35	37,659	19,669	114.35	35,869	21,459	114.35	35,454	21,874
26,000	237.84	59,622	118.92	39,163	20,459	118.92	37,302	22,320	118.92	36,870	22,752
27,000	246.98	61,913	123.49	40,667	21,246	123.49	38,735	23,178	123.49	38,286	23,627
28,000	256.13	64,207	128.07	42,177	22,030	128.07	40,173	24,034	128.07	39,708	24,499
29,000	265.28	66,501	132.64	43,681	22,820	132.64	41,605	24,896	132.64	41,124	25,377
30,000	274.43	68,795	137.22	45,191	23,604	137.22	43,043	25,752	137.22	42,545	26,250
32,500	297.30	74,528	148.65	48,954	25,574	148.65	46,627	27,901	148.65	46,088	28,440
35,000	320.16	80,258	160.08	52,717	27,541	160.08	50,212	30,046	160.08	49,630	30,628
40,000	365.90	91,724	182.95	60,249	31,475	182.95	57,386	34,338	182.95	56,721	35,003
45,000	411.64	103,190	205.82	67,780	35,410	205.82	64,559	38,631	205.82	63,812	39,378
50,000	457.37	114,653	228.69	75,312	39,341	228.69	71,733	42,920	228.69	70,903	43,750
55,000	503.11	126,120	251.56	82,844	43,276	251.56	78,907	47,213	251.56	77,994	48,126
60,000	548.85	137,586	274.43	90,377	47,210	274.43	86,081	51,505	274.43	85,085	52,501
65,000	594.59	149,052	297.30	97,907	51,145	297.30	93,255	55,797	297.30	92,175	56,877
70,000	640.32	160,515	320.16	105,434	55,081	320.16	100,423	60,092	320.16	99,261	61,254
75,000	686.06	171,982	343.03	112,965	59,017	343.03	107,597	64,385	343.03	106,352	65,630
80,000	731.80	183,448	365.90	120,497	62,951	365.90	114,771	68,677	365.90	113,443	70,005
85,000	777.53	194,911	388.77	128,029	66,882	388.77	121,945	72,966	388.77	120,533	74,378
90,000	823.27	206,377	411.64	135,561	70,816	411.64	129,119	77,258	411.64	127,624	78,753
95,000	869.01	217,844	434.51	143,092	74,752	434.51	136,293	81,551	434.51	134,715	83,129
100,000	914.74	229,306	457.37	150,619	78,687	457.37	143,461	85,845	457.37	141,801	87,505
105,000	960.48	240,773	480.24	158,150	82,623	480.24	150,635	90,138	480.24	148,891	91,882
110,000	1,006.22	252,239	503.11	165,682	86,557	503.11	157,809	94,430	503.11	155,982	96,257
115,000	1,051.96	263,706	525.98	173,214	90,492	525.98	164,983	98,723	525.98	163,073	100,633
120,000	1,097.69	275,168	548.85	180,740	94,428	548.85	172,157	103,011	548.85	170,164	105,004
125,000	1,143.43	286,635	571.72	188,277	98,358	571.72	179,331	107,304	571.72	177,255	109,380
130,000	1,189.17	298,101	594.59	195,809	102,292	594.59	186,504	111,597	594.59	184,345	113,756
135,000	1,234.90	309,564	617.45	203,335	106,229	617.45	193,673	115,891	617.45	191,431	118,133
140,000	1,280.64	321,030	640.32	210,867	110,163	640.32	200,847	120,183	640.32	198,522	122,508
145,000	1,326.38	332,497	663.19	218,399	114,098	663.19	208,021	124,476	663.19	205,613	126,884
150,000	1,372.11	343,960	686.06	225,931	118,029	686.06	215,195	128,765	686.06	212,703	131,257
155,000	1,417.85	355,426	708.93	233,462	121,964	708.93	222,368	133,058	708.93	219,794	135,632
160,000	1,463.59	366,892	731.80	240,994	125,898	731.80	229,542	137,350	731.80	226,885	140,007
165,000	1,509.32	378,355	754.66	248,520	129,835	754.66	236,711	141,644	754.66	233,971	144,384
170,000	1,555.06	389,822	777.53	256,052	133,770	777.53	243,885	145,937	777.53	241,061	148,761
175,000	1,600.80	401,288	800.40	263,584	137,704	800.40	251,059	150,229	800.40	248,152	153,136
180,000	1,646.54	412,754	823.27	271,116	141,638	823.27	258,232	154,522	823.27	255,243	157,511
185,000	1,692.27	424,217	846.14	278,647	145,570	846.14	265,406	158,811	846.14	262,334	161,883
190,000	1,738.01	435,684	869.01	286,179	149,505	869.01	272,580	163,104	869.01	269,425	166,259
195,000	1,783.75	447,150	891.88	293,711	153,439	891.88	279,754	167,396	891.88	276,516	170,634
200,000	1,829.48	458,613	914.74	301,237	157,376	914.74	286,923	171,690	914.74	283,601	175,012

AMOUNT OF LOAN	30 YEARS		360 DAY BASIS 541.823 PAYMENTS			364 DAY BASIS 525.977 PAYMENTS			365 DAY BASIS 522.307 PAYMENTS		
	MONTHLY PAYMENT	TOTAL INTRST	BWEEKLY PAYMENT	TOTAL INTRST	INTRST SAVED	BWEEKLY PAYMENT	TOTAL INTRST	INTRST SAVED	BWEEKLY PAYMENT	TOTAL INTRST	INTRST SAVED
$ 50	0.47	119	0.24	80	39	0.24	76	43	0.24	75	44
100	0.94	238	0.47	155	83	0.47	147	91	0.47	145	93
200	1.87	473	0.94	309	164	0.94	294	179	0.94	291	182
300	2.81	712	1.41	464	248	1.41	442	270	1.41	436	276
400	3.74	946	1.87	613	333	1.87	584	362	1.87	577	369
500	4.67	1,181	2.34	768	413	2.34	731	450	2.34	722	459
600	5.61	1,420	2.81	923	497	2.81	878	542	2.81	868	552
700	6.54	1,654	3.27	1,072	582	3.27	1,020	634	3.27	1,008	646
800	7.47	1,889	3.74	1,226	663	3.74	1,167	722	3.74	1,153	736
900	8.41	2,128	4.21	1,381	747	4.21	1,314	814	4.21	1,299	829
1,000	9.34	2,362	4.67	1,530	832	4.67	1,456	906	4.67	1,439	923
2,000	18.67	4,721	9.34	3,061	1,660	9.34	2,913	1,808	9.34	2,878	1,843
3,000	28.01	7,084	14.01	4,591	2,493	14.01	4,369	2,715	14.01	4,318	2,766
4,000	37.34	9,442	18.67	6,116	3,326	18.67	5,820	3,622	18.67	5,751	3,691
5,000	46.68	11,805	23.34	7,646	4,159	23.34	7,276	4,529	23.34	7,191	4,614
6,000	56.01	14,164	28.01	9,176	4,988	28.01	8,733	5,431	28.01	8,630	5,534
7,000	65.35	16,526	32.68	10,707	5,819	32.68	10,189	6,337	32.68	10,069	6,457
8,000	74.68	18,885	37.34	12,232	6,653	37.34	11,640	7,245	37.34	11,503	7,382
9,000	84.02	21,247	42.01	13,762	7,485	42.01	13,096	8,151	42.01	12,942	8,305
10,000	93.35	23,606	46.68	15,292	8,314	46.68	14,553	9,053	46.68	14,381	9,225
11,000	102.69	25,968	51.35	16,823	9,145	51.35	16,009	9,959	51.35	15,820	10,148
12,000	112.02	28,327	56.01	18,348	9,979	56.01	17,460	10,867	56.01	17,254	11,073
13,000	121.36	30,690	60.68	19,878	10,812	60.68	18,916	11,774	60.68	18,694	11,996
14,000	130.69	33,048	65.35	21,408	11,640	65.35	20,373	12,675	65.35	20,133	12,915
15,000	140.03	35,411	70.02	22,938	12,473	70.02	21,829	13,582	70.02	21,572	13,839
16,000	149.36	37,770	74.68	24,463	13,307	74.68	23,280	14,490	74.68	23,006	14,764
17,000	158.70	40,132	79.35	25,994	14,138	79.35	24,736	15,396	79.35	24,445	15,687
18,000	168.03	42,491	84.02	27,524	14,967	84.02	26,193	16,298	84.02	25,884	16,607
19,000	177.37	44,853	88.69	29,054	15,799	88.69	27,649	17,204	88.69	27,323	17,530
20,000	186.70	47,212	93.35	30,579	16,633	93.35	29,100	18,112	93.35	28,757	18,455
21,000	196.04	49,574	98.02	32,109	17,465	98.02	30,556	19,018	98.02	30,197	19,377
22,000	205.37	51,933	102.69	33,640	18,293	102.69	32,013	19,920	102.69	31,636	20,297
23,000	214.71	54,296	107.36	35,170	19,126	107.36	33,469	20,827	107.36	33,075	21,221
24,000	224.04	56,654	112.02	36,695	19,959	112.02	34,920	21,734	112.02	34,509	22,145
25,000	233.38	59,017	116.69	38,225	20,792	116.69	36,376	22,641	116.69	35,948	23,069
26,000	242.71	61,376	121.36	39,756	21,620	121.36	37,833	23,543	121.36	37,387	23,989
27,000	252.04	63,734	126.02	41,281	22,453	126.02	39,284	24,450	126.02	38,821	24,913
28,000	261.38	66,097	130.69	42,811	23,286	130.69	40,740	25,357	130.69	40,260	25,837
29,000	270.71	68,456	135.36	44,341	24,115	135.36	42,196	26,260	135.36	41,699	26,757
30,000	280.05	70,818	140.03	45,871	24,947	140.03	43,653	27,165	140.03	43,139	27,679
32,500	303.39	76,720	151.70	49,695	27,025	151.70	47,291	29,429	151.70	46,734	29,986
35,000	326.72	82,619	163.36	53,512	29,107	163.36	50,924	31,695	163.36	50,324	32,295
40,000	373.40	94,424	186.70	61,158	33,266	186.70	58,200	36,224	186.70	57,515	36,909
45,000	420.07	106,225	210.04	68,805	37,420	210.04	65,476	40,749	210.04	64,705	41,520
50,000	466.75	118,030	233.38	76,451	41,579	233.38	72,753	45,277	233.38	71,896	46,134
55,000	513.42	129,831	256.71	84,091	45,740	256.71	80,024	49,807	256.71	79,081	50,750
60,000	560.09	141,632	280.05	91,738	49,894	280.05	87,300	54,332	280.05	86,272	55,360
65,000	606.77	153,437	303.39	99,384	54,053	303.39	94,576	58,861	303.39	93,463	59,974
70,000	653.44	165,238	326.72	107,024	58,214	326.72	101,847	63,391	326.72	100,648	64,590
75,000	700.12	177,043	350.06	114,671	62,372	350.06	109,124	67,919	350.06	107,839	69,204
80,000	746.79	188,844	373.40	122,317	66,527	373.40	116,400	72,444	373.40	115,029	73,815
85,000	793.46	200,646	396.73	129,957	70,689	396.73	123,671	76,975	396.73	122,215	78,431
90,000	840.14	212,450	420.07	137,604	74,846	420.07	130,947	81,503	420.07	129,406	83,044
95,000	886.81	224,252	443.41	145,250	79,002	443.41	138,223	86,029	443.41	136,596	87,656
100,000	933.49	236,056	466.75	152,896	83,160	466.75	145,500	90,556	466.75	143,787	92,269
105,000	980.16	247,858	490.08	160,537	87,321	490.08	152,771	95,087	490.08	150,972	96,886
110,000	1,026.83	259,659	513.42	168,183	91,476	513.42	160,047	99,612	513.42	158,163	101,496
115,000	1,073.51	271,464	536.76	175,829	95,635	536.76	167,323	104,141	536.76	165,354	106,110
120,000	1,120.18	283,265	560.09	183,470	99,795	560.09	174,594	108,671	560.09	172,539	110,726
125,000	1,166.86	295,070	583.43	191,116	103,954	583.43	181,871	113,199	583.43	179,730	115,340
130,000	1,213.53	306,871	606.77	198,762	108,109	606.77	189,147	117,724	606.77	186,920	119,951
135,000	1,260.20	318,672	630.10	206,403	112,269	630.10	196,418	122,254	630.10	194,106	124,566
140,000	1,306.88	330,477	653.44	214,049	116,428	653.44	203,694	126,783	653.44	201,296	129,181
145,000	1,353.55	342,278	676.78	221,695	120,583	676.78	210,971	131,307	676.78	208,487	133,791
150,000	1,400.23	354,083	700.12	229,341	124,742	700.12	218,247	135,836	700.12	215,678	138,405
155,000	1,446.90	365,884	723.45	236,982	128,902	723.45	225,518	140,366	723.45	222,863	143,021
160,000	1,493.58	377,689	746.79	244,628	133,061	746.79	232,794	144,895	746.79	230,054	147,635
165,000	1,540.25	389,490	770.13	252,274	137,216	770.13	240,071	149,419	770.13	237,244	152,246
170,000	1,586.92	401,291	793.46	259,915	141,376	793.46	247,342	153,949	793.46	244,430	156,861
175,000	1,633.60	413,096	816.80	267,561	145,535	816.80	254,618	158,478	816.80	251,620	161,476
180,000	1,680.27	424,897	840.14	275,207	149,690	840.14	261,894	163,003	840.14	258,811	166,086
185,000	1,726.95	436,702	863.48	282,853	153,849	863.48	269,171	167,531	863.48	266,002	170,700
190,000	1,773.62	448,503	886.81	290,494	158,009	886.81	276,442	172,061	886.81	273,187	175,316
195,000	1,820.29	460,304	910.15	298,140	162,164	910.15	283,718	176,586	910.15	280,378	179,926
200,000	1,866.97	472,109	933.49	305,786	166,323	933.49	290,994	181,115	933.49	287,568	184,541

11.00% BIWEEKLY MORTGAGES

AMOUNT OF LOAN	30 YEARS		360 DAY BASIS 535.670 PAYMENTS			364 DAY BASIS 519.647 PAYMENTS			365 DAY BASIS 515.941 PAYMENTS		
	MONTHLY PAYMENT	TOTAL INTRST	BWEEKLY PAYMENT	TOTAL INTRST	INTRST SAVED	BWEEKLY PAYMENT	TOTAL INTRST	INTRST SAVED	BWEEKLY PAYMENT	TOTAL INTRST	INTRST SAVED
$ 50	0.48	123	0.24	79	44	0.24	75	48	0.24	74	49
100	0.96	246	0.48	157	89	0.48	149	97	0.48	148	98
200	1.91	488	0.96	314	174	0.96	299	189	0.96	295	193
300	2.86	730	1.43	466	264	1.43	443	287	1.43	438	292
400	3.81	972	1.91	623	349	1.91	593	379	1.91	585	387
500	4.77	1,217	2.39	780	437	2.39	742	475	2.39	733	484
600	5.72	1,459	2.86	932	527	2.86	886	573	2.86	876	583
700	6.67	1,701	3.34	1,089	612	3.34	1,036	665	3.34	1,023	678
800	7.62	1,943	3.81	1,241	702	3.81	1,180	763	3.81	1,166	777
900	8.58	2,189	4.29	1,398	791	4.29	1,329	860	4.29	1,313	876
1,000	9.53	2,431	4.77	1,555	876	4.77	1,479	952	4.77	1,461	970
2,000	19.05	4,858	9.53	3,105	1,753	9.53	2,952	1,906	9.53	2,917	1,941
3,000	28.57	7,285	14.29	4,655	2,630	14.29	4,426	2,859	14.29	4,373	2,912
4,000	38.10	9,716	19.05	6,205	3,511	19.05	5,899	3,817	19.05	5,829	3,887
5,000	47.62	12,143	23.81	7,754	4,389	23.81	7,373	4,770	23.81	7,285	4,858
6,000	57.14	14,570	28.57	9,304	5,266	28.57	8,846	5,724	28.57	8,740	5,830
7,000	66.67	17,001	33.34	10,859	6,142	33.34	10,325	6,676	33.34	10,201	6,800
8,000	76.19	19,428	38.10	12,409	7,019	38.10	11,799	7,629	38.10	11,657	7,771
9,000	85.71	21,856	42.86	13,959	7,897	42.86	13,272	8,584	42.86	13,113	8,743
10,000	95.24	24,286	47.62	15,509	8,777	47.62	14,746	9,540	47.62	14,569	9,717
11,000	104.76	26,714	52.38	17,058	9,656	52.38	16,219	10,495	52.38	16,025	10,689
12,000	114.28	29,141	57.14	18,608	10,533	57.14	17,693	11,448	57.14	17,481	11,660
13,000	123.81	31,572	61.91	20,163	11,409	61.91	19,171	12,401	61.91	18,942	12,630
14,000	133.33	33,999	66.67	21,713	12,286	66.67	20,645	13,354	66.67	20,398	13,601
15,000	142.85	36,426	71.43	23,263	13,163	71.43	22,118	14,308	71.43	21,854	14,572
16,000	152.38	38,857	76.19	24,813	14,044	76.19	23,592	15,265	76.19	23,310	15,547
17,000	161.90	41,284	80.95	26,362	14,922	80.95	25,065	16,219	80.95	24,765	16,519
18,000	171.42	43,711	85.71	27,912	15,799	85.71	26,539	17,172	85.71	26,221	17,490
19,000	180.95	46,142	90.48	29,467	16,675	90.48	28,018	18,124	90.48	27,682	18,460
20,000	190.47	48,569	95.24	31,017	17,552	95.24	29,491	19,078	95.24	29,138	19,431
21,000	199.99	50,996	100.00	32,567	18,429	100.00	30,965	20,031	100.00	30,594	20,402
22,000	209.52	53,427	104.76	34,117	19,310	104.76	32,438	20,989	104.76	32,050	21,377
23,000	219.04	55,854	109.52	35,667	20,187	109.52	33,912	21,942	109.52	33,506	22,348
24,000	228.56	58,282	114.28	37,216	21,066	114.28	35,385	22,897	114.28	34,962	23,320
25,000	238.09	60,712	119.05	38,772	21,940	119.05	36,864	23,848	119.05	36,423	24,289
26,000	247.61	63,140	123.81	40,321	22,819	123.81	38,337	24,803	123.81	37,879	25,261
27,000	257.13	65,567	128.57	41,871	23,696	128.57	39,811	25,756	128.57	39,335	26,232
28,000	266.66	67,998	133.33	43,421	24,577	133.33	41,285	26,713	133.33	40,790	27,208
29,000	276.18	70,425	138.09	44,971	25,454	138.09	42,758	27,667	138.09	42,246	28,179
30,000	285.70	72,852	142.85	46,520	26,332	142.85	44,232	28,620	142.85	43,702	29,150
32,500	309.51	78,924	154.76	50,400	28,524	154.76	47,921	31,003	154.76	47,347	31,577
35,000	333.32	84,995	166.66	54,275	30,720	166.66	51,604	33,391	166.66	50,987	34,008
40,000	380.93	97,135	190.47	62,029	35,106	190.47	58,977	38,158	190.47	58,271	38,864
45,000	428.55	109,278	214.28	69,783	39,495	214.28	66,350	42,928	214.28	65,556	43,722
50,000	476.17	121,421	238.09	77,538	43,883	238.09	73,723	47,698	238.09	72,840	48,581
55,000	523.78	133,561	261.89	85,287	48,274	261.89	81,090	52,471	261.89	80,120	53,441
60,000	571.40	145,704	285.70	93,041	52,663	285.70	88,463	57,241	285.70	87,404	58,300
65,000	619.02	157,847	309.51	100,795	57,052	309.51	95,836	62,011	309.51	94,689	63,158
70,000	666.63	169,987	333.32	108,550	61,437	333.32	103,209	66,778	333.32	101,973	68,014
75,000	714.25	182,130	357.13	116,304	65,826	357.13	110,582	71,548	357.13	109,258	72,872
80,000	761.86	194,270	380.93	124,053	70,217	380.93	117,949	76,321	380.93	116,537	77,733
85,000	809.48	206,413	404.74	131,807	74,606	404.74	125,322	81,091	404.74	123,822	82,591
90,000	857.10	218,556	428.55	139,561	78,995	428.55	132,695	85,861	428.55	131,107	87,449
95,000	904.71	230,696	452.36	147,316	83,380	452.36	140,068	90,628	452.36	138,391	92,305
100,000	952.33	242,839	476.17	155,070	87,769	476.17	147,440	95,399	476.17	145,676	97,163
105,000	999.94	254,978	499.97	162,819	92,159	499.97	154,808	100,170	499.97	152,955	102,023
110,000	1,047.56	267,122	523.78	170,573	96,549	523.78	162,181	104,941	523.78	160,240	106,882
115,000	1,095.18	279,265	547.59	178,328	100,937	547.59	169,554	109,711	547.59	167,524	111,741
120,000	1,142.79	291,404	571.40	186,082	105,322	571.40	176,926	114,478	571.40	174,809	116,595
125,000	1,190.41	303,548	595.21	193,836	109,712	595.21	184,299	119,249	595.21	182,093	121,455
130,000	1,238.03	315,691	619.02	201,590	114,101	619.02	191,672	124,019	619.02	189,378	126,313
135,000	1,285.64	327,830	642.82	209,339	118,491	642.82	199,039	128,791	642.82	196,657	131,173
140,000	1,333.26	339,974	666.63	217,094	122,880	666.63	206,412	133,562	666.63	203,942	136,032
145,000	1,380.87	352,113	690.44	224,848	127,265	690.44	213,785	138,328	690.44	211,226	140,887
150,000	1,428.49	364,256	714.25	232,602	131,654	714.25	221,158	143,098	714.25	218,511	145,745
155,000	1,476.11	376,400	738.06	240,357	136,043	738.06	228,531	147,869	738.06	225,795	150,605
160,000	1,523.72	388,539	761.86	248,106	140,433	761.86	235,898	152,641	761.86	233,075	155,464
165,000	1,571.34	400,682	785.67	255,860	144,822	785.67	243,271	157,411	785.67	240,359	160,323
170,000	1,618.95	412,822	809.48	263,614	149,208	809.48	250,644	162,178	809.48	247,644	165,178
175,000	1,666.57	424,965	833.29	271,368	153,597	833.29	258,017	166,948	833.29	254,928	170,037
180,000	1,714.19	437,108	857.10	279,123	157,985	857.10	265,389	171,719	857.10	262,213	174,895
185,000	1,761.80	449,248	880.90	286,872	162,376	880.90	272,757	176,491	880.90	269,492	179,756
190,000	1,809.42	461,391	904.71	294,626	166,765	904.71	280,130	181,261	904.71	276,777	184,614
195,000	1,857.04	473,534	928.52	302,380	171,154	928.52	287,503	186,031	928.52	284,062	189,472
200,000	1,904.65	485,674	952.33	310,135	175,539	952.33	294,875	190,799	952.33	291,346	194,328

68

AMOUNT OF LOAN	30 YEARS		360 DAY BASIS 529.505 PAYMENTS			364 DAY BASIS 513.324 PAYMENTS			365 DAY BASIS 509.588 PAYMENTS		
	MONTHLY PAYMENT	TOTAL INTRST	BWEEKLY PAYMENT	TOTAL INTRST	INTRST SAVED	BWEEKLY PAYMENT	TOTAL INTRST	INTRST SAVED	BWEEKLY PAYMENT	TOTAL INTRST	INTRST SAVED
$ 50	0.49	126	0.25	82	44	0.25	78	48	0.25	77	49
100	0.98	253	0.49	159	94	0.49	152	101	0.49	150	103
200	1.95	502	0.98	319	183	0.98	303	199	0.98	299	203
300	2.92	751	1.46	473	278	1.46	449	302	1.46	444	307
400	3.89	1,000	1.95	633	367	1.95	601	399	1.95	594	406
500	4.86	1,250	2.43	787	463	2.43	747	503	2.43	738	512
600	5.83	1,499	2.92	946	553	2.92	899	600	2.92	888	611
700	6.80	1,748	3.40	1,100	648	3.40	1,045	703	3.40	1,033	715
800	7.78	2,001	3.89	1,260	741	3.89	1,197	804	3.89	1,182	819
900	8.75	2,250	4.38	1,419	831	4.38	1,348	902	4.38	1,332	918
1,000	9.72	2,499	4.86	1,573	926	4.86	1,495	1,004	4.86	1,477	1,022
2,000	19.43	4,995	9.72	3,147	1,848	9.72	2,990	2,005	9.72	2,953	2,042
3,000	29.14	7,490	14.57	4,715	2,775	14.57	4,479	3,011	14.57	4,425	3,065
4,000	38.86	9,990	19.43	6,288	3,702	19.43	5,974	4,016	19.43	5,901	4,089
5,000	48.57	12,485	24.29	7,862	4,623	24.29	7,469	5,016	24.29	7,378	5,107
6,000	58.28	14,981	29.14	9,430	5,551	29.14	8,958	6,023	29.14	8,849	6,132
7,000	67.99	17,476	34.00	11,003	6,473	34.00	10,453	7,023	34.00	10,326	7,150
8,000	77.71	19,976	38.86	12,577	7,399	38.86	11,948	8,028	38.86	11,803	8,173
9,000	87.42	22,471	43.71	14,145	8,326	43.71	13,437	9,034	43.71	13,274	9,197
10,000	97.13	24,967	48.57	15,718	9,249	48.57	14,932	10,035	48.57	14,751	10,216
11,000	106.84	27,462	53.42	17,286	10,176	53.42	16,422	11,040	53.42	16,222	11,240
12,000	116.56	29,962	58.28	18,860	11,102	58.28	17,917	12,045	58.28	17,699	12,263
13,000	126.27	32,457	63.14	20,433	12,024	63.14	19,411	13,046	63.14	19,175	13,282
14,000	135.98	34,953	67.99	22,001	12,952	67.99	20,901	14,052	67.99	20,647	14,306
15,000	145.69	37,448	72.85	23,574	13,874	72.85	22,396	15,052	72.85	22,123	15,325
16,000	155.41	39,948	77.71	25,148	14,800	77.71	23,890	16,058	77.71	23,600	16,348
17,000	165.12	42,443	82.56	26,716	15,727	82.56	25,380	17,063	82.56	25,072	17,371
18,000	174.83	44,939	87.42	28,289	16,650	87.42	26,875	18,064	87.42	26,548	18,391
19,000	184.54	47,434	92.27	29,857	17,577	92.27	28,364	19,070	92.27	28,020	19,414
20,000	194.26	49,934	97.13	31,431	18,503	97.13	29,859	20,075	97.13	29,496	20,438
21,000	203.97	52,429	101.99	33,004	19,425	101.99	31,354	21,075	101.99	30,973	21,456
22,000	213.68	54,925	106.84	34,572	20,353	106.84	32,844	22,081	106.84	32,444	22,481
23,000	223.40	57,424	111.70	36,146	21,278	111.70	34,338	23,086	111.70	33,921	23,503
24,000	233.11	59,920	116.56	37,719	22,201	116.56	35,833	24,087	116.56	35,398	24,522
25,000	242.82	62,415	121.41	39,287	23,128	121.41	37,323	25,092	121.41	36,869	25,546
26,000	252.53	64,911	126.27	40,861	24,050	126.27	38,817	26,094	126.27	38,346	26,565
27,000	262.25	67,410	131.13	42,434	24,976	131.13	40,312	27,098	131.13	39,822	27,588
28,000	271.96	69,906	135.98	44,002	25,904	135.98	41,802	28,104	135.98	41,294	28,612
29,000	281.67	72,401	140.84	45,575	26,826	140.84	43,297	29,104	140.84	42,770	29,631
30,000	291.38	74,897	145.69	47,144	27,753	145.69	44,786	30,111	145.69	44,242	30,655
32,500	315.66	81,138	157.83	51,072	30,066	157.83	48,518	32,620	157.83	47,928	33,210
35,000	339.95	87,382	169.98	55,005	32,377	169.98	52,255	35,127	169.98	51,620	35,762
40,000	388.51	99,864	194.26	62,862	37,002	194.26	59,718	40,146	194.26	58,993	40,871
45,000	437.07	112,345	218.54	70,718	41,627	218.54	67,182	45,163	218.54	66,365	45,980
50,000	485.64	124,830	242.82	78,574	46,256	242.82	74,645	50,185	242.82	73,738	51,092
55,000	534.20	137,312	267.10	86,431	50,881	267.10	82,109	55,203	267.10	81,111	56,201
60,000	582.76	149,794	291.38	94,287	55,507	291.38	89,572	60,222	291.38	88,484	61,310
65,000	631.32	162,275	315.66	102,144	60,131	315.66	97,036	65,239	315.66	95,857	66,418
70,000	679.89	174,760	339.95	110,005	64,755	339.95	104,504	70,256	339.95	103,234	71,526
75,000	728.45	187,242	364.23	117,862	69,380	364.23	111,968	75,274	364.23	110,607	76,635
80,000	777.01	199,724	388.51	125,718	74,006	388.51	119,432	80,292	388.51	117,980	81,744
85,000	825.58	212,209	412.79	133,574	78,635	412.79	126,895	85,314	412.79	125,353	86,856
90,000	874.14	224,690	437.07	141,431	83,259	437.07	134,359	90,331	437.07	132,726	91,964
95,000	922.70	237,172	461.35	149,287	87,885	461.35	141,822	95,350	461.35	140,098	97,074
100,000	971.27	249,657	485.64	157,149	92,508	485.64	149,291	100,366	485.64	147,476	102,181
105,000	1,019.83	262,139	509.92	165,005	97,134	509.92	156,754	105,385	509.92	154,849	107,290
110,000	1,068.39	274,620	534.20	172,862	101,758	534.20	164,218	110,402	534.20	162,222	112,398
115,000	1,116.96	287,106	558.48	180,718	106,388	558.48	171,681	115,425	558.48	169,595	117,511
120,000	1,165.52	299,587	582.76	188,574	111,013	582.76	179,145	120,442	582.76	176,968	122,619
125,000	1,214.08	312,069	607.04	196,431	115,638	607.04	186,608	125,461	607.04	184,340	127,729
130,000	1,262.64	324,550	631.32	204,287	120,263	631.32	194,072	130,478	631.32	191,713	132,837
135,000	1,311.21	337,036	655.61	212,149	124,887	655.61	201,540	135,496	655.61	199,091	137,945
140,000	1,359.77	349,517	679.89	220,005	129,512	679.89	209,004	140,513	679.89	206,464	143,053
145,000	1,408.33	361,999	704.17	227,862	134,137	704.17	216,467	145,532	704.17	213,837	148,162
150,000	1,456.90	374,484	728.45	235,718	138,766	728.45	223,931	150,553	728.45	221,209	153,275
155,000	1,505.46	386,966	752.73	243,574	143,392	752.73	231,394	155,572	752.73	228,582	158,384
160,000	1,554.02	399,447	777.01	251,431	148,016	777.01	238,858	160,589	777.01	235,955	163,492
165,000	1,602.59	411,932	801.30	259,292	152,640	801.30	246,327	165,605	801.30	243,333	168,599
170,000	1,651.15	424,414	825.58	267,149	157,265	825.58	253,790	170,624	825.58	250,706	173,708
175,000	1,699.71	436,896	849.86	275,005	161,891	849.86	261,254	175,642	849.86	258,078	178,818
180,000	1,748.28	449,381	874.14	282,862	166,519	874.14	268,717	180,664	874.14	265,451	183,930
185,000	1,796.84	461,862	898.42	290,718	171,144	898.42	276,181	185,681	898.42	272,824	189,038
190,000	1,845.40	474,344	922.70	298,574	175,770	922.70	283,644	190,700	922.70	280,197	194,147
195,000	1,893.96	486,826	946.98	306,431	180,395	946.98	291,108	195,718	946.98	287,570	199,256
200,000	1,942.53	499,311	971.27	314,292	185,019	971.27	298,576	200,735	971.27	294,948	204,363

BIWEEKLY MORTGAGES

AMOUNT OF LOAN	30 YEARS		360 DAY BASIS 523.334 PAYMENTS			364 DAY BASIS 507.015 PAYMENTS			365 DAY BASIS 503.253 PAYMENTS		
	MONTHLY PAYMENT	TOTAL INTRST	BWEEKLY PAYMENT	TOTAL INTRST	INTRST SAVED	BWEEKLY PAYMENT	TOTAL INTRST	INTRST SAVED	BWEEKLY PAYMENT	TOTAL INTRST	INTRST SAVED
$ 50	0.50	130	0.25	81	49	0.25	77	53	0.25	76	54
100	1.00	260	0.50	162	98	0.50	154	106	0.50	152	108
200	1.99	516	1.00	323	193	1.00	307	209	1.00	303	213
300	2.98	773	1.49	480	293	1.49	455	318	1.49	450	323
400	3.97	1,029	1.99	641	388	1.99	609	420	1.99	601	428
500	4.96	1,286	2.48	798	488	2.48	757	529	2.48	748	538
600	5.95	1,542	2.98	960	582	2.98	911	631	2.98	900	642
700	6.94	1,798	3.47	1,116	682	3.47	1,059	739	3.47	1,046	752
800	7.93	2,055	3.97	1,278	777	3.97	1,213	842	3.97	1,198	857
900	8.92	2,311	4.46	1,434	877	4.46	1,361	950	4.46	1,345	966
1,000	9.91	2,568	4.96	1,596	972	4.96	1,515	1,053	4.96	1,496	1,072
2,000	19.81	5,132	9.91	3,186	1,946	9.91	3,025	2,107	9.91	2,987	2,145
3,000	29.71	7,696	14.86	4,777	2,919	14.86	4,534	3,162	14.86	4,478	3,218
4,000	39.62	10,263	19.81	6,367	3,896	19.81	6,044	4,219	19.81	5,969	4,294
5,000	49.52	12,827	24.76	7,958	4,869	24.76	7,554	5,273	24.76	7,461	5,366
6,000	59.42	15,391	29.71	9,548	5,843	29.71	9,063	6,328	29.71	8,952	6,439
7,000	69.33	17,959	34.67	11,144	6,815	34.67	10,578	7,381	34.67	10,448	7,511
8,000	79.23	20,523	39.62	12,734	7,789	39.62	12,088	8,435	39.62	11,939	8,584
9,000	89.13	23,087	44.57	14,325	8,762	44.57	13,598	9,489	44.57	13,430	9,657
10,000	99.03	25,651	49.52	15,915	9,736	49.52	15,107	10,544	49.52	14,921	10,730
11,000	108.94	28,218	54.47	17,506	10,712	54.47	16,617	11,601	54.47	16,412	11,806
12,000	118.84	30,782	59.42	19,097	11,685	59.42	18,127	12,655	59.42	17,903	12,879
13,000	128.74	33,346	64.37	20,687	12,659	64.37	19,637	13,709	64.37	19,394	13,952
14,000	138.65	35,914	69.33	22,283	13,631	69.33	21,151	14,763	69.33	20,891	15,023
15,000	148.55	38,478	74.28	23,873	14,605	74.28	22,661	15,817	74.28	22,382	16,096
16,000	158.45	41,042	79.23	25,464	15,578	79.23	24,171	16,871	79.23	23,873	17,169
17,000	168.35	43,606	84.18	27,054	16,552	84.18	25,681	17,925	84.18	25,364	18,242
18,000	178.26	46,174	89.13	28,645	17,529	89.13	27,190	18,984	89.13	26,855	19,319
19,000	188.16	48,738	94.08	30,235	18,503	94.08	28,700	20,038	94.08	28,346	20,392
20,000	198.06	51,302	99.03	31,826	19,476	99.03	30,210	21,092	99.03	29,837	21,465
21,000	207.97	53,869	103.99	33,422	20,447	103.99	31,724	22,145	103.99	31,333	22,536
22,000	217.87	56,433	108.94	35,012	21,421	108.94	33,234	23,199	108.94	32,824	23,609
23,000	227.77	58,997	113.89	36,603	22,394	113.89	34,744	24,253	113.89	34,315	24,682
24,000	237.67	61,561	118.84	38,193	23,368	118.84	36,254	25,307	118.84	35,807	25,754
25,000	247.58	64,129	123.79	39,784	24,345	123.79	37,763	26,366	123.79	37,298	26,831
26,000	257.48	66,693	128.74	41,374	25,319	128.74	39,273	27,420	128.74	38,789	27,904
27,000	267.38	69,257	133.69	42,965	26,292	133.69	40,783	28,474	133.69	40,280	28,977
28,000	277.29	71,824	138.65	44,560	27,264	138.65	42,298	29,526	138.65	41,776	30,048
29,000	287.19	74,388	143.60	46,151	28,237	143.60	43,807	30,581	143.60	43,267	31,121
30,000	297.09	76,952	148.55	47,741	29,211	148.55	45,317	31,635	148.55	44,758	32,194
32,500	321.85	83,469	160.93	51,720	31,646	160.93	49,094	34,272	160.93	48,489	34,877
35,000	346.61	89,780	173.31	55,699	34,081	173.31	52,871	36,909	173.31	52,219	37,561
40,000	396.12	102,603	198.06	63,652	38,951	198.06	60,419	42,184	198.06	59,674	42,929
45,000	445.64	115,430	222.82	71,609	43,821	222.82	67,973	47,457	222.82	67,135	48,295
50,000	495.15	128,254	247.58	79,567	48,687	247.58	75,527	52,727	247.58	74,595	53,659
55,000	544.67	141,081	272.34	87,525	53,556	272.34	83,080	58,001	272.34	82,056	59,025
60,000	594.18	153,905	297.09	95,477	58,428	297.09	90,629	63,276	297.09	89,511	64,394
65,000	643.69	166,728	321.85	103,435	63,293	321.85	98,183	68,545	321.85	96,972	69,756
70,000	693.21	179,556	346.61	111,393	68,163	346.61	105,736	73,820	346.61	104,433	75,123
75,000	742.72	192,379	371.36	119,345	73,034	371.36	113,285	79,094	371.36	111,888	80,491
80,000	792.24	205,206	396.12	127,303	77,903	396.12	120,839	84,367	396.12	119,349	85,857
85,000	841.75	218,030	420.88	135,261	82,769	420.88	128,392	89,638	420.88	126,809	91,221
90,000	891.27	230,857	445.64	143,219	87,638	445.64	135,946	94,911	445.64	134,270	96,587
95,000	940.78	243,681	470.39	151,171	92,510	470.39	143,495	100,186	470.39	141,725	101,956
100,000	990.30	256,508	495.15	159,129	97,379	495.15	151,048	105,460	495.15	149,186	107,322
105,000	1,039.81	269,332	519.91	167,087	102,245	519.91	158,602	110,730	519.91	156,646	112,686
110,000	1,089.33	282,159	544.67	175,044	107,115	544.67	166,156	116,003	544.67	164,107	118,052
115,000	1,138.84	294,982	569.42	182,997	111,985	569.42	173,704	121,278	569.42	171,562	123,420
120,000	1,188.35	307,806	594.18	190,955	116,851	594.18	181,258	126,548	594.18	179,023	128,783
125,000	1,237.87	320,633	618.94	198,912	121,721	618.94	188,812	131,821	618.94	186,483	134,150
130,000	1,287.38	333,457	643.69	206,865	126,592	643.69	196,360	137,097	643.69	193,939	139,518
135,000	1,336.90	346,284	668.45	214,823	131,461	668.45	203,914	142,370	668.45	201,399	144,885
140,000	1,386.41	359,108	693.21	222,780	136,328	693.21	211,468	147,640	693.21	208,860	150,248
145,000	1,435.93	371,935	717.97	230,738	141,197	717.97	219,022	152,913	717.97	216,321	155,614
150,000	1,485.44	384,758	742.72	238,691	146,067	742.72	226,570	158,188	742.72	223,776	160,982
155,000	1,534.96	397,586	767.48	246,648	150,938	767.48	234,124	163,462	767.48	231,237	166,349
160,000	1,584.47	410,409	792.24	254,606	155,803	792.24	241,678	168,731	792.24	238,697	171,712
165,000	1,633.99	423,236	817.00	262,564	160,672	817.00	249,231	174,005	817.00	246,158	177,078
170,000	1,683.50	436,060	841.75	270,516	165,544	841.75	256,780	179,280	841.75	253,613	182,447
175,000	1,733.02	448,887	866.51	278,474	170,413	866.51	264,334	184,553	866.51	261,074	187,813
180,000	1,782.53	461,711	891.27	286,432	175,279	891.27	271,887	189,824	891.27	268,534	193,177
185,000	1,832.04	474,534	916.02	294,384	180,150	916.02	279,436	195,098	916.02	275,990	198,544
190,000	1,881.56	487,362	940.78	302,342	185,020	940.78	286,990	200,372	940.78	283,450	203,912
195,000	1,931.07	500,185	965.54	310,300	189,885	965.54	294,543	205,642	965.54	290,911	209,274
200,000	1,980.59	513,012	990.30	318,258	194,754	990.30	302,097	210,915	990.30	298,371	214,641

AMOUNT OF LOAN	30 YEARS		360 DAY BASIS 517.166 PAYMENTS			364 DAY BASIS 500.728 PAYMENTS			365 DAY BASIS 496.944 PAYMENTS		
	MONTHLY PAYMENT	TOTAL INTRST	BWEEKLY PAYMENT	TOTAL INTRST	INTRST SAVED	BWEEKLY PAYMENT	TOTAL INTRST	INTRST SAVED	BWEEKLY PAYMENT	TOTAL INTRST	INTRST SAVED
$ 50	0.51	134	0.26	84	50	0.26	80	54	0.26	79	55
100	1.01	264	0.51	164	100	0.51	155	109	0.51	153	111
200	2.02	527	1.01	322	205	1.01	306	221	1.01	302	225
300	3.03	791	1.52	486	305	1.52	461	330	1.52	455	336
400	4.04	1,054	2.02	645	409	2.02	611	443	2.02	604	450
500	5.05	1,318	2.53	808	510	2.53	767	551	2.53	757	561
600	6.06	1,582	3.03	967	615	3.03	917	665	3.03	906	676
700	7.07	1,845	3.54	1,131	714	3.54	1,073	772	3.54	1,059	786
800	8.08	2,109	4.04	1,289	820	4.04	1,223	886	4.04	1,208	901
900	9.09	2,372	4.55	1,453	919	4.55	1,378	994	4.55	1,361	1,011
1,000	10.10	2,636	5.05	1,612	1,024	5.05	1,529	1,107	5.05	1,510	1,126
2,000	20.19	5,268	10.10	3,223	2,045	10.10	3,057	2,211	10.10	3,019	2,249
3,000	30.29	7,904	15.15	4,835	3,069	15.15	4,586	3,318	15.15	4,529	3,375
4,000	40.38	10,537	20.19	6,442	4,095	20.19	6,110	4,427	20.19	6,033	4,504
5,000	50.48	13,173	25.24	8,053	5,120	25.24	7,638	5,535	25.24	7,543	5,630
6,000	60.57	15,805	30.29	9,665	6,140	30.29	9,167	6,638	30.29	9,052	6,753
7,000	70.66	18,438	35.33	11,271	7,167	35.33	10,691	7,747	35.33	10,557	7,881
8,000	80.76	21,074	40.38	12,883	8,191	40.38	12,219	8,855	40.38	12,067	9,007
9,000	90.85	23,706	45.43	14,495	9,211	45.43	13,748	9,958	45.43	13,576	10,130
10,000	100.95	26,342	50.48	16,107	10,235	50.48	15,277	11,065	50.48	15,086	11,256
11,000	111.04	28,974	55.52	17,713	11,261	55.52	16,800	12,174	55.52	16,590	12,384
12,000	121.13	31,607	60.57	19,325	12,282	60.57	18,329	13,278	60.57	18,100	13,507
13,000	131.23	34,243	65.62	20,936	13,307	65.62	19,858	14,385	65.62	19,609	14,634
14,000	141.32	36,875	70.66	22,543	14,332	70.66	21,381	15,494	70.66	21,114	15,761
15,000	151.42	39,511	75.71	24,155	15,356	75.71	22,910	16,601	75.71	22,624	16,887
16,000	161.51	42,144	80.76	25,766	16,378	80.76	24,439	17,705	80.76	24,133	18,011
17,000	171.60	44,776	85.80	27,373	17,403	85.80	25,962	18,814	85.80	25,638	19,138
18,000	181.70	47,412	90.85	28,985	18,427	90.85	27,491	19,921	90.85	27,147	20,265
19,000	191.79	50,048	95.90	30,596	19,448	95.90	29,020	21,024	95.90	28,657	21,387
20,000	201.89	52,680	100.95	32,208	20,472	100.95	30,548	22,132	100.95	30,166	22,514
21,000	211.98	55,313	105.99	33,814	21,499	105.99	32,072	23,241	105.99	31,671	23,642
22,000	222.08	57,949	111.04	35,426	22,523	111.04	33,601	24,348	111.04	33,181	24,768
23,000	232.17	60,581	116.09	37,038	23,543	116.09	35,130	25,451	116.09	34,690	25,891
24,000	242.26	63,214	121.13	38,644	24,570	121.13	36,653	26,561	121.13	36,195	27,019
25,000	252.36	65,850	126.18	40,256	25,594	126.18	38,182	27,668	126.18	37,704	28,146
26,000	262.45	68,482	131.23	41,866	26,614	131.23	39,711	28,771	131.23	39,214	29,268
27,000	272.55	71,118	136.28	43,479	27,639	136.28	41,239	29,879	136.28	40,724	30,394
28,000	282.64	73,750	141.32	45,086	28,664	141.32	42,763	30,987	141.32	42,228	31,522
29,000	292.73	76,383	146.37	46,698	29,685	146.37	44,292	32,091	146.37	43,738	32,645
30,000	302.83	79,019	151.42	48,309	30,710	151.42	45,820	33,199	151.42	45,247	33,772
32,500	328.06	85,602	164.03	52,331	33,271	164.03	49,634	35,968	164.03	49,014	36,588
35,000	353.30	92,188	176.65	56,357	35,831	176.65	53,454	38,734	176.65	52,785	39,403
40,000	403.77	105,357	201.89	64,444	40,946	201.89	61,092	44,265	201.89	60,328	45,029
45,000	454.24	118,526	227.12	72,459	46,067	227.12	68,725	49,801	227.12	67,866	50,660
50,000	504.71	131,696	252.36	80,512	51,184	252.36	76,364	55,332	252.36	75,409	56,287
55,000	555.18	144,865	277.59	88,560	56,305	277.59	83,997	60,868	277.59	82,947	61,918
60,000	605.65	158,034	302.83	96,613	61,421	302.83	91,635	66,399	302.83	90,490	67,544
65,000	656.12	171,203	328.06	104,661	66,542	328.06	99,269	71,934	328.06	98,027	73,176
70,000	706.59	184,372	353.30	112,715	71,657	353.30	106,907	77,465	353.30	105,570	78,802
75,000	757.06	197,542	378.53	120,763	76,779	378.53	114,541	83,001	378.53	113,108	84,434
80,000	807.53	210,711	403.77	128,816	81,895	403.77	122,179	88,532	403.77	120,651	90,060
85,000	858.00	223,880	429.00	136,864	87,016	429.00	129,812	94,068	429.00	128,189	95,691
90,000	908.47	237,049	454.24	144,917	92,132	454.24	137,451	99,598	454.24	135,732	101,317
95,000	958.94	250,218	479.47	152,966	97,252	479.47	145,084	105,134	479.47	143,270	106,948
100,000	1,009.41	263,388	504.71	161,019	102,369	504.71	152,722	110,666	504.71	150,813	112,575
105,000	1,059.89	276,560	529.95	169,072	107,488	529.95	160,361	116,199	529.95	158,355	118,205
110,000	1,110.36	289,730	555.18	177,120	112,610	555.18	167,994	121,736	555.18	165,893	123,837
115,000	1,160.83	302,899	580.42	185,173	117,726	580.42	175,633	127,266	580.42	173,436	129,463
120,000	1,211.30	316,068	605.65	193,222	122,846	605.65	183,266	132,802	605.65	180,974	135,094
125,000	1,261.77	329,237	630.89	201,275	127,962	630.89	190,904	138,333	630.89	188,517	140,720
130,000	1,312.24	342,406	656.12	209,323	133,083	656.12	198,538	143,868	656.12	196,055	146,351
135,000	1,362.71	355,576	681.36	217,376	138,200	681.36	206,176	149,400	681.36	203,598	151,978
140,000	1,413.18	368,745	706.59	225,424	143,321	706.59	213,809	154,936	706.59	211,136	157,609
145,000	1,463.65	381,914	731.83	233,478	148,436	731.83	221,448	160,466	731.83	218,679	163,235
150,000	1,514.12	395,083	757.06	241,526	153,557	757.06	229,081	166,002	757.06	226,216	168,867
155,000	1,564.59	408,252	782.30	249,579	158,673	782.30	236,720	171,532	782.30	233,759	174,493
160,000	1,615.06	421,422	807.53	257,627	163,795	807.53	244,353	177,069	807.53	241,297	180,125
165,000	1,665.53	434,591	832.77	265,680	168,911	832.77	251,991	182,600	832.77	248,840	185,751
170,000	1,716.00	447,760	858.00	273,728	174,032	858.00	259,625	188,135	858.00	256,378	191,382
175,000	1,766.47	460,929	883.24	281,782	179,147	883.24	267,263	193,666	883.24	263,921	197,008
180,000	1,816.94	474,098	908.47	289,830	184,268	908.47	274,896	199,202	908.47	271,459	202,639
185,000	1,867.41	487,268	933.71	297,883	189,385	933.71	282,535	204,733	933.71	279,002	208,266
190,000	1,917.88	500,437	958.94	305,931	194,506	958.94	290,168	210,269	958.94	286,539	213,898
195,000	1,968.35	513,606	984.18	313,984	199,622	984.18	297,806	215,800	984.18	294,082	219,524
200,000	2,018.82	526,775	1,009.41	322,033	204,742	1,009.41	305,440	221,335	1,009.41	301,620	225,155

12.00%   BIWEEKLY MORTGAGES

AMOUNT OF LOAN	30 YEARS		360 DAY BASIS 511.007 PAYMENTS			364 DAY BASIS 494.470 PAYMENTS			365 DAY BASIS 490.669 PAYMENTS		
	MONTHLY PAYMENT	TOTAL INTRST	BWEEKLY PAYMENT	TOTAL INTRST	INTRST SAVED	BWEEKLY PAYMENT	TOTAL INTRST	INTRST SAVED	BWEEKLY PAYMENT	TOTAL INTRST	INTRST SAVED
$ 50	0.52	137	0.26	83	54	0.26	79	58	0.26	78	59
100	1.03	271	0.52	166	105	0.52	157	114	0.52	155	116
200	2.06	542	1.03	326	216	1.03	309	233	1.03	305	237
300	3.09	812	1.55	492	320	1.55	466	346	1.55	461	351
400	4.12	1,083	2.06	653	430	2.06	619	464	2.06	611	472
500	5.15	1,354	2.58	818	536	2.58	776	578	2.58	766	588
600	6.18	1,625	3.09	979	646	3.09	928	697	3.09	916	709
700	7.21	1,896	3.61	1,145	751	3.61	1,085	811	3.61	1,071	825
800	8.23	2,163	4.12	1,305	858	4.12	1,237	926	4.12	1,222	941
900	9.26	2,434	4.63	1,466	968	4.63	1,389	1,045	4.63	1,372	1,062
1,000	10.29	2,704	5.15	1,632	1,072	5.15	1,547	1,157	5.15	1,527	1,177
2,000	20.58	5,409	10.29	3,258	2,151	10.29	3,088	2,321	10.29	3,049	2,360
3,000	30.86	8,110	15.43	4,885	3,225	15.43	4,630	3,480	15.43	4,571	3,539
4,000	41.15	10,814	20.58	6,517	4,297	20.58	6,176	4,638	20.58	6,098	4,716
5,000	51.44	13,518	25.72	8,143	5,375	25.72	7,718	5,800	25.72	7,620	5,898
6,000	61.72	16,219	30.86	9,770	6,449	30.86	9,259	6,960	30.86	9,142	7,077
7,000	72.01	18,924	36.01	11,401	7,523	36.01	10,806	8,118	36.01	10,669	8,255
8,000	82.29	21,624	41.15	13,028	8,596	41.15	12,347	9,277	41.15	12,191	9,433
9,000	92.58	24,329	46.29	14,655	9,674	46.29	13,889	10,440	46.29	13,713	10,616
10,000	102.87	27,033	51.44	16,286	10,747	51.44	15,436	11,597	51.44	15,240	11,793
11,000	113.15	29,734	56.58	17,913	11,821	56.58	16,977	12,757	56.58	16,762	12,972
12,000	123.44	32,438	61.72	19,539	12,899	61.72	18,519	13,919	61.72	18,284	14,154
13,000	133.72	35,139	66.86	21,166	13,973	66.86	20,060	15,079	66.86	19,806	15,333
14,000	144.01	37,844	72.01	22,798	15,046	72.01	21,607	16,237	72.01	21,333	16,511
15,000	154.30	40,548	77.15	24,424	16,124	77.15	23,148	17,400	77.15	22,855	17,693
16,000	164.58	43,249	82.29	26,051	17,198	82.29	24,690	18,559	82.29	24,377	18,872
17,000	174.87	45,953	87.44	27,682	18,271	87.44	26,236	19,717	87.44	25,904	20,049
18,000	185.16	48,658	92.58	29,309	19,349	92.58	27,778	20,880	92.58	27,426	21,232
19,000	195.44	51,358	97.72	30,936	20,422	97.72	29,320	22,038	97.72	28,948	22,410
20,000	205.73	54,063	102.87	32,567	21,496	102.87	30,866	23,197	102.87	30,475	23,588
21,000	216.01	56,764	108.01	34,194	22,570	108.01	32,408	24,356	108.01	31,997	24,767
22,000	226.30	59,468	113.15	35,820	23,648	113.15	33,949	25,519	113.15	33,519	25,949
23,000	236.59	62,172	118.30	37,452	24,720	118.30	35,496	26,676	118.30	35,046	27,126
24,000	246.87	64,873	123.44	39,079	25,794	123.44	37,037	27,836	123.44	36,568	28,305
25,000	257.16	67,578	128.58	40,705	26,873	128.58	38,579	28,999	128.58	38,090	29,488
26,000	267.44	70,278	133.72	42,332	27,946	133.72	40,121	30,157	133.72	39,612	30,666
27,000	277.73	72,983	138.87	43,964	29,019	138.87	41,667	31,316	138.87	41,139	31,844
28,000	288.02	75,687	144.01	45,590	30,097	144.01	43,209	32,478	144.01	42,661	33,026
29,000	298.30	78,388	149.15	47,217	31,171	149.15	44,750	33,638	149.15	44,183	34,205
30,000	308.59	81,092	154.30	48,848	32,244	154.30	46,297	34,795	154.30	45,710	35,382
32,500	334.30	87,848	167.15	52,915	34,933	167.15	50,151	37,697	167.15	49,515	38,333
35,000	360.02	94,607	180.01	56,986	37,621	180.01	54,010	40,597	180.01	53,325	41,282
40,000	411.45	108,122	205.73	65,129	42,993	205.73	61,727	46,395	205.73	60,945	47,177
45,000	462.88	121,637	231.44	73,267	48,370	231.44	69,440	52,197	231.44	68,560	53,077
50,000	514.31	135,152	257.16	81,411	53,741	257.16	77,158	57,994	257.16	76,180	58,972
55,000	565.74	148,666	282.87	89,549	59,117	282.87	84,871	63,795	282.87	83,796	64,870
60,000	617.17	162,181	308.59	97,692	64,489	308.59	92,588	69,593	308.59	91,416	70,765
65,000	668.60	175,696	334.30	105,830	69,866	334.30	100,301	75,395	334.30	99,031	76,665
70,000	720.03	189,211	360.02	113,973	75,238	360.02	108,019	81,192	360.02	106,651	82,560
75,000	771.46	202,726	385.73	122,111	80,615	385.73	115,732	86,994	385.73	114,266	88,460
80,000	822.90	216,244	411.45	130,254	85,990	411.45	123,450	92,794	411.45	121,886	94,358
85,000	874.33	229,759	437.17	138,397	91,362	437.17	131,167	98,592	437.17	129,506	100,253
90,000	925.76	243,274	462.88	146,535	96,739	462.88	138,880	104,394	462.88	137,121	106,153
95,000	977.19	256,788	488.60	154,678	102,110	488.60	146,598	110,190	488.60	144,741	112,047
100,000	1,028.62	270,303	514.31	162,816	107,487	514.31	154,311	115,992	514.31	152,356	117,947
105,000	1,080.05	283,818	540.03	170,959	112,859	540.03	162,029	121,789	540.03	159,976	123,842
110,000	1,131.48	297,333	565.74	179,097	118,236	565.74	169,741	127,592	565.74	167,591	129,742
115,000	1,182.91	310,848	591.46	187,240	123,608	591.46	177,459	133,389	591.46	175,211	135,637
120,000	1,234.34	324,362	617.17	195,378	128,984	617.17	185,172	139,190	617.17	182,826	141,536
125,000	1,285.77	337,877	642.89	203,521	134,356	642.89	192,890	144,987	642.89	190,446	147,431
130,000	1,337.20	351,392	668.60	211,659	139,733	668.60	200,603	150,789	668.60	198,061	153,331
135,000	1,388.63	364,907	694.32	219,802	145,105	694.32	208,320	156,587	694.32	205,681	159,226
140,000	1,440.06	378,422	720.03	227,940	150,482	720.03	216,033	162,389	720.03	213,296	165,126
145,000	1,491.49	391,936	745.75	236,083	155,853	745.75	223,751	168,185	745.75	220,916	171,020
150,000	1,542.92	405,451	771.46	244,221	161,230	771.46	231,464	173,987	771.46	228,532	176,919
155,000	1,594.35	418,966	797.18	252,365	166,601	797.18	239,182	179,784	797.18	236,152	182,814
160,000	1,645.79	432,484	822.90	260,508	171,976	822.90	246,899	185,585	822.90	243,772	188,712
165,000	1,697.22	445,999	848.61	268,646	177,353	848.61	254,612	191,387	848.61	251,387	194,612
170,000	1,748.65	459,514	874.33	276,789	182,725	874.33	262,330	197,184	874.33	259,007	200,507
175,000	1,800.08	473,029	900.04	284,927	188,102	900.04	270,043	202,986	900.04	266,622	206,407
180,000	1,851.51	486,544	925.76	293,070	193,474	925.76	277,761	208,783	925.76	274,242	212,302
185,000	1,902.94	500,058	951.47	301,208	198,850	951.47	285,473	214,585	951.47	281,857	218,201
190,000	1,954.37	513,573	977.19	309,351	204,222	977.19	293,191	220,382	977.19	289,477	224,096
195,000	2,005.80	527,088	1,002.90	317,489	209,599	1,002.90	300,904	226,184	1,002.90	297,092	229,996
200,000	2,057.23	540,603	1,028.62	325,632	214,971	1,028.62	308,622	231,981	1,028.62	304,712	235,891

72

BIWEEKLY MORTGAGES 12.25%

AMOUNT OF LOAN	30 YEARS MONTHLY PAYMENT	30 YEARS TOTAL INTRST	360 DAY BASIS 504.866 PAYMENTS BWEEKLY PAYMENT	TOTAL INTRST	INTRST SAVED	364 DAY BASIS 488.247 PAYMENTS BWEEKLY PAYMENT	TOTAL INTRST	INTRST SAVED	365 DAY BASIS 484.432 PAYMENTS BWEEKLY PAYMENT	TOTAL INTRST	INTRST SAVED
$ 50	0.53	141	0.27	86	55	0.27	82	59	0.27	81	60
100	1.05	278	0.53	168	110	0.53	159	119	0.53	157	121
200	2.10	556	1.05	330	226	1.05	313	243	1.05	309	247
300	3.15	834	1.58	498	336	1.58	471	363	1.58	465	369
400	4.20	1,112	2.10	660	452	2.10	625	487	2.10	617	495
500	5.24	1,386	2.62	823	563	2.62	779	607	2.62	769	617
600	6.29	1,664	3.15	990	674	3.15	938	726	3.15	926	738
700	7.34	1,942	3.67	1,153	789	3.67	1,092	850	3.67	1,078	864
800	8.39	2,220	4.20	1,320	900	4.20	1,251	969	4.20	1,235	985
900	9.44	2,498	4.72	1,483	1,015	4.72	1,405	1,093	4.72	1,387	1,111
1,000	10.48	2,773	5.24	1,645	1,128	5.24	1,558	1,215	5.24	1,538	1,235
2,000	20.96	5,546	10.48	3,291	2,255	10.48	3,117	2,429	10.48	3,077	2,469
3,000	31.44	8,318	15.72	4,936	3,382	15.72	4,675	3,643	15.72	4,615	3,703
4,000	41.92	11,091	20.96	6,582	4,509	20.96	6,234	4,857	20.96	6,154	4,937
5,000	52.40	13,864	26.20	8,227	5,637	26.20	7,792	6,072	26.20	7,692	6,172
6,000	62.88	16,637	31.44	9,873	6,764	31.44	9,350	7,287	31.44	9,231	7,406
7,000	73.36	19,410	36.68	11,518	7,892	36.68	10,909	8,501	36.68	10,769	8,641
8,000	83.84	22,182	41.92	13,164	9,018	41.92	12,467	9,715	41.92	12,307	9,875
9,000	94.32	24,955	47.16	14,809	10,146	47.16	14,026	10,929	47.16	13,846	11,109
10,000	104.79	27,724	52.40	16,455	11,269	52.40	15,584	12,140	52.40	15,384	12,340
11,000	115.27	30,497	57.64	18,100	12,397	57.64	17,143	13,354	57.64	16,923	13,574
12,000	125.75	33,270	62.88	19,746	13,524	62.88	18,701	14,569	62.88	18,461	14,809
13,000	136.23	36,043	68.12	21,391	14,652	68.12	20,259	15,784	68.12	20,000	16,043
14,000	146.71	38,816	73.36	23,037	15,779	73.36	21,818	16,998	73.36	21,538	17,278
15,000	157.19	41,588	78.60	24,682	16,906	78.60	23,376	18,212	78.60	23,076	18,512
16,000	167.67	44,361	83.84	26,328	18,033	83.84	24,935	19,426	83.84	24,615	19,746
17,000	178.15	47,134	89.08	27,973	19,161	89.08	26,493	20,641	89.08	26,153	20,981
18,000	188.63	49,907	94.32	29,619	20,288	94.32	28,051	21,856	94.32	27,692	22,215
19,000	199.11	52,680	99.56	31,264	21,416	99.56	29,610	23,070	99.56	29,230	23,450
20,000	209.58	55,449	104.79	32,905	22,544	104.79	31,163	24,286	104.79	30,764	24,685
21,000	220.06	58,222	110.03	34,550	23,672	110.03	32,722	25,500	110.03	32,302	25,920
22,000	230.54	60,994	115.27	36,196	24,798	115.27	34,280	26,714	115.27	33,840	27,154
23,000	241.02	63,767	120.51	37,841	25,926	120.51	35,839	27,928	120.51	35,379	28,388
24,000	251.50	66,540	125.75	39,487	27,053	125.75	37,397	29,143	125.75	36,917	29,623
25,000	261.98	69,313	130.99	41,132	28,181	130.99	38,955	30,358	130.99	38,456	30,857
26,000	272.46	72,086	136.23	42,778	29,308	136.23	40,514	31,572	136.23	39,994	32,092
27,000	282.94	74,858	141.47	44,423	30,435	141.47	42,072	32,786	141.47	41,533	33,325
28,000	293.42	77,631	146.71	46,069	31,562	146.71	43,631	34,000	146.71	43,071	34,560
29,000	303.89	80,400	151.95	47,714	32,686	151.95	45,189	35,211	151.95	44,609	35,791
30,000	314.37	83,173	157.19	49,360	33,813	157.19	46,748	36,425	157.19	46,148	37,025
32,500	340.57	90,105	170.29	53,474	36,631	170.29	50,644	39,461	170.29	49,994	40,111
35,000	366.77	97,037	183.39	57,587	39,450	183.39	54,540	42,497	183.39	53,840	43,197
40,000	419.16	110,898	209.58	65,810	45,088	209.58	62,327	48,571	209.58	61,527	49,371
45,000	471.56	124,762	235.78	74,037	50,725	235.78	70,119	54,643	235.78	69,219	55,543
50,000	523.95	138,622	261.98	82,265	56,357	261.98	77,911	60,711	261.98	76,911	61,711
55,000	576.35	152,486	288.18	90,492	61,994	288.18	85,703	66,783	288.18	84,604	67,882
60,000	628.74	166,346	314.37	98,715	67,631	314.37	93,490	72,856	314.37	92,291	74,055
65,000	681.14	180,210	340.57	106,942	73,268	340.57	101,282	78,928	340.57	99,983	80,227
70,000	733.53	194,071	366.77	115,170	78,901	366.77	109,074	84,997	366.77	107,675	86,396
75,000	785.93	207,935	392.97	123,397	84,538	392.97	116,866	91,069	392.97	115,367	92,568
80,000	838.32	221,795	419.16	131,620	90,175	419.16	124,654	97,141	419.16	123,055	98,740
85,000	890.72	235,659	445.36	139,847	95,812	445.36	132,446	103,213	445.36	130,747	104,912
90,000	943.11	249,520	471.56	148,075	101,445	471.56	140,238	109,282	471.56	138,439	111,081
95,000	995.51	263,384	497.76	156,302	107,082	497.76	148,030	115,354	497.76	146,131	117,253
100,000	1,047.90	277,244	523.95	164,525	112,719	523.95	155,817	121,427	523.95	153,818	123,426
105,000	1,100.30	291,108	550.15	172,752	118,356	550.15	163,609	127,499	550.15	161,510	129,598
110,000	1,152.69	304,968	576.35	180,980	123,988	576.35	171,401	133,567	576.35	169,202	135,766
115,000	1,205.09	318,832	602.55	189,207	129,625	602.55	179,193	139,639	602.55	176,895	141,937
120,000	1,257.48	332,693	628.74	197,429	135,264	628.74	186,980	145,713	628.74	184,582	148,111
125,000	1,309.88	346,557	654.94	205,657	140,900	654.94	194,772	151,785	654.94	192,274	154,283
130,000	1,362.27	360,417	681.14	213,884	146,533	681.14	202,565	157,852	681.14	199,966	160,451
135,000	1,414.61	374,281	707.34	222,112	152,169	707.34	210,357	163,924	707.34	207,658	166,623
140,000	1,467.06	388,142	733.53	230,334	157,808	733.53	218,144	169,998	733.53	215,345	172,797
145,000	1,519.45	402,002	759.73	238,562	163,440	759.73	225,936	176,066	759.73	223,038	178,964
150,000	1,571.85	415,866	785.93	246,789	169,077	785.93	233,728	182,138	785.93	230,730	185,136
155,000	1,624.24	429,726	812.12	255,012	174,714	812.12	241,515	188,211	812.12	238,417	191,309
160,000	1,676.64	443,590	838.32	263,239	180,351	838.32	249,307	194,283	838.32	246,109	197,481
165,000	1,729.03	457,451	864.52	271,467	185,984	864.52	257,099	200,352	864.52	253,801	203,650
170,000	1,781.43	471,315	890.72	279,694	191,621	890.72	264,891	206,424	890.72	261,493	209,822
175,000	1,833.82	485,175	916.91	287,917	197,258	916.91	272,679	212,496	916.91	269,181	215,994
180,000	1,886.22	499,039	943.11	296,144	202,895	943.11	280,471	218,568	943.11	276,873	222,166
185,000	1,938.61	512,900	969.31	304,372	208,528	969.31	288,263	224,637	969.31	284,565	228,335
190,000	1,991.01	526,764	995.51	312,599	214,165	995.51	296,055	230,709	995.51	292,257	234,507
195,000	2,043.40	540,624	1,021.70	320,822	219,802	1,021.70	303,842	236,782	1,021.70	299,944	240,680
200,000	2,095.80	554,488	1,047.90	329,049	225,439	1,047.90	311,634	242,854	1,047.90	307,636	246,852

73

12.50% BIWEEKLY MORTGAGES

AMOUNT OF LOAN	30 YEARS		360 DAY BASIS 498.749 PAYMENTS			364 DAY BASIS 482.064 PAYMENTS			365 DAY BASIS 478.239 PAYMENTS		
	MONTHLY PAYMENT	TOTAL INTRST	BWEEKLY PAYMENT	TOTAL INTRST	INTRST SAVED	BWEEKLY PAYMENT	TOTAL INTRST	INTRST SAVED	BWEEKLY PAYMENT	TOTAL INTRST	INTRST SAVED
$ 50	0.54	144	0.27	85	59	0.27	80	64	0.27	79	65
100	1.07	285	0.54	169	116	0.54	160	125	0.54	158	127
200	2.14	570	1.07	334	236	1.07	316	254	1.07	312	258
300	3.21	856	1.61	503	353	1.61	476	380	1.61	470	386
400	4.27	1,137	2.14	667	470	2.14	632	505	2.14	623	514
500	5.34	1,422	2.67	832	590	2.67	787	635	2.67	777	645
600	6.41	1,708	3.21	1,001	707	3.21	947	761	3.21	935	773
700	7.48	1,993	3.74	1,165	828	3.74	1,103	890	3.74	1,089	904
800	8.54	2,274	4.27	1,330	944	4.27	1,258	1,016	4.27	1,242	1,032
900	9.61	2,560	4.81	1,499	1,061	4.81	1,419	1,141	4.81	1,400	1,160
1,000	10.68	2,845	5.34	1,663	1,182	5.34	1,574	1,271	5.34	1,554	1,291
2,000	21.35	5,686	10.68	3,327	2,359	10.68	3,148	2,538	10.68	3,108	2,578
3,000	32.02	8,527	16.01	4,985	3,542	16.01	4,718	3,809	16.01	4,657	3,870
4,000	42.70	11,372	21.35	6,648	4,724	21.35	6,292	5,080	21.35	6,210	5,162
5,000	53.37	14,213	26.69	8,312	5,901	26.69	7,866	6,347	26.69	7,764	6,449
6,000	64.04	17,054	32.02	9,970	7,084	32.02	9,436	7,618	32.02	9,313	7,741
7,000	74.71	19,896	37.36	11,633	8,263	37.36	11,010	8,886	37.36	10,867	9,029
8,000	85.39	22,740	42.70	13,297	9,443	42.70	12,584	10,156	42.70	12,421	10,319
9,000	96.06	25,582	48.03	14,955	10,627	48.03	14,154	11,428	48.03	13,970	11,612
10,000	106.73	28,423	53.37	16,618	11,805	53.37	15,728	12,695	53.37	15,524	12,899
11,000	117.40	31,264	58.70	18,277	12,987	58.70	17,297	13,967	58.70	17,073	14,191
12,000	128.08	34,109	64.04	19,940	14,169	64.04	18,871	15,238	64.04	18,626	15,483
13,000	138.75	36,950	69.38	21,603	15,347	69.38	20,446	16,504	69.38	20,180	16,770
14,000	149.42	39,791	74.71	23,262	16,529	74.71	22,015	17,776	74.71	21,729	18,062
15,000	160.09	42,632	80.05	24,925	17,707	80.05	23,589	19,043	80.05	23,283	19,349
16,000	170.77	45,477	85.39	26,588	18,889	85.39	25,163	20,314	85.39	24,837	20,640
17,000	181.44	48,318	90.72	28,247	20,071	90.72	26,733	21,585	90.72	26,386	21,932
18,000	192.11	51,160	96.06	29,910	21,250	96.06	28,307	22,853	96.06	27,940	23,220
19,000	202.78	54,001	101.39	31,568	22,433	101.39	29,876	24,125	101.39	29,489	24,512
20,000	213.46	56,846	106.73	33,231	23,615	106.73	31,451	25,395	106.73	31,042	25,804
21,000	224.13	59,687	112.07	34,895	24,792	112.07	33,025	26,662	112.07	32,596	27,091
22,000	234.80	62,528	117.40	36,553	25,975	117.40	34,594	27,934	117.40	34,145	28,383
23,000	245.47	65,369	122.74	38,216	27,153	122.74	36,169	29,200	122.74	35,699	29,670
24,000	256.15	68,214	128.08	39,880	28,334	128.08	37,743	30,471	128.08	37,253	30,961
25,000	266.82	71,055	133.41	41,538	29,517	133.41	39,312	31,743	133.41	38,802	32,253
26,000	277.49	73,896	138.75	43,201	30,695	138.75	40,886	33,010	138.75	40,356	33,540
27,000	288.16	76,738	144.08	44,860	31,878	144.08	42,456	34,282	144.08	41,905	34,833
28,000	298.84	79,582	149.42	46,523	33,059	149.42	44,030	35,552	149.42	43,458	36,124
29,000	309.51	82,424	154.76	48,186	34,238	154.76	45,604	36,820	154.76	45,012	37,412
30,000	320.18	85,265	160.09	49,845	35,420	160.09	47,174	38,091	160.09	46,561	38,704
32,500	346.86	92,370	173.43	53,998	38,372	173.43	51,104	41,266	173.43	50,441	41,929
35,000	373.55	99,478	186.78	58,156	41,322	186.78	55,040	44,438	186.78	54,325	45,153
40,000	426.91	113,688	213.46	66,463	47,225	213.46	62,901	50,787	213.46	62,085	51,603
45,000	480.27	127,897	240.14	74,770	53,127	240.14	70,763	57,134	240.14	69,844	58,053
50,000	533.63	142,107	266.82	83,076	59,031	266.82	78,624	63,483	266.82	77,604	64,503
55,000	587.00	156,320	293.50	91,383	64,937	293.50	86,486	69,834	293.50	85,363	70,957
60,000	640.36	170,530	320.18	89,689	70,841	320.18	94,347	76,183	320.18	93,123	77,407
65,000	693.72	184,739	346.86	107,996	76,743	346.86	102,209	82,530	346.86	100,882	83,857
70,000	747.09	198,952	373.55	116,308	82,644	373.55	110,075	88,877	373.55	108,646	90,306
75,000	800.45	213,162	400.23	124,614	88,548	400.23	117,936	95,226	400.23	116,406	96,756
80,000	853.81	227,372	426.91	132,921	94,451	426.91	125,798	101,574	426.91	124,165	103,207
85,000	907.17	241,581	453.59	141,228	100,353	453.59	133,659	107,922	453.59	131,924	109,657
90,000	960.54	255,794	480.27	149,534	106,260	480.27	141,521	114,273	480.27	139,684	116,110
95,000	1,013.90	270,004	506.95	157,841	112,163	506.95	149,382	120,622	506.95	147,443	122,561
100,000	1,067.26	284,214	533.63	166,147	118,067	533.63	157,244	126,970	533.63	155,203	129,011
105,000	1,120.63	298,427	560.32	174,459	123,968	560.32	165,110	133,317	560.32	162,967	135,460
110,000	1,173.99	312,636	587.00	182,766	129,870	587.00	172,972	139,664	587.00	170,726	141,910
115,000	1,227.35	326,846	613.68	191,072	135,774	613.68	180,833	146,013	613.68	178,486	148,360
120,000	1,280.71	341,056	640.36	199,379	141,677	640.36	188,695	152,361	640.36	186,245	154,811
125,000	1,334.08	355,269	667.04	207,686	147,583	667.04	196,556	158,713	667.04	194,005	161,264
130,000	1,387.44	369,478	693.72	215,992	153,486	693.72	204,417	165,061	693.72	201,764	167,714
135,000	1,440.80	383,688	720.40	224,299	159,389	720.40	212,279	171,409	720.40	209,523	174,165
140,000	1,494.17	397,901	747.09	232,610	165,291	747.09	220,145	177,756	747.09	217,288	180,613
145,000	1,547.53	412,111	773.77	240,917	171,194	773.77	228,007	184,104	773.77	225,047	187,064
150,000	1,600.89	426,320	800.45	249,224	177,096	800.45	235,868	190,452	800.45	232,806	193,514
155,000	1,654.25	440,530	827.13	257,530	183,000	827.13	243,730	196,800	827.13	240,566	199,964
160,000	1,707.62	454,743	853.81	265,837	188,906	853.81	251,591	203,152	853.81	248,325	206,418
165,000	1,760.98	468,953	880.49	274,144	194,809	880.49	259,453	209,500	880.49	256,085	212,868
170,000	1,814.34	483,162	907.17	282,450	200,712	907.17	267,314	215,848	907.17	263,844	219,318
175,000	1,867.71	497,376	933.86	290,762	206,614	933.86	275,180	222,196	933.86	271,608	225,768
180,000	1,921.07	511,585	960.54	299,068	212,517	960.54	283,042	228,543	960.54	279,368	232,217
185,000	1,974.43	525,795	987.22	307,375	218,420	987.22	290,903	234,892	987.22	287,127	238,668
190,000	2,027.79	540,004	1,013.90	315,682	224,322	1,013.90	298,765	241,239	1,013.90	294,887	245,117
195,000	2,081.16	554,218	1,040.58	323,988	230,230	1,040.58	306,626	247,592	1,040.58	302,646	251,572
200,000	2,134.52	568,427	1,067.26	332,295	236,132	1,067.26	314,488	253,939	1,067.26	310,405	258,022

74

AMOUNT OF LOAN	30 YEARS		360 DAY BASIS 492.661 PAYMENTS			364 DAY BASIS 475.928 PAYMENTS			365 DAY BASIS 472.097 PAYMENTS		
	MONTHLY PAYMENT	TOTAL INTRST	BWEEKLY PAYMENT	TOTAL INTRST	INTRST SAVED	BWEEKLY PAYMENT	TOTAL INTRST	INTRST SAVED	BWEEKLY PAYMENT	TOTAL INTRST	INTRST SAVED
$ 50	0.55	148	0.28	88	60	0.28	83	65	0.28	82	66
100	1.09	292	0.55	171	121	0.55	162	130	0.55	160	132
200	2.18	585	1.09	337	248	1.09	319	266	1.09	315	270
300	3.27	877	1.64	508	369	1.64	481	396	1.64	474	403
400	4.35	1,166	2.18	674	492	2.18	638	528	2.18	629	537
500	5.44	1,458	2.72	840	618	2.72	795	663	2.72	784	674
600	6.53	1,751	3.27	1,011	740	3.27	956	795	3.27	944	807
700	7.61	2,040	3.81	1,177	863	3.81	1,113	927	3.81	1,099	941
800	8.70	2,332	4.35	1,343	989	4.35	1,270	1,062	4.35	1,254	1,078
900	9.79	2,624	4.90	1,514	1,110	4.90	1,432	1,192	4.90	1,413	1,211
1,000	10.87	2,913	5.44	1,680	1,233	5.44	1,589	1,324	5.44	1,568	1,345
2,000	21.74	5,826	10.87	3,355	2,471	10.87	3,173	2,653	10.87	3,132	2,694
3,000	32.61	8,740	16.31	5,035	3,705	16.31	4,762	3,978	16.31	4,700	4,040
4,000	43.47	11,649	21.74	6,710	4,939	21.74	6,347	5,302	21.74	6,263	5,386
5,000	54.34	14,562	27.17	8,386	6,176	27.17	7,931	6,631	27.17	7,827	6,735
6,000	65.21	17,476	32.61	10,066	7,410	32.61	9,520	7,956	32.61	9,395	8,081
7,000	76.07	20,385	38.04	11,741	8,644	38.04	11,104	9,281	38.04	10,959	9,426
8,000	86.94	23,298	43.47	13,416	9,882	43.47	12,689	10,609	43.47	12,522	10,776
9,000	97.81	26,212	48.91	15,096	11,116	48.91	14,278	11,934	48.91	14,090	12,122
10,000	108.67	29,121	54.34	16,771	12,350	54.34	15,862	13,259	54.34	15,654	13,467
11,000	119.54	32,034	59.77	18,446	13,588	59.77	17,446	14,588	59.77	17,217	14,817
12,000	130.41	34,948	65.21	20,126	14,822	65.21	19,035	15,913	65.21	18,785	16,163
13,000	141.28	37,861	70.64	21,802	16,059	70.64	20,620	17,241	70.64	20,349	17,512
14,000	152.14	40,770	76.07	23,477	17,293	76.07	22,204	18,566	76.07	21,912	18,858
15,000	163.01	43,684	81.51	25,157	18,527	81.51	23,793	19,891	81.51	23,481	20,203
16,000	173.88	46,597	86.94	26,832	19,765	86.94	25,377	21,220	86.94	25,044	21,553
17,000	184.74	49,506	92.37	28,507	20,999	92.37	26,961	22,545	92.37	26,608	22,898
18,000	195.61	52,420	97.81	30,187	22,233	97.81	28,551	23,869	97.81	28,176	24,244
19,000	206.48	55,333	103.24	31,862	23,471	103.24	30,135	25,198	103.24	29,739	25,594
20,000	217.34	58,242	108.67	33,537	24,705	108.67	31,719	26,523	108.67	31,303	26,939
21,000	228.21	61,156	114.11	35,218	25,938	114.11	33,308	27,848	114.11	32,871	28,285
22,000	239.08	64,069	119.54	36,893	27,176	119.54	34,892	29,177	119.54	34,434	29,635
23,000	249.94	66,978	124.97	38,568	28,410	124.97	36,477	30,501	124.97	35,998	30,980
24,000	260.81	69,892	130.41	40,248	29,644	130.41	38,066	31,826	130.41	37,566	32,326
25,000	271.68	72,805	135.84	41,923	30,882	135.84	39,650	33,155	135.84	39,130	33,675
26,000	282.55	75,718	141.28	43,603	32,115	141.28	41,239	34,479	141.28	40,698	35,020
27,000	293.41	78,628	146.71	45,278	33,350	146.71	42,823	35,805	146.71	42,261	36,367
28,000	304.28	81,541	152.14	46,953	34,588	152.14	44,408	37,133	152.14	43,825	37,716
29,000	315.15	84,454	157.58	48,634	35,820	157.58	45,997	38,457	157.58	45,393	39,061
30,000	326.01	87,364	163.01	50,309	37,055	163.01	47,581	39,783	163.01	46,957	40,407
32,500	353.18	94,645	176.59	54,499	40,146	176.59	51,544	43,101	176.59	50,868	43,777
35,000	380.35	101,926	190.18	58,694	43,232	190.18	55,512	46,414	190.18	54,783	47,143
40,000	434.68	116,485	217.34	67,075	49,410	217.34	63,438	53,047	217.34	62,606	53,879
45,000	489.02	131,047	244.51	75,461	55,586	244.51	71,369	59,678	244.51	70,432	60,615
50,000	543.35	145,606	271.68	83,846	61,760	271.68	79,300	66,306	271.68	78,259	67,347
55,000	597.69	160,168	298.85	92,232	67,936	298.85	87,231	72,937	298.85	86,086	74,082
60,000	652.02	174,727	326.01	100,612	74,115	326.01	95,157	79,570	326.01	93,908	80,819
65,000	706.36	189,290	353.18	108,998	80,292	353.18	103,088	86,202	353.18	101,735	87,555
70,000	760.69	203,848	380.35	117,384	86,464	380.35	111,019	92,829	380.35	109,562	94,286
75,000	815.02	218,407	407.51	125,764	92,643	407.51	118,945	99,462	407.51	117,384	101,023
80,000	869.36	232,970	434.68	134,150	98,820	434.68	126,876	106,094	434.68	125,211	107,759
85,000	923.69	247,528	461.85	142,535	104,993	461.85	134,807	112,721	461.85	133,038	114,490
90,000	978.03	262,091	489.02	150,921	111,170	489.02	142,738	119,353	489.02	140,865	121,226
95,000	1,032.36	276,650	516.18	159,302	117,348	516.18	150,665	125,985	516.18	148,687	127,963
100,000	1,086.70	291,212	543.35	167,687	123,525	543.35	158,595	132,617	543.35	156,514	134,698
105,000	1,141.03	305,771	570.52	176,073	129,698	570.52	166,526	139,245	570.52	164,341	141,430
110,000	1,195.37	320,333	597.69	184,459	135,874	597.69	174,457	145,876	597.69	172,168	148,165
115,000	1,249.70	334,892	624.85	192,839	142,053	624.85	182,384	152,508	624.85	179,990	154,902
120,000	1,304.04	349,454	652.02	201,225	148,229	652.02	190,315	159,139	652.02	187,817	161,637
125,000	1,358.37	364,013	679.19	209,610	154,403	679.19	198,246	165,767	679.19	195,644	168,369
130,000	1,412.71	378,576	706.36	217,996	160,580	706.36	206,177	172,399	706.36	203,470	175,106
135,000	1,467.04	393,134	733.52	226,377	166,757	733.52	214,103	179,031	733.52	211,293	181,841
140,000	1,521.38	407,697	760.69	234,762	172,935	760.69	222,034	185,663	760.69	219,119	188,578
145,000	1,575.71	422,256	787.86	243,148	179,108	787.86	229,965	192,291	787.86	226,946	195,310
150,000	1,630.04	436,814	815.02	251,529	185,285	815.02	237,891	198,923	815.02	234,768	202,046
155,000	1,684.38	451,377	842.19	259,914	191,463	842.19	245,822	205,555	842.19	242,595	208,782
160,000	1,738.71	465,936	869.36	268,300	197,636	869.36	253,753	212,183	869.36	250,422	215,514
165,000	1,793.05	480,498	896.53	276,685	203,813	896.53	261,684	218,814	896.53	258,249	222,249
170,000	1,847.38	495,057	923.69	285,066	209,991	923.69	269,610	225,447	923.69	266,071	228,986
175,000	1,901.72	509,619	950.86	293,452	216,167	950.86	277,541	232,078	950.86	273,898	235,721
180,000	1,956.05	524,178	978.03	301,837	222,341	978.03	285,472	238,706	978.03	281,725	242,453
185,000	2,010.39	538,740	1,005.20	310,223	228,517	1,005.20	293,403	245,337	1,005.20	289,552	249,188
190,000	2,064.72	553,299	1,032.36	318,604	234,695	1,032.36	301,329	251,970	1,032.36	297,374	255,925
195,000	2,119.06	567,862	1,059.53	326,989	240,873	1,059.53	309,260	258,602	1,059.53	305,201	262,661
200,000	2,173.39	582,420	1,086.70	335,375	247,045	1,086.70	317,191	265,229	1,086.70	313,028	269,392

BIWEEKLY MORTGAGES

AMOUNT OF LOAN	30 YEARS		360 DAY BASIS 486.609 PAYMENTS			364 DAY BASIS 469.844 PAYMENTS			365 DAY BASIS 466.011 PAYMENTS		
	MONTHLY PAYMENT	TOTAL INTRST	BWEEKLY PAYMENT	TOTAL INTRST	INTRST SAVED	BWEEKLY PAYMENT	TOTAL INTRST	INTRST SAVED	BWEEKLY PAYMENT	TOTAL INTRST	INTRST SAVED
$ 50	0.56	152	0.28	86	66	0.28	82	70	0.28	80	72
100	1.11	300	0.56	173	127	0.56	163	137	0.56	161	139
200	2.22	599	1.11	340	259	1.11	322	277	1.11	317	282
300	3.32	895	1.66	508	387	1.66	480	415	1.66	474	421
400	4.43	1,195	2.22	680	515	2.22	643	552	2.22	635	560
500	5.54	1,494	2.77	848	646	2.77	801	693	2.77	791	703
600	6.64	1,790	3.32	1,016	774	3.32	960	830	3.32	947	843
700	7.75	2,090	3.88	1,188	902	3.88	1,123	967	3.88	1,108	982
800	8.85	2,386	4.43	1,356	1,030	4.43	1,281	1,105	4.43	1,264	1,122
900	9.96	2,686	4.98	1,523	1,163	4.98	1,440	1,246	4.98	1,421	1,265
1,000	11.07	2,985	5.54	1,696	1,289	5.54	1,603	1,382	5.54	1,582	1,403
2,000	22.13	5,967	11.07	3,387	2,580	11.07	3,201	2,766	11.07	3,159	2,808
3,000	33.19	8,948	16.60	5,078	3,870	16.60	4,799	4,149	16.60	4,736	4,212
4,000	44.25	11,930	22.13	6,769	5,161	22.13	6,398	5,532	22.13	6,313	5,617
5,000	55.31	14,912	27.66	8,460	6,452	27.66	7,996	6,916	27.66	7,890	7,022
6,000	66.38	17,897	33.19	10,151	7,746	33.19	9,594	8,303	33.19	9,467	8,430
7,000	77.44	20,878	38.72	11,842	9,036	38.72	11,192	9,686	38.72	11,044	9,834
8,000	88.50	23,860	44.25	13,532	10,328	44.25	12,791	11,069	44.25	12,621	11,239
9,000	99.56	26,842	49.78	15,223	11,619	49.78	14,389	12,453	49.78	14,198	12,644
10,000	110.62	29,823	55.31	16,914	12,909	55.31	15,987	13,836	55.31	15,775	14,048
11,000	121.69	32,808	60.85	18,610	14,198	60.85	17,590	15,218	60.85	17,357	15,451
12,000	132.75	35,790	66.38	20,301	15,489	66.38	19,188	16,602	66.38	18,934	16,856
13,000	143.81	38,772	71.91	21,992	16,780	71.91	20,786	17,986	71.91	20,511	18,261
14,000	154.87	41,753	77.44	23,683	18,070	77.44	22,385	19,368	77.44	22,088	19,665
15,000	165.93	44,735	82.97	25,374	19,361	82.97	23,983	20,752	82.97	23,665	21,070
16,000	177.00	47,720	88.50	27,065	20,655	88.50	25,581	22,139	88.50	25,242	22,478
17,000	188.06	50,702	94.03	28,756	21,946	94.03	27,179	23,523	94.03	26,819	23,883
18,000	199.12	53,683	99.56	30,447	23,236	99.56	28,778	24,905	99.56	28,396	25,287
19,000	210.18	56,665	105.09	32,138	24,527	105.09	30,376	26,289	105.09	29,973	26,692
20,000	221.24	59,646	110.62	33,829	25,817	110.62	31,974	27,672	110.62	31,550	28,096
21,000	232.31	62,632	116.16	35,525	27,107	116.16	33,577	29,055	116.16	33,132	29,500
22,000	243.37	65,613	121.69	37,215	28,398	121.69	35,175	30,438	121.69	34,709	30,904
23,000	254.43	68,595	127.22	38,906	29,689	127.22	36,774	31,821	127.22	36,286	32,309
24,000	265.49	71,576	132.75	40,597	30,979	132.75	38,372	33,204	132.75	37,863	33,713
25,000	276.55	74,558	138.28	42,288	32,270	138.28	39,970	34,588	138.28	39,440	35,118
26,000	287.62	77,543	143.81	43,979	33,564	143.81	41,568	35,975	143.81	41,017	36,526
27,000	298.68	80,525	149.34	45,670	34,855	149.34	43,167	37,358	149.34	42,594	37,931
28,000	309.74	83,506	154.87	47,361	36,145	154.87	44,765	38,741	154.87	44,171	39,335
29,000	320.80	86,488	160.40	49,052	37,436	160.40	46,363	40,125	160.40	45,748	40,740
30,000	331.86	89,470	165.93	50,743	38,727	165.93	47,961	41,509	165.93	47,325	42,145
32,500	359.52	96,927	179.76	54,973	41,954	179.76	51,959	44,968	179.76	51,270	45,657
35,000	387.17	104,381	193.59	59,203	45,178	193.59	55,957	48,424	193.59	55,215	49,166
40,000	442.48	119,293	221.24	67,663	51,636	221.24	63,948	55,345	221.24	63,100	56,193
45,000	497.79	134,204	248.90	76,117	58,087	248.90	71,944	62,260	248.90	70,990	63,214
50,000	553.10	149,116	276.55	84,572	64,544	276.55	79,935	69,181	276.55	78,875	70,241
55,000	608.41	164,028	304.21	93,031	70,997	304.21	87,931	76,097	304.21	86,765	77,263
60,000	663.72	178,939	331.86	101,486	77,453	331.86	95,922	83,017	331.86	94,650	84,289
65,000	719.03	193,851	359.52	109,946	83,905	359.52	103,918	89,933	359.52	102,540	91,311
70,000	774.34	208,762	387.17	118,400	90,362	387.17	111,910	96,852	387.17	110,425	98,337
75,000	829.65	223,674	414.83	126,860	96,814	414.83	119,905	103,769	414.83	118,315	105,359
80,000	884.96	238,586	442.48	135,315	103,271	442.48	127,897	110,689	442.48	126,201	112,385
85,000	940.27	253,497	470.14	143,774	109,723	470.14	135,892	117,605	470.14	134,090	119,407
90,000	995.58	268,409	497.79	152,229	116,180	497.79	143,884	124,525	497.79	141,976	126,433
95,000	1,050.89	283,320	525.45	160,689	122,631	525.45	151,880	131,440	525.45	149,865	133,455
100,000	1,106.20	298,232	553.10	169,143	129,089	553.10	159,871	138,361	553.10	157,751	140,481
105,000	1,161.51	313,144	580.76	177,603	135,541	580.76	167,867	145,277	580.76	165,641	147,503
110,000	1,216.82	328,055	608.41	186,058	141,997	608.41	175,858	152,197	608.41	173,526	154,529
115,000	1,272.13	342,967	636.07	194,517	148,450	636.07	183,854	159,113	636.07	181,416	161,551
120,000	1,327.44	357,878	663.72	202,972	154,906	663.72	191,845	166,033	663.72	189,301	168,577
125,000	1,382.75	372,790	691.38	211,432	161,358	691.38	199,841	172,949	691.38	197,191	175,599
130,000	1,438.06	387,702	719.03	219,886	167,816	719.03	207,832	179,870	719.03	205,076	182,626
135,000	1,493.37	402,613	746.69	228,346	174,267	746.69	215,828	186,785	746.69	212,966	189,647
140,000	1,548.68	417,525	774.34	236,801	180,724	774.34	223,819	193,706	774.34	220,851	196,674
145,000	1,603.99	432,436	802.00	245,261	187,176	802.00	231,815	200,621	802.00	228,741	203,695
150,000	1,659.30	447,348	829.65	253,715	193,633	829.65	239,806	207,542	829.65	236,626	210,722
155,000	1,714.61	462,260	857.31	262,175	200,085	857.31	247,802	214,458	857.31	244,516	217,744
160,000	1,769.92	477,171	884.96	270,630	206,541	884.96	255,793	221,378	884.96	252,401	224,770
165,000	1,825.23	492,083	912.62	279,089	212,994	912.62	263,789	228,294	912.62	260,291	231,792
170,000	1,880.54	506,994	940.27	287,544	219,450	940.27	271,780	235,214	940.27	268,176	238,818
175,000	1,935.85	521,906	967.93	296,003	225,903	967.93	279,776	242,130	967.93	276,066	245,840
180,000	1,991.16	536,818	995.58	304,458	232,360	995.58	287,767	249,051	995.58	283,951	252,867
185,000	2,046.47	551,729	1,023.24	312,918	238,811	1,023.24	295,763	255,966	1,023.24	291,841	259,888
190,000	2,101.78	566,641	1,050.89	321,373	245,268	1,050.89	303,754	262,887	1,050.89	299,726	266,915
195,000	2,157.09	581,552	1,078.55	329,832	251,720	1,078.55	311,750	269,802	1,078.55	307,616	273,936
200,000	2,212.40	596,464	1,106.20	338,287	258,177	1,106.20	319,741	276,723	1,106.20	315,501	280,963

AMOUNT OF LOAN	30 YEARS		360 DAY BASIS 480.599 PAYMENTS			364 DAY BASIS 463.817 PAYMENTS			365 DAY BASIS 459.984 PAYMENTS		
	MONTHLY PAYMENT	TOTAL INTRST	BWEEKLY PAYMENT	TOTAL INTRST	INTRST SAVED	BWEEKLY PAYMENT	TOTAL INTRST	INTRST SAVED	BWEEKLY PAYMENT	TOTAL INTRST	INTRST SAVED
$ 50	0.57	155	0.29	89	66	0.29	85	70	0.29	83	72
100	1.13	307	0.57	174	133	0.57	164	143	0.57	162	145
200	2.26	614	1.13	343	271	1.13	324	290	1.13	320	294
300	3.38	917	1.69	512	405	1.69	484	433	1.69	477	440
400	4.51	1,224	2.26	686	538	2.26	648	576	2.26	640	584
500	5.63	1,527	2.82	855	672	2.82	808	719	2.82	797	730
600	6.76	1,834	3.38	1,024	810	3.38	968	866	3.38	955	879
700	7.89	2,140	3.95	1,198	942	3.95	1,132	1,008	3.95	1,117	1,023
800	9.01	2,444	4.51	1,368	1,076	4.51	1,292	1,152	4.51	1,275	1,169
900	10.14	2,750	5.07	1,537	1,213	5.07	1,452	1,298	5.07	1,432	1,318
1,000	11.26	3,054	5.63	1,706	1,348	5.63	1,611	1,443	5.63	1,590	1,464
2,000	22.52	6,107	11.26	3,412	2,695	11.26	3,223	2,884	11.26	3,179	2,928
3,000	33.78	9,161	16.89	5,117	4,044	16.89	4,834	4,327	16.89	4,769	4,392
4,000	45.04	12,214	22.52	6,823	5,391	22.52	6,445	5,769	22.52	6,359	5,855
5,000	56.29	15,264	28.15	8,529	6,735	28.15	8,056	7,208	28.15	7,949	7,315
6,000	67.55	18,318	33.78	10,235	8,083	33.78	9,668	8,650	33.78	9,538	8,780
7,000	78.81	21,372	39.41	11,940	9,432	39.41	11,279	10,093	39.41	11,128	10,244
8,000	90.07	24,425	45.04	13,646	10,779	45.04	12,890	11,535	45.04	12,718	11,707
9,000	101.32	27,475	50.66	15,347	12,128	50.66	14,497	12,978	50.66	14,303	13,172
10,000	112.58	30,529	56.29	17,053	13,476	56.29	16,108	14,421	56.29	15,892	14,637
11,000	123.84	33,582	61.92	18,759	14,823	61.92	17,720	15,862	61.92	17,482	16,100
12,000	135.10	36,636	67.55	20,464	16,172	67.55	19,331	17,305	67.55	19,072	17,564
13,000	146.36	39,690	73.18	22,170	17,520	73.18	20,942	18,748	73.18	20,662	19,028
14,000	157.61	42,740	78.81	23,876	18,864	78.81	22,553	20,187	78.81	22,251	20,489
15,000	168.87	45,793	84.44	25,582	20,211	84.44	24,165	21,628	84.44	23,841	21,952
16,000	180.13	48,847	90.07	27,288	21,559	90.07	25,776	23,071	90.07	25,431	23,416
17,000	191.39	51,900	95.70	28,993	22,907	95.70	27,387	24,513	95.70	27,020	24,880
18,000	202.64	54,950	101.32	30,694	24,256	101.32	28,994	25,956	101.32	28,606	26,344
19,000	213.90	58,004	106.95	32,400	25,604	106.95	30,605	27,399	106.95	30,195	27,809
20,000	225.16	61,058	112.58	34,106	26,952	112.58	32,217	28,841	112.58	31,785	29,273
21,000	236.42	64,111	118.21	35,812	28,299	118.21	33,828	30,283	118.21	33,375	30,736
22,000	247.68	67,165	123.84	37,517	29,648	123.84	35,439	31,726	123.84	34,964	32,201
23,000	258.93	70,215	129.47	39,223	30,992	129.47	37,050	33,165	129.47	36,554	33,661
24,000	270.19	73,268	135.10	40,929	32,339	135.10	38,662	34,606	135.10	38,144	35,124
25,000	281.45	76,322	140.73	42,635	33,687	140.73	40,273	36,049	140.73	39,734	36,588
26,000	292.71	79,376	146.36	44,340	35,036	146.36	41,884	37,492	146.36	41,323	38,053
27,000	303.96	82,426	151.98	46,041	36,385	151.98	43,491	38,935	151.98	42,908	39,518
28,000	315.22	85,479	157.61	47,747	37,732	157.61	45,102	40,377	157.61	44,498	40,981
29,000	326.48	88,533	163.24	49,453	39,080	163.24	46,713	41,820	163.24	46,088	42,445
30,000	337.74	91,586	168.87	51,159	40,427	168.87	48,325	43,261	168.87	47,677	43,909
32,500	365.88	99,217	182.94	55,421	43,796	182.94	52,351	46,866	182.94	51,649	47,568
35,000	394.03	106,851	197.02	59,688	47,163	197.02	56,381	50,470	197.02	55,626	51,225
40,000	450.31	122,112	225.16	68,212	53,900	225.16	64,433	57,679	225.16	63,570	58,542
45,000	506.60	137,376	253.30	76,736	60,640	253.30	72,485	64,891	253.30	71,514	65,862
50,000	562.89	152,640	281.45	85,265	67,375	281.45	80,541	72,099	281.45	79,462	73,178
55,000	619.18	167,905	309.59	93,789	74,116	309.59	88,593	79,312	309.59	87,406	80,499
60,000	675.47	183,169	337.74	102,318	80,851	337.74	96,650	86,519	337.74	95,355	87,814
65,000	731.76	198,434	365.88	110,842	87,592	365.88	104,701	93,733	365.88	103,299	95,135
70,000	788.05	213,698	394.03	119,370	94,328	394.03	112,758	100,940	394.03	111,247	102,451
75,000	844.34	228,962	422.17	127,894	101,068	422.17	120,810	108,152	422.17	119,191	109,771
80,000	900.62	244,223	450.31	136,419	107,804	450.31	128,861	115,362	450.31	127,135	117,088
85,000	956.91	259,488	478.46	144,947	114,541	478.46	136,918	122,570	478.46	135,084	124,404
90,000	1,013.20	274,752	506.60	153,471	121,281	506.60	144,970	129,782	506.60	143,028	131,724
95,000	1,069.49	290,016	534.75	162,000	128,016	534.75	153,026	136,990	534.75	150,976	139,040
100,000	1,125.78	305,281	562.89	170,524	134,757	562.89	161,078	144,203	562.89	158,920	146,361
105,000	1,182.07	320,545	591.04	179,053	141,492	591.04	169,134	151,411	591.04	166,869	153,676
110,000	1,238.36	335,810	619.18	187,577	148,233	619.18	177,186	158,624	619.18	174,813	160,997
115,000	1,294.64	351,070	647.32	196,101	154,969	647.32	185,238	165,832	647.32	182,757	168,313
120,000	1,350.93	366,335	675.47	204,630	161,705	675.47	193,294	173,041	675.47	190,705	175,630
125,000	1,407.22	381,599	703.61	213,154	168,445	703.61	201,346	180,253	703.61	198,649	182,950
130,000	1,463.51	396,864	731.76	221,683	175,181	731.76	209,403	187,461	731.76	206,598	190,266
135,000	1,519.80	412,128	759.90	230,207	181,921	759.90	217,455	194,673	759.90	214,542	197,586
140,000	1,576.09	427,392	788.05	238,736	188,656	788.05	225,511	201,881	788.05	222,490	204,902
145,000	1,632.38	442,657	816.19	247,260	195,397	816.19	233,563	209,094	816.19	230,434	212,223
150,000	1,688.67	457,921	844.34	255,789	202,132	844.34	241,619	216,302	844.34	238,383	219,538
155,000	1,744.95	473,182	872.48	264,313	208,869	872.48	249,671	223,511	872.48	246,327	226,855
160,000	1,801.24	488,446	900.62	272,837	215,609	900.62	257,723	230,723	900.62	254,271	234,175
165,000	1,857.53	503,711	928.77	281,366	222,345	928.77	265,779	237,932	928.77	262,219	241,492
170,000	1,913.82	518,975	956.91	289,890	229,085	956.91	273,831	245,144	956.91	270,163	248,812
175,000	1,970.11	534,240	985.06	298,419	235,821	985.06	281,888	252,352	985.06	278,112	256,128
180,000	2,026.40	549,504	1,013.20	306,943	242,561	1,013.20	289,939	259,565	1,013.20	286,056	263,448
185,000	2,082.69	564,768	1,041.35	315,472	249,296	1,041.35	297,996	266,772	1,041.35	294,004	270,764
190,000	2,138.97	580,029	1,069.49	323,996	256,033	1,069.49	306,048	273,981	1,069.49	301,948	278,081
195,000	2,195.26	595,294	1,097.63	332,520	262,774	1,097.63	314,099	281,195	1,097.63	309,892	285,402
200,000	2,251.55	610,558	1,125.78	341,049	269,509	1,125.78	322,156	288,402	1,125.78	317,841	292,717

AMOUNT OF LOAN	30 YEARS		360 DAY BASIS 474.635 PAYMENTS			364 DAY BASIS 457.851 PAYMENTS			365 DAY BASIS 454.022 PAYMENTS		
	MONTHLY PAYMENT	TOTAL INTRST	BWEEKLY PAYMENT	TOTAL INTRST	INTRST SAVED	BWEEKLY PAYMENT	TOTAL INTRST	INTRST SAVED	BWEEKLY PAYMENT	TOTAL INTRST	INTRST SAVED
$ 50	0.58	159	0.29	88	71	0.29	83	76	0.29	82	77
100	1.15	314	0.58	175	139	0.58	166	148	0.58	163	151
200	2.30	628	1.15	346	282	1.15	327	301	1.15	322	306
300	3.44	938	1.72	516	422	1.72	488	450	1.72	481	457
400	4.59	1,252	2.30	692	560	2.30	653	599	2.30	644	608
500	5.73	1,563	2.87	862	701	2.87	814	749	2.87	803	760
600	6.88	1,877	3.44	1,033	844	3.44	975	902	3.44	962	915
700	8.02	2,187	4.01	1,203	984	4.01	1,136	1,051	4.01	1,121	1,066
800	9.17	2,501	4.59	1,379	1,122	4.59	1,302	1,199	4.59	1,284	1,217
900	10.31	2,812	5.16	1,549	1,263	5.16	1,463	1,349	5.16	1,443	1,369
1,000	11.46	3,126	5.73	1,720	1,406	5.73	1,623	1,503	5.73	1,602	1,524
2,000	22.91	6,248	11.46	3,439	2,809	11.46	3,247	3,001	11.46	3,203	3,045
3,000	34.37	9,373	17.19	5,159	4,214	17.19	4,870	4,503	17.19	4,805	4,568
4,000	45.82	12,495	22.91	6,874	5,621	22.91	6,489	6,006	22.91	6,402	6,093
5,000	57.28	15,621	28.64	8,594	7,027	28.64	8,113	7,508	28.64	8,003	7,618
6,000	68.73	18,743	34.37	10,313	8,430	34.37	9,736	9,007	34.37	9,605	9,138
7,000	80.18	21,865	40.09	12,028	9,837	40.09	11,355	10,510	40.09	11,202	10,663
8,000	91.64	24,990	45.82	13,748	11,242	45.82	12,979	12,011	45.82	12,803	12,187
9,000	103.09	28,112	51.55	15,467	12,645	51.55	14,602	13,510	51.55	14,405	13,707
10,000	114.55	31,238	57.28	17,187	14,051	57.28	16,226	15,012	57.28	16,006	15,232
11,000	126.00	34,360	63.00	18,902	15,458	63.00	17,845	16,515	63.00	17,603	16,757
12,000	137.45	37,482	68.73	20,622	16,860	68.73	19,468	18,014	68.73	19,205	18,277
13,000	148.91	40,608	74.46	22,341	18,267	74.46	21,092	19,516	74.46	20,806	19,802
14,000	160.36	43,730	80.18	24,056	19,674	80.18	22,710	21,020	80.18	22,403	21,327
15,000	171.82	46,855	85.91	25,776	21,079	85.91	24,334	22,521	85.91	24,005	22,850
16,000	183.27	49,977	91.64	27,496	22,481	91.64	25,957	24,020	91.64	25,607	24,370
17,000	194.73	53,103	97.37	29,215	23,888	97.37	27,581	25,522	97.37	27,208	25,895
18,000	206.18	56,225	103.09	30,930	25,295	103.09	29,200	27,025	103.09	28,805	27,420
19,000	217.63	59,347	108.82	32,650	26,697	108.82	30,823	28,524	108.82	30,407	28,940
20,000	229.09	62,472	114.55	34,369	28,103	114.55	32,447	30,025	114.55	32,008	30,464
21,000	240.54	65,594	120.27	36,084	29,510	120.27	34,066	31,528	120.27	33,605	31,989
22,000	252.00	68,720	126.00	37,804	30,916	126.00	35,689	33,031	126.00	35,207	33,513
23,000	263.45	71,842	131.73	39,524	32,318	131.73	37,313	34,529	131.73	36,808	35,034
24,000	274.90	74,964	137.45	41,239	33,725	137.45	38,932	36,032	137.45	38,405	36,559
25,000	286.36	78,090	143.18	42,958	35,132	143.18	40,555	37,535	143.18	40,007	38,083
26,000	297.81	81,212	148.91	44,678	36,534	148.91	42,179	39,033	148.91	41,608	39,604
27,000	309.27	84,337	154.64	46,398	37,939	154.64	43,802	40,535	154.64	43,210	41,127
28,000	320.72	87,459	160.36	48,112	39,347	160.36	45,421	42,038	160.36	44,807	42,652
29,000	332.17	90,581	166.09	49,834	40,747	166.09	47,044	43,537	166.09	46,409	44,172
30,000	343.63	93,707	171.82	51,552	42,155	171.82	48,668	45,039	171.82	48,010	45,697
32,500	372.26	101,514	186.13	55,844	45,670	186.13	52,720	48,794	186.13	52,007	49,507
35,000	400.90	109,324	200.45	60,141	49,183	200.45	56,776	52,548	200.45	56,009	53,315
40,000	458.17	124,941	229.09	68,734	56,207	229.09	64,889	60,052	229.09	64,012	60,929
45,000	515.44	140,558	257.72	77,323	63,235	257.72	72,997	67,561	257.72	72,011	68,547
50,000	572.71	156,176	286.36	85,916	70,260	286.36	81,110	75,066	286.36	80,014	76,162
55,000	629.98	171,793	314.99	94,505	77,288	314.99	89,218	82,575	314.99	88,012	83,781
60,000	687.25	187,410	343.63	103,099	84,311	343.63	97,331	90,079	343.63	96,016	91,394
65,000	744.52	203,027	372.26	111,688	91,339	372.26	105,440	97,587	372.26	104,014	99,013
70,000	801.79	218,644	400.90	120,281	98,363	400.90	113,552	105,092	400.90	112,017	106,627
75,000	859.06	234,262	429.53	128,870	105,392	429.53	121,661	112,601	429.53	120,016	114,246
80,000	916.33	249,879	458.17	137,464	112,415	458.17	129,774	120,105	458.17	128,019	121,860
85,000	973.61	265,500	486.81	146,058	119,443	486.81	137,886	127,614	486.81	136,022	129,478
90,000	1,030.88	281,117	515.44	154,646	126,471	515.44	145,995	135,122	515.44	144,021	137,096
95,000	1,088.15	296,734	544.08	163,239	133,495	544.08	154,108	142,626	544.08	152,024	144,710
100,000	1,145.42	312,351	572.71	171,828	140,523	572.71	162,216	150,135	572.71	160,023	152,328
105,000	1,202.69	327,968	601.35	180,422	147,546	601.35	170,329	157,639	601.35	168,026	159,942
110,000	1,259.96	343,586	629.98	189,011	154,575	629.98	178,437	165,149	629.98	176,025	167,561
115,000	1,317.23	359,203	658.62	197,604	161,599	658.62	186,550	172,653	658.62	184,028	175,175
120,000	1,374.50	374,820	687.25	206,193	168,627	687.25	194,658	180,162	687.25	192,027	182,793
125,000	1,431.77	390,437	715.89	214,786	175,651	715.89	202,771	187,666	715.89	200,030	190,407
130,000	1,489.04	406,054	744.52	223,375	182,679	744.52	210,879	195,175	744.52	208,029	198,026
135,000	1,546.31	421,672	773.16	231,969	189,703	773.16	218,992	202,680	773.16	216,032	205,640
140,000	1,603.58	437,289	801.79	240,558	196,731	801.79	227,100	210,189	801.79	224,030	213,259
145,000	1,660.85	452,906	830.43	249,151	203,755	830.43	235,213	217,693	830.43	232,033	220,873
150,000	1,718.12	468,523	859.06	257,740	210,783	859.06	243,321	225,202	859.06	240,032	228,491
155,000	1,775.39	484,140	887.70	266,333	217,807	887.70	251,434	232,706	887.70	248,035	236,105
160,000	1,832.66	499,758	916.33	274,922	224,836	916.33	259,543	240,215	916.33	256,034	243,724
165,000	1,889.94	515,378	944.97	283,516	231,862	944.97	267,655	247,723	944.97	264,037	251,341
170,000	1,947.21	530,996	973.61	292,109	238,887	973.61	275,768	255,228	973.61	272,040	258,956
175,000	2,004.48	546,613	1,002.24	300,698	245,915	1,002.24	283,877	262,736	1,002.24	280,039	266,574
180,000	2,061.75	562,230	1,030.88	309,292	252,938	1,030.88	291,989	270,241	1,030.88	288,042	274,188
185,000	2,119.02	577,847	1,059.51	317,881	259,966	1,059.51	300,098	277,749	1,059.51	296,041	281,806
190,000	2,176.29	593,464	1,088.15	326,474	266,990	1,088.15	308,211	285,253	1,088.15	304,044	289,420
195,000	2,233.56	609,082	1,116.78	335,063	274,019	1,116.78	316,319	292,763	1,116.78	312,043	297,039
200,000	2,290.83	624,699	1,145.42	343,656	281,043	1,145.42	324,432	300,267	1,145.42	320,046	304,653

AMOUNT OF LOAN	30 YEARS		360 DAY BASIS 468.723 PAYMENTS			364 DAY BASIS 451.951 PAYMENTS			365 DAY BASIS 448.129 PAYMENTS		
	MONTHLY PAYMENT	TOTAL INTRST	BWEEKLY PAYMENT	TOTAL INTRST	INTRST SAVED	BWEEKLY PAYMENT	TOTAL INTRST	INTRST SAVED	BWEEKLY PAYMENT	TOTAL INTRST	INTRST SAVED
$ 50	0.59	162	0.30	91	71	0.30	86	76	0.30	84	78
100	1.17	321	0.59	177	144	0.59	167	154	0.59	164	157
200	2.34	642	1.17	348	294	1.17	329	313	1.17	324	318
300	3.50	960	1.75	520	440	1.75	491	469	1.75	484	476
400	4.67	1,281	2.34	697	584	2.34	658	623	2.34	649	632
500	5.83	1,599	2.92	869	730	2.92	820	779	2.92	809	790
600	7.00	1,920	3.50	1,041	879	3.50	982	938	3.50	968	952
700	8.16	2,238	4.08	1,212	1,026	4.08	1,144	1,094	4.08	1,128	1,110
800	9.33	2,559	4.67	1,389	1,170	4.67	1,311	1,248	4.67	1,293	1,266
900	10.49	2,876	5.25	1,561	1,315	5.25	1,473	1,403	5.25	1,453	1,423
1,000	11.66	3,198	5.83	1,733	1,465	5.83	1,635	1,563	5.83	1,613	1,585
2,000	23.31	6,392	11.66	3,465	2,927	11.66	3,270	3,122	11.66	3,225	3,167
3,000	34.96	9,586	17.48	5,193	4,393	17.48	4,900	4,686	17.48	4,833	4,753
4,000	46.61	12,780	23.31	6,926	5,854	23.31	6,535	6,245	23.31	6,446	6,334
5,000	58.26	15,974	29.13	8,654	7,320	29.13	8,165	7,809	29.13	8,054	7,920
6,000	69.91	19,168	34.96	10,387	8,781	34.96	9,800	9,368	34.96	9,667	9,501
7,000	81.56	22,362	40.78	12,115	10,247	40.78	11,431	10,931	40.78	11,275	11,087
8,000	93.21	25,556	46.61	13,847	11,709	46.61	13,065	12,491	46.61	12,887	12,669
9,000	104.87	28,753	52.44	15,580	13,173	52.44	14,700	14,053	52.44	14,500	14,253
10,000	116.52	31,947	58.26	17,308	14,639	58.26	16,331	15,616	58.26	16,108	15,839
11,000	128.17	35,141	64.09	19,040	16,101	64.09	17,966	17,175	64.09	17,721	17,420
12,000	139.82	38,335	69.91	20,768	17,567	69.91	19,596	18,739	69.91	19,329	19,006
13,000	151.47	41,529	75.74	22,501	19,028	75.74	21,231	20,298	75.74	20,941	20,588
14,000	163.12	44,723	81.56	24,229	20,494	81.56	22,861	21,862	81.56	22,549	22,174
15,000	174.77	47,917	87.39	25,962	21,955	87.39	24,496	23,421	87.39	24,162	23,755
16,000	186.42	51,111	93.21	27,690	23,421	93.21	26,126	24,985	93.21	25,770	25,341
17,000	198.07	54,305	99.04	29,422	24,883	99.04	27,761	26,544	99.04	27,383	26,922
18,000	209.73	57,503	104.87	31,155	26,348	104.87	29,396	28,107	104.87	28,995	28,508
19,000	221.38	60,697	110.69	32,883	27,814	110.69	31,026	29,671	110.69	30,603	30,094
20,000	233.03	63,891	116.52	34,616	29,275	116.52	32,661	31,230	116.52	32,216	31,675
21,000	244.68	67,085	122.34	36,344	30,741	122.34	34,292	32,793	122.34	33,824	33,261
22,000	256.33	70,279	128.17	38,076	32,203	128.17	35,927	34,352	128.17	35,437	34,842
23,000	267.98	73,473	133.99	39,804	33,669	133.99	37,557	35,916	133.99	37,045	36,428
24,000	279.63	76,667	139.82	41,537	35,130	139.82	39,192	37,475	139.82	38,657	38,010
25,000	291.28	79,861	145.64	43,265	36,596	145.64	40,822	39,039	145.64	40,266	39,595
26,000	302.93	83,055	151.47	44,997	38,058	151.47	42,457	40,598	151.47	41,878	41,177
27,000	314.59	86,252	157.30	46,730	39,522	157.30	44,092	42,160	157.30	43,491	42,761
28,000	326.24	89,446	163.12	48,458	40,988	163.12	45,722	43,724	163.12	45,099	44,347
29,000	337.89	92,640	168.95	50,191	42,449	168.95	47,357	45,283	168.95	46,711	45,929
30,000	349.54	95,834	174.77	51,919	43,915	174.77	48,987	46,847	174.77	48,320	47,514
32,500	378.67	103,821	189.34	56,248	47,573	189.34	53,072	50,749	189.34	52,349	51,472
35,000	407.79	111,804	203.90	60,573	51,231	203.90	57,153	54,651	203.90	56,374	55,430
40,000	466.05	127,778	233.03	69,227	58,551	233.03	65,318	62,460	233.03	64,428	63,350
45,000	524.31	143,752	262.16	77,880	65,872	262.16	73,483	70,269	262.16	72,481	71,271
50,000	582.56	159,722	291.28	86,530	73,192	291.28	81,644	78,078	291.28	80,531	79,191
55,000	640.82	175,695	320.41	95,184	80,511	320.41	89,810	85,885	320.41	88,585	87,110
60,000	699.07	191,665	349.54	103,837	87,828	349.54	97,975	93,690	349.54	96,639	95,026
65,000	757.33	207,639	378.67	112,491	95,148	378.67	106,140	101,499	378.67	104,693	102,946
70,000	815.58	223,609	407.79	121,141	102,468	407.79	114,301	109,308	407.79	112,743	110,866
75,000	873.84	239,582	436.92	129,794	109,788	436.92	122,466	117,116	436.92	120,797	118,785
80,000	932.10	255,556	466.05	138,448	117,108	466.05	130,632	124,924	466.05	128,851	126,705
85,000	990.35	271,526	495.18	147,102	124,424	495.18	138,797	132,729	495.18	136,905	134,621
90,000	1,048.61	287,500	524.31	155,756	131,744	524.31	146,962	140,538	524.31	144,959	142,541
95,000	1,106.86	303,470	553.43	164,405	139,065	553.43	155,123	148,347	553.43	153,008	150,462
100,000	1,165.12	319,443	582.56	173,059	146,384	582.56	163,289	156,154	582.56	161,062	158,381
105,000	1,223.37	335,413	611.69	181,713	153,700	611.69	171,454	163,959	611.69	169,116	166,297
110,000	1,281.63	351,387	640.82	190,367	161,020	640.82	179,619	171,768	640.82	177,170	174,217
115,000	1,339.88	367,357	669.94	199,016	168,341	669.94	187,780	179,577	669.94	185,220	182,137
120,000	1,398.14	383,330	699.07	207,670	175,660	699.07	195,945	187,385	699.07	193,274	190,056
125,000	1,456.40	399,304	728.20	216,324	182,980	728.20	204,111	195,193	728.20	201,328	197,976
130,000	1,514.65	415,274	757.33	224,978	190,296	757.33	212,276	202,998	757.33	209,382	205,892
135,000	1,572.91	431,248	786.46	233,632	197,616	786.46	220,441	210,807	786.46	217,436	213,812
140,000	1,631.16	447,218	815.58	242,281	204,937	815.58	228,602	218,616	815.58	225,485	221,733
145,000	1,689.42	463,191	844.71	250,935	212,256	844.71	236,768	226,423	844.71	233,539	229,652
150,000	1,747.67	479,161	873.84	259,589	219,572	873.84	244,933	234,228	873.84	241,593	237,568
155,000	1,805.93	495,135	902.97	268,243	226,892	902.97	253,098	242,037	902.97	249,647	245,488
160,000	1,864.19	511,108	932.10	276,897	234,211	932.10	261,264	249,844	932.10	257,701	253,407
165,000	1,922.44	527,078	961.22	285,546	241,532	961.22	269,424	257,654	961.22	265,751	261,327
170,000	1,980.70	543,052	990.35	294,200	248,852	990.35	277,590	265,462	990.35	273,805	269,247
175,000	2,038.95	559,022	1,019.48	302,854	256,168	1,019.48	285,755	273,267	1,019.48	281,859	277,153
180,000	2,097.21	574,996	1,048.61	311,508	263,488	1,048.61	293,920	281,076	1,048.61	289,913	285,083
185,000	2,155.46	590,966	1,077.73	320,157	270,809	1,077.73	302,081	288,885	1,077.73	297,962	293,004
190,000	2,213.72	606,939	1,106.86	328,811	278,128	1,106.86	310,246	296,693	1,106.86	306,016	300,923
195,000	2,271.97	622,909	1,135.99	337,465	285,444	1,135.99	318,412	304,497	1,135.99	314,070	308,839
200,000	2,330.23	638,883	1,165.12	346,119	292,764	1,165.12	326,577	312,306	1,165.12	322,124	316,759

14.00% BIWEEKLY MORTGAGES

AMOUNT OF LOAN	30 YEARS		360 DAY BASIS 462.868 PAYMENTS			364 DAY BASIS 446.119 PAYMENTS			365 DAY BASIS 442.307 PAYMENTS		
	MONTHLY PAYMENT	TOTAL INTRST	BWEEKLY PAYMENT	TOTAL INTRST	INTRST SAVED	BWEEKLY PAYMENT	TOTAL INTRST	INTRST SAVED	BWEEKLY PAYMENT	TOTAL INTRST	INTRST SAVED
$ 50	0.60	166	0.30	89	77	0.30	84	82	0.30	83	83
100	1.19	328	0.60	178	150	0.60	168	160	0.60	165	163
200	2.37	653	1.19	351	302	1.19	331	322	1.19	326	327
300	3.56	982	1.78	524	458	1.78	494	488	1.78	487	495
400	4.74	1,306	2.37	697	609	2.37	657	649	2.37	648	658
500	5.93	1,635	2.97	875	760	2.97	825	810	2.97	814	821
600	7.11	1,960	3.56	1,048	912	3.56	988	972	3.56	975	985
700	8.30	2,288	4.15	1,221	1,067	4.15	1,151	1,137	4.15	1,136	1,152
800	9.48	2,613	4.74	1,394	1,219	4.74	1,315	1,298	4.74	1,297	1,316
900	10.67	2,941	5.34	1,572	1,369	5.34	1,482	1,459	5.34	1,462	1,479
1,000	11.85	3,266	5.93	1,745	1,521	5.93	1,645	1,621	5.93	1,623	1,643
2,000	23.70	6,532	11.85	3,485	3,047	11.85	3,287	3,245	11.85	3,241	3,291
3,000	35.55	9,798	17.78	5,230	4,568	17.78	4,932	4,866	17.78	4,864	4,934
4,000	47.40	13,064	23.70	6,970	6,094	23.70	6,573	6,491	23.70	6,483	6,581
5,000	59.25	16,330	29.63	8,715	7,615	29.63	8,219	8,111	29.63	8,106	8,224
6,000	71.10	19,596	35.55	10,455	9,141	35.55	9,860	9,736	35.55	9,724	9,872
7,000	82.95	22,862	41.48	12,200	10,662	41.48	11,505	11,357	41.48	11,347	11,515
8,000	94.79	26,124	47.40	13,940	12,184	47.40	13,146	12,978	47.40	12,965	13,159
9,000	106.64	29,390	53.32	15,680	13,710	53.32	14,787	14,603	53.32	14,584	14,806
10,000	118.49	32,656	59.25	17,425	15,231	59.25	16,433	16,223	59.25	16,207	16,449
11,000	130.34	35,922	65.17	19,165	16,757	65.17	18,074	17,848	65.17	17,825	18,097
12,000	142.19	39,188	71.10	20,910	18,278	71.10	19,719	19,469	71.10	19,448	19,740
13,000	154.04	42,454	77.02	22,650	19,804	77.02	21,360	21,094	77.02	21,066	21,388
14,000	165.89	45,720	82.95	24,395	21,325	82.95	23,006	22,714	82.95	22,689	23,031
15,000	177.74	48,986	88.87	26,135	22,851	88.87	24,647	24,339	88.87	24,308	24,678
16,000	189.58	52,249	94.79	27,875	24,374	94.79	26,288	25,961	94.79	25,926	26,323
17,000	201.43	55,515	100.72	29,620	25,895	100.72	27,933	27,582	100.72	27,549	27,966
18,000	213.28	58,781	106.64	31,360	27,421	106.64	29,574	29,207	106.64	29,168	29,613
19,000	225.13	62,047	112.57	33,105	28,942	112.57	31,220	30,827	112.57	30,790	31,257
20,000	236.98	65,313	118.49	34,845	30,468	118.49	32,861	32,452	118.49	32,409	32,904
21,000	248.83	68,579	124.42	36,590	31,989	124.42	34,506	34,073	124.42	34,032	34,547
22,000	260.68	71,845	130.34	38,330	33,515	130.34	36,147	35,698	130.34	35,650	36,195
23,000	272.53	75,111	136.27	40,075	35,036	136.27	37,793	37,318	136.27	37,273	37,838
24,000	284.37	78,373	142.19	41,815	36,558	142.19	39,434	38,939	142.19	38,892	39,481
25,000	296.22	81,639	148.11	43,555	38,084	148.11	41,075	40,564	148.11	40,510	41,129
26,000	308.07	84,905	154.04	45,300	39,605	154.04	42,720	42,185	154.04	42,133	42,772
27,000	319.92	88,171	159.96	47,040	41,131	159.96	44,361	43,810	159.96	43,751	44,420
28,000	331.77	91,437	165.89	48,785	42,652	165.89	46,007	45,430	165.89	45,374	46,063
29,000	343.62	94,703	171.81	50,525	44,178	171.81	47,648	47,055	171.81	46,993	47,710
30,000	355.47	97,969	177.74	52,270	45,699	177.74	49,293	48,676	177.74	48,616	49,353
32,500	385.09	106,132	192.55	56,625	49,507	192.55	53,400	52,732	192.55	52,666	53,466
35,000	414.71	114,296	207.36	60,980	53,316	207.36	57,507	56,789	207.36	56,717	57,579
40,000	473.95	130,622	236.98	69,690	60,932	236.98	65,721	64,901	236.98	64,818	65,804
45,000	533.20	146,952	266.60	78,401	68,551	266.60	73,935	73,017	266.60	72,919	74,033
50,000	592.44	163,278	296.22	87,111	76,167	296.22	82,149	81,129	296.22	81,020	82,258
55,000	651.68	179,605	325.84	95,821	83,784	325.84	90,363	89,242	325.84	89,121	90,484
60,000	710.93	195,935	355.47	104,536	91,399	355.47	98,582	97,353	355.47	97,227	98,708
65,000	770.17	212,261	385.09	113,246	99,015	385.09	106,796	105,465	385.09	105,328	106,933
70,000	829.42	228,591	414.71	121,956	106,633	414.71	115,010	113,581	414.71	113,429	115,162
75,000	888.66	244,918	444.33	130,666	114,252	444.33	123,224	121,694	444.33	121,530	123,388
80,000	947.90	261,244	473.95	139,376	121,868	473.95	131,438	129,806	473.95	129,631	131,613
85,000	1,007.15	277,574	503.58	148,091	129,483	503.58	139,657	137,917	503.58	137,737	139,837
90,000	1,066.39	293,900	533.20	156,801	137,099	533.20	147,871	146,029	533.20	145,838	148,062
95,000	1,125.63	310,227	562.82	165,511	144,716	562.82	156,085	154,142	562.82	153,939	156,288
100,000	1,184.88	326,557	592.44	174,222	152,335	592.44	164,299	162,258	592.44	162,040	164,517
105,000	1,244.12	342,883	622.06	182,932	159,951	622.06	172,513	170,370	622.06	170,141	172,742
110,000	1,303.36	359,210	651.68	191,642	167,568	651.68	180,727	178,483	651.68	178,243	180,967
115,000	1,362.61	375,540	681.31	200,357	175,183	681.31	188,946	186,595	681.31	186,348	189,192
120,000	1,421.85	391,866	710.93	209,067	182,799	710.93	197,159	194,707	710.93	194,449	197,417
125,000	1,481.09	408,192	740.55	217,777	190,415	740.55	205,373	202,819	740.55	202,550	205,642
130,000	1,540.34	424,522	770.17	226,487	198,035	770.17	213,587	210,935	770.17	210,652	213,870
135,000	1,599.58	440,849	799.79	235,197	205,652	799.79	221,802	219,047	799.79	218,753	222,096
140,000	1,658.83	457,179	829.42	243,912	213,267	829.42	230,020	227,159	829.42	226,858	230,321
145,000	1,718.07	473,505	859.04	252,622	220,883	859.04	238,234	235,271	859.04	234,959	238,546
150,000	1,777.31	489,832	888.66	261,332	228,500	888.66	246,448	243,384	888.66	243,061	246,771
155,000	1,836.56	506,162	918.28	270,042	236,120	918.28	254,662	251,500	918.28	251,162	255,000
160,000	1,895.80	522,488	947.90	278,753	243,735	947.90	262,876	259,612	947.90	259,263	263,225
165,000	1,955.04	538,814	977.52	287,463	251,351	977.52	271,090	267,724	977.52	267,364	271,450
170,000	2,014.29	555,144	1,007.15	296,178	258,966	1,007.15	279,309	275,835	1,007.15	275,469	279,675
175,000	2,073.53	571,471	1,036.77	304,888	266,583	1,036.77	287,523	283,948	1,036.77	283,571	287,900
180,000	2,132.77	587,797	1,066.39	313,598	274,199	1,066.39	295,737	292,060	1,066.39	291,672	296,125
185,000	2,192.02	604,127	1,096.01	322,308	281,819	1,096.01	303,951	300,176	1,096.01	299,773	304,354
190,000	2,251.26	620,454	1,125.63	331,018	289,436	1,125.63	312,165	308,289	1,125.63	307,874	312,580
195,000	2,310.50	636,780	1,155.25	339,722	297,052	1,155.25	320,379	316,401	1,155.25	315,975	320,805
200,000	2,369.75	653,110	1,184.88	348,443	304,667	1,184.88	328,597	324,513	1,184.88	324,081	329,029

80

AMOUNT OF LOAN	30 YEARS		360 DAY BASIS 457.072 PAYMENTS			364 DAY BASIS 440.360 PAYMENTS			365 DAY BASIS 436.559 PAYMENTS		
	MONTHLY PAYMENT	TOTAL INTRST	BWEEKLY PAYMENT	TOTAL INTRST	INTRST SAVED	BWEEKLY PAYMENT	TOTAL INTRST	INTRST SAVED	BWEEKLY PAYMENT	TOTAL INTRST	INTRST SAVED
$ 50	0.61	170	0.31	92	78	0.31	87	83	0.31	85	85
100	1.21	336	0.61	179	157	0.61	169	167	0.61	166	170
200	2.41	668	1.21	353	315	1.21	333	335	1.21	328	340
300	3.62	1,003	1.81	527	476	1.81	497	506	1.81	490	513
400	4.82	1,335	2.41	702	633	2.41	661	674	2.41	652	683
500	6.03	1,671	3.02	880	791	3.02	830	841	3.02	818	853
600	7.23	2,003	3.62	1,055	948	3.62	994	1,009	3.62	980	1,023
700	8.44	2,338	4.22	1,229	1,109	4.22	1,158	1,180	4.22	1,142	1,196
800	9.64	2,670	4.82	1,403	1,267	4.82	1,323	1,347	4.82	1,304	1,366
900	10.85	3,006	5.43	1,582	1,424	5.43	1,491	1,515	5.43	1,471	1,535
1,000	12.05	3,338	6.03	1,756	1,582	6.03	1,655	1,683	6.03	1,632	1,706
2,000	24.10	6,676	12.05	3,508	3,168	12.05	3,306	3,370	12.05	3,261	3,415
3,000	36.15	10,014	18.08	5,264	4,750	18.08	4,962	5,052	18.08	4,893	5,121
4,000	48.19	13,348	24.10	7,015	6,333	24.10	6,613	6,735	24.10	6,521	6,827
5,000	60.24	16,686	30.12	8,767	7,919	30.12	8,264	8,422	30.12	8,149	8,537
6,000	72.29	20,024	36.15	10,523	9,501	36.15	9,919	10,105	36.15	9,782	10,242
7,000	84.33	23,359	42.17	12,275	11,084	42.17	11,570	11,789	42.17	11,410	11,949
8,000	96.38	26,697	48.19	14,026	12,671	48.19	13,221	13,476	48.19	13,038	13,659
9,000	108.43	30,035	54.22	15,782	14,253	54.22	14,876	15,159	54.22	14,670	15,365
10,000	120.47	33,369	60.24	17,534	15,835	60.24	16,527	16,842	60.24	16,298	17,071
11,000	132.52	36,707	66.26	19,286	17,421	66.26	18,178	18,529	66.26	17,926	18,781
12,000	144.57	40,045	72.29	21,042	19,003	72.29	19,834	20,211	72.29	19,559	20,486
13,000	156.61	43,380	78.31	22,793	20,587	78.31	21,485	21,895	78.31	21,187	22,193
14,000	168.66	46,718	84.33	24,545	22,173	84.33	23,136	23,582	84.33	22,815	23,903
15,000	180.71	50,056	90.36	26,301	23,755	90.36	24,791	25,265	90.36	24,447	25,609
16,000	192.75	53,390	96.38	28,053	25,337	96.38	26,442	26,948	96.38	26,076	27,314
17,000	204.80	56,728	102.40	29,804	26,924	102.40	28,093	28,635	102.40	27,704	29,024
18,000	216.85	60,066	108.43	31,560	28,506	108.43	29,748	30,318	108.43	29,336	30,730
19,000	228.90	63,404	114.45	33,312	30,092	114.45	31,399	32,005	114.45	30,964	32,440
20,000	240.94	66,738	120.47	35,063	31,675	120.47	33,050	33,688	120.47	32,592	34,146
21,000	252.99	70,076	126.50	36,820	33,256	126.50	34,706	35,370	126.50	34,225	35,851
22,000	265.04	73,414	132.52	38,571	34,843	132.52	36,357	37,057	132.52	35,853	37,561
23,000	277.08	76,749	138.54	40,323	36,426	138.54	38,007	38,742	138.54	37,481	39,268
24,000	289.13	80,087	144.57	42,079	38,008	144.57	39,663	40,424	144.57	39,113	40,974
25,000	301.18	83,425	150.59	43,830	39,595	150.59	41,314	42,111	150.59	40,741	42,684
26,000	313.22	86,759	156.61	45,582	41,177	156.61	42,965	43,794	156.61	42,370	44,389
27,000	325.27	90,097	162.64	47,338	42,759	162.64	44,620	45,477	162.64	44,002	46,095
28,000	337.32	93,435	168.66	49,090	44,345	168.66	46,271	47,164	168.66	45,630	47,805
29,000	349.36	96,770	174.68	50,841	45,929	174.68	47,922	48,848	174.68	47,258	49,512
30,000	361.41	100,108	180.71	52,597	47,511	180.71	49,577	50,531	180.71	48,891	51,217
32,500	391.53	108,451	195.77	56,981	51,470	195.77	53,709	54,742	195.77	52,965	55,486
35,000	421.65	116,794	210.83	61,364	55,430	210.83	57,841	58,953	210.83	57,040	59,754
40,000	481.88	133,477	240.94	70,127	63,350	240.94	66,100	67,377	240.94	65,185	68,292
45,000	542.11	150,160	271.06	78,894	71,266	271.06	74,364	75,796	271.06	73,334	76,826
50,000	602.35	166,846	301.18	87,661	79,185	301.18	82,628	84,218	301.18	81,483	85,363
55,000	662.58	183,529	331.29	96,423	87,106	331.29	90,887	92,642	331.29	89,628	93,901
60,000	722.82	200,215	361.41	105,190	95,025	361.41	99,151	101,064	361.41	97,777	102,438
65,000	783.05	216,898	391.53	113,957	102,941	391.53	107,410	109,484	391.53	105,926	110,972
70,000	843.29	233,584	421.65	122,724	110,860	421.65	115,678	117,906	421.65	114,075	119,509
75,000	903.52	250,267	451.76	131,487	118,780	451.76	123,937	126,330	451.76	122,220	128,047
80,000	963.75	266,950	481.88	140,254	126,696	481.88	132,201	134,749	481.88	130,369	136,581
85,000	1,023.99	283,636	512.00	149,021	134,615	512.00	140,464	143,172	512.00	138,518	145,118
90,000	1,084.22	300,319	542.11	157,783	142,536	542.11	148,724	151,595	542.11	146,663	153,656
95,000	1,144.46	317,006	572.23	166,550	150,456	572.23	156,987	160,019	572.23	154,812	162,194
100,000	1,204.69	333,688	602.35	175,317	158,371	602.35	165,251	168,437	602.35	162,961	170,727
105,000	1,264.93	350,375	632.47	184,084	166,291	632.47	173,514	176,861	632.47	171,110	179,265
110,000	1,325.16	367,058	662.58	192,847	174,211	662.58	181,774	185,284	662.58	179,255	187,803
115,000	1,385.40	383,744	692.70	201,614	182,130	692.70	190,037	193,707	692.70	187,404	196,340
120,000	1,445.63	400,427	722.82	210,381	190,046	722.82	198,301	202,126	722.82	195,554	204,873
125,000	1,505.86	417,110	752.93	219,143	197,967	752.93	206,560	210,550	752.93	203,698	213,412
130,000	1,566.10	433,796	783.05	227,910	205,886	783.05	214,824	218,972	783.05	211,848	221,948
135,000	1,626.33	450,479	813.17	236,677	213,802	813.17	223,088	227,391	813.17	219,997	230,482
140,000	1,686.57	467,165	843.29	245,444	221,721	843.29	231,351	235,814	843.29	228,146	239,019
145,000	1,746.80	483,848	873.40	254,207	229,641	873.40	239,610	244,238	873.40	236,291	247,557
150,000	1,807.04	500,534	903.52	262,974	237,560	903.52	247,874	252,660	903.52	244,440	256,094
155,000	1,867.27	517,217	933.64	271,741	245,476	933.64	256,138	261,079	933.64	252,589	264,628
160,000	1,927.50	533,900	963.75	280,503	253,397	963.75	264,397	269,503	963.75	260,734	273,166
165,000	1,987.74	550,586	993.87	289,270	261,316	993.87	272,661	277,925	993.87	268,883	281,703
170,000	2,047.97	567,269	1,023.99	298,037	269,232	1,023.99	280,924	286,345	1,023.99	277,032	290,237
175,000	2,108.21	583,956	1,054.11	306,804	277,152	1,054.11	289,188	294,768	1,054.11	285,181	298,775
180,000	2,168.44	600,638	1,084.22	315,567	285,071	1,084.22	297,447	303,191	1,084.22	293,326	307,312
185,000	2,228.68	617,325	1,114.34	324,334	292,991	1,114.34	305,711	311,614	1,114.34	301,475	315,850
190,000	2,288.91	634,008	1,144.46	333,101	300,907	1,144.46	313,974	320,034	1,144.46	309,624	324,384
195,000	2,349.14	650,690	1,174.57	341,863	308,827	1,174.57	322,234	328,456	1,174.57	317,769	332,921
200,000	2,409.38	667,377	1,204.69	350,630	316,747	1,204.69	330,497	336,880	1,204.69	325,918	341,459

14.50% BIWEEKLY MORTGAGES

AMOUNT OF LOAN	30 YEARS		360 DAY BASIS 451.342 PAYMENTS			364 DAY BASIS 434.676 PAYMENTS			365 DAY BASIS 430.889 PAYMENTS		
	MONTHLY PAYMENT	TOTAL INTRST	BWEEKLY PAYMENT	TOTAL INTRST	INTRST SAVED	BWEEKLY PAYMENT	TOTAL INTRST	INTRST SAVED	BWEEKLY PAYMENT	TOTAL INTRST	INTRST SAVED
$ 50	0.62	173	0.31	90	83	0.31	85	88	0.31	84	89
100	1.23	343	0.62	180	163	0.62	169	174	0.62	167	176
200	2.45	682	1.23	355	327	1.23	335	347	1.23	330	352
300	3.68	1,025	1.84	530	495	1.84	500	525	1.84	493	532
400	4.90	1,364	2.45	706	658	2.45	665	699	2.45	656	708
500	6.13	1,707	3.07	886	821	3.07	834	873	3.07	823	884
600	7.35	2,046	3.68	1,061	985	3.68	1,000	1,046	3.68	986	1,060
700	8.58	2,389	4.29	1,236	1,153	4.29	1,165	1,224	4.29	1,149	1,240
800	9.80	2,728	4.90	1,412	1,316	4.90	1,330	1,398	4.90	1,311	1,417
900	11.03	3,071	5.52	1,591	1,480	5.52	1,499	1,572	5.52	1,479	1,592
1,000	12.25	3,410	6.13	1,767	1,643	6.13	1,665	1,745	6.13	1,641	1,769
2,000	24.50	6,820	12.25	3,529	3,291	12.25	3,325	3,495	12.25	3,278	3,542
3,000	36.74	10,226	18.37	5,291	4,935	18.37	4,985	5,241	18.37	4,915	5,311
4,000	48.99	13,636	24.50	7,058	6,578	24.50	6,650	6,986	24.50	6,557	7,079
5,000	61.23	17,043	30.62	8,820	8,223	30.62	8,310	8,733	30.62	8,194	8,849
6,000	73.48	20,453	36.74	10,582	9,871	36.74	9,970	10,483	36.74	9,831	10,622
7,000	85.72	23,859	42.86	12,345	11,514	42.86	11,630	12,229	42.86	11,468	12,391
8,000	97.97	27,269	48.99	14,111	13,158	48.99	13,295	13,974	48.99	13,109	14,160
9,000	110.22	30,679	55.11	15,873	14,806	55.11	14,955	15,724	55.11	14,746	15,933
10,000	122.46	34,086	61.23	17,636	16,450	61.23	16,615	17,471	61.23	16,383	17,703
11,000	134.71	37,496	67.36	19,402	18,094	67.36	18,280	19,216	67.36	18,025	19,471
12,000	146.95	40,902	73.48	21,165	19,737	73.48	19,940	20,962	73.48	19,662	21,240
13,000	159.20	44,312	79.60	22,927	21,385	79.60	21,600	22,712	79.60	21,299	23,013
14,000	171.44	47,718	85.72	24,689	23,029	85.72	23,260	24,458	85.72	22,936	24,782
15,000	183.69	51,128	91.85	26,456	24,672	91.85	24,925	26,203	91.85	24,577	26,551
16,000	195.93	54,535	97.97	28,218	26,317	97.97	26,585	27,950	97.97	26,214	28,321
17,000	208.18	57,945	104.09	29,980	27,965	104.09	28,245	29,700	104.09	27,851	30,094
18,000	220.43	61,355	110.22	31,747	29,608	110.22	29,910	31,445	110.22	29,493	31,862
19,000	232.67	64,761	116.34	33,509	31,252	116.34	31,570	33,191	116.34	31,130	33,631
20,000	244.92	68,171	122.46	35,271	32,900	122.46	33,230	34,941	122.46	32,767	35,404
21,000	257.16	71,578	128.58	37,034	34,544	128.58	34,891	36,687	128.58	34,404	37,174
22,000	269.41	74,988	134.71	38,800	36,188	134.71	36,555	38,433	134.71	36,045	38,943
23,000	281.65	78,394	140.83	40,562	37,832	140.83	38,215	40,179	140.83	37,682	40,712
24,000	293.90	81,804	146.95	42,325	39,479	146.95	39,876	41,928	146.95	39,319	42,485
25,000	306.14	85,210	153.07	44,087	41,123	153.07	41,536	43,674	153.07	40,956	44,254
26,000	318.39	88,620	159.20	45,854	42,766	159.20	43,200	45,420	159.20	42,598	46,022
27,000	330.64	92,030	165.32	47,616	44,414	165.32	44,861	47,169	165.32	44,235	47,795
28,000	342.88	95,437	171.44	49,378	46,059	171.44	46,521	48,916	171.44	45,872	49,565
29,000	355.13	98,847	177.57	51,145	47,702	177.57	48,185	50,662	177.57	47,513	51,334
30,000	367.37	102,253	183.69	52,907	49,346	183.69	49,846	52,407	183.69	49,150	53,103
32,500	397.99	110,776	199.00	57,317	53,459	199.00	54,001	56,775	199.00	53,247	57,529
35,000	428.60	119,296	214.30	61,723	57,573	214.30	58,151	61,145	214.30	57,340	61,956
40,000	489.83	136,339	244.92	70,543	65,795	244.92	66,461	69,878	244.92	65,533	70,806
45,000	551.06	153,382	275.53	79,358	74,024	275.53	74,766	78,616	275.53	73,723	79,659
50,000	612.28	170,421	306.14	88,174	82,247	306.14	83,072	87,349	306.14	81,912	88,509
55,000	673.51	187,464	336.76	96,994	90,474	336.76	91,381	96,083	336.76	90,106	97,358
60,000	734.74	204,506	367.37	105,810	98,696	367.37	99,687	104,819	367.37	98,296	106,210
65,000	795.97	221,549	397.99	114,630	106,919	397.99	107,997	113,552	397.99	106,490	115,059
70,000	857.19	238,588	428.60	123,445	115,143	428.60	116,302	122,286	428.60	114,679	123,909
75,000	918.42	255,631	459.21	132,261	123,370	459.21	124,608	131,023	459.21	122,869	132,762
80,000	979.65	272,674	489.83	141,081	131,593	489.83	132,917	139,757	489.83	131,062	141,612
85,000	1,040.88	289,717	520.44	149,896	139,821	520.44	141,223	148,494	520.44	139,252	150,465
90,000	1,102.11	306,760	551.06	158,717	148,043	551.06	149,533	157,227	551.06	147,446	159,314
95,000	1,163.33	323,799	581.67	167,532	156,267	581.67	157,838	165,961	581.67	155,635	168,164
100,000	1,224.56	340,842	612.28	176,348	164,494	612.28	166,143	174,699	612.28	163,825	177,017
105,000	1,285.79	357,884	642.90	185,168	172,716	642.90	174,453	183,431	642.90	172,019	185,865
110,000	1,347.02	374,927	673.51	193,983	180,944	673.51	182,759	192,168	673.51	180,208	194,719
115,000	1,408.24	391,966	704.12	202,799	189,167	704.12	191,064	200,902	704.12	188,398	203,568
120,000	1,469.47	409,009	734.74	211,619	197,390	734.74	199,374	209,635	734.74	196,591	212,418
125,000	1,530.70	426,052	765.35	220,435	205,617	765.35	207,679	218,373	765.35	204,781	221,271
130,000	1,591.93	443,095	795.97	229,255	213,840	795.97	215,989	227,106	795.97	212,975	230,120
135,000	1,653.16	460,138	826.58	238,070	222,068	826.58	224,294	235,844	826.58	221,164	238,974
140,000	1,714.38	477,177	857.19	246,886	230,291	857.19	232,600	244,577	857.19	229,354	247,823
145,000	1,775.61	494,220	887.81	255,706	238,514	887.81	240,910	253,310	887.81	237,548	256,672
150,000	1,836.84	511,262	918.42	264,522	246,740	918.42	249,215	262,047	918.42	245,737	265,525
155,000	1,898.07	528,305	949.04	273,342	254,963	949.04	257,525	270,780	949.04	253,931	274,374
160,000	1,959.29	545,344	979.65	282,157	263,187	979.65	265,830	279,514	979.65	262,120	283,224
165,000	2,020.52	562,387	1,010.26	290,973	271,414	1,010.26	274,136	288,251	1,010.26	270,310	292,077
170,000	2,081.75	579,430	1,040.88	299,793	279,637	1,040.88	282,446	296,984	1,040.88	278,504	300,926
175,000	2,142.98	596,473	1,071.49	308,608	287,865	1,071.49	290,751	305,722	1,071.49	286,693	309,780
180,000	2,204.21	613,516	1,102.11	317,429	296,087	1,102.11	299,061	314,455	1,102.11	294,887	318,629
185,000	2,265.43	630,555	1,132.72	326,244	304,311	1,132.72	307,366	323,189	1,132.72	303,077	327,478
190,000	2,326.66	647,598	1,163.33	335,060	312,538	1,163.33	315,672	331,926	1,163.33	311,266	336,332
195,000	2,387.89	664,640	1,193.95	343,880	320,760	1,193.95	323,981	340,659	1,193.95	319,460	345,180
200,000	2,449.12	681,683	1,224.56	352,695	328,988	1,224.56	332,287	349,396	1,224.56	327,649	354,034

AMOUNT OF LOAN	30 YEARS		360 DAY BASIS 445.678 PAYMENTS			364 DAY BASIS 429.069 PAYMENTS			365 DAY BASIS 425.299 PAYMENTS		
	MONTHLY PAYMENT	TOTAL INTRST	BWEEKLY PAYMENT	TOTAL INTRST	INTRST SAVED	BWEEKLY PAYMENT	TOTAL INTRST	INTRST SAVED	BWEEKLY PAYMENT	TOTAL INTRST	INTRST SAVED
$ 50	0.63	177	0.32	93	84	0.32	87	90	0.32	86	91
100	1.25	350	0.63	181	169	0.63	170	180	0.63	168	182
200	2.49	696	1.25	357	339	1.25	336	360	1.25	332	364
300	3.74	1,046	1.87	533	513	1.87	502	544	1.87	495	551
400	4.98	1,393	2.49	710	683	2.49	668	725	2.49	659	734
500	6.23	1,743	3.12	891	852	3.12	839	904	3.12	827	916
600	7.47	2,089	3.74	1,067	1,022	3.74	1,005	1,084	3.74	991	1,098
700	8.72	2,439	4.36	1,243	1,196	4.36	1,171	1,268	4.36	1,154	1,285
800	9.96	2,786	4.98	1,419	1,367	4.98	1,337	1,449	4.98	1,318	1,468
900	11.21	3,136	5.61	1,600	1,536	5.61	1,507	1,629	5.61	1,486	1,650
1,000	12.45	3,482	6.23	1,777	1,705	6.23	1,673	1,809	6.23	1,650	1,832
2,000	24.89	6,960	12.45	3,549	3,411	12.45	3,342	3,618	12.45	3,295	3,665
3,000	37.34	10,442	18.67	5,321	5,121	18.67	5,011	5,431	18.67	4,940	5,502
4,000	49.78	13,921	24.89	7,093	6,828	24.89	6,680	7,241	24.89	6,586	7,335
5,000	62.23	17,403	31.12	8,869	8,534	31.12	8,353	9,050	31.12	8,235	9,168
6,000	74.67	20,881	37.34	10,642	10,239	37.34	10,021	10,860	37.34	9,881	11,000
7,000	87.12	24,363	43.56	12,414	11,949	43.56	11,690	12,673	43.56	11,526	12,837
8,000	99.56	27,842	49.78	14,186	13,656	49.78	13,359	14,483	49.78	13,171	14,671
9,000	112.01	31,324	56.01	15,962	15,362	56.01	15,032	16,292	56.01	14,821	16,503
10,000	124.45	34,802	62.23	17,735	17,067	62.23	16,701	18,101	62.23	16,466	18,336
11,000	136.90	38,284	68.45	19,507	18,777	68.45	18,370	19,914	68.45	18,112	20,172
12,000	149.34	41,762	74.67	21,279	20,483	74.67	20,039	21,723	74.67	19,757	22,005
13,000	161.79	45,244	80.90	23,055	22,189	80.90	21,712	23,532	80.90	21,407	23,837
14,000	174.23	48,723	87.12	24,827	23,896	87.12	23,380	25,343	87.12	23,052	25,671
15,000	186.68	52,205	93.34	26,600	25,605	93.34	25,049	27,156	93.34	24,697	27,508
16,000	199.12	55,683	99.56	28,372	27,311	99.56	26,718	28,965	99.56	26,343	29,340
17,000	211.57	59,165	105.79	30,148	29,017	105.79	28,391	30,774	105.79	27,992	31,173
18,000	224.01	62,644	112.01	31,920	30,724	112.01	30,060	32,584	112.01	29,638	33,006
19,000	236.46	66,126	118.23	33,693	32,433	118.23	31,729	34,397	118.23	31,283	34,843
20,000	248.90	69,604	124.45	35,465	34,139	124.45	33,398	36,206	124.45	32,928	36,676
21,000	261.34	73,082	130.67	37,237	35,845	130.67	35,066	38,016	130.67	34,574	38,508
22,000	273.79	76,564	136.90	39,013	37,551	136.90	36,740	39,824	136.90	36,223	40,341
23,000	286.23	80,043	143.12	40,785	39,258	143.12	38,408	41,635	143.12	37,869	42,174
24,000	298.68	83,525	149.34	42,558	40,967	149.34	40,077	43,448	149.34	39,514	44,011
25,000	311.12	87,003	155.56	44,330	42,673	155.56	41,746	45,257	155.56	41,160	45,843
26,000	323.57	90,485	161.79	46,106	44,379	161.79	43,419	47,066	161.79	42,809	47,676
27,000	336.01	93,964	168.01	47,878	46,086	168.01	45,088	48,876	168.01	44,454	49,510
28,000	348.46	97,446	174.23	49,650	47,796	174.23	46,757	50,689	174.23	46,100	51,346
29,000	360.90	100,924	180.45	51,423	49,501	180.45	48,426	52,498	180.45	47,745	53,179
30,000	373.35	104,406	186.68	53,199	51,207	186.68	50,099	54,307	186.68	49,395	55,011
32,500	404.46	113,106	202.23	57,629	55,477	202.23	54,271	58,835	202.23	53,508	59,598
35,000	435.57	121,805	217.79	62,064	59,741	217.79	58,447	63,358	217.79	57,626	64,179
40,000	497.80	139,208	248.90	70,929	68,279	248.90	66,795	72,413	248.90	65,857	73,351
45,000	560.02	156,607	280.01	79,794	76,813	280.01	75,144	81,463	280.01	74,088	82,519
50,000	622.24	174,006	311.12	88,659	85,347	311.12	83,492	90,514	311.12	82,319	91,687
55,000	684.47	191,409	342.24	97,529	93,880	342.24	91,845	99,564	342.24	90,554	100,855
60,000	746.69	208,808	373.35	106,394	102,414	373.35	100,193	108,615	373.35	98,785	110,023
65,000	808.91	226,208	404.46	115,259	110,949	404.46	108,541	117,667	404.46	107,016	119,192
70,000	871.14	243,610	435.57	124,124	119,486	435.57	116,890	126,720	435.57	115,247	128,363
75,000	933.36	261,010	466.68	132,989	128,021	466.68	125,238	135,772	466.68	123,479	137,531
80,000	995.59	278,412	497.80	141,859	136,553	497.80	133,591	144,821	497.80	131,714	146,698
85,000	1,057.81	295,812	528.91	150,724	145,088	528.91	141,939	153,873	528.91	139,945	155,867
90,000	1,120.03	313,211	560.02	159,589	153,622	560.02	150,287	162,924	560.02	148,176	165,035
95,000	1,182.26	330,614	591.13	168,454	162,160	591.13	158,636	171,978	591.13	156,407	174,207
100,000	1,244.48	348,013	622.24	177,319	170,694	622.24	166,984	181,029	622.24	164,638	183,375
105,000	1,306.70	365,412	653.35	186,184	179,228	653.35	175,332	190,080	653.35	172,869	192,543
110,000	1,368.93	382,815	684.47	195,053	187,762	684.47	183,685	199,130	684.47	181,104	201,711
115,000	1,431.15	400,214	715.58	203,918	196,296	715.58	192,033	208,181	715.58	189,335	210,879
120,000	1,493.38	417,617	746.69	212,783	204,834	746.69	200,382	217,235	746.69	197,567	220,050
125,000	1,555.60	435,016	777.80	221,648	213,368	777.80	208,730	226,286	777.80	205,798	229,218
130,000	1,617.82	452,415	808.91	230,513	221,902	808.91	217,078	235,337	808.91	214,029	238,386
135,000	1,680.05	469,818	840.03	239,383	230,435	840.03	225,431	244,387	840.03	222,264	247,554
140,000	1,742.27	487,217	871.14	248,248	238,969	871.14	233,779	253,438	871.14	230,495	256,722
145,000	1,804.49	504,616	902.25	257,113	247,503	902.25	242,128	262,488	902.25	238,726	265,890
150,000	1,866.72	522,019	933.36	265,978	256,041	933.36	250,476	271,543	933.36	246,957	275,062
155,000	1,928.94	539,418	964.47	274,843	264,575	964.47	258,824	280,594	964.47	255,188	284,230
160,000	1,991.17	556,821	995.59	283,713	273,108	995.59	267,177	289,644	995.59	263,423	293,398
165,000	2,053.39	574,220	1,026.70	292,578	281,642	1,026.70	275,525	298,695	1,026.70	271,654	302,566
170,000	2,115.61	591,620	1,057.81	301,443	290,177	1,057.81	283,873	307,747	1,057.81	279,886	311,734
175,000	2,177.84	609,022	1,088.92	310,308	298,714	1,088.92	292,222	316,800	1,088.92	288,117	320,905
180,000	2,240.06	626,422	1,120.03	319,173	307,249	1,120.03	300,570	325,852	1,120.03	296,348	330,074
185,000	2,302.29	643,824	1,151.15	328,042	315,782	1,151.15	308,923	334,901	1,151.15	304,583	339,241
190,000	2,364.51	661,224	1,182.26	336,907	324,317	1,182.26	317,271	343,953	1,182.26	312,814	348,410
195,000	2,426.73	678,623	1,213.37	345,772	332,851	1,213.37	325,619	353,004	1,213.37	321,045	357,578
200,000	2,488.96	696,026	1,244.48	354,637	341,389	1,244.48	333,968	362,058	1,244.48	329,276	366,750

BIWEEKLY MORTGAGES

AMOUNT OF LOAN	30 YEARS		360 DAY BASIS 440.084 PAYMENTS			364 DAY BASIS 423.542 PAYMENTS			365 DAY BASIS 419.790 PAYMENTS		
	MONTHLY PAYMENT	TOTAL INTRST	BWEEKLY PAYMENT	TOTAL INTRST	INTRST SAVED	BWEEKLY PAYMENT	TOTAL INTRST	INTRST SAVED	BWEEKLY PAYMENT	TOTAL INTRST	INTRST SAVED
$ 50	0.64	180	0.32	91	89	0.32	86	94	0.32	84	96
100	1.27	357	0.64	182	175	0.64	171	186	0.64	169	188
200	2.53	711	1.27	359	352	1.27	338	373	1.27	333	378
300	3.80	1,068	1.90	536	532	1.90	505	563	1.90	498	570
400	5.06	1,422	2.53	713	709	2.53	672	750	2.53	662	760
500	6.33	1,779	3.17	895	884	3.17	843	936	3.17	831	948
600	7.59	2,132	3.80	1,072	1,060	3.80	1,009	1,123	3.80	995	1,137
700	8.86	2,490	4.43	1,250	1,240	4.43	1,176	1,314	4.43	1,160	1,330
800	10.12	2,843	5.06	1,427	1,416	5.06	1,343	1,500	5.06	1,324	1,519
900	11.38	3,197	5.69	1,604	1,593	5.69	1,510	1,687	5.69	1,489	1,708
1,000	12.65	3,554	6.33	1,786	1,768	6.33	1,681	1,873	6.33	1,657	1,897
2,000	25.29	7,104	12.65	3,567	3,537	12.65	3,358	3,746	12.65	3,310	3,794
3,000	37.94	10,658	18.97	5,348	5,310	18.97	5,035	5,623	18.97	4,963	5,695
4,000	50.58	14,209	25.29	7,130	7,079	25.29	6,711	7,498	25.29	6,616	7,593
5,000	63.23	17,763	31.62	8,915	8,848	31.62	8,392	9,371	31.62	8,274	9,489
6,000	75.87	21,313	37.94	10,697	10,616	37.94	10,069	11,244	37.94	9,927	11,386
7,000	88.52	24,867	44.26	12,478	12,389	44.26	11,746	13,121	44.26	11,580	13,287
8,000	101.16	28,418	50.58	14,259	14,159	50.58	13,423	14,995	50.58	13,233	15,185
9,000	113.80	31,968	56.90	16,041	15,927	56.90	15,100	16,868	56.90	14,886	17,082
10,000	126.45	35,522	63.23	17,827	17,695	63.23	16,781	18,741	63.23	16,543	18,979
11,000	139.09	39,072	69.55	19,608	19,464	69.55	18,457	20,615	69.55	18,196	20,876
12,000	151.74	42,626	75.87	21,389	21,237	75.87	20,134	22,492	75.87	19,849	22,777
13,000	164.38	46,177	82.19	23,171	23,006	82.19	21,811	24,366	82.19	21,503	24,674
14,000	177.03	49,731	88.52	24,956	24,775	88.52	23,492	26,239	88.52	23,160	26,571
15,000	189.67	53,281	94.84	26,738	26,543	94.84	25,169	28,112	94.84	24,813	28,468
16,000	202.32	56,835	101.16	28,519	28,316	101.16	26,846	29,989	101.16	26,466	30,369
17,000	214.96	60,386	107.48	30,300	30,086	107.48	28,522	31,864	107.48	28,119	32,267
18,000	227.60	63,936	113.80	32,082	31,854	113.80	30,199	33,737	113.80	29,772	34,164
19,000	240.25	67,490	120.13	33,867	33,623	120.13	31,880	35,610	120.13	31,429	36,061
20,000	252.89	71,040	126.45	35,649	35,391	126.45	33,557	37,483	126.45	33,082	37,958
21,000	265.54	74,594	132.77	37,430	37,164	132.77	35,234	39,360	132.77	34,736	39,858
22,000	278.18	78,145	139.09	39,211	38,934	139.09	36,910	41,235	139.09	36,389	41,756
23,000	290.83	81,699	145.42	40,997	40,702	145.42	38,591	43,108	145.42	38,046	43,653
24,000	303.47	85,249	151.74	42,778	42,471	151.74	40,268	44,981	151.74	39,699	45,550
25,000	316.12	88,803	158.06	44,560	44,243	158.06	41,945	46,858	158.06	41,352	47,451
26,000	328.76	92,354	164.38	46,341	46,013	164.38	43,622	48,732	164.38	43,005	49,349
27,000	341.40	95,904	170.70	48,122	47,782	170.70	45,299	50,605	170.70	44,658	51,246
28,000	354.05	99,458	177.03	49,908	49,550	177.03	46,980	52,478	177.03	46,315	53,143
29,000	366.69	103,008	183.35	51,689	51,319	183.35	48,656	54,352	183.35	47,968	55,040
30,000	379.34	106,562	189.67	53,471	53,091	189.67	50,333	56,229	189.67	49,622	56,940
32,500	410.91	115,442	205.48	57,928	57,514	205.48	54,529	60,913	205.48	53,758	61,684
35,000	442.56	124,322	221.28	62,382	61,940	221.28	58,721	65,601	221.28	57,891	66,431
40,000	505.78	142,081	252.89	71,293	70,788	252.89	67,110	74,971	252.89	66,161	75,920
45,000	569.00	159,840	284.50	80,204	79,636	284.50	75,498	84,342	284.50	74,430	85,410
50,000	632.23	177,603	316.12	89,119	88,484	316.12	83,890	93,713	316.12	82,704	94,899
55,000	695.45	195,362	347.73	98,030	97,332	347.73	92,278	103,084	347.73	90,974	104,388
60,000	758.67	213,121	379.34	106,941	106,180	379.34	100,666	112,455	379.34	99,243	113,878
65,000	821.89	230,880	410.95	115,853	115,027	410.95	109,055	121,825	410.95	107,513	123,367
70,000	885.12	248,643	442.56	124,764	123,879	442.56	117,443	131,200	442.56	115,782	132,861
75,000	948.34	266,402	474.17	133,675	132,727	474.17	125,831	140,571	474.17	124,052	142,350
80,000	1,011.56	284,162	505.78	142,586	141,576	505.78	134,219	149,943	505.78	132,321	151,841
85,000	1,074.78	301,921	537.39	151,497	150,424	537.39	142,607	159,314	537.39	140,591	161,330
90,000	1,138.00	319,680	569.00	160,408	159,272	569.00	150,995	168,685	569.00	148,861	170,819
95,000	1,201.23	337,443	600.62	169,323	168,120	600.62	159,388	178,055	600.62	157,134	180,309
100,000	1,264.45	355,202	632.23	178,234	176,968	632.23	167,776	187,426	632.23	165,404	189,798
105,000	1,327.67	372,961	663.84	187,145	185,816	663.84	176,164	196,797	663.84	173,673	199,288
110,000	1,390.89	390,720	695.45	196,056	194,664	695.45	184,552	206,168	695.45	181,943	208,777
115,000	1,454.12	408,483	727.06	204,967	203,516	727.06	192,940	215,543	727.06	190,213	218,270
120,000	1,517.34	426,242	758.67	213,879	212,363	758.67	201,329	224,913	758.67	198,482	227,760
125,000	1,580.56	444,002	790.28	222,790	221,212	790.28	209,717	234,285	790.28	206,752	237,250
130,000	1,643.78	461,761	821.89	231,701	230,060	821.89	218,105	243,656	821.89	215,021	246,740
135,000	1,707.00	479,520	853.50	240,612	238,908	853.50	226,493	253,027	853.50	223,291	256,229
140,000	1,770.23	497,283	885.12	249,527	247,756	885.12	234,885	262,398	885.12	231,565	265,718
145,000	1,833.45	515,042	916.73	258,438	256,604	916.73	243,274	271,768	916.73	239,834	275,208
150,000	1,896.67	532,801	948.34	267,349	265,452	948.34	251,662	281,139	948.34	248,104	284,697
155,000	1,959.89	550,560	979.95	276,260	274,300	979.95	260,050	290,510	979.95	256,373	294,187
160,000	2,023.12	568,323	1,011.56	285,171	283,152	1,011.56	268,438	299,885	1,011.56	264,643	303,680
165,000	2,086.34	586,082	1,043.17	294,082	292,000	1,043.17	276,826	309,256	1,043.17	272,912	313,170
170,000	2,149.56	603,842	1,074.78	302,993	300,849	1,074.78	285,214	318,628	1,074.78	281,182	322,660
175,000	2,212.78	621,601	1,106.39	311,905	309,696	1,106.39	293,603	327,998	1,106.39	289,451	332,150
180,000	2,276.00	639,360	1,138.00	320,816	318,544	1,138.00	301,991	337,369	1,138.00	297,721	341,639
185,000	2,339.22	657,123	1,169.62	329,731	327,392	1,169.62	310,383	346,740	1,169.62	305,995	351,128
190,000	2,402.45	674,882	1,201.23	338,642	336,240	1,201.23	318,771	356,111	1,201.23	314,264	360,618
195,000	2,465.67	692,641	1,232.84	347,553	345,088	1,232.84	327,160	365,481	1,232.84	322,534	370,107
200,000	2,528.89	710,400	1,264.45	356,464	353,936	1,264.45	335,548	374,852	1,264.45	330,803	379,597

AMOUNT OF LOAN	30 YEARS		360 DAY BASIS 434.563 PAYMENTS			364 DAY BASIS 418.096 PAYMENTS			365 DAY BASIS 414.365 PAYMENTS		
	MONTHLY PAYMENT	TOTAL INTRST	BWEEKLY PAYMENT	TOTAL INTRST	INTRST SAVED	BWEEKLY PAYMENT	TOTAL INTRST	INTRST SAVED	BWEEKLY PAYMENT	TOTAL INTRST	INTRST SAVED
$ 50	0.65	184	0.33	93	91	0.33	88	96	0.33	87	97
100	1.29	364	0.65	182	182	0.65	172	192	0.65	169	195
200	2.57	725	1.29	361	364	1.29	339	386	1.29	335	390
300	3.86	1,090	1.93	539	551	1.93	507	583	1.93	500	590
400	5.14	1,450	2.57	717	733	2.57	675	775	2.57	665	785
500	6.43	1,815	3.22	899	916	3.22	846	969	3.22	834	981
600	7.71	2,176	3.86	1,077	1,099	3.86	1,014	1,162	3.86	999	1,177
700	9.00	2,540	4.50	1,256	1,284	4.50	1,181	1,359	4.50	1,165	1,375
800	10.28	2,901	5.14	1,434	1,467	5.14	1,349	1,552	5.14	1,330	1,571
900	11.57	3,265	5.79	1,616	1,649	5.79	1,521	1,744	5.79	1,499	1,766
1,000	12.85	3,626	6.43	1,794	1,832	6.43	1,688	1,938	6.43	1,664	1,962
2,000	25.69	7,248	12.85	3,584	3,664	12.85	3,373	3,875	12.85	3,325	3,923
3,000	38.54	10,874	19.27	5,374	5,500	19.27	5,057	5,817	19.27	4,985	5,889
4,000	51.38	14,497	25.69	7,164	7,333	25.69	6,741	7,756	25.69	6,645	7,852
5,000	64.23	18,123	32.12	8,958	9,165	32.12	8,429	9,694	32.12	8,309	9,814
6,000	77.07	21,745	38.54	10,748	10,997	38.54	10,113	11,632	38.54	9,970	11,775
7,000	89.92	25,371	44.96	12,538	12,833	44.96	11,798	13,573	44.96	11,630	13,741
8,000	102.76	28,994	51.38	14,328	14,666	51.38	13,482	15,512	51.38	13,290	15,704
9,000	115.61	32,620	57.81	16,122	16,498	57.81	15,170	17,450	57.81	14,954	17,666
10,000	128.45	36,242	64.23	17,912	18,330	64.23	16,854	19,388	64.23	16,615	19,627
11,000	141.30	39,868	70.65	19,702	20,166	70.65	18,538	21,330	70.65	18,275	21,593
12,000	154.14	43,490	77.07	21,492	21,998	77.07	20,223	23,267	77.07	19,935	23,555
13,000	166.98	47,113	83.49	23,282	23,831	83.49	21,907	25,206	83.49	21,595	25,518
14,000	179.83	50,739	89.92	25,076	25,663	89.92	23,595	27,144	89.92	23,260	27,479
15,000	192.67	54,361	96.34	26,866	27,495	96.34	25,279	29,082	96.34	24,920	29,441
16,000	205.52	57,987	102.76	28,656	29,331	102.76	26,964	31,023	102.76	26,580	31,407
17,000	218.36	61,610	109.18	30,446	31,164	109.18	28,648	32,962	109.18	28,240	33,370
18,000	231.21	65,236	115.61	32,240	32,996	115.61	30,336	34,900	115.61	29,905	35,331
19,000	244.05	68,858	122.03	34,030	34,828	122.03	32,020	36,838	122.03	31,565	37,293
20,000	256.90	72,484	128.45	35,820	36,664	128.45	33,704	38,780	128.45	33,225	39,259
21,000	269.74	76,106	134.87	37,610	38,496	134.87	35,389	40,717	134.87	34,885	41,221
22,000	282.59	79,732	141.30	39,404	40,328	141.30	37,077	42,655	141.30	36,550	43,182
23,000	295.43	83,355	147.72	41,194	42,161	147.72	38,761	44,594	147.72	38,210	45,145
24,000	308.28	86,981	154.14	42,984	43,997	154.14	40,445	46,536	154.14	39,870	47,111
25,000	321.12	90,603	160.56	44,773	45,830	160.56	42,129	48,474	160.56	41,530	49,073
26,000	333.96	94,226	166.98	46,563	47,663	166.98	43,814	50,412	166.98	43,191	51,035
27,000	346.81	97,852	173.41	48,358	49,494	173.41	45,502	52,350	173.41	44,855	52,997
28,000	359.65	101,474	179.83	50,148	51,327	179.83	47,186	54,288	179.83	46,515	54,959
29,000	372.50	105,100	186.25	51,937	53,163	186.25	48,870	56,230	186.25	48,175	56,925
30,000	385.34	108,722	192.67	53,727	54,995	192.67	50,555	58,167	192.67	49,836	58,886
32,500	417.45	117,782	208.73	58,206	59,576	208.73	54,769	63,013	208.73	53,990	63,792
35,000	449.57	126,845	224.79	62,685	64,160	224.79	58,984	67,861	224.79	58,145	68,700
40,000	513.79	144,964	256.90	71,639	73,325	256.90	67,409	77,555	256.90	66,450	78,514
45,000	578.01	163,084	289.01	80,593	82,491	289.01	75,834	87,250	289.01	74,756	88,328
50,000	642.23	181,203	321.12	89,547	91,656	321.12	84,259	96,944	321.12	83,061	98,142
55,000	706.46	199,326	353.23	98,501	100,825	353.23	92,684	106,642	353.23	91,366	107,960
60,000	770.68	217,445	385.34	107,455	109,990	385.34	101,109	116,336	385.34	99,671	117,774
65,000	834.90	235,564	417.45	116,408	119,156	417.45	109,534	126,030	417.45	107,977	127,587
70,000	899.13	253,687	449.57	125,366	128,321	449.57	117,963	135,724	449.57	116,286	137,401
75,000	963.35	271,806	481.68	134,320	137,486	481.68	126,388	145,418	481.68	124,591	147,215
80,000	1,027.57	289,925	513.79	143,274	146,651	513.79	134,814	155,111	513.79	132,897	157,028
85,000	1,091.79	308,044	545.90	152,228	155,816	545.90	143,239	164,805	545.90	141,202	166,842
90,000	1,156.02	326,167	578.01	161,182	164,985	578.01	151,664	174,503	578.01	149,507	176,660
95,000	1,220.24	344,286	610.12	170,136	174,150	610.12	160,089	184,197	610.12	157,812	186,474
100,000	1,284.46	362,406	642.23	179,089	183,317	642.23	168,514	193,892	642.23	166,118	196,288
105,000	1,348.69	380,528	674.35	188,048	192,480	674.35	176,942	203,585	674.35	174,427	206,101
110,000	1,412.91	398,648	706.46	197,001	201,647	706.46	185,368	213,280	706.46	182,732	215,916
115,000	1,477.13	416,767	738.57	205,955	210,812	738.57	193,793	222,974	738.57	191,038	225,729
120,000	1,541.36	434,890	770.68	214,909	219,981	770.68	202,218	232,672	770.68	199,343	235,547
125,000	1,605.58	453,009	802.79	223,863	229,146	802.79	210,643	242,366	802.79	207,648	245,361
130,000	1,669.80	471,128	834.90	232,817	238,311	834.90	219,068	252,060	834.90	215,953	255,175
135,000	1,734.02	489,247	867.01	241,770	247,477	867.01	227,493	261,754	867.01	224,259	264,988
140,000	1,798.25	507,370	899.13	250,729	256,641	899.13	235,923	271,447	899.13	232,568	274,802
145,000	1,862.47	525,489	931.24	259,682	265,807	931.24	244,348	281,141	931.24	240,873	284,616
150,000	1,926.69	543,608	963.35	268,636	274,972	963.35	252,773	290,835	963.35	249,179	294,429
155,000	1,990.92	561,731	995.46	277,590	284,141	995.46	261,198	300,533	995.46	257,484	304,247
160,000	2,055.14	579,850	1,027.57	286,544	293,306	1,027.57	269,623	310,227	1,027.57	265,789	314,061
165,000	2,119.36	597,970	1,059.68	295,498	302,472	1,059.68	278,048	319,922	1,059.68	274,094	323,876
170,000	2,183.58	616,089	1,091.79	304,452	311,637	1,091.79	286,473	329,616	1,091.79	282,400	333,689
175,000	2,247.81	634,212	1,123.91	313,410	320,802	1,123.91	294,902	339,310	1,123.91	290,709	343,503
180,000	2,312.03	652,331	1,156.02	322,364	329,967	1,156.02	303,327	349,004	1,156.02	299,014	353,317
185,000	2,376.25	670,450	1,188.13	331,317	339,133	1,188.13	311,752	358,698	1,188.13	307,319	363,131
190,000	2,440.48	688,573	1,220.24	340,271	348,302	1,220.24	320,177	368,396	1,220.24	315,625	372,948
195,000	2,504.70	706,692	1,252.35	349,225	357,467	1,252.35	328,603	378,089	1,252.35	323,930	382,762
200,000	2,568.92	724,811	1,284.46	358,179	366,632	1,284.46	337,028	387,783	1,284.46	332,235	392,576

AMOUNT OF LOAN	30 YEARS		360 DAY BASIS 429.118 PAYMENTS			364 DAY BASIS 412.734 PAYMENTS			365 DAY BASIS 409.023 PAYMENTS		
	MONTHLY PAYMENT	TOTAL INTRST	BWEEKLY PAYMENT	TOTAL INTRST	INTRST SAVED	BWEEKLY PAYMENT	TOTAL INTRST	INTRST SAVED	BWEEKLY PAYMENT	TOTAL INTRST	INTRST SAVED
$ 50	0.66	188	0.33	92	96	0.33	86	102	0.33	85	103
100	1.31	372	0.66	183	189	0.66	172	200	0.66	170	202
200	2.61	740	1.31	362	378	1.31	341	399	1.31	336	404
300	3.92	1,111	1.96	541	570	1.96	509	602	1.96	502	609
400	5.22	1,479	2.61	720	759	2.61	677	802	2.61	668	811
500	6.53	1,851	3.27	903	948	3.27	850	1,001	3.27	838	1,013
600	7.83	2,219	3.92	1,082	1,137	3.92	1,018	1,201	3.92	1,003	1,216
700	9.14	2,590	4.57	1,261	1,329	4.57	1,186	1,404	4.57	1,169	1,421
800	10.44	2,958	5.22	1,440	1,518	5.22	1,354	1,604	5.22	1,335	1,623
900	11.75	3,330	5.88	1,623	1,707	5.88	1,527	1,803	5.88	1,505	1,825
1,000	13.05	3,698	6.53	1,802	1,896	6.53	1,695	2,003	6.53	1,671	2,027
2,000	26.10	7,396	13.05	3,600	3,796	13.05	3,386	4,010	13.05	3,338	4,058
3,000	39.14	11,090	19.57	5,398	5,692	19.57	5,077	6,013	19.57	5,005	6,085
4,000	52.19	14,788	26.10	7,200	7,588	26.10	6,772	8,016	26.10	6,676	8,112
5,000	65.23	18,483	32.62	8,998	9,485	32.62	8,463	10,020	32.62	8,342	10,141
6,000	78.28	22,181	39.14	10,796	11,385	39.14	10,154	12,027	39.14	10,009	12,172
7,000	91.32	25,875	45.66	12,594	13,281	45.66	11,845	14,030	45.66	11,676	14,199
8,000	104.37	29,573	52.19	14,396	15,177	52.19	13,541	16,032	52.19	13,347	16,226
9,000	117.41	33,268	58.71	16,194	17,074	58.71	15,232	18,036	58.71	15,014	18,254
10,000	130.46	36,966	65.23	17,991	18,975	65.23	16,923	20,043	65.23	16,681	20,285
11,000	143.50	40,660	71.75	19,789	20,871	71.75	18,614	22,046	71.75	18,347	22,313
12,000	156.55	44,358	78.28	21,591	22,767	78.28	20,309	24,049	78.28	20,018	24,340
13,000	169.59	48,052	84.80	23,389	24,663	84.80	22,000	26,052	84.80	21,685	26,367
14,000	182.64	51,750	91.32	25,187	26,563	91.32	23,691	28,059	91.32	23,352	28,398
15,000	195.68	55,445	97.84	26,985	28,460	97.84	25,382	30,063	97.84	25,019	30,426
16,000	208.73	59,143	104.37	28,787	30,356	104.37	27,077	32,066	104.37	26,690	32,453
17,000	221.77	62,837	110.89	30,585	32,252	110.89	28,768	34,069	110.89	28,357	34,480
18,000	234.82	66,535	117.41	32,383	34,152	117.41	30,459	36,076	117.41	30,023	36,512
19,000	247.86	70,230	123.93	34,181	36,049	123.93	32,150	38,080	123.93	31,690	38,540
20,000	260.91	73,928	130.46	35,983	37,945	130.46	33,845	40,083	130.46	33,361	40,567
21,000	273.95	77,622	136.98	37,781	39,841	136.98	35,536	42,086	136.98	35,028	42,594
22,000	287.00	81,320	143.50	39,578	41,742	143.50	37,227	44,093	143.50	36,695	44,625
23,000	300.04	85,014	150.02	41,376	43,638	150.02	38,918	46,096	150.02	38,362	46,652
24,000	313.09	88,712	156.55	43,178	45,534	156.55	40,614	48,098	156.55	40,033	48,679
25,000	326.13	92,407	163.07	44,976	47,431	163.07	42,305	50,102	163.07	41,699	50,708
26,000	339.18	96,105	169.59	46,774	49,331	169.59	43,996	52,109	169.59	43,366	52,739
27,000	352.22	99,799	176.11	48,572	51,227	176.11	45,687	54,112	176.11	45,033	54,766
28,000	365.27	103,497	182.64	50,374	53,123	182.64	47,382	56,115	182.64	46,704	56,793
29,000	378.31	107,192	189.16	52,172	55,020	189.16	49,073	58,119	189.16	48,371	58,821
30,000	391.36	110,890	195.68	53,970	56,920	195.68	50,764	60,126	195.68	50,038	60,852
32,500	423.97	120,129	211.99	58,469	61,660	211.99	54,995	65,134	211.99	54,209	65,920
35,000	456.59	129,372	228.30	62,968	66,404	228.30	59,227	70,145	228.30	58,380	70,992
40,000	521.81	147,852	260.91	71,961	75,891	260.91	67,686	80,166	260.91	66,718	81,134
45,000	587.04	166,334	293.52	80,955	85,379	293.52	76,146	90,188	293.52	75,056	91,278
50,000	652.26	184,814	326.13	89,948	94,866	326.13	84,605	100,209	326.13	83,395	101,419
55,000	717.49	203,296	358.75	98,946	104,350	358.75	93,068	110,228	358.75	91,737	111,559
60,000	782.72	221,779	391.36	107,940	113,839	391.36	101,528	120,251	391.36	100,075	121,704
65,000	847.94	240,258	423.97	116,933	123,325	423.97	109,987	130,271	423.97	108,413	131,845
70,000	913.17	258,741	456.59	125,931	132,810	456.59	118,450	140,291	456.59	116,756	141,985
75,000	978.39	277,220	489.20	134,925	142,295	489.20	126,909	150,311	489.20	125,094	152,126
80,000	1,043.62	295,703	521.81	143,918	151,785	521.81	135,369	160,334	521.81	133,432	162,271
85,000	1,108.84	314,182	554.42	152,912	161,270	554.42	143,828	170,354	554.42	141,771	172,411
90,000	1,174.07	332,665	587.04	161,909	170,756	587.04	152,291	180,374	587.04	150,113	182,552
95,000	1,239.30	351,148	619.65	170,903	180,245	619.65	160,751	190,397	619.65	158,451	192,697
100,000	1,304.52	369,627	652.26	179,897	189,730	652.26	169,210	200,417	652.26	166,789	202,838
105,000	1,369.75	388,110	684.88	188,894	199,216	684.88	177,673	210,437	684.88	175,132	212,978
110,000	1,434.97	406,589	717.49	197,888	208,701	717.49	186,133	220,456	717.49	183,470	223,119
115,000	1,500.20	425,072	750.10	206,881	218,191	750.10	194,592	230,480	750.10	191,808	233,264
120,000	1,565.43	443,555	782.72	215,879	227,676	782.72	203,055	240,500	782.72	200,150	243,405
125,000	1,630.65	462,034	815.33	224,873	237,161	815.33	211,514	250,520	815.33	208,489	253,545
130,000	1,695.88	480,517	847.94	233,866	246,651	847.94	219,974	260,543	847.94	216,827	263,690
135,000	1,761.10	498,996	880.55	242,860	256,136	880.55	228,433	270,563	880.55	225,165	273,831
140,000	1,826.33	517,479	913.17	251,858	265,621	913.17	236,896	280,583	913.17	233,508	283,971
145,000	1,891.55	535,958	945.78	260,851	275,107	945.78	245,356	290,602	945.78	241,846	294,112
150,000	1,956.78	554,441	978.39	269,845	284,596	978.39	253,815	300,626	978.39	250,184	304,257
155,000	2,022.01	572,924	1,011.01	278,843	294,081	1,011.01	262,278	310,646	1,011.01	258,526	314,398
160,000	2,087.23	591,403	1,043.62	287,836	303,567	1,043.62	270,737	320,666	1,043.62	266,865	324,538
165,000	2,152.46	609,886	1,076.23	296,830	313,056	1,076.23	279,197	330,689	1,076.23	275,203	334,683
170,000	2,217.68	628,365	1,108.84	305,823	322,542	1,108.84	287,656	340,709	1,108.84	283,541	344,824
175,000	2,282.91	646,848	1,141.46	314,821	332,027	1,141.46	296,119	350,729	1,141.46	291,883	354,965
180,000	2,348.14	665,330	1,174.07	323,815	341,515	1,174.07	304,579	360,751	1,174.07	300,222	365,108
185,000	2,413.36	683,810	1,206.68	332,808	351,002	1,206.68	313,039	370,772	1,206.68	308,560	375,250
190,000	2,478.59	702,292	1,239.30	341,806	360,486	1,239.30	321,501	380,791	1,239.30	316,902	385,390
195,000	2,543.81	720,772	1,271.91	350,799	369,973	1,271.91	329,961	390,811	1,271.91	325,240	395,532
200,000	2,609.04	739,254	1,304.52	359,793	379,461	1,304.52	338,420	400,834	1,304.52	333,579	405,675

BIWEEKLY MORTGAGES 15.75%

AMOUNT OF LOAN	30 YEARS		360 DAY BASIS 423.749 PAYMENTS			364 DAY BASIS 407.456 PAYMENTS			365 DAY BASIS 403.769 PAYMENTS		
	MONTHLY PAYMENT	TOTAL INTRST	BWEEKLY PAYMENT	TOTAL INTRST	INTRST SAVED	BWEEKLY PAYMENT	TOTAL INTRST	INTRST SAVED	BWEEKLY PAYMENT	TOTAL INTRST	INTRST SAVED
$ 50	0.67	191	0.34	94	97	0.34	89	102	0.34	87	104
100	1.33	379	0.67	184	195	0.67	173	206	0.67	171	208
200	2.65	754	1.33	364	390	1.33	342	412	1.33	337	417
300	3.98	1,133	1.99	543	590	1.99	511	622	1.99	504	629
400	5.30	1,508	2.65	723	785	2.65	680	828	2.65	670	838
500	6.63	1,887	3.32	907	980	3.32	853	1,034	3.32	841	1,046
600	7.95	2,262	3.98	1,087	1,175	3.98	1,022	1,240	3.98	1,007	1,255
700	9.28	2,641	4.64	1,266	1,375	4.64	1,191	1,450	4.64	1,173	1,468
800	10.60	3,016	5.30	1,446	1,570	5.30	1,360	1,656	5.30	1,340	1,676
900	11.93	3,395	5.97	1,630	1,765	5.97	1,533	1,862	5.97	1,511	1,884
1,000	13.25	3,770	6.63	1,809	1,961	6.63	1,701	2,069	6.63	1,677	2,093
2,000	26.50	7,540	13.25	3,615	3,925	13.25	3,399	4,141	13.25	3,350	4,190
3,000	39.74	11,306	19.87	5,420	5,886	19.87	5,096	6,210	19.87	5,023	6,283
4,000	52.99	15,076	26.50	7,229	7,847	26.50	6,798	8,278	26.50	6,700	8,376
5,000	66.24	18,846	33.12	9,035	9,811	33.12	8,495	10,351	33.12	8,373	10,473
6,000	79.48	22,613	39.74	10,840	11,773	39.74	10,192	12,421	39.74	10,046	12,567
7,000	92.73	26,383	46.37	12,649	13,734	46.37	11,894	14,489	46.37	11,723	14,660
8,000	105.97	30,149	52.99	14,454	15,695	52.99	13,591	16,558	52.99	13,396	16,753
9,000	119.22	33,919	59.61	16,260	17,659	59.61	15,288	18,631	59.61	15,069	18,850
10,000	132.47	37,689	66.24	18,069	19,620	66.24	16,990	20,699	66.24	16,746	20,943
11,000	145.71	41,456	72.86	19,874	21,582	72.86	18,687	22,769	72.86	18,419	23,037
12,000	158.96	45,226	79.48	21,680	23,546	79.48	20,385	24,841	79.48	20,092	25,134
13,000	172.21	48,996	86.11	23,489	25,507	86.11	22,086	26,910	86.11	21,769	27,227
14,000	185.45	52,762	92.73	25,294	27,468	92.73	23,783	28,979	92.73	23,441	29,321
15,000	198.70	56,532	99.35	27,099	29,433	99.35	25,481	31,051	99.35	25,114	31,418
16,000	211.94	60,298	105.97	28,905	31,393	105.97	27,178	33,120	105.97	26,787	33,511
17,000	225.19	64,068	112.60	30,714	33,354	112.60	28,880	35,188	112.60	28,464	35,604
18,000	238.44	67,838	119.22	32,519	35,319	119.22	30,577	37,261	119.22	30,137	37,701
19,000	251.68	71,605	125.84	34,325	37,280	125.84	32,274	39,331	125.84	31,810	39,795
20,000	264.93	75,375	132.47	36,134	39,241	132.47	33,976	41,399	132.47	33,487	41,888
21,000	278.17	79,141	139.09	37,939	41,202	139.09	35,673	43,468	139.09	35,160	43,981
22,000	291.42	82,911	145.71	39,744	43,167	145.71	37,370	45,541	145.71	36,833	46,078
23,000	304.67	86,681	152.34	41,554	45,127	152.34	39,072	47,609	152.34	38,510	48,171
24,000	317.91	90,448	158.96	43,359	47,089	158.96	40,769	49,679	158.96	40,183	50,265
25,000	331.16	94,218	165.58	45,164	49,054	165.58	42,467	51,751	165.58	41,856	52,362
26,000	344.41	97,988	172.21	46,974	51,014	172.21	44,168	53,820	172.21	43,533	54,455
27,000	357.65	101,754	178.83	48,779	52,975	178.83	45,865	55,889	178.83	45,206	56,548
28,000	370.90	105,524	185.45	50,584	54,940	185.45	47,563	57,961	185.45	46,879	58,645
29,000	384.14	109,290	192.07	52,389	56,901	192.07	49,260	60,030	192.07	48,552	60,738
30,000	397.39	113,060	198.70	54,199	58,861	198.70	50,962	62,098	198.70	50,229	62,831
32,500	430.51	122,484	215.26	58,716	63,768	215.26	55,209	67,275	215.26	54,415	68,069
35,000	463.62	131,903	231.81	63,229	68,674	231.81	59,452	72,451	231.81	58,598	73,305
40,000	529.85	150,750	264.93	72,264	78,482	264.93	67,947	82,799	264.93	66,971	83,775
45,000	596.08	169,589	298.04	81,294	88,295	298.04	76,438	93,151	298.04	75,339	94,250
50,000	662.31	188,432	331.16	90,329	98,103	331.16	84,933	103,499	331.16	83,712	104,720
55,000	728.54	207,274	364.27	99,359	107,915	364.27	93,424	113,850	364.27	92,081	115,193
60,000	794.78	226,121	397.39	108,394	117,727	397.39	101,919	124,202	397.39	100,454	125,667
65,000	861.01	244,964	430.51	117,428	127,536	430.51	110,414	134,550	430.51	108,827	136,137
70,000	927.24	263,806	463.62	126,459	137,347	463.62	118,905	144,901	463.62	117,195	146,611
75,000	993.47	282,649	496.74	135,493	147,156	496.74	127,400	155,249	496.74	125,568	157,081
80,000	1,059.70	301,492	529.85	144,523	156,969	529.85	135,891	165,601	529.85	133,937	167,555
85,000	1,125.93	320,335	562.97	153,558	166,777	562.97	144,386	175,949	562.97	142,310	178,025
90,000	1,192.16	339,178	596.08	162,588	176,590	596.08	152,876	186,302	596.08	150,679	188,499
95,000	1,258.39	358,020	629.20	171,623	186,397	629.20	161,371	196,649	629.20	159,051	198,969
100,000	1,324.62	376,863	662.31	180,653	196,210	662.31	169,862	207,001	662.31	167,420	209,443
105,000	1,390.85	395,706	695.43	189,688	206,018	695.43	178,357	217,349	695.43	175,793	219,913
110,000	1,457.08	414,549	728.54	198,718	215,831	728.54	186,848	227,701	728.54	184,162	230,387
115,000	1,523.31	433,392	761.66	207,753	225,639	761.66	195,343	238,049	761.66	192,535	240,857
120,000	1,589.55	452,238	794.78	216,787	235,451	794.78	203,834	248,400	794.78	200,908	251,330
125,000	1,655.78	471,081	827.89	225,818	245,263	827.89	212,329	258,752	827.89	209,276	261,805
130,000	1,722.01	489,924	861.01	234,852	255,072	861.01	220,824	269,100	861.01	217,649	272,275
135,000	1,788.24	508,766	894.12	243,882	264,884	894.12	229,315	279,451	894.12	226,018	282,748
140,000	1,854.47	527,609	927.24	252,917	274,692	927.24	237,810	289,799	927.24	234,391	293,218
145,000	1,920.70	546,452	960.35	261,947	284,505	960.35	246,300	300,152	960.35	242,760	303,692
150,000	1,986.93	565,295	993.47	270,982	294,313	993.47	254,795	310,500	993.47	251,132	314,163
155,000	2,053.16	584,138	1,026.58	280,012	304,126	1,026.58	263,286	320,852	1,026.58	259,501	324,637
160,000	2,119.39	602,980	1,059.70	289,047	313,933	1,059.70	271,781	331,199	1,059.70	267,874	335,106
165,000	2,185.62	621,823	1,092.81	298,077	323,746	1,092.81	280,272	341,551	1,092.81	276,243	345,580
170,000	2,251.85	640,666	1,125.93	307,112	333,554	1,125.93	288,767	351,899	1,125.93	284,616	356,050
175,000	2,318.08	659,509	1,159.04	316,142	343,367	1,159.04	297,258	362,251	1,159.04	292,984	366,525
180,000	2,384.32	678,355	1,192.16	325,177	353,178	1,192.16	305,753	372,602	1,192.16	301,357	376,998
185,000	2,450.55	697,198	1,225.28	334,211	362,987	1,225.28	314,248	382,950	1,225.28	309,730	387,468
190,000	2,516.78	716,041	1,258.39	343,242	372,799	1,258.39	322,739	393,302	1,258.39	318,099	397,942
195,000	2,583.01	734,884	1,291.51	352,276	382,608	1,291.51	331,233	403,651	1,291.51	326,472	408,412
200,000	2,649.24	753,726	1,324.62	361,306	392,420	1,324.62	339,724	414,002	1,324.62	334,840	418,886

16.00%   BIWEEKLY MORTGAGES

AMOUNT OF LOAN	30 YEARS		360 DAY BASIS 418.460 PAYMENTS			364 DAY BASIS 402.263 PAYMENTS			365 DAY BASIS 398.600 PAYMENTS		
	MONTHLY PAYMENT	TOTAL INTRST	BWEEKLY PAYMENT	TOTAL INTRST	INTRST SAVED	BWEEKLY PAYMENT	TOTAL INTRST	INTRST SAVED	BWEEKLY PAYMENT	TOTAL INTRST	INTRST SAVED
$ 50	0.68	195	0.34	92	103	0.34	87	108	0.34	86	109
100	1.35	386	0.68	185	201	0.68	174	212	0.68	171	215
200	2.69	768	1.35	365	403	1.35	343	425	1.35	338	430
300	4.04	1,154	2.02	545	609	2.02	513	641	2.02	505	649
400	5.38	1,537	2.69	726	811	2.69	682	855	2.69	672	865
500	6.73	1,923	3.37	910	1,013	3.37	856	1,067	3.37	843	1,080
600	8.07	2,305	4.04	1,091	1,214	4.04	1,025	1,280	4.04	1,010	1,295
700	9.42	2,691	4.71	1,271	1,420	4.71	1,195	1,496	4.71	1,177	1,514
800	10.76	3,074	5.38	1,451	1,623	5.38	1,364	1,710	5.38	1,344	1,730
900	12.11	3,460	6.06	1,636	1,824	6.06	1,538	1,922	6.06	1,516	1,944
1,000	13.45	3,842	6.73	1,816	2,026	6.73	1,707	2,135	6.73	1,683	2,159
2,000	26.90	7,684	13.45	3,628	4,056	13.45	3,410	4,274	13.45	3,361	4,323
3,000	40.35	11,526	20.18	5,445	6,081	20.18	5,118	6,408	20.18	5,044	6,482
4,000	53.80	15,368	26.90	7,257	8,111	26.90	6,821	8,547	26.90	6,722	8,646
5,000	67.24	19,206	33.62	9,069	10,137	33.62	8,524	10,682	33.62	8,401	10,805
6,000	80.69	23,048	40.35	10,885	12,163	40.35	10,231	12,817	40.35	10,084	12,964
7,000	94.14	26,890	47.07	12,697	14,193	47.07	11,935	14,955	47.07	11,762	15,128
8,000	107.59	30,732	53.80	14,513	16,219	53.80	13,642	17,090	53.80	13,445	17,287
9,000	121.03	34,571	60.52	16,325	18,246	60.52	15,345	19,226	60.52	15,123	19,448
10,000	134.48	38,413	67.24	18,137	20,276	67.24	17,048	21,365	67.24	16,802	21,611
11,000	147.93	42,255	73.97	19,953	22,302	73.97	18,755	23,500	73.97	18,484	23,771
12,000	161.38	46,097	80.69	21,766	24,331	80.69	20,459	25,638	80.69	20,163	25,934
13,000	174.82	49,935	87.41	23,578	26,357	87.41	22,162	27,773	87.41	21,842	28,093
14,000	188.27	53,777	94.14	25,394	28,383	94.14	23,869	29,908	94.14	23,524	30,253
15,000	201.72	57,619	100.86	27,206	30,413	100.86	25,572	32,047	100.86	25,203	32,416
16,000	215.17	61,461	107.59	29,022	32,439	107.59	27,279	34,182	107.59	26,885	34,576
17,000	228.61	65,300	114.31	30,834	34,466	114.31	28,983	36,317	114.31	28,564	36,736
18,000	242.06	69,142	121.03	32,646	36,496	121.03	30,686	38,456	121.03	30,243	38,899
19,000	255.51	72,984	127.76	34,462	38,522	127.76	32,393	40,591	127.76	31,925	41,059
20,000	268.96	76,826	134.48	36,275	40,551	134.48	34,096	42,730	134.48	33,604	43,222
21,000	282.40	80,664	141.20	38,087	42,577	141.20	35,800	44,864	141.20	35,282	45,382
22,000	295.85	84,506	147.93	39,903	44,603	147.93	37,507	46,999	147.93	36,965	47,541
23,000	309.30	88,348	154.65	41,715	46,633	154.65	39,210	49,138	154.65	38,643	49,705
24,000	322.75	92,190	161.38	43,531	48,659	161.38	40,917	51,273	161.38	40,326	51,864
25,000	336.19	96,028	168.10	45,343	50,685	168.10	42,620	53,408	168.10	42,005	54,023
26,000	349.64	99,870	174.82	47,155	52,715	174.82	44,324	55,546	174.82	43,683	56,187
27,000	363.09	103,712	181.55	48,971	54,741	181.55	46,031	57,681	181.55	45,366	58,346
28,000	376.54	107,554	188.27	50,783	56,771	188.27	47,734	59,820	188.27	47,044	60,510
29,000	389.98	111,393	194.99	52,596	58,797	194.99	49,437	61,956	194.99	48,723	62,670
30,000	403.43	115,235	201.72	54,412	60,823	201.72	51,144	64,091	201.72	50,406	64,829
32,500	437.05	124,838	218.53	58,946	65,892	218.53	55,407	69,431	218.53	54,606	70,232
35,000	470.67	134,441	235.34	63,480	70,961	235.34	59,669	74,772	235.34	58,807	75,634
40,000	537.91	153,648	268.96	72,549	81,099	268.96	68,193	85,455	268.96	67,207	86,441
45,000	605.15	172,854	302.58	81,618	91,236	302.58	76,717	96,137	302.58	75,608	97,246
50,000	672.38	192,057	336.19	90,682	101,375	336.19	85,237	106,820	336.19	84,005	108,052
55,000	739.62	211,263	369.81	99,751	111,512	369.81	93,761	117,502	369.81	92,406	118,857
60,000	806.86	230,470	403.43	108,819	121,651	403.43	102,285	128,185	403.43	100,807	129,663
65,000	874.10	249,676	437.05	117,888	131,788	437.05	110,809	138,867	437.05	109,208	140,468
70,000	941.33	268,879	470.67	126,957	141,922	470.67	119,333	149,546	470.67	117,609	151,270
75,000	1,008.57	288,085	504.29	136,025	152,060	504.29	127,857	160,228	504.29	126,010	162,075
80,000	1,075.81	307,292	537.91	145,094	162,198	537.91	136,381	170,911	537.91	134,411	172,881
85,000	1,143.05	326,498	571.53	154,162	172,336	571.53	144,905	181,593	571.53	142,812	183,686
90,000	1,210.29	345,704	605.15	163,231	182,473	605.15	153,429	192,275	605.15	151,213	194,491
95,000	1,277.52	364,907	638.76	172,296	192,611	638.76	161,950	202,957	638.76	159,610	205,297
100,000	1,344.76	384,114	672.38	181,364	202,750	672.38	170,474	213,640	672.38	168,011	216,103
105,000	1,412.00	403,320	706.00	190,433	212,887	706.00	178,998	224,322	706.00	176,412	226,908
110,000	1,479.24	422,526	739.62	199,501	223,025	739.62	187,522	235,004	739.62	184,813	237,713
115,000	1,546.48	441,733	773.24	208,570	233,163	773.24	196,046	245,687	773.24	193,213	248,520
120,000	1,613.71	460,936	806.86	217,639	243,297	806.86	204,570	256,366	806.86	201,614	259,322
125,000	1,680.95	480,142	840.48	226,707	253,435	840.48	213,094	267,048	840.48	210,015	270,127
130,000	1,748.19	499,348	874.10	235,776	263,572	874.10	221,618	277,730	874.10	218,416	280,932
135,000	1,815.43	518,555	907.72	244,845	273,710	907.72	230,142	288,413	907.72	226,817	291,738
140,000	1,882.66	537,758	941.33	253,909	283,849	941.33	238,662	299,096	941.33	235,214	302,544
145,000	1,949.90	556,964	974.95	262,978	293,986	974.95	247,186	309,778	974.95	243,615	313,349
150,000	2,017.14	576,170	1,008.57	272,046	304,124	1,008.57	255,710	320,460	1,008.57	252,016	324,154
155,000	2,084.38	595,377	1,042.19	281,115	314,262	1,042.19	264,234	331,143	1,042.19	260,417	334,960
160,000	2,151.62	614,583	1,075.81	290,183	324,400	1,075.81	272,759	341,824	1,075.81	268,818	345,765
165,000	2,218.85	633,786	1,109.43	299,252	334,534	1,109.43	281,283	352,503	1,109.43	277,219	356,567
170,000	2,286.09	652,992	1,143.05	308,321	344,671	1,143.05	289,807	363,185	1,143.05	285,620	367,372
175,000	2,353.33	672,199	1,176.67	317,389	354,810	1,176.67	298,331	373,868	1,176.67	294,021	378,178
180,000	2,420.57	691,405	1,210.29	326,458	364,947	1,210.29	306,855	384,550	1,210.29	302,422	388,983
185,000	2,487.81	710,612	1,243.91	335,527	375,085	1,243.91	315,379	395,233	1,243.91	310,823	399,789
190,000	2,555.04	729,814	1,277.52	344,591	385,223	1,277.52	323,899	405,915	1,277.52	319,219	410,595
195,000	2,622.28	749,021	1,311.14	353,660	395,361	1,311.14	332,423	416,598	1,311.14	327,620	421,401
200,000	2,689.52	768,227	1,344.76	362,728	405,499	1,344.76	340,947	427,280	1,344.76	336,021	432,206

88

AMOUNT OF LOAN	30 YEARS		360 DAY BASIS 413.250 PAYMENTS			364 DAY BASIS 397.156 PAYMENTS			365 DAY BASIS 393.519 PAYMENTS		
	MONTHLY PAYMENT	TOTAL INTREST	BWEEKLY PAYMENT	TOTAL INTRST	INTRST SAVED	BWEEKLY PAYMENT	TOTAL INTRST	INTRST SAVED	BWEEKLY PAYMENT	TOTAL INTRST	INTRST SAVED
$ 50	0.69	198	0.35	95	103	0.35	89	109	0.35	88	110
100	1.37	393	0.69	185	208	0.69	174	219	0.69	172	221
200	2.73	783	1.37	366	417	1.37	344	439	1.37	339	444
300	4.10	1,176	2.05	547	629	2.05	514	662	2.05	507	669
400	5.46	1,566	2.73	728	838	2.73	684	882	2.73	674	892
500	6.83	1,959	3.42	913	1,046	3.42	858	1,101	3.42	846	1,113
600	8.19	2,348	4.10	1,094	1,254	4.10	1,028	1,320	4.10	1,013	1,335
700	9.56	2,742	4.78	1,275	1,467	4.78	1,198	1,544	4.78	1,181	1,561
800	10.92	3,131	5.46	1,456	1,675	5.46	1,368	1,763	5.46	1,349	1,782
900	12.29	3,524	6.15	1,641	1,883	6.15	1,543	1,981	6.15	1,520	2,004
1,000	13.65	3,914	6.83	1,822	2,092	6.83	1,713	2,201	6.83	1,688	2,226
2,000	27.30	7,828	13.65	3,641	4,187	13.65	3,421	4,407	13.65	3,372	4,456
3,000	40.95	11,742	20.48	5,463	6,279	20.48	5,134	6,608	20.48	5,059	6,683
4,000	54.60	15,656	27.30	7,282	8,374	27.30	6,842	8,814	27.30	6,743	8,913
5,000	68.25	19,570	34.13	9,104	10,466	34.13	8,555	11,015	34.13	8,431	11,139
6,000	81.90	23,484	40.95	10,923	12,561	40.95	10,264	13,220	40.95	10,115	13,369
7,000	95.55	27,398	47.78	12,745	14,653	47.78	11,976	15,422	47.78	11,802	15,596
8,000	109.20	31,312	54.60	14,563	16,749	54.60	13,685	17,627	54.60	13,486	17,826
9,000	122.85	35,226	61.43	16,386	18,840	61.43	15,397	19,829	61.43	15,174	20,052
10,000	136.50	39,140	68.25	18,204	20,936	68.25	17,106	22,034	68.25	16,858	22,282
11,000	150.15	43,054	75.08	20,027	23,027	75.08	18,818	24,236	75.08	18,545	24,509
12,000	163.80	46,968	81.90	21,845	25,123	81.90	20,527	26,441	81.90	20,229	26,739
13,000	177.45	50,882	88.73	23,668	27,214	88.73	22,240	28,642	88.73	21,917	28,965
14,000	191.10	54,796	95.55	25,486	29,310	95.55	23,948	30,848	95.55	23,601	31,195
15,000	204.75	58,710	102.38	27,309	31,401	102.38	25,661	33,049	102.38	25,288	33,422
16,000	218.39	62,620	109.20	29,127	33,493	109.20	27,369	35,251	109.20	26,972	35,648
17,000	232.04	66,534	116.02	30,945	35,589	116.02	29,078	37,456	116.02	28,656	37,878
18,000	245.69	70,448	122.85	32,768	37,680	122.85	30,791	39,657	122.85	30,344	40,104
19,000	259.34	74,362	129.67	34,586	39,776	129.67	32,499	41,863	129.67	32,028	42,334
20,000	272.99	78,276	136.50	36,409	41,867	136.50	34,212	44,064	136.50	33,715	44,561
21,000	286.64	82,190	143.32	38,227	43,963	143.32	35,920	46,270	143.32	35,399	46,791
22,000	300.29	86,104	150.15	40,049	46,055	150.15	37,633	48,471	150.15	37,087	49,017
23,000	313.94	90,018	156.97	41,868	48,150	156.97	39,342	50,676	156.97	38,771	51,247
24,000	327.59	93,932	163.80	43,690	50,242	163.80	41,054	52,878	163.80	40,458	53,474
25,000	341.24	97,846	170.62	45,509	52,337	170.62	42,763	55,083	170.62	42,142	55,704
26,000	354.89	101,760	177.45	47,331	54,429	177.45	44,475	57,285	177.45	43,830	57,930
27,000	368.54	105,674	184.27	49,150	56,524	184.27	46,184	59,490	184.27	45,514	60,160
28,000	382.19	109,588	191.10	50,972	58,616	191.10	47,897	61,691	191.10	47,201	62,387
29,000	395.84	113,502	197.92	52,790	60,712	197.92	49,605	63,897	197.92	48,885	64,617
30,000	409.49	117,416	204.75	54,613	62,803	204.75	51,318	66,098	204.75	50,573	66,843
32,500	443.61	127,200	221.81	59,163	68,037	221.81	55,593	71,607	221.81	54,786	72,414
35,000	477.73	136,983	238.87	63,713	73,270	238.87	59,869	77,114	238.87	59,000	77,983
40,000	545.98	156,553	272.99	72,813	83,740	272.99	68,420	88,133	272.99	67,427	89,126
45,000	614.23	176,123	307.12	81,917	94,206	307.12	76,975	99,148	307.12	75,858	100,265
50,000	682.47	195,689	341.24	91,017	104,672	341.24	85,526	110,163	341.24	84,284	111,405
55,000	750.72	215,259	375.36	100,118	115,141	375.36	94,076	121,183	375.36	92,711	122,548
60,000	818.97	234,829	409.49	109,222	125,607	409.49	102,631	132,198	409.49	101,142	133,687
65,000	887.21	254,396	443.61	118,322	136,074	443.61	111,182	143,214	443.61	109,569	144,827
70,000	955.46	273,966	477.73	127,422	146,544	477.73	119,733	154,233	477.73	117,996	155,970
75,000	1,023.71	293,536	511.86	136,526	157,010	511.86	128,288	165,248	511.86	126,427	167,109
80,000	1,091.95	313,102	545.98	145,626	167,476	545.98	136,839	176,263	545.98	134,854	178,248
85,000	1,160.20	332,672	580.10	154,726	177,946	580.10	145,390	187,282	580.10	143,280	189,392
90,000	1,228.45	352,242	614.23	163,831	188,411	614.23	153,945	198,297	614.23	151,711	200,531
95,000	1,296.69	371,808	648.35	172,931	198,877	648.35	162,496	209,312	648.35	160,138	211,670
100,000	1,364.94	391,378	682.47	182,031	209,347	682.47	171,047	220,331	682.47	168,565	222,813
105,000	1,433.19	410,948	716.60	191,135	219,813	716.60	179,602	231,346	716.60	176,996	233,952
110,000	1,501.43	430,515	750.72	200,235	230,280	750.72	188,153	242,362	750.72	185,423	245,092
115,000	1,569.68	450,085	784.84	209,335	240,750	784.84	196,704	253,381	784.84	193,849	256,236
120,000	1,637.93	469,655	818.97	218,439	251,216	818.97	205,259	264,396	818.97	202,280	267,375
125,000	1,706.17	489,221	853.09	227,539	261,682	853.09	213,810	275,411	853.09	210,707	278,514
130,000	1,774.42	508,791	887.21	236,640	272,151	887.21	222,361	286,430	887.21	219,134	289,657
135,000	1,842.67	528,361	921.34	245,744	282,617	921.34	230,916	297,445	921.34	227,565	300,796
140,000	1,910.91	547,928	955.46	254,844	293,084	955.46	239,467	308,461	955.46	235,992	311,936
145,000	1,979.16	567,498	989.58	263,944	303,554	989.58	248,018	319,480	989.58	244,419	323,079
150,000	2,047.41	587,068	1,023.71	273,048	314,020	1,023.71	256,573	330,495	1,023.71	252,849	334,219
155,000	2,115.65	606,634	1,057.83	282,148	324,486	1,057.83	265,124	341,510	1,057.83	261,276	345,358
160,000	2,183.90	626,204	1,091.95	291,248	334,956	1,091.95	273,674	352,530	1,091.95	269,703	356,501
165,000	2,252.15	645,774	1,126.08	300,353	345,421	1,126.08	282,229	363,545	1,126.08	278,134	367,640
170,000	2,320.39	665,340	1,160.20	309,453	355,887	1,160.20	290,780	374,560	1,160.20	286,561	378,779
175,000	2,388.64	684,910	1,194.32	318,553	366,357	1,194.32	299,331	385,579	1,194.32	294,988	389,922
180,000	2,456.89	704,480	1,228.45	327,657	376,823	1,228.45	307,886	396,594	1,228.45	303,418	401,062
185,000	2,525.13	724,047	1,262.57	336,757	387,290	1,262.57	316,437	407,610	1,262.57	311,845	412,202
190,000	2,593.38	743,617	1,296.69	345,857	397,760	1,296.69	324,988	418,629	1,296.69	320,272	423,345
195,000	2,661.63	763,187	1,330.82	354,961	408,226	1,330.82	333,543	429,644	1,330.82	328,703	434,484
200,000	2,729.87	782,753	1,364.94	364,061	418,692	1,364.94	342,094	440,659	1,364.94	337,130	445,623

16.50% BIWEEKLY MORTGAGES

AMOUNT OF LOAN	30 YEARS MONTHLY PAYMENT	30 YEARS TOTAL INTRST	360 DAY BASIS 408.121 PAYMENTS BWEEKLY PAYMENT	TOTAL INTRST	INTRST SAVED	364 DAY BASIS 392.135 PAYMENTS BWEEKLY PAYMENT	TOTAL INTRST	INTRST SAVED	365 DAY BASIS 388.524 PAYMENTS BWEEKLY PAYMENT	TOTAL INTRST	INTRST SAVED
$ 50	0.70	202	0.35	93	109	0.35	87	115	0.35	86	116
100	1.39	400	0.70	186	214	0.70	174	226	0.70	172	228
200	2.78	801	1.39	367	434	1.39	345	456	1.39	340	461
300	4.16	1,198	2.08	549	649	2.08	516	682	2.08	508	690
400	5.55	1,598	2.78	735	863	2.78	690	908	2.78	680	918
500	6.93	1,995	3.47	916	1,079	3.47	861	1,134	3.47	848	1,147
600	8.32	2,395	4.16	1,098	1,297	4.16	1,031	1,364	4.16	1,016	1,379
700	9.70	2,792	4.85	1,279	1,513	4.85	1,202	1,590	4.85	1,184	1,608
800	11.09	3,192	5.55	1,465	1,727	5.55	1,376	1,816	5.55	1,356	1,836
900	12.47	3,589	6.24	1,647	1,942	6.24	1,547	2,042	6.24	1,524	2,065
1,000	13.86	3,990	6.93	1,828	2,162	6.93	1,717	2,273	6.93	1,692	2,298
2,000	27.71	7,976	13.86	3,657	4,319	13.86	3,435	4,541	13.86	3,385	4,591
3,000	41.56	11,962	20.78	5,481	6,481	20.78	5,149	6,813	20.78	5,074	6,888
4,000	55.41	15,948	27.71	7,309	8,639	27.71	6,866	9,082	27.71	6,766	9,182
5,000	69.26	19,934	34.63	9,133	10,801	34.63	8,580	11,354	34.63	8,455	11,479
6,000	83.11	23,920	41.56	10,962	12,958	41.56	10,297	13,623	41.56	10,147	13,773
7,000	96.97	27,909	48.49	12,790	15,119	48.49	12,015	15,894	48.49	11,840	16,069
8,000	110.82	31,895	55.41	14,619	17,281	55.41	13,728	18,167	55.41	13,528	18,367
9,000	124.67	35,881	62.34	16,442	19,439	62.34	15,446	20,435	62.34	15,221	20,660
10,000	138.52	39,867	69.26	18,266	21,601	69.26	17,159	22,708	69.26	16,909	22,958
11,000	152.37	43,853	76.19	20,095	23,758	76.19	18,877	24,976	76.19	18,602	25,251
12,000	166.22	47,839	83.11	21,919	25,920	83.11	20,590	27,249	83.11	20,290	27,549
13,000	180.07	51,825	90.04	23,747	28,078	90.04	22,308	29,517	90.04	21,983	29,842
14,000	193.93	55,815	96.97	25,575	30,240	96.97	24,025	31,790	96.97	23,675	32,140
15,000	207.78	59,801	103.89	27,400	32,401	103.89	25,739	34,062	103.89	25,364	34,437
16,000	221.63	63,787	110.82	29,228	34,559	110.82	27,456	36,331	110.82	27,056	36,731
17,000	235.48	67,773	117.74	31,052	36,721	117.74	29,170	38,603	117.74	28,745	39,028
18,000	249.33	71,759	124.67	32,880	38,879	124.67	30,887	40,872	124.67	30,437	41,322
19,000	263.18	75,745	131.59	34,705	41,040	131.59	32,601	43,144	131.59	32,126	43,619
20,000	277.03	79,731	138.52	36,533	43,198	138.52	34,319	45,412	138.52	33,818	45,913
21,000	290.89	83,720	145.45	38,361	45,359	145.45	36,036	47,684	145.45	35,511	48,209
22,000	304.74	87,706	152.37	40,185	47,521	152.37	37,750	49,956	152.37	37,199	50,507
23,000	318.59	91,692	159.30	42,014	49,678	159.30	39,467	52,225	159.30	38,892	52,800
24,000	332.44	95,678	166.22	43,838	51,840	166.22	41,181	54,497	166.22	40,580	55,098
25,000	346.29	99,664	173.15	45,666	53,998	173.15	42,898	56,766	173.15	42,273	57,391
26,000	360.14	103,650	180.07	47,490	56,160	180.07	44,612	59,038	180.07	43,962	59,688
27,000	373.99	107,636	187.00	49,319	58,317	187.00	46,329	61,307	187.00	45,654	61,982
28,000	387.85	111,626	193.93	51,147	60,479	193.93	48,047	63,579	193.93	47,346	64,280
29,000	401.70	115,612	200.85	52,971	62,641	200.85	49,760	65,852	200.85	49,035	66,577
30,000	415.55	119,598	207.78	54,799	64,799	207.78	51,478	68,120	207.78	50,728	68,870
32,500	450.18	129,565	225.09	59,364	70,201	225.09	55,766	73,799	225.09	54,953	74,612
35,000	484.81	139,532	242.41	63,933	75,599	242.41	60,057	79,475	242.41	59,182	80,350
40,000	554.06	159,462	277.03	73,062	86,400	277.03	68,633	90,829	277.03	67,633	91,829
45,000	623.32	179,395	311.66	82,193	97,200	311.66	77,213	102,182	311.66	76,087	103,308
50,000	692.58	199,329	346.29	91,328	108,001	346.29	85,792	113,537	346.29	84,542	114,787
55,000	761.84	219,262	380.92	100,461	118,801	380.92	94,372	124,890	380.92	92,997	126,265
60,000	831.09	239,192	415.55	109,593	129,597	415.55	102,952	136,240	415.55	101,451	137,741
65,000	900.35	259,126	450.18	118,728	140,398	450.18	111,531	147,595	450.18	109,906	149,220
70,000	969.61	279,060	484.81	127,861	151,199	484.81	120,111	158,949	484.81	118,360	160,700
75,000	1,038.87	298,993	519.44	136,994	161,999	519.44	128,691	170,302	519.44	126,815	172,178
80,000	1,108.12	318,923	554.06	146,124	172,799	554.06	137,266	181,657	554.06	135,266	183,657
85,000	1,177.38	338,857	588.69	155,257	183,600	588.69	145,846	193,011	588.69	143,720	195,137
90,000	1,246.64	358,790	623.32	164,390	194,400	623.32	154,426	204,364	623.32	152,175	206,615
95,000	1,315.90	378,724	657.95	173,523	205,201	657.95	163,005	215,719	657.95	160,629	218,095
100,000	1,385.15	398,654	692.58	182,656	215,998	692.58	171,585	227,069	692.58	169,084	229,570
105,000	1,454.41	418,588	727.21	191,790	226,798	727.21	180,164	238,424	727.21	177,539	241,049
110,000	1,523.67	438,521	761.84	200,923	237,598	761.84	188,744	249,777	761.84	185,993	252,528
115,000	1,592.93	458,455	796.47	210,056	248,399	796.47	197,324	261,131	796.47	194,448	264,007
120,000	1,662.18	478,385	831.09	219,185	259,200	831.09	205,899	272,486	831.09	202,898	275,487
125,000	1,731.44	498,318	865.72	228,319	269,999	865.72	214,479	283,839	865.72	211,353	286,965
130,000	1,800.70	518,252	900.35	237,452	280,800	900.35	223,059	295,193	900.35	219,808	298,444
135,000	1,869.95	538,182	934.98	246,585	291,597	934.98	231,638	306,544	934.98	228,262	309,920
140,000	1,939.21	558,116	969.61	255,718	302,398	969.61	240,218	317,898	969.61	236,717	321,399
145,000	2,008.47	578,049	1,004.24	264,851	313,198	1,004.24	248,798	329,251	1,004.24	245,171	332,878
150,000	2,077.73	597,983	1,038.87	273,985	323,998	1,038.87	257,377	340,606	1,038.87	253,626	344,357
155,000	2,146.98	617,913	1,073.49	283,114	334,799	1,073.49	265,953	351,960	1,073.49	262,077	355,836
160,000	2,216.24	637,846	1,108.12	292,247	345,599	1,108.12	274,533	363,313	1,108.12	270,531	367,315
165,000	2,285.50	657,780	1,142.75	301,380	356,400	1,142.75	283,112	374,668	1,142.75	278,986	378,794
170,000	2,354.76	677,714	1,177.38	310,514	367,200	1,177.38	291,692	386,022	1,177.38	287,440	390,274
175,000	2,424.01	697,644	1,212.01	319,647	377,997	1,212.01	300,272	397,372	1,212.01	295,895	401,749
180,000	2,493.27	717,577	1,246.64	328,780	388,797	1,246.64	308,851	408,726	1,246.64	304,350	413,227
185,000	2,562.53	737,511	1,281.27	337,913	399,598	1,281.27	317,431	420,080	1,281.27	312,804	424,707
190,000	2,631.79	757,444	1,315.90	347,046	410,398	1,315.90	326,010	431,434	1,315.90	321,259	436,185
195,000	2,701.04	777,374	1,350.52	356,176	421,198	1,350.52	334,586	442,788	1,350.52	329,709	447,665
200,000	2,770.30	797,308	1,385.15	365,309	431,999	1,385.15	343,166	454,142	1,385.15	338,164	459,144

90

AMOUNT OF LOAN	30 YEARS		360 DAY BASIS 403.074 PAYMENTS			364 DAY BASIS 387.201 PAYMENTS			365 DAY BASIS 383.617 PAYMENTS		
	MONTHLY PAYMENT	TOTAL INTRST	BWEEKLY PAYMENT	TOTAL INTRST	INTRST SAVED	BWEEKLY PAYMENT	TOTAL INTRST	INTRST SAVED	BWEEKLY PAYMENT	TOTAL INTRST	INTRST SAVED
$ 50	0.71	206	0.36	95	111	0.36	89	117	0.36	88	118
100	1.41	408	0.71	186	222	0.71	175	233	0.71	172	236
200	2.82	815	1.41	368	447	1.41	346	469	1.41	341	474
300	4.22	1,219	2.11	550	669	2.11	517	702	2.11	509	710
400	5.63	1,627	2.82	737	890	2.82	692	935	2.82	682	945
500	7.03	2,031	3.52	919	1,112	3.52	863	1,168	3.52	850	1,181
600	8.44	2,438	4.22	1,101	1,337	4.22	1,034	1,404	4.22	1,019	1,419
700	9.84	2,842	4.92	1,283	1,559	4.92	1,205	1,637	4.92	1,187	1,655
800	11.25	3,250	5.63	1,469	1,781	5.63	1,380	1,870	5.63	1,360	1,890
900	12.65	3,654	6.33	1,651	2,003	6.33	1,551	2,103	6.33	1,528	2,126
1,000	14.06	4,062	7.03	1,834	2,228	7.03	1,722	2,340	7.03	1,697	2,365
2,000	28.11	8,120	14.06	3,667	4,453	14.06	3,444	4,676	14.06	3,394	4,726
3,000	42.17	12,181	21.09	5,501	6,680	21.09	5,166	7,015	21.09	5,090	7,091
4,000	56.22	16,239	28.11	7,330	8,909	28.11	6,884	9,355	28.11	6,783	9,456
5,000	70.27	20,297	35.14	9,164	11,133	35.14	8,606	11,691	35.14	8,480	11,817
6,000	84.33	24,359	42.17	10,998	13,361	42.17	10,328	14,031	42.17	10,177	14,182
7,000	98.38	28,417	49.19	12,827	15,590	49.19	12,046	16,371	49.19	11,870	16,547
8,000	112.44	32,478	56.22	14,661	17,817	56.22	13,768	18,710	56.22	13,567	18,911
9,000	126.49	36,536	63.25	16,494	20,042	63.25	15,490	21,046	63.25	15,264	21,272
10,000	140.54	40,594	70.27	18,324	22,270	70.27	17,209	23,385	70.27	16,957	23,637
11,000	154.60	44,656	77.30	20,158	24,498	77.30	18,931	25,725	77.30	18,654	26,002
12,000	168.65	48,714	84.33	21,991	26,723	84.33	20,653	28,061	84.33	20,350	28,364
13,000	182.71	52,776	91.36	23,825	28,951	91.36	22,375	30,401	91.36	22,047	30,729
14,000	196.76	56,834	98.38	25,654	31,180	98.38	24,093	32,741	98.38	23,740	33,094
15,000	210.81	60,892	105.41	27,488	33,404	105.41	25,815	35,077	105.41	25,437	35,455
16,000	224.87	64,953	112.44	29,322	35,631	112.44	27,537	37,416	112.44	27,134	37,819
17,000	238.92	69,011	119.46	31,151	37,860	119.46	29,255	39,756	119.46	28,827	40,184
18,000	252.98	73,073	126.49	32,984	40,088	126.49	30,977	42,096	126.49	30,524	42,549
19,000	267.03	77,131	133.52	34,818	42,313	133.52	32,699	44,432	133.52	32,221	44,910
20,000	281.08	81,189	140.54	36,648	44,541	140.54	34,417	46,772	140.54	33,914	47,275
21,000	295.14	85,250	147.57	38,482	46,768	147.57	36,139	49,111	147.57	35,610	49,640
22,000	309.19	89,308	154.60	40,315	48,993	154.60	37,861	51,447	154.60	37,307	52,001
23,000	323.25	93,370	161.63	42,149	51,221	161.63	39,583	53,787	161.63	39,004	54,366
24,000	337.30	97,428	168.65	43,978	53,450	168.65	41,301	56,127	168.65	40,697	56,731
25,000	351.35	101,486	175.68	45,812	55,674	175.68	43,023	58,463	175.68	42,394	59,092
26,000	365.41	105,548	182.71	47,646	57,902	182.71	44,745	60,803	182.71	44,091	61,457
27,000	379.46	109,606	189.73	49,475	60,131	189.73	46,464	63,142	189.73	45,784	63,822
28,000	393.52	113,667	196.76	51,309	62,358	196.76	48,186	65,481	196.76	47,480	66,187
29,000	407.57	117,725	203.79	53,142	64,583	203.79	49,908	67,817	203.79	49,177	68,548
30,000	421.62	121,783	210.81	54,972	66,811	210.81	51,626	70,157	210.81	50,870	70,913
32,500	456.76	131,934	228.38	59,554	72,380	228.38	55,929	76,005	228.38	55,110	76,824
35,000	491.89	142,080	245.95	64,136	77,944	245.95	60,232	81,848	245.95	59,351	82,729
40,000	562.16	162,378	281.08	73,296	89,082	281.08	68,834	93,544	281.08	67,827	94,551
45,000	632.43	182,675	316.22	82,460	100,215	316.22	77,441	105,234	316.22	76,307	106,368
50,000	702.70	202,972	351.35	91,620	111,352	351.35	86,043	116,929	351.35	84,784	118,188
55,000	772.97	223,269	386.49	100,784	122,485	386.49	94,649	128,620	386.49	93,264	130,005
60,000	843.24	243,566	421.62	109,944	133,622	421.62	103,252	140,314	421.62	101,741	141,825
65,000	913.51	263,864	456.76	119,108	144,756	456.76	111,858	152,006	456.76	110,221	153,643
70,000	983.78	284,161	491.89	128,268	155,893	491.89	120,460	163,701	491.89	118,697	165,464
75,000	1,054.05	304,458	527.03	137,432	167,026	527.03	129,067	175,391	527.03	127,178	177,280
80,000	1,124.32	324,755	562.16	146,592	178,163	562.16	137,669	187,086	562.16	135,654	189,101
85,000	1,194.59	345,052	597.30	155,756	189,296	597.30	146,275	198,777	597.30	144,134	200,918
90,000	1,264.86	365,350	632.43	164,916	200,434	632.43	154,878	210,472	632.43	152,611	212,739
95,000	1,335.13	385,647	667.57	174,080	211,567	667.57	163,484	222,163	667.57	161,091	224,556
100,000	1,405.40	405,944	702.70	183,240	222,704	702.70	172,086	233,858	702.70	169,568	236,376
105,000	1,475.67	426,241	737.84	192,404	233,837	737.84	180,692	245,549	737.84	178,048	248,193
110,000	1,545.94	446,538	772.97	201,564	244,974	772.97	189,295	257,243	772.97	186,524	260,014
115,000	1,616.21	466,836	808.11	210,728	256,108	808.11	197,901	268,935	808.11	195,005	271,831
120,000	1,686.48	487,133	843.24	219,888	267,245	843.24	206,503	280,630	843.24	203,481	283,652
125,000	1,756.75	507,430	878.38	229,052	278,378	878.38	215,110	292,320	878.38	211,962	295,468
130,000	1,827.02	527,727	913.51	238,212	289,515	913.51	223,712	304,015	913.51	220,438	307,289
135,000	1,897.29	548,024	948.65	247,376	300,648	948.65	232,318	315,706	948.65	228,918	319,106
140,000	1,967.56	568,322	983.78	256,536	311,786	983.78	240,921	327,401	983.78	237,395	330,927
145,000	2,037.83	588,619	1,018.92	265,700	322,919	1,018.92	249,527	339,092	1,018.92	245,875	342,744
150,000	2,108.10	608,916	1,054.05	274,860	334,056	1,054.05	258,129	350,787	1,054.05	254,351	354,565
155,000	2,178.37	629,213	1,089.19	284,024	345,189	1,089.19	266,735	362,478	1,089.19	262,832	366,381
160,000	2,248.64	649,510	1,124.32	293,184	356,326	1,124.32	275,338	374,172	1,124.32	271,308	378,202
165,000	2,318.91	669,808	1,159.46	302,348	367,460	1,159.46	283,944	385,864	1,159.46	279,789	390,019
170,000	2,389.18	690,105	1,194.59	311,508	378,597	1,194.59	292,546	397,559	1,194.59	288,265	401,840
175,000	2,459.45	710,402	1,229.73	320,672	389,730	1,229.73	301,153	409,249	1,229.73	296,745	413,657
180,000	2,529.72	730,699	1,264.86	329,832	400,867	1,264.86	309,755	420,944	1,264.86	305,222	425,477
185,000	2,599.99	750,996	1,300.00	338,996	412,000	1,300.00	318,361	432,635	1,300.00	313,702	437,294
190,000	2,670.26	771,294	1,335.13	348,156	423,138	1,335.13	326,964	444,330	1,335.13	322,179	449,115
195,000	2,740.53	791,591	1,370.27	357,320	434,271	1,370.27	335,570	456,021	1,370.27	330,659	460,932
200,000	2,810.80	811,888	1,405.40	366,480	445,408	1,405.40	344,172	467,716	1,405.40	339,135	472,753

BIWEEKLY MORTGAGES

AMOUNT OF LOAN	30 YEARS MONTHLY PAYMENT	TOTAL INTRST	360 DAY BASIS 398.110 PAYMENTS BWEEKLY PAYMENT	TOTAL INTRST	INTRST SAVED	364 DAY BASIS 382.353 PAYMENTS BWEEKLY PAYMENT	TOTAL INTRST	INTRST SAVED	365 DAY BASIS 378.797 PAYMENTS BWEEKLY PAYMENT	TOTAL INTRST	INTRST SAVED
$ 50	0.72	209	0.36	93	116	0.36	88	121	0.36	86	123
100	1.43	415	0.72	187	228	0.72	175	240	0.72	173	242
200	2.86	830	1.43	369	461	1.43	347	483	1.43	342	488
300	4.28	1,241	2.14	552	689	2.14	518	723	2.14	511	730
400	5.71	1,656	2.86	739	917	2.86	694	962	2.86	683	973
500	7.13	2,067	3.57	921	1,146	3.57	865	1,202	3.57	852	1,215
600	8.56	2,482	4.28	1,104	1,378	4.28	1,036	1,446	4.28	1,021	1,461
700	9.98	2,893	4.99	1,287	1,606	4.99	1,208	1,685	4.99	1,190	1,703
800	11.41	3,308	5.71	1,473	1,835	5.71	1,383	1,925	5.71	1,363	1,945
900	12.84	3,722	6.42	1,656	2,066	6.42	1,555	2,167	6.42	1,532	2,190
1,000	14.26	4,134	7.13	1,839	2,295	7.13	1,726	2,408	7.13	1,701	2,433
2,000	28.52	8,267	14.26	3,677	4,590	14.26	3,452	4,815	14.26	3,402	4,865
3,000	42.78	12,401	21.39	5,516	6,885	21.39	5,179	7,222	21.39	5,102	7,299
4,000	57.03	16,531	28.52	7,354	9,177	28.52	6,905	9,626	28.52	6,803	9,728
5,000	71.29	20,664	35.65	9,193	11,471	35.65	8,631	12,033	35.65	8,504	12,160
6,000	85.55	24,798	42.78	11,031	13,767	42.78	10,357	14,441	42.78	10,205	14,593
7,000	99.80	28,928	49.90	12,866	16,062	49.90	12,079	16,849	49.90	11,902	17,026
8,000	114.06	33,062	57.03	14,704	18,358	57.03	13,806	19,256	57.03	13,603	19,459
9,000	128.32	37,195	64.16	16,543	20,652	64.16	15,532	21,663	64.16	15,304	21,891
10,000	142.57	41,325	71.29	18,381	22,944	71.29	17,258	24,067	71.29	17,004	24,321
11,000	156.83	45,459	78.42	20,220	25,239	78.42	18,984	26,475	78.42	18,705	26,754
12,000	171.09	49,592	85.55	22,058	27,534	85.55	20,710	28,882	85.55	20,406	29,186
13,000	185.34	53,722	92.67	23,893	29,829	92.67	22,433	31,289	92.67	22,103	31,619
14,000	199.60	57,856	99.80	25,731	32,125	99.80	24,159	33,697	99.80	23,804	34,052
15,000	213.86	61,990	106.93	27,570	34,420	106.93	25,885	36,105	106.93	25,505	36,485
16,000	228.11	66,120	114.06	29,408	36,712	114.06	27,611	38,509	114.06	27,206	38,914
17,000	242.37	70,253	121.19	31,247	39,006	121.19	29,337	40,916	121.19	28,906	41,347
18,000	256.63	74,387	128.32	33,085	41,302	128.32	31,064	43,323	128.32	30,607	43,780
19,000	270.88	78,517	135.44	34,920	43,597	135.44	32,786	45,731	135.44	32,304	46,213
20,000	285.14	82,650	142.57	36,759	45,891	142.57	34,512	48,138	142.57	34,005	48,645
21,000	299.40	86,784	149.70	38,597	48,187	149.70	36,238	50,546	149.70	35,706	51,078
22,000	313.65	90,914	156.83	40,436	50,478	156.83	37,964	52,950	156.83	37,407	53,507
23,000	327.91	95,048	163.96	42,274	52,774	163.96	39,691	55,357	163.96	39,108	55,940
24,000	342.17	99,181	171.09	44,113	55,068	171.09	41,417	57,764	171.09	40,808	58,373
25,000	356.42	103,311	178.21	45,947	57,364	178.21	43,139	60,172	178.21	42,505	60,806
26,000	370.68	107,445	185.34	47,786	59,659	185.34	44,865	62,580	185.34	44,206	63,239
27,000	384.94	111,578	192.47	49,624	61,954	192.47	46,591	64,987	192.47	45,907	65,671
28,000	399.19	115,708	199.60	51,463	64,245	199.60	48,318	67,390	199.60	47,608	68,100
29,000	413.45	119,842	206.73	53,301	66,541	206.73	50,044	69,798	206.73	49,309	70,533
30,000	427.71	123,976	213.86	55,140	68,836	213.86	51,770	72,206	213.86	51,010	72,966
32,500	463.35	134,306	231.68	59,734	74,572	231.68	56,084	78,222	231.68	55,260	79,046
35,000	498.99	144,636	249.50	64,328	80,308	249.50	60,397	84,239	249.50	59,510	85,126
40,000	570.28	165,301	285.14	73,517	91,784	285.14	69,024	96,277	285.14	68,010	97,291
45,000	641.56	185,962	320.78	82,706	103,256	320.78	77,651	108,311	320.78	76,511	109,451
50,000	712.84	206,622	356.42	91,896	114,728	356.42	86,278	120,344	356.42	85,011	121,611
55,000	784.13	227,287	392.07	101,087	126,200	392.07	94,909	132,378	392.07	93,515	133,772
60,000	855.41	247,948	427.71	110,276	137,672	427.71	103,536	144,412	427.71	102,015	145,933
65,000	926.69	268,608	463.35	119,464	149,144	463.35	112,163	156,445	463.35	110,516	158,092
70,000	997.98	289,273	498.99	128,653	160,620	498.99	120,790	168,483	498.99	119,016	170,257
75,000	1,069.26	309,934	534.63	137,842	172,092	534.63	129,417	180,517	534.63	127,516	182,418
80,000	1,140.55	330,598	570.28	147,034	183,564	570.28	138,048	192,550	570.28	136,020	194,578
85,000	1,211.83	351,259	605.92	156,223	195,036	605.92	146,675	204,584	605.92	144,521	206,738
90,000	1,283.11	371,920	641.56	165,411	206,509	641.56	155,302	216,618	641.56	153,021	218,899
95,000	1,354.40	392,584	677.20	174,600	217,984	677.20	163,929	228,655	677.20	161,521	231,063
100,000	1,425.68	413,245	712.84	183,789	229,456	712.84	172,557	240,688	712.84	170,022	243,223
105,000	1,496.96	433,906	748.48	192,977	240,929	748.48	181,184	252,722	748.48	178,522	255,384
110,000	1,568.25	454,570	784.13	202,170	252,400	784.13	189,814	264,756	784.13	187,026	267,544
115,000	1,639.53	475,231	819.77	211,359	263,872	819.77	198,442	276,789	819.77	195,526	279,705
120,000	1,710.82	495,895	855.41	220,547	275,348	855.41	207,069	288,826	855.41	204,027	291,868
125,000	1,782.10	516,556	891.05	229,736	286,820	891.05	215,696	300,860	891.05	212,527	304,029
130,000	1,853.38	537,217	926.69	238,925	298,292	926.69	224,323	312,894	926.69	221,027	316,190
135,000	1,924.67	557,881	962.34	248,117	309,764	962.34	232,954	324,927	962.34	229,532	328,349
140,000	1,995.95	578,542	997.98	257,306	321,236	997.98	241,581	336,961	997.98	238,032	340,510
145,000	2,067.23	599,203	1,033.62	266,494	332,709	1,033.62	250,208	348,995	1,033.62	246,532	352,671
150,000	2,138.52	619,867	1,069.26	275,683	344,184	1,069.26	258,835	361,032	1,069.26	255,032	364,835
155,000	2,209.80	640,528	1,104.90	284,872	355,656	1,104.90	267,462	373,066	1,104.90	263,533	376,995
160,000	2,281.09	661,192	1,140.55	294,064	367,128	1,140.55	276,093	385,099	1,140.55	272,037	389,155
165,000	2,352.37	681,853	1,176.19	303,253	378,600	1,176.19	284,720	397,133	1,176.19	280,537	401,316
170,000	2,423.65	702,514	1,211.83	312,442	390,072	1,211.83	293,347	409,167	1,211.83	289,038	413,476
175,000	2,494.94	723,178	1,247.47	321,630	401,548	1,247.47	301,974	421,204	1,247.47	297,538	425,640
180,000	2,566.22	743,839	1,283.11	330,819	413,020	1,283.11	310,601	433,238	1,283.11	306,038	437,801
185,000	2,637.50	764,500	1,318.75	340,008	424,492	1,318.75	319,228	445,272	1,318.75	314,539	449,961
190,000	2,708.79	785,164	1,354.40	349,200	435,964	1,354.40	327,859	457,305	1,354.40	323,043	462,121
195,000	2,780.07	805,825	1,390.04	358,389	447,436	1,390.04	336,486	469,339	1,390.04	331,543	474,282
200,000	2,851.36	826,490	1,425.68	367,577	458,913	1,425.68	345,113	481,377	1,425.68	340,043	486,447

AMOUNT OF LOAN	30 YEARS		360 DAY BASIS 393.228 PAYMENTS			364 DAY BASIS 377.592 PAYMENTS			365 DAY BASIS 374.064 PAYMENTS		
	MONTHLY PAYMENT	TOTAL INTRST	BWEEKLY PAYMENT	TOTAL INTRST	INTRST SAVED	BWEEKLY PAYMENT	TOTAL INTRST	INTRST SAVED	BWEEKLY PAYMENT	TOTAL INTRST	INTRST SAVED
$ 50	0.73	213	0.37	95	118	0.37	90	123	0.37	88	125
100	1.45	422	0.73	187	235	0.73	176	246	0.73	173	249
200	2.90	844	1.45	370	474	1.45	348	496	1.45	342	502
300	4.34	1,262	2.17	553	709	2.17	519	743	2.17	512	750
400	5.79	1,684	2.90	740	944	2.90	695	989	2.90	685	999
500	7.23	2,103	3.62	923	1,180	3.62	867	1,236	3.62	854	1,249
600	8.68	2,525	4.34	1,107	1,418	4.34	1,039	1,486	4.34	1,023	1,502
700	10.13	2,947	5.07	1,294	1,653	5.07	1,214	1,733	5.07	1,197	1,750
800	11.57	3,365	5.79	1,477	1,888	5.79	1,386	1,979	5.79	1,366	1,999
900	13.02	3,787	6.51	1,660	2,127	6.51	1,558	2,229	6.51	1,535	2,252
1,000	14.46	4,206	7.23	1,843	2,363	7.23	1,730	2,476	7.23	1,704	2,502
2,000	28.92	8,411	14.46	3,686	4,725	14.46	3,460	4,951	14.46	3,409	5,002
3,000	43.38	12,617	21.69	5,529	7,088	21.69	5,190	7,427	21.69	5,113	7,504
4,000	57.84	16,822	28.92	7,372	9,450	28.92	6,920	9,902	28.92	6,818	10,004
5,000	72.30	21,028	36.15	9,215	11,813	36.15	8,650	12,378	36.15	8,522	12,506
6,000	86.76	25,234	43.38	11,058	14,176	43.38	10,380	14,854	43.38	10,227	15,007
7,000	101.22	29,439	50.61	12,901	16,538	50.61	12,110	17,329	50.61	11,931	17,508
8,000	115.68	33,645	57.84	14,744	18,901	57.84	13,840	19,805	57.84	13,636	20,009
9,000	130.14	37,850	65.07	16,587	21,263	65.07	15,570	22,280	65.07	15,340	22,510
10,000	144.60	42,056	72.30	18,430	23,626	72.30	17,300	24,756	72.30	17,045	25,011
11,000	159.06	46,262	79.53	20,273	25,989	79.53	19,030	27,232	79.53	18,749	27,513
12,000	173.52	50,467	86.76	22,116	28,351	86.76	20,760	29,707	86.76	20,454	30,013
13,000	187.98	54,673	93.99	23,959	30,714	93.99	22,490	32,183	93.99	22,158	32,515
14,000	202.44	58,878	101.22	25,803	33,075	101.22	24,220	34,658	101.22	23,863	35,015
15,000	216.90	63,084	108.45	27,646	35,438	108.45	25,950	37,134	108.45	25,567	37,517
16,000	231.36	67,290	115.68	29,489	37,801	115.68	27,680	39,610	115.68	27,272	40,018
17,000	245.82	71,495	122.91	31,332	40,163	122.91	29,410	42,085	122.91	28,976	42,519
18,000	260.28	75,701	130.14	33,175	42,526	130.14	31,140	44,561	130.14	30,681	45,020
19,000	274.74	79,906	137.37	35,018	44,888	137.37	32,870	47,036	137.37	32,385	47,521
20,000	289.20	84,112	144.60	36,861	47,251	144.60	34,600	49,512	144.60	34,090	50,022
21,000	303.66	88,318	151.83	38,704	49,614	151.83	36,330	51,988	151.83	35,794	52,524
22,000	318.12	92,523	159.06	40,547	51,976	159.06	38,060	54,463	159.06	37,499	55,024
23,000	332.58	96,729	166.29	42,390	54,339	166.29	39,790	56,939	166.29	39,203	57,526
24,000	347.04	100,934	173.52	44,233	56,701	173.52	41,520	59,414	173.52	40,908	60,026
25,000	361.50	105,140	180.75	46,076	59,064	180.75	43,250	61,890	180.75	42,612	62,528
26,000	375.96	109,346	187.98	47,919	61,427	187.98	44,980	64,366	187.98	44,317	65,029
27,000	390.42	113,551	195.21	49,762	63,789	195.21	46,710	66,841	195.21	46,021	67,530
28,000	404.88	117,757	202.44	51,605	66,152	202.44	48,440	69,317	202.44	47,726	70,031
29,000	419.34	121,962	209.67	53,448	68,514	209.67	50,170	71,792	209.67	49,430	72,532
30,000	433.80	126,168	216.90	55,291	70,877	216.90	51,900	74,268	216.90	51,134	75,034
32,500	469.95	136,682	234.98	59,901	76,781	234.98	56,227	80,455	234.98	55,398	81,284
35,000	506.10	147,196	253.05	64,506	82,690	253.05	60,550	86,646	253.05	59,657	87,539
40,000	578.40	168,224	289.20	73,722	94,502	289.20	69,200	99,024	289.20	68,179	100,045
45,000	650.70	189,252	325.35	82,937	106,315	325.35	77,850	111,402	325.35	76,702	112,550
50,000	723.00	210,280	361.50	92,152	118,128	361.50	86,500	123,780	361.50	85,224	125,056
55,000	795.30	231,308	397.65	101,367	129,941	397.65	95,149	136,159	397.65	93,747	137,561
60,000	867.60	252,336	433.80	110,582	141,754	433.80	103,799	148,537	433.80	102,269	150,067
65,000	939.90	273,364	469.95	119,797	153,567	469.95	112,449	160,915	469.95	110,791	162,573
70,000	1,012.20	294,392	506.10	129,013	165,379	506.10	121,099	173,293	506.10	119,314	175,078
75,000	1,084.49	315,416	542.25	138,228	177,188	542.25	129,749	185,667	542.25	127,836	187,580
80,000	1,156.79	336,444	578.40	147,443	189,001	578.40	138,399	198,045	578.40	136,359	200,085
85,000	1,229.09	357,472	614.55	156,658	200,814	614.55	147,049	210,423	614.55	144,881	212,591
90,000	1,301.39	378,500	650.70	165,873	212,627	650.70	155,699	222,801	650.70	153,403	225,097
95,000	1,373.69	399,528	686.85	175,089	224,439	686.85	164,349	235,179	686.85	161,926	237,602
100,000	1,445.99	420,556	723.00	184,304	236,252	723.00	172,999	247,557	723.00	170,448	250,108
105,000	1,518.29	441,584	759.15	193,519	248,065	759.15	181,649	259,935	759.15	178,971	262,613
110,000	1,590.59	462,612	795.30	202,734	259,878	795.30	190,299	272,313	795.30	187,493	275,119
115,000	1,662.89	483,640	831.45	211,949	271,691	831.45	198,949	284,691	831.45	196,016	287,624
120,000	1,735.19	504,668	867.60	221,165	283,503	867.60	207,599	297,069	867.60	204,538	300,130
125,000	1,807.49	525,696	903.75	230,380	295,316	903.75	216,249	309,447	903.75	213,060	312,636
130,000	1,879.79	546,724	939.90	239,595	307,129	939.90	224,899	321,825	939.90	221,583	325,141
135,000	1,952.09	567,752	976.05	248,810	318,942	976.05	233,549	334,203	976.05	230,105	337,647
140,000	2,024.39	588,780	1,012.20	258,025	330,755	1,012.20	242,199	346,581	1,012.20	238,628	350,152
145,000	2,096.68	609,805	1,048.34	267,237	342,568	1,048.34	250,845	358,960	1,048.34	247,146	362,659
150,000	2,168.98	630,833	1,084.49	276,452	354,381	1,084.49	259,495	371,338	1,084.49	255,669	375,164
155,000	2,241.28	651,861	1,120.64	285,667	366,194	1,120.64	268,145	383,716	1,120.64	264,191	387,670
160,000	2,313.58	672,889	1,156.79	294,882	378,007	1,156.79	276,795	396,094	1,156.79	272,713	400,176
165,000	2,385.88	693,917	1,192.94	304,097	389,820	1,192.94	285,445	408,472	1,192.94	281,236	412,681
170,000	2,458.18	714,943	1,229.09	313,313	401,632	1,229.09	294,095	420,850	1,229.09	289,758	425,187
175,000	2,530.48	735,973	1,265.24	322,528	413,445	1,265.24	302,745	433,228	1,265.24	298,281	437,692
180,000	2,602.78	757,001	1,301.39	331,743	425,258	1,301.39	311,394	445,607	1,301.39	306,803	450,198
185,000	2,675.08	778,029	1,337.54	340,958	437,071	1,337.54	320,044	457,985	1,337.54	315,326	462,703
190,000	2,747.38	799,057	1,373.69	350,173	448,884	1,373.69	328,694	470,363	1,373.69	323,848	475,209
195,000	2,819.68	820,085	1,409.84	359,389	460,696	1,409.84	337,344	482,741	1,409.84	332,370	487,715
200,000	2,891.98	841,113	1,445.99	368,604	472,509	1,445.99	345,994	495,119	1,445.99	340,893	500,220

17.50%   BIWEEKLY MORTGAGES

AMOUNT OF LOAN	30 YEARS		360 DAY BASIS 388.429 PAYMENTS			364 DAY BASIS 372.915 PAYMENTS			365 DAY BASIS 369.418 PAYMENTS		
	MONTHLY PAYMENT	TOTAL INTRST	BWEEKLY PAYMENT	TOTAL INTRST	INTRST SAVED	BWEEKLY PAYMENT	TOTAL INTRST	INTRST SAVED	BWEEKLY PAYMENT	TOTAL INTRST	INTRST SAVED
$ 50	0.74	216	0.37	94	122	0.37	88	128	0.37	87	129
100	1.47	429	0.74	187	242	0.74	176	253	0.74	173	256
200	2.94	858	1.47	371	487	1.47	348	510	1.47	343	515
300	4.40	1,284	2.20	555	729	2.20	520	764	2.20	513	771
400	5.87	1,713	2.94	742	971	2.94	696	1,017	2.94	686	1,027
500	7.34	2,142	3.67	926	1,216	3.67	869	1,273	3.67	856	1,286
600	8.80	2,568	4.40	1,109	1,459	4.40	1,041	1,527	4.40	1,025	1,543
700	10.27	2,997	5.14	1,297	1,700	5.14	1,217	1,780	5.14	1,199	1,798
800	11.74	3,426	5.87	1,480	1,946	5.87	1,389	2,037	5.87	1,368	2,058
900	13.20	3,852	6.60	1,664	2,188	6.60	1,561	2,291	6.60	1,538	2,314
1,000	14.67	4,281	7.34	1,851	2,430	7.34	1,737	2,544	7.34	1,712	2,569
2,000	29.33	8,559	14.67	3,698	4,861	14.67	3,471	5,088	14.67	3,419	5,140
3,000	43.99	12,836	22.00	5,545	7,291	22.00	5,204	7,632	22.00	5,127	7,709
4,000	58.66	17,118	29.33	7,393	9,725	29.33	6,938	10,180	29.33	6,835	10,283
5,000	73.32	21,395	36.66	9,240	12,155	36.66	8,671	12,724	36.66	8,543	12,852
6,000	87.98	25,673	43.99	11,087	14,586	43.99	10,405	15,268	43.99	10,251	15,422
7,000	102.65	29,954	51.33	12,938	17,016	51.33	12,142	17,812	51.33	11,962	17,992
8,000	117.31	34,232	58.66	14,785	19,447	58.66	13,875	20,357	58.66	13,670	20,562
9,000	131.97	38,509	65.99	16,632	21,877	65.99	15,609	22,900	65.99	15,378	23,131
10,000	146.64	42,790	73.32	18,480	24,310	73.32	17,342	25,448	73.32	17,086	25,704
11,000	161.30	47,068	80.65	20,327	26,741	80.65	19,076	27,992	80.65	18,794	28,274
12,000	175.96	51,346	87.98	22,174	29,172	87.98	20,809	30,537	87.98	20,501	30,845
13,000	190.63	55,627	95.32	24,025	31,602	95.32	22,544	33,081	95.32	22,213	33,414
14,000	205.29	59,904	102.65	25,872	34,032	102.65	24,280	35,624	102.65	23,921	35,983
15,000	219.95	64,182	109.98	27,719	36,463	109.98	26,013	38,169	109.98	25,629	38,553
16,000	234.62	68,463	117.31	29,567	38,896	117.31	27,747	40,716	117.31	27,336	41,127
17,000	249.28	72,741	124.64	31,414	41,327	124.64	29,480	43,261	124.64	29,044	43,697
18,000	263.94	77,018	131.97	33,261	43,757	131.97	31,214	45,804	131.97	30,752	46,266
19,000	278.61	81,300	139.31	35,112	46,188	139.31	32,951	48,349	139.31	32,464	48,836
20,000	293.27	85,577	146.64	36,959	48,618	146.64	34,684	50,893	146.64	34,171	51,406
21,000	307.93	89,855	153.97	38,806	51,049	153.97	36,418	53,437	153.97	35,879	53,976
22,000	322.60	94,136	161.30	40,654	53,482	161.30	38,151	55,985	161.30	37,587	56,549
23,000	337.26	98,414	168.63	42,501	55,913	168.63	39,885	58,529	168.63	39,295	59,119
24,000	351.92	102,691	175.96	44,348	58,343	175.96	41,618	61,073	175.96	41,003	61,688
25,000	366.59	106,972	183.30	46,199	60,773	183.30	43,355	63,617	183.30	42,714	64,258
26,000	381.25	111,250	190.63	48,046	63,204	190.63	45,089	66,161	190.63	44,422	66,828
27,000	395.91	115,528	197.96	49,893	65,635	197.96	46,822	68,706	197.96	46,130	69,398
28,000	410.58	119,809	205.29	51,741	68,068	205.29	48,556	71,253	205.29	47,838	71,971
29,000	425.24	124,086	212.62	53,588	70,498	212.62	50,289	73,797	212.62	49,546	74,540
30,000	439.90	128,364	219.95	55,435	72,929	219.95	52,023	76,341	219.95	51,253	77,111
32,500	476.56	139,062	238.28	60,055	79,007	238.28	56,358	82,704	238.28	55,525	83,537
35,000	513.22	149,759	256.61	64,675	85,084	256.61	60,694	89,065	256.61	59,796	89,963
40,000	586.54	171,154	293.27	73,915	97,239	293.27	69,365	101,789	293.27	68,339	102,815
45,000	659.85	192,546	329.93	83,154	109,392	329.93	78,036	114,510	329.93	76,882	115,664
50,000	733.17	213,941	366.59	92,394	121,547	366.59	86,707	127,234	366.59	85,425	128,516
55,000	806.48	235,333	403.24	101,630	133,703	403.24	95,374	139,959	403.24	93,964	141,369
60,000	879.80	256,728	439.90	110,870	145,858	439.90	104,045	152,683	439.90	102,507	154,221
65,000	953.12	278,123	476.56	120,110	158,013	476.56	112,716	165,407	476.56	111,050	167,073
70,000	1,026.43	299,515	513.22	129,350	170,165	513.22	121,387	178,128	513.22	119,593	179,922
75,000	1,099.75	320,910	549.88	138,589	182,321	549.88	130,059	190,851	549.88	128,136	192,774
80,000	1,173.07	342,305	586.54	147,829	194,476	586.54	138,730	203,575	586.54	136,678	205,627
85,000	1,246.38	363,697	623.19	157,065	206,632	623.19	147,397	216,300	623.19	145,218	218,479
90,000	1,319.70	385,092	659.85	166,305	218,787	659.85	156,068	229,024	659.85	153,760	231,332
95,000	1,393.01	406,484	696.51	175,545	230,939	696.51	164,739	241,745	696.51	162,303	244,181
100,000	1,466.33	427,879	733.17	184,784	243,095	733.17	173,410	254,469	733.17	170,846	257,033
105,000	1,539.65	449,274	769.83	194,024	255,250	769.83	182,081	267,193	769.83	179,389	269,885
110,000	1,612.96	470,666	806.48	203,260	267,406	806.48	190,748	279,918	806.48	187,928	282,738
115,000	1,686.28	492,061	843.14	212,500	279,561	843.14	199,420	292,641	843.14	196,471	295,590
120,000	1,759.60	513,456	879.80	221,740	291,716	879.80	208,091	305,365	879.80	205,014	308,442
125,000	1,832.91	534,848	916.46	230,980	303,868	916.46	216,762	318,086	916.46	213,557	321,291
130,000	1,906.23	556,243	953.12	240,219	316,024	953.12	225,433	330,810	953.12	222,100	334,143
135,000	1,979.54	577,634	989.77	249,455	328,179	989.77	234,100	343,534	989.77	230,639	346,995
140,000	2,052.86	599,030	1,026.43	258,695	340,335	1,026.43	242,771	356,259	1,026.43	239,182	359,848
145,000	2,126.18	620,425	1,063.09	267,935	352,490	1,063.09	251,442	368,983	1,063.09	247,725	372,700
150,000	2,199.49	641,816	1,099.75	277,175	364,641	1,099.75	260,113	381,703	1,099.75	256,267	385,549
155,000	2,272.81	663,212	1,136.41	286,415	376,797	1,136.41	268,784	394,428	1,136.41	264,810	398,402
160,000	2,346.13	684,607	1,173.07	295,654	388,953	1,173.07	277,455	407,152	1,173.07	273,353	411,254
165,000	2,419.44	705,998	1,209.72	304,890	401,108	1,209.72	286,123	419,875	1,209.72	281,892	424,106
170,000	2,492.76	727,394	1,246.38	314,130	413,264	1,246.38	294,794	432,600	1,246.38	290,435	436,959
175,000	2,566.07	748,785	1,283.04	323,370	425,415	1,283.04	303,465	445,320	1,283.04	298,978	449,807
180,000	2,639.39	770,180	1,319.70	332,610	437,570	1,319.70	312,136	458,044	1,319.70	307,521	462,659
185,000	2,712.71	791,576	1,356.36	341,850	449,726	1,356.36	320,807	470,769	1,356.36	316,064	475,512
190,000	2,786.02	812,967	1,393.01	351,085	461,882	1,393.01	329,474	483,493	1,393.01	324,603	488,364
195,000	2,859.34	834,362	1,429.67	360,325	474,037	1,429.67	338,145	496,217	1,429.67	333,146	501,216
200,000	2,932.66	855,758	1,466.33	369,565	486,193	1,466.33	346,816	508,942	1,466.33	341,689	514,069

94

BIWEEKLY MORTGAGES 17.75%

AMOUNT OF LOAN	30 YEARS MONTHLY PAYMENT	30 YEARS TOTAL INTRST	360 DAY BASIS 383.713 PAYMENTS BWEEKLY PAYMENT	TOTAL INTRST	INTRST SAVED	364 DAY BASIS 368.325 PAYMENTS BWEEKLY PAYMENT	TOTAL INTRST	INTRST SAVED	365 DAY BASIS 364.857 PAYMENTS BWEEKLY PAYMENT	TOTAL INTRST	INTRST SAVED
$ 50	0.75	220	0.38	96	124	0.38	90	130	0.38	89	131
100	1.49	436	0.75	188	248	0.75	176	260	0.75	174	262
200	2.98	873	1.49	372	501	1.49	349	524	1.49	344	529
300	4.47	1,309	2.24	560	749	2.24	525	784	2.24	517	792
400	5.95	1,742	2.98	743	999	2.98	698	1,044	2.98	687	1,055
500	7.44	2,178	3.72	927	1,251	3.72	870	1,308	3.72	857	1,321
600	8.93	2,615	4.47	1,115	1,500	4.47	1,046	1,569	4.47	1,031	1,584
700	10.41	3,048	5.21	1,299	1,749	5.21	1,219	1,829	5.21	1,201	1,847
800	11.90	3,484	5.95	1,483	2,001	5.95	1,392	2,092	5.95	1,371	2,113
900	13.39	3,920	6.70	1,671	2,249	6.70	1,568	2,352	6.70	1,545	2,375
1,000	14.87	4,353	7.44	1,855	2,498	7.44	1,740	2,613	7.44	1,715	2,638
2,000	29.74	8,706	14.87	3,706	5,000	14.87	3,477	5,229	14.87	3,425	5,281
3,000	44.61	13,060	22.31	5,561	7,499	22.31	5,217	7,843	22.31	5,140	7,920
4,000	59.47	17,409	29.74	7,412	9,997	29.74	6,954	10,455	29.74	6,851	10,558
5,000	74.34	21,762	37.17	9,263	12,499	37.17	8,691	13,071	37.17	8,562	13,200
6,000	89.21	26,116	44.61	11,117	14,999	44.61	10,431	15,685	44.61	10,276	15,840
7,000	104.07	30,465	52.04	12,968	17,497	52.04	12,168	18,297	52.04	11,987	18,478
8,000	118.94	34,818	59.47	14,819	19,999	59.47	13,904	20,914	59.47	13,698	21,120
9,000	133.81	39,172	66.91	16,674	22,498	66.91	15,645	23,527	66.91	15,413	23,759
10,000	148.67	43,521	74.34	18,525	24,996	74.34	17,381	26,140	74.34	17,123	26,398
11,000	163.54	47,874	81.77	20,376	27,498	81.77	19,118	28,756	81.77	18,834	29,040
12,000	178.41	52,228	89.21	22,231	29,997	89.21	20,858	31,370	89.21	20,549	31,679
13,000	193.27	56,577	96.64	24,082	32,495	96.64	22,595	33,982	96.64	22,260	34,317
14,000	208.14	60,930	104.07	25,933	34,997	104.07	24,332	36,598	104.07	23,971	36,959
15,000	223.01	65,284	111.51	27,788	37,496	111.51	26,072	39,212	111.51	25,685	39,599
16,000	237.88	69,637	118.94	29,639	39,998	118.94	27,809	41,828	118.94	27,396	42,241
17,000	252.74	73,986	126.37	31,490	42,496	126.37	29,545	44,441	126.37	29,107	44,879
18,000	267.61	78,340	133.81	33,345	44,995	133.81	31,286	47,054	133.81	30,822	47,518
19,000	282.48	82,693	141.24	35,196	47,497	141.24	33,022	49,671	141.24	32,532	50,161
20,000	297.34	87,042	148.67	37,047	49,995	148.67	34,759	52,283	148.67	34,243	52,799
21,000	312.21	91,396	156.11	38,901	52,495	156.11	36,499	54,897	156.11	35,958	55,438
22,000	327.08	95,749	163.54	40,752	54,997	163.54	38,236	57,513	163.54	37,669	58,080
23,000	341.94	100,098	170.97	42,603	57,495	170.97	39,973	60,125	170.97	39,380	60,718
24,000	356.81	104,452	178.41	44,458	59,994	178.41	41,713	62,739	178.41	41,094	63,358
25,000	371.68	108,805	185.84	46,309	62,496	185.84	43,450	65,355	185.84	42,805	66,000
26,000	386.54	113,154	193.27	48,160	64,994	193.27	45,186	67,968	193.27	44,516	68,638
27,000	401.41	117,508	200.71	50,015	67,493	200.71	46,927	70,581	200.71	46,230	71,278
28,000	416.28	121,861	208.14	51,866	69,995	208.14	48,663	73,198	208.14	47,941	73,920
29,000	431.15	126,214	215.58	53,721	72,493	215.58	50,404	75,810	215.58	49,656	76,558
30,000	446.01	130,564	223.01	55,572	74,992	223.01	52,140	78,424	223.01	51,367	79,197
32,500	483.18	141,445	241.59	60,201	81,244	241.59	56,484	84,961	241.59	55,646	85,799
35,000	520.35	152,326	260.18	64,834	87,492	260.18	60,831	91,495	260.18	59,928	92,398
40,000	594.68	174,085	297.34	74,093	99,992	297.34	69,518	104,567	297.34	68,487	105,598
45,000	669.02	195,847	334.51	83,356	112,491	334.51	78,208	117,639	334.51	77,048	118,799
50,000	743.35	217,606	371.68	92,618	124,988	371.68	86,899	130,707	371.68	85,610	131,996
55,000	817.69	239,368	408.85	101,881	137,487	408.85	95,590	143,778	408.85	94,172	145,196
60,000	892.02	261,127	446.01	111,140	149,987	446.01	104,277	156,850	446.01	102,730	158,397
65,000	966.35	282,886	483.18	120,402	162,484	483.18	112,967	169,919	483.18	111,292	171,594
70,000	1,040.69	304,648	520.35	129,665	174,983	520.35	121,658	182,990	520.35	119,853	184,795
75,000	1,115.02	326,407	557.51	138,924	187,483	557.51	130,345	196,062	557.51	128,411	197,996
80,000	1,189.36	348,170	594.68	148,186	199,984	594.68	139,036	209,134	594.68	136,973	211,197
85,000	1,263.69	369,928	631.85	157,449	212,479	631.85	147,726	222,202	631.85	145,535	224,393
90,000	1,338.03	391,691	669.02	166,712	224,979	669.02	156,417	235,274	669.02	154,097	237,594
95,000	1,412.36	413,450	706.18	175,970	237,480	706.18	165,104	248,346	706.18	162,655	250,795
100,000	1,486.70	435,212	743.35	185,233	249,979	743.35	173,794	261,418	743.35	171,216	263,996
105,000	1,561.03	456,971	780.52	194,496	262,475	780.52	182,485	274,486	780.52	179,778	277,193
110,000	1,635.37	478,733	817.69	203,758	274,975	817.69	191,176	287,557	817.69	188,340	290,393
115,000	1,709.70	500,492	854.85	213,017	287,475	854.85	199,863	300,629	854.85	196,898	303,594
120,000	1,784.04	522,254	892.02	222,280	299,974	892.02	208,553	313,701	892.02	205,460	316,794
125,000	1,858.37	544,013	929.19	231,542	312,471	929.19	217,244	326,769	929.19	214,021	329,992
130,000	1,932.70	565,772	966.35	240,801	324,971	966.35	225,931	339,841	966.35	222,580	343,192
135,000	2,007.04	587,534	1,003.52	250,064	337,470	1,003.52	234,622	352,912	1,003.52	231,141	356,393
140,000	2,081.37	609,293	1,040.69	259,326	349,967	1,040.69	243,312	365,981	1,040.69	239,703	369,590
145,000	2,155.71	631,056	1,077.86	268,589	362,467	1,077.86	252,003	379,053	1,077.86	248,265	382,791
150,000	2,230.04	652,814	1,115.02	277,848	374,966	1,115.02	260,690	392,124	1,115.02	256,823	395,991
155,000	2,304.38	674,577	1,152.19	287,110	387,467	1,152.19	269,380	405,197	1,152.19	265,385	409,192
160,000	2,378.71	696,336	1,189.36	296,373	399,963	1,189.36	278,071	418,265	1,189.36	273,946	422,390
165,000	2,453.05	718,098	1,226.53	305,636	412,462	1,226.53	286,762	431,336	1,226.53	282,508	435,590
170,000	2,527.38	739,857	1,263.69	314,894	424,963	1,263.69	295,449	444,408	1,263.69	291,066	448,791
175,000	2,601.72	761,619	1,300.86	324,157	437,462	1,300.86	304,139	457,480	1,300.86	299,628	461,991
180,000	2,676.05	783,378	1,338.03	333,420	449,958	1,338.03	312,830	470,548	1,338.03	308,190	475,188
185,000	2,750.39	805,140	1,375.20	342,682	462,458	1,375.20	321,521	483,619	1,375.20	316,751	488,389
190,000	2,824.72	826,899	1,412.36	351,941	474,958	1,412.36	330,207	496,692	1,412.36	325,309	501,590
195,000	2,899.05	848,658	1,449.53	361,204	487,454	1,449.53	338,898	509,760	1,449.53	333,871	514,787
200,000	2,973.39	870,420	1,486.70	370,466	499,954	1,486.70	347,589	522,831	1,486.70	342,433	527,987

95

18.00% BIWEEKLY MORTGAGES

AMOUNT OF LOAN	30 YEARS		360 DAY BASIS 379.079 PAYMENTS			364 DAY BASIS 363.819 PAYMENTS			365 DAY BASIS 360.382 PAYMENTS		
	MONTHLY PAYMENT	TOTAL INTRST	BWEEKLY PAYMENT	TOTAL INTRST	INTRST SAVED	BWEEKLY PAYMENT	TOTAL INTRST	INTRST SAVED	BWEEKLY PAYMENT	TOTAL INTRST	INTRST SAVED
$ 50	0.76	224	0.38	94	130	0.38	88	136	0.38	87	137
100	1.51	444	0.76	188	256	0.76	177	267	0.76	174	270
200	3.02	887	1.51	372	515	1.51	349	538	1.51	344	543
300	4.53	1,331	2.27	561	770	2.27	526	805	2.27	518	813
400	6.03	1,771	3.02	745	1,026	3.02	699	1,072	3.02	688	1,083
500	7.54	2,214	3.77	929	1,285	3.77	872	1,342	3.77	859	1,355
600	9.05	2,658	4.53	1,117	1,541	4.53	1,048	1,610	4.53	1,033	1,625
700	10.55	3,098	5.28	1,302	1,796	5.28	1,221	1,877	5.28	1,203	1,895
800	12.06	3,542	6.03	1,486	2,056	6.03	1,394	2,148	6.03	1,373	2,169
900	13.57	3,985	6.79	1,674	2,311	6.79	1,570	2,415	6.79	1,547	2,438
1,000	15.08	4,429	7.54	1,858	2,571	7.54	1,743	2,686	7.54	1,717	2,712
2,000	30.15	8,854	15.08	3,717	5,137	15.08	3,486	5,368	15.08	3,435	5,419
3,000	45.22	13,279	22.61	5,571	7,708	22.61	5,226	8,053	22.61	5,148	8,131
4,000	60.29	17,704	30.15	7,429	10,275	30.15	6,969	10,735	30.15	6,866	10,838
5,000	75.36	22,130	37.68	9,284	12,846	37.68	8,709	13,421	37.68	8,579	13,551
6,000	90.43	26,555	45.22	11,142	15,413	45.22	10,452	16,103	45.22	10,296	16,259
7,000	105.50	30,980	52.75	12,996	17,984	52.75	12,191	18,789	52.75	12,010	18,970
8,000	120.57	35,405	60.29	14,855	20,550	60.29	13,935	21,470	60.29	13,727	21,678
9,000	135.64	39,830	67.82	16,709	23,121	67.82	15,674	24,156	67.82	15,441	24,389
10,000	150.71	44,256	75.36	18,567	25,689	75.36	17,417	26,839	75.36	17,158	27,098
11,000	165.78	48,681	82.89	20,422	28,259	82.89	19,157	29,524	82.89	18,872	29,809
12,000	180.86	53,110	90.43	22,280	30,830	90.43	20,900	32,210	90.43	20,589	32,521
13,000	195.93	57,535	97.97	24,138	33,397	97.97	22,643	34,892	97.97	22,307	35,228
14,000	211.00	61,960	105.50	25,993	35,967	105.50	24,383	37,577	105.50	24,020	37,940
15,000	226.07	66,385	113.04	27,851	38,534	113.04	26,126	40,259	113.04	25,738	40,647
16,000	241.14	70,810	120.57	29,706	41,104	120.57	27,866	42,944	120.57	27,451	43,359
17,000	256.21	75,236	128.11	31,564	43,672	128.11	29,609	45,627	128.11	29,169	46,067
18,000	271.28	79,661	135.64	33,418	46,243	135.64	31,348	48,313	135.64	30,882	48,779
19,000	286.35	84,086	143.18	35,277	48,809	143.18	33,092	50,994	143.18	32,599	51,487
20,000	301.42	88,511	150.71	37,131	51,380	150.71	34,831	53,680	150.71	34,313	54,198
21,000	316.49	92,936	158.25	38,989	53,947	158.25	36,574	56,362	158.25	36,030	56,906
22,000	331.56	97,362	165.78	40,844	56,518	165.78	38,314	59,048	165.78	37,744	59,618
23,000	346.63	101,787	173.32	42,702	59,085	173.32	40,057	61,730	173.32	39,461	62,326
24,000	361.71	106,216	180.86	44,560	61,656	180.86	41,800	64,416	180.86	41,179	65,037
25,000	376.78	110,641	188.39	46,415	64,226	188.39	43,540	67,101	188.39	42,892	67,749
26,000	391.85	115,066	195.93	48,273	66,793	195.93	45,283	69,783	195.93	44,610	70,456
27,000	406.92	119,491	203.46	50,127	69,364	203.46	47,023	72,468	203.46	46,323	73,168
28,000	421.99	123,916	211.00	51,986	71,930	211.00	48,766	75,150	211.00	48,041	75,875
29,000	437.06	128,342	218.53	53,840	74,502	218.53	50,505	77,837	218.53	49,754	78,588
30,000	452.13	132,767	226.07	55,698	77,069	226.07	52,249	80,518	226.07	51,472	81,295
32,500	489.81	143,832	244.91	60,340	83,492	244.91	56,603	87,229	244.91	55,761	88,071
35,000	527.48	154,893	263.74	64,978	89,915	263.74	60,954	93,939	263.74	60,047	94,846
40,000	602.84	177,022	301.42	74,262	102,760	301.42	69,662	107,360	301.42	68,626	108,396
45,000	678.19	199,148	339.10	83,546	115,602	339.10	78,371	120,777	339.10	77,206	121,942
50,000	753.55	221,278	376.78	92,829	128,449	376.78	87,080	134,198	376.78	85,785	135,493
55,000	828.90	243,404	414.45	102,109	141,295	414.45	95,785	147,619	414.45	94,360	149,044
60,000	904.26	265,534	452.13	111,393	154,141	452.13	104,493	161,041	452.13	102,940	162,594
65,000	979.61	287,660	489.81	120,677	166,983	489.81	113,202	174,458	489.81	111,519	176,141
70,000	1,054.96	309,786	527.48	129,957	179,829	527.48	121,907	187,879	527.48	120,094	189,692
75,000	1,130.32	331,915	565.16	139,240	192,675	565.16	130,616	201,299	565.16	128,673	203,242
80,000	1,205.67	354,041	602.84	148,524	205,517	602.84	139,325	214,716	602.84	137,253	216,788
85,000	1,281.03	376,171	640.52	157,808	218,363	640.52	148,033	228,138	640.52	145,832	230,339
90,000	1,356.38	398,297	678.19	167,088	231,209	678.19	156,738	241,559	678.19	154,407	243,890
95,000	1,431.74	420,426	715.87	176,371	244,055	715.87	165,447	254,979	715.87	162,987	257,439
100,000	1,507.09	442,552	753.55	185,655	256,897	753.55	174,156	268,396	753.55	171,566	270,986
105,000	1,582.44	464,678	791.22	194,935	269,743	791.22	182,861	281,817	791.22	180,141	284,537
110,000	1,657.80	486,808	828.90	204,219	282,589	828.90	191,570	295,238	828.90	188,721	298,087
115,000	1,733.15	508,934	866.58	213,502	295,432	866.58	200,278	308,656	866.58	197,300	311,634
120,000	1,808.51	531,064	904.26	222,786	308,278	904.26	208,987	322,077	904.26	205,879	325,185
125,000	1,883.86	553,190	941.93	232,066	321,124	941.93	217,692	335,498	941.93	214,455	338,735
130,000	1,959.22	575,319	979.61	241,350	333,969	979.61	226,401	348,918	979.61	223,034	352,285
135,000	2,034.57	597,445	1,017.29	250,633	346,812	1,017.29	235,109	362,336	1,017.29	231,613	365,832
140,000	2,109.92	619,571	1,054.96	259,913	359,658	1,054.96	243,814	375,757	1,054.96	240,189	379,382
145,000	2,185.28	641,701	1,092.64	269,197	372,504	1,092.64	252,523	389,178	1,092.64	248,768	392,933
150,000	2,260.63	663,827	1,130.32	278,481	385,346	1,130.32	261,232	402,595	1,130.32	257,347	406,480
155,000	2,335.99	685,956	1,168.00	287,764	398,192	1,168.00	269,941	416,015	1,168.00	265,926	420,030
160,000	2,411.34	708,082	1,205.67	297,044	411,038	1,205.67	278,646	429,436	1,205.67	274,502	433,580
165,000	2,486.70	730,212	1,243.35	306,328	423,884	1,243.35	287,354	442,858	1,243.35	283,081	447,131
170,000	2,562.05	752,338	1,281.03	315,612	436,726	1,281.03	296,063	456,275	1,281.03	291,660	460,678
175,000	2,637.40	774,464	1,318.70	324,891	449,573	1,318.70	304,768	469,696	1,318.70	300,236	474,228
180,000	2,712.76	796,594	1,356.38	334,175	462,419	1,356.38	313,477	483,117	1,356.38	308,815	487,779
185,000	2,788.11	818,720	1,394.06	343,459	475,261	1,394.06	322,186	496,534	1,394.06	317,394	501,326
190,000	2,863.47	840,849	1,431.74	352,743	488,106	1,431.74	330,894	509,955	1,431.74	325,973	514,876
195,000	2,938.82	862,975	1,469.41	362,022	500,953	1,469.41	339,599	523,376	1,469.41	334,549	528,426
200,000	3,014.18	885,105	1,507.09	371,306	513,799	1,507.09	348,308	536,797	1,507.09	343,128	541,977

96

GROWING EQUITY MORTGAGES

Generally, growing equity mortgages (GEMs) call for a fixed percentage increase in the mortgage payment each year until the loan is paid off. The first year's GEM payment is the same as the widely used 30-year mortgage payment. There are a variety of GEM plans available to borrowers. We have included six of the most popular ones in this table: GEMs with increases per year of 1%, 2%, 3%, 4%, 5%, and 6%.

Each interest rate within this table appears on two facing pages. On each page, we show four mortgage plans; the benchmark 30-year monthly payment mortgage and three of the GEM plans. On the left-facing page, we show the benchmark 30-year mortgage along with the 1%, 2%, and 3% GEM plans. On the right-facing page, we repeat the 30-year mortgage along with the 4%, 5%, and 6% GEM plans. The annual payment percentage increase at the top of each GEM's group of columns identifies the GEM plan. Directly below each annual payment percentage increase, we show the number of payments required to pay off the GEM. The number of payments includes a fractional last payment. The very last payment required to pay off the GEM is somewhat less than the last year's full monthly payment. There is no need to show the first year's payment for each GEM plan, since the first year's GEM payment is identical to the 30-year mortgage payment shown. We display the last year's monthly payment for each GEM plan so that you can see how large the payment has grown at the time the GEM pays off.

Here is how to use this table. First, find the page with the interest rate and the GEM plan for the desired loan. Look down the first column to find your loan amount. Then read across the page and find the columns which represent the 30-year plan and the desired alternative GEM plan. The first group of columns represents the 30-year loan plan. Within this group, you find both the monthly payment and the total interest paid through the life of the loan. Each GEM plan's group of columns shows the last year's payment, the total interest paid, and the all-important third column, the interest saved. This third column is the difference between the interest paid on the 30-year loan and the desired GEM plan loan.

EXAMPLE

How much interest will you save on a $64,900 mortgage at 13.5% interest if you choose a GEM based upon a 4% increase per year in payment? What is the complete payment schedule? How long will it take to pay off this GEM?

First find the 13.5% mortgage plans on pages 152 and 153. Note that the 4% GEM is displayed as the first of the GEM plans on page 153. Move down the loan amount column until you find a row entry for $64,900. Since there is no row entry for exactly this loan amount, you must combine the three entries from $900, $4,000, and $60,000 to get the interest saved. The interest-saved entries for the 4% GEM are $1,659, $7,370, and $110,545; and their sum is $119,574.

The first year's GEM payment is the same as for the benchmark 30-year mortgage. The corresponding entries for the 30-year mortgage are $10.31, $45.82, and $687.25; and their sum is $743.38. The last year's payment entries for the 4% GEM are $16.51, $73.36, and $1,100.31; and their sum is $1,190.18. Thus the 4% GEM payments start at $743.38 and go up 4% per year until the 13th year when they reach $1,190.18. At the top of the page, under the 4% per year GEM plan, you will find that 155.767 payments are needed to pay off this mortgage. Multiply the fraction 0.767 times $1,190.18 to get $912.87, the very last payment. To give you a better picture of how this GEM loan works, here is the complete payment schedule. Each loan year's payment is 4% higher than the prior year's payment.

LOAN YEAR	PAYMENT SCHEDULE
1	12 @ $743.38
2	12 @ 773.12
3	12 @ 804.04
4	12 @ 836.20
5	12 @ 869.65
6	12 @ 904.44
7	12 @ 940.62
8	12 @ 978.24
9	12 @ 1017.37
10	12 @ 1058.06
11	12 @ 1100.38
12	12 @ 1144.40
13	11 @ 1190.18
	1 @ 912.87

The 4% GEM loan plan starts with the same payment as the 30-year mortgage plan. But since the borrower is making ever-increasing payments, the loan pays off in slightly less than 13 years.

7.00% GROWING EQUITY MORTGAGES

AMOUNT OF LOAN	30 YEARS		1% PMT INCR/YR 282.422 PAYMENTS			2% PMT INCR/YR 241.390 PAYMENTS			3% PMT INCR/YR 214.510 PAYMENTS		
	MONTHLY PAYMENT	TOTAL INTRST	LAST YR MON PMT	TOTAL INTRST	INTRST SAVED	LAST YR MON PMT	TOTAL INTRST	INTRST SAVED	LAST YR MON PMT	TOTAL INTRST	INTRST SAVED
$ 50	0.34	72	0.43	58	14	0.51	50	22	0.56	45	27
100	0.67	141	0.84	112	29	1.00	97	44	1.11	87	54
200	1.34	282	1.68	224	58	1.99	193	89	2.21	173	109
300	2.00	420	2.51	333	87	2.97	287	133	3.31	257	163
400	2.67	561	3.36	446	115	3.97	384	177	4.41	344	217
500	3.33	699	4.19	555	144	4.95	478	221	5.50	427	272
600	4.00	840	5.03	667	173	5.94	575	265	6.61	514	326
700	4.66	978	5.86	776	202	6.92	668	310	7.70	598	380
800	5.33	1,119	6.70	888	231	7.92	765	354	8.81	684	435
900	5.99	1,256	7.53	997	259	8.90	859	397	9.90	768	488
1,000	6.66	1,398	8.37	1,109	289	9.90	956	442	11.01	855	543
2,000	13.31	2,792	16.73	2,215	577	19.78	1,908	884	22.00	1,707	1,085
3,000	19.96	4,186	25.09	3,321	865	29.66	2,861	1,325	32.99	2,559	1,627
4,000	26.62	5,583	33.47	4,430	1,153	39.56	3,817	1,766	44.00	3,414	2,169
5,000	33.27	6,977	41.83	5,536	1,441	49.44	4,769	2,208	54.99	4,266	2,711
6,000	39.92	8,371	50.19	6,641	1,730	59.32	5,722	2,649	65.98	5,118	3,253
7,000	46.58	9,769	58.56	7,750	2,019	69.22	6,677	3,092	76.99	5,973	3,796
8,000	53.23	11,163	66.92	8,856	2,307	79.10	7,630	3,533	87.98	6,825	4,338
9,000	59.88	12,557	75.28	9,962	2,595	88.98	8,583	3,974	98.97	7,677	4,880
10,000	66.54	13,954	83.65	11,071	2,883	98.87	9,538	4,416	109.98	8,532	5,422
11,000	73.19	15,348	92.01	12,177	3,171	108.76	10,491	4,857	120.97	9,384	5,964
12,000	79.84	16,742	100.37	13,283	3,459	118.64	11,444	5,298	131.96	10,236	6,506
13,000	86.49	18,136	108.73	14,389	3,747	128.52	12,396	5,740	142.95	11,088	7,048
14,000	93.15	19,534	117.10	15,498	4,036	138.42	13,352	6,182	153.96	11,943	7,591
15,000	99.80	20,928	125.46	16,604	4,324	148.30	14,305	6,623	164.95	12,795	8,133
16,000	106.45	22,322	133.83	17,709	4,613	158.18	15,257	7,065	175.95	13,647	8,675
17,000	113.11	23,720	142.20	18,818	4,902	168.08	16,213	7,507	186.95	14,502	9,218
18,000	119.76	25,114	150.56	19,924	5,190	177.96	17,166	7,948	197.95	15,354	9,760
19,000	126.41	26,508	158.92	21,030	5,478	187.84	18,118	8,390	208.94	16,207	10,301
20,000	133.07	27,905	167.29	22,139	5,766	197.74	19,074	8,831	219.94	17,061	10,844
21,000	139.72	29,299	175.65	23,245	6,054	207.62	20,027	9,272	230.94	17,913	11,386
22,000	146.37	30,693	184.01	24,351	6,342	217.50	20,979	9,714	241.93	18,766	11,927
23,000	153.02	32,087	192.37	25,457	6,630	227.38	21,932	10,155	252.92	19,618	12,469
24,000	159.68	33,485	200.74	26,566	6,919	237.28	22,887	10,598	263.93	20,473	13,012
25,000	166.33	34,879	209.10	27,672	7,207	247.16	23,840	11,039	274.92	21,325	13,554
26,000	172.98	36,273	217.46	28,777	7,496	257.04	24,793	11,480	285.91	22,177	14,096
27,000	179.64	37,670	225.84	29,886	7,784	266.94	25,748	11,922	296.92	23,032	14,638
28,000	186.29	39,064	234.20	30,992	8,072	276.82	26,701	12,363	307.91	23,884	15,180
29,000	192.94	40,458	242.56	32,098	8,360	286.70	27,654	12,804	318.90	24,736	15,722
30,000	199.60	41,856	250.93	33,207	8,649	296.60	28,609	13,247	329.91	25,591	16,265
32,500	216.23	45,343	271.84	35,973	9,370	321.31	30,992	14,351	357.40	27,722	17,621
35,000	232.86	48,830	292.74	38,740	10,090	346.02	33,376	15,454	384.88	29,854	18,976
40,000	266.13	55,807	334.57	44,275	11,532	395.46	38,145	17,662	439.87	34,120	21,687
45,000	299.39	62,780	376.38	49,808	12,972	444.88	42,911	19,869	494.85	38,383	24,397
50,000	332.66	69,758	418.21	55,343	14,415	494.32	47,680	22,078	549.84	42,649	27,109
55,000	365.92	76,731	460.02	60,876	15,855	543.74	52,447	24,284	604.81	46,913	29,818
60,000	399.19	83,708	501.85	66,411	17,297	593.18	57,216	26,492	659.80	51,179	32,529
65,000	432.45	90,682	543.66	71,944	18,738	642.60	61,982	28,700	714.77	55,442	35,240
70,000	465.72	97,659	585.49	77,479	20,180	692.04	66,751	30,908	769.76	59,708	37,951
75,000	498.98	104,633	627.30	83,012	21,621	741.46	71,517	33,116	824.74	63,971	40,662
80,000	532.25	111,610	669.13	88,547	23,063	790.90	76,287	35,323	879.73	68,237	43,373
85,000	565.51	118,584	710.94	94,080	24,504	840.32	81,053	37,531	934.70	72,500	46,084
90,000	598.78	125,561	752.76	99,615	25,946	889.76	85,822	39,739	989.69	76,767	48,794
95,000	632.04	132,534	794.58	105,148	27,386	939.18	90,588	41,946	1,044.67	81,030	51,504
100,000	665.31	139,512	836.40	110,683	28,829	988.62	95,358	44,154	1,099.66	85,296	54,216
105,000	698.57	146,485	878.22	116,216	30,269	1,038.04	100,124	46,361	1,154.63	89,559	56,926
110,000	731.84	153,462	920.04	121,751	31,711	1,087.48	104,893	48,569	1,209.62	93,825	59,637
115,000	765.10	160,436	961.86	127,284	33,152	1,135.90	109,659	50,777	1,264.59	98,088	62,348
120,000	798.37	167,413	1,003.68	132,819	34,594	1,186.34	114,429	52,984	1,319.58	102,354	65,059
125,000	831.63	174,387	1,045.49	138,352	36,035	1,235.76	119,195	55,192	1,374.56	106,618	67,769
130,000	864.90	181,364	1,087.32	143,887	37,477	1,285.20	123,964	57,400	1,429.55	110,884	70,480
135,000	898.16	188,338	1,129.13	149,420	38,918	1,334.62	128,730	59,608	1,484.52	115,147	73,191
140,000	931.43	195,315	1,170.96	154,955	40,360	1,384.06	133,499	61,816	1,539.51	119,413	75,902
145,000	964.69	202,288	1,212.77	160,488	41,800	1,433.48	138,266	64,022	1,594.49	123,676	78,612
150,000	997.96	209,266	1,254.60	166,023	43,243	1,482.92	143,035	66,231	1,649.48	127,942	81,324
155,000	1,031.22	216,239	1,296.41	171,556	44,683	1,532.34	147,801	68,438	1,704.45	132,206	84,033
160,000	1,064.49	223,216	1,338.24	177,091	46,125	1,581.78	152,570	70,646	1,759.44	136,472	86,744
165,000	1,097.75	230,190	1,380.05	182,624	47,566	1,631.20	157,337	72,853	1,814.41	140,735	89,455
170,000	1,131.02	237,167	1,421.88	188,159	49,008	1,680.64	162,106	75,061	1,869.40	145,001	92,166
175,000	1,164.28	244,141	1,463.69	193,692	50,449	1,730.06	166,872	77,269	1,924.38	149,264	94,877
180,000	1,197.55	251,118	1,505.52	199,227	51,891	1,779.50	171,641	79,477	1,979.37	153,530	97,588
185,000	1,230.81	258,092	1,547.33	204,760	53,332	1,828.92	176,408	81,684	2,034.34	157,793	100,299
190,000	1,264.08	265,069	1,589.15	210,295	54,774	1,878.36	181,177	83,892	2,089.33	162,060	103,009
195,000	1,297.34	272,042	1,630.97	215,828	56,214	1,927.78	185,943	86,099	2,144.31	166,323	105,719
200,000	1,330.61	279,020	1,672.79	221,363	57,657	1,977.22	190,712	88,308	2,199.30	170,589	108,431

GROWING EQUITY MORTGAGES 7.00%

AMOUNT OF LOAN	30 YEARS		4% PMT INCR/YR 195.007 PAYMENTS			5% PMT INCR/YR 180.054 PAYMENTS			6% PMT INCR/YR 168.031 PAYMENTS		
	MONTHLY PAYMENT	TOTAL INTRST	LAST YR MON PMT	TOTAL INTRST	INTRST SAVED	LAST YR MON PMT	TOTAL INTRST	INTRST SAVED	LAST YR MON PMT	TOTAL INTRST	INTRST SAVED
$ 50	0.34	72	0.64	41	31	0.71	38	34	0.77	36	36
100	0.67	141	1.25	79	62	1.39	74	67	1.51	69	72
200	1.34	282	2.51	158	124	2.79	147	135	3.03	138	144
300	2.00	420	3.75	235	185	4.16	218	202	4.52	205	215
400	2.67	561	5.00	314	247	5.55	292	269	6.04	274	287
500	3.33	699	6.24	391	308	6.92	363	336	7.53	340	359
600	4.00	840	7.49	470	370	8.32	436	404	9.04	409	431
700	4.66	978	8.73	547	431	9.69	507	471	10.54	475	503
800	5.33	1,119	9.98	626	493	11.08	581	538	12.05	544	575
900	5.99	1,256	11.22	702	554	12.45	652	604	13.54	611	645
1,000	6.66	1,398	12.47	782	616	13.85	725	673	15.06	680	718
2,000	13.31	2,792	24.93	1,561	1,231	27.67	1,448	1,344	30.09	1,357	1,435
3,000	19.96	4,186	37.38	2,340	1,846	41.50	2,171	2,015	45.13	2,035	2,151
4,000	26.62	5,583	49.86	3,122	2,461	55.34	2,896	2,687	60.19	2,715	2,868
5,000	33.27	6,977	62.31	3,901	3,076	69.17	3,619	3,358	75.22	3,392	3,585
6,000	39.92	8,371	74.77	4,680	3,691	82.99	4,341	4,030	90.26	4,070	4,301
7,000	46.58	9,769	87.24	5,461	4,308	96.84	5,067	4,702	105.31	4,750	5,019
8,000	53.23	11,163	99.70	6,240	4,923	110.66	5,789	5,374	120.35	5,427	5,736
9,000	59.88	12,557	112.15	7,019	5,538	124.49	6,512	6,045	135.38	6,105	6,452
10,000	66.54	13,954	124.63	7,801	6,153	138.33	7,238	6,716	150.44	6,785	7,169
11,000	73.19	15,348	137.08	8,580	6,768	152.16	7,960	7,388	165.48	7,462	7,886
12,000	79.84	16,742	149.54	9,359	7,383	165.98	8,683	8,059	180.51	8,140	8,602
13,000	86.49	18,136	161.99	10,138	7,998	179.81	9,406	8,730	195.55	8,817	9,319
14,000	93.15	19,534	174.47	10,920	8,614	193.65	10,131	9,403	210.60	9,497	10,037
15,000	99.80	20,928	186.92	11,699	9,229	207.48	10,854	10,074	225.64	10,175	10,753
16,000	106.45	22,322	199.38	12,478	9,844	221.30	11,576	10,746	240.67	10,852	11,470
17,000	113.11	23,720	211.85	13,260	10,460	235.15	12,302	11,418	255.73	11,532	12,188
18,000	119.76	25,114	224.31	14,039	11,075	248.97	13,024	12,090	270.77	12,210	12,904
19,000	126.41	26,508	236.76	14,818	11,690	262.80	13,747	12,761	285.80	12,887	13,621
20,000	133.07	27,905	249.24	15,600	12,305	276.64	14,472	13,433	300.86	13,567	14,338
21,000	139.72	29,299	261.69	16,379	12,920	290.47	15,195	14,104	315.89	14,244	15,055
22,000	146.37	30,693	274.15	17,158	13,535	304.29	15,918	14,775	330.93	14,922	15,771
23,000	153.02	32,087	286.60	17,937	14,150	318.12	16,641	15,446	345.96	15,599	16,488
24,000	159.68	33,485	299.08	18,719	14,766	331.96	17,366	16,119	361.02	16,279	17,206
25,000	166.33	34,879	311.53	19,498	15,381	345.79	18,089	16,790	376.06	16,957	17,922
26,000	172.98	36,273	323.99	20,277	15,996	359.61	18,811	17,462	391.09	17,634	18,639
27,000	179.64	37,670	336.46	21,058	16,612	373.46	19,537	18,133	406.15	18,314	19,356
28,000	186.29	39,064	348.92	21,837	17,227	387.28	20,259	18,805	421.18	18,992	20,072
29,000	192.94	40,458	361.37	22,617	17,841	401.11	20,982	19,476	436.22	19,669	20,789
30,000	199.60	41,856	373.85	23,398	18,458	414.95	21,707	20,149	451.28	20,349	21,507
32,500	216.23	45,343	404.99	25,347	19,996	449.53	23,515	21,828	488.88	22,044	23,299
35,000	232.86	48,830	436.14	27,296	21,534	484.10	25,324	23,506	526.47	23,739	25,091
40,000	266.13	55,807	498.46	31,197	24,610	553.27	28,942	26,865	601.69	27,132	28,675
45,000	299.39	62,780	560.75	35,095	27,685	622.41	32,558	30,222	676.89	30,521	32,259
50,000	332.66	69,758	623.07	38,995	30,763	691.58	36,177	33,581	752.11	33,914	35,844
55,000	365.92	76,731	685.36	42,893	33,838	760.72	39,793	36,938	827.31	37,304	39,427
60,000	399.19	83,708	747.68	46,794	36,914	829.89	43,412	40,296	902.53	40,696	43,012
65,000	432.45	90,682	809.97	50,692	39,990	899.03	47,028	43,654	977.73	44,086	46,596
70,000	465.72	97,659	872.28	54,592	43,067	968.20	50,647	47,012	1,052.95	47,478	50,181
75,000	498.98	104,633	934.58	58,490	46,143	1,037.34	54,263	50,370	1,128.15	50,868	53,765
80,000	532.25	111,610	996.89	62,391	49,219	1,106.51	57,882	53,728	1,203.37	54,261	57,349
85,000	565.51	118,584	1,059.19	66,289	52,295	1,175.65	61,499	57,086	1,278.56	57,650	60,934
90,000	598.78	125,561	1,121.50	70,189	55,372	1,244.82	65,117	60,444	1,353.78	61,043	64,518
95,000	632.04	132,534	1,183.80	74,087	58,447	1,313.97	68,733	63,801	1,428.98	64,433	68,101
100,000	665.31	139,512	1,246.11	77,988	61,524	1,383.13	72,352	67,160	1,504.20	67,825	71,687
105,000	698.57	146,485	1,308.41	81,886	64,599	1,452.28	75,968	70,517	1,579.40	71,215	75,270
110,000	731.84	153,462	1,370.72	85,787	67,675	1,521.44	79,587	73,875	1,654.62	74,607	78,855
115,000	765.10	160,436	1,433.02	89,684	70,752	1,590.59	83,203	77,233	1,729.82	77,997	82,439
120,000	798.37	167,413	1,495.33	93,585	73,828	1,659.75	86,822	80,591	1,805.04	81,390	86,023
125,000	831.63	174,387	1,557.63	97,483	76,904	1,728.90	90,438	83,949	1,880.24	84,779	89,608
130,000	864.90	181,364	1,619.94	101,384	79,980	1,798.06	94,057	87,307	1,955.46	88,172	93,192
135,000	898.16	188,338	1,682.24	105,282	83,056	1,867.21	97,673	90,665	2,030.65	91,562	96,776
140,000	931.43	195,315	1,744.55	109,182	86,133	1,936.38	101,292	94,023	2,105.87	94,954	100,361
145,000	964.69	202,288	1,806.85	113,080	89,208	2,005.52	104,908	97,380	2,181.07	98,344	103,944
150,000	997.96	209,266	1,869.16	116,981	92,285	2,074.69	108,527	100,739	2,256.29	101,736	107,530
155,000	1,031.22	216,239	1,931.46	120,879	95,360	2,143.83	112,143	104,096	2,331.49	105,126	111,113
160,000	1,064.49	223,216	1,993.77	124,779	98,437	2,213.00	115,761	107,455	2,406.71	108,519	114,697
165,000	1,097.75	230,190	2,056.07	128,677	101,513	2,282.14	119,378	110,812	2,481.91	111,908	118,282
170,000	1,131.02	237,167	2,118.38	132,578	104,589	2,351.31	122,996	114,171	2,557.13	115,301	121,866
175,000	1,164.28	244,141	2,180.67	136,476	107,665	2,420.45	126,615	117,528	2,632.33	118,691	125,450
180,000	1,197.55	251,118	2,242.99	140,376	110,742	2,489.62	130,231	120,887	2,707.55	122,083	129,035
185,000	1,230.81	258,092	2,305.28	144,274	113,818	2,558.77	133,848	124,244	2,782.74	125,473	132,619
190,000	1,264.08	265,069	2,367.60	148,175	116,894	2,627.93	137,466	127,603	2,857.96	128,865	136,204
195,000	1,297.34	272,042	2,429.89	152,073	119,969	2,697.08	141,082	130,960	2,933.16	132,255	139,787
200,000	1,330.61	279,020	2,492.21	155,973	123,047	2,766.24	144,701	134,319	3,008.38	135,648	143,372

7.25% GROWING EQUITY MORTGAGES

AMOUNT OF LOAN	30 YEARS		1% PMT INCR/YR 280.840 PAYMENTS			2% PMT INCR/YR 239.622 PAYMENTS			3% PMT INCR/YR 212.748 PAYMENTS		
	MONTHLY PAYMENT	TOTAL INTRST	LAST YR MON PMT	TOTAL INTRST	INTRST SAVED	LAST YR MON PMT	TOTAL INTRST	INTRST SAVED	LAST YR MON PMT	TOTAL INTRST	INTRST SAVED
$ 50	0.35	76	0.44	60	16	0.51	52	24	0.58	46	30
100	0.69	148	0.87	117	31	1.01	101	47	1.14	90	58
200	1.37	293	1.72	231	62	2.00	199	94	2.26	178	115
300	2.05	438	2.58	345	93	2.99	297	141	3.39	265	173
400	2.73	583	3.43	459	124	3.98	394	189	4.51	352	231
500	3.42	731	4.30	576	155	4.98	495	236	5.65	443	288
600	4.10	876	5.15	690	186	5.97	593	283	6.78	530	346
700	4.78	1,021	6.01	804	217	6.96	691	330	7.90	617	404
800	5.46	1,166	6.86	918	248	7.95	789	377	9.02	705	461
900	6.14	1,310	7.72	1,032	278	8.94	887	423	10.15	792	518
1,000	6.83	1,459	8.59	1,149	310	9.95	988	471	11.29	882	577
2,000	13.65	2,914	17.16	2,295	619	19.89	1,972	942	22.56	1,762	1,152
3,000	20.47	4,369	25.73	3,442	927	29.82	2,957	1,412	33.83	2,641	1,728
4,000	27.29	5,824	34.31	4,588	1,236	39.76	3,942	1,882	45.11	3,521	2,303
5,000	34.11	7,280	42.88	5,734	1,546	49.69	4,927	2,353	56.38	4,401	2,879
6,000	40.94	8,738	51.47	6,883	1,855	59.64	5,914	2,824	67.67	5,283	3,455
7,000	47.76	10,194	60.04	8,029	2,165	69.58	6,899	3,295	78.94	6,163	4,031
8,000	54.58	11,649	68.62	9,175	2,474	79.51	7,884	3,765	90.21	7,042	4,607
9,000	61.40	13,104	77.19	10,321	2,783	89.45	8,868	4,236	101.48	7,922	5,182
10,000	68.22	14,559	85.76	11,467	3,092	99.38	9,853	4,706	112.76	8,801	5,758
11,000	75.04	16,014	94.34	12,614	3,400	109.32	10,838	5,176	124.03	9,681	6,333
12,000	81.87	17,473	102.92	13,763	3,710	119.27	11,826	5,647	135.32	10,563	6,910
13,000	88.69	18,928	111.50	14,909	4,019	129.20	12,810	6,118	146.59	11,443	7,485
14,000	95.51	20,384	120.07	16,055	4,329	139.14	13,795	6,589	157.86	12,322	8,062
15,000	102.33	21,839	128.65	17,201	4,638	149.08	14,780	7,059	169.14	13,202	8,637
16,000	109.15	23,294	137.22	18,347	4,947	159.01	15,764	7,529	180.41	14,082	9,212
17,000	115.97	24,749	145.79	19,493	5,256	168.95	16,749	8,000	191.68	14,961	9,788
18,000	122.80	26,208	154.38	20,643	5,565	178.90	17,737	8,471	202.97	15,843	10,365
19,000	129.62	27,663	162.95	21,789	5,874	188.83	18,722	8,941	214.24	16,723	10,940
20,000	136.44	29,118	171.53	22,935	6,183	198.77	19,706	9,412	225.51	17,603	11,515
21,000	143.26	30,574	180.10	24,081	6,493	208.70	20,691	9,883	236.79	18,482	12,092
22,000	150.08	32,029	188.68	25,227	6,802	218.64	21,676	10,353	248.06	19,362	12,667
23,000	156.91	33,488	197.26	26,376	7,112	228.59	22,664	10,824	259.35	20,244	13,244
24,000	163.73	34,943	205.84	27,523	7,420	238.52	23,648	11,295	270.62	21,124	13,819
25,000	170.55	36,398	214.41	28,669	7,729	248.46	24,633	11,765	281.89	22,003	14,395
26,000	177.37	37,853	222.98	29,815	8,038	258.39	25,618	12,235	293.17	22,883	14,970
27,000	184.19	39,308	231.56	30,961	8,347	268.33	26,603	12,705	304.44	23,762	15,546
28,000	191.01	40,764	240.13	32,107	8,657	278.27	27,587	13,177	315.71	24,642	16,122
29,000	197.84	42,222	248.72	33,256	8,966	288.22	28,575	13,647	327.00	25,524	16,698
30,000	204.66	43,678	257.29	34,402	9,276	298.15	29,560	14,118	338.27	26,404	17,274
32,500	221.71	47,316	278.73	37,268	10,048	322.99	32,022	15,294	366.45	28,603	18,713
35,000	238.77	50,957	300.17	40,136	10,821	347.84	34,486	16,471	394.65	30,805	20,153
40,000	272.88	58,237	343.05	45,870	12,367	397.53	39,413	18,824	451.03	35,205	23,032
45,000	306.98	65,513	385.92	51,601	13,912	447.21	44,337	21,176	507.39	39,603	25,910
50,000	341.09	72,792	428.81	57,334	15,458	496.90	49,263	23,529	563.77	44,004	28,788
55,000	375.20	80,072	471.69	63,068	17,004	546.60	54,190	25,882	620.15	48,404	31,668
60,000	409.31	87,352	514.57	68,802	18,550	596.29	59,116	28,236	676.53	52,805	34,547
65,000	443.42	94,631	557.45	74,536	20,095	645.98	64,043	30,588	732.91	57,206	37,425
70,000	477.53	101,911	600.33	80,269	21,642	695.67	68,970	32,941	789.28	61,606	40,305
75,000	511.64	109,190	643.21	86,003	23,187	745.36	73,896	35,294	845.66	66,007	43,183
80,000	545.75	116,470	686.10	91,737	24,733	795.05	78,823	37,647	902.04	70,408	46,062
85,000	579.85	123,746	728.97	97,467	26,279	844.73	83,747	39,999	958.40	74,806	48,940
90,000	613.96	131,026	771.85	103,201	27,825	894.42	88,673	42,353	1,014.78	79,206	51,820
95,000	648.07	138,305	814.73	108,935	29,370	944.12	93,600	44,705	1,071.16	83,607	54,698
100,000	682.18	145,585	857.61	114,669	30,916	993.81	98,526	47,059	1,127.54	88,008	57,577
105,000	716.29	152,864	900.49	120,402	32,462	1,043.50	103,453	49,411	1,183.92	92,408	60,456
110,000	750.40	160,144	943.38	126,136	34,008	1,093.19	108,380	51,764	1,240.30	96,809	63,335
115,000	784.51	167,424	986.26	131,870	35,554	1,142.88	113,306	54,118	1,296.68	101,210	66,214
120,000	818.62	174,703	1,029.14	137,604	37,099	1,192.57	118,233	56,470	1,353.05	105,610	69,093
125,000	852.73	181,983	1,072.02	143,337	38,646	1,242.27	123,160	58,823	1,409.43	110,011	71,972
130,000	886.83	189,259	1,114.89	149,068	40,191	1,291.94	128,083	61,176	1,465.79	114,409	74,850
135,000	920.94	196,538	1,157.77	154,802	41,736	1,341.64	133,010	63,528	1,522.17	118,809	77,729
140,000	955.05	203,818	1,200.65	160,535	43,283	1,391.33	137,937	65,881	1,578.55	123,210	80,608
145,000	989.16	211,098	1,243.54	166,269	44,829	1,441.02	142,863	68,235	1,634.93	127,611	83,487
150,000	1,023.27	218,377	1,286.42	172,003	46,374	1,490.71	147,790	70,587	1,691.31	132,011	86,366
155,000	1,057.38	225,657	1,329.30	177,737	47,920	1,540.40	152,716	72,941	1,747.69	136,412	89,245
160,000	1,091.49	232,936	1,372.18	183,470	49,466	1,590.09	157,643	75,293	1,804.07	140,813	92,123
165,000	1,125.60	240,216	1,415.06	189,204	51,012	1,639.79	162,570	77,646	1,860.45	145,213	95,003
170,000	1,159.70	247,492	1,457.93	194,935	52,557	1,689.46	167,493	79,999	1,916.81	149,611	97,881
175,000	1,193.81	254,772	1,500.81	200,668	54,104	1,739.16	172,420	82,352	1,973.19	154,012	100,760
180,000	1,227.92	262,051	1,543.70	206,402	55,649	1,788.85	177,347	84,704	2,029.56	158,412	103,639
185,000	1,262.03	269,331	1,586.58	212,136	57,195	1,838.54	182,273	87,058	2,085.94	162,813	106,518
190,000	1,296.14	276,610	1,629.46	217,869	58,740	1,888.23	187,200	89,410	2,142.32	167,214	109,396
195,000	1,330.25	283,890	1,672.34	223,603	60,287	1,937.92	192,126	91,764	2,198.70	171,614	112,276
200,000	1,364.36	291,170	1,715.22	229,337	61,833	1,987.61	197,053	94,117	2,255.08	176,015	115,155

102

GROWING EQUITY MORTGAGES 7.25%

AMOUNT OF LOAN	30 YEARS		4% PMT INCR/YR 193.363 PAYMENTS			5% PMT INCR/YR 178.446 PAYMENTS			6% PMT INCR/YR 166.503 PAYMENTS		
	MONTHLY PAYMENT	TOTAL INTRST	LAST YR MON PMT	TOTAL INTRST	INTRST SAVED	LAST YR MON PMT	TOTAL INTRST	INTRST SAVED	LAST YR MON PMT	TOTAL INTRST	INTRST SAVED
$ 50	0.35	76	0.66	43	33	0.69	40	36	0.75	37	39
100	0.69	148	1.29	82	66	1.37	77	71	1.47	72	76
200	1.37	293	2.57	162	131	2.71	151	142	2.92	141	152
300	2.05	438	3.84	242	196	4.06	225	213	4.37	210	228
400	2.73	583	5.11	322	261	5.41	299	284	5.82	280	303
500	3.42	731	6.41	404	327	6.77	375	356	7.29	352	379
600	4.10	876	7.68	484	392	8.12	449	427	8.75	421	455
700	4.78	1,021	8.95	564	457	9.46	523	498	10.20	490	531
800	5.46	1,166	10.23	644	522	10.81	597	569	11.65	559	607
900	6.14	1,310	11.50	724	586	12.16	671	639	13.10	629	681
1,000	6.83	1,459	12.79	806	653	13.52	748	711	14.57	701	758
2,000	13.65	2,914	25.57	1,610	1,304	27.03	1,493	1,421	29.11	1,399	1,515
3,000	20.47	4,369	38.34	2,413	1,956	40.53	2,238	2,131	43.66	2,097	2,272
4,000	27.29	5,824	51.11	3,217	2,607	54.03	2,983	2,841	58.21	2,795	3,029
5,000	34.11	7,280	63.89	4,020	3,260	67.54	3,728	3,552	72.75	3,493	3,787
6,000	40.94	8,738	76.68	4,826	3,912	81.06	4,475	4,263	87.32	4,194	4,544
7,000	47.76	10,194	89.45	5,630	4,564	94.56	5,220	4,974	101.87	4,892	5,302
8,000	54.58	11,649	102.23	6,434	5,215	108.06	5,965	5,684	116.42	5,590	6,059
9,000	61.40	13,104	115.00	7,237	5,867	121.57	6,710	6,394	130.96	6,288	6,816
10,000	68.22	14,559	127.77	8,041	6,518	135.07	7,455	7,104	145.51	6,986	7,573
11,000	75.04	16,014	140.55	8,844	7,170	148.57	8,200	7,814	160.05	7,684	8,330
12,000	81.87	17,473	153.34	9,650	7,823	162.10	8,948	8,525	174.62	8,385	9,088
13,000	88.69	18,928	166.11	10,454	8,474	175.60	9,693	9,235	189.17	9,083	9,845
14,000	95.51	20,384	178.89	11,257	9,127	189.10	10,438	9,946	203.72	9,781	10,603
15,000	102.33	21,839	191.66	12,061	9,778	202.61	11,183	10,656	218.26	10,479	11,360
16,000	109.15	23,294	204.44	12,864	10,430	216.11	11,928	11,366	232.81	11,177	12,117
17,000	115.97	24,749	217.21	13,668	11,081	229.61	12,673	12,076	247.36	11,875	12,874
18,000	122.80	26,208	230.00	14,474	11,734	243.14	13,420	12,788	261.92	12,576	13,632
19,000	129.62	27,663	242.78	15,278	12,385	256.64	14,165	13,498	276.47	13,274	14,389
20,000	136.44	29,118	255.55	16,081	13,037	270.14	14,910	14,208	291.02	13,972	15,146
21,000	143.26	30,574	268.32	16,885	13,689	283.65	15,655	14,919	305.56	14,670	15,904
22,000	150.08	32,029	281.10	17,688	14,341	297.15	16,400	15,629	320.11	15,368	16,661
23,000	156.91	33,488	293.89	18,494	14,994	310.67	17,146	16,340	334.68	16,069	17,419
24,000	163.73	34,943	306.66	19,298	15,645	324.17	17,893	17,050	349.22	16,767	18,176
25,000	170.55	36,398	319.44	20,101	16,297	337.68	18,638	17,760	363.77	17,465	18,933
26,000	177.37	37,853	332.21	20,905	16,948	351.18	19,383	18,470	378.32	18,163	19,690
27,000	184.19	39,308	344.98	21,709	17,599	364.68	20,128	19,180	392.86	18,861	20,447
28,000	191.01	40,764	357.76	22,512	18,252	378.19	20,873	19,891	407.41	19,559	21,205
29,000	197.84	42,222	370.55	23,318	18,904	391.71	21,621	20,601	421.98	20,260	21,962
30,000	204.66	43,678	383.32	24,122	19,556	405.21	22,366	21,312	436.53	20,958	22,720
32,500	221.71	47,316	415.26	26,131	21,185	438.97	24,228	23,088	472.89	22,703	24,613
35,000	238.77	50,957	447.21	28,142	22,815	472.75	26,093	24,864	509.28	24,451	26,506
40,000	272.88	58,237	511.10	32,162	26,075	540.28	29,821	28,416	582.03	27,944	30,293
45,000	306.98	65,513	574.97	36,180	29,333	607.80	33,546	31,967	654.77	31,434	34,077
50,000	341.09	72,792	638.86	40,200	32,592	675.33	37,273	35,519	727.52	34,927	37,865
55,000	375.20	80,072	702.74	44,221	35,851	742.87	41,001	39,071	800.27	38,420	41,652
60,000	409.31	87,352	766.63	48,241	39,111	810.41	44,728	42,624	873.03	41,913	45,439
65,000	443.42	94,631	830.52	52,261	42,370	877.94	48,456	46,175	945.78	45,406	49,225
70,000	477.53	101,911	894.40	56,281	45,630	945.48	52,184	49,727	1,018.54	48,899	53,012
75,000	511.64	109,190	958.29	60,302	48,888	1,013.01	55,911	53,279	1,091.29	52,392	56,798
80,000	545.75	116,470	1,022.18	64,322	52,148	1,080.55	59,639	56,831	1,164.05	55,885	60,585
85,000	579.85	123,746	1,086.05	68,340	55,406	1,148.06	63,364	60,382	1,236.78	59,376	64,367
90,000	613.96	131,026	1,149.94	72,360	58,666	1,215.60	67,091	63,935	1,309.53	62,869	68,157
95,000	648.07	138,305	1,213.82	76,380	61,925	1,283.13	70,819	67,486	1,382.29	66,362	71,943
100,000	682.18	145,585	1,277.71	80,401	65,184	1,350.67	74,547	71,038	1,455.04	69,854	75,731
105,000	716.29	152,864	1,341.60	84,421	68,443	1,418.21	78,274	74,590	1,527.80	73,347	79,517
110,000	750.40	160,144	1,405.49	88,441	71,703	1,485.74	82,002	78,142	1,600.55	76,840	83,304
115,000	784.51	167,424	1,469.37	92,462	74,962	1,553.28	85,729	81,695	1,673.30	80,333	87,091
120,000	818.62	174,703	1,533.26	96,482	78,221	1,620.81	89,457	85,246	1,746.06	83,826	90,877
125,000	852.73	181,983	1,597.15	100,502	81,481	1,688.35	93,185	88,798	1,818.81	87,319	94,664
130,000	886.83	189,259	1,661.02	104,520	84,739	1,755.86	96,910	92,349	1,891.54	90,810	98,449
135,000	920.94	196,538	1,724.90	108,540	87,998	1,823.40	100,637	95,901	1,964.30	94,303	102,235
140,000	955.05	203,818	1,788.79	112,560	91,258	1,890.93	104,365	99,453	2,037.05	97,796	106,022
145,000	989.16	211,098	1,852.68	116,581	94,517	1,958.47	108,092	103,005	2,109.81	101,289	109,809
150,000	1,023.27	218,377	1,916.57	120,601	97,776	2,026.00	111,820	106,557	2,182.56	104,782	113,595
155,000	1,057.38	225,657	1,980.45	124,621	101,036	2,093.54	115,548	110,109	2,255.32	108,275	117,382
160,000	1,091.49	232,936	2,044.34	128,642	104,294	2,161.08	119,275	113,661	2,328.07	111,768	121,168
165,000	1,125.60	240,216	2,108.23	132,662	107,554	2,228.61	123,003	117,213	2,400.82	115,261	124,955
170,000	1,159.70	247,492	2,172.10	136,679	110,813	2,296.13	126,728	120,764	2,473.56	118,751	128,741
175,000	1,193.81	254,772	2,235.98	140,700	114,072	2,363.66	130,455	124,317	2,546.31	122,244	132,528
180,000	1,227.92	262,051	2,299.87	144,720	117,331	2,431.20	134,183	127,868	2,619.07	125,737	136,314
185,000	1,262.03	269,331	2,363.76	148,740	120,591	2,498.73	137,911	131,420	2,691.82	129,230	140,101
190,000	1,296.14	276,610	2,427.65	152,761	123,849	2,566.27	141,638	134,972	2,764.57	132,723	143,887
195,000	1,330.25	283,890	2,491.53	156,781	127,109	2,633.80	145,366	138,524	2,837.33	136,216	147,674
200,000	1,364.36	291,170	2,555.42	160,801	130,369	2,701.34	149,093	142,077	2,910.08	139,709	151,461

GROWING EQUITY MORTGAGES

AMOUNT OF LOAN	30 YEARS		1% PMT INCR/YR 279.239 PAYMENTS			2% PMT INCR/YR 237.825 PAYMENTS			3% PMT INCR/YR 210.995 PAYMENTS		
	MONTHLY PAYMENT	TOTAL INTRST	LAST YR MON PMT	TOTAL INTRST	INTRST SAVED	LAST YR MON PMT	TOTAL INTRST	INTRST SAVED	LAST YR MON PMT	TOTAL INTRST	INTRST SAVED
$ 50	0.35	76	0.44	59	17	0.51	51	25	0.58	45	31
100	0.70	152	0.88	119	33	1.02	102	50	1.16	91	61
200	1.40	304	1.76	238	66	2.04	204	100	2.31	182	122
300	2.10	456	2.64	357	99	3.06	306	150	3.47	273	183
400	2.80	608	3.52	475	133	4.08	408	200	4.63	364	244
500	3.50	760	4.40	594	166	5.10	509	251	5.78	454	306
600	4.20	912	5.28	713	199	6.12	611	301	6.94	545	367
700	4.90	1,064	6.16	832	232	7.14	713	351	8.10	636	428
800	5.60	1,216	7.04	951	265	8.16	815	401	9.26	727	489
900	6.30	1,368	7.92	1,070	298	9.18	917	451	10.41	818	550
1,000	7.00	1,520	8.80	1,189	331	10.20	1,019	501	11.57	909	611
2,000	13.99	3,036	17.59	2,374	662	20.38	2,035	1,001	23.12	1,815	1,221
3,000	20.98	4,553	26.38	3,560	993	30.56	3,051	1,502	34.68	2,721	1,832
4,000	27.97	6,069	35.16	4,745	1,324	40.75	4,067	2,002	46.23	3,627	2,442
5,000	34.97	7,589	43.96	5,934	1,655	50.94	5,085	2,504	57.80	4,536	3,053
6,000	41.96	9,106	52.75	7,120	1,986	61.13	6,101	3,005	69.35	5,443	3,663
7,000	48.95	10,622	61.54	8,305	2,317	71.31	7,117	3,505	80.91	6,349	4,273
8,000	55.94	12,138	70.33	9,491	2,647	81.49	8,133	4,005	92.46	7,255	4,883
9,000	62.93	13,655	79.11	10,676	2,979	91.68	9,149	4,506	104.01	8,161	5,494
10,000	69.93	15,175	87.91	11,865	3,310	101.87	10,168	5,007	115.58	9,070	6,105
11,000	76.92	16,691	96.70	13,050	3,641	112.06	11,184	5,507	127.14	9,976	6,715
12,000	83.91	18,208	105.49	14,236	3,972	122.24	12,200	6,008	138.69	10,882	7,326
13,000	90.90	19,724	114.28	15,421	4,303	132.42	13,216	6,508	150.24	11,788	7,936
14,000	97.90	21,244	123.08	16,610	4,634	142.62	14,234	7,010	161.81	12,697	8,547
15,000	104.89	22,760	131.86	17,796	4,964	152.80	15,250	7,510	173.37	13,604	9,156
16,000	111.88	24,277	140.65	18,981	5,296	162.99	16,266	8,011	184.92	14,510	9,767
17,000	118.87	25,793	149.44	20,167	5,626	173.17	17,282	8,511	196.47	15,416	10,377
18,000	125.86	27,310	158.23	21,352	5,958	183.35	18,298	9,012	208.03	16,322	10,988
19,000	132.86	28,830	167.03	22,541	6,289	193.55	19,317	9,513	219.60	17,231	11,599
20,000	139.85	30,346	175.81	23,727	6,619	203.74	20,333	10,013	231.15	18,137	12,209
21,000	146.84	31,862	184.60	24,912	6,950	213.92	21,349	10,513	242.70	19,043	12,819
22,000	153.83	33,379	193.39	26,098	7,281	224.10	22,365	11,014	254.26	19,950	13,429
23,000	160.82	34,895	202.18	27,283	7,612	234.28	23,380	11,515	265.81	20,856	14,039
24,000	167.82	36,415	210.98	28,472	7,943	244.48	24,399	12,016	277.38	21,765	14,650
25,000	174.81	37,932	219.76	29,657	8,275	254.67	25,415	12,517	288.93	22,671	15,261
26,000	181.80	39,448	228.55	30,843	8,605	264.85	26,431	13,017	300.49	23,577	15,871
27,000	188.79	40,964	237.34	32,029	8,935	275.03	27,447	13,517	312.04	24,483	16,481
28,000	195.79	42,484	246.14	33,217	9,267	285.23	28,466	14,018	323.61	25,392	17,092
29,000	202.78	44,001	254.93	34,403	9,598	295.41	29,482	14,519	335.16	26,298	17,703
30,000	209.77	45,517	263.72	35,588	9,929	305.60	30,498	15,019	346.72	27,204	18,313
32,500	227.25	49,310	285.69	38,554	10,756	331.06	33,039	16,271	375.61	29,471	19,839
35,000	244.73	53,103	307.67	41,519	11,584	356.53	35,580	17,523	404.50	31,738	21,365
40,000	279.69	60,688	351.62	47,451	13,238	407.46	40,663	20,025	462.28	36,272	24,416
45,000	314.65	68,274	395.57	53,381	14,893	458.39	45,745	22,529	520.07	40,805	27,469
50,000	349.61	75,860	439.52	59,312	16,548	509.32	50,827	25,033	577.85	45,339	30,521
55,000	384.57	83,445	483.47	65,243	18,202	560.25	55,910	27,535	635.64	49,873	33,572
60,000	419.53	91,031	527.42	71,173	19,858	611.18	60,992	30,039	693.42	54,406	36,625
65,000	454.49	98,616	571.37	77,104	21,512	662.11	66,075	32,541	751.20	58,940	39,676
70,000	489.46	106,206	615.33	83,038	23,168	713.05	71,160	35,046	809.00	63,476	42,730
75,000	524.42	113,791	659.28	88,969	24,822	763.98	76,243	37,548	866.79	68,010	45,781
80,000	559.38	121,377	703.23	94,900	26,477	814.91	81,325	40,052	924.57	72,543	48,834
85,000	594.34	128,962	747.18	100,831	28,131	865.84	86,408	42,554	982.35	77,077	51,885
90,000	629.30	136,548	791.13	106,762	29,786	916.77	91,490	45,058	1,040.14	81,611	54,937
95,000	664.26	144,134	835.08	112,693	31,441	967.70	96,572	47,562	1,097.92	86,144	57,990
100,000	699.22	151,719	879.03	118,623	33,096	1,018.63	101,655	50,064	1,155.70	90,678	61,041
105,000	734.18	159,305	922.98	124,554	34,751	1,069.56	106,737	52,568	1,213.49	95,211	64,094
110,000	769.14	166,890	966.93	130,485	36,405	1,120.49	111,820	55,070	1,271.27	99,745	67,145
115,000	804.10	174,476	1,010.88	136,416	38,060	1,171.42	116,902	57,574	1,329.05	104,279	70,197
120,000	839.06	182,062	1,054.84	142,347	39,715	1,222.35	121,985	60,077	1,386.84	108,812	73,250
125,000	874.02	189,647	1,098.79	148,278	41,369	1,273.28	127,067	62,580	1,444.62	113,346	76,301
130,000	908.98	197,233	1,142.74	154,209	43,024	1,324.21	132,150	65,083	1,502.41	117,880	79,353
135,000	943.94	204,818	1,186.69	160,139	44,679	1,375.14	137,232	67,586	1,560.19	122,413	82,405
140,000	978.91	212,408	1,230.65	166,073	46,335	1,426.09	142,317	70,090	1,617.99	126,949	85,459
145,000	1,013.87	219,993	1,274.60	172,004	47,989	1,477.02	147,400	72,593	1,675.77	131,483	88,510
150,000	1,048.83	227,579	1,318.55	177,935	49,644	1,527.95	152,482	75,097	1,733.56	136,017	91,562
155,000	1,083.79	235,164	1,362.50	183,866	51,298	1,578.88	157,565	77,599	1,791.34	140,550	94,614
160,000	1,118.75	242,750	1,406.45	189,797	52,953	1,629.81	162,647	80,103	1,849.12	145,084	97,666
165,000	1,153.71	250,336	1,450.40	195,728	54,608	1,680.74	167,730	82,606	1,906.91	149,618	100,718
170,000	1,188.67	257,921	1,494.35	201,659	56,262	1,731.67	172,812	85,109	1,964.69	154,151	103,770
175,000	1,223.63	265,507	1,538.30	207,589	57,918	1,782.60	177,895	87,612	2,022.47	158,685	106,822
180,000	1,258.59	273,092	1,582.25	213,520	59,572	1,833.53	182,977	90,115	2,080.26	163,218	109,874
185,000	1,293.55	280,678	1,626.20	219,451	61,227	1,884.46	188,060	92,618	2,138.04	167,752	112,926
190,000	1,328.51	288,264	1,670.15	225,382	62,882	1,935.39	193,142	95,122	2,195.82	172,286	115,978
195,000	1,363.47	295,849	1,714.10	231,313	64,536	1,986.32	198,225	97,624	2,253.61	176,819	119,030
200,000	1,398.43	303,435	1,758.05	237,244	66,191	2,037.25	203,307	100,128	2,311.39	181,353	122,082

AMOUNT OF LOAN	30 YEARS MONTHLY PAYMENT	30 YEARS TOTAL INTRST	4% PMT INCR/YR 191.723 PAYMENTS LAST YR MON PMT	TOTAL INTRST	INTRST SAVED	5% PMT INCR/YR 176.856 PAYMENTS LAST YR MON PMT	TOTAL INTRST	INTRST SAVED	6% PMT INCR/YR 164.996 PAYMENTS LAST YR MON PMT	TOTAL INTRST	INTRST SAVED
$ 50	0.35	76	0.63	41	35	0.69	38	38	0.75	36	40
100	0.70	152	1.26	83	69	1.39	77	75	1.49	72	80
200	1.40	304	2.52	166	138	2.77	154	150	2.99	144	160
300	2.10	456	3.78	249	207	4.16	231	225	4.48	216	240
400	2.80	608	5.04	332	276	5.54	308	300	5.97	288	320
500	3.50	760	6.30	415	345	6.93	385	375	7.47	360	400
600	4.20	912	7.56	498	414	8.32	461	451	8.96	432	480
700	4.90	1,064	8.82	581	483	9.70	538	526	10.45	504	560
800	5.60	1,216	10.09	664	552	11.09	615	601	11.94	576	640
900	6.30	1,368	11.35	747	621	12.47	692	676	13.44	648	720
1,000	7.00	1,520	12.61	830	690	13.86	769	751	14.93	720	800
2,000	13.99	3,036	25.20	1,657	1,379	27.70	1,536	1,500	29.84	1,438	1,598
3,000	20.98	4,553	37.78	2,484	2,069	41.54	2,302	2,251	44.75	2,156	2,397
4,000	27.97	6,069	50.37	3,311	2,758	55.38	3,069	3,000	59.66	2,874	3,195
5,000	34.97	7,589	62.98	4,141	3,448	69.24	3,838	3,751	74.59	3,595	3,994
6,000	41.96	9,106	75.57	4,968	4,138	83.08	4,604	4,502	89.50	4,313	4,793
7,000	48.95	10,622	88.16	5,795	4,827	96.92	5,371	5,251	104.41	5,031	5,591
8,000	55.94	12,138	100.74	6,622	5,516	110.76	6,137	6,001	119.32	5,749	6,389
9,000	62.93	13,655	113.33	7,450	6,205	124.60	6,904	6,751	134.23	6,467	7,188
10,000	69.93	15,175	125.94	8,279	6,896	138.46	7,673	7,502	149.16	7,187	7,988
11,000	76.92	16,691	138.53	9,107	7,584	152.30	8,439	8,252	164.06	7,905	8,786
12,000	83.91	18,208	151.12	9,934	8,274	166.14	9,206	9,002	178.97	8,623	9,585
13,000	90.90	19,724	163.71	10,761	8,963	179.98	9,972	9,752	193.88	9,341	10,383
14,000	97.90	21,244	176.31	11,591	9,653	193.84	10,741	10,503	208.81	10,061	11,183
15,000	104.89	22,760	188.90	12,418	10,342	207.68	11,508	11,252	223.72	10,779	11,981
16,000	111.88	24,277	201.49	13,245	11,032	221.51	12,274	12,003	238.63	11,497	12,780
17,000	118.87	25,793	214.08	14,072	11,721	235.35	13,041	12,752	253.54	12,215	13,578
18,000	125.86	27,310	226.67	14,899	12,411	249.19	13,807	13,503	268.45	12,933	14,377
19,000	132.86	28,830	239.27	15,729	13,101	263.05	14,576	14,254	283.38	13,653	15,177
20,000	139.85	30,346	251.86	16,556	13,790	276.89	15,343	15,003	298.29	14,371	15,975
21,000	146.84	31,862	264.45	17,383	14,479	290.73	16,109	15,753	313.20	15,089	16,773
22,000	153.83	33,379	277.04	18,210	15,169	304.57	16,876	16,503	328.11	15,807	17,572
23,000	160.82	34,895	289.63	19,038	15,857	318.41	17,642	17,253	343.02	16,525	18,370
24,000	167.82	36,415	302.23	19,867	16,548	332.27	18,411	18,004	357.95	17,246	19,169
25,000	174.81	37,932	314.82	20,695	17,237	346.11	19,178	18,754	372.86	17,964	19,968
26,000	181.80	39,448	327.41	21,522	17,926	359.95	19,944	19,504	387.77	18,682	20,766
27,000	188.79	40,964	340.00	22,349	18,615	373.79	20,711	20,253	402.68	19,400	21,564
28,000	195.79	42,484	352.61	23,179	19,305	387.65	21,480	21,004	417.61	20,120	22,364
29,000	202.78	44,001	365.20	24,006	19,995	401.49	22,246	21,755	432.52	20,838	23,163
30,000	209.77	45,517	377.78	24,833	20,684	415.33	23,013	22,504	447.42	21,556	23,961
32,500	227.25	49,310	409.26	26,902	22,408	449.94	24,930	24,380	484.71	23,352	25,958
35,000	244.73	53,103	440.74	28,971	24,132	484.55	26,848	26,255	521.99	25,148	27,955
40,000	279.69	60,688	503.71	33,110	27,578	553.77	30,683	30,005	596.56	28,740	31,948
45,000	314.65	68,274	566.67	37,248	31,026	622.99	34,518	33,756	671.13	32,333	35,941
50,000	349.61	75,860	629.63	41,386	34,474	692.20	38,353	37,507	745.69	35,925	39,935
55,000	384.57	83,445	692.59	45,525	37,922	761.42	42,188	41,257	820.26	39,517	43,928
60,000	419.53	91,031	755.55	49,663	41,368	830.64	46,023	45,008	894.83	43,109	47,922
65,000	454.49	98,616	818.51	53,802	44,814	899.86	49,858	48,758	969.39	46,702	51,914
70,000	489.46	106,206	881.49	57,943	48,263	969.10	53,695	52,511	1,043.98	50,296	55,910
75,000	524.42	113,791	944.45	62,081	51,710	1,038.32	57,530	56,261	1,118.55	53,889	59,902
80,000	559.38	121,377	1,007.41	66,219	55,158	1,107.53	61,365	60,012	1,193.12	57,481	63,896
85,000	594.34	128,962	1,070.37	70,358	58,604	1,176.75	65,200	63,762	1,267.68	61,073	67,889
90,000	629.30	136,548	1,133.33	74,496	62,052	1,245.97	69,035	67,513	1,342.25	64,665	71,883
95,000	664.26	144,134	1,196.29	78,635	65,499	1,315.19	72,870	71,264	1,416.82	68,257	75,877
100,000	699.22	151,719	1,259.26	82,773	68,946	1,384.41	76,705	75,014	1,491.39	71,850	79,869
105,000	734.18	159,305	1,322.22	86,911	72,394	1,453.63	80,540	78,765	1,565.95	75,442	83,863
110,000	769.14	166,890	1,385.18	91,050	75,840	1,522.84	84,375	82,515	1,640.52	79,034	87,856
115,000	804.10	174,476	1,448.14	95,188	79,288	1,592.06	88,210	86,266	1,715.09	82,626	91,850
120,000	839.06	182,062	1,511.10	99,327	82,735	1,661.28	92,045	90,017	1,789.65	86,219	95,843
125,000	874.02	189,647	1,574.06	103,465	86,182	1,730.50	95,880	93,767	1,864.22	89,811	99,836
130,000	908.98	197,233	1,637.02	107,603	89,630	1,799.72	99,715	97,518	1,938.79	93,403	103,830
135,000	943.94	204,818	1,699.98	111,742	93,076	1,868.94	103,550	101,268	2,013.36	96,995	107,823
140,000	978.91	212,408	1,762.96	115,883	96,525	1,938.17	107,388	105,020	2,087.94	100,590	111,818
145,000	1,013.87	219,993	1,825.92	120,021	99,972	2,007.39	111,223	108,770	2,162.51	104,182	115,811
150,000	1,048.83	227,579	1,888.88	124,159	103,420	2,076.61	115,058	112,521	2,237.08	107,775	119,804
155,000	1,083.79	235,164	1,951.84	128,298	106,866	2,145.83	118,893	116,271	2,311.65	111,367	123,797
160,000	1,118.75	242,750	2,014.81	132,436	110,314	2,215.05	122,728	120,022	2,386.21	114,959	127,791
165,000	1,153.71	250,336	2,077.77	136,575	113,761	2,284.27	126,563	123,773	2,460.78	118,551	131,785
170,000	1,188.67	257,921	2,140.73	140,713	117,208	2,353.49	130,398	127,523	2,535.35	122,144	135,777
175,000	1,223.63	265,507	2,203.69	144,851	120,656	2,422.70	134,233	131,274	2,609.92	125,736	139,771
180,000	1,258.59	273,092	2,266.65	148,990	124,102	2,491.92	138,068	135,024	2,684.48	129,328	143,764
185,000	1,293.55	280,678	2,329.61	153,128	127,550	2,561.14	141,903	138,775	2,759.05	132,920	147,758
190,000	1,328.51	288,264	2,392.57	157,267	130,997	2,630.36	145,738	142,526	2,833.62	136,513	151,751
195,000	1,363.47	295,849	2,455.53	161,405	134,444	2,699.58	149,573	146,276	2,908.18	140,105	155,744
200,000	1,398.43	303,435	2,518.49	165,543	137,892	2,768.80	153,408	150,027	2,982.75	143,697	159,738

105

7.75% GROWING EQUITY MORTGAGES

AMOUNT OF LOAN	30 YEARS MONTHLY PAYMENT	30 YEARS TOTAL INTRST	1% PMT INCR/YR 277.618 PAYMENTS LAST YR MON PMT	TOTAL INTRST	INTRST SAVED	2% PMT INCR/YR 236.028 PAYMENTS LAST YR MON PMT	TOTAL INTRST	INTRST SAVED	3% PMT INCR/YR 209.255 PAYMENTS LAST YR MON PMT	TOTAL INTRST	INTRST SAVED
$ 50	0.36	80	0.45	62	18	0.52	53	27	0.60	47	33
100	0.72	159	0.91	124	35	1.05	106	53	1.19	94	65
200	1.44	318	1.81	247	71	2.10	212	106	2.38	189	129
300	2.15	474	2.70	368	106	3.13	314	160	3.55	280	194
400	2.87	633	3.61	492	141	4.18	420	213	4.74	374	259
500	3.59	792	4.51	615	177	5.23	526	266	5.93	469	323
600	4.30	948	5.41	736	212	6.26	629	319	7.11	560	388
700	5.02	1,107	6.31	859	248	7.31	735	372	8.30	655	452
800	5.74	1,266	7.22	983	283	8.36	840	426	9.49	749	517
900	6.45	1,422	8.11	1,104	318	9.40	943	479	10.66	840	582
1,000	7.17	1,581	9.01	1,227	354	10.45	1,049	532	11.85	935	646
2,000	14.33	3,159	18.02	2,451	708	20.88	2,095	1,064	23.69	1,867	1,292
3,000	21.50	4,740	27.03	3,679	1,061	31.32	3,144	1,596	35.54	2,801	1,939
4,000	28.66	6,318	36.03	4,903	1,415	41.75	4,191	2,127	47.37	3,733	2,585
5,000	35.83	7,899	45.04	6,130	1,769	52.20	5,240	2,659	59.22	4,668	3,231
6,000	42.99	9,476	54.05	7,354	2,122	62.63	6,286	3,190	71.06	5,600	3,876
7,000	50.15	11,054	63.05	8,578	2,476	73.06	7,332	3,722	82.89	6,532	4,522
8,000	57.32	12,635	72.06	9,805	2,830	83.50	8,381	4,254	94.74	7,466	5,169
9,000	64.48	14,213	81.06	11,029	3,184	93.94	9,427	4,786	106.58	8,398	5,815
10,000	71.65	15,794	90.08	12,257	3,537	104.38	10,476	5,318	118.43	9,333	6,461
11,000	78.81	17,372	99.08	13,481	3,891	114.81	11,522	5,850	130.26	10,265	7,107
12,000	85.97	18,949	108.08	14,705	4,244	125.24	12,569	6,380	142.10	11,197	7,752
13,000	93.14	20,530	117.09	15,932	4,598	135.69	13,618	6,912	153.95	12,131	8,399
14,000	100.30	22,108	126.09	17,156	4,952	146.12	14,664	7,444	165.78	13,063	9,045
15,000	107.47	23,689	135.11	18,383	5,306	156.56	15,713	7,976	177.63	13,998	9,691
16,000	114.63	25,267	144.11	19,607	5,660	166.99	16,759	8,508	189.47	14,930	10,337
17,000	121.80	26,848	153.12	20,835	6,013	177.44	17,808	9,040	201.32	15,865	10,983
18,000	128.96	28,426	162.12	22,059	6,367	187.87	18,854	9,572	213.15	16,797	11,629
19,000	136.12	30,003	171.13	23,283	6,720	198.30	19,901	10,102	224.99	17,729	12,274
20,000	143.29	31,584	180.14	24,510	7,074	208.75	20,950	10,634	236.84	18,663	12,921
21,000	150.45	33,162	189.14	25,734	7,428	219.18	21,996	11,166	248.67	19,595	13,567
22,000	157.62	34,743	198.15	26,961	7,782	229.62	23,045	11,698	260.52	20,530	14,213
23,000	164.78	36,321	207.16	28,186	8,135	240.05	24,091	12,230	272.36	21,462	14,859
24,000	171.94	37,898	216.16	29,410	8,488	250.48	25,137	12,761	284.19	22,394	15,504
25,000	179.11	39,480	225.17	30,637	8,843	260.93	26,186	13,294	296.04	23,328	16,152
26,000	186.27	41,057	234.17	31,861	9,196	271.36	27,233	13,824	307.88	24,260	16,797
27,000	193.44	42,638	243.19	33,088	9,550	281.81	28,282	14,356	319.73	25,195	17,443
28,000	200.60	44,216	252.19	34,312	9,904	292.24	29,328	14,888	331.56	26,127	18,089
29,000	207.76	45,794	261.19	35,536	10,258	302.67	30,374	15,420	343.40	27,059	18,735
30,000	214.93	47,375	270.20	36,764	10,611	313.11	31,423	15,952	355.25	27,993	19,382
32,500	232.84	51,322	292.72	39,827	11,495	339.20	34,041	17,281	384.85	30,326	20,996
35,000	250.75	55,270	315.23	42,890	12,380	365.30	36,660	18,610	414.45	32,659	22,611
40,000	286.57	63,165	360.27	49,017	14,148	417.48	41,897	21,268	473.66	37,324	25,841
45,000	322.39	71,060	405.30	55,144	15,916	469.66	47,133	23,927	532.86	41,989	29,071
50,000	358.21	78,956	450.33	61,271	17,685	521.84	52,370	26,586	592.07	46,654	32,302
55,000	394.03	86,851	495.36	67,397	19,454	574.03	57,607	29,244	651.27	51,319	35,532
60,000	429.85	94,746	540.39	73,524	21,222	626.21	62,843	31,903	710.48	55,984	38,762
65,000	465.67	102,641	585.42	79,651	22,990	678.39	68,080	34,561	769.68	60,649	41,992
70,000	501.49	110,536	630.45	85,778	24,758	730.58	73,317	37,219	828.89	65,314	45,222
75,000	537.31	118,432	675.49	91,904	26,528	782.76	78,554	39,878	888.09	69,980	48,452
80,000	573.13	126,327	720.52	98,031	28,296	834.94	83,790	42,537	947.30	74,645	51,682
85,000	608.96	134,226	765.56	104,161	30,065	887.14	89,030	45,196	1,006.52	79,312	54,914
90,000	644.78	142,121	810.59	110,288	31,833	939.32	94,267	47,854	1,065.72	83,978	58,143
95,000	680.60	150,016	855.63	116,415	33,601	991.51	99,503	50,513	1,124.93	88,643	61,373
100,000	716.42	157,911	900.66	122,541	35,370	1,043.69	104,740	53,171	1,184.13	93,308	64,603
105,000	752.24	165,806	945.69	128,668	37,138	1,095.87	109,977	55,829	1,243.34	97,973	67,833
110,000	788.06	173,702	990.72	134,795	38,907	1,148.05	115,213	58,489	1,302.54	102,638	71,064
115,000	823.88	181,597	1,035.75	140,922	40,675	1,200.24	120,450	61,147	1,361.75	107,303	74,294
120,000	859.70	189,492	1,080.78	147,048	42,444	1,252.42	125,687	63,805	1,420.95	111,968	77,524
125,000	895.52	197,387	1,125.81	153,175	44,212	1,304.60	130,923	66,464	1,480.16	116,633	80,754
130,000	931.34	205,282	1,170.85	159,302	45,980	1,356.79	136,160	69,122	1,539.36	121,299	83,983
135,000	967.16	213,178	1,215.88	165,429	47,749	1,408.97	141,397	71,781	1,598.57	125,964	87,214
140,000	1,002.98	221,073	1,260.91	171,555	49,518	1,461.15	146,634	74,439	1,657.77	130,629	90,444
145,000	1,038.80	228,968	1,305.94	177,682	51,286	1,513.34	151,870	77,098	1,716.98	135,294	93,674
150,000	1,074.62	236,863	1,350.97	183,809	53,054	1,565.52	157,107	79,756	1,776.18	139,959	96,904
155,000	1,110.44	244,758	1,396.00	189,936	54,822	1,617.70	162,344	82,414	1,835.39	144,624	100,134
160,000	1,146.26	252,654	1,441.04	196,062	56,590	1,669.88	167,580	85,074	1,894.59	149,289	103,365
165,000	1,182.09	260,552	1,486.08	202,192	58,360	1,722.08	172,820	87,732	1,953.81	153,957	106,595
170,000	1,217.91	268,448	1,531.11	208,319	60,129	1,774.26	178,057	90,391	2,013.02	158,622	109,826
175,000	1,253.73	276,343	1,576.14	214,446	61,897	1,826.45	183,293	93,050	2,072.22	163,287	113,056
180,000	1,289.55	284,238	1,621.17	220,573	63,665	1,878.63	188,530	95,708	2,131.43	167,953	116,285
185,000	1,325.37	292,133	1,666.21	226,699	65,434	1,930.81	193,767	98,366	2,190.63	172,618	119,515
190,000	1,361.19	300,028	1,711.24	232,826	67,202	1,983.00	199,004	101,024	2,249.84	177,283	122,745
195,000	1,397.01	307,924	1,756.27	238,953	68,971	2,035.18	204,240	103,684	2,309.04	181,948	125,976
200,000	1,432.83	315,819	1,801.30	245,080	70,739	2,087.36	209,477	106,342	2,368.25	186,613	129,206

106

GROWING EQUITY MORTGAGES 7.75%

AMOUNT OF LOAN	30 YEARS		4% PMT INCR/YR 190.046 PAYMENTS			5% PMT INCR/YR 175.288 PAYMENTS			6% PMT INCR/YR 163.514 PAYMENTS		
	MONTHLY PAYMENT	TOTAL INTRST	LAST YR MON PMT	TOTAL INTRST	INTRST SAVED	LAST YR MON PMT	TOTAL INTRST	INTRST SAVED	LAST YR MON PMT	TOTAL INTRST	INTRST SAVED
$ 50	0.36	80	0.65	43	37	0.71	40	40	0.77	37	43
100	0.72	159	1.30	86	73	1.43	80	79	1.54	75	84
200	1.44	318	2.59	172	146	2.85	159	159	3.07	149	169
300	2.15	474	3.87	256	218	4.26	237	237	4.59	222	252
400	2.87	633	5.17	342	291	5.68	316	317	6.12	296	337
500	3.59	792	6.47	428	364	7.11	396	396	7.66	371	421
600	4.30	948	7.74	511	437	8.51	473	475	9.17	443	505
700	5.02	1,107	9.04	597	510	9.94	553	554	10.71	518	589
800	5.74	1,266	10.34	683	583	11.36	633	633	12.24	593	673
900	6.45	1,422	11.62	767	655	12.77	710	712	13.76	665	757
1,000	7.17	1,581	12.91	853	728	14.20	790	791	15.29	740	841
2,000	14.33	3,159	25.81	1,703	1,456	28.37	1,577	1,582	30.56	1,477	1,682
3,000	21.50	4,740	38.72	2,555	2,185	42.57	2,367	2,373	45.86	2,216	2,524
4,000	28.66	6,318	51.62	3,405	2,913	56.74	3,154	3,164	61.13	2,953	3,365
5,000	35.83	7,899	64.53	4,258	3,641	70.94	3,944	3,955	76.42	3,693	4,206
6,000	42.99	9,476	77.42	5,108	4,368	85.12	4,731	4,745	91.69	4,430	5,046
7,000	50.15	11,054	90.32	5,958	5,096	99.29	5,518	5,536	106.97	5,167	5,887
8,000	57.32	12,635	103.23	6,810	5,825	113.49	6,308	6,327	122.26	5,907	6,728
9,000	64.48	14,213	116.12	7,660	6,553	127.67	7,095	7,118	137.53	6,644	7,569
10,000	71.65	15,794	129.04	8,513	7,281	141.86	7,885	7,909	152.82	7,383	8,411
11,000	78.81	17,372	141.93	9,363	8,009	156.04	8,672	8,700	168.10	8,120	9,252
12,000	85.97	18,949	154.83	10,213	8,736	170.21	9,459	9,490	183.37	8,857	10,092
13,000	93.14	20,530	167.74	11,065	9,465	184.41	10,249	10,281	198.66	9,597	10,933
14,000	100.30	22,108	180.63	11,915	10,193	198.59	11,036	11,072	213.93	10,334	11,774
15,000	107.47	23,689	193.55	12,768	10,921	212.78	11,826	11,863	229.23	11,074	12,615
16,000	114.63	25,267	206.44	13,618	11,649	226.96	12,613	12,654	244.50	11,811	13,456
17,000	121.80	26,848	219.35	14,470	12,378	241.16	13,403	13,445	259.79	12,550	14,298
18,000	128.96	28,426	232.25	15,320	13,106	255.33	14,190	14,236	275.06	13,287	15,139
19,000	136.12	30,003	245.14	16,170	13,833	269.51	14,977	15,026	290.33	14,024	15,979
20,000	143.29	31,584	258.06	17,023	14,561	283.70	15,767	15,817	305.63	14,764	16,820
21,000	150.45	33,162	270.95	17,873	15,289	297.88	16,554	16,608	320.90	15,501	17,661
22,000	157.62	34,743	283.86	18,725	16,018	312.08	17,344	17,399	336.19	16,241	18,502
23,000	164.78	36,321	296.76	19,575	16,746	326.25	18,131	18,190	351.46	16,978	19,343
24,000	171.94	37,898	309.65	20,425	17,473	340.43	18,919	18,979	366.74	17,715	20,183
25,000	179.11	39,480	322.57	21,278	18,202	354.63	19,708	19,772	382.03	18,454	21,026
26,000	186.27	41,057	335.46	22,128	18,929	368.80	20,495	20,562	397.30	19,191	21,866
27,000	193.44	42,638	348.37	22,980	19,658	383.00	21,285	21,353	412.59	19,931	22,707
28,000	200.60	44,216	361.27	23,830	20,386	397.17	22,072	22,144	427.87	20,668	23,548
29,000	207.76	45,794	374.16	24,680	21,114	411.35	22,860	22,934	443.14	21,405	24,389
30,000	214.93	47,375	387.08	25,533	21,842	425.55	23,649	23,726	458.43	22,145	25,230
32,500	232.84	51,322	419.33	27,660	23,662	461.01	25,620	25,702	496.63	23,990	27,332
35,000	250.75	55,270	451.59	29,788	25,482	496.47	27,591	27,679	534.83	25,835	29,435
40,000	286.57	63,165	516.10	34,043	29,122	567.39	31,533	31,633	611.23	29,525	33,640
45,000	322.39	71,060	580.61	38,298	32,762	638.31	35,473	35,587	687.63	33,216	37,844
50,000	358.21	78,956	645.12	42,553	36,403	709.23	39,414	39,542	764.04	36,906	42,050
55,000	394.03	86,851	709.63	46,808	40,043	780.15	43,355	43,496	840.44	40,597	46,254
60,000	429.85	94,746	774.14	51,063	43,683	851.07	47,296	47,450	916.84	44,287	50,459
65,000	465.67	102,641	838.65	55,318	47,323	921.99	51,237	51,404	993.24	47,977	54,664
70,000	501.49	110,536	903.16	59,573	50,963	992.92	55,179	55,357	1,069.64	51,668	58,868
75,000	537.31	118,432	967.66	63,828	54,604	1,063.84	59,120	59,312	1,146.04	55,358	63,074
80,000	573.13	126,327	1,032.17	68,083	58,244	1,134.76	63,061	63,266	1,222.45	59,048	67,279
85,000	608.96	134,226	1,096.70	72,340	61,886	1,205.70	67,005	67,221	1,298.87	62,741	71,485
90,000	644.78	142,121	1,161.21	76,595	65,526	1,276.62	70,946	71,175	1,375.27	66,432	75,689
95,000	680.60	150,016	1,225.72	80,850	69,166	1,347.54	74,887	75,129	1,451.67	70,122	79,894
100,000	716.42	157,911	1,290.23	85,105	72,806	1,418.46	78,828	79,083	1,528.07	73,812	84,099
105,000	752.24	165,806	1,354.74	89,360	76,446	1,489.38	82,769	83,037	1,604.47	77,503	88,303
110,000	788.06	173,702	1,419.25	93,615	80,087	1,560.30	86,710	86,992	1,680.88	81,193	92,509
115,000	823.88	181,597	1,483.76	97,870	83,727	1,631.23	90,651	90,946	1,757.28	84,884	96,713
120,000	859.70	189,492	1,548.27	102,125	87,367	1,702.15	94,593	94,899	1,833.68	88,574	100,918
125,000	895.52	197,387	1,612.78	106,380	91,007	1,773.07	98,534	98,853	1,910.08	92,264	105,123
130,000	931.34	205,282	1,677.29	110,635	94,647	1,843.99	102,475	102,807	1,986.48	95,955	109,327
135,000	967.16	213,178	1,741.80	114,890	98,288	1,914.91	106,416	106,762	2,062.88	99,645	113,533
140,000	1,002.98	221,073	1,806.31	119,145	101,928	1,985.83	110,357	110,716	2,139.28	103,335	117,738
145,000	1,038.80	228,968	1,870.82	123,400	105,568	2,056.75	114,298	114,670	2,215.69	107,026	121,942
150,000	1,074.62	236,863	1,935.33	127,655	109,208	2,127.67	118,239	118,624	2,292.09	110,716	126,147
155,000	1,110.44	244,758	1,999.84	131,910	112,848	2,198.60	122,181	122,577	2,368.49	114,407	130,351
160,000	1,146.26	252,654	2,064.35	136,165	116,489	2,269.52	126,532	126,532	2,444.89	118,097	134,557
165,000	1,182.09	260,552	2,128.88	140,423	120,129	2,340.46	130,065	130,487	2,521.31	121,790	138,762
170,000	1,217.91	268,448	2,193.39	144,678	123,770	2,411.38	134,007	134,441	2,597.71	125,480	142,968
175,000	1,253.73	276,343	2,257.90	148,933	127,410	2,482.30	137,948	138,395	2,674.12	129,171	147,172
180,000	1,289.55	284,238	2,322.41	153,188	131,050	2,553.22	141,889	142,349	2,750.52	132,861	151,377
185,000	1,325.37	292,133	2,386.92	157,443	134,690	2,624.14	145,830	146,303	2,826.92	136,551	155,582
190,000	1,361.19	300,028	2,451.43	161,698	138,330	2,695.06	149,771	150,257	2,903.32	140,242	159,786
195,000	1,397.01	307,924	2,515.94	165,953	141,971	2,765.98	153,712	154,212	2,979.72	143,932	163,992
200,000	1,432.83	315,819	2,580.45	170,208	145,611	2,836.91	157,653	158,166	3,056.12	147,622	168,197

107

8.00% GROWING EQUITY MORTGAGES

AMOUNT OF LOAN	30 YEARS MONTHLY PAYMENT	30 YEARS TOTAL INTRST	1% PMT INCR/YR 275.977 PAYMENTS LAST YR MON PMT	TOTAL INTRST	INTRST SAVED	2% PMT INCR/YR 234.232 PAYMENTS LAST YR MON PMT	TOTAL INTRST	INTRST SAVED	3% PMT INCR/YR 207.527 PAYMENTS LAST YR MON PMT	TOTAL INTRST	INTRST SAVED
$ 50	0.37	83	0.46	64	19	0.54	55	28	0.61	49	34
100	0.74	166	0.92	128	38	1.08	110	56	1.22	98	68
200	1.47	329	1.83	254	75	2.14	216	113	2.43	192	137
300	2.21	496	2.75	382	114	3.22	326	170	3.65	290	206
400	2.94	658	3.66	507	151	4.28	433	225	4.86	385	273
500	3.67	821	4.57	632	189	5.35	539	282	6.07	480	341
600	4.41	988	5.49	761	227	6.42	649	339	7.29	577	411
700	5.14	1,150	6.40	886	264	7.49	755	395	8.50	672	478
800	5.88	1,317	7.32	1,014	303	8.57	865	452	9.72	770	547
900	6.61	1,480	8.23	1,140	340	9.63	972	508	10.93	865	615
1,000	7.34	1,642	9.14	1,265	377	10.69	1,078	564	12.13	960	682
2,000	14.68	3,285	18.27	2,530	755	21.39	2,157	1,128	24.26	1,919	1,366
3,000	22.02	4,927	27.41	3,795	1,132	32.08	3,235	1,692	36.40	2,879	2,048
4,000	29.36	6,570	36.54	5,060	1,510	42.77	4,314	2,256	48.53	3,838	2,732
5,000	36.69	8,208	45.67	6,321	1,887	53.45	5,389	2,819	60.64	4,795	3,413
6,000	44.03	9,851	54.80	7,586	2,265	64.14	6,468	3,383	72.77	5,755	4,096
7,000	51.37	11,493	63.94	8,851	2,642	74.84	7,546	3,947	84.91	6,714	4,779
8,000	58.71	13,136	73.08	10,116	3,020	85.53	8,625	4,511	97.04	7,674	5,462
9,000	66.04	14,774	82.20	11,378	3,396	96.21	9,700	5,074	109.15	8,631	6,143
10,000	73.38	16,417	91.34	12,643	3,774	106.90	10,779	5,638	121.29	9,590	6,827
11,000	80.72	18,059	100.47	13,908	4,151	117.59	11,857	6,202	133.42	10,550	7,509
12,000	88.06	19,702	109.61	15,172	4,530	128.29	12,936	6,766	145.55	11,509	8,193
13,000	95.39	21,340	118.73	16,434	4,906	138.97	14,011	7,329	157.67	12,466	8,874
14,000	102.73	22,983	127.87	17,699	5,284	149.66	15,090	7,893	169.80	13,426	9,557
15,000	110.07	24,625	137.01	18,964	5,661	160.35	16,168	8,457	181.93	14,385	10,240
16,000	117.41	26,268	146.14	20,229	6,039	171.04	17,246	9,022	194.06	15,345	10,923
17,000	124.74	27,906	155.27	21,491	6,415	181.72	18,322	9,584	206.18	16,302	11,604
18,000	132.08	29,549	164.40	22,756	6,793	192.42	19,401	10,148	218.31	17,261	12,288
19,000	139.42	31,191	173.54	24,020	7,171	203.11	20,479	10,712	230.44	18,221	12,970
20,000	146.76	32,834	182.67	25,285	7,549	213.80	21,557	11,277	242.57	19,180	13,654
21,000	154.10	34,476	191.81	26,550	7,926	224.49	22,636	11,840	254.70	20,140	14,336
22,000	161.43	36,115	200.93	27,812	8,303	235.17	23,711	12,404	266.82	21,097	15,018
23,000	168.77	37,757	210.07	29,077	8,680	245.87	24,790	12,967	278.95	22,056	15,701
24,000	176.11	39,400	219.21	30,342	9,058	256.56	25,868	13,532	291.08	23,016	16,384
25,000	183.45	41,042	228.34	31,607	9,435	267.25	26,947	14,095	303.21	23,975	17,067
26,000	190.78	42,681	237.47	32,868	9,813	277.93	28,022	14,659	315.33	24,932	17,749
27,000	198.12	44,323	246.60	34,133	10,190	288.62	29,101	15,222	327.46	25,892	18,431
28,000	205.46	45,966	255.74	35,398	10,568	299.32	30,179	15,787	339.59	26,851	19,115
29,000	212.80	47,608	264.88	36,663	10,945	310.01	31,258	16,350	351.73	27,811	19,797
30,000	220.13	49,247	274.00	37,925	11,322	320.69	32,333	16,914	363.84	28,768	20,479
32,500	238.48	53,353	296.84	41,087	12,266	347.42	35,029	18,324	394.17	31,167	22,186
35,000	256.82	57,455	319.67	44,246	13,209	374.14	37,723	19,732	424.48	33,563	23,892
40,000	293.51	65,664	365.34	50,567	15,097	427.59	43,112	22,552	485.13	38,358	27,306
45,000	330.20	73,872	411.01	56,889	16,983	481.04	48,501	25,371	545.77	43,153	30,719
50,000	366.89	82,080	456.67	63,210	18,870	534.49	53,891	28,189	606.41	47,948	34,132
55,000	403.58	90,289	502.34	69,531	20,758	587.94	59,280	31,009	667.06	52,743	37,546
60,000	440.26	98,494	548.00	75,850	22,644	641.38	64,666	33,828	727.68	57,536	40,958
65,000	476.95	106,702	593.67	82,171	24,531	694.83	70,056	36,646	788.33	62,331	44,371
70,000	513.64	114,910	639.34	88,492	26,418	748.28	75,445	39,465	848.97	67,126	47,784
75,000	550.33	123,119	685.00	94,814	28,305	801.73	80,834	42,285	909.61	71,921	51,198
80,000	587.02	131,327	730.67	101,135	30,192	855.18	86,224	45,103	970.25	76,716	54,611
85,000	623.70	139,532	776.33	107,453	32,079	908.61	91,610	47,922	1,030.88	81,508	58,024
90,000	660.39	147,740	822.00	113,775	33,965	962.06	97,000	50,740	1,091.52	86,303	61,437
95,000	697.08	155,949	867.67	120,096	35,853	1,015.51	102,389	53,560	1,152.17	91,099	64,850
100,000	733.77	164,157	913.34	126,417	37,740	1,068.96	107,778	56,379	1,212.81	95,894	68,263
105,000	770.46	172,366	959.00	132,739	39,627	1,122.41	113,168	59,198	1,273.45	100,689	71,677
110,000	807.15	180,574	1,004.67	139,060	41,514	1,175.87	118,557	62,017	1,334.10	105,484	75,090
115,000	843.83	188,779	1,050.33	145,378	43,401	1,229.30	123,944	64,835	1,394.72	110,276	78,503
120,000	880.52	196,987	1,096.00	151,699	45,288	1,282.75	129,333	67,654	1,455.37	115,071	81,916
125,000	917.21	205,196	1,141.67	158,021	47,175	1,336.20	134,722	70,474	1,516.01	119,866	85,330
130,000	953.90	213,404	1,187.33	164,342	49,062	1,389.65	140,112	73,292	1,576.65	124,661	88,743
135,000	990.59	221,612	1,233.00	170,663	50,949	1,443.10	145,501	76,111	1,637.29	129,456	92,156
140,000	1,027.28	229,821	1,278.67	176,985	52,836	1,496.55	150,890	78,931	1,697.94	134,252	95,569
145,000	1,063.96	238,026	1,324.33	183,303	54,723	1,549.99	156,277	81,749	1,758.56	139,044	98,982
150,000	1,100.65	246,234	1,370.00	189,624	56,610	1,603.44	161,666	84,568	1,819.21	143,839	102,395
155,000	1,137.34	254,442	1,415.67	195,946	58,496	1,656.89	167,056	87,386	1,879.85	148,634	105,808
160,000	1,174.03	262,651	1,461.33	202,267	60,384	1,710.34	172,445	90,206	1,940.49	153,429	109,222
165,000	1,210.72	270,859	1,507.00	208,588	62,271	1,763.79	177,834	93,025	2,001.14	158,224	112,635
170,000	1,247.40	279,064	1,552.66	214,906	64,158	1,817.23	183,221	95,843	2,061.76	163,017	116,047
175,000	1,284.09	287,272	1,598.33	221,228	66,044	1,870.68	188,610	98,662	2,122.41	167,812	119,460
180,000	1,320.78	295,481	1,644.00	227,549	67,932	1,924.13	193,999	101,482	2,183.05	172,607	122,874
185,000	1,357.47	303,689	1,689.66	233,870	69,819	1,977.58	199,389	104,300	2,243.69	177,402	126,287
190,000	1,394.16	311,898	1,735.33	240,192	71,706	2,031.03	204,777	107,120	2,304.33	182,197	129,701
195,000	1,430.85	320,106	1,781.00	246,513	73,593	2,084.48	210,167	109,939	2,364.98	186,992	133,114
200,000	1,467.53	328,311	1,826.66	252,831	75,480	2,137.91	215,554	112,757	2,425.60	191,784	136,527

GROWING EQUITY MORTGAGES 8.00%

AMOUNT OF LOAN	30 YEARS MONTHLY PAYMENT	30 YEARS TOTAL INTRST	4% PMT INCR/YR 188.388 PAYMENTS LAST YR MON PMT	4% TOTAL INTRST	4% INTRST SAVED	5% PMT INCR/YR 173.741 PAYMENTS LAST YR MON PMT	5% TOTAL INTRST	5% INTRST SAVED	6% PMT INCR/YR 162.054 PAYMENTS LAST YR MON PMT	6% TOTAL INTRST	6% INTRST SAVED
$ 50	0.37	83	0.67	44	39	0.73	41	42	0.79	39	44
100	0.74	166	1.33	89	77	1.47	82	84	1.58	77	89
200	1.47	329	2.65	175	154	2.91	162	167	3.14	152	177
300	2.21	496	3.98	264	232	4.38	245	251	4.71	229	267
400	2.94	658	5.29	351	307	5.82	325	333	6.27	304	354
500	3.67	821	6.61	437	384	7.27	405	416	7.83	379	442
600	4.41	988	7.94	526	462	8.73	487	501	9.41	456	532
700	5.14	1,150	9.26	613	537	10.18	567	583	10.96	531	619
800	5.88	1,317	10.59	702	615	11.64	650	667	12.54	608	709
900	6.61	1,480	11.90	788	692	13.09	730	750	14.10	683	797
1,000	7.34	1,642	13.22	875	767	14.53	810	832	15.66	758	884
2,000	14.68	3,285	26.44	1,749	1,536	29.07	1,619	1,666	31.31	1,516	1,769
3,000	22.02	4,927	39.66	2,624	2,303	43.60	2,429	2,498	46.97	2,274	2,653
4,000	29.36	6,570	52.88	3,498	3,072	58.13	3,239	3,331	62.62	3,032	3,538
5,000	36.69	8,208	66.08	4,370	3,838	72.64	4,046	4,162	78.26	3,787	4,421
6,000	44.03	9,851	79.30	5,245	4,606	87.18	4,856	4,995	93.91	4,545	5,306
7,000	51.37	11,493	92.51	6,119	5,374	101.71	5,665	5,828	109.57	5,303	6,190
8,000	58.71	13,136	105.73	6,994	6,142	116.24	6,475	6,661	125.22	6,061	7,075
9,000	66.04	14,774	118.93	7,866	6,908	130.75	7,282	7,492	140.86	6,816	7,958
10,000	73.38	16,417	132.15	8,740	7,677	145.29	8,092	8,325	156.51	7,574	8,843
11,000	80.72	18,059	145.37	9,615	8,444	159.82	8,902	9,157	172.17	8,332	9,727
12,000	88.06	19,702	158.59	10,490	9,212	174.35	9,711	9,991	187.83	9,090	10,612
13,000	95.39	21,340	171.79	11,362	9,978	188.87	10,518	10,822	203.46	9,846	11,494
14,000	102.73	22,983	185.01	12,236	10,747	203.40	11,328	11,655	219.12	10,604	12,379
15,000	110.07	24,625	198.23	13,111	11,514	217.93	12,138	12,487	234.77	11,362	13,263
16,000	117.41	26,268	211.45	13,985	12,283	232.46	12,947	13,321	250.43	12,120	14,148
17,000	124.74	27,906	224.65	14,857	13,049	246.98	13,755	14,151	266.06	12,875	15,031
18,000	132.08	29,549	237.87	15,732	13,817	261.51	14,564	14,985	281.72	13,633	15,916
19,000	139.42	31,191	251.09	16,606	14,585	276.04	15,374	15,817	297.37	14,391	16,800
20,000	146.76	32,834	264.31	17,481	15,353	290.57	16,184	16,650	313.03	15,149	17,685
21,000	154.10	34,476	277.53	18,356	16,120	305.11	16,993	17,483	328.68	15,907	18,569
22,000	161.43	36,115	290.73	19,228	16,887	319.62	17,801	18,314	344.32	16,662	19,453
23,000	168.77	37,757	303.95	20,102	17,655	334.15	18,610	19,147	359.97	17,420	20,337
24,000	176.11	39,400	317.16	20,977	18,423	348.69	19,420	19,980	375.63	18,178	21,222
25,000	183.45	41,042	330.38	21,851	19,191	363.22	20,230	20,812	391.29	18,936	22,106
26,000	190.78	42,681	343.58	22,723	19,958	377.73	21,037	21,644	406.92	19,692	22,989
27,000	198.12	44,323	356.80	23,598	20,725	392.26	21,847	22,476	422.58	20,449	23,874
28,000	205.46	45,966	370.02	24,472	21,494	406.80	22,656	23,310	438.23	21,207	24,759
29,000	212.80	47,608	383.24	25,347	22,261	421.33	23,466	24,142	453.89	21,965	25,643
30,000	220.13	49,247	396.44	26,219	23,028	435.84	24,273	24,974	469.52	22,721	26,526
32,500	238.48	53,353	429.49	28,405	24,948	472.17	26,297	27,056	508.66	24,616	28,737
35,000	256.82	57,455	462.52	30,589	26,866	508.49	28,319	29,136	547.78	26,508	30,947
40,000	293.51	65,664	528.59	34,959	30,705	581.13	32,365	33,299	626.04	30,295	35,369
45,000	330.20	73,872	594.67	39,330	34,542	653.77	36,411	37,461	704.29	34,082	39,790
50,000	366.89	82,080	660.75	43,700	38,380	726.42	40,457	41,623	782.55	37,870	44,210
55,000	403.58	90,289	726.82	48,070	42,219	799.06	44,503	45,786	860.81	41,657	48,632
60,000	440.26	98,494	792.88	52,438	46,056	871.68	48,546	49,948	939.04	45,442	53,052
65,000	476.95	106,702	858.96	56,808	49,894	944.33	52,592	54,110	1,017.30	49,229	57,473
70,000	513.64	114,910	925.04	61,178	53,732	1,016.97	56,638	58,272	1,095.56	53,016	61,894
75,000	550.33	123,119	991.11	65,548	57,571	1,089.62	60,684	62,435	1,173.81	56,803	66,316
80,000	587.02	131,327	1,057.19	69,919	61,408	1,162.26	64,730	66,597	1,252.07	60,590	70,737
85,000	623.70	139,532	1,123.25	74,286	65,246	1,234.88	68,773	70,759	1,330.31	64,375	75,157
90,000	660.39	147,740	1,189.33	78,657	69,083	1,307.53	72,819	74,921	1,408.56	68,162	79,578
95,000	697.08	155,949	1,255.40	83,027	72,922	1,380.17	76,865	79,084	1,486.82	71,950	83,999
100,000	733.77	164,157	1,321.48	87,397	76,760	1,452.81	80,911	83,246	1,565.08	75,737	88,420
105,000	770.46	172,366	1,387.55	91,767	80,599	1,525.46	84,957	87,409	1,643.34	79,524	92,842
110,000	807.15	180,574	1,453.63	96,138	84,436	1,598.10	89,003	91,571	1,721.59	83,311	97,263
115,000	843.83	188,779	1,519.69	100,505	88,274	1,670.73	93,047	95,732	1,799.83	87,096	101,683
120,000	880.52	196,987	1,585.77	104,875	92,112	1,743.37	97,093	99,894	1,878.09	90,883	106,104
125,000	917.21	205,196	1,651.84	109,246	95,950	1,816.01	101,138	104,058	1,956.34	94,670	110,526
130,000	953.90	213,404	1,717.92	113,616	99,788	1,888.66	105,184	108,220	2,034.60	98,458	114,946
135,000	990.59	221,612	1,784.00	117,986	103,626	1,961.30	109,230	112,382	2,112.86	102,245	119,367
140,000	1,027.28	229,821	1,850.07	122,356	107,465	2,033.94	113,276	116,545	2,191.11	106,032	123,789
145,000	1,063.96	238,026	1,916.13	126,724	111,302	2,106.57	117,320	120,706	2,269.35	109,817	128,209
150,000	1,100.65	246,234	1,982.21	131,094	115,140	2,179.21	121,366	124,868	2,347.61	113,604	132,630
155,000	1,137.34	254,442	2,048.29	135,465	118,977	2,251.86	125,412	129,030	2,425.86	117,391	137,051
160,000	1,174.03	262,651	2,114.36	139,835	122,816	2,324.50	129,458	133,193	2,504.12	121,178	141,473
165,000	1,210.72	270,859	2,180.44	144,205	126,654	2,397.14	133,503	137,356	2,582.38	124,966	145,893
170,000	1,247.40	279,064	2,246.50	148,573	130,491	2,469.77	137,547	141,517	2,660.61	128,750	150,314
175,000	1,284.09	287,272	2,312.57	152,943	134,329	2,542.41	141,593	145,679	2,738.87	132,538	154,734
180,000	1,320.78	295,481	2,378.65	157,313	138,168	2,615.05	145,639	149,842	2,817.13	136,325	159,156
185,000	1,357.47	303,689	2,444.73	161,683	142,006	2,687.70	149,685	154,004	2,895.39	140,112	163,577
190,000	1,394.16	311,898	2,510.80	166,054	145,844	2,760.34	153,731	158,167	2,973.64	143,899	167,999
195,000	1,430.85	320,106	2,576.88	170,424	149,682	2,832.99	157,777	162,329	3,051.90	147,686	172,420
200,000	1,467.53	328,311	2,642.94	174,792	153,519	2,905.61	161,820	166,491	3,130.14	151,471	176,840

AMOUNT OF LOAN	30 YEARS		1% PMT INCR/YR 274.304 PAYMENTS			2% PMT INCR/YR 232.439 PAYMENTS			3% PMT INCR/YR 205.810 PAYMENTS		
	MONTHLY PAYMENT	TOTAL INTRST	LAST YR MON PMT	TOTAL INTRST	INTRST SAVED	LAST YR MON PMT	TOTAL INTRST	INTRST SAVED	LAST YR MON PMT	TOTAL INTRST	INTRST SAVED
$ 50	0.38	87	0.47	66	21	0.55	57	30	0.63	50	37
100	0.76	174	0.95	133	41	1.11	113	61	1.26	101	73
200	1.51	344	1.88	263	81	2.20	224	120	2.50	199	145
300	2.26	514	2.81	393	121	3.29	334	180	3.74	297	217
400	3.01	684	3.75	523	161	4.39	444	240	4.98	395	289
500	3.76	854	4.68	652	202	5.48	555	299	6.21	493	361
600	4.51	1,024	5.61	782	242	6.57	665	359	7.45	591	433
700	5.26	1,194	6.55	912	282	7.66	776	418	8.69	689	505
800	6.02	1,367	7.49	1,045	322	8.77	889	478	9.95	790	577
900	6.77	1,537	8.43	1,175	362	9.86	999	538	11.19	888	649
1,000	7.52	1,707	9.36	1,305	402	10.96	1,110	597	12.43	986	721
2,000	15.03	3,411	18.71	2,606	805	21.90	2,217	1,194	24.84	1,970	1,441
3,000	22.54	5,114	28.06	3,908	1,206	32.84	3,324	1,790	37.26	2,954	2,160
4,000	30.06	6,822	37.42	5,213	1,609	43.79	4,433	2,389	49.68	3,940	2,882
5,000	37.57	8,525	46.76	6,515	2,010	54.73	5,540	2,985	62.10	4,923	3,602
6,000	45.08	10,229	56.11	7,816	2,413	65.67	6,647	3,582	74.51	5,907	4,322
7,000	52.59	11,932	65.46	9,118	2,814	76.61	7,754	4,178	86.92	6,891	5,041
8,000	60.11	13,640	74.82	10,423	3,217	87.57	8,864	4,776	99.35	7,877	5,763
9,000	67.62	15,343	84.17	11,724	3,619	98.51	9,971	5,372	111.77	8,861	6,482
10,000	75.13	17,047	93.52	13,026	4,021	109.45	11,078	5,969	124.18	9,844	7,203
11,000	82.64	18,750	102.86	14,328	4,422	120.39	12,185	6,565	136.59	10,828	7,922
12,000	90.16	20,458	112.22	15,633	4,825	131.35	13,295	7,163	149.02	11,814	8,644
13,000	97.67	22,161	121.57	16,934	5,227	142.29	14,402	7,759	161.43	12,798	9,363
14,000	105.18	23,865	130.92	18,236	5,629	153.23	15,509	8,356	173.85	13,781	10,084
15,000	112.69	25,568	140.27	19,538	6,030	164.17	16,616	8,952	186.26	14,765	10,803
16,000	120.21	27,276	149.63	20,843	6,433	175.12	17,725	9,551	198.69	15,751	11,525
17,000	127.72	28,979	158.98	22,144	6,835	186.06	18,832	10,147	211.10	16,735	12,244
18,000	135.23	30,683	168.32	23,446	7,237	197.00	19,939	10,744	223.51	17,718	12,965
19,000	142.75	32,390	177.68	24,751	7,639	207.96	21,049	11,341	235.94	18,705	13,685
20,000	150.26	34,094	187.03	26,052	8,042	218.90	22,156	11,938	248.36	19,688	14,406
21,000	157.77	35,797	196.38	27,354	8,443	229.84	23,263	12,534	260.77	20,672	15,125
22,000	165.28	37,501	205.73	28,656	8,845	240.78	24,370	13,131	273.18	21,656	15,845
23,000	172.80	39,208	215.09	29,961	9,247	251.74	25,480	13,728	285.61	22,642	16,566
24,000	180.31	40,912	224.43	31,262	9,650	262.68	26,587	14,325	298.02	23,625	17,287
25,000	187.82	42,615	233.78	32,564	10,051	273.62	27,694	14,921	310.44	24,609	18,006
26,000	195.33	44,319	243.13	33,866	10,453	284.56	28,801	15,518	322.85	25,593	18,726
27,000	202.85	46,026	252.49	35,170	10,856	295.51	29,910	16,116	335.28	26,579	19,447
28,000	210.36	47,730	261.84	36,472	11,258	306.45	31,017	16,713	347.69	27,563	20,167
29,000	217.87	49,433	271.19	37,774	11,659	317.40	32,124	17,309	360.11	28,546	20,887
30,000	225.38	51,137	280.53	39,075	12,062	328.34	33,231	17,906	372.52	29,530	21,607
32,500	244.17	55,401	303.92	42,334	13,067	355.71	36,003	19,398	403.58	31,993	23,408
35,000	262.95	59,662	327.30	45,590	14,072	383.07	38,772	20,890	434.62	34,453	25,209
40,000	300.51	68,184	374.05	52,102	16,082	437.79	44,309	23,875	496.70	39,374	28,810
45,000	338.07	76,705	420.80	58,613	18,092	492.50	49,847	26,858	558.78	44,295	32,410
50,000	375.64	85,230	467.57	65,128	20,102	547.24	55,387	29,843	620.88	49,218	36,012
55,000	413.20	93,752	514.32	71,639	22,113	601.95	60,925	32,827	682.96	54,139	39,613
60,000	450.76	102,274	561.07	78,151	24,123	656.67	66,462	35,812	745.04	59,060	43,214
65,000	488.33	110,799	607.83	84,666	26,133	711.40	72,003	38,796	807.14	63,983	46,816
70,000	525.89	119,320	654.58	91,177	28,143	766.12	77,540	41,780	869.22	68,904	50,416
75,000	563.45	127,842	701.34	97,689	30,153	820.84	83,078	44,764	931.30	73,824	54,018
80,000	601.02	136,367	748.10	104,203	32,164	875.57	88,618	47,749	993.39	78,748	57,619
85,000	638.58	144,889	794.85	110,715	34,174	930.29	94,156	50,733	1,055.48	83,669	61,220
90,000	676.14	153,410	841.60	117,226	36,184	985.01	99,693	53,717	1,117.56	88,589	64,821
95,000	713.71	161,936	888.37	123,741	38,195	1,039.74	105,234	56,702	1,179.65	93,513	68,423
100,000	751.27	170,457	935.12	130,253	40,204	1,094.46	110,771	59,686	1,241.73	98,433	72,024
105,000	788.83	178,979	981.87	136,764	42,215	1,149.18	116,309	62,670	1,303.82	103,354	75,625
110,000	826.40	187,504	1,028.63	143,279	44,225	1,203.91	121,849	65,655	1,365.91	108,278	79,226
115,000	863.96	196,026	1,075.38	149,790	46,236	1,258.63	127,387	68,639	1,427.99	113,198	82,828
120,000	901.52	204,547	1,122.14	156,302	48,245	1,313.34	132,925	71,622	1,490.08	118,119	86,428
125,000	939.09	213,072	1,168.90	162,817	50,255	1,368.08	138,465	74,607	1,552.17	123,043	90,029
130,000	976.65	221,594	1,215.65	169,328	52,266	1,422.79	144,003	77,591	1,614.25	127,963	93,631
135,000	1,014.21	230,116	1,262.40	175,840	54,276	1,477.51	149,540	80,576	1,676.33	132,884	97,232
140,000	1,051.78	238,641	1,309.17	182,354	56,287	1,532.24	155,081	83,560	1,738.43	137,807	100,834
145,000	1,089.34	247,162	1,355.92	188,866	58,297	1,586.96	160,618	86,544	1,800.51	142,728	104,434
150,000	1,126.90	255,684	1,402.67	195,377	60,307	1,641.68	166,156	89,528	1,862.59	147,649	108,035
155,000	1,164.47	264,209	1,449.43	201,892	62,317	1,696.41	171,696	92,513	1,924.69	152,572	111,637
160,000	1,202.03	272,731	1,496.19	208,404	64,327	1,751.13	177,234	95,497	1,986.77	157,493	115,238
165,000	1,239.59	281,252	1,542.94	214,915	66,337	1,805.85	182,771	98,481	2,048.85	162,414	118,838
170,000	1,277.16	289,778	1,589.70	221,430	68,348	1,860.58	188,312	101,466	2,110.95	167,337	122,441
175,000	1,314.72	298,299	1,636.45	227,941	70,358	1,915.30	193,849	104,450	2,173.03	172,258	126,041
180,000	1,352.28	306,821	1,683.20	234,453	72,368	1,970.02	199,387	107,434	2,235.11	177,179	129,642
185,000	1,389.85	315,346	1,729.97	240,968	74,378	2,024.75	204,927	110,419	2,297.21	182,102	133,244
190,000	1,427.41	323,868	1,776.72	247,479	76,389	2,079.47	210,465	113,403	2,359.29	187,023	136,845
195,000	1,464.97	332,389	1,823.47	253,991	78,398	2,134.18	216,002	116,387	2,421.37	191,944	140,445
200,000	1,502.54	340,914	1,870.24	260,505	80,409	2,188.92	221,543	119,371	2,483.47	196,867	144,047

AMOUNT OF LOAN	30 YEARS		4% PMT INCR/YR 186.749 PAYMENTS			5% PMT INCR/YR 172.215 PAYMENTS			6% PMT INCR/YR 160.619 PAYMENTS		
	MONTHLY PAYMENT	TOTAL INTRST	LAST YR MON PMT	TOTAL INTRST	INTRST SAVED	LAST YR MON PMT	TOTAL INTRST	INTRST SAVED	LAST YR MON PMT	TOTAL INTRST	INTRST SAVED
$ 50	0.38	87	0.68	46	41	0.75	43	44	0.81	40	47
100	0.76	174	1.37	92	82	1.50	85	89	1.62	80	94
200	1.51	344	2.72	181	163	2.99	168	176	3.22	157	187
300	2.26	514	4.07	271	243	4.47	250	264	4.82	234	280
400	3.01	684	5.42	360	324	5.96	333	351	6.42	312	372
500	3.76	854	6.77	449	405	7.44	416	438	8.02	389	465
600	4.51	1,024	8.12	538	486	8.93	498	526	9.62	466	558
700	5.26	1,194	9.47	628	566	10.41	581	613	11.22	544	650
800	6.02	1,367	10.84	720	647	11.92	666	701	12.84	623	744
900	6.77	1,537	12.19	809	728	13.40	749	788	14.44	701	836
1,000	7.52	1,707	13.54	898	809	14.89	831	876	16.04	778	929
2,000	15.03	3,411	27.07	1,794	1,617	29.76	1,660	1,751	32.06	1,554	1,857
3,000	22.54	5,114	40.59	2,690	2,424	44.63	2,489	2,625	48.08	2,329	2,785
4,000	30.06	6,822	54.14	3,588	3,234	59.52	3,320	3,502	64.12	3,107	3,715
5,000	37.57	8,525	67.66	4,484	4,041	74.39	4,149	4,376	80.13	3,883	4,642
6,000	45.08	10,229	81.19	5,380	4,849	89.26	4,978	5,251	96.15	4,659	5,570
7,000	52.59	11,932	94.71	6,276	5,656	104.12	5,807	6,125	112.17	5,434	6,498
8,000	60.11	13,640	108.25	7,174	6,466	119.01	6,639	7,001	128.21	6,212	7,428
9,000	67.62	15,343	121.78	8,070	7,273	133.88	7,467	7,876	144.23	6,988	8,355
10,000	75.13	17,047	135.30	8,966	8,081	148.75	8,296	8,751	160.25	7,764	9,283
11,000	82.64	18,750	148.83	9,861	8,889	163.62	9,125	9,625	176.27	8,539	10,211
12,000	90.16	20,458	162.37	10,760	9,698	178.51	9,957	10,501	192.30	9,317	11,141
13,000	97.67	22,161	175.90	11,656	10,505	193.38	10,785	11,376	208.32	10,093	12,068
14,000	105.18	23,865	189.42	12,551	11,314	208.25	11,614	12,251	224.34	10,869	12,996
15,000	112.69	25,568	202.95	13,447	12,121	223.12	12,443	13,125	240.36	11,644	13,924
16,000	120.21	27,276	216.49	14,346	12,930	238.01	13,275	14,001	256.40	12,422	14,854
17,000	127.72	28,979	230.02	15,241	13,738	252.88	14,104	14,875	272.42	13,198	15,781
18,000	135.23	30,683	243.54	16,137	14,546	267.75	14,932	15,751	288.44	13,973	16,710
19,000	142.75	32,390	257.08	17,035	15,355	282.64	15,764	16,626	304.48	14,751	17,639
20,000	150.26	34,094	270.61	17,931	16,163	297.50	16,593	17,501	320.49	15,527	18,567
21,000	157.77	35,797	284.13	18,827	16,970	312.37	17,422	18,375	336.51	16,303	19,494
22,000	165.28	37,501	297.66	19,723	17,778	327.24	18,250	19,251	352.53	17,078	20,423
23,000	172.80	39,208	311.20	20,621	18,587	342.13	19,082	20,126	368.57	17,856	21,352
24,000	180.31	40,912	324.73	21,517	19,395	357.00	19,911	21,001	384.59	18,632	22,280
25,000	187.82	42,615	338.25	22,413	20,202	371.87	20,740	21,875	400.61	19,408	23,207
26,000	195.33	44,319	351.78	23,309	21,010	386.74	21,569	22,750	416.62	20,183	24,136
27,000	202.85	46,026	365.32	24,207	21,819	401.63	22,400	23,626	432.66	20,961	25,065
28,000	210.36	47,730	378.85	25,103	22,627	416.50	23,229	24,501	448.68	21,737	25,993
29,000	217.87	49,433	392.37	25,999	23,434	431.37	24,058	25,375	464.70	22,513	26,920
30,000	225.38	51,137	405.90	26,894	24,243	446.24	24,887	26,250	480.72	23,288	27,849
32,500	244.17	55,401	439.74	29,138	26,263	483.44	26,962	28,439	520.80	25,231	30,170
35,000	262.95	59,662	473.56	31,378	28,284	520.62	29,036	30,626	560.85	27,171	32,491
40,000	300.51	68,184	541.20	35,860	32,324	594.99	33,183	35,001	640.97	31,052	37,132
45,000	338.07	76,705	608.84	40,342	36,363	669.36	37,330	39,375	721.08	34,932	41,773
50,000	375.64	85,230	676.51	44,826	40,404	743.74	41,479	43,751	801.21	38,815	46,415
55,000	413.20	93,752	744.15	49,307	44,445	818.11	45,626	48,126	881.33	42,696	51,056
60,000	450.76	102,274	811.79	53,789	48,485	892.47	49,773	52,501	961.44	46,577	55,697
65,000	488.33	110,799	879.45	58,273	52,526	966.86	53,923	56,876	1,041.57	50,460	60,339
70,000	525.89	119,320	947.10	62,754	56,566	1,041.23	58,069	61,251	1,121.69	54,340	64,980
75,000	563.45	127,842	1,014.74	67,236	60,606	1,115.59	62,216	65,626	1,201.80	58,221	69,621
80,000	601.02	136,367	1,082.40	71,720	64,647	1,189.98	66,366	70,001	1,281.93	62,104	74,263
85,000	638.58	144,889	1,150.05	76,202	68,687	1,264.34	70,513	74,376	1,362.05	65,984	78,905
90,000	676.14	153,410	1,217.69	80,683	72,727	1,338.71	74,660	78,750	1,442.16	69,865	83,545
95,000	713.71	161,936	1,285.35	85,167	76,769	1,413.10	78,809	83,127	1,522.29	73,748	88,188
100,000	751.27	170,457	1,352.99	89,649	80,808	1,487.46	82,956	87,501	1,602.41	77,629	92,828
105,000	788.83	178,979	1,420.64	94,130	84,849	1,561.83	87,103	91,876	1,682.52	81,509	97,470
110,000	826.40	187,504	1,488.30	98,614	88,890	1,636.22	91,252	96,252	1,762.65	85,392	102,112
115,000	863.96	196,026	1,555.94	103,096	92,930	1,710.58	95,399	100,627	1,842.76	89,273	106,753
120,000	901.52	204,547	1,623.59	107,578	96,969	1,784.95	99,546	105,001	1,922.88	93,153	111,394
125,000	939.09	213,072	1,691.25	112,062	101,010	1,859.33	103,696	109,376	2,003.01	97,036	116,036
130,000	976.65	221,594	1,758.89	116,543	105,051	1,933.70	107,843	113,751	2,083.12	100,917	120,677
135,000	1,014.21	230,116	1,826.53	121,025	109,091	2,008.07	111,990	118,126	2,163.24	104,797	125,319
140,000	1,051.78	238,641	1,894.20	125,509	113,132	2,082.45	116,139	122,502	2,243.37	108,680	129,961
145,000	1,089.34	247,162	1,961.84	129,990	117,172	2,156.82	120,286	126,876	2,323.48	112,561	134,601
150,000	1,126.90	255,684	2,029.48	134,472	121,212	2,231.18	124,433	131,251	2,403.60	116,442	139,242
155,000	1,164.47	264,209	2,097.14	138,956	125,253	2,305.57	128,582	135,627	2,483.73	120,325	143,884
160,000	1,202.03	272,731	2,164.79	143,438	129,293	2,379.94	132,729	140,002	2,563.84	124,205	148,526
165,000	1,239.59	281,252	2,232.43	147,919	133,333	2,454.30	136,876	144,376	2,643.96	128,086	153,166
170,000	1,277.16	289,778	2,300.09	152,403	137,375	2,528.69	141,025	148,753	2,724.09	131,969	157,809
175,000	1,314.72	298,299	2,367.74	156,885	141,414	2,603.06	145,172	153,127	2,804.20	135,849	162,450
180,000	1,352.28	306,821	2,435.38	161,366	145,455	2,677.42	149,319	157,502	2,884.32	139,730	167,091
185,000	1,389.85	315,346	2,503.04	165,850	149,496	2,751.81	153,469	161,877	2,964.45	143,613	171,733
190,000	1,427.41	323,868	2,570.68	170,332	153,536	2,826.17	157,616	166,252	3,044.56	147,493	176,375
195,000	1,464.97	332,389	2,638.33	174,814	157,575	2,900.54	161,763	170,626	3,124.68	151,374	181,015
200,000	1,502.54	340,914	2,705.99	179,298	161,616	2,974.93	165,912	175,002	3,204.81	155,257	185,657

8.50% GROWING EQUITY MORTGAGES

AMOUNT OF LOAN	30 YEARS		1% PMT INCR/YR 272.614 PAYMENTS			2% PMT INCR/YR 230.648 PAYMENTS			3% PMT INCR/YR 204.107 PAYMENTS		
	MONTHLY PAYMENT	TOTAL INTRST	LAST YR MON PMT	TOTAL INTRST	INTRST SAVED	LAST YR MON PMT	TOTAL INTRST	INTRST SAVED	LAST YR MON PMT	TOTAL INTRST	INTRST SAVED
$ 50	0.39	90	0.49	69	21	0.57	58	32	0.64	52	38
100	0.77	177	0.96	134	43	1.12	114	63	1.27	101	76
200	1.54	354	1.92	269	85	2.24	228	126	2.55	202	152
300	2.31	532	2.88	403	129	3.37	342	190	3.82	304	228
400	3.08	709	3.83	537	172	4.49	456	253	5.09	405	304
500	3.85	886	4.79	672	214	5.61	570	316	6.36	506	380
600	4.62	1,063	5.75	806	257	6.73	684	379	7.64	607	456
700	5.39	1,240	6.71	941	299	7.85	798	442	8.91	708	532
800	6.16	1,418	7.67	1,075	343	8.97	912	506	10.18	810	608
900	6.93	1,595	8.63	1,209	386	10.10	1,026	569	11.45	911	684
1,000	7.69	1,768	9.57	1,341	427	11.20	1,137	631	12.71	1,010	758
2,000	15.38	3,537	19.14	2,681	856	22.41	2,275	1,262	25.42	2,019	1,518
3,000	23.07	5,305	28.72	4,022	1,283	33.61	3,412	1,893	38.13	3,029	2,276
4,000	30.76	7,074	38.29	5,363	1,711	44.81	4,550	2,524	50.84	4,038	3,036
5,000	38.45	8,842	47.86	6,703	2,139	56.01	5,687	3,155	63.55	5,048	3,794
6,000	46.14	10,610	57.43	8,044	2,566	67.22	6,824	3,786	76.26	6,057	4,553
7,000	53.83	12,379	67.00	9,385	2,994	78.42	7,962	4,417	88.97	7,067	5,312
8,000	61.52	14,147	76.57	10,726	3,421	89.62	9,099	5,048	101.68	8,076	6,071
9,000	69.21	15,916	86.15	12,066	3,850	100.83	10,237	5,679	114.39	9,086	6,830
10,000	76.90	17,684	95.72	13,407	4,277	112.03	11,374	6,310	127.10	10,095	7,589
11,000	84.59	19,452	105.29	14,748	4,704	123.23	12,511	6,941	139.81	11,105	8,347
12,000	92.27	21,217	114.85	16,085	5,132	134.42	13,646	7,571	152.51	12,112	9,105
13,000	99.96	22,986	124.42	17,426	5,560	145.62	14,783	8,203	165.22	13,121	9,865
14,000	107.65	24,754	133.99	18,767	5,987	156.83	15,921	8,833	177.93	14,131	10,623
15,000	115.34	26,522	143.57	20,107	6,415	168.03	17,058	9,464	190.64	15,140	11,382
16,000	123.03	28,291	153.14	21,448	6,843	179.23	18,195	10,096	203.35	16,150	12,141
17,000	130.72	30,059	162.71	22,789	7,270	190.43	19,333	10,726	216.06	17,159	12,900
18,000	138.41	31,828	172.28	24,129	7,699	201.64	20,470	11,358	228.77	18,169	13,659
19,000	146.10	33,596	181.85	25,470	8,126	212.84	21,608	11,988	241.48	19,178	14,418
20,000	153.79	35,364	191.42	26,811	8,553	224.04	22,745	12,619	254.19	20,188	15,176
21,000	161.48	37,133	201.00	28,151	8,982	235.25	23,882	13,251	266.90	21,197	15,936
22,000	169.17	38,901	210.57	29,492	9,409	246.45	25,020	13,881	279.61	22,207	16,694
23,000	176.86	40,670	220.14	30,833	9,837	257.65	26,157	14,513	292.32	23,216	17,454
24,000	184.54	42,434	229.70	32,170	10,264	268.84	27,292	15,142	305.02	24,223	18,211
25,000	192.23	44,203	239.27	33,511	10,692	280.04	28,429	15,774	317.73	25,233	18,970
26,000	199.92	45,971	248.84	34,852	11,119	291.25	29,567	16,404	330.44	26,242	19,729
27,000	207.61	47,740	258.42	36,193	11,547	302.45	30,704	17,036	343.15	27,252	20,488
28,000	215.30	49,508	267.99	37,533	11,975	313.65	31,841	17,667	355.86	28,261	21,247
29,000	222.99	51,276	277.56	38,874	12,402	324.85	32,979	18,297	368.57	29,271	22,005
30,000	230.68	53,045	287.13	40,215	12,830	336.06	34,116	18,929	381.28	30,280	22,765
32,500	249.90	57,464	311.05	43,565	13,899	364.06	36,958	20,506	413.05	32,803	24,661
35,000	269.12	61,883	334.98	46,915	14,968	392.06	39,800	22,083	444.81	35,325	26,558
40,000	307.57	70,725	382.84	53,618	17,107	448.07	45,487	25,238	508.37	40,373	30,352
45,000	346.02	79,567	430.70	60,322	19,245	504.09	51,174	28,393	571.92	45,421	34,146
50,000	384.46	88,406	478.54	67,022	21,384	560.09	56,858	31,548	635.45	50,466	37,940
55,000	422.91	97,248	526.40	73,726	23,522	616.10	62,545	34,703	699.01	55,513	41,735
60,000	461.35	106,086	574.25	80,426	25,660	672.10	68,230	37,856	762.54	60,558	45,528
65,000	499.80	114,928	622.11	87,130	27,798	728.11	73,917	41,011	826.09	65,606	49,322
70,000	538.24	123,766	669.96	93,830	29,936	784.11	79,601	44,165	889.63	70,651	53,115
75,000	576.69	132,608	717.82	100,533	32,075	840.13	85,288	47,320	953.18	75,698	56,910
80,000	615.14	141,450	765.67	107,237	34,213	896.14	90,975	50,475	1,016.73	80,746	60,704
85,000	653.58	150,289	813.52	113,937	36,352	952.14	96,659	53,630	1,080.27	85,791	64,498
90,000	692.03	159,131	861.38	120,641	38,490	1,008.16	102,346	56,785	1,143.82	90,838	68,293
95,000	730.47	167,969	909.23	127,341	40,628	1,064.16	108,030	59,939	1,207.36	95,883	72,086
100,000	768.92	176,811	957.09	134,045	42,766	1,120.17	113,717	63,094	1,270.91	100,931	75,880
105,000	807.36	185,650	1,004.93	140,745	44,905	1,176.17	119,401	66,249	1,334.44	105,976	79,674
110,000	845.81	194,492	1,052.79	147,449	47,043	1,232.19	125,088	69,404	1,398.00	111,024	83,468
115,000	884.26	203,334	1,100.65	154,152	49,182	1,288.20	130,775	72,559	1,461.55	116,071	87,263
120,000	922.70	212,172	1,148.50	160,852	51,320	1,344.20	136,459	75,713	1,525.08	121,116	91,056
125,000	961.15	221,014	1,196.36	167,556	53,458	1,400.21	142,146	78,868	1,588.63	126,164	94,850
130,000	999.59	229,852	1,244.21	174,256	55,596	1,456.21	147,830	82,022	1,652.17	131,209	98,643
135,000	1,038.04	238,694	1,292.06	180,960	57,734	1,512.23	153,517	85,177	1,715.72	136,256	102,438
140,000	1,076.48	247,533	1,339.91	187,660	59,873	1,568.23	159,202	88,331	1,779.26	141,301	106,232
145,000	1,114.93	256,375	1,387.77	194,364	62,011	1,624.24	164,888	91,487	1,842.81	146,349	110,026
150,000	1,153.38	265,217	1,435.63	201,067	64,150	1,680.26	170,575	94,642	1,906.36	151,397	113,820
155,000	1,191.82	274,055	1,483.48	207,767	66,288	1,736.26	176,260	97,795	1,969.90	156,442	117,613
160,000	1,230.27	282,897	1,531.34	214,471	68,426	1,792.27	181,947	100,950	2,033.45	161,489	121,408
165,000	1,268.71	291,736	1,579.18	221,171	70,565	1,848.27	187,631	104,105	2,096.98	166,534	125,202
170,000	1,307.16	300,578	1,627.04	227,875	72,703	1,904.29	193,318	107,260	2,160.54	171,582	128,996
175,000	1,345.60	309,416	1,674.89	234,575	74,841	1,960.29	199,002	110,414	2,224.07	176,627	132,789
180,000	1,384.05	318,258	1,722.75	241,279	76,979	2,016.30	204,689	113,569	2,287.62	181,674	136,584
185,000	1,422.49	327,096	1,770.60	247,979	79,117	2,072.30	210,373	116,723	2,351.16	186,719	140,377
190,000	1,460.94	335,938	1,818.46	254,682	81,256	2,128.31	216,060	119,878	2,414.71	191,767	144,171
195,000	1,499.39	344,780	1,866.31	261,386	83,394	2,184.33	221,747	123,033	2,478.26	196,814	147,966
200,000	1,537.83	353,619	1,914.16	268,086	85,533	2,240.33	227,431	126,188	2,541.80	201,859	151,760

GROWING EQUITY MORTGAGES 8.50%

AMOUNT OF LOAN	30 YEARS		4% PMT INCR/YR 185.129 PAYMENTS			5% PMT INCR/YR 170.713 PAYMENTS			6% PMT INCR/YR 159.207 PAYMENTS		
	MONTHLY PAYMENT	TOTAL INTRST	LAST YR MON PMT	TOTAL INTRST	INTRST SAVED	LAST YR MON PMT	TOTAL INTRST	INTRST SAVED	LAST YR MON PMT	TOTAL INTRST	INTRST SAVED
$ 50	0.39	90	0.70	47	43	0.77	44	46	0.83	41	49
100	0.77	177	1.39	92	85	1.52	85	92	1.64	80	97
200	1.54	354	2.77	184	170	3.05	170	184	3.28	159	195
300	2.31	532	4.16	276	256	4.57	256	276	4.93	239	293
400	3.08	709	5.55	369	340	6.10	341	368	6.57	319	390
500	3.85	886	6.93	461	425	7.62	426	460	8.21	399	487
600	4.62	1,063	8.32	553	510	9.15	511	552	9.85	478	585
700	5.39	1,240	9.71	645	595	10.67	597	643	11.50	558	682
800	6.16	1,418	11.09	737	681	12.20	682	736	13.14	638	780
900	6.93	1,595	12.48	829	766	13.72	767	828	14.78	718	877
1,000	7.69	1,768	13.85	919	849	15.23	850	918	16.40	795	973
2,000	15.38	3,537	27.70	1,838	1,699	30.45	1,700	1,837	32.80	1,590	1,947
3,000	23.07	5,305	41.55	2,756	2,549	45.68	2,550	2,755	49.21	2,385	2,920
4,000	30.76	7,074	55.40	3,675	3,399	60.90	3,399	3,675	65.61	3,180	3,894
5,000	38.45	8,842	69.25	4,594	4,248	76.13	4,249	4,593	82.01	3,975	4,867
6,000	46.14	10,610	83.10	5,513	5,097	91.35	5,099	5,511	98.41	4,770	5,840
7,000	53.83	12,379	96.94	6,432	5,947	106.58	5,949	6,430	114.82	5,565	6,814
8,000	61.52	14,147	110.79	7,350	6,797	121.81	6,799	7,348	131.22	6,360	7,787
9,000	69.21	15,916	124.64	8,269	7,647	137.03	7,649	8,267	147.62	7,155	8,761
10,000	76.90	17,684	138.49	9,188	8,496	152.26	8,499	9,185	164.02	7,950	9,734
11,000	84.59	19,452	152.34	10,107	9,345	167.48	9,349	10,103	180.42	8,746	10,706
12,000	92.27	21,217	166.17	11,023	10,194	182.69	10,196	11,021	196.81	9,538	11,679
13,000	99.96	22,986	180.02	11,942	11,044	197.91	11,046	11,940	213.21	10,333	12,653
14,000	107.65	24,754	193.87	12,861	11,893	213.14	11,896	12,858	229.61	11,128	13,626
15,000	115.34	26,522	207.72	13,780	12,742	228.37	12,746	13,776	246.01	11,923	14,599
16,000	123.03	28,291	221.57	14,698	13,593	243.59	13,595	14,696	262.41	12,718	15,573
17,000	130.72	30,059	235.42	15,617	14,442	258.82	14,445	15,614	278.82	13,513	16,546
18,000	138.41	31,828	249.27	16,536	15,292	274.04	15,295	16,533	295.22	14,308	17,520
19,000	146.10	33,596	263.12	17,455	16,141	289.27	16,145	17,451	311.62	15,104	18,492
20,000	153.79	35,364	276.97	18,374	16,990	304.49	16,995	18,369	328.02	15,899	19,465
21,000	161.48	37,133	290.82	19,293	17,840	319.72	17,845	19,288	344.43	16,694	20,439
22,000	169.17	38,901	304.67	20,211	18,690	334.95	18,695	20,206	360.83	17,489	21,412
23,000	176.86	40,670	318.51	21,130	19,540	350.17	19,545	21,125	377.23	18,284	22,386
24,000	184.54	42,434	332.35	22,046	20,388	365.38	20,392	22,042	393.61	19,076	23,358
25,000	192.23	44,203	346.20	22,965	21,238	380.60	21,242	22,961	410.01	19,871	24,332
26,000	199.92	45,971	360.04	23,884	22,087	395.83	22,092	23,879	426.42	20,667	25,304
27,000	207.61	47,740	373.89	24,803	22,937	411.05	22,942	24,798	442.82	21,462	26,278
28,000	215.30	49,508	387.74	25,722	23,786	426.28	23,792	25,716	459.22	22,257	27,251
29,000	222.99	51,276	401.59	26,640	24,636	441.50	24,641	26,635	475.62	23,052	28,224
30,000	230.68	53,045	415.44	27,559	25,486	456.73	25,491	27,554	492.02	23,847	29,198
32,500	249.90	57,464	450.06	29,855	27,609	494.78	27,615	29,849	533.02	25,833	31,631
35,000	269.12	61,883	484.67	32,151	29,732	532.84	29,738	32,145	574.01	27,820	34,063
40,000	307.57	70,725	553.92	36,745	33,980	608.97	33,988	36,737	656.02	31,795	38,930
45,000	346.02	79,567	623.16	41,339	38,228	685.10	38,237	41,330	738.04	35,770	43,797
50,000	384.46	88,406	692.39	45,930	42,476	761.20	42,484	45,922	820.03	39,743	48,663
55,000	422.91	97,248	761.64	50,525	46,723	837.33	46,733	50,515	902.04	43,718	53,530
60,000	461.35	106,086	830.87	55,116	50,970	913.44	50,980	55,106	984.03	47,691	58,395
65,000	499.80	114,928	900.11	59,710	55,218	989.57	55,229	59,699	1,066.04	51,666	63,262
70,000	538.24	123,766	969.34	64,302	59,464	1,065.68	59,476	64,290	1,148.03	55,639	68,127
75,000	576.69	132,608	1,038.59	68,896	63,712	1,141.81	63,726	68,882	1,230.04	59,614	72,994
80,000	615.14	141,450	1,107.83	73,490	67,960	1,217.94	67,975	73,475	1,312.05	63,590	77,860
85,000	653.58	150,289	1,177.06	78,081	72,208	1,294.04	72,222	78,067	1,394.04	67,563	82,726
90,000	692.03	159,131	1,246.31	82,675	76,456	1,370.17	76,471	82,660	1,476.05	71,538	87,593
95,000	730.47	167,969	1,315.54	87,267	80,702	1,446.28	80,718	87,251	1,558.04	75,511	92,458
100,000	768.92	176,811	1,384.78	91,861	84,950	1,522.41	84,968	91,843	1,640.05	79,486	97,325
105,000	807.36	185,650	1,454.01	96,453	89,197	1,598.52	89,215	96,435	1,722.04	83,459	102,191
110,000	845.81	194,492	1,523.26	101,047	93,445	1,674.65	93,464	101,028	1,804.05	87,434	107,058
115,000	884.26	203,334	1,592.50	105,641	97,693	1,750.77	97,713	105,621	1,886.06	91,409	111,925
120,000	922.70	212,172	1,661.73	110,232	101,940	1,826.88	101,960	110,212	1,968.05	95,382	116,790
125,000	961.15	221,014	1,730.98	114,826	106,188	1,903.01	106,210	114,804	2,050.06	99,357	121,657
130,000	999.59	229,852	1,800.21	119,418	110,434	1,979.12	110,457	119,395	2,132.05	103,330	126,522
135,000	1,038.04	238,694	1,869.45	124,012	114,682	2,055.25	114,706	123,988	2,214.06	107,305	131,389
140,000	1,076.48	247,533	1,938.68	128,603	118,930	2,131.36	118,953	128,580	2,296.05	111,278	136,255
145,000	1,114.93	256,375	2,007.93	133,197	123,178	2,207.49	123,202	133,173	2,378.07	115,254	141,121
150,000	1,153.38	265,217	2,077.17	137,791	127,426	2,283.61	127,451	137,766	2,460.08	119,229	145,988
155,000	1,191.82	274,055	2,146.40	142,383	131,672	2,359.72	131,698	142,357	2,542.07	123,202	150,853
160,000	1,230.27	282,897	2,215.65	146,977	135,920	2,435.85	135,948	146,949	2,624.08	127,177	155,720
165,000	1,268.71	291,735	2,284.88	151,569	140,167	2,511.96	140,195	151,541	2,706.07	131,150	160,586
170,000	1,307.16	300,578	2,354.12	156,163	144,415	2,588.09	144,444	156,134	2,788.08	135,125	165,453
175,000	1,345.60	309,416	2,423.35	160,754	148,662	2,664.20	148,691	160,725	2,870.07	139,098	170,318
180,000	1,384.05	318,258	2,492.60	165,348	152,910	2,740.32	152,940	165,318	2,952.08	143,073	175,185
185,000	1,422.49	327,096	2,561.82	169,940	157,156	2,816.43	157,187	169,909	3,034.07	147,046	180,050
190,000	1,460.94	335,938	2,631.07	174,534	161,404	2,892.56	161,437	174,501	3,116.08	151,021	184,917
195,000	1,499.39	344,780	2,700.32	179,128	165,652	2,968.69	165,686	179,094	3,198.09	154,997	189,783
200,000	1,537.83	353,619	2,769.54	183,719	169,900	3,044.80	169,933	183,686	3,280.08	158,969	194,650

113

8.75%   GROWING EQUITY MORTGAGES

AMOUNT OF LOAN	30 YEARS		1% PMT INCR/YR 270.908 PAYMENTS			2% PMT INCR/YR 228.860 PAYMENTS			3% PMT INCR/YR 202.371 PAYMENTS		
	MONTHLY PAYMENT	TOTAL INTRST	LAST YR MON PMT	TOTAL INTRST	INTRST SAVED	LAST YR MON PMT	TOTAL INTRST	INTRST SAVED	LAST YR MON PMT	TOTAL INTRST	INTRST SAVED
$ 50	0.40	94	0.50	71	23	0.58	60	34	0.64	53	41
100	0.79	184	0.98	139	45	1.15	118	66	1.27	104	80
200	1.58	369	1.97	278	91	2.30	235	134	2.54	208	161
300	2.37	553	2.95	416	137	3.45	353	200	3.80	313	240
400	3.15	734	3.92	552	182	4.59	467	267	5.05	414	320
500	3.94	918	4.90	691	227	5.74	585	333	6.32	519	399
600	4.73	1,103	5.89	830	273	6.89	702	401	7.59	623	480
700	5.51	1,284	6.86	965	319	8.03	817	467	8.84	724	560
800	6.30	1,468	7.84	1,104	364	9.18	935	533	10.11	829	639
900	7.09	1,652	8.83	1,243	409	10.33	1,052	600	11.38	933	719
1,000	7.87	1,833	9.80	1,379	454	11.47	1,167	666	12.63	1,035	798
2,000	15.74	3,666	19.59	2,758	908	22.93	2,334	1,332	25.26	2,069	1,597
3,000	23.61	5,500	29.39	4,136	1,364	34.40	3,501	1,999	37.89	3,104	2,396
4,000	31.47	7,329	39.17	5,512	1,817	45.85	4,665	2,664	50.50	4,136	3,193
5,000	39.34	9,162	48.97	6,891	2,271	57.31	5,832	3,330	63.13	5,170	3,992
6,000	47.21	10,996	58.76	8,270	2,726	68.78	6,999	3,997	75.76	6,205	4,791
7,000	55.07	12,825	68.55	9,645	3,180	80.23	8,163	4,662	88.37	7,237	5,588
8,000	62.94	14,658	78.34	11,024	3,634	91.69	9,330	5,328	101.00	8,272	6,386
9,000	70.81	16,492	88.14	12,403	4,089	103.16	10,497	5,995	113.63	9,306	7,186
10,000	78.68	18,325	97.93	13,782	4,543	114.62	11,664	6,661	126.26	10,341	7,984
11,000	86.54	20,154	107.72	15,157	4,997	126.07	12,828	7,326	138.87	11,373	8,781
12,000	94.41	21,988	117.51	16,536	5,452	137.54	13,995	7,993	151.50	12,407	9,581
13,000	102.28	23,821	127.31	17,915	5,906	149.00	15,162	8,659	164.13	13,442	10,379
14,000	110.14	25,650	137.09	19,291	6,359	160.45	16,326	9,324	176.74	14,474	11,176
15,000	118.01	27,484	146.89	20,669	6,815	171.92	17,493	9,991	189.37	15,509	11,975
16,000	125.88	29,317	156.68	22,048	7,269	183.38	18,660	10,657	202.00	16,543	12,774
17,000	133.74	31,146	166.47	23,424	7,722	194.83	19,824	11,322	214.61	17,575	13,571
18,000	141.61	32,980	176.26	24,803	8,177	206.30	20,991	11,989	227.24	18,610	14,370
19,000	149.48	34,813	186.06	26,181	8,632	217.76	22,158	12,655	239.87	19,644	15,169
20,000	157.35	36,646	195.86	27,560	9,086	229.23	23,325	13,321	252.50	20,679	15,967
21,000	165.21	38,476	205.64	28,936	9,540	240.68	24,489	13,987	265.11	21,711	16,765
22,000	173.08	40,309	215.44	30,315	9,994	252.14	25,656	14,653	277.74	22,746	17,563
23,000	180.95	42,142	225.23	31,693	10,449	263.61	26,823	15,319	290.37	23,780	18,362
24,000	188.81	43,972	235.01	33,069	10,903	275.06	27,987	15,985	302.98	24,812	19,160
25,000	196.68	45,805	244.81	34,448	11,357	286.53	29,154	16,651	315.61	25,847	19,958
26,000	204.55	47,638	254.61	35,827	11,811	297.99	30,321	17,317	328.24	26,881	20,757
27,000	212.41	49,468	264.39	37,203	12,265	309.44	31,485	17,983	340.86	27,913	21,555
28,000	220.28	51,301	274.19	38,581	12,720	320.91	32,652	18,649	353.48	28,948	22,353
29,000	228.15	53,134	283.98	39,960	13,174	332.37	33,819	19,315	366.11	29,982	23,152
30,000	236.02	54,967	293.78	41,339	13,628	343.84	34,986	19,981	378.74	31,017	23,950
32,500	255.68	59,545	318.25	44,781	14,764	372.48	37,899	21,646	410.29	33,600	25,945
35,000	275.35	64,126	342.73	48,227	15,899	401.13	40,815	23,311	441.86	36,185	27,941
40,000	314.69	73,288	391.70	55,117	18,171	458.44	46,647	26,641	504.99	41,355	31,933
45,000	354.02	82,447	440.65	62,005	20,442	515.74	52,476	29,971	568.10	46,523	35,924
50,000	393.36	91,610	489.62	68,896	22,714	573.05	58,308	33,302	631.23	51,693	39,917
55,000	432.69	100,768	538.58	75,784	24,984	630.35	64,137	36,631	694.34	56,861	43,907
60,000	472.03	109,931	587.54	82,675	27,256	687.66	69,969	39,962	757.47	62,032	47,899
65,000	511.36	119,090	636.50	89,562	29,528	744.95	75,798	43,292	820.58	67,199	51,891
70,000	550.70	128,252	685.47	96,453	31,799	802.27	81,629	46,623	883.71	72,370	55,882
75,000	590.03	137,411	734.42	103,341	34,070	859.56	87,459	49,952	946.82	77,537	59,874
80,000	629.37	146,573	783.39	110,232	36,341	916.87	93,290	53,283	1,009.95	82,708	63,865
85,000	668.70	155,732	832.34	117,120	38,612	974.17	99,120	56,612	1,073.07	87,876	67,856
90,000	708.04	164,894	881.31	124,010	40,884	1,031.48	104,951	59,943	1,136.20	93,046	71,848
95,000	747.37	174,053	930.26	130,898	43,155	1,088.78	110,781	63,272	1,199.31	98,214	75,839
100,000	786.71	183,216	979.23	137,789	45,427	1,146.09	116,612	66,604	1,262.44	103,384	79,832
105,000	826.04	192,374	1,028.19	144,677	47,697	1,203.38	122,441	69,933	1,325.55	108,552	83,822
110,000	865.38	201,537	1,077.15	151,568	49,969	1,260.70	128,273	73,264	1,388.68	113,722	87,815
115,000	904.71	210,696	1,126.11	158,455	52,241	1,317.99	134,102	76,594	1,451.79	118,890	91,806
120,000	944.05	219,858	1,175.07	165,346	54,512	1,375.30	139,934	79,924	1,514.92	124,061	95,799
125,000	983.38	229,017	1,224.03	172,234	56,783	1,432.60	145,763	83,254	1,578.04	129,228	99,789
130,000	1,022.72	238,179	1,273.00	179,125	59,054	1,489.91	151,595	86,584	1,641.17	134,399	103,780
135,000	1,062.05	247,338	1,321.95	186,013	61,325	1,547.21	157,424	89,914	1,704.28	139,566	107,772
140,000	1,101.39	256,500	1,370.92	192,903	63,597	1,604.52	163,256	93,244	1,767.41	144,737	111,763
145,000	1,140.72	265,659	1,419.87	199,791	65,868	1,661.81	169,085	96,574	1,830.52	149,905	115,754
150,000	1,180.06	274,822	1,468.84	206,682	68,140	1,719.12	174,917	99,905	1,893.65	155,075	119,747
155,000	1,219.39	283,980	1,517.79	213,570	70,410	1,776.42	180,746	103,234	1,956.76	160,243	123,737
160,000	1,258.73	293,143	1,566.76	220,461	72,682	1,833.73	186,578	106,565	2,019.89	165,413	127,730
165,000	1,298.06	302,302	1,615.72	227,348	74,954	1,891.03	192,407	109,895	2,083.01	170,581	131,721
170,000	1,337.40	311,464	1,664.68	234,239	77,225	1,948.34	198,239	113,225	2,146.13	175,751	135,713
175,000	1,376.73	320,623	1,713.64	241,127	79,496	2,005.64	204,068	116,555	2,209.25	180,919	139,704
180,000	1,416.07	329,785	1,762.60	248,018	81,767	2,062.95	209,900	119,885	2,272.38	186,089	143,696
185,000	1,455.40	338,944	1,811.56	254,906	84,038	2,120.24	215,729	123,215	2,335.49	191,257	147,687
190,000	1,494.74	348,106	1,860.53	261,796	86,310	2,177.55	221,561	126,545	2,398.62	196,428	151,678
195,000	1,534.07	357,265	1,909.48	268,684	88,581	2,234.85	227,390	129,875	2,461.73	201,595	155,670
200,000	1,573.41	366,428	1,958.45	275,575	90,853	2,292.16	233,222	133,206	2,524.86	206,766	159,662

114

GROWING EQUITY MORTGAGES 8.75%

AMOUNT OF LOAN	30 YEARS MONTHLY PAYMENT	30 YEARS TOTAL INTRST	4% PMT INCR/YR 183.529 PAYMENTS LAST YR MON PMT	4% TOTAL INTRST	4% INTRST SAVED	5% PMT INCR/YR 169.231 PAYMENTS LAST YR MON PMT	5% TOTAL INTRST	5% INTRST SAVED	6% PMT INCR/YR 157.818 PAYMENTS LAST YR MON PMT	6% TOTAL INTRST	6% INTRST SAVED
$ 50	0.40	94	0.72	49	45	0.79	45	49	0.85	42	52
100	0.79	184	1.42	95	89	1.56	88	96	1.69	82	102
200	1.58	369	2.85	190	179	3.13	175	194	3.37	164	205
300	2.37	553	4.27	285	268	4.69	263	290	5.06	246	307
400	3.15	734	5.67	377	357	6.24	349	385	6.72	326	408
500	3.94	918	7.10	472	446	7.80	436	482	8.40	408	510
600	4.73	1,103	8.52	567	536	9.37	524	579	10.09	490	613
700	5.51	1,284	9.92	659	625	10.91	609	675	11.75	570	714
800	6.30	1,468	11.35	754	714	12.47	697	771	13.44	652	816
900	7.09	1,652	12.77	849	803	14.04	785	867	15.12	734	918
1,000	7.87	1,833	14.17	941	892	15.58	870	963	16.79	814	1,019
2,000	15.74	3,666	28.35	1,882	1,784	31.16	1,740	1,926	33.57	1,627	2,039
3,000	23.61	5,500	42.52	2,823	2,677	46.75	2,610	2,890	50.36	2,441	3,059
4,000	31.47	7,329	56.68	3,762	3,567	62.31	3,478	3,851	67.12	3,253	4,076
5,000	39.34	9,162	70.85	4,703	4,459	77.89	4,348	4,814	83.91	4,066	5,096
6,000	47.21	10,996	85.02	5,644	5,352	93.47	5,218	5,778	100.70	4,880	6,116
7,000	55.07	12,825	99.18	6,582	6,243	109.03	6,086	6,739	117.46	5,692	7,133
8,000	62.94	14,658	113.35	7,523	7,135	124.62	6,956	7,702	134.25	6,505	8,153
9,000	70.81	16,492	127.52	8,464	8,028	140.20	7,826	8,666	151.03	7,319	9,173
10,000	78.68	18,325	141.70	9,406	8,919	155.78	8,696	9,629	167.82	8,133	10,192
11,000	86.54	20,154	155.85	10,344	9,810	171.34	9,564	10,590	184.58	8,944	11,210
12,000	94.41	21,988	170.03	11,285	10,703	186.93	10,434	11,554	201.37	9,758	12,230
13,000	102.28	23,821	184.20	12,226	11,595	202.51	11,304	12,517	218.16	10,572	13,249
14,000	110.14	25,650	198.36	13,165	12,485	218.07	12,172	13,478	234.92	11,383	14,267
15,000	118.01	27,484	212.53	14,106	13,378	233.65	13,042	14,442	251.71	12,197	15,287
16,000	125.88	29,317	226.70	15,047	14,270	249.23	13,912	15,405	268.49	13,011	16,306
17,000	133.74	31,146	240.86	15,985	15,161	264.80	14,779	16,367	285.26	13,822	17,324
18,000	141.61	32,980	255.03	16,926	16,054	280.38	15,649	17,331	302.04	14,636	18,344
19,000	149.48	34,813	269.21	17,868	16,945	295.96	16,520	18,293	318.83	15,450	19,363
20,000	157.35	36,646	283.38	18,809	17,837	311.54	17,390	19,256	335.62	16,263	20,383
21,000	165.21	38,476	297.53	19,747	18,729	327.10	18,257	20,219	352.38	17,075	21,401
22,000	173.08	40,309	311.71	20,688	19,621	342.69	19,127	21,182	369.17	17,889	22,420
23,000	180.95	42,142	325.88	21,629	20,513	358.27	19,997	22,145	385.95	18,702	23,440
24,000	188.81	43,972	340.04	22,568	21,404	373.83	20,865	23,107	402.72	19,514	24,458
25,000	196.68	45,805	354.21	23,509	22,296	389.41	21,735	24,070	419.50	20,328	25,477
26,000	204.55	47,638	368.38	24,450	23,188	405.00	22,605	25,033	436.29	21,141	26,497
27,000	212.41	49,468	382.54	25,389	24,079	420.56	23,473	25,995	453.06	21,953	27,515
28,000	220.28	51,301	396.71	26,330	24,971	436.14	24,343	26,958	469.84	22,766	28,535
29,000	228.15	53,134	410.89	27,271	25,863	451.72	25,213	27,921	486.63	23,580	29,554
30,000	236.02	54,967	425.06	28,212	26,755	467.30	26,083	28,884	503.41	24,394	30,573
32,500	255.68	59,545	460.47	30,561	28,984	506.23	28,255	31,290	545.35	26,425	33,120
35,000	275.35	64,126	495.89	32,912	31,214	545.17	30,429	33,697	587.30	28,458	35,668
40,000	314.69	73,288	566.74	37,615	35,673	623.06	34,777	38,511	671.21	32,525	40,763
45,000	354.02	82,447	637.57	42,315	40,132	700.94	39,123	43,311	755.10	36,589	45,858
50,000	393.36	91,610	708.42	47,018	44,592	778.83	43,471	48,139	839.01	40,655	50,955
55,000	432.69	100,768	779.25	51,718	49,050	856.70	47,816	52,952	922.90	44,719	56,049
60,000	472.03	109,931	850.10	56,421	53,510	934.59	52,164	57,767	1,006.81	48,786	61,145
65,000	511.36	119,090	920.93	61,121	57,969	1,012.46	56,510	62,580	1,090.69	52,850	66,240
70,000	550.70	128,252	991.78	65,824	62,428	1,090.35	60,858	67,393	1,174.60	56,916	71,336
75,000	590.03	137,411	1,062.61	70,524	66,887	1,168.22	65,203	72,208	1,258.49	60,980	76,431
80,000	629.37	146,573	1,133.46	75,227	71,346	1,246.11	69,551	77,022	1,342.40	65,047	81,526
85,000	668.70	155,732	1,204.29	79,927	75,805	1,323.98	73,897	81,835	1,426.29	69,111	86,621
90,000	708.04	164,894	1,275.14	84,630	80,264	1,401.87	78,245	86,649	1,510.20	73,177	91,717
95,000	747.37	174,053	1,345.97	89,330	84,723	1,479.74	82,591	91,462	1,594.09	77,241	96,812
100,000	786.71	183,216	1,416.82	94,033	89,183	1,557.63	86,939	96,277	1,678.00	81,308	101,908
105,000	826.04	192,374	1,487.65	98,733	93,641	1,635.50	91,284	101,090	1,761.88	85,372	107,002
110,000	865.38	201,537	1,558.50	103,436	98,101	1,713.39	95,632	105,905	1,845.79	89,438	112,099
115,000	904.71	210,696	1,629.33	108,136	102,560	1,791.26	99,978	110,718	1,929.68	93,502	117,194
120,000	944.05	219,858	1,700.18	112,839	107,019	1,869.15	104,326	115,532	2,013.59	97,569	122,289
125,000	983.38	229,017	1,771.01	117,539	111,478	1,947.03	108,672	120,345	2,097.48	101,633	127,384
130,000	1,022.72	238,179	1,841.86	122,242	115,937	2,024.92	113,020	125,159	2,181.39	105,699	132,480
135,000	1,062.05	247,338	1,912.69	126,943	120,395	2,102.79	117,366	129,973	2,265.28	109,764	137,574
140,000	1,101.39	256,500	1,983.54	131,645	124,855	2,180.68	121,713	134,787	2,349.19	113,830	142,670
145,000	1,140.72	265,659	2,054.37	136,346	129,313	2,258.55	126,059	139,600	2,433.07	117,894	147,765
150,000	1,180.06	274,822	2,125.22	141,048	133,774	2,336.44	130,407	144,415	2,516.98	121,961	152,861
155,000	1,219.39	283,980	2,196.05	145,749	138,231	2,414.31	134,753	149,227	2,600.87	126,025	157,955
160,000	1,258.73	293,143	2,266.90	150,451	142,692	2,492.20	139,101	154,042	2,684.78	130,091	163,052
165,000	1,298.06	302,302	2,337.73	155,152	147,150	2,570.07	143,446	158,856	2,768.67	134,155	168,147
170,000	1,337.40	311,464	2,408.58	159,854	151,610	2,647.96	147,794	163,670	2,852.58	138,222	173,242
175,000	1,376.73	320,623	2,479.41	164,555	156,068	2,725.83	152,140	168,483	2,936.47	142,286	178,337
180,000	1,416.07	329,785	2,550.26	169,257	160,528	2,803.72	156,488	173,297	3,020.38	146,352	183,433
185,000	1,455.40	338,944	2,621.09	173,958	164,986	2,881.59	160,833	178,111	3,104.26	150,416	188,528
190,000	1,494.74	348,106	2,691.94	178,661	169,445	2,959.48	165,181	182,925	3,188.17	154,483	193,623
195,000	1,534.07	357,265	2,762.77	183,361	173,904	3,037.35	169,527	187,738	3,272.06	158,547	198,718
200,000	1,573.41	366,428	2,833.62	188,064	178,364	3,115.24	173,875	192,553	3,355.97	162,613	203,815

115

9.00% GROWING EQUITY MORTGAGES

AMOUNT OF LOAN	30 YEARS MONTHLY PAYMENT	30 YEARS TOTAL INTRST	1% PMT INCR/YR 269.188 PAYMENTS LAST YR MON PMT	TOTAL INTRST	INTRST SAVED	2% PMT INCR/YR 227.060 PAYMENTS LAST YR MON PMT	TOTAL INTRST	INTRST SAVED	3% PMT INCR/YR 200.647 PAYMENTS LAST YR MON PMT	TOTAL INTRST	INTRST SAVED
$ 50	0.41	98	0.51	73	25	0.59	62	36	0.66	55	43
100	0.81	192	1.01	143	49	1.16	121	71	1.30	107	85
200	1.61	380	2.00	283	97	2.30	239	141	2.58	212	168
300	2.42	571	3.01	426	145	3.46	360	211	3.88	319	252
400	3.22	759	4.01	566	193	4.60	478	281	5.17	424	335
500	4.03	951	5.02	709	242	5.76	599	352	6.47	531	420
600	4.83	1,139	6.01	850	289	6.90	717	422	7.75	635	504
700	5.64	1,330	7.02	993	337	8.06	838	492	9.05	742	588
800	6.44	1,518	8.02	1,133	385	9.20	956	562	10.33	847	671
900	7.25	1,710	9.02	1,276	434	10.35	1,077	633	11.63	954	756
1,000	8.05	1,898	10.02	1,416	482	11.50	1,196	702	12.92	1,059	839
2,000	16.10	3,796	20.04	2,832	964	22.99	2,391	1,405	25.84	2,118	1,678
3,000	24.14	5,690	30.05	4,245	1,445	34.48	3,584	2,106	38.74	3,174	2,516
4,000	32.19	7,588	40.07	5,661	1,927	45.98	4,780	2,808	51.66	4,233	3,355
5,000	40.24	9,486	50.09	7,077	2,409	57.47	5,975	3,511	64.57	5,292	4,194
6,000	48.28	11,381	60.09	8,490	2,891	68.96	7,168	4,213	77.48	6,348	5,033
7,000	56.33	13,279	70.11	9,906	3,373	80.45	8,364	4,915	90.39	7,407	5,872
8,000	64.37	15,173	80.12	11,319	3,854	91.94	9,557	5,616	103.29	8,463	6,710
9,000	72.42	17,071	90.14	12,734	4,337	103.43	10,752	6,319	116.21	9,522	7,549
10,000	80.47	18,969	100.16	14,150	4,819	114.93	11,948	7,021	129.13	10,581	8,388
11,000	88.51	20,864	110.17	15,563	5,301	126.41	13,141	7,723	142.03	11,637	9,227
12,000	96.56	22,762	120.19	16,979	5,783	137.91	14,336	8,426	154.95	12,696	10,066
13,000	104.61	24,660	130.21	18,395	6,265	149.41	15,532	9,128	167.87	13,755	10,905
14,000	112.65	26,554	140.22	19,808	6,746	160.89	16,725	9,829	180.77	14,811	11,743
15,000	120.70	28,452	150.24	21,224	7,228	172.39	17,920	10,532	193.69	15,870	12,582
16,000	128.74	30,346	160.24	22,637	7,709	183.87	19,113	11,233	206.59	16,926	13,420
17,000	136.79	32,244	170.26	24,053	8,191	195.37	20,309	11,935	219.51	17,985	14,259
18,000	144.84	34,142	180.28	25,469	8,673	206.87	21,504	12,638	232.43	19,044	15,098
19,000	152.88	36,037	190.29	26,882	9,155	218.35	22,697	13,340	245.33	20,100	15,937
20,000	160.93	37,935	200.31	28,298	9,637	229.85	23,893	14,042	258.25	21,159	16,776
21,000	168.98	39,833	210.33	29,714	10,119	241.35	25,088	14,745	271.16	22,218	17,615
22,000	177.02	41,727	220.34	31,127	10,600	252.83	26,281	15,446	284.07	23,274	18,453
23,000	185.07	43,625	230.36	32,543	11,082	264.33	27,477	16,148	296.98	24,333	19,292
24,000	193.11	45,520	240.37	33,956	11,564	275.81	28,670	16,850	309.88	25,390	20,130
25,000	201.16	47,418	250.39	35,371	12,047	287.31	29,865	17,553	322.80	26,448	20,970
26,000	209.21	49,316	260.41	36,787	12,529	298.80	31,061	18,255	335.72	27,507	21,809
27,000	217.25	51,210	270.41	38,200	13,010	310.29	32,254	18,956	348.62	28,564	22,646
28,000	225.30	53,108	280.43	39,616	13,492	321.78	33,449	19,659	361.54	29,622	23,486
29,000	233.35	55,006	290.45	41,032	13,974	333.28	34,645	20,361	374.46	30,681	24,325
30,000	241.39	56,900	300.46	42,445	14,455	344.76	35,838	21,062	387.36	31,738	25,162
32,500	261.51	61,644	325.51	45,983	15,661	373.50	38,825	22,819	419.65	34,383	27,261
35,000	281.62	66,383	350.54	49,519	16,864	402.22	41,810	24,573	451.92	37,027	29,356
40,000	321.85	75,866	400.61	56,593	19,273	459.68	47,783	28,083	516.47	42,316	33,550
45,000	362.09	85,352	450.70	63,669	21,683	517.15	53,758	31,594	581.05	47,608	37,744
50,000	402.32	94,835	500.77	70,743	24,092	574.61	59,730	35,105	645.61	52,897	41,938
55,000	442.55	104,318	550.85	77,817	26,501	632.07	65,703	38,615	710.16	58,186	46,132
60,000	482.78	113,801	600.92	84,890	28,911	689.53	71,675	42,126	774.72	63,475	50,326
65,000	523.01	123,284	651.00	91,964	31,320	746.99	77,648	45,636	839.28	68,764	54,520
70,000	563.24	132,766	701.07	99,038	33,728	804.45	83,620	49,146	903.83	74,053	58,713
75,000	603.47	142,249	751.15	106,111	36,138	861.90	89,593	52,656	968.39	79,343	62,906
80,000	643.70	151,732	801.22	113,185	38,547	919.36	95,565	56,167	1,032.95	84,632	67,100
85,000	683.93	161,215	851.30	120,259	40,956	976.82	101,538	59,677	1,097.51	89,921	71,294
90,000	724.17	170,701	901.39	127,335	43,366	1,034.29	107,513	63,188	1,162.08	95,213	75,488
95,000	764.40	180,184	951.46	134,409	45,775	1,091.75	113,486	66,698	1,226.64	100,502	79,682
100,000	804.63	189,667	1,001.54	141,483	48,184	1,149.21	119,458	70,209	1,291.19	105,791	83,876
105,000	844.86	199,150	1,051.61	148,557	50,593	1,206.67	125,431	73,719	1,355.75	111,080	88,070
110,000	885.09	208,632	1,101.69	155,630	53,002	1,264.13	131,403	77,229	1,420.31	116,369	92,263
115,000	925.32	218,115	1,151.76	162,704	55,411	1,321.58	137,376	80,739	1,484.87	121,658	96,457
120,000	965.55	227,598	1,201.84	169,778	57,820	1,379.04	143,348	84,250	1,549.42	126,948	100,650
125,000	1,005.78	237,081	1,251.91	176,851	60,229	1,436.50	149,321	87,760	1,613.98	132,237	104,844
130,000	1,046.01	246,564	1,301.99	183,925	62,639	1,493.96	155,293	91,271	1,678.54	137,526	109,038
135,000	1,086.25	256,050	1,352.07	191,002	65,048	1,551.43	161,268	94,782	1,743.11	142,818	113,232
140,000	1,126.48	265,533	1,402.15	198,075	67,458	1,608.89	167,241	98,292	1,807.67	148,107	117,426
145,000	1,166.71	275,016	1,452.22	205,149	69,867	1,666.35	173,213	101,803	1,872.23	153,396	121,620
150,000	1,206.94	284,498	1,502.30	212,223	72,275	1,723.81	179,186	105,312	1,936.78	158,685	125,813
155,000	1,247.17	293,981	1,552.37	219,296	74,685	1,781.27	185,158	108,823	2,001.34	163,974	130,007
160,000	1,287.40	303,464	1,602.45	226,370	77,094	1,838.72	191,131	112,333	2,065.90	169,263	134,201
165,000	1,327.63	312,947	1,652.52	233,444	79,503	1,896.18	197,103	115,844	2,130.46	174,553	138,394
170,000	1,367.86	322,430	1,702.60	240,518	81,912	1,953.64	203,076	119,354	2,195.01	179,842	142,588
175,000	1,408.09	331,912	1,752.67	247,591	84,321	2,011.10	209,048	122,864	2,259.57	185,131	146,781
180,000	1,448.33	341,399	1,802.76	254,668	86,731	2,068.57	215,024	126,375	2,324.14	190,423	150,976
185,000	1,488.56	350,882	1,852.83	261,742	89,140	2,126.03	220,996	129,886	2,388.70	195,712	155,170
190,000	1,528.79	360,364	1,902.91	268,815	91,549	2,183.49	226,969	133,395	2,453.26	201,001	159,363
195,000	1,569.02	369,847	1,952.98	275,889	93,958	2,240.95	232,941	136,906	2,517.82	206,290	163,557
200,000	1,609.25	379,330	2,003.06	282,963	96,367	2,298.41	238,914	140,416	2,582.37	211,579	167,751

116

GROWING EQUITY MORTGAGES 9.00%

AMOUNT OF LOAN	30 YEARS		4% PMT INCR/YR 181.948 PAYMENTS			5% PMT INCR/YR 167.761 PAYMENTS			6% PMT INCR/YR 156.454 PAYMENTS		
	MONTHLY PAYMENT	TOTAL INTRST	LAST YR MON PMT	TOTAL INTRST	INTRST SAVED	LAST YR MON PMT	TOTAL INTRST	INTRST SAVED	LAST YR MON PMT	TOTAL INTRST	INTRST SAVED
$ 50	0.41	98	0.74	50	48	0.77	46	52	0.87	43	55
100	0.81	192	1.46	97	95	1.53	90	102	1.73	84	108
200	1.61	380	2.90	193	187	3.04	178	202	3.43	166	214
300	2.42	571	4.36	290	281	4.56	268	303	5.16	251	320
400	3.22	759	5.80	385	374	6.07	356	403	6.87	333	426
500	4.03	951	7.26	482	469	7.60	446	505	8.60	417	534
600	4.83	1,139	8.70	578	561	9.11	534	605	10.30	499	640
700	5.64	1,330	10.16	675	655	10.64	624	706	12.03	583	747
800	6.44	1,518	11.60	770	748	12.14	712	806	13.74	665	853
900	7.25	1,710	13.06	867	843	13.67	802	908	15.46	750	960
1,000	8.05	1,898	14.50	963	935	15.18	890	1,008	17.17	832	1,066
2,000	16.10	3,796	29.00	1,925	1,871	30.36	1,779	2,017	34.34	1,664	2,132
3,000	24.14	5,690	43.47	2,885	2,805	45.52	2,666	3,024	51.49	2,493	3,197
4,000	32.19	7,588	57.97	3,848	3,740	60.70	3,556	4,032	68.66	3,325	4,263
5,000	40.24	9,486	72.47	4,810	4,676	75.88	4,446	5,040	85.83	4,157	5,329
6,000	48.28	11,381	86.95	5,770	5,611	91.04	5,333	6,048	102.98	4,986	6,395
7,000	56.33	13,279	101.45	6,733	6,546	106.22	6,223	7,056	120.15	5,818	7,461
8,000	64.37	15,173	115.93	7,693	7,480	121.38	7,110	8,063	137.30	6,648	8,525
9,000	72.42	17,071	130.42	8,655	8,416	136.56	7,999	9,072	154.47	7,479	9,592
10,000	80.47	18,969	144.92	9,618	9,351	151.74	8,889	10,080	171.64	8,311	10,658
11,000	88.51	20,864	159.40	10,578	10,286	166.90	9,776	11,088	188.79	9,141	11,723
12,000	96.56	22,762	173.90	11,540	11,222	182.08	10,666	12,096	205.96	9,973	12,789
13,000	104.61	24,660	188.40	12,503	12,157	197.26	11,555	13,105	223.13	10,804	13,856
14,000	112.65	26,554	202.88	13,463	13,091	212.42	12,443	14,111	240.27	11,634	14,920
15,000	120.70	28,452	217.37	14,426	14,026	227.60	13,332	15,120	257.44	12,466	15,986
16,000	128.74	30,346	231.85	15,386	14,960	242.76	14,220	16,126	274.59	13,295	17,051
17,000	136.79	32,244	246.35	16,348	15,896	257.94	15,109	17,135	291.76	14,127	18,117
18,000	144.84	34,142	260.85	17,311	16,831	273.12	15,999	18,143	308.93	14,959	19,183
19,000	152.88	36,037	275.33	18,271	17,766	288.28	16,886	19,151	326.08	15,788	20,249
20,000	160.93	37,935	289.83	19,233	18,702	303.46	17,776	20,159	343.25	16,620	21,315
21,000	168.98	39,833	304.32	20,196	19,637	318.64	18,665	21,168	360.42	17,452	22,381
22,000	177.02	41,727	318.80	21,156	20,571	333.80	19,552	22,175	377.57	18,282	23,445
23,000	185.07	43,625	333.30	22,118	21,507	348.98	20,442	23,183	394.74	19,113	24,512
24,000	193.11	45,520	347.78	23,079	22,441	364.14	21,329	24,191	411.89	19,943	25,577
25,000	201.16	47,418	362.28	24,041	23,377	379.32	22,219	25,199	429.06	20,775	26,643
26,000	209.21	49,316	376.78	25,004	24,312	394.50	23,108	26,208	446.23	21,607	27,709
27,000	217.25	51,210	391.25	25,964	25,246	409.66	23,996	27,214	463.38	22,436	28,774
28,000	225.30	53,108	405.75	26,926	26,182	424.84	24,885	28,223	480.55	23,268	29,840
29,000	233.35	55,006	420.25	27,889	27,117	440.02	25,775	29,231	497.72	24,100	30,906
30,000	241.39	56,900	434.73	28,849	28,051	455.18	26,662	30,238	514.87	24,929	31,971
32,500	261.51	61,644	470.96	31,254	30,390	493.12	28,885	32,759	557.78	27,008	34,636
35,000	281.62	66,383	507.18	33,657	32,726	531.04	31,105	35,278	600.68	29,084	37,299
40,000	321.85	75,866	579.63	38,464	37,402	606.90	35,549	40,317	686.48	33,238	42,628
45,000	362.09	85,352	652.10	43,274	42,078	682.77	39,994	45,358	772.31	37,395	47,957
50,000	402.32	94,835	724.56	48,082	46,753	758.63	44,438	50,397	858.12	41,550	53,285
55,000	442.55	104,318	797.01	52,890	51,428	834.49	48,881	55,437	943.93	45,704	58,614
60,000	482.78	113,801	869.46	57,698	56,103	910.35	53,324	60,477	1,029.74	49,859	63,942
65,000	523.01	123,284	941.91	62,505	60,779	986.21	57,768	65,516	1,115.54	54,013	69,271
70,000	563.24	132,766	1,014.36	67,313	65,453	1,062.07	62,211	70,555	1,201.35	58,168	74,598
75,000	603.47	142,249	1,086.82	72,121	70,128	1,137.93	66,654	75,595	1,287.16	62,322	79,927
80,000	643.70	151,732	1,159.27	76,928	74,804	1,213.79	71,098	80,634	1,372.97	66,477	85,255
85,000	683.93	161,215	1,231.72	81,736	79,479	1,289.65	75,541	85,674	1,458.77	70,631	90,584
90,000	724.17	170,701	1,304.19	86,546	84,155	1,365.53	79,987	90,714	1,544.60	74,788	95,913
95,000	764.40	180,184	1,376.64	91,354	88,830	1,441.39	84,430	95,754	1,630.41	78,942	101,242
100,000	804.63	189,667	1,449.09	96,162	93,505	1,517.25	88,873	100,794	1,716.22	83,097	106,570
105,000	844.86	199,150	1,521.55	100,970	98,180	1,593.11	93,316	105,834	1,802.03	87,251	111,899
110,000	885.09	208,632	1,594.00	105,777	102,855	1,668.97	97,760	110,872	1,887.83	91,406	117,226
115,000	925.32	218,115	1,666.45	110,585	107,530	1,744.83	102,203	115,912	1,973.64	95,560	122,555
120,000	965.55	227,598	1,738.90	115,393	112,205	1,820.69	106,646	120,952	2,059.45	99,715	127,883
125,000	1,005.78	237,081	1,811.35	120,200	116,881	1,896.55	111,090	125,991	2,145.26	103,869	133,212
130,000	1,046.01	246,564	1,883.80	125,008	121,556	1,972.41	115,533	131,031	2,231.06	108,024	138,540
135,000	1,086.25	256,050	1,956.27	129,818	126,232	2,048.29	119,979	136,071	2,316.89	112,181	143,869
140,000	1,126.48	265,533	2,028.73	134,626	130,907	2,124.15	124,422	141,111	2,402.70	116,335	149,198
145,000	1,166.71	275,016	2,101.18	139,434	135,582	2,200.01	128,865	146,151	2,488.51	120,490	154,526
150,000	1,206.94	284,498	2,173.63	144,241	140,257	2,275.87	133,309	151,189	2,574.32	124,644	159,854
155,000	1,247.17	293,981	2,246.08	149,049	144,932	2,351.73	137,752	156,229	2,660.12	128,799	165,182
160,000	1,287.40	303,464	2,318.53	153,857	149,607	2,427.58	142,195	161,269	2,745.93	132,953	170,511
165,000	1,327.63	312,947	2,390.99	158,665	154,282	2,503.44	146,638	166,309	2,831.74	137,108	175,839
170,000	1,367.86	322,430	2,463.44	163,472	158,958	2,579.30	151,082	171,348	2,917.55	141,262	181,168
175,000	1,408.09	331,912	2,535.89	168,280	163,632	2,655.16	155,525	176,387	3,003.35	145,417	186,495
180,000	1,448.33	341,399	2,608.36	173,090	168,309	2,731.04	159,971	181,428	3,089.18	149,573	191,826
185,000	1,488.56	350,882	2,680.81	177,898	172,984	2,806.90	164,414	186,468	3,174.99	153,728	197,154
190,000	1,528.79	360,364	2,753.26	182,706	177,658	2,882.76	168,857	191,507	3,260.80	157,882	202,482
195,000	1,569.02	369,847	2,825.72	187,513	182,334	2,958.62	173,301	196,546	3,346.61	162,037	207,810
200,000	1,609.25	379,330	2,898.17	192,321	187,009	3,034.48	177,744	201,586	3,432.41	166,191	213,139

117

9.25% GROWING EQUITY MORTGAGES

AMOUNT OF LOAN	30 YEARS		1% PMT INCR/YR 267.454 PAYMENTS			2% PMT INCR/YR 225.249 PAYMENTS			3% PMT INCR/YR 198.939 PAYMENTS		
	MONTHLY PAYMENT	TOTAL INTRST	LAST YR MON PMT	TOTAL INTRST	INTRST SAVED	LAST YR MON PMT	TOTAL INTRST	INTRST SAVED	LAST YR MON PMT	TOTAL INTRST	INTRST SAVED
$ 50	0.42	101	0.52	75	26	0.60	63	38	0.67	56	45
100	0.83	199	1.03	147	52	1.19	124	75	1.33	110	89
200	1.65	394	2.05	292	102	2.36	246	148	2.65	217	177
300	2.47	589	3.07	436	153	3.53	367	222	3.96	325	264
400	3.30	788	4.11	583	205	4.71	492	296	5.30	435	353
500	4.12	983	5.13	728	255	5.88	613	370	6.61	542	441
600	4.94	1,178	6.15	872	306	7.06	735	443	7.93	650	528
700	5.76	1,374	7.17	1,016	358	8.23	856	518	9.24	757	617
800	6.59	1,572	8.20	1,164	408	9.41	980	592	10.58	867	705
900	7.41	1,768	9.22	1,308	460	10.58	1,102	666	11.89	975	793
1,000	8.23	1,963	10.24	1,452	511	11.75	1,223	740	13.21	1,082	881
2,000	16.46	3,926	20.49	2,904	1,022	23.51	2,447	1,479	26.41	2,165	1,761
3,000	24.69	5,888	30.73	4,357	1,531	35.26	3,670	2,218	39.62	3,247	2,641
4,000	32.91	7,848	40.96	5,806	2,042	47.00	4,891	2,957	52.81	4,327	3,521
5,000	41.14	9,810	51.21	7,258	2,552	58.76	6,114	3,696	66.02	5,409	4,401
6,000	49.37	11,773	61.45	8,710	3,063	70.51	7,338	4,435	79.22	6,491	5,282
7,000	57.59	13,732	71.68	10,159	3,573	82.25	8,558	5,174	92.42	7,571	6,161
8,000	65.82	15,695	81.93	11,612	4,083	94.01	9,782	5,913	105.62	8,654	7,041
9,000	74.05	17,658	92.17	13,064	4,594	105.76	11,005	6,653	118.83	9,736	7,922
10,000	82.27	19,617	102.40	14,513	5,104	117.50	12,226	7,391	132.02	10,816	8,801
11,000	90.50	21,580	112.65	15,965	5,615	129.26	13,449	8,131	145.23	11,898	9,682
12,000	98.73	23,543	122.89	17,417	6,126	141.01	14,673	8,870	158.43	12,980	10,563
13,000	106.95	25,502	133.12	18,867	6,635	152.75	15,893	9,609	171.62	14,060	11,442
14,000	115.18	27,465	143.37	20,319	7,146	164.51	17,117	10,348	184.83	15,143	12,322
15,000	123.41	29,428	153.61	21,771	7,657	176.26	18,340	11,088	198.04	16,225	13,203
16,000	131.63	31,387	163.84	23,220	8,167	188.00	19,561	11,826	211.23	17,305	14,082
17,000	139.86	33,350	174.09	24,672	8,678	199.75	20,784	12,566	224.43	18,387	14,963
18,000	148.09	35,312	184.33	26,125	9,187	211.51	22,008	13,304	237.64	19,469	15,843
19,000	156.31	37,272	194.56	27,574	9,698	223.25	23,228	14,044	250.83	20,549	16,723
20,000	164.54	39,234	204.81	29,026	10,208	235.00	24,452	14,782	264.04	21,632	17,602
21,000	172.77	41,197	215.05	30,478	10,719	246.76	25,675	15,522	277.25	22,714	18,483
22,000	180.99	43,156	225.28	31,927	11,229	258.50	26,896	16,260	290.44	23,794	19,362
23,000	189.22	45,119	235.53	33,380	11,739	270.25	28,119	17,000	303.64	24,876	20,243
24,000	197.45	47,082	245.77	34,832	12,250	282.01	29,343	17,739	316.85	25,958	21,124
25,000	205.67	49,041	256.00	36,281	12,760	293.75	30,563	18,478	330.04	27,038	22,003
26,000	213.90	51,004	266.24	37,733	13,271	305.50	31,787	19,217	343.25	28,120	22,884
27,000	222.13	52,967	276.49	39,185	13,782	317.26	33,010	19,957	356.45	29,203	23,764
28,000	230.35	54,926	286.72	40,635	14,291	329.00	34,231	20,695	369.64	30,283	24,643
29,000	238.58	56,889	296.96	42,087	14,802	340.75	35,454	21,435	382.85	31,365	25,524
30,000	246.81	58,852	307.21	43,539	15,313	352.51	36,678	22,174	396.06	32,447	26,405
32,500	267.37	63,753	332.80	47,165	16,588	381.87	39,732	24,021	429.05	35,149	28,604
35,000	287.94	68,658	358.40	50,794	17,864	411.25	42,789	25,869	462.06	37,854	30,804
40,000	329.08	78,469	409.61	58,052	20,417	470.01	48,903	29,566	528.08	43,263	35,206
45,000	370.21	88,276	460.81	65,307	22,969	528.75	55,015	33,261	594.08	48,670	39,606
50,000	411.34	98,082	512.00	72,562	25,520	587.49	61,127	36,955	660.08	54,076	44,006
55,000	452.48	107,893	563.21	79,820	28,073	646.25	67,241	40,652	726.10	59,485	48,408
60,000	493.61	117,700	614.40	87,075	30,625	705.00	73,352	44,348	792.10	64,892	52,808
65,000	534.74	127,506	665.60	94,330	33,176	763.74	79,464	48,042	858.10	70,299	57,207
70,000	575.88	137,317	716.81	101,588	35,729	822.50	85,578	51,739	924.12	75,708	61,609
75,000	617.01	147,124	768.00	108,843	38,281	881.24	91,690	55,434	990.12	81,114	66,010
80,000	658.15	156,934	819.21	116,101	40,833	940.00	97,804	59,130	1,056.14	86,524	70,410
85,000	699.28	166,741	870.40	123,356	43,385	998.74	103,916	62,825	1,122.14	91,930	74,811
90,000	740.41	176,548	921.60	130,611	45,937	1,057.49	110,027	66,521	1,188.14	97,337	79,211
95,000	781.55	186,358	972.81	137,869	48,489	1,116.25	116,142	70,216	1,254.16	102,746	83,612
100,000	822.68	196,165	1,024.00	145,124	51,041	1,174.99	122,253	73,912	1,320.16	108,153	88,012
105,000	863.81	205,972	1,075.20	152,379	53,593	1,233.73	128,365	77,607	1,386.16	113,559	92,413
110,000	904.95	215,782	1,126.41	159,637	56,145	1,292.49	134,479	81,303	1,452.18	118,968	96,814
115,000	946.08	225,589	1,177.60	166,892	58,697	1,351.24	140,591	84,998	1,518.18	124,375	101,214
120,000	987.22	235,399	1,228.81	174,150	61,249	1,409.99	146,705	88,694	1,584.20	129,784	105,615
125,000	1,028.35	245,206	1,280.00	181,405	63,801	1,468.74	152,817	92,389	1,650.20	135,191	110,015
130,000	1,069.48	255,013	1,331.20	188,660	66,353	1,527.48	158,928	96,085	1,716.20	140,597	114,416
135,000	1,110.62	264,823	1,382.41	195,918	68,905	1,586.24	165,043	99,781	1,782.22	146,006	118,817
140,000	1,151.75	274,630	1,433.60	203,173	71,457	1,644.98	171,154	103,476	1,848.22	151,413	123,217
145,000	1,192.88	284,437	1,484.80	210,428	74,009	1,703.73	177,266	107,171	1,914.22	156,820	127,617
150,000	1,234.02	294,247	1,536.00	217,686	76,561	1,762.48	183,380	110,867	1,980.24	162,229	132,018
155,000	1,275.15	304,054	1,587.20	224,942	79,112	1,821.23	189,491	114,563	2,046.24	167,635	136,419
160,000	1,316.29	313,864	1,638.41	232,200	81,664	1,879.99	195,606	118,258	2,112.26	173,045	140,819
165,000	1,357.42	323,671	1,689.60	239,455	84,216	1,938.73	201,717	121,954	2,178.26	178,451	145,220
170,000	1,398.55	333,478	1,740.80	246,710	86,768	1,997.47	207,829	125,649	2,244.26	183,858	149,620
175,000	1,439.69	343,288	1,792.00	253,968	89,320	2,056.23	213,943	129,345	2,310.28	189,267	154,021
180,000	1,480.82	353,095	1,843.20	261,223	91,872	2,114.98	220,055	133,040	2,376.28	194,674	158,421
185,000	1,521.95	362,902	1,894.40	268,478	94,424	2,173.72	226,166	136,736	2,442.28	200,080	162,822
190,000	1,563.09	372,712	1,945.60	275,736	96,976	2,232.48	232,281	140,431	2,508.30	205,489	167,223
195,000	1,604.22	382,519	1,996.80	282,991	99,528	2,291.22	238,392	144,127	2,574.30	210,896	171,623
200,000	1,645.36	392,330	2,048.01	290,249	102,081	2,349.98	244,507	147,823	2,640.32	216,305	176,025

118

AMOUNT OF LOAN	30 YEARS		4% PMT INCR/YR 180.388 PAYMENTS			5% PMT INCR/YR 166.253 PAYMENTS			6% PMT INCR/YR 155.058 PAYMENTS		
	MONTHLY PAYMENT	TOTAL INTRST	LAST YR MON PMT	TOTAL INTRST	INTRST SAVED	LAST YR MON PMT	TOTAL INTRST	INTRST SAVED	LAST YR MON PMT	TOTAL INTRST	INTRST SAVED
$ 50	0.42	101	0.76	51	50	0.79	47	54	0.85	44	57
100	0.83	199	1.49	100	99	1.57	92	107	1.67	86	113
200	1.65	394	2.97	198	196	3.11	183	211	3.32	171	223
300	2.47	589	4.45	295	294	4.66	273	316	4.97	255	334
400	3.30	788	5.94	395	393	6.22	365	423	6.64	341	447
500	4.12	983	7.42	493	490	7.77	455	528	8.29	426	557
600	4.94	1,178	8.90	590	588	9.32	546	632	9.94	510	668
700	5.76	1,374	10.37	688	686	10.86	636	738	11.59	594	780
800	6.59	1,572	11.87	788	784	12.43	728	844	13.26	681	891
900	7.41	1,768	13.34	886	882	13.97	818	950	14.91	765	1,003
1,000	8.23	1,963	14.82	983	980	15.52	908	1,055	16.56	849	1,114
2,000	16.46	3,926	29.64	1,967	1,959	31.04	1,817	2,109	33.12	1,698	2,228
3,000	24.69	5,888	44.47	2,950	2,938	46.56	2,725	3,163	49.68	2,548	3,340
4,000	32.91	7,848	59.27	3,931	3,917	62.06	3,631	4,217	66.22	3,395	4,453
5,000	41.14	9,810	74.09	4,914	4,896	77.58	4,540	5,270	82.78	4,244	5,566
6,000	49.37	11,773	88.91	5,897	5,876	93.09	5,448	6,325	99.34	5,093	6,680
7,000	57.59	13,732	103.72	6,878	6,854	108.59	6,355	7,377	115.88	5,940	7,792
8,000	65.82	15,695	118.54	7,861	7,834	124.11	7,263	8,432	132.44	6,789	8,906
9,000	74.05	17,658	133.36	8,845	8,813	139.63	8,171	9,487	149.00	7,638	10,020
10,000	82.27	19,617	148.16	9,826	9,791	155.13	9,078	10,539	165.54	8,485	11,132
11,000	90.50	21,580	162.99	10,809	10,771	170.65	9,986	11,594	182.10	9,334	12,246
12,000	98.73	23,543	177.81	11,792	11,751	186.17	10,894	12,649	198.66	10,184	13,359
13,000	106.95	25,502	192.61	12,773	12,729	201.67	11,801	13,701	215.20	11,031	14,471
14,000	115.18	27,465	207.43	13,756	13,709	217.19	12,709	14,756	231.76	11,880	15,585
15,000	123.41	29,428	222.25	14,740	14,688	232.71	13,617	15,811	248.33	12,729	16,699
16,000	131.63	31,387	237.06	15,720	15,667	248.21	14,524	16,863	264.87	13,576	17,811
17,000	139.86	33,350	251.88	16,704	16,646	263.73	15,432	17,918	281.43	14,425	18,925
18,000	148.09	35,312	266.70	17,687	17,625	279.25	16,340	18,972	297.99	15,274	20,038
19,000	156.31	37,272	281.51	18,668	18,604	294.75	17,247	20,025	314.53	16,121	21,151
20,000	164.54	39,234	296.33	19,651	19,583	310.26	18,155	21,079	331.09	16,971	22,263
21,000	172.77	41,197	311.15	20,634	20,563	325.78	19,064	22,133	347.65	17,820	23,377
22,000	180.99	43,156	325.95	21,615	21,541	341.28	19,970	23,186	364.19	18,667	24,489
23,000	189.22	45,119	340.77	22,599	22,520	356.80	20,878	24,241	380.75	19,516	25,603
24,000	197.45	47,082	355.60	23,582	23,500	372.32	21,787	25,295	397.31	20,365	26,717
25,000	205.67	49,041	370.40	24,563	24,478	387.82	22,693	26,348	413.85	21,212	27,829
26,000	213.90	51,004	385.22	25,546	25,458	403.34	23,601	27,403	430.41	22,061	28,943
27,000	222.13	52,967	400.04	26,529	26,438	418.86	24,510	28,457	446.97	22,910	30,057
28,000	230.35	54,926	414.85	27,510	27,416	434.36	25,416	29,510	463.51	23,757	31,169
29,000	238.58	56,889	429.67	28,493	28,396	449.88	26,324	30,565	480.07	24,607	32,282
30,000	246.81	58,852	444.49	29,477	29,375	465.40	27,233	31,619	496.63	25,456	33,396
32,500	267.37	63,753	481.52	31,931	31,822	504.17	29,500	34,253	538.00	27,575	36,178
35,000	287.94	68,658	518.56	34,388	34,270	542.95	31,770	36,888	579.39	29,697	38,961
40,000	329.08	78,469	592.65	39,302	39,167	620.53	36,310	42,159	662.17	33,941	44,528
45,000	370.21	88,276	666.73	44,214	44,062	698.09	40,848	47,428	744.94	38,183	50,093
50,000	411.34	98,082	740.80	49,125	48,957	775.64	45,385	52,697	827.70	42,424	55,658
55,000	452.48	107,893	814.89	54,039	53,854	853.22	49,925	57,968	910.48	46,668	61,225
60,000	493.61	117,700	888.96	58,951	58,749	930.78	54,463	63,237	993.24	50,909	66,791
65,000	534.74	127,506	963.04	63,863	63,643	1,008.33	59,001	68,505	1,076.00	55,151	72,355
70,000	575.88	137,317	1,037.13	68,777	68,540	1,085.91	63,540	73,777	1,158.78	59,395	77,922
75,000	617.01	147,124	1,111.20	73,688	73,436	1,163.46	68,078	79,046	1,241.55	63,636	83,488
80,000	658.15	156,934	1,185.29	78,602	78,332	1,241.04	72,618	84,316	1,324.33	67,880	89,054
85,000	699.28	166,741	1,259.36	83,514	83,227	1,318.60	77,156	89,585	1,407.09	72,121	94,620
90,000	740.41	176,548	1,333.44	88,425	88,123	1,396.15	81,693	94,855	1,489.85	76,363	100,185
95,000	781.55	186,358	1,407.53	93,339	93,019	1,473.73	86,233	100,125	1,572.63	80,607	105,751
100,000	822.68	196,165	1,481.60	98,251	97,914	1,551.29	90,771	105,394	1,655.39	84,848	111,317
105,000	863.81	205,972	1,555.67	103,163	102,809	1,628.84	95,308	110,664	1,738.16	89,090	116,882
110,000	904.95	215,782	1,629.76	108,076	107,706	1,706.42	99,848	115,934	1,820.94	93,333	122,449
115,000	946.08	225,589	1,703.84	112,988	112,601	1,783.97	104,386	121,203	1,903.70	97,575	128,014
120,000	987.22	235,399	1,777.93	117,902	117,497	1,861.55	108,926	126,473	1,986.48	101,819	133,580
125,000	1,028.35	245,206	1,852.00	122,814	122,392	1,939.11	113,463	131,743	2,069.24	106,060	139,146
130,000	1,069.48	255,013	1,926.07	127,725	127,288	2,016.66	118,001	137,012	2,152.00	110,302	144,711
135,000	1,110.62	264,823	2,000.16	132,639	132,184	2,094.24	122,541	142,282	2,234.79	114,545	150,278
140,000	1,151.75	274,630	2,074.24	137,551	137,079	2,171.80	127,079	147,551	2,317.55	118,787	155,843
145,000	1,192.88	284,437	2,148.31	142,462	141,975	2,249.35	131,615	152,821	2,400.31	123,028	161,409
150,000	1,234.02	294,247	2,222.40	147,376	146,871	2,326.93	136,156	158,091	2,483.09	127,272	166,975
155,000	1,275.15	304,054	2,296.47	152,288	151,766	2,404.49	140,694	163,360	2,565.85	131,514	172,540
160,000	1,316.29	313,864	2,370.56	157,202	156,662	2,482.06	145,234	168,630	2,648.63	135,757	178,107
165,000	1,357.42	323,671	2,444.64	162,114	161,557	2,559.62	149,771	173,900	2,731.40	139,999	183,672
170,000	1,398.55	333,478	2,518.71	167,025	166,453	2,637.17	154,309	179,169	2,814.16	144,240	189,238
175,000	1,439.69	343,288	2,592.80	171,939	171,349	2,714.75	158,849	184,439	2,896.94	148,484	194,804
180,000	1,480.82	353,095	2,666.87	176,851	176,244	2,792.31	163,386	189,709	2,979.70	152,726	200,369
185,000	1,521.95	362,902	2,740.95	181,762	181,140	2,869.86	167,924	194,978	3,062.46	156,967	205,935
190,000	1,563.09	372,712	2,815.04	186,676	186,036	2,947.44	172,464	200,248	3,145.24	161,211	211,501
195,000	1,604.22	382,519	2,889.11	191,588	190,931	3,025.00	177,002	205,517	3,228.01	165,452	217,067
200,000	1,645.36	392,330	2,963.20	196,502	195,828	3,102.57	181,541	210,789	3,310.79	169,696	222,634

AMOUNT OF LOAN	30 YEARS		1% PMT INCR/YR 265.708 PAYMENTS			2% PMT INCR/YR 223.446 PAYMENTS			3% PMT INCR/YR 197.248 PAYMENTS		
	MONTHLY PAYMENT	TOTAL INTRST	LAST YR MON PMT	TOTAL INTRST	INTRST SAVED	LAST YR MON PMT	TOTAL INTRST	INTRST SAVED	LAST YR MON PMT	TOTAL INTRST	INTRST SAVED
$ 50	0.43	105	0.54	77	28	0.61	65	40	0.69	58	47
100	0.85	206	1.06	151	55	1.21	127	79	1.36	113	93
200	1.69	408	2.10	300	108	2.41	252	156	2.71	223	185
300	2.53	611	3.15	448	163	3.61	377	234	4.06	333	278
400	3.37	813	4.19	597	216	4.81	502	311	5.41	444	369
500	4.21	1,016	5.24	745	271	6.01	627	389	6.76	554	462
600	5.05	1,218	6.29	894	324	7.21	751	467	8.10	664	554
700	5.89	1,420	7.33	1,042	378	8.41	876	544	9.45	774	646
800	6.73	1,623	8.38	1,191	432	9.61	1,001	622	10.80	885	738
900	7.57	1,825	9.42	1,339	486	10.81	1,126	699	12.15	995	830
1,000	8.41	2,028	10.47	1,488	540	12.01	1,250	778	13.50	1,105	923
2,000	16.82	4,055	20.94	2,975	1,080	24.02	2,501	1,554	26.99	2,210	1,845
3,000	25.23	6,083	31.40	4,463	1,620	36.03	3,751	2,332	40.49	3,315	2,768
4,000	33.64	8,110	41.87	5,950	2,160	48.05	5,001	3,109	53.98	4,420	3,690
5,000	42.05	10,138	52.34	7,438	2,700	60.06	6,252	3,886	67.48	5,525	4,613
6,000	50.46	12,166	62.81	8,925	3,241	72.07	7,502	4,664	80.97	6,630	5,536
7,000	58.86	14,190	73.26	10,410	3,780	84.07	8,750	5,440	94.45	7,733	6,457
8,000	67.27	16,217	83.73	11,897	4,320	96.08	10,000	6,217	107.95	8,838	7,379
9,000	75.68	18,245	94.20	13,385	4,860	108.09	11,251	6,994	121.44	9,943	8,302
10,000	84.09	20,272	104.67	14,873	5,399	120.10	12,501	7,771	134.94	11,048	9,224
11,000	92.50	22,300	115.14	16,360	5,940	132.11	13,751	8,549	148.44	12,153	10,147
12,000	100.91	24,328	125.60	17,848	6,480	144.12	15,002	9,326	161.93	13,258	11,070
13,000	109.32	26,355	136.07	19,335	7,020	156.14	16,252	10,103	175.43	14,363	11,992
14,000	117.72	28,379	146.53	20,820	7,559	168.13	17,500	10,879	188.91	15,466	12,913
15,000	126.13	30,407	157.00	22,307	8,100	180.14	18,750	11,657	202.40	16,571	13,836
16,000	134.54	32,434	167.46	23,795	8,639	192.16	20,001	12,433	215.90	17,676	14,758
17,000	142.95	34,462	177.93	25,282	9,180	204.17	21,251	13,211	229.39	18,781	15,681
18,000	151.36	36,490	188.40	26,770	9,720	216.18	22,501	13,989	242.89	19,886	16,604
19,000	159.77	38,517	198.87	28,258	10,259	228.19	23,752	14,765	256.38	20,991	17,526
20,000	168.18	40,545	209.34	29,745	10,800	240.20	25,002	15,543	269.88	22,096	18,449
21,000	176.58	42,569	219.79	31,230	11,339	252.20	26,250	16,319	283.36	23,199	19,370
22,000	184.99	44,596	230.26	32,717	11,879	264.21	27,500	17,096	296.85	24,304	20,292
23,000	193.40	46,624	240.73	34,205	12,419	276.22	28,750	17,874	310.35	25,409	21,215
24,000	201.81	48,652	251.20	35,692	12,960	288.23	30,001	18,651	323.85	26,514	22,138
25,000	210.22	50,679	261.66	37,180	13,499	300.25	31,251	19,428	337.34	27,619	23,060
26,000	218.63	52,707	272.13	38,667	14,040	312.26	32,502	20,205	350.84	28,724	23,983
27,000	227.04	54,734	282.60	40,155	14,579	324.27	33,752	20,982	364.33	29,829	24,905
28,000	235.44	56,758	293.06	41,640	15,118	336.27	35,000	21,758	377.81	30,932	25,826
29,000	243.85	58,786	303.52	43,127	15,659	348.28	36,250	22,536	391.31	32,037	26,749
30,000	252.26	60,814	313.99	44,615	16,199	360.29	37,500	23,314	404.80	33,142	27,672
32,500	273.28	65,881	340.16	48,332	17,549	390.31	40,625	25,256	438.53	35,903	29,978
35,000	294.30	70,948	366.32	52,050	18,898	420.33	43,750	27,198	472.27	38,664	32,284
40,000	336.35	81,086	418.66	59,487	21,599	480.39	50,001	31,085	539.74	44,190	36,896
45,000	378.39	91,220	470.99	66,922	24,298	540.43	56,251	34,969	607.20	49,713	41,507
50,000	420.43	101,355	523.32	74,357	26,998	600.48	62,500	38,855	674.67	55,235	46,120
55,000	462.47	111,489	575.64	81,792	29,697	660.52	68,749	42,740	742.13	60,758	50,731
60,000	504.52	121,627	627.98	89,229	32,398	720.58	75,001	46,626	809.61	66,283	55,344
65,000	546.56	131,762	680.31	96,664	35,098	780.62	81,250	50,512	877.07	71,806	59,956
70,000	588.60	141,896	732.64	104,099	37,797	840.67	87,499	54,397	944.53	77,329	64,567
75,000	630.65	152,034	784.98	111,537	40,497	900.72	93,751	58,283	1,012.01	82,854	69,180
80,000	672.69	162,168	837.31	118,972	43,196	960.77	100,000	62,168	1,079.47	88,377	73,791
85,000	714.73	172,303	889.64	126,406	45,897	1,020.81	106,249	66,054	1,146.93	93,900	78,403
90,000	756.77	182,437	941.96	133,841	48,596	1,080.85	112,498	69,939	1,214.39	99,423	83,014
95,000	798.82	192,575	994.30	141,279	51,296	1,140.91	118,750	73,825	1,281.87	104,948	87,627
100,000	840.86	202,710	1,046.63	148,714	53,996	1,200.96	124,999	77,711	1,349.33	110,471	92,239
105,000	882.90	212,844	1,098.96	156,149	56,695	1,261.00	131,249	81,595	1,416.80	115,993	96,851
110,000	924.94	222,978	1,151.29	163,583	59,395	1,321.04	137,498	85,480	1,484.26	121,516	101,462
115,000	966.99	233,116	1,203.63	171,021	62,095	1,381.10	143,750	89,366	1,551.74	127,042	106,074
120,000	1,009.03	243,251	1,255.96	178,456	64,795	1,441.14	149,999	93,252	1,619.20	132,564	110,687
125,000	1,051.07	253,385	1,308.28	185,891	67,494	1,501.19	156,248	97,137	1,686.66	138,087	115,298
130,000	1,093.12	263,523	1,360.62	193,329	70,194	1,561.24	162,500	101,023	1,754.14	143,612	119,911
135,000	1,135.16	273,658	1,412.95	200,763	72,895	1,621.29	168,749	104,909	1,821.60	149,135	124,523
140,000	1,177.20	283,792	1,465.28	208,198	75,594	1,681.33	174,998	108,794	1,889.06	154,658	129,134
145,000	1,219.24	293,926	1,517.61	215,633	78,293	1,741.37	181,247	112,679	1,956.52	160,181	133,745
150,000	1,261.29	304,064	1,569.95	223,071	80,993	1,801.43	187,499	116,565	2,024.00	165,706	138,358
155,000	1,303.33	314,199	1,622.28	230,505	83,694	1,861.48	193,748	120,451	2,091.46	171,229	142,970
160,000	1,345.37	324,333	1,674.60	237,939	86,393	1,921.52	199,997	124,336	2,158.92	176,752	147,581
165,000	1,387.41	334,468	1,726.93	245,375	89,093	1,981.56	206,247	128,221	2,226.39	182,274	152,194
170,000	1,429.46	344,606	1,779.27	252,813	91,793	2,041.62	212,498	132,108	2,293.86	187,800	156,806
175,000	1,471.50	354,740	1,831.60	260,248	94,492	2,101.66	218,748	135,992	2,361.33	193,322	161,418
180,000	1,513.54	364,874	1,883.93	267,682	97,192	2,161.71	224,997	139,877	2,428.79	198,845	166,029
185,000	1,555.59	375,012	1,936.27	275,120	99,892	2,221.77	231,247	143,763	2,496.27	204,371	170,641
190,000	1,597.63	385,147	1,988.60	282,555	102,592	2,281.81	237,498	147,649	2,563.73	209,893	175,254
195,000	1,639.67	395,281	2,040.92	289,990	105,291	2,341.85	243,747	151,534	2,631.19	215,416	179,865
200,000	1,681.71	405,416	2,093.25	297,425	107,991	2,401.90	249,996	155,420	2,698.65	220,939	184,477

GROWING EQUITY MORTGAGES 9.50%

AMOUNT OF LOAN	30 YEARS MONTHLY PAYMENT	30 YEARS TOTAL INTRST	4% PMT INCR/YR 178.802 PAYMENTS LAST YR MON PMT	4% TOTAL INTRST	4% INTRST SAVED	5% PMT INCR/YR 164.769 PAYMENTS LAST YR MON PMT	5% TOTAL INTRST	5% INTRST SAVED	6% PMT INCR/YR 153.663 PAYMENTS LAST YR MON PMT	6% TOTAL INTRST	6% INTRST SAVED
$ 50	0.43	105	0.74	52	53	0.81	49	56	0.87	45	60
100	0.85	206	1.47	102	104	1.60	95	111	1.71	89	117
200	1.69	408	2.93	203	205	3.19	187	221	3.40	175	233
300	2.53	611	4.38	303	308	4.77	280	331	5.09	261	350
400	3.37	813	5.84	403	410	6.35	372	441	6.78	348	465
500	4.21	1,016	7.29	503	513	7.94	464	552	8.47	434	582
600	5.05	1,218	8.74	603	615	9.52	557	661	10.16	521	697
700	5.89	1,420	10.20	703	717	11.11	649	771	11.85	607	813
800	6.73	1,623	11.65	803	820	12.69	742	881	13.54	693	930
900	7.57	1,825	13.11	903	922	14.27	834	991	15.23	780	1,045
1,000	8.41	2,028	14.56	1,003	1,025	15.86	927	1,101	16.92	866	1,162
2,000	16.82	4,055	29.13	2,007	2,048	31.72	1,853	2,202	33.85	1,732	2,323
3,000	25.23	6,083	43.69	3,010	3,073	47.57	2,780	3,303	50.77	2,598	3,485
4,000	33.64	8,110	58.25	4,013	4,097	63.43	3,707	4,403	67.69	3,464	4,646
5,000	42.05	10,138	72.82	5,017	5,121	79.29	4,633	5,505	84.61	4,330	5,808
6,000	50.46	12,166	87.38	6,020	6,146	95.15	5,560	6,606	101.54	5,196	6,970
7,000	58.86	14,190	101.93	7,021	7,169	110.99	6,484	7,706	118.44	6,060	8,130
8,000	67.27	16,217	116.49	8,024	8,193	126.85	7,411	8,806	135.36	6,926	9,291
9,000	75.68	18,245	131.05	9,028	9,217	142.71	8,338	9,907	152.28	7,792	10,453
10,000	84.09	20,272	145.62	10,031	10,241	158.56	9,264	11,008	169.21	8,658	11,614
11,000	92.50	22,300	160.18	11,034	11,266	174.42	10,191	12,109	186.13	9,524	12,776
12,000	100.91	24,328	174.74	12,038	12,290	190.28	11,118	13,210	203.05	10,390	13,938
13,000	109.32	26,355	189.31	13,041	13,314	206.14	12,044	14,311	219.97	11,256	15,099
14,000	117.72	28,379	203.85	14,042	14,337	221.98	12,969	15,410	236.88	12,120	16,259
15,000	126.13	30,407	218.42	15,045	15,362	237.84	13,895	16,512	253.80	12,986	17,421
16,000	134.54	32,434	232.98	16,049	16,385	253.70	14,822	17,612	270.72	13,852	18,582
17,000	142.95	34,462	247.54	17,052	17,410	269.55	15,749	18,713	287.64	14,718	19,744
18,000	151.36	36,490	262.11	18,055	18,435	285.41	16,675	19,815	304.57	15,584	20,906
19,000	159.77	38,517	276.67	19,059	19,458	301.27	17,602	20,915	321.49	16,450	22,067
20,000	168.18	40,545	291.23	20,062	20,483	317.13	18,529	22,016	338.41	17,316	23,229
21,000	176.58	42,569	305.78	21,063	21,506	332.97	19,453	23,116	355.31	18,180	24,389
22,000	184.99	44,596	320.34	22,066	22,530	348.83	20,380	24,216	372.24	19,046	25,550
23,000	193.40	46,624	334.91	23,070	23,554	364.68	21,306	25,318	389.16	19,912	26,712
24,000	201.81	48,652	349.47	24,073	24,579	380.54	22,233	26,419	406.08	20,778	27,874
25,000	210.22	50,679	364.03	25,076	25,603	396.40	23,160	27,519	423.00	21,644	29,035
26,000	218.63	52,707	378.60	26,080	26,627	412.26	24,086	28,621	439.93	22,510	30,197
27,000	227.04	54,734	393.16	27,083	27,651	428.12	25,013	29,721	456.85	23,376	31,358
28,000	235.44	56,758	407.71	28,084	28,674	443.96	25,937	30,821	473.75	24,240	32,518
29,000	243.85	58,786	422.27	29,087	29,699	459.82	26,864	31,922	490.67	25,106	33,680
30,000	252.26	60,814	436.83	30,090	30,724	475.67	27,791	33,023	507.60	25,972	34,842
32,500	273.28	65,881	473.23	32,598	33,283	515.31	30,106	35,775	549.89	28,136	37,745
35,000	294.30	70,948	509.63	35,105	35,843	554.95	32,421	38,527	592.19	30,300	40,648
40,000	336.35	81,086	582.45	40,121	40,965	634.24	37,055	44,031	676.80	34,630	46,456
45,000	378.39	91,220	655.25	45,136	46,084	713.51	41,686	49,534	761.40	38,958	52,262
50,000	420.43	101,355	728.05	50,150	51,205	792.78	46,317	55,038	845.99	43,286	58,069
55,000	462.47	111,489	800.85	55,164	56,325	872.06	50,948	60,541	930.58	47,614	63,875
60,000	504.52	121,627	873.67	60,181	61,446	951.35	55,581	66,046	1,015.19	51,944	69,683
65,000	546.56	131,762	946.47	65,195	66,567	1,030.62	60,212	71,550	1,099.79	56,272	75,490
70,000	588.60	141,896	1,019.26	70,210	71,686	1,109.89	64,843	77,053	1,184.38	60,600	81,296
75,000	630.65	152,034	1,092.08	75,226	76,808	1,189.18	69,476	82,558	1,268.99	64,931	87,103
80,000	672.69	162,168	1,164.88	80,240	81,928	1,268.46	74,107	88,061	1,353.58	69,259	92,909
85,000	714.73	172,303	1,237.68	85,255	87,048	1,347.73	78,738	93,565	1,438.18	73,587	98,716
90,000	756.77	182,437	1,310.48	90,269	92,168	1,427.00	83,369	99,066	1,522.77	77,915	104,522
95,000	798.82	192,575	1,383.30	95,286	97,289	1,506.29	88,003	104,572	1,607.38	82,245	110,330
100,000	840.86	202,710	1,456.10	100,300	102,410	1,585.57	92,634	110,076	1,691.98	86,573	116,137
105,000	882.90	212,844	1,528.90	105,314	107,530	1,664.84	97,264	115,580	1,776.57	90,901	121,943
110,000	924.94	222,978	1,601.70	110,329	112,649	1,744.11	101,895	121,083	1,861.16	95,229	127,749
115,000	966.99	233,116	1,674.51	115,345	117,771	1,823.40	106,529	126,587	1,945.77	99,559	133,557
120,000	1,009.03	243,251	1,747.31	120,360	122,891	1,902.68	111,160	132,091	2,030.37	103,887	139,364
125,000	1,051.07	253,385	1,820.11	125,374	128,011	1,981.95	115,791	137,594	2,114.96	108,215	145,170
130,000	1,093.12	263,523	1,892.93	130,390	133,133	2,061.24	120,424	143,099	2,199.57	112,545	150,978
135,000	1,135.16	273,658	1,965.73	135,405	138,253	2,140.51	125,055	148,603	2,284.16	116,873	156,785
140,000	1,177.20	283,792	2,038.53	140,419	143,373	2,219.79	129,686	154,106	2,368.76	121,201	162,591
145,000	1,219.24	293,926	2,111.33	145,433	148,493	2,299.06	134,317	159,609	2,453.35	125,529	168,397
150,000	1,261.29	304,064	2,184.15	150,450	153,614	2,378.35	138,950	165,114	2,537.96	129,859	174,205
155,000	1,303.33	314,199	2,256.95	155,464	158,735	2,457.62	143,581	170,618	2,622.56	134,187	180,012
160,000	1,345.37	324,333	2,329.75	160,479	163,854	2,536.90	148,212	176,121	2,707.15	138,515	185,818
165,000	1,387.41	334,468	2,402.55	165,493	168,975	2,616.17	152,843	181,625	2,791.74	142,843	191,625
170,000	1,429.46	344,606	2,475.36	170,510	174,096	2,695.46	157,476	187,131	2,876.35	147,173	197,433
175,000	1,471.50	354,740	2,548.16	175,524	179,216	2,774.73	162,107	192,633	2,960.95	151,501	203,239
180,000	1,513.54	364,874	2,620.96	180,538	184,336	2,854.01	166,738	198,136	3,045.54	155,829	209,045
185,000	1,555.59	375,012	2,693.78	185,555	189,457	2,933.30	171,372	203,643	3,130.15	160,159	214,853
190,000	1,597.63	385,147	2,766.58	190,569	194,578	3,012.57	176,003	209,144	3,214.75	164,487	220,660
195,000	1,639.67	395,281	2,839.38	195,583	199,698	3,091.84	180,634	214,647	3,299.34	168,815	226,466
200,000	1,681.71	405,416	2,912.18	200,598	204,818	3,171.12	185,265	220,151	3,383.93	173,143	232,273

GROWING EQUITY MORTGAGES

AMOUNT OF LOAN	30 YEARS		1% PMT INCR/YR 263.949 PAYMENTS			2% PMT INCR/YR 221.652 PAYMENTS			3% PMT INCR/YR 195.575 PAYMENTS		
	MONTHLY PAYMENT	TOTAL INTRST	LAST YR MON PMT	TOTAL INTRST	INTRST SAVED	LAST YR MON PMT	TOTAL INTRST	INTRST SAVED	LAST YR MON PMT	TOTAL INTRST	INTRST SAVED
$ 50	0.43	105	0.53	76	29	0.61	64	41	0.69	56	49
100	0.86	210	1.06	152	58	1.23	128	82	1.38	113	97
200	1.72	419	2.12	305	114	2.46	256	163	2.76	226	193
300	2.58	629	3.18	457	172	3.68	384	245	4.14	339	290
400	3.44	838	4.24	610	228	4.91	512	326	5.52	452	386
500	4.30	1,048	5.30	762	286	6.14	640	408	6.90	565	483
600	5.16	1,258	6.36	915	343	7.37	768	490	8.28	678	580
700	6.02	1,467	7.42	1,067	400	8.60	895	572	9.66	791	676
800	6.88	1,677	8.48	1,220	457	9.83	1,023	654	11.04	904	773
900	7.74	1,886	9.54	1,372	514	11.05	1,151	735	12.42	1,017	869
1,000	8.60	2,096	10.60	1,525	571	12.28	1,279	817	13.80	1,130	966
2,000	17.19	4,188	21.18	3,047	1,141	24.55	2,556	1,632	27.58	2,257	1,931
3,000	25.78	6,281	31.77	4,569	1,712	36.82	3,832	2,449	41.37	3,384	2,897
4,000	34.37	8,373	42.36	6,091	2,282	49.09	5,109	3,264	55.15	4,511	3,862
5,000	42.96	10,466	52.94	7,613	2,853	61.36	6,385	4,081	68.94	5,638	4,828
6,000	51.55	12,558	63.53	9,135	3,423	73.63	7,662	4,896	82.72	6,765	5,793
7,000	60.15	14,654	74.13	10,660	3,994	85.91	8,941	5,713	96.52	7,894	6,760
8,000	68.74	16,746	84.71	12,182	4,564	98.18	10,217	6,529	110.31	9,021	7,725
9,000	77.33	18,839	95.30	13,704	5,135	110.45	11,494	7,345	124.09	10,148	8,691
10,000	85.92	20,931	105.89	15,226	5,705	122.71	12,771	8,160	137.88	11,275	9,656
11,000	94.51	23,024	116.47	16,748	6,276	134.98	14,047	8,977	151.66	12,403	10,621
12,000	103.10	25,116	127.06	18,270	6,846	147.25	15,324	9,792	165.45	13,530	11,586
13,000	111.70	27,212	137.66	19,795	7,417	159.54	16,603	10,609	179.25	14,659	12,553
14,000	120.29	29,304	148.24	21,317	7,987	171.80	17,879	11,425	193.03	15,786	13,518
15,000	128.88	31,397	158.83	22,839	8,558	184.07	19,156	12,241	206.81	16,913	14,484
16,000	137.47	33,489	169.42	24,361	9,128	196.34	20,432	13,057	220.60	18,040	15,449
17,000	146.06	35,582	180.00	25,883	9,699	208.61	21,709	13,873	234.38	19,167	16,415
18,000	154.65	37,674	190.59	27,405	10,269	220.88	22,985	14,689	248.17	20,294	17,380
19,000	163.24	39,766	201.18	28,927	10,839	233.15	24,262	15,504	261.95	21,421	18,345
20,000	171.84	41,862	211.77	30,452	11,410	245.43	25,541	16,321	275.75	22,551	19,311
21,000	180.43	43,955	222.36	31,974	11,981	257.70	26,818	17,137	289.54	23,678	20,277
22,000	189.02	46,047	232.95	33,496	12,551	269.97	28,094	17,953	303.32	24,805	21,242
23,000	197.61	48,140	243.53	35,018	13,122	282.24	29,371	18,769	317.11	25,932	22,208
24,000	206.20	50,232	254.12	36,540	13,692	294.50	30,647	19,585	330.89	27,059	23,173
25,000	214.79	52,324	264.71	38,062	14,262	306.77	31,924	20,400	344.67	28,186	24,138
26,000	223.39	54,420	275.30	39,586	14,834	319.06	33,203	21,217	358.48	29,316	25,104
27,000	231.98	56,513	285.89	41,108	15,405	331.32	34,479	22,034	372.26	30,443	26,070
28,000	240.57	58,605	296.48	42,630	15,975	343.59	35,756	22,849	386.04	31,570	27,035
29,000	249.16	60,698	307.06	44,152	16,546	355.86	37,032	23,666	399.83	32,697	28,001
30,000	257.75	62,790	317.65	45,674	17,116	368.13	38,309	24,481	413.61	33,824	28,966
32,500	279.23	68,023	344.12	49,481	18,542	398.81	41,502	26,521	448.08	36,643	31,380
35,000	300.71	73,256	370.59	53,287	19,969	429.49	44,694	28,562	482.55	39,462	33,794
40,000	343.67	83,721	423.54	60,900	22,821	490.85	51,079	32,642	551.49	45,099	38,622
45,000	386.62	94,183	476.47	68,510	25,673	552.19	57,462	36,721	620.41	50,735	43,448
50,000	429.58	104,649	529.41	76,123	28,526	613.55	63,847	40,802	689.35	56,372	48,277
55,000	472.54	115,114	582.35	83,736	31,378	674.90	70,233	44,881	758.29	62,010	53,104
60,000	515.50	125,580	635.30	91,349	34,231	736.26	76,618	48,962	827.23	67,648	57,932
65,000	558.46	136,046	688.24	98,962	37,084	797.62	83,003	53,043	896.16	73,286	62,760
70,000	601.41	146,508	741.17	106,572	39,936	858.96	89,386	57,122	965.09	78,921	67,587
75,000	644.37	156,973	794.12	114,185	42,788	920.32	95,771	61,202	1,034.02	84,559	72,414
80,000	687.33	167,439	847.06	121,797	45,642	981.68	102,156	65,283	1,102.96	90,196	77,243
85,000	730.29	177,904	900.00	129,410	48,494	1,043.03	108,542	69,362	1,171.90	95,834	82,070
90,000	773.24	188,366	952.93	137,020	51,346	1,104.38	114,924	73,442	1,240.82	101,469	86,897
95,000	816.20	198,832	1,005.88	144,633	54,199	1,165.73	121,309	77,523	1,309.76	107,107	91,725
100,000	859.16	209,298	1,058.82	152,246	57,052	1,227.09	127,695	81,603	1,378.70	112,745	96,553
105,000	902.12	219,763	1,111.77	159,859	59,904	1,288.45	134,080	85,683	1,447.64	118,382	101,381
110,000	945.07	230,225	1,164.70	167,469	62,756	1,349.79	140,463	89,762	1,516.56	124,018	106,207
115,000	988.03	240,691	1,217.64	175,082	65,609	1,411.15	146,848	93,843	1,585.50	129,655	111,036
120,000	1,030.99	251,156	1,270.58	182,695	68,461	1,472.51	153,233	97,923	1,654.44	135,293	115,863
125,000	1,073.95	261,622	1,323.53	190,308	71,314	1,533.87	159,618	102,004	1,723.37	140,931	120,691
130,000	1,116.91	272,088	1,376.47	197,921	74,167	1,595.22	166,004	106,084	1,792.31	146,569	125,519
135,000	1,159.86	282,550	1,429.40	205,530	77,020	1,656.57	172,386	110,164	1,861.23	152,204	130,346
140,000	1,202.82	293,015	1,482.35	213,143	79,872	1,717.92	178,772	114,243	1,930.17	157,842	135,173
145,000	1,245.78	303,481	1,535.29	220,756	82,725	1,779.28	185,157	118,324	1,999.11	163,479	140,002
150,000	1,288.74	313,946	1,588.23	228,369	85,577	1,840.64	191,542	122,404	2,068.05	169,117	144,829
155,000	1,331.69	324,408	1,641.16	235,979	88,429	1,901.98	197,925	126,483	2,136.97	174,752	149,656
160,000	1,374.65	334,874	1,694.11	243,592	91,282	1,963.34	204,310	130,564	2,205.91	180,390	154,484
165,000	1,417.61	345,340	1,747.05	251,205	94,135	2,024.70	210,695	134,645	2,274.85	186,028	159,312
170,000	1,460.57	355,805	1,799.99	258,818	96,987	2,086.05	217,081	138,724	2,343.79	191,665	164,140
175,000	1,503.53	366,271	1,852.94	266,431	99,840	2,147.41	223,466	142,805	2,412.72	197,303	168,968
180,000	1,546.48	376,733	1,905.87	274,041	102,692	2,208.75	229,848	146,885	2,481.65	202,938	173,795
185,000	1,589.44	387,199	1,958.81	281,654	105,544	2,270.11	236,234	150,964	2,550.58	208,576	178,622
190,000	1,632.40	397,664	2,011.76	289,266	108,398	2,331.47	242,619	155,045	2,619.52	214,214	183,450
195,000	1,675.36	408,130	2,064.70	296,879	111,251	2,392.83	249,004	159,126	2,688.46	219,852	188,278
200,000	1,718.31	418,592	2,117.63	304,489	114,103	2,454.17	255,387	163,205	2,757.38	225,487	193,105

GROWING EQUITY MORTGAGES 9.75%

AMOUNT OF LOAN	30 YEARS		4% PMT INCR/YR 177.223 PAYMENTS			5% PMT INCR/YR 163.309 PAYMENTS			6% PMT INCR/YR 152.291 PAYMENTS		
	MONTHLY PAYMENT	TOTAL INTRST	LAST YR MON PMT	TOTAL INTRST	INTRST SAVED	LAST YR MON PMT	TOTAL INTRST	INTRST SAVED	LAST YR MON PMT	TOTAL INTRST	INTRST SAVED
$ 50	0.43	105	0.74	51	54	0.81	47	58	0.87	44	61
100	0.86	210	1.49	103	107	1.62	95	115	1.73	88	122
200	1.72	419	2.98	205	214	3.24	189	230	3.46	177	242
300	2.58	629	4.47	308	321	4.86	284	345	5.19	265	364
400	3.44	838	5.96	410	428	6.49	379	459	6.92	354	484
500	4.30	1,048	7.45	513	535	8.11	473	575	8.65	442	606
600	5.16	1,258	8.94	615	643	9.73	568	690	10.38	531	727
700	6.02	1,467	10.42	718	749	11.35	663	804	12.11	619	848
800	6.88	1,677	11.91	820	857	12.97	757	920	13.84	708	969
900	7.74	1,886	13.40	923	963	14.59	852	1,034	15.57	796	1,090
1,000	8.60	2,096	14.89	1,025	1,071	16.22	947	1,149	17.30	884	1,212
2,000	17.19	4,188	29.77	2,048	2,140	32.41	1,891	2,297	34.59	1,767	2,421
3,000	25.78	6,281	44.64	3,071	3,210	48.61	2,835	3,446	51.87	2,649	3,632
4,000	34.37	8,373	59.52	4,093	4,280	64.81	3,779	4,594	69.16	3,531	4,842
5,000	42.96	10,466	74.39	5,116	5,350	81.01	4,723	5,743	86.44	4,413	6,053
6,000	51.55	12,558	89.27	6,139	6,419	97.21	5,668	6,890	103.73	5,296	7,262
7,000	60.15	14,654	104.16	7,164	7,490	113.42	6,614	8,040	121.03	6,180	8,474
8,000	68.74	16,746	119.04	8,186	8,560	129.62	7,558	9,188	138.32	7,062	9,684
9,000	77.33	18,839	133.91	9,209	9,630	145.82	8,503	10,336	155.60	7,945	10,894
10,000	85.92	20,931	148.79	10,232	10,699	162.01	9,447	11,484	172.89	8,827	12,104
11,000	94.51	23,024	163.66	11,255	11,769	178.21	10,391	12,633	190.17	9,709	13,315
12,000	103.10	25,116	178.54	12,277	12,839	194.41	11,335	13,781	207.46	10,592	14,524
13,000	111.70	27,212	193.43	13,302	13,910	210.63	12,282	14,930	224.76	11,476	15,736
14,000	120.29	29,304	208.30	14,325	14,979	226.82	13,226	16,078	242.05	12,358	16,946
15,000	128.88	31,397	223.18	15,348	16,049	243.02	14,170	17,227	259.33	13,240	18,157
16,000	137.47	33,489	238.05	16,371	17,118	259.22	15,115	18,374	276.62	14,123	19,366
17,000	146.06	35,582	252.93	17,393	18,189	275.42	16,059	19,523	293.90	15,005	20,577
18,000	154.65	37,674	267.80	18,416	19,258	291.62	17,003	20,671	311.19	15,887	21,787
19,000	163.24	39,766	282.68	19,439	20,327	307.81	17,947	21,819	328.47	16,770	22,996
20,000	171.84	41,862	297.57	20,464	21,398	324.03	18,894	22,968	345.78	17,654	24,208
21,000	180.43	43,955	312.45	21,487	22,468	340.23	19,838	24,117	363.06	18,536	25,419
22,000	189.02	46,047	327.32	22,509	23,538	356.43	20,782	25,265	380.35	19,419	26,628
23,000	197.61	48,140	342.20	23,532	24,608	372.62	21,727	26,413	397.63	20,301	27,839
24,000	206.20	50,232	357.07	24,555	25,677	388.82	22,671	27,561	414.91	21,183	29,049
25,000	214.79	52,324	371.95	25,578	26,746	405.02	23,615	28,709	432.20	22,065	30,259
26,000	223.39	54,420	386.84	26,603	27,817	421.24	24,562	29,858	449.50	22,950	31,470
27,000	231.98	56,513	401.71	27,625	28,888	437.43	25,506	31,007	466.79	23,832	32,681
28,000	240.57	58,605	416.59	28,648	29,957	453.63	26,450	32,155	484.07	24,714	33,891
29,000	249.16	60,698	431.46	29,671	31,027	469.83	27,394	33,304	501.36	25,597	35,101
30,000	257.75	62,790	446.34	30,693	32,097	486.03	28,339	34,451	518.64	26,479	36,311
32,500	279.23	68,023	483.54	33,251	34,772	526.53	30,700	37,323	561.87	28,686	39,337
35,000	300.71	73,256	520.73	35,809	37,447	567.03	33,062	40,194	605.09	30,892	42,364
40,000	343.67	83,721	595.13	40,925	42,796	648.04	37,766	45,935	691.53	35,306	48,415
45,000	386.62	94,183	669.50	46,039	48,144	729.03	42,507	51,676	777.96	39,717	54,466
50,000	429.58	104,649	743.89	51,155	53,494	810.04	47,230	57,419	864.40	44,131	60,518
55,000	472.54	115,114	818.29	56,271	58,843	891.04	51,954	63,160	950.84	48,544	66,570
60,000	515.50	125,580	892.68	61,387	64,193	972.05	56,677	68,903	1,037.29	52,958	72,622
65,000	558.46	136,046	967.07	66,503	69,543	1,053.06	61,401	74,645	1,123.73	57,371	78,675
70,000	601.41	146,508	1,041.45	71,617	74,891	1,134.05	66,122	80,386	1,210.16	61,782	84,726
75,000	644.37	156,973	1,115.84	76,733	80,241	1,215.06	70,845	86,128	1,296.60	66,196	90,777
80,000	687.33	167,439	1,190.23	81,848	85,591	1,296.05	75,569	91,870	1,383.04	70,609	96,830
85,000	730.29	177,904	1,264.63	86,964	90,940	1,377.07	80,292	97,612	1,469.49	75,023	102,881
90,000	773.24	188,366	1,339.00	92,078	96,288	1,458.06	85,014	103,352	1,555.91	79,434	108,932
95,000	816.20	198,832	1,413.39	97,194	101,638	1,539.07	89,737	109,095	1,642.35	83,848	114,984
100,000	859.16	209,298	1,487.79	102,310	106,988	1,620.07	94,461	114,837	1,728.80	88,261	121,037
105,000	902.12	219,763	1,562.18	107,426	112,337	1,701.08	99,184	120,579	1,815.24	92,675	127,088
110,000	945.07	230,225	1,636.56	112,540	117,685	1,782.07	103,905	126,320	1,901.67	97,086	133,139
115,000	988.03	240,691	1,710.95	117,656	123,035	1,863.08	108,629	132,062	1,988.11	101,500	139,191
120,000	1,030.99	251,156	1,785.34	122,772	128,384	1,944.09	113,352	137,804	2,074.55	105,913	145,243
125,000	1,073.95	261,622	1,859.73	127,888	133,734	2,025.09	118,076	143,546	2,161.00	110,327	151,295
130,000	1,116.91	272,088	1,934.13	133,003	139,085	2,106.10	122,799	149,289	2,247.44	114,740	157,348
135,000	1,159.86	282,550	2,008.50	138,117	144,433	2,187.09	127,520	155,030	2,333.87	119,151	163,399
140,000	1,202.82	293,015	2,082.90	143,233	149,782	2,268.10	132,244	160,771	2,420.31	123,565	169,450
145,000	1,245.78	303,481	2,157.29	148,349	155,132	2,349.10	136,967	166,514	2,506.75	127,978	175,503
150,000	1,288.74	313,946	2,231.68	153,465	160,481	2,430.11	141,691	172,255	2,593.20	132,392	181,554
155,000	1,331.69	324,408	2,306.06	158,579	165,829	2,511.10	146,412	177,996	2,679.62	136,803	187,605
160,000	1,374.65	334,874	2,380.45	163,695	171,179	2,592.11	151,136	183,738	2,766.07	141,217	193,657
165,000	1,417.61	345,340	2,454.84	168,811	176,529	2,673.12	155,859	189,481	2,852.51	145,630	199,710
170,000	1,460.57	355,805	2,529.23	173,927	181,878	2,754.12	160,582	195,223	2,938.95	150,044	205,761
175,000	1,503.53	366,271	2,603.63	179,043	187,228	2,835.13	165,306	200,965	3,025.40	154,457	211,814
180,000	1,546.48	376,733	2,678.00	184,156	192,577	2,916.12	170,027	206,706	3,111.82	158,868	217,865
185,000	1,589.44	387,198	2,752.40	189,272	197,926	2,997.13	174,751	212,449	3,198.27	163,282	223,916
190,000	1,632.40	397,664	2,826.79	194,388	203,276	3,078.13	179,474	218,190	3,284.71	167,695	229,969
195,000	1,675.36	408,130	2,901.18	199,504	208,626	3,159.14	184,198	223,932	3,371.15	172,109	236,021
200,000	1,718.31	418,592	2,975.56	204,618	213,974	3,240.13	188,919	229,673	3,457.58	176,520	242,072

AMOUNT OF LOAN	30 YEARS		1% PMT INCR/YR 262.165 PAYMENTS			2% PMT INCR/YR 219.866 PAYMENTS			3% PMT INCR/YR 193.919 PAYMENTS		
	MONTHLY PAYMENT	TOTAL INTRST	LAST YR MON PMT	TOTAL INTRST	INTRST SAVED	LAST YR MON PMT	TOTAL INTRST	INTRST SAVED	LAST YR MON PMT	TOTAL INTRST	INTRST SAVED
$ 50	0.44	108	0.54	78	30	0.63	65	43	0.71	58	50
100	0.88	217	1.08	156	61	1.26	131	86	1.41	116	101
200	1.76	434	2.17	313	121	2.51	262	172	2.82	231	203
300	2.64	650	3.25	469	181	3.77	393	257	4.24	347	303
400	3.52	867	4.34	626	241	5.03	524	343	5.65	462	405
500	4.39	1,080	5.41	779	301	6.27	652	428	7.04	575	505
600	5.27	1,297	6.49	936	361	7.53	783	514	8.46	691	606
700	6.15	1,514	7.58	1,092	422	8.78	914	600	9.87	807	707
800	7.03	1,731	8.66	1,249	482	10.04	1,045	686	11.28	922	809
900	7.90	1,944	9.74	1,402	542	11.28	1,174	770	12.68	1,035	909
1,000	8.78	2,161	10.82	1,558	603	12.54	1,304	857	14.09	1,151	1,010
2,000	17.56	4,322	21.64	3,117	1,205	25.08	2,609	1,713	28.18	2,302	2,020
3,000	26.33	6,479	32.45	4,672	1,807	37.61	3,911	2,568	42.25	3,450	3,029
4,000	35.11	8,640	43.27	6,231	2,409	50.15	5,215	3,425	56.34	4,601	4,039
5,000	43.88	10,797	54.08	7,787	3,010	62.67	6,517	4,280	70.41	5,749	5,048
6,000	52.66	12,958	64.90	9,345	3,613	75.21	7,822	5,136	84.50	6,900	6,058
7,000	61.44	15,118	75.72	10,903	4,215	87.75	9,126	5,992	98.59	8,050	7,068
8,000	70.21	17,276	86.53	12,459	4,817	100.28	10,428	6,848	112.67	9,199	8,077
9,000	78.99	19,436	97.35	14,017	5,419	112.82	11,732	7,704	126.76	10,350	9,086
10,000	87.76	21,594	108.15	15,573	6,021	125.34	13,034	8,560	140.83	11,498	10,096
11,000	96.54	23,754	118.98	17,132	6,622	137.88	14,339	9,415	154.92	12,649	11,105
12,000	105.31	25,912	129.78	18,687	7,225	150.41	15,641	10,271	168.99	13,797	12,115
13,000	114.09	28,072	140.60	20,246	7,826	162.95	16,945	11,127	183.08	14,948	13,124
14,000	122.87	30,233	151.42	21,804	8,429	175.49	18,250	11,983	197.17	16,098	14,135
15,000	131.64	32,390	162.23	23,360	9,030	188.01	19,551	12,839	211.24	17,247	15,143
16,000	140.42	34,551	173.05	24,918	9,633	200.55	20,856	13,695	225.33	18,398	16,153
17,000	149.19	36,708	183.86	26,474	10,234	213.08	22,158	14,550	239.41	19,546	17,162
18,000	157.97	38,869	194.68	28,032	10,837	225.62	23,462	15,407	253.50	20,697	18,172
19,000	166.74	41,026	205.49	29,588	11,438	238.15	24,764	16,262	267.57	21,845	19,181
20,000	175.52	43,187	216.31	31,146	12,041	250.69	26,069	17,118	281.66	22,996	20,191
21,000	184.30	45,348	227.13	32,705	12,643	263.23	27,373	17,975	295.75	24,146	21,202
22,000	193.07	47,505	237.94	34,260	13,245	275.75	28,675	18,830	309.82	25,295	22,210
23,000	201.85	49,666	248.76	35,819	13,847	288.29	29,979	19,687	323.91	26,446	23,220
24,000	210.62	51,823	259.57	37,374	14,449	300.82	31,281	20,542	337.98	27,594	24,229
25,000	219.40	53,984	270.39	38,933	15,051	313.36	32,586	21,398	352.07	28,745	25,239
26,000	228.17	56,141	281.19	40,488	15,653	325.88	33,888	22,253	366.15	29,893	26,248
27,000	236.95	58,302	292.02	42,047	16,255	338.42	35,192	23,110	380.24	31,044	27,258
28,000	245.73	60,463	302.84	43,605	16,858	350.96	36,497	23,966	394.32	32,195	28,268
29,000	254.50	62,620	313.64	45,161	17,459	363.49	37,798	24,822	408.40	33,343	29,277
30,000	263.28	64,781	324.46	46,719	18,062	376.03	39,103	25,678	422.49	34,494	30,287
32,500	285.22	70,179	351.50	50,612	19,567	407.36	42,362	27,817	457.69	37,368	32,811
35,000	307.16	75,578	378.54	54,506	21,072	438.70	45,620	29,958	492.90	40,243	35,335
40,000	351.03	86,371	432.61	62,289	24,082	501.36	52,135	34,236	563.30	45,989	40,383
45,000	394.91	97,168	486.68	70,076	27,092	564.03	58,652	38,516	633.71	51,738	45,430
50,000	438.79	107,964	540.76	77,862	30,102	626.70	65,169	42,795	704.13	57,487	50,477
55,000	482.67	118,761	594.84	85,649	33,112	689.37	71,686	47,075	774.54	63,236	55,525
60,000	526.55	129,558	648.92	93,435	36,123	752.04	78,203	51,355	844.96	68,985	60,573
65,000	570.43	140,355	702.99	101,222	39,133	814.71	84,720	55,635	915.37	74,734	65,621
70,000	614.31	151,152	757.07	109,008	42,144	877.39	91,238	59,914	985.79	80,483	70,669
75,000	658.18	161,945	811.14	116,792	45,153	940.04	97,752	64,193	1,056.19	86,229	75,716
80,000	702.06	172,742	865.21	124,579	48,163	1,002.71	104,269	68,473	1,126.60	91,978	80,764
85,000	745.94	183,538	919.29	132,365	51,173	1,065.39	110,786	72,752	1,197.01	97,727	85,811
90,000	789.82	194,335	973.37	140,152	54,183	1,128.06	117,304	77,031	1,267.43	103,476	90,859
95,000	833.70	205,132	1,027.45	147,938	57,194	1,190.73	123,821	81,311	1,337.84	109,225	95,907
100,000	877.58	215,929	1,081.52	155,725	60,204	1,253.40	130,338	85,591	1,408.26	114,974	100,955
105,000	921.46	226,726	1,135.60	163,511	63,215	1,316.07	136,855	89,871	1,478.67	120,723	106,003
110,000	965.33	237,519	1,189.66	171,295	66,224	1,378.73	143,370	94,149	1,549.07	126,469	111,050
115,000	1,009.21	248,316	1,243.74	179,081	69,235	1,441.40	149,887	98,429	1,619.49	132,218	116,098
120,000	1,053.09	259,112	1,297.82	186,868	72,244	1,504.07	156,404	102,708	1,689.90	137,967	121,145
125,000	1,096.97	269,909	1,351.90	194,654	75,255	1,566.74	162,921	106,988	1,760.31	143,716	126,193
130,000	1,140.85	280,706	1,405.97	202,441	78,265	1,629.41	169,438	111,268	1,830.73	149,465	131,241
135,000	1,184.73	291,503	1,460.05	210,227	81,276	1,692.09	175,955	115,548	1,901.14	155,214	136,289
140,000	1,228.61	302,300	1,514.13	218,014	84,286	1,754.76	182,472	119,828	1,971.56	160,963	141,337
145,000	1,272.48	313,093	1,568.19	225,798	87,295	1,817.41	188,987	124,106	2,041.96	166,709	146,384
150,000	1,316.36	323,890	1,622.27	233,584	90,306	1,880.09	195,504	128,386	2,112.37	172,458	151,432
155,000	1,360.24	334,686	1,676.35	241,371	93,315	1,942.76	202,021	132,665	2,182.79	178,207	156,479
160,000	1,404.12	345,483	1,730.43	249,157	96,326	2,005.43	208,538	136,945	2,253.20	183,956	161,527
165,000	1,448.00	356,280	1,784.50	256,944	99,336	2,068.10	215,056	141,224	2,323.61	189,705	166,575
170,000	1,491.88	367,077	1,838.58	264,730	102,347	2,130.77	221,573	145,504	2,394.03	195,454	171,623
175,000	1,535.76	377,874	1,892.66	272,517	105,357	2,193.44	228,090	149,784	2,464.44	201,203	176,671
180,000	1,579.63	388,667	1,946.72	280,300	108,367	2,256.10	234,604	154,063	2,534.84	206,949	181,718
185,000	1,623.51	399,464	2,000.80	288,087	111,377	2,318.77	241,122	158,342	2,605.26	212,698	186,766
190,000	1,667.39	410,260	2,054.88	295,873	114,387	2,381.44	247,639	162,621	2,675.67	218,447	191,813
195,000	1,711.27	421,057	2,108.96	303,660	117,397	2,444.11	254,156	166,901	2,746.09	224,196	196,861
200,000	1,755.15	431,854	2,163.03	311,446	120,408	2,506.79	260,673	171,181	2,816.50	229,945	201,909

GROWING EQUITY MORTGAGES 10.00%

AMOUNT OF LOAN	30 YEARS		4% PMT INCR/YR 175.667 PAYMENTS			5% PMT INCR/YR 161.873 PAYMENTS			6% PMT INCR/YR 150.944 PAYMENTS		
	MONTHLY PAYMENT	TOTAL INTRST	LAST YR MON PMT	TOTAL INTRST	INTRST SAVED	LAST YR MON PMT	TOTAL INTRST	INTRST SAVED	LAST YR MON PMT	TOTAL INTRST	INTRST SAVED
$ 50	0.44	108	0.76	52	56	0.83	48	60	0.89	45	63
100	0.88	217	1.52	105	112	1.66	97	120	1.77	90	127
200	1.76	434	3.05	210	224	3.32	194	240	3.54	181	253
300	2.64	650	4.57	315	335	4.98	290	360	5.31	271	379
400	3.52	867	6.10	419	448	6.64	387	480	7.08	362	505
500	4.39	1,080	7.60	522	558	8.28	482	598	8.83	450	630
600	5.27	1,297	9.13	627	670	9.94	579	718	10.60	540	757
700	6.15	1,514	10.65	732	782	11.60	675	839	12.38	631	883
800	7.03	1,731	12.17	836	895	13.26	772	959	14.15	721	1,010
900	7.90	1,944	13.68	939	1,005	14.90	867	1,077	15.90	810	1,134
1,000	8.78	2,161	15.20	1,044	1,117	16.56	963	1,198	17.67	900	1,261
2,000	17.56	4,322	30.41	2,088	2,234	33.11	1,927	2,395	35.33	1,800	2,522
3,000	26.33	6,479	45.60	3,129	3,350	49.65	2,888	3,591	52.98	2,698	3,781
4,000	35.11	8,640	60.80	4,173	4,467	66.21	3,852	4,788	70.65	3,598	5,042
5,000	43.88	10,797	75.99	5,214	5,583	82.74	4,813	5,984	88.30	4,496	6,301
6,000	52.66	12,958	91.19	6,258	6,700	99.30	5,776	7,182	105.96	5,396	7,562
7,000	61.44	15,118	106.39	7,302	7,816	115.85	6,740	8,378	123.63	6,296	8,822
8,000	70.21	17,276	121.58	8,343	8,933	132.39	7,701	9,575	141.28	7,194	10,082
9,000	78.99	19,436	136.79	9,387	10,049	148.95	8,665	10,771	158.94	8,094	11,342
10,000	87.76	21,594	151.97	10,429	11,165	165.48	9,626	11,968	176.59	8,992	12,602
11,000	96.54	23,754	167.18	11,473	12,281	182.04	10,589	13,165	194.26	9,892	13,862
12,000	105.31	25,912	182.36	12,514	13,398	198.58	11,550	14,362	211.90	10,790	15,122
13,000	114.09	28,072	197.57	13,558	14,514	215.13	12,514	15,558	229.57	11,690	16,382
14,000	122.87	30,233	212.77	14,602	15,631	231.69	13,477	16,756	247.24	12,591	17,642
15,000	131.64	32,390	227.96	15,643	16,747	248.23	14,439	17,951	264.89	13,488	18,902
16,000	140.42	34,551	243.16	16,687	17,864	264.78	15,402	19,149	282.55	14,389	20,162
17,000	149.19	36,708	258.35	17,728	18,980	281.32	16,363	20,345	300.20	15,287	21,421
18,000	157.97	38,869	273.55	18,772	20,097	297.88	17,327	21,542	317.87	16,187	22,682
19,000	166.74	41,026	288.74	19,814	21,212	314.41	18,288	22,738	335.51	17,085	23,941
20,000	175.52	43,187	303.94	20,857	22,330	330.97	19,252	23,935	353.18	17,985	25,202
21,000	184.30	45,348	319.15	21,901	23,447	347.53	20,215	25,133	370.85	18,885	26,463
22,000	193.07	47,505	334.33	22,943	24,562	364.06	21,176	26,329	388.49	19,783	27,722
23,000	201.85	49,666	349.54	23,987	25,679	380.62	22,140	27,526	406.16	20,683	28,983
24,000	210.62	51,823	364.73	25,028	26,795	397.16	23,101	28,722	423.81	21,581	30,242
25,000	219.40	53,984	379.93	26,072	27,912	413.71	24,064	29,920	441.48	22,481	31,503
26,000	228.17	56,141	395.12	27,113	29,028	430.25	25,026	31,115	459.12	23,379	32,762
27,000	236.95	58,302	410.32	28,157	30,145	446.80	25,989	32,313	476.79	24,279	34,023
28,000	245.73	60,463	425.52	29,201	31,262	463.36	26,953	33,510	494.46	25,179	35,284
29,000	254.50	62,620	440.71	30,242	32,378	479.90	27,914	34,706	512.10	26,077	36,543
30,000	263.28	64,781	455.92	31,286	33,495	496.45	28,877	35,904	529.77	26,977	37,804
32,500	285.22	70,179	493.91	33,893	36,286	537.82	31,284	38,895	573.92	29,225	40,954
35,000	307.16	75,578	531.90	36,501	39,077	579.20	33,690	41,888	618.07	31,473	44,105
40,000	351.03	86,371	607.87	41,713	44,658	661.92	38,501	47,870	706.34	35,967	50,404
45,000	394.91	97,168	683.86	46,927	50,241	744.66	43,314	53,854	794.64	40,463	56,705
50,000	438.79	107,964	759.84	52,141	55,823	827.40	48,127	59,837	882.93	44,959	63,005
55,000	482.67	118,761	835.83	57,356	61,405	910.15	52,940	65,821	971.23	49,456	69,305
60,000	526.55	129,558	911.81	62,570	66,988	992.89	57,752	71,806	1,059.52	53,952	75,606
65,000	570.43	140,355	987.80	67,785	72,570	1,075.63	62,565	77,790	1,147.82	58,448	81,907
70,000	614.31	151,152	1,063.79	72,999	78,153	1,158.37	67,378	83,774	1,236.11	62,944	88,208
75,000	658.18	161,945	1,139.75	78,211	83,734	1,241.10	72,189	89,756	1,324.39	67,438	94,507
80,000	702.06	172,742	1,215.74	83,425	89,317	1,323.84	77,002	95,740	1,412.68	71,934	100,808
85,000	745.94	183,538	1,291.73	88,640	94,898	1,406.58	81,815	101,723	1,500.98	76,430	107,108
90,000	789.82	194,335	1,367.71	93,854	100,481	1,489.32	86,628	107,707	1,589.27	80,927	113,408
95,000	833.70	205,132	1,443.70	99,068	106,064	1,572.07	91,441	113,691	1,677.57	85,423	119,709
100,000	877.58	215,929	1,519.68	104,283	111,646	1,654.81	96,253	119,676	1,765.86	89,919	126,010
105,000	921.46	226,726	1,595.67	109,497	117,229	1,737.55	101,066	125,660	1,854.16	94,415	132,311
110,000	965.33	237,519	1,671.64	114,709	122,810	1,820.27	105,877	131,642	1,942.43	98,909	138,610
115,000	1,009.21	248,316	1,747.63	119,924	128,392	1,903.02	110,690	137,626	2,030.73	103,405	144,911
120,000	1,053.09	259,112	1,823.61	125,138	133,974	1,985.76	115,503	143,609	2,119.02	107,901	151,211
125,000	1,096.97	269,909	1,899.60	130,352	139,557	2,068.50	120,316	149,593	2,207.32	112,397	157,512
130,000	1,140.85	280,706	1,975.58	135,567	145,139	2,151.24	125,129	155,577	2,295.61	116,894	163,812
135,000	1,184.73	291,503	2,051.57	140,781	150,722	2,233.99	129,941	161,562	2,383.91	121,390	170,113
140,000	1,228.61	302,300	2,127.56	145,995	156,305	2,316.73	134,754	167,546	2,472.20	125,886	176,414
145,000	1,272.48	313,093	2,203.52	151,208	161,885	2,399.45	139,565	173,528	2,560.48	130,380	182,713
150,000	1,316.36	323,890	2,279.51	156,422	167,468	2,482.19	144,378	179,512	2,648.77	134,876	189,014
155,000	1,360.24	334,686	2,355.50	161,636	173,050	2,564.94	149,191	185,495	2,737.07	139,372	195,314
160,000	1,404.12	345,483	2,431.48	166,851	178,632	2,647.68	154,004	191,479	2,825.37	143,868	201,615
165,000	1,448.00	356,280	2,507.47	172,065	184,215	2,730.42	158,817	197,463	2,913.66	148,365	207,915
170,000	1,491.88	367,077	2,583.45	177,279	189,798	2,813.16	163,629	203,448	3,001.96	152,861	214,216
175,000	1,535.76	377,874	2,659.44	182,494	195,380	2,895.90	168,442	209,432	3,090.25	157,357	220,517
180,000	1,579.63	388,667	2,735.41	187,706	200,961	2,978.63	173,253	215,414	3,178.53	161,851	226,816
185,000	1,623.51	399,464	2,811.39	192,920	206,544	3,061.37	178,066	221,398	3,266.82	166,347	233,117
190,000	1,667.39	410,260	2,887.38	198,135	212,125	3,144.11	182,879	227,381	3,355.12	170,843	239,417
195,000	1,711.27	421,057	2,963.37	203,349	217,708	3,226.85	187,692	233,365	3,443.41	175,339	245,718
200,000	1,755.15	431,854	3,039.35	208,563	223,291	3,309.60	192,505	239,349	3,531.71	179,835	252,019

10.25%   GROWING EQUITY MORTGAGES

AMOUNT OF LOAN	30 YEARS		1% PMT INCR/YR 260.372 PAYMENTS			2% PMT INCR/YR 218.091 PAYMENTS			3% PMT INCR/YR 192.281 PAYMENTS		
	MONTHLY PAYMENT	TOTAL INTRST	LAST YR MON PMT	TOTAL INTRST	INTRST SAVED	LAST YR MON PMT	TOTAL INTRST	INTRST SAVED	LAST YR MON PMT	TOTAL INTRST	INTRST SAVED
$ 50	0.45	112	0.55	80	32	0.64	67	45	0.72	59	53
100	0.90	224	1.11	160	64	1.29	134	90	1.44	118	106
200	1.80	448	2.22	321	127	2.57	268	180	2.89	236	212
300	2.69	668	3.32	478	190	3.84	399	269	4.32	352	316
400	3.59	892	4.42	638	254	5.13	533	359	5.76	470	422
500	4.49	1,116	5.53	798	318	6.41	667	449	7.21	588	528
600	5.38	1,337	6.63	956	381	7.68	798	539	8.63	704	633
700	6.28	1,561	7.74	1,116	445	8.97	932	629	10.08	822	739
800	7.17	1,781	8.84	1,273	508	10.24	1,064	717	11.51	938	843
900	8.07	2,005	9.95	1,434	571	11.53	1,198	807	12.95	1,056	949
1,000	8.97	2,229	11.05	1,594	635	12.81	1,332	897	14.39	1,174	1,055
2,000	17.93	4,455	22.10	3,185	1,270	25.61	2,661	1,794	28.77	2,345	2,110
3,000	26.89	6,680	33.14	4,776	1,904	38.41	3,990	2,690	43.15	3,516	3,164
4,000	35.85	8,906	44.18	6,367	2,539	51.20	5,319	3,587	57.53	4,688	4,218
5,000	44.81	11,132	55.22	7,959	3,173	64.00	6,648	4,484	71.91	5,859	5,273
6,000	53.77	13,357	66.27	9,550	3,807	76.80	7,977	5,380	86.29	7,030	6,327
7,000	62.73	15,583	77.31	11,141	4,442	89.59	9,306	6,277	100.66	8,202	7,381
8,000	71.69	17,808	88.35	12,732	5,076	102.39	10,635	7,173	115.04	9,373	8,435
9,000	80.65	20,034	99.39	14,323	5,711	115.19	11,964	8,070	129.42	10,544	9,490
10,000	89.62	22,263	110.45	15,917	6,346	128.00	13,295	8,968	143.81	11,718	10,545
11,000	98.58	24,489	121.49	17,508	6,981	140.80	14,624	9,865	158.19	12,889	11,600
12,000	107.54	26,714	132.53	19,099	7,615	153.59	15,953	10,761	172.57	14,061	12,653
13,000	116.50	28,940	143.57	20,690	8,250	166.39	17,282	11,658	186.95	15,232	13,708
14,000	125.46	31,166	154.62	22,282	8,884	179.19	18,611	12,555	201.33	16,403	14,763
15,000	134.42	33,391	165.66	23,873	9,518	191.98	19,940	13,451	215.70	17,574	15,817
16,000	143.38	35,617	176.70	25,464	10,153	204.78	21,269	14,348	230.08	18,746	16,871
17,000	152.34	37,842	187.74	27,055	10,787	217.58	22,598	15,244	244.46	19,917	17,925
18,000	161.30	40,068	198.78	28,646	11,422	230.38	23,927	16,141	258.84	21,088	18,980
19,000	170.26	42,294	209.83	30,237	12,057	243.17	25,256	17,038	273.22	22,260	20,034
20,000	179.23	44,523	220.88	31,831	12,692	255.98	26,588	17,935	287.61	23,433	21,090
21,000	188.19	46,748	231.92	33,422	13,326	268.78	27,917	18,831	301.99	24,605	22,143
22,000	197.15	48,974	242.97	35,013	13,961	281.58	29,246	19,728	316.37	25,776	23,198
23,000	206.11	51,200	254.01	36,605	14,595	294.38	30,575	20,625	330.75	26,947	24,253
24,000	215.07	53,425	265.05	38,196	15,229	307.17	31,904	21,521	345.12	28,119	25,306
25,000	224.03	55,651	276.09	39,787	15,864	319.97	33,233	22,418	359.50	29,290	26,361
26,000	232.99	57,876	287.13	41,378	16,498	332.77	34,562	23,314	373.88	30,461	27,415
27,000	241.95	60,102	298.18	42,969	17,133	345.56	35,891	24,211	388.26	31,633	28,469
28,000	250.91	62,328	309.22	44,560	17,768	358.36	37,220	25,108	402.64	32,804	29,524
29,000	259.87	64,553	320.26	46,151	18,402	371.16	38,549	26,004	417.02	33,975	30,578
30,000	268.84	66,782	331.32	47,745	19,037	383.97	39,881	26,901	431.41	35,149	31,633
32,500	291.24	72,346	358.92	51,723	20,623	415.96	43,203	29,143	467.35	38,077	34,269
35,000	313.64	77,910	386.53	55,701	22,209	447.96	46,526	31,384	503.30	41,005	36,905
40,000	358.45	89,042	441.75	63,659	25,383	511.95	53,173	35,869	575.21	46,864	42,178
45,000	403.25	100,170	496.96	71,615	28,555	575.94	59,818	40,353	647.10	52,721	47,449
50,000	448.06	111,302	552.19	79,574	31,728	639.94	66,466	44,836	719.00	58,580	52,722
55,000	492.86	122,430	607.40	87,529	34,901	703.93	73,111	49,319	790.90	64,436	57,994
60,000	537.67	133,561	662.62	95,488	38,073	767.93	79,759	53,802	862.80	70,295	63,266
65,000	582.47	144,689	717.83	103,443	41,246	831.91	86,404	58,285	934.69	76,152	68,537
70,000	627.28	155,821	773.05	111,402	44,419	895.91	93,052	62,769	1,006.60	82,011	73,810
75,000	672.08	166,949	828.27	119,357	47,592	959.90	99,697	67,252	1,078.49	87,867	79,082
80,000	716.89	178,080	883.49	127,316	50,764	1,023.90	106,344	71,736	1,150.40	93,726	84,354
85,000	761.69	189,208	938.70	135,272	53,936	1,087.88	112,989	76,219	1,222.29	99,583	89,625
90,000	806.50	200,340	993.92	143,230	57,110	1,151.88	119,637	80,703	1,294.20	105,442	94,898
95,000	851.30	211,468	1,049.14	151,186	60,282	1,215.87	126,282	85,186	1,366.09	111,299	100,169
100,000	896.11	222,600	1,104.36	159,144	63,456	1,279.87	132,930	89,670	1,437.99	117,157	105,443
105,000	940.91	233,728	1,159.57	167,100	66,628	1,343.85	139,575	94,153	1,509.88	123,014	110,714
110,000	985.72	244,859	1,214.79	175,058	69,801	1,407.85	146,222	98,637	1,581.79	128,873	115,986
115,000	1,030.52	255,987	1,270.01	183,014	72,973	1,471.84	152,867	103,120	1,653.68	134,730	121,257
120,000	1,075.33	267,119	1,325.23	190,972	76,147	1,535.84	159,515	107,604	1,725.59	140,588	126,531
125,000	1,120.13	278,247	1,380.44	198,928	79,319	1,599.82	166,160	112,087	1,797.48	146,445	131,802
130,000	1,164.94	289,378	1,435.66	206,887	82,491	1,663.82	172,808	116,570	1,869.39	152,304	137,074
135,000	1,209.74	300,506	1,490.87	214,842	85,664	1,727.81	179,453	121,053	1,941.28	158,161	142,345
140,000	1,254.55	311,638	1,546.10	222,801	88,837	1,791.81	186,100	125,538	2,013.18	164,019	147,619
145,000	1,299.35	322,766	1,601.31	230,756	92,010	1,855.79	192,746	130,020	2,085.08	169,876	152,890
150,000	1,344.16	333,898	1,656.53	238,715	95,183	1,919.79	199,393	134,505	2,156.98	175,735	158,163
155,000	1,388.96	345,026	1,711.74	246,670	98,356	1,983.78	206,038	138,988	2,228.87	181,592	163,434
160,000	1,433.77	356,157	1,766.97	254,629	101,528	2,047.78	212,686	143,471	2,300.78	187,450	168,707
165,000	1,478.57	367,285	1,822.18	262,585	104,700	2,111.76	219,331	147,954	2,372.67	193,307	173,978
170,000	1,523.38	378,417	1,877.40	270,543	107,874	2,175.76	225,979	152,438	2,444.58	199,166	179,251
175,000	1,568.18	389,545	1,932.61	278,499	111,046	2,239.75	232,624	156,921	2,516.47	205,023	184,522
180,000	1,612.99	400,676	1,987.84	286,457	114,219	2,303.75	239,271	161,405	2,588.38	210,882	189,794
185,000	1,657.79	411,804	2,043.05	294,413	117,391	2,367.73	245,916	165,888	2,660.27	216,738	195,066
190,000	1,702.60	422,936	2,098.27	302,371	120,565	2,431.73	252,564	170,372	2,732.17	222,597	200,339
195,000	1,747.40	434,064	2,153.48	310,327	123,737	2,495.72	259,209	174,855	2,804.06	228,454	205,610
200,000	1,792.21	445,196	2,208.71	318,285	126,911	2,559.72	265,857	179,339	2,875.97	234,313	210,883

126

AMOUNT OF LOAN	30 YEARS		4% PMT INCR/YR 174.132 PAYMENTS			5% PMT INCR/YR 160.461 PAYMENTS			6% PMT INCR/YR 149.623 PAYMENTS		
	MONTHLY PAYMENT	TOTAL INTRST	LAST YR MON PMT	TOTAL INTRST	INTRST SAVED	LAST YR MON PMT	TOTAL INTRST	INTRST SAVED	LAST YR MON PMT	TOTAL INTRST	INTRST SAVED
$ 50	0.45	112	0.78	54	58	0.85	49	63	0.91	46	66
100	0.90	224	1.56	107	117	1.70	99	125	1.81	92	132
200	1.80	448	3.12	214	234	3.39	198	250	3.62	185	263
300	2.69	668	4.66	319	349	5.07	294	374	5.41	275	393
400	3.59	892	6.22	426	466	6.77	393	499	7.22	367	525
500	4.49	1,116	7.78	533	583	8.47	492	624	9.03	460	656
600	5.38	1,337	9.32	638	699	10.14	589	748	10.83	550	787
700	6.28	1,561	10.87	745	816	11.84	688	873	12.64	642	919
800	7.17	1,781	12.42	850	931	13.52	784	997	14.43	733	1,048
900	8.07	2,005	13.97	957	1,048	15.22	883	1,122	16.24	825	1,180
1,000	8.97	2,229	15.53	1,064	1,165	16.91	982	1,247	18.05	917	1,312
2,000	17.93	4,455	31.05	2,126	2,329	33.81	1,962	2,493	36.08	1,833	2,622
3,000	26.89	6,680	46.56	3,188	3,492	50.71	2,942	3,738	54.11	2,748	3,932
4,000	35.85	8,906	62.08	4,250	4,656	67.60	3,922	4,984	72.14	3,663	5,243
5,000	44.81	11,132	77.60	5,312	5,820	84.50	4,902	6,230	90.17	4,578	6,554
6,000	53.77	13,357	93.11	6,374	6,983	101.39	5,881	7,476	108.20	5,494	7,863
7,000	62.73	15,583	108.63	7,436	8,147	118.29	6,861	8,722	126.23	6,409	9,174
8,000	71.69	17,808	124.14	8,497	9,311	135.18	7,841	9,967	144.25	7,324	10,484
9,000	80.65	20,034	139.66	9,559	10,475	152.08	8,821	11,213	162.28	8,239	11,795
10,000	89.62	22,263	155.19	10,623	11,640	168.99	9,803	12,460	180.33	9,157	13,106
11,000	98.58	24,489	170.71	11,685	12,804	185.89	10,783	13,706	198.36	10,072	14,417
12,000	107.54	26,714	186.22	12,747	13,967	202.78	11,763	14,951	216.39	10,987	15,727
13,000	116.50	28,940	201.74	13,809	15,131	219.68	12,743	16,197	234.42	11,902	17,038
14,000	125.46	31,166	217.26	14,871	16,295	236.57	13,723	17,443	252.45	12,818	18,348
15,000	134.42	33,391	232.77	15,933	17,458	253.47	14,702	18,689	270.48	13,733	19,658
16,000	143.38	35,617	248.29	16,995	18,622	270.36	15,682	19,935	288.51	14,648	20,969
17,000	152.34	37,842	263.80	18,057	19,785	287.26	16,662	21,180	306.54	15,563	22,279
18,000	161.30	40,068	279.32	19,119	20,949	304.16	17,642	22,426	324.57	16,479	23,589
19,000	170.26	42,294	294.84	20,180	22,114	321.05	18,622	23,672	342.60	17,394	24,900
20,000	179.23	44,523	310.37	21,245	23,278	337.96	19,604	24,919	360.65	18,311	26,212
21,000	188.19	46,748	325.88	22,307	24,441	354.86	20,584	26,164	378.68	19,226	27,522
22,000	197.15	48,974	341.40	23,368	25,606	371.76	21,564	27,410	396.70	20,142	28,832
23,000	206.11	51,200	356.92	24,430	26,770	388.65	22,544	28,656	414.73	21,057	30,143
24,000	215.07	53,425	372.43	25,492	27,933	405.55	23,524	29,901	432.76	21,972	31,453
25,000	224.03	55,651	387.95	26,554	29,097	422.44	24,503	31,148	450.79	22,887	32,764
26,000	232.99	57,876	403.46	27,616	30,260	439.34	25,483	32,393	468.82	23,803	34,073
27,000	241.95	60,102	418.98	28,678	31,424	456.23	26,463	33,639	486.85	24,718	35,384
28,000	250.91	62,328	434.49	29,740	32,588	473.13	27,443	34,885	504.88	25,633	36,695
29,000	259.87	64,553	450.01	30,802	33,751	490.02	28,423	36,130	522.91	26,548	38,005
30,000	268.84	66,782	465.54	31,866	34,916	506.94	29,405	37,377	540.96	27,466	39,316
32,500	291.24	72,346	504.33	34,521	37,825	549.18	31,855	40,491	586.03	29,754	42,592
35,000	313.64	77,910	543.12	37,175	40,735	591.41	34,304	43,606	631.11	32,042	45,868
40,000	358.45	89,042	620.72	42,487	46,555	675.91	39,206	49,836	721.27	36,620	52,422
45,000	403.25	100,170	698.30	47,797	52,373	760.39	44,105	56,065	811.42	41,196	58,974
50,000	448.06	111,302	775.89	53,108	58,194	844.88	49,007	62,295	901.58	45,775	65,527
55,000	492.86	122,430	853.47	58,418	64,012	929.36	53,906	68,524	991.73	50,351	72,079
60,000	537.67	133,561	931.07	63,729	69,832	1,013.86	58,808	74,753	1,081.90	54,929	78,632
65,000	582.47	144,689	1,008.65	69,039	75,650	1,098.33	63,707	80,982	1,172.04	59,505	85,184
70,000	627.28	155,821	1,086.25	74,351	81,470	1,182.83	68,609	87,212	1,262.21	64,084	91,737
75,000	672.08	166,949	1,163.83	79,660	87,289	1,267.31	73,508	93,441	1,352.36	68,660	98,289
80,000	716.89	178,080	1,241.42	84,972	93,108	1,351.80	78,410	99,670	1,442.52	73,238	104,842
85,000	761.69	189,208	1,319.00	90,282	98,927	1,436.28	83,309	105,899	1,532.67	77,814	111,394
90,000	806.50	200,340	1,396.60	95,593	104,747	1,520.78	88,210	112,130	1,622.84	82,393	117,947
95,000	851.30	211,468	1,474.18	100,902	110,566	1,605.25	93,110	118,358	1,712.98	86,969	124,499
100,000	896.11	222,600	1,551.77	106,214	116,386	1,689.75	98,011	124,589	1,803.15	91,547	131,053
105,000	940.91	233,728	1,629.35	111,524	122,204	1,774.23	102,911	130,817	1,893.30	96,123	137,605
110,000	985.72	244,859	1,706.95	116,835	128,024	1,858.72	107,812	137,047	1,983.46	100,701	144,158
115,000	1,030.52	255,987	1,784.53	122,145	133,842	1,943.20	112,712	143,275	2,073.61	105,278	150,709
120,000	1,075.33	267,119	1,862.12	127,457	139,662	2,027.70	117,613	149,506	2,163.78	109,856	157,263
125,000	1,120.13	278,247	1,939.70	132,766	145,481	2,112.17	122,513	155,734	2,253.92	114,432	163,815
130,000	1,164.94	289,378	2,017.30	138,078	151,300	2,196.67	127,414	161,964	2,344.09	119,010	170,368
135,000	1,209.74	300,506	2,094.88	143,387	157,119	2,281.15	132,313	168,193	2,434.23	123,587	176,919
140,000	1,254.55	311,638	2,172.47	148,699	162,939	2,365.64	137,214	174,423	2,524.40	128,165	183,473
145,000	1,299.35	322,766	2,250.05	154,008	168,758	2,450.12	142,114	180,652	2,614.55	132,741	190,025
150,000	1,344.16	333,898	2,327.65	159,320	174,578	2,534.61	147,016	186,882	2,704.71	137,319	196,579
155,000	1,388.96	345,026	2,405.23	164,630	180,396	2,619.09	151,915	193,111	2,794.86	141,896	203,130
160,000	1,433.77	356,157	2,482.83	169,941	186,216	2,703.59	156,817	199,340	2,885.03	146,474	209,683
165,000	1,478.57	367,285	2,560.40	175,251	192,034	2,788.06	161,716	205,569	2,975.17	151,050	216,235
170,000	1,523.38	378,417	2,638.00	180,563	197,854	2,872.56	166,618	211,799	3,065.34	155,628	222,789
175,000	1,568.18	389,545	2,715.58	185,872	203,673	2,957.04	171,517	218,028	3,155.49	160,205	229,340
180,000	1,612.99	400,676	2,793.18	191,184	209,492	3,041.53	176,419	224,257	3,245.65	164,783	235,893
185,000	1,657.79	411,804	2,870.76	196,493	215,311	3,126.01	181,318	230,486	3,335.80	169,359	242,445
190,000	1,702.60	422,936	2,948.35	201,805	221,131	3,210.51	186,220	236,716	3,425.97	173,937	248,999
195,000	1,747.40	434,064	3,025.93	207,114	226,950	3,294.98	191,119	242,945	3,516.11	178,514	255,550
200,000	1,792.21	445,196	3,103.53	212,426	232,770	3,379.48	196,020	249,176	3,606.28	183,092	262,104

127

10.50% GROWING EQUITY MORTGAGES

AMOUNT OF LOAN	30 YEARS		1% PMT INCR/YR 258.571 PAYMENTS			2% PMT INCR/YR 216.328 PAYMENTS			3% PMT INCR/YR 190.623 PAYMENTS		
	MONTHLY PAYMENT	TOTAL INTRST	LAST YR MON PMT	TOTAL INTRST	INTRST SAVED	LAST YR MON PMT	TOTAL INTRST	INTRST SAVED	LAST YR MON PMT	TOTAL INTRST	INTRST SAVED
$ 50	0.46	116	0.57	82	34	0.66	68	48	0.72	60	56
100	0.92	231	1.13	164	67	1.31	137	94	1.43	121	110
200	1.83	459	2.26	325	134	2.61	271	188	2.85	239	220
300	2.75	690	3.39	489	201	3.93	408	282	4.28	359	331
400	3.66	918	4.51	650	268	5.23	542	376	5.70	477	441
500	4.58	1,149	5.64	814	335	6.54	679	470	7.14	598	551
600	5.49	1,376	6.77	975	401	7.84	813	563	8.55	716	660
700	6.41	1,608	7.90	1,139	469	9.16	950	658	9.99	837	771
800	7.32	1,835	9.02	1,301	534	10.45	1,084	751	11.40	955	880
900	8.24	2,066	10.15	1,465	601	11.77	1,221	845	12.84	1,075	991
1,000	9.15	2,294	11.28	1,626	668	13.07	1,355	939	14.26	1,194	1,100
2,000	18.30	4,588	22.55	3,252	1,336	26.14	2,711	1,877	28.51	2,387	2,201
3,000	27.45	6,882	33.83	4,877	2,005	39.21	4,066	2,816	42.77	3,581	3,301
4,000	36.59	9,172	45.09	6,500	2,672	52.26	5,419	3,753	57.01	4,772	4,400
5,000	45.74	11,466	56.37	8,126	3,340	65.33	6,774	4,692	71.26	5,966	5,500
6,000	54.89	13,760	67.65	9,752	4,008	78.40	8,130	5,630	85.52	7,159	6,601
7,000	64.04	16,054	78.92	11,377	4,677	91.46	9,485	6,569	99.77	8,353	7,701
8,000	73.18	18,345	90.19	13,000	5,345	104.52	10,838	7,507	114.01	9,544	8,801
9,000	82.33	20,639	101.46	14,626	6,013	117.59	12,193	8,446	128.27	10,738	9,901
10,000	91.48	22,933	112.74	16,252	6,681	130.66	13,548	9,385	142.52	11,931	11,002
11,000	100.63	25,227	124.02	17,878	7,349	143.72	14,904	10,323	156.78	13,125	12,102
12,000	109.77	27,517	135.28	19,501	8,016	156.78	16,257	11,260	171.02	14,316	13,201
13,000	118.92	29,811	146.56	21,126	8,685	169.85	17,612	12,199	185.27	15,510	14,301
14,000	128.07	32,105	157.83	22,752	9,353	182.92	18,967	13,138	199.53	16,703	15,402
15,000	137.22	34,399	169.11	24,378	10,021	195.98	20,323	14,076	213.78	17,897	16,502
16,000	146.36	36,690	180.37	26,001	10,689	209.04	21,675	15,015	228.02	19,088	17,602
17,000	155.51	38,984	191.65	27,626	11,358	222.11	23,031	15,953	242.28	20,282	18,702
18,000	164.66	41,278	202.93	29,252	12,026	235.18	24,386	16,892	256.53	21,475	19,803
19,000	173.81	43,572	214.20	30,878	12,694	248.24	25,742	17,830	270.79	22,669	20,903
20,000	182.95	45,862	225.47	32,501	13,361	261.30	27,094	18,768	285.03	23,860	22,002
21,000	192.10	48,156	236.74	34,127	14,029	274.37	28,450	19,706	299.29	25,054	23,102
22,000	201.25	50,450	248.02	35,752	14,698	287.43	29,805	20,645	313.54	26,247	24,203
23,000	210.40	52,744	259.30	37,378	15,366	300.50	31,160	21,584	327.80	27,441	25,303
24,000	219.54	55,034	270.56	39,001	16,033	313.56	32,513	22,521	342.04	28,632	26,402
25,000	228.69	57,328	281.84	40,627	16,701	326.63	33,869	23,459	356.29	29,826	27,502
26,000	237.84	59,622	293.11	42,253	17,369	339.69	35,224	24,398	370.55	31,019	28,603
27,000	246.98	61,913	304.38	43,875	18,038	352.75	36,577	25,336	384.79	32,210	29,703
28,000	256.13	64,207	315.65	45,501	18,706	365.82	37,932	26,275	399.04	33,404	30,803
29,000	265.28	66,501	326.93	47,127	19,374	378.89	39,287	27,214	413.30	34,597	31,904
30,000	274.43	68,795	338.21	48,753	20,042	391.95	40,643	28,152	427.55	35,791	33,004
32,500	297.30	74,528	366.39	52,816	21,712	424.62	44,030	30,498	463.18	38,774	35,754
35,000	320.16	80,258	394.56	56,876	23,382	457.27	47,414	32,844	498.80	41,754	38,504
40,000	365.90	91,724	450.93	65,002	26,722	522.60	54,189	37,535	570.06	47,720	44,004
45,000	411.64	103,190	507.30	73,128	30,062	587.92	60,963	42,227	641.32	53,685	49,505
50,000	457.37	114,653	563.66	81,251	33,402	653.24	67,734	46,919	712.57	59,649	55,004
55,000	503.11	126,120	620.03	89,377	36,743	718.56	74,509	51,611	783.83	65,614	60,506
60,000	548.85	137,586	676.40	97,503	40,083	783.89	81,283	56,303	855.09	71,580	66,006
65,000	594.59	149,052	732.77	105,629	43,423	849.22	88,057	60,995	926.35	77,545	71,507
70,000	640.32	160,515	789.13	113,752	46,763	914.53	94,829	65,686	997.60	83,509	77,006
75,000	686.06	171,982	845.49	121,878	50,104	979.86	101,603	70,379	1,068.86	89,474	82,508
80,000	731.80	183,448	901.86	130,003	53,445	1,045.19	108,377	75,071	1,140.12	95,440	88,008
85,000	777.53	194,911	958.22	138,127	56,784	1,110.50	115,149	79,762	1,211.37	101,403	93,508
90,000	823.27	206,377	1,014.59	146,252	60,125	1,175.83	121,923	84,454	1,282.63	107,368	99,009
95,000	869.01	217,844	1,070.96	154,378	63,466	1,241.16	128,697	89,147	1,353.89	113,334	104,510
100,000	914.74	229,306	1,127.32	162,501	66,805	1,306.47	135,469	93,837	1,425.14	119,297	110,009
105,000	960.48	240,773	1,183.69	170,627	70,146	1,371.80	142,243	98,530	1,496.40	125,263	115,510
110,000	1,006.22	252,239	1,240.06	178,753	73,486	1,437.13	149,017	103,222	1,567.66	131,228	121,011
115,000	1,051.96	263,706	1,296.43	186,879	76,827	1,502.46	155,792	107,914	1,638.92	137,194	126,512
120,000	1,097.69	275,168	1,352.78	195,002	80,166	1,567.77	162,563	112,605	1,710.17	143,157	132,011
125,000	1,143.43	286,635	1,409.15	203,128	83,507	1,633.10	169,337	117,298	1,781.43	149,123	137,512
130,000	1,189.17	298,101	1,465.52	211,254	86,847	1,698.43	176,112	121,989	1,852.69	155,088	143,013
135,000	1,234.90	309,564	1,521.88	219,377	90,187	1,763.74	182,883	126,681	1,923.93	161,052	148,512
140,000	1,280.64	321,030	1,578.25	227,503	93,527	1,829.07	189,657	131,373	1,995.20	167,017	154,013
145,000	1,326.38	332,497	1,634.62	235,629	96,868	1,894.40	196,432	136,065	2,066.46	172,983	159,514
150,000	1,372.11	343,960	1,690.98	243,752	100,208	1,959.71	203,203	140,757	2,137.70	178,946	165,014
155,000	1,417.85	355,426	1,747.35	251,878	103,548	2,025.04	209,978	145,448	2,208.96	184,911	170,515
160,000	1,463.59	366,892	1,803.72	260,004	106,888	2,090.37	216,752	150,140	2,280.23	190,877	176,015
165,000	1,509.32	378,355	1,860.07	268,127	110,228	2,155.68	223,523	154,832	2,351.47	196,840	181,515
170,000	1,555.06	389,822	1,916.44	276,253	113,569	2,221.01	230,298	159,524	2,422.73	202,806	187,016
175,000	1,600.80	401,288	1,972.81	284,379	116,909	2,286.34	237,072	164,216	2,493.99	208,771	192,517
180,000	1,646.54	412,754	2,029.18	292,505	120,249	2,351.66	243,846	168,908	2,565.24	214,737	198,017
185,000	1,692.27	424,217	2,085.54	300,628	123,589	2,416.98	250,618	173,599	2,636.50	220,700	203,517
190,000	1,738.01	435,684	2,141.91	308,754	126,930	2,482.31	257,392	178,292	2,707.76	226,666	209,018
195,000	1,783.75	447,150	2,198.28	316,880	130,270	2,547.63	264,166	182,984	2,779.02	232,631	214,519
200,000	1,829.48	458,613	2,254.64	325,003	133,610	2,612.95	270,938	187,675	2,850.27	238,595	220,018

128

GROWING EQUITY MORTGAGES 10.50%

AMOUNT OF LOAN	30 YEARS MONTHLY PAYMENT	30 YEARS TOTAL INTRST	4% PMT INCR/YR 172.621 PAYMENTS LAST YR MON PMT	4% TOTAL INTRST	4% INTRST SAVED	5% PMT INCR/YR 159.072 PAYMENTS LAST YR MON PMT	5% TOTAL INTRST	5% INTRST SAVED	6% PMT INCR/YR 148.325 PAYMENTS LAST YR MON PMT	6% TOTAL INTRST	6% INTRST SAVED
$ 50	0.46	116	0.80	55	61	0.87	50	66	0.93	47	69
100	0.92	231	1.59	109	122	1.73	101	130	1.85	94	137
200	1.83	459	3.17	216	243	3.45	200	259	3.68	186	273
300	2.75	690	4.76	326	364	5.19	300	390	5.53	281	409
400	3.66	918	6.34	433	485	6.90	399	519	7.36	373	545
500	4.58	1,149	7.93	542	607	8.64	500	649	9.22	467	682
600	5.49	1,376	9.51	649	727	10.35	599	777	11.05	559	817
700	6.41	1,608	11.10	758	850	12.09	700	908	12.90	653	955
800	7.32	1,835	12.68	865	970	13.80	798	1,037	14.73	746	1,089
900	8.24	2,066	14.27	975	1,091	15.54	899	1,167	16.58	840	1,226
1,000	9.15	2,294	15.84	1,082	1,212	17.25	998	1,296	18.41	932	1,362
2,000	18.30	4,588	31.69	2,163	2,425	34.51	1,996	2,592	36.82	1,864	2,724
3,000	27.45	6,882	47.53	3,245	3,637	51.76	2,994	3,888	55.23	2,796	4,086
4,000	36.59	9,172	63.36	4,324	4,848	69.00	3,989	5,183	73.63	3,726	5,446
5,000	45.74	11,466	79.21	5,406	6,060	86.25	4,987	6,479	92.04	4,658	6,808
6,000	54.89	13,760	95.05	6,488	7,272	103.50	5,985	7,775	110.45	5,590	8,170
7,000	64.04	16,054	110.90	7,569	8,485	120.76	6,983	9,071	128.86	6,522	9,532
8,000	73.18	18,345	126.72	8,649	9,696	137.99	7,979	10,366	147.25	7,451	10,894
9,000	82.33	20,639	142.57	9,730	10,909	155.25	8,977	11,662	165.66	8,383	12,256
10,000	91.48	22,933	158.41	10,812	12,121	172.50	9,975	12,958	184.08	9,315	13,618
11,000	100.63	25,227	174.26	11,894	13,333	189.75	10,972	14,255	202.49	10,247	14,980
12,000	109.77	27,517	190.09	12,973	14,544	206.99	11,968	15,549	220.88	11,177	16,340
13,000	118.92	29,811	205.93	14,055	15,756	224.24	12,966	16,845	239.29	12,109	17,702
14,000	128.07	32,105	221.78	15,137	16,968	241.50	13,964	18,141	257.70	13,041	19,064
15,000	137.22	34,399	237.62	16,218	18,181	258.75	14,962	19,437	276.11	13,973	20,426
16,000	146.36	36,690	253.45	17,298	19,392	275.98	15,957	20,733	294.51	14,903	21,787
17,000	155.51	38,984	269.29	18,379	20,605	293.24	16,955	22,029	312.92	15,835	23,149
18,000	164.66	41,278	285.14	19,461	21,817	310.49	17,953	23,325	331.33	16,767	24,511
19,000	173.81	43,572	300.98	20,543	23,029	327.74	18,951	24,621	349.74	17,699	25,873
20,000	182.95	45,862	316.81	21,622	24,240	344.98	19,947	25,915	368.13	18,628	27,234
21,000	192.10	48,156	332.66	22,704	25,452	362.23	20,945	27,211	386.54	19,560	28,596
22,000	201.25	50,450	348.50	23,785	26,665	379.49	21,943	28,507	404.95	20,492	29,958
23,000	210.40	52,744	364.34	24,867	27,877	396.74	22,941	29,803	423.37	21,424	31,320
24,000	219.54	55,034	380.17	25,946	29,088	413.98	23,936	31,098	441.76	22,354	32,680
25,000	228.69	57,328	396.02	27,028	30,300	431.23	24,934	32,394	460.17	23,286	34,042
26,000	237.84	59,622	411.86	28,110	31,512	448.48	25,932	33,690	478.58	24,218	35,404
27,000	246.98	61,913	427.69	29,189	32,724	465.72	26,928	34,985	496.97	25,148	36,765
28,000	256.13	64,207	443.53	30,271	33,936	482.97	27,926	36,281	515.38	26,080	38,127
29,000	265.28	66,501	459.38	31,353	35,148	500.23	28,923	37,578	533.80	27,012	39,489
30,000	274.43	68,795	475.22	32,434	36,361	517.48	29,921	38,874	552.21	27,944	40,851
32,500	297.30	74,528	514.83	35,137	39,391	560.60	32,415	42,113	598.23	30,273	44,255
35,000	320.16	80,258	554.41	37,838	42,420	603.71	34,906	45,352	644.22	32,599	47,659
40,000	365.90	91,724	633.62	43,244	48,480	689.96	39,894	51,830	736.26	37,257	54,467
45,000	411.64	103,190	712.83	48,650	54,540	776.21	44,881	58,309	828.30	41,915	61,275
50,000	457.37	114,653	792.02	54,054	60,599	862.44	49,866	64,787	920.32	46,570	68,083
55,000	503.11	126,120	871.22	59,460	66,660	948.69	54,853	71,267	1,012.36	51,228	74,892
60,000	548.85	137,586	950.43	64,866	72,720	1,034.94	59,841	77,745	1,104.39	55,885	81,701
65,000	594.59	149,052	1,029.64	70,272	78,780	1,121.19	64,828	84,224	1,196.43	60,543	88,509
70,000	640.32	160,515	1,108.83	75,676	84,839	1,207.42	69,813	90,702	1,288.45	65,198	95,317
75,000	686.06	171,982	1,188.03	81,082	90,900	1,293.67	74,800	97,182	1,380.49	69,856	102,126
80,000	731.80	183,448	1,267.24	86,488	96,960	1,379.92	79,787	103,661	1,472.53	74,514	108,934
85,000	777.53	194,911	1,346.43	91,892	103,019	1,466.15	84,773	110,138	1,564.54	79,169	115,742
90,000	823.27	206,377	1,425.64	97,298	109,079	1,552.40	89,760	116,617	1,656.58	83,827	122,550
95,000	869.01	217,844	1,504.84	102,704	115,140	1,638.65	94,747	123,097	1,748.62	88,485	129,359
100,000	914.74	229,306	1,584.03	108,108	121,198	1,724.88	99,732	129,574	1,840.64	93,140	136,166
105,000	960.48	240,773	1,663.24	113,514	127,259	1,811.13	104,719	136,054	1,932.67	97,798	142,975
110,000	1,006.22	252,239	1,742.45	118,920	133,319	1,897.38	109,707	142,532	2,024.71	102,455	149,784
115,000	1,051.96	263,706	1,821.65	124,326	139,380	1,983.63	114,694	149,012	2,116.75	107,113	156,593
120,000	1,097.69	275,168	1,900.84	129,730	145,438	2,069.86	119,679	155,489	2,208.77	111,769	163,399
125,000	1,143.43	286,635	1,980.05	135,136	151,499	2,156.11	124,666	161,969	2,300.81	116,426	170,209
130,000	1,189.17	298,101	2,059.26	140,542	157,559	2,242.36	129,653	168,448	2,392.84	121,084	177,017
135,000	1,234.90	309,564	2,138.45	145,946	163,618	2,328.59	134,639	174,925	2,484.86	125,739	183,825
140,000	1,280.64	321,030	2,217.65	151,352	169,678	2,414.84	139,626	181,404	2,576.90	130,397	190,633
145,000	1,326.38	332,497	2,296.86	156,758	175,739	2,501.09	144,613	187,884	2,668.94	135,055	197,442
150,000	1,372.11	343,960	2,376.05	162,162	181,798	2,587.32	149,598	194,362	2,760.95	139,710	204,250
155,000	1,417.85	355,426	2,455.26	167,568	187,858	2,673.57	154,585	200,841	2,852.99	144,368	211,058
160,000	1,463.59	366,892	2,534.46	172,974	193,918	2,759.82	159,573	207,319	2,945.03	149,025	217,867
165,000	1,509.32	378,355	2,613.65	178,378	199,977	2,846.05	164,558	213,797	3,037.05	153,681	224,674
170,000	1,555.06	389,822	2,692.86	183,784	206,038	2,932.30	169,545	220,277	3,129.09	158,339	231,483
175,000	1,600.80	401,288	2,772.06	189,190	212,098	3,018.55	174,532	226,756	3,221.12	162,996	238,292
180,000	1,646.54	412,754	2,851.27	194,596	218,158	3,104.80	179,520	233,234	3,313.16	167,654	245,100
185,000	1,692.27	424,217	2,930.46	200,000	224,217	3,191.03	184,505	239,712	3,405.18	172,309	251,908
190,000	1,738.01	435,684	3,009.67	205,406	230,278	3,277.28	189,492	246,192	3,497.22	176,967	258,717
195,000	1,783.75	447,150	3,088.88	210,812	236,338	3,363.53	194,479	252,671	3,589.26	181,625	265,525
200,000	1,829.48	458,613	3,168.07	216,216	242,397	3,449.76	199,464	259,149	3,681.27	186,280	272,333

129

10.75%   GROWING EQUITY MORTGAGES

AMOUNT OF LOAN	30 YEARS		1% PMT INCR/YR 256.764 PAYMENTS			2% PMT INCR/YR 214.549 PAYMENTS			3% PMT INCR/YR 188.974 PAYMENTS		
	MONTHLY PAYMENT	TOTAL INTRST	LAST YR MON PMT	TOTAL INTRST	INTRST SAVED	LAST YR MON PMT	TOTAL INTRST	INTRST SAVED	LAST YR MON PMT	TOTAL INTRST	INTRST SAVED
$ 50	0.47	119	0.58	84	35	0.66	70	49	0.73	61	58
100	0.94	238	1.16	168	70	1.32	140	98	1.46	123	115
200	1.87	473	2.30	332	141	2.62	277	196	2.91	244	229
300	2.81	712	3.46	500	212	3.93	416	296	4.38	366	346
400	3.74	946	4.61	665	281	5.24	553	393	5.83	487	459
500	4.67	1,181	5.76	830	351	6.54	690	491	7.28	608	573
600	5.61	1,420	6.91	997	423	7.86	830	590	8.74	731	689
700	6.54	1,654	8.06	1,162	492	9.16	967	687	10.19	851	803
800	7.47	1,889	9.21	1,327	562	10.46	1,104	785	11.64	972	917
900	8.41	2,128	10.36	1,495	633	11.78	1,244	884	13.10	1,095	1,033
1,000	9.34	2,362	11.51	1,659	703	13.08	1,381	981	14.55	1,215	1,147
2,000	18.67	4,721	23.01	3,316	1,405	26.14	2,759	1,962	29.09	2,428	2,293
3,000	28.01	7,084	34.52	4,976	2,108	39.22	4,140	2,944	43.64	3,643	3,441
4,000	37.34	9,442	46.02	6,632	2,810	52.29	5,519	3,923	58.17	4,856	4,586
5,000	46.68	11,805	57.53	8,292	3,513	65.36	6,899	4,906	72.73	6,071	5,734
6,000	56.01	14,164	69.03	9,948	4,216	78.43	8,278	5,886	87.26	7,284	6,880
7,000	65.35	16,526	80.54	11,608	4,918	91.51	9,659	6,867	101.81	8,499	8,027
8,000	74.68	18,885	92.04	13,264	5,621	104.57	11,037	7,848	116.35	9,712	9,173
9,000	84.02	21,247	103.55	14,924	6,323	117.65	12,418	8,829	130.90	10,927	10,320
10,000	93.35	23,606	115.04	16,581	7,025	130.71	13,796	9,810	145.44	12,140	11,466
11,000	102.69	25,968	126.55	18,240	7,728	143.79	15,177	10,791	159.99	13,355	12,613
12,000	112.02	28,327	138.05	19,897	8,430	156.86	16,556	11,771	174.52	14,568	13,759
13,000	121.36	30,690	149.56	21,556	9,134	169.93	17,937	12,753	189.07	15,783	14,907
14,000	130.69	33,048	161.06	23,213	9,835	183.00	19,315	13,733	203.61	16,996	16,052
15,000	140.03	35,411	172.57	24,872	10,539	196.08	20,696	14,715	218.16	18,211	17,200
16,000	149.36	37,770	184.07	26,529	11,241	209.14	22,074	15,696	232.70	19,423	18,347
17,000	158.70	40,132	195.58	28,188	11,944	222.22	23,455	16,677	247.25	20,639	19,493
18,000	168.03	42,491	207.08	29,845	12,646	235.28	24,834	17,657	261.79	21,851	20,640
19,000	177.37	44,853	218.59	31,505	13,348	248.36	26,214	18,639	276.34	23,067	21,786
20,000	186.70	47,212	230.09	33,161	14,051	261.43	27,593	19,619	290.87	24,279	22,933
21,000	196.04	49,574	241.60	34,821	14,753	274.50	28,974	20,600	305.42	25,494	24,080
22,000	205.37	51,933	253.10	36,477	15,456	287.57	30,352	21,581	319.96	26,707	25,226
23,000	214.71	54,296	264.61	38,137	16,159	300.65	31,733	22,563	334.51	27,922	26,374
24,000	224.04	56,654	276.11	39,793	16,861	313.71	33,111	23,543	349.05	29,135	27,519
25,000	233.38	59,017	287.62	41,453	17,564	326.79	34,492	24,525	363.60	30,350	28,667
26,000	242.71	61,376	299.11	43,110	18,266	339.85	35,871	25,505	378.13	31,563	29,813
27,000	252.04	63,734	310.61	44,766	18,968	352.92	37,249	26,485	392.67	32,776	30,958
28,000	261.38	66,097	322.12	46,426	19,671	366.00	38,630	27,467	407.22	33,991	32,106
29,000	270.71	68,456	333.62	48,082	20,374	379.06	40,008	28,448	421.76	35,204	33,252
30,000	280.05	70,818	345.13	49,742	21,076	392.14	41,389	29,429	436.31	36,419	34,399
32,500	303.39	76,720	373.90	53,888	22,832	424.82	44,839	31,881	472.67	39,454	37,266
35,000	326.72	82,619	402.65	58,031	24,588	457.49	48,286	34,333	509.02	42,488	40,131
40,000	373.40	94,424	460.18	66,322	28,102	522.85	55,186	39,238	581.75	48,559	45,865
45,000	420.07	106,225	517.69	74,611	31,614	588.20	62,083	44,142	654.46	54,627	51,598
50,000	466.75	118,030	575.22	82,903	35,127	653.56	68,982	49,048	727.18	60,698	57,332
55,000	513.42	129,831	632.73	91,192	38,639	718.91	75,879	53,952	799.89	66,767	63,064
60,000	560.09	141,632	690.25	99,481	42,151	784.26	82,776	58,856	872.60	72,836	68,796
65,000	606.77	153,437	747.78	107,773	45,664	849.62	89,675	63,762	945.33	78,907	74,530
70,000	653.44	165,238	805.29	116,061	49,177	914.97	96,572	68,666	1,018.04	84,975	80,263
75,000	700.12	177,043	862.82	124,353	52,690	980.34	103,472	73,571	1,090.76	91,046	85,997
80,000	746.79	188,844	920.34	132,642	56,202	1,045.69	110,369	78,475	1,163.47	97,115	91,729
85,000	793.46	200,646	977.85	140,931	59,715	1,111.04	117,266	83,380	1,236.18	103,183	97,463
90,000	840.14	212,450	1,035.38	149,223	63,227	1,176.40	124,165	88,285	1,308.91	109,254	103,196
95,000	886.81	224,252	1,092.90	157,512	66,740	1,241.75	131,062	93,190	1,381.62	115,323	108,929
100,000	933.49	236,056	1,150.43	165,803	70,253	1,307.11	137,962	98,094	1,454.35	121,394	114,662
105,000	980.16	247,858	1,207.94	174,092	73,766	1,372.46	144,858	103,000	1,527.06	127,463	120,395
110,000	1,026.83	259,659	1,265.46	182,381	77,278	1,437.81	151,755	107,904	1,599.77	133,531	126,128
115,000	1,073.51	271,464	1,322.99	190,673	80,791	1,503.17	158,655	112,809	1,672.49	139,602	131,862
120,000	1,120.18	283,265	1,380.50	198,962	84,303	1,568.52	165,552	117,713	1,745.20	145,671	137,594
125,000	1,166.86	295,070	1,438.03	207,253	87,817	1,633.89	172,451	122,619	1,817.93	151,742	143,328
130,000	1,213.53	306,871	1,495.54	215,542	91,329	1,699.23	179,348	127,523	1,890.64	157,811	149,060
135,000	1,260.20	318,672	1,553.06	223,831	94,841	1,764.58	186,245	132,427	1,963.35	163,879	154,793
140,000	1,306.88	330,477	1,610.59	232,123	98,354	1,829.95	193,145	137,332	2,036.08	169,950	160,527
145,000	1,353.55	342,278	1,668.10	240,412	101,866	1,895.30	200,042	142,236	2,108.79	176,019	166,259
150,000	1,400.23	354,083	1,725.63	248,704	105,379	1,960.66	206,941	147,142	2,181.51	182,090	171,993
155,000	1,446.90	365,884	1,783.15	256,992	108,892	2,026.01	213,838	152,046	2,254.22	188,159	177,725
160,000	1,493.58	377,689	1,840.68	265,284	112,405	2,091.37	220,737	156,952	2,326.95	194,230	183,459
165,000	1,540.25	389,490	1,898.19	273,573	115,917	2,156.72	227,634	161,856	2,399.66	200,298	189,192
170,000	1,586.92	401,291	1,955.71	281,862	119,429	2,222.07	234,531	166,760	2,472.37	206,367	194,924
175,000	1,633.60	413,096	2,013.24	290,154	122,942	2,287.43	241,431	171,665	2,545.10	212,438	200,658
180,000	1,680.27	424,897	2,070.75	298,443	126,454	2,352.78	248,328	176,569	2,617.81	218,507	206,390
185,000	1,726.95	436,702	2,128.28	306,734	129,968	2,418.15	255,227	181,475	2,690.53	224,578	212,124
190,000	1,773.62	448,503	2,185.79	315,023	133,480	2,483.50	262,124	186,379	2,763.24	230,646	217,857
195,000	1,820.29	460,304	2,243.31	323,312	136,992	2,548.85	269,021	191,283	2,835.95	236,715	223,589
200,000	1,866.97	472,109	2,300.84	331,604	140,505	2,614.21	275,921	196,188	2,908.68	242,786	229,323

AMOUNT OF LOAN	30 YEARS		4% PMT INCR/YR 171.132 PAYMENTS			5% PMT INCR/YR 157.707 PAYMENTS			6% PMT INCR/YR 147.051 PAYMENTS		
	MONTHLY PAYMENT	TOTAL INTRST	LAST YR MON PMT	TOTAL INTRST	INTRST SAVED	LAST YR MON PMT	TOTAL INTRST	INTRST SAVED	LAST YR MON PMT	TOTAL INTRST	INTRST SAVED
$ 50	0.47	119	0.81	56	63	0.89	51	68	0.95	48	71
100	0.94	238	1.63	111	127	1.77	103	135	1.89	96	142
200	1.87	473	3.24	221	252	3.53	203	270	3.76	190	283
300	2.81	712	4.87	332	380	5.30	306	406	5.65	286	426
400	3.74	946	6.48	441	505	7.05	407	539	7.53	380	566
500	4.67	1,181	8.09	550	631	8.81	508	673	9.40	474	707
600	5.61	1,420	9.71	662	758	10.58	610	810	11.29	570	850
700	6.54	1,654	11.33	771	883	12.33	711	943	13.16	664	990
800	7.47	1,889	12.94	880	1,009	14.09	812	1,077	15.03	758	1,131
900	8.41	2,128	14.56	992	1,136	15.86	915	1,213	16.92	854	1,274
1,000	9.34	2,362	16.17	1,101	1,261	17.61	1,015	1,347	18.79	948	1,414
2,000	18.67	4,721	32.33	2,199	2,522	35.21	2,029	2,692	37.57	1,894	2,827
3,000	28.01	7,084	48.50	3,300	3,784	52.82	3,044	4,040	56.36	2,842	4,242
4,000	37.34	9,442	64.66	4,399	5,043	70.41	4,057	5,385	75.14	3,788	5,654
5,000	46.68	11,805	80.83	5,500	6,305	88.02	5,072	6,733	93.93	4,736	7,069
6,000	56.01	14,164	96.99	6,598	7,566	105.62	6,086	8,078	112.70	5,682	8,482
7,000	65.35	16,526	113.17	7,699	8,827	123.23	7,101	9,425	131.50	6,631	9,895
8,000	74.68	18,885	129.32	8,798	10,087	140.82	8,114	10,771	150.27	7,577	11,308
9,000	84.02	21,247	145.50	9,898	11,349	158.43	9,129	12,118	169.06	8,525	12,722
10,000	93.35	23,606	161.65	10,997	12,609	176.03	10,143	13,463	187.84	9,471	14,135
11,000	102.69	25,968	177.83	12,098	13,870	193.64	11,158	14,810	206.63	10,419	15,549
12,000	112.02	28,327	193.98	13,196	15,131	211.23	12,171	16,156	225.41	11,365	16,962
13,000	121.36	30,690	210.16	14,297	16,393	228.84	13,186	17,504	244.20	12,313	18,377
14,000	130.69	33,048	226.31	15,396	17,652	246.44	14,200	18,848	262.97	13,259	19,789
15,000	140.03	35,411	242.49	16,496	18,915	264.05	15,215	20,196	281.77	14,207	21,204
16,000	149.36	37,770	258.64	17,595	20,175	281.64	16,228	21,542	300.54	15,153	22,617
17,000	158.70	40,132	274.82	18,696	21,436	299.25	17,243	22,889	319.34	16,101	24,031
18,000	168.03	42,491	290.97	19,794	22,697	316.85	18,257	24,234	338.11	17,047	25,444
19,000	177.37	44,853	307.15	20,895	23,958	334.46	19,272	25,581	356.90	17,996	26,857
20,000	186.70	47,212	323.30	21,994	25,218	352.05	20,285	26,927	375.68	18,942	28,270
21,000	196.04	49,574	339.48	23,095	26,479	369.66	21,300	28,274	394.47	19,890	29,684
22,000	205.37	51,933	355.63	24,193	27,740	387.26	22,314	29,619	413.24	20,836	31,097
23,000	214.71	54,296	371.81	25,294	29,002	404.87	23,329	30,967	432.04	21,784	32,512
24,000	224.04	56,654	387.96	26,393	30,261	422.46	24,342	32,312	450.81	22,730	33,924
25,000	233.38	59,017	404.14	27,493	31,524	440.07	25,357	33,660	469.61	23,678	35,339
26,000	242.71	61,376	420.30	28,592	32,784	457.67	26,371	35,005	488.38	24,624	36,752
27,000	252.04	63,734	436.45	29,690	34,044	475.26	27,384	36,350	507.15	25,570	38,164
28,000	261.38	66,097	452.63	30,791	35,306	492.87	28,399	37,698	525.95	26,518	39,579
29,000	270.71	68,456	468.78	31,890	36,566	510.46	29,412	39,044	544.72	27,464	40,992
30,000	280.05	70,818	484.96	32,991	37,827	528.08	30,428	40,390	563.52	28,412	42,406
32,500	303.39	76,720	525.37	35,740	40,980	572.09	32,964	43,756	610.48	30,781	45,939
35,000	326.72	82,619	565.77	38,488	44,131	616.08	35,498	47,121	657.42	33,147	49,472
40,000	373.40	94,424	646.61	43,988	50,436	704.10	40,570	53,854	751.35	37,883	56,541
45,000	420.07	106,225	727.43	49,485	56,740	792.10	45,640	60,585	845.26	42,618	63,607
50,000	466.75	118,030	808.26	54,984	63,046	880.13	50,713	67,317	939.19	47,354	70,676
55,000	513.42	129,831	889.08	60,482	69,349	968.13	55,783	74,048	1,033.10	52,088	77,743
60,000	560.09	141,632	969.89	65,979	75,653	1,056.13	60,853	80,779	1,127.01	56,823	84,809
65,000	606.77	153,437	1,050.73	71,479	81,958	1,144.16	65,926	87,511	1,220.94	61,559	91,878
70,000	653.44	165,238	1,131.55	76,976	88,262	1,232.16	70,996	94,242	1,314.85	66,294	98,944
75,000	700.12	177,043	1,212.38	82,476	94,567	1,320.18	76,068	100,975	1,408.78	71,030	106,013
80,000	746.79	188,844	1,293.20	87,973	100,871	1,408.18	81,138	107,706	1,502.69	75,764	113,080
85,000	793.46	200,646	1,374.02	93,470	107,176	1,496.19	86,209	114,437	1,596.60	80,499	120,147
90,000	840.14	212,450	1,454.85	98,970	113,480	1,584.21	91,281	121,169	1,690.53	85,235	127,215
95,000	886.81	224,252	1,535.67	104,467	119,785	1,672.21	96,351	127,901	1,784.44	89,970	134,282
100,000	933.49	236,056	1,616.50	109,967	126,089	1,760.23	101,423	134,633	1,878.37	94,706	141,350
105,000	980.16	247,858	1,697.32	115,464	132,394	1,848.24	106,494	141,364	1,972.27	99,440	148,418
110,000	1,026.83	259,659	1,778.14	120,961	138,698	1,936.24	111,564	148,095	2,066.18	104,175	155,484
115,000	1,073.51	271,464	1,858.97	126,461	145,003	2,024.26	116,636	154,828	2,160.11	108,911	162,553
120,000	1,120.18	283,265	1,939.79	131,958	151,307	2,112.27	121,706	161,559	2,254.02	113,645	169,620
125,000	1,166.86	295,070	2,020.62	137,458	157,612	2,200.29	126,779	168,291	2,347.95	118,382	176,688
130,000	1,213.53	306,871	2,101.44	142,955	163,916	2,288.29	131,849	175,022	2,441.86	123,116	183,755
135,000	1,260.20	318,672	2,182.26	148,453	170,220	2,376.30	136,919	181,753	2,535.77	127,851	190,821
140,000	1,306.88	330,477	2,263.09	153,952	176,525	2,464.32	141,992	188,485	2,629.70	132,587	197,890
145,000	1,353.55	342,278	2,343.91	159,449	182,829	2,552.32	147,062	195,216	2,723.61	137,321	204,957
150,000	1,400.23	354,083	2,424.75	164,949	189,134	2,640.34	152,134	201,949	2,817.54	142,058	212,025
155,000	1,446.90	365,884	2,505.56	170,446	195,438	2,728.35	157,204	208,680	2,911.45	146,792	219,092
160,000	1,493.58	377,689	2,586.40	175,946	201,743	2,816.37	162,277	215,412	3,005.38	151,529	226,160
165,000	1,540.25	389,490	2,667.21	181,443	208,047	2,904.37	167,347	222,143	3,099.29	156,263	233,227
170,000	1,586.92	401,291	2,748.03	186,940	214,351	2,992.37	172,417	228,874	3,193.19	160,997	240,294
175,000	1,633.60	413,096	2,828.87	192,440	220,656	3,080.40	177,489	235,607	3,287.12	165,734	247,362
180,000	1,680.27	424,897	2,909.68	197,937	226,960	3,168.40	182,560	242,337	3,381.03	170,468	254,429
185,000	1,726.95	436,702	2,990.52	203,437	233,265	3,256.42	187,632	249,070	3,474.96	175,205	261,497
190,000	1,773.62	448,503	3,071.34	208,934	239,569	3,344.43	192,702	255,801	3,568.87	179,939	268,564
195,000	1,820.29	460,304	3,152.15	214,432	245,872	3,432.43	197,772	262,532	3,662.78	184,673	275,631
200,000	1,866.97	472,109	3,232.99	219,931	252,178	3,520.45	202,845	269,264	3,756.71	189,410	282,699

11.00% GROWING EQUITY MORTGAGES

AMOUNT OF LOAN	30 YEARS		1% PMT INCR/YR 254.951 PAYMENTS			2% PMT INCR/YR 212.775 PAYMENTS			3% PMT INCR/YR 187.348 PAYMENTS		
	MONTHLY PAYMENT	TOTAL INTRST	LAST YR MON PMT	TOTAL INTRST	INTRST SAVED	LAST YR MON PMT	TOTAL INTRST	INTRST SAVED	LAST YR MON PMT	TOTAL INTRST	INTRST SAVED
$ 50	0.48	123	0.59	86	37	0.67	71	52	0.75	63	60
100	0.96	246	1.18	171	75	1.34	142	104	1.50	125	121
200	1.91	488	2.35	340	148	2.67	282	206	2.98	248	240
300	2.86	730	3.52	508	222	4.00	422	308	4.46	371	359
400	3.81	972	4.70	676	296	5.33	562	410	5.94	494	478
500	4.77	1,217	5.88	848	369	6.68	704	513	7.43	619	598
600	5.72	1,459	7.05	1,016	443	8.01	844	615	8.91	742	717
700	6.67	1,701	8.22	1,184	517	9.34	984	717	10.39	865	836
800	7.62	1,943	9.39	1,353	590	10.67	1,124	819	11.87	988	955
900	8.58	2,189	10.57	1,524	665	12.01	1,266	923	13.37	1,113	1,076
1,000	9.53	2,431	11.74	1,692	739	13.34	1,406	1,025	14.85	1,236	1,195
2,000	19.05	4,858	23.48	3,382	1,476	26.67	2,809	2,049	29.68	2,470	2,388
3,000	28.57	7,285	35.21	5,071	2,214	40.00	4,212	3,073	44.51	3,704	3,581
4,000	38.10	9,716	46.95	6,764	2,952	53.35	5,618	4,098	59.36	4,940	4,776
5,000	47.62	12,143	58.69	8,453	3,690	66.68	7,021	5,122	74.19	6,173	5,970
6,000	57.14	14,570	70.42	10,142	4,428	80.01	8,424	6,146	89.02	7,407	7,163
7,000	66.67	17,001	82.16	11,835	5,166	93.35	9,830	7,171	103.87	8,643	8,358
8,000	76.19	19,428	93.90	13,524	5,904	106.68	11,233	8,195	118.70	9,877	9,551
9,000	85.71	21,856	105.63	15,214	6,642	120.01	12,636	9,220	133.53	11,111	10,745
10,000	95.24	24,286	117.37	16,906	7,380	133.36	14,042	10,244	148.38	12,347	11,939
11,000	104.76	26,714	129.11	18,595	8,119	146.69	15,445	11,269	163.21	13,580	13,134
12,000	114.28	29,141	140.84	20,285	8,856	160.02	16,848	12,293	178.04	14,814	14,327
13,000	123.81	31,572	152.58	21,977	9,595	173.36	18,254	13,318	192.89	16,050	15,522
14,000	133.33	33,999	164.31	23,667	10,332	186.69	19,657	14,342	207.72	17,284	16,715
15,000	142.85	36,426	176.05	25,356	11,070	200.02	21,060	15,366	222.56	18,518	17,908
16,000	152.38	38,857	187.79	27,048	11,809	213.37	22,466	16,391	237.40	19,754	19,103
17,000	161.90	41,284	199.52	28,738	12,546	226.70	23,869	17,415	252.23	20,987	20,297
18,000	171.42	43,711	211.26	30,427	13,284	240.03	25,272	18,439	267.07	22,221	21,490
19,000	180.95	46,142	223.00	32,120	14,022	253.37	26,678	19,464	281.91	23,457	22,685
20,000	190.47	48,569	234.73	33,809	14,760	266.70	28,081	20,488	296.75	24,691	23,878
21,000	199.99	50,996	246.47	35,499	15,497	280.03	29,484	21,512	311.58	25,925	25,071
22,000	209.52	53,427	258.21	37,191	16,236	293.38	30,890	22,537	326.43	27,161	26,266
23,000	219.04	55,854	269.94	38,880	16,974	306.71	32,293	23,561	341.26	28,394	27,460
24,000	228.56	58,282	281.68	40,570	17,712	320.04	33,696	24,586	356.09	29,628	28,654
25,000	238.09	60,712	293.42	42,262	18,450	333.38	35,102	25,610	370.94	30,864	29,848
26,000	247.61	63,140	305.15	43,952	19,188	346.71	36,505	26,635	385.77	32,098	31,042
27,000	257.13	65,567	316.88	45,641	19,926	360.04	37,908	27,659	400.60	33,332	32,235
28,000	266.66	67,998	328.63	47,333	20,665	373.39	39,314	28,684	415.45	34,568	33,430
29,000	276.18	70,425	340.36	49,023	21,402	386.72	40,717	29,708	430.28	35,801	34,624
30,000	285.70	72,852	352.09	50,712	22,140	400.05	42,120	30,732	445.11	37,035	35,817
32,500	309.51	78,924	381.44	54,939	23,985	433.39	45,630	33,294	482.21	40,122	38,802
35,000	333.32	84,995	410.78	59,165	25,830	466.73	49,141	35,854	519.30	43,209	41,786
40,000	380.93	97,135	469.46	67,615	29,520	533.39	56,159	40,976	593.48	49,379	47,756
45,000	428.55	109,278	528.14	76,068	33,210	600.07	63,180	46,098	667.67	55,553	53,725
50,000	476.17	121,421	586.83	84,521	36,900	666.75	70,201	51,220	741.86	61,726	59,695
55,000	523.78	133,561	645.50	92,972	40,589	733.42	77,219	56,342	816.03	67,897	65,664
60,000	571.40	145,704	704.19	101,425	44,279	800.10	84,240	61,464	890.22	74,070	71,634
65,000	619.02	157,847	762.88	109,878	47,969	866.78	91,260	66,587	964.41	80,244	77,603
70,000	666.63	169,987	821.55	118,328	51,659	933.44	98,279	71,708	1,038.59	86,415	83,572
75,000	714.25	182,130	880.24	126,781	55,349	1,000.12	105,300	76,830	1,112.78	92,588	89,542
80,000	761.86	194,270	938.91	135,231	59,039	1,066.79	112,318	81,952	1,186.95	98,759	95,511
85,000	809.48	206,413	997.60	143,684	62,729	1,133.47	119,339	87,074	1,261.14	104,932	101,481
90,000	857.10	218,556	1,056.28	152,137	66,419	1,200.15	126,359	92,197	1,335.33	111,106	107,450
95,000	904.71	230,696	1,114.96	160,587	70,109	1,266.81	133,378	97,319	1,409.51	117,277	113,419
100,000	952.33	242,839	1,173.64	169,040	73,799	1,333.49	140,399	102,440	1,483.70	123,450	119,389
105,000	999.94	254,978	1,232.32	177,490	77,488	1,400.16	147,417	107,561	1,557.87	129,621	125,357
110,000	1,047.56	267,122	1,291.00	185,943	81,179	1,466.84	154,438	112,684	1,632.06	135,794	131,328
115,000	1,095.18	279,265	1,349.69	194,396	84,869	1,533.52	161,458	117,807	1,706.25	141,967	137,298
120,000	1,142.79	291,404	1,408.37	202,846	88,558	1,600.18	168,477	122,927	1,780.43	148,138	143,266
125,000	1,190.41	303,548	1,467.05	211,299	92,249	1,666.86	175,498	128,050	1,854.62	154,312	149,236
130,000	1,238.03	315,691	1,525.74	219,752	95,939	1,733.54	182,518	133,173	1,928.81	160,485	155,206
135,000	1,285.64	327,830	1,584.41	228,202	99,628	1,800.21	189,537	138,293	2,002.99	166,656	161,174
140,000	1,333.26	339,974	1,643.10	236,655	103,319	1,866.89	196,557	143,417	2,077.18	172,829	167,145
145,000	1,380.87	352,113	1,701.77	245,106	107,007	1,933.55	203,576	148,537	2,151.35	179,000	173,113
150,000	1,428.49	364,256	1,760.46	253,559	110,697	2,000.23	210,597	153,659	2,225.54	185,174	179,082
155,000	1,476.11	376,400	1,819.15	262,012	114,388	2,066.91	217,617	158,783	2,299.73	191,347	185,053
160,000	1,523.72	388,539	1,877.82	270,462	118,077	2,133.58	224,636	163,903	2,373.91	197,518	191,021
165,000	1,571.34	400,682	1,936.51	278,915	121,767	2,200.26	231,656	169,026	2,448.10	203,691	196,991
170,000	1,618.95	412,822	1,995.18	287,365	125,457	2,266.92	238,675	174,147	2,522.27	209,862	202,960
175,000	1,666.57	424,965	2,053.87	295,818	129,147	2,333.60	245,696	179,269	2,596.46	216,036	208,929
180,000	1,714.19	437,108	2,112.55	304,271	132,837	2,400.28	252,716	184,392	2,670.65	222,209	214,899
185,000	1,761.80	449,248	2,171.23	312,721	136,527	2,466.95	259,735	189,513	2,744.83	228,380	220,868
190,000	1,809.42	461,391	2,229.91	321,174	140,217	2,533.62	266,755	194,636	2,819.02	234,553	226,838
195,000	1,857.04	473,534	2,288.60	329,627	143,907	2,600.30	273,776	199,758	2,893.21	240,726	232,808
200,000	1,904.65	485,674	2,347.28	338,077	147,597	2,666.97	280,795	204,879	2,967.38	246,897	238,777

132

AMOUNT OF LOAN	30 YEARS		4% PMT INCR/YR 169.666 PAYMENTS			5% PMT INCR/YR 156.365 PAYMENTS			6% PMT INCR/YR 145.802 PAYMENTS		
	MONTHLY PAYMENT	TOTAL INTRST	LAST YR MON PMT	TOTAL INTRST	INTRST SAVED	LAST YR MON PMT	TOTAL INTRST	INTRST SAVED	LAST YR MON PMT	TOTAL INTRST	INTRST SAVED
$ 50	0.48	123	0.83	57	66	0.91	52	71	0.97	49	74
100	0.96	246	1.66	113	133	1.81	105	141	1.93	98	148
200	1.91	488	3.31	225	263	3.60	207	281	3.84	194	294
300	2.86	730	4.95	336	394	5.39	310	420	5.75	289	441
400	3.81	972	6.60	447	525	7.18	412	560	7.67	385	587
500	4.77	1,217	8.26	561	656	8.99	517	700	9.60	483	734
600	5.72	1,459	9.91	672	787	10.79	620	839	11.51	579	880
700	6.67	1,701	11.55	783	918	12.58	722	979	13.42	674	1,027
800	7.62	1,943	13.20	895	1,048	14.37	825	1,118	15.33	770	1,173
900	8.58	2,189	14.86	1,008	1,181	16.18	930	1,259	17.26	868	1,321
1,000	9.53	2,431	16.50	1,119	1,312	17.97	1,032	1,399	19.18	964	1,467
2,000	19.05	4,858	32.99	2,236	2,622	35.92	2,062	2,796	38.33	1,926	2,932
3,000	28.57	7,285	49.47	3,354	3,931	53.87	3,092	4,193	57.49	2,887	4,398
4,000	38.10	9,716	65.98	4,473	5,243	71.84	4,125	5,591	76.66	3,851	5,865
5,000	47.62	12,143	82.46	5,590	6,553	89.79	5,155	6,988	95.82	4,813	7,330
6,000	57.14	14,570	98.95	6,707	7,863	107.75	6,185	8,385	114.98	5,775	8,795
7,000	66.67	17,001	115.45	7,827	9,174	125.72	7,217	9,784	134.15	6,738	10,263
8,000	76.19	19,428	131.94	8,944	10,484	143.67	8,247	11,181	153.31	7,700	11,728
9,000	85.71	21,856	148.42	10,061	11,795	161.62	9,277	12,579	172.47	8,662	13,194
10,000	95.24	24,286	164.92	11,180	13,106	179.59	10,309	13,977	191.64	9,626	14,660
11,000	104.76	26,714	181.41	12,297	14,417	197.54	11,339	15,375	210.80	10,587	16,127
12,000	114.28	29,141	197.90	13,414	15,727	215.49	12,370	16,771	229.95	11,549	17,592
13,000	123.81	31,572	214.40	14,534	17,038	233.46	13,402	18,170	249.13	12,513	19,059
14,000	133.33	33,999	230.88	15,651	18,348	251.41	14,432	19,567	268.29	13,475	20,524
15,000	142.85	36,426	247.37	16,768	19,658	269.36	15,462	20,964	287.44	14,436	21,990
16,000	152.38	38,857	263.87	17,887	20,970	287.34	16,494	22,363	306.62	15,400	23,457
17,000	161.90	41,284	280.36	19,005	22,279	305.29	17,524	23,760	325.77	16,362	24,922
18,000	171.42	43,711	296.84	20,122	23,589	323.24	18,554	25,157	344.93	17,324	26,387
19,000	180.95	46,142	313.35	21,241	24,901	341.21	19,587	26,555	364.11	18,288	27,854
20,000	190.47	48,569	329.83	22,358	26,211	359.16	20,617	27,952	383.26	19,249	29,320
21,000	199.99	50,996	346.32	23,475	27,521	377.11	21,647	29,349	402.42	20,211	30,785
22,000	209.52	53,427	362.82	24,595	28,832	395.08	22,679	30,748	421.60	21,175	32,252
23,000	219.04	55,854	379.31	25,712	30,142	413.03	23,709	32,145	440.75	22,137	33,717
24,000	228.56	58,282	395.79	26,829	31,453	430.98	24,739	33,543	459.91	23,098	35,184
25,000	238.09	60,712	412.29	27,948	32,764	448.95	25,771	34,941	479.08	24,062	36,650
26,000	247.61	63,140	428.78	29,065	34,075	466.91	26,801	36,339	498.24	25,024	38,116
27,000	257.13	65,567	445.27	30,183	35,384	484.86	27,831	37,736	517.40	25,986	39,581
28,000	266.66	67,998	461.77	31,302	36,696	502.83	28,864	39,134	536.57	26,949	41,049
29,000	276.18	70,425	478.25	32,419	38,006	520.78	29,894	40,531	555.73	27,911	42,514
30,000	285.70	72,852	494.74	33,536	39,316	538.73	30,924	41,928	574.88	28,873	43,979
32,500	309.51	78,924	535.97	36,331	42,593	583.63	33,501	45,23	622.79	31,279	47,645
35,000	333.32	84,995	577.20	39,126	45,869	628.52	36,079	48,916	670.71	33,685	51,309
40,000	380.93	97,135	659.65	44,714	52,421	718.30	41,231	55,900	766.51	38,496	58,639
45,000	428.55	109,278	742.11	50,304	58,974	808.09	46,386	62,892	862.33	43,309	65,969
50,000	476.17	121,421	824.57	55,894	65,527	897.89	51,540	69,881	958.15	48,122	73,299
55,000	523.78	133,561	907.02	61,482	72,079	987.67	56,693	76,868	1,053.95	52,933	80,628
60,000	571.40	145,704	989.48	67,072	78,632	1,077.46	61,848	83,856	1,149.77	57,746	87,958
65,000	619.02	157,847	1,071.94	72,663	85,184	1,167.25	67,002	90,845	1,245.59	62,559	95,288
70,000	666.63	169,987	1,154.39	78,250	91,737	1,257.03	72,155	97,832	1,341.39	67,369	102,618
75,000	714.25	182,130	1,236.85	83,841	98,289	1,346.82	77,310	104,820	1,437.21	72,182	109,948
80,000	761.86	194,270	1,319.30	89,428	104,842	1,436.60	82,462	111,808	1,533.01	76,993	117,277
85,000	809.48	206,413	1,401.76	95,019	111,394	1,526.40	87,617	118,796	1,628.83	81,806	124,607
90,000	857.10	218,556	1,484.22	100,609	117,947	1,616.19	92,771	125,785	1,724.65	86,619	131,937
95,000	904.71	230,696	1,566.66	106,197	124,499	1,705.97	97,924	132,772	1,820.45	91,429	139,267
100,000	952.33	242,839	1,649.13	111,787	131,052	1,795.76	103,079	139,760	1,916.28	96,242	146,597
105,000	999.94	254,978	1,731.57	117,375	137,603	1,885.54	108,231	146,747	2,012.08	101,053	153,925
110,000	1,047.56	267,122	1,814.03	122,965	144,157	1,975.33	113,386	153,736	2,107.90	105,866	161,256
115,000	1,095.18	279,265	1,896.50	128,555	150,710	2,065.13	118,541	160,724	2,203.72	110,679	168,586
120,000	1,142.79	291,404	1,978.94	134,143	157,261	2,154.90	123,693	167,711	2,299.52	115,489	175,915
125,000	1,190.41	303,548	2,061.40	139,733	163,815	2,244.70	128,848	174,700	2,395.34	120,302	183,246
130,000	1,238.03	315,691	2,143.87	145,323	170,368	2,334.49	134,003	181,688	2,491.16	125,115	190,576
135,000	1,285.64	327,830	2,226.31	150,911	176,919	2,424.27	139,155	188,675	2,586.96	129,926	197,904
140,000	1,333.26	339,974	2,308.77	156,501	183,473	2,514.06	144,310	195,664	2,682.78	134,739	205,235
145,000	1,380.87	352,113	2,391.22	162,089	190,024	2,603.84	149,462	202,651	2,778.58	139,549	212,564
150,000	1,428.49	364,256	2,473.68	167,679	196,577	2,693.63	154,617	209,639	2,874.40	144,362	219,894
155,000	1,476.11	376,400	2,556.14	173,269	203,131	2,783.43	159,772	216,628	2,970.22	149,175	227,225
160,000	1,523.72	388,539	2,638.59	178,857	209,682	2,873.20	164,924	223,615	3,066.02	153,986	234,553
165,000	1,571.34	400,682	2,721.05	184,447	216,235	2,963.00	170,079	230,603	3,161.84	158,799	241,883
170,000	1,618.95	412,822	2,803.50	190,035	222,787	3,052.77	175,231	237,591	3,257.65	163,609	249,213
175,000	1,666.57	424,965	2,885.96	195,625	229,340	3,142.57	180,386	244,579	3,353.47	168,422	256,543
180,000	1,714.19	437,108	2,968.42	201,215	235,893	3,232.36	185,541	251,567	3,449.29	173,235	263,873
185,000	1,761.80	449,248	3,050.87	206,803	242,445	3,322.14	190,693	258,554	3,545.09	178,046	271,202
190,000	1,809.42	461,391	3,133.33	212,393	248,998	3,411.93	195,848	265,543	3,640.91	182,859	278,532
195,000	1,857.04	473,534	3,215.79	217,983	255,551	3,501.73	201,003	272,531	3,736.73	187,671	285,863
200,000	1,904.65	485,674	3,298.24	223,571	262,103	3,591.50	206,155	279,519	3,832.53	192,482	293,192

AMOUNT OF LOAN	30 YEARS		1% PMT INCR/YR 253.135 PAYMENTS			2% PMT INCR/YR 211.016 PAYMENTS			3% PMT INCR/YR 185.742 PAYMENTS		
	MONTHLY PAYMENT	TOTAL INTRST	LAST YR MON PMT	TOTAL INTRST	INTRST SAVED	LAST YR MON PMT	TOTAL INTRST	INTRST SAVED	LAST YR MON PMT	TOTAL INTRST	INTRST SAVED
$ 50	0.49	126	0.60	87	39	0.69	72	54	0.76	64	62
100	0.98	253	1.21	175	78	1.37	145	108	1.53	127	126
200	1.95	502	2.40	347	155	2.73	287	215	3.04	253	249
300	2.92	751	3.60	518	233	4.09	430	321	4.55	378	373
400	3.89	1,000	4.79	690	310	5.45	572	428	6.06	503	497
500	4.86	1,250	5.99	862	388	6.81	715	535	7.57	628	622
600	5.83	1,499	7.18	1,034	465	8.16	857	642	9.08	753	746
700	6.80	1,748	8.38	1,206	542	9.52	1,000	748	10.59	879	869
800	7.78	2,001	9.59	1,380	621	10.89	1,145	856	12.12	1,006	995
900	8.75	2,250	10.78	1,552	698	12.25	1,287	963	13.63	1,131	1,119
1,000	9.72	2,499	11.98	1,724	775	13.61	1,430	1,069	15.14	1,256	1,243
2,000	19.43	4,995	23.95	3,446	1,549	27.21	2,857	2,138	30.27	2,510	2,485
3,000	29.14	7,490	35.91	5,167	2,323	40.80	4,284	3,206	45.40	3,764	3,726
4,000	38.86	9,990	47.89	6,891	3,099	54.41	5,714	4,276	60.54	5,021	4,969
5,000	48.57	12,485	59.86	8,613	3,872	68.01	7,141	5,344	75.67	6,275	6,210
6,000	58.28	14,981	71.82	10,334	4,647	81.61	8,568	6,413	90.80	7,529	7,452
7,000	67.99	17,476	83.79	12,055	5,421	95.20	9,995	7,481	105.93	8,783	8,693
8,000	77.71	19,976	95.77	13,780	6,196	108.81	11,425	8,551	121.07	10,039	9,937
9,000	87.42	22,471	107.74	15,501	6,970	122.41	12,852	9,619	136.20	11,293	11,178
10,000	97.13	24,967	119.70	17,223	7,744	136.01	14,279	10,688	151.33	12,547	12,420
11,000	106.84	27,462	131.67	18,944	8,518	149.60	15,707	11,755	166.45	13,801	13,661
12,000	116.56	29,962	143.65	20,668	9,294	163.21	17,136	12,826	181.60	15,057	14,905
13,000	126.27	32,457	155.61	22,390	10,067	176.81	18,564	13,893	196.72	16,311	16,146
14,000	135.98	34,953	167.58	24,111	10,842	190.40	19,991	14,962	211.85	17,565	17,388
15,000	145.69	37,448	179.55	25,832	11,616	204.00	21,418	16,030	226.98	18,819	18,629
16,000	155.41	39,948	191.53	27,557	12,391	217.61	22,848	17,100	242.12	20,076	19,872
17,000	165.12	42,443	203.49	29,278	13,165	231.21	24,275	18,168	257.25	21,330	21,113
18,000	174.83	44,939	215.46	30,999	13,940	244.80	25,702	19,237	272.38	22,584	22,355
19,000	184.54	47,434	227.43	32,721	14,713	258.40	27,129	20,305	287.51	23,838	23,596
20,000	194.26	49,934	239.40	34,445	15,489	272.01	28,559	21,375	302.65	25,094	24,840
21,000	203.97	52,429	251.37	36,166	16,263	285.61	29,986	22,443	317.78	26,348	26,081
22,000	213.68	54,925	263.34	37,888	17,037	299.20	31,413	23,512	332.91	27,602	27,323
23,000	223.40	57,424	275.32	39,612	17,812	312.81	32,843	24,581	348.05	28,858	28,566
24,000	233.11	59,920	287.28	41,334	18,586	326.41	34,270	25,650	363.18	30,112	29,808
25,000	242.82	62,415	299.25	43,055	19,360	340.01	35,697	26,718	378.31	31,366	31,049
26,000	252.53	64,911	311.22	44,776	20,135	353.60	37,125	27,786	393.43	32,620	32,291
27,000	262.25	67,410	323.19	46,501	20,909	367.21	38,554	28,856	408.58	33,877	33,533
28,000	271.96	69,906	335.16	48,222	21,684	380.81	39,982	29,924	423.70	35,131	34,775
29,000	281.67	72,401	347.13	49,943	22,458	394.41	41,409	30,992	438.83	36,385	36,016
30,000	291.38	74,897	359.09	51,665	23,232	408.00	42,836	32,061	453.96	37,639	37,258
32,500	315.66	81,138	389.02	55,970	25,168	442.00	46,405	34,733	491.79	40,775	40,363
35,000	339.95	87,382	418.95	60,277	27,105	476.01	49,977	37,405	529.63	43,914	43,468
40,000	388.51	99,864	478.80	68,887	30,977	544.01	57,115	42,749	605.29	50,186	49,678
45,000	437.07	112,345	538.64	77,497	34,848	612.00	64,254	48,091	680.94	56,458	55,887
50,000	485.64	124,830	598.50	86,110	38,720	680.01	71,395	53,435	756.61	62,733	62,097
55,000	534.20	137,312	658.34	94,720	42,592	748.01	78,533	58,779	832.27	69,005	68,307
60,000	582.76	149,794	718.19	103,330	46,464	816.00	85,672	64,122	907.92	75,278	74,516
65,000	631.32	162,275	778.03	111,939	50,336	884.00	92,810	69,465	983.58	81,550	80,725
70,000	679.89	174,760	837.89	120,552	54,208	952.01	99,951	74,809	1,059.25	87,825	86,935
75,000	728.45	187,242	897.74	129,162	58,080	1,020.01	107,090	80,152	1,134.90	94,097	93,145
80,000	777.01	199,724	957.58	137,772	61,952	1,088.00	114,228	85,496	1,210.56	100,370	99,354
85,000	825.58	212,209	1,017.44	146,385	65,824	1,156.01	121,369	90,840	1,286.23	106,644	105,565
90,000	874.14	224,690	1,077.28	154,994	69,696	1,224.01	128,508	96,182	1,361.88	112,917	111,773
95,000	922.70	237,172	1,137.13	163,604	73,568	1,292.00	135,646	101,526	1,437.54	119,189	117,983
100,000	971.27	249,657	1,196.99	172,217	77,440	1,360.01	142,787	106,870	1,513.21	125,464	124,193
105,000	1,019.83	262,139	1,256.83	180,827	81,312	1,428.01	149,926	112,213	1,588.86	131,736	130,403
110,000	1,068.39	274,620	1,316.68	189,437	85,183	1,496.00	157,064	117,556	1,664.52	138,008	136,612
115,000	1,116.96	287,106	1,376.53	198,049	89,057	1,564.01	164,205	122,901	1,740.19	144,283	142,823
120,000	1,165.52	299,587	1,436.38	206,659	92,928	1,632.01	171,344	128,243	1,815.84	150,555	149,032
125,000	1,214.08	312,069	1,496.22	215,269	96,800	1,700.01	178,482	133,587	1,891.50	156,828	155,241
130,000	1,262.64	324,550	1,556.07	223,879	100,671	1,768.00	185,621	138,929	1,967.15	163,100	161,450
135,000	1,311.21	337,036	1,615.92	232,492	104,544	1,836.01	192,762	144,274	2,042.82	169,375	167,661
140,000	1,359.77	349,517	1,675.77	241,102	108,415	1,904.01	199,900	149,617	2,118.48	175,647	173,870
145,000	1,408.33	361,999	1,735.61	249,711	112,288	1,972.00	207,039	154,960	2,194.13	181,920	180,079
150,000	1,456.90	374,484	1,795.47	258,324	116,160	2,040.01	214,180	160,304	2,269.80	188,194	186,290
155,000	1,505.46	386,966	1,855.32	266,934	120,032	2,108.01	221,318	165,648	2,345.46	194,467	192,499
160,000	1,554.02	399,447	1,915.16	275,544	123,903	2,176.00	228,457	170,990	2,421.11	200,739	198,708
165,000	1,602.59	411,932	1,975.02	284,156	127,776	2,244.01	235,598	176,334	2,496.78	207,014	204,918
170,000	1,651.15	424,414	2,034.86	292,766	131,648	2,312.01	242,736	181,678	2,572.44	213,286	211,128
175,000	1,699.71	436,896	2,094.71	301,376	135,520	2,380.00	249,875	187,021	2,648.09	219,558	217,338
180,000	1,748.28	449,381	2,154.57	309,989	139,392	2,448.01	257,016	192,365	2,723.76	225,833	223,548
185,000	1,796.84	461,862	2,214.41	318,599	143,263	2,516.01	264,154	197,708	2,799.42	232,106	229,756
190,000	1,845.40	474,344	2,274.26	327,209	147,135	2,584.01	271,293	203,051	2,875.07	238,378	235,966
195,000	1,893.96	486,826	2,334.10	335,818	151,008	2,652.00	278,431	208,395	2,950.73	244,650	242,176
200,000	1,942.53	499,311	2,393.96	344,431	154,880	2,720.01	285,572	213,739	3,026.40	250,925	248,386

AMOUNT OF LOAN	30 YEARS		4% PMT INCR/YR 168.221 PAYMENTS			5% PMT INCR/YR 154.998 PAYMENTS			6% PMT INCR/YR 144.576 PAYMENTS		
	MONTHLY PAYMENT	TOTAL INTRST	LAST YR MON PMT	TOTAL INTRST	INTRST SAVED	LAST YR MON PMT	TOTAL INTRST	INTRST SAVED	LAST YR MON PMT	TOTAL INTRST	INTRST SAVED
$ 50	0.49	126	0.85	58	68	0.88	53	73	0.99	50	76
100	0.98	253	1.70	115	138	1.76	107	146	1.97	100	153
200	1.95	502	3.38	229	273	3.50	211	291	3.92	197	305
300	2.92	751	5.06	342	409	5.24	315	436	5.88	295	456
400	3.89	1,000	6.74	455	545	6.99	420	580	7.83	392	608
500	4.86	1,250	8.42	569	681	8.73	524	726	9.78	489	761
600	5.83	1,499	10.10	682	817	10.47	629	870	11.73	587	912
700	6.80	1,748	11.78	795	953	12.21	733	1,015	13.68	684	1,064
800	7.78	2,001	13.47	911	1,090	13.97	840	1,161	15.65	784	1,217
900	8.75	2,250	15.15	1,024	1,226	15.71	944	1,306	17.61	881	1,369
1,000	9.72	2,499	16.83	1,137	1,362	17.46	1,049	1,450	19.56	979	1,520
2,000	19.43	4,995	33.65	2,272	2,723	34.89	2,095	2,900	39.10	1,956	3,039
3,000	29.14	7,490	50.46	3,407	4,083	52.33	3,141	4,349	58.64	2,933	4,557
4,000	38.86	9,990	67.29	4,545	5,445	69.79	4,190	5,800	78.19	3,912	6,078
5,000	48.57	12,485	84.11	5,680	6,805	87.22	5,236	7,249	97.73	4,889	7,596
6,000	58.28	14,981	100.92	6,815	8,166	104.66	6,283	8,698	117.27	5,866	9,115
7,000	67.99	17,476	117.74	7,950	9,526	122.10	7,329	10,147	136.81	6,843	10,633
8,000	77.71	19,976	134.57	9,087	10,889	139.56	8,378	11,598	156.37	7,822	12,154
9,000	87.42	22,471	151.38	10,222	12,249	156.99	9,424	13,047	175.91	8,799	13,672
10,000	97.13	24,967	168.20	11,357	13,610	174.43	10,471	14,496	195.44	9,776	15,191
11,000	106.84	27,462	185.01	12,493	14,969	191.87	11,517	15,945	214.98	10,752	16,710
12,000	116.56	29,962	201.84	13,630	16,332	209.33	12,560	17,396	234.54	11,731	18,231
13,000	126.27	32,457	218.66	14,765	17,692	226.76	13,612	18,845	254.08	12,708	19,749
14,000	135.98	34,953	235.47	15,900	19,053	244.20	14,659	20,294	273.62	13,685	21,268
15,000	145.69	37,448	252.29	17,035	20,413	261.64	15,705	21,743	293.16	14,662	22,786
16,000	155.41	39,948	269.12	18,172	21,776	279.09	16,754	23,194	312.72	15,641	24,307
17,000	165.12	42,443	285.93	19,308	23,135	296.53	17,800	24,643	332.25	16,618	25,825
18,000	174.83	44,939	302.75	20,443	24,496	313.97	18,847	26,092	351.79	17,595	27,344
19,000	184.54	47,434	319.56	21,578	25,856	331.41	19,893	27,541	371.33	18,572	28,862
20,000	194.26	49,934	336.40	22,715	27,219	348.86	20,942	28,992	390.89	19,551	30,383
21,000	203.97	52,429	353.21	23,850	28,579	366.30	21,988	30,441	410.43	20,528	31,901
22,000	213.68	54,925	370.02	24,985	29,940	383.74	23,034	31,891	429.97	21,505	33,420
23,000	223.40	57,424	386.86	26,122	31,302	401.19	24,083	33,341	449.52	22,484	34,940
24,000	233.11	59,920	403.67	27,258	32,662	418.63	25,129	34,791	469.06	23,461	36,459
25,000	242.82	62,415	420.49	28,393	34,022	436.07	26,176	36,239	488.60	24,438	37,977
26,000	252.53	64,911	437.30	29,528	35,383	453.51	27,222	37,689	508.14	25,415	39,496
27,000	262.25	67,410	454.13	30,665	36,745	470.96	28,271	39,139	527.70	26,394	41,016
28,000	271.96	69,906	470.95	31,800	38,106	488.40	29,317	40,589	547.24	27,371	42,535
29,000	281.67	72,401	487.76	32,935	39,466	505.84	30,364	42,037	566.78	28,348	44,053
30,000	291.38	74,897	504.58	34,070	40,827	523.28	31,410	43,487	586.31	29,324	45,573
32,500	315.66	81,138	546.62	36,899	44,229	566.88	34,027	47,111	635.17	31,768	49,370
35,000	339.95	87,382	588.68	39,750	47,632	610.50	36,647	50,735	684.05	34,213	53,169
40,000	388.51	99,864	672.77	45,428	54,436	697.71	41,881	57,983	781.76	39,100	60,764
45,000	437.07	112,345	756.86	51,105	61,240	784.91	47,115	65,230	879.47	43,987	68,358
50,000	485.64	124,830	840.97	56,785	68,045	872.14	52,352	72,478	977.20	48,875	75,955
55,000	534.20	137,312	925.06	62,463	74,849	959.35	57,586	79,726	1,074.92	53,762	83,550
60,000	582.76	149,794	1,009.15	68,141	81,653	1,046.55	62,820	86,974	1,172.63	58,649	91,145
65,000	631.32	162,275	1,093.24	73,818	88,457	1,133.76	68,055	94,220	1,270.34	63,536	98,739
70,000	679.89	174,760	1,177.35	79,498	95,262	1,220.98	73,291	101,469	1,368.07	68,424	106,336
75,000	728.45	187,242	1,261.44	85,176	102,066	1,308.19	78,525	108,717	1,465.78	73,311	113,931
80,000	777.01	199,724	1,345.53	90,853	108,871	1,395.40	83,760	115,964	1,563.50	78,198	121,526
85,000	825.58	212,209	1,429.64	96,533	115,676	1,482.62	88,996	123,213	1,661.23	83,087	129,122
90,000	874.14	224,690	1,513.73	102,211	122,479	1,569.83	94,231	130,459	1,758.94	87,973	136,717
95,000	922.70	237,172	1,597.82	107,888	129,284	1,657.04	99,465	137,707	1,856.65	92,860	144,312
100,000	971.27	249,657	1,681.93	113,568	136,089	1,744.26	104,701	144,956	1,954.39	97,749	151,908
105,000	1,019.83	262,139	1,766.02	119,246	142,893	1,831.47	109,936	152,203	2,052.10	102,636	159,503
110,000	1,068.39	274,620	1,850.11	124,924	149,696	1,918.67	115,170	159,450	2,149.81	107,522	167,098
115,000	1,116.96	287,106	1,934.21	130,603	156,503	2,005.90	120,406	166,700	2,247.54	112,411	174,695
120,000	1,165.52	299,587	2,018.30	136,281	163,306	2,093.11	125,641	173,946	2,345.26	117,298	182,289
125,000	1,214.08	312,069	2,102.39	141,959	170,110	2,180.31	130,875	181,194	2,442.97	122,185	189,884
130,000	1,262.64	324,550	2,186.48	147,636	176,914	2,267.52	136,109	188,441	2,540.68	127,071	197,479
135,000	1,311.21	337,036	2,270.59	153,316	183,720	2,354.74	141,346	195,690	2,638.41	131,960	205,076
140,000	1,359.77	349,517	2,354.68	158,994	190,523	2,441.95	146,580	202,937	2,736.12	136,847	212,670
145,000	1,408.33	361,999	2,438.77	164,672	197,327	2,529.16	151,814	210,185	2,833.84	141,734	220,265
150,000	1,456.90	374,484	2,522.88	170,351	204,133	2,616.38	157,051	217,433	2,931.57	146,622	227,862
155,000	1,505.46	386,966	2,606.97	176,029	210,937	2,703.59	162,285	224,681	3,029.28	151,509	235,457
160,000	1,554.02	399,447	2,691.06	181,707	217,740	2,790.80	167,520	231,927	3,126.99	156,396	243,051
165,000	1,602.59	411,932	2,775.17	187,387	224,545	2,878.02	172,756	239,176	3,224.73	161,285	250,647
170,000	1,651.15	424,414	2,859.26	193,064	231,350	2,965.23	177,990	246,424	3,322.44	166,171	258,243
175,000	1,699.71	436,896	2,943.35	198,742	238,154	3,052.43	183,225	253,671	3,420.15	171,058	265,838
180,000	1,748.28	449,381	3,027.46	204,422	244,959	3,139.66	188,461	260,920	3,517.88	175,947	273,434
185,000	1,796.84	461,862	3,111.55	210,099	251,763	3,226.87	193,695	268,167	3,615.60	180,834	281,029
190,000	1,845.40	474,344	3,195.64	215,777	258,567	3,314.09	198,930	275,414	3,713.31	185,720	288,624
195,000	1,893.96	486,826	3,279.73	221,455	265,371	3,401.28	204,164	282,662	3,811.02	190,607	296,219
200,000	1,942.53	499,311	3,363.83	227,134	272,177	3,488.50	209,401	289,910	3,908.75	195,496	303,815

11.50% GROWING EQUITY MORTGAGES

AMOUNT OF LOAN	30 YEARS		1% PMT INCR/YR 251.311 PAYMENTS			2% PMT INCR/YR 209.273 PAYMENTS			3% PMT INCR/YR 184.157 PAYMENTS		
	MONTHLY PAYMENT	TOTAL INTRST	LAST YR MON PMT	TOTAL INTRST	INTRST SAVED	LAST YR MON PMT	TOTAL INTRST	INTRST SAVED	LAST YR MON PMT	TOTAL INTRST	INTRST SAVED
$ 50	0.50	130	0.61	89	41	0.70	74	56	0.78	65	65
100	1.00	260	1.22	178	82	1.40	148	112	1.56	130	130
200	1.99	516	2.43	353	163	2.79	293	223	3.10	257	259
300	2.98	773	3.64	529	244	4.17	438	335	4.64	384	389
400	3.97	1,029	4.84	704	325	5.56	583	446	6.19	512	517
500	4.96	1,286	6.05	879	407	6.95	728	558	7.73	639	647
600	5.95	1,542	7.26	1,054	488	8.33	873	669	9.27	766	776
700	6.94	1,798	8.47	1,230	568	9.72	1,018	780	10.81	894	904
800	7.93	2,055	9.68	1,405	650	11.10	1,163	892	12.35	1,021	1,034
900	8.92	2,311	10.88	1,580	731	12.49	1,308	1,003	13.90	1,149	1,162
1,000	9.91	2,568	12.09	1,755	813	13.88	1,453	1,115	15.44	1,276	1,292
2,000	19.81	5,132	24.17	3,508	1,624	27.74	2,904	2,228	30.86	2,550	2,582
3,000	29.71	7,696	36.25	5,260	2,436	41.60	4,354	3,342	46.29	3,823	3,873
4,000	39.62	10,263	48.34	7,016	3,247	55.48	5,807	4,456	61.73	5,099	5,164
5,000	49.52	12,827	60.42	8,768	4,059	69.34	7,258	5,569	77.15	6,373	6,454
6,000	59.42	15,391	72.50	10,521	4,870	83.20	8,708	6,683	92.57	7,647	7,744
7,000	69.33	17,959	84.60	12,276	5,683	97.08	10,161	7,798	108.01	8,923	9,036
8,000	79.23	20,523	96.68	14,028	6,495	110.94	11,612	8,911	123.44	10,196	10,327
9,000	89.13	23,087	108.76	15,781	7,306	124.80	13,062	10,025	138.86	11,470	11,617
10,000	99.03	25,651	120.84	17,533	8,118	138.67	14,513	11,138	154.29	12,744	12,907
11,000	108.94	28,218	132.93	19,289	8,929	152.54	15,966	12,252	169.72	14,020	14,198
12,000	118.84	30,782	145.01	21,041	9,741	166.40	17,416	13,366	185.15	15,293	15,489
13,000	128.74	33,346	157.09	22,794	10,552	180.27	18,867	14,479	200.57	16,567	16,779
14,000	138.65	35,914	169.18	24,549	11,365	194.14	20,320	15,594	216.01	17,843	18,071
15,000	148.55	38,478	181.26	26,301	12,177	208.01	21,770	16,708	231.44	19,117	19,361
16,000	158.45	41,042	193.34	28,054	12,988	221.87	23,221	17,821	246.86	20,390	20,652
17,000	168.35	43,606	205.42	29,806	13,800	235.73	24,671	18,935	262.28	21,664	21,942
18,000	178.26	46,174	217.51	31,562	14,612	249.61	26,124	20,050	277.72	22,940	23,234
19,000	188.16	48,738	229.59	33,314	15,424	263.47	27,575	21,163	293.15	24,213	24,525
20,000	198.06	51,302	241.67	35,067	16,235	277.33	29,025	22,277	308.57	25,487	25,815
21,000	207.97	53,869	253.76	36,822	17,047	291.21	30,478	23,391	324.01	26,763	27,106
22,000	217.87	56,433	265.84	38,574	17,859	305.07	31,929	24,504	339.43	28,037	28,396
23,000	227.77	58,997	277.92	40,327	18,670	318.93	33,380	25,617	354.86	29,310	29,687
24,000	237.67	61,561	290.00	42,079	19,482	332.80	34,830	26,731	370.28	30,584	30,977
25,000	247.58	64,129	302.09	43,835	20,294	346.67	36,283	27,846	385.72	31,860	32,269
26,000	257.48	66,693	314.17	45,587	21,106	360.53	37,734	28,959	401.15	33,134	33,559
27,000	267.38	69,257	326.25	47,340	21,917	374.40	39,184	30,073	416.57	34,407	34,850
28,000	277.29	71,824	338.35	49,095	22,729	388.27	40,637	31,187	432.01	35,683	36,141
29,000	287.19	74,388	350.43	50,847	23,541	402.14	42,088	32,300	447.43	36,957	37,431
30,000	297.09	76,952	362.51	52,600	24,352	416.00	43,538	33,414	462.86	38,231	38,721
32,500	321.85	83,366	392.72	56,984	26,382	450.67	47,167	36,199	501.43	41,417	41,949
35,000	346.61	89,780	422.93	61,368	28,412	485.34	50,796	38,984	540.01	44,604	45,176
40,000	396.12	102,603	483.34	70,133	32,470	554.66	58,051	44,552	617.14	50,974	51,629
45,000	445.64	115,430	543.77	78,901	36,529	624.00	65,309	50,121	694.29	57,347	58,083
50,000	495.15	128,254	604.18	87,666	40,588	693.33	72,564	55,690	771.43	63,718	64,536
55,000	544.67	141,081	664.60	96,434	44,647	762.67	79,821	61,260	848.58	70,091	70,990
60,000	594.18	153,905	725.01	105,200	48,705	832.00	87,076	66,829	925.71	76,461	77,444
65,000	643.69	166,728	785.42	113,965	52,763	901.32	94,332	72,396	1,002.85	82,832	83,896
70,000	693.21	179,556	845.85	122,733	56,823	970.66	101,589	77,967	1,079.99	89,205	90,351
75,000	742.72	192,379	906.26	131,498	60,881	1,039.99	108,844	83,535	1,157.13	95,576	96,803
80,000	792.24	205,206	966.68	140,266	64,940	1,109.33	116,102	89,104	1,234.28	101,949	103,257
85,000	841.75	218,030	1,027.09	149,031	68,999	1,178.65	123,357	94,673	1,311.42	108,319	109,711
90,000	891.27	230,857	1,087.52	157,799	73,058	1,247.99	130,615	100,242	1,388.57	114,692	116,165
95,000	940.78	243,681	1,147.93	166,565	77,116	1,317.32	137,870	105,811	1,465.70	121,063	122,618
100,000	990.30	256,508	1,208.35	175,333	81,175	1,386.66	145,127	111,381	1,542.86	127,436	129,072
105,000	1,039.81	269,332	1,268.77	184,098	85,234	1,455.99	152,382	116,950	1,619.99	133,806	135,526
110,000	1,089.33	282,159	1,329.19	192,866	89,293	1,525.32	159,640	122,519	1,697.14	140,179	141,980
115,000	1,138.84	294,982	1,389.60	201,631	93,351	1,594.65	166,895	128,087	1,774.28	146,550	148,432
120,000	1,188.35	307,806	1,450.01	210,396	97,410	1,663.98	174,150	133,656	1,851.41	152,921	154,885
125,000	1,237.87	320,633	1,510.44	219,165	101,468	1,733.32	181,408	139,225	1,928.56	159,293	161,340
130,000	1,287.38	333,457	1,570.85	227,930	105,527	1,802.64	188,663	144,794	2,005.70	165,664	167,793
135,000	1,336.90	346,284	1,631.27	236,698	109,586	1,871.98	195,921	150,363	2,082.85	172,037	174,247
140,000	1,386.41	359,108	1,691.68	245,463	113,645	1,941.31	203,176	155,932	2,159.98	178,408	180,700
145,000	1,435.93	371,935	1,752.11	254,231	117,704	2,010.65	210,433	161,502	2,237.13	184,781	187,154
150,000	1,485.44	384,758	1,812.52	262,996	121,762	2,079.97	217,688	167,070	2,314.27	191,151	193,607
155,000	1,534.96	397,586	1,872.94	271,764	125,822	2,149.31	224,946	172,640	2,391.42	197,524	200,062
160,000	1,584.47	410,409	1,933.35	280,530	129,879	2,218.64	232,201	178,208	2,468.55	203,895	206,514
165,000	1,633.99	423,236	1,993.78	289,298	133,938	2,287.98	239,459	183,777	2,545.70	210,268	212,968
170,000	1,683.50	436,060	2,054.19	298,063	137,997	2,357.31	246,714	189,346	2,622.84	216,638	219,422
175,000	1,733.02	448,887	2,114.61	306,831	142,056	2,426.65	253,972	194,916	2,699.99	223,011	225,876
180,000	1,782.53	461,711	2,175.03	315,596	146,115	2,495.97	261,227	200,484	2,777.12	229,382	232,329
185,000	1,832.04	474,534	2,235.44	324,361	150,173	2,565.30	268,482	206,052	2,854.26	235,753	238,781
190,000	1,881.56	487,362	2,295.86	333,129	154,233	2,634.64	275,740	211,623	2,931.41	242,126	245,236
195,000	1,931.07	500,185	2,356.27	341,895	158,290	2,703.96	282,995	217,190	3,008.54	248,496	251,689
200,000	1,980.59	513,012	2,416.70	350,663	162,349	2,773.30	290,252	222,760	3,085.69	254,869	258,143

136

AMOUNT OF LOAN	30 YEARS		4% PMT INCR/YR 166.752 PAYMENTS			5% PMT INCR/YR 153.640 PAYMENTS			6% PMT INCR/YR 143.335 PAYMENTS		
	MONTHLY PAYMENT	TOTAL INTRST	LAST YR MON PMT	TOTAL INTRST	INTRST SAVED	LAST YR MON PMT	TOTAL INTRST	INTRST SAVED	LAST YR MON PMT	TOTAL INTRST	INTRST SAVED
$ 50	0.50	130	0.83	59	71	0.90	54	76	0.95	51	79
100	1.00	260	1.67	117	143	1.80	108	152	1.90	101	159
200	1.99	516	3.31	233	283	3.57	215	301	3.78	200	316
300	2.98	773	4.96	348	425	5.35	321	452	5.66	300	473
400	3.97	1,029	6.61	463	566	7.13	427	602	7.54	399	630
500	4.96	1,286	8.26	578	708	8.91	533	753	9.42	498	788
600	5.95	1,542	9.91	694	848	10.69	639	903	11.29	597	945
700	6.94	1,798	11.56	809	989	12.46	746	1,052	13.17	696	1,102
800	7.93	2,055	13.20	924	1,131	14.24	852	1,203	15.05	795	1,260
900	8.92	2,311	14.85	1,039	1,272	16.02	958	1,353	16.93	894	1,417
1,000	9.91	2,568	16.50	1,155	1,413	17.80	1,064	1,504	18.81	994	1,574
2,000	19.81	5,132	32.99	2,307	2,825	35.58	2,127	3,005	37.61	1,985	3,147
3,000	29.71	7,696	49.47	3,460	4,236	53.35	3,189	4,507	56.40	2,977	4,719
4,000	39.62	10,263	65.97	4,614	5,649	71.15	4,254	6,009	75.21	3,971	6,292
5,000	49.52	12,827	82.45	5,767	7,060	88.93	5,316	7,511	94.00	4,962	7,865
6,000	59.42	15,391	98.94	6,919	8,472	106.71	6,378	9,013	112.80	5,954	9,437
7,000	69.33	17,959	115.44	8,074	9,885	124.51	7,443	10,516	131.61	6,948	11,011
8,000	79.23	20,523	131.92	9,227	11,296	142.29	8,505	12,018	150.40	7,939	12,584
9,000	89.13	23,087	148.41	10,379	12,708	160.06	9,567	13,520	169.20	8,931	14,156
10,000	99.03	25,651	164.89	11,532	14,119	177.84	10,630	15,021	187.99	9,923	15,728
11,000	108.94	28,218	181.39	12,686	15,532	195.64	11,694	16,524	206.80	10,916	17,302
12,000	118.84	30,782	197.88	13,839	16,943	213.42	12,756	18,026	225.59	11,908	18,874
13,000	128.74	33,346	214.36	14,991	18,355	231.20	13,819	19,527	244.39	12,900	20,446
14,000	138.65	35,914	230.86	16,146	19,768	249.00	14,883	21,031	263.20	13,893	22,021
15,000	148.55	38,478	247.35	17,298	21,180	266.77	15,946	22,532	281.99	14,885	23,593
16,000	158.45	41,042	263.83	18,451	22,591	284.55	17,008	24,034	300.79	15,876	25,166
17,000	168.35	43,606	280.32	19,604	24,003	302.33	18,070	25,536	319.58	16,868	26,738
18,000	178.26	46,174	296.82	20,758	25,416	320.13	19,135	27,039	338.39	17,862	28,312
19,000	188.16	48,738	313.30	21,911	26,827	337.91	20,197	28,541	357.18	18,853	29,885
20,000	198.06	51,302	329.78	23,063	28,239	355.69	21,259	30,043	375.98	19,845	31,457
21,000	207.97	53,869	346.29	24,218	29,651	373.48	22,324	31,545	394.79	20,839	33,030
22,000	217.87	56,433	362.77	25,370	31,063	391.26	23,386	33,047	413.58	21,830	34,603
23,000	227.77	58,997	379.25	26,523	32,474	409.04	24,448	34,549	432.38	22,822	36,175
24,000	237.67	61,561	395.74	27,675	33,886	426.82	25,511	36,050	451.17	23,814	37,747
25,000	247.58	64,129	412.24	28,830	35,299	444.62	26,575	37,554	469.98	24,807	39,322
26,000	257.48	66,693	428.72	29,983	36,710	462.40	27,638	39,055	488.77	25,799	40,894
27,000	267.38	69,257	445.21	31,135	38,122	480.18	28,700	40,557	507.57	26,791	42,466
28,000	277.29	71,824	461.71	32,290	39,534	497.97	29,764	42,060	526.38	27,784	44,040
29,000	287.19	74,388	478.19	33,442	40,946	515.75	30,827	43,561	545.17	28,776	45,612
30,000	297.09	76,952	494.68	34,595	42,357	533.53	31,889	45,063	563.97	29,768	47,184
32,500	321.85	83,366	535.90	37,478	45,888	578.00	34,547	48,819	610.97	32,249	51,117
35,000	346.61	89,780	577.13	40,362	49,418	622.46	37,205	52,575	657.97	34,730	55,050
40,000	396.12	102,603	659.57	46,126	56,477	711.37	42,519	60,084	751.95	39,690	62,913
45,000	445.64	115,430	742.02	51,893	63,537	800.31	47,835	67,595	845.96	44,652	70,778
50,000	495.15	128,254	824.46	57,658	70,596	889.22	53,148	75,106	939.94	49,613	78,641
55,000	544.67	141,081	906.92	63,425	77,656	978.15	58,464	82,617	1,033.95	54,575	86,506
60,000	594.18	153,905	989.35	69,190	84,715	1,067.06	63,778	90,127	1,127.93	59,535	94,370
65,000	643.69	166,728	1,071.79	74,954	91,774	1,155.97	69,092	97,636	1,221.92	64,496	102,232
70,000	693.21	179,556	1,154.25	80,721	98,835	1,244.91	74,408	105,148	1,315.92	69,458	110,098
75,000	742.72	192,379	1,236.68	86,486	105,893	1,333.82	79,722	112,657	1,409.90	74,418	117,961
80,000	792.24	205,206	1,319.14	92,253	112,953	1,422.75	85,038	120,168	1,503.91	79,380	125,826
85,000	841.75	218,030	1,401.58	98,017	120,013	1,511.66	90,351	127,679	1,597.89	84,341	133,689
90,000	891.27	230,857	1,484.03	103,784	127,073	1,600.59	95,667	135,190	1,691.90	89,303	141,554
95,000	940.78	243,681	1,566.47	109,549	134,132	1,689.51	100,981	142,700	1,785.88	94,263	149,418
100,000	990.30	256,508	1,648.92	115,316	141,192	1,778.44	106,297	150,211	1,879.89	99,226	157,282
105,000	1,039.81	269,332	1,731.36	121,081	148,251	1,867.35	111,611	157,721	1,973.87	104,186	165,146
110,000	1,089.33	282,159	1,813.81	126,847	155,312	1,956.28	116,927	165,232	2,067.87	109,148	173,011
115,000	1,138.84	294,982	1,896.25	132,612	162,370	2,045.19	122,240	172,742	2,161.86	114,108	180,874
120,000	1,188.35	307,806	1,978.69	138,377	169,429	2,134.11	127,554	180,252	2,255.84	119,069	188,737
125,000	1,237.87	320,633	2,061.14	144,144	176,489	2,223.04	132,870	187,763	2,349.85	124,031	196,602
130,000	1,287.38	333,457	2,143.58	149,908	183,549	2,311.95	138,184	195,273	2,443.83	128,991	204,466
135,000	1,336.90	346,284	2,226.04	155,675	190,609	2,400.88	143,500	202,784	2,537.84	133,953	212,331
140,000	1,386.41	359,108	2,308.47	161,440	197,668	2,489.79	148,814	210,294	2,631.82	138,914	220,194
145,000	1,435.93	371,935	2,390.93	167,207	204,728	2,578.72	154,129	217,806	2,725.82	143,876	228,059
150,000	1,485.44	384,758	2,473.37	172,972	211,786	2,667.64	159,443	225,315	2,819.81	148,836	235,922
155,000	1,534.96	397,586	2,555.82	178,739	218,847	2,756.57	164,759	232,827	2,913.81	153,799	243,787
160,000	1,584.47	410,409	2,638.26	184,503	225,906	2,845.48	170,073	240,336	3,007.80	158,759	251,650
165,000	1,633.99	423,236	2,720.71	190,270	232,966	2,934.41	175,389	247,847	3,101.80	163,721	259,515
170,000	1,683.50	436,060	2,803.15	196,035	240,025	3,023.32	180,703	255,357	3,195.79	168,681	267,379
175,000	1,733.02	448,887	2,885.61	201,802	247,085	3,112.25	186,019	262,868	3,289.79	173,644	275,243
180,000	1,782.53	461,711	2,968.04	207,566	254,145	3,201.17	191,332	270,379	3,383.77	178,604	283,107
185,000	1,832.04	474,534	3,050.48	213,331	261,203	3,290.08	196,646	277,888	3,477.76	183,564	290,970
190,000	1,881.56	487,362	3,132.94	219,098	268,264	3,379.01	201,962	285,400	3,571.76	188,526	298,836
195,000	1,931.07	500,185	3,215.37	224,863	275,322	3,467.92	207,276	292,909	3,665.75	193,487	306,698
200,000	1,980.59	513,012	3,297.83	230,630	282,382	3,556.86	212,592	300,420	3,759.75	198,449	314,563

11.75% GROWING EQUITY MORTGAGES

AMOUNT OF LOAN	30 YEARS		1% PMT INCR/YR 249.473 PAYMENTS			2% PMT INCR/YR 207.545 PAYMENTS			3% PMT INCR/YR 182.593 PAYMENTS		
	MONTHLY PAYMENT	TOTAL INTRST	LAST YR MON PMT	TOTAL INTRST	INTRST SAVED	LAST YR MON PMT	TOTAL INTRST	INTRST SAVED	LAST YR MON PMT	TOTAL INTRST	INTRST SAVED
$ 50	0.51	134	0.62	91	43	0.71	75	59	0.79	66	68
100	1.01	264	1.23	179	85	1.41	148	116	1.57	129	135
200	2.02	527	2.46	357	170	2.83	295	232	3.15	259	268
300	3.03	791	3.70	536	255	4.24	443	348	4.72	388	403
400	4.04	1,054	4.93	714	340	5.66	590	464	6.29	518	536
500	5.05	1,318	6.16	893	425	7.07	738	580	7.87	647	671
600	6.06	1,582	7.39	1,071	511	8.49	885	697	9.44	777	805
700	7.07	1,845	8.63	1,250	595	9.90	1,033	812	11.01	906	939
800	8.08	2,109	9.86	1,428	681	11.31	1,180	929	12.59	1,036	1,073
900	9.09	2,372	11.09	1,607	765	12.73	1,328	1,044	14.16	1,165	1,207
1,000	10.10	2,636	12.32	1,785	851	14.14	1,476	1,160	15.74	1,295	1,341
2,000	20.19	5,268	24.64	3,568	1,700	28.27	2,949	2,319	31.46	2,588	2,680
3,000	30.29	7,904	36.96	5,354	2,550	42.41	4,424	3,480	47.19	3,883	4,021
4,000	40.38	10,537	49.27	7,136	3,401	56.54	5,897	4,640	62.91	5,175	5,362
5,000	50.48	13,173	61.60	8,922	4,251	70.68	7,373	5,800	78.65	6,470	6,703
6,000	60.57	15,805	73.91	10,704	5,101	84.81	8,846	6,959	94.37	7,763	8,042
7,000	70.66	18,438	86.22	12,487	5,951	98.94	10,319	8,119	110.09	9,056	9,382
8,000	80.76	21,074	98.54	14,273	6,801	113.08	11,795	9,279	125.82	10,351	10,723
9,000	90.85	23,706	110.85	16,055	7,651	127.21	13,268	10,438	141.54	11,644	12,062
10,000	100.95	26,342	123.18	17,841	8,501	141.35	14,744	11,598	157.28	12,939	13,403
11,000	111.04	28,974	135.49	19,623	9,351	155.48	16,217	12,757	173.00	14,231	14,743
12,000	121.13	31,607	147.80	21,406	10,201	169.61	17,690	13,917	188.72	15,524	16,083
13,000	131.23	34,243	160.13	23,192	11,051	183.75	19,166	15,077	204.45	16,819	17,424
14,000	141.32	36,875	172.44	24,974	11,901	197.88	20,639	16,236	220.17	18,112	18,763
15,000	151.42	39,511	184.76	26,760	12,751	212.02	22,114	17,397	235.91	19,407	20,104
16,000	161.51	42,144	197.07	28,542	13,602	226.15	23,588	18,556	251.63	20,699	21,445
17,000	171.60	44,776	209.38	30,325	14,451	240.28	25,061	19,715	267.35	21,992	22,784
18,000	181.70	47,412	221.71	32,110	15,302	254.42	26,536	20,876	283.08	23,287	24,125
19,000	191.79	50,044	234.02	33,893	16,151	268.55	28,009	22,035	298.80	24,580	25,464
20,000	201.89	52,680	246.34	35,679	17,001	282.69	29,485	23,195	314.54	25,875	26,805
21,000	211.98	55,313	258.66	37,461	17,852	296.82	30,958	24,355	330.26	27,168	28,145
22,000	222.08	57,949	270.98	39,247	18,702	310.97	32,434	25,515	345.99	28,463	29,486
23,000	232.17	60,581	283.29	41,029	19,552	325.09	33,907	26,674	361.71	29,755	30,826
24,000	242.26	63,214	295.60	42,812	20,402	339.22	35,380	27,834	377.43	31,048	32,166
25,000	252.36	65,850	307.93	44,598	21,252	353.36	36,856	28,994	393.17	32,343	33,507
26,000	262.45	68,482	320.24	46,380	22,102	367.49	38,329	30,153	408.89	33,636	34,846
27,000	272.55	71,118	332.56	48,166	22,952	381.64	39,804	31,314	424.62	34,931	36,187
28,000	282.64	73,750	344.87	49,948	23,802	395.76	41,278	32,472	440.34	36,223	37,527
29,000	292.73	76,383	357.19	51,731	24,652	409.89	42,751	33,632	456.06	37,516	38,867
30,000	302.83	79,019	369.51	53,517	25,502	424.04	44,226	34,793	471.80	38,811	40,208
32,500	328.06	85,602	400.30	57,975	27,627	459.36	47,910	37,692	511.11	42,044	43,558
35,000	353.30	92,188	431.09	62,436	29,752	494.71	51,597	40,591	550.43	45,279	46,909
40,000	403.77	105,357	492.68	71,354	34,003	565.38	58,968	46,389	629.06	51,747	53,610
45,000	454.24	118,526	554.26	80,273	38,253	636.05	66,338	52,188	707.69	58,215	60,311
50,000	504.71	131,696	615.84	89,192	42,504	706.72	73,709	57,987	786.32	64,684	67,012
55,000	555.18	144,865	677.43	98,111	46,754	777.39	81,079	63,786	864.95	71,152	73,713
60,000	605.65	158,034	739.01	107,030	51,004	848.06	88,450	69,584	943.58	77,620	80,414
65,000	656.12	171,203	800.59	115,949	55,254	918.73	95,821	75,382	1,022.21	84,088	87,115
70,000	706.59	184,372	862.17	124,868	59,504	989.40	103,191	81,181	1,100.84	90,556	93,816
75,000	757.06	197,542	923.76	133,787	63,755	1,060.07	110,562	86,980	1,179.47	97,024	100,518
80,000	807.53	210,711	985.34	142,706	68,005	1,130.74	117,933	92,778	1,258.11	103,492	107,219
85,000	858.00	223,880	1,046.92	151,625	72,255	1,201.41	125,303	98,577	1,336.74	109,961	113,919
90,000	908.47	237,049	1,108.51	160,544	76,505	1,272.08	132,674	104,375	1,415.37	116,429	120,620
95,000	958.94	250,218	1,170.09	169,463	80,755	1,342.75	140,045	110,173	1,494.00	122,897	127,321
100,000	1,009.41	263,388	1,231.67	178,382	85,006	1,413.42	147,415	115,973	1,572.63	129,365	134,023
105,000	1,059.89	276,560	1,293.27	187,304	89,256	1,484.10	154,788	121,772	1,651.27	135,835	140,725
110,000	1,110.36	289,730	1,354.85	196,223	93,507	1,554.77	162,159	127,571	1,729.90	142,304	147,426
115,000	1,160.83	302,899	1,416.43	205,142	97,757	1,625.44	169,530	133,369	1,808.54	148,772	154,127
120,000	1,211.30	316,068	1,478.02	214,061	102,007	1,696.11	176,900	139,168	1,887.17	155,240	160,828
125,000	1,261.77	329,237	1,539.60	222,980	106,257	1,766.78	184,271	144,966	1,965.80	161,708	167,529
130,000	1,312.24	342,406	1,601.18	231,899	110,507	1,837.45	191,641	150,765	2,044.43	168,176	174,230
135,000	1,362.71	355,576	1,662.77	240,818	114,758	1,908.12	199,012	156,564	2,123.06	174,644	180,932
140,000	1,413.18	368,745	1,724.35	249,737	119,008	1,978.79	206,383	162,362	2,201.69	181,112	187,633
145,000	1,463.65	381,914	1,785.93	258,656	123,258	2,049.46	213,753	168,161	2,280.32	187,580	194,334
150,000	1,514.12	395,083	1,847.51	267,574	127,509	2,120.13	221,124	173,959	2,358.95	194,049	201,034
155,000	1,564.59	408,252	1,909.10	276,493	131,759	2,190.80	228,495	179,757	2,437.58	200,517	207,735
160,000	1,615.06	421,422	1,970.68	285,412	136,010	2,261.47	235,865	185,557	2,516.21	206,985	214,437
165,000	1,665.53	434,591	2,032.26	294,331	140,260	2,332.14	243,236	191,355	2,594.84	213,453	221,138
170,000	1,716.00	447,760	2,093.85	303,250	144,510	2,402.81	250,607	197,153	2,673.47	219,921	227,839
175,000	1,766.47	460,929	2,155.43	312,169	148,760	2,473.48	257,977	202,952	2,752.10	226,389	234,540
180,000	1,816.94	474,098	2,217.01	321,088	153,010	2,544.15	265,348	208,750	2,830.73	232,857	241,241
185,000	1,867.41	487,268	2,278.60	330,007	157,261	2,614.82	272,718	214,550	2,909.36	239,326	247,942
190,000	1,917.88	500,437	2,340.18	338,926	161,511	2,685.50	280,090	220,348	2,987.99	245,794	254,643
195,000	1,968.35	513,606	2,401.76	347,845	165,761	2,756.17	287,460	226,146	3,066.63	252,262	261,344
200,000	2,018.82	526,775	2,463.34	356,764	170,011	2,826.84	294,830	231,945	3,145.26	258,730	268,045

GROWING EQUITY MORTGAGES 11.75%

AMOUNT OF LOAN	30 YEARS		4% PMT INCR/YR 165.298 PAYMENTS			5% PMT INCR/YR 152.305 PAYMENTS			6% PMT INCR/YR 142.084 PAYMENTS		
	MONTHLY PAYMENT	TOTAL INTRST	LAST YR MON PMT	TOTAL INTRST	INTRST SAVED	LAST YR MON PMT	TOTAL INTRST	INTRST SAVED	LAST YR MON PMT	TOTAL INTRST	INTRST SAVED
$ 50	0.51	134	0.85	60	74	0.92	55	79	0.97	51	83
100	1.01	264	1.68	117	147	1.81	108	156	1.92	101	163
200	2.02	527	3.36	234	293	3.63	216	311	3.83	202	325
300	3.03	791	5.05	351	440	5.44	324	467	5.75	302	489
400	4.04	1,054	6.73	469	585	7.26	432	622	7.67	403	651
500	5.05	1,318	8.41	586	732	9.07	540	778	9.59	504	814
600	6.06	1,582	10.09	703	879	10.88	648	934	11.50	605	977
700	7.07	1,845	11.77	820	1,025	12.70	756	1,089	13.42	706	1,139
800	8.08	2,109	13.45	937	1,172	14.51	864	1,245	15.34	806	1,303
900	9.09	2,372	15.14	1,054	1,318	16.32	972	1,400	17.26	907	1,465
1,000	10.10	2,636	16.82	1,172	1,464	18.14	1,080	1,556	19.17	1,008	1,628
2,000	20.19	5,268	33.62	2,341	2,927	36.26	2,158	3,110	38.33	2,014	3,254
3,000	30.29	7,904	50.44	3,512	4,392	54.40	3,237	4,667	57.50	3,022	4,882
4,000	40.38	10,537	67.24	4,682	5,855	72.52	4,315	6,222	76.65	4,028	6,509
5,000	50.48	13,173	84.05	5,853	7,320	90.65	5,395	7,778	95.83	5,036	8,137
6,000	60.57	15,805	100.85	7,023	8,782	108.78	6,473	9,332	114.98	6,041	9,764
7,000	70.66	18,438	117.65	8,192	10,246	126.90	7,550	10,888	134.13	7,047	11,391
8,000	80.76	21,074	134.47	9,364	11,710	145.03	8,630	12,444	153.31	8,055	13,019
9,000	90.85	23,706	151.27	10,533	13,173	163.15	9,708	13,998	172.46	9,061	14,645
10,000	100.95	26,342	168.09	11,705	14,637	181.29	10,788	15,554	191.63	10,069	16,273
11,000	111.04	28,974	184.89	12,874	16,100	199.41	11,865	17,109	210.79	11,075	17,899
12,000	121.13	31,607	201.69	14,043	17,564	217.53	12,943	18,664	229.94	12,081	19,526
13,000	131.23	34,243	218.51	15,215	19,028	235.67	14,023	20,220	249.11	13,089	21,154
14,000	141.32	36,875	235.31	16,384	20,491	253.79	15,101	21,774	268.27	14,095	22,780
15,000	151.42	39,511	252.13	17,556	21,955	271.93	16,180	23,331	287.44	15,103	24,408
16,000	161.51	42,144	268.93	18,725	23,419	290.05	17,258	24,886	306.59	16,109	26,035
17,000	171.60	44,776	285.73	19,895	24,881	308.17	18,336	26,440	325.75	17,114	27,662
18,000	181.70	47,412	302.54	21,066	26,346	326.31	19,416	27,996	344.92	18,122	29,290
19,000	191.79	50,044	319.34	22,236	27,808	344.43	20,493	29,551	364.07	19,128	30,916
20,000	201.89	52,680	336.16	23,407	29,273	362.57	21,573	31,107	383.25	20,136	32,544
21,000	211.98	55,313	352.96	24,577	30,736	380.69	22,651	32,662	402.40	21,142	34,171
22,000	222.08	57,949	369.78	25,748	32,201	398.82	23,731	34,218	421.57	22,150	35,799
23,000	232.17	60,581	386.58	26,917	33,664	416.94	24,808	35,773	440.73	23,156	37,425
24,000	242.26	63,214	403.38	28,087	35,127	435.06	25,886	37,329	459.88	24,162	39,052
25,000	252.36	65,850	420.20	29,258	36,592	453.20	26,966	38,884	479.05	25,170	40,680
26,000	262.45	68,482	437.00	30,428	38,054	471.32	28,044	40,438	498.21	26,176	42,306
27,000	272.55	71,118	453.82	31,599	39,519	489.46	29,124	41,994	517.38	27,184	43,934
28,000	282.64	73,750	470.62	32,769	40,981	507.58	30,201	43,549	536.54	28,189	45,561
29,000	292.73	76,383	487.42	33,938	42,445	525.70	31,279	45,104	555.69	29,195	47,188
30,000	302.83	79,019	504.23	35,110	43,909	543.84	32,359	46,660	574.86	30,203	48,816
32,500	328.06	85,602	546.24	38,034	47,568	589.15	35,054	50,548	622.76	32,719	52,883
35,000	353.30	92,188	588.27	40,961	51,227	634.48	37,752	54,436	670.67	35,237	56,951
40,000	403.77	105,357	672.31	46,812	58,545	725.11	43,144	62,213	766.48	40,270	65,087
45,000	454.24	118,526	756.34	52,663	65,863	815.75	48,537	69,989	862.28	45,304	73,222
50,000	504.71	131,696	840.38	58,515	73,181	906.39	53,930	77,766	958.09	50,337	81,359
55,000	555.18	144,865	924.42	64,366	80,499	997.02	59,323	85,542	1,053.90	55,371	89,494
60,000	605.65	158,034	1,008.45	70,217	87,817	1,087.66	64,716	93,319	1,149.70	60,405	97,629
65,000	656.12	171,203	1,092.49	76,068	95,135	1,178.30	70,108	101,095	1,245.51	65,438	105,765
70,000	706.59	184,372	1,176.52	81,920	102,452	1,268.93	75,501	108,871	1,341.32	70,472	113,900
75,000	757.06	197,542	1,260.56	87,771	109,771	1,359.57	80,894	116,648	1,437.13	75,505	122,037
80,000	807.53	210,711	1,344.60	93,622	117,089	1,450.21	86,287	124,424	1,532.93	80,539	130,172
85,000	858.00	223,880	1,428.63	99,473	124,407	1,540.84	91,679	132,201	1,628.74	85,572	138,308
90,000	908.47	237,049	1,512.67	105,325	131,724	1,631.48	97,072	139,977	1,724.55	90,606	146,443
95,000	958.94	250,218	1,596.71	111,176	139,042	1,722.12	102,465	147,753	1,820.35	95,639	154,579
100,000	1,009.41	263,388	1,680.74	117,027	146,361	1,812.76	107,858	155,530	1,916.16	100,673	162,715
105,000	1,059.89	276,560	1,764.79	122,880	153,680	1,903.41	113,253	163,307	2,011.99	105,708	170,852
110,000	1,110.36	289,730	1,848.83	128,732	160,998	1,994.05	118,645	171,085	2,107.79	110,742	178,988
115,000	1,160.83	302,899	1,932.87	134,583	168,316	2,084.68	124,038	178,861	2,203.60	115,776	187,123
120,000	1,211.30	316,068	2,016.90	140,434	175,634	2,175.32	129,431	186,637	2,299.41	120,809	195,259
125,000	1,261.77	329,237	2,100.94	146,285	182,952	2,265.96	134,824	194,413	2,395.22	125,843	203,394
130,000	1,312.24	342,406	2,184.98	152,137	190,269	2,356.59	140,217	202,189	2,491.02	130,876	211,530
135,000	1,362.71	355,576	2,269.01	157,988	197,588	2,447.23	145,609	209,967	2,586.83	135,910	219,666
140,000	1,413.18	368,745	2,353.05	163,839	204,906	2,537.87	151,002	217,743	2,682.64	140,943	227,802
145,000	1,463.65	381,914	2,437.08	169,690	212,224	2,628.51	156,395	225,519	2,778.44	145,977	235,937
150,000	1,514.12	395,083	2,521.12	175,542	219,541	2,719.14	161,788	233,295	2,874.25	151,010	244,073
155,000	1,564.59	408,252	2,605.16	181,393	226,859	2,809.78	167,181	241,071	2,970.06	156,044	252,208
160,000	1,615.06	421,422	2,689.19	187,244	234,178	2,900.42	172,573	248,849	3,065.87	161,077	260,345
165,000	1,665.53	434,591	2,773.23	193,095	241,496	2,991.05	177,966	256,625	3,161.67	166,111	268,480
170,000	1,716.00	447,760	2,857.27	198,947	248,813	3,081.69	183,359	264,401	3,257.48	171,144	276,616
175,000	1,766.47	460,929	2,941.30	204,798	256,131	3,172.33	188,752	272,177	3,353.29	176,178	284,751
180,000	1,816.94	474,098	3,025.34	210,649	263,449	3,262.96	194,144	279,954	3,449.09	181,212	292,886
185,000	1,867.41	487,268	3,109.37	216,500	270,768	3,353.60	199,537	287,731	3,544.90	186,245	301,023
190,000	1,917.88	500,437	3,193.41	222,352	278,085	3,444.24	204,930	295,507	3,640.71	191,279	309,158
195,000	1,968.35	513,606	3,277.45	228,203	285,403	3,534.87	210,323	303,283	3,736.52	196,312	317,294
200,000	2,018.82	526,775	3,361.48	234,054	292,721	3,625.51	215,716	311,059	3,832.32	201,346	325,429

139

12.00% GROWING EQUITY MORTGAGES

AMOUNT OF LOAN	30 YEARS		1% PMT INCR/YR 247.636 PAYMENTS			2% PMT INCR/YR 205.832 PAYMENTS			3% PMT INCR/YR 181.049 PAYMENTS		
	MONTHLY PAYMENT	TOTAL INTRST	LAST YR MON PMT	TOTAL INTRST	INTRST SAVED	LAST YR MON PMT	TOTAL INTRST	INTRST SAVED	LAST YR MON PMT	TOTAL INTRST	INTRST SAVED
$ 50	0.52	137	0.63	92	45	0.73	76	61	0.81	67	70
100	1.03	271	1.26	182	89	1.44	150	121	1.60	132	139
200	2.06	542	2.51	364	178	2.88	300	242	3.21	263	279
300	3.09	812	3.77	545	267	4.33	450	362	4.81	395	417
400	4.12	1,083	5.03	727	356	5.77	600	483	6.42	526	557
500	5.15	1,354	6.28	909	445	7.21	750	604	8.02	658	696
600	6.18	1,625	7.54	1,091	534	8.65	900	725	9.63	789	836
700	7.21	1,896	8.80	1,272	624	10.10	1,050	846	11.23	921	975
800	8.23	2,163	10.04	1,451	712	11.52	1,198	965	12.82	1,050	1,113
900	9.26	2,434	11.30	1,633	801	12.97	1,347	1,087	14.43	1,182	1,252
1,000	10.29	2,704	12.56	1,815	889	14.41	1,497	1,207	16.03	1,313	1,391
2,000	20.58	5,409	25.11	3,630	1,779	28.82	2,995	2,414	32.06	2,627	2,782
3,000	30.86	8,110	37.66	5,442	2,668	43.21	4,490	3,620	48.08	3,938	4,172
4,000	41.15	10,814	50.21	7,256	3,558	57.62	5,988	4,826	64.11	5,251	5,563
5,000	51.44	13,518	62.77	9,071	4,447	72.03	7,485	6,033	80.14	6,565	6,953
6,000	61.72	16,219	75.31	10,883	5,336	86.42	8,980	7,239	96.16	7,876	8,343
7,000	72.01	18,924	87.87	12,698	6,226	100.83	10,478	8,446	112.19	9,189	9,735
8,000	82.29	21,624	100.41	14,510	7,114	115.23	11,973	9,651	128.21	10,501	11,123
9,000	92.58	24,329	112.97	16,325	8,004	129.63	13,470	10,859	144.24	11,814	12,515
10,000	102.87	27,033	125.52	18,140	8,893	144.04	14,968	12,065	160.27	13,127	13,906
11,000	113.15	29,734	138.06	19,952	9,782	158.44	16,463	13,271	176.28	14,439	15,295
12,000	123.44	32,438	150.62	21,766	10,672	172.85	17,960	14,478	192.32	15,752	16,686
13,000	133.72	35,139	163.16	23,578	11,561	187.24	19,455	15,684	208.33	17,063	18,076
14,000	144.01	37,844	175.72	25,393	12,451	201.65	20,953	16,891	224.36	18,377	19,467
15,000	154.30	40,548	188.28	27,208	13,340	216.06	22,450	18,098	240.39	19,690	20,858
16,000	164.58	43,249	200.82	29,020	14,229	230.45	23,945	19,304	256.41	21,001	22,248
17,000	174.87	45,953	213.37	30,835	15,118	244.86	25,443	20,510	272.44	22,314	23,639
18,000	185.16	48,658	225.93	32,650	16,008	259.27	26,940	21,718	288.47	23,628	25,030
19,000	195.44	51,358	238.47	34,462	16,896	273.66	28,435	22,923	304.49	24,939	26,419
20,000	205.73	54,063	251.03	36,276	17,787	288.07	29,933	24,130	320.52	26,252	27,811
21,000	216.01	56,764	263.57	38,089	18,675	302.47	31,428	25,336	336.54	27,564	29,200
22,000	226.30	59,468	276.13	39,903	19,565	316.87	32,925	26,543	352.57	28,877	30,591
23,000	236.59	62,172	288.68	41,718	20,454	331.28	34,423	27,749	368.60	30,190	31,982
24,000	246.87	64,873	301.23	43,530	21,343	345.68	35,918	28,955	384.62	31,502	33,371
25,000	257.16	67,578	313.78	45,345	22,233	360.09	37,415	30,163	400.65	32,815	34,763
26,000	267.44	70,278	326.33	47,157	23,121	374.48	38,910	31,368	416.66	34,126	36,152
27,000	277.73	72,983	338.88	48,972	24,011	388.89	40,408	32,575	432.69	35,440	37,543
28,000	288.02	75,687	351.44	50,787	24,900	403.30	41,905	33,782	448.73	36,753	38,934
29,000	298.30	78,388	363.98	52,599	25,789	417.69	43,400	34,988	464.74	38,064	40,324
30,000	308.59	81,092	376.54	54,413	26,679	432.10	44,898	36,194	480.77	39,378	41,714
32,500	334.30	87,848	407.91	58,946	28,902	468.10	48,638	39,210	520.83	42,658	45,190
35,000	360.02	94,607	439.29	63,482	31,125	504.11	52,380	42,227	560.90	45,940	48,667
40,000	411.45	108,122	502.05	72,550	35,572	576.13	59,863	48,259	641.03	52,503	55,619
45,000	462.88	121,637	564.80	81,619	40,018	648.14	67,346	54,291	721.15	59,065	62,572
50,000	514.31	135,152	627.56	90,687	44,465	720.16	74,828	60,324	801.28	65,628	69,524
55,000	565.74	148,666	690.31	99,756	48,910	792.17	82,311	66,355	881.40	72,190	76,476
60,000	617.17	162,181	753.06	108,824	53,357	864.19	89,793	72,388	961.53	78,753	83,428
65,000	668.60	175,696	815.82	117,892	57,804	936.20	97,276	78,420	1,041.66	85,316	90,380
70,000	720.03	189,211	878.57	126,961	62,250	1,008.22	104,759	84,452	1,121.78	91,878	97,333
75,000	771.46	202,726	941.33	136,029	66,697	1,080.23	112,241	90,485	1,201.91	98,441	104,285
80,000	822.90	216,244	1,004.09	145,101	71,143	1,152.26	119,726	96,518	1,282.05	105,005	111,239
85,000	874.33	229,759	1,066.85	154,169	75,590	1,224.27	127,209	102,550	1,362.18	111,568	118,191
90,000	925.76	243,274	1,129.60	163,237	80,037	1,296.29	134,691	108,583	1,442.30	118,131	125,143
95,000	977.19	256,788	1,192.36	172,306	84,482	1,368.30	142,174	114,614	1,522.43	124,693	132,095
100,000	1,028.62	270,303	1,255.11	181,374	88,929	1,440.32	149,656	120,647	1,602.56	131,256	139,047
105,000	1,080.05	283,818	1,317.87	190,443	93,375	1,512.33	157,139	126,679	1,682.69	137,818	146,000
110,000	1,131.48	297,333	1,380.62	199,511	97,822	1,584.35	164,622	132,711	1,762.81	144,381	152,952
115,000	1,182.91	310,848	1,443.38	208,580	102,268	1,656.36	172,104	138,744	1,842.94	150,943	159,905
120,000	1,234.34	324,362	1,506.13	217,648	106,714	1,728.37	179,587	144,775	1,923.06	157,506	166,856
125,000	1,285.77	337,877	1,568.88	226,716	111,161	1,800.39	187,069	150,808	2,003.19	164,068	173,809
130,000	1,337.20	351,392	1,631.64	235,785	115,607	1,872.40	194,552	156,840	2,083.31	170,631	180,761
135,000	1,388.63	364,907	1,694.39	244,853	120,054	1,944.42	202,035	162,872	2,163.44	177,194	187,713
140,000	1,440.06	378,422	1,757.15	253,922	124,500	2,016.43	209,517	168,905	2,243.57	183,756	194,666
145,000	1,491.49	391,936	1,819.90	262,990	128,946	2,088.45	217,000	174,936	2,323.69	190,319	201,617
150,000	1,542.92	405,451	1,882.66	272,059	133,392	2,160.46	224,482	180,969	2,403.82	196,881	208,570
155,000	1,594.35	418,966	1,945.41	281,127	137,839	2,232.47	231,965	187,001	2,483.95	203,444	215,522
160,000	1,645.79	432,484	2,008.18	290,198	142,286	2,304.50	239,450	193,034	2,564.09	210,009	222,475
165,000	1,697.22	445,999	2,070.93	299,267	146,732	2,376.52	246,932	199,067	2,644.21	216,571	229,428
170,000	1,748.65	459,514	2,133.69	308,335	151,179	2,448.53	254,415	205,099	2,724.34	223,134	236,380
175,000	1,800.08	473,029	2,196.44	317,404	155,625	2,520.55	261,898	211,131	2,804.47	229,696	243,333
180,000	1,851.51	486,544	2,259.19	326,472	160,072	2,592.56	269,380	217,164	2,884.59	236,259	250,285
185,000	1,902.94	500,058	2,321.95	335,541	164,517	2,664.58	276,863	223,195	2,964.72	242,821	257,237
190,000	1,954.37	513,573	2,384.70	344,609	168,964	2,736.59	284,345	229,228	3,044.84	249,384	264,189
195,000	2,005.80	527,088	2,447.46	353,677	173,411	2,808.60	291,828	235,260	3,124.97	255,947	271,141
200,000	2,057.23	540,603	2,510.21	362,746	177,857	2,880.62	299,310	241,293	3,205.10	262,509	278,094

140

AMOUNT OF LOAN	30 YEARS		4% PMT INCR/YR 163.867 PAYMENTS			5% PMT INCR/YR 150.993 PAYMENTS			6% PMT INCR/YR 140.858 PAYMENTS		
	MONTHLY PAYMENT	TOTAL INTRST	LAST YR MON PMT	TOTAL INTRST	INTRST SAVED	LAST YR MON PMT	TOTAL INTRST	INTRST SAVED	LAST YR MON PMT	TOTAL INTRST	INTRST SAVED
$ 50	0.52	137	0.87	61	76	0.93	56	81	0.99	52	85
100	1.03	271	1.72	119	152	1.85	110	161	1.96	102	169
200	2.06	542	3.43	238	304	3.70	219	323	3.91	205	337
300	3.09	812	5.15	357	455	5.55	329	483	5.87	307	505
400	4.12	1,083	6.86	476	607	7.40	439	644	7.82	409	674
500	5.15	1,354	8.58	595	759	9.25	548	806	9.78	512	842
600	6.18	1,625	10.29	714	911	11.10	658	967	11.73	614	1,011
700	7.21	1,896	12.01	833	1,063	12.95	768	1,128	13.69	717	1,179
800	8.23	2,163	13.70	950	1,213	14.78	875	1,288	15.62	817	1,346
900	9.26	2,434	15.42	1,069	1,365	16.63	985	1,449	17.58	919	1,515
1,000	10.29	2,704	17.13	1,188	1,516	18.48	1,095	1,609	19.53	1,022	1,682
2,000	20.58	5,409	34.27	2,376	3,033	36.96	2,189	3,220	39.07	2,043	3,366
3,000	30.86	8,110	51.38	3,561	4,549	55.42	3,282	4,828	58.58	3,063	5,047
4,000	41.15	10,814	68.52	4,749	6,065	73.90	4,377	6,437	78.11	4,085	6,729
5,000	51.44	13,518	85.65	5,937	7,581	92.38	5,471	8,047	97.65	5,107	8,411
6,000	61.72	16,219	102.77	7,123	9,096	110.84	6,564	9,655	117.16	6,126	10,093
7,000	72.01	18,924	119.90	8,311	10,613	129.32	7,659	11,265	136.70	7,148	11,776
8,000	82.29	21,624	137.02	9,497	12,127	147.78	8,751	12,873	156.21	8,168	13,456
9,000	92.58	24,329	154.15	10,686	13,645	166.26	9,846	14,483	175.74	9,190	15,139
10,000	102.87	27,033	171.29	11,872	15,161	184.74	10,941	16,092	195.28	10,211	16,822
11,000	113.15	29,734	188.40	13,058	16,676	203.20	12,033	17,701	214.79	11,231	18,503
12,000	123.44	32,438	205.54	14,246	18,192	221.68	13,128	19,310	234.33	12,253	20,185
13,000	133.72	35,139	222.65	15,432	19,707	240.14	14,221	20,918	253.84	13,273	21,866
14,000	144.01	37,844	239.79	16,620	21,224	258.62	15,315	22,529	273.37	14,294	23,550
15,000	154.30	40,548	256.92	17,807	22,741	277.10	16,410	24,138	292.90	15,316	25,232
16,000	164.58	43,249	274.04	18,993	24,256	295.56	17,503	25,746	312.42	16,336	26,913
17,000	174.87	45,953	291.17	20,181	25,772	314.04	18,597	27,356	331.96	17,358	28,595
18,000	185.16	48,658	308.31	21,369	27,289	332.52	19,692	28,966	351.49	18,379	30,279
19,000	195.44	51,358	325.42	22,555	28,803	350.98	20,785	30,573	371.00	19,399	31,959
20,000	205.73	54,063	342.56	23,743	30,320	369.46	21,879	32,184	390.54	20,421	33,642
21,000	216.01	56,764	359.67	24,928	31,836	387.92	22,972	33,792	410.05	21,441	35,323
22,000	226.30	59,468	376.81	26,116	33,352	406.40	24,067	35,401	429.58	22,462	37,006
23,000	236.59	62,172	393.94	27,304	34,868	424.88	25,161	37,011	449.12	23,484	38,688
24,000	246.87	64,873	411.06	28,490	36,383	443.34	26,254	38,619	468.63	24,504	40,369
25,000	257.16	67,578	428.19	29,678	37,900	461.82	27,349	40,229	488.17	25,525	42,053
26,000	267.44	70,278	445.31	30,863	39,415	480.28	28,441	41,837	507.68	26,545	43,733
27,000	277.73	72,983	462.44	32,051	40,932	498.76	29,536	43,447	527.21	27,567	45,416
28,000	288.02	75,687	479.57	33,239	42,448	517.24	30,630	45,057	546.75	28,589	47,098
29,000	298.30	78,388	496.69	34,425	43,963	535.70	31,723	46,665	566.26	29,608	48,780
30,000	308.59	81,092	513.83	35,613	45,479	554.18	32,818	48,274	585.80	30,630	50,462
32,500	334.30	87,848	556.63	38,579	49,269	600.35	35,551	52,297	634.60	33,182	54,666
35,000	360.02	94,607	599.46	41,548	53,059	646.54	38,287	56,320	683.43	35,735	58,872
40,000	411.45	108,122	685.09	47,483	60,639	738.91	43,756	64,366	781.05	40,840	67,282
45,000	462.88	121,637	770.73	53,418	68,219	831.27	49,226	72,411	878.68	45,944	75,693
50,000	514.31	135,152	856.36	59,353	75,799	923.63	54,695	80,457	976.31	51,049	84,103
55,000	565.74	148,666	942.00	65,288	83,378	1,015.99	60,164	88,502	1,073.94	56,154	92,512
60,000	617.17	162,181	1,027.63	71,223	90,958	1,108.35	65,634	96,547	1,171.57	61,258	100,923
65,000	668.60	175,696	1,113.27	77,159	98,537	1,200.71	71,103	104,593	1,269.20	66,363	109,333
70,000	720.03	189,211	1,198.90	83,094	106,117	1,293.07	76,572	112,639	1,366.83	71,468	117,743
75,000	771.46	202,726	1,284.54	89,029	113,697	1,385.43	82,041	120,685	1,464.46	76,572	126,154
80,000	822.90	216,244	1,370.19	94,966	121,278	1,477.81	87,512	128,731	1,562.11	81,679	134,565
85,000	874.33	229,759	1,455.82	100,901	128,858	1,570.17	92,982	136,777	1,659.74	86,784	142,975
90,000	925.76	243,274	1,541.46	106,836	136,438	1,662.53	98,451	144,823	1,757.37	91,889	151,385
95,000	977.19	256,788	1,627.09	112,771	144,017	1,754.89	103,921	152,867	1,855.00	96,993	159,795
100,000	1,028.62	270,303	1,712.73	118,706	151,597	1,847.25	109,390	160,913	1,952.63	102,098	168,205
105,000	1,080.05	283,818	1,798.36	124,642	159,176	1,939.61	114,859	168,959	2,050.26	107,203	176,615
110,000	1,131.48	297,333	1,884.00	130,577	166,756	2,031.98	120,329	177,004	2,147.89	112,307	185,026
115,000	1,182.91	310,848	1,969.63	136,512	174,336	2,124.34	125,798	185,050	2,245.52	117,412	193,436
120,000	1,234.34	324,362	2,055.27	142,447	181,915	2,216.70	131,267	193,095	2,343.15	122,517	201,846
125,000	1,285.77	337,877	2,140.90	148,382	189,495	2,309.06	136,736	201,141	2,440.78	127,621	210,256
130,000	1,337.20	351,392	2,226.54	154,317	197,075	2,401.42	142,206	209,186	2,538.40	132,726	218,666
135,000	1,388.63	364,907	2,312.17	160,252	204,655	2,493.78	147,675	217,232	2,636.03	137,831	227,076
140,000	1,440.06	378,422	2,397.81	166,187	212,235	2,586.14	153,144	225,278	2,733.66	142,936	235,486
145,000	1,491.49	391,936	2,483.44	172,122	219,814	2,678.50	158,614	233,322	2,831.29	148,040	243,896
150,000	1,542.92	405,451	2,569.08	178,057	227,394	2,770.86	164,083	241,368	2,928.92	153,145	252,306
155,000	1,594.35	418,966	2,654.71	183,993	234,973	2,863.22	169,552	249,414	3,026.55	158,250	260,716
160,000	1,645.79	432,484	2,740.36	189,930	242,554	2,955.60	175,023	257,461	3,124.20	163,356	269,128
165,000	1,697.22	445,999	2,826.00	195,865	250,134	3,047.96	180,493	265,506	3,221.83	168,461	277,538
170,000	1,748.65	459,514	2,911.63	201,800	257,714	3,140.32	185,962	273,552	3,319.46	173,566	285,948
175,000	1,800.08	473,029	2,997.27	207,735	265,294	3,232.69	191,431	281,598	3,417.09	178,670	294,359
180,000	1,851.51	486,544	3,082.90	213,670	272,874	3,325.05	196,901	289,643	3,514.72	183,775	302,769
185,000	1,902.94	500,058	3,168.53	219,605	280,453	3,417.41	202,370	297,688	3,612.35	188,880	311,178
190,000	1,954.37	513,573	3,254.17	225,540	288,033	3,509.77	207,839	305,734	3,709.98	193,985	319,588
195,000	2,005.80	527,088	3,339.80	231,476	295,612	3,602.13	213,309	313,779	3,807.61	199,089	327,999
200,000	2,057.23	540,603	3,425.44	237,411	303,192	3,694.49	218,778	321,825	3,905.24	204,194	336,409

12.25% GROWING EQUITY MORTGAGES

AMOUNT OF LOAN	30 YEARS MONTHLY PAYMENT	30 YEARS TOTAL INTRST	1% PMT INCR/YR 245.799 PAYMENTS LAST YR MON PMT	TOTAL INTRST	INTRST SAVED	2% PMT INCR/YR 204.137 PAYMENTS LAST YR MON PMT	TOTAL INTRST	INTRST SAVED	3% PMT INCR/YR 179.515 PAYMENTS LAST YR MON PMT	TOTAL INTRST	INTRST SAVED
$ 50	0.53	141	0.65	94	47	0.74	77	64	0.80	68	73
100	1.05	278	1.28	185	93	1.47	152	126	1.59	134	144
200	2.10	556	2.56	370	186	2.94	305	251	3.18	267	289
300	3.15	834	3.84	555	279	4.41	457	377	4.76	401	433
400	4.20	1,112	5.12	739	373	5.88	609	503	6.35	534	578
500	5.24	1,386	6.39	922	464	7.34	759	627	7.93	666	720
600	6.29	1,664	7.67	1,107	557	8.81	912	752	9.51	799	865
700	7.34	1,942	8.96	1,291	651	10.28	1,064	878	11.10	933	1,009
800	8.39	2,220	10.24	1,476	744	11.75	1,216	1,004	12.69	1,066	1,154
900	9.44	2,498	11.52	1,661	837	13.22	1,369	1,129	14.28	1,200	1,298
1,000	10.48	2,773	12.79	1,843	930	14.67	1,519	1,254	15.85	1,331	1,442
2,000	20.96	5,546	25.58	3,687	1,859	29.35	3,037	2,509	31.70	2,663	2,883
3,000	31.44	8,318	38.36	5,530	2,788	44.02	4,556	3,762	47.56	3,994	4,324
4,000	41.92	11,091	51.15	7,373	3,718	58.70	6,075	5,016	63.41	5,325	5,766
5,000	52.40	13,864	63.94	9,216	4,648	73.37	7,594	6,270	79.26	6,657	7,207
6,000	62.88	16,637	76.73	11,060	5,577	88.05	9,112	7,525	95.11	7,988	8,649
7,000	73.36	19,410	89.51	12,903	6,507	102.72	10,631	8,779	110.96	9,319	10,091
8,000	83.84	22,182	102.30	14,746	7,436	117.40	12,150	10,032	126.82	10,650	11,532
9,000	94.32	24,955	115.09	16,589	8,366	132.07	13,669	11,286	142.67	11,982	12,973
10,000	104.79	27,724	127.86	18,430	9,294	146.73	15,185	12,539	158.50	13,311	14,413
11,000	115.27	30,497	140.65	20,273	10,224	161.41	16,704	13,793	174.36	14,642	15,855
12,000	125.75	33,270	153.44	22,116	11,154	176.08	18,222	15,048	190.21	15,974	17,296
13,000	136.23	36,043	166.23	23,960	12,083	190.75	19,741	16,302	206.06	17,305	18,738
14,000	146.71	38,816	179.01	25,803	13,013	205.43	21,260	17,556	221.91	18,636	20,180
15,000	157.19	41,588	191.80	27,646	13,942	220.10	22,779	18,809	237.76	19,967	21,621
16,000	167.67	44,361	204.59	29,490	14,871	234.78	24,297	20,064	253.62	21,299	23,062
17,000	178.15	47,134	217.38	31,333	15,801	249.45	25,816	21,318	269.47	22,630	24,504
18,000	188.63	49,907	230.16	33,176	16,731	264.13	27,335	22,572	285.32	23,961	25,946
19,000	199.11	52,680	242.95	35,019	17,661	278.80	28,853	23,827	301.17	25,293	27,387
20,000	209.58	55,449	255.73	36,860	18,589	293.46	30,370	25,079	317.01	26,622	28,827
21,000	220.06	58,222	268.52	38,703	19,519	308.14	31,888	26,334	332.86	27,953	30,269
22,000	230.54	60,994	281.30	40,546	20,448	322.81	33,407	27,587	348.71	29,284	31,710
23,000	241.02	63,767	294.09	42,390	21,377	337.49	34,926	28,841	364.56	30,616	33,151
24,000	251.50	66,540	306.88	44,233	22,307	352.16	36,445	30,095	380.42	31,947	34,593
25,000	261.98	69,313	319.67	46,076	23,237	366.84	37,963	31,350	396.27	33,278	36,035
26,000	272.46	72,086	332.45	47,919	24,167	381.51	39,482	32,604	412.12	34,610	37,476
27,000	282.94	74,858	345.24	49,763	25,095	396.18	41,001	33,857	427.97	35,941	38,917
28,000	293.42	77,631	358.03	51,606	26,025	410.86	42,520	35,111	443.82	37,272	40,359
29,000	303.89	80,400	370.80	53,447	26,953	425.52	44,036	36,364	459.66	38,601	41,799
30,000	314.37	83,173	383.59	55,290	27,883	440.19	45,555	37,618	475.51	39,933	43,240
32,500	340.57	90,105	415.56	59,898	30,207	476.88	49,351	40,754	515.14	43,261	46,844
35,000	366.77	97,037	447.53	64,506	32,531	513.57	53,148	43,889	554.77	46,589	50,448
40,000	419.16	110,898	511.45	73,720	37,178	586.93	60,740	50,158	634.02	53,244	57,654
45,000	471.56	124,762	575.39	82,936	41,826	660.30	68,333	56,429	713.28	59,900	64,862
50,000	523.95	138,622	639.32	92,150	46,472	733.66	75,924	62,698	792.52	66,554	72,068
55,000	576.35	152,486	703.26	101,366	51,120	807.03	83,518	68,968	871.78	73,211	79,275
60,000	628.74	166,346	767.18	110,580	55,766	880.39	91,109	75,237	951.03	79,865	86,481
65,000	681.14	180,210	831.12	119,796	60,414	953.76	98,703	81,507	1,030.29	86,522	93,688
70,000	733.53	194,071	895.05	129,010	65,061	1,027.12	106,294	87,777	1,109.53	93,176	100,895
75,000	785.93	207,935	958.98	138,226	69,709	1,100.49	113,888	94,047	1,188.79	99,833	108,102
80,000	838.32	221,795	1,022.91	147,440	74,355	1,173.85	121,479	100,316	1,268.03	106,487	115,308
85,000	890.72	235,659	1,086.85	156,656	79,003	1,247.22	129,073	106,586	1,347.29	113,144	122,515
90,000	943.11	249,520	1,150.77	165,869	83,651	1,320.58	136,664	112,856	1,426.54	119,798	129,722
95,000	995.51	263,384	1,214.71	175,086	88,298	1,393.95	144,258	119,126	1,505.80	126,455	136,929
100,000	1,047.90	277,244	1,278.64	184,299	92,945	1,467.31	151,849	125,395	1,585.04	133,109	144,135
105,000	1,100.30	291,108	1,342.58	193,516	97,592	1,540.69	159,442	131,666	1,664.30	139,765	151,343
110,000	1,152.69	304,968	1,406.50	202,729	102,239	1,614.04	167,034	137,934	1,743.55	146,420	158,548
115,000	1,205.09	318,832	1,470.44	211,946	106,886	1,687.42	174,627	144,205	1,822.81	153,076	165,756
120,000	1,257.48	332,693	1,534.36	221,159	111,534	1,760.78	182,219	150,474	1,902.05	159,731	172,962
125,000	1,309.88	346,557	1,598.30	230,376	116,181	1,834.15	189,812	156,745	1,981.31	166,387	180,170
130,000	1,362.27	360,417	1,662.23	239,589	120,828	1,907.51	197,403	163,014	2,060.56	173,042	187,375
135,000	1,414.67	374,281	1,726.17	248,806	125,475	1,980.88	204,997	169,284	2,139.82	179,698	194,583
140,000	1,467.06	388,142	1,790.09	258,019	130,123	2,054.24	212,588	175,554	2,219.06	186,352	201,790
145,000	1,519.45	402,002	1,854.02	267,233	134,769	2,127.60	220,180	181,822	2,298.30	193,007	208,995
150,000	1,571.85	415,866	1,917.96	276,449	139,417	2,200.97	227,773	188,093	2,377.56	199,663	216,203
155,000	1,624.24	429,726	1,981.88	285,663	144,063	2,274.33	235,364	194,362	2,456.81	206,318	223,408
160,000	1,676.64	443,590	2,045.82	294,879	148,711	2,347.70	242,958	200,632	2,536.07	212,974	230,616
165,000	1,729.03	457,451	2,109.75	304,093	153,358	2,421.06	250,549	206,902	2,615.31	219,629	237,822
170,000	1,781.43	471,315	2,173.68	313,309	158,006	2,494.43	258,143	213,172	2,694.57	226,285	245,030
175,000	1,833.82	485,175	2,237.61	322,523	162,652	2,567.79	265,734	219,441	2,773.82	232,939	252,236
180,000	1,886.22	499,039	2,301.55	331,739	167,300	2,641.16	273,328	225,711	2,853.06	239,596	259,443
185,000	1,938.61	512,900	2,365.47	340,953	171,947	2,714.52	280,919	231,981	2,932.32	246,250	266,650
190,000	1,991.01	526,764	2,429.41	350,169	176,595	2,787.89	288,513	238,251	3,011.58	252,907	273,857
195,000	2,043.40	540,624	2,493.34	359,382	181,242	2,861.25	296,104	244,520	3,090.83	259,561	281,063
200,000	2,095.80	554,488	2,557.27	368,599	185,890	2,934.63	303,698	250,790	3,170.09	266,218	288,270

AMOUNT OF LOAN	30 YEARS		4% PMT INCR/YR 162.461 PAYMENTS			5% PMT INCR/YR 149.707 PAYMENTS			6% PMT INCR/YR 139.656 PAYMENTS		
	MONTHLY PAYMENT	TOTAL INTRST	LAST YR MON PMT	TOTAL INTRST	INTRST SAVED	LAST YR MON PMT	TOTAL INTRST	INTRST SAVED	LAST YR MON PMT	TOTAL INTRST	INTRST SAVED
$ 50	0.53	141	0.88	61	80	0.95	57	84	1.01	53	88
100	1.05	278	1.75	121	157	1.89	111	167	1.99	104	174
200	2.10	556	3.50	242	314	3.77	223	333	3.99	208	348
300	3.15	834	5.24	362	472	5.66	334	500	5.98	312	522
400	4.20	1,112	6.99	483	629	7.54	445	667	7.97	416	696
500	5.24	1,386	8.72	602	784	9.41	555	831	9.95	518	868
600	6.29	1,664	10.47	723	941	11.30	666	998	11.94	621	1,043
700	7.34	1,942	12.22	843	1,099	13.18	777	1,165	13.93	725	1,217
800	8.39	2,220	13.97	964	1,256	15.07	889	1,331	15.93	829	1,391
900	9.44	2,498	15.72	1,085	1,413	16.95	1,000	1,498	17.92	933	1,565
1,000	10.48	2,773	17.45	1,204	1,569	18.82	1,109	1,664	19.89	1,035	1,738
2,000	20.96	5,546	34.90	2,407	3,139	37.64	2,218	3,328	39.79	2,070	3,476
3,000	31.44	8,318	52.35	3,611	4,707	56.46	3,327	4,991	59.68	3,105	5,213
4,000	41.92	11,091	69.80	4,815	6,276	75.28	4,437	6,654	79.58	4,141	6,950
5,000	52.40	13,864	87.25	6,019	7,845	94.10	5,546	8,318	99.47	5,176	8,688
6,000	62.88	16,637	104.70	7,222	9,415	112.92	6,655	9,982	119.37	6,211	10,426
7,000	73.36	19,410	122.15	8,426	10,984	131.74	7,764	11,646	139.26	7,246	12,164
8,000	83.84	22,182	139.60	9,630	12,552	150.56	8,873	13,309	159.15	8,281	13,901
9,000	94.32	24,955	157.05	10,834	14,121	169.39	9,982	14,973	179.05	9,316	15,639
10,000	104.79	27,724	174.48	12,035	15,689	188.19	11,089	16,635	198.92	10,349	17,375
11,000	115.27	30,497	191.93	13,239	17,258	207.01	12,199	18,298	218.82	11,385	19,112
12,000	125.75	33,270	209.38	14,443	18,827	225.83	13,308	19,962	238.71	12,420	20,850
13,000	136.23	36,043	226.83	15,646	20,397	244.65	14,417	21,626	258.61	13,455	22,588
14,000	146.71	38,816	244.28	16,850	21,966	263.47	15,526	23,290	278.50	14,490	24,326
15,000	157.19	41,588	261.73	18,054	23,534	282.29	16,635	24,953	298.39	15,525	26,063
16,000	167.67	44,361	279.18	19,258	25,103	301.11	17,744	26,617	318.29	16,560	27,801
17,000	178.15	47,134	296.63	20,461	26,673	319.93	18,853	28,281	338.18	17,595	29,539
18,000	188.63	49,907	314.08	21,665	28,242	338.75	19,963	29,944	358.08	18,631	31,276
19,000	199.11	52,680	331.53	22,869	29,811	357.57	21,072	31,608	377.97	19,666	33,014
20,000	209.58	55,449	348.97	24,071	31,378	376.38	22,179	33,270	397.85	20,699	34,750
21,000	220.06	58,222	366.42	25,274	32,948	395.20	23,288	34,934	417.74	21,734	36,488
22,000	230.54	60,994	383.87	26,478	34,516	414.02	24,397	36,597	437.63	22,769	38,225
23,000	241.02	63,767	401.32	27,682	36,085	432.84	25,506	38,261	457.53	23,804	39,963
24,000	251.50	66,540	418.77	28,885	37,655	451.66	26,615	39,925	477.42	24,840	41,700
25,000	261.98	69,313	436.22	30,089	39,224	470.48	27,725	41,588	497.32	25,875	43,438
26,000	272.46	72,086	453.67	31,293	40,793	489.30	28,834	43,252	517.21	26,910	45,176
27,000	282.94	74,858	471.12	32,497	42,361	508.12	29,943	44,915	537.10	27,945	46,913
28,000	293.42	77,631	488.57	33,700	43,931	526.94	31,052	46,579	557.00	28,980	48,651
29,000	303.89	80,400	506.00	34,902	45,498	545.74	32,159	48,241	576.87	30,013	50,387
30,000	314.37	83,173	523.45	36,106	47,067	564.56	33,268	49,905	596.77	31,048	52,125
32,500	340.57	90,105	567.07	39,115	50,990	611.61	36,041	54,064	646.50	33,636	56,469
35,000	366.77	97,037	610.70	42,124	54,913	658.67	38,814	58,223	696.24	36,224	60,813
40,000	419.16	110,898	697.93	48,141	62,757	752.75	44,358	66,540	795.69	41,398	69,500
45,000	471.56	124,762	785.18	54,160	70,602	846.85	49,904	74,858	895.16	46,574	78,188
50,000	523.95	138,622	872.42	60,176	78,446	940.94	55,447	83,175	994.61	51,747	86,875
55,000	576.35	152,486	959.67	66,195	86,291	1,035.04	60,993	91,493	1,094.08	56,923	95,563
60,000	628.74	166,346	1,046.90	72,212	94,134	1,129.13	66,537	99,809	1,193.54	62,097	104,249
65,000	681.14	180,210	1,134.15	78,230	101,980	1,223.23	72,082	108,128	1,293.01	67,273	112,937
70,000	733.53	194,071	1,221.38	84,247	109,824	1,317.31	77,626	116,445	1,392.46	72,446	121,625
75,000	785.93	207,935	1,308.63	90,265	117,670	1,411.42	83,172	124,763	1,491.93	77,622	130,313
80,000	838.32	221,795	1,395.86	96,282	125,513	1,505.50	88,716	133,079	1,591.38	82,796	138,999
85,000	890.72	235,659	1,483.11	102,301	133,358	1,599.61	94,261	141,398	1,690.85	87,972	147,687
90,000	943.11	249,520	1,570.35	108,317	141,203	1,693.69	99,805	149,715	1,790.30	93,145	156,375
95,000	995.51	263,384	1,657.60	114,336	149,048	1,787.79	105,351	158,033	1,889.78	98,321	165,063
100,000	1,047.90	277,244	1,744.83	120,353	156,891	1,881.88	110,895	166,349	1,989.23	103,495	173,749
105,000	1,100.30	291,108	1,832.08	126,371	164,737	1,975.98	116,440	174,668	2,088.70	108,671	182,437
110,000	1,152.69	304,968	1,919.31	132,388	172,580	2,070.07	121,984	182,984	2,188.15	113,844	191,124
115,000	1,205.09	318,832	2,006.56	138,406	180,426	2,164.17	127,530	191,302	2,287.62	119,020	199,812
120,000	1,257.48	332,693	2,093.80	144,423	188,270	2,258.25	133,073	199,620	2,387.07	124,194	208,499
125,000	1,309.88	346,557	2,181.05	150,442	196,115	2,352.36	138,619	207,938	2,486.54	129,370	217,187
130,000	1,362.27	360,417	2,268.28	156,458	203,959	2,446.44	144,163	216,254	2,586.00	134,543	225,874
135,000	1,414.67	374,281	2,355.53	162,477	211,804	2,540.54	149,709	224,572	2,685.47	139,719	234,562
140,000	1,467.06	388,142	2,442.76	168,494	219,648	2,634.63	155,252	232,890	2,784.92	144,893	243,249
145,000	1,519.45	402,002	2,530.00	174,510	227,492	2,728.71	160,796	241,206	2,884.37	150,067	251,935
150,000	1,571.85	415,866	2,617.25	180,529	235,337	2,822.82	166,342	249,524	2,983.84	155,242	260,624
155,000	1,624.24	429,726	2,704.48	186,545	243,181	2,916.90	171,886	257,840	3,083.29	160,416	269,310
160,000	1,676.64	443,590	2,791.73	192,564	251,026	3,011.00	177,431	266,159	3,182.76	165,592	277,998
165,000	1,729.03	457,451	2,878.96	198,581	258,870	3,105.09	182,975	274,476	3,282.22	170,766	286,685
170,000	1,781.43	471,315	2,966.21	204,599	266,716	3,199.19	188,521	282,794	3,381.69	175,941	295,374
175,000	1,833.82	485,175	3,053.45	210,616	274,559	3,293.28	194,064	291,111	3,481.14	181,115	304,060
180,000	1,886.22	499,039	3,140.69	216,635	282,404	3,387.38	199,610	299,429	3,580.61	186,291	312,748
185,000	1,938.61	512,900	3,227.93	222,651	290,249	3,481.47	205,154	307,746	3,680.06	191,465	321,435
190,000	1,991.01	526,764	3,315.18	228,670	298,094	3,575.57	210,700	316,064	3,779.53	196,640	330,124
195,000	2,043.40	540,624	3,402.41	234,686	305,938	3,669.65	216,243	324,381	3,878.98	201,814	338,810
200,000	2,095.80	554,488	3,489.66	240,705	313,783	3,763.76	221,789	332,699	3,978.45	206,990	347,498

143

GROWING EQUITY MORTGAGES

AMOUNT OF LOAN	30 YEARS		1% PMT INCR/YR 243.965 PAYMENTS			2% PMT INCR/YR 202.428 PAYMENTS			3% PMT INCR/YR 177.969 PAYMENTS		
	MONTHLY PAYMENT	TOTAL INTRST	LAST YR MON PMT	TOTAL INTRST	INTRST SAVED	LAST YR MON PMT	TOTAL INTRST	INTRST SAVED	LAST YR MON PMT	TOTAL INTRST	INTRST SAVED
$ 50	0.54	144	0.66	95	49	0.74	79	65	0.82	69	75
100	1.07	285	1.31	188	97	1.47	155	130	1.62	136	149
200	2.14	570	2.61	376	194	2.94	309	261	3.24	271	299
300	3.21	856	3.92	564	292	4.41	464	392	4.86	407	449
400	4.27	1,137	5.21	749	388	5.86	616	521	6.46	540	597
500	5.34	1,422	6.52	937	485	7.33	771	651	8.08	675	747
600	6.41	1,708	7.82	1,125	583	8.80	925	783	9.70	811	897
700	7.48	1,993	9.13	1,313	680	10.27	1,080	913	11.31	946	1,047
800	8.54	2,274	10.42	1,498	776	11.72	1,232	1,042	12.92	1,080	1,194
900	9.61	2,560	11.73	1,686	874	13.19	1,387	1,173	14.54	1,215	1,345
1,000	10.68	2,845	13.03	1,874	971	14.66	1,542	1,303	16.15	1,351	1,494
2,000	21.35	5,686	26.05	3,745	1,941	29.31	3,081	2,605	32.29	2,699	2,987
3,000	32.02	8,527	39.07	5,615	2,912	43.96	4,620	3,907	48.43	4,048	4,479
4,000	42.70	11,372	52.10	7,489	3,883	58.62	6,162	5,210	64.59	5,399	5,973
5,000	53.37	14,213	65.12	9,360	4,853	73.27	7,701	6,512	80.73	6,748	7,465
6,000	64.04	17,054	78.14	11,231	5,823	87.91	9,241	7,813	96.87	8,096	8,958
7,000	74.71	19,896	91.16	13,102	6,794	102.56	10,780	9,116	113.01	9,445	10,451
8,000	85.39	22,740	104.19	14,976	7,764	117.22	12,322	10,418	129.16	10,796	11,944
9,000	96.06	25,582	117.21	16,846	8,736	131.87	13,861	11,721	145.30	12,144	13,438
10,000	106.73	28,423	130.23	18,717	9,706	146.52	15,400	13,023	161.44	13,493	14,930
11,000	117.40	31,264	143.25	20,588	10,676	161.17	16,940	14,324	177.58	14,841	16,423
12,000	128.08	34,109	156.28	22,462	11,647	175.83	18,481	15,628	193.73	16,192	17,917
13,000	138.75	36,950	169.30	24,333	12,617	190.47	20,021	16,929	209.87	17,541	19,409
14,000	149.42	39,791	182.32	26,204	13,587	205.12	21,560	18,231	226.01	18,890	20,901
15,000	160.09	42,632	195.34	28,075	14,557	219.77	23,099	19,533	242.15	20,238	22,394
16,000	170.77	45,477	208.37	29,948	15,529	234.43	24,641	20,836	258.30	21,589	23,888
17,000	181.44	48,318	221.39	31,819	16,499	249.08	26,180	22,138	274.44	22,938	25,380
18,000	192.11	51,160	234.41	33,690	17,470	263.73	27,720	23,440	290.58	24,286	26,874
19,000	202.78	54,001	247.43	35,561	18,440	278.37	29,259	24,742	306.72	25,635	28,366
20,000	213.46	56,846	260.46	37,435	19,411	293.03	30,801	26,045	322.88	26,986	29,860
21,000	224.13	59,687	273.48	39,306	20,381	307.68	32,340	27,347	339.02	28,334	31,353
22,000	234.80	62,528	286.50	41,177	21,351	322.33	33,879	28,649	355.16	29,683	32,845
23,000	245.47	65,369	299.52	43,048	22,321	336.98	35,419	29,950	371.30	31,032	34,337
24,000	256.15	68,214	312.55	44,921	23,293	351.64	36,960	31,254	387.45	32,382	35,832
25,000	266.82	71,055	325.57	46,792	24,263	366.29	38,500	32,555	403.59	33,731	37,324
26,000	277.49	73,896	338.59	48,663	25,233	380.93	40,039	33,857	419.73	35,080	38,816
27,000	288.16	76,738	351.61	50,534	26,204	395.58	41,578	35,160	435.87	36,428	40,310
28,000	298.84	79,582	364.64	52,408	27,174	410.24	43,120	36,462	452.02	37,779	41,803
29,000	309.51	82,424	377.66	54,279	28,145	424.89	44,659	37,765	468.16	39,128	43,296
30,000	320.18	85,265	390.68	56,150	29,115	439.54	46,199	39,066	484.30	40,476	44,789
32,500	346.86	92,370	423.24	60,828	31,542	476.16	50,048	42,322	524.66	43,849	48,521
35,000	373.55	99,478	455.80	65,510	33,968	512.80	53,900	45,578	565.03	47,224	52,254
40,000	426.91	113,688	520.91	74,867	38,821	586.06	61,599	52,089	645.74	53,969	59,719
45,000	480.27	127,897	586.02	84,224	43,673	659.31	69,298	58,599	726.45	60,715	67,182
50,000	533.63	142,107	651.13	93,582	48,525	732.56	76,997	65,110	807.16	67,460	74,647
55,000	587.00	156,320	716.25	102,942	53,378	805.83	84,698	71,622	887.89	74,207	82,113
60,000	640.36	170,530	781.36	112,299	58,231	879.08	92,397	78,133	968.60	80,953	89,577
65,000	693.72	184,739	846.47	121,657	63,082	952.33	100,096	84,643	1,049.31	87,698	97,041
70,000	747.09	198,952	911.59	131,017	67,935	1,025.59	107,798	91,154	1,130.04	94,446	104,506
75,000	800.45	213,162	976.70	140,374	72,788	1,098.85	115,497	97,665	1,210.75	101,191	111,971
80,000	853.81	227,372	1,041.81	149,731	77,641	1,172.10	123,196	104,176	1,291.46	107,936	119,436
85,000	907.17	241,581	1,106.92	159,089	82,492	1,245.35	130,895	110,686	1,372.18	114,682	126,899
90,000	960.54	255,794	1,172.04	168,449	87,345	1,318.62	138,596	117,198	1,452.90	121,429	134,365
95,000	1,013.90	270,004	1,237.15	177,806	92,198	1,391.87	146,295	123,709	1,533.61	128,174	141,830
100,000	1,067.26	284,214	1,302.26	187,163	97,051	1,465.12	153,994	130,220	1,614.33	134,920	149,294
105,000	1,120.63	298,427	1,367.38	196,524	101,903	1,538.38	161,695	136,732	1,695.05	141,667	156,760
110,000	1,173.99	312,636	1,432.49	205,881	106,755	1,611.64	169,394	143,242	1,775.77	148,413	164,223
115,000	1,227.35	326,846	1,497.60	215,238	111,608	1,684.89	177,093	149,753	1,856.48	155,158	171,688
120,000	1,280.71	341,056	1,562.71	224,596	116,460	1,758.14	184,792	156,264	1,937.19	161,903	179,153
125,000	1,334.08	355,269	1,627.83	233,956	121,313	1,831.41	192,493	162,776	2,017.92	168,651	186,618
130,000	1,387.44	369,478	1,692.94	243,313	126,165	1,904.66	200,192	169,286	2,098.63	175,396	194,082
135,000	1,440.80	383,688	1,758.05	252,670	131,018	1,977.91	207,891	175,797	2,179.34	182,142	201,546
140,000	1,494.17	397,901	1,823.17	262,030	135,871	2,051.18	215,593	182,308	2,260.07	188,889	209,012
145,000	1,547.53	412,111	1,888.28	271,388	140,723	2,124.43	223,292	188,819	2,340.78	195,634	216,477
150,000	1,600.89	426,320	1,953.39	280,745	145,575	2,197.68	230,991	195,329	2,421.49	202,380	223,940
155,000	1,654.25	440,530	2,018.50	290,103	150,427	2,270.93	238,690	201,840	2,502.20	209,125	231,405
160,000	1,707.62	454,743	2,083.62	299,463	155,280	2,344.20	246,391	208,352	2,582.93	215,873	238,870
165,000	1,760.98	468,953	2,148.73	308,820	160,133	2,417.45	254,090	214,863	2,663.64	222,618	246,335
170,000	1,814.34	483,162	2,213.84	318,177	164,985	2,490.70	261,789	221,373	2,744.35	229,363	253,799
175,000	1,867.71	497,376	2,278.96	327,537	169,839	2,563.97	269,490	227,886	2,825.08	236,111	261,265
180,000	1,921.07	511,585	2,344.07	336,895	174,690	2,637.22	277,189	234,396	2,905.79	242,856	268,729
185,000	1,974.43	525,795	2,409.18	346,252	179,543	2,710.47	284,888	240,907	2,986.50	249,601	276,194
190,000	2,027.79	540,004	2,474.29	355,610	184,394	2,783.72	292,587	247,417	3,067.21	256,347	283,657
195,000	2,081.16	554,218	2,539.41	364,970	189,248	2,856.99	300,289	253,929	3,147.94	263,094	291,124
200,000	2,134.52	568,427	2,604.52	374,327	194,100	2,930.24	307,988	260,439	3,228.65	269,840	298,587

AMOUNT OF LOAN	30 YEARS		4% PMT INCR/YR 161.077 PAYMENTS			5% PMT INCR/YR 148.444 PAYMENTS			6% PMT INCR/YR 138.478 PAYMENTS		
	MONTHLY PAYMENT	TOTAL INTRST	LAST YR MON PMT	TOTAL INTRST	INTRST SAVED	LAST YR MON PMT	TOTAL INTRST	INTRST SAVED	LAST YR MON PMT	TOTAL INTRST	INTRST SAVED
$ 50	0.54	144	0.90	62	82	0.97	57	87	1.03	54	90
100	1.07	285	1.78	123	162	1.92	113	172	2.03	105	180
200	2.14	570	3.56	245	325	3.84	226	344	4.06	211	359
300	3.21	856	5.34	368	488	5.76	339	517	6.09	316	540
400	4.27	1,137	7.11	488	649	7.67	450	687	8.11	420	717
500	5.34	1,422	8.89	611	811	9.59	563	859	10.14	525	897
600	6.41	1,708	10.67	733	975	11.51	676	1,032	12.17	630	1,078
700	7.48	1,993	12.45	856	1,137	13.43	788	1,205	14.20	736	1,257
800	8.54	2,274	14.22	976	1,298	15.34	899	1,375	16.21	839	1,435
900	9.61	2,560	16.00	1,099	1,461	17.26	1,012	1,548	18.24	945	1,615
1,000	10.68	2,845	17.78	1,221	1,624	19.18	1,125	1,720	20.27	1,050	1,795
2,000	21.35	5,686	35.55	2,440	3,246	38.34	2,248	3,438	40.53	2,098	3,588
3,000	32.02	8,527	53.32	3,659	4,868	57.50	3,372	5,155	60.78	3,146	5,381
4,000	42.70	11,372	71.10	4,881	6,491	76.68	4,497	6,875	81.06	4,197	7,175
5,000	53.37	14,213	88.86	6,100	8,113	95.84	5,620	8,593	101.31	5,245	8,968
6,000	64.04	17,054	106.63	7,319	9,735	115.01	6,743	10,311	121.57	6,293	10,761
7,000	74.71	19,896	124.40	8,538	11,358	134.17	7,866	12,030	141.82	7,341	12,555
8,000	85.39	22,740	142.18	9,759	12,981	153.35	8,991	13,749	162.10	8,391	14,349
9,000	96.06	25,582	159.95	10,978	14,604	172.51	10,115	15,467	182.35	9,439	16,143
10,000	106.73	28,423	177.71	12,197	16,226	191.67	11,238	17,185	202.61	10,488	17,935
11,000	117.40	31,264	195.48	13,416	17,848	210.83	12,361	18,903	222.86	11,536	19,728
12,000	128.08	34,109	213.26	14,638	19,471	230.01	13,486	20,623	243.13	12,586	21,523
13,000	138.75	36,950	231.03	15,857	21,093	249.18	14,609	22,341	263.39	13,634	23,316
14,000	149.42	39,791	248.80	17,076	22,715	268.34	15,733	24,058	283.64	14,682	25,109
15,000	160.09	42,632	266.56	18,295	24,337	287.50	16,856	25,776	303.90	15,730	26,902
16,000	170.77	45,477	284.34	19,516	25,961	306.68	17,981	27,496	324.17	16,780	28,697
17,000	181.44	48,318	302.11	20,735	27,583	325.84	19,104	29,214	344.43	17,829	30,489
18,000	192.11	51,160	319.88	21,954	29,206	345.00	20,227	30,933	364.68	18,877	32,283
19,000	202.78	54,001	337.64	23,173	30,828	364.16	21,350	32,651	384.94	19,925	34,076
20,000	213.46	56,846	355.43	24,394	32,452	383.34	22,476	34,370	405.21	20,975	35,871
21,000	224.13	59,687	373.19	25,614	34,073	402.51	23,599	36,088	425.47	22,023	37,664
22,000	234.80	62,528	390.96	26,833	35,695	421.67	24,722	37,806	445.72	23,071	39,457
23,000	245.47	65,369	408.73	28,052	37,317	440.83	25,845	39,524	465.98	24,120	41,249
24,000	256.15	68,214	426.51	29,273	38,941	460.01	26,970	41,244	486.25	25,170	43,044
25,000	266.82	71,055	444.27	30,492	40,563	479.17	28,094	42,961	506.50	26,218	44,837
26,000	277.49	73,896	462.04	31,711	42,185	498.33	29,217	44,679	526.76	27,266	46,630
27,000	288.16	76,738	479.81	32,930	43,808	517.49	30,340	46,398	547.01	28,314	48,424
28,000	298.84	79,582	497.59	34,151	45,431	536.67	31,465	48,117	567.29	29,364	50,218
29,000	309.51	82,424	515.36	35,371	47,053	555.84	32,588	49,836	587.54	30,413	52,011
30,000	320.18	85,265	533.12	36,590	48,675	575.00	33,711	51,554	607.80	31,461	53,804
32,500	346.86	92,370	577.55	39,638	52,732	622.91	36,520	55,850	658.44	34,082	58,288
35,000	373.55	99,478	621.99	42,689	56,789	670.84	39,331	60,147	709.11	36,705	62,773
40,000	426.91	113,688	710.84	48,787	64,901	766.67	44,949	68,739	810.40	41,948	71,740
45,000	480.27	127,897	799.68	54,884	73,013	862.50	50,567	77,330	911.70	47,191	80,706
50,000	533.63	142,107	888.53	60,982	81,125	958.32	56,185	85,922	1,012.99	52,434	89,673
55,000	587.00	156,320	977.40	67,082	89,238	1,054.17	61,805	94,515	1,114.30	57,679	98,641
60,000	640.36	170,530	1,066.25	73,179	97,351	1,149.99	67,423	103,107	1,215.59	62,922	107,608
65,000	693.72	184,739	1,155.09	79,277	105,462	1,245.82	73,041	111,698	1,316.89	68,164	116,575
70,000	747.09	198,952	1,243.96	85,377	113,575	1,341.67	78,661	120,291	1,418.20	73,409	125,543
75,000	800.45	213,162	1,332.81	91,474	121,688	1,437.49	84,279	128,883	1,519.49	78,652	134,510
80,000	853.81	227,372	1,421.66	97,572	129,800	1,533.32	89,896	137,476	1,620.79	83,895	143,477
85,000	907.17	241,581	1,510.50	103,669	137,912	1,629.15	95,514	146,067	1,722.08	89,138	152,443
90,000	960.54	255,794	1,599.37	109,769	146,025	1,724.99	101,134	154,660	1,823.39	94,382	161,412
95,000	1,013.90	270,004	1,688.22	115,866	154,138	1,820.82	106,752	163,252	1,924.68	99,625	170,379
100,000	1,067.26	284,214	1,777.07	121,964	162,250	1,916.65	112,370	171,844	2,025.98	104,868	179,346
105,000	1,120.63	298,427	1,865.93	128,064	170,363	2,012.49	117,990	180,437	2,127.29	110,113	188,314
110,000	1,173.99	312,636	1,954.78	134,161	178,475	2,108.32	123,608	189,028	2,228.58	115,355	197,281
115,000	1,227.35	326,846	2,043.63	140,259	186,587	2,204.14	129,226	197,620	2,329.88	120,598	206,248
120,000	1,280.71	341,056	2,132.48	146,356	194,700	2,299.97	134,844	206,212	2,431.17	125,841	215,215
125,000	1,334.08	355,269	2,221.34	152,456	202,813	2,395.82	140,464	214,805	2,532.48	131,086	224,183
130,000	1,387.44	369,478	2,310.19	158,554	210,924	2,491.64	146,082	223,396	2,633.78	136,329	233,149
135,000	1,440.80	383,688	2,399.04	164,651	219,037	2,587.47	151,699	231,989	2,735.07	141,571	242,117
140,000	1,494.17	397,901	2,487.90	170,751	227,150	2,683.31	157,319	240,582	2,836.38	146,816	251,085
145,000	1,547.53	412,111	2,576.75	176,849	235,262	2,779.14	162,937	249,174	2,937.67	152,059	260,052
150,000	1,600.89	426,320	2,665.60	182,946	243,374	2,874.97	168,555	257,765	3,038.97	157,302	269,018
155,000	1,654.25	440,530	2,754.45	189,044	251,486	2,970.80	174,173	266,357	3,140.26	162,545	277,985
160,000	1,707.62	454,743	2,843.31	195,143	259,600	3,066.64	179,793	274,950	3,241.57	167,789	286,954
165,000	1,760.98	468,953	2,932.16	201,241	267,712	3,162.47	185,411	283,542	3,342.87	173,032	295,921
170,000	1,814.34	483,162	3,021.01	207,339	275,823	3,258.29	191,029	292,133	3,444.16	178,275	304,887
175,000	1,867.71	497,376	3,109.87	213,438	283,938	3,354.14	196,649	300,727	3,545.47	183,520	313,856
180,000	1,921.07	511,585	3,198.72	219,536	292,049	3,449.97	202,267	309,318	3,646.76	188,763	322,822
185,000	1,974.43	525,795	3,287.57	225,633	300,162	3,545.79	207,885	317,910	3,748.06	194,005	331,790
190,000	2,027.79	540,004	3,376.42	231,731	308,273	3,641.62	213,502	326,502	3,849.35	199,248	340,756
195,000	2,081.16	554,218	3,465.28	237,831	316,387	3,737.46	219,122	335,096	3,950.66	204,493	349,725
200,000	2,134.52	568,427	3,554.13	243,928	324,499	3,833.29	224,740	343,687	4,051.96	209,736	358,691

12.75% GROWING EQUITY MORTGAGES

AMOUNT OF LOAN	30 YEARS MONTHLY PAYMENT	30 YEARS TOTAL INTRST	1% PMT INCR/YR 242.135 PAYMENTS LAST YR MON PMT	1% TOTAL INTRST	1% INTRST SAVED	2% PMT INCR/YR 200.735 PAYMENTS LAST YR MON PMT	2% TOTAL INTRST	2% INTRST SAVED	3% PMT INCR/YR 176.448 PAYMENTS LAST YR MON PMT	3% TOTAL INTRST	3% INTRST SAVED
$ 50	0.55	148	0.67	97	51	0.76	80	68	0.83	70	78
100	1.09	292	1.33	191	101	1.50	157	135	1.65	137	155
200	2.18	585	2.66	382	203	2.99	314	271	3.30	275	310
300	3.27	877	3.99	573	304	4.49	471	406	4.95	412	465
400	4.35	1,166	5.31	761	405	5.97	625	541	6.58	547	619
500	5.44	1,458	6.64	952	506	7.47	782	676	8.23	685	773
600	6.53	1,751	7.97	1,142	609	8.96	939	812	9.88	822	929
700	7.61	2,040	9.29	1,331	709	10.45	1,093	947	11.51	958	1,082
800	8.70	2,332	10.62	1,521	811	11.94	1,250	1,082	13.16	1,095	1,237
900	9.79	2,624	11.95	1,712	912	13.44	1,407	1,217	14.81	1,232	1,392
1,000	10.87	2,913	13.26	1,900	1,013	14.92	1,562	1,351	16.44	1,368	1,545
2,000	21.74	5,826	26.53	3,801	2,025	29.84	3,123	2,703	32.88	2,735	3,091
3,000	32.61	8,740	39.79	5,701	3,039	44.77	4,685	4,055	49.33	4,103	4,637
4,000	43.47	11,649	53.04	7,599	4,050	59.67	6,244	5,405	65.75	5,468	6,181
5,000	54.34	14,562	66.31	9,500	5,062	74.60	7,806	6,756	82.19	6,836	7,726
6,000	65.21	17,476	79.57	11,400	6,076	89.52	9,368	8,108	98.64	8,204	9,272
7,000	76.07	20,385	92.82	13,298	7,087	104.43	10,927	9,458	115.06	9,569	10,816
8,000	86.94	23,298	106.08	15,198	8,100	119.35	12,489	10,809	131.50	10,937	12,361
9,000	97.81	26,212	119.35	17,099	9,113	134.27	14,050	12,162	147.95	12,304	13,908
10,000	108.67	29,121	132.60	18,997	10,124	149.18	15,609	13,512	164.37	13,670	15,451
11,000	119.54	32,034	145.86	20,897	11,137	164.10	17,171	14,863	180.81	15,038	16,996
12,000	130.41	34,948	159.12	22,798	12,150	179.02	18,733	16,215	197.26	16,405	18,543
13,000	141.28	37,861	172.39	24,698	13,163	193.95	20,294	17,567	213.70	17,773	20,088
14,000	152.14	40,770	185.64	26,596	14,174	208.86	21,854	18,916	230.13	19,138	21,632
15,000	163.01	43,684	198.90	28,496	15,188	223.78	23,415	20,269	246.57	20,506	23,178
16,000	173.88	46,597	212.17	30,397	16,200	238.70	24,977	21,620	263.01	21,874	24,723
17,000	184.74	49,506	225.42	32,295	17,211	253.61	26,536	22,970	279.44	23,239	26,267
18,000	195.61	52,420	238.68	34,195	18,225	268.53	28,098	24,322	295.88	24,607	27,813
19,000	206.48	55,333	251.94	36,096	19,237	283.45	29,660	25,673	312.32	25,974	29,359
20,000	217.34	58,242	265.20	37,994	20,248	298.36	31,219	27,023	328.75	27,340	30,902
21,000	228.21	61,156	278.46	39,894	21,262	313.28	32,781	28,375	345.19	28,707	32,449
22,000	239.08	64,069	291.72	41,794	22,275	328.21	34,342	29,727	361.63	30,075	33,994
23,000	249.94	66,978	304.97	43,692	23,286	343.11	35,902	31,076	378.06	31,440	35,538
24,000	260.81	69,892	318.24	45,593	24,299	358.04	37,463	32,429	394.50	32,808	37,084
25,000	271.68	72,805	331.50	47,493	25,312	372.96	39,025	33,780	410.94	34,176	38,629
26,000	282.55	75,718	344.76	49,394	26,324	387.88	40,586	35,132	427.38	35,543	40,175
27,000	293.41	78,628	358.02	51,292	27,336	402.79	42,146	36,482	443.81	36,909	41,719
28,000	304.28	81,541	371.28	53,192	28,349	417.71	43,707	37,834	460.25	38,277	43,264
29,000	315.15	84,454	384.54	55,092	29,362	432.63	45,269	39,185	476.69	39,644	44,810
30,000	326.01	87,364	397.79	56,990	30,374	447.54	46,828	40,536	493.12	41,010	46,354
32,500	353.18	94,645	430.95	61,740	32,905	484.84	50,731	43,914	534.22	44,428	50,217
35,000	380.35	101,926	464.10	66,490	35,436	522.14	54,634	47,292	575.31	47,846	54,080
40,000	434.68	116,485	530.39	75,987	40,498	596.72	62,438	54,047	657.49	54,679	61,806
45,000	489.02	131,047	596.70	85,487	45,560	671.32	70,244	60,803	739.69	61,516	69,531
50,000	543.35	145,606	662.99	94,984	50,622	745.90	78,047	67,559	821.87	68,349	77,257
55,000	597.69	160,168	729.30	104,484	55,684	820.50	85,853	74,315	904.06	75,185	84,983
60,000	652.02	174,727	795.59	113,981	60,746	895.08	93,657	81,070	986.24	82,019	92,708
65,000	706.36	189,290	861.89	123,481	65,810	969.68	101,463	87,827	1,068.43	88,855	100,435
70,000	760.69	203,848	928.19	132,977	70,871	1,044.26	109,266	94,582	1,150.61	95,689	108,159
75,000	815.02	218,407	994.48	142,474	75,933	1,118.85	117,070	101,337	1,232.79	102,523	115,884
80,000	869.36	232,970	1,060.78	151,974	80,996	1,193.44	124,876	108,094	1,314.99	109,359	123,611
85,000	923.69	247,528	1,127.08	161,471	86,057	1,268.03	132,679	114,849	1,397.16	116,193	131,335
90,000	978.03	262,091	1,193.38	170,971	91,120	1,342.63	140,485	121,606	1,479.36	123,029	139,062
95,000	1,032.36	276,650	1,259.68	180,468	96,182	1,417.21	148,289	128,361	1,561.54	129,863	146,787
100,000	1,086.70	291,212	1,325.98	189,968	101,244	1,491.81	156,095	135,117	1,643.73	136,699	154,513
105,000	1,141.03	305,771	1,392.27	199,465	106,306	1,566.39	163,898	141,873	1,725.91	143,533	162,238
110,000	1,195.37	320,333	1,458.58	208,964	111,369	1,640.99	171,704	148,629	1,808.10	150,369	169,964
115,000	1,249.70	334,892	1,524.87	218,461	116,431	1,715.57	179,508	155,384	1,890.28	157,202	177,690
120,000	1,304.04	349,454	1,591.18	227,961	121,493	1,790.17	187,314	162,141	1,972.48	164,038	185,416
125,000	1,358.37	364,013	1,657.47	237,458	126,555	1,864.75	195,117	168,896	2,054.66	170,872	193,141
130,000	1,412.71	378,576	1,723.77	246,958	131,618	1,939.35	202,923	175,653	2,136.85	177,708	200,868
135,000	1,467.04	393,134	1,790.07	256,455	136,679	2,013.93	210,727	182,407	2,219.03	184,542	208,592
140,000	1,521.38	407,697	1,856.37	265,955	141,742	2,088.53	218,533	189,164	2,301.22	191,378	216,319
145,000	1,575.71	422,256	1,922.67	275,452	146,804	2,163.11	226,336	195,920	2,383.40	198,212	224,044
150,000	1,630.04	436,814	1,988.96	284,949	151,865	2,237.70	234,140	202,674	2,465.58	205,046	231,768
155,000	1,684.38	451,377	2,055.26	294,448	156,929	2,312.29	241,946	209,431	2,547.78	211,882	239,495
160,000	1,738.71	465,936	2,121.56	303,945	161,991	2,386.88	249,749	216,187	2,629.95	218,716	247,220
165,000	1,793.05	480,498	2,187.86	313,445	167,053	2,461.47	257,555	222,943	2,712.15	225,552	254,946
170,000	1,847.38	495,057	2,254.15	322,942	172,115	2,536.06	265,359	229,698	2,794.33	232,386	262,671
175,000	1,901.72	509,619	2,320.46	332,442	177,177	2,610.65	273,164	236,455	2,876.52	239,222	270,397
180,000	1,956.05	524,178	2,386.75	341,939	182,239	2,685.24	280,968	243,210	2,958.70	246,056	278,122
185,000	2,010.39	538,740	2,453.06	351,439	187,301	2,759.83	288,774	249,966	3,040.90	252,892	285,848
190,000	2,064.72	553,299	2,519.35	360,936	192,363	2,834.42	296,578	256,721	3,123.07	259,725	293,574
195,000	2,119.06	567,862	2,585.66	370,435	197,427	2,909.02	304,383	263,479	3,205.27	266,561	301,301
200,000	2,173.39	582,420	2,651.95	379,933	202,487	2,983.60	312,187	270,233	3,287.45	273,395	309,025

146

AMOUNT OF LOAN	30 YEARS		4% PMT INCR/YR 159.718 PAYMENTS			5% PMT INCR/YR 147.203 PAYMENTS			6% PMT INCR/YR 137.322 PAYMENTS		
	MONTHLY PAYMENT	TOTAL INTRST	LAST YR MON PMT	TOTAL INTRST	INTRST SAVED	LAST YR MON PMT	TOTAL INTRST	INTRST SAVED	LAST YR MON PMT	TOTAL INTRST	INTRST SAVED
$ 50	0.55	148	0.92	63	85	0.99	58	90	1.04	54	94
100	1.09	292	1.81	124	168	1.96	114	178	2.07	107	185
200	2.18	585	3.63	248	337	3.91	229	356	4.14	214	371
300	3.27	877	5.44	373	504	5.87	343	534	6.21	321	556
400	4.35	1,166	7.24	495	671	7.81	456	710	8.26	425	741
500	5.44	1,458	9.06	619	839	9.77	570	888	10.33	532	926
600	6.53	1,751	10.87	743	1,008	11.73	685	1,066	12.40	639	1,112
700	7.61	2,040	12.67	865	1,175	13.67	797	1,243	14.45	744	1,296
800	8.70	2,332	14.49	990	1,342	15.62	912	1,420	16.52	851	1,481
900	9.79	2,624	16.30	1,114	1,510	17.58	1,026	1,598	18.58	958	1,666
1,000	10.87	2,913	18.10	1,236	1,677	19.52	1,139	1,774	20.63	1,063	1,850
2,000	21.74	5,826	36.20	2,472	3,354	39.04	2,278	3,548	41.27	2,125	3,701
3,000	32.61	8,740	54.30	3,708	5,032	58.56	3,416	5,324	61.90	3,188	5,552
4,000	43.47	11,649	72.38	4,942	6,707	78.07	4,553	7,096	82.52	4,249	7,400
5,000	54.34	14,562	90.48	6,178	8,384	97.59	5,692	8,870	103.15	5,312	9,250
6,000	65.21	17,476	108.58	7,415	10,061	117.11	6,831	10,645	123.79	6,374	11,102
7,000	76.07	20,385	126.66	8,649	11,736	136.61	7,967	12,418	144.40	7,435	12,950
8,000	86.94	23,298	144.76	9,885	13,413	156.13	9,106	14,192	165.04	8,498	14,800
9,000	97.81	26,212	162.86	11,121	15,091	175.65	10,245	15,967	185.67	9,561	16,651
10,000	108.67	29,121	180.94	12,355	16,766	195.16	11,382	17,739	206.29	10,621	18,500
11,000	119.54	32,034	199.04	13,591	18,443	214.68	12,520	19,514	226.92	11,684	20,350
12,000	130.41	34,948	217.14	14,827	20,121	234.20	13,659	21,289	247.56	12,747	22,201
13,000	141.28	37,861	235.24	16,063	21,798	253.72	14,798	23,063	268.19	13,810	24,051
14,000	152.14	40,770	253.32	17,297	23,473	273.22	15,935	24,835	288.81	14,870	25,900
15,000	163.01	43,684	271.42	18,533	25,151	292.74	17,073	26,611	309.44	15,933	27,751
16,000	173.88	46,597	289.52	19,769	26,828	312.26	18,212	28,385	330.08	16,996	29,601
17,000	184.74	49,506	307.61	21,003	28,503	331.77	19,349	30,157	350.69	18,057	31,449
18,000	195.61	52,420	325.71	22,239	30,181	351.29	20,488	31,932	371.33	19,119	33,301
19,000	206.48	55,333	343.80	23,476	31,857	370.81	21,627	33,706	391.96	20,182	35,151
20,000	217.34	58,242	361.89	24,710	33,532	390.31	22,763	35,479	412.58	21,243	36,999
21,000	228.21	61,156	379.99	25,946	35,210	409.83	23,902	37,254	433.21	22,306	38,850
22,000	239.08	64,069	398.09	27,182	36,887	429.35	25,041	39,028	453.85	23,368	40,701
23,000	249.94	66,978	416.17	28,416	38,562	448.86	26,178	40,800	474.46	24,429	42,549
24,000	260.81	69,892	434.27	29,652	40,240	468.38	27,316	42,576	495.10	25,492	44,400
25,000	271.68	72,805	452.37	30,888	41,917	487.90	28,455	44,350	515.73	26,555	46,250
26,000	282.55	75,718	470.47	32,124	43,594	507.42	29,594	46,124	536.36	27,617	48,101
27,000	293.41	78,628	488.55	33,358	45,270	526.92	30,731	47,897	556.98	28,678	49,950
28,000	304.28	81,541	506.65	34,594	46,947	546.44	31,869	49,672	577.61	29,741	51,800
29,000	315.15	84,454	524.75	35,830	48,624	565.96	33,008	51,446	598.25	30,804	53,650
30,000	326.01	87,364	542.83	37,064	50,300	585.47	34,145	53,219	618.86	31,864	55,500
32,500	353.18	94,645	588.07	40,154	54,491	634.26	36,991	57,654	670.44	34,520	60,125
35,000	380.35	101,926	633.31	43,243	58,683	683.05	39,837	62,089	722.02	37,176	64,750
40,000	434.68	116,485	723.77	49,419	67,064	780.62	45,527	70,958	825.15	42,486	73,999
45,000	489.02	131,047	814.25	55,598	75,449	878.21	51,218	79,829	928.31	47,798	83,249
50,000	543.35	145,606	904.72	61,774	83,832	975.78	56,908	88,698	1,031.44	53,107	92,499
55,000	597.69	160,168	995.20	67,952	92,216	1,073.37	62,600	97,568	1,134.59	58,419	101,749
60,000	652.02	174,727	1,085.66	74,129	100,598	1,170.93	68,290	106,437	1,237.73	63,729	110,998
65,000	706.36	189,290	1,176.14	80,307	108,983	1,268.52	73,982	115,308	1,340.88	69,041	120,249
70,000	760.69	203,848	1,266.60	86,484	117,364	1,366.09	79,672	124,176	1,444.02	74,350	129,498
75,000	815.02	218,407	1,357.07	92,660	125,747	1,463.66	85,361	133,046	1,547.15	79,660	138,747
80,000	869.36	232,970	1,447.55	98,838	134,132	1,561.25	91,053	141,917	1,650.30	84,972	147,998
85,000	923.69	247,528	1,538.01	105,015	142,513	1,658.81	96,743	150,785	1,753.44	90,282	157,246
90,000	978.03	262,091	1,628.49	111,193	150,898	1,756.40	102,435	159,656	1,856.59	95,593	166,498
95,000	1,032.36	276,650	1,718.96	117,370	159,280	1,853.97	108,125	168,525	1,959.73	100,903	175,747
100,000	1,086.70	291,212	1,809.44	123,548	167,664	1,951.56	113,817	177,395	2,062.88	106,215	184,997
105,000	1,141.03	305,771	1,899.90	129,724	176,047	2,049.13	119,506	186,265	2,166.02	111,525	194,246
110,000	1,195.37	320,333	1,990.38	135,903	184,430	2,146.71	125,198	195,135	2,269.17	116,836	203,497
115,000	1,249.70	334,892	2,080.84	142,079	192,813	2,244.28	130,888	204,004	2,372.30	122,146	212,746
120,000	1,304.04	349,454	2,171.32	148,258	201,196	2,341.87	136,580	212,874	2,475.46	127,458	221,996
125,000	1,358.37	364,013	2,261.79	154,434	209,579	2,439.44	142,270	221,743	2,578.59	132,768	231,245
130,000	1,412.71	378,576	2,352.27	160,613	217,963	2,537.02	147,961	230,615	2,681.75	138,079	240,497
135,000	1,467.04	393,134	2,442.73	166,789	226,345	2,634.59	153,651	239,483	2,784.88	143,389	249,745
140,000	1,521.38	407,697	2,533.21	172,967	234,730	2,732.18	159,343	248,354	2,888.03	148,701	258,996
145,000	1,575.71	422,256	2,623.67	179,144	243,112	2,829.75	165,033	257,223	2,991.17	154,011	268,245
150,000	1,630.04	436,814	2,714.14	185,320	251,494	2,927.32	170,723	266,091	3,094.30	159,320	277,494
155,000	1,684.38	451,377	2,804.62	191,499	259,878	3,024.90	176,415	274,962	3,197.46	164,632	286,745
160,000	1,738.71	465,936	2,895.08	197,675	268,261	3,122.47	182,104	283,832	3,300.59	169,942	295,994
165,000	1,793.05	480,498	2,985.56	203,853	276,645	3,220.06	187,796	292,702	3,403.74	175,254	305,244
170,000	1,847.38	495,057	3,076.02	210,030	285,027	3,317.63	193,486	301,571	3,506.88	180,563	314,494
175,000	1,901.72	509,619	3,166.50	216,208	293,411	3,415.22	199,178	310,441	3,610.03	185,875	323,744
180,000	1,956.05	524,178	3,256.97	222,385	301,793	3,512.78	204,868	319,310	3,713.17	191,185	332,993
185,000	2,010.39	538,740	3,347.45	228,563	310,177	3,610.37	210,560	328,180	3,816.32	196,497	342,243
190,000	2,064.72	553,299	3,437.91	234,739	318,560	3,707.94	216,249	337,050	3,919.45	201,806	351,493
195,000	2,119.06	567,862	3,528.39	240,918	326,944	3,805.53	221,941	345,921	4,022.61	207,118	360,744
200,000	2,173.39	582,420	3,618.85	247,094	335,326	3,903.10	227,631	354,789	4,125.74	212,428	369,992

GROWING EQUITY MORTGAGES

AMOUNT OF LOAN	30 YEARS		1% PMT INCR/YR 240.311 PAYMENTS			2% PMT INCR/YR 199.060 PAYMENTS			3% PMT INCR/YR 174.948 PAYMENTS		
	MONTHLY PAYMENT	TOTAL INTRST	LAST YR MON PMT	TOTAL INTRST	INTRST SAVED	LAST YR MON PMT	TOTAL INTRST	INTRST SAVED	LAST YR MON PMT	TOTAL INTRST	INTRST SAVED
$ 50	0.56	152	0.68	98	54	0.77	81	71	0.85	71	81
100	1.11	300	1.35	194	106	1.52	159	141	1.68	139	161
200	2.22	599	2.71	387	212	3.05	318	281	3.36	279	320
300	3.32	895	4.05	578	317	4.56	475	420	5.02	416	479
400	4.43	1,195	5.41	772	423	6.08	634	561	6.70	555	640
500	5.54	1,494	6.76	966	528	7.61	793	701	8.38	694	800
600	6.64	1,790	8.10	1,157	633	9.12	950	840	10.04	831	959
700	7.75	2,090	9.46	1,351	739	10.64	1,109	981	11.72	970	1,120
800	8.85	2,386	10.80	1,542	844	12.15	1,265	1,121	13.39	1,108	1,278
900	9.96	2,686	12.15	1,735	951	13.67	1,424	1,262	15.07	1,247	1,439
1,000	11.07	2,985	13.51	1,929	1,056	15.20	1,583	1,402	16.74	1,386	1,599
2,000	22.13	5,967	27.00	3,856	2,111	30.38	3,164	2,803	33.47	2,770	3,197
3,000	33.19	8,948	40.50	5,782	3,166	45.56	4,745	4,203	50.20	4,154	4,794
4,000	44.25	11,930	53.99	7,709	4,221	60.75	6,326	5,604	66.93	5,538	6,392
5,000	55.31	14,912	67.49	9,635	5,277	75.93	7,907	7,005	83.66	6,922	7,990
6,000	66.38	17,897	81.00	11,565	6,332	91.13	9,491	8,406	100.41	8,308	9,589
7,000	77.44	20,878	94.49	13,491	7,387	106.31	11,072	9,806	117.13	9,692	11,186
8,000	88.50	23,860	107.99	15,418	8,442	121.49	12,653	11,207	133.86	11,076	12,784
9,000	99.56	26,842	121.48	17,344	9,498	136.67	14,234	12,608	150.59	12,460	14,382
10,000	110.62	29,823	134.98	19,271	10,552	151.86	15,815	14,008	167.32	13,844	15,979
11,000	121.69	32,808	148.48	21,200	11,608	167.05	17,398	15,410	184.07	15,230	17,578
12,000	132.75	35,790	161.98	23,127	12,663	182.24	18,979	16,811	200.80	16,614	19,176
13,000	143.81	38,772	175.48	25,053	13,719	197.42	20,560	18,212	217.53	17,998	20,774
14,000	154.87	41,753	188.97	26,980	14,773	212.60	22,141	19,612	234.25	19,382	22,371
15,000	165.93	44,735	202.47	28,906	15,829	227.79	23,722	21,013	250.98	20,765	23,970
16,000	177.00	47,720	215.97	30,836	16,884	242.98	25,305	22,415	267.73	22,152	25,568
17,000	188.06	50,702	229.47	32,762	17,940	258.17	26,886	23,816	284.46	23,535	27,167
18,000	199.12	53,683	242.96	34,689	18,994	273.35	28,467	25,216	301.19	24,919	28,764
19,000	210.18	56,665	256.46	36,615	20,050	288.53	30,048	26,617	317.92	26,303	30,362
20,000	221.24	59,646	269.95	38,542	21,104	303.72	31,629	28,017	334.65	27,687	31,959
21,000	232.31	62,632	283.46	40,471	22,161	318.91	33,213	29,419	351.39	29,073	33,559
22,000	243.37	65,613	296.96	42,398	23,215	334.09	34,794	30,819	368.12	30,457	35,156
23,000	254.43	68,595	310.45	44,324	24,271	349.28	36,375	32,220	384.85	31,841	36,754
24,000	265.49	71,576	323.95	46,251	25,325	364.46	37,956	33,620	401.58	33,225	38,351
25,000	276.55	74,558	337.44	48,177	26,381	379.64	39,537	35,021	418.31	34,609	39,949
26,000	287.62	77,543	350.95	50,106	27,437	394.84	41,120	36,423	435.05	35,995	41,548
27,000	298.68	80,525	364.45	52,033	28,492	410.02	42,701	37,824	451.78	37,379	43,146
28,000	309.74	83,506	377.94	53,960	29,546	425.21	44,282	39,224	468.51	38,763	44,743
29,000	320.80	86,488	391.44	55,886	30,602	440.39	45,863	40,625	485.24	40,147	46,341
30,000	331.86	89,470	404.93	57,813	31,657	455.57	47,444	42,026	501.97	41,531	47,939
32,500	359.52	96,927	438.68	62,632	34,295	493.54	51,399	45,528	543.81	44,993	51,934
35,000	387.17	104,381	472.42	67,448	36,933	531.50	55,351	49,030	585.63	48,453	55,928
40,000	442.48	119,293	539.91	77,084	42,209	607.43	63,259	56,034	669.29	55,375	63,918
45,000	497.79	134,204	607.40	86,719	47,485	683.36	71,166	63,038	752.95	62,296	71,908
50,000	553.10	149,116	674.89	96,354	52,762	759.29	79,073	70,043	836.61	69,218	79,898
55,000	608.41	164,028	742.38	105,990	58,038	835.22	86,981	77,047	920.27	76,140	87,888
60,000	663.72	178,939	809.86	115,625	63,314	911.15	94,888	84,051	1,003.94	83,062	95,877
65,000	719.03	193,851	877.35	125,261	68,590	987.07	102,795	91,056	1,087.60	89,984	103,867
70,000	774.34	208,762	944.84	134,896	73,866	1,063.00	110,703	98,060	1,171.26	96,905	111,857
75,000	829.65	223,674	1,012.33	144,532	79,142	1,138.93	118,610	105,064	1,254.92	103,827	119,847
80,000	884.96	238,586	1,079.82	154,167	84,419	1,214.86	126,517	112,069	1,338.58	110,749	127,837
85,000	940.27	253,497	1,147.31	163,803	89,694	1,290.79	134,425	119,072	1,422.24	117,671	135,826
90,000	995.58	268,409	1,214.80	173,438	94,971	1,366.72	142,332	126,077	1,505.90	124,593	143,816
95,000	1,050.89	283,320	1,282.29	183,073	100,247	1,442.65	150,239	133,081	1,589.57	131,514	151,806
100,000	1,106.20	298,232	1,349.77	192,709	105,523	1,518.58	158,146	140,086	1,673.23	138,436	159,796
105,000	1,161.51	313,144	1,417.26	202,344	110,800	1,594.50	166,054	147,090	1,756.89	145,358	167,786
110,000	1,216.82	328,055	1,484.75	211,980	116,075	1,670.43	173,961	154,094	1,840.55	152,280	175,775
115,000	1,272.13	342,967	1,552.24	221,615	121,352	1,746.36	181,868	161,099	1,924.21	159,202	183,765
120,000	1,327.44	357,878	1,619.73	231,251	126,627	1,822.29	189,776	168,102	2,007.87	166,124	191,754
125,000	1,382.75	372,790	1,687.22	240,886	131,904	1,898.22	197,683	175,107	2,091.53	173,045	199,745
130,000	1,438.06	387,702	1,754.71	250,522	137,180	1,974.15	205,590	182,112	2,175.19	179,967	207,735
135,000	1,493.37	402,613	1,822.20	260,157	142,456	2,050.08	213,498	189,115	2,258.86	186,889	215,724
140,000	1,548.68	417,525	1,889.68	269,792	147,733	2,126.01	221,405	196,120	2,342.52	193,811	223,714
145,000	1,603.99	432,436	1,957.17	279,428	153,008	2,201.93	229,312	203,124	2,426.18	200,733	231,703
150,000	1,659.30	447,348	2,024.66	289,063	158,285	2,277.86	237,220	210,128	2,509.84	207,654	239,694
155,000	1,714.61	462,260	2,092.15	298,699	163,561	2,353.79	245,127	217,133	2,593.50	214,576	247,684
160,000	1,769.92	477,171	2,159.64	308,334	168,837	2,429.72	253,034	224,137	2,677.16	221,498	255,673
165,000	1,825.23	492,083	2,227.13	317,970	174,113	2,505.65	260,942	231,141	2,760.82	228,420	263,663
170,000	1,880.54	506,994	2,294.62	327,605	179,389	2,581.58	268,849	238,145	2,844.49	235,342	271,652
175,000	1,935.85	521,906	2,362.10	337,240	184,666	2,657.51	276,756	245,150	2,928.15	242,263	279,643
180,000	1,991.16	536,818	2,429.59	346,876	189,942	2,733.44	284,664	252,154	3,011.81	249,185	287,633
185,000	2,046.47	551,729	2,497.08	356,511	195,218	2,809.36	292,571	259,158	3,095.47	256,107	295,622
190,000	2,101.78	566,641	2,564.57	366,147	200,494	2,885.29	300,478	266,163	3,179.13	263,029	303,612
195,000	2,157.09	581,552	2,632.06	375,782	205,770	2,961.22	308,386	273,166	3,262.79	269,951	311,601
200,000	2,212.40	596,464	2,699.55	385,418	211,046	3,037.15	316,293	280,171	3,346.45	276,873	319,591

AMOUNT OF LOAN	30 YEARS		4% PMT INCR/YR 158.382 PAYMENTS			5% PMT INCR/YR 145.985 PAYMENTS			6% PMT INCR/YR 136.190 PAYMENTS		
	MONTHLY PAYMENT	TOTAL INTRST	LAST YR MON PMT	TOTAL INTRST	INTRST SAVED	LAST YR MON PMT	TOTAL INTRST	INTRST SAVED	LAST YR MON PMT	TOTAL INTRST	INTRST SAVED
$ 50	0.56	152	0.93	64	88	1.01	59	93	1.06	55	97
100	1.11	300	1.85	126	174	1.99	116	184	2.11	108	192
200	2.22	599	3.70	252	347	3.99	232	367	4.21	217	382
300	3.32	895	5.53	376	519	5.96	346	549	6.30	323	572
400	4.43	1,195	7.38	501	694	7.96	462	733	8.41	431	764
500	5.54	1,494	9.22	627	867	9.95	578	916	10.52	539	955
600	6.64	1,790	11.06	751	1,039	11.92	692	1,098	12.60	646	1,144
700	7.75	2,090	12.90	877	1,213	13.92	808	1,282	14.71	754	1,336
800	8.85	2,386	14.74	1,001	1,385	15.89	922	1,464	16.80	860	1,526
900	9.96	2,686	16.58	1,127	1,559	17.89	1,038	1,648	18.91	969	1,717
1,000	11.07	2,985	18.43	1,253	1,732	19.88	1,154	1,831	21.01	1,077	1,908
2,000	22.13	5,967	36.85	2,503	3,464	39.74	2,306	3,661	42.01	2,152	3,815
3,000	33.19	8,948	55.26	3,754	5,194	59.60	3,458	5,490	63.00	3,227	5,721
4,000	44.25	11,930	73.68	5,004	6,926	79.47	4,610	7,320	84.00	4,302	7,628
5,000	55.31	14,912	92.10	6,255	8,657	99.33	5,762	9,150	104.99	5,377	9,535
6,000	66.38	17,897	110.53	7,508	10,389	119.21	6,916	10,981	126.01	6,454	11,443
7,000	77.44	20,878	128.94	8,758	12,120	139.07	8,068	12,810	147.00	7,529	13,349
8,000	88.50	23,860	147.36	10,008	13,851	158.93	9,219	14,641	168.00	8,604	15,256
9,000	99.56	26,842	165.77	11,259	15,583	178.80	10,371	16,471	188.99	9,679	17,163
10,000	110.62	29,823	184.19	12,510	17,313	198.66	11,523	18,300	209.99	10,754	19,069
11,000	121.69	32,808	202.62	13,762	19,046	218.54	12,677	20,131	231.00	11,831	20,977
12,000	132.75	35,790	221.04	15,013	20,777	238.40	13,829	21,961	252.00	12,906	22,884
13,000	143.81	38,772	239.45	16,264	22,508	258.26	14,981	23,791	272.99	13,981	24,791
14,000	154.87	41,753	257.87	17,514	24,239	278.12	16,133	25,620	293.99	15,056	26,697
15,000	165.93	44,735	276.29	18,765	25,970	297.99	17,285	27,450	314.98	16,131	28,604
16,000	177.00	47,720	294.72	20,017	27,703	317.87	18,439	29,281	336.00	17,208	30,512
17,000	188.06	50,702	313.13	21,268	29,434	337.73	19,591	31,111	356.99	18,283	32,419
18,000	199.12	53,683	331.55	22,519	31,164	357.59	20,743	32,940	377.99	19,358	34,325
19,000	210.18	56,665	349.97	23,769	32,896	377.45	21,895	34,770	398.98	20,433	36,232
20,000	221.24	59,646	368.38	25,020	34,626	397.32	23,047	36,599	419.98	21,508	38,138
21,000	232.31	62,632	386.81	26,272	36,360	417.20	24,201	38,431	440.99	22,585	40,047
22,000	243.37	65,613	405.23	27,523	38,090	437.06	25,353	40,260	461.99	23,660	41,953
23,000	254.43	68,595	423.64	28,774	39,821	456.92	26,505	42,090	482.98	24,735	43,860
24,000	265.49	71,576	442.06	30,024	41,552	476.78	27,656	43,920	503.98	25,810	45,766
25,000	276.55	74,558	460.48	31,275	43,283	496.64	28,808	45,750	524.97	26,885	47,673
26,000	287.62	77,543	478.91	32,527	45,016	516.52	29,962	47,581	545.99	27,961	49,582
27,000	298.68	80,525	497.32	33,778	46,747	536.39	31,114	49,411	566.98	29,036	51,489
28,000	309.74	83,506	515.74	35,028	48,478	556.25	32,266	51,240	587.98	30,111	53,395
29,000	320.80	86,488	534.16	36,279	50,209	576.11	33,418	53,070	608.97	31,186	55,302
30,000	331.86	89,470	552.57	37,530	51,940	595.97	34,570	54,900	629.97	32,261	57,209
32,500	359.52	96,927	598.63	40,658	56,269	645.65	37,452	59,475	682.48	34,951	61,976
35,000	387.17	104,381	644.67	43,785	60,596	695.30	40,332	64,049	734.96	37,638	66,743
40,000	442.48	119,293	736.76	50,039	69,254	794.63	46,093	73,200	839.96	43,015	76,278
45,000	497.79	134,204	828.86	56,294	77,910	893.96	51,855	82,349	944.95	48,392	85,812
50,000	553.10	149,116	920.95	62,549	86,567	993.29	57,617	91,499	1,049.95	53,769	95,347
55,000	608.41	164,028	1,013.05	68,804	95,224	1,092.62	63,379	100,649	1,154.94	59,146	104,882
60,000	663.72	178,939	1,105.14	75,059	103,880	1,191.95	69,140	109,799	1,259.94	64,523	114,416
65,000	719.03	193,851	1,197.24	81,314	112,537	1,291.27	74,902	118,949	1,364.93	69,900	123,951
70,000	774.34	208,762	1,289.32	87,569	121,193	1,390.60	80,664	128,098	1,469.93	75,277	133,485
75,000	829.65	223,674	1,381.43	93,824	129,850	1,489.93	86,425	137,249	1,574.92	80,654	143,020
80,000	884.96	238,586	1,473.52	100,079	138,507	1,589.26	92,187	146,399	1,679.92	86,031	152,555
85,000	940.27	253,497	1,565.62	106,334	147,163	1,688.59	97,949	155,548	1,784.91	91,407	162,090
90,000	995.58	268,409	1,657.71	112,589	155,820	1,787.92	103,710	164,699	1,889.91	96,784	171,625
95,000	1,050.89	283,320	1,749.81	118,844	164,476	1,887.25	109,472	173,849	1,994.90	102,161	181,159
100,000	1,106.20	298,232	1,841.90	125,099	173,133	1,986.58	115,234	182,998	2,099.90	107,538	190,694
105,000	1,161.51	313,144	1,934.00	131,354	181,790	2,085.91	120,995	192,149	2,204.89	112,915	200,229
110,000	1,216.82	328,055	2,026.09	137,609	190,446	2,185.23	126,757	201,298	2,309.89	118,292	209,763
115,000	1,272.13	342,967	2,118.19	143,864	199,103	2,284.56	132,519	210,448	2,414.88	123,669	219,298
120,000	1,327.44	357,878	2,210.29	150,118	207,760	2,383.89	138,280	219,598	2,519.88	129,046	228,832
125,000	1,382.75	372,790	2,302.38	156,373	216,417	2,483.22	144,042	228,748	2,624.87	134,423	238,367
130,000	1,438.06	387,702	2,394.48	162,628	225,074	2,582.55	149,804	237,898	2,729.87	139,800	247,902
135,000	1,493.37	402,613	2,486.57	168,883	233,730	2,681.88	155,565	247,048	2,834.86	145,176	257,437
140,000	1,548.68	417,525	2,578.67	175,138	242,387	2,781.21	161,327	256,198	2,939.86	150,553	266,972
145,000	1,603.99	432,436	2,670.76	181,393	251,043	2,880.54	167,089	265,347	3,044.85	155,930	276,506
150,000	1,659.30	447,348	2,762.86	187,648	259,700	2,979.86	172,850	274,498	3,149.85	161,307	286,041
155,000	1,714.61	462,260	2,854.95	193,903	268,357	3,079.19	178,612	283,648	3,254.84	166,684	295,576
160,000	1,769.92	477,171	2,947.05	200,158	277,013	3,178.52	184,374	292,797	3,359.84	172,061	305,110
165,000	1,825.23	492,083	3,039.14	206,413	285,670	3,277.85	190,136	301,947	3,464.83	177,438	314,645
170,000	1,880.54	506,994	3,131.24	212,668	294,326	3,377.18	195,897	311,097	3,569.83	182,815	324,179
175,000	1,935.85	521,906	3,223.33	218,923	302,983	3,476.51	201,659	320,247	3,674.82	188,192	333,714
180,000	1,991.16	536,818	3,315.43	225,178	311,640	3,575.84	207,421	329,397	3,779.82	193,569	343,249
185,000	2,046.47	551,729	3,407.52	231,433	320,296	3,675.17	213,182	338,547	3,884.81	198,946	352,783
190,000	2,101.78	566,641	3,499.62	237,688	328,953	3,774.49	218,944	347,697	3,989.81	204,322	362,319
195,000	2,157.09	581,552	3,591.71	243,942	337,610	3,873.82	224,706	356,846	4,094.80	209,699	371,853
200,000	2,212.40	596,464	3,683.81	250,197	346,267	3,973.15	230,467	365,997	4,199.80	215,076	381,388

GROWING EQUITY MORTGAGES

AMOUNT OF LOAN	30 YEARS		1% PMT INCR/YR 238.476 PAYMENTS			2% PMT INCR/YR 197.405 PAYMENTS			3% PMT INCR/YR 173.472 PAYMENTS		
	MONTHLY PAYMENT	TOTAL INTRST	LAST YR MON PMT	TOTAL INTRST	INTRST SAVED	LAST YR MON PMT	TOTAL INTRST	INTRST SAVED	LAST YR MON PMT	TOTAL INTRST	INTRST SAVED
$ 50	0.57	155	0.69	100	55	0.78	82	73	0.86	72	83
100	1.13	307	1.37	196	111	1.55	161	146	1.71	141	166
200	2.26	614	2.73	393	221	3.10	322	292	3.42	282	332
300	3.38	917	4.08	587	330	4.64	481	436	5.11	421	496
400	4.51	1,224	5.45	783	441	6.19	642	582	6.82	562	662
500	5.63	1,527	6.80	977	550	7.73	801	726	8.52	701	826
600	6.76	1,834	8.17	1,174	660	9.28	962	872	10.23	842	992
700	7.89	2,140	9.53	1,370	770	10.83	1,123	1,017	11.93	983	1,157
800	9.01	2,444	10.89	1,564	880	12.37	1,282	1,162	13.63	1,122	1,322
900	10.14	2,750	12.25	1,761	989	13.92	1,443	1,307	15.34	1,263	1,487
1,000	11.26	3,054	13.60	1,954	1,100	15.46	1,602	1,452	17.03	1,402	1,652
2,000	22.52	6,107	27.21	3,909	2,198	30.92	3,204	2,903	34.06	2,804	3,303
3,000	33.78	9,161	40.81	5,863	3,298	46.37	4,806	4,355	51.10	4,206	4,955
4,000	45.04	12,214	54.41	7,818	4,396	61.83	6,408	5,806	68.13	5,608	6,606
5,000	56.29	15,264	68.00	9,770	5,494	77.27	8,008	7,256	85.14	7,007	8,257
6,000	67.55	18,318	81.61	11,724	6,594	92.73	9,610	8,708	102.18	8,409	9,909
7,000	78.81	21,372	95.21	13,679	7,693	108.19	11,212	10,160	119.21	9,811	11,561
8,000	90.07	24,425	108.81	15,633	8,792	123.65	12,814	11,611	136.24	11,213	13,212
9,000	101.32	27,475	122.41	17,585	9,890	139.09	14,414	13,061	153.26	12,613	14,862
10,000	112.58	30,529	136.01	19,540	10,989	154.55	16,016	14,513	170.29	14,015	16,514
11,000	123.84	33,582	149.61	21,494	12,088	170.01	17,618	15,964	187.32	15,417	18,165
12,000	135.10	36,636	163.22	23,448	13,188	185.46	19,220	17,416	204.35	16,819	19,817
13,000	146.36	39,690	176.82	25,403	14,287	200.92	20,823	18,867	221.38	18,220	21,470
14,000	157.61	42,740	190.41	27,355	15,385	216.36	22,422	20,318	238.40	19,620	23,120
15,000	168.87	45,793	204.01	29,309	16,484	231.82	24,024	21,769	255.43	21,022	24,771
16,000	180.13	48,847	217.62	31,264	17,583	247.28	25,626	23,221	272.46	22,424	26,423
17,000	191.39	51,900	231.22	33,218	18,682	262.74	27,229	24,671	289.49	23,826	28,074
18,000	202.64	54,950	244.81	35,170	19,780	278.18	28,828	26,122	306.51	25,226	29,724
19,000	213.90	58,004	258.41	37,125	20,879	293.64	30,430	27,574	323.54	26,628	31,376
20,000	225.16	61,058	272.02	39,079	21,979	309.10	32,033	29,025	340.57	28,030	33,028
21,000	236.42	64,111	285.62	41,034	23,077	324.55	33,635	30,476	357.61	29,431	34,680
22,000	247.68	67,165	299.22	42,988	24,177	340.01	35,237	31,928	374.64	30,833	36,332
23,000	258.93	70,215	312.82	44,940	25,275	355.46	36,836	33,379	391.65	32,233	37,982
24,000	270.19	73,268	326.42	46,894	26,374	370.91	38,439	34,829	408.69	33,635	39,633
25,000	281.45	76,322	340.02	48,849	27,473	386.37	40,041	36,281	425.72	35,037	41,285
26,000	292.71	79,376	353.63	50,803	28,573	401.83	41,643	37,733	442.75	36,439	42,937
27,000	303.96	82,426	367.22	52,755	29,671	417.27	43,243	39,183	459.77	37,839	44,587
28,000	315.22	85,479	380.82	54,710	30,769	432.73	44,845	40,634	476.80	39,240	46,239
29,000	326.48	88,533	394.42	56,664	31,869	448.19	46,447	42,086	493.83	40,642	47,891
30,000	337.74	91,586	408.03	58,619	32,967	463.64	48,049	43,537	510.86	42,044	49,542
32,500	365.88	99,217	442.02	63,502	35,715	502.27	52,052	47,165	553.43	45,547	53,670
35,000	394.03	106,851	476.03	68,388	38,463	540.92	56,057	50,794	596.01	49,052	57,799
40,000	450.31	122,112	544.02	78,155	43,957	618.18	64,063	58,049	681.13	56,057	66,055
45,000	506.60	137,376	612.03	87,925	49,451	695.45	72,071	65,305	766.28	63,064	74,312
50,000	562.89	152,640	680.03	97,695	54,945	772.73	80,079	72,561	851.42	70,072	82,568
55,000	619.18	167,905	748.04	107,465	60,440	850.00	88,087	79,818	936.57	77,079	90,826
60,000	675.47	183,169	816.04	117,234	65,935	927.28	96,095	87,074	1,021.71	84,086	99,083
65,000	731.76	198,434	884.05	127,004	71,430	1,004.55	104,103	94,331	1,106.85	91,094	107,340
70,000	788.05	213,698	952.05	136,774	76,924	1,081.82	112,112	101,586	1,192.00	98,101	115,597
75,000	844.34	228,962	1,020.05	146,544	82,418	1,159.10	120,120	108,842	1,277.14	105,109	123,853
80,000	900.62	244,223	1,088.05	156,311	87,912	1,236.36	128,125	116,098	1,362.27	112,114	132,109
85,000	956.91	259,488	1,156.05	166,081	93,407	1,313.63	136,134	123,354	1,447.41	119,121	140,367
90,000	1,013.20	274,752	1,224.06	175,850	98,902	1,390.91	144,142	130,610	1,532.56	126,129	148,623
95,000	1,069.49	290,016	1,292.06	185,620	104,396	1,468.18	152,150	137,866	1,617.70	133,136	156,880
100,000	1,125.78	305,281	1,360.06	195,390	109,891	1,545.45	160,158	145,123	1,702.84	140,143	165,138
105,000	1,182.07	320,545	1,428.07	205,160	115,385	1,622.73	168,166	152,379	1,787.99	147,151	173,394
110,000	1,238.36	335,810	1,496.07	214,929	120,881	1,700.00	176,174	159,636	1,873.13	154,158	181,652
115,000	1,294.64	351,070	1,564.07	224,697	126,373	1,777.26	184,180	166,890	1,958.26	161,163	189,907
120,000	1,350.93	366,335	1,632.07	234,466	131,869	1,854.54	192,188	174,147	2,043.40	168,171	198,164
125,000	1,407.22	381,599	1,700.08	244,236	137,363	1,931.81	200,196	181,403	2,128.55	175,178	206,421
130,000	1,463.51	396,864	1,768.08	254,006	142,858	2,009.09	208,204	188,660	2,213.69	182,185	214,679
135,000	1,519.80	412,128	1,836.08	263,776	148,352	2,086.36	216,213	195,915	2,298.83	189,193	222,935
140,000	1,576.09	427,392	1,904.09	273,545	153,847	2,163.63	224,221	203,171	2,383.98	196,200	231,192
145,000	1,632.38	442,657	1,972.09	283,315	159,342	2,240.91	232,229	210,428	2,469.12	203,208	239,449
150,000	1,688.67	457,921	2,040.10	293,085	164,836	2,318.18	240,237	217,684	2,554.26	210,215	247,706
155,000	1,744.95	473,182	2,108.09	302,852	170,330	2,395.44	248,243	224,939	2,639.39	217,220	255,962
160,000	1,801.24	488,446	2,176.09	312,622	175,824	2,472.72	256,251	232,195	2,724.54	224,228	264,218
165,000	1,857.53	503,711	2,244.10	322,392	181,319	2,549.99	264,259	239,452	2,809.68	231,235	272,476
170,000	1,913.82	518,975	2,312.10	332,161	186,814	2,627.26	272,267	246,708	2,894.82	238,242	280,733
175,000	1,970.11	534,240	2,380.11	341,931	192,309	2,704.54	280,275	253,965	2,979.97	245,250	288,990
180,000	2,026.40	549,504	2,448.11	351,701	197,803	2,781.81	288,283	261,221	3,065.11	252,257	297,247
185,000	2,082.69	564,768	2,516.12	361,471	203,297	2,859.09	296,292	268,476	3,150.26	259,264	305,504
190,000	2,138.97	580,029	2,584.11	371,240	208,791	2,936.35	304,297	275,732	3,235.39	266,270	313,759
195,000	2,195.26	595,294	2,652.11	381,007	214,287	3,013.62	312,306	282,988	3,320.53	273,277	322,017
200,000	2,251.55	610,558	2,720.12	390,777	219,781	3,090.90	320,314	290,244	3,405.67	280,284	330,274

GROWING EQUITY MORTGAGES 13.25%

AMOUNT OF LOAN	30 YEARS		4% PMT INCR/YR 157.067 PAYMENTS			5% PMT INCR/YR 144.791 PAYMENTS			6% PMT INCR/YR 135.079 PAYMENTS		
	MONTHLY PAYMENT	TOTAL INTRST	LAST YR MON PMT	TOTAL INTRST	INTRST SAVED	LAST YR MON PMT	TOTAL INTRST	INTRST SAVED	LAST YR MON PMT	TOTAL INTRST	INTRST SAVED
$ 50	0.57	155	0.95	65	90	1.02	60	95	1.08	56	99
100	1.13	307	1.88	127	180	2.03	117	190	2.15	110	197
200	2.26	614	3.76	255	359	4.06	235	379	4.29	219	395
300	3.38	917	5.63	380	537	6.07	350	567	6.42	327	590
400	4.51	1,224	7.51	508	716	8.10	468	756	8.56	437	787
500	5.63	1,527	9.37	633	894	10.11	583	944	10.69	544	983
600	6.76	1,834	11.26	761	1,073	12.14	701	1,133	12.83	654	1,180
700	7.89	2,140	13.14	888	1,252	14.17	818	1,322	14.98	764	1,376
800	9.01	2,444	15.00	1,014	1,430	16.18	934	1,510	17.10	871	1,573
900	10.14	2,750	16.88	1,141	1,609	18.21	1,051	1,699	19.25	981	1,769
1,000	11.26	3,054	18.75	1,267	1,787	20.22	1,167	1,887	21.37	1,089	1,965
2,000	22.52	6,107	37.50	2,533	3,574	40.44	2,333	3,774	42.75	2,178	3,929
3,000	33.78	9,161	56.25	3,800	5,361	60.66	3,500	5,661	64.12	3,266	5,895
4,000	45.04	12,214	74.99	5,066	7,148	80.89	4,667	7,547	85.50	4,355	7,859
5,000	56.29	15,264	93.73	6,331	8,933	101.09	5,832	9,432	106.86	5,442	9,822
6,000	67.55	18,318	112.48	7,598	10,720	121.31	6,998	11,320	128.23	6,531	11,787
7,000	78.81	21,372	131.22	8,864	12,508	141.53	8,165	13,207	149.60	7,620	13,752
8,000	90.07	24,425	149.97	10,131	14,294	161.75	9,332	15,093	170.98	8,708	15,717
9,000	101.32	27,475	168.71	11,396	16,079	181.96	10,497	16,978	192.34	9,795	17,680
10,000	112.58	30,529	187.45	12,662	17,867	202.18	11,663	18,866	213.71	10,884	19,645
11,000	123.84	33,582	206.20	13,929	19,653	222.40	12,830	20,752	235.09	11,973	21,609
12,000	135.10	36,636	224.95	15,195	21,441	242.62	13,997	22,639	256.46	13,062	23,574
13,000	146.36	39,690	243.70	16,462	23,228	262.84	15,163	24,527	277.83	14,150	25,540
14,000	157.61	42,740	262.43	17,727	25,013	283.04	16,328	26,412	299.19	15,237	27,503
15,000	168.87	45,793	281.18	18,993	26,800	303.27	17,495	28,298	320.57	16,326	29,467
16,000	180.13	48,847	299.93	20,260	28,587	323.49	18,662	30,185	341.94	17,415	31,432
17,000	191.39	51,900	318.68	21,527	30,373	343.71	19,828	32,072	363.32	18,504	33,396
18,000	202.64	54,950	337.41	22,791	32,159	363.91	20,993	33,957	384.67	19,591	35,359
19,000	213.90	58,004	356.16	24,058	33,946	384.13	22,160	35,844	406.05	20,679	37,325
20,000	225.16	61,058	374.91	25,324	35,734	404.36	23,327	37,731	427.42	21,768	39,290
21,000	236.42	64,111	393.66	26,591	37,520	424.58	24,493	39,618	448.80	22,857	41,254
22,000	247.68	67,165	412.41	27,858	39,307	444.80	25,660	41,505	470.17	23,946	43,219
23,000	258.93	70,215	431.14	29,122	41,093	465.00	26,825	43,390	491.53	25,033	45,182
24,000	270.19	73,268	449.89	30,389	42,879	485.22	27,992	45,276	512.90	26,121	47,147
25,000	281.45	76,322	468.63	31,656	44,666	505.44	29,158	47,164	534.28	27,210	49,112
26,000	292.71	79,376	487.38	32,922	46,454	525.67	30,325	49,051	555.65	28,299	51,077
27,000	303.96	82,426	506.12	34,187	48,239	545.87	31,490	50,936	577.01	29,386	53,040
28,000	315.22	85,479	524.86	35,453	50,025	566.09	32,657	52,822	598.38	30,475	55,004
29,000	326.48	88,533	543.61	36,720	51,813	586.31	33,823	54,710	619.76	31,564	56,969
30,000	337.74	91,586	562.36	37,987	53,599	606.53	34,990	56,596	641.13	32,652	58,934
32,500	365.88	99,217	609.22	41,151	58,066	657.07	37,905	61,312	694.55	35,372	63,845
35,000	394.03	106,851	656.09	44,318	62,533	707.62	40,822	66,029	747.99	38,094	68,757
40,000	450.31	122,112	749.80	50,647	71,465	808.69	46,651	75,461	854.82	43,535	78,577
45,000	506.60	137,376	843.53	56,978	80,398	909.78	52,483	84,893	961.68	48,977	88,399
50,000	562.89	152,640	937.25	63,309	89,331	1,010.87	58,315	94,325	1,068.53	54,419	98,221
55,000	619.18	167,905	1,030.98	69,640	98,265	1,111.96	64,146	103,759	1,175.39	59,861	108,044
60,000	675.47	183,169	1,124.71	75,971	107,198	1,213.05	69,978	113,191	1,282.24	65,303	117,866
65,000	731.76	198,434	1,218.43	82,302	116,132	1,314.14	75,810	122,624	1,389.10	70,745	127,689
70,000	788.05	213,698	1,312.16	88,633	125,065	1,415.22	81,641	132,057	1,495.95	76,187	137,511
75,000	844.34	228,962	1,405.89	94,965	133,997	1,516.31	87,473	141,489	1,602.81	81,629	147,333
80,000	900.62	244,223	1,499.60	101,294	142,929	1,617.38	93,303	150,920	1,709.65	87,069	157,154
85,000	956.91	259,488	1,593.33	107,625	151,863	1,718.47	99,134	160,354	1,816.50	92,511	166,977
90,000	1,013.20	274,752	1,687.05	113,956	160,796	1,819.56	104,966	169,786	1,923.36	97,953	176,799
95,000	1,069.49	290,016	1,780.78	120,287	169,729	1,920.65	110,798	179,218	2,030.21	103,395	186,621
100,000	1,125.78	305,281	1,874.51	126,618	178,663	2,021.74	116,629	188,652	2,137.07	108,837	196,444
105,000	1,182.07	320,545	1,968.23	132,949	187,596	2,122.83	122,461	198,084	2,243.92	114,279	206,266
110,000	1,238.36	335,810	2,061.96	139,280	196,530	2,223.92	128,293	207,517	2,350.78	119,721	216,089
115,000	1,294.64	351,070	2,155.67	145,609	205,461	2,324.99	134,122	216,948	2,457.61	125,162	225,908
120,000	1,350.93	366,335	2,249.40	151,940	214,395	2,426.08	139,954	226,381	2,564.47	130,604	235,731
125,000	1,407.22	381,599	2,343.12	158,272	223,327	2,527.16	145,786	235,813	2,671.32	136,046	245,553
130,000	1,463.51	396,864	2,436.85	164,603	232,261	2,628.25	151,617	245,247	2,778.18	141,488	255,376
135,000	1,519.80	412,128	2,530.58	170,934	241,194	2,729.34	157,449	254,679	2,885.03	146,930	265,198
140,000	1,576.09	427,392	2,624.31	177,265	250,127	2,830.43	163,281	264,111	2,991.89	152,372	275,020
145,000	1,632.38	442,657	2,718.03	183,596	259,061	2,931.52	169,112	273,545	3,098.74	157,814	284,843
150,000	1,688.67	457,921	2,811.76	189,927	267,994	3,032.61	174,944	282,977	3,205.60	163,256	294,665
155,000	1,744.95	473,182	2,905.47	196,256	276,926	3,133.68	180,774	292,408	3,312.44	168,696	304,486
160,000	1,801.24	488,446	2,999.20	202,587	285,859	3,234.77	186,606	301,841	3,419.29	174,138	314,308
165,000	1,857.53	503,711	3,092.92	208,918	294,793	3,335.86	192,437	311,274	3,526.15	179,580	324,131
170,000	1,913.82	518,975	3,186.65	215,249	303,726	3,436.95	198,269	320,706	3,633.00	185,022	333,953
175,000	1,970.11	534,240	3,280.38	221,581	312,659	3,538.03	204,100	330,140	3,739.86	190,464	343,776
180,000	2,026.40	549,504	3,374.10	227,912	321,592	3,639.12	209,932	339,572	3,846.71	195,906	353,598
185,000	2,082.69	564,768	3,467.83	234,243	330,525	3,740.21	215,764	349,004	3,953.57	201,349	363,419
190,000	2,138.97	580,029	3,561.54	240,572	339,457	3,841.28	221,594	358,435	4,060.40	206,789	373,240
195,000	2,195.26	595,294	3,655.27	246,903	348,391	3,942.37	227,425	367,869	4,167.26	212,231	383,063
200,000	2,251.55	610,558	3,749.00	253,234	357,324	4,043.46	233,257	377,301	4,274.11	217,673	392,885

151

13.50% GROWING EQUITY MORTGAGES

AMOUNT OF LOAN	30 YEARS		1% PMT INCR/YR 236.646 PAYMENTS			2% PMT INCR/YR 195.769 PAYMENTS			3% PMT INCR/YR 172.017 PAYMENTS		
	MONTHLY PAYMENT	TOTAL INTRST	LAST YR MON PMT	TOTAL INTRST	INTRST SAVED	LAST YR MON PMT	TOTAL INTRST	INTRST SAVED	LAST YR MON PMT	TOTAL INTRST	INTRST SAVED
$ 50	0.58	159	0.70	101	58	0.80	83	76	0.88	72	87
100	1.15	314	1.39	199	115	1.58	163	151	1.74	143	171
200	2.30	628	2.78	398	230	3.16	326	302	3.48	286	342
300	3.44	938	4.16	595	343	4.72	487	451	5.20	426	512
400	4.59	1,252	5.55	794	458	6.30	650	602	6.94	569	683
500	5.73	1,563	6.92	991	572	7.87	811	752	8.67	710	853
600	6.88	1,877	8.31	1,190	687	9.44	974	903	10.41	852	1,025
700	8.02	2,187	9.69	1,387	800	11.01	1,135	1,052	12.13	993	1,194
800	9.17	2,501	11.08	1,586	915	12.59	1,299	1,202	13.87	1,136	1,365
900	10.31	2,812	12.46	1,782	1,030	14.15	1,459	1,353	15.59	1,277	1,535
1,000	11.46	3,126	13.84	1,982	1,144	15.73	1,623	1,503	17.33	1,419	1,707
2,000	22.91	6,248	27.68	3,961	2,287	31.45	3,243	3,005	34.65	2,837	3,411
3,000	34.37	9,373	41.52	5,942	3,431	47.18	4,865	4,508	51.99	4,256	5,117
4,000	45.82	12,495	55.36	7,921	4,574	62.90	6,486	6,009	69.31	5,673	6,822
5,000	57.28	15,621	69.20	9,903	5,718	78.63	8,108	7,513	86.64	7,092	8,529
6,000	68.73	18,743	83.03	11,882	6,861	94.35	9,729	9,014	103.96	8,510	10,233
7,000	80.18	21,865	96.87	13,861	8,004	110.07	11,349	10,516	121.28	9,927	11,938
8,000	91.64	24,990	110.71	15,843	9,147	125.80	12,971	12,019	138.61	11,346	13,644
9,000	103.09	28,112	124.54	17,822	10,290	141.52	14,592	13,520	155.93	12,764	15,348
10,000	114.55	31,238	138.39	19,803	11,435	157.25	16,214	15,024	173.27	14,183	17,055
11,000	126.00	34,360	152.22	21,782	12,578	172.97	17,835	16,525	190.59	15,600	18,760
12,000	137.45	37,482	166.05	23,761	13,721	188.69	19,455	18,027	207.91	17,017	20,465
13,000	148.91	40,608	179.90	25,743	14,865	204.42	21,077	19,531	225.24	18,437	22,171
14,000	160.36	43,730	193.73	27,722	16,008	220.14	22,698	21,032	242.56	19,854	23,876
15,000	171.82	46,855	207.58	29,703	17,152	235.87	24,320	22,535	259.89	21,273	25,582
16,000	183.27	49,977	221.41	31,682	18,295	251.59	25,941	24,036	277.21	22,690	27,287
17,000	194.73	53,103	235.26	33,664	19,439	267.32	27,563	25,540	294.55	24,110	28,993
18,000	206.18	56,225	249.09	35,643	20,582	283.04	29,183	27,042	311.87	25,527	30,698
19,000	217.63	59,347	262.92	37,622	21,725	298.76	30,804	28,543	329.18	26,944	32,403
20,000	229.09	62,472	276.77	39,604	22,868	314.49	32,426	30,046	346.52	28,364	34,108
21,000	240.54	65,594	290.60	41,583	24,011	330.21	34,046	31,548	363.84	29,781	35,813
22,000	252.00	68,720	304.44	43,564	25,156	345.94	35,669	33,051	381.17	31,200	37,520
23,000	263.45	71,842	318.28	45,543	26,299	361.66	37,289	34,553	398.49	32,617	39,225
24,000	274.90	74,964	332.11	47,522	27,442	377.38	38,910	36,054	415.81	34,035	40,929
25,000	286.36	78,090	345.95	49,504	28,586	393.11	40,532	37,558	433.15	35,454	42,636
26,000	297.81	81,212	359.79	51,483	29,729	408.83	42,152	39,060	450.46	36,871	44,341
27,000	309.27	84,337	373.63	53,465	30,872	424.56	43,775	40,562	467.80	38,291	46,046
28,000	320.72	87,459	387.46	55,444	32,015	440.28	45,395	42,064	485.12	39,708	47,751
29,000	332.17	90,581	401.30	57,423	33,158	456.00	47,016	43,565	502.44	41,125	49,456
30,000	343.63	93,707	415.14	59,404	34,303	471.73	48,638	45,069	519.77	42,544	51,163
32,500	372.26	101,514	449.73	64,353	37,161	511.03	52,690	48,824	563.08	46,089	55,425
35,000	400.90	109,324	484.33	69,305	40,019	550.35	56,744	52,580	606.40	49,635	59,689
40,000	458.17	124,941	553.52	79,205	45,736	628.97	64,850	60,091	693.02	56,725	68,216
45,000	515.44	140,558	622.71	89,105	51,453	707.59	72,956	67,602	779.65	63,816	76,742
50,000	572.71	156,176	691.90	99,005	57,171	786.21	81,062	75,114	866.28	70,966	85,270
55,000	629.98	171,793	761.08	108,906	62,887	864.83	89,168	82,625	952.90	77,996	93,797
60,000	687.25	187,410	830.27	118,806	68,604	943.45	97,274	90,136	1,039.53	85,087	102,323
65,000	744.52	203,027	899.46	128,706	74,321	1,022.07	105,380	97,647	1,126.15	92,177	110,850
70,000	801.79	218,644	968.65	138,607	80,037	1,100.69	113,486	105,158	1,212.78	99,267	119,377
75,000	859.06	234,262	1,037.84	148,507	85,755	1,179.31	121,592	112,670	1,299.41	106,358	127,904
80,000	916.33	249,879	1,107.03	158,407	91,472	1,257.92	129,698	120,181	1,386.03	113,448	136,431
85,000	973.61	265,500	1,176.23	168,310	97,190	1,336.56	137,806	127,694	1,472.67	120,541	144,959
90,000	1,030.88	281,117	1,245.42	178,210	102,907	1,415.18	145,912	135,205	1,559.30	127,631	153,486
95,000	1,088.15	296,734	1,314.60	188,111	108,623	1,493.80	154,018	142,716	1,645.92	134,721	162,013
100,000	1,145.42	312,351	1,383.79	198,011	114,340	1,572.42	162,124	150,227	1,732.55	141,812	170,539
105,000	1,202.69	327,968	1,452.98	207,911	120,057	1,651.04	170,230	157,738	1,819.18	148,902	179,066
110,000	1,259.96	343,586	1,522.17	217,811	125,775	1,729.66	178,336	165,250	1,905.80	155,993	187,593
115,000	1,317.23	359,203	1,591.36	227,712	131,491	1,808.27	186,442	172,761	1,992.43	163,083	196,120
120,000	1,374.50	374,820	1,660.55	237,612	137,208	1,886.89	194,548	180,272	2,079.05	170,173	204,647
125,000	1,431.77	390,437	1,729.73	247,512	142,925	1,965.51	202,654	187,783	2,165.68	177,264	213,173
130,000	1,489.04	406,054	1,798.92	257,413	148,641	2,044.13	210,760	195,294	2,252.31	184,354	221,700
135,000	1,546.31	421,672	1,868.11	267,313	154,359	2,122.75	218,866	202,806	2,338.93	191,445	230,227
140,000	1,603.58	437,289	1,937.30	277,213	160,076	2,201.37	226,972	210,317	2,425.56	198,535	238,754
145,000	1,660.85	452,906	2,006.49	287,113	165,793	2,279.99	235,078	217,828	2,512.18	205,625	247,281
150,000	1,718.12	468,523	2,075.68	297,014	171,509	2,358.61	243,184	225,339	2,598.81	212,716	255,807
155,000	1,775.39	484,140	2,144.86	306,914	177,226	2,437.23	251,290	232,850	2,685.44	219,806	264,334
160,000	1,832.66	499,758	2,214.05	316,814	182,944	2,515.85	259,396	240,362	2,772.06	226,896	272,862
165,000	1,889.94	515,378	2,283.25	326,717	188,661	2,594.48	267,504	247,874	2,858.70	233,989	281,389
170,000	1,947.21	530,996	2,352.44	336,617	194,379	2,673.10	275,610	255,386	2,945.33	241,079	289,917
175,000	2,004.48	546,613	2,421.63	346,518	200,095	2,751.72	283,716	262,897	3,031.96	248,170	298,443
180,000	2,061.75	562,230	2,490.82	356,418	205,812	2,830.34	291,822	270,408	3,118.58	255,260	306,970
185,000	2,119.02	577,847	2,560.01	366,318	211,529	2,908.96	299,928	277,919	3,205.21	262,350	315,497
190,000	2,176.29	593,464	2,629.20	376,219	217,245	2,987.58	308,034	285,430	3,291.83	269,441	324,023
195,000	2,233.56	609,082	2,698.38	386,119	222,963	3,066.20	316,140	292,942	3,378.46	276,531	332,551
200,000	2,290.83	624,699	2,767.57	396,019	228,680	3,144.82	324,246	300,453	3,465.09	283,622	341,077

AMOUNT OF LOAN	30 YEARS		4% PMT INCR/YR 155.767 PAYMENTS			5% PMT INCR/YR 143.600 PAYMENTS			6% PMT INCR/YR 133.990 PAYMENTS		
	MONTHLY PAYMENT	TOTAL INTRST	LAST YR MON PMT	TOTAL INTRST	INTRST SAVED	LAST YR MON PMT	TOTAL INTRST	INTRST SAVED	LAST YR MON PMT	TOTAL INTRST	INTRST SAVED
$ 50	0.58	159	0.93	66	93	0.99	60	99	1.10	56	103
100	1.15	314	1.84	129	185	1.97	119	195	2.18	111	203
200	2.30	628	3.68	258	370	3.93	238	390	4.37	222	406
300	3.44	938	5.51	385	553	5.88	355	583	6.53	331	607
400	4.59	1,252	7.35	514	738	7.85	474	778	8.71	442	810
500	5.73	1,563	9.17	641	922	9.80	591	972	10.88	551	1,012
600	6.88	1,877	11.02	770	1,107	11.77	709	1,168	13.06	662	1,215
700	8.02	2,187	12.84	897	1,290	13.72	826	1,361	15.22	771	1,416
800	9.17	2,501	14.68	1,026	1,475	15.68	945	1,556	17.41	882	1,619
900	10.31	2,812	16.51	1,153	1,659	17.63	1,062	1,750	19.57	991	1,821
1,000	11.46	3,126	18.35	1,282	1,844	19.60	1,181	1,945	21.75	1,102	2,024
2,000	22.91	6,248	36.68	2,563	3,685	39.18	2,360	3,888	43.49	2,203	4,045
3,000	34.37	9,373	55.03	3,845	5,528	58.78	3,541	5,832	65.24	3,305	6,068
4,000	45.82	12,495	73.36	5,125	7,370	78.37	4,721	7,774	86.98	4,405	8,090
5,000	57.28	15,621	91.71	6,407	9,214	97.97	5,902	9,719	108.73	5,507	10,114
6,000	68.73	18,743	110.04	7,688	11,055	117.55	7,081	11,662	130.47	6,608	12,135
7,000	80.18	21,865	128.37	8,968	12,897	137.14	8,260	13,605	152.21	7,708	14,157
8,000	91.64	24,990	146.72	10,250	14,740	156.74	9,441	15,549	173.96	8,810	16,180
9,000	103.09	28,112	165.05	11,530	16,582	176.32	10,620	17,492	195.70	9,911	18,201
10,000	114.55	31,238	183.40	12,813	18,425	195.92	11,801	19,437	217.45	11,013	20,225
11,000	126.00	34,360	201.73	14,093	20,267	215.50	12,980	21,380	239.19	12,113	22,247
12,000	137.45	37,482	220.06	15,373	22,109	235.09	14,160	23,322	260.92	13,213	24,269
13,000	148.91	40,608	238.41	16,655	23,953	254.69	15,341	25,267	282.68	14,316	26,292
14,000	160.36	43,730	256.74	17,936	25,794	274.27	16,520	27,210	304.41	15,416	28,314
15,000	171.82	46,855	275.09	19,218	27,637	293.87	17,701	29,154	326.17	16,518	30,337
16,000	183.27	49,977	293.42	20,498	29,479	313.45	18,880	31,097	347.90	17,619	32,358
17,000	194.73	53,103	311.77	21,780	31,323	333.05	20,061	33,042	369.66	18,721	34,382
18,000	206.18	56,225	330.10	23,061	33,164	352.64	21,240	34,985	391.39	19,821	36,404
19,000	217.63	59,347	348.43	24,341	35,006	372.22	22,420	36,927	413.13	20,921	38,426
20,000	229.09	62,472	366.78	25,623	36,849	391.82	23,601	38,871	434.88	22,024	40,448
21,000	240.54	65,594	385.11	26,903	38,691	411.41	24,780	40,814	456.62	23,124	42,470
22,000	252.00	68,720	403.46	28,186	40,534	431.01	25,961	42,759	478.37	24,226	44,494
23,000	263.45	71,842	421.79	29,466	42,376	450.59	27,140	44,702	500.11	25,327	46,515
24,000	274.90	74,964	440.12	30,746	44,218	470.17	28,319	46,645	521.84	26,427	48,537
25,000	286.36	78,090	458.47	32,028	46,062	489.77	29,500	48,590	543.60	27,529	50,561
26,000	297.81	81,212	476.80	33,309	47,903	509.36	30,681	50,532	565.33	28,629	52,583
27,000	309.27	84,337	495.15	34,591	49,746	528.96	31,861	52,476	587.09	29,732	54,605
28,000	320.72	87,459	513.48	35,871	51,588	548.54	33,040	54,419	608.82	30,832	56,627
29,000	332.17	90,581	531.81	37,151	53,430	568.12	34,219	56,362	630.56	31,932	58,649
30,000	343.63	93,707	550.16	38,434	55,273	587.72	35,400	58,307	652.31	33,035	60,672
32,500	372.26	101,514	596.00	41,635	59,879	636.69	38,349	63,165	706.66	35,786	65,728
35,000	400.90	109,324	641.85	44,839	64,485	685.68	41,300	68,024	761.03	38,540	70,784
40,000	458.17	124,941	733.54	51,244	73,697	783.63	47,200	77,741	869.74	44,045	80,896
45,000	515.44	140,558	825.24	57,649	82,909	881.58	53,099	87,459	978.46	49,551	91,007
50,000	572.71	156,176	916.93	64,055	92,121	979.53	58,999	97,177	1,087.17	55,056	101,120
55,000	629.98	171,793	1,008.62	70,460	101,333	1,077.48	64,899	106,894	1,195.89	60,562	111,231
60,000	687.25	187,410	1,100.31	76,865	110,545	1,175.43	70,798	116,612	1,304.61	66,067	121,343
65,000	744.52	203,027	1,192.00	83,270	119,757	1,273.38	76,698	126,329	1,413.32	71,573	131,454
70,000	801.79	218,644	1,283.69	89,676	128,968	1,371.33	82,598	136,046	1,522.04	77,078	141,566
75,000	859.06	234,262	1,375.38	96,081	138,181	1,469.28	88,497	145,765	1,630.75	82,584	151,678
80,000	916.33	249,879	1,467.07	102,486	147,393	1,567.24	94,397	155,482	1,739.47	88,089	161,790
85,000	973.61	265,500	1,558.78	108,893	156,607	1,665.20	100,299	165,201	1,848.20	93,596	171,904
90,000	1,030.88	281,117	1,650.47	115,299	165,818	1,763.15	106,199	174,918	1,956.92	99,102	182,015
95,000	1,088.15	296,734	1,742.16	121,704	175,030	1,861.11	112,098	184,636	2,065.63	104,607	192,127
100,000	1,145.42	312,351	1,833.85	128,109	184,242	1,959.06	117,998	194,353	2,174.35	110,113	202,238
105,000	1,202.69	327,968	1,925.55	134,515	193,453	2,057.01	123,898	204,070	2,283.06	115,618	212,350
110,000	1,259.96	343,586	2,017.24	140,920	202,666	2,154.96	129,797	213,789	2,391.78	121,124	222,462
115,000	1,317.23	359,203	2,108.93	147,325	211,878	2,252.91	135,697	223,506	2,500.50	126,629	232,574
120,000	1,374.50	374,820	2,200.62	153,730	221,090	2,350.86	141,597	233,223	2,609.21	132,135	242,685
125,000	1,431.77	390,437	2,292.31	160,136	230,301	2,448.81	147,496	242,941	2,717.93	137,640	252,797
130,000	1,489.04	406,054	2,384.00	166,541	239,513	2,546.76	153,396	252,658	2,826.64	143,146	262,908
135,000	1,546.31	421,672	2,475.69	172,946	248,726	2,644.71	159,296	262,376	2,935.36	148,651	273,021
140,000	1,603.58	437,289	2,567.38	179,351	257,938	2,742.67	165,196	272,093	3,044.07	154,156	283,133
145,000	1,660.85	452,906	2,659.07	185,757	267,149	2,840.62	171,095	281,811	3,152.79	159,662	293,244
150,000	1,718.12	468,523	2,750.77	192,162	276,361	2,938.57	176,995	291,528	3,261.50	165,167	303,356
155,000	1,775.39	484,140	2,842.46	198,567	285,573	3,036.52	182,895	301,245	3,370.22	170,673	313,467
160,000	1,832.66	499,758	2,934.15	204,972	294,786	3,134.47	188,794	310,964	3,478.94	176,178	323,580
165,000	1,889.94	515,378	3,025.85	211,380	303,998	3,232.44	194,696	320,682	3,587.67	181,686	333,692
170,000	1,947.21	530,996	3,117.55	217,785	313,211	3,330.39	200,596	330,400	3,696.39	187,191	343,805
175,000	2,004.48	546,613	3,209.24	224,190	322,423	3,428.34	206,495	340,118	3,805.10	192,696	353,917
180,000	2,061.75	562,230	3,300.93	230,595	331,635	3,526.29	212,395	349,835	3,913.82	198,202	364,028
185,000	2,119.02	577,847	3,392.62	237,001	340,846	3,624.24	218,295	359,552	4,022.53	203,707	374,140
190,000	2,176.29	593,464	3,484.31	243,406	350,058	3,722.19	224,194	369,269	4,131.25	209,213	384,251
195,000	2,233.56	609,082	3,576.00	249,811	359,271	3,820.15	230,094	378,988	4,239.96	214,718	394,364
200,000	2,290.83	624,699	3,667.69	256,217	368,482	3,918.10	235,994	388,705	4,348.68	220,224	404,475

13.75% GROWING EQUITY MORTGAGES

AMOUNT OF LOAN	30 YEARS MONTHLY PAYMENT	TOTAL INTRST	1% PMT INCR/YR 234.823 PAYMENTS LAST YR MON PMT	TOTAL INTRST	INTRST SAVED	2% PMT INCR/YR 194.153 PAYMENTS LAST YR MON PMT	TOTAL INTRST	INTRST SAVED	3% PMT INCR/YR 170.586 PAYMENTS LAST YR MON PMT	TOTAL INTRST	INTRST SAVED
$ 50	0.59	162	0.71	102	60	0.81	84	78	0.89	73	89
100	1.17	321	1.41	202	119	1.61	165	156	1.77	144	177
200	2.34	642	2.83	404	238	3.21	330	312	3.54	289	353
300	3.50	960	4.23	603	357	4.80	493	467	5.29	431	529
400	4.67	1,281	5.64	805	476	6.41	658	623	7.06	576	705
500	5.83	1,599	7.04	1,004	595	8.00	821	778	8.82	718	881
600	7.00	1,920	8.46	1,206	714	9.61	986	934	10.59	863	1,057
700	8.16	2,238	9.86	1,405	833	11.20	1,149	1,089	12.34	1,005	1,233
800	9.33	2,559	11.27	1,607	952	12.81	1,314	1,245	14.11	1,149	1,410
900	10.49	2,876	12.67	1,806	1,070	14.40	1,477	1,399	15.87	1,292	1,584
1,000	11.66	3,198	14.09	2,008	1,190	16.01	1,642	1,556	17.64	1,436	1,762
2,000	23.31	6,392	28.16	4,013	2,379	32.00	3,283	3,109	35.26	2,871	3,521
3,000	34.96	9,586	42.24	6,019	3,567	47.99	4,923	4,663	52.88	4,305	5,281
4,000	46.61	12,780	56.31	8,024	4,756	63.99	6,563	6,217	70.50	5,739	7,041
5,000	58.26	15,974	70.38	10,030	5,944	79.98	8,203	7,771	88.12	7,173	8,801
6,000	69.91	19,168	84.46	12,035	7,133	95.97	9,843	9,325	105.75	8,608	10,560
7,000	81.56	22,362	98.53	14,040	8,322	111.96	11,484	10,878	123.37	10,042	12,320
8,000	93.21	25,556	112.61	16,046	9,510	127.96	13,124	12,432	140.99	11,476	14,080
9,000	104.87	28,755	126.69	18,054	10,699	143.96	14,766	13,987	158.63	12,912	15,841
10,000	116.52	31,947	140.77	20,059	11,888	159.96	16,407	15,540	176.25	14,347	17,600
11,000	128.17	35,141	154.84	22,064	13,077	175.95	18,047	17,094	193.87	15,781	19,360
12,000	139.82	38,335	168.92	24,070	14,265	191.94	19,687	18,648	211.49	17,215	21,120
13,000	151.47	41,529	182.99	26,075	15,454	207.94	21,327	20,202	229.11	18,649	22,880
14,000	163.12	44,723	197.07	28,081	16,642	223.93	22,967	21,756	246.73	20,084	24,639
15,000	174.77	47,917	211.14	30,086	17,831	239.92	24,608	23,309	264.36	21,518	26,399
16,000	186.42	51,111	225.22	32,091	19,020	255.91	26,248	24,863	281.98	22,952	28,159
17,000	198.07	54,305	239.29	34,097	20,208	271.91	27,888	26,417	299.60	24,386	29,919
18,000	209.73	57,503	253.38	36,105	21,398	287.91	29,530	27,973	317.24	25,823	31,680
19,000	221.38	60,697	267.45	38,110	22,587	303.91	31,171	29,526	334.86	27,257	33,440
20,000	233.03	63,891	281.53	40,116	23,775	319.90	32,811	31,080	352.48	28,691	35,200
21,000	244.68	67,085	295.60	42,121	24,964	335.89	34,451	32,634	370.10	30,125	36,960
22,000	256.33	70,279	309.67	44,126	26,153	351.89	36,091	34,188	387.72	31,559	38,720
23,000	267.98	73,473	323.75	46,132	27,341	367.88	37,732	35,741	405.34	32,994	40,479
24,000	279.63	76,667	337.82	48,137	28,530	383.87	39,372	37,295	422.97	34,428	42,239
25,000	291.28	79,861	351.90	50,143	29,718	399.87	41,012	38,849	440.59	35,862	43,999
26,000	302.93	83,055	365.97	52,148	30,907	415.86	42,652	40,403	458.21	37,296	45,759
27,000	314.59	86,252	380.06	54,156	32,096	431.86	44,295	41,957	475.85	38,733	47,519
28,000	326.24	89,446	394.13	56,161	33,285	447.86	45,935	43,511	493.47	40,167	49,279
29,000	337.89	92,640	408.21	58,167	34,473	463.85	47,575	45,065	511.09	41,601	51,039
30,000	349.54	95,834	422.28	60,172	35,662	479.84	49,215	46,619	528.71	43,035	52,799
32,500	378.67	103,821	457.47	65,187	38,634	519.83	53,317	50,504	572.77	46,622	57,199
35,000	407.79	111,804	492.65	70,199	41,605	559.81	57,416	54,388	616.82	50,207	61,597
40,000	466.05	127,778	563.04	80,229	47,549	639.79	65,620	62,158	704.94	57,380	70,398
45,000	524.31	143,752	633.42	90,258	53,494	719.77	73,823	69,929	793.07	64,553	79,199
50,000	582.56	159,722	703.80	100,285	59,437	799.73	82,024	77,698	881.17	71,724	87,998
55,000	640.82	175,695	774.18	110,315	65,380	879.71	90,227	85,468	969.30	78,898	96,797
60,000	699.07	191,665	844.55	120,342	71,323	959.67	98,428	93,237	1,057.41	86,069	105,596
65,000	757.33	207,639	914.94	130,371	77,268	1,039.65	106,631	101,008	1,145.53	93,242	114,397
70,000	815.58	223,609	985.31	140,398	83,211	1,119.62	114,832	108,777	1,233.64	100,413	123,196
75,000	873.84	239,582	1,055.69	150,428	89,154	1,199.60	123,036	116,546	1,321.76	107,587	131,995
80,000	932.10	255,556	1,126.08	160,457	95,099	1,279.57	131,239	124,317	1,409.88	114,760	140,796
85,000	990.35	271,526	1,196.45	170,484	101,042	1,359.54	139,440	132,086	1,497.99	121,931	149,595
90,000	1,048.61	287,500	1,266.84	180,514	106,986	1,439.52	147,643	139,857	1,586.12	129,104	158,396
95,000	1,106.86	303,470	1,337.21	190,541	112,929	1,519.48	155,844	147,626	1,674.23	136,276	167,194
100,000	1,165.12	319,443	1,407.59	200,570	118,873	1,599.46	164,048	155,395	1,762.35	143,449	175,994
105,000	1,223.37	335,413	1,477.96	210,597	124,816	1,679.42	172,249	163,164	1,850.46	150,620	184,793
110,000	1,281.63	351,387	1,548.35	220,627	130,760	1,759.40	180,452	170,935	1,938.58	157,793	193,594
115,000	1,339.88	367,357	1,618.72	230,654	136,703	1,839.37	188,653	178,704	2,026.69	164,965	202,392
120,000	1,398.14	383,330	1,689.11	240,683	142,647	1,919.35	196,856	186,474	2,114.81	172,138	211,192
125,000	1,456.40	399,304	1,759.49	250,713	148,591	1,999.33	205,060	194,244	2,202.94	179,311	219,993
130,000	1,514.65	415,274	1,829.86	260,740	154,534	2,079.29	213,261	202,013	2,291.04	186,482	228,792
135,000	1,572.91	431,248	1,900.25	270,769	160,479	2,159.27	221,464	209,784	2,379.17	193,656	237,592
140,000	1,631.16	447,218	1,970.62	280,796	166,422	2,239.23	229,665	217,553	2,467.28	200,827	246,391
145,000	1,689.42	463,191	2,041.00	290,826	172,365	2,319.21	237,868	225,323	2,555.40	208,000	255,191
150,000	1,747.67	479,161	2,111.38	300,853	178,308	2,399.18	246,069	233,092	2,643.51	215,171	263,990
155,000	1,805.93	495,135	2,181.76	310,882	184,253	2,479.15	254,273	240,862	2,731.63	222,344	272,791
160,000	1,864.19	511,108	2,252.14	320,912	190,196	2,559.13	262,476	248,632	2,819.75	229,518	281,590
165,000	1,922.44	527,078	2,322.52	330,939	196,139	2,639.10	270,677	256,401	2,907.86	236,689	290,389
170,000	1,980.70	543,052	2,392.90	340,968	202,084	2,719.08	278,880	264,172	2,995.99	243,862	299,190
175,000	2,038.95	559,022	2,463.27	350,995	208,027	2,799.04	287,081	271,941	3,084.09	251,033	307,989
180,000	2,097.21	574,996	2,533.66	361,025	213,971	2,879.02	295,284	279,712	3,172.22	258,207	316,789
185,000	2,155.46	590,966	2,604.03	371,052	219,914	2,958.98	303,485	287,481	3,260.33	265,378	325,588
190,000	2,213.72	606,939	2,674.41	381,081	225,858	3,038.96	311,689	295,250	3,348.45	272,551	334,388
195,000	2,271.97	622,909	2,744.79	391,108	231,801	3,118.93	319,890	303,019	3,436.56	279,722	343,187
200,000	2,330.23	638,883	2,815.17	401,138	237,745	3,198.91	328,093	310,790	3,524.68	286,896	351,987

154

GROWING EQUITY MORTGAGES 13.75%

AMOUNT OF LOAN	30 YEARS		4% PMT INCR/YR 154.448 PAYMENTS			5% PMT INCR/YR 142.393 PAYMENTS			6% PMT INCR/YR 132.923 PAYMENTS		
	MONTHLY PAYMENT	TOTAL INTRST	LAST YR MON PMT	TOTAL INTRST	INTRST SAVED	LAST YR MON PMT	TOTAL INTRST	INTRST SAVED	LAST YR MON PMT	TOTAL INTRST	INTRST SAVED
$ 50	0.59	162	0.94	66	96	1.01	61	101	1.12	57	105
100	1.17	321	1.87	131	190	2.00	120	201	2.22	112	209
200	2.34	642	3.75	261	381	4.00	241	401	4.44	225	417
300	3.50	960	5.60	390	570	5.99	359	601	6.64	335	625
400	4.67	1,281	7.48	520	761	7.99	479	802	8.87	447	834
500	5.83	1,599	9.33	649	950	9.97	598	1,001	11.07	558	1,041
600	7.00	1,920	11.21	779	1,141	11.97	718	1,202	13.29	670	1,250
700	8.16	2,238	13.06	908	1,330	13.96	836	1,402	15.49	780	1,458
800	9.33	2,559	14.94	1,038	1,521	15.96	956	1,603	17.71	893	1,666
900	10.49	2,876	16.79	1,167	1,709	17.94	1,075	1,801	19.91	1,003	1,873
1,000	11.66	3,198	18.67	1,297	1,901	19.94	1,195	2,003	22.13	1,115	2,083
2,000	23.31	6,392	37.32	2,593	3,799	39.87	2,388	4,004	44.25	2,229	4,163
3,000	34.96	9,586	55.97	3,888	5,698	59.79	3,581	6,005	66.36	3,342	6,244
4,000	46.61	12,780	74.62	5,184	7,596	79.72	4,775	8,005	88.48	4,456	8,324
5,000	58.26	15,974	93.28	6,479	9,495	99.64	5,968	10,006	110.59	5,569	10,405
6,000	69.91	19,168	111.93	7,775	11,393	119.57	7,161	12,007	132.71	6,683	12,485
7,000	81.56	22,362	130.58	9,070	13,292	139.50	8,354	14,008	154.83	7,796	14,566
8,000	93.21	25,556	149.23	10,366	15,190	159.42	9,547	16,009	176.94	8,909	16,647
9,000	104.87	28,753	167.90	11,663	17,090	179.36	10,743	18,010	199.07	10,025	18,728
10,000	116.52	31,947	186.55	12,959	18,988	199.29	11,936	20,011	221.19	11,138	20,809
11,000	128.17	35,141	205.20	14,254	20,887	219.21	13,129	22,012	243.30	12,252	22,889
12,000	139.82	38,335	223.86	15,550	22,785	239.14	14,322	24,013	265.42	13,365	24,970
13,000	151.47	41,529	242.51	16,845	24,684	259.07	15,515	26,014	287.54	14,478	27,051
14,000	163.12	44,723	261.16	18,141	26,582	278.99	16,708	28,015	309.65	15,592	29,131
15,000	174.77	47,917	279.81	19,436	28,481	298.92	17,902	30,015	331.77	16,705	31,212
16,000	186.42	51,111	298.46	20,732	30,379	318.84	19,095	32,016	353.88	17,819	33,292
17,000	198.07	54,305	317.12	22,027	32,278	338.77	20,288	34,017	376.00	18,932	35,373
18,000	209.73	57,503	335.78	23,325	34,178	358.71	21,483	36,020	398.13	20,048	37,455
19,000	221.38	60,697	354.44	24,620	36,077	378.63	22,676	38,021	420.25	21,161	39,536
20,000	233.03	63,891	373.09	25,916	37,975	398.56	23,870	40,021	442.36	22,274	41,617
21,000	244.68	67,085	391.74	27,211	39,874	418.49	25,063	42,022	464.48	23,388	43,697
22,000	256.33	70,279	410.39	28,507	41,772	438.41	26,256	44,023	486.59	24,501	45,778
23,000	267.98	73,473	429.04	29,802	43,671	458.34	27,449	46,024	508.71	25,615	47,858
24,000	279.63	76,667	447.70	31,098	45,569	478.26	28,642	48,025	530.82	26,728	49,939
25,000	291.28	79,861	466.35	32,393	47,468	498.19	29,835	50,026	552.94	27,842	52,019
26,000	302.93	83,055	485.00	33,688	49,367	518.11	31,029	52,026	575.05	28,955	54,100
27,000	314.59	86,252	503.67	34,986	51,266	538.06	32,224	54,028	597.19	30,070	56,182
28,000	326.24	89,446	522.32	36,281	53,165	557.98	33,417	56,029	619.30	31,184	58,262
29,000	337.89	92,640	540.97	37,577	55,063	577.91	34,610	58,030	641.42	32,297	60,343
30,000	349.54	95,834	559.62	38,872	56,962	597.83	35,803	60,031	663.53	33,411	62,423
32,500	378.67	103,821	606.26	42,112	61,709	647.65	38,781	65,034	718.83	36,195	67,626
35,000	407.79	111,804	652.88	45,350	66,454	697.46	41,769	70,035	774.11	38,978	72,826
40,000	466.05	127,778	746.16	51,829	75,949	797.10	47,737	80,041	884.70	44,547	83,231
45,000	524.31	143,752	839.44	58,309	85,443	896.75	53,705	90,047	995.30	50,116	93,636
50,000	582.56	159,722	932.70	64,786	94,936	996.38	59,671	100,051	1,105.87	55,683	104,039
55,000	640.82	175,695	1,025.97	71,265	104,430	1,096.02	65,639	110,056	1,216.47	61,252	114,443
60,000	699.07	191,665	1,119.23	77,743	113,922	1,195.65	71,605	120,060	1,327.04	66,820	124,845
65,000	757.33	207,639	1,212.51	84,222	123,417	1,295.29	77,573	130,066	1,437.64	72,389	135,250
70,000	815.58	223,609	1,305.77	90,700	132,909	1,394.92	83,539	140,070	1,548.21	77,956	145,653
75,000	873.84	239,582	1,399.05	97,179	142,403	1,494.56	89,506	150,076	1,658.81	83,525	156,057
80,000	932.10	255,556	1,492.32	103,658	151,898	1,594.21	95,474	160,082	1,769.40	89,094	166,462
85,000	990.35	271,526	1,585.58	110,136	161,390	1,693.83	101,440	170,086	1,879.98	94,661	176,865
90,000	1,048.61	287,500	1,678.86	116,615	170,885	1,793.48	107,408	180,092	1,990.57	100,230	187,270
95,000	1,106.86	303,470	1,772.12	123,093	180,377	1,893.11	113,374	190,096	2,101.15	105,798	197,672
100,000	1,165.12	319,443	1,865.39	129,572	189,871	1,992.75	119,342	200,101	2,211.75	111,367	208,076
105,000	1,223.37	335,413	1,958.65	136,049	199,364	2,092.38	125,308	210,105	2,322.32	116,934	218,479
110,000	1,281.63	351,387	2,051.93	142,529	208,858	2,192.02	131,276	220,111	2,432.92	122,503	228,884
115,000	1,339.88	367,357	2,145.19	149,006	218,351	2,291.65	137,242	230,115	2,543.49	128,070	239,287
120,000	1,398.14	383,330	2,238.47	155,486	227,844	2,391.29	143,210	240,120	2,654.09	133,639	249,691
125,000	1,456.40	399,304	2,331.74	161,965	237,339	2,490.94	149,177	250,127	2,764.68	139,208	260,096
130,000	1,514.65	415,274	2,425.00	168,442	246,832	2,590.57	155,143	260,131	2,875.26	144,775	270,499
135,000	1,572.91	431,248	2,518.28	174,922	256,326	2,690.21	161,111	270,137	2,985.85	150,344	280,904
140,000	1,631.16	447,218	2,611.54	181,399	265,819	2,789.84	167,077	280,141	3,096.43	155,912	291,306
145,000	1,689.42	463,191	2,704.82	187,879	275,312	2,889.48	173,045	290,146	3,207.02	161,481	301,710
150,000	1,747.67	479,161	2,798.08	194,356	284,805	2,989.11	179,011	300,150	3,317.60	167,048	312,113
155,000	1,805.93	495,135	2,891.35	200,835	294,300	3,088.75	184,979	310,156	3,428.19	172,617	322,518
160,000	1,864.19	511,108	2,984.63	207,315	303,793	3,188.40	190,947	320,161	3,538.79	178,186	332,922
165,000	1,922.44	527,078	3,077.89	213,792	313,286	3,288.02	196,913	330,165	3,649.37	183,753	343,325
170,000	1,980.70	543,052	3,171.16	220,272	322,780	3,387.67	202,881	340,171	3,759.96	189,322	353,730
175,000	2,038.95	559,022	3,264.42	226,749	332,273	3,487.30	208,847	350,175	3,870.54	194,890	364,132
180,000	2,097.21	574,996	3,357.70	233,228	341,768	3,586.94	214,814	360,182	3,981.13	200,459	374,537
185,000	2,155.46	590,966	3,450.96	239,706	351,260	3,686.57	220,780	370,186	4,091.71	206,026	384,940
190,000	2,213.72	606,939	3,544.24	246,185	360,754	3,786.21	226,748	380,191	4,202.30	211,595	395,344
195,000	2,271.97	622,909	3,637.50	252,663	370,246	3,885.84	232,714	390,195	4,312.88	217,162	405,747
200,000	2,330.23	638,883	3,730.77	259,142	379,741	3,985.48	238,682	400,201	4,423.47	222,731	416,152

155

14.00% GROWING EQUITY MORTGAGES

AMOUNT OF LOAN	30 YEARS		1% PMT INCR/YR 233.010 PAYMENTS			2% PMT INCR/YR 192.557 PAYMENTS			3% PMT INCR/YR 169.177 PAYMENTS		
	MONTHLY PAYMENT	TOTAL INTRST	LAST YR MON PMT	TOTAL INTRST	INTRST SAVED	LAST YR MON PMT	TOTAL INTRST	INTRST SAVED	LAST YR MON PMT	TOTAL INTRST	INTRST SAVED
$ 50	0.60	166	0.72	103	63	0.82	85	81	0.91	74	92
100	1.19	328	1.44	204	124	1.63	167	161	1.80	146	182
200	2.37	653	2.86	406	247	3.25	332	321	3.58	290	363
300	3.56	982	4.30	611	371	4.89	499	483	5.38	436	546
400	4.74	1,306	5.73	812	494	6.51	664	642	7.17	580	726
500	5.93	1,635	7.16	1,017	618	8.14	831	804	8.97	726	909
600	7.11	1,960	8.59	1,219	741	9.76	996	964	10.75	870	1,090
700	8.30	2,288	10.03	1,423	865	11.39	1,163	1,125	12.55	1,017	1,271
800	9.48	2,613	11.45	1,625	988	13.01	1,328	1,285	14.34	1,161	1,452
900	10.67	2,941	12.89	1,829	1,112	14.65	1,495	1,446	16.14	1,307	1,634
1,000	11.85	3,266	14.32	2,031	1,235	16.27	1,660	1,606	17.92	1,451	1,815
2,000	23.70	6,532	28.63	4,062	2,470	32.54	3,319	3,213	35.85	2,902	3,630
3,000	35.55	9,798	42.95	6,093	3,705	48.80	4,979	4,819	53.77	4,352	5,446
4,000	47.40	13,064	57.26	8,124	4,940	65.07	6,638	6,426	71.70	5,803	7,261
5,000	59.25	16,330	71.58	10,155	6,175	81.34	8,298	8,032	89.62	7,254	9,076
6,000	71.10	19,596	85.90	12,186	7,410	97.61	9,957	9,639	107.55	8,705	10,891
7,000	82.95	22,862	100.21	14,217	8,645	113.87	11,617	11,245	125.47	10,155	12,707
8,000	94.79	26,124	114.52	16,246	9,878	130.13	13,274	12,850	143.39	11,604	14,520
9,000	106.64	29,390	128.83	18,277	11,113	146.39	14,934	14,456	161.30	13,055	16,335
10,000	118.49	32,656	143.15	20,308	12,348	162.66	16,593	16,063	179.23	14,506	18,150
11,000	130.34	35,922	157.46	22,339	13,583	178.93	18,253	17,669	197.15	15,956	19,966
12,000	142.19	39,188	171.78	24,370	14,818	195.20	19,913	19,275	215.08	17,407	21,781
13,000	154.04	42,454	186.10	26,401	16,053	211.46	21,572	20,882	233.00	18,858	23,596
14,000	165.89	45,720	200.41	28,432	17,288	227.73	23,232	22,488	250.92	20,309	25,411
15,000	177.74	48,986	214.73	30,463	18,523	244.00	24,891	24,095	268.85	21,760	27,226
16,000	189.58	52,249	229.03	32,491	19,758	260.25	26,549	25,700	286.76	23,208	29,041
17,000	201.43	55,515	243.35	34,522	20,993	276.52	28,208	27,307	304.68	24,659	30,856
18,000	213.28	58,781	257.67	36,553	22,228	292.79	29,868	28,913	322.61	26,110	32,671
19,000	225.13	62,047	271.98	38,585	23,462	309.06	31,527	30,520	340.53	27,561	34,486
20,000	236.98	65,313	286.30	40,616	24,697	325.32	33,187	32,126	358.45	29,011	36,302
21,000	248.83	68,579	300.61	42,647	25,932	341.59	34,846	33,733	376.38	30,462	38,117
22,000	260.68	71,845	314.93	44,678	27,167	357.86	36,506	35,339	394.30	31,913	39,932
23,000	272.53	75,111	329.25	46,709	28,402	374.13	38,166	36,945	412.23	33,364	41,747
24,000	284.37	78,373	343.55	48,737	29,636	390.38	39,823	38,550	430.14	34,812	43,561
25,000	296.22	81,639	357.87	50,768	30,871	406.65	41,482	40,157	448.06	36,263	45,376
26,000	308.07	84,905	372.18	52,799	32,106	422.91	43,142	41,763	465.98	37,714	47,191
27,000	319.92	88,171	386.50	54,830	33,341	439.18	44,802	43,369	483.91	39,165	49,006
28,000	331.77	91,437	400.81	56,861	34,576	455.45	46,461	44,976	501.83	40,615	50,822
29,000	343.62	94,703	415.13	58,892	35,811	471.72	48,121	46,582	519.76	42,066	52,637
30,000	355.47	97,969	429.45	60,923	37,046	487.98	49,780	48,189	537.68	43,517	54,452
32,500	385.09	106,132	465.23	66,000	40,132	528.65	53,928	52,204	582.48	47,143	58,989
35,000	414.71	114,296	501.01	71,076	43,220	569.31	58,076	56,220	627.29	50,769	63,527
40,000	473.95	130,622	572.58	81,229	49,393	650.63	66,371	64,251	716.89	58,021	72,601
45,000	533.20	146,952	644.16	91,384	55,568	731.97	74,669	72,283	806.51	65,274	81,678
50,000	592.44	163,278	715.73	101,536	61,742	813.29	82,965	80,313	896.12	72,526	90,752
55,000	651.68	179,605	787.30	111,689	67,916	894.62	91,260	88,345	985.72	79,778	99,827
60,000	710.93	195,935	858.88	121,844	74,091	975.95	99,558	96,377	1,075.35	87,032	108,903
65,000	770.17	212,261	930.45	131,997	80,264	1,057.28	107,854	104,407	1,164.95	94,284	117,977
70,000	829.42	228,591	1,002.03	142,152	86,439	1,138.62	116,152	112,439	1,254.57	101,537	127,054
75,000	888.66	244,918	1,073.60	152,304	92,614	1,219.94	124,447	120,471	1,344.18	108,789	136,129
80,000	947.90	261,244	1,145.17	162,457	98,787	1,301.26	132,743	128,501	1,433.78	116,041	145,203
85,000	1,007.15	277,574	1,216.75	172,612	104,962	1,382.60	141,041	136,533	1,523.40	123,295	154,279
90,000	1,066.39	293,900	1,288.32	182,765	111,135	1,463.92	149,336	144,564	1,613.01	130,547	163,353
95,000	1,125.63	310,227	1,359.88	192,917	117,310	1,545.25	157,632	152,595	1,702.62	137,799	172,428
100,000	1,184.88	326,557	1,431.46	203,073	123,484	1,626.59	165,930	160,627	1,792.24	145,052	181,505
105,000	1,244.12	342,883	1,503.03	213,225	129,658	1,707.91	174,225	168,658	1,881.84	152,304	190,579
110,000	1,303.36	359,210	1,574.60	223,378	135,832	1,789.23	182,521	176,689	1,971.45	159,556	199,653
115,000	1,362.61	375,540	1,646.18	233,533	142,007	1,870.57	190,819	184,721	2,061.07	166,810	208,730
120,000	1,421.85	391,866	1,717.75	243,686	148,180	1,951.90	199,114	192,752	2,150.68	174,062	217,804
125,000	1,481.09	408,192	1,789.32	253,838	154,354	2,033.22	207,410	200,782	2,240.28	181,313	226,879
130,000	1,540.34	424,522	1,860.90	263,993	160,529	2,114.56	215,708	208,814	2,329.90	188,567	235,955
135,000	1,599.58	440,849	1,932.47	274,146	166,703	2,195.88	224,003	216,846	2,419.51	195,819	245,030
140,000	1,658.83	457,179	2,004.05	284,301	172,878	2,277.22	232,301	224,878	2,509.13	203,073	254,106
145,000	1,718.07	473,505	2,075.62	294,454	179,051	2,358.54	240,597	232,908	2,598.74	210,325	263,180
150,000	1,777.31	489,832	2,147.18	304,606	185,226	2,439.87	248,892	240,940	2,688.34	217,577	272,255
155,000	1,836.56	506,162	2,218.76	314,761	191,401	2,521.20	257,190	248,972	2,777.96	224,830	281,332
160,000	1,895.80	522,488	2,290.33	324,914	197,574	2,602.53	265,486	257,002	2,867.57	232,082	290,406
165,000	1,955.04	538,814	2,361.90	335,067	203,747	2,683.85	273,781	265,033	2,957.17	239,334	299,480
170,000	2,014.29	555,144	2,433.48	345,222	209,922	2,765.19	282,079	273,065	3,046.79	246,588	308,556
175,000	2,073.53	571,471	2,505.05	355,374	216,097	2,846.51	290,375	281,096	3,136.40	253,840	317,631
180,000	2,132.77	587,797	2,576.62	365,527	222,270	2,927.84	298,671	289,126	3,226.01	261,091	326,706
185,000	2,192.02	604,127	2,648.20	375,682	228,445	3,009.17	306,968	297,159	3,315.63	268,345	335,782
190,000	2,251.26	620,454	2,719.77	385,835	234,619	3,090.50	315,264	305,190	3,405.23	275,597	344,857
195,000	2,310.50	636,780	2,791.34	395,987	240,793	3,171.82	323,560	313,220	3,494.84	282,849	353,931
200,000	2,369.75	653,110	2,862.92	406,143	246,967	3,253.16	331,857	321,253	3,584.46	290,103	363,007

156

AMOUNT OF LOAN	30 YEARS		4% PMT INCR/YR 153.152 PAYMENTS			5% PMT INCR/YR 141.208 PAYMENTS			6% PMT INCR/YR 131.870 PAYMENTS		
	MONTHLY PAYMENT	TOTAL INTRST	LAST YR MON PMT	TOTAL INTRST	INTRST SAVED	LAST YR MON PMT	TOTAL INTRST	INTRST SAVED	LAST YR MON PMT	TOTAL INTRST	INTRST SAVED
$ 50	0.60	166	0.96	67	99	1.03	62	104	1.07	58	108
100	1.19	328	1.91	132	196	2.04	122	206	2.13	114	214
200	2.37	653	3.79	262	391	4.05	241	412	4.24	225	428
300	3.56	982	5.70	394	588	6.09	363	619	6.38	339	643
400	4.74	1,306	7.59	524	782	8.11	483	823	8.49	450	856
500	5.93	1,635	9.49	656	979	10.14	604	1,031	10.62	564	1,071
600	7.11	1,960	11.38	786	1,174	12.16	724	1,236	12.73	676	1,284
700	8.30	2,288	13.29	918	1,370	14.20	846	1,442	14.86	789	1,499
800	9.48	2,613	15.18	1,048	1,565	16.21	965	1,648	16.98	901	1,712
900	10.67	2,941	17.08	1,180	1,761	18.25	1,087	1,854	19.11	1,014	1,927
1,000	11.85	3,266	18.97	1,310	1,956	20.27	1,207	2,059	21.22	1,126	2,140
2,000	23.70	6,532	37.94	2,621	3,911	40.54	2,414	4,118	42.44	2,252	4,280
3,000	35.55	9,798	56.92	3,931	5,867	60.80	3,620	6,178	63.66	3,379	6,419
4,000	47.40	13,064	75.89	5,241	7,823	81.07	4,827	8,237	84.89	4,505	8,559
5,000	59.25	16,330	94.86	6,552	9,778	101.34	6,034	10,296	106.11	5,631	10,699
6,000	71.10	19,596	113.83	7,862	11,734	121.61	7,241	12,355	127.33	6,757	12,839
7,000	82.95	22,862	132.81	9,172	13,690	141.87	8,448	14,414	148.55	7,883	14,979
8,000	94.79	26,124	151.76	10,480	15,644	162.12	9,653	16,471	169.75	9,008	17,116
9,000	106.64	29,390	170.73	11,791	17,599	182.39	10,860	18,530	190.98	10,134	19,256
10,000	118.49	32,656	189.71	13,101	19,555	202.66	12,066	20,590	212.20	11,260	21,396
11,000	130.34	35,922	208.68	14,411	21,511	222.93	13,273	22,649	233.42	12,387	23,535
12,000	142.19	39,188	227.65	15,722	23,466	243.19	14,480	24,708	254.64	13,513	25,675
13,000	154.04	42,454	246.62	17,032	25,422	263.46	15,687	26,767	275.86	14,639	27,815
14,000	165.89	45,720	265.60	18,342	27,378	283.73	16,894	28,826	297.08	15,765	29,955
15,000	177.74	48,986	284.57	19,653	29,333	304.00	18,101	30,885	318.31	16,891	32,095
16,000	189.58	52,249	303.52	20,961	31,288	324.25	19,306	32,943	339.51	18,016	34,233
17,000	201.43	55,515	322.50	22,271	33,244	344.51	20,512	35,003	360.73	19,142	36,373
18,000	213.28	58,781	341.47	23,582	35,199	364.78	21,719	37,062	381.95	20,268	38,513
19,000	225.13	62,047	360.44	24,892	37,155	385.05	22,926	39,121	403.17	21,394	40,653
20,000	236.98	65,313	379.41	26,202	39,111	405.32	24,133	41,180	424.40	22,521	42,792
21,000	248.83	68,579	398.38	27,512	41,067	425.58	25,340	43,239	445.62	23,647	44,932
22,000	260.68	71,845	417.36	28,823	43,022	445.85	26,547	45,298	466.84	24,773	47,072
23,000	272.53	75,111	436.33	30,133	44,978	466.12	27,753	47,358	488.06	25,899	49,212
24,000	284.37	78,373	455.29	31,441	46,932	486.37	28,958	49,415	509.26	27,024	51,349
25,000	296.22	81,639	474.26	32,752	48,887	506.64	30,165	51,474	530.48	28,150	53,489
26,000	308.07	84,905	493.23	34,062	50,843	526.90	31,372	53,533	551.71	29,276	55,629
27,000	319.92	88,171	512.20	35,372	52,799	547.17	32,579	55,592	572.93	30,402	57,769
28,000	331.77	91,437	531.17	36,683	54,754	567.44	33,786	57,651	594.15	31,528	59,909
29,000	343.62	94,703	550.15	37,993	56,710	587.70	34,992	59,711	615.37	32,655	62,048
30,000	355.47	97,969	569.12	39,303	58,666	607.97	36,199	61,770	636.59	33,781	64,188
32,500	385.09	106,132	616.54	42,578	63,554	658.63	39,215	66,917	689.64	36,596	69,539
35,000	414.71	114,296	663.96	45,853	68,443	709.29	42,232	72,064	742.68	39,410	74,886
40,000	473.95	130,622	758.81	52,402	78,220	810.62	48,264	82,358	848.77	45,039	85,583
45,000	533.20	146,952	853.67	58,954	87,998	911.95	54,298	92,654	954.88	50,670	96,282
50,000	592.44	163,278	948.52	65,503	97,775	1,013.27	60,330	102,948	1,060.97	56,300	106,978
55,000	651.68	179,605	1,043.36	72,053	107,552	1,114.59	66,363	113,242	1,167.06	61,929	117,676
60,000	710.93	195,935	1,138.22	78,605	117,330	1,215.93	72,397	123,538	1,273.17	67,561	128,375
65,000	770.17	212,261	1,233.07	85,154	127,107	1,317.25	78,429	133,832	1,379.26	73,189	139,072
70,000	829.42	228,591	1,327.93	91,706	136,885	1,418.59	84,463	144,128	1,485.36	78,820	149,771
75,000	888.66	244,918	1,422.77	98,255	146,663	1,519.91	90,495	154,423	1,591.45	84,450	160,468
80,000	947.90	261,244	1,517.62	104,805	156,439	1,621.23	96,528	164,716	1,697.54	90,079	171,166
85,000	1,007.15	277,574	1,612.48	111,356	166,218	1,722.57	102,562	175,012	1,803.65	95,710	181,864
90,000	1,066.39	293,900	1,707.32	117,906	175,994	1,823.89	108,594	185,306	1,909.74	101,339	192,561
95,000	1,125.63	310,227	1,802.17	124,455	185,772	1,925.21	114,626	195,601	2,015.83	106,968	203,259
100,000	1,184.88	326,557	1,897.03	131,007	195,550	2,026.55	120,660	205,897	2,121.94	112,599	213,958
105,000	1,244.12	342,883	1,991.88	137,557	205,326	2,127.87	126,693	216,190	2,228.03	118,229	224,654
110,000	1,303.36	359,210	2,086.72	144,107	215,104	2,229.19	132,725	226,485	2,334.12	123,858	235,352
115,000	1,362.61	375,540	2,181.58	150,658	224,882	2,330.53	138,759	236,781	2,440.23	129,489	246,051
120,000	1,421.85	391,866	2,276.43	157,207	234,659	2,431.85	144,791	247,075	2,546.32	135,118	256,748
125,000	1,481.09	408,192	2,371.27	163,757	244,435	2,533.17	150,824	257,368	2,652.41	140,747	267,445
130,000	1,540.34	424,522	2,466.13	170,308	254,214	2,634.50	156,858	267,664	2,758.51	146,378	278,144
135,000	1,599.58	440,849	2,560.98	176,858	263,991	2,735.82	162,890	277,959	2,864.60	152,008	288,841
140,000	1,658.83	457,179	2,655.84	183,409	273,770	2,837.16	168,924	288,255	2,970.71	157,639	299,540
145,000	1,718.07	473,505	2,750.69	189,959	283,546	2,938.48	174,957	298,549	3,076.80	163,268	310,237
150,000	1,777.31	489,832	2,845.53	196,508	293,324	3,039.80	180,989	308,843	3,182.89	168,897	320,935
155,000	1,836.56	506,162	2,940.39	203,060	303,102	3,141.14	187,023	319,139	3,289.00	174,528	331,634
160,000	1,895.80	522,488	3,035.24	209,610	312,878	3,242.46	193,055	329,433	3,395.09	180,158	342,330
165,000	1,955.04	538,814	3,130.08	216,159	322,655	3,343.78	199,088	339,726	3,501.18	185,787	353,027
170,000	2,014.29	555,144	3,224.94	222,711	332,433	3,445.12	205,122	350,022	3,607.29	191,418	363,726
175,000	2,073.53	571,471	3,319.79	229,260	342,211	3,546.44	211,154	360,317	3,713.38	197,047	374,424
180,000	2,132.77	587,797	3,414.63	235,810	351,987	3,647.76	217,186	370,611	3,819.47	202,676	385,121
185,000	2,192.02	604,127	3,509.49	242,361	361,766	3,749.10	223,220	380,907	3,925.57	208,307	395,820
190,000	2,251.26	620,454	3,604.34	248,911	371,543	3,850.42	229,253	391,201	4,031.66	213,937	406,517
195,000	2,310.50	636,780	3,699.18	255,460	381,320	3,951.74	235,285	401,495	4,137.75	219,566	417,214
200,000	2,369.75	653,110	3,794.05	262,012	391,098	4,053.08	241,319	411,791	4,243.86	225,197	427,913

14.25% GROWING EQUITY MORTGAGES

AMOUNT OF LOAN	30 YEARS		1% PMT INCR/YR 231.208 PAYMENTS			2% PMT INCR/YR 190.960 PAYMENTS			3% PMT INCR/YR 167.783 PAYMENTS		
	MONTHLY PAYMENT	TOTAL INTRST	LAST YR MON PMT	TOTAL INTRST	INTRST SAVED	LAST YR MON PMT	TOTAL INTRST	INTRST SAVED	LAST YR MON PMT	TOTAL INTRST	INTRST SAVED
$ 50	0.61	170	0.74	105	65	0.82	86	84	0.90	75	95
100	1.21	336	1.46	207	129	1.63	169	167	1.78	148	188
200	2.41	668	2.91	411	257	3.24	336	332	3.54	293	375
300	3.62	1,003	4.37	618	385	4.87	505	498	5.32	441	562
400	4.82	1,335	5.82	822	513	6.49	671	664	7.08	587	748
500	6.03	1,671	7.28	1,029	642	8.12	840	831	8.86	734	937
600	7.23	2,003	8.73	1,234	769	9.73	1,007	996	10.62	880	1,123
700	8.44	2,338	10.20	1,440	898	11.36	1,176	1,162	12.39	1,028	1,310
800	9.64	2,670	11.65	1,645	1,025	12.97	1,343	1,327	14.16	1,173	1,497
900	10.85	3,006	13.11	1,852	1,154	14.60	1,512	1,494	15.93	1,321	1,685
1,000	12.05	3,338	14.56	2,056	1,282	16.22	1,678	1,660	17.70	1,467	1,871
2,000	24.10	6,676	29.12	4,112	2,564	32.44	3,357	3,319	35.39	2,934	3,742
3,000	36.15	10,014	43.67	6,168	3,846	48.65	5,035	4,979	53.09	4,401	5,613
4,000	48.19	13,348	58.22	8,221	5,127	64.86	6,711	6,637	70.77	5,865	7,483
5,000	60.24	16,686	72.78	10,277	6,409	81.08	8,390	8,296	88.46	7,332	9,354
6,000	72.29	20,024	87.33	12,333	7,691	97.29	10,068	9,956	106.16	8,799	11,225
7,000	84.33	23,359	101.88	14,387	8,972	113.50	11,744	11,615	123.84	10,264	13,095
8,000	96.38	26,697	116.44	16,443	10,254	129.71	13,423	13,274	141.54	11,731	14,966
9,000	108.43	30,035	131.00	18,499	11,536	145.93	15,101	14,934	159.23	13,197	16,838
10,000	120.47	33,369	145.54	20,552	12,817	162.14	16,777	16,592	176.91	14,662	18,707
11,000	132.52	36,707	160.10	22,608	14,099	178.35	18,455	18,252	194.61	16,129	20,578
12,000	144.57	40,045	174.66	24,664	15,381	194.57	20,134	19,911	212.31	17,596	22,449
13,000	156.61	43,380	189.20	26,717	16,663	210.78	21,810	21,570	229.99	19,061	24,319
14,000	168.66	46,718	203.76	28,773	17,945	226.99	23,488	23,230	247.68	20,528	26,190
15,000	180.71	50,056	218.32	30,829	19,227	243.21	25,167	24,889	265.38	21,994	28,062
16,000	192.75	53,390	232.86	32,883	20,507	259.42	26,843	26,547	283.06	23,459	29,931
17,000	204.80	56,728	247.42	34,939	21,789	275.63	28,521	28,207	300.76	24,926	31,802
18,000	216.85	60,066	261.98	36,995	23,071	291.85	30,200	29,866	318.45	26,393	33,673
19,000	228.90	63,404	276.54	39,050	24,354	308.07	31,878	31,526	336.15	27,860	35,544
20,000	240.94	66,738	291.08	41,104	25,634	324.27	33,554	33,184	353.83	29,325	37,413
21,000	252.99	70,076	305.64	43,160	26,916	340.49	35,233	34,843	371.52	30,791	39,285
22,000	265.04	73,414	320.20	45,216	28,198	356.71	36,911	36,503	389.22	32,258	41,156
23,000	277.08	76,749	334.74	47,269	29,480	372.91	38,587	38,162	406.90	33,723	43,026
24,000	289.13	80,087	349.30	49,325	30,762	389.13	40,265	39,822	424.60	35,190	44,897
25,000	301.18	83,425	363.86	51,381	32,044	405.35	41,944	41,481	442.29	36,657	46,768
26,000	313.22	86,759	378.40	53,435	33,324	421.55	43,620	43,139	459.97	38,122	48,637
27,000	325.27	90,097	392.96	55,491	34,606	437.77	45,298	44,799	477.67	39,588	50,509
28,000	337.32	93,435	407.52	57,546	35,889	453.99	46,977	46,458	495.37	41,055	52,380
29,000	349.36	96,770	422.06	59,600	37,170	470.19	48,653	48,117	513.05	42,520	54,250
30,000	361.41	100,108	436.62	61,656	38,452	486.41	50,331	49,777	530.74	43,987	56,121
32,500	391.53	108,451	473.01	66,794	41,657	526.95	54,526	53,925	574.98	47,653	60,798
35,000	421.65	116,794	509.40	71,933	44,861	567.49	58,721	58,073	619.21	51,319	65,475
40,000	481.88	133,477	582.16	82,208	51,269	648.55	67,108	66,369	707.66	58,649	74,828
45,000	542.11	150,160	654.93	92,483	57,677	729.61	75,496	74,664	796.11	65,979	84,181
50,000	602.35	166,846	727.70	102,760	64,086	810.68	83,885	82,961	884.57	73,311	93,535
55,000	662.58	183,529	800.47	113,034	70,495	891.75	92,273	91,256	973.02	80,642	102,887
60,000	722.82	200,215	873.25	123,312	76,903	972.82	100,662	99,553	1,061.49	87,974	112,241
65,000	783.05	216,898	946.01	133,586	83,312	1,053.88	109,050	107,848	1,149.94	95,304	121,594
70,000	843.29	233,584	1,018.79	143,864	89,720	1,134.96	117,440	116,144	1,238.40	102,636	130,948
75,000	903.52	250,267	1,091.55	154,138	96,129	1,216.02	125,827	124,440	1,326.85	109,966	140,301
80,000	963.75	266,950	1,164.32	164,413	102,537	1,297.08	134,214	132,736	1,415.30	117,296	149,654
85,000	1,023.99	283,636	1,237.09	174,690	108,946	1,378.16	142,604	141,032	1,503.76	124,628	159,008
90,000	1,084.22	300,319	1,309.86	184,965	115,354	1,459.22	150,991	149,328	1,592.21	131,959	168,360
95,000	1,144.46	317,006	1,382.63	195,242	121,764	1,540.29	159,381	157,625	1,680.68	139,291	177,715
100,000	1,204.69	333,688	1,455.40	205,517	128,171	1,621.35	167,769	165,919	1,769.13	146,621	187,067
105,000	1,264.93	350,375	1,528.17	215,794	134,581	1,702.43	176,158	174,217	1,857.59	153,953	196,422
110,000	1,325.16	367,058	1,600.94	226,069	140,989	1,783.49	184,546	182,512	1,946.04	161,283	205,775
115,000	1,385.40	383,744	1,673.71	236,346	147,398	1,864.57	192,935	190,809	2,034.51	168,615	215,129
120,000	1,445.63	400,427	1,746.48	246,621	153,806	1,945.63	201,323	199,104	2,122.96	175,945	224,482
125,000	1,505.86	417,110	1,819.24	256,896	160,214	2,026.69	209,710	207,400	2,211.41	183,275	233,835
130,000	1,566.10	433,796	1,892.02	267,173	166,623	2,107.76	218,100	215,696	2,299.87	190,608	243,188
135,000	1,626.33	450,479	1,964.78	277,448	173,031	2,188.83	226,487	223,992	2,388.32	197,938	252,541
140,000	1,686.57	467,165	2,037.56	287,725	179,440	2,269.90	234,877	232,288	2,476.78	205,270	261,895
145,000	1,746.80	483,848	2,110.32	298,000	185,848	2,350.96	243,264	240,584	2,565.23	212,600	271,248
150,000	1,807.04	500,534	2,183.10	308,277	192,257	2,432.04	251,654	248,880	2,653.70	219,932	280,602
155,000	1,867.27	517,217	2,255.87	318,552	198,665	2,513.10	260,041	257,176	2,742.15	227,262	289,955
160,000	1,927.50	533,900	2,328.63	328,826	205,074	2,594.16	268,429	265,471	2,830.60	234,592	299,308
165,000	1,987.74	550,586	2,401.41	339,103	211,483	2,675.24	276,818	273,768	2,919.06	241,925	308,661
170,000	2,047.97	567,269	2,474.17	349,378	217,891	2,756.30	285,206	282,063	3,007.51	249,255	318,014
175,000	2,108.21	583,956	2,546.95	359,655	224,301	2,837.37	293,596	290,361	3,095.98	256,588	327,369
180,000	2,168.44	600,638	2,619.71	369,930	230,708	2,918.43	301,983	298,655	3,184.43	263,917	336,721
185,000	2,228.68	617,325	2,692.49	380,207	237,118	2,999.51	310,373	306,952	3,272.89	271,249	346,076
190,000	2,288.91	634,008	2,765.25	390,482	243,526	3,080.57	318,761	315,248	3,361.34	278,579	355,429
195,000	2,349.14	650,690	2,838.02	400,757	249,933	3,161.63	327,147	323,543	3,449.79	285,909	364,781
200,000	2,409.38	667,377	2,910.79	411,034	256,343	3,242.71	335,537	331,840	3,538.26	293,242	374,135

GROWING EQUITY MORTGAGES 14.25%

AMOUNT OF LOAN	30 YEARS MONTHLY PAYMENT	30 YEARS TOTAL INTRST	4% PMT INCR/YR 151.879 PAYMENTS LAST YR MON PMT	TOTAL INTRST	INTRST SAVED	5% PMT INCR/YR 140.045 PAYMENTS LAST YR MON PMT	TOTAL INTRST	INTRST SAVED	6% PMT INCR/YR 130.784 PAYMENTS LAST YR MON PMT	TOTAL INTRST	INTRST SAVED
$ 50	0.61	170	0.98	68	102	1.04	62	108	1.09	58	112
100	1.21	336	1.94	133	203	2.07	123	213	2.17	115	221
200	2.41	668	3.86	265	403	4.12	244	424	4.32	228	440
300	3.62	1,003	5.80	398	605	6.19	367	636	6.48	342	661
400	4.82	1,335	7.72	530	805	8.24	488	847	8.63	455	880
500	6.03	1,671	9.65	663	1,008	10.31	611	1,060	10.80	570	1,101
600	7.23	2,003	11.58	795	1,208	12.37	732	1,271	12.95	683	1,320
700	8.44	2,338	13.51	928	1,410	14.44	855	1,483	15.11	798	1,540
800	9.64	2,670	15.43	1,060	1,610	16.49	976	1,694	17.26	911	1,759
900	10.85	3,006	17.37	1,193	1,813	18.56	1,099	1,907	19.43	1,026	1,980
1,000	12.05	3,338	19.29	1,325	2,013	20.61	1,220	2,118	21.58	1,139	2,199
2,000	24.10	6,676	38.58	2,649	4,027	41.22	2,440	4,236	43.16	2,277	4,399
3,000	36.15	10,014	57.88	3,974	6,040	61.83	3,660	6,354	64.74	3,416	6,598
4,000	48.19	13,348	77.15	5,297	8,051	82.42	4,879	8,469	86.30	4,553	8,795
5,000	60.24	16,686	96.45	6,622	10,064	103.03	6,099	10,587	107.88	5,692	10,994
6,000	72.29	20,024	115.74	7,946	12,078	123.64	7,319	12,705	129.46	6,830	13,194
7,000	84.33	23,359	135.02	9,269	14,090	144.23	8,537	14,822	151.02	7,967	15,392
8,000	96.38	26,697	154.31	10,594	16,103	164.84	9,757	16,940	172.60	9,106	17,591
9,000	108.43	30,035	173.60	11,919	18,116	185.45	10,977	19,058	194.18	10,244	19,791
10,000	120.47	33,369	192.88	13,242	20,127	206.04	12,196	21,173	215.74	11,381	21,988
11,000	132.52	36,707	212.17	14,566	22,141	226.65	13,416	23,291	237.32	12,520	24,187
12,000	144.57	40,045	231.46	15,891	24,154	247.26	14,636	25,409	258.90	13,659	26,386
13,000	156.61	43,380	250.74	17,214	26,166	267.86	15,854	27,526	280.46	14,795	28,585
14,000	168.66	46,718	270.03	18,539	28,179	288.47	17,074	29,644	302.04	15,934	30,784
15,000	180.71	50,056	289.32	19,863	30,193	309.08	18,294	31,762	323.62	17,073	32,983
16,000	192.75	53,390	308.60	21,186	32,204	329.67	19,512	33,878	345.19	18,210	35,180
17,000	204.80	56,728	327.89	22,511	34,217	350.28	20,733	35,995	366.77	19,348	37,380
18,000	216.85	60,066	347.18	23,836	36,230	370.89	21,953	38,113	388.35	20,487	39,579
19,000	228.90	63,404	366.48	25,160	38,244	391.50	23,173	40,231	409.93	21,626	41,778
20,000	240.94	66,738	385.75	26,483	40,255	412.09	24,391	42,347	431.49	22,763	43,975
21,000	252.99	70,076	405.05	27,808	42,268	432.70	25,611	44,465	453.07	23,901	46,175
22,000	265.04	73,414	424.34	29,133	44,281	453.31	26,831	46,583	474.65	25,040	48,374
23,000	277.08	76,749	443.61	30,455	46,294	473.90	28,050	48,699	496.21	26,177	50,572
24,000	289.13	80,087	462.91	31,780	48,307	494.51	29,270	50,817	517.79	27,315	52,772
25,000	301.18	83,425	482.20	33,105	50,320	515.12	30,490	52,935	539.37	28,454	54,971
26,000	313.22	86,759	501.48	34,428	52,331	535.71	31,708	55,051	560.93	29,591	57,168
27,000	325.27	90,097	520.77	35,752	54,345	556.32	32,928	57,169	582.51	30,730	59,367
28,000	337.32	93,435	540.06	37,077	56,358	576.93	34,148	59,287	604.09	31,868	61,567
29,000	349.36	96,770	559.34	38,400	58,370	597.52	35,366	61,404	625.65	33,005	63,765
30,000	361.41	100,108	578.63	39,725	60,383	618.13	36,587	63,521	647.23	34,144	65,964
32,500	391.53	108,451	626.85	43,036	65,415	669.65	39,636	68,815	701.17	36,990	71,461
35,000	421.65	116,794	675.08	46,346	70,448	721.16	42,685	74,109	755.11	39,835	76,959
40,000	481.88	133,477	771.51	52,966	80,511	824.18	48,782	84,695	862.97	45,525	87,952
45,000	542.11	150,160	867.94	59,586	90,574	927.19	54,879	95,281	970.84	51,215	98,945
50,000	602.35	166,846	964.38	66,208	100,638	1,030.22	60,978	105,868	1,078.72	56,906	109,940
55,000	662.58	183,529	1,060.81	72,828	110,701	1,133.24	67,074	116,455	1,186.58	62,596	120,933
60,000	722.82	200,215	1,157.26	79,449	120,766	1,236.27	73,173	127,042	1,294.46	68,288	131,927
65,000	783.05	216,898	1,253.69	86,069	130,829	1,339.28	79,270	137,628	1,402.32	73,977	142,921
70,000	843.29	233,584	1,350.13	92,691	140,893	1,442.31	85,369	148,215	1,510.20	79,669	153,915
75,000	903.52	250,267	1,446.56	99,311	150,956	1,545.33	91,466	158,801	1,618.07	85,359	164,908
80,000	963.75	266,950	1,542.99	105,931	161,019	1,648.34	97,562	169,388	1,725.93	91,048	175,902
85,000	1,023.99	283,636	1,639.44	112,552	171,084	1,751.37	103,661	179,975	1,833.81	96,740	186,896
90,000	1,084.22	300,319	1,735.87	119,172	181,147	1,854.38	109,758	190,561	1,941.67	102,430	197,889
95,000	1,144.46	317,006	1,832.32	125,794	191,212	1,957.41	115,857	201,149	2,049.55	108,121	208,885
100,000	1,204.69	333,688	1,928.75	132,414	201,274	2,060.43	121,953	211,735	2,157.42	113,811	219,877
105,000	1,264.93	350,375	2,025.19	139,036	211,339	2,163.46	128,052	222,323	2,265.30	119,502	230,873
110,000	1,325.16	367,058	2,121.62	145,655	221,403	2,266.47	134,149	232,909	2,373.16	125,192	241,866
115,000	1,385.40	383,744	2,218.07	152,277	231,467	2,369.50	140,248	243,496	2,481.04	130,884	252,860
120,000	1,445.63	400,427	2,314.50	158,897	241,530	2,472.52	146,344	254,083	2,588.90	136,573	263,854
125,000	1,505.86	417,110	2,410.93	165,517	251,593	2,575.53	152,441	264,669	2,696.77	142,263	274,847
130,000	1,566.10	433,796	2,507.38	172,139	261,657	2,678.56	158,540	275,256	2,804.65	147,955	285,841
135,000	1,626.33	450,479	2,603.81	178,758	271,721	2,781.58	164,637	285,842	2,912.51	153,644	296,835
140,000	1,686.57	467,165	2,700.25	185,380	281,785	2,884.61	170,736	296,429	3,020.39	159,336	307,829
145,000	1,746.80	483,848	2,796.68	192,000	291,848	2,987.62	176,832	307,016	3,128.25	165,026	318,822
150,000	1,807.04	500,534	2,893.13	198,622	301,912	3,090.65	182,931	317,603	3,236.13	170,717	329,817
155,000	1,867.27	517,217	2,989.56	205,242	311,975	3,193.67	189,028	328,189	3,344.00	176,407	340,810
160,000	1,927.50	533,900	3,085.99	211,861	322,039	3,296.68	195,125	338,775	3,451.86	182,097	351,803
165,000	1,987.74	550,586	3,182.44	218,483	332,103	3,399.71	201,223	349,363	3,559.74	187,788	362,798
170,000	2,047.97	567,269	3,278.87	225,103	342,166	3,502.72	207,320	359,949	3,667.60	193,478	373,791
175,000	2,108.21	583,956	3,375.31	231,725	352,231	3,605.75	213,419	370,537	3,775.48	199,169	384,787
180,000	2,168.44	600,638	3,471.74	238,345	362,293	3,708.77	219,516	381,122	3,883.34	204,859	395,779
185,000	2,228.68	617,325	3,568.19	244,966	372,359	3,811.80	225,615	391,710	3,991.23	210,551	406,774
190,000	2,288.91	634,008	3,664.62	251,586	382,422	3,914.81	231,711	402,297	4,099.09	216,240	417,768
195,000	2,349.14	650,690	3,761.05	258,206	392,484	4,017.83	237,808	412,882	4,206.95	221,930	428,760
200,000	2,409.38	667,377	3,857.50	264,828	402,549	4,120.86	243,907	423,470	4,314.83	227,622	439,755

159

14.50% GROWING EQUITY MORTGAGES

AMOUNT OF LOAN	30 YEARS		1% PMT INCR/YR 229.416 PAYMENTS			2% PMT INCR/YR 189.375 PAYMENTS			3% PMT INCR/YR 166.378 PAYMENTS		
	MONTHLY PAYMENT	TOTAL INTRST	LAST YR MON PMT	TOTAL INTRST	INTRST SAVED	LAST YR MON PMT	TOTAL INTRST	INTRST SAVED	LAST YR MON PMT	TOTAL INTRST	INTRST SAVED
$ 50	0.62	173	0.75	106	67	0.83	86	87	0.91	76	97
100	1.23	343	1.49	209	134	1.66	171	172	1.81	149	194
200	2.45	682	2.96	416	266	3.30	339	343	3.60	297	385
300	3.68	1,025	4.45	625	400	4.95	510	515	5.40	446	579
400	4.90	1,364	5.92	832	532	6.59	679	685	7.20	593	771
500	6.13	1,707	7.41	1,041	666	8.25	849	858	9.00	742	965
600	7.35	2,046	8.88	1,248	798	9.89	1,018	1,028	10.79	890	1,156
700	8.58	2,389	10.37	1,457	932	11.55	1,189	1,200	12.60	1,039	1,350
800	9.80	2,728	11.84	1,664	1,064	13.19	1,357	1,371	14.39	1,186	1,542
900	11.03	3,071	13.33	1,873	1,198	14.84	1,528	1,543	16.20	1,335	1,736
1,000	12.25	3,410	14.80	2,080	1,330	16.49	1,697	1,713	17.99	1,483	1,927
2,000	24.50	6,820	29.60	4,160	2,660	32.97	3,393	3,427	35.98	2,965	3,855
3,000	36.74	10,226	44.39	6,238	3,988	49.45	5,088	5,138	53.95	4,446	5,780
4,000	48.99	13,636	59.19	8,318	5,318	65.93	6,785	6,851	71.94	5,928	7,708
5,000	61.23	17,043	73.97	10,396	6,647	82.41	8,479	8,564	89.92	7,409	9,634
6,000	73.48	20,453	88.77	12,476	7,977	98.89	10,176	10,277	107.91	8,891	11,562
7,000	85.72	23,859	103.56	14,554	9,305	115.37	11,870	11,989	125.88	10,371	13,488
8,000	97.97	27,269	118.36	16,634	10,635	131.85	13,567	13,702	143.87	11,854	15,415
9,000	110.22	30,679	133.16	18,714	11,965	148.34	15,264	15,415	161.86	13,337	17,342
10,000	122.46	34,086	147.95	20,792	13,294	164.82	16,958	17,128	179.84	14,817	19,269
11,000	134.71	37,496	162.74	22,872	14,624	181.30	18,655	18,841	197.83	16,300	21,196
12,000	146.95	40,902	177.53	24,949	15,953	197.78	20,349	20,553	215.80	17,780	23,122
13,000	159.20	44,312	192.33	27,029	17,283	214.26	22,046	22,266	233.79	19,263	25,049
14,000	171.44	47,718	207.12	29,107	18,611	230.74	23,741	23,977	251.77	20,743	26,975
15,000	183.69	51,128	221.92	31,187	19,941	247.22	25,437	25,691	269.75	22,226	28,902
16,000	195.93	54,535	236.70	33,265	21,270	263.70	27,132	27,403	287.73	23,706	30,829
17,000	208.18	57,945	251.50	35,345	22,600	280.18	28,828	29,117	305.72	25,188	32,757
18,000	220.43	61,355	266.30	37,425	23,930	296.67	30,525	30,830	323.71	26,671	34,684
19,000	232.67	64,761	281.09	39,503	25,258	313.14	32,220	32,541	341.68	28,151	36,610
20,000	244.92	68,171	295.89	41,583	26,588	329.63	33,916	34,255	359.67	29,634	38,537
21,000	257.16	71,578	310.68	43,661	27,917	346.10	35,611	35,967	377.65	31,114	40,464
22,000	269.41	74,988	325.48	45,741	29,247	362.59	37,308	37,680	395.64	32,597	42,391
23,000	281.65	78,394	340.26	47,818	30,576	379.06	39,002	39,392	413.61	34,077	44,317
24,000	293.90	81,804	355.06	49,899	31,905	395.55	40,699	41,105	431.60	35,560	46,244
25,000	306.14	85,210	369.85	51,976	33,234	412.02	42,393	42,817	449.58	37,040	48,170
26,000	318.39	88,620	384.65	54,056	34,564	428.51	44,090	44,530	467.57	38,523	50,097
27,000	330.64	92,030	399.45	56,137	35,893	445.00	45,787	46,243	485.56	40,005	52,025
28,000	342.88	95,437	414.24	58,214	37,223	461.47	47,481	47,956	503.53	41,486	53,951
29,000	355.13	98,847	429.04	60,294	38,553	477.96	49,178	49,669	521.52	42,968	55,879
30,000	367.37	102,253	443.82	62,372	39,881	494.43	50,872	51,381	539.50	44,449	57,804
32,500	397.99	110,776	480.82	67,571	43,205	535.64	55,113	55,663	584.46	48,154	62,622
35,000	428.60	119,296	517.80	72,768	46,528	576.84	59,351	59,945	629.41	51,857	67,439
40,000	489.83	136,339	591.77	83,164	53,175	659.25	67,830	68,509	719.33	59,266	77,073
45,000	551.06	153,382	665.74	93,559	59,823	741.65	76,310	77,072	809.25	66,674	86,708
50,000	612.28	170,421	739.70	103,953	66,468	824.05	84,786	85,635	899.15	74,081	96,340
55,000	673.51	187,464	813.67	114,349	73,116	906.46	93,265	94,199	989.07	81,489	105,975
60,000	734.74	204,506	887.65	124,744	79,762	988.86	101,745	102,761	1,078.99	88,898	115,608
65,000	795.97	221,549	961.62	135,140	86,409	1,071.27	110,224	111,325	1,168.91	96,306	125,243
70,000	857.19	238,588	1,035.58	145,533	93,055	1,153.66	118,701	119,887	1,258.81	103,713	134,875
75,000	918.42	255,631	1,109.55	155,929	99,702	1,236.07	127,180	128,451	1,348.73	111,121	144,510
80,000	979.65	272,674	1,183.52	166,325	106,349	1,318.48	135,659	137,015	1,438.65	118,530	154,144
85,000	1,040.88	289,717	1,257.50	176,720	112,997	1,400.89	144,138	145,579	1,528.57	125,938	163,779
90,000	1,102.11	306,760	1,331.47	187,116	119,644	1,483.29	152,617	154,143	1,618.49	133,347	173,413
95,000	1,163.33	323,799	1,405.43	197,509	126,290	1,565.69	161,094	162,705	1,708.39	140,753	183,046
100,000	1,224.56	340,842	1,479.40	207,905	132,937	1,648.10	169,573	171,269	1,798.31	148,162	192,680
105,000	1,285.79	357,882	1,553.37	218,301	139,583	1,730.50	178,052	179,832	1,888.23	155,570	202,314
110,000	1,347.02	374,927	1,627.35	228,697	146,230	1,812.91	186,531	188,396	1,978.14	162,979	211,948
115,000	1,408.24	391,966	1,701.31	239,090	152,876	1,895.31	195,008	196,958	2,068.05	170,385	221,581
120,000	1,469.47	409,009	1,775.28	249,486	159,523	1,977.71	203,487	205,522	2,157.97	177,794	231,215
125,000	1,530.70	426,052	1,849.25	259,881	166,171	2,060.12	211,966	214,086	2,247.88	185,202	240,850
130,000	1,591.93	443,095	1,923.22	270,277	172,818	2,142.53	220,445	222,650	2,337.80	192,611	250,484
135,000	1,653.16	460,138	1,997.20	280,673	179,465	2,224.94	228,924	231,214	2,427.72	200,019	260,119
140,000	1,714.38	477,177	2,071.16	291,066	186,111	2,307.33	237,401	239,776	2,517.62	207,426	269,751
145,000	1,775.61	494,220	2,145.13	301,462	192,758	2,389.74	245,880	248,340	2,607.54	214,834	279,386
150,000	1,836.84	511,262	2,219.10	311,858	199,404	2,472.14	254,359	256,903	2,697.46	222,243	289,019
155,000	1,898.07	528,305	2,293.08	322,253	206,052	2,554.55	262,838	265,467	2,787.38	229,651	298,654
160,000	1,959.29	545,344	2,367.04	332,647	212,697	2,636.95	271,315	274,029	2,877.28	237,058	308,286
165,000	2,020.52	562,387	2,441.01	343,042	219,345	2,719.35	279,794	282,593	2,967.20	244,466	317,921
170,000	2,081.75	579,430	2,514.98	353,438	225,992	2,801.76	288,273	291,157	3,057.12	251,875	327,555
175,000	2,142.98	596,473	2,588.95	363,834	232,639	2,884.17	296,752	299,721	3,147.04	259,283	337,190
180,000	2,204.21	613,516	2,662.93	374,230	239,286	2,966.58	305,232	308,284	3,236.96	266,692	346,824
185,000	2,265.43	630,555	2,736.89	384,623	245,932	3,048.97	313,708	316,847	3,326.86	274,098	356,457
190,000	2,326.66	647,598	2,810.86	395,019	252,579	3,131.38	322,187	325,411	3,416.78	281,507	366,091
195,000	2,387.89	664,640	2,884.83	405,414	259,226	3,213.79	330,667	333,973	3,506.70	288,915	375,725
200,000	2,449.12	681,683	2,958.80	415,810	265,873	3,296.19	339,146	342,537	3,596.62	296,324	385,359

AMOUNT OF LOAN	30 YEARS		4% PMT INCR/YR 150.630 PAYMENTS			5% PMT INCR/YR 138.906 PAYMENTS			6% PMT INCR/YR 129.719 PAYMENTS		
	MONTHLY PAYMENT	TOTAL INTRST	LAST YR MON PMT	TOTAL INTRST	INTRST SAVED	LAST YR MON PMT	TOTAL INTRST	INTRST SAVED	LAST YR MON PMT	TOTAL INTRST	INTRST SAVED
$ 50	0.62	173	0.99	68	105	1.06	63	110	1.11	59	114
100	1.23	343	1.97	135	208	2.10	124	219	2.20	116	227
200	2.45	682	3.92	268	414	4.19	247	435	4.39	230	452
300	3.68	1,025	5.89	403	622	6.29	371	654	6.59	346	679
400	4.90	1,364	7.85	536	828	8.38	493	871	8.78	460	904
500	6.13	1,707	9.81	670	1,037	10.48	617	1,090	10.98	576	1,131
600	7.35	2,046	11.77	803	1,243	12.57	740	1,306	13.16	690	1,356
700	8.58	2,389	13.74	938	1,451	14.67	864	1,525	15.37	806	1,583
800	9.80	2,728	15.69	1,071	1,657	16.76	986	1,742	17.55	921	1,807
900	11.03	3,071	17.66	1,206	1,865	18.87	1,111	1,960	19.75	1,037	2,034
1,000	12.25	3,410	19.61	1,339	2,071	20.95	1,233	2,177	21.94	1,151	2,259
2,000	24.50	6,820	39.23	2,678	4,142	41.90	2,466	4,354	43.88	2,302	4,518
3,000	36.74	10,226	58.82	4,015	6,211	62.84	3,697	6,529	65.80	3,451	6,775
4,000	48.99	13,636	78.43	5,353	8,283	83.79	4,931	8,705	87.73	4,601	9,035
5,000	61.23	17,043	98.03	6,690	10,353	104.72	6,162	10,881	109.65	5,750	11,293
6,000	73.48	20,453	117.64	8,029	12,424	125.68	7,395	13,058	131.59	6,901	13,552
7,000	85.72	23,859	137.24	9,366	14,493	146.61	8,626	15,233	153.51	8,050	15,809
8,000	97.97	27,269	156.85	10,705	16,564	167.56	9,859	17,410	175.45	9,201	18,068
9,000	110.22	30,679	176.47	12,044	18,635	188.51	11,092	19,587	197.39	10,352	20,327
10,000	122.46	34,086	196.06	13,381	20,705	209.45	12,324	21,762	219.31	11,501	22,585
11,000	134.71	37,496	215.68	14,719	22,777	230.40	13,557	23,939	241.25	12,652	24,844
12,000	146.95	40,902	235.27	16,056	24,846	251.33	14,788	26,114	263.17	13,801	27,101
13,000	159.20	44,312	254.88	17,395	26,917	272.29	16,021	28,291	285.10	14,952	29,360
14,000	171.44	47,718	274.48	18,732	28,986	293.22	17,252	30,466	307.02	16,101	31,617
15,000	183.69	51,128	294.09	20,071	31,057	314.17	18,485	32,643	328.96	17,251	33,877
16,000	195.93	54,535	313.69	21,408	33,127	335.11	19,717	34,818	350.88	18,400	36,135
17,000	208.18	57,945	333.30	22,747	35,198	356.06	20,950	36,995	372.82	19,551	38,394
18,000	220.43	61,355	352.92	24,085	37,270	377.01	22,183	39,172	394.76	20,702	40,653
19,000	232.67	64,761	372.51	25,422	39,339	397.94	23,414	41,347	416.68	21,851	42,910
20,000	244.92	68,171	392.12	26,761	41,410	418.90	24,647	43,524	438.61	23,002	45,169
21,000	257.16	71,578	411.72	28,098	43,480	439.83	25,878	45,700	460.53	24,151	47,427
22,000	269.41	74,988	431.33	29,437	45,551	460.78	27,112	47,876	482.47	25,302	49,686
23,000	281.65	78,394	450.93	30,774	47,620	481.72	28,343	50,051	504.39	26,451	51,943
24,000	293.90	81,804	470.54	32,113	49,691	502.67	29,576	52,228	526.33	27,601	54,203
25,000	306.14	85,210	490.14	33,450	51,760	523.60	30,807	54,403	548.25	28,750	56,460
26,000	318.39	88,620	509.75	34,788	53,832	544.55	32,040	56,580	570.19	29,901	58,719
27,000	330.64	92,030	529.37	36,127	55,903	565.51	33,273	58,757	592.13	31,052	60,978
28,000	342.88	95,437	548.96	37,464	57,973	586.44	34,505	60,932	614.05	32,201	63,236
29,000	355.13	98,847	568.57	38,803	60,044	607.39	35,738	63,109	635.98	33,352	65,495
30,000	367.37	102,253	588.17	40,140	62,113	628.33	36,969	65,284	657.90	34,501	67,752
32,500	397.99	110,776	637.19	43,486	67,290	680.70	40,051	70,725	712.74	37,377	73,399
35,000	428.60	119,296	686.20	46,830	72,466	733.05	43,131	76,165	767.56	40,251	79,045
40,000	489.83	136,339	784.23	53,521	82,818	837.78	49,293	87,046	877.21	46,002	90,337
45,000	551.06	153,382	882.26	60,211	93,171	942.50	55,451	97,928	986.86	51,752	101,630
50,000	612.28	170,421	980.28	66,899	103,522	1,047.21	61,614	108,807	1,096.50	57,501	112,920
55,000	673.51	187,464	1,078.31	73,590	113,874	1,151.93	67,776	119,688	1,206.15	63,251	124,213
60,000	734.74	204,506	1,176.34	80,280	124,226	1,256.65	73,938	130,568	1,315.81	69,002	135,504
65,000	795.97	221,549	1,274.37	86,970	134,579	1,361.38	80,100	141,449	1,425.46	74,752	146,797
70,000	857.19	238,588	1,372.39	93,659	144,929	1,466.09	86,260	152,328	1,535.10	80,501	158,087
75,000	918.42	255,631	1,470.42	100,349	155,282	1,570.81	92,422	163,209	1,644.75	86,251	169,380
80,000	979.65	272,674	1,568.45	107,039	165,635	1,675.53	98,583	174,091	1,754.40	92,002	180,672
85,000	1,040.88	289,717	1,666.48	113,730	175,987	1,780.26	104,745	184,972	1,864.06	97,752	191,965
90,000	1,102.11	306,760	1,764.51	120,420	186,340	1,884.98	110,907	195,853	1,973.71	103,503	203,257
95,000	1,163.33	323,799	1,862.53	127,108	196,691	1,989.69	117,067	206,732	2,083.35	109,251	214,548
100,000	1,224.56	340,842	1,960.56	133,799	207,043	2,094.41	123,229	217,613	2,193.00	115,002	225,840
105,000	1,285.79	357,884	2,058.59	140,489	217,395	2,199.14	129,391	228,493	2,302.65	120,752	237,132
110,000	1,347.02	374,927	2,156.62	147,179	227,748	2,303.86	135,552	239,375	2,412.31	126,503	248,424
115,000	1,408.24	391,966	2,254.64	153,868	238,098	2,408.57	141,712	250,254	2,521.94	132,251	259,715
120,000	1,469.47	409,009	2,352.67	160,558	248,451	2,513.29	147,874	261,135	2,631.60	138,002	271,007
125,000	1,530.70	426,052	2,450.70	167,248	258,804	2,618.02	154,036	272,016	2,741.25	143,752	282,300
130,000	1,591.93	443,095	2,548.73	173,938	269,157	2,722.74	160,198	282,897	2,850.90	149,503	293,592
135,000	1,653.16	460,138	2,646.76	180,629	279,509	2,827.46	166,360	293,778	2,960.56	155,253	304,885
140,000	1,714.38	477,177	2,744.78	187,317	289,860	2,932.17	172,520	304,657	3,070.19	161,002	316,175
145,000	1,775.61	494,220	2,842.81	194,007	300,213	3,036.90	178,681	315,539	3,179.85	166,752	327,468
150,000	1,836.84	511,262	2,940.84	200,698	310,564	3,141.62	184,843	326,419	3,289.50	172,503	338,759
155,000	1,898.07	528,305	3,038.87	207,388	320,917	3,246.34	191,005	337,300	3,399.15	178,253	350,052
160,000	1,959.29	545,344	3,136.89	214,076	331,268	3,351.05	197,165	348,179	3,508.79	184,002	361,342
165,000	2,020.52	562,387	3,234.92	220,767	341,620	3,455.77	203,327	359,060	3,618.44	189,752	372,635
170,000	2,081.75	579,430	3,332.95	227,457	351,973	3,560.50	209,489	369,941	3,728.10	195,503	383,927
175,000	2,142.98	596,473	3,430.98	234,147	362,326	3,665.22	215,650	380,823	3,837.75	201,253	395,220
180,000	2,204.21	613,516	3,529.01	240,838	372,678	3,769.95	221,812	391,704	3,947.40	207,004	406,512
185,000	2,265.43	630,555	3,627.03	247,526	383,029	3,874.65	227,972	402,583	4,057.04	212,752	417,803
190,000	2,326.66	647,598	3,725.06	254,216	393,382	3,979.38	234,134	413,464	4,166.69	218,503	429,095
195,000	2,387.89	664,640	3,823.09	260,907	403,733	4,084.10	240,296	424,344	4,276.35	224,253	440,387
200,000	2,449.12	681,683	3,921.12	267,597	414,086	4,188.83	246,458	435,225	4,386.00	230,004	451,679

14.75% GROWING EQUITY MORTGAGES

AMOUNT OF LOAN	30 YEARS		1% PMT INCR/YR 227.632 PAYMENTS			2% PMT INCR/YR 187.809 PAYMENTS			3% PMT INCR/YR 164.994 PAYMENTS		
	MONTHLY PAYMENT	TOTAL INTRST	LAST YR MON PMT	TOTAL INTRST	INTRST SAVED	LAST YR MON PMT	TOTAL INTRST	INTRST SAVED	LAST YR MON PMT	TOTAL INTRST	INTRST SAVED
$ 50	0.63	177	0.75	107	70	0.85	87	90	0.93	76	101
100	1.25	350	1.50	212	138	1.68	173	177	1.84	151	199
200	2.49	696	2.98	421	275	3.35	343	353	3.66	300	396
300	3.74	1,046	4.47	632	414	5.03	515	531	5.49	450	596
400	4.98	1,393	5.96	841	552	6.70	686	707	7.31	599	794
500	6.23	1,743	7.45	1,053	690	8.38	858	885	9.15	750	993
600	7.47	2,089	8.94	1,262	827	10.05	1,029	1,060	10.97	899	1,190
700	8.72	2,439	10.43	1,474	965	11.74	1,201	1,238	12.81	1,049	1,390
800	9.96	2,786	11.91	1,683	1,103	13.40	1,372	1,414	14.63	1,198	1,588
900	11.21	3,136	13.41	1,895	1,241	15.09	1,544	1,592	16.46	1,349	1,787
1,000	12.45	3,482	14.89	2,104	1,378	16.76	1,714	1,768	18.28	1,498	1,984
2,000	24.89	6,960	29.77	4,205	2,755	33.50	3,427	3,533	36.55	2,993	3,967
3,000	37.34	10,442	44.66	6,309	4,133	50.25	5,141	5,301	54.84	4,491	5,951
4,000	49.78	13,921	59.54	8,410	5,511	67.00	6,854	7,067	73.10	5,987	7,934
5,000	62.23	17,403	74.44	10,513	6,890	83.75	8,568	8,835	91.39	7,485	9,918
6,000	74.67	20,881	89.32	12,615	8,266	100.50	10,280	10,601	109.66	8,980	11,901
7,000	87.12	24,363	104.21	14,718	9,645	117.25	11,995	12,368	127.94	10,478	13,885
8,000	99.56	27,842	119.09	16,819	11,023	133.99	13,707	14,135	146.21	11,974	15,868
9,000	112.01	31,324	133.98	18,923	12,401	150.75	15,422	15,902	164.49	13,472	17,852
10,000	124.45	34,802	148.86	21,024	13,778	167.49	17,134	17,668	182.76	14,967	19,835
11,000	136.90	38,284	163.75	23,128	15,156	184.25	18,848	19,436	201.04	16,465	21,819
12,000	149.34	41,762	178.63	25,229	16,533	200.99	20,561	21,201	219.31	17,961	23,801
13,000	161.79	45,244	193.52	27,333	17,911	217.75	22,275	22,969	237.59	19,459	25,785
14,000	174.23	48,723	208.40	29,434	19,289	234.49	23,988	24,735	255.86	20,954	27,769
15,000	186.68	52,205	223.30	31,538	20,667	251.25	25,702	26,503	274.15	22,452	29,753
16,000	199.12	55,683	238.18	33,639	22,044	267.99	27,414	28,269	292.41	23,948	31,735
17,000	211.57	59,165	253.07	35,742	23,423	284.75	29,129	30,036	310.70	25,445	33,720
18,000	224.01	62,644	267.95	37,844	24,800	301.49	30,841	31,803	328.97	26,941	35,703
19,000	236.46	66,126	282.84	39,947	26,179	318.24	32,556	33,570	347.25	28,439	37,687
20,000	248.90	69,604	297.72	42,048	27,556	334.99	34,268	35,336	365.52	29,935	39,669
21,000	261.34	73,082	312.60	44,150	28,932	351.73	35,980	37,102	383.79	31,430	41,652
22,000	273.79	76,564	327.49	46,253	30,311	368.49	37,695	38,869	402.07	32,928	43,636
23,000	286.23	80,043	342.37	48,354	31,689	385.23	39,407	40,636	420.34	34,424	45,619
24,000	298.68	83,525	357.27	50,458	33,067	401.98	41,121	42,404	438.62	35,922	47,603
25,000	311.12	87,003	372.15	52,559	34,444	418.73	42,834	44,169	456.89	37,417	49,586
26,000	323.57	90,485	387.04	54,663	35,822	435.48	44,548	45,937	475.17	38,915	51,570
27,000	336.01	93,964	401.92	56,764	37,200	452.23	46,261	47,703	493.44	40,411	53,553
28,000	348.46	97,446	416.81	58,868	38,578	468.98	47,975	49,471	511.73	41,909	55,537
29,000	360.90	100,924	431.69	60,969	39,955	485.72	49,687	51,237	529.99	43,404	57,520
30,000	373.35	104,406	446.58	63,073	41,333	502.48	51,402	53,004	548.28	44,902	59,504
32,500	404.46	113,106	483.79	68,328	44,778	544.35	55,685	57,421	593.96	48,643	64,463
35,000	435.57	121,805	521.01	73,583	48,222	586.22	59,968	61,837	639.65	52,385	69,422
40,000	497.80	139,208	595.44	84,097	55,111	669.97	68,536	70,672	731.04	59,869	79,339
45,000	560.02	156,607	669.87	94,608	61,999	753.71	77,102	79,505	822.41	67,352	89,255
50,000	622.24	174,006	744.29	105,119	68,887	837.45	85,668	88,338	913.78	74,835	99,171
55,000	684.47	191,409	818.73	115,632	75,777	921.21	94,236	97,173	1,005.17	82,319	109,090
60,000	746.69	208,808	893.15	126,143	82,665	1,004.95	102,801	106,007	1,096.54	89,802	119,006
65,000	808.91	226,208	967.58	136,654	89,554	1,088.69	111,367	114,841	1,187.91	97,285	128,923
70,000	871.14	243,610	1,042.01	147,167	96,443	1,172.44	119,935	123,675	1,279.30	104,769	138,841
75,000	933.36	261,010	1,116.44	157,678	103,332	1,256.18	128,501	132,509	1,370.67	112,252	148,758
80,000	995.59	278,412	1,190.87	168,191	110,221	1,339.93	137,069	141,343	1,462.06	119,737	158,675
85,000	1,057.81	295,812	1,265.30	178,702	117,110	1,423.67	145,635	150,177	1,553.43	127,219	168,593
90,000	1,120.03	313,211	1,339.72	189,213	123,998	1,507.41	154,201	159,010	1,644.80	134,702	178,509
95,000	1,182.26	330,614	1,414.16	199,726	130,888	1,591.17	162,769	167,845	1,736.19	142,187	188,427
100,000	1,244.48	348,013	1,488.58	210,237	137,776	1,674.91	171,335	176,678	1,827.56	149,669	198,344
105,000	1,306.70	365,412	1,563.01	220,748	144,664	1,758.65	179,901	185,511	1,918.93	157,152	208,260
110,000	1,368.93	382,815	1,637.44	231,261	151,554	1,842.40	188,469	194,346	2,010.32	164,637	218,178
115,000	1,431.15	400,214	1,711.87	241,772	158,442	1,926.14	197,035	203,179	2,101.69	172,119	228,095
120,000	1,493.38	417,617	1,786.30	252,286	165,331	2,009.89	205,603	212,014	2,193.08	179,604	238,013
125,000	1,555.60	435,016	1,860.73	262,796	172,220	2,093.63	214,169	220,847	2,284.45	187,087	247,929
130,000	1,617.82	452,415	1,935.15	273,307	179,108	2,177.37	222,735	229,680	2,375.82	194,569	257,846
135,000	1,680.05	469,818	2,009.59	283,821	185,997	2,261.13	231,303	238,515	2,467.21	202,054	267,764
140,000	1,742.27	487,217	2,084.01	294,331	192,886	2,344.87	239,869	247,348	2,558.58	209,537	277,680
145,000	1,804.49	504,616	2,158.44	304,842	199,774	2,428.61	248,435	256,181	2,649.95	217,019	287,597
150,000	1,866.72	522,019	2,232.87	315,356	206,663	2,512.36	257,003	265,016	2,741.34	224,504	297,515
155,000	1,928.94	539,418	2,307.30	325,867	213,551	2,596.10	265,569	273,849	2,832.71	231,987	307,431
160,000	1,991.17	556,821	2,381.73	336,380	220,441	2,679.85	274,137	282,684	2,924.10	239,471	317,350
165,000	2,053.39	574,220	2,456.16	346,891	227,329	2,763.59	282,702	291,518	3,015.47	246,954	327,266
170,000	2,115.61	591,620	2,530.58	357,402	234,218	2,847.33	291,268	300,352	3,106.84	254,437	337,183
175,000	2,177.84	609,022	2,605.02	367,915	241,107	2,931.09	299,836	309,186	3,198.23	261,921	347,101
180,000	2,240.06	626,422	2,679.44	378,426	247,996	3,014.83	308,402	318,020	3,289.60	269,404	357,018
185,000	2,302.29	643,824	2,753.88	388,939	254,885	3,098.58	316,970	326,854	3,380.99	276,889	366,935
190,000	2,364.51	661,223	2,828.30	399,450	261,774	3,182.32	325,536	335,688	3,472.36	284,371	376,853
195,000	2,426.73	678,623	2,902.73	409,961	268,662	3,266.06	334,102	344,521	3,563.73	291,854	386,769
200,000	2,488.96	696,026	2,977.16	420,474	275,552	3,349.81	342,670	353,356	3,655.12	299,339	396,687

162

AMOUNT OF LOAN	30 YEARS		4% PMT INCR/YR 149.403 PAYMENTS			5% PMT INCR/YR 137.789 PAYMENTS			6% PMT INCR/YR 128.676 PAYMENTS		
	MONTHLY PAYMENT	TOTAL INTRST	LAST YR MON PMT	TOTAL INTRST	INTRST SAVED	LAST YR MON PMT	TOTAL INTRST	INTRST SAVED	LAST YR MON PMT	TOTAL INTRST	INTRST SAVED
$ 50	0.63	177	1.01	69	108	1.08	64	113	1.13	59	118
100	1.25	350	2.00	136	214	2.14	125	225	2.24	117	233
200	2.49	696	3.99	271	425	4.26	249	447	4.46	233	463
300	3.74	1,046	5.99	407	639	6.40	375	671	6.70	350	696
400	4.98	1,393	7.97	541	852	8.52	498	895	8.92	465	928
500	6.23	1,743	9.97	677	1,066	10.66	624	1,119	11.16	582	1,161
600	7.47	2,089	11.96	812	1,277	12.78	747	1,342	13.38	698	1,391
700	8.72	2,439	13.96	948	1,491	14.91	873	1,566	15.62	815	1,624
800	9.96	2,786	15.95	1,082	1,704	17.03	997	1,789	17.84	930	1,856
900	11.21	3,136	17.95	1,218	1,918	19.17	1,122	2,014	20.08	1,047	2,089
1,000	12.45	3,482	19.93	1,353	2,129	21.29	1,246	2,236	22.30	1,163	2,319
2,000	24.89	6,960	39.85	2,703	4,257	42.57	2,490	4,470	44.57	2,324	4,636
3,000	37.34	10,442	59.78	4,056	6,386	63.86	3,735	6,707	66.87	3,486	6,956
4,000	49.78	13,921	79.70	5,406	8,515	85.14	4,979	8,942	89.15	4,647	9,274
5,000	62.23	17,403	99.63	6,759	10,644	106.43	6,225	11,178	111.44	5,810	11,593
6,000	74.67	20,881	119.55	8,110	12,771	127.71	7,469	13,412	133.72	6,971	13,910
7,000	87.12	24,363	139.48	9,462	14,901	149.00	8,715	15,648	156.02	8,133	16,230
8,000	99.56	27,842	159.40	10,813	17,029	170.28	9,959	17,883	178.30	9,294	18,548
9,000	112.01	31,324	179.33	12,165	19,159	191.58	11,205	20,119	200.59	10,457	20,867
10,000	124.45	34,802	199.25	13,516	21,286	212.85	12,449	22,353	222.87	11,618	23,184
11,000	136.90	38,284	219.18	14,869	23,415	234.15	13,694	24,590	245.17	12,780	25,504
12,000	149.34	41,762	239.10	16,219	25,543	255.42	14,938	26,824	267.45	13,941	27,821
13,000	161.79	45,244	259.03	17,572	27,672	276.72	16,184	29,060	289.74	15,104	30,140
14,000	174.23	48,723	278.95	18,923	29,800	297.99	17,428	31,295	312.02	16,265	32,458
15,000	186.68	52,205	298.88	20,275	31,930	319.29	18,674	33,531	334.32	17,428	34,777
16,000	199.12	55,683	318.80	21,626	34,057	340.56	19,918	35,765	356.59	18,589	37,094
17,000	211.57	59,165	338.73	22,978	36,187	361.86	21,164	38,001	378.89	19,751	39,414
18,000	224.01	62,644	358.65	24,329	38,315	383.13	22,408	40,236	401.17	20,912	41,732
19,000	236.46	66,126	378.58	25,681	40,445	404.43	23,653	42,473	423.46	22,075	44,051
20,000	248.90	69,604	398.50	27,032	42,572	425.70	24,897	44,707	445.74	23,236	46,368
21,000	261.34	73,082	418.41	28,383	44,699	446.98	26,141	46,941	468.02	24,397	48,685
22,000	273.79	76,564	438.35	29,735	46,829	468.27	27,387	49,177	490.32	25,559	51,005
23,000	286.23	80,043	458.26	31,086	48,957	489.55	28,631	51,412	512.59	26,720	53,323
24,000	298.68	83,525	478.20	32,439	51,086	510.84	29,877	53,648	534.89	27,883	55,643
25,000	311.12	87,003	498.11	33,789	53,214	532.12	31,121	55,882	557.17	29,044	57,959
26,000	323.57	90,485	518.05	35,142	55,343	553.41	32,366	58,119	579.46	30,206	60,279
27,000	336.01	93,964	537.96	36,492	57,472	574.69	33,610	60,354	601.74	31,367	62,597
28,000	348.46	97,446	557.90	37,845	59,601	595.98	34,856	62,590	624.04	32,530	64,916
29,000	360.90	100,924	577.81	39,196	61,728	617.26	36,100	64,824	646.32	33,691	67,233
30,000	373.35	104,406	597.75	40,548	63,858	638.56	37,346	67,060	668.61	34,853	69,553
32,500	404.46	113,106	647.55	43,927	69,179	691.76	40,458	72,648	724.33	37,758	75,348
35,000	435.57	121,805	697.36	47,305	74,500	744.97	43,569	78,236	780.04	40,662	81,143
40,000	497.80	139,208	796.99	54,064	85,144	851.41	49,794	89,414	891.48	46,471	92,737
45,000	560.02	156,607	896.61	60,821	95,786	957.82	56,018	100,589	1,002.91	52,279	104,328
50,000	622.24	174,006	996.23	67,578	106,428	1,064.24	62,241	111,765	1,114.34	58,087	115,919
55,000	684.47	191,409	1,095.86	74,337	117,072	1,170.68	68,466	122,943	1,225.78	63,897	127,512
60,000	746.69	208,808	1,195.47	81,095	127,713	1,277.09	74,690	134,118	1,337.21	69,705	139,103
65,000	808.91	226,208	1,295.09	87,852	138,356	1,383.51	80,913	145,295	1,448.63	75,513	150,695
70,000	871.14	243,610	1,394.72	94,611	148,999	1,489.95	87,138	156,472	1,560.08	81,323	162,287
75,000	933.36	261,010	1,494.34	101,368	159,642	1,596.36	93,362	167,648	1,671.51	87,131	173,879
80,000	995.59	278,412	1,593.97	108,127	170,285	1,702.80	99,587	178,825	1,782.95	92,941	185,471
85,000	1,057.81	295,812	1,693.59	114,884	180,928	1,809.21	105,811	190,001	1,894.38	98,749	197,063
90,000	1,120.03	313,211	1,793.20	121,641	191,570	1,915.63	112,034	201,177	2,005.80	104,557	208,654
95,000	1,182.26	330,614	1,892.84	128,400	202,214	2,022.07	118,259	212,355	2,117.25	110,367	220,247
100,000	1,244.48	348,013	1,992.45	135,157	212,856	2,128.48	124,483	223,530	2,228.67	116,175	231,838
105,000	1,306.70	365,412	2,092.07	141,914	223,498	2,234.90	130,706	234,706	2,340.10	121,983	243,429
110,000	1,368.93	382,815	2,191.70	148,673	234,142	2,341.33	136,931	245,884	2,451.55	127,793	255,022
115,000	1,431.15	400,214	2,291.32	155,430	244,784	2,447.75	143,155	257,059	2,562.97	133,601	266,613
120,000	1,493.38	417,617	2,390.95	162,189	255,428	2,554.19	149,380	268,237	2,674.42	139,410	278,207
125,000	1,555.60	435,016	2,490.57	168,946	266,070	2,660.60	155,603	279,413	2,785.84	145,219	289,797
130,000	1,617.82	452,415	2,590.18	175,703	276,712	2,767.02	161,827	290,588	2,897.27	151,027	301,388
135,000	1,680.05	469,818	2,689.81	182,462	287,356	2,873.46	168,052	301,766	3,008.71	156,836	312,982
140,000	1,742.27	487,217	2,789.43	189,219	297,998	2,979.87	174,275	312,942	3,120.14	162,644	324,573
145,000	1,804.49	504,616	2,889.05	195,977	308,639	3,086.29	180,499	324,117	3,231.57	168,452	336,164
150,000	1,866.72	522,019	2,988.68	202,735	319,284	3,192.72	186,724	335,295	3,343.01	174,262	347,757
155,000	1,928.94	539,418	3,088.30	209,493	329,925	3,299.14	192,947	346,471	3,454.44	180,070	359,348
160,000	1,991.17	556,821	3,187.93	216,252	340,569	3,405.58	199,172	357,649	3,565.88	185,880	370,941
165,000	2,053.39	574,220	3,287.54	223,009	351,211	3,511.99	205,396	368,824	3,677.31	191,688	382,532
170,000	2,115.61	591,620	3,387.16	229,766	361,854	3,618.41	211,619	380,001	3,788.74	197,496	394,124
175,000	2,177.84	609,022	3,486.79	236,525	372,497	3,724.85	217,844	391,178	3,900.18	203,306	405,716
180,000	2,240.06	626,422	3,586.41	243,282	383,140	3,831.26	224,068	402,354	4,011.61	209,114	417,308
185,000	2,302.29	643,824	3,686.04	250,041	393,783	3,937.70	230,293	413,531	4,123.05	214,924	428,900
190,000	2,364.51	661,224	3,785.66	256,798	404,426	4,044.11	236,516	424,708	4,234.48	220,732	440,492
195,000	2,426.73	678,623	3,885.27	263,555	415,068	4,150.53	242,740	435,883	4,345.90	226,540	452,083
200,000	2,488.96	696,026	3,984.91	270,314	425,712	4,256.97	248,965	447,061	4,457.35	232,350	463,676

163

GROWING EQUITY MORTGAGES

AMOUNT OF LOAN	30 YEARS		1% PMT INCR/YR 225.846 PAYMENTS			2% PMT INCR/YR 186.266 PAYMENTS			3% PMT INCR/YR 163.636 PAYMENTS		
	MONTHLY PAYMENT	TOTAL INTRST	LAST YR MON PMT	TOTAL INTRST	INTRST SAVED	LAST YR MON PMT	TOTAL INTRST	INTRST SAVED	LAST YR MON PMT	TOTAL INTRST	INTRST SAVED
$ 50	0.64	180	0.77	108	72	0.86	88	92	0.94	77	103
100	1.27	357	1.52	214	143	1.71	174	183	1.87	152	205
200	2.53	711	3.03	425	286	3.41	346	365	3.72	303	408
300	3.80	1,068	4.55	639	429	5.11	521	547	5.58	455	613
400	5.06	1,422	6.05	851	571	6.81	693	729	7.43	605	817
500	6.33	1,779	7.57	1,064	715	8.52	867	912	9.30	757	1,022
600	7.59	2,132	9.08	1,276	856	10.22	1,039	1,093	11.15	908	1,224
700	8.86	2,490	10.60	1,490	1,000	11.92	1,213	1,277	13.01	1,060	1,430
800	10.12	2,843	12.11	1,701	1,142	13.62	1,385	1,458	14.86	1,210	1,633
900	11.38	3,197	13.61	1,913	1,284	15.32	1,558	1,639	16.71	1,360	1,837
1,000	12.65	3,554	15.13	2,127	1,427	17.03	1,732	1,822	18.58	1,513	2,041
2,000	25.29	7,104	30.25	4,251	2,853	34.04	3,461	3,643	37.14	3,023	4,081
3,000	37.94	10,658	45.38	6,377	4,281	51.06	5,193	5,465	55.72	4,536	6,122
4,000	50.58	14,209	60.50	8,501	5,708	68.07	6,923	7,286	74.28	6,047	8,162
5,000	63.23	17,763	75.63	10,628	7,135	85.10	8,655	9,108	92.86	7,559	10,204
6,000	75.87	21,313	90.75	12,752	8,561	102.11	10,384	10,929	111.42	9,070	12,243
7,000	88.52	24,867	105.88	14,878	9,989	119.14	12,116	12,751	129.99	10,582	14,285
8,000	101.16	28,418	121.00	17,002	11,416	136.15	13,846	14,572	148.56	12,093	16,325
9,000	113.80	31,968	136.12	19,126	12,842	153.16	15,576	16,392	167.12	13,604	18,364
10,000	126.45	35,522	151.25	21,253	14,269	170.19	17,307	18,215	185.70	15,116	20,406
11,000	139.09	39,072	166.37	23,377	15,695	187.20	19,037	20,035	204.26	16,627	22,445
12,000	151.74	42,626	181.50	25,503	17,123	204.22	20,769	21,857	222.84	18,140	24,486
13,000	164.38	46,177	196.62	27,627	18,550	221.23	22,499	23,678	241.40	19,650	26,527
14,000	177.03	49,731	211.75	29,754	19,977	238.26	24,230	25,501	259.97	21,163	28,568
15,000	189.67	53,281	226.87	31,878	21,403	255.27	25,960	27,321	278.54	22,674	30,607
16,000	202.32	56,835	242.00	34,004	22,831	272.30	27,692	29,143	297.11	24,186	32,649
17,000	214.96	60,386	257.12	36,128	24,258	289.31	29,422	30,964	315.68	25,697	34,689
18,000	227.60	63,936	272.24	38,252	25,684	306.32	31,151	32,785	334.24	27,208	36,728
19,000	240.25	67,490	287.37	40,379	27,111	323.34	32,883	34,607	352.82	28,720	38,770
20,000	252.89	71,040	302.49	42,503	28,537	340.36	34,613	36,427	371.38	30,231	40,809
21,000	265.54	74,594	317.63	44,629	29,965	357.38	36,344	38,250	389.95	31,743	42,851
22,000	278.18	78,145	332.74	46,753	31,392	374.39	38,074	40,071	408.52	33,254	44,891
23,000	290.83	81,699	347.88	48,880	32,819	391.42	39,806	41,893	427.09	34,767	46,932
24,000	303.47	85,249	362.99	51,004	34,245	408.43	41,536	43,713	445.66	36,277	48,972
25,000	316.12	88,803	378.13	53,130	35,673	425.46	43,267	45,536	464.23	37,790	51,013
26,000	328.76	92,354	393.25	55,254	37,100	442.47	44,997	47,357	482.80	39,301	53,053
27,000	341.40	95,904	408.36	57,378	38,526	459.48	46,727	49,177	501.36	40,811	55,093
28,000	354.05	99,458	423.50	59,505	39,953	476.50	48,459	50,999	519.93	42,324	57,134
29,000	366.69	103,008	438.62	61,629	41,379	493.52	50,188	52,820	538.50	43,835	59,173
30,000	379.34	106,562	453.75	63,755	42,807	510.54	51,920	54,642	557.07	45,347	61,215
32,500	410.95	115,442	491.56	69,068	46,374	553.08	56,246	59,196	603.49	49,126	66,316
35,000	442.56	124,322	529.37	74,381	49,941	595.63	60,573	63,749	649.91	52,904	71,418
40,000	505.78	142,081	604.99	85,006	57,075	680.71	69,225	72,856	742.75	60,462	81,619
45,000	569.00	159,840	680.61	95,631	64,209	765.80	77,878	81,962	835.60	68,019	91,821
50,000	632.23	177,603	756.24	106,258	71,345	850.90	86,533	91,070	928.45	75,578	102,025
55,000	695.45	195,362	831.86	116,883	78,479	935.98	95,185	100,177	1,021.29	83,135	112,227
60,000	758.67	213,121	907.48	127,509	85,612	1,021.07	103,838	109,283	1,114.13	90,693	122,428
65,000	821.89	230,880	983.10	138,134	92,746	1,106.16	112,491	118,389	1,206.97	98,250	132,630
70,000	885.12	248,643	1,058.73	148,761	99,882	1,191.25	121,145	127,498	1,299.83	105,809	142,834
75,000	948.34	266,402	1,134.35	159,386	107,016	1,276.34	129,798	136,604	1,392.67	113,366	153,036
80,000	1,011.56	284,162	1,209.97	170,011	114,151	1,361.43	138,451	145,711	1,485.51	120,923	163,239
85,000	1,074.78	301,921	1,285.60	180,636	121,285	1,446.51	147,103	154,818	1,578.35	128,481	173,440
90,000	1,138.00	319,680	1,361.22	191,262	128,418	1,531.60	155,756	163,924	1,671.19	136,038	183,642
95,000	1,201.23	337,443	1,436.85	201,889	135,554	1,616.70	164,411	173,032	1,764.05	143,597	193,846
100,000	1,264.45	355,202	1,512.47	212,514	142,688	1,701.78	173,063	182,139	1,856.89	151,154	204,048
105,000	1,327.67	372,961	1,588.09	223,139	149,822	1,786.87	181,716	191,245	1,949.73	158,711	214,250
110,000	1,390.89	390,720	1,663.71	233,764	156,955	1,871.95	190,369	200,351	2,042.57	166,269	224,451
115,000	1,454.12	408,483	1,739.34	244,392	164,091	1,957.05	199,023	209,460	2,135.42	173,828	234,655
120,000	1,517.34	426,242	1,814.96	255,017	171,225	2,042.14	207,676	218,566	2,228.26	181,385	244,857
125,000	1,580.56	444,002	1,890.58	265,642	178,360	2,127.23	216,329	227,673	2,321.11	188,942	255,060
130,000	1,643.78	461,761	1,966.20	276,267	185,494	2,212.31	224,981	236,780	2,413.95	196,499	265,262
135,000	1,707.00	479,520	2,041.82	286,892	192,628	2,297.40	233,634	245,886	2,506.79	204,057	275,463
140,000	1,770.23	497,283	2,117.46	297,520	199,763	2,382.50	242,289	254,994	2,599.64	211,616	285,667
145,000	1,833.45	515,042	2,193.08	308,145	206,897	2,467.58	250,941	264,101	2,692.48	219,173	295,869
150,000	1,896.67	532,801	2,268.70	318,770	214,031	2,552.67	259,594	273,207	2,785.32	226,730	306,071
155,000	1,959.89	550,560	2,344.32	329,395	221,165	2,637.75	268,247	282,313	2,878.16	234,287	316,273
160,000	2,023.12	568,323	2,419.95	340,023	228,300	2,722.85	276,901	291,422	2,971.02	241,847	326,476
165,000	2,086.34	586,082	2,495.57	350,648	235,434	2,807.94	285,554	300,528	3,063.86	249,404	336,678
170,000	2,149.56	603,842	2,571.19	361,273	242,569	2,893.02	294,207	309,635	3,156.70	256,961	346,881
175,000	2,212.78	621,601	2,646.81	371,898	249,703	2,978.11	302,859	318,742	3,249.54	264,518	357,083
180,000	2,276.00	639,360	2,722.43	382,523	256,837	3,063.20	311,512	327,848	3,342.38	272,076	367,284
185,000	2,339.23	657,123	2,798.06	393,151	263,972	3,148.30	320,167	336,956	3,435.24	279,635	377,488
190,000	2,402.45	674,882	2,873.68	403,776	271,106	3,233.38	328,819	346,063	3,528.08	287,192	387,690
195,000	2,465.67	692,641	2,949.30	414,401	278,240	3,318.47	337,472	355,169	3,620.92	294,749	397,892
200,000	2,528.89	710,400	3,024.93	425,026	285,374	3,403.55	346,124	364,276	3,713.76	302,306	408,094

GROWING EQUITY MORTGAGES 15.00%

AMOUNT OF LOAN	30 YEARS		4% PMT INCR/YR 148.197 PAYMENTS			5% PMT INCR/YR 136.693 PAYMENTS			6% PMT INCR/YR 127.654 PAYMENTS		
	MONTHLY PAYMENT	TOTAL INTRST	LAST YR MON PMT	TOTAL INTRST	INTRST SAVED	LAST YR MON PMT	TOTAL INTRST	INTRST SAVED	LAST YR MON PMT	TOTAL INTRST	INTRST SAVED
$ 50	0.64	180	1.02	70	110	1.09	64	116	1.15	60	120
100	1.27	357	2.03	138	219	2.17	127	230	2.27	118	239
200	2.53	711	4.05	273	438	4.33	252	459	4.53	235	476
300	3.80	1,068	6.08	411	657	6.50	378	690	6.81	353	715
400	5.06	1,422	8.10	546	876	8.65	503	919	9.06	470	952
500	6.33	1,779	10.13	684	1,095	10.83	630	1,149	11.34	588	1,191
600	7.59	2,132	12.15	820	1,312	12.98	755	1,377	13.59	705	1,427
700	8.86	2,490	14.19	957	1,533	15.15	882	1,608	15.87	823	1,667
800	10.12	2,843	16.20	1,093	1,750	17.31	1,007	1,836	18.12	939	1,904
900	11.38	3,197	18.22	1,228	1,969	19.46	1,131	2,066	20.38	1,056	2,141
1,000	12.65	3,554	20.25	1,366	2,188	21.64	1,258	2,296	22.65	1,174	2,380
2,000	25.29	7,104	40.49	2,730	4,374	43.25	2,514	4,590	45.29	2,347	4,757
3,000	37.94	10,658	60.74	4,096	6,562	64.89	3,773	6,885	67.94	3,521	7,137
4,000	50.58	14,209	80.98	5,460	8,749	86.51	5,029	9,180	90.58	4,694	9,515
5,000	63.23	17,763	101.23	6,826	10,937	108.14	6,287	11,476	113.24	5,868	11,895
6,000	75.87	21,313	121.47	8,190	13,123	129.76	7,543	13,770	135.87	7,040	14,273
7,000	88.52	24,867	141.72	9,556	15,311	151.40	8,802	16,065	158.53	8,215	16,652
8,000	101.16	28,418	161.96	10,920	17,498	173.02	10,058	18,360	181.16	9,387	19,031
9,000	113.80	31,968	182.20	12,284	19,684	194.64	11,314	20,654	203.80	10,560	21,408
10,000	126.45	35,522	202.45	13,650	21,872	216.27	12,572	22,950	226.45	11,734	23,788
11,000	139.09	39,072	222.69	15,014	24,058	237.89	13,829	25,243	249.09	12,906	26,166
12,000	151.74	42,626	242.94	16,380	26,246	259.53	15,087	27,539	271.74	14,081	28,545
13,000	164.38	46,177	263.18	17,744	28,433	281.15	16,343	29,834	294.38	15,253	30,924
14,000	177.03	49,731	283.43	19,110	30,621	302.78	17,601	32,130	317.03	16,427	33,304
15,000	189.67	53,281	303.67	20,474	32,807	324.40	18,858	34,423	339.67	17,600	35,681
16,000	202.32	56,835	323.92	21,840	34,995	346.04	20,116	36,719	362.32	18,774	38,061
17,000	214.96	60,386	344.16	23,204	37,182	367.65	21,372	39,014	384.96	19,947	40,439
18,000	227.60	63,936	364.39	24,568	39,368	389.27	22,628	41,308	407.60	21,119	42,817
19,000	240.25	67,490	384.65	25,934	41,556	410.91	23,887	43,603	430.25	22,293	45,197
20,000	252.89	71,040	404.89	27,298	43,742	432.53	25,143	45,897	452.89	23,466	47,574
21,000	265.54	74,594	425.14	28,664	45,930	454.16	26,401	48,193	475.54	24,640	49,954
22,000	278.18	78,145	445.38	30,028	48,117	475.78	27,657	50,488	498.18	25,813	52,332
23,000	290.83	81,699	465.63	31,394	50,305	497.42	28,916	52,783	520.83	26,987	54,712
24,000	303.47	85,249	485.87	32,758	52,491	519.04	30,172	55,077	543.47	28,159	57,090
25,000	316.12	88,803	506.12	34,124	54,679	540.67	31,430	57,373	566.12	29,334	59,469
26,000	328.76	92,354	526.36	35,488	56,866	562.29	32,686	59,668	588.76	30,506	61,848
27,000	341.40	95,904	546.59	36,852	59,052	583.91	33,943	61,961	611.40	31,679	64,225
28,000	354.05	99,458	566.85	38,218	61,240	605.55	35,201	64,257	634.05	32,853	66,605
29,000	366.69	103,008	587.08	39,582	63,426	627.16	36,457	66,551	656.69	34,025	68,983
30,000	379.34	106,562	607.34	40,948	65,614	648.80	37,715	68,847	679.34	35,200	71,362
32,500	410.95	115,442	657.94	44,360	71,082	702.86	40,858	74,584	735.95	38,133	77,309
35,000	442.56	124,322	708.55	47,772	76,550	756.93	44,001	80,321	792.56	41,066	83,256
40,000	505.78	142,081	809.77	54,596	87,485	865.06	50,286	91,795	905.77	46,932	95,149
45,000	569.00	159,840	910.99	61,420	98,420	973.18	56,571	103,269	1,018.99	52,798	107,042
50,000	632.23	177,603	1,012.22	68,245	109,358	1,081.33	62,858	114,745	1,132.23	58,666	118,937
55,000	695.45	195,362	1,113.44	75,069	120,293	1,189.46	69,143	126,219	1,245.45	64,532	130,830
60,000	758.67	213,121	1,214.66	81,893	131,228	1,297.58	75,429	137,692	1,358.66	70,398	142,723
65,000	821.89	230,880	1,315.87	88,717	142,163	1,405.71	81,714	149,166	1,471.88	76,264	154,616
70,000	885.12	248,643	1,417.11	95,543	153,100	1,513.86	88,001	160,642	1,585.12	82,131	166,512
75,000	948.34	266,402	1,518.32	102,367	164,035	1,621.98	94,286	172,116	1,698.33	87,998	178,404
80,000	1,011.56	284,162	1,619.54	109,191	194,971	1,730.11	100,572	183,590	1,811.55	93,864	190,298
85,000	1,074.78	301,921	1,720.76	116,015	185,906	1,838.24	106,857	195,064	1,924.77	99,730	202,191
90,000	1,138.00	319,680	1,821.97	122,839	196,841	1,946.37	113,142	206,538	2,037.98	105,596	214,084
95,000	1,201.23	337,443	1,923.21	129,665	207,778	2,054.51	119,429	218,014	2,151.22	111,463	225,980
100,000	1,264.45	355,202	2,024.43	136,489	218,713	2,162.64	125,715	229,487	2,264.44	117,329	237,873
105,000	1,327.67	372,961	2,125.64	143,313	229,648	2,270.77	132,000	240,961	2,377.65	123,196	249,765
110,000	1,390.89	390,720	2,226.86	150,137	240,583	2,378.89	138,285	252,435	2,490.87	129,062	261,658
115,000	1,454.12	408,483	2,328.09	156,963	251,520	2,487.04	144,572	263,911	2,604.11	134,929	273,554
120,000	1,517.34	426,242	2,429.31	163,787	262,455	2,595.17	150,857	275,385	2,717.32	140,795	285,447
125,000	1,580.56	444,002	2,530.53	170,611	273,391	2,703.29	157,143	286,859	2,830.54	146,661	297,341
130,000	1,643.78	461,761	2,631.74	177,435	284,326	2,811.42	163,428	298,333	2,943.76	152,527	309,234
135,000	1,707.00	479,520	2,732.96	184,259	295,261	2,919.55	169,713	309,807	3,056.98	158,394	321,126
140,000	1,770.23	497,283	2,834.20	191,085	306,198	3,027.69	176,000	321,283	3,170.21	164,261	333,022
145,000	1,833.45	515,042	2,935.41	197,909	317,133	3,135.82	182,286	332,756	3,283.43	170,127	344,915
150,000	1,896.67	532,801	3,036.63	204,733	328,068	3,243.95	188,571	344,230	3,396.65	175,993	356,808
155,000	1,959.89	550,560	3,137.85	211,557	339,003	3,352.08	194,856	355,704	3,509.86	181,859	368,701
160,000	2,023.12	568,323	3,239.08	218,383	349,940	3,460.22	201,143	367,180	3,623.10	187,727	380,596
165,000	2,086.34	586,082	3,340.30	225,206	360,876	3,568.35	207,429	378,653	3,736.32	193,593	392,489
170,000	2,149.56	603,842	3,441.51	232,030	371,812	3,676.48	213,714	390,128	3,849.53	199,459	404,383
175,000	2,212.78	621,601	3,542.73	238,854	382,747	3,784.60	219,999	401,602	3,962.75	205,325	416,276
180,000	2,276.00	639,360	3,643.95	245,678	393,682	3,892.73	226,284	413,076	4,075.97	211,191	428,169
185,000	2,339.23	657,123	3,745.18	252,504	404,619	4,000.88	232,571	424,552	4,189.20	217,059	440,064
190,000	2,402.45	674,882	3,846.40	259,328	415,554	4,109.00	238,857	436,025	4,302.42	222,925	451,957
195,000	2,465.67	692,641	3,947.62	266,152	426,489	4,217.13	245,142	447,499	4,415.64	228,791	463,850
200,000	2,528.89	710,400	4,048.83	272,976	437,424	4,325.26	251,427	458,973	4,528.86	234,657	475,743

15.25% GROWING EQUITY MORTGAGES

AMOUNT OF LOAN	30 YEARS		1% PMT INCR/YR 224.074 PAYMENTS			2% PMT INCR/YR 184.744 PAYMENTS			3% PMT INCR/YR 162.299 PAYMENTS		
	MONTHLY PAYMENT	TOTAL INTRST	LAST YR MON PMT	TOTAL INTRST	INTRST SAVED	LAST YR MON PMT	TOTAL INTRST	INTRST SAVED	LAST YR MON PMT	TOTAL INTRST	INTRST SAVED
$ 50	0.65	184	0.78	109	75	0.87	89	95	0.95	78	106
100	1.29	364	1.54	216	148	1.74	176	188	1.89	154	210
200	2.57	725	3.07	430	295	3.46	350	375	3.77	305	420
300	3.86	1,090	4.62	646	444	5.20	526	564	5.67	459	631
400	5.14	1,450	6.15	859	591	6.92	699	751	7.55	611	839
500	6.43	1,815	7.69	1,076	739	8.65	875	940	9.44	765	1,050
600	7.71	2,176	9.22	1,289	887	10.38	1,049	1,127	11.32	916	1,260
700	9.00	2,540	10.77	1,505	1,035	12.11	1,225	1,315	13.22	1,070	1,470
800	10.28	2,901	12.30	1,719	1,182	13.84	1,399	1,502	15.10	1,222	1,679
900	11.57	3,265	13.84	1,935	1,330	15.57	1,575	1,690	16.99	1,375	1,890
1,000	12.85	3,626	15.37	2,149	1,477	17.29	1,749	1,877	18.87	1,527	2,099
2,000	25.69	7,248	30.73	4,295	2,953	34.58	3,495	3,753	37.73	3,052	4,196
3,000	38.54	10,874	46.10	6,444	4,430	51.87	5,244	5,630	56.60	4,579	6,295
4,000	51.38	14,497	61.46	8,590	5,907	69.15	6,990	7,507	75.45	6,105	8,392
5,000	64.23	18,123	76.83	10,739	7,384	86.45	8,739	9,384	94.32	7,632	10,491
6,000	77.07	21,745	92.19	12,885	8,860	103.73	10,486	11,259	113.18	9,157	12,588
7,000	89.92	25,371	107.56	15,034	10,337	121.02	12,234	13,137	132.05	10,684	14,687
8,000	102.76	28,994	122.92	17,180	11,814	138.30	13,981	15,013	150.91	12,209	16,785
9,000	115.61	32,620	138.29	19,328	13,292	155.60	15,730	16,890	169.78	13,736	18,884
10,000	128.45	36,242	153.65	21,475	14,767	172.88	17,476	18,766	188.63	15,261	20,981
11,000	141.30	39,868	169.02	23,623	16,245	190.17	19,225	20,643	207.50	16,789	23,079
12,000	154.14	43,490	184.37	25,770	17,720	207.45	20,971	22,519	226.36	18,314	25,176
13,000	166.98	47,113	199.73	27,916	19,197	224.73	22,718	24,395	245.22	19,839	27,274
14,000	179.83	50,739	215.10	30,065	20,674	242.03	24,467	26,272	264.09	21,366	29,373
15,000	192.67	54,361	230.46	32,211	22,150	259.31	26,213	28,148	282.94	22,891	31,470
16,000	205.52	57,987	245.83	34,360	23,627	276.60	27,962	30,025	301.81	24,418	33,569
17,000	218.36	61,610	261.19	36,506	25,104	293.88	29,708	31,902	320.67	25,944	35,666
18,000	231.21	65,236	276.56	38,654	26,582	311.18	31,457	33,779	339.54	27,471	37,765
19,000	244.05	68,858	291.92	40,801	28,057	328.46	33,204	35,654	358.40	28,996	39,862
20,000	256.90	72,484	307.29	42,949	29,535	345.75	34,952	37,532	377.27	30,523	41,961
21,000	269.74	76,106	322.65	45,096	31,010	363.03	36,699	39,407	396.12	32,048	44,058
22,000	282.59	79,732	338.02	47,244	32,488	380.33	38,448	41,284	414.99	33,575	46,157
23,000	295.43	83,355	353.38	49,391	33,964	397.61	40,194	43,161	433.85	35,100	48,255
24,000	308.28	86,981	368.75	51,539	35,442	414.90	41,943	45,038	452.72	36,628	50,353
25,000	321.12	90,603	384.11	53,686	36,917	432.19	43,689	46,914	471.58	38,153	52,450
26,000	333.96	94,226	399.47	55,832	38,394	449.47	45,436	48,790	490.43	39,678	54,548
27,000	346.81	97,852	414.84	57,980	39,872	466.76	47,185	50,667	509.30	41,205	56,647
28,000	359.65	101,474	430.19	60,127	41,347	484.04	48,931	52,543	528.16	42,730	58,744
29,000	372.50	105,100	445.56	62,275	42,825	501.34	50,680	54,420	547.03	44,257	60,843
30,000	385.34	108,722	460.92	64,422	44,300	518.62	52,426	56,296	565.88	45,782	62,940
32,500	417.45	117,782	499.33	69,790	47,992	561.83	56,795	60,987	613.04	49,597	68,185
35,000	449.57	126,845	537.75	75,160	51,685	605.06	61,166	65,679	660.21	53,414	73,431
40,000	513.79	144,964	614.57	85,896	59,068	691.49	69,903	75,061	754.52	61,044	83,920
45,000	578.01	163,084	691.39	96,632	66,452	777.93	78,640	84,444	848.83	68,674	94,410
50,000	642.23	181,203	768.20	107,369	73,834	864.36	87,377	93,826	943.14	76,303	104,900
55,000	706.46	199,326	845.03	118,107	81,219	950.80	96,116	103,210	1,037.46	83,935	115,391
60,000	770.68	217,445	921.85	128,843	88,602	1,037.23	104,853	112,592	1,131.77	91,565	125,880
65,000	834.90	235,564	998.66	139,579	95,985	1,123.67	113,590	121,974	1,226.08	99,195	136,369
70,000	899.13	253,687	1,075.49	150,318	103,369	1,210.11	122,329	131,358	1,320.40	106,826	146,860
75,000	963.35	271,806	1,152.31	161,054	110,752	1,296.54	131,066	140,740	1,414.71	114,456	157,350
80,000	1,027.57	289,925	1,229.13	171,790	118,135	1,382.97	139,803	150,122	1,509.02	122,086	167,839
85,000	1,091.79	308,044	1,305.94	182,526	125,518	1,469.41	148,540	159,504	1,603.33	129,716	178,328
90,000	1,156.02	326,167	1,382.77	193,265	132,902	1,555.85	157,279	168,888	1,697.65	137,347	188,820
95,000	1,220.24	344,286	1,459.59	204,001	140,285	1,642.28	166,016	178,270	1,791.96	144,977	199,309
100,000	1,284.46	362,406	1,536.40	214,737	147,669	1,728.71	174,753	187,653	1,886.27	152,607	209,799
105,000	1,348.69	380,528	1,613.23	225,476	155,052	1,815.16	183,493	197,035	1,980.60	160,238	220,290
110,000	1,412.91	398,648	1,690.05	236,212	162,436	1,901.59	192,230	206,418	2,074.91	167,868	230,780
115,000	1,477.13	416,767	1,766.87	246,948	169,819	1,988.02	200,967	215,800	2,169.22	175,498	241,269
120,000	1,541.36	434,890	1,843.69	257,687	177,203	2,074.47	209,706	225,184	2,263.54	183,130	251,760
125,000	1,605.58	453,009	1,920.51	268,423	184,586	2,160.90	218,443	234,566	2,357.85	190,759	262,250
130,000	1,669.80	471,128	1,997.33	279,159	191,969	2,247.33	227,180	243,948	2,452.16	198,389	272,739
135,000	1,734.02	489,247	2,074.14	289,895	199,352	2,333.76	235,917	253,330	2,546.47	206,019	283,228
140,000	1,798.25	507,370	2,150.97	300,634	206,736	2,420.21	244,656	262,714	2,640.79	213,651	293,719
145,000	1,862.47	525,489	2,227.79	311,370	214,119	2,506.64	253,393	272,096	2,735.10	221,280	304,209
150,000	1,926.69	543,608	2,304.61	322,106	221,502	2,593.07	262,130	281,478	2,829.41	228,910	314,698
155,000	1,990.92	561,731	2,381.43	332,844	228,887	2,679.52	270,869	290,862	2,923.73	236,542	325,189
160,000	2,055.14	579,850	2,458.25	343,581	236,269	2,765.95	279,606	300,244	3,018.04	244,172	335,678
165,000	2,119.36	597,970	2,535.07	354,317	243,653	2,852.38	288,343	309,627	3,112.35	251,801	346,169
170,000	2,183.58	616,089	2,611.88	365,053	251,036	2,938.81	297,080	319,009	3,206.66	259,431	356,658
175,000	2,247.81	634,212	2,688.71	375,791	258,421	3,025.26	305,820	328,392	3,300.98	267,063	367,149
180,000	2,312.03	652,331	2,765.53	386,527	265,804	3,111.69	314,557	337,774	3,395.29	274,693	377,638
185,000	2,376.25	670,450	2,842.35	397,264	273,186	3,198.12	323,294	347,156	3,489.60	282,322	388,128
190,000	2,440.48	688,573	2,919.17	408,002	280,571	3,284.56	332,033	356,540	3,583.93	289,954	398,619
195,000	2,504.70	706,692	2,995.99	418,738	287,954	3,371.00	340,770	365,922	3,678.24	297,584	409,108
200,000	2,568.92	724,811	3,072.81	429,474	295,337	3,457.43	349,507	375,304	3,772.55	305,214	419,597

GROWING EQUITY MORTGAGES 15.25%

AMOUNT OF LOAN	30 YEARS MONTHLY PAYMENT	30 YEARS TOTAL INTRST	4% LAST YR MON PMT	4% TOTAL INTRST	4% INTRST SAVED	5% LAST YR MON PMT	5% TOTAL INTRST	5% INTRST SAVED	6% LAST YR MON PMT	6% TOTAL INTRST	6% INTRST SAVED
$ 50	0.65	184	1.04	70	114	1.11	65	119	1.16	61	123
100	1.29	364	2.07	139	225	2.21	128	236	2.31	119	245
200	2.57	725	4.11	276	449	4.40	254	471	4.60	237	488
300	3.86	1,090	6.18	415	675	6.60	382	708	6.91	357	733
400	5.14	1,450	8.23	552	898	8.79	508	942	9.20	474	976
500	6.43	1,815	10.29	690	1,125	11.00	636	1,179	11.52	594	1,221
600	7.71	2,176	12.34	827	1,349	13.19	762	1,414	13.81	711	1,465
700	9.00	2,540	14.41	966	1,574	15.39	890	1,650	16.12	831	1,709
800	10.28	2,901	16.46	1,103	1,798	17.58	1,016	1,885	18.41	948	1,953
900	11.57	3,265	18.52	1,242	2,023	19.79	1,144	2,121	20.72	1,068	2,197
1,000	12.85	3,626	20.57	1,379	2,247	21.98	1,270	2,356	23.01	1,186	2,440
2,000	25.69	7,248	41.13	2,756	4,492	43.94	2,539	4,709	46.01	2,369	4,879
3,000	38.54	10,874	61.70	4,135	6,739	65.92	3,809	7,065	69.02	3,555	7,319
4,000	51.38	14,497	82.26	5,512	8,985	87.88	5,077	9,420	92.01	4,739	9,758
5,000	64.23	18,123	102.83	6,891	11,232	109.86	6,347	11,776	115.03	5,924	12,199
6,000	77.07	21,745	123.39	8,268	13,477	131.82	7,616	14,129	138.02	7,108	14,637
7,000	89.92	25,371	143.96	9,647	15,724	153.79	8,886	16,485	161.03	8,294	17,077
8,000	102.76	28,994	164.52	11,024	17,970	175.75	10,155	18,839	184.03	9,478	19,516
9,000	115.61	32,620	185.10	12,403	20,217	197.73	11,425	21,195	207.04	10,663	21,957
10,000	128.45	36,242	205.65	13,780	22,462	219.69	12,693	23,549	230.03	11,847	24,395
11,000	141.30	39,868	226.23	15,159	24,709	241.67	13,963	25,905	253.05	13,033	26,835
12,000	154.14	43,490	246.78	16,536	26,954	263.63	15,232	28,258	276.04	14,217	29,273
13,000	166.98	47,113	267.34	17,914	29,199	285.59	16,500	30,613	299.04	15,401	31,712
14,000	179.83	50,739	287.91	19,293	31,446	307.57	17,770	32,969	322.05	16,586	34,153
15,000	192.67	54,361	308.47	20,670	33,691	329.53	19,039	35,322	345.04	17,770	36,591
16,000	205.52	57,987	329.04	22,049	35,938	351.51	20,309	37,678	368.06	18,956	39,031
17,000	218.36	61,610	349.60	23,426	38,184	373.47	21,578	40,032	391.05	20,140	41,470
18,000	231.21	65,236	370.17	24,805	40,431	395.45	22,848	42,388	414.06	21,325	43,911
19,000	244.05	68,858	390.73	26,182	42,676	417.41	24,116	44,742	437.06	22,509	46,349
20,000	256.90	72,484	411.31	27,561	44,923	439.39	25,386	47,098	460.07	23,695	48,789
21,000	269.74	76,106	431.86	28,938	47,168	461.35	26,655	49,451	483.06	24,878	51,228
22,000	282.59	79,732	452.44	30,317	49,415	483.32	27,925	51,807	506.08	26,064	53,668
23,000	295.43	83,355	472.99	31,694	51,661	505.29	29,193	54,162	529.07	27,248	56,107
24,000	308.28	86,981	493.57	33,073	53,908	527.26	30,464	56,517	552.08	28,434	58,547
25,000	321.12	90,603	514.12	34,450	56,153	549.22	31,732	58,871	575.08	29,617	60,986
26,000	333.96	94,226	534.68	35,827	58,399	571.18	33,001	61,225	598.07	30,801	63,425
27,000	346.81	97,852	555.25	37,206	60,646	593.16	34,271	63,581	621.08	31,987	65,865
28,000	359.65	101,474	575.81	38,583	62,891	615.12	35,539	65,935	644.08	33,171	68,303
29,000	372.50	105,100	596.38	39,962	65,138	637.10	36,809	68,291	667.09	34,356	70,744
30,000	385.34	108,722	616.94	41,339	67,383	659.06	38,078	70,644	690.09	35,540	73,182
32,500	417.45	117,782	668.35	44,784	72,998	713.98	41,251	76,531	747.59	38,502	79,280
35,000	449.57	126,845	719.78	48,231	78,614	768.92	44,425	82,420	805.11	41,465	85,380
40,000	513.79	144,964	822.59	55,120	89,844	878.76	50,771	94,193	920.12	47,387	97,577
45,000	578.01	163,084	925.41	62,009	101,075	988.59	57,117	105,967	1,035.13	53,310	109,774
50,000	642.23	181,203	1,028.23	68,898	112,305	1,098.43	63,462	117,741	1,150.14	59,233	121,970
55,000	706.46	199,326	1,131.07	75,789	123,537	1,208.29	69,810	129,516	1,265.16	65,158	134,168
60,000	770.68	217,445	1,233.88	82,679	134,766	1,318.12	76,156	141,289	1,380.17	71,080	146,365
65,000	834.90	235,564	1,336.70	89,568	145,996	1,427.96	82,501	153,063	1,495.18	77,003	158,561
70,000	899.13	253,687	1,439.54	96,459	157,228	1,537.82	88,849	164,838	1,610.20	82,928	170,759
75,000	963.35	271,806	1,542.35	103,348	168,458	1,647.66	95,195	176,611	1,725.21	88,850	182,956
80,000	1,027.57	289,925	1,645.17	110,238	179,687	1,757.49	101,540	188,385	1,840.22	94,773	195,152
85,000	1,091.79	308,044	1,747.99	117,127	190,917	1,867.33	107,886	200,158	1,955.23	100,696	207,348
90,000	1,156.02	326,167	1,850.83	124,018	202,149	1,977.19	114,233	211,934	2,070.26	106,621	219,546
95,000	1,220.24	344,286	1,953.64	130,907	213,379	2,087.02	120,579	223,707	2,185.26	112,543	231,743
100,000	1,284.46	362,406	2,056.46	137,797	224,609	2,196.86	126,925	235,481	2,300.27	118,466	243,940
105,000	1,348.69	380,528	2,159.30	144,688	235,840	2,306.72	133,272	247,256	2,415.30	124,391	256,137
110,000	1,412.91	398,648	2,262.11	151,577	247,071	2,416.56	139,619	259,030	2,530.31	130,313	268,333
115,000	1,477.13	416,767	2,364.93	158,466	258,301	2,526.39	145,964	270,803	2,645.31	136,236	280,531
120,000	1,541.36	434,890	2,467.77	165,357	269,533	2,636.25	152,311	282,579	2,760.34	142,161	292,729
125,000	1,605.58	453,009	2,570.59	172,247	280,762	2,746.09	158,657	294,352	2,875.35	148,084	304,925
130,000	1,669.80	471,128	2,673.40	179,136	291,992	2,855.92	165,003	306,125	2,990.36	154,006	317,122
135,000	1,734.02	489,247	2,776.22	186,025	303,222	2,965.76	171,348	317,899	3,105.37	159,929	329,318
140,000	1,798.25	507,370	2,879.06	192,916	314,454	3,075.62	177,696	329,674	3,220.39	165,854	341,516
145,000	1,862.47	525,489	2,981.87	199,806	325,683	3,185.46	184,042	341,447	3,335.40	171,776	353,713
150,000	1,926.69	543,608	3,084.69	206,695	336,913	3,295.29	190,387	353,221	3,450.41	177,699	365,909
155,000	1,990.92	561,731	3,187.53	213,586	348,145	3,405.15	196,735	364,996	3,565.43	183,624	378,107
160,000	2,055.14	579,850	3,290.35	220,475	359,375	3,514.99	203,080	376,770	3,680.44	189,547	390,303
165,000	2,119.36	597,970	3,393.16	227,365	370,605	3,624.82	209,426	388,544	3,795.45	195,469	402,501
170,000	2,183.58	616,089	3,495.98	234,254	381,835	3,734.66	215,772	400,317	3,910.46	201,392	414,697
175,000	2,247.81	634,212	3,598.82	241,145	393,067	3,844.52	222,119	412,093	4,025.49	207,317	426,895
180,000	2,312.03	652,331	3,701.63	248,034	404,297	3,954.36	228,465	423,866	4,140.49	213,239	439,092
185,000	2,376.25	670,450	3,804.45	254,924	415,526	4,064.19	234,811	435,639	4,255.50	219,162	451,288
190,000	2,440.48	688,573	3,907.29	261,815	426,758	4,174.05	241,158	447,415	4,370.53	225,087	463,486
195,000	2,504.70	706,692	4,010.11	268,704	437,988	4,283.89	247,504	459,188	4,485.54	231,010	475,682
200,000	2,568.92	724,811	4,112.92	275,593	449,218	4,393.72	253,850	470,961	4,600.54	236,932	487,879

167

GROWING EQUITY MORTGAGES

AMOUNT OF LOAN	30 YEARS		1% PMT INCR/YR 222.318 PAYMENTS			2% PMT INCR/YR 183.243 PAYMENTS			3% PMT INCR/YR 160.983 PAYMENTS		
	MONTHLY PAYMENT	TOTAL INTRST	LAST YR MON PMT	TOTAL INTRST	INTRST SAVED	LAST YR MON PMT	TOTAL INTRST	INTRST SAVED	LAST YR MON PMT	TOTAL INTRST	INTRST SAVED
$ 50	0.66	188	0.79	110	78	0.89	90	98	0.97	79	109
100	1.31	372	1.57	218	154	1.76	178	194	1.92	155	217
200	2.61	740	3.12	434	306	3.51	353	387	3.83	308	432
300	3.92	1,111	4.69	652	459	5.28	531	580	5.76	463	648
400	5.22	1,479	6.24	868	611	7.03	706	773	7.67	616	863
500	6.53	1,851	7.81	1,086	765	8.79	884	967	9.59	772	1,079
600	7.83	2,219	9.37	1,302	917	10.54	1,059	1,160	11.50	925	1,294
700	9.14	2,590	10.93	1,520	1,070	12.30	1,237	1,353	13.42	1,080	1,510
800	10.44	2,958	12.49	1,736	1,222	14.05	1,412	1,546	15.33	1,233	1,725
900	11.75	3,330	14.05	1,954	1,376	15.81	1,590	1,740	17.26	1,388	1,942
1,000	13.05	3,698	15.61	2,170	1,528	17.56	1,765	1,933	19.16	1,541	2,157
2,000	26.10	7,396	31.22	4,341	3,055	35.13	3,530	3,866	38.33	3,082	4,314
3,000	39.14	11,090	46.82	6,508	4,582	52.68	5,293	5,797	57.48	4,622	6,468
4,000	52.19	14,788	62.43	8,679	6,109	70.24	7,058	7,730	76.64	6,163	8,625
5,000	65.23	18,483	78.02	10,847	7,636	87.79	8,821	9,662	95.79	7,702	10,781
6,000	78.28	22,181	93.63	13,017	9,164	105.35	10,586	11,595	114.96	9,244	12,937
7,000	91.32	25,875	109.23	15,185	10,690	122.90	12,349	13,526	134.11	10,783	15,092
8,000	104.37	29,573	124.84	17,355	12,218	140.47	14,115	15,458	153.27	12,324	17,249
9,000	117.41	33,268	140.44	19,523	13,745	158.02	15,877	17,391	172.42	13,863	19,405
10,000	130.46	36,966	156.05	21,693	15,273	175.58	17,643	19,323	191.58	15,405	21,561
11,000	143.50	40,660	171.65	23,861	16,799	193.13	19,406	21,254	210.73	16,944	23,716
12,000	156.55	44,358	187.26	26,031	18,327	210.70	21,171	23,187	229.90	18,485	25,873
13,000	169.59	48,052	202.85	28,199	19,853	228.25	22,934	25,118	249.05	20,024	28,028
14,000	182.64	51,750	218.46	30,370	21,380	245.81	24,699	27,051	268.21	21,566	30,184
15,000	195.68	55,445	234.06	32,537	22,908	263.36	26,462	28,983	287.36	23,105	32,340
16,000	208.73	59,143	249.67	34,708	24,435	280.92	28,227	30,916	306.53	24,646	34,497
17,000	221.77	62,837	265.27	36,876	25,961	298.47	29,990	32,847	325.68	26,186	36,651
18,000	234.82	66,535	280.88	39,046	27,489	316.04	31,755	34,780	344.84	27,727	38,808
19,000	247.86	70,230	296.48	41,214	29,016	333.59	33,518	36,712	363.99	29,266	40,964
20,000	260.91	73,928	312.09	43,384	30,544	351.15	35,283	38,645	383.16	30,807	43,121
21,000	273.95	77,622	327.68	45,552	32,070	368.70	37,046	40,576	402.30	32,347	45,275
22,000	287.00	81,320	343.29	47,722	33,598	386.26	38,811	42,509	421.47	33,888	47,432
23,000	300.04	85,014	358.89	49,890	35,124	403.81	40,574	44,440	440.62	35,427	49,587
24,000	313.09	88,712	374.50	52,060	36,652	421.38	42,339	46,373	459.78	36,968	51,744
25,000	326.13	92,407	390.10	54,228	38,179	438.93	44,102	48,305	478.93	38,508	53,899
26,000	339.18	96,105	405.71	56,398	39,707	456.49	45,867	50,238	498.10	40,049	56,056
27,000	352.22	99,799	421.31	58,566	41,233	474.04	47,630	52,169	517.25	41,588	58,211
28,000	365.27	103,497	436.92	60,737	42,760	491.61	49,395	54,102	536.41	43,129	60,368
29,000	378.31	107,192	452.51	62,904	44,288	509.16	51,158	56,034	555.56	44,669	62,523
30,000	391.36	110,890	468.12	65,075	45,815	526.72	52,924	57,966	574.73	46,210	64,680
32,500	423.97	120,129	507.13	70,490	49,632	570.61	57,333	62,796	622.61	50,060	70,069
35,000	456.59	129,372	546.15	75,921	53,451	614.51	61,745	67,627	670.52	53,912	75,460
40,000	521.81	147,852	624.16	86,766	61,086	702.29	70,564	77,288	766.30	61,613	86,239
45,000	587.04	166,334	702.19	97,612	68,722	790.08	79,385	86,949	862.09	69,315	97,019
50,000	652.26	184,814	780.20	108,456	76,358	877.86	88,205	96,609	957.87	77,015	107,799
55,000	717.49	203,296	858.22	119,303	83,993	965.65	97,026	106,270	1,053.66	84,718	118,578
60,000	782.72	221,779	936.25	130,149	91,630	1,053.44	105,847	115,932	1,149.45	92,420	129,359
65,000	847.94	240,258	1,014.26	140,994	99,264	1,141.22	114,666	125,592	1,245.23	100,120	140,138
70,000	913.17	258,741	1,092.29	151,840	106,901	1,229.01	123,488	135,253	1,341.02	107,823	150,919
75,000	978.39	277,220	1,170.30	162,684	114,536	1,316.78	132,307	144,913	1,436.80	115,523	161,697
80,000	1,043.62	295,703	1,248.32	173,531	122,172	1,404.58	141,128	154,575	1,532.59	123,225	172,478
85,000	1,108.84	314,182	1,326.34	184,375	129,807	1,492.35	149,947	164,235	1,628.37	130,926	183,256
90,000	1,174.07	332,665	1,404.36	195,222	137,443	1,580.14	158,769	173,896	1,724.16	138,628	194,037
95,000	1,239.30	351,148	1,482.39	206,068	145,080	1,667.93	167,590	183,558	1,819.95	146,330	204,818
100,000	1,304.52	369,627	1,560.40	216,913	152,714	1,755.71	176,409	193,218	1,915.73	154,031	215,596
105,000	1,369.75	388,110	1,638.42	227,759	160,351	1,843.50	185,230	202,880	2,011.52	161,733	226,377
110,000	1,434.97	406,589	1,716.44	238,603	167,986	1,931.28	194,050	212,539	2,107.30	169,433	237,156
115,000	1,500.20	425,072	1,794.46	249,450	175,622	2,019.07	202,871	222,201	2,203.09	177,136	247,936
120,000	1,565.43	443,555	1,872.49	260,297	183,258	2,106.86	211,692	231,863	2,298.89	184,838	258,717
125,000	1,630.65	462,034	1,950.50	271,141	190,893	2,194.64	220,511	241,523	2,394.66	192,538	269,496
130,000	1,695.88	480,517	2,028.52	281,987	198,530	2,282.43	229,333	251,184	2,490.46	200,241	280,276
135,000	1,761.10	498,996	2,106.54	292,831	206,165	2,370.21	238,152	260,844	2,586.23	207,941	291,055
140,000	1,826.33	517,479	2,184.56	303,678	213,801	2,458.00	246,973	270,506	2,682.03	215,643	301,836
145,000	1,891.55	535,958	2,262.57	314,522	221,436	2,545.78	255,793	280,166	2,777.80	223,344	312,614
150,000	1,956.78	554,441	2,340.60	325,369	229,072	2,633.57	264,614	289,827	2,873.60	231,046	323,395
155,000	2,022.01	572,924	2,418.62	336,215	236,709	2,721.36	273,435	299,489	2,969.39	238,748	334,176
160,000	2,087.23	591,403	2,496.63	347,060	244,343	2,809.14	282,254	309,149	3,065.17	246,449	344,954
165,000	2,152.46	609,886	2,574.66	357,906	251,980	2,896.93	291,075	318,811	3,160.96	254,151	355,735
170,000	2,217.68	628,365	2,652.67	368,750	259,615	2,984.71	299,895	328,470	3,256.74	261,851	366,514
175,000	2,282.91	646,848	2,730.70	379,597	267,251	3,072.50	308,716	338,132	3,352.53	269,554	377,294
180,000	2,348.14	665,330	2,808.72	390,444	274,886	3,160.29	317,537	347,793	3,448.32	277,256	388,074
185,000	2,413.36	683,810	2,886.73	401,288	282,522	3,248.06	326,356	357,454	3,544.10	284,956	398,854
190,000	2,478.59	702,292	2,964.76	412,134	290,158	3,335.86	335,178	367,114	3,639.89	292,659	409,633
195,000	2,543.81	720,772	3,042.77	422,979	297,793	3,423.63	343,997	376,775	3,735.67	300,359	420,413
200,000	2,609.04	739,254	3,120.80	433,825	305,429	3,511.42	352,818	386,436	3,831.46	308,061	431,193

GROWING EQUITY MORTGAGES 15.50%

AMOUNT OF LOAN	30 YEARS		4% PMT INCR/YR 145.852 PAYMENTS			5% PMT INCR/YR 134.563 PAYMENTS			6% PMT INCR/YR 125.671 PAYMENTS		
	MONTHLY PAYMENT	TOTAL INTRST	LAST YR MON PMT	TOTAL INTRST	INTRST SAVED	LAST YR MON PMT	TOTAL INTRST	INTRST SAVED	LAST YR MON PMT	TOTAL INTRST	INTRST SAVED
$ 50	0.66	188	1.06	71	117	1.13	65	123	1.18	61	127
100	1.31	372	2.10	140	232	2.24	129	243	2.35	121	251
200	2.61	740	4.18	278	462	4.46	256	484	4.67	239	501
300	3.92	1,111	6.28	418	693	6.70	385	726	7.02	360	751
400	5.22	1,479	8.36	557	922	8.93	513	966	9.35	479	1,000
500	6.53	1,851	10.45	697	1,154	11.17	642	1,209	11.69	599	1,252
600	7.83	2,219	12.54	835	1,384	13.39	769	1,450	14.02	718	1,501
700	9.14	2,590	14.63	975	1,615	15.63	898	1,692	16.37	838	1,752
800	10.44	2,958	16.71	1,113	1,845	17.86	1,026	1,932	18.70	957	2,001
900	11.75	3,330	18.81	1,253	2,077	20.10	1,155	2,175	21.04	1,078	2,252
1,000	13.05	3,698	20.89	1,392	2,306	22.32	1,282	2,416	23.37	1,197	2,501
2,000	26.10	7,396	41.79	2,783	4,613	44.64	2,564	4,832	46.74	2,393	5,003
3,000	39.14	11,090	62.66	4,173	6,917	66.94	3,844	7,246	70.09	3,588	7,502
4,000	52.19	14,788	83.56	5,565	9,223	89.26	5,126	9,662	93.46	4,785	10,003
5,000	65.23	18,483	104.44	6,955	11,528	111.57	6,406	12,077	116.82	5,980	12,503
6,000	78.28	22,181	125.33	8,347	13,834	133.89	7,688	14,493	140.19	7,177	15,004
7,000	91.32	25,875	146.21	9,737	16,138	156.19	8,969	16,906	163.54	8,371	17,504
8,000	104.37	29,573	167.10	11,128	18,445	178.51	10,251	19,322	186.91	9,568	20,005
9,000	117.41	33,268	187.98	12,518	20,750	200.81	11,531	21,737	210.26	10,763	22,505
10,000	130.46	36,966	208.87	13,910	23,056	223.13	12,813	24,153	233.63	11,960	25,006
11,000	143.50	40,660	229.75	15,300	25,360	245.43	14,093	26,567	256.99	13,155	27,505
12,000	156.55	44,358	250.64	16,692	27,666	267.75	15,375	28,983	280.36	14,351	30,007
13,000	169.59	48,052	271.52	18,082	29,970	290.06	16,655	31,397	303.71	15,546	32,506
14,000	182.64	51,750	292.41	19,473	32,277	312.38	17,937	33,813	327.08	16,743	35,007
15,000	195.68	55,445	313.29	20,863	34,582	334.68	19,218	36,227	350.43	17,938	37,507
16,000	208.73	59,143	334.18	22,255	36,888	357.00	20,500	38,643	373.80	19,135	40,008
17,000	221.77	62,837	355.06	23,645	39,192	379.30	21,780	41,057	397.16	20,330	42,507
18,000	234.82	66,535	375.95	25,037	41,498	401.62	23,062	43,473	420.53	21,526	45,009
19,000	247.86	70,230	396.83	26,426	43,804	423.92	24,342	45,888	443.88	22,721	47,509
20,000	260.91	73,928	417.73	27,818	46,110	446.24	25,624	48,304	467.25	23,918	50,010
21,000	273.95	77,622	438.60	29,208	48,414	468.55	26,904	50,718	490.60	25,113	52,509
22,000	287.00	81,320	459.50	30,600	50,720	490.87	28,186	53,134	513.97	26,309	55,011
23,000	300.04	85,014	480.37	31,990	53,024	513.17	29,467	55,547	537.33	27,504	57,510
24,000	313.09	88,712	501.27	33,382	55,330	535.49	30,748	57,964	560.70	28,701	60,011
25,000	326.13	92,407	522.14	34,771	57,636	557.79	32,029	60,378	584.05	29,896	62,511
26,000	339.18	96,105	543.04	36,163	59,942	580.11	33,311	62,794	607.42	31,093	65,012
27,000	352.22	99,799	563.92	37,553	62,246	602.42	34,591	65,208	630.77	32,288	67,511
28,000	365.27	103,497	584.81	38,945	64,552	624.74	35,873	67,624	654.14	33,484	70,013
29,000	378.31	107,192	605.69	40,335	66,857	647.04	37,153	70,039	677.50	34,679	72,513
30,000	391.36	110,890	626.58	41,726	69,164	669.36	38,435	72,455	700.87	35,876	75,014
32,500	423.97	120,129	678.79	45,203	74,926	725.13	41,638	78,491	759.27	38,865	81,264
35,000	456.59	129,372	731.02	48,681	80,691	780.92	44,842	84,530	817.68	41,856	87,516
40,000	521.81	147,852	835.43	55,635	92,217	892.47	51,246	96,606	934.48	47,834	100,018
45,000	587.04	166,334	939.87	62,590	103,744	1,004.04	57,653	108,681	1,051.30	53,814	112,520
50,000	652.26	184,814	1,044.29	69,543	115,271	1,115.59	64,057	120,757	1,168.10	59,792	125,022
55,000	717.49	203,296	1,148.72	76,498	126,798	1,227.15	70,464	132,832	1,284.92	65,772	137,524
60,000	782.72	221,779	1,253.16	83,453	138,326	1,338.72	76,870	144,909	1,401.73	71,752	150,027
65,000	847.94	240,258	1,357.58	90,406	149,852	1,450.27	83,275	156,983	1,518.53	77,730	162,528
70,000	913.17	258,741	1,462.01	97,361	161,380	1,561.83	89,682	169,059	1,635.35	83,710	175,031
75,000	978.39	277,220	1,566.43	104,314	172,906	1,673.38	96,086	181,134	1,752.15	89,688	187,532
80,000	1,043.62	295,703	1,670.87	111,269	184,434	1,784.94	102,493	193,210	1,868.96	95,668	200,035
85,000	1,108.84	314,182	1,775.29	118,222	195,960	1,896.49	108,897	205,285	1,985.76	101,646	212,536
90,000	1,174.07	332,665	1,879.72	125,177	207,488	2,008.06	115,304	217,361	2,102.58	107,626	225,039
95,000	1,239.30	351,148	1,984.16	132,132	219,016	2,119.62	121,710	229,438	2,219.40	113,606	237,542
100,000	1,304.52	369,627	2,088.58	139,086	230,541	2,231.17	128,115	241,512	2,336.20	119,584	250,043
105,000	1,369.75	388,110	2,193.01	146,041	242,069	2,342.74	134,521	253,589	2,453.01	125,564	262,546
110,000	1,434.97	406,589	2,297.43	152,994	253,595	2,454.29	140,926	265,663	2,569.81	131,542	275,047
115,000	1,500.20	425,072	2,401.87	159,949	265,123	2,565.85	147,333	277,739	2,686.63	137,522	287,550
120,000	1,565.43	443,555	2,506.30	166,904	276,651	2,677.42	153,739	289,816	2,803.45	143,502	300,053
125,000	1,630.65	462,034	2,610.72	173,857	288,177	2,788.96	160,144	301,890	2,920.25	149,480	312,554
130,000	1,695.88	480,517	2,715.16	180,812	299,705	2,900.53	166,550	313,967	3,037.06	155,460	325,057
135,000	1,761.10	498,996	2,819.58	187,765	311,231	3,012.08	172,955	326,041	3,153.86	161,438	337,558
140,000	1,826.33	517,479	2,924.01	194,720	322,759	3,123.64	179,361	338,118	3,270.68	167,418	350,061
145,000	1,891.55	535,958	3,028.43	201,673	334,285	3,235.19	185,766	350,192	3,387.48	173,396	362,562
150,000	1,956.78	554,441	3,132.87	208,628	345,813	3,346.76	192,172	362,269	3,504.29	179,376	375,065
155,000	2,022.01	572,924	3,237.30	215,583	357,341	3,458.32	198,579	374,345	3,621.11	185,356	387,568
160,000	2,087.23	591,403	3,341.72	222,537	368,866	3,569.87	204,984	386,419	3,737.91	191,334	400,069
165,000	2,152.46	609,886	3,446.16	229,492	380,394	3,681.44	211,390	398,496	3,854.73	197,314	412,572
170,000	2,217.68	628,365	3,550.58	236,445	391,920	3,792.99	217,795	410,572	3,971.53	203,292	425,073
175,000	2,282.91	646,848	3,655.01	243,400	403,448	3,904.55	224,201	422,647	4,088.34	209,272	437,576
180,000	2,348.14	665,330	3,759.45	250,355	414,975	4,016.12	230,608	434,722	4,205.16	215,252	450,078
185,000	2,413.36	683,810	3,863.87	257,308	426,502	4,127.66	237,012	446,798	4,321.96	221,230	462,580
190,000	2,478.59	702,292	3,968.30	264,263	438,029	4,239.23	243,419	458,873	4,438.78	227,210	475,082
195,000	2,543.81	720,772	4,072.72	271,216	449,556	4,350.78	249,823	470,949	4,555.58	233,188	487,584
200,000	2,609.04	739,254	4,177.16	278,171	461,083	4,462.34	256,230	483,024	4,672.39	239,168	500,086

GROWING EQUITY MORTGAGES

AMOUNT OF LOAN	30 YEARS		1% PMT INCR/YR 220.576 PAYMENTS			2% PMT INCR/YR 181.764 PAYMENTS			3% PMT INCR/YR 159.691 PAYMENTS		
	MONTHLY PAYMENT	TOTAL INTRST	LAST YR MON PMT	TOTAL INTRST	INTRST SAVED	LAST YR MON PMT	TOTAL INTRST	INTRST SAVED	LAST YR MON PMT	TOTAL INTRST	INTRST SAVED
$ 50	0.67	191	0.80	111	80	0.90	91	100	0.98	79	112
100	1.33	379	1.59	220	159	1.79	179	200	1.95	156	223
200	2.65	754	3.17	438	316	3.57	356	398	3.89	311	443
300	3.98	1,133	4.76	659	474	5.36	535	598	5.84	467	666
400	5.30	1,508	6.34	877	631	7.13	712	796	7.78	622	886
500	6.63	1,887	7.93	1,097	790	8.92	892	995	9.74	778	1,109
600	7.95	2,262	9.51	1,315	947	10.70	1,069	1,193	11.67	933	1,329
700	9.28	2,641	11.10	1,535	1,106	12.49	1,248	1,393	13.63	1,089	1,552
800	10.60	3,016	12.68	1,753	1,263	14.27	1,425	1,591	15.57	1,244	1,772
900	11.93	3,395	14.27	1,973	1,422	16.06	1,604	1,791	17.52	1,401	1,994
1,000	13.25	3,770	15.85	2,191	1,579	17.83	1,781	1,989	19.46	1,555	2,215
2,000	26.50	7,540	31.70	4,383	3,157	35.67	3,562	3,978	38.92	3,110	4,430
3,000	39.74	11,306	47.53	6,571	4,735	53.48	5,341	5,965	58.36	4,663	6,643
4,000	52.99	15,076	63.38	8,763	6,313	71.32	7,122	7,954	77.82	6,218	8,858
5,000	66.24	18,846	79.23	10,954	7,892	89.15	8,903	9,943	97.28	7,773	11,073
6,000	79.48	22,613	95.07	13,143	9,470	106.97	10,682	11,931	116.72	9,326	13,287
7,000	92.73	26,383	110.92	15,334	11,049	124.80	12,464	13,919	136.18	10,881	15,502
8,000	105.97	30,149	126.76	17,523	12,626	142.62	14,243	15,906	155.62	12,435	17,714
9,000	119.22	33,919	142.60	19,714	14,205	160.45	16,024	17,895	175.08	13,990	19,929
10,000	132.47	37,689	158.45	21,905	15,784	178.29	17,805	19,884	194.54	15,545	22,144
11,000	145.71	41,456	174.29	24,094	17,362	196.11	19,584	21,872	213.98	17,098	24,358
12,000	158.96	45,226	190.14	26,286	18,940	213.94	21,365	23,861	233.44	18,653	26,573
13,000	172.21	48,996	205.99	28,477	20,519	231.77	23,146	25,850	252.90	20,208	28,788
14,000	185.45	52,762	221.83	30,666	22,096	249.59	24,925	27,837	272.34	21,761	31,001
15,000	198.70	56,532	237.67	32,857	23,675	267.42	26,706	29,826	291.80	23,316	33,216
16,000	211.94	60,298	253.51	35,046	25,252	285.24	28,485	31,813	311.24	24,869	35,429
17,000	225.19	64,068	269.36	37,237	26,831	303.08	30,266	33,802	330.70	26,424	37,644
18,000	238.44	67,838	285.21	39,428	28,410	320.91	32,047	35,791	350.16	27,979	39,859
19,000	251.68	71,605	301.05	41,617	29,988	338.73	33,826	37,779	369.60	29,532	42,073
20,000	264.93	75,375	316.90	43,809	31,566	356.56	35,608	39,767	389.06	31,087	44,288
21,000	278.17	79,141	332.73	45,997	33,144	374.38	37,387	41,754	408.50	32,641	46,500
22,000	291.42	82,911	348.58	48,189	34,722	392.21	39,168	43,743	427.96	34,196	48,715
23,000	304.67	86,681	364.43	50,380	36,301	410.05	40,949	45,732	447.42	35,751	50,930
24,000	317.91	90,448	380.27	52,569	37,879	427.87	42,728	47,720	466.86	37,304	53,144
25,000	331.16	94,218	396.12	54,760	39,458	445.70	44,509	49,709	486.32	38,859	55,359
26,000	344.41	97,988	411.97	56,951	41,037	463.53	46,290	51,698	505.78	40,414	57,574
27,000	357.65	101,754	427.80	59,140	42,614	481.35	48,069	53,685	525.22	41,967	59,787
28,000	370.90	105,524	443.65	61,331	44,193	499.18	49,850	55,674	544.68	43,522	62,002
29,000	384.14	109,290	459.49	63,520	45,770	517.00	51,629	57,661	564.12	45,075	64,215
30,000	397.39	113,060	475.34	65,712	47,348	534.83	53,410	59,650	583.58	46,630	66,430
32,500	430.51	122,484	514.95	71,189	51,295	579.41	57,862	64,622	632.22	50,517	71,967
35,000	463.62	131,903	554.56	76,663	55,240	623.97	62,312	69,591	680.84	54,402	77,501
40,000	529.85	150,746	633.78	87,615	63,131	713.11	71,213	79,533	778.10	62,173	88,573
45,000	596.08	169,589	713.00	98,566	71,023	802.25	80,114	89,475	875.36	69,944	99,645
50,000	662.31	188,432	792.22	109,518	78,914	891.38	89,016	99,416	972.62	77,716	110,716
55,000	728.54	207,274	871.44	120,469	86,805	980.52	97,917	109,357	1,069.89	85,487	121,787
60,000	794.78	226,121	950.67	131,423	94,698	1,069.67	106,820	119,301	1,167.16	93,260	132,861
65,000	861.01	244,964	1,029.89	142,375	102,589	1,158.81	115,722	129,242	1,264.42	101,032	143,932
70,000	927.24	263,806	1,109.12	153,326	110,480	1,247.94	124,123	139,183	1,361.68	108,803	155,003
75,000	993.47	282,649	1,188.34	164,278	118,371	1,337.08	133,524	149,125	1,458.94	116,575	166,074
80,000	1,059.70	301,492	1,267.56	175,229	126,263	1,426.22	142,426	159,066	1,556.21	124,346	177,146
85,000	1,125.93	320,334	1,346.78	186,181	134,154	1,515.35	151,327	169,008	1,653.47	132,117	188,218
90,000	1,192.16	339,178	1,426.00	197,132	142,046	1,604.49	160,229	178,949	1,750.73	139,889	199,289
95,000	1,258.39	358,020	1,505.22	208,084	149,936	1,693.63	169,130	188,890	1,847.99	147,660	210,360
100,000	1,324.62	376,863	1,584.44	219,035	157,828	1,782.76	178,031	198,832	1,945.25	155,432	221,431
105,000	1,390.85	395,706	1,663.66	229,987	165,719	1,871.90	186,933	208,773	2,042.51	163,203	232,503
110,000	1,457.08	414,549	1,742.88	240,939	173,610	1,961.04	195,834	218,715	2,139.77	170,974	243,575
115,000	1,523.31	433,392	1,822.10	251,890	181,502	2,050.17	204,735	228,657	2,237.03	178,746	254,646
120,000	1,589.55	452,238	1,901.34	262,844	189,394	2,139.33	213,639	238,599	2,334.31	186,519	265,719
125,000	1,655.78	471,081	1,980.56	273,796	197,285	2,228.46	222,540	248,541	2,431.57	194,290	276,791
130,000	1,722.01	489,924	2,059.78	284,747	205,177	2,317.60	231,441	258,483	2,528.83	202,062	287,862
135,000	1,788.24	508,766	2,139.00	295,699	213,067	2,406.74	240,343	268,423	2,626.09	209,833	298,933
140,000	1,854.47	527,609	2,218.22	306,652	220,959	2,495.87	249,244	278,365	2,723.35	217,605	310,004
145,000	1,920.70	546,452	2,297.44	317,602	228,850	2,585.01	258,146	288,306	2,820.61	225,376	321,076
150,000	1,986.93	565,295	2,376.66	328,553	236,742	2,674.15	267,047	298,248	2,917.87	233,147	332,148
155,000	2,053.16	584,138	2,455.88	339,505	244,633	2,763.28	275,948	308,190	3,015.13	240,919	343,219
160,000	2,119.39	602,980	2,535.10	350,456	252,524	2,852.42	284,850	318,130	3,112.40	248,690	354,290
165,000	2,185.62	621,823	2,614.32	361,408	260,415	2,941.56	293,751	328,072	3,209.66	256,462	365,361
170,000	2,251.85	640,666	2,693.54	372,359	268,307	3,030.69	302,652	338,014	3,306.92	264,233	376,433
175,000	2,318.08	659,509	2,772.77	383,311	276,198	3,119.83	311,554	347,955	3,404.18	272,004	387,505
180,000	2,384.32	678,355	2,852.00	394,265	284,090	3,208.98	320,457	357,898	3,501.45	279,778	398,577
185,000	2,450.55	697,198	2,931.22	405,216	291,982	3,298.12	329,358	367,840	3,598.72	287,549	409,649
190,000	2,516.78	716,041	3,010.44	416,168	299,873	3,387.25	338,260	377,781	3,695.98	295,320	420,721
195,000	2,583.01	734,884	3,089.66	427,119	307,765	3,476.39	347,161	387,723	3,793.24	303,092	431,792
200,000	2,649.24	753,726	3,168.88	438,071	315,655	3,565.53	356,063	397,663	3,890.50	310,863	442,863

GROWING EQUITY MORTGAGES 15.75%

AMOUNT OF LOAN	30 YEARS		4% PMT INCR/YR 144.711 PAYMENTS			5% PMT INCR/YR 133.528 PAYMENTS			6% PMT INCR/YR 124.709 PAYMENTS		
	MONTHLY PAYMENT	TOTAL INTRST	LAST YR MON PMT	TOTAL INTRST	INTRST SAVED	LAST YR MON PMT	TOTAL INTRST	INTRST SAVED	LAST YR MON PMT	TOTAL INTRST	INTRST SAVED
$ 50	0.67	191	1.07	72	119	1.15	66	125	1.20	62	129
100	1.33	379	2.13	141	238	2.27	130	249	2.38	122	257
200	2.65	754	4.24	281	473	4.53	259	495	4.75	241	513
300	3.98	1,133	6.37	422	711	6.81	389	744	7.13	363	770
400	5.30	1,508	8.49	562	946	9.06	517	991	9.49	483	1,025
500	6.63	1,887	10.61	703	1,184	11.34	648	1,239	11.87	605	1,282
600	7.95	2,262	12.73	843	1,419	13.60	776	1,486	14.24	724	1,538
700	9.28	2,641	14.86	984	1,657	15.87	906	1,735	16.62	846	1,795
800	10.60	3,016	16.97	1,123	1,893	18.13	1,035	1,981	18.98	966	2,050
900	11.93	3,395	19.10	1,265	2,130	20.40	1,165	2,230	21.36	1,088	2,307
1,000	13.25	3,770	21.21	1,404	2,366	22.66	1,294	2,476	23.73	1,207	2,563
2,000	26.50	7,540	42.43	2,808	4,732	45.32	2,587	4,953	47.46	2,415	5,125
3,000	39.74	11,306	63.63	4,211	7,095	67.97	3,879	7,427	71.17	3,621	7,685
4,000	52.99	15,076	84.84	5,615	9,461	90.63	5,172	9,904	94.90	4,828	10,248
5,000	66.24	18,846	106.05	7,019	11,827	113.29	6,466	12,380	118.63	6,036	12,810
6,000	79.48	22,613	127.25	8,421	14,192	135.94	7,758	14,855	142.34	7,242	15,371
7,000	92.73	26,383	148.46	9,826	16,557	158.60	9,051	17,332	166.07	8,449	17,934
8,000	105.97	30,149	169.66	11,228	18,921	181.24	10,343	19,806	189.78	9,655	20,494
9,000	119.22	33,919	190.88	12,632	21,287	203.91	11,636	22,283	213.50	10,862	23,057
10,000	132.47	37,689	212.09	14,036	23,653	226.57	12,930	24,759	237.23	12,070	25,619
11,000	145.71	41,456	233.29	15,439	26,017	249.21	14,222	27,234	260.94	13,276	28,180
12,000	158.96	45,226	254.50	16,843	28,383	271.88	15,515	29,711	284.67	14,483	30,743
13,000	172.21	48,996	275.71	18,247	30,749	294.54	16,809	32,187	308.40	15,691	33,305
14,000	185.45	52,762	296.91	19,650	33,112	317.18	18,100	34,662	332.11	16,896	35,866
15,000	198.70	56,532	318.13	21,054	35,478	339.84	19,394	37,138	355.84	18,104	38,428
16,000	211.94	60,298	339.32	22,456	37,842	362.49	20,686	39,612	379.55	19,310	40,988
17,000	225.19	64,068	360.54	23,860	40,208	385.15	21,979	42,089	403.28	20,517	43,551
18,000	238.44	67,838	381.75	25,264	42,574	407.81	23,273	44,565	427.01	21,725	46,113
19,000	251.68	71,605	402.95	26,667	44,938	430.46	24,565	47,040	450.72	22,931	48,674
20,000	264.93	75,375	424.16	28,071	47,304	453.12	25,858	49,517	474.45	24,138	51,237
21,000	278.17	79,141	445.36	29,473	49,668	475.77	27,150	51,991	498.16	25,344	53,797
22,000	291.42	82,911	466.57	30,878	52,033	498.43	28,443	54,468	521.89	26,551	56,360
23,000	304.67	86,681	487.79	32,282	54,399	521.09	29,737	56,944	545.62	27,759	58,922
24,000	317.91	90,448	508.98	33,684	56,764	543.73	31,029	59,419	569.33	28,965	61,483
25,000	331.16	94,218	530.20	35,088	59,130	566.40	32,322	61,896	593.06	30,172	64,046
26,000	344.41	97,988	551.41	36,493	61,495	589.06	33,616	64,372	616.79	31,380	66,608
27,000	357.65	101,754	572.61	37,895	63,859	611.70	34,907	66,847	640.50	32,585	69,169
28,000	370.90	105,524	593.82	39,299	66,225	634.36	36,201	69,323	664.23	33,793	71,731
29,000	384.14	109,290	615.02	40,701	68,589	657.01	37,493	71,797	687.94	34,999	74,291
30,000	397.39	113,060	636.23	42,106	70,954	679.67	38,786	74,274	711.66	36,206	76,854
32,500	430.51	122,484	689.26	45,615	76,869	736.32	42,019	80,465	770.98	39,224	83,250
35,000	463.62	131,903	742.27	49,123	82,780	792.95	45,250	86,653	830.27	42,240	89,663
40,000	529.85	150,746	848.31	56,140	94,606	906.22	51,714	99,032	948.88	48,274	102,472
45,000	596.08	169,589	954.34	63,157	106,431	1,019.50	58,178	111,411	1,067.49	54,309	115,280
50,000	662.31	188,432	1,060.38	70,175	118,257	1,132.77	64,642	123,790	1,186.10	60,343	128,089
55,000	728.54	207,274	1,166.42	77,192	130,082	1,246.05	71,106	136,167	1,304.70	66,377	140,897
60,000	794.78	226,121	1,272.47	84,211	141,910	1,359.34	77,572	148,549	1,423.33	72,412	153,709
65,000	861.01	244,964	1,378.50	91,229	153,735	1,472.62	84,036	160,928	1,541.94	78,447	166,517
70,000	927.24	263,806	1,484.54	98,246	165,560	1,585.90	90,500	173,306	1,660.55	84,481	179,325
75,000	993.47	282,649	1,590.58	105,263	177,386	1,699.17	96,965	185,684	1,779.15	90,515	192,134
80,000	1,059.70	301,492	1,696.61	112,280	189,212	1,812.45	103,429	198,063	1,897.76	96,549	204,943
85,000	1,125.93	320,335	1,802.65	119,298	201,037	1,925.72	109,893	210,442	2,016.37	102,583	217,752
90,000	1,192.16	339,178	1,908.69	126,315	212,863	2,039.00	116,357	222,821	2,134.98	108,617	230,561
95,000	1,258.39	358,020	2,014.72	133,332	224,688	2,152.27	122,821	235,199	2,253.58	114,651	243,369
100,000	1,324.62	376,863	2,120.76	140,350	236,513	2,265.55	129,285	247,578	2,372.19	120,685	256,178
105,000	1,390.85	395,706	2,226.80	147,367	248,339	2,378.83	135,749	259,957	2,490.80	126,719	268,987
110,000	1,457.08	414,549	2,332.83	154,384	260,165	2,492.10	142,213	272,336	2,609.41	132,753	281,796
115,000	1,523.31	433,392	2,438.87	161,402	271,990	2,605.38	148,677	284,715	2,728.02	138,787	294,605
120,000	1,589.55	452,238	2,544.92	168,421	283,817	2,718.67	155,143	297,095	2,846.64	144,823	307,415
125,000	1,655.78	471,081	2,650.96	175,438	295,643	2,831.95	161,607	309,474	2,965.25	150,857	320,224
130,000	1,722.01	489,924	2,756.99	182,455	307,469	2,945.22	168,071	321,853	3,083.86	156,891	333,033
135,000	1,788.24	508,766	2,863.03	189,473	319,293	3,058.50	174,535	334,231	3,202.47	162,926	345,840
140,000	1,854.47	527,609	2,969.07	196,490	331,119	3,171.77	180,999	346,610	3,321.07	168,960	358,649
145,000	1,920.70	546,452	3,075.10	203,507	342,945	3,285.05	187,463	358,989	3,439.68	174,994	371,458
150,000	1,986.93	565,295	3,181.14	210,524	354,771	3,398.32	193,927	371,368	3,558.29	181,028	384,267
155,000	2,053.16	584,138	3,287.18	217,542	366,596	3,511.60	200,391	383,747	3,676.90	187,062	397,076
160,000	2,119.39	602,980	3,393.21	224,559	378,421	3,624.88	206,855	396,125	3,795.50	193,096	409,884
165,000	2,185.62	621,823	3,499.25	231,576	390,247	3,738.15	213,320	408,503	3,914.11	199,130	422,693
170,000	2,251.85	640,666	3,605.28	238,594	402,072	3,851.43	219,784	420,882	4,032.72	205,164	435,502
175,000	2,318.08	659,509	3,711.32	245,611	413,898	3,964.71	226,248	433,261	4,151.33	211,198	448,311
180,000	2,384.32	678,355	3,817.37	252,630	425,725	4,078.00	232,713	445,642	4,269.95	217,234	461,121
185,000	2,450.55	697,198	3,923.41	259,647	437,551	4,191.27	239,178	458,020	4,388.56	223,268	473,930
190,000	2,516.78	716,041	4,029.45	266,665	449,376	4,304.55	245,642	470,399	4,507.17	229,302	486,739
195,000	2,583.01	734,884	4,135.48	273,682	461,202	4,417.82	252,106	482,778	4,625.78	235,336	499,548
200,000	2,649.24	753,726	4,241.52	280,699	473,027	4,531.10	258,570	495,156	4,744.39	241,370	512,356

AMOUNT OF LOAN	30 YEARS		1% PMT INCR/YR 218.848 PAYMENTS			2% PMT INCR/YR 180.306 PAYMENTS			3% PMT INCR/YR 158.420 PAYMENTS		
	MONTHLY PAYMENT	TOTAL INTRST	LAST YR MON PMT	TOTAL INTRST	INTRST SAVED	LAST YR MON PMT	TOTAL INTRST	INTRST SAVED	LAST YR MON PMT	TOTAL INTRST	INTRST SAVED
$ 50	0.68	195	0.81	112	83	0.92	91	104	1.00	80	115
100	1.35	386	1.61	222	164	1.82	181	205	1.98	158	228
200	2.69	768	3.22	442	326	3.62	359	409	3.95	314	454
300	4.04	1,154	4.83	665	489	5.44	540	614	5.93	472	682
400	5.38	1,537	6.44	885	652	7.24	719	818	7.90	627	910
500	6.73	1,923	8.05	1,107	816	9.06	899	1,024	9.88	785	1,138
600	8.07	2,305	9.65	1,327	978	10.86	1,078	1,227	11.85	941	1,364
700	9.42	2,691	11.27	1,549	1,142	12.68	1,259	1,432	13.83	1,099	1,592
800	10.76	3,074	12.87	1,769	1,305	14.48	1,437	1,637	15.80	1,255	1,819
900	12.11	3,460	14.49	1,992	1,468	16.30	1,618	1,842	17.78	1,413	2,047
1,000	13.45	3,842	16.09	2,212	1,630	18.10	1,797	2,045	19.75	1,569	2,273
2,000	26.90	7,684	32.18	4,423	3,261	36.20	3,593	4,091	39.50	3,137	4,547
3,000	40.35	11,526	48.26	6,635	4,891	54.31	5,390	6,136	59.26	4,706	6,820
4,000	53.80	15,368	64.35	8,847	6,521	72.41	7,187	8,181	79.01	6,274	9,094
5,000	67.24	19,206	80.43	11,056	8,150	90.50	8,981	10,225	98.74	7,841	11,365
6,000	80.69	23,048	96.52	13,267	9,781	108.60	10,778	12,270	118.50	9,409	13,639
7,000	94.14	26,890	112.61	15,479	11,411	126.70	12,575	14,315	138.25	10,978	15,912
8,000	107.59	30,732	128.69	17,691	13,041	144.80	14,371	16,361	158.00	12,546	18,186
9,000	121.03	34,571	144.77	19,900	14,671	162.89	16,166	18,405	177.74	14,113	20,458
10,000	134.48	38,413	160.86	22,112	16,301	180.99	17,963	20,450	197.49	15,681	22,732
11,000	147.93	42,255	176.95	24,323	17,932	199.09	19,760	22,495	217.24	17,250	25,005
12,000	161.38	46,097	193.03	26,535	19,562	217.20	21,556	24,541	236.99	18,818	27,279
13,000	174.82	49,935	209.11	28,744	21,191	235.28	23,351	26,584	256.73	20,385	29,553
14,000	188.27	53,777	225.20	30,956	22,821	253.39	25,148	28,629	276.48	21,953	31,824
15,000	201.72	57,619	241.29	33,167	24,452	271.49	26,944	30,675	296.23	23,522	34,097
16,000	215.17	61,461	257.38	35,379	26,082	289.59	28,741	32,720	315.98	25,090	36,371
17,000	228.61	65,300	273.45	37,588	27,712	307.68	30,536	34,764	335.72	26,657	38,643
18,000	242.06	69,142	289.54	39,800	29,342	325.78	32,332	36,810	355.47	28,226	40,916
19,000	255.51	72,984	305.63	42,012	30,972	343.88	34,129	38,855	375.23	29,794	43,190
20,000	268.96	76,826	321.72	44,223	32,603	361.98	35,926	40,900	394.98	31,363	45,463
21,000	282.40	80,664	337.79	46,432	34,232	380.07	37,720	42,944	414.71	32,929	47,735
22,000	295.85	84,506	353.88	48,644	35,862	398.18	39,517	44,989	434.47	34,498	50,008
23,000	309.30	88,348	369.97	50,856	37,492	416.28	41,314	47,034	454.22	36,066	52,282
24,000	322.75	92,190	386.06	53,067	39,123	434.38	43,110	49,080	473.97	37,635	54,555
25,000	336.19	96,028	402.13	55,277	40,751	452.47	44,905	51,123	493.71	39,201	56,827
26,000	349.64	99,870	418.22	57,488	42,382	470.57	46,702	53,168	513.46	40,770	59,100
27,000	363.09	103,712	434.31	59,700	44,012	488.67	48,498	55,214	533.21	42,338	61,374
28,000	376.54	107,554	450.40	61,912	45,642	506.77	50,295	57,259	552.96	43,907	63,647
29,000	389.98	111,393	466.47	64,121	47,272	524.86	52,090	59,303	572.70	45,473	65,920
30,000	403.43	115,235	482.56	66,332	48,903	542.96	53,886	61,349	592.45	47,042	68,193
32,500	437.05	124,838	522.78	71,860	52,978	588.21	58,377	66,461	641.82	50,962	73,876
35,000	470.67	134,441	562.99	77,388	57,053	633.46	62,868	71,573	691.19	54,883	79,558
40,000	537.91	153,648	643.42	88,444	65,204	723.96	71,849	81,799	789.94	62,723	90,925
45,000	605.15	172,854	723.85	99,500	73,354	814.45	80,831	92,023	888.68	70,564	102,290
50,000	672.38	192,057	804.27	110,553	81,504	904.93	89,810	102,247	987.41	78,403	113,654
55,000	739.62	211,263	884.69	121,609	89,654	995.43	98,791	112,472	1,086.16	86,243	125,020
60,000	806.86	230,470	965.12	132,665	97,805	1,085.93	107,773	122,697	1,184.90	94,084	136,386
65,000	874.10	249,676	1,045.55	143,721	105,955	1,176.42	116,754	132,922	1,283.65	101,925	147,751
70,000	941.33	268,879	1,125.97	154,774	114,105	1,266.91	125,733	143,146	1,382.37	109,763	159,116
75,000	1,008.57	288,085	1,206.40	165,830	122,255	1,357.40	134,715	153,370	1,481.12	117,604	170,481
80,000	1,075.81	307,292	1,286.83	176,886	130,406	1,447.90	143,696	163,596	1,579.86	125,445	181,847
85,000	1,143.05	326,498	1,367.26	187,942	138,556	1,538.39	152,678	173,820	1,678.61	133,285	193,213
90,000	1,210.29	345,704	1,447.69	198,997	146,707	1,628.89	161,659	184,045	1,777.35	141,126	204,578
95,000	1,277.52	364,907	1,528.10	210,051	154,856	1,719.37	170,638	194,269	1,876.08	148,965	215,942
100,000	1,344.76	384,114	1,608.53	221,107	163,007	1,809.87	179,620	204,494	1,974.83	156,805	227,309
105,000	1,412.00	403,320	1,688.96	232,162	171,158	1,900.37	188,601	214,719	2,073.57	164,646	238,674
110,000	1,479.24	422,526	1,769.39	243,218	179,308	1,990.86	197,583	224,943	2,172.31	172,487	250,039
115,000	1,546.48	441,733	1,849.82	254,274	187,459	2,081.36	206,564	235,169	2,271.06	180,327	261,406
120,000	1,613.71	460,936	1,930.24	265,321	195,609	2,171.84	215,543	245,393	2,369.79	188,166	272,770
125,000	1,680.95	480,142	2,010.66	276,383	203,759	2,262.34	224,525	255,617	2,468.53	196,007	284,135
130,000	1,748.19	499,348	2,091.09	287,439	211,909	2,352.83	233,506	265,842	2,567.28	203,847	295,501
135,000	1,815.43	518,555	2,171.52	298,495	220,060	2,443.33	242,488	276,067	2,666.02	211,688	306,867
140,000	1,882.66	537,758	2,251.94	309,548	228,210	2,533.81	251,467	286,291	2,764.75	219,527	318,231
145,000	1,949.90	556,964	2,332.37	320,604	236,360	2,624.31	260,448	296,516	2,863.49	227,367	329,597
150,000	2,017.14	576,170	2,412.80	331,660	244,510	2,714.80	269,430	306,740	2,962.24	235,208	340,962
155,000	2,084.38	595,377	2,493.23	342,716	252,661	2,805.30	278,411	316,966	3,060.98	243,048	352,329
160,000	2,151.62	614,583	2,573.65	353,772	260,811	2,895.80	287,392	327,191	3,159.73	250,889	363,694
165,000	2,218.85	633,786	2,654.07	364,825	268,961	2,986.28	296,372	337,414	3,258.46	258,728	375,058
170,000	2,286.09	652,992	2,734.50	375,881	277,111	3,076.78	305,353	347,639	3,357.20	266,569	386,423
175,000	2,353.33	672,199	2,814.93	386,937	285,262	3,167.27	314,335	357,864	3,455.94	274,409	397,790
180,000	2,420.57	691,405	2,895.36	397,992	293,413	3,257.77	323,316	368,089	3,554.69	282,250	409,155
185,000	2,487.81	710,612	2,975.79	409,048	301,564	3,348.26	332,297	378,315	3,653.43	290,090	420,522
190,000	2,555.04	729,814	3,056.20	420,102	309,712	3,438.75	341,277	388,537	3,752.16	297,929	431,885
195,000	2,622.28	749,021	3,136.63	431,157	317,864	3,529.24	350,258	398,763	3,850.91	305,770	443,251
200,000	2,689.52	768,227	3,217.06	442,213	326,014	3,619.74	359,240	408,987	3,949.65	313,610	454,617

AMOUNT OF LOAN	30 YEARS		4% PMT INCR/YR 143.575 PAYMENTS			5% PMT INCR/YR 132.513 PAYMENTS			6% PMT INCR/YR 123.766 PAYMENTS		
	MONTHLY PAYMENT	TOTAL INTRST	LAST YR MON PMT	TOTAL INTRST	INTRST SAVED	LAST YR MON PMT	TOTAL INTRST	INTRST SAVED	LAST YR MON PMT	TOTAL INTRST	INTRST SAVED
$ 50	0.68	195	1.05	72	123	1.16	67	128	1.22	62	133
100	1.35	386	2.08	143	243	2.31	131	255	2.42	123	263
200	2.69	768	4.14	283	485	4.60	261	507	4.82	244	524
300	4.04	1,154	6.22	426	728	6.91	392	762	7.24	366	788
400	5.38	1,537	8.28	567	970	9.20	522	1,015	9.63	487	1,050
500	6.73	1,923	10.36	709	1,214	11.51	653	1,270	12.05	610	1,313
600	8.07	2,305	12.42	850	1,455	13.80	783	1,522	14.45	731	1,574
700	9.42	2,691	14.50	992	1,699	16.11	914	1,777	16.87	853	1,838
800	10.76	3,074	16.56	1,133	1,941	18.40	1,044	2,030	19.27	974	2,100
900	12.11	3,460	18.64	1,276	2,184	20.71	1,175	2,285	21.69	1,097	2,363
1,000	13.45	3,842	20.71	1,416	2,426	23.00	1,305	2,537	24.09	1,218	2,624
2,000	26.90	7,684	41.41	2,833	4,851	46.01	2,610	5,074	48.17	2,436	5,248
3,000	40.35	11,526	62.12	4,249	7,277	69.01	3,914	7,612	72.26	3,654	7,872
4,000	53.80	15,368	82.82	5,665	9,703	92.02	5,219	10,149	96.35	4,872	10,496
5,000	67.24	19,206	103.51	7,080	12,126	115.00	6,522	12,684	120.42	6,089	13,117
6,000	80.69	23,048	124.22	8,496	14,552	138.01	7,827	15,221	144.50	7,307	15,741
7,000	94.14	26,890	144.92	9,913	16,977	161.01	9,132	17,758	168.59	8,525	18,365
8,000	107.59	30,732	165.63	11,329	19,403	184.02	10,436	20,296	192.68	9,743	20,989
9,000	121.03	34,571	186.32	12,744	21,827	207.00	11,740	22,831	216.75	10,960	23,611
10,000	134.48	38,413	207.03	14,160	24,253	230.01	13,044	25,369	240.83	12,178	26,235
11,000	147.93	42,255	227.73	15,576	26,679	253.01	14,349	27,906	264.92	13,396	28,859
12,000	161.38	46,097	248.44	16,993	29,104	276.01	15,654	30,443	289.01	14,614	31,483
13,000	174.82	49,935	269.13	18,407	31,528	299.00	16,957	32,978	313.08	15,830	34,105
14,000	188.27	53,777	289.83	19,824	33,953	322.01	18,262	35,515	337.16	17,048	36,729
15,000	201.72	57,619	310.54	21,240	36,379	345.01	19,567	38,052	361.25	18,266	39,353
16,000	215.17	61,461	331.24	22,656	38,805	368.01	20,871	40,590	385.34	19,485	41,976
17,000	228.61	65,300	351.93	24,071	41,229	391.01	22,174	43,126	409.41	20,701	44,599
18,000	242.06	69,142	372.64	25,487	43,655	414.00	23,479	45,663	433.49	21,919	47,223
19,000	255.51	72,984	393.35	26,904	46,080	437.01	24,784	48,200	457.58	23,137	49,847
20,000	268.96	76,826	414.05	28,320	48,506	460.01	26,089	50,737	481.67	24,355	52,471
21,000	282.40	80,664	434.74	29,735	50,929	483.00	27,392	53,272	505.74	25,572	55,092
22,000	295.85	84,506	455.45	31,151	53,355	506.00	28,697	55,809	529.82	26,790	57,716
23,000	309.30	88,348	476.15	32,567	55,781	529.01	30,001	58,347	553.91	28,008	60,340
24,000	322.75	92,190	496.86	33,984	58,206	552.01	31,306	60,884	578.00	29,226	62,964
25,000	336.19	96,028	517.55	35,398	60,630	575.00	32,609	63,419	602.07	30,442	65,586
26,000	349.64	99,870	538.25	36,815	63,055	598.00	33,914	65,956	626.15	31,660	68,210
27,000	363.09	103,712	558.96	38,231	65,481	621.01	35,219	68,493	650.24	32,879	70,833
28,000	376.54	107,554	579.67	39,647	67,907	644.01	36,523	71,031	674.33	34,097	73,457
29,000	389.98	111,393	600.36	41,062	70,331	667.00	37,827	73,566	698.39	35,313	76,080
30,000	403.43	115,235	621.06	42,478	72,757	690.00	39,131	76,104	722.48	36,531	78,704
32,500	437.05	124,838	672.82	46,018	78,820	747.50	42,392	82,446	782.69	39,576	85,262
35,000	470.67	134,441	724.57	49,558	84,883	805.01	45,653	88,788	842.90	42,620	91,821
40,000	537.91	153,648	828.09	56,638	97,010	920.01	52,176	101,472	963.31	48,709	104,939
45,000	605.15	172,854	931.60	63,718	109,136	1,035.01	58,698	114,156	1,083.73	54,798	118,056
50,000	672.38	192,057	1,035.10	70,797	121,260	1,150.00	65,218	126,839	1,204.13	60,885	131,172
55,000	739.62	211,263	1,138.61	77,877	133,386	1,265.00	71,740	139,523	1,324.55	66,974	144,289
60,000	806.86	230,470	1,242.12	84,957	145,513	1,380.00	78,263	152,207	1,444.96	73,062	157,408
65,000	874.10	249,676	1,345.64	92,037	157,639	1,495.01	84,785	164,891	1,565.38	79,151	170,525
70,000	941.33	268,879	1,449.13	99,115	169,764	1,609.99	91,305	177,574	1,685.78	85,238	183,641
75,000	1,008.57	288,085	1,552.65	106,195	181,890	1,725.00	97,827	190,258	1,806.20	91,327	196,758
80,000	1,075.81	307,292	1,656.16	113,275	194,017	1,840.00	104,350	202,942	1,926.61	97,416	209,876
85,000	1,143.05	326,498	1,759.67	120,355	206,143	1,955.00	110,872	215,626	2,047.03	103,505	222,993
90,000	1,210.29	345,704	1,863.19	127,435	218,269	2,070.01	117,394	228,310	2,167.45	109,594	236,110
95,000	1,277.52	364,907	1,966.68	134,513	230,394	2,184.99	123,914	240,993	2,287.84	115,681	249,226
100,000	1,344.76	384,114	2,070.20	141,593	242,521	2,300.00	130,437	253,677	2,408.26	121,770	262,344
105,000	1,412.00	403,320	2,173.71	148,673	254,647	2,415.00	136,959	266,361	2,528.68	127,858	275,462
110,000	1,479.24	422,526	2,277.22	155,753	266,773	2,530.00	143,481	279,045	2,649.09	133,947	288,579
115,000	1,546.48	441,733	2,380.73	162,833	278,900	2,645.01	150,003	291,730	2,769.51	140,036	301,697
120,000	1,613.71	460,936	2,484.23	169,912	291,024	2,759.99	156,523	304,413	2,889.91	146,123	314,813
125,000	1,680.95	480,142	2,587.75	176,992	303,150	2,874.99	163,046	317,096	3,010.33	152,212	327,930
130,000	1,748.19	499,348	2,691.26	184,072	315,276	2,990.00	169,568	329,780	3,130.74	158,301	341,047
135,000	1,815.43	518,555	2,794.77	191,152	327,403	3,105.00	176,090	342,465	3,251.16	164,390	354,165
140,000	1,882.66	537,758	2,898.27	198,230	339,528	3,219.99	182,610	355,148	3,371.56	170,477	367,281
145,000	1,949.90	556,964	3,001.78	205,310	351,654	3,334.99	189,133	367,831	3,491.97	176,566	380,398
150,000	2,017.14	576,170	3,105.29	212,390	363,780	3,449.98	195,655	380,515	3,612.39	182,654	393,516
155,000	2,084.38	595,377	3,208.81	219,470	375,907	3,565.00	202,177	393,200	3,732.81	188,743	406,634
160,000	2,151.62	614,583	3,312.32	226,550	388,033	3,680.00	208,699	405,884	3,853.22	194,832	419,751
165,000	2,218.85	633,786	3,415.82	233,628	400,158	3,794.99	215,220	418,566	3,973.62	200,919	432,867
170,000	2,286.09	652,992	3,519.33	240,708	412,284	3,909.99	221,742	431,250	4,094.04	207,008	445,984
175,000	2,353.32	672,199	3,622.84	247,788	424,411	4,024.99	228,264	443,935	4,214.46	213,097	459,102
180,000	2,420.57	691,405	3,726.36	254,868	436,537	4,140.00	234,786	456,619	4,334.87	219,186	472,219
185,000	2,487.81	710,612	3,829.87	261,948	448,664	4,255.00	241,308	469,304	4,455.29	225,274	485,338
190,000	2,555.04	729,814	3,933.37	269,027	460,787	4,369.99	247,829	481,985	4,575.69	231,362	498,452
195,000	2,622.28	749,021	4,036.88	276,107	472,914	4,484.99	254,351	494,670	4,696.10	237,450	511,571
200,000	2,689.52	768,227	4,140.39	283,187	485,040	4,599.99	260,873	507,354	4,816.52	243,539	524,688

173

GROWING EQUITY MORTGAGES

AMOUNT OF LOAN	30 YEARS		1% PMT INCR/YR 217.137 PAYMENTS			2% PMT INCR/YR 178.846 PAYMENTS			3% PMT INCR/YR 157.170 PAYMENTS		
	MONTHLY PAYMENT	TOTAL INTRST	LAST YR MON PMT	TOTAL INTRST	INTRST SAVED	LAST YR MON PMT	TOTAL INTRST	INTRST SAVED	LAST YR MON PMT	TOTAL INTRST	INTRST SAVED
$ 50	0.69	198	0.83	113	85	0.91	92	106	1.01	81	117
100	1.37	393	1.64	224	169	1.81	182	211	2.01	159	234
200	2.73	783	3.27	446	337	3.60	362	421	4.01	316	467
300	4.10	1,176	4.90	671	505	5.41	545	631	6.02	475	701
400	5.46	1,566	6.53	893	673	7.20	725	841	8.02	633	933
500	6.83	1,959	8.17	1,117	842	9.01	907	1,052	10.03	792	1,167
600	8.19	2,348	9.80	1,339	1,009	10.81	1,087	1,261	12.03	949	1,399
700	9.56	2,742	11.44	1,563	1,179	12.61	1,269	1,473	14.04	1,108	1,634
800	10.92	3,131	13.06	1,785	1,346	14.41	1,450	1,681	16.04	1,265	1,866
900	12.29	3,524	14.70	2,009	1,515	16.22	1,632	1,892	18.05	1,424	2,100
1,000	13.65	3,914	16.33	2,231	1,683	18.01	1,812	2,102	20.05	1,582	2,332
2,000	27.30	7,828	32.65	4,463	3,365	36.02	3,624	4,204	40.09	3,163	4,665
3,000	40.95	11,742	48.98	6,694	5,048	54.03	5,436	6,306	60.14	4,745	6,997
4,000	54.60	15,656	65.31	8,926	6,730	72.04	7,248	8,408	80.18	6,327	9,329
5,000	68.25	19,570	81.64	11,157	8,413	90.05	9,059	10,511	100.23	7,908	11,662
6,000	81.90	23,484	97.96	13,389	10,095	108.07	10,871	12,613	120.27	9,490	13,994
7,000	95.55	27,398	114.29	15,620	11,778	126.08	12,683	14,715	140.32	11,072	16,326
8,000	109.20	31,312	130.62	17,852	13,460	144.09	14,495	16,817	160.36	12,653	18,659
9,000	122.85	35,226	146.95	20,083	15,143	162.10	16,307	18,919	180.41	14,235	20,991
10,000	136.50	39,140	163.27	22,315	16,825	180.11	18,119	21,021	200.45	15,816	23,324
11,000	150.15	43,054	179.60	24,546	18,508	198.12	19,931	23,123	220.50	17,398	25,656
12,000	163.80	46,968	195.93	26,778	20,190	216.13	21,743	25,225	240.55	18,980	27,988
13,000	177.45	50,882	212.26	29,009	21,873	234.14	23,554	27,328	260.59	20,561	30,321
14,000	191.10	54,796	228.58	31,240	23,556	252.15	25,366	29,430	280.64	22,143	32,653
15,000	204.75	58,710	244.91	33,472	25,238	270.16	27,178	31,532	300.68	23,725	34,985
16,000	218.39	62,620	261.23	35,701	26,919	288.16	28,988	33,632	320.71	25,304	37,316
17,000	232.04	66,534	277.55	37,932	28,602	306.17	30,800	35,734	340.76	26,886	39,648
18,000	245.69	70,448	293.88	40,164	30,284	324.18	32,612	37,836	360.80	28,468	41,980
19,000	259.34	74,362	310.21	42,395	31,967	342.19	34,424	39,938	380.85	30,049	44,313
20,000	272.99	78,276	326.54	44,627	33,649	360.20	36,235	42,041	400.90	31,631	46,645
21,000	286.64	82,190	342.86	46,858	35,332	378.22	38,047	44,143	420.94	33,213	48,977
22,000	300.29	86,104	359.19	49,090	37,014	396.23	39,859	46,245	440.99	34,794	51,310
23,000	313.94	90,018	375.52	51,321	38,697	414.24	41,671	48,347	461.03	36,376	53,642
24,000	327.59	93,932	391.85	53,553	40,379	432.25	43,483	50,449	481.08	37,958	55,974
25,000	341.24	97,846	408.17	55,784	42,062	450.26	45,295	52,551	501.12	39,539	58,307
26,000	354.89	101,760	424.50	58,016	43,744	468.27	47,107	54,653	521.17	41,121	60,639
27,000	368.54	105,674	440.83	60,247	45,427	486.28	48,919	56,755	541.21	42,703	62,971
28,000	382.19	109,588	457.16	62,479	47,109	504.29	50,730	58,858	561.26	44,284	65,304
29,000	395.84	113,502	473.48	64,710	48,792	522.30	52,542	60,960	581.30	45,866	67,636
30,000	409.49	117,416	489.81	66,941	50,475	540.31	54,354	63,062	601.35	47,448	69,968
32,500	443.61	127,200	530.62	72,519	54,681	585.33	58,883	68,317	651.46	51,401	75,799
35,000	477.73	136,983	571.44	78,096	58,887	630.35	63,412	73,571	701.56	55,354	81,629
40,000	545.98	156,553	653.07	89,254	67,299	720.41	72,471	84,082	801.79	63,262	93,291
45,000	614.23	176,123	734.71	100,411	75,712	810.46	81,530	94,593	902.02	71,170	104,953
50,000	682.47	195,689	816.33	111,566	84,123	900.50	90,588	105,101	1,002.23	79,077	116,612
55,000	750.72	215,259	897.97	122,723	92,536	990.56	99,647	115,612	1,102.46	86,985	128,274
60,000	818.97	234,829	979.61	133,880	100,949	1,080.61	108,706	126,123	1,202.69	94,893	139,936
65,000	887.21	254,396	1,061.23	145,035	109,361	1,170.65	117,764	136,632	1,302.90	102,800	151,596
70,000	955.46	273,966	1,142.87	156,193	117,773	1,260.71	126,823	147,143	1,403.13	110,708	163,258
75,000	1,023.71	293,536	1,224.51	167,350	126,186	1,350.76	135,883	157,653	1,503.35	118,616	174,920
80,000	1,091.95	313,102	1,306.13	178,505	134,597	1,440.80	144,940	168,162	1,603.57	126,522	186,580
85,000	1,160.20	332,672	1,387.77	189,662	143,010	1,530.86	153,999	178,673	1,703.79	134,431	198,241
90,000	1,228.45	352,242	1,469.41	200,820	151,422	1,620.91	163,059	189,183	1,804.02	142,339	209,903
95,000	1,296.69	371,808	1,551.03	211,974	159,834	1,710.95	172,116	199,692	1,904.23	150,245	221,563
100,000	1,364.94	391,378	1,632.67	223,132	168,246	1,801.01	181,175	210,203	2,004.46	158,153	233,225
105,000	1,433.19	410,948	1,714.31	234,289	176,659	1,891.06	190,235	220,713	2,104.69	166,062	244,886
110,000	1,501.43	430,515	1,795.93	245,444	185,071	1,981.10	199,292	231,223	2,204.90	173,968	256,547
115,000	1,569.68	450,085	1,877.57	256,601	193,484	2,071.16	208,351	241,734	2,305.13	181,876	268,209
120,000	1,637.93	469,655	1,959.21	267,759	201,896	2,161.21	217,411	252,244	2,405.36	189,784	279,871
125,000	1,706.17	489,221	2,040.83	278,914	210,307	2,251.26	226,468	262,753	2,505.57	197,691	291,530
130,000	1,774.42	508,791	2,122.47	290,071	218,720	2,341.31	235,528	273,263	2,605.80	205,599	303,192
135,000	1,842.67	528,361	2,204.11	301,228	227,133	2,431.36	244,587	283,774	2,706.02	213,507	314,854
140,000	1,910.91	547,928	2,285.73	312,383	235,545	2,521.41	253,644	294,284	2,806.24	221,414	326,514
145,000	1,979.16	567,498	2,367.37	323,540	243,958	2,611.46	262,704	304,794	2,906.46	229,322	338,176
150,000	2,047.41	587,068	2,449.00	334,698	252,370	2,701.51	271,763	315,305	3,006.69	237,230	349,838
155,000	2,115.65	606,634	2,530.63	345,853	260,781	2,791.56	280,820	325,814	3,106.90	245,136	361,498
160,000	2,183.90	626,204	2,612.27	357,010	269,194	2,881.61	289,880	336,324	3,207.13	253,045	373,159
165,000	2,252.15	645,774	2,693.90	368,167	277,607	2,971.66	298,939	346,835	3,307.36	260,953	384,821
170,000	2,320.39	665,340	2,775.53	379,322	286,018	3,061.71	307,996	357,344	3,407.57	268,859	396,481
175,000	2,388.64	684,910	2,857.17	390,479	294,431	3,151.76	317,056	367,854	3,507.80	276,767	408,143
180,000	2,456.89	704,480	2,938.80	401,637	302,843	3,241.81	326,115	378,365	3,608.03	284,676	419,804
185,000	2,525.13	724,047	3,020.43	412,792	311,255	3,331.86	335,173	388,874	3,708.24	292,582	431,465
190,000	2,593.38	743,617	3,102.06	423,949	319,668	3,421.91	344,232	399,385	3,808.47	300,490	443,127
195,000	2,661.63	763,187	3,183.70	435,106	328,081	3,511.96	353,291	409,896	3,908.69	308,399	454,788
200,000	2,729.87	782,753	3,265.33	446,261	336,492	3,602.01	362,349	420,404	4,008.91	316,305	466,448

GROWING EQUITY MORTGAGES 16.25%

AMOUNT OF LOAN	30 YEARS		4% PMT INCR/YR 142.431 PAYMENTS			5% PMT INCR/YR 131.493 PAYMENTS			6% PMT INCR/YR 122.841 PAYMENTS		
	MONTHLY PAYMENT	TOTAL INTRST	LAST YR MON PMT	TOTAL INTRST	INTRST SAVED	LAST YR MON PMT	TOTAL INTRST	INTRST SAVED	LAST YR MON PMT	TOTAL INTRST	INTRST SAVED
$ 50	0.69	198	1.06	73	125	1.12	67	131	1.24	63	135
100	1.37	393	2.11	144	249	2.23	132	261	2.45	124	269
200	2.73	783	4.20	286	497	4.45	263	520	4.89	246	537
300	4.10	1,176	6.31	429	747	6.68	396	780	7.34	369	807
400	5.46	1,566	8.41	571	995	8.89	526	1,040	9.78	491	1,075
500	6.83	1,959	10.51	715	1,244	11.13	659	1,300	12.23	615	1,344
600	8.19	2,348	12.61	857	1,491	13.34	789	1,559	14.67	737	1,611
700	9.56	2,742	14.72	1,001	1,741	15.57	922	1,820	17.12	861	1,881
800	10.92	3,131	16.81	1,143	1,988	17.79	1,053	2,078	19.56	983	2,148
900	12.29	3,524	18.92	1,286	2,238	20.02	1,185	2,339	22.01	1,106	2,418
1,000	13.65	3,914	21.01	1,428	2,486	22.23	1,316	2,598	24.45	1,228	2,686
2,000	27.30	7,828	42.03	2,857	4,971	44.47	2,632	5,196	48.89	2,457	5,371
3,000	40.95	11,742	63.04	4,285	7,457	66.70	3,947	7,795	73.34	3,685	8,057
4,000	54.60	15,656	84.05	5,713	9,943	88.94	5,263	10,393	97.78	4,914	10,742
5,000	68.25	19,570	105.07	7,141	12,429	111.17	6,579	12,991	122.23	6,142	13,428
6,000	81.90	23,484	126.08	8,570	14,914	133.41	7,895	15,589	146.67	7,371	16,113
7,000	95.55	27,398	147.09	9,998	17,400	155.64	9,211	18,187	171.12	8,599	18,799
8,000	109.20	31,312	168.11	11,426	19,886	177.88	10,526	20,786	195.56	9,828	21,484
9,000	122.85	35,226	189.12	12,854	22,372	200.11	11,842	23,384	220.01	11,056	24,170
10,000	136.50	39,140	210.14	14,283	24,857	222.34	13,158	25,982	244.45	12,285	26,855
11,000	150.15	43,054	231.15	15,711	27,343	244.58	14,474	28,580	268.90	13,513	29,541
12,000	163.80	46,968	252.16	17,139	29,829	266.81	15,790	31,178	293.34	14,742	32,226
13,000	177.45	50,882	273.18	18,567	32,315	289.05	17,105	33,777	317.79	15,970	34,912
14,000	191.10	54,796	294.19	19,996	34,800	311.28	18,421	36,375	342.23	17,198	37,598
15,000	204.75	58,710	315.20	21,424	37,286	333.52	19,737	38,973	366.68	18,427	40,283
16,000	218.39	62,620	336.20	22,850	39,770	355.73	21,051	41,569	391.10	19,654	42,966
17,000	232.04	66,534	357.21	24,279	42,255	377.97	22,367	44,167	415.55	20,882	45,652
18,000	245.69	70,448	378.23	25,707	44,741	400.20	23,683	46,765	439.99	22,111	48,337
19,000	259.34	74,362	399.24	27,135	47,227	422.44	24,998	49,364	464.44	23,339	51,023
20,000	272.99	78,276	420.26	28,563	49,713	444.67	26,314	51,962	488.88	24,568	53,708
21,000	286.64	82,190	441.27	29,992	52,198	466.91	27,630	54,560	513.33	25,796	56,394
22,000	300.29	86,104	462.28	31,420	54,684	489.14	28,946	57,158	537.77	27,025	59,079
23,000	313.94	90,018	483.30	32,848	57,170	511.38	30,262	59,756	562.22	28,253	61,765
24,000	327.59	93,932	504.31	34,276	59,656	533.61	31,577	62,355	586.66	29,481	64,451
25,000	341.24	97,846	525.32	35,705	62,141	555.84	32,893	64,953	611.11	30,710	67,136
26,000	354.89	101,760	546.34	37,133	64,627	578.08	34,209	67,551	635.55	31,938	69,822
27,000	368.54	105,674	567.35	38,561	67,113	600.31	35,525	70,149	660.00	33,167	72,507
28,000	382.19	109,588	588.36	39,989	69,599	622.55	36,841	72,747	684.44	34,395	75,193
29,000	395.84	113,502	609.38	41,418	72,084	644.78	38,156	75,346	708.89	35,624	77,878
30,000	409.49	117,416	630.39	42,846	74,570	667.02	39,472	77,944	733.33	36,852	80,564
32,500	443.61	127,200	682.92	46,416	80,784	722.59	42,761	84,439	794.44	39,923	87,277
35,000	477.73	136,983	735.44	49,985	86,998	778.17	46,050	90,933	855.54	42,993	93,990
40,000	545.98	156,553	840.51	57,127	99,426	889.34	52,629	103,924	977.77	49,135	107,418
45,000	614.23	176,123	945.58	64,268	111,855	1,000.52	59,208	116,915	1,099.99	55,278	120,845
50,000	682.47	195,689	1,050.65	71,407	124,282	1,111.67	65,785	129,904	1,222.20	61,418	134,271
55,000	750.72	215,259	1,155.70	78,549	136,710	1,222.84	72,364	142,895	1,344.43	67,561	147,698
60,000	818.97	234,829	1,260.77	85,690	149,139	1,334.02	78,943	155,886	1,466.65	73,703	161,126
65,000	887.21	254,396	1,365.82	92,830	161,566	1,445.17	85,520	168,876	1,588.86	79,844	174,552
70,000	955.46	273,966	1,470.89	99,971	173,995	1,556.34	92,099	181,867	1,711.08	85,986	187,980
75,000	1,023.71	293,536	1,575.95	107,112	186,424	1,667.52	98,678	194,858	1,833.31	92,128	201,408
80,000	1,091.95	313,102	1,681.01	114,252	198,850	1,778.67	105,255	207,847	1,955.52	98,269	214,833
85,000	1,160.20	332,672	1,786.07	121,393	211,279	1,889.84	111,834	220,838	2,077.74	104,411	228,261
90,000	1,228.45	352,242	1,891.14	128,534	223,708	2,001.02	118,413	233,829	2,199.97	110,553	241,689
95,000	1,296.69	371,808	1,996.19	135,674	236,134	2,112.17	124,991	246,817	2,322.17	116,694	255,114
100,000	1,364.94	391,378	2,101.26	142,815	248,563	2,223.34	131,570	259,808	2,444.40	122,836	268,542
105,000	1,433.19	410,948	2,206.33	149,956	260,992	2,334.52	138,149	272,799	2,566.63	128,979	281,969
110,000	1,501.43	430,515	2,311.38	157,096	273,419	2,445.67	144,726	285,789	2,688.83	135,119	295,396
115,000	1,569.68	450,085	2,416.45	164,237	285,848	2,556.84	151,305	298,780	2,811.06	141,262	308,823
120,000	1,637.93	469,655	2,521.52	171,378	298,277	2,668.02	157,884	311,771	2,933.28	147,404	322,251
125,000	1,706.17	489,221	2,626.57	178,518	310,703	2,779.17	164,461	324,760	3,055.49	153,545	335,676
130,000	1,774.42	508,791	2,731.64	185,659	323,132	2,890.34	171,040	337,751	3,177.72	159,687	349,104
135,000	1,842.67	528,361	2,836.71	192,800	335,561	3,001.52	177,619	350,742	3,299.94	165,829	362,532
140,000	1,910.91	547,928	2,941.76	199,940	347,988	3,112.67	184,197	363,731	3,422.15	171,970	375,958
145,000	1,979.16	567,498	3,046.83	207,081	360,417	3,223.84	190,776	376,722	3,544.37	178,112	389,386
150,000	2,047.41	587,068	3,151.89	214,222	372,846	3,335.02	197,355	389,713	3,666.60	184,255	402,813
155,000	2,115.65	606,634	3,256.95	221,362	385,272	3,446.17	203,932	402,702	3,788.81	190,395	416,239
160,000	2,183.90	626,204	3,362.01	228,503	397,701	3,557.34	210,511	415,693	3,911.03	196,538	429,666
165,000	2,252.15	645,774	3,467.08	235,645	410,129	3,668.52	217,090	428,684	4,033.26	202,680	443,094
170,000	2,320.39	665,340	3,572.13	242,784	422,556	3,779.67	223,667	441,673	4,155.47	208,821	456,519
175,000	2,388.64	684,910	3,677.20	249,925	434,985	3,890.84	230,246	454,664	4,277.69	214,963	469,947
180,000	2,456.89	704,480	3,782.27	257,067	447,413	4,002.01	236,825	467,655	4,399.92	221,105	483,375
185,000	2,525.13	724,047	3,887.32	264,206	459,841	4,113.17	243,402	480,645	4,522.12	227,246	496,801
190,000	2,593.38	743,617	3,992.39	271,347	472,270	4,224.34	249,981	493,636	4,644.35	233,388	510,229
195,000	2,661.63	763,187	4,097.46	278,489	484,698	4,335.51	256,560	506,627	4,766.57	239,531	523,656
200,000	2,729.87	782,753	4,202.51	285,628	497,125	4,446.67	263,138	519,615	4,888.78	245,671	537,082

175

AMOUNT OF LOAN	30 YEARS		1% PMT INCR/YR 215.438 PAYMENTS			2% PMT INCR/YR 177.403 PAYMENTS			3% PMT INCR/YR 155.939 PAYMENTS		
	MONTHLY PAYMENT	TOTAL INTRST	LAST YR MON PMT	TOTAL INTRST	INTRST SAVED	LAST YR MON PMT	TOTAL INTRST	INTRST SAVED	LAST YR MON PMT	TOTAL INTRST	INTRST SAVED
$ 50	0.70	202	0.83	114	88	0.92	93	109	1.00	81	121
100	1.39	400	1.65	226	174	1.83	184	216	1.98	160	240
200	2.78	801	3.29	452	349	3.67	367	434	3.96	321	480
300	4.16	1,198	4.93	676	522	5.49	549	649	5.93	479	719
400	5.55	1,598	6.57	903	695	7.32	733	865	7.91	640	958
500	6.93	1,995	8.21	1,127	868	9.14	914	1,081	9.88	798	1,197
600	8.32	2,395	9.85	1,353	1,042	10.98	1,098	1,297	11.86	959	1,436
700	9.70	2,792	11.49	1,577	1,215	12.80	1,280	1,512	13.83	1,117	1,675
800	11.09	3,192	13.13	1,803	1,389	14.63	1,463	1,729	15.81	1,277	1,915
900	12.47	3,589	14.77	2,027	1,562	16.45	1,645	1,944	17.78	1,436	2,153
1,000	13.86	3,990	16.41	2,253	1,737	18.29	1,829	2,161	19.76	1,596	2,394
2,000	27.71	7,976	32.82	4,504	3,472	36.56	3,655	4,321	39.51	3,191	4,785
3,000	41.56	11,962	49.22	6,755	5,207	54.84	5,482	6,480	59.25	4,785	7,177
4,000	55.41	15,948	65.62	9,005	6,943	73.11	7,309	8,639	79.00	6,380	9,568
5,000	69.26	19,934	82.02	11,256	8,678	91.39	9,136	10,798	98.75	7,974	11,960
6,000	83.11	23,920	98.43	13,507	10,413	109.66	10,962	12,958	118.49	9,569	14,351
7,000	96.97	27,909	114.84	15,760	12,149	127.95	12,791	15,118	138.26	11,165	16,744
8,000	110.82	31,895	131.24	18,011	13,884	146.22	14,618	17,277	158.00	12,760	19,135
9,000	124.67	35,881	147.65	20,261	15,620	164.50	16,444	19,437	177.75	14,354	21,527
10,000	138.52	39,867	164.05	22,512	17,355	182.77	18,271	21,596	197.50	15,948	23,919
11,000	152.37	43,853	180.45	24,763	19,090	201.05	20,098	23,755	217.24	17,543	26,310
12,000	166.22	47,839	196.86	27,014	20,825	219.32	21,925	25,914	236.99	19,137	28,702
13,000	180.07	51,825	213.26	29,264	22,561	237.60	23,751	28,074	256.74	20,732	31,093
14,000	193.93	55,815	229.67	31,518	24,297	255.89	25,580	30,235	276.50	22,328	33,487
15,000	207.78	59,801	246.07	33,768	26,033	274.16	27,407	32,394	296.24	23,923	35,878
16,000	221.63	63,787	262.48	36,019	27,768	292.44	29,233	34,554	315.99	25,517	38,270
17,000	235.48	67,773	278.88	38,270	29,503	310.71	31,060	36,713	335.74	27,112	40,661
18,000	249.33	71,759	295.28	40,521	31,238	328.99	32,887	38,872	355.48	28,706	43,053
19,000	263.18	75,745	311.69	42,771	32,974	347.26	34,714	41,031	375.23	30,301	45,444
20,000	277.03	79,731	328.09	45,022	34,709	365.54	36,540	43,191	394.98	31,895	47,836
21,000	290.89	83,720	344.50	47,275	36,445	383.82	38,369	45,351	414.74	33,491	50,229
22,000	304.74	87,706	360.90	49,526	38,180	402.10	40,196	47,510	434.49	35,086	52,620
23,000	318.59	91,692	377.31	51,777	39,915	420.37	42,022	49,670	454.23	36,680	55,012
24,000	332.44	95,678	393.71	54,027	41,651	438.65	43,849	51,829	473.98	38,275	57,403
25,000	346.29	99,664	410.11	56,278	43,386	456.92	45,676	53,988	493.73	39,869	59,795
26,000	360.14	103,650	426.52	58,529	45,121	475.20	47,503	56,147	513.47	41,464	62,186
27,000	373.99	107,636	442.92	60,780	46,856	493.47	49,329	58,307	533.22	43,058	64,578
28,000	387.85	111,626	459.33	63,033	48,593	511.76	51,158	60,468	552.98	44,655	66,971
29,000	401.70	115,612	475.74	65,284	50,328	530.03	52,985	62,627	572.73	46,249	69,363
30,000	415.55	119,598	492.14	67,534	52,064	548.31	54,811	64,787	592.47	47,844	71,754
32,500	450.18	129,565	533.15	73,162	56,403	594.00	59,379	70,186	641.85	51,831	77,734
35,000	484.81	139,532	574.16	78,790	60,742	639.70	63,947	75,585	691.22	55,818	83,714
40,000	554.06	159,462	656.18	90,044	69,418	731.07	73,080	86,382	789.96	63,790	95,672
45,000	623.32	179,395	738.20	101,300	78,095	822.46	82,216	97,179	888.71	71,764	107,631
50,000	692.58	199,329	820.23	112,556	86,773	913.84	91,352	107,977	987.45	79,739	119,590
55,000	761.84	219,262	902.25	123,813	95,449	1,005.23	100,487	118,775	1,086.20	87,713	131,549
60,000	831.09	239,192	984.26	135,066	104,126	1,096.61	109,621	129,571	1,184.94	95,685	143,507
65,000	900.35	259,126	1,066.29	146,322	112,804	1,187.99	118,756	140,370	1,283.68	103,659	155,467
70,000	969.61	279,060	1,148.31	157,579	121,481	1,279.38	127,892	151,168	1,382.43	111,634	167,426
75,000	1,038.87	298,993	1,230.34	168,835	130,158	1,370.77	137,027	161,966	1,481.18	119,608	179,385
80,000	1,108.12	318,923	1,312.35	180,088	138,835	1,462.14	146,161	172,762	1,579.91	127,580	191,343
85,000	1,177.38	338,857	1,394.38	191,344	147,513	1,553.53	155,297	183,560	1,678.66	135,554	203,303
90,000	1,246.64	358,790	1,476.40	202,601	156,189	1,644.92	164,432	194,358	1,777.41	143,529	215,261
95,000	1,315.90	378,724	1,558.43	213,857	164,867	1,736.30	173,568	205,156	1,876.16	151,503	227,221
100,000	1,385.15	398,654	1,640.44	225,110	173,544	1,827.68	182,701	215,953	1,974.89	159,475	239,179
105,000	1,454.41	418,588	1,722.46	236,367	182,221	1,919.05	191,837	226,751	2,073.64	167,450	251,138
110,000	1,523.67	438,521	1,804.49	247,623	190,898	2,010.45	200,972	237,549	2,172.39	175,424	263,097
115,000	1,592.93	458,455	1,886.51	258,879	199,576	2,101.84	210,108	248,347	2,271.14	183,398	275,057
120,000	1,662.18	478,385	1,968.53	270,133	208,252	2,193.21	219,241	259,144	2,369.87	191,370	287,015
125,000	1,731.44	498,318	2,050.55	281,389	216,929	2,284.60	228,377	269,941	2,468.62	199,345	298,973
130,000	1,800.70	518,252	2,132.58	292,645	225,607	2,375.99	237,513	280,739	2,567.37	207,319	310,933
135,000	1,869.95	538,182	2,214.59	303,899	234,283	2,467.36	246,646	291,536	2,666.10	215,291	322,891
140,000	1,939.21	558,116	2,296.61	315,155	242,961	2,558.75	255,782	302,334	2,764.85	223,265	334,851
145,000	2,008.47	578,049	2,378.64	326,411	251,638	2,650.13	264,917	313,132	2,863.60	231,240	346,809
150,000	2,077.73	597,983	2,460.66	337,667	260,316	2,741.52	274,053	323,930	2,962.35	239,214	358,769
155,000	2,146.98	617,913	2,542.68	348,921	268,992	2,832.89	283,186	334,727	3,061.08	247,186	370,727
160,000	2,216.24	637,846	2,624.70	360,177	277,669	2,924.28	292,322	345,524	3,159.83	255,161	382,685
165,000	2,285.50	657,780	2,706.73	371,433	286,347	3,015.67	301,458	356,322	3,258.58	263,135	394,645
170,000	2,354.76	677,714	2,788.75	382,689	295,025	3,107.06	310,593	367,121	3,357.32	271,109	406,605
175,000	2,424.01	697,644	2,870.77	393,943	303,701	3,198.43	319,727	377,917	3,456.06	279,081	418,563
180,000	2,493.27	717,577	2,952.79	405,199	312,378	3,289.82	328,862	388,715	3,554.81	287,056	430,521
185,000	2,562.53	737,511	3,034.82	416,455	321,056	3,381.20	337,998	399,513	3,653.56	295,030	442,481
190,000	2,631.79	757,443	3,116.84	427,711	329,733	3,472.59	347,133	410,311	3,752.30	303,004	454,440
195,000	2,701.04	777,374	3,198.85	438,965	338,409	3,563.96	356,267	421,107	3,851.04	310,976	466,398
200,000	2,770.30	797,308	3,280.88	450,221	347,087	3,655.35	365,402	431,906	3,949.79	318,951	478,357

GROWING EQUITY MORTGAGES 16.50%

AMOUNT OF LOAN	30 YEARS		4% PMT INCR/YR 141.308 PAYMENTS			5% PMT INCR/YR 130.468 PAYMENTS			6% PMT INCR/YR 121.935 PAYMENTS		
	MONTHLY PAYMENT	TOTAL INTRST	LAST YR MON PMT	TOTAL INTRST	INTRST SAVED	LAST YR MON PMT	TOTAL INTRST	INTRST SAVED	LAST YR MON PMT	TOTAL INTRST	INTRST SAVED
$ 50	0.70	202	1.08	73	129	1.14	68	134	1.25	63	139
100	1.39	400	2.14	145	255	2.26	134	266	2.49	125	275
200	2.78	801	4.28	290	511	4.53	267	534	4.98	249	552
300	4.16	1,198	6.40	433	765	6.78	399	799	7.45	372	826
400	5.55	1,598	8.54	578	1,020	9.04	532	1,066	9.94	497	1,101
500	6.93	1,995	10.67	721	1,274	11.29	664	1,331	12.41	620	1,375
600	8.32	2,395	12.81	866	1,529	13.55	798	1,597	14.90	745	1,650
700	9.70	2,792	14.93	1,009	1,783	15.80	929	1,863	17.37	868	1,924
800	11.09	3,192	17.07	1,154	2,038	18.06	1,063	2,129	19.86	993	2,199
900	12.47	3,589	19.20	1,297	2,292	20.31	1,195	2,394	22.33	1,116	2,473
1,000	13.86	3,990	21.34	1,442	2,548	22.58	1,328	2,662	24.82	1,240	2,750
2,000	27.71	7,976	42.66	2,882	5,094	45.14	2,655	5,321	49.62	2,479	5,497
3,000	41.56	11,962	63.98	4,321	7,641	67.70	3,981	7,981	74.43	3,718	8,244
4,000	55.41	15,948	85.30	5,761	10,187	90.26	5,308	10,640	99.23	4,956	10,992
5,000	69.26	19,934	106.62	7,201	12,733	112.82	6,635	13,299	124.03	6,195	13,739
6,000	83.11	23,920	127.94	8,641	15,279	135.38	7,961	15,959	148.84	7,433	16,487
7,000	96.97	27,909	149.28	10,083	17,826	157.95	9,290	18,619	173.66	8,674	19,235
8,000	110.82	31,895	170.60	11,523	20,372	180.51	10,616	21,279	198.46	9,912	21,983
9,000	124.67	35,881	191.92	12,963	22,918	203.07	11,943	23,938	223.26	11,151	24,730
10,000	138.52	39,867	213.25	14,402	25,465	225.63	13,269	26,598	248.07	12,390	27,477
11,000	152.37	43,853	234.57	15,842	28,011	248.19	14,596	29,257	272.87	13,628	30,225
12,000	166.22	47,839	255.89	17,282	30,557	270.75	15,923	31,916	297.67	14,867	32,972
13,000	180.07	51,825	277.21	18,722	33,103	293.32	17,249	34,576	322.48	16,106	35,719
14,000	193.93	55,815	298.55	20,164	35,651	315.89	18,578	37,237	347.30	17,346	38,469
15,000	207.78	59,801	319.87	21,604	38,197	338.45	19,904	39,897	372.10	18,584	41,217
16,000	221.63	63,787	341.19	23,044	40,743	361.01	21,231	42,556	396.91	19,823	43,964
17,000	235.48	67,773	362.51	24,483	43,290	383.57	22,557	45,216	421.71	21,062	46,711
18,000	249.33	71,759	383.83	25,923	45,836	406.13	23,884	47,875	446.51	22,300	49,459
19,000	263.18	75,745	405.15	27,363	48,382	428.69	25,211	50,534	471.32	23,539	52,206
20,000	277.03	79,731	426.47	28,803	50,928	451.25	26,537	53,194	496.12	24,778	54,953
21,000	290.89	83,720	447.81	30,245	53,475	473.83	27,865	55,855	520.94	26,018	57,702
22,000	304.74	87,706	469.13	31,685	56,021	496.39	29,192	58,514	545.74	27,257	60,449
23,000	318.59	91,692	490.45	33,125	58,567	518.95	30,519	61,173	570.55	28,495	63,197
24,000	332.44	95,678	511.78	34,564	61,114	541.51	31,845	63,833	595.35	29,734	65,944
25,000	346.29	99,664	533.10	36,004	63,660	564.07	33,172	66,492	620.15	30,973	68,691
26,000	360.14	103,650	554.42	37,444	66,206	586.63	34,498	69,152	644.96	32,211	71,439
27,000	373.99	107,636	575.74	38,884	68,752	609.19	35,825	71,811	669.76	33,450	74,186
28,000	387.85	111,626	597.08	40,326	71,300	631.77	37,153	74,473	694.58	34,690	76,936
29,000	401.70	115,612	618.40	41,766	73,846	654.33	38,480	77,132	719.38	35,929	79,683
30,000	415.55	119,598	639.72	43,206	76,392	676.89	39,807	79,791	744.19	37,167	82,431
32,500	450.18	129,565	693.03	46,806	82,759	733.30	43,124	86,441	806.20	40,265	89,300
35,000	484.81	139,532	746.34	50,407	89,125	789.70	46,441	93,091	868.22	43,362	96,170
40,000	554.06	159,462	852.95	57,606	101,856	902.51	53,074	106,388	992.24	49,555	109,907
45,000	623.32	179,395	959.57	64,807	114,588	1,015.32	59,709	119,686	1,116.27	55,750	123,645
50,000	692.58	199,329	1,066.20	72,009	127,320	1,128.14	66,344	132,985	1,240.31	61,945	137,384
55,000	761.84	219,262	1,172.82	79,210	140,052	1,240.96	72,978	146,284	1,364.34	68,140	151,122
60,000	831.09	239,192	1,279.42	86,409	152,783	1,353.76	79,611	159,581	1,488.36	74,333	164,859
65,000	900.35	259,126	1,386.05	93,611	165,515	1,466.58	86,246	172,880	1,612.39	80,528	178,598
70,000	969.61	279,060	1,492.67	100,812	178,248	1,579.39	92,881	186,179	1,736.42	86,723	192,337
75,000	1,038.87	298,993	1,599.29	108,013	190,980	1,692.21	99,516	199,477	1,860.46	92,918	206,075
80,000	1,108.12	318,923	1,705.90	115,212	203,711	1,805.01	106,149	212,774	1,984.47	99,111	219,812
85,000	1,177.38	338,857	1,812.52	122,414	216,443	1,917.83	112,783	226,074	2,108.51	105,306	233,551
90,000	1,246.64	358,790	1,919.15	129,615	229,175	2,030.65	119,418	239,372	2,232.54	111,500	247,290
95,000	1,315.90	378,724	2,025.77	136,816	241,908	2,143.46	126,053	252,671	2,356.58	117,695	261,029
100,000	1,385.15	398,654	2,132.37	144,016	254,638	2,256.26	132,686	265,968	2,480.59	123,888	274,766
105,000	1,454.41	418,588	2,239.00	151,217	267,371	2,369.08	139,320	279,268	2,604.63	130,083	288,505
110,000	1,523.67	438,521	2,345.62	158,418	280,103	2,481.90	145,955	292,566	2,728.66	136,278	302,243
115,000	1,592.93	458,455	2,452.24	165,619	292,836	2,594.72	152,590	305,865	2,852.70	142,473	315,982
120,000	1,662.18	478,385	2,558.85	172,819	305,566	2,707.52	159,223	319,162	2,976.71	148,666	329,719
125,000	1,731.44	498,318	2,665.47	180,020	318,298	2,820.33	165,858	332,460	3,100.75	154,861	343,457
130,000	1,800.70	518,252	2,772.09	187,221	331,031	2,933.15	172,492	345,760	3,224.78	161,056	357,196
135,000	1,869.95	538,182	2,878.70	194,421	343,761	3,045.95	179,125	359,057	3,348.80	167,249	370,933
140,000	1,939.21	558,116	2,985.32	201,622	356,494	3,158.77	185,760	372,356	3,472.83	173,444	384,672
145,000	2,008.47	578,049	3,091.95	208,823	369,226	3,271.59	192,395	385,654	3,596.86	179,639	398,410
150,000	2,077.73	597,983	3,198.57	216,024	381,959	3,384.40	199,030	398,953	3,720.90	185,834	412,149
155,000	2,146.98	617,913	3,305.18	223,224	394,689	3,497.20	205,663	412,250	3,844.91	192,027	425,886
160,000	2,216.24	637,846	3,411.80	230,425	407,421	3,610.02	212,297	425,549	3,968.95	198,222	439,624
165,000	2,285.50	657,780	3,518.42	237,626	420,154	3,722.84	218,932	438,848	4,092.98	204,416	453,364
170,000	2,354.76	677,714	3,625.04	244,827	432,887	3,835.66	225,567	452,147	4,217.02	210,611	467,103
175,000	2,424.01	697,644	3,731.65	252,027	445,617	3,948.46	232,200	465,444	4,341.03	216,804	480,840
180,000	2,493.27	717,577	3,838.27	259,228	458,349	4,061.27	238,834	478,743	4,465.07	222,999	494,578
185,000	2,562.53	737,511	3,944.90	266,429	471,082	4,174.09	245,469	492,042	4,589.10	229,194	508,317
190,000	2,631.79	757,444	4,051.52	273,630	483,814	4,286.91	252,104	505,340	4,713.14	235,389	522,055
195,000	2,701.04	777,374	4,158.13	280,830	496,544	4,399.71	258,737	518,637	4,837.15	241,582	535,792
200,000	2,770.30	797,308	4,264.75	288,031	509,277	4,512.53	265,372	531,936	4,961.19	247,777	549,531

177

GROWING EQUITY MORTGAGES

AMOUNT OF LOAN	30 YEARS		1% PMT INCR/YR 213.743 PAYMENTS			2% PMT INCR/YR 175.980 PAYMENTS			3% PMT INCR/YR 154.697 PAYMENTS		
	MONTHLY PAYMENT	TOTAL INTRST	LAST YR MON PMT	TOTAL INTRST	INTRST SAVED	LAST YR MON PMT	TOTAL INTRST	INTRST SAVED	LAST YR MON PMT	TOTAL INTRST	INTRST SAVED
$ 50	0.71	206	0.84	115	91	0.94	94	112	1.01	82	124
100	1.41	408	1.67	228	180	1.86	185	223	2.01	162	246
200	2.82	815	3.34	456	359	3.72	370	445	4.02	323	492
300	4.22	1,219	5.00	682	537	5.57	553	666	6.02	483	736
400	5.63	1,627	6.67	910	717	7.43	738	889	8.03	645	982
500	7.03	2,031	8.33	1,136	895	9.28	922	1,109	10.02	804	1,227
600	8.44	2,438	10.00	1,364	1,074	11.14	1,107	1,331	12.03	966	1,472
700	9.84	2,842	11.65	1,590	1,252	12.98	1,290	1,552	14.03	1,126	1,716
800	11.25	3,250	13.32	1,818	1,432	14.84	1,475	1,775	16.04	1,288	1,962
900	12.65	3,654	14.98	2,044	1,610	16.69	1,658	1,996	18.04	1,447	2,207
1,000	14.06	4,062	16.65	2,272	1,790	18.55	1,843	2,219	20.05	1,609	2,453
2,000	28.11	8,120	33.29	4,541	3,579	37.09	3,684	4,436	40.08	3,216	4,904
3,000	42.17	12,181	49.94	6,813	5,368	55.64	5,527	6,654	60.12	4,825	7,356
4,000	56.22	16,239	66.58	9,083	7,156	74.18	7,369	8,870	80.16	6,432	9,807
5,000	70.27	20,297	83.22	11,352	8,945	92.72	9,210	11,087	100.19	8,039	12,258
6,000	84.33	24,359	99.87	13,624	10,735	111.27	11,053	13,306	120.23	9,648	14,711
7,000	98.38	28,417	116.51	15,893	12,524	129.81	12,894	15,523	140.27	11,255	17,162
8,000	112.44	32,478	133.16	18,165	14,313	148.36	14,737	17,741	160.31	12,864	19,614
9,000	126.49	36,536	149.80	20,435	16,101	166.90	16,578	19,958	180.34	14,471	22,065
10,000	140.54	40,594	166.44	22,704	17,890	185.44	18,420	22,174	200.38	16,078	24,516
11,000	154.60	44,656	183.09	24,976	19,680	203.99	20,263	24,393	220.42	17,687	26,969
12,000	168.65	48,714	199.73	27,246	21,468	222.53	22,104	26,610	240.45	19,294	29,420
13,000	182.71	52,776	216.38	29,517	23,259	241.08	23,947	28,829	260.50	20,903	31,873
14,000	196.76	56,834	233.02	31,787	25,047	259.62	25,788	31,046	280.53	22,510	34,324
15,000	210.81	60,892	249.66	34,056	26,836	278.16	27,629	33,263	300.56	24,117	36,775
16,000	224.87	64,953	266.31	36,328	28,625	296.71	29,472	35,481	320.61	25,726	39,227
17,000	238.92	69,011	282.95	38,598	30,413	315.25	31,314	37,697	340.64	27,333	41,678
18,000	252.98	73,073	299.61	40,869	32,204	333.80	33,157	39,916	360.69	28,942	44,131
19,000	267.03	77,131	316.24	43,139	33,992	352.34	34,998	42,133	380.72	30,549	46,582
20,000	281.08	81,189	332.88	45,408	35,781	370.88	36,839	44,350	400.75	32,156	49,033
21,000	295.14	85,250	349.54	47,680	37,570	389.43	38,682	46,568	420.80	33,765	51,485
22,000	309.19	89,308	366.18	49,950	39,358	407.97	40,523	48,785	440.83	35,372	53,936
23,000	323.25	93,370	382.83	52,222	41,148	426.52	42,367	51,003	460.88	36,981	56,389
24,000	337.30	97,428	399.47	54,491	42,937	445.06	44,208	53,220	480.91	38,588	58,840
25,000	351.35	101,486	416.11	56,761	44,725	463.60	46,049	55,437	500.94	40,195	61,291
26,000	365.41	105,548	432.76	59,032	46,516	482.15	47,892	57,656	520.99	41,804	63,744
27,000	379.46	109,606	449.40	61,302	48,304	500.69	49,733	59,873	541.02	43,411	66,195
28,000	393.52	113,667	466.05	63,574	50,093	519.24	51,576	62,091	561.07	45,020	68,647
29,000	407.57	117,725	482.69	65,843	51,882	537.78	53,417	64,308	581.10	46,627	71,098
30,000	421.62	121,783	499.33	68,113	53,670	556.32	55,259	66,524	601.13	48,234	73,549
32,500	456.76	131,934	540.94	73,790	58,144	602.69	59,864	72,070	651.23	52,254	79,680
35,000	491.89	142,080	582.55	79,465	62,615	649.04	64,468	77,612	701.32	56,273	85,807
40,000	562.16	162,378	665.77	90,817	71,561	741.76	73,678	88,700	801.51	64,312	98,066
45,000	632.43	182,675	748.99	102,169	80,506	834.48	82,888	99,787	901.69	72,351	110,324
50,000	702.70	202,972	832.21	113,521	89,451	927.20	92,098	110,874	1,001.88	80,390	122,582
55,000	772.97	223,269	915.43	124,873	98,396	1,019.92	101,307	121,962	1,102.07	88,429	134,840
60,000	843.24	243,566	998.65	136,225	107,341	1,112.64	110,517	133,049	1,202.26	96,468	147,098
65,000	913.51	263,864	1,081.87	147,577	116,287	1,205.36	119,727	144,137	1,302.45	104,507	159,357
70,000	983.78	284,161	1,165.10	158,930	125,231	1,298.08	128,937	155,224	1,402.64	112,546	171,615
75,000	1,054.05	304,458	1,248.32	170,282	134,176	1,390.80	138,147	166,311	1,502.82	120,585	183,873
80,000	1,124.32	324,755	1,331.54	181,634	143,121	1,483.52	147,356	177,399	1,603.01	128,624	196,131
85,000	1,194.59	345,052	1,414.76	192,986	152,066	1,576.24	156,566	188,486	1,703.20	136,663	208,389
90,000	1,264.86	365,350	1,497.98	204,338	161,012	1,668.96	165,776	199,574	1,803.39	144,702	220,648
95,000	1,335.13	385,647	1,581.20	215,690	169,957	1,761.68	174,986	210,661	1,903.58	152,741	232,906
100,000	1,405.40	405,944	1,664.42	227,042	178,902	1,854.40	184,195	221,749	2,003.76	160,780	245,164
105,000	1,475.67	426,241	1,747.64	238,394	187,847	1,947.12	193,405	232,836	2,103.95	168,819	257,422
110,000	1,545.94	446,538	1,830.86	249,746	196,792	2,039.83	202,615	243,923	2,204.14	176,858	269,680
115,000	1,616.21	466,836	1,914.08	261,099	205,737	2,132.55	211,825	255,011	2,304.33	184,897	281,939
120,000	1,686.48	487,133	1,997.31	272,451	214,682	2,225.27	221,034	266,099	2,404.52	192,936	294,197
125,000	1,756.75	507,430	2,080.53	283,803	223,627	2,317.99	230,244	277,186	2,504.71	200,975	306,455
130,000	1,827.02	527,727	2,163.75	295,155	232,572	2,410.71	239,454	288,273	2,604.89	209,014	318,713
135,000	1,897.29	548,024	2,246.97	306,507	241,517	2,503.43	248,664	299,360	2,705.08	217,053	330,971
140,000	1,967.56	568,322	2,330.19	317,859	250,463	2,596.15	257,873	310,449	2,805.27	225,092	343,230
145,000	2,037.83	588,619	2,413.41	329,211	259,408	2,688.87	267,083	321,536	2,905.46	233,131	355,488
150,000	2,108.10	608,916	2,496.63	340,563	268,353	2,781.59	276,293	332,623	3,005.65	241,170	367,746
155,000	2,178.37	629,213	2,579.85	351,915	277,298	2,874.31	285,503	343,710	3,105.83	249,209	380,004
160,000	2,248.64	649,510	2,663.07	363,268	286,242	2,967.03	294,713	354,797	3,206.02	257,248	392,262
165,000	2,318.91	669,808	2,746.30	374,620	295,188	3,059.75	303,922	365,886	3,306.21	265,287	404,521
170,000	2,389.18	690,105	2,829.52	385,972	304,133	3,152.47	313,132	376,973	3,406.40	273,326	416,779
175,000	2,459.45	710,402	2,912.74	397,324	313,078	3,245.19	322,342	388,060	3,506.59	281,365	429,037
180,000	2,529.72	730,699	2,995.96	408,676	322,023	3,337.91	331,552	399,147	3,606.78	289,404	441,295
185,000	2,599.99	750,996	3,079.18	420,028	330,968	3,430.63	340,761	410,235	3,706.96	297,443	453,553
190,000	2,670.26	771,294	3,162.40	431,380	339,914	3,523.35	349,971	421,323	3,807.15	305,482	465,812
195,000	2,740.53	791,591	3,245.62	442,732	348,859	3,616.07	359,181	432,410	3,907.34	313,521	478,070
200,000	2,810.80	811,888	3,328.84	454,084	357,804	3,708.79	368,391	443,497	4,007.53	321,560	490,328

GROWING EQUITY MORTGAGES 16.75%

AMOUNT OF LOAN	30 YEARS		4% PMT INCR/YR 140.206 PAYMENTS			5% PMT INCR/YR 129.463 PAYMENTS			6% PMT INCR/YR 121.046 PAYMENTS		
	MONTHLY PAYMENT	TOTAL INTRST	LAST YR MON PMT	TOTAL INTRST	INTRST SAVED	LAST YR MON PMT	TOTAL INTRST	INTRST SAVED	LAST YR MON PMT	TOTAL INTRST	INTRST SAVED
$ 50	0.71	206	1.09	74	132	1.16	68	138	1.27	64	142
100	1.41	408	2.17	146	262	2.30	135	273	2.53	126	282
200	2.82	815	4.34	292	523	4.59	269	546	5.05	251	564
300	4.22	1.219	6.50	436	783	6.87	402	817	7.56	375	844
400	5.63	1.627	8.67	582	1.045	9.17	537	1.090	10.08	501	1.126
500	7.03	2.031	10.82	727	1.304	11.45	669	1.362	12.59	625	1.406
600	8.44	2.438	12.99	873	1.565	13.75	804	1.634	15.11	751	1.687
700	9.84	2.842	15.15	1.017	1.825	16.03	937	1.905	17.62	875	1.967
800	11.25	3.250	17.32	1.163	2.087	18.33	1.071	2.179	20.15	1.000	2.250
900	12.65	3.654	19.47	1.307	2.347	20.61	1.204	2.450	22.65	1.125	2.529
1,000	14.06	4.062	21.64	1.453	2.609	22.90	1.339	2.723	25.18	1.250	2.812
2,000	28.11	8.120	43.27	2.904	5.216	45.79	2.676	5.444	50.34	2.499	5.621
3,000	42.17	12.181	64.92	4.357	7.824	68.69	4.015	8.166	75.52	3.749	8.432
4,000	56.22	16.239	86.55	5.809	10.433	91.58	5.352	10.887	100.68	4.998	11.241
5,000	70.27	20.297	108.18	7.260	13.037	114.46	6.689	13.608	125.84	6.246	14.051
6,000	84.33	24.359	129.82	8.713	15.646	137.36	8.028	16.331	151.02	7.496	16.863
7,000	98.38	28.417	151.45	10.164	18.253	160.25	9.365	19.052	176.18	8.745	19.672
8,000	112.44	32.478	173.10	11.617	20.861	183.15	10.704	21.774	201.36	9.995	22.483
9,000	126.49	36.536	194.73	13.069	23.467	206.04	12.041	24.495	226.52	11.244	25.292
10,000	140.54	40.594	216.35	14.520	26.074	228.92	13.379	27.215	251.69	12.492	28.102
11,000	154.60	44.656	238.00	15.973	28.683	251.83	14.718	29.938	276.87	13.743	30.913
12,000	168.65	48.714	259.63	17.424	31.290	274.71	16.055	32.659	302.03	14.991	33.723
13,000	182.71	52.776	281.27	18.877	33.899	297.62	17.394	35.382	327.21	16.241	36.535
14,000	196.76	56.834	302.90	20.329	36.505	320.50	18.731	38.103	352.37	17.490	39.344
15,000	210.81	60.892	324.53	21.780	39.112	343.39	20.068	40.824	377.53	18.739	42.153
16,000	224.87	64.953	346.18	23.233	41.720	366.29	21.407	43.546	402.71	19.989	44.964
17,000	238.92	69.011	367.81	24.684	44.327	389.18	22.744	46.267	427.87	21.237	47.774
18,000	252.98	73.073	389.45	26.137	46.936	412.08	24.083	48.990	453.05	22.488	50.585
19,000	267.03	77.131	411.08	27.588	49.543	434.96	25.420	51.711	478.21	23.736	53.395
20,000	281.08	81.189	432.71	29.040	52.149	457.85	26.757	54.432	503.37	24.985	56.204
21,000	295.14	85.250	454.35	30.493	54.757	480.75	28.096	57.154	528.55	26.235	59.015
22,000	309.19	89.308	475.98	31.944	57.364	503.64	29.433	59.875	553.71	27.484	61.824
23,000	323.25	93.370	497.63	33.397	59.973	526.54	30.772	62.598	578.89	28.734	64.636
24,000	337.30	97.428	519.26	34.848	62.580	549.43	32.109	65.319	604.05	29.982	67.446
25,000	351.35	101.486	540.89	36.300	65.186	572.31	33.447	68.039	629.21	31.231	70.255
26,000	365.41	105.548	562.53	37.753	67.795	595.21	34.786	70.762	654.39	32.481	73.067
27,000	379.46	109.606	584.16	39.204	70.402	618.10	36.123	73.483	679.56	33.730	75.876
28,000	393.52	113.667	605.81	40.657	73.010	641.00	37.462	76.205	704.73	34.980	78.687
29,000	407.57	117.725	627.44	42.108	75.617	663.89	38.799	78.926	729.90	36.229	81.496
30,000	421.62	121.783	649.06	43.560	78.223	686.77	40.136	81.647	755.06	37.477	84.306
32,500	456.76	131.934	703.16	47.190	84.744	744.01	43.482	88.452	817.99	40.601	91.333
35,000	491.89	142.080	757.24	50.820	91.260	801.24	46.825	95.255	880.90	43.723	98.357
40,000	562.16	162.378	865.42	58.079	104.299	915.70	53.515	108.863	1,006.74	49.970	112.408
45,000	632.43	182.675	973.60	65.339	117.336	1,030.16	60.204	122.471	1,132.59	56.216	126.459
50,000	702.70	202.972	1,081.77	72.599	130.373	1,144.62	66.893	136.079	1,258.43	62.462	140.510
55,000	772.97	223.269	1,189.95	79.859	143.410	1,259.09	73.583	149.686	1,384.27	68.708	154.561
60,000	843.24	243.566	1,298.13	87.119	156.447	1,373.55	80.272	163.294	1,510.11	74.954	168.612
65,000	913.51	263.864	1,406.31	94.379	169.485	1,488.01	86.961	176.903	1,635.96	81.201	182.663
70,000	983.78	284.161	1,514.48	101.639	182.522	1,602.47	93.651	190.510	1,761.80	87.447	196.714
75,000	1,054.05	304.458	1,622.66	108.899	195.559	1,716.94	100.340	204.118	1,887.64	93.693	210.765
80,000	1,124.32	324.755	1,730.84	116.159	208.596	1,831.40	107.029	217.726	2,013.49	99.939	224.816
85,000	1,194.59	345.052	1,839.02	123.419	221.633	1,945.86	113.719	231.333	2,139.33	106.185	238.867
90,000	1,264.86	365.350	1,947.19	130.679	234.671	2,060.32	120.408	244.942	2,265.17	112.432	252.918
95,000	1,335.13	385.647	2,055.37	137.939	247.708	2,174.79	127.097	258.550	2,391.01	118.678	266.969
100,000	1,405.40	405.944	2,163.55	145.199	260.745	2,289.25	133.787	272.157	2,516.86	124.924	281.020
105,000	1,475.67	426.241	2,271.73	152.459	273.782	2,403.71	140.476	285.765	2,642.70	131.170	295.071
110,000	1,545.94	446.538	2,379.90	159.719	286.819	2,518.17	147.165	299.373	2,768.54	137.417	309.121
115,000	1,616.21	466.836	2,488.08	166.979	299.857	2,632.64	153.855	312.981	2,894.39	143.663	323.173
120,000	1,686.48	487.133	2,596.26	174.238	312.895	2,747.10	160.544	326.589	3,020.23	149.909	337.224
125,000	1,756.75	507.430	2,704.44	181.498	325.932	2,861.56	167.234	340.196	3,146.07	156.155	351.275
130,000	1,827.02	527.727	2,812.61	188.758	338.969	2,976.02	173.923	353.804	3,271.91	162.401	365.326
135,000	1,897.29	548.024	2,920.79	196.018	352.006	3,090.49	180.612	367.412	3,397.76	168.648	379.376
140,000	1,967.56	568.322	3,028.97	203.278	365.044	3,204.95	187.302	381.020	3,523.60	174.894	393.428
145,000	2,037.83	588.619	3,137.15	210.538	378.081	3,319.41	193.991	394.628	3,649.44	181.140	407.479
150,000	2,108.10	608.916	3,245.32	217.798	391.118	3,433.87	200.680	408.236	3,775.29	187.386	421.530
155,000	2,178.37	629.213	3,353.50	225.058	404.155	3,548.34	207.370	421.843	3,901.13	193.632	435.581
160,000	2,248.64	649.510	3,461.68	232.318	417.192	3,662.80	214.059	435.451	4,026.97	199.879	449.631
165,000	2,318.91	669.808	3,569.86	239.578	430.230	3,777.26	220.748	449.060	4,152.81	206.125	463.683
170,000	2,389.18	690.105	3,678.03	246.838	443.267	3,891.72	227.438	462.667	4,278.66	212.371	477.734
175,000	2,459.45	710.402	3,786.21	254.098	456.304	4,006.18	234.127	476.275	4,404.50	218.617	491.785
180,000	2,529.72	730.699	3,894.39	261.358	469.341	4,120.65	240.816	489.883	4,530.34	224.863	505.836
185,000	2,599.99	750.996	4,002.57	268.618	482.378	4,235.11	247.506	503.490	4,656.19	231.110	519.886
190,000	2,670.26	771.294	4,110.74	275.878	495.416	4,349.57	254.195	517.099	4,782.03	237.356	533.938
195,000	2,740.53	791.591	4,218.92	283.137	508.454	4,464.03	260.884	530.707	4,907.87	243.602	547.989
200,000	2,810.80	811.888	4,327.10	290.397	521.491	4,578.50	267.574	544.314	5,033.71	249.848	562.040

179

17.00% GROWING EQUITY MORTGAGES

AMOUNT OF LOAN	30 YEARS		1% PMT INCR/YR 212.066 PAYMENTS			2% PMT INCR/YR 174.582 PAYMENTS			3% PMT INCR/YR 153.475 PAYMENTS		
	MONTHLY PAYMENT	TOTAL INTRST	LAST YR MON PMT	TOTAL INTRST	INTRST SAVED	LAST YR MON PMT	TOTAL INTRST	INTRST SAVED	LAST YR MON PMT	TOTAL INTRST	INTRST SAVED
$ 50	0.72	209	0.85	116	93	0.95	94	115	1.03	82	127
100	1.43	415	1.69	230	185	1.89	187	228	2.04	163	252
200	2.86	830	3.39	460	370	3.77	373	457	4.08	326	504
300	4.28	1,241	5.07	687	554	5.65	558	683	6.10	487	754
400	5.71	1,656	6.76	917	739	7.53	744	912	8.14	650	1,006
500	7.13	2,067	8.44	1,145	922	9.41	929	1,138	10.17	811	1,256
600	8.56	2,482	10.14	1,375	1,107	11.29	1,115	1,367	12.20	973	1,509
700	9.98	2,893	11.82	1,603	1,290	13.17	1,300	1,593	14.23	1,134	1,759
800	11.41	3,308	13.51	1,832	1,476	15.06	1,486	1,822	16.27	1,297	2,011
900	12.84	3,722	15.21	2,062	1,660	16.94	1,673	2,049	18.31	1,460	2,262
1,000	14.26	4,134	16.89	2,290	1,844	18.82	1,857	2,277	20.33	1,621	2,513
2,000	28.52	8,267	33.78	4,580	3,687	37.63	3,715	4,552	40.66	3,242	5,025
3,000	42.78	12,401	50.66	6,870	5,531	56.45	5,572	6,829	60.99	4,864	7,537
4,000	57.03	16,531	67.54	9,158	7,373	75.25	7,427	9,104	81.31	6,483	10,048
5,000	71.29	20,664	84.43	11,448	9,216	94.07	9,285	11,379	101.64	8,104	12,560
6,000	85.55	24,798	101.32	13,738	11,060	112.88	11,142	13,656	121.97	9,725	15,073
7,000	99.80	28,928	118.19	16,026	12,902	131.68	12,997	15,931	142.29	11,345	17,583
8,000	114.06	33,062	135.08	18,316	14,746	150.50	14,854	18,208	162.62	12,966	20,096
9,000	128.32	37,195	151.97	20,606	16,589	169.32	16,712	20,483	182.95	14,587	22,608
10,000	142.57	41,325	168.85	22,893	18,432	188.12	18,567	22,758	203.27	16,206	25,119
11,000	156.83	45,459	185.73	25,183	20,276	206.93	20,424	25,035	223.60	17,827	27,632
12,000	171.09	49,592	202.62	27,474	22,118	225.75	22,282	27,310	243.93	19,449	30,143
13,000	185.34	53,722	219.50	29,761	23,961	244.55	24,137	29,585	264.25	21,068	32,654
14,000	199.60	57,856	236.39	32,051	25,805	263.37	25,994	31,862	284.58	22,689	35,167
15,000	213.86	61,990	253.28	34,341	27,649	282.18	27,852	34,138	304.91	24,310	37,680
16,000	228.11	66,120	270.15	36,629	29,491	300.99	29,707	36,413	325.23	25,930	40,190
17,000	242.37	70,253	287.04	38,919	31,334	319.80	31,564	38,689	345.56	27,551	42,702
18,000	256.63	74,387	303.93	41,209	33,178	338.62	33,421	40,966	365.89	29,172	45,215
19,000	270.88	78,517	320.80	43,497	35,020	357.42	35,277	43,240	386.21	30,791	47,726
20,000	285.14	82,650	337.69	45,787	36,863	376.24	37,134	45,516	406.54	32,413	50,237
21,000	299.40	86,784	354.58	48,077	38,707	395.05	38,991	47,793	426.87	34,034	52,750
22,000	313.65	90,914	371.46	50,365	40,549	413.85	40,847	50,067	447.19	35,653	55,261
23,000	327.91	95,048	388.35	52,655	42,393	432.67	42,704	52,344	467.52	37,274	57,774
24,000	342.17	99,181	405.23	54,945	44,236	451.49	44,561	54,620	487.85	38,895	60,286
25,000	356.42	103,311	422.11	57,232	46,079	470.29	46,417	56,894	508.17	40,515	62,796
26,000	370.68	107,445	439.00	59,523	47,922	489.10	48,274	59,171	528.50	42,136	65,309
27,000	384.94	111,578	455.89	61,813	49,765	507.92	50,131	61,447	548.83	43,757	67,821
28,000	399.19	115,708	472.76	64,100	51,608	526.72	51,987	63,721	569.15	45,376	70,332
29,000	413.45	119,842	489.65	66,390	53,452	545.54	53,844	65,998	589.48	46,998	72,844
30,000	427.71	123,976	506.54	68,680	55,296	564.35	55,701	68,275	609.81	48,619	75,357
32,500	463.35	134,306	548.75	74,403	59,903	611.38	60,342	73,964	660.63	52,670	81,636
35,000	498.99	144,636	590.96	80,126	64,510	658.41	64,984	79,652	711.44	56,721	87,915
40,000	570.28	165,301	675.39	91,574	73,727	752.47	74,268	91,033	813.08	64,825	100,476
45,000	641.56	185,962	759.80	103,019	82,943	846.52	83,551	102,411	914.71	72,927	113,035
50,000	712.84	206,622	844.22	114,465	92,157	940.58	92,833	113,789	1,016.34	81,030	125,592
55,000	784.13	227,287	928.65	125,913	101,374	1,034.64	102,118	125,169	1,117.98	89,134	138,153
60,000	855.41	247,948	1,013.07	137,358	110,590	1,128.70	111,400	136,548	1,219.61	97,236	150,712
65,000	926.69	268,608	1,097.48	148,804	119,804	1,222.75	120,683	147,925	1,321.24	105,338	163,270
70,000	997.98	289,273	1,181.91	160,252	129,021	1,316.81	129,967	159,306	1,422.88	113,442	175,831
75,000	1,069.26	309,934	1,266.33	171,697	138,237	1,410.87	139,250	170,684	1,524.51	121,544	188,390
80,000	1,140.55	330,598	1,350.76	183,145	147,453	1,504.93	148,534	182,064	1,626.15	129,648	200,950
85,000	1,211.83	351,259	1,435.18	194,591	156,668	1,598.98	157,817	193,442	1,727.78	137,751	213,508
90,000	1,283.11	371,920	1,519.59	206,036	165,884	1,693.04	167,099	204,821	1,829.41	145,853	226,067
95,000	1,354.40	392,584	1,604.02	217,484	175,100	1,787.10	176,384	216,200	1,931.05	153,957	238,627
100,000	1,425.68	413,245	1,688.44	228,930	184,315	1,881.15	185,666	227,579	2,032.68	162,059	251,186
105,000	1,496.96	433,906	1,772.86	240,375	193,531	1,975.21	194,949	238,957	2,134.31	170,161	263,745
110,000	1,568.25	454,570	1,857.29	251,823	202,747	2,069.27	204,233	250,337	2,235.95	178,265	276,305
115,000	1,639.53	475,231	1,941.70	263,269	211,962	2,163.33	213,516	261,715	2,337.58	186,368	288,863
120,000	1,710.82	495,895	2,026.13	274,717	221,178	2,257.39	222,801	273,094	2,439.22	194,472	301,423
125,000	1,782.10	516,556	2,110.55	286,162	230,394	2,351.44	232,083	284,473	2,540.85	202,574	313,982
130,000	1,853.38	537,217	2,194.97	297,608	239,609	2,445.50	241,366	295,851	2,642.48	210,676	326,541
135,000	1,924.67	557,881	2,279.40	309,056	248,825	2,539.56	250,650	307,231	2,744.12	218,780	339,101
140,000	1,995.95	578,542	2,363.81	320,501	258,041	2,633.61	259,933	318,609	2,845.75	226,882	351,660
145,000	2,067.23	599,203	2,448.23	331,947	267,256	2,727.67	269,215	329,988	2,947.38	234,985	364,218
150,000	2,138.52	619,867	2,532.66	343,395	276,472	2,821.73	278,500	341,367	3,049.02	243,089	376,778
155,000	2,209.80	640,528	2,617.08	354,840	285,688	2,915.78	287,782	352,746	3,150.65	251,191	389,337
160,000	2,281.09	661,192	2,701.50	366,288	294,904	3,009.85	297,067	364,125	3,252.29	259,295	401,897
165,000	2,352.37	681,853	2,785.92	377,734	304,119	3,103.90	306,349	375,504	3,353.92	267,397	414,456
170,000	2,423.65	702,514	2,870.34	389,179	313,335	3,197.95	315,632	386,882	3,455.55	275,499	427,015
175,000	2,494.94	723,178	2,954.77	400,627	322,551	3,292.02	324,916	398,262	3,557.19	283,604	439,574
180,000	2,566.22	743,839	3,039.19	412,073	331,766	3,386.07	334,199	409,640	3,658.82	291,706	452,133
185,000	2,637.50	764,500	3,123.60	423,519	340,981	3,480.13	343,481	421,019	3,760.44	299,808	464,692
190,000	2,708.79	785,164	3,208.03	434,966	350,198	3,574.19	352,765	432,398	3,862.09	307,912	477,252
195,000	2,780.07	805,825	3,292.45	446,412	359,413	3,668.24	362,048	443,777	3,963.72	316,014	489,811
200,000	2,851.36	826,490	3,376.88	457,860	368,630	3,762.31	371,333	455,157	4,065.36	324,118	502,372

GROWING EQUITY MORTGAGES 17.00%

AMOUNT OF LOAN	30 YEARS		4% PMT INCR/YR 139.124 PAYMENTS			5% PMT INCR/YR 128.477 PAYMENTS			6% PMT INCR/YR 120.176 PAYMENTS		
	MONTHLY PAYMENT	TOTAL INTRST	LAST YR MON PMT	TOTAL INTRST	INTRST SAVED	LAST YR MON PMT	TOTAL INTRST	INTRST SAVED	LAST YR MON PMT	TOTAL INTRST	INTRST SAVED
$ 50	0.72	209	1.11	74	135	1.17	69	140	1.29	64	145
100	1.43	415	2.20	147	268	2.33	136	279	2.56	127	288
200	2.86	830	4.40	294	536	4.66	271	559	5.12	253	577
300	4.28	1,241	6.59	440	801	6.97	405	836	7.66	378	863
400	5.71	1,656	8.79	587	1,069	9.30	541	1,115	10.23	505	1,151
500	7.13	2,067	10.98	732	1,335	11.61	675	1,392	12.77	630	1,437
600	8.56	2,482	13.18	879	1,603	13.94	810	1,672	15.33	757	1,725
700	9.98	2,893	15.36	1,025	1,868	16.26	944	1,949	17.87	882	2,011
800	11.41	3,308	17.57	1,172	2,136	18.59	1,080	2,228	20.43	1,008	2,300
900	12.84	3,722	19.77	1,319	2,403	20.92	1,215	2,507	22.99	1,135	2,587
1,000	14.26	4,134	21.95	1,464	2,670	23.23	1,349	2,785	25.54	1,260	2,874
2,000	28.52	8,267	43.91	2,928	5,339	46.46	2,698	5,569	51.07	2,520	5,747
3,000	42.78	12,401	65.86	4,393	8,008	69.68	4,048	8,353	76.61	3,780	8,621
4,000	57.03	16,531	87.80	5,855	10,676	92.90	5,395	11,136	102.13	5,038	11,493
5,000	71.29	20,664	109.75	7,319	13,345	116.12	6,745	13,919	127.67	6,298	14,366
6,000	85.55	24,798	131.70	8,783	16,015	139.35	8,094	16,704	153.21	7,558	17,240
7,000	99.80	28,928	153.64	10,246	18,682	162.56	9,441	19,487	178.73	8,817	20,111
8,000	114.06	33,062	175.59	11,710	21,352	185.79	10,791	22,271	204.26	10,077	22,985
9,000	128.32	37,195	197.54	13,174	24,021	209.02	12,140	25,055	229.80	11,337	25,858
10,000	142.57	41,325	219.48	14,637	26,688	232.23	13,487	27,838	255.32	12,595	28,730
11,000	156.83	45,459	241.43	16,101	29,358	255.46	14,837	30,622	280.86	13,855	31,604
12,000	171.09	49,592	263.39	17,565	32,027	278.69	16,186	33,406	306.40	15,115	34,477
13,000	185.34	53,722	285.32	19,027	34,695	301.90	17,533	36,189	331.92	16,374	37,348
14,000	199.60	57,856	307.28	20,492	37,364	325.13	18,883	38,973	357.45	17,634	40,222
15,000	213.86	61,990	329.23	21,956	40,034	348.36	20,232	41,758	382.99	18,894	43,096
16,000	228.11	66,120	351.16	23,418	42,702	371.57	21,579	44,541	408.51	20,152	45,968
17,000	242.37	70,253	373.12	24,882	45,371	394.80	22,929	47,324	434.05	21,412	48,841
18,000	256.63	74,387	395.07	26,347	48,040	418.02	24,278	50,109	459.59	22,672	51,715
19,000	270.88	78,517	417.01	27,809	50,708	441.23	25,626	52,891	485.10	23,930	54,587
20,000	285.14	82,650	438.96	29,273	53,377	464.46	26,975	55,675	510.64	25,190	57,460
21,000	299.40	86,784	460.91	30,737	56,047	487.69	28,324	58,460	536.18	26,450	60,334
22,000	313.65	90,914	482.85	32,200	58,714	510.90	29,672	61,242	561.70	27,709	63,205
23,000	327.91	95,048	504.80	33,664	61,384	534.13	31,021	64,027	587.24	28,969	66,079
24,000	342.17	99,181	526.75	35,128	64,053	557.36	32,370	66,811	612.77	30,229	68,952
25,000	356.42	103,311	548.69	36,591	66,720	580.57	33,718	69,593	638.29	31,487	71,824
26,000	370.68	107,445	570.64	38,055	69,390	603.80	35,067	72,378	663.83	32,747	74,698
27,000	384.94	111,578	592.60	39,519	72,059	627.03	36,416	75,162	689.37	34,007	77,571
28,000	399.19	115,708	614.53	40,981	74,727	650.24	37,764	77,944	714.89	35,266	80,442
29,000	413.45	119,842	636.49	42,446	77,396	673.47	39,113	80,729	740.43	36,526	83,316
30,000	427.71	123,976	658.44	43,910	80,066	696.69	40,462	83,514	765.96	37,786	86,190
32,500	463.35	134,306	713.31	47,568	86,738	754.75	43,834	90,472	829.79	40,934	93,372
35,000	498.99	144,636	768.17	51,227	93,409	812.80	47,205	97,431	893.62	44,082	100,554
40,000	570.28	165,301	877.92	58,545	106,755	928.93	53,950	111,351	1,021.28	50,381	114,920
45,000	641.56	185,962	987.65	65,864	120,098	1,045.03	60,692	125,270	1,148.94	56,677	129,285
50,000	712.84	206,622	1,097.38	73,181	133,441	1,161.14	67,435	139,187	1,276.59	62,974	143,648
55,000	784.13	227,287	1,207.13	80,500	146,787	1,277.27	74,180	153,107	1,404.26	69,273	158,014
60,000	855.41	247,948	1,316.86	87,818	160,130	1,393.37	80,923	167,025	1,531.91	75,569	172,379
65,000	926.69	268,608	1,426.60	95,135	173,473	1,509.48	87,666	180,942	1,659.56	81,866	186,742
70,000	997.98	289,273	1,536.34	102,454	186,819	1,625.60	94,410	194,863	1,787.23	88,163	201,108
75,000	1,069.26	309,934	1,646.08	109,772	200,162	1,741.71	101,153	208,781	1,914.88	94,461	215,473
80,000	1,140.55	330,598	1,755.82	117,091	213,507	1,857.84	107,897	222,701	2,042.55	100,760	229,838
85,000	1,211.83	351,259	1,865.56	124,408	226,851	1,973.94	114,640	236,619	2,170.20	107,057	244,202
90,000	1,283.11	371,920	1,975.29	131,726	240,194	2,090.05	121,383	250,537	2,297.85	113,353	258,567
95,000	1,354.40	392,584	2,085.04	139,045	253,539	2,206.17	128,128	264,456	2,425.52	119,652	272,932
100,000	1,425.68	413,245	2,194.77	146,362	266,883	2,322.28	134,871	278,374	2,553.18	125,949	287,296
105,000	1,496.96	433,906	2,304.50	153,680	280,226	2,438.39	141,613	292,293	2,680.83	132,245	301,661
110,000	1,568.25	454,570	2,414.25	160,999	293,571	2,554.51	148,358	306,212	2,808.50	138,544	316,026
115,000	1,639.53	475,231	2,523.98	168,316	306,915	2,670.62	155,101	320,130	2,936.15	144,840	330,391
120,000	1,710.82	495,895	2,633.73	175,635	320,260	2,786.75	161,845	334,050	3,063.82	151,139	344,756
125,000	1,782.10	516,556	2,743.46	182,953	333,603	2,902.85	168,588	347,968	3,191.47	157,436	359,120
130,000	1,853.38	537,217	2,853.19	190,270	346,947	3,018.96	175,331	361,886	3,319.12	163,732	373,485
135,000	1,924.67	557,881	2,962.94	197,589	360,292	3,135.08	182,076	375,805	3,446.79	170,031	387,850
140,000	1,995.95	578,542	3,072.67	204,907	373,635	3,251.19	188,818	389,724	3,574.44	176,328	402,214
145,000	2,067.23	599,203	3,182.41	212,224	386,979	3,367.30	195,561	403,642	3,702.09	182,624	416,579
150,000	2,138.52	619,867	3,292.15	219,543	400,324	3,483.42	202,306	417,561	3,829.76	188,923	430,944
155,000	2,209.80	640,528	3,401.89	226,861	413,667	3,599.53	209,049	431,479	3,957.42	195,220	445,308
160,000	2,281.09	661,192	3,511.63	234,180	427,012	3,715.66	215,793	445,399	4,085.08	201,518	459,674
165,000	2,352.37	681,853	3,621.37	241,497	440,356	3,831.76	222,536	459,317	4,212.74	207,815	474,038
170,000	2,423.65	702,514	3,731.10	248,815	453,699	3,947.87	229,279	473,235	4,340.39	214,112	488,402
175,000	2,494.94	723,178	3,840.85	256,134	467,044	4,063.99	236,024	487,154	4,468.06	220,410	502,768
180,000	2,566.22	743,839	3,950.58	263,451	480,388	4,180.10	242,766	501,073	4,595.71	226,707	517,132
185,000	2,637.50	764,500	4,060.31	270,769	493,731	4,296.21	249,509	514,991	4,723.36	233,003	531,497
190,000	2,708.79	785,164	4,170.06	278,088	507,076	4,412.33	256,254	528,910	4,851.03	239,302	545,862
195,000	2,780.07	805,825	4,279.79	285,405	520,420	4,528.44	262,997	542,828	4,978.68	245,599	560,226
200,000	2,851.36	826,490	4,389.54	292,724	533,766	4,644.56	269,741	556,749	5,106.35	251,897	574,593

181

17.25%   GROWING EQUITY MORTGAGES

AMOUNT OF LOAN	30 YEARS		1% PMT INCR/YR 210.409 PAYMENTS			2% PMT INCR/YR 173.203 PAYMENTS			3% PMT INCR/YR 152.274 PAYMENTS		
	MONTHLY PAYMENT	TOTAL INTRST	LAST YR MON PMT	TOTAL INTRST	INTRST SAVED	LAST YR MON PMT	TOTAL INTRST	INTRST SAVED	LAST YR MON PMT	TOTAL INTRST	INTRST SAVED
$ 50	0.73	213	0.86	117	96	0.96	95	118	1.04	83	130
100	1.45	422	1.72	232	190	1.91	188	234	2.07	164	258
200	2.90	844	3.43	463	381	3.83	376	468	4.13	328	516
300	4.34	1.262	5.14	693	569	5.73	562	700	6.19	490	772
400	5.79	1.684	6.86	924	760	7.64	750	934	8.26	654	1.030
500	7.23	2.103	8.56	1.154	949	9.54	936	1.167	10.31	817	1.286
600	8.68	2.525	10.28	1.386	1.139	11.45	1.123	1.402	12.38	981	1.544
700	10.13	2.947	12.00	1.617	1.330	13.37	1.311	1.636	14.44	1.145	1.802
800	11.57	3.365	13.70	1.847	1.518	15.27	1.497	1.868	16.50	1.307	2.058
900	13.02	3.787	15.42	2.078	1.709	17.18	1.685	2.102	18.56	1.471	2.316
1,000	14.46	4.206	17.13	2.308	1.898	19.08	1.871	2.335	20.62	1.633	2.573
2,000	28.92	8.411	34.25	4.616	3.795	38.16	3.742	4.669	41.23	3.266	5.145
3,000	43.38	12.617	51.38	6.923	5.694	57.24	5.613	7.004	61.85	4.900	7.717
4,000	57.84	16.822	68.50	9.231	7.591	76.32	7.484	9.338	82.47	6.533	10.289
5,000	72.30	21.028	85.63	11.539	9.489	95.40	9.355	11.673	103.08	8.166	12.862
6,000	86.76	25.234	102.75	13.847	11.387	114.48	11.226	14.008	123.70	9.799	15.435
7,000	101.22	29.439	119.88	16.155	13.284	133.56	13.097	16.342	144.32	11.432	18.007
8,000	115.68	33.645	137.00	18.462	15.183	152.64	14.969	18.676	164.93	13.065	20.580
9,000	130.14	37.850	154.13	20.770	17.080	171.72	16.840	21.010	185.55	14.699	23.151
10,000	144.60	42.056	171.25	23.078	18.978	190.80	18.711	23.345	206.17	16.332	25.724
11,000	159.06	46.262	188.38	25.386	20.876	209.88	20.582	25.680	226.78	17.965	28.297
12,000	173.52	50.467	205.50	27.694	22.773	228.96	22.453	28.014	247.40	19.598	30.869
13,000	187.98	54.673	222.63	30.001	24.672	248.04	24.324	30.349	268.01	21.231	33.442
14,000	202.44	58.878	239.75	32.309	26.569	267.12	26.195	32.683	288.63	22.865	36.013
15,000	216.90	63.084	256.88	34.617	28.467	286.19	28.066	35.018	309.25	24.498	38.586
16,000	231.36	67.290	274.00	36.925	30.365	305.27	29.937	37.353	329.86	26.131	41.159
17,000	245.82	71.495	291.13	39.233	32.262	324.35	31.808	39.687	350.48	27.764	43.731
18,000	260.28	75.701	308.25	41.540	34.161	343.43	33.679	42.022	371.10	29.397	46.304
19,000	274.74	79.906	325.38	43.848	36.058	362.51	35.550	44.356	391.71	31.030	48.876
20,000	289.20	84.112	342.50	46.156	37.956	381.59	37.421	46.691	412.33	32.664	51.448
21,000	303.66	88.318	359.63	48.464	39.854	400.67	39.292	49.026	432.95	34.297	54.021
22,000	318.12	92.523	376.75	50.772	41.751	419.75	41.164	51.359	453.56	35.930	56.593
23,000	332.58	96.729	393.88	53.080	43.649	438.83	43.035	53.694	474.18	37.563	59.166
24,000	347.04	100.934	411.00	55.387	45.547	457.91	44.906	56.028	494.80	39.196	61.738
25,000	361.50	105.140	428.13	57.695	47.445	476.99	46.777	58.363	515.41	40.830	64.310
26,000	375.96	109.346	445.25	60.003	49.343	496.07	48.648	60.698	536.03	42.463	66.883
27,000	390.42	113.551	462.38	62.311	51.240	515.15	50.519	63.032	556.65	44.096	69.455
28,000	404.88	117.757	479.50	64.619	53.138	534.23	52.390	65.367	577.26	45.729	72.028
29,000	419.34	121.962	496.63	66.926	55.036	553.31	54.261	67.701	597.88	47.362	74.600
30,000	433.80	126.168	513.75	69.234	56.934	572.39	56.132	70.036	618.50	48.995	77.173
32,500	469.95	136.682	556.56	75.004	61.678	620.09	60.810	75.872	670.04	53.078	83.604
35,000	506.10	147.196	599.38	80.773	66.423	667.79	65.487	81.709	721.58	57.161	90.035
40,000	578.40	168.224	685.00	92.312	75.912	763.19	74.843	93.381	824.66	65.327	102.897
45,000	650.70	189.252	770.63	103.851	85.401	858.58	84.198	105.054	927.74	73.493	115.759
50,000	723.00	210.280	856.25	115.390	94.890	953.98	93.553	116.727	1.030.83	81.659	128.621
55,000	795.30	231.308	941.88	126.929	104.379	1.049.38	102.909	128.399	1.133.91	89.825	141.483
60,000	867.60	252.336	1.027.50	138.468	113.868	1.144.78	112.264	140.072	1.236.99	97.991	154.345
65,000	939.90	273.364	1.113.13	150.007	123.357	1.240.18	121.620	151.744	1.340.07	106.157	167.207
70,000	1.012.20	294.392	1.198.75	161.546	132.846	1.335.58	130.975	163.417	1.443.16	114.323	180.069
75,000	1.084.49	315.416	1.284.37	173.083	142.333	1.430.96	140.328	175.088	1.546.22	122.487	192.929
80,000	1.156.79	336.444	1.369.99	184.622	151.822	1.526.36	149.684	186.760	1.649.31	130.653	205.791
85,000	1.229.09	357.472	1.455.62	196.161	161.311	1.621.76	159.039	198.433	1.752.39	138.819	218.653
90,000	1.301.39	378.500	1.541.24	207.700	170.800	1.717.16	168.394	210.106	1.855.47	146.985	231.515
95,000	1.373.69	399.528	1.626.87	219.239	180.289	1.812.55	177.750	221.778	1.958.55	155.150	244.379
100,000	1.445.99	420.556	1.712.49	230.778	189.778	1.907.95	187.105	233.451	2.061.64	163.316	257.240
105,000	1.518.29	441.584	1.798.12	242.317	199.267	2.003.35	196.460	245.124	2.164.72	171.482	270.102
110,000	1.590.59	462.612	1.883.74	253.856	208.756	2.098.75	205.816	256.796	2.267.80	179.648	282.964
115,000	1.662.89	483.640	1.969.37	265.395	218.245	2.194.15	215.171	268.469	2.370.88	187.814	295.826
120,000	1.735.19	504.668	2.054.99	276.934	227.734	2.289.55	224.526	280.142	2.473.97	195.980	308.688
125,000	1.807.49	525.696	2.140.62	288.473	237.223	2.384.94	233.882	291.814	2.577.05	204.146	321.550
130,000	1.879.79	546.724	2.226.24	300.012	246.712	2.480.34	243.237	303.487	2.680.13	212.312	334.412
135,000	1.952.09	567.752	2.311.87	311.551	256.201	2.575.74	252.592	315.160	2.783.21	220.478	347.274
140,000	2.024.39	588.780	2.397.49	323.090	265.690	2.671.14	261.948	326.832	2.886.30	228.644	360.136
145,000	2.096.68	609.805	2.483.11	334.627	275.178	2.766.52	271.303	338.504	2.989.36	236.808	372.997
150,000	2.168.98	630.833	2.568.73	346.166	284.667	2.861.92	280.656	350.177	3.092.45	244.974	385.859
155,000	2.241.28	651.861	2.654.36	357.705	294.156	2.957.32	290.012	361.849	3.195.53	253.140	398.721
160,000	2.313.58	672.889	2.739.98	369.244	303.645	3.052.72	299.367	373.522	3.298.61	261.305	411.584
165,000	2.385.88	693.917	2.825.61	380.783	313.134	3.148.12	308.722	385.195	3.401.69	269.471	424.446
170,000	2.458.18	714.945	2.911.23	392.322	322.623	3.243.52	318.078	396.867	3.504.78	277.637	437.308
175,000	2.530.48	735.973	2.996.86	403.861	332.112	3.338.91	327.433	408.540	3.607.86	285.803	450.170
180,000	2.602.78	757.001	3.082.48	415.400	341.601	3.434.31	336.788	420.213	3.710.94	293.969	463.032
185,000	2.675.08	778.029	3.168.11	426.939	351.090	3.529.71	346.144	431.885	3.814.02	302.135	475.894
190,000	2.747.38	799.057	3.253.73	438.478	360.579	3.625.11	355.499	443.558	3.917.11	310.301	488.756
195,000	2.819.68	820.085	3.339.36	450.017	370.068	3.720.51	364.855	455.230	4.020.19	318.467	501.618
200,000	2.891.98	841.113	3.424.98	461.556	379.557	3.815.91	374.210	466.903	4.123.27	326.633	514.480

GROWING EQUITY MORTGAGES 17.25%

AMOUNT OF LOAN	30 YEARS		4% PMT INCR/YR 138.063 PAYMENTS			5% PMT INCR/YR 127.510 PAYMENTS			6% PMT INCR/YR 119.282 PAYMENTS		
	MONTHLY PAYMENT	TOTAL INTRST	LAST YR MON PMT	TOTAL INTRST	INTRST SAVED	LAST YR MON PMT	TOTAL INTRST	INTRST SAVED	LAST YR MON PMT	TOTAL INTRST	INTRST SAVED
$ 50	0.73	213	1.12	75	138	1.19	69	144	1.23	65	148
100	1.45	422	2.23	148	274	2.36	137	285	2.45	128	294
200	2.90	844	4.46	296	548	4.72	273	571	4.90	255	589
300	4.34	1.262	6.68	443	819	7.07	408	854	7.33	381	881
400	5.79	1.684	8.91	591	1.093	9.43	545	1.139	9.78	509	1.175
500	7.23	2.103	11.13	738	1.365	11.78	680	1.423	12.21	635	1.468
600	8.68	2.525	13.36	886	1.639	14.14	816	1.709	14.66	762	1.763
700	10.13	2.947	15.59	1.034	1.913	16.50	953	1.994	17.11	890	2.057
800	11.57	3.365	17.81	1.180	2.185	18.85	1.088	2.277	19.55	1.016	2.349
900	13.02	3.787	20.04	1.329	2.458	21.21	1.224	2.563	22.00	1.144	2.643
1,000	14.46	4.206	22.26	1.475	2.731	23.55	1.359	2.847	24.43	1.270	2.936
2,000	28.92	8.411	44.52	2.950	5.461	47.11	2.719	5.692	48.86	2.539	5.872
3,000	43.38	12.617	66.78	4.425	8.192	70.66	4.078	8.539	73.29	3.809	8.808
4,000	57.84	16.822	89.04	5.900	10.922	94.22	5.438	11.384	97.72	5.078	11.744
5,000	72.30	21.028	111.30	7.376	13.652	117.77	6.797	14.231	122.15	6.348	14.680
6,000	86.76	25.234	133.56	8.851	16.383	141.32	8.156	17.078	146.58	7.618	17.616
7,000	101.22	29.439	155.82	10.326	19.113	164.88	9.516	19.923	171.01	8.887	20.552
8,000	115.68	33.645	178.08	11.801	21.844	188.43	10.875	22.770	195.44	10.157	23.488
9,000	130.14	37.850	200.34	13.276	24.574	211.98	12.235	25.615	219.87	11.426	26.424
10,000	144.60	42.056	222.61	14.751	27.305	235.54	13.594	28.462	244.30	12.696	29.360
11,000	159.06	46.262	244.87	16.226	30.036	259.09	14.953	31.309	268.73	13.965	32.297
12,000	173.52	50.467	267.13	17.701	32.766	282.65	16.313	34.154	293.16	15.235	35.232
13,000	187.98	54.673	289.39	19.177	35.496	306.20	17.672	37.001	317.59	16.505	38.168
14,000	202.44	58.878	311.65	20.652	38.226	329.75	19.032	39.846	342.02	17.774	41.104
15,000	216.90	63.084	333.91	22.127	40.957	353.31	20.391	42.693	366.45	19.044	44.040
16,000	231.36	67.290	356.17	23.602	43.688	376.86	21.750	45.540	390.88	20.313	46.977
17,000	245.82	71.495	378.43	25.077	46.418	400.41	23.110	48.385	415.31	21.583	49.912
18,000	260.28	75.701	400.69	26.552	49.149	423.97	24.469	51.232	439.74	22.853	52.848
19,000	274.74	79.906	422.95	28.027	51.879	447.52	25.829	54.077	464.17	24.122	55.784
20,000	289.20	84.112	445.21	29.502	54.610	471.08	27.188	56.924	488.60	25.392	58.720
21,000	303.66	88.318	467.47	30.977	57.341	494.63	28.548	59.770	513.03	26.661	61.657
22,000	318.12	92.523	489.73	32.453	60.070	518.18	29.907	62.616	537.46	27.931	64.592
23,000	332.58	96.729	511.99	33.928	62.801	541.74	31.266	65.463	561.89	29.201	67.528
24,000	347.04	100.934	534.25	35.403	65.531	565.29	32.626	68.308	586.32	30.470	70.464
25,000	361.50	105.140	556.51	36.878	68.262	588.85	33.985	71.155	610.75	31.740	73.400
26,000	375.96	109.346	578.77	38.353	70.993	612.40	35.345	74.001	635.18	33.009	76.337
27,000	390.42	113.551	601.03	39.828	73.723	635.95	36.704	76.847	659.61	34.279	79.272
28,000	404.88	117.757	623.29	41.303	76.454	659.51	38.063	79.694	684.04	35.548	82.208
29,000	419.34	121.962	645.55	42.778	79.184	683.06	39.423	82.539	708.47	36.818	85.144
30,000	433.80	126.168	667.82	44.254	81.914	706.61	40.782	85.386	732.90	38.088	88.080
32,500	469.95	136.682	723.47	47.941	88.741	765.50	44.181	92.501	793.97	41.262	95.420
35,000	506.10	147.196	779.12	51.629	95.567	824.38	47.579	99.617	855.05	44.436	102.760
40,000	578.40	168.224	890.42	59.005	109.219	942.15	54.376	113.848	977.19	50.784	117.440
45,000	650.70	189.252	1.001.72	66.380	122.872	1.059.92	61.173	128.079	1.099.34	57.132	132.120
50,000	723.00	210.280	1.113.03	73.756	136.524	1.177.69	67.970	142.310	1.221.49	63.480	146.800
55,000	795.30	231.308	1.224.33	81.131	150.177	1.295.46	74.767	156.541	1.343.64	69.827	161.481
60,000	867.60	252.336	1.335.63	88.507	163.829	1.413.23	81.564	170.772	1.465.79	76.175	176.161
65,000	939.90	273.364	1.446.93	95.883	177.481	1.531.00	88.361	185.003	1.587.94	82.523	190.841
70,000	1.012.20	294.392	1.558.24	103.258	191.134	1.648.77	95.158	199.234	1.710.09	88.871	205.521
75,000	1.084.49	315.416	1.669.52	110.632	204.784	1.766.52	101.954	213.462	1.832.22	95.218	220.198
80,000	1.156.79	336.444	1.780.83	118.008	218.436	1.884.29	108.751	227.693	1.954.37	101.566	234.878
85,000	1.229.09	357.472	1.892.13	125.383	232.089	2.002.06	115.548	241.924	2.076.52	107.914	249.558
90,000	1.301.39	378.500	2.003.43	132.759	245.741	2.119.83	122.345	256.155	2.198.67	114.262	264.238
95,000	1.373.69	399.528	2.114.73	140.134	259.394	2.237.60	129.142	270.386	2.320.82	120.610	278.918
100,000	1.445.99	420.556	2.226.04	147.510	273.046	2.355.37	135.939	284.617	2.442.97	126.958	293.598
105,000	1.518.29	441.584	2.337.34	154.886	286.698	2.473.13	142.736	298.848	2.565.12	133.305	308.279
110,000	1.590.59	462.612	2.448.64	162.261	300.351	2.590.90	149.533	313.079	2.687.27	139.653	322.959
115,000	1.662.89	483.640	2.559.94	169.637	314.003	2.708.67	156.330	327.310	2.809.42	146.001	337.639
120,000	1.735.19	504.668	2.671.25	177.012	327.656	2.826.44	163.127	341.541	2.931.57	152.349	352.319
125,000	1.807.49	525.696	2.782.55	184.388	341.308	2.944.21	169.924	355.772	3.053.72	158.697	366.999
130,000	1.879.79	546.724	2.893.85	191.764	354.960	3.061.98	176.721	370.003	3.175.87	165.045	381.679
135,000	1.952.09	567.752	3.005.15	199.139	368.613	3.179.75	183.518	384.234	3.298.01	171.393	396.359
140,000	2.024.39	588.780	3.116.46	206.515	382.265	3.297.52	190.315	398.465	3.420.16	177.741	411.039
145,000	2.096.68	609.805	3.227.74	213.889	395.916	3.415.27	197.110	412.695	3.542.30	184.088	425.717
150,000	2.168.98	630.833	3.339.05	221.264	409.569	3.533.04	203.907	426.926	3.664.45	190.435	440.398
155,000	2.241.28	651.861	3.450.35	228.640	423.221	3.650.81	210.705	441.156	3.786.60	196.783	455.078
160,000	2.313.58	672.889	3.561.65	236.015	436.874	3.768.58	217.502	455.387	3.908.74	203.131	469.758
165,000	2.385.88	693.917	3.672.95	243.391	450.526	3.886.35	224.299	469.618	4.030.89	209.479	484.438
170,000	2.458.18	714.945	3.784.26	250.766	464.179	4.004.12	231.096	483.849	4.153.04	215.827	499.118
175,000	2.530.48	735.973	3.895.56	258.142	477.831	4.121.89	237.893	498.080	4.275.19	222.175	513.798
180,000	2.602.78	757.001	4.006.86	265.518	491.483	4.239.65	244.690	512.311	4.397.34	228.523	528.478
185,000	2.675.08	778.029	4.118.16	272.893	505.136	4.357.42	251.487	526.542	4.519.49	234.871	543.158
190,000	2.747.38	799.057	4.229.47	280.269	518.788	4.475.19	258.284	540.773	4.641.64	241.219	557.838
195,000	2.819.68	820.085	4.340.77	287.644	532.441	4.592.96	265.081	555.004	4.763.79	247.567	572.518
200,000	2.891.98	841.113	4.452.07	295.020	546.093	4.710.73	271.878	569.235	4.885.94	253.915	587.198

183

17.50%   GROWING EQUITY MORTGAGES

AMOUNT OF LOAN	30 YEARS		1% PMT INCR/YR 208.768 PAYMENTS			2% PMT INCR/YR 171.845 PAYMENTS			3% PMT INCR/YR 151.093 PAYMENTS		
	MONTHLY PAYMENT	TOTAL INTRST	LAST YR MON PMT	TOTAL INTRST	INTRST SAVED	LAST YR MON PMT	TOTAL INTRST	INTRST SAVED	LAST YR MON PMT	TOTAL INTRST	INTRST SAVED
$ 50	0.74	216	0.88	118	98	0.98	96	120	1.06	84	132
100	1.47	429	1.74	233	196	1.94	189	240	2.10	165	264
200	2.94	858	3.48	467	391	3.88	378	480	4.19	330	528
300	4.40	1,284	5.21	698	586	5.81	566	718	6.27	494	790
400	5.87	1,713	6.95	931	782	7.75	755	958	8.37	659	1,054
500	7.34	2,142	8.69	1,165	977	9.68	944	1,198	10.47	824	1,318
600	8.80	2,568	10.42	1,396	1,172	11.61	1,131	1,437	12.55	988	1,580
700	10.27	2,997	12.16	1,629	1,368	13.55	1,321	1,676	14.64	1,153	1,844
800	11.74	3,426	13.90	1,863	1,563	15.49	1,510	1,916	16.74	1,318	2,108
900	13.20	3,852	15.63	2,094	1,758	17.42	1,697	2,155	18.82	1,482	2,370
1,000	14.67	4,281	17.37	2,327	1,954	19.36	1,886	2,395	20.92	1,647	2,634
2,000	29.33	8,559	34.74	4,652	3,907	38.70	3,771	4,788	41.82	3,292	5,267
3,000	43.99	12,836	52.10	6,977	5,859	58.04	5,656	7,180	62.72	4,937	7,899
4,000	58.66	17,118	69.47	9,305	7,813	77.40	7,542	9,576	83.64	6,583	10,535
5,000	73.32	21,395	86.83	11,630	9,765	96.74	9,426	11,969	104.54	8,228	13,167
6,000	87.98	25,673	104.20	13,955	11,718	116.09	11,311	14,362	125.44	9,873	15,800
7,000	102.65	29,954	121.57	16,282	13,672	135.44	13,197	16,757	146.35	11,520	18,434
8,000	117.31	34,232	138.93	18,607	15,625	154.79	15,082	19,150	167.26	13,165	21,067
9,000	131.97	38,509	156.29	20,932	17,577	174.13	16,967	21,542	188.16	14,810	23,699
10,000	146.64	42,790	173.67	23,260	19,530	193.49	18,853	23,937	209.07	16,456	26,334
11,000	161.30	47,068	191.03	25,585	21,483	212.83	20,737	26,331	229.98	18,101	28,967
12,000	175.96	51,346	208.39	27,910	23,436	232.18	22,622	28,724	250.88	19,746	31,600
13,000	190.63	55,627	225.76	30,237	25,390	251.53	24,508	31,119	271.79	21,393	34,234
14,000	205.29	59,904	243.13	32,562	27,342	270.88	26,393	33,511	292.69	23,038	36,866
15,000	219.95	64,182	260.49	34,887	29,295	290.22	28,278	35,904	313.60	24,683	39,499
16,000	234.62	68,463	277.86	37,215	31,248	309.58	30,164	38,299	334.51	26,330	42,133
17,000	249.28	72,741	295.22	39,540	33,201	328.92	32,048	40,693	355.41	27,974	44,767
18,000	263.94	77,018	312.59	41,865	35,153	348.26	33,933	43,085	376.32	29,619	47,399
19,000	278.61	81,300	329.96	44,192	37,108	367.62	35,819	45,481	397.23	31,266	50,034
20,000	293.27	85,577	347.32	46,517	39,060	386.96	37,704	47,873	418.13	32,911	52,666
21,000	307.93	89,855	364.68	48,842	41,013	406.31	39,589	50,266	439.03	34,556	55,299
22,000	322.60	94,136	382.06	51,170	42,966	425.66	41,475	52,661	459.95	36,203	57,933
23,000	337.26	98,414	399.42	53,495	44,919	445.01	43,360	55,055	480.85	37,848	60,566
24,000	351.92	102,691	416.78	55,820	46,871	464.35	45,244	57,447	501.75	39,492	63,199
25,000	366.59	106,972	434.15	58,147	48,825	483.71	47,130	59,842	522.67	41,139	65,833
26,000	381.25	111,250	451.52	60,472	50,778	503.05	49,015	62,235	543.57	42,784	68,466
27,000	395.91	115,528	468.88	62,797	52,731	522.39	50,900	64,628	564.47	44,429	71,099
28,000	410.58	119,809	486.25	65,125	54,684	541.75	52,786	67,023	585.39	46,076	73,733
29,000	425.24	124,086	503.61	67,450	56,636	561.10	54,671	69,415	606.29	47,721	76,365
30,000	439.90	128,364	520.98	69,775	58,589	580.44	56,555	71,809	627.19	49,366	78,998
32,500	476.56	139,062	564.39	75,590	63,472	628.81	61,268	77,794	679.46	53,480	85,582
35,000	513.22	149,759	607.81	81,404	68,355	677.18	65,982	83,777	731.73	57,594	92,165
40,000	586.54	171,154	694.64	93,034	78,120	773.93	75,408	95,746	836.27	65,822	105,332
45,000	659.85	192,546	781.46	104,662	87,884	870.66	84,833	107,713	940.79	74,048	118,498
50,000	733.17	213,941	868.30	116,292	97,649	967.40	94,259	119,682	1,045.33	82,277	131,664
55,000	806.48	235,333	955.12	127,919	107,414	1,064.13	103,684	131,649	1,149.85	90,503	144,830
60,000	879.80	256,728	1,041.95	139,549	117,179	1,160.88	113,110	143,649	1,254.38	98,731	157,997
65,000	953.12	278,123	1,128.78	151,179	126,944	1,257.62	122,537	155,586	1,358.92	106,959	171,164
70,000	1,026.43	299,515	1,215.61	162,807	136,708	1,354.35	131,961	167,554	1,463.45	115,186	184,329
75,000	1,099.75	320,910	1,302.44	174,437	146,473	1,451.10	141,388	179,522	1,567.98	123,414	197,496
80,000	1,173.07	342,305	1,389.27	186,066	156,239	1,547.84	150,814	191,491	1,672.52	131,642	210,663
85,000	1,246.38	363,697	1,476.09	197,694	166,003	1,644.57	160,239	203,458	1,777.04	139,868	223,829
90,000	1,319.70	385,092	1,562.93	209,324	175,768	1,741.32	169,665	215,427	1,881.58	148,097	236,995
95,000	1,393.01	406,484	1,649.75	220,951	185,533	1,838.05	179,090	227,394	1,986.10	156,323	250,161
100,000	1,466.33	427,879	1,736.58	232,581	195,298	1,934.79	188,516	239,363	2,090.64	164,551	263,328
105,000	1,539.65	449,274	1,823.41	244,211	205,063	2,031.54	197,943	251,331	2,195.17	172,779	276,495
110,000	1,612.96	470,666	1,910.24	255,839	214,827	2,128.27	207,367	263,299	2,299.70	181,006	289,660
115,000	1,686.28	492,061	1,997.07	267,469	224,592	2,225.01	216,794	275,267	2,404.23	189,234	302,827
120,000	1,759.60	513,456	2,083.90	279,099	234,357	2,321.75	226,220	287,235	2,508.77	197,462	315,994
125,000	1,832.91	534,848	2,170.72	290,726	244,122	2,418.49	235,645	299,203	2,613.29	205,689	329,159
130,000	1,906.23	556,243	2,257.56	302,356	253,887	2,515.23	245,071	311,172	2,717.83	213,917	342,326
135,000	1,979.54	577,634	2,344.38	313,984	263,650	2,611.96	254,496	323,138	2,822.35	222,143	355,491
140,000	2,052.86	599,030	2,431.21	325,613	273,417	2,708.71	263,922	335,108	2,926.89	230,371	368,659
145,000	2,126.18	620,425	2,518.04	337,243	283,182	2,805.45	273,349	347,076	3,031.42	238,600	381,825
150,000	2,199.49	641,816	2,604.87	348,871	292,945	2,902.18	282,773	359,043	3,135.95	246,826	394,990
155,000	2,272.81	663,212	2,691.70	360,501	302,711	2,998.92	292,200	371,012	3,240.48	255,054	408,158
160,000	2,346.13	684,607	2,778.53	372,131	312,476	3,095.67	301,626	382,981	3,345.02	263,282	421,325
165,000	2,419.44	705,998	2,865.35	383,758	322,240	3,192.40	311,051	394,947	3,449.54	271,509	434,489
170,000	2,492.76	727,393	2,952.19	395,388	332,006	3,289.14	320,477	406,917	3,554.08	279,737	447,657
175,000	2,566.07	748,785	3,039.01	407,016	341,769	3,385.87	329,902	418,883	3,658.60	287,963	460,822
180,000	2,639.39	770,180	3,125.84	418,646	351,534	3,482.62	339,328	430,852	3,763.14	296,192	473,988
185,000	2,712.71	791,576	3,212.67	430,275	361,301	3,579.36	348,755	442,821	3,867.68	304,420	487,156
190,000	2,786.02	812,967	3,299.50	441,903	371,064	3,676.09	358,179	454,788	3,972.20	312,646	500,321
195,000	2,859.34	834,362	3,386.33	453,533	380,829	3,772.84	367,606	466,756	4,076.74	320,874	513,488
200,000	2,932.66	855,758	3,473.16	465,163	390,595	3,869.58	377,032	478,726	4,181.27	329,103	526,655

AMOUNT OF LOAN	30 YEARS		4% PMT INCR/YR 137.020 PAYMENTS			5% PMT INCR/YR 126.562 PAYMENTS			6% PMT INCR/YR 118.395 PAYMENTS		
	MONTHLY PAYMENT	TOTAL INTRST	LAST YR MON PMT	TOTAL INTRST	INTRST SAVED	LAST YR MON PMT	TOTAL INTRST	INTRST SAVED	LAST YR MON PMT	TOTAL INTRST	INTRST SAVED
$ 50	0.74	216	1.14	75	141	1.21	70	146	1.25	65	151
100	1.47	429	2.26	149	280	2.39	138	291	2.48	129	300
200	2.94	858	4.53	299	559	4.79	275	583	4.97	257	601
300	4.40	1,284	6.77	446	838	7.17	411	873	7.43	384	900
400	5.87	1,713	9.04	595	1,118	9.56	549	1,164	9.92	513	1,200
500	7.34	2,142	11.30	745	1,397	11.96	686	1,456	12.40	641	1,501
600	8.80	2,568	13.55	892	1,676	14.33	822	1,746	14.87	768	1,800
700	10.27	2,997	15.81	1,041	1,956	16.73	960	2,037	17.35	897	2,100
800	11.74	3,426	18.07	1,191	2,235	19.12	1,097	2,329	19.83	1,025	2,401
900	13.20	3,852	20.32	1,338	2,514	21.50	1,233	2,619	22.30	1,152	2,700
1,000	14.67	4,281	22.58	1,488	2,793	23.90	1,371	2,910	24.78	1,281	3,000
2,000	29.33	8,559	45.15	2,973	5,586	47.78	2,740	5,819	49.55	2,560	5,999
3,000	43.99	12,836	67.72	4,459	8,377	71.66	4,110	8,726	74.33	3,839	8,997
4,000	58.66	17,118	90.30	5,947	11,171	95.55	5,481	11,637	99.10	5,119	11,999
5,000	73.32	21,395	112.87	7,432	13,963	119.43	6,850	14,545	123.87	6,398	14,997
6,000	87.98	25,673	135.44	8,918	16,755	143.31	8,220	17,453	148.64	7,677	17,996
7,000	102.65	29,954	158.02	10,406	19,548	167.21	9,591	20,363	173.43	8,958	20,996
8,000	117.31	34,232	180.59	11,892	22,340	191.09	10,960	23,272	198.19	10,237	23,995
9,000	131.97	38,509	203.16	13,377	25,132	214.97	12,329	26,180	222.96	11,516	26,993
10,000	146.64	42,790	225.75	14,865	27,925	238.86	13,700	29,090	247.75	12,796	29,994
11,000	161.30	47,068	248.31	16,351	30,717	262.74	15,070	31,998	272.51	14,075	32,993
12,000	175.96	51,346	270.88	17,837	33,509	286.62	16,439	34,907	297.28	15,354	35,992
13,000	190.63	55,627	293.47	19,324	36,303	310.52	17,810	37,817	322.07	16,635	38,992
14,000	205.29	59,904	316.03	20,810	39,094	334.40	19,180	40,724	346.83	17,914	41,990
15,000	219.95	64,182	338.60	22,296	41,886	358.28	20,549	43,633	371.60	19,193	44,989
16,000	234.62	68,463	361.19	23,783	44,680	382.17	21,920	46,543	396.39	20,474	47,989
17,000	249.28	72,741	383.76	25,269	47,472	406.05	23,290	49,451	421.15	21,753	50,988
18,000	263.94	77,018	406.32	26,755	50,263	429.93	24,659	52,359	445.92	23,032	53,986
19,000	278.61	81,300	428.91	28,242	53,058	453.83	26,030	55,270	470.71	24,312	56,988
20,000	293.27	85,577	451.48	29,728	55,849	477.71	27,399	58,178	495.47	25,591	59,986
21,000	307.93	89,855	474.04	31,214	58,641	501.59	28,769	61,086	520.24	26,870	62,985
22,000	322.60	94,136	496.63	32,701	61,435	525.48	30,140	63,996	545.03	28,151	65,985
23,000	337.26	98,414	519.20	34,187	64,227	549.36	31,509	66,905	569.79	29,430	68,984
24,000	351.92	102,691	541.76	35,673	67,018	573.24	32,879	69,812	594.56	30,709	71,982
25,000	366.59	106,972	564.35	37,161	69,811	597.14	34,250	72,722	619.35	31,989	74,983
26,000	381.25	111,250	586.92	38,646	72,604	621.02	35,619	75,631	644.11	33,268	77,982
27,000	395.91	115,528	609.49	40,132	75,396	644.90	36,988	78,540	668.88	34,547	80,981
28,000	410.58	119,809	632.07	41,620	78,189	668.79	38,359	81,450	693.67	35,828	83,981
29,000	425.24	124,086	654.64	43,106	80,980	692.67	39,729	84,357	718.43	37,107	86,979
30,000	439.90	128,364	677.21	44,591	83,773	716.55	41,098	87,266	743.20	38,386	89,978
32,500	476.56	139,062	733.64	48,308	90,754	776.27	44,523	94,539	805.14	41,585	97,477
35,000	513.22	149,759	790.08	52,024	97,735	835.98	47,948	101,811	867.07	44,784	104,975
40,000	586.54	171,154	902.95	59,456	111,698	955.41	54,799	116,355	990.95	51,182	119,972
45,000	659.85	192,546	1,015.81	66,887	125,659	1,074.83	61,647	130,912	1,114.80	57,579	134,967
50,000	733.17	213,941	1,128.68	74,319	139,622	1,194.26	68,498	145,443	1,238.68	63,977	149,964
55,000	806.48	235,333	1,241.54	81,750	153,583	1,313.67	75,346	159,987	1,362.53	70,374	164,959
60,000	879.80	256,728	1,354.41	89,183	167,545	1,433.10	82,196	174,532	1,486.40	76,772	179,956
65,000	953.12	278,123	1,467.28	96,615	181,508	1,552.53	89,047	189,076	1,610.28	83,170	194,953
70,000	1,026.43	299,515	1,580.14	104,046	195,469	1,671.95	95,895	203,620	1,734.13	89,567	209,948
75,000	1,099.75	320,910	1,693.01	111,478	209,432	1,791.38	102,745	218,165	1,858.00	95,965	224,945
80,000	1,173.07	342,305	1,805.89	118,911	223,394	1,910.81	109,596	232,709	1,981.88	102,363	239,942
85,000	1,246.38	363,697	1,918.74	126,342	237,355	2,030.22	116,444	247,253	2,105.73	108,760	254,937
90,000	1,319.70	385,092	2,031.62	133,774	251,318	2,149.65	123,295	261,797	2,229.61	115,158	269,934
95,000	1,393.01	406,484	2,144.47	141,205	265,279	2,269.07	130,143	276,341	2,353.46	121,554	284,930
100,000	1,466.33	427,879	2,257.35	148,637	279,242	2,388.50	136,993	290,886	2,477.33	127,953	299,926
105,000	1,539.65	449,274	2,370.22	156,070	293,204	2,507.93	143,844	305,430	2,601.21	134,351	314,923
110,000	1,612.96	470,666	2,483.08	163,500	307,166	2,627.34	150,692	319,973	2,725.06	140,747	329,919
115,000	1,686.28	492,061	2,595.95	170,933	321,128	2,746.77	157,543	334,518	2,848.93	147,146	344,915
120,000	1,759.60	513,456	2,708.82	178,365	335,091	2,866.20	164,393	349,063	2,972.81	153,544	359,912
125,000	1,832.91	534,848	2,821.68	185,796	349,052	2,985.62	171,241	363,607	3,096.66	159,940	374,908
130,000	1,906.23	556,243	2,934.55	193,229	363,014	3,105.05	178,092	378,151	3,220.54	166,339	389,904
135,000	1,979.54	577,634	3,047.41	200,659	376,975	3,224.46	184,940	392,694	3,344.39	172,735	404,899
140,000	2,052.86	599,030	3,160.28	208,092	390,938	3,343.89	191,790	407,240	3,468.26	179,133	419,897
145,000	2,126.18	620,425	3,273.16	215,524	404,901	3,463.32	198,641	421,784	3,592.14	185,532	434,893
150,000	2,199.49	641,816	3,386.01	222,955	418,861	3,582.74	205,489	436,327	3,715.99	191,928	449,888
155,000	2,272.81	663,212	3,498.89	230,387	432,825	3,702.17	212,340	450,872	3,839.86	198,326	464,886
160,000	2,346.13	684,607	3,611.76	237,820	446,787	3,821.60	219,190	465,417	3,963.74	204,725	479,882
165,000	2,419.44	705,998	3,724.62	245,251	460,747	3,941.01	226,038	479,960	4,087.59	211,121	494,877
170,000	2,492.76	727,394	3,837.49	252,683	474,711	4,060.44	232,889	494,505	4,211.47	217,519	509,875
175,000	2,566.07	748,785	3,950.35	260,114	488,671	4,179.86	239,737	509,048	4,335.32	223,916	524,869
180,000	2,639.39	770,180	4,063.22	267,546	502,634	4,299.29	246,587	523,593	4,459.19	230,314	539,866
185,000	2,712.71	791,576	4,176.09	274,979	516,597	4,418.72	253,438	538,138	4,583.07	236,712	554,864
190,000	2,786.02	812,967	4,288.95	282,409	530,558	4,538.13	260,286	552,681	4,706.92	243,109	569,858
195,000	2,859.34	834,362	4,401.82	289,842	544,520	4,657.56	267,137	567,225	4,830.79	249,507	584,855
200,000	2,932.66	855,758	4,514.70	297,274	558,484	4,776.99	273,987	581,771	4,954.67	255,905	599,853

17.75% GROWING EQUITY MORTGAGES

AMOUNT OF LOAN	30 YEARS		1% PMT INCR/YR 207.147 PAYMENTS			2% PMT INCR/YR 170.510 PAYMENTS			3% PMT INCR/YR 149.933 PAYMENTS		
	MONTHLY PAYMENT	TOTAL INTRST	LAST YR MON PMT	TOTAL INTRST	INTRST SAVED	LAST YR MON PMT	TOTAL INTRST	INTRST SAVED	LAST YR MON PMT	TOTAL INTRST	INTRST SAVED
$ 50	0.75	220	0.89	119	101	0.99	96	124	1.07	84	136
100	1.49	436	1.76	235	201	1.97	191	245	2.12	166	270
200	2.98	873	3.53	470	403	3.93	381	492	4.25	333	540
300	4.47	1,309	5.29	705	604	5.90	572	737	6.37	499	810
400	5.95	1,742	7.05	938	804	7.85	760	982	8.48	664	1,078
500	7.44	2,178	8.81	1,173	1,005	9.82	951	1,227	10.61	830	1,348
600	8.93	2,615	10.58	1,408	1,207	11.78	1,141	1,474	12.73	996	1,619
700	10.41	3,048	12.33	1,641	1,407	13.74	1,330	1,718	14.84	1,161	1,887
800	11.90	3,484	14.09	1,876	1,608	15.70	1,520	1,964	16.97	1,327	2,157
900	13.39	3,920	15.86	2,111	1,809	17.67	1,711	2,209	19.09	1,494	2,426
1,000	14.87	4,353	17.61	2,344	2,009	19.62	1,900	2,453	21.20	1,658	2,695
2,000	29.74	8,706	35.22	4,688	4,018	39.24	3,799	4,907	42.40	3,316	5,390
3,000	44.61	13,060	52.83	7,032	6,028	58.86	5,699	7,361	63.60	4,975	8,085
4,000	59.47	17,409	70.43	9,374	8,035	78.47	7,597	9,812	84.79	6,631	10,778
5,000	74.34	21,762	88.04	11,718	10,044	98.09	9,496	12,266	105.99	8,289	13,473
6,000	89.21	26,116	105.65	14,063	12,053	117.71	11,396	14,720	127.19	9,947	16,169
7,000	104.07	30,465	123.25	16,405	14,060	137.32	13,294	17,171	148.38	11,604	18,861
8,000	118.94	34,818	140.86	18,749	16,069	156.94	15,193	19,625	169.58	13,262	21,556
9,000	133.81	39,172	158.47	21,093	18,079	176.56	17,093	22,079	190.78	14,920	24,252
10,000	148.67	43,521	176.07	23,435	20,086	196.17	18,991	24,530	211.97	16,577	26,944
11,000	163.54	47,874	193.68	25,779	22,095	215.79	20,890	26,984	233.17	18,235	29,639
12,000	178.41	52,228	211.29	28,123	24,105	235.41	22,790	29,438	254.37	19,893	32,335
13,000	193.27	56,577	228.89	30,465	26,112	255.02	24,687	31,890	275.56	21,550	35,027
14,000	208.14	60,930	246.50	32,809	28,121	274.64	26,587	34,343	296.76	23,208	37,722
15,000	223.01	65,284	264.11	35,153	30,131	294.26	28,487	36,797	317.96	24,866	40,418
16,000	237.88	69,637	281.72	37,497	32,140	313.88	30,386	39,251	339.16	26,524	43,113
17,000	252.74	73,986	299.32	39,839	34,147	333.49	32,284	41,702	360.35	28,181	45,805
18,000	267.61	78,340	316.93	42,183	36,157	353.11	34,184	44,156	381.55	29,839	48,501
19,000	282.48	82,693	334.54	44,527	38,165	372.73	36,083	46,610	402.75	31,497	51,196
20,000	297.34	87,042	352.14	46,869	40,173	392.33	37,981	49,061	423.94	33,154	53,888
21,000	312.21	91,396	369.75	49,214	42,182	411.95	39,881	51,515	445.14	34,812	56,584
22,000	327.08	95,749	387.36	51,558	44,191	431.58	41,780	53,969	466.34	36,470	59,279
23,000	341.94	100,098	404.96	53,900	46,198	451.18	43,678	56,420	487.52	38,126	61,972
24,000	356.81	104,452	422.57	56,244	48,208	470.80	45,578	58,874	508.73	39,785	64,667
25,000	371.68	108,805	440.18	58,588	50,217	490.42	47,477	61,328	529.93	41,443	67,362
26,000	386.54	113,154	457.78	60,930	52,224	510.03	49,375	63,779	551.11	43,099	70,055
27,000	401.41	117,508	475.39	63,274	54,234	529.65	51,275	66,233	572.31	44,757	72,751
28,000	416.28	121,861	493.00	65,618	56,243	549.27	53,174	68,687	593.52	46,416	75,445
29,000	431.15	126,214	510.61	67,962	58,252	568.89	55,074	71,140	614.72	48,074	78,140
30,000	446.01	130,564	528.21	70,304	60,260	588.50	56,972	73,592	635.90	49,730	80,834
32,500	483.18	141,445	572.23	76,163	65,282	637.55	61,720	79,725	688.90	53,875	87,570
35,000	520.35	152,326	616.25	82,023	70,303	686.59	66,468	85,858	741.89	58,020	94,306
40,000	594.68	174,085	704.28	93,739	80,346	784.67	75,962	98,123	847.87	66,307	107,778
45,000	669.02	195,847	792.32	105,457	90,390	882.76	85,458	110,389	953.86	74,596	121,251
50,000	743.35	217,606	880.35	117,174	100,432	980.83	94,953	122,653	1,059.84	82,884	134,722
55,000	817.69	239,368	968.39	128,892	110,476	1,078.92	104,449	134,919	1,165.83	91,173	148,195
60,000	892.02	261,127	1,056.42	140,608	120,519	1,177.00	113,943	147,184	1,271.81	99,461	161,666
65,000	966.35	282,886	1,144.45	152,325	130,561	1,275.08	123,437	159,449	1,377.78	107,748	175,138
70,000	1,040.69	304,648	1,232.49	164,043	140,605	1,373.17	132,934	171,714	1,483.78	116,037	188,611
75,000	1,115.02	326,407	1,320.52	175,759	150,648	1,471.25	142,428	183,979	1,589.75	124,325	202,082
80,000	1,189.36	348,170	1,408.56	187,478	160,692	1,569.34	151,924	196,246	1,695.74	132,614	215,556
85,000	1,263.69	369,928	1,496.59	199,194	170,734	1,667.41	161,418	208,510	1,801.72	140,902	229,026
90,000	1,338.03	391,691	1,584.63	210,913	180,778	1,765.50	170,915	220,776	1,907.71	149,191	242,500
95,000	1,412.36	413,450	1,672.66	222,629	190,821	1,863.58	180,409	233,041	2,013.69	157,478	255,972
100,000	1,486.70	435,212	1,760.71	234,347	200,865	1,961.67	189,905	245,307	2,119.68	165,768	269,444
105,000	1,561.03	456,971	1,848.73	246,064	210,907	2,059.75	199,400	257,571	2,225.66	174,055	282,916
110,000	1,635.37	478,733	1,936.78	257,782	220,951	2,157.84	208,896	269,837	2,331.65	182,344	296,389
115,000	1,709.70	500,492	2,024.81	269,498	230,994	2,255.91	218,390	282,102	2,437.62	190,632	309,860
120,000	1,784.04	522,254	2,112.85	281,217	241,037	2,354.00	227,886	294,368	2,543.61	198,921	323,333
125,000	1,858.37	544,013	2,200.88	292,933	251,080	2,452.08	237,381	306,632	2,649.59	207,209	336,804
130,000	1,932.70	565,772	2,288.91	304,649	261,123	2,550.16	246,875	318,897	2,755.57	215,496	350,276
135,000	2,007.04	587,534	2,376.95	316,368	271,166	2,648.25	256,371	331,163	2,861.56	223,785	363,749
140,000	2,081.37	609,293	2,464.98	328,084	281,209	2,746.32	265,865	343,428	2,967.54	232,073	377,220
145,000	2,155.71	631,056	2,553.02	339,803	291,253	2,844.41	275,362	355,694	3,073.53	240,362	390,694
150,000	2,230.04	652,814	2,641.05	351,519	301,295	2,942.49	284,856	367,958	3,179.50	248,650	404,164
155,000	2,304.38	674,577	2,729.09	363,237	311,340	3,040.58	294,352	380,225	3,285.49	256,939	417,638
160,000	2,378.71	696,336	2,817.12	374,954	321,382	3,138.66	303,846	392,490	3,391.47	265,226	431,110
165,000	2,453.05	718,098	2,905.16	386,672	331,426	3,236.75	313,343	404,755	3,497.46	273,516	444,582
170,000	2,527.38	739,857	2,993.19	398,388	341,469	3,334.82	322,837	417,020	3,603.44	281,803	458,054
175,000	2,601.72	761,619	3,081.23	410,107	351,512	3,432.91	332,333	429,286	3,709.43	290,092	471,527
180,000	2,676.05	783,378	3,169.26	421,823	361,555	3,530.99	341,827	441,551	3,815.41	298,380	484,998
185,000	2,750.39	805,140	3,257.30	433,542	371,598	3,629.08	351,324	453,816	3,921.40	306,669	498,471
190,000	2,824.72	826,899	3,345.33	445,258	381,641	3,727.16	360,818	466,081	4,027.38	314,957	511,942
195,000	2,899.05	848,658	3,433.36	456,974	391,684	3,825.23	370,312	478,346	4,133.35	323,244	525,414
200,000	2,973.39	870,420	3,521.40	468,693	401,727	3,923.32	379,809	490,611	4,239.34	331,533	538,887

GROWING EQUITY MORTGAGES 17.75%

AMOUNT OF LOAN	30 YEARS MONTHLY PAYMENT	30 YEARS TOTAL INTRST	4% PMT INCR/YR 135.998 PAYMENTS LAST YR MON PMT	TOTAL INTRST	INTRST SAVED	5% PMT INCR/YR 125.632 PAYMENTS LAST YR MON PMT	TOTAL INTRST	INTRST SAVED	6% PMT INCR/YR 117.525 PAYMENTS LAST YR MON PMT	TOTAL INTRST	INTRST SAVED
$ 50	0.75	220	1.15	76	144	1.22	70	150	1.27	65	155
100	1.49	436	2.29	150	286	2.43	139	297	2.52	129	307
200	2.98	873	4.59	301	572	4.85	277	596	5.03	259	614
300	4.47	1,309	6.88	451	858	7.28	416	893	7.55	388	921
400	5.95	1,742	9.16	600	1,142	9.69	553	1,189	10.05	516	1,226
500	7.44	2,178	11.45	750	1,428	12.12	691	1,487	12.57	646	1,532
600	8.93	2,615	13.75	900	1,715	14.55	830	1,785	15.09	775	1,840
700	10.41	3,048	16.03	1,049	1,999	16.96	967	2,081	17.59	903	2,145
800	11.90	3,484	18.32	1,199	2,285	19.38	1,105	2,379	20.10	1,032	2,452
900	13.39	3,920	20.61	1,349	2,571	21.81	1,244	2,676	22.62	1,162	2,758
1,000	14.87	4,353	22.89	1,498	2,855	24.22	1,381	2,972	25.12	1,290	3,063
2,000	29.74	8,706	45.78	2,996	5,710	48.44	2,762	5,944	50.25	2,580	6,126
3,000	44.61	13,060	68.68	4,494	8,566	72.66	4,142	8,918	75.37	3,869	9,191
4,000	59.47	17,409	91.55	5,990	11,419	96.87	5,522	11,887	100.47	5,158	12,251
5,000	74.34	21,762	114.44	7,488	14,274	121.09	6,902	14,860	125.60	6,447	15,315
6,000	89.21	26,116	137.33	8,986	17,130	145.31	8,283	17,833	150.72	7,737	18,379
7,000	104.07	30,465	160.21	10,483	19,982	169.52	9,663	20,802	175.82	9,026	21,439
8,000	118.94	34,818	183.10	11,981	22,837	193.74	11,043	23,775	200.95	10,315	24,503
9,000	133.81	39,172	205.99	13,479	25,693	217.96	12,424	26,748	226.07	11,605	27,567
10,000	148.67	43,521	228.87	14,975	28,546	242.17	13,803	29,718	251.17	12,893	30,628
11,000	163.54	47,874	251.76	16,473	31,401	266.39	15,184	32,690	276.30	14,183	33,691
12,000	178.41	52,228	274.65	17,971	34,257	290.61	16,565	35,663	301.42	15,473	36,755
13,000	193.27	56,577	297.53	19,468	37,109	314.82	17,944	38,633	326.53	16,761	39,816
14,000	208.14	60,930	320.42	20,966	39,964	339.04	19,325	41,605	351.65	18,051	42,879
15,000	223.01	65,284	343.31	22,464	42,820	363.26	20,706	44,578	376.77	19,341	45,943
16,000	237.88	69,637	366.21	23,962	45,675	387.48	22,087	47,550	401.89	20,631	49,006
17,000	252.74	73,986	389.08	25,458	48,528	411.69	23,466	50,520	427.00	21,919	52,067
18,000	267.61	78,340	411.97	26,956	51,384	435.91	24,847	53,493	452.12	23,209	55,131
19,000	282.48	82,693	434.86	28,454	54,239	460.13	26,227	56,466	477.24	24,499	58,194
20,000	297.34	87,042	457.74	29,950	57,092	484.34	27,607	59,435	502.35	25,787	61,255
21,000	312.21	91,396	480.63	31,448	59,948	508.56	28,988	62,408	527.47	27,077	64,319
22,000	327.08	95,749	503.52	32,946	62,803	532.78	30,368	65,381	552.59	28,366	67,383
23,000	341.94	100,098	526.40	34,443	65,655	556.98	31,748	68,350	577.70	29,655	70,443
24,000	356.81	104,452	549.29	35,941	68,511	581.21	33,128	71,324	602.82	30,944	73,508
25,000	371.68	108,805	572.18	37,439	71,366	605.43	34,509	74,296	627.95	32,234	76,571
26,000	386.54	113,154	595.06	38,935	74,219	629.63	35,888	77,266	653.05	33,523	79,631
27,000	401.41	117,508	617.95	40,433	77,075	653.85	37,269	80,239	678.17	34,812	82,696
28,000	416.28	121,861	640.84	41,931	79,930	678.08	38,650	83,211	703.30	36,102	85,759
29,000	431.15	126,214	663.74	43,429	82,785	702.30	40,031	86,183	728.42	37,392	88,822
30,000	446.01	130,564	686.61	44,926	85,638	726.50	41,410	89,154	753.52	38,680	91,884
32,500	483.18	141,445	743.83	48,670	92,775	787.05	44,861	96,584	816.32	41,904	99,541
35,000	520.35	152,326	801.05	52,414	99,912	847.60	48,313	104,013	879.12	45,128	107,198
40,000	594.68	174,085	915.48	59,901	114,184	968.67	55,213	118,872	1,004.70	51,574	122,511
45,000	669.02	195,847	1,029.93	67,389	128,458	1,089.76	62,116	133,731	1,130.30	58,021	137,826
50,000	743.35	217,606	1,144.35	74,876	142,730	1,210.84	69,017	148,589	1,255.87	64,467	153,139
55,000	817.69	239,368	1,258.80	82,365	157,003	1,331.93	75,919	163,449	1,381.47	70,915	168,453
60,000	892.02	261,127	1,373.22	89,851	171,276	1,453.01	82,820	178,307	1,507.05	77,360	183,767
65,000	966.35	282,886	1,487.65	97,338	185,548	1,574.08	89,721	193,165	1,632.63	83,806	199,080
70,000	1,040.69	304,648	1,602.09	104,827	199,821	1,695.17	96,623	208,025	1,758.22	90,254	214,394
75,000	1,115.02	326,407	1,716.52	112,313	214,094	1,816.25	103,524	222,883	1,883.80	96,700	229,707
80,000	1,189.36	348,170	1,830.97	119,802	228,368	1,937.34	110,427	237,743	2,009.40	103,147	245,023
85,000	1,263.69	369,928	1,945.39	127,288	242,640	2,058.42	117,328	252,600	2,134.98	109,593	260,335
90,000	1,338.03	391,691	2,059.84	134,777	256,914	2,179.51	124,230	267,461	2,260.57	116,041	275,650
95,000	1,412.36	413,450	2,174.26	142,264	271,186	2,300.59	131,131	282,319	2,386.15	122,487	290,963
100,000	1,486.70	435,212	2,288.71	149,752	285,460	2,421.68	138,034	297,178	2,511.75	128,934	306,278
105,000	1,561.03	456,971	2,403.13	157,239	299,732	2,542.75	144,934	312,037	2,637.33	135,380	321,591
110,000	1,635.37	478,733	2,517.58	164,727	314,006	2,663.85	151,837	326,896	2,762.92	141,827	336,906
115,000	1,709.70	500,492	2,632.00	172,214	328,278	2,784.92	158,738	341,754	2,888.50	148,273	352,219
120,000	1,784.04	522,254	2,746.45	179,703	342,551	2,906.01	165,640	356,614	3,014.10	154,721	367,533
125,000	1,858.37	544,013	2,860.88	187,189	356,824	3,027.09	172,541	371,472	3,139.68	161,167	382,846
130,000	1,932.70	565,772	2,975.30	194,676	371,096	3,148.16	179,442	386,330	3,265.26	167,613	398,159
135,000	2,007.04	587,534	3,089.75	202,165	385,369	3,269.26	186,344	401,190	3,390.85	174,060	413,474
140,000	2,081.37	609,293	3,204.17	209,651	399,642	3,390.33	193,245	416,048	3,516.43	180,506	428,787
145,000	2,155.71	631,056	3,318.62	217,140	413,916	3,511.42	200,148	430,908	3,642.03	186,954	444,102
150,000	2,230.04	652,814	3,433.04	224,627	428,187	3,632.50	207,049	445,765	3,767.61	193,400	459,414
155,000	2,304.38	674,577	3,547.49	232,115	442,462	3,753.59	213,951	460,626	3,893.20	199,847	474,730
160,000	2,378.71	696,336	3,661.91	239,602	456,734	3,874.67	220,852	475,484	4,018.78	206,293	490,043
165,000	2,453.05	718,098	3,776.36	247,091	471,008	3,995.76	227,755	490,343	4,144.38	212,740	505,358
170,000	2,527.38	739,857	3,890.79	254,577	485,280	4,116.84	234,655	505,202	4,269.96	219,186	520,671
175,000	2,601.72	761,619	4,005.23	262,065	499,554	4,237.93	241,558	520,061	4,395.55	225,634	535,985
180,000	2,676.05	783,378	4,119.66	269,552	513,826	4,359.00	248,459	534,919	4,521.13	232,080	551,298
185,000	2,750.39	805,140	4,234.10	277,041	528,099	4,480.10	255,361	549,779	4,646.73	238,527	566,613
190,000	2,824.72	826,899	4,348.53	284,527	542,372	4,601.17	262,262	564,637	4,772.31	244,973	581,926
195,000	2,899.05	848,658	4,462.95	292,014	556,644	4,722.25	269,163	579,495	4,897.88	251,419	597,239
200,000	2,973.39	870,420	4,577.40	299,503	570,917	4,843.34	276,065	594,355	5,023.48	257,867	612,553

GROWING EQUITY MORTGAGES

AMOUNT OF LOAN	30 YEARS		1% PMT INCR/YR 205.545 PAYMENTS			2% PMT INCR/YR 169.194 PAYMENTS			3% PMT INCR/YR 148.795 PAYMENTS		
	MONTHLY PAYMENT	TOTAL INTRST	LAST YR MON PMT	TOTAL INTRST	INTRST SAVED	LAST YR MON PMT	TOTAL INTRST	INTRST SAVED	LAST YR MON PMT	TOTAL INTRST	INTRST SAVED
$ 50	0.76	224	0.90	119	105	1.00	97	127	1.08	85	139
100	1.51	444	1.79	237	207	1.99	192	252	2.15	167	277
200	3.02	887	3.58	473	414	3.98	384	503	4.31	335	552
300	4.53	1,331	5.36	710	621	5.98	575	756	6.46	502	829
400	6.03	1,771	7.14	945	826	7.96	765	1,006	8.60	668	1,103
500	7.54	2,214	8.93	1,181	1,033	9.95	957	1,257	10.75	836	1,378
600	9.05	2,658	10.72	1,418	1,240	11.94	1,149	1,509	12.90	1,003	1,655
700	10.55	3,098	12.49	1,653	1,445	13.92	1,339	1,759	15.04	1,169	1,929
800	12.06	3,542	14.28	1,889	1,653	15.91	1,531	2,011	17.19	1,336	2,206
900	13.57	3,985	16.07	2,126	1,859	17.91	1,723	2,262	19.35	1,504	2,481
1,000	15.08	4,429	17.86	2,363	2,066	19.90	1,914	2,515	21.50	1,671	2,758
2,000	30.15	8,854	35.71	4,723	4,131	39.78	3,827	5,027	42.99	3,341	5,513
3,000	45.22	13,279	53.55	7,084	6,195	59.67	5,739	7,540	64.47	5,010	8,269
4,000	60.29	17,704	71.40	9,444	8,260	79.55	7,652	10,052	85.96	6,680	11,024
5,000	75.36	22,130	89.25	11,805	10,325	99.44	9,564	12,566	107.45	8,349	13,781
6,000	90.43	26,555	107.10	14,165	12,390	119.32	11,477	15,078	128.93	10,019	16,536
7,000	105.50	30,980	124.94	16,526	14,454	139.21	13,389	17,591	150.42	11,688	19,292
8,000	120.57	35,405	142.79	18,887	16,518	159.09	15,302	20,103	171.90	13,358	22,047
9,000	135.64	39,830	160.64	21,247	18,583	178.97	17,214	22,616	193.39	15,027	24,803
10,000	150.71	44,256	178.49	23,608	20,648	198.86	19,127	25,129	214.88	16,697	27,559
11,000	165.78	48,681	196.33	25,968	22,713	218.74	21,039	27,642	236.36	18,366	30,315
12,000	180.86	53,110	214.19	28,331	24,779	238.64	22,953	30,157	257.86	20,038	33,072
13,000	195.93	57,535	232.04	30,691	26,844	258.53	24,866	32,669	279.35	21,707	35,828
14,000	211.00	61,960	249.89	33,052	28,908	278.41	26,778	35,182	300.84	23,377	38,583
15,000	226.07	66,385	267.74	35,412	30,973	298.29	28,691	37,694	322.32	25,046	41,339
16,000	241.14	70,810	285.58	37,773	33,037	318.18	30,603	40,207	343.81	26,716	44,094
17,000	256.21	75,236	303.43	40,134	35,102	338.06	32,516	42,720	365.29	28,385	46,851
18,000	271.28	79,661	321.28	42,494	37,167	357.95	34,428	45,233	386.78	30,055	49,606
19,000	286.35	84,086	339.13	44,855	39,231	377.83	36,341	47,745	408.27	31,724	52,362
20,000	301.42	88,511	356.97	47,215	41,296	397.72	38,253	50,258	429.75	33,394	55,117
21,000	316.49	92,936	374.82	49,576	43,360	417.60	40,166	52,770	451.24	35,063	57,873
22,000	331.56	97,362	392.67	51,936	45,426	437.49	42,078	55,284	472.73	36,733	60,629
23,000	346.63	101,787	410.52	54,297	47,490	457.37	43,991	57,796	494.21	38,402	63,385
24,000	361.71	106,216	428.37	56,660	49,556	477.27	45,906	60,311	515.71	40,074	66,142
25,000	376.78	110,641	446.22	59,020	51,621	497.15	47,818	62,823	537.20	41,743	68,898
26,000	391.85	115,066	464.07	61,381	53,685	517.04	49,730	65,336	558.68	43,413	71,653
27,000	406.92	119,491	481.92	63,741	55,750	536.92	51,642	67,849	580.17	45,082	74,409
28,000	421.99	123,916	499.76	66,102	57,814	556.81	53,555	70,361	601.66	46,752	77,164
29,000	437.06	128,342	517.61	68,462	59,880	576.69	55,467	72,875	623.14	48,421	79,921
30,000	452.13	132,767	535.46	70,823	61,944	596.58	57,380	75,387	644.63	50,091	82,676
32,500	489.81	143,832	580.08	76,725	67,107	646.29	62,162	81,670	698.35	54,265	89,567
35,000	527.48	154,893	624.70	82,625	72,268	696.00	66,942	87,951	752.06	58,438	96,455
40,000	602.84	177,022	713.95	94,430	82,592	795.43	76,506	100,516	859.51	66,788	110,234
45,000	678.19	199,148	803.18	106,233	92,915	894.86	86,069	113,079	966.94	75,135	124,013
50,000	753.55	221,278	892.43	118,038	103,240	994.29	95,633	125,645	1,074.38	83,485	137,793
55,000	828.90	243,404	981.67	129,841	113,563	1,093.72	105,195	138,209	1,181.81	91,832	151,572
60,000	904.26	265,534	1,070.92	141,646	123,888	1,193.15	114,760	150,774	1,289.26	100,181	165,353
65,000	979.61	287,660	1,160.16	153,448	134,212	1,292.57	124,322	163,338	1,396.69	108,529	179,131
70,000	1,054.96	309,786	1,249.39	165,251	144,535	1,392.00	133,884	175,902	1,504.12	116,877	192,909
75,000	1,130.32	331,915	1,338.64	177,056	154,859	1,491.43	143,449	188,466	1,611.57	125,226	206,689
80,000	1,205.67	354,041	1,427.88	188,858	165,183	1,590.86	153,011	201,030	1,719.00	133,573	220,468
85,000	1,281.03	376,171	1,517.13	200,663	175,508	1,690.29	162,575	213,596	1,826.43	141,923	234,248
90,000	1,356.38	398,297	1,606.37	212,466	185,831	1,789.71	172,138	226,159	1,933.87	150,270	248,027
95,000	1,431.74	420,426	1,695.62	224,271	196,155	1,889.15	181,702	238,724	2,041.32	158,620	261,806
100,000	1,507.09	442,552	1,784.85	236,074	206,478	1,988.57	191,264	251,288	2,148.75	166,967	275,585
105,000	1,582.44	464,678	1,874.09	247,876	216,802	2,088.00	200,827	263,851	2,256.18	175,315	289,363
110,000	1,657.80	486,808	1,963.34	259,681	227,127	2,187.43	210,391	276,417	2,363.63	183,664	303,144
115,000	1,733.15	508,934	2,052.58	271,484	237,450	2,286.85	219,953	288,981	2,471.06	192,012	316,922
120,000	1,808.51	531,064	2,141.83	283,289	247,775	2,386.29	229,518	301,546	2,578.50	200,361	330,703
125,000	1,883.86	553,190	2,231.06	295,091	258,099	2,485.71	239,080	314,110	2,685.93	208,709	344,481
130,000	1,959.22	575,319	2,320.31	306,896	268,423	2,585.15	248,644	326,675	2,793.38	217,058	358,261
135,000	2,034.57	597,445	2,409.55	318,699	278,746	2,684.57	258,207	339,238	2,900.81	225,406	372,039
140,000	2,109.92	619,571	2,498.79	330,502	289,069	2,783.99	267,769	351,802	3,008.24	233,753	385,818
145,000	2,185.28	641,701	2,588.04	342,307	299,394	2,883.43	277,333	364,368	3,115.69	242,102	399,599
150,000	2,260.63	663,827	2,677.27	354,109	309,718	2,982.85	286,895	376,932	3,223.12	250,450	413,377
155,000	2,335.99	685,956	2,766.52	365,914	320,042	3,082.29	296,460	389,496	3,330.56	258,799	427,157
160,000	2,411.34	708,082	2,855.76	377,717	330,365	3,181.71	306,022	402,060	3,437.99	267,147	440,935
165,000	2,486.70	730,212	2,945.01	389,522	340,690	3,281.15	315,586	414,626	3,545.44	275,496	454,716
170,000	2,562.05	752,338	3,034.25	401,325	351,013	3,380.57	325,149	427,189	3,652.87	283,844	468,494
175,000	2,637.40	774,464	3,123.48	413,127	361,337	3,479.99	334,711	439,753	3,760.30	292,191	482,273
180,000	2,712.76	796,594	3,212.73	424,932	371,662	3,579.43	344,275	452,319	3,867.75	300,541	496,053
185,000	2,788.11	818,720	3,301.97	436,735	381,985	3,678.85	353,838	464,882	3,975.18	308,888	509,832
190,000	2,863.47	840,849	3,391.22	448,540	392,309	3,778.29	363,402	477,449	4,082.62	317,238	523,611
195,000	2,938.82	862,975	3,480.46	460,342	402,633	3,877.71	372,964	490,011	4,190.05	325,585	537,390
200,000	3,014.18	885,105	3,569.71	472,147	412,958	3,977.15	382,529	502,576	4,297.50	333,934	551,171

GROWING EQUITY MORTGAGES 18.00%

AMOUNT OF LOAN	30 YEARS		4% PMT INCR/YR 134.993 PAYMENTS			5% PMT INCR/YR 124.719 PAYMENTS			6% PMT INCR/YR 116.672 PAYMENTS		
	MONTHLY PAYMENT	TOTAL INTRST	LAST YR MON PMT	TOTAL INTRST	INTRST SAVED	LAST YR MON PMT	TOTAL INTRST	INTRST SAVED	LAST YR MON PMT	TOTAL INTRST	INTRST SAVED
$ 50	0.76	224	1.17	76	148	1.24	71	153	1.28	66	158
100	1.51	444	2.32	151	293	2.46	140	304	2.55	130	314
200	3.02	887	4.65	303	584	4.92	279	608	5.10	261	626
300	4.53	1,331	6.97	454	877	7.38	419	912	7.65	391	940
400	6.03	1,771	9.28	604	1,167	9.82	556	1,215	10.19	520	1,251
500	7.54	2,214	11.61	755	1,459	12.28	696	1,518	12.74	650	1,564
600	9.05	2,658	13.93	906	1,752	14.74	836	1,822	15.29	781	1,877
700	10.55	3,098	16.24	1,056	2,042	17.18	973	2,125	17.82	909	2,189
800	12.06	3,542	18.57	1,207	2,335	19.64	1,113	2,429	20.38	1,040	2,502
900	13.57	3,985	20.89	1,359	2,626	22.10	1,252	2,733	22.93	1,170	2,815
1,000	15.08	4,429	23.21	1,510	2,919	24.56	1,392	3,037	25.48	1,300	3,129
2,000	30.15	8,854	46.41	3,018	5,836	49.11	2,782	6,072	50.94	2,599	6,255
3,000	45.22	13,279	69.61	4,527	8,752	73.66	4,173	9,106	76.40	3,898	9,381
4,000	60.29	17,704	92.81	6,035	11,669	98.21	5,563	12,141	101.86	5,197	12,507
5,000	75.36	22,130	116.01	7,543	14,587	122.75	6,954	15,176	127.32	6,496	15,634
6,000	90.43	26,555	139.21	9,052	17,503	147.30	8,344	18,211	152.78	7,795	18,760
7,000	105.50	30,980	162.41	10,560	20,420	171.85	9,735	21,245	178.24	9,094	21,886
8,000	120.57	35,405	185.61	12,068	23,337	196.40	11,125	24,280	203.70	10,393	25,012
9,000	135.64	39,830	208.81	13,576	26,254	220.94	12,515	27,315	229.16	11,691	28,139
10,000	150.71	44,256	232.01	15,085	29,171	245.49	13,906	30,350	254.62	12,990	31,266
11,000	165.78	48,681	255.21	16,593	32,088	270.04	15,296	33,385	280.08	14,289	34,392
12,000	180.86	53,110	278.43	18,103	35,007	294.60	16,688	36,422	305.56	15,590	37,520
13,000	195.93	57,535	301.63	19,611	37,924	319.15	18,079	39,456	331.02	16,889	40,646
14,000	211.00	61,960	324.82	21,120	40,840	343.70	19,469	42,491	356.48	18,187	43,773
15,000	226.07	66,385	348.02	22,628	43,757	368.24	20,860	45,525	381.94	19,486	46,899
16,000	241.14	70,810	371.22	24,136	46,674	392.79	22,250	48,560	407.40	20,785	50,025
17,000	256.21	75,236	394.42	25,645	49,591	417.34	23,640	51,596	432.86	22,084	53,152
18,000	271.28	79,661	417.62	27,153	52,508	441.89	25,031	54,630	458.32	23,383	56,278
19,000	286.35	84,086	440.82	28,661	55,425	466.43	26,421	57,665	483.78	24,682	59,404
20,000	301.42	88,511	464.02	30,169	58,342	490.98	27,812	60,699	509.24	25,981	62,530
21,000	316.49	92,936	487.22	31,678	61,258	515.53	29,202	63,734	534.70	27,280	65,656
22,000	331.56	97,362	510.42	33,186	64,176	540.08	30,593	66,769	560.16	28,578	68,784
23,000	346.63	101,787	533.62	34,694	67,093	564.62	31,983	69,804	585.62	29,877	71,910
24,000	361.71	106,216	556.84	36,204	70,012	589.19	33,375	72,841	611.10	31,178	75,038
25,000	376.78	110,641	580.04	37,713	72,928	613.73	34,765	75,876	636.56	32,477	78,164
26,000	391.85	115,066	603.24	39,221	75,845	638.28	36,156	78,910	662.02	33,776	81,290
27,000	406.92	119,491	626.43	40,729	78,762	662.83	37,546	81,945	687.48	35,074	84,417
28,000	421.99	123,916	649.63	42,238	81,678	687.38	38,937	84,979	712.94	36,373	87,543
29,000	437.06	128,342	672.83	43,746	84,596	711.92	40,327	88,015	738.40	37,672	90,670
30,000	452.13	132,767	696.03	45,254	87,513	736.47	41,718	91,049	763.86	38,971	93,796
32,500	489.81	143,832	754.04	49,026	94,806	797.85	45,194	98,638	827.52	42,219	101,613
35,000	527.48	154,893	812.03	52,796	102,097	859.21	48,670	106,223	891.17	45,465	109,428
40,000	602.84	177,022	928.04	60,339	116,683	981.96	55,623	121,399	1,018.49	51,961	125,061
45,000	678.19	199,148	1,044.04	67,881	131,267	1,104.70	62,575	136,573	1,145.79	58,456	140,692
50,000	753.55	221,278	1,160.06	75,424	145,854	1,227.45	69,529	151,749	1,273.11	64,952	156,326
55,000	828.90	243,404	1,276.05	82,965	160,439	1,350.19	76,481	166,923	1,400.41	71,446	171,958
60,000	904.26	265,534	1,392.07	90,508	175,026	1,472.94	83,435	182,099	1,527.73	77,942	187,592
65,000	979.61	287,660	1,508.06	98,050	189,610	1,595.68	90,387	197,273	1,655.03	84,437	203,223
70,000	1,054.96	309,786	1,624.06	105,592	204,194	1,718.42	97,339	212,447	1,782.33	90,931	218,855
75,000	1,130.32	331,915	1,740.08	113,135	218,780	1,841.17	104,293	227,622	1,909.65	97,427	234,488
80,000	1,205.67	354,041	1,856.07	120,676	233,365	1,963.91	111,245	242,796	2,036.95	103,921	250,120
85,000	1,281.03	376,171	1,972.09	128,220	247,951	2,086.66	118,199	257,972	2,164.27	110,417	265,754
90,000	1,356.38	398,297	2,088.08	135,761	262,536	2,209.40	125,151	273,146	2,291.58	116,912	281,385
95,000	1,431.74	420,426	2,204.10	143,304	277,122	2,332.15	132,105	288,321	2,418.89	123,408	297,018
100,000	1,507.09	442,552	2,320.10	150,846	291,706	2,454.89	139,057	303,495	2,546.20	129,902	312,650
105,000	1,582.44	464,678	2,436.09	158,387	306,291	2,577.63	146,009	318,669	2,673.50	136,396	328,282
110,000	1,657.80	486,808	2,552.11	165,931	320,877	2,700.38	152,963	333,845	2,800.82	142,892	343,916
115,000	1,733.15	508,934	2,668.10	173,472	335,462	2,823.12	159,915	349,019	2,928.12	149,387	359,547
120,000	1,808.51	531,064	2,784.12	181,015	350,049	2,945.87	166,869	364,195	3,055.44	155,883	375,181
125,000	1,883.86	553,190	2,900.12	188,557	364,633	3,068.61	173,821	379,369	3,182.74	162,377	390,813
130,000	1,959.22	575,319	3,016.13	196,100	379,219	3,191.36	180,774	394,545	3,310.06	168,873	406,446
135,000	2,034.57	597,445	3,132.13	203,642	393,803	3,314.10	187,726	409,719	3,437.36	175,367	422,078
140,000	2,109.92	619,571	3,248.12	211,183	408,388	3,436.84	194,679	424,892	3,564.67	181,862	437,709
145,000	2,185.28	641,701	3,364.14	218,726	422,975	3,559.59	201,632	440,069	3,691.98	188,358	453,343
150,000	2,260.63	663,827	3,480.14	226,268	437,559	3,682.33	208,584	455,243	3,819.29	194,852	468,975
155,000	2,335.99	685,956	3,596.15	233,811	452,145	3,805.08	215,538	470,418	3,946.61	201,348	484,608
160,000	2,411.34	708,082	3,712.15	241,353	466,729	3,927.82	222,490	485,592	4,073.91	207,843	500,239
165,000	2,486.70	730,212	3,828.16	248,896	481,316	4,050.57	229,444	500,768	4,201.23	214,339	515,873
170,000	2,562.05	752,338	3,944.16	256,437	495,901	4,173.31	236,396	515,942	4,328.53	220,833	531,505
175,000	2,637.40	774,464	4,060.16	263,979	510,485	4,296.05	243,348	531,116	4,455.83	227,327	547,137
180,000	2,712.76	796,594	4,176.17	271,522	525,072	4,418.80	250,302	546,292	4,583.15	233,823	562,771
185,000	2,788.11	818,720	4,292.17	279,064	539,656	4,541.54	257,254	561,466	4,710.45	240,318	578,402
190,000	2,863.47	840,849	4,408.18	286,607	554,242	4,664.29	264,208	576,641	4,837.77	246,814	594,035
195,000	2,938.82	862,975	4,524.18	294,148	568,827	4,787.03	271,160	591,815	4,965.07	253,308	609,667
200,000	3,014.18	885,105	4,640.19	301,692	583,413	4,909.78	278,114	606,991	5,092.39	259,804	625,301

189

AUGMENTED PAYMENT MORTGAGES

Generally, augmented payment mortgages (APMs) call for a one-time percentage increase in the mortgage payment over the widely used 30-year mortgage payment. The larger payment results in the shortening of your mortgage term. There are a variety of APM plans available to borrowers. We have included six of the most popular ones in this table: APMs with one-time increases of 2%, 4%, 6%, 8%, 10%, and 12%.

Each interest rate within this table appears on two facing pages. On each page, we show four mortgage plans; the benchmark 30-year mortgage and three of the APM plans. On the left-facing page, we show the benchmark 30-year mortgage along with the 2%, 4%, and 6% APM plans. On the right-facing page, we repeat the 30-year mortgage along with the 8%, 10%, and 12% APM plans. The percentage increase at the top of each APM's group of columns identifies the APM plan. Directly below each payment percentage increase, we show the number of payments required to pay off the APM. The number of payments includes a fractional last payment. The very last payment required to pay off the APM is somewhat less than the other monthly payments.

Here is how to use this table. First, find the page with the interest rate and the APM plan for the desired loan. Look down the first column to find your loan amount. Then read across the page and find the columns which represent the 30-year plan and the desired alternative APM plan. The first group of columns represent the 30-year loan plan. Within this group, you find both the monthly payment and the total interest paid through the life of the loan. Each APM plan's group of columns shows the monthly payment, the total interest paid, and the all-important third column, the interest saved. This third column is the difference between the interest paid on the 30-year loan and the desired APM plan loan.

EXAMPLE

How much interest will you save on a $68,300 mortgage at 12.25% interest if you choose an APM plan based upon a one-time 2% increase in the 30-year mortgage payment? How much is the difference in the payments between the two plans? How long will it take to pay off this APM?

First, find the 12.25% mortgage plans on pages 236 and 237. Note that the 2% APM is displayed as the first of the APM plans on page 236. Move down the loan amount column until you find a row entry for $68,300. Since there is no row entry for exactly this loan amount, you must combine the three entries from $300, $8,000, and $60,000 to get the interest saved. The interest-saved entries for the 2% APMs are $153, $4,057, and $30,433; and their sum is $34,643.

The corresponding payment entries for the 30-year mortgage are $3.15, $83.84, and $628.74; and their sum is $715.73. The corresponding payment entries for the 2% APM are $3.21, $85.52, and $641.31; and their sum is $730.04. At the top of the page, under the 2% APM plan, you find that 305.488 payments are needed to pay off this mortgage. Multipy the fraction 0.488 times $730.04, to get $356.26, the very last payment. Therefore you will make 305 payments of $730.04 and one final payment of $356.26 on your alternative APM plan. The difference in the monthly payment between the two mortgage plans is $730.04 less $715.73, or $14.31. As a result of this difference, the 2% APM loan plan pays off in 25½ years.

7.00% AUGMENTED PAYMENT MORTGAGES

AMOUNT OF LOAN	30 YEARS		2% PMT INCREASE 337.543 PAYMENTS			4% PMT INCREASE 318.405 PAYMENTS			6% PMT INCREASE 301.805 PAYMENTS		
	MONTHLY PAYMENT	TOTAL INTRST	MONTHLY PAYMENT	TOTAL INTRST	INTRST SAVED	MONTHLY PAYMENT	TOTAL INTRST	INTRST SAVED	MONTHLY PAYMENT	TOTAL INTRST	INTRST SAVED
$ 50	0.34	72	0.35	68	4	0.35	61	11	0.36	59	13
100	0.67	141	0.68	130	11	0.70	123	18	0.71	114	27
200	1.34	282	1.37	262	20	1.39	243	39	1.42	229	53
300	2.00	420	2.04	389	31	2.08	362	58	2.12	340	80
400	2.67	561	2.72	518	43	2.78	485	76	2.83	454	107
500	3.33	699	3.40	648	51	3.46	602	97	3.53	565	134
600	4.00	840	4.08	777	63	4.16	725	115	4.24	680	160
700	4.66	978	4.75	903	75	4.85	844	134	4.94	791	187
800	5.33	1,119	5.44	1,036	83	5.54	964	155	5.65	905	214
900	5.99	1,256	6.11	1,162	94	6.23	1,084	172	6.35	1,016	240
1,000	6.66	1,398	6.79	1,292	106	6.93	1,207	191	7.06	1,131	267
2,000	13.31	2,792	13.58	2,584	208	13.84	2,407	385	14.11	2,258	534
3,000	19.96	4,186	20.36	3,872	314	20.76	3,610	576	21.16	3,386	800
4,000	26.62	5,583	27.15	5,164	419	27.68	4,813	770	28.22	4,517	1,066
5,000	33.27	6,977	33.94	6,456	521	34.60	6,017	960	35.27	5,645	1,332
6,000	39.92	8,371	40.72	7,745	626	41.52	7,220	1,151	42.32	6,772	1,599
7,000	46.58	9,769	47.51	9,037	732	48.44	8,424	1,345	49.37	7,900	1,869
8,000	53.23	11,163	54.29	10,325	838	55.36	9,627	1,536	56.42	9,028	2,135
9,000	59.88	12,557	61.08	11,617	940	62.28	10,830	1,727	63.47	10,156	2,401
10,000	66.54	13,954	67.87	12,909	1,045	69.20	12,034	1,920	70.53	11,286	2,668
11,000	73.19	15,348	74.65	14,198	1,150	76.12	13,237	2,111	77.58	12,414	2,934
12,000	79.84	16,742	81.44	15,490	1,252	83.03	14,437	2,305	84.63	13,542	3,200
13,000	86.49	18,136	88.22	16,778	1,358	89.95	15,641	2,495	91.68	14,669	3,467
14,000	93.15	19,534	95.01	18,070	1,464	96.88	16,847	2,687	98.74	15,800	3,734
15,000	99.80	20,928	101.80	19,362	1,566	103.79	18,047	2,881	105.79	16,928	4,000
16,000	106.45	22,322	108.58	20,650	1,672	110.71	19,251	3,071	112.84	18,056	4,266
17,000	113.11	23,720	115.37	21,942	1,778	117.63	20,454	3,266	119.90	19,186	4,534
18,000	119.76	25,114	122.16	23,234	1,880	124.55	21,657	3,457	126.95	20,314	4,800
19,000	126.41	26,508	128.94	24,523	1,985	131.47	22,861	3,647	133.99	21,439	5,069
20,000	133.07	27,905	135.73	25,815	2,090	138.39	24,064	3,841	141.05	22,570	5,335
21,000	139.72	29,299	142.51	27,103	2,196	145.31	25,267	4,032	148.10	23,697	5,602
22,000	146.37	30,693	149.30	28,395	2,298	152.22	26,468	4,225	155.15	24,825	5,868
23,000	153.02	32,087	156.08	29,684	2,403	159.14	27,671	4,416	162.20	25,953	6,134
24,000	159.68	33,485	162.87	30,976	2,509	166.07	28,878	4,607	169.26	27,084	6,401
25,000	166.33	34,879	169.66	32,268	2,611	172.98	30,078	4,801	176.31	28,211	6,668
26,000	172.98	36,273	176.44	33,556	2,717	179.90	31,281	4,992	183.36	29,339	6,934
27,000	179.64	37,670	183.23	34,848	2,822	186.83	32,488	5,182	190.42	30,470	7,200
28,000	186.29	39,064	190.02	36,140	2,924	193.74	33,688	5,376	197.47	31,597	7,467
29,000	192.94	40,458	196.80	37,428	3,030	200.66	34,891	5,567	204.52	32,725	7,733
30,000	199.60	41,856	203.59	38,720	3,136	207.58	36,095	5,761	211.58	33,856	8,000
32,500	216.23	45,343	220.55	41,945	3,398	224.88	39,103	6,240	229.20	36,674	8,669
35,000	232.86	48,830	237.52	45,173	3,657	242.17	42,108	6,722	246.83	39,495	9,335
40,000	266.13	55,807	271.45	51,626	4,181	276.78	48,128	7,679	282.10	45,139	10,668
45,000	299.39	62,780	305.38	58,079	4,701	311.37	54,142	8,638	317.35	50,778	12,002
50,000	332.66	69,758	339.31	64,532	5,226	345.97	60,159	9,599	352.62	56,422	13,336
55,000	365.92	76,731	373.24	70,985	5,746	380.56	66,172	10,559	387.88	62,064	14,667
60,000	399.19	83,708	407.17	77,437	6,271	415.16	72,189	11,519	423.14	67,706	16,002
65,000	432.45	90,682	441.10	83,890	6,792	449.75	78,203	12,479	458.40	73,347	17,335
70,000	465.72	97,659	475.03	90,343	7,316	484.35	84,219	13,440	493.66	78,989	18,670
75,000	498.98	104,633	508.96	96,796	7,837	518.94	90,233	14,400	528.92	84,631	20,002
80,000	532.25	111,610	542.90	103,252	8,358	553.54	96,250	15,360	564.19	90,275	21,335
85,000	565.51	118,584	576.82	109,702	8,882	588.13	102,264	16,320	599.44	95,914	22,670
90,000	598.78	125,561	610.76	116,158	9,403	622.73	108,280	17,281	634.71	101,559	24,002
95,000	632.04	132,534	644.68	122,607	9,927	657.32	114,294	18,240	669.96	107,197	25,337
100,000	665.31	139,512	678.62	129,063	10,449	691.92	120,311	19,201	705.23	112,842	26,670
105,000	698.57	146,485	712.54	135,513	10,972	726.51	126,324	20,161	740.48	118,481	28,004
110,000	731.84	153,462	746.48	141,969	11,493	761.11	132,341	21,121	775.75	124,125	29,337
115,000	765.10	160,436	780.40	148,419	12,017	795.70	138,355	22,081	811.01	129,767	30,669
120,000	798.37	167,413	814.34	154,875	12,538	830.30	144,372	23,041	846.27	135,409	32,004
125,000	831.63	174,387	848.26	161,324	13,063	864.90	150,388	23,999	881.53	141,050	33,337
130,000	864.90	181,364	882.20	167,780	13,584	899.50	156,405	24,959	916.79	146,692	34,672
135,000	898.16	188,338	916.12	174,230	14,108	934.09	162,419	25,919	952.05	152,333	36,005
140,000	931.43	195,315	950.06	180,686	14,629	968.69	168,436	26,879	987.32	157,978	37,337
145,000	964.69	202,288	983.98	187,136	15,152	1,003.28	174,449	27,839	1,022.57	163,617	38,671
150,000	997.96	209,266	1,017.92	193,592	15,674	1,037.88	180,466	28,800	1,057.84	169,261	40,005
155,000	1,031.22	216,239	1,051.84	200,041	16,198	1,072.47	186,480	29,759	1,093.09	174,900	41,339
160,000	1,064.49	223,216	1,085.78	206,497	16,719	1,107.07	192,497	30,719	1,128.36	180,545	42,671
165,000	1,097.75	230,190	1,119.71	212,950	17,240	1,141.66	198,510	31,680	1,163.62	186,186	44,004
170,000	1,131.02	237,167	1,153.64	219,403	17,764	1,176.26	204,527	32,640	1,198.88	191,828	45,339
175,000	1,164.28	244,141	1,187.57	225,856	18,285	1,210.85	210,541	33,600	1,234.14	197,470	46,671
180,000	1,197.55	251,118	1,221.50	232,309	18,809	1,245.45	216,558	34,560	1,269.40	203,111	48,007
185,000	1,230.81	258,092	1,255.43	238,762	19,330	1,280.04	222,571	35,521	1,304.66	208,753	49,339
190,000	1,264.08	265,069	1,289.36	245,214	19,855	1,314.64	228,588	36,481	1,339.92	214,395	50,674
195,000	1,297.34	272,042	1,323.29	251,667	20,375	1,349.23	234,602	37,440	1,375.18	220,036	52,006
200,000	1,330.61	279,020	1,357.22	258,120	20,900	1,383.83	240,618	38,402	1,410.45	225,681	53,339

194

AUGMENTED PAYMENT MORTGAGES 7.00%

AMOUNT OF LOAN	30 YEARS MONTHLY PAYMENT	30 YEARS TOTAL INTRST	8% PMT INCREASE 287.206 PAYMENTS MONTHLY PAYMENT	TOTAL INTRST	INTRST SAVED	10% PMT INCREASE 274.221 PAYMENTS MONTHLY PAYMENT	TOTAL INTRST	INTRST SAVED	12% PMT INCREASE 262.565 PAYMENTS MONTHLY PAYMENT	TOTAL INTRST	INTRST SAVED
$ 50	0.34	72	0.37	56	16	0.37	51	21	0.38	50	22
100	0.67	141	0.72	107	34	0.74	103	38	0.75	97	44
200	1.34	282	1.45	216	66	1.47	203	79	1.50	194	88
300	2.00	420	2.16	320	100	2.20	303	117	2.24	288	132
400	2.67	561	2.88	427	134	2.94	406	155	2.99	385	176
500	3.33	699	3.60	534	165	3.66	504	195	3.73	479	220
600	4.00	840	4.32	641	199	4.40	607	233	4.48	576	264
700	4.66	978	5.03	745	233	5.13	707	271	5.22	671	307
800	5.33	1,119	5.76	854	265	5.86	807	312	5.97	768	351
900	5.99	1,256	6.47	958	298	6.59	907	349	6.71	862	394
1,000	6.66	1,398	7.19	1,065	333	7.33	1,010	388	7.46	959	439
2,000	13.31	2,792	14.37	2,127	665	14.64	2,015	777	14.91	1,915	877
3,000	19.96	4,186	21.56	3,192	994	21.96	3,022	1,164	22.36	2,871	1,315
4,000	26.62	5,583	28.75	4,257	1,326	29.28	4,029	1,554	29.81	3,827	1,756
5,000	33.27	6,977	35.93	5,319	1,658	36.60	5,036	1,941	37.26	4,783	2,194
6,000	39.92	8,371	43.11	6,381	1,990	43.91	6,041	2,330	44.71	5,739	2,632
7,000	46.58	9,769	50.31	7,449	2,320	51.24	7,051	2,718	52.17	6,698	3,071
8,000	53.23	11,163	57.49	8,511	2,652	58.55	8,056	3,107	59.62	7,654	3,509
9,000	59.88	12,557	64.67	9,574	2,983	65.87	9,063	3,494	67.07	8,610	3,947
10,000	66.54	13,954	71.86	10,639	3,315	73.19	10,070	3,884	74.52	9,566	4,388
11,000	73.19	15,348	79.05	11,704	3,644	80.51	11,078	4,270	81.97	10,522	4,826
12,000	79.84	16,742	86.23	12,766	3,976	87.82	12,082	4,660	89.42	11,479	5,263
13,000	86.49	18,136	93.41	13,828	4,308	95.14	13,089	5,047	96.87	12,435	5,701
14,000	93.15	19,534	100.60	14,893	4,641	102.47	14,099	5,435	104.33	13,393	6,141
15,000	99.80	20,928	107.78	15,955	4,973	109.78	15,104	5,824	111.78	14,350	6,578
16,000	106.45	22,322	114.97	17,020	5,302	117.10	16,111	6,211	119.22	15,303	7,019
17,000	113.11	23,720	122.16	18,085	5,635	124.42	17,119	6,601	126.68	16,262	7,458
18,000	119.76	25,114	129.34	19,147	5,967	131.74	18,126	6,988	134.13	17,218	7,896
19,000	126.41	26,508	136.52	20,209	6,299	139.05	19,130	7,378	141.58	18,174	8,334
20,000	133.07	27,905	143.72	21,277	6,628	146.38	20,140	7,765	149.04	19,133	8,772
21,000	139.72	29,299	150.90	22,339	6,960	153.69	21,145	8,154	156.49	20,089	9,210
22,000	146.37	30,693	158.08	23,402	7,291	161.01	22,152	8,541	163.93	21,042	9,651
23,000	153.02	32,087	165.26	24,464	7,623	168.32	23,157	8,930	171.38	21,998	10,089
24,000	159.68	33,485	172.45	25,529	7,956	175.65	24,167	9,318	178.84	22,957	10,528
25,000	166.33	34,879	179.64	26,594	8,285	182.96	25,171	9,708	186.29	23,913	10,966
26,000	172.98	36,273	186.82	27,656	8,617	190.28	26,179	10,094	193.74	24,869	11,404
27,000	179.64	37,670	194.01	28,721	8,949	197.60	27,186	10,484	201.20	25,828	11,842
28,000	186.29	39,064	201.19	29,783	9,281	204.92	28,193	10,871	208.64	26,782	12,282
29,000	192.94	40,458	208.38	30,848	9,610	212.23	29,198	11,260	216.09	27,738	12,720
30,000	199.60	41,856	215.57	31,913	9,943	219.56	30,208	11,648	223.55	28,696	13,160
32,500	216.23	45,343	233.53	34,571	10,772	237.85	32,723	12,620	242.18	31,088	14,255
35,000	232.86	48,830	251.49	37,229	11,601	256.15	35,242	13,588	260.80	33,477	15,353
40,000	266.13	55,807	287.42	42,549	13,258	292.74	40,275	15,532	298.07	38,263	17,544
45,000	299.39	62,780	323.34	47,865	14,915	329.33	45,309	17,471	335.32	43,043	19,737
50,000	332.66	69,758	359.27	53,184	16,574	365.93	50,346	19,412	372.58	47,826	21,932
55,000	365.92	76,731	395.19	58,501	18,230	402.51	55,377	21,354	409.83	52,607	24,124
60,000	399.19	83,708	431.13	63,823	19,885	439.11	60,413	23,295	447.09	57,390	26,318
65,000	432.45	90,682	467.05	69,140	21,542	475.70	65,447	25,235	484.34	62,171	28,511
70,000	465.72	97,659	502.98	74,459	23,200	512.29	70,481	27,178	521.61	66,957	30,702
75,000	498.98	104,633	538.90	79,775	24,858	548.88	75,514	29,119	558.86	71,737	32,896
80,000	532.25	111,610	574.83	85,095	26,515	585.48	80,551	31,059	596.12	76,520	35,090
85,000	565.51	118,584	610.75	90,411	28,173	622.06	85,582	33,002	633.37	81,301	37,283
90,000	598.78	125,561	646.68	95,730	29,831	658.66	90,618	34,943	670.63	86,084	39,477
95,000	632.04	132,534	682.60	101,047	31,487	695.24	95,649	36,885	707.88	90,865	41,669
100,000	665.31	139,512	718.53	106,366	33,146	731.84	100,686	38,826	745.15	95,650	43,862
105,000	698.57	146,485	754.46	111,685	34,800	768.43	105,720	40,765	782.40	100,431	46,054
110,000	731.84	153,462	790.39	117,005	36,457	805.02	110,753	42,709	819.66	105,214	48,248
115,000	765.10	160,436	826.31	122,321	38,115	841.61	115,787	44,649	856.91	109,995	50,441
120,000	798.37	167,413	862.24	127,641	39,772	878.21	120,824	46,589	894.17	114,778	52,635
125,000	831.63	174,387	898.16	132,957	41,430	914.79	125,855	48,532	931.43	119,561	54,826
130,000	864.90	181,364	934.09	138,276	43,088	951.39	130,891	50,473	968.69	124,344	57,020
135,000	898.16	188,338	970.01	143,593	44,745	987.98	135,925	52,413	1,005.94	129,125	59,213
140,000	931.43	195,315	1,005.94	148,912	46,403	1,024.57	140,959	54,356	1,043.20	133,908	61,407
145,000	964.69	202,288	1,041.87	154,231	48,057	1,061.16	145,993	56,296	1,080.45	138,688	63,600
150,000	997.96	209,266	1,077.80	159,551	49,715	1,097.76	151,029	58,237	1,117.72	143,474	65,792
155,000	1,031.22	216,239	1,113.72	164,867	51,372	1,134.34	156,060	60,179	1,154.97	148,255	67,984
160,000	1,064.49	223,216	1,149.65	170,186	53,030	1,170.94	161,096	62,120	1,192.23	153,038	70,178
165,000	1,097.75	230,190	1,185.57	175,503	54,687	1,207.53	166,130	64,060	1,229.48	157,818	72,372
170,000	1,131.02	237,167	1,221.50	180,822	56,345	1,244.12	171,164	66,003	1,266.74	162,602	74,565
175,000	1,164.28	244,141	1,257.42	186,139	58,002	1,280.71	176,198	67,943	1,303.99	167,382	76,759
180,000	1,197.55	251,118	1,293.35	191,458	59,660	1,317.31	181,234	69,884	1,341.26	172,168	78,950
185,000	1,230.81	258,092	1,329.27	196,774	61,318	1,353.89	186,261	71,827	1,378.51	176,948	81,144
190,000	1,264.08	265,069	1,365.21	202,097	62,972	1,390.49	191,302	73,767	1,415.77	181,732	83,337
195,000	1,297.34	272,042	1,401.13	207,413	64,629	1,427.07	196,333	75,709	1,453.02	186,512	85,530
200,000	1,330.61	279,020	1,437.06	212,732	66,288	1,463.67	201,369	77,651	1,490.28	191,295	87,725

195

7.25% AUGMENTED PAYMENT MORTGAGES

AMOUNT OF LOAN	30 YEARS		2% PMT INCREASE 336.530 PAYMENTS			4% PMT INCREASE 316.715 PAYMENTS			6% PMT INCREASE 299.650 PAYMENTS		
	MONTHLY PAYMENT	TOTAL INTRST	MONTHLY PAYMENT	TOTAL INTRST	INTRST SAVED	MONTHLY PAYMENT	TOTAL INTRST	INTRST SAVED	MONTHLY PAYMENT	TOTAL INTRST	INTRST SAVED
$ 50	0.35	76	0.36	71	5	0.36	64	12	0.37	61	15
100	0.69	148	0.70	136	12	0.72	128	20	0.73	119	29
200	1.37	293	1.40	271	22	1.42	250	43	1.45	234	59
300	2.05	438	2.09	403	35	2.13	375	63	2.17	350	88
400	2.73	583	2.78	536	47	2.84	499	84	2.89	466	117
500	3.42	731	3.49	674	57	3.56	628	103	3.63	588	143
600	4.10	876	4.18	807	69	4.26	749	127	4.35	703	173
700	4.78	1,021	4.88	942	79	4.97	874	147	5.07	819	202
800	5.46	1,166	5.57	1,074	92	5.68	999	167	5.79	935	231
900	6.14	1,310	6.26	1,207	103	6.39	1,124	186	6.51	1,051	259
1,000	6.83	1,459	6.97	1,346	113	7.10	1,249	210	7.24	1,169	290
2,000	13.65	2,914	13.92	2,684	230	14.20	2,497	417	14.47	2,336	578
3,000	20.47	4,369	20.88	4,027	342	21.29	3,743	626	21.70	3,502	867
4,000	27.29	5,824	27.84	5,369	455	28.38	4,988	836	28.93	4,669	1,155
5,000	34.11	7,280	34.79	6,708	572	35.47	6,234	1,046	36.16	5,835	1,445
6,000	40.94	8,738	41.76	8,053	685	42.58	7,486	1,252	43.40	7,005	1,733
7,000	47.76	10,194	48.72	9,396	798	49.67	8,731	1,463	50.63	8,171	2,023
8,000	54.58	11,649	55.67	10,735	914	56.76	9,977	1,672	57.85	9,335	2,314
9,000	61.40	13,104	62.63	12,077	1,027	63.86	11,225	1,879	65.08	10,501	2,603
10,000	68.22	14,559	69.58	13,416	1,143	70.95	12,471	2,088	72.31	11,668	2,891
11,000	75.04	16,014	76.54	14,758	1,256	78.04	13,716	2,298	79.54	12,834	3,180
12,000	81.87	17,473	83.51	16,104	1,369	85.14	14,965	2,508	86.78	14,004	3,469
13,000	88.69	18,928	90.46	17,443	1,485	92.24	16,214	2,714	94.01	15,170	3,758
14,000	95.51	20,384	97.42	18,785	1,599	99.33	17,459	2,925	101.24	16,337	4,047
15,000	102.33	21,839	104.38	20,127	1,712	106.42	18,705	3,134	108.47	17,503	4,336
16,000	109.15	23,294	111.33	21,466	1,828	113.52	19,953	3,341	115.70	18,670	4,624
17,000	115.97	24,749	118.29	22,808	1,941	120.61	21,199	3,550	122.93	19,836	4,913
18,000	122.80	26,208	125.26	24,154	2,054	127.71	22,448	3,760	130.17	21,005	5,203
19,000	129.62	27,663	132.21	25,493	2,170	134.80	23,693	3,970	137.40	22,172	5,491
20,000	136.44	29,118	139.17	26,835	2,283	141.90	24,942	4,176	144.63	23,338	5,780
21,000	143.26	30,574	146.13	28,177	2,397	148.99	26,187	4,387	151.86	24,505	6,069
22,000	150.08	32,029	153.08	29,516	2,513	156.08	27,433	4,596	159.08	25,668	6,361
23,000	156.91	33,488	160.05	30,862	2,626	163.19	28,685	4,803	166.32	26,838	6,650
24,000	163.73	34,943	167.00	32,201	2,742	170.28	29,930	5,013	173.55	28,004	6,939
25,000	170.55	36,398	173.96	33,543	2,855	177.37	31,176	5,222	180.78	29,171	7,227
26,000	177.37	37,853	180.92	34,885	2,968	184.46	32,421	5,432	188.01	30,337	7,516
27,000	184.19	39,308	187.87	36,224	3,084	191.56	33,670	5,638	195.24	31,504	7,804
28,000	191.01	40,764	194.83	37,566	3,198	198.65	34,915	5,849	202.47	32,670	8,094
29,000	197.84	42,222	201.80	38,912	3,310	205.75	36,164	6,058	209.71	33,840	8,382
30,000	204.66	43,678	208.75	40,251	3,427	212.85	37,413	6,265	216.94	35,006	8,672
32,500	221.71	47,316	226.14	43,603	3,713	230.58	40,528	6,788	235.01	37,921	9,395
35,000	238.77	50,957	243.55	46,962	3,995	248.32	43,647	7,310	253.10	40,841	10,116
40,000	272.88	58,237	278.34	53,670	4,567	283.80	49,884	8,353	289.25	46,674	11,563
45,000	306.98	65,513	313.12	60,374	5,139	319.26	56,114	9,399	325.40	52,506	13,007
50,000	341.09	72,792	347.91	67,082	5,710	354.73	62,348	10,444	361.56	58,341	14,451
55,000	375.20	80,072	382.70	73,790	6,282	390.21	68,585	11,487	397.71	64,174	15,898
60,000	409.31	87,352	417.50	80,501	6,851	425.68	74,819	12,533	433.87	70,009	17,343
65,000	443.42	94,631	452.29	87,209	7,422	461.16	81,056	13,575	470.03	75,844	18,787
70,000	477.53	101,911	487.08	93,917	7,994	496.63	87,290	14,621	506.18	81,677	20,234
75,000	511.64	109,190	521.87	100,625	8,565	532.11	93,527	15,663	542.34	87,512	21,678
80,000	545.75	116,470	556.67	107,336	9,134	567.58	99,761	16,709	578.50	93,348	23,122
85,000	579.85	123,746	591.45	114,041	9,705	603.04	105,992	17,754	614.64	99,177	24,569
90,000	613.96	131,026	626.24	120,749	10,277	638.52	112,229	18,797	650.80	105,012	26,014
95,000	648.07	138,305	661.03	127,456	10,849	673.99	118,463	19,842	686.95	110,845	27,460
100,000	682.18	145,585	695.82	134,164	11,421	709.47	124,700	20,885	723.11	116,680	28,905
105,000	716.29	152,864	730.62	140,876	11,988	744.94	130,934	21,930	759.27	122,515	30,349
110,000	750.40	160,144	765.41	147,583	12,561	780.42	137,171	22,973	795.42	128,348	31,796
115,000	784.51	167,424	800.20	154,291	13,133	815.89	143,405	24,019	831.58	134,183	33,241
120,000	818.62	174,703	834.99	160,999	13,704	851.36	149,638	25,065	867.74	140,018	34,685
125,000	852.73	181,983	869.78	167,707	14,276	886.84	155,876	26,107	903.89	145,851	36,132
130,000	886.83	189,259	904.57	174,415	14,844	922.30	162,106	27,153	940.04	151,683	37,576
135,000	920.94	196,538	939.36	181,123	15,415	957.78	168,343	28,195	976.20	157,518	39,020
140,000	955.05	203,818	974.15	187,831	15,987	993.25	174,577	29,241	1,012.35	163,351	40,467
145,000	989.16	211,098	1,008.94	194,539	16,559	1,028.73	180,814	30,284	1,048.51	169,186	41,912
150,000	1,023.27	218,377	1,043.74	201,250	17,127	1,064.20	187,048	31,329	1,084.67	175,021	43,356
155,000	1,057.38	225,657	1,078.53	207,958	17,699	1,099.68	193,285	32,372	1,120.82	180,854	44,803
160,000	1,091.49	232,936	1,113.32	214,666	18,270	1,135.15	199,519	33,417	1,156.98	186,689	46,247
165,000	1,125.60	240,216	1,148.11	221,373	18,843	1,170.62	205,753	34,463	1,193.14	192,524	47,692
170,000	1,159.70	247,492	1,182.89	228,079	19,414	1,206.09	211,987	35,505	1,229.28	198,354	49,138
175,000	1,193.81	254,772	1,217.69	234,789	19,983	1,241.56	218,221	36,551	1,265.44	204,189	50,583
180,000	1,227.92	262,051	1,252.48	241,497	20,554	1,277.04	224,458	37,593	1,301.60	210,024	52,027
185,000	1,262.03	269,331	1,287.27	248,205	21,126	1,312.51	230,692	38,639	1,337.75	215,857	53,474
190,000	1,296.14	276,610	1,322.06	254,913	21,697	1,347.99	236,929	39,681	1,373.91	221,692	54,918
195,000	1,330.25	283,890	1,356.86	261,624	22,266	1,383.46	243,163	40,727	1,410.07	227,527	56,363
200,000	1,364.36	291,170	1,391.65	268,332	22,838	1,418.93	249,396	41,774	1,446.22	233,360	57,810

AUGMENTED PAYMENT MORTGAGES 7.25%

AMOUNT OF LOAN	30 YEARS		8% PMT INCREASE 284.72 PAYMENTS			10% PMT INCREASE 271.511 PAYMENTS			12% PMT INCREASE 259.692 PAYMENTS		
	MONTHLY PAYMENT	TOTAL INTRST	MONTHLY PAYMENT	TOTAL INTRST	INTRST SAVED	MONTHLY PAYMENT	TOTAL INTRST	INTRST SAVED	MONTHLY PAYMENT	TOTAL INTRST	INTRST SAVED
$ 50	0.35	76	0.38	58	18	0.39	56	20	0.39	51	25
100	0.69	148	0.75	114	34	0.76	106	42	0.77	100	48
200	1.37	293	1.48	221	72	1.51	210	83	1.53	197	96
300	2.05	438	2.21	329	109	2.26	314	124	2.30	297	141
400	2.73	583	2.95	440	143	3.00	415	168	3.06	395	188
500	3.42	731	3.69	551	180	3.76	521	210	3.83	495	236
600	4.10	876	4.43	661	215	4.51	625	251	4.59	592	284
700	4.78	1,021	5.16	769	252	5.26	728	293	5.35	689	332
800	5.46	1,166	5.90	880	286	6.01	832	334	6.12	789	377
900	6.14	1,310	6.63	988	322	6.75	933	377	6.88	887	423
1,000	6.83	1,459	7.38	1,101	358	7.51	1,039	420	7.65	987	472
2,000	13.65	2,914	14.74	2,197	717	15.02	2,078	836	15.29	1,971	943
3,000	20.47	4,369	22.11	3,295	1,074	22.52	3,114	1,255	22.93	2,955	1,414
4,000	27.29	5,824	29.47	4,391	1,433	30.02	4,151	1,673	30.56	3,936	1,888
5,000	34.11	7,280	36.84	5,489	1,791	37.52	5,187	2,093	38.20	4,920	2,360
6,000	40.94	8,738	44.22	6,591	2,147	45.03	6,226	2,512	45.85	5,907	2,831
7,000	47.76	10,194	51.58	7,686	2,508	52.54	7,265	2,929	53.49	6,891	3,303
8,000	54.58	11,649	58.95	8,785	2,864	60.04	8,302	3,347	61.13	7,875	3,774
9,000	61.40	13,104	66.31	9,880	3,224	67.54	9,338	3,766	68.77	8,859	4,245
10,000	68.22	14,559	73.68	10,979	3,580	75.04	10,374	4,185	76.41	9,843	4,716
11,000	75.04	16,014	81.04	12,074	3,940	82.54	11,411	4,603	84.04	10,825	5,189
12,000	81.87	17,473	88.42	13,175	4,298	90.06	12,452	5,021	91.69	11,811	5,662
13,000	88.69	18,928	95.79	14,274	4,654	97.56	13,489	5,439	99.33	12,795	6,133
14,000	95.51	20,384	103.15	15,369	5,015	105.06	14,525	5,859	106.97	13,779	6,605
15,000	102.33	21,839	110.52	16,468	5,371	112.56	15,561	6,278	114.61	14,763	7,076
16,000	109.15	23,294	117.88	17,563	5,731	120.07	16,600	6,694	122.25	15,747	7,547
17,000	115.97	24,749	125.25	18,662	6,087	127.57	17,637	7,112	129.89	16,731	8,018
18,000	122.80	26,208	132.62	19,760	6,448	135.08	18,676	7,532	137.54	17,718	8,490
19,000	129.62	27,663	139.99	20,859	6,804	142.58	19,712	7,951	145.17	18,699	8,964
20,000	136.44	29,118	147.36	21,957	7,161	150.08	20,748	8,370	152.81	19,684	9,434
21,000	143.26	30,574	154.72	23,053	7,521	157.59	21,787	8,787	160.45	20,668	9,906
22,000	150.08	32,029	162.09	24,151	7,878	165.09	22,824	9,205	168.09	21,652	10,377
23,000	156.91	33,488	169.46	25,249	8,239	172.60	23,863	9,625	175.74	22,638	10,850
24,000	163.73	34,943	176.83	26,348	8,595	180.10	24,899	10,044	183.38	23,622	11,321
25,000	170.55	36,398	184.19	27,443	8,955	187.61	25,938	10,460	191.02	24,606	11,792
26,000	177.37	37,853	191.56	28,542	9,311	195.11	26,975	10,878	198.66	25,588	12,265
27,000	184.19	39,308	198.93	29,640	9,668	202.61	28,011	11,297	206.29	26,572	12,736
28,000	191.01	40,764	206.29	30,736	10,028	210.11	29,047	11,717	213.93	27,556	13,208
29,000	197.84	42,222	213.67	31,837	10,385	217.62	30,086	12,136	221.58	28,543	13,679
30,000	204.66	43,678	221.03	32,933	10,745	225.13	31,125	12,553	229.22	29,527	14,151
32,500	221.71	47,316	239.45	35,677	11,639	243.88	33,716	13,600	248.32	31,987	15,329
35,000	238.77	50,957	257.87	38,422	12,535	262.65	36,312	14,645	267.42	34,447	16,510
40,000	272.88	58,237	294.71	43,911	14,326	300.17	41,499	16,738	305.63	39,370	18,867
45,000	306.98	65,513	331.54	49,398	16,115	337.68	46,684	18,829	343.82	44,287	21,226
50,000	341.09	72,792	368.38	54,887	17,905	375.20	51,871	20,921	382.02	49,208	23,584
55,000	375.20	80,072	405.22	60,376	19,696	412.72	57,058	23,014	420.22	54,128	25,944
60,000	409.31	87,352	442.05	65,863	21,489	450.24	62,245	25,107	458.43	59,051	28,301
65,000	443.42	94,631	478.89	71,352	23,279	487.76	67,432	27,199	496.63	63,971	30,660
70,000	477.53	101,911	515.73	76,841	25,070	525.28	72,619	29,292	534.83	68,891	33,020
75,000	511.64	109,190	552.57	82,330	26,860	562.80	77,806	31,384	573.04	73,814	35,376
80,000	545.75	116,470	589.41	87,820	28,650	600.33	82,996	33,474	611.24	78,734	37,736
85,000	579.85	123,746	626.24	93,306	30,440	637.84	88,181	35,565	649.43	83,652	40,094
90,000	613.96	131,026	663.08	98,795	32,231	675.36	93,368	37,658	687.64	88,575	42,451
95,000	648.07	138,305	699.92	104,285	34,020	712.88	98,555	39,750	725.84	93,495	44,810
100,000	682.18	145,585	736.75	109,771	35,814	750.40	103,742	41,843	764.04	98,415	47,170
105,000	716.29	152,864	773.59	115,260	37,604	787.92	108,929	43,935	802.24	103,335	49,529
110,000	750.40	160,144	810.43	120,750	39,394	825.44	114,116	46,028	840.45	108,258	51,886
115,000	784.51	167,424	847.27	126,239	41,185	862.96	119,303	48,121	878.65	113,178	54,246
120,000	818.62	174,703	884.11	131,732	42,975	900.48	124,490	50,213	916.85	118,099	56,604
125,000	852.73	181,983	920.95	137,217	44,766	938.00	129,677	52,306	955.06	123,021	58,962
130,000	886.83	189,259	957.78	142,704	46,555	975.51	134,862	54,397	993.25	127,939	61,320
135,000	920.94	196,538	994.62	148,193	48,345	1,013.03	140,049	56,489	1,031.45	132,859	63,679
140,000	955.05	203,818	1,031.45	153,680	50,138	1,050.56	145,239	58,579	1,069.66	137,782	66,036
145,000	989.16	211,098	1,068.29	159,169	51,929	1,088.08	150,426	60,672	1,107.86	142,702	68,396
150,000	1,023.27	218,377	1,105.13	164,658	53,719	1,125.60	155,613	62,764	1,146.06	147,623	70,754
155,000	1,057.38	225,657	1,141.97	170,147	55,510	1,163.12	160,800	64,857	1,184.27	152,545	73,112
160,000	1,091.49	232,936	1,178.81	175,637	57,299	1,200.64	165,987	66,949	1,222.47	157,466	75,470
165,000	1,125.60	240,216	1,215.65	181,126	59,090	1,238.16	171,174	69,042	1,260.67	162,386	77,830
170,000	1,159.70	247,492	1,252.48	186,612	60,880	1,275.67	176,358	71,134	1,298.86	167,304	80,188
175,000	1,193.81	254,772	1,289.31	192,099	62,673	1,313.19	181,546	73,226	1,337.07	172,226	82,546
180,000	1,227.92	262,051	1,326.15	197,588	64,463	1,350.71	186,733	75,318	1,375.27	177,147	84,904
185,000	1,262.03	269,331	1,362.99	203,077	66,254	1,388.23	191,920	77,411	1,413.47	182,067	87,264
190,000	1,296.14	276,610	1,399.83	208,567	68,043	1,425.75	197,107	79,503	1,451.68	186,990	89,620
195,000	1,330.25	283,890	1,436.67	214,056	69,834	1,463.28	202,297	81,593	1,489.88	191,910	91,980
200,000	1,364.36	291,170	1,473.51	219,545	71,625	1,500.80	207,484	83,686	1,528.08	196,830	94,340

AUGMENTED PAYMENT MORTGAGES

AMOUNT OF LOAN	30 YEARS		2% PMT INCREASE 335.471 PAYMENTS			4% PMT INCREASE 314.966 PAYMENTS			6% PMT INCREASE 297.438 PAYMENTS		
	MONTHLY PAYMENT	TOTAL INTRST	MONTHLY PAYMENT	TOTAL INTRST	INTRST SAVED	MONTHLY PAYMENT	TOTAL INTRST	INTRST SAVED	MONTHLY PAYMENT	TOTAL INTRST	INTRST SAVED
$ 50	0.35	76	0.36	71	5	0.36	63	13	0.37	60	16
100	0.70	152	0.71	138	14	0.73	130	22	0.74	120	32
200	1.40	304	1.43	280	24	1.46	260	44	1.48	240	64
300	2.10	456	2.14	418	38	2.18	387	69	2.23	363	93
400	2.80	608	2.86	559	49	2.91	517	91	2.97	483	125
500	3.50	760	3.57	698	62	3.64	646	114	3.71	603	157
600	4.20	912	4.28	836	76	4.37	776	136	4.45	724	188
700	4.90	1,064	5.00	977	87	5.10	906	158	5.19	844	220
800	5.60	1,216	5.71	1,116	100	5.82	1,033	183	5.94	967	249
900	6.30	1,368	6.43	1,257	111	6.55	1,163	205	6.68	1,087	281
1,000	7.00	1,520	7.14	1,395	125	7.28	1,293	227	7.42	1,207	313
2,000	13.99	3,036	14.27	2,787	249	14.55	2,583	453	14.83	2,411	625
3,000	20.98	4,553	21.40	4,179	374	21.82	3,873	680	22.24	3,615	938
4,000	27.97	6,069	28.53	5,571	498	29.09	5,162	907	29.65	4,819	1,250
5,000	34.97	7,589	35.67	6,966	623	36.37	6,455	1,134	37.07	6,026	1,563
6,000	41.96	9,106	42.80	8,358	748	43.64	7,745	1,361	44.48	7,230	1,876
7,000	48.95	10,622	49.93	9,750	872	50.91	9,035	1,587	51.89	8,434	2,188
8,000	55.94	12,138	57.06	11,142	996	58.18	10,325	1,813	59.30	9,638	2,500
9,000	62.93	13,655	64.19	12,534	1,121	65.45	11,615	2,040	66.71	10,842	2,813
10,000	69.93	15,175	71.33	13,929	1,246	72.73	12,907	2,268	74.13	12,049	3,126
11,000	76.92	16,691	78.46	15,321	1,370	80.00	14,197	2,494	81.54	13,253	3,438
12,000	83.91	18,208	85.59	16,713	1,495	87.27	15,487	2,721	88.94	14,454	3,754
13,000	90.90	19,724	92.72	18,105	1,619	94.54	16,777	2,947	96.35	15,658	4,066
14,000	97.90	21,244	99.86	19,500	1,744	101.82	18,070	3,174	103.77	16,865	4,379
15,000	104.89	22,760	106.99	20,892	1,868	109.09	19,360	3,400	111.18	18,069	4,691
16,000	111.88	24,277	114.12	22,284	1,993	116.36	20,649	3,628	118.59	19,273	5,004
17,000	118.87	25,793	121.25	23,676	2,117	123.62	21,936	3,857	126.00	20,477	5,316
18,000	125.86	27,310	128.38	25,068	2,242	130.89	23,226	4,084	133.41	21,681	5,629
19,000	132.86	28,830	135.52	26,463	2,367	138.17	24,519	4,311	140.83	22,888	5,942
20,000	139.85	30,346	142.65	27,855	2,491	145.44	25,809	4,537	148.24	24,092	6,254
21,000	146.84	31,862	149.78	29,247	2,615	152.71	27,098	4,764	155.65	25,296	6,566
22,000	153.83	33,379	156.91	30,639	2,740	159.98	28,388	4,991	163.06	26,500	6,879
23,000	160.82	34,895	164.04	32,031	2,864	167.25	29,678	5,217	170.47	27,704	7,191
24,000	167.82	36,415	171.18	33,426	2,989	174.53	30,971	5,444	177.89	28,911	7,504
25,000	174.81	37,932	178.31	34,818	3,114	181.80	32,261	5,671	185.30	30,115	7,817
26,000	181.80	39,448	185.44	36,210	3,238	189.07	33,551	5,897	192.71	31,319	8,129
27,000	188.79	40,964	192.57	37,602	3,362	196.34	34,840	6,124	200.12	32,523	8,441
28,000	195.79	42,484	199.71	38,997	3,487	203.62	36,133	6,351	207.54	33,730	8,754
29,000	202.78	44,001	206.84	40,389	3,612	210.89	37,423	6,578	214.95	34,934	9,067
30,000	209.77	45,517	213.97	41,781	3,736	218.16	38,713	6,804	222.36	36,138	9,379
32,500	227.25	49,310	231.80	45,262	4,048	236.34	41,939	7,371	240.89	39,150	10,160
35,000	244.73	53,103	249.62	48,740	4,363	254.52	45,165	7,938	259.41	42,158	10,945
40,000	279.69	60,688	285.28	55,703	4,985	290.88	51,617	9,071	296.47	48,181	12,507
45,000	314.65	68,274	320.94	62,666	5,608	327.24	58,069	10,205	333.53	54,204	14,070
50,000	349.61	75,860	356.60	69,629	6,231	363.59	64,518	11,342	370.59	60,228	15,632
55,000	384.57	83,445	392.26	76,592	6,853	399.95	70,971	12,474	407.64	66,248	17,197
60,000	419.53	91,031	427.92	83,555	7,476	436.31	77,423	13,608	444.70	72,271	18,760
65,000	454.49	98,616	463.58	90,518	8,098	472.67	83,875	14,741	481.76	78,294	20,322
70,000	489.46	106,206	499.25	97,484	8,722	509.04	90,330	15,876	518.83	84,320	21,886
75,000	524.42	113,791	534.91	104,447	9,344	545.40	96,782	17,009	555.89	90,343	23,448
80,000	559.38	121,377	570.57	111,410	9,967	581.76	103,235	18,142	592.94	96,363	25,014
85,000	594.34	128,962	606.23	118,373	10,589	618.11	109,684	19,278	630.00	102,386	26,576
90,000	629.30	136,548	641.89	125,335	11,213	654.47	116,136	20,412	667.06	108,409	28,139
95,000	664.26	144,134	677.55	132,298	11,836	690.83	122,588	21,546	704.12	114,432	29,702
100,000	699.22	151,719	713.20	139,261	12,461	727.19	129,040	22,679	741.17	120,452	31,267
105,000	734.18	159,305	748.86	146,221	13,084	763.55	135,492	23,813	778.23	126,475	32,830
110,000	769.14	166,890	784.52	153,184	13,706	799.91	141,944	24,946	815.29	132,498	34,392
115,000	804.10	174,476	820.18	160,147	14,329	836.26	148,393	26,083	852.35	138,521	35,955
120,000	839.06	182,062	855.84	167,110	14,952	872.62	154,846	27,216	889.40	144,541	37,521
125,000	874.02	189,647	891.50	174,072	15,575	908.98	161,297	28,349	926.46	150,564	39,083
130,000	908.98	197,233	927.16	181,035	16,198	945.34	167,750	29,483	963.52	156,587	40,646
135,000	943.94	204,818	962.82	187,998	16,820	981.70	174,202	30,616	1,000.58	162,611	42,207
140,000	978.91	212,408	998.49	194,961	17,444	1,018.07	180,655	31,751	1,037.64	168,634	43,774
145,000	1,013.87	219,993	1,034.15	201,927	18,066	1,054.42	187,106	32,887	1,074.70	174,657	45,336
150,000	1,048.83	227,579	1,069.81	208,890	18,689	1,090.78	193,559	34,020	1,111.76	180,680	46,899
155,000	1,083.79	235,164	1,105.47	215,853	19,311	1,127.14	200,011	35,153	1,148.82	186,703	48,461
160,000	1,118.75	242,750	1,141.13	222,816	19,934	1,163.50	206,463	36,287	1,185.88	192,726	50,024
165,000	1,153.71	250,336	1,176.78	229,779	20,560	1,199.86	212,915	37,421	1,222.93	198,746	51,590
170,000	1,188.67	257,921	1,212.44	236,738	21,183	1,236.22	219,367	38,554	1,259.99	204,769	53,152
175,000	1,223.63	265,507	1,248.10	243,701	21,806	1,272.58	225,819	39,688	1,297.05	210,792	54,715
180,000	1,258.59	273,092	1,283.76	250,664	22,428	1,308.93	232,268	40,824	1,334.11	216,815	56,277
185,000	1,293.55	280,678	1,319.42	257,627	23,051	1,345.29	238,721	41,957	1,371.16	222,835	57,843
190,000	1,328.51	288,264	1,355.08	264,591	23,674	1,381.65	245,173	43,091	1,408.22	228,858	59,406
195,000	1,363.47	295,849	1,390.74	271,553	24,296	1,418.01	251,625	44,224	1,445.28	234,881	60,968
200,000	1,398.43	303,435	1,426.40	278,516	24,919	1,454.37	258,077	45,358	1,482.34	240,904	62,531

AUGMENTED PAYMENT MORTGAGES 7.50%

AMOUNT OF LOAN	30 YEARS		8% PMT INCREASE 282.194 PAYMENTS			10% PMT INCREASE 268.759 PAYMENTS			12% PMT INCREASE 256.789 PAYMENTS		
	MONTHLY PAYMENT	TOTAL INTRST	MONTHLY PAYMENT	TOTAL INTRST	INTRST SAVED	MONTHLY PAYMENT	TOTAL INTRST	INTRST SAVED	MONTHLY PAYMENT	TOTAL INTRST	INTRST SAVED
$ 50	0.35	76	0.38	57	19	0.39	55	21	0.39	50	26
100	0.70	152	0.76	114	38	0.77	107	45	0.78	100	52
200	1.40	304	1.51	226	78	1.54	214	90	1.57	203	101
300	2.10	456	2.27	341	115	2.31	321	135	2.35	303	153
400	2.80	608	3.02	452	156	3.08	428	180	3.14	406	202
500	3.50	760	3.78	567	193	3.85	535	225	3.92	507	253
600	4.20	912	4.54	681	231	4.62	642	270	4.70	607	305
700	4.90	1,064	5.29	793	271	5.39	749	315	5.49	710	354
800	5.60	1,216	6.05	907	309	6.16	856	360	6.27	810	406
900	6.30	1,368	6.80	1,019	349	6.93	962	406	7.06	913	455
1,000	7.00	1,520	7.56	1,133	387	7.70	1,069	451	7.84	1,013	507
2,000	13.99	3,036	15.11	2,264	772	15.39	2,136	900	15.67	2,024	1,012
3,000	20.98	4,553	22.66	3,395	1,158	23.08	3,203	1,350	23.50	3,035	1,518
4,000	27.97	6,069	30.21	4,525	1,544	30.77	4,270	1,799	31.33	4,045	2,024
5,000	34.97	7,589	37.77	5,658	1,931	38.47	5,339	2,250	39.17	5,058	2,531
6,000	41.96	9,106	45.32	6,789	2,317	46.16	6,406	2,700	47.00	6,069	3,037
7,000	48.95	10,622	52.87	7,920	2,702	53.85	7,473	3,149	54.82	7,077	3,545
8,000	55.94	12,138	60.42	9,050	3,088	61.53	8,537	3,601	62.65	8,088	4,050
9,000	62.93	13,655	67.96	10,178	3,477	69.22	9,603	4,052	70.48	9,098	4,557
10,000	69.93	15,175	75.52	11,311	3,864	76.92	10,673	4,502	78.32	10,112	5,063
11,000	76.92	16,691	83.07	12,442	4,249	84.61	11,740	4,951	86.15	11,122	5,569
12,000	83.91	18,208	90.62	13,572	4,636	92.30	12,806	5,402	93.98	12,133	6,075
13,000	90.90	19,724	98.17	14,703	5,021	99.99	13,873	5,851	101.81	13,144	6,580
14,000	97.90	21,244	105.73	15,836	5,408	107.69	14,943	6,301	109.65	14,157	7,087
15,000	104.89	22,760	113.28	16,967	5,793	115.38	16,009	6,751	117.48	15,168	7,592
16,000	111.88	24,277	120.83	18,098	6,179	123.07	17,076	7,201	125.31	16,178	8,099
17,000	118.87	25,793	128.38	19,228	6,565	130.76	18,143	7,650	133.13	17,186	8,607
18,000	125.86	27,310	135.93	20,359	6,951	138.45	19,210	8,100	140.96	18,197	9,113
19,000	132.86	28,830	143.49	21,492	7,338	146.15	20,279	8,551	148.80	19,210	9,620
20,000	139.85	30,346	151.04	22,623	7,723	153.84	21,346	9,000	156.63	20,221	10,125
21,000	146.84	31,862	158.59	23,753	8,109	161.52	22,410	9,452	164.46	21,232	10,630
22,000	153.83	33,379	166.14	24,884	8,495	169.21	23,477	9,902	172.29	22,242	11,137
23,000	160.82	34,895	173.69	26,014	8,881	176.90	24,543	10,352	180.12	23,253	11,642
24,000	167.82	36,415	181.25	27,148	9,267	184.60	25,613	10,802	187.96	24,266	12,149
25,000	174.81	37,932	188.79	28,275	9,657	192.29	26,680	11,252	195.79	25,277	12,655
26,000	181.80	39,448	196.34	29,406	10,042	199.98	27,746	11,702	203.62	26,287	13,161
27,000	188.79	40,964	203.89	30,537	10,427	207.67	28,813	12,151	211.44	27,295	13,669
28,000	195.79	42,484	211.45	31,670	10,814	215.37	29,883	12,601	219.28	28,309	14,175
29,000	202.78	44,001	219.00	32,800	11,201	223.06	30,949	13,052	227.11	29,319	14,682
30,000	209.77	45,517	226.55	33,931	11,586	230.75	32,016	13,501	234.94	30,330	15,187
32,500	227.25	49,310	245.43	36,759	12,551	249.98	34,684	14,626	254.52	32,858	16,452
35,000	244.73	53,103	264.31	39,587	13,516	269.20	37,353	15,750	274.10	35,386	17,717
40,000	279.69	60,688	302.07	45,242	15,446	307.66	42,686	18,002	313.25	40,439	20,249
45,000	314.65	68,274	339.82	50,895	17,379	346.12	48,023	20,251	352.41	45,495	22,779
50,000	349.61	75,860	377.58	56,551	19,309	384.57	53,357	22,503	391.56	50,548	25,312
55,000	384.57	83,445	415.34	62,206	21,239	423.03	58,693	24,752	430.72	55,604	27,841
60,000	419.53	91,031	453.09	67,859	23,172	461.48	64,027	27,004	469.87	60,657	30,374
65,000	454.49	98,616	490.85	73,515	25,101	499.94	69,363	29,253	509.03	65,713	32,903
70,000	489.46	106,206	528.62	79,172	27,033	538.41	74,703	31,503	548.20	70,772	35,434
75,000	524.42	113,791	566.37	84,826	28,965	576.86	80,036	33,755	587.35	75,825	37,966
80,000	559.38	121,377	604.13	90,482	30,895	615.32	85,373	36,004	626.51	80,881	40,496
85,000	594.34	128,962	641.89	96,138	32,824	653.77	90,707	38,255	665.66	85,934	43,028
90,000	629.30	136,548	679.64	101,790	34,758	692.23	96,043	40,505	704.82	90,990	45,558
95,000	664.26	144,134	717.40	107,446	36,688	730.69	101,380	42,754	743.97	96,043	48,091
100,000	699.22	151,719	755.16	113,102	38,617	769.14	106,713	45,006	783.13	101,099	50,620
105,000	734.18	159,305	792.91	118,754	40,551	807.60	112,050	47,255	822.28	106,152	53,153
110,000	769.14	166,890	830.67	124,410	42,480	846.05	117,384	49,506	861.44	111,208	55,682
115,000	804.10	174,476	868.43	130,066	44,410	884.51	122,720	51,756	900.59	116,262	58,214
120,000	839.06	182,062	906.18	135,719	46,343	922.97	128,056	54,006	939.75	121,317	60,745
125,000	874.02	189,647	943.94	141,374	48,273	961.42	133,390	56,257	978.90	126,371	63,276
130,000	908.98	197,233	981.70	147,030	50,203	999.88	138,727	58,506	1,018.06	131,427	65,806
135,000	943.94	204,818	1,019.46	152,685	52,133	1,038.33	144,061	60,757	1,057.21	136,480	68,338
140,000	978.91	212,408	1,057.22	158,341	54,067	1,076.80	149,400	63,008	1,096.38	141,538	70,870
145,000	1,013.87	219,993	1,094.98	163,997	55,996	1,115.26	154,736	65,257	1,135.53	146,592	73,401
150,000	1,048.83	227,579	1,132.74	169,652	57,927	1,153.71	160,070	67,509	1,174.69	151,647	75,932
155,000	1,083.79	235,164	1,170.49	175,305	59,859	1,192.17	165,406	69,758	1,213.84	156,701	78,463
160,000	1,118.75	242,750	1,208.25	180,961	61,789	1,230.63	170,743	72,007	1,253.00	161,757	80,993
165,000	1,153.71	250,336	1,246.01	186,617	63,719	1,269.08	176,812	74,256	1,292.16	166,812	83,524
170,000	1,188.67	257,921	1,283.76	192,269	65,652	1,307.54	181,413	76,508	1,331.31	171,866	86,055
175,000	1,223.63	265,507	1,321.52	197,925	67,582	1,345.99	186,747	78,760	1,370.47	176,922	88,585
180,000	1,258.59	273,092	1,359.28	203,581	69,511	1,384.45	192,083	81,009	1,409.62	181,975	91,117
185,000	1,293.55	280,678	1,397.03	209,233	71,445	1,422.91	197,420	83,258	1,448.78	187,031	93,647
190,000	1,328.51	288,264	1,434.79	214,889	73,375	1,461.36	202,754	85,510	1,487.93	192,084	96,180
195,000	1,363.47	295,849	1,472.55	220,545	75,304	1,499.82	208,090	87,759	1,527.09	197,140	98,709
200,000	1,398.43	303,435	1,510.30	226,198	77,237	1,538.27	213,424	90,011	1,566.24	202,193	101,242

199

7.75%   AUGMENTED PAYMENT MORTGAGES

AMOUNT OF LOAN	30 YEARS		2% PMT INCREASE 334.366 PAYMENTS			4% PMT INCREASE 313.159 PAYMENTS			6% PMT INCREASE 295.168 PAYMENTS		
	MONTHLY PAYMENT	TOTAL INTRST	MONTHLY PAYMENT	TOTAL INTRST	INTRST SAVED	MONTHLY PAYMENT	TOTAL INTRST	INTRST SAVED	MONTHLY PAYMENT	TOTAL INTRST	INTRST SAVED
$ 50	0.36	80	0.37	74	6	0.37	66	14	0.38	62	18
100	0.72	159	0.73	144	15	0.75	135	24	0.76	124	35
200	1.44	318	1.47	292	26	1.50	270	48	1.53	252	66
300	2.15	474	2.19	432	42	2.24	401	73	2.28	373	101
400	2.87	633	2.93	580	53	2.98	533	100	3.04	497	136
500	3.59	792	3.66	724	68	3.73	668	124	3.81	625	167
600	4.30	948	4.39	868	80	4.47	800	148	4.56	746	202
700	5.02	1,107	5.12	1,012	95	5.22	935	172	5.32	870	237
800	5.74	1,266	5.85	1,156	110	5.97	1,070	196	6.08	995	271
900	6.45	1,422	6.58	1,300	122	6.71	1,201	221	6.84	1,119	303
1,000	7.17	1,581	7.31	1,444	137	7.46	1,336	245	7.60	1,243	338
2,000	14.33	3,159	14.62	2,888	271	14.90	2,666	493	15.19	2,484	675
3,000	21.50	4,740	21.93	4,333	407	22.36	4,002	738	22.79	3,727	1,013
4,000	28.66	6,318	29.23	5,774	544	29.81	5,335	983	30.38	4,967	1,351
5,000	35.83	7,899	36.55	7,221	678	37.26	6,668	1,231	37.98	6,210	1,689
6,000	42.99	9,476	43.85	8,662	814	44.71	8,001	1,475	45.57	7,451	2,025
7,000	50.15	11,054	51.15	10,103	951	52.16	9,334	1,720	53.16	8,691	2,363
8,000	57.32	12,635	58.47	11,550	1,085	59.61	10,667	1,968	60.76	9,934	2,701
9,000	64.48	14,213	65.77	12,991	1,222	67.06	12,000	2,213	68.35	11,175	3,038
10,000	71.65	15,794	73.08	14,435	1,359	74.52	13,337	2,457	75.95	12,418	3,376
11,000	78.81	17,372	80.39	15,880	1,492	81.96	14,667	2,705	83.54	13,658	3,714
12,000	85.97	18,949	87.69	17,321	1,628	89.41	16,000	2,949	91.13	14,899	4,050
13,000	93.14	20,530	95.00	18,765	1,765	96.87	17,336	3,194	98.73	16,142	4,388
14,000	100.30	22,108	102.31	20,209	1,899	104.31	18,666	3,442	106.32	17,382	4,726
15,000	107.47	23,689	109.62	21,653	2,036	111.77	20,002	3,687	113.92	18,626	5,063
16,000	114.63	25,267	116.92	23,094	2,173	119.22	21,335	3,932	121.51	19,866	5,401
17,000	121.80	26,848	124.24	24,542	2,306	126.67	22,668	4,180	129.11	21,109	5,739
18,000	128.96	28,426	131.54	25,983	2,443	134.12	24,001	4,425	136.70	22,349	6,077
19,000	136.12	30,003	138.84	27,423	2,580	141.56	25,331	4,672	144.29	23,590	6,413
20,000	143.29	31,584	146.16	28,871	2,713	149.02	26,667	4,917	151.89	24,833	6,751
21,000	150.45	33,162	153.46	30,312	2,850	156.47	28,000	5,162	159.48	26,073	7,089
22,000	157.62	34,743	160.77	31,756	2,987	163.92	29,333	5,410	167.08	27,317	7,426
23,000	164.78	36,321	168.08	33,200	3,121	171.37	30,666	5,655	174.67	28,557	7,764
24,000	171.94	37,898	175.38	34,641	3,257	178.82	31,999	5,899	182.26	29,797	8,101
25,000	179.11	39,480	182.69	36,085	3,395	186.27	33,332	6,148	189.86	31,041	8,439
26,000	186.27	41,057	190.00	37,530	3,527	193.72	34,665	6,392	197.45	32,281	8,776
27,000	193.44	42,638	197.31	38,974	3,664	201.18	36,001	6,637	205.05	33,524	9,114
28,000	200.60	44,216	204.61	40,415	3,801	208.62	37,331	6,885	212.64	34,765	9,451
29,000	207.76	45,794	211.92	41,859	3,935	216.07	38,664	7,130	220.23	36,005	9,789
30,000	214.93	47,375	219.23	43,303	4,072	223.53	40,000	7,375	227.83	37,248	10,127
32,500	232.84	51,322	237.50	46,912	4,410	242.15	43,331	7,991	246.81	40,350	10,972
35,000	250.75	55,270	255.77	50,521	4,749	260.78	46,666	8,604	265.80	43,456	11,814
40,000	286.57	63,165	292.30	57,735	5,430	298.03	53,331	9,834	303.76	49,660	13,505
45,000	322.39	71,060	328.84	64,953	6,107	335.29	59,999	11,061	341.73	55,868	15,192
50,000	358.21	78,956	365.37	72,167	6,789	372.54	66,664	12,292	379.70	62,075	16,881
55,000	394.03	86,851	401.91	79,385	7,466	409.79	73,329	13,522	417.67	68,283	18,568
60,000	429.85	94,746	438.45	86,603	8,143	447.04	79,995	14,751	455.64	74,490	20,256
65,000	465.67	102,641	474.98	93,817	8,824	484.30	86,663	15,978	493.61	80,698	21,943
70,000	501.49	110,536	511.52	101,035	9,501	521.55	93,328	17,208	531.58	86,905	23,631
75,000	537.31	118,432	548.06	108,253	10,179	558.80	99,993	18,439	569.55	93,113	25,319
80,000	573.13	126,327	584.59	115,467	10,860	596.06	106,662	19,665	607.52	99,320	27,007
85,000	608.96	134,226	621.14	122,688	11,538	633.32	113,330	20,896	645.50	105,531	28,695
90,000	644.78	142,121	657.68	129,906	12,215	670.57	119,995	22,126	683.47	111,738	30,383
95,000	680.60	150,016	694.21	137,120	12,896	707.82	126,660	23,356	721.44	117,946	32,070
100,000	716.42	157,911	730.75	144,338	13,573	745.08	133,329	24,582	759.41	124,154	33,757
105,000	752.24	165,806	767.28	151,552	14,254	782.33	139,994	25,812	797.37	130,358	35,448
110,000	788.06	173,702	803.82	158,770	14,932	819.58	146,659	27,043	835.34	136,566	37,136
115,000	823.88	181,597	840.36	165,988	15,609	856.84	153,327	28,270	873.31	142,773	38,824
120,000	859.70	189,492	876.89	173,202	16,290	894.09	159,992	29,500	911.28	148,981	40,511
125,000	895.52	197,387	913.43	180,420	16,967	931.34	166,658	30,729	949.25	155,188	42,199
130,000	931.34	205,282	949.97	187,638	17,644	968.59	173,323	31,959	987.22	161,396	43,886
135,000	967.16	213,178	986.50	194,852	18,326	1,005.85	179,991	33,187	1,025.19	167,603	45,575
140,000	1,002.98	221,073	1,023.04	202,070	19,003	1,043.10	186,656	34,417	1,063.16	173,811	47,262
145,000	1,038.80	228,968	1,059.58	209,288	19,680	1,080.35	193,321	35,647	1,101.13	180,018	48,950
150,000	1,074.62	236,863	1,096.11	216,502	20,361	1,117.60	199,986	36,877	1,139.10	186,226	50,637
155,000	1,110.44	244,758	1,132.65	223,720	21,038	1,154.86	206,655	38,103	1,177.07	192,433	52,325
160,000	1,146.26	252,654	1,169.19	230,937	21,717	1,192.11	213,320	39,334	1,215.04	198,641	54,013
165,000	1,182.09	260,552	1,205.73	238,155	22,397	1,229.37	219,988	40,564	1,253.02	204,851	55,701
170,000	1,217.91	268,448	1,242.27	245,373	23,075	1,266.63	226,657	41,791	1,290.98	211,056	57,392
175,000	1,253.73	276,343	1,278.80	252,587	23,756	1,303.88	233,322	43,021	1,328.95	217,264	59,079
180,000	1,289.55	284,238	1,315.34	259,805	24,433	1,341.13	239,987	44,251	1,366.92	223,471	60,767
185,000	1,325.37	292,133	1,351.88	267,023	25,110	1,378.38	246,652	45,481	1,404.89	229,679	62,454
190,000	1,361.19	300,028	1,388.41	274,237	25,791	1,415.64	253,320	46,708	1,442.86	235,886	64,142
195,000	1,397.01	307,924	1,424.95	281,455	26,469	1,452.89	259,986	47,938	1,480.83	242,094	65,830
200,000	1,432.83	315,819	1,461.49	288,673	27,146	1,490.14	266,651	49,168	1,518.80	248,301	67,518

AUGMENTED PAYMENT MORTGAGES 7.75%

AMOUNT OF LOAN	30 YEARS		8% PMT INCREASE 279.614 PAYMENTS			10% PMT INCREASE 265.969 PAYMENTS			12% PMT INCREASE 253.857 PAYMENTS		
	MONTHLY PAYMENT	TOTAL INTRST	MONTHLY PAYMENT	TOTAL INTRST	INTRST SAVED	MONTHLY PAYMENT	TOTAL INTRST	INTRST SAVED	MONTHLY PAYMENT	TOTAL INTRST	INTRST SAVED
$ 50	0.36	80	0.39	59	21	0.40	56	24	0.40	52	28
100	0.72	159	0.78	118	41	0.79	110	49	0.81	106	53
200	1.44	318	1.56	236	82	1.58	220	98	1.61	209	109
300	2.15	474	2.32	349	125	2.37	330	144	2.41	312	162
400	2.87	633	3.10	467	166	3.16	440	193	3.21	415	218
500	3.59	792	3.88	585	207	3.95	551	241	4.02	521	271
600	4.30	948	4.64	697	251	4.73	658	290	4.82	624	324
700	5.02	1,107	5.42	816	291	5.52	768	339	5.62	727	380
800	5.74	1,266	6.20	934	332	6.31	878	388	6.43	832	434
900	6.45	1,422	6.97	1,049	373	7.10	988	434	7.22	933	489
1,000	7.17	1,581	7.74	1,164	417	7.89	1,098	483	8.03	1,038	543
2,000	14.33	3,159	15.48	2,328	831	15.76	2,192	967	16.05	2,074	1,085
3,000	21.50	4,740	23.22	3,493	1,247	23.65	3,290	1,450	24.08	3,113	1,627
4,000	28.66	6,318	30.95	4,654	1,664	31.53	4,386	1,932	32.10	4,149	2,169
5,000	35.83	7,899	38.70	5,821	2,078	39.41	5,482	2,417	40.13	5,187	2,712
6,000	42.99	9,476	46.43	6,982	2,494	47.29	6,578	2,898	48.15	6,223	3,253
7,000	50.15	11,054	54.16	8,144	2,910	55.17	7,674	3,380	56.17	7,259	3,795
8,000	57.32	12,635	61.91	9,311	3,324	63.05	8,769	3,866	64.20	8,298	4,337
9,000	64.48	14,213	69.64	10,472	3,741	70.93	9,865	4,348	72.22	9,334	4,879
10,000	71.65	15,794	77.38	11,637	4,157	78.82	10,964	4,830	80.25	10,372	5,422
11,000	78.81	17,372	85.11	12,798	4,574	86.69	12,057	5,315	88.27	11,408	5,964
12,000	85.97	18,949	92.85	13,962	4,987	94.57	13,153	5,796	96.29	12,444	6,505
13,000	93.14	20,530	100.59	15,126	5,404	102.45	14,249	6,281	104.32	13,482	7,048
14,000	100.30	22,108	108.32	16,288	5,820	110.33	15,344	6,764	112.34	14,518	7,590
15,000	107.47	23,689	116.07	17,455	6,234	118.22	16,443	7,246	120.37	15,557	8,132
16,000	114.63	25,267	123.80	18,616	6,651	126.09	17,536	7,731	128.39	16,593	8,674
17,000	121.80	26,848	131.54	19,780	7,068	133.98	18,635	8,213	136.42	17,631	9,217
18,000	128.96	28,426	139.28	20,945	7,481	141.86	19,730	8,696	144.44	18,667	9,759
19,000	136.12	30,003	147.01	22,106	7,897	149.73	20,824	9,179	152.45	19,700	10,303
20,000	143.29	31,584	154.75	23,270	8,314	157.62	21,922	9,662	160.48	20,739	10,845
21,000	150.45	33,162	162.49	24,434	8,728	165.50	23,018	10,144	168.50	21,775	11,387
22,000	157.62	34,743	170.23	25,599	9,144	173.38	24,114	10,629	176.53	22,813	11,930
23,000	164.78	36,321	177.96	26,760	9,561	181.26	25,210	11,111	184.55	23,849	12,472
24,000	171.94	37,898	185.70	27,924	9,974	189.13	26,303	11,595	192.57	24,885	13,013
25,000	179.11	39,480	193.44	29,089	10,391	197.02	27,401	12,079	200.60	25,924	13,556
26,000	186.27	41,057	201.17	30,250	10,807	204.90	28,497	12,560	208.62	26,960	14,097
27,000	193.44	42,638	208.92	31,417	11,221	212.78	29,593	13,045	216.65	27,998	14,640
28,000	200.60	44,216	216.65	32,578	11,638	220.66	30,689	13,527	224.67	29,034	15,182
29,000	207.76	45,794	224.38	33,740	12,054	228.54	31,785	14,009	232.69	30,070	15,724
30,000	214.93	47,375	232.12	34,904	12,471	236.42	32,880	14,495	240.72	31,108	16,267
32,500	232.84	51,322	251.47	37,815	13,507	256.12	35,620	15,702	260.78	33,701	17,621
35,000	250.75	55,270	270.81	40,722	14,548	275.83	38,362	16,908	280.84	36,293	18,977
40,000	286.57	63,165	309.50	46,541	16,624	315.23	43,841	19,324	320.96	41,478	21,687
45,000	322.39	71,060	348.18	52,356	18,704	354.63	49,321	21,739	361.08	46,663	24,397
50,000	358.21	78,956	386.87	58,174	20,782	394.03	54,800	24,156	401.20	51,847	27,109
55,000	394.03	86,851	425.55	63,990	22,861	433.43	60,279	26,572	441.31	57,030	29,821
60,000	429.85	94,746	464.24	69,808	24,938	472.84	65,761	28,985	481.43	62,214	32,532
65,000	465.67	102,641	502.92	75,623	27,018	512.24	71,240	31,401	521.55	67,399	35,242
70,000	501.49	110,536	541.61	81,442	29,094	551.64	76,719	33,817	561.67	72,584	37,952
75,000	537.31	118,432	580.29	87,257	31,175	591.04	82,198	36,234	601.79	77,769	40,663
80,000	573.13	126,327	618.98	93,075	33,252	630.44	87,677	38,650	641.91	82,953	43,374
85,000	608.96	134,226	657.68	98,897	35,329	669.86	93,162	41,064	682.04	88,141	46,085
90,000	644.78	142,121	696.36	104,712	37,409	709.26	98,641	43,480	722.15	93,323	48,798
95,000	680.60	150,016	735.05	110,530	39,486	748.66	104,120	45,896	762.27	98,508	51,508
100,000	716.42	157,911	773.73	116,346	41,565	788.06	109,600	48,311	802.39	103,692	54,219
105,000	752.24	165,806	812.42	122,164	43,642	827.46	115,079	50,727	842.51	108,877	56,929
110,000	788.06	173,702	851.10	127,979	45,723	866.87	120,561	53,141	882.63	114,062	59,640
115,000	823.88	181,597	889.79	133,798	47,799	906.27	126,040	55,557	922.75	119,247	62,350
120,000	859.70	189,492	928.48	139,616	49,876	945.67	131,519	57,973	962.86	124,429	65,063
125,000	895.52	197,387	967.16	145,431	51,956	985.07	136,998	60,389	1,002.98	129,613	67,774
130,000	931.34	205,282	1,005.85	151,250	54,032	1,024.47	142,477	62,805	1,043.10	134,798	70,484
135,000	967.16	213,178	1,044.53	157,065	56,113	1,063.88	147,959	65,219	1,083.22	139,983	73,195
140,000	1,002.98	221,073	1,083.22	162,883	58,190	1,103.28	153,438	67,635	1,123.34	145,168	75,905
145,000	1,038.80	228,968	1,121.90	168,699	60,269	1,142.68	158,917	70,051	1,163.46	150,352	78,616
150,000	1,074.62	236,863	1,160.59	174,517	62,346	1,182.08	164,397	72,466	1,203.57	155,535	81,328
155,000	1,110.44	244,758	1,199.28	180,335	64,423	1,221.48	169,876	74,882	1,243.69	160,719	84,039
160,000	1,146.26	252,654	1,237.96	186,151	66,503	1,260.89	175,358	77,296	1,283.81	165,904	86,750
165,000	1,182.09	260,552	1,276.66	191,972	68,580	1,300.30	180,839	79,713	1,323.94	171,091	89,461
170,000	1,217.91	268,448	1,315.34	197,787	70,661	1,339.70	186,319	82,129	1,364.06	176,276	92,172
175,000	1,253.73	276,343	1,354.03	203,606	72,737	1,379.10	191,798	84,545	1,404.18	181,461	94,882
180,000	1,289.55	284,238	1,392.71	209,421	74,817	1,418.51	197,280	86,958	1,444.30	186,646	97,592
185,000	1,325.37	292,133	1,431.40	215,239	76,894	1,457.91	202,759	89,374	1,484.41	191,828	100,305
190,000	1,361.19	300,028	1,470.09	221,058	78,970	1,497.31	208,238	91,790	1,524.53	197,013	103,015
195,000	1,397.01	307,924	1,508.77	226,873	81,051	1,536.71	213,717	94,207	1,564.65	202,197	105,727
200,000	1,432.83	315,819	1,547.46	232,691	83,128	1,576.11	219,196	96,623	1,604.77	207,382	108,437

8.00% AUGMENTED PAYMENT MORTGAGES

AMOUNT OF LOAN	30 YEARS		2% PMT INCREASE 333.213 PAYMENTS			4% PMT INCREASE 311.294 PAYMENTS			6% PMT INCREASE 292.844 PAYMENTS		
	MONTHLY PAYMENT	TOTAL INTRST	MONTHLY PAYMENT	TOTAL INTRST	INTRST SAVED	MONTHLY PAYMENT	TOTAL INTRST	INTRST SAVED	MONTHLY PAYMENT	TOTAL INTRST	INTRST SAVED
$ 50	0.37	83	0.38	77	6	0.38	68	15	0.39	64	19
100	0.74	166	0.75	150	16	0.77	140	26	0.78	128	38
200	1.47	329	1.50	300	29	1.53	276	53	1.56	257	72
300	2.21	496	2.25	450	46	2.30	416	80	2.34	385	111
400	2.94	658	3.00	600	58	3.06	553	105	3.12	514	144
500	3.67	821	3.74	746	75	3.82	689	132	3.89	639	182
600	4.41	988	4.50	899	89	4.59	829	159	4.67	768	220
700	5.14	1,150	5.24	1,046	104	5.35	965	185	5.45	896	254
800	5.88	1,317	6.00	1,199	118	6.12	1,105	212	6.23	1,024	293
900	6.61	1,480	6.74	1,346	134	6.87	1,239	241	7.01	1,153	327
1,000	7.34	1,642	7.49	1,496	146	7.63	1,375	267	7.78	1,278	364
2,000	14.68	3,285	14.97	2,988	297	15.27	2,753	532	15.56	2,557	728
3,000	22.02	4,927	22.46	4,484	443	22.90	4,129	798	23.34	3,835	1,092
4,000	29.36	6,570	29.95	5,980	590	30.53	5,504	1,066	31.12	5,113	1,457
5,000	36.69	8,208	37.42	7,469	739	38.16	6,879	1,329	38.89	6,389	1,819
6,000	44.03	9,851	44.91	8,965	886	45.79	8,254	1,597	46.67	7,667	2,184
7,000	51.37	11,493	52.40	10,460	1,033	53.42	9,629	1,864	54.45	8,945	2,548
8,000	58.71	13,136	59.88	11,953	1,183	61.06	11,008	2,128	62.23	10,224	2,912
9,000	66.04	14,774	67.36	13,445	1,329	68.68	12,380	2,394	70.00	11,499	3,275
10,000	73.38	16,417	74.85	14,941	1,476	76.32	13,758	2,659	77.78	12,777	3,640
11,000	80.72	18,059	82.33	16,433	1,626	83.95	15,133	2,926	85.56	14,056	4,003
12,000	88.06	19,702	89.82	17,929	1,773	91.58	16,508	3,194	93.34	15,334	4,368
13,000	95.39	21,340	97.30	19,422	1,918	99.21	17,883	3,457	101.11	16,609	4,731
14,000	102.73	22,983	104.78	20,914	2,069	106.84	19,259	3,724	108.89	17,888	5,095
15,000	110.07	24,625	112.27	22,410	2,215	114.47	20,634	3,991	116.67	19,166	5,459
16,000	117.41	26,268	119.76	23,906	2,362	122.11	22,012	4,256	124.45	20,444	5,824
17,000	124.74	27,906	127.23	25,395	2,511	129.73	23,384	4,522	132.22	21,720	6,186
18,000	132.08	29,549	134.72	26,890	2,659	137.36	24,759	4,790	140.00	22,998	6,551
19,000	139.42	31,191	142.21	28,386	2,805	145.00	26,138	5,053	147.79	24,279	6,912
20,000	146.76	32,834	149.70	29,882	2,952	152.63	27,513	5,321	155.57	25,558	7,276
21,000	154.10	34,476	157.18	31,374	3,102	160.26	28,888	5,588	163.35	26,836	7,640
22,000	161.43	36,115	164.66	32,867	3,248	167.89	30,263	5,852	171.12	28,111	8,004
23,000	168.77	37,757	172.15	34,363	3,394	175.52	31,638	6,119	178.90	29,390	8,367
24,000	176.11	39,400	179.63	35,855	3,545	183.15	33,013	6,387	186.68	30,668	8,732
25,000	183.45	41,042	187.12	37,351	3,691	190.79	34,392	6,650	194.46	31,946	9,096
26,000	190.78	42,681	194.60	38,843	3,838	198.41	35,764	6,917	202.23	33,222	9,459
27,000	198.12	44,323	202.08	40,336	3,987	206.04	37,139	7,184	210.01	34,500	9,823
28,000	205.46	45,966	209.57	41,831	4,135	213.68	38,517	7,449	217.79	35,778	10,188
29,000	212.80	47,608	217.06	43,327	4,281	221.31	39,892	7,716	225.57	37,057	10,551
30,000	220.13	49,247	224.53	44,816	4,431	228.94	41,268	7,979	233.34	38,332	10,915
32,500	238.48	53,353	243.25	48,554	4,799	248.02	44,707	8,646	252.79	41,528	11,825
35,000	256.82	57,455	261.96	52,288	5,167	267.09	48,144	9,311	272.23	44,721	12,734
40,000	293.51	65,664	299.38	59,757	5,907	305.25	55,022	10,642	311.12	51,110	14,554
45,000	330.20	73,872	336.80	67,226	6,646	343.41	61,901	11,971	350.01	57,498	16,374
50,000	366.89	82,080	374.23	74,698	7,382	381.57	68,780	13,300	388.90	63,887	18,193
55,000	403.58	90,289	411.65	82,167	8,122	419.72	75,656	14,633	427.79	70,276	20,013
60,000	440.26	98,494	449.07	89,636	8,858	457.87	82,532	15,962	466.68	76,664	21,830
65,000	476.95	106,702	486.49	97,105	9,597	496.03	89,411	17,291	505.57	83,053	23,649
70,000	513.64	114,910	523.91	104,574	10,336	534.19	96,290	18,620	544.45	89,442	25,468
75,000	550.33	123,119	561.34	112,046	11,073	572.34	103,166	19,953	583.35	95,831	27,288
80,000	587.02	131,327	598.76	119,515	11,812	610.50	110,045	21,282	622.24	102,219	29,108
85,000	623.70	139,532	636.17	126,980	12,552	648.65	116,921	22,611	661.12	108,605	30,927
90,000	660.39	147,740	673.60	134,452	13,288	686.81	123,800	23,940	700.01	114,994	32,746
95,000	697.08	155,949	711.02	141,921	14,028	724.96	130,676	25,273	738.90	121,382	34,567
100,000	733.77	164,157	748.45	149,393	14,764	763.12	137,555	26,602	777.80	127,774	36,383
105,000	770.46	172,366	785.87	156,862	15,504	801.28	144,434	27,932	816.69	134,163	38,203
110,000	807.15	180,574	823.29	164,331	16,243	839.44	151,313	29,261	855.58	140,551	40,023
115,000	843.83	188,779	860.71	171,800	16,979	877.58	158,185	30,594	933.35	153,326	41,842
120,000	880.52	196,987	898.13	179,269	17,718	915.74	165,064	31,923	933.35	153,326	43,661
125,000	917.21	205,196	935.55	186,737	18,459	953.90	171,943	33,253	972.24	159,715	45,481
130,000	953.90	213,404	972.98	194,210	19,194	992.06	178,822	34,582	1,011.13	166,103	47,301
135,000	990.59	221,612	1,010.40	201,678	19,934	1,030.21	185,698	35,914	1,050.03	172,491	49,117
140,000	1,027.28	229,821	1,047.83	209,151	20,670	1,068.37	192,577	37,244	1,088.92	178,884	50,937
145,000	1,063.96	238,026	1,085.24	216,616	21,410	1,106.52	199,453	38,573	1,127.80	185,269	52,757
150,000	1,100.65	246,234	1,122.66	224,085	22,149	1,144.68	206,332	39,902	1,166.69	191,658	54,576
155,000	1,137.34	254,442	1,160.09	231,557	22,885	1,182.83	213,208	41,234	1,205.58	198,047	56,395
160,000	1,174.03	262,651	1,197.51	239,026	23,625	1,220.99	220,087	42,564	1,244.47	204,436	58,215
165,000	1,210.72	270,859	1,234.93	246,495	24,364	1,259.15	226,966	43,893	1,283.36	210,824	60,035
170,000	1,247.40	279,064	1,272.35	253,964	25,100	1,297.30	233,842	45,222	1,322.24	217,210	61,854
175,000	1,284.09	287,272	1,309.77	261,432	25,840	1,335.45	240,718	46,554	1,361.14	223,602	63,670
180,000	1,320.78	295,481	1,347.20	268,905	26,576	1,373.61	247,597	47,884	1,400.03	229,990	65,491
185,000	1,357.47	303,689	1,384.62	276,373	27,316	1,411.77	254,476	49,213	1,438.92	236,379	67,310
190,000	1,394.16	311,898	1,422.04	283,842	28,056	1,449.93	261,355	50,543	1,477.81	242,768	69,130
195,000	1,430.85	320,106	1,459.47	291,314	28,792	1,488.08	268,230	51,876	1,516.70	249,156	70,950
200,000	1,467.53	328,311	1,496.88	298,780	29,531	1,526.23	275,106	53,205	1,555.58	255,542	72,769

AUGMENTED PAYMENT MORTGAGES 8.00%

AMOUNT OF LOAN	30 YEARS		8% PMT INCREASE 276.989 PAYMENTS			10% PMT INCREASE 263.145 PAYMENTS			12% PMT INCREASE 250.902 PAYMENTS		
	MONTHLY PAYMENT	TOTAL INTRST	MONTHLY PAYMENT	TOTAL INTRST	INTRST SAVED	MONTHLY PAYMENT	TOTAL INTRST	INTRST SAVED	MONTHLY PAYMENT	TOTAL INTRST	INTRST SAVED
$ 50	0.37	83	0.40	61	22	0.41	58	25	0.41	53	30
100	0.74	166	0.80	122	44	0.81	113	53	0.83	108	58
200	1.47	329	1.59	240	89	1.62	226	103	1.65	214	115
300	2.21	496	2.39	362	134	2.43	339	157	2.48	322	174
400	2.94	658	3.18	481	177	3.23	450	208	3.29	425	233
500	3.67	821	3.96	597	224	4.04	563	258	4.11	531	290
600	4.41	988	4.76	718	270	4.85	676	312	4.94	639	349
700	5.14	1,150	5.55	837	313	5.65	787	363	5.76	745	405
800	5.88	1,317	6.35	959	358	6.47	903	414	6.59	853	464
900	6.61	1,480	7.14	1,078	402	7.27	1,013	467	7.40	957	523
1,000	7.34	1,642	7.93	1,197	445	8.07	1,124	518	8.22	1,062	580
2,000	14.68	3,285	15.85	2,390	895	16.15	2,250	1,035	16.44	2,125	1,160
3,000	22.02	4,927	23.78	3,587	1,340	24.22	3,373	1,554	24.66	3,187	1,740
4,000	29.36	6,570	31.71	4,783	1,787	32.30	4,500	2,070	32.88	4,250	2,320
5,000	36.69	8,208	39.63	5,977	2,231	40.36	5,621	2,587	41.09	5,310	2,898
6,000	44.03	9,851	47.55	7,171	2,680	48.43	6,744	3,107	49.31	6,372	3,479
7,000	51.37	11,493	55.48	8,367	3,126	56.51	7,870	3,623	57.53	7,434	4,059
8,000	58.71	13,136	63.41	9,564	3,572	64.58	8,994	4,142	65.76	8,499	4,637
9,000	66.04	14,774	71.32	10,755	4,019	72.64	10,115	4,659	73.96	9,557	5,217
10,000	73.38	16,417	79.25	11,951	4,466	80.72	11,241	5,176	82.19	10,622	5,795
11,000	80.72	18,059	87.18	13,148	4,911	88.79	12,365	5,694	90.41	11,684	6,375
12,000	88.06	19,702	95.10	14,342	5,360	96.87	13,491	6,211	98.63	12,746	6,956
13,000	95.39	21,340	103.02	15,535	5,805	104.93	14,612	6,728	106.84	13,806	7,534
14,000	102.73	22,983	110.95	16,732	6,251	113.00	15,735	7,248	115.06	14,869	8,114
15,000	110.07	24,625	118.88	17,928	6,697	121.08	16,862	7,763	123.28	15,931	8,694
16,000	117.41	26,268	126.80	19,122	7,146	129.15	17,985	8,283	131.50	16,994	9,274
17,000	124.74	27,906	134.72	20,316	7,590	137.21	19,106	8,800	139.71	18,054	9,852
18,000	132.08	29,549	142.65	21,512	8,037	145.29	20,232	9,317	147.93	19,116	10,433
19,000	139.42	31,191	150.57	22,706	8,485	153.36	21,356	9,835	156.15	20,178	11,013
20,000	146.76	32,834	158.50	23,903	8,931	161.44	22,482	10,352	164.37	21,241	11,593
21,000	154.10	34,476	166.43	25,099	9,377	169.51	23,606	10,870	172.59	22,303	12,173
22,000	161.43	36,115	174.34	26,290	9,825	177.57	24,727	11,388	180.80	23,363	12,752
23,000	168.77	37,757	182.27	27,487	10,270	185.65	25,853	11,904	189.02	24,425	13,332
24,000	176.11	39,400	190.20	28,683	10,717	193.72	26,976	12,424	197.24	25,488	13,912
25,000	183.45	41,042	198.13	29,880	11,162	201.80	28,103	12,939	205.46	26,550	14,492
26,000	190.78	42,681	206.04	31,071	11,610	209.86	29,224	13,457	213.67	27,610	15,071
27,000	198.12	44,323	213.97	32,267	12,056	217.93	30,347	13,976	221.89	28,673	15,650
28,000	205.46	45,966	221.90	33,464	12,502	226.01	31,473	14,493	230.12	29,738	16,228
29,000	212.80	47,608	229.82	34,658	12,950	234.08	32,597	15,011	238.34	30,800	16,808
30,000	220.13	49,247	237.74	35,851	13,396	242.14	33,718	15,529	246.55	31,860	17,387
32,500	238.48	53,353	257.56	38,841	14,512	262.33	36,531	16,822	267.10	34,516	18,837
35,000	256.82	57,455	277.37	41,828	15,627	282.50	39,338	18,117	287.64	37,169	20,286
40,000	293.51	65,664	316.99	47,803	17,861	322.86	44,999	20,705	328.73	42,479	23,185
45,000	330.20	73,872	356.62	53,780	20,092	363.22	50,580	23,292	369.82	47,789	26,083
50,000	366.89	82,060	396.24	59,754	22,326	403.58	56,200	25,880	410.92	53,101	28,979
55,000	403.58	90,289	435.87	65,731	24,558	443.94	61,821	28,468	452.01	58,410	31,879
60,000	440.26	98,494	475.48	71,703	26,791	484.29	67,438	31,056	493.09	63,717	34,777
65,000	476.95	106,702	515.11	77,680	29,022	524.65	73,059	33,643	534.18	69,027	37,675
70,000	513.64	114,910	554.73	83,654	31,256	565.00	78,677	36,233	575.28	74,339	40,571
75,000	550.33	123,119	594.36	89,631	33,488	605.36	84,297	38,822	616.37	79,648	43,471
80,000	587.02	131,327	633.98	95,605	35,722	645.72	89,918	41,409	657.46	84,958	46,369
85,000	623.70	139,532	673.60	101,580	37,952	686.07	95,536	43,996	698.54	90,265	49,267
90,000	660.39	147,740	713.22	107,554	40,186	726.43	101,156	46,584	739.63	95,577	52,163
95,000	697.08	155,949	752.85	113,531	42,418	766.79	106,777	49,172	780.73	100,887	55,062
100,000	733.77	164,157	792.47	119,505	44,652	807.15	112,397	51,760	821.82	106,196	57,961
105,000	770.46	172,366	832.10	125,483	46,883	847.51	118,018	54,348	862.92	111,508	60,858
110,000	807.15	180,574	871.72	131,457	49,117	887.87	123,639	56,935	904.01	116,818	63,756
115,000	843.83	188,779	911.34	137,431	51,348	928.21	129,254	59,525	945.09	122,125	66,654
120,000	880.52	196,987	950.96	143,405	53,582	968.57	134,874	62,113	986.18	127,435	69,552
125,000	917.21	205,196	990.59	149,383	55,813	1,008.93	140,495	64,701	1,027.28	132,747	72,449
130,000	953.90	213,404	1,030.21	155,357	58,047	1,049.29	146,115	67,289	1,068.37	138,056	75,348
135,000	990.59	221,612	1,069.84	161,335	60,278	1,089.65	151,736	69,876	1,109.46	143,366	78,246
140,000	1,027.28	229,821	1,109.46	167,308	62,513	1,130.01	157,356	72,465	1,150.55	148,675	81,146
145,000	1,063.96	238,026	1,149.08	173,283	64,743	1,170.36	162,974	75,052	1,191.64	153,985	84,041
150,000	1,100.65	246,234	1,188.70	179,257	66,977	1,210.72	168,595	77,639	1,232.73	159,294	86,940
155,000	1,137.34	254,442	1,228.33	185,234	69,208	1,251.07	174,213	80,229	1,273.82	164,604	89,838
160,000	1,174.03	262,651	1,267.95	191,208	71,443	1,291.43	179,833	82,818	1,314.91	169,914	92,737
165,000	1,210.72	270,859	1,307.58	197,185	73,674	1,331.79	185,454	85,405	1,356.01	175,226	95,633
170,000	1,247.40	279,064	1,347.19	203,157	75,907	1,372.14	191,072	87,992	1,397.09	180,533	98,531
175,000	1,284.09	287,272	1,386.82	209,134	78,138	1,412.50	196,692	90,580	1,438.18	185,842	101,430
180,000	1,320.78	295,481	1,426.44	215,108	80,373	1,452.86	202,313	93,168	1,479.27	191,152	104,329
185,000	1,357.47	303,689	1,466.07	221,085	82,604	1,493.22	207,933	95,756	1,520.37	196,464	107,225
190,000	1,394.16	311,898	1,505.69	227,060	84,838	1,533.58	213,554	98,344	1,561.46	201,773	110,125
195,000	1,430.85	320,106	1,545.32	233,037	87,069	1,573.94	219,174	100,932	1,602.55	207,083	113,023
200,000	1,467.53	328,311	1,584.93	239,008	89,303	1,614.28	224,790	103,521	1,643.63	212,390	115,921

AMOUNT OF LOAN	30 YEARS		2% PMT INCREASE 332.009 PAYMENTS			4% PMT INCREASE 309.370 PAYMENTS			6% PMT INCREASE 290.468 PAYMENTS		
	MONTHLY PAYMENT	TOTAL INTRST	MONTHLY PAYMENT	TOTAL INTRST	INTRST SAVED	MONTHLY PAYMENT	TOTAL INTRST	INTRST SAVED	MONTHLY PAYMENT	TOTAL INTRST	INTRST SAVED
$ 50	0.38	87	0.39	79	8	0.40	74	13	0.40	66	21
100	0.76	174	0.78	159	15	0.79	144	30	0.81	135	39
200	1.51	344	1.54	311	33	1.57	286	58	1.60	265	79
300	2.26	514	2.31	467	47	2.35	427	87	2.40	397	117
400	3.01	684	3.07	619	65	3.13	568	116	3.19	527	157
500	3.76	854	3.84	775	79	3.91	710	144	3.99	659	195
600	4.51	1,024	4.60	927	97	4.69	851	173	4.78	788	236
700	5.26	1,194	5.37	1,083	111	5.47	992	202	5.58	921	273
800	6.02	1,367	6.14	1,239	128	6.26	1,137	230	6.38	1,053	314
900	6.77	1,537	6.91	1,394	143	7.04	1,278	259	7.18	1,186	351
1,000	7.52	1,707	7.67	1,547	160	7.82	1,419	288	7.97	1,315	392
2,000	15.03	3,411	15.33	3,090	321	15.63	2,835	576	15.93	2,627	784
3,000	22.54	5,114	22.99	4,633	481	23.44	4,252	862	23.89	3,939	1,175
4,000	30.06	6,822	30.66	6,179	643	31.26	5,671	1,151	31.86	5,254	1,568
5,000	37.57	8,525	38.32	7,723	802	39.07	7,087	1,438	39.82	6,566	1,959
6,000	45.08	10,229	45.98	9,266	963	46.88	8,503	1,726	47.78	7,879	2,350
7,000	52.59	11,932	53.64	10,809	1,123	54.69	9,919	2,013	55.75	9,194	2,738
8,000	60.11	13,640	61.31	12,355	1,285	62.51	11,339	2,301	63.72	10,509	3,131
9,000	67.62	15,343	68.97	13,899	1,444	70.32	12,755	2,588	71.68	11,821	3,522
10,000	75.13	17,047	76.63	15,442	1,605	78.14	14,174	2,873	79.64	13,133	3,914
11,000	82.64	18,750	84.29	16,985	1,765	85.95	15,590	3,160	87.60	14,445	4,305
12,000	90.16	20,458	91.96	18,532	1,926	93.77	17,010	3,448	95.57	15,760	4,698
13,000	97.67	22,161	99.62	20,075	2,086	101.58	18,426	3,735	103.53	17,072	5,089
14,000	105.18	23,865	107.28	21,618	2,247	109.39	19,842	4,023	111.49	18,384	5,481
15,000	112.69	25,568	114.94	23,161	2,407	117.20	21,258	4,310	119.45	19,696	5,872
16,000	120.21	27,276	122.61	24,708	2,568	125.02	22,677	4,599	127.42	21,011	6,265
17,000	127.72	28,979	130.27	26,251	2,728	132.83	24,094	4,885	135.38	22,324	6,655
18,000	135.23	30,683	137.93	27,794	2,889	140.64	25,510	5,173	143.34	23,636	7,047
19,000	142.75	32,390	145.61	29,344	3,046	148.46	26,929	5,461	151.32	24,954	7,436
20,000	150.26	34,094	153.27	30,887	3,207	156.27	28,345	5,749	159.28	26,266	7,828
21,000	157.77	35,797	160.93	32,430	3,367	164.08	29,761	6,036	167.24	27,578	8,219
22,000	165.28	37,501	168.59	33,973	3,528	171.89	31,178	6,323	175.20	28,890	8,611
23,000	172.80	39,208	176.26	35,520	3,688	179.71	32,597	6,611	183.17	30,205	9,003
24,000	180.31	40,912	183.92	37,063	3,849	187.52	34,013	6,899	191.13	31,517	9,395
25,000	187.82	42,615	191.58	38,606	4,009	195.33	35,429	7,186	199.09	32,829	9,786
26,000	195.33	44,319	199.24	40,149	4,170	203.14	36,845	7,474	207.05	34,141	10,178
27,000	202.85	46,026	206.91	41,696	4,330	210.96	38,265	7,761	215.02	35,456	10,570
28,000	210.36	47,730	214.57	43,239	4,491	218.77	39,681	8,049	222.98	36,769	10,961
29,000	217.87	49,433	222.23	44,782	4,651	226.58	41,097	8,336	230.94	38,081	11,352
30,000	225.38	51,137	229.89	46,326	4,811	234.40	42,516	8,621	238.90	39,393	11,744
32,500	244.17	55,401	249.05	50,187	5,214	253.94	46,061	9,340	258.82	42,679	12,722
35,000	262.95	59,662	268.21	54,048	5,614	273.47	49,603	10,059	278.73	45,962	13,700
40,000	300.51	68,184	306.52	61,767	6,417	312.53	56,687	11,497	318.54	52,526	15,658
45,000	338.07	76,705	344.83	69,487	7,218	351.59	63,771	12,934	358.35	59,089	17,616
50,000	375.64	85,230	383.15	77,209	8,021	390.67	70,862	14,368	398.18	65,659	19,571
55,000	413.20	93,752	421.46	84,929	8,823	429.73	77,946	15,806	437.99	72,222	21,530
60,000	450.76	102,274	459.78	92,651	9,623	468.79	85,031	17,244	477.81	78,789	23,485
65,000	488.33	110,799	498.10	100,374	10,425	507.86	92,117	18,682	517.63	85,355	25,444
70,000	525.89	119,320	536.41	108,093	11,227	546.93	99,204	20,116	557.44	91,918	27,402
75,000	563.45	127,842	574.72	115,812	12,030	585.99	106,288	21,554	597.26	98,485	29,357
80,000	601.02	136,367	613.04	123,535	12,832	625.06	113,375	22,992	637.08	105,051	31,316
85,000	638.58	144,889	651.35	131,234	13,655	664.12	120,459	24,430	676.89	111,615	33,274
90,000	676.14	153,410	689.66	138,973	14,437	703.19	127,546	25,864	716.71	118,181	35,229
95,000	713.71	161,936	727.98	146,696	15,240	742.26	134,633	27,303	756.53	124,748	37,188
100,000	751.27	170,457	766.30	154,418	16,039	781.32	141,717	28,740	796.35	131,314	39,143
105,000	788.83	178,979	804.61	162,138	16,841	820.38	148,801	30,178	836.16	137,878	41,101
110,000	826.40	187,504	842.93	169,860	17,644	859.46	155,891	31,613	875.98	144,444	43,060
115,000	863.96	196,026	881.24	177,580	18,446	898.52	162,975	33,051	915.80	151,011	45,015
120,000	901.52	204,547	919.55	185,299	19,248	937.58	170,059	34,488	955.61	157,574	46,973
125,000	939.09	213,072	957.87	193,021	20,051	976.65	177,146	35,926	995.44	164,143	48,929
130,000	976.65	221,594	996.18	200,741	20,853	1,015.72	184,233	37,361	1,035.25	170,707	50,887
135,000	1,014.21	230,116	1,034.49	208,460	21,656	1,054.78	191,317	38,799	1,075.06	177,271	52,845
140,000	1,051.78	238,641	1,072.82	216,186	22,455	1,093.85	198,404	40,237	1,114.89	183,840	54,801
145,000	1,089.34	247,162	1,111.13	223,905	23,257	1,132.91	205,488	41,674	1,154.70	190,403	56,759
150,000	1,126.90	255,684	1,149.44	231,624	24,060	1,171.98	212,575	43,109	1,194.51	196,967	58,717
155,000	1,164.47	264,209	1,187.76	239,347	24,862	1,211.05	219,663	44,546	1,234.34	203,536	60,673
160,000	1,202.03	272,731	1,226.07	247,066	25,665	1,250.11	226,747	45,984	1,274.15	210,100	62,631
165,000	1,239.59	281,252	1,264.38	254,786	26,466	1,289.17	233,831	47,421	1,313.97	216,666	64,586
170,000	1,277.16	289,778	1,302.70	262,508	27,270	1,328.25	240,921	48,857	1,353.79	223,233	66,545
175,000	1,314.72	298,299	1,341.01	270,227	28,072	1,367.31	248,005	50,294	1,393.60	229,796	68,503
180,000	1,352.28	306,821	1,379.33	277,950	28,871	1,406.37	255,089	51,732	1,433.42	236,363	70,458
185,000	1,389.85	315,346	1,417.65	285,673	29,673	1,445.44	262,176	53,170	1,473.24	242,929	72,417
190,000	1,427.41	323,868	1,455.96	293,392	30,476	1,484.51	269,263	54,605	1,513.05	249,493	74,375
195,000	1,464.97	332,389	1,494.27	301,111	31,278	1,523.57	276,347	56,042	1,552.87	256,059	76,330
200,000	1,502.54	340,914	1,532.59	308,834	32,080	1,562.64	283,434	57,480	1,592.69	262,625	78,289

AMOUNT OF LOAN	30 YEARS		8% PMT INCREASE 274.322 PAYMENTS			10% PMT INCREASE 260.290 PAYMENTS			12% PMT INCREASE 247.927 PAYMENTS		
	MONTHLY PAYMENT	TOTAL INTRST	MONTHLY PAYMENT	TOTAL INTRST	INTRST SAVED	MONTHLY PAYMENT	TOTAL INTRST	INTRST SAVED	MONTHLY PAYMENT	TOTAL INTRST	INTRST SAVED
$ 50	0.38	87	0.41	62	25	0.42	59	28	0.43	57	30
100	0.76	174	0.82	125	49	0.84	119	55	0.85	111	63
200	1.51	344	1.63	247	97	1.66	232	112	1.69	219	125
300	2.26	514	2.44	369	145	2.49	348	166	2.53	327	187
400	3.01	684	3.25	492	192	3.31	462	222	3.37	436	248
500	3.76	854	4.06	614	240	4.14	578	276	4.21	544	310
600	4.51	1,024	4.87	736	288	4.96	691	333	5.05	652	372
700	5.26	1,194	5.68	858	336	5.79	807	387	5.89	760	434
800	6.02	1,367	6.50	983	384	6.62	923	444	6.74	871	496
900	6.77	1,537	7.31	1,105	432	7.45	1,039	498	7.58	979	558
1,000	7.52	1,707	8.12	1,227	480	8.27	1,153	554	8.42	1,088	619
2,000	15.03	3,411	16.23	2,452	959	16.53	2,303	1,108	16.83	2,173	1,238
3,000	22.54	5,114	24.34	3,677	1,437	24.79	3,453	1,661	25.24	3,258	1,856
4,000	30.06	6,822	32.46	4,904	1,918	33.07	4,608	2,214	33.67	4,348	2,474
5,000	37.57	8,525	40.58	6,132	2,393	41.33	5,758	2,767	42.08	5,433	3,092
6,000	45.08	10,229	48.69	7,357	2,872	49.59	6,908	3,321	50.49	6,518	3,711
7,000	52.59	11,932	56.80	8,581	3,351	57.85	8,058	3,874	58.90	7,603	4,329
8,000	60.11	13,640	64.92	9,809	3,831	66.12	9,210	4,430	67.32	8,690	4,950
9,000	67.62	15,343	73.03	11,034	4,309	74.38	10,360	4,983	75.73	9,776	5,567
10,000	75.13	17,047	81.14	12,258	4,789	82.64	11,510	5,537	84.15	10,863	6,184
11,000	82.64	18,750	89.25	13,483	5,267	90.90	12,660	6,090	92.56	11,948	6,802
12,000	90.16	20,458	97.37	14,711	5,747	99.18	13,816	6,642	100.98	13,036	7,422
13,000	97.67	22,161	105.48	15,935	6,226	107.44	14,966	7,195	109.39	14,121	8,040
14,000	105.18	23,865	113.59	17,160	6,705	115.70	16,116	7,749	117.80	15,206	8,659
15,000	112.69	25,568	121.71	18,388	7,180	123.96	17,266	8,302	126.21	16,291	9,277
16,000	120.21	27,276	129.83	19,615	7,661	132.23	18,418	8,858	134.64	17,381	9,895
17,000	127.72	28,979	137.94	20,840	8,139	140.49	19,568	9,411	143.05	18,466	10,513
18,000	135.23	30,683	146.05	22,065	8,618	148.75	20,718	9,965	151.46	19,551	11,132
19,000	142.75	32,390	154.17	23,292	9,098	157.03	21,873	10,517	159.88	20,639	11,751
20,000	150.26	34,094	162.28	24,517	9,577	165.29	23,023	11,071	168.29	21,724	12,370
21,000	157.77	35,797	170.39	25,742	10,055	173.55	24,173	11,624	176.70	22,809	12,988
22,000	165.28	37,501	178.50	26,966	10,535	181.81	25,323	12,178	185.11	23,894	13,607
23,000	172.80	39,208	186.62	28,194	11,014	190.08	26,476	12,732	193.54	24,984	14,224
24,000	180.31	40,912	194.73	29,419	11,493	198.34	27,626	13,286	201.95	26,069	14,843
25,000	187.82	42,615	202.84	30,646	11,969	206.60	28,776	13,839	210.36	27,154	15,461
26,000	195.33	44,319	210.96	31,871	12,448	214.86	29,926	14,393	218.77	28,239	16,080
27,000	202.85	46,026	219.08	33,098	12,928	223.14	31,081	14,945	227.19	29,327	16,699
28,000	210.36	47,730	227.19	34,323	13,407	231.40	32,231	15,499	235.60	30,412	17,318
29,000	217.87	49,433	235.30	35,548	13,885	239.66	33,381	16,052	244.01	31,497	17,936
30,000	225.38	51,137	243.41	36,773	14,364	247.92	34,531	16,606	252.43	32,584	18,553
32,500	244.17	55,401	263.70	39,839	15,562	268.59	37,411	17,990	273.47	35,301	20,100
35,000	262.95	59,662	283.99	42,905	16,757	289.25	40,289	19,373	294.50	38,015	21,647
40,000	300.51	68,184	324.55	49,031	19,153	330.56	46,041	22,143	336.57	43,445	24,739
45,000	338.07	76,705	365.12	55,160	21,545	371.88	51,797	24,908	378.64	48,875	27,830
50,000	375.64	85,230	405.69	61,290	23,940	413.20	57,552	27,678	420.72	54,308	30,922
55,000	413.20	93,752	446.26	67,419	26,333	454.52	63,307	30,445	462.78	59,736	34,016
60,000	450.76	102,274	486.82	73,545	28,729	495.84	69,062	33,212	504.85	65,166	37,108
65,000	488.33	110,799	527.40	79,677	31,122	537.16	74,817	35,982	546.93	70,599	40,200
70,000	525.89	119,320	567.96	85,804	33,516	578.48	80,573	38,747	589.00	76,029	43,291
75,000	563.45	127,842	608.53	91,933	35,909	619.80	86,328	41,514	631.06	81,457	46,385
80,000	601.02	136,367	649.10	98,062	38,305	661.12	92,083	44,284	673.14	86,890	49,477
85,000	638.58	144,889	689.67	104,191	40,697	702.44	97,838	47,051	715.21	92,320	52,569
90,000	676.14	153,410	730.23	110,318	43,092	743.75	103,591	49,819	757.28	97,750	55,660
95,000	713.71	161,936	770.81	116,450	45,486	785.08	109,348	52,588	799.36	103,183	58,753
100,000	751.27	170,457	811.37	122,577	47,880	826.40	115,104	55,353	841.42	108,611	61,846
105,000	788.83	178,979	851.94	128,706	50,273	867.71	120,856	58,123	883.49	114,041	64,938
110,000	826.40	187,504	892.51	134,835	52,669	909.04	126,614	60,890	925.57	119,474	68,030
115,000	863.96	196,026	933.08	140,964	55,062	950.36	132,369	63,657	967.64	124,904	71,122
120,000	901.52	204,547	973.64	147,091	57,456	991.67	138,122	66,425	1,009.70	130,332	74,215
125,000	939.09	213,072	1,014.22	153,223	59,849	1,033.00	143,880	69,192	1,051.78	135,765	77,307
130,000	976.65	221,594	1,054.78	159,349	62,245	1,074.32	149,635	71,959	1,093.85	141,195	80,399
135,000	1,014.21	230,116	1,095.35	165,479	64,637	1,115.63	155,387	74,729	1,135.92	146,625	83,491
140,000	1,051.78	238,641	1,135.92	171,608	67,033	1,156.96	161,145	77,496	1,177.99	152,056	86,585
145,000	1,089.34	247,162	1,176.49	177,737	69,425	1,198.27	166,898	80,264	1,220.06	157,486	89,676
150,000	1,126.90	255,684	1,217.05	183,864	71,820	1,239.59	172,653	83,031	1,262.13	162,916	92,768
155,000	1,164.47	264,209	1,257.63	189,996	74,213	1,280.92	178,411	85,798	1,304.21	168,349	95,860
160,000	1,202.03	272,731	1,298.19	196,122	76,609	1,322.23	184,163	88,568	1,346.27	173,777	98,954
165,000	1,239.59	281,252	1,338.76	202,251	79,001	1,363.55	189,918	91,334	1,388.34	179,207	102,045
170,000	1,277.16	289,777	1,379.33	208,381	81,397	1,404.88	195,676	94,102	1,430.42	184,640	105,138
175,000	1,314.72	298,299	1,419.90	214,510	83,789	1,446.19	201,429	96,870	1,472.49	190,070	108,229
180,000	1,352.28	306,821	1,460.46	220,636	86,185	1,487.51	207,184	99,637	1,514.55	195,498	111,323
185,000	1,389.85	315,346	1,501.04	226,769	88,578	1,528.84	212,942	102,404	1,556.63	200,931	114,415
190,000	1,427.41	323,868	1,541.60	232,895	90,973	1,570.15	218,694	105,174	1,598.70	206,361	117,507
195,000	1,464.97	332,389	1,582.17	239,024	93,365	1,611.47	224,450	107,939	1,640.77	211,791	120,598
200,000	1,502.54	340,914	1,622.74	245,153	95,761	1,652.79	230,205	110,709	1,682.84	217,221	123,693

8.50% AUGMENTED PAYMENT MORTGAGES

AMOUNT OF LOAN	30 YEARS		2% PMT INCREASE 330.756 PAYMENTS			4% PMT INCREASE 307.387 PAYMENTS			6% PMT INCREASE 288.039 PAYMENTS		
	MONTHLY PAYMENT	TOTAL INTRST	MONTHLY PAYMENT	TOTAL INTRST	INTRST SAVED	MONTHLY PAYMENT	TOTAL INTRST	INTRST SAVED	MONTHLY PAYMENT	TOTAL INTRST	INTRST SAVED
$ 50	0.39	90	0.40	82	8	0.41	76	14	0.41	68	22
100	0.77	177	0.79	161	16	0.80	146	31	0.82	136	41
200	1.54	354	1.57	319	35	1.60	292	62	1.63	270	84
300	2.31	532	2.36	481	51	2.40	438	94	2.45	406	126
400	3.08	709	3.14	639	70	3.20	584	125	3.26	539	170
500	3.85	886	3.93	800	86	4.00	730	156	4.08	675	211
600	4.62	1,063	4.71	958	105	4.80	875	188	4.90	811	252
700	5.39	1,240	5.50	1,119	121	5.61	1,024	216	5.71	945	295
800	6.16	1,418	6.28	1,277	141	6.41	1,170	248	6.53	1,081	337
900	6.93	1,595	7.07	1,438	157	7.21	1,316	279	7.35	1,217	378
1,000	7.69	1,768	7.84	1,593	175	8.00	1,459	309	8.15	1,348	420
2,000	15.38	3,537	15.69	3,190	347	16.00	2,918	619	16.30	2,695	842
3,000	23.07	5,305	23.53	4,783	522	23.99	4,374	931	24.45	4,043	1,262
4,000	30.76	7,074	31.38	6,379	695	31.99	5,833	1,241	32.61	5,393	1,681
5,000	38.45	8,842	39.22	7,972	870	39.99	7,292	1,550	40.76	6,740	2,102
6,000	46.14	10,610	47.06	9,565	1,045	47.99	8,752	1,858	48.91	8,088	2,522
7,000	53.83	12,379	54.91	11,162	1,217	55.98	10,208	2,171	57.06	9,436	2,943
8,000	61.52	14,147	62.75	12,755	1,392	63.98	11,667	2,480	65.21	10,783	3,364
9,000	69.21	15,916	70.59	14,348	1,568	71.98	13,126	2,790	73.36	12,131	3,785
10,000	76.90	17,684	78.44	15,945	1,739	79.98	14,585	3,099	81.51	13,478	4,206
11,000	84.59	19,452	86.28	17,538	1,914	87.97	16,041	3,411	89.67	14,828	4,624
12,000	92.27	21,217	94.12	19,131	2,086	95.96	17,497	3,720	97.81	16,173	5,044
13,000	99.96	22,986	101.96	20,724	2,262	103.96	18,956	4,030	105.96	17,521	5,465
14,000	107.65	24,754	109.80	22,317	2,437	111.96	20,415	4,339	114.11	18,868	5,886
15,000	115.34	26,522	117.65	23,913	2,609	119.95	21,871	4,651	122.26	20,216	6,306
16,000	123.03	28,291	125.49	25,507	2,784	127.95	23,330	4,961	130.41	21,563	6,728
17,000	130.72	30,059	133.33	27,100	2,959	135.95	24,789	5,270	138.56	22,911	7,148
18,000	138.41	31,828	141.18	28,696	3,132	143.95	26,248	5,580	146.71	24,258	7,570
19,000	146.10	33,596	149.02	30,289	3,307	151.94	27,704	5,892	154.87	25,609	7,987
20,000	153.79	35,364	156.87	31,886	3,478	159.94	29,163	6,201	163.02	26,956	8,408
21,000	161.48	37,133	164.71	33,479	3,654	167.94	30,623	6,510	171.17	28,304	8,829
22,000	169.17	38,901	172.55	35,072	3,829	175.94	32,082	6,819	179.32	29,651	9,250
23,000	176.86	40,670	180.40	36,668	4,002	183.93	33,538	7,132	187.47	30,999	9,671
24,000	184.54	42,434	188.23	38,258	4,176	191.92	34,994	7,440	195.61	32,343	10,091
25,000	192.23	44,203	196.07	39,851	4,352	199.92	36,453	7,750	203.76	33,691	10,512
26,000	199.92	45,971	203.92	41,448	4,523	207.92	37,912	8,059	211.92	35,041	10,930
27,000	207.61	47,740	211.76	43,041	4,699	215.91	39,368	8,372	220.07	36,389	11,351
28,000	215.30	49,508	219.61	44,637	4,871	223.91	40,827	8,681	228.22	37,736	11,772
29,000	222.99	51,276	227.45	46,230	5,046	231.91	42,286	8,990	236.37	39,084	12,192
30,000	230.68	53,045	235.29	47,824	5,221	239.91	43,745	9,300	244.52	40,431	12,614
32,500	249.90	57,464	254.90	51,810	5,654	259.90	47,390	10,074	264.89	43,799	13,665
35,000	269.12	61,883	274.50	55,793	6,090	279.88	51,031	10,852	285.27	47,169	14,714
40,000	307.57	70,725	313.72	63,765	6,960	319.87	58,324	12,401	326.02	53,906	16,819
45,000	346.02	79,567	352.94	71,737	7,830	359.86	65,616	13,951	366.78	60,647	18,920
50,000	384.46	88,406	392.15	79,706	8,700	399.84	72,906	15,500	407.53	67,385	21,021
55,000	422.91	97,248	431.37	87,678	9,570	439.83	80,198	17,050	448.28	74,122	23,126
60,000	461.35	106,086	470.58	95,647	10,439	479.80	87,484	18,602	489.03	80,860	25,226
65,000	499.80	114,928	509.80	103,619	11,309	519.79	94,777	20,151	529.79	87,600	27,328
70,000	538.24	123,766	549.00	111,585	12,181	559.77	102,066	21,700	570.53	94,335	29,431
75,000	576.69	132,608	588.22	119,557	13,051	599.76	109,358	23,250	611.29	101,075	31,533
80,000	615.14	141,450	627.44	127,530	13,920	639.75	116,651	24,799	652.05	107,816	33,634
85,000	653.58	150,289	666.65	135,498	14,791	679.72	123,937	26,352	692.79	114,551	35,738
90,000	692.03	159,131	705.87	143,471	15,660	719.71	131,229	27,902	733.55	121,291	37,840
95,000	730.47	167,969	745.08	151,440	16,529	759.69	138,519	29,450	774.30	128,029	39,940
100,000	768.92	176,811	784.30	159,412	17,399	799.68	145,811	31,000	815.06	134,769	42,042
105,000	807.36	185,650	823.51	167,381	18,269	839.65	153,097	32,553	855.80	141,504	44,146
110,000	845.81	194,492	862.73	175,353	19,139	879.64	160,390	34,102	896.56	148,244	46,248
115,000	884.26	203,334	901.95	183,325	20,009	919.63	167,682	35,652	937.32	154,985	48,349
120,000	922.70	212,172	941.15	191,291	20,881	959.61	174,972	37,200	978.06	161,719	50,453
125,000	961.15	221,014	980.37	199,263	21,751	999.60	182,264	38,750	1,018.82	168,460	52,554
130,000	999.59	229,852	1,019.58	207,232	22,620	1,039.57	189,550	40,302	1,059.57	175,197	54,655
135,000	1,038.04	238,694	1,058.80	215,204	23,490	1,079.56	196,843	41,851	1,100.32	181,935	56,759
140,000	1,076.48	247,533	1,098.01	223,173	24,360	1,119.54	204,132	43,401	1,141.07	188,673	58,860
145,000	1,114.93	256,375	1,137.23	231,146	25,229	1,159.53	211,424	44,951	1,181.83	195,413	60,962
150,000	1,153.38	265,217	1,176.45	239,118	26,099	1,199.52	218,717	46,500	1,222.58	202,151	63,066
155,000	1,191.82	274,055	1,215.66	247,087	26,968	1,239.49	226,003	48,052	1,263.33	208,888	65,167
160,000	1,230.27	282,897	1,254.88	255,059	27,838	1,279.48	233,296	49,601	1,304.09	215,629	67,268
165,000	1,268.71	291,736	1,294.08	263,025	28,711	1,319.46	240,585	51,151	1,344.83	222,363	69,373
170,000	1,307.16	300,578	1,333.30	270,997	29,581	1,359.45	247,877	52,701	1,385.59	229,104	71,474
175,000	1,345.60	309,416	1,372.51	278,966	30,450	1,399.42	255,164	54,252	1,426.34	235,842	73,574
180,000	1,384.05	318,258	1,411.73	286,938	31,320	1,439.41	262,456	55,802	1,467.09	242,579	75,679
185,000	1,422.49	327,096	1,450.94	294,907	32,189	1,479.39	269,745	57,351	1,507.84	249,317	77,779
190,000	1,460.94	335,938	1,490.16	302,879	33,059	1,519.38	277,038	58,900	1,548.60	256,057	79,881
195,000	1,499.39	344,780	1,529.38	310,852	33,928	1,559.37	284,330	60,450	1,589.35	262,795	81,985
200,000	1,537.83	353,619	1,568.59	318,821	34,798	1,599.34	291,616	62,003	1,630.10	269,532	84,087

206

AUGMENTED PAYMENT MORTGAGES 8.50%

AMOUNT OF LOAN	30 YEARS		8% PMT INCREASE 271.615 PAYMENTS			10% PMT INCREASE 257.408 PAYMENTS			12% PMT INCREASE 244.937 PAYMENTS		
	MONTHLY PAYMENT	TOTAL INTRST	MONTHLY PAYMENT	TOTAL INTRST	INTRST SAVED	MONTHLY PAYMENT	TOTAL INTRST	INTRST SAVED	MONTHLY PAYMENT	TOTAL INTRST	INTRST SAVED
$ 50	0.39	90	0.42	64	26	0.43	61	29	0.44	58	32
100	0.77	177	0.83	125	52	0.85	119	58	0.86	111	66
200	1.54	354	1.66	251	103	1.69	235	119	1.72	221	133
300	2.31	532	2.49	376	156	2.54	354	178	2.59	334	198
400	3.08	709	3.33	504	205	3.39	473	236	3.45	445	264
500	3.85	886	4.16	630	256	4.24	591	295	4.31	556	330
600	4.62	1,063	4.99	755	308	5.08	708	355	5.17	666	397
700	5.39	1,240	5.82	881	359	5.93	826	414	6.04	779	461
800	6.16	1,418	6.65	1,006	412	6.78	945	473	6.90	890	528
900	6.93	1,595	7.48	1,132	463	7.62	1,061	534	7.76	1,001	594
1,000	7.69	1,768	8.31	1,257	511	8.46	1,178	590	8.61	1,109	659
2,000	15.38	3,537	16.61	2,512	1,025	16.92	2,355	1,182	17.23	2,220	1,317
3,000	23.07	5,305	24.92	3,769	1,536	25.38	3,533	1,772	25.84	3,329	1,976
4,000	30.76	7,074	33.22	5,023	2,051	33.84	4,711	2,363	34.45	4,438	2,636
5,000	38.45	8,842	41.53	6,280	2,562	42.30	5,888	2,954	43.06	5,547	3,295
6,000	46.14	10,610	49.83	7,535	3,075	50.75	7,063	3,547	51.68	6,658	3,952
7,000	53.83	12,379	58.14	8,792	3,587	59.21	8,241	4,138	60.29	7,767	4,612
8,000	61.52	14,147	66.44	10,046	4,101	67.67	9,419	4,728	68.90	8,876	5,271
9,000	69.21	15,916	74.75	11,303	4,613	76.13	10,596	5,320	77.52	9,988	5,928
10,000	76.90	17,684	83.05	12,558	5,126	84.59	11,774	5,910	86.13	11,096	6,588
11,000	84.59	19,452	91.36	13,815	5,637	93.05	12,952	6,500	94.74	12,205	7,247
12,000	92.27	21,217	99.65	15,066	6,151	101.50	14,127	7,090	103.34	13,312	7,905
13,000	99.96	22,986	107.96	16,324	6,662	109.96	15,305	7,681	111.96	14,423	8,563
14,000	107.65	24,754	116.26	17,578	7,176	118.42	16,482	8,272	120.57	15,532	9,222
15,000	115.34	26,522	124.57	18,835	7,687	126.87	17,657	8,865	129.18	16,641	9,881
16,000	123.03	28,291	132.87	20,089	8,202	135.33	18,835	9,456	137.79	17,750	10,541
17,000	130.72	30,059	141.18	21,347	8,712	143.79	20,013	10,046	146.41	18,861	11,198
18,000	138.41	31,828	149.48	22,601	9,227	152.25	21,190	10,638	155.02	19,970	11,858
19,000	146.10	33,596	157.79	23,858	9,738	160.71	22,368	11,228	163.63	21,079	12,517
20,000	153.79	35,364	166.09	25,113	10,251	169.17	23,546	11,818	172.24	22,188	13,176
21,000	161.48	37,133	174.40	26,370	10,763	177.63	24,723	12,410	180.86	23,299	13,834
22,000	169.17	38,901	182.70	27,624	11,277	186.09	25,901	13,000	189.47	24,408	14,493
23,000	176.86	40,670	191.01	28,881	11,789	194.55	27,079	13,591	198.08	25,517	15,153
24,000	184.54	42,434	199.30	30,133	12,301	202.99	28,251	14,183	206.68	26,624	15,810
25,000	192.23	44,203	207.61	31,390	12,813	211.45	29,429	14,774	215.30	27,735	16,468
26,000	199.92	45,971	215.91	32,644	13,327	219.91	30,607	15,364	223.91	28,844	17,127
27,000	207.61	47,740	224.22	33,902	13,838	228.37	31,784	15,956	232.52	29,953	17,787
28,000	215.30	49,508	232.52	35,156	14,352	236.83	32,962	16,546	241.14	31,064	18,444
29,000	222.99	51,276	240.83	36,413	14,863	245.29	34,140	17,136	249.76	32,173	19,103
30,000	230.68	53,045	249.13	37,667	15,378	253.75	35,317	17,728	258.36	33,282	19,763
32,500	249.90	57,464	269.89	40,806	16,658	274.89	38,259	19,205	279.89	36,055	21,409
35,000	269.12	61,883	290.65	43,945	17,938	296.03	41,200	20,683	301.41	38,826	23,057
40,000	307.57	70,725	332.18	50,225	20,500	338.33	47,089	23,636	344.48	44,376	26,349
45,000	346.02	79,567	373.70	56,503	23,064	380.62	52,975	26,592	387.54	49,923	29,644
50,000	384.46	88,406	415.22	62,780	25,626	422.91	58,860	29,546	430.60	55,470	32,936
55,000	422.91	97,248	456.74	69,057	28,191	465.20	64,746	32,502	473.66	61,017	36,231
60,000	461.35	106,086	498.26	75,335	30,751	507.49	70,632	35,454	516.71	66,561	39,525
65,000	499.80	114,928	539.78	81,612	33,316	549.78	76,518	38,410	559.78	72,111	42,817
70,000	538.24	123,766	581.30	87,890	35,876	592.06	82,401	41,365	602.83	77,655	46,111
75,000	576.69	132,608	622.83	94,170	38,438	634.36	88,289	44,319	645.89	83,202	49,406
80,000	615.14	141,450	664.35	100,447	41,003	676.65	94,175	47,275	688.96	88,752	52,698
85,000	653.58	150,289	705.87	106,725	43,564	718.94	100,061	50,228	732.01	94,296	55,993
90,000	692.03	159,131	747.39	113,002	46,129	761.23	105,947	53,184	775.07	99,843	59,288
95,000	730.47	167,969	788.91	119,280	48,689	803.52	111,832	56,137	818.13	105,390	62,579
100,000	768.92	176,811	830.43	125,557	51,254	845.81	117,718	59,093	861.19	110,937	65,874
105,000	807.36	185,650	871.95	131,835	53,815	888.10	123,604	62,046	904.24	116,482	69,168
110,000	845.81	194,492	913.47	138,112	56,380	930.39	129,490	65,002	947.31	122,031	72,461
115,000	884.26	203,334	955.00	144,392	58,942	972.69	135,378	67,956	990.37	127,578	75,756
120,000	922.70	212,172	996.52	150,670	61,502	1,014.97	141,261	70,911	1,033.42	133,123	79,049
125,000	961.15	221,014	1,038.04	156,947	64,067	1,057.27	147,150	73,864	1,076.49	138,672	82,342
130,000	999.59	229,852	1,079.56	163,225	66,627	1,099.55	153,033	76,819	1,119.54	144,217	85,635
135,000	1,038.04	238,694	1,121.08	169,502	69,192	1,141.84	158,919	79,775	1,162.60	149,764	88,930
140,000	1,076.48	247,533	1,162.60	175,780	71,753	1,184.13	164,805	82,728	1,205.66	155,311	92,222
145,000	1,114.93	256,375	1,204.12	182,057	74,318	1,226.42	170,690	85,685	1,248.72	160,858	95,517
150,000	1,153.38	265,217	1,245.65	188,337	76,880	1,268.72	176,579	88,638	1,291.79	166,407	98,810
155,000	1,191.82	274,055	1,287.17	194,615	79,440	1,311.00	182,462	91,593	1,334.84	171,952	102,103
160,000	1,230.27	282,897	1,328.69	200,892	82,005	1,353.30	188,350	94,547	1,377.90	177,499	105,398
165,000	1,268.71	291,736	1,370.21	207,170	84,566	1,395.58	194,233	97,503	1,420.96	183,046	108,690
170,000	1,307.16	300,578	1,411.73	213,447	87,131	1,437.88	200,122	100,456	1,464.02	188,593	111,985
175,000	1,345.60	309,416	1,453.25	219,724	89,692	1,480.16	206,005	103,411	1,507.07	194,137	115,279
180,000	1,384.05	318,258	1,494.77	226,002	92,256	1,522.46	211,893	106,365	1,550.14	199,687	118,571
185,000	1,422.49	327,096	1,536.29	232,279	94,817	1,564.74	217,775	109,319	1,593.19	205,231	121,865
190,000	1,460.94	335,938	1,577.82	238,560	97,378	1,607.03	223,662	112,276	1,636.25	210,778	125,160
195,000	1,499.39	344,780	1,619.34	244,837	99,943	1,649.33	229,551	115,229	1,679.32	216,328	128,452
200,000	1,537.83	353,619	1,660.86	251,114	102,505	1,691.61	235,434	118,185	1,722.37	221,872	131,747

207

AUGMENTED PAYMENT MORTGAGES

AMOUNT OF LOAN	30 YEARS		2% PMT INCREASE 329.452 PAYMENTS			4% PMT INCREASE 305.348 PAYMENTS			6% PMT INCREASE 285.564 PAYMENTS		
	MONTHLY PAYMENT	TOTAL INTRST	MONTHLY PAYMENT	TOTAL INTRST	INTRST SAVED	MONTHLY PAYMENT	TOTAL INTRST	INTRST SAVED	MONTHLY PAYMENT	TOTAL INTRST	INTRST SAVED
$ 50	0.40	94	0.41	85	9	0.42	78	16	0.42	70	24
100	0.79	184	0.81	167	17	0.82	150	34	0.84	140	44
200	1.58	369	1.61	330	39	1.64	301	68	1.67	277	92
300	2.37	553	2.42	497	56	2.46	451	102	2.51	417	136
400	3.15	734	3.21	658	76	3.28	602	132	3.34	554	180
500	3.94	918	4.02	824	94	4.10	752	166	4.18	694	224
600	4.73	1,103	4.82	988	115	4.92	902	201	5.01	831	272
700	5.51	1,284	5.62	1,152	132	5.73	1,050	234	5.84	968	316
800	6.30	1,468	6.43	1,318	150	6.55	1,200	268	6.68	1,108	360
900	7.09	1,652	7.23	1,482	170	7.37	1,350	302	7.52	1,247	405
1,000	7.87	1,833	8.03	1,645	188	8.18	1,498	335	8.34	1,382	451
2,000	15.74	3,666	16.05	3,288	378	16.37	2,999	667	16.68	2,763	903
3,000	23.61	5,500	24.08	4,933	567	24.55	4,496	1,004	25.03	4,148	1,352
4,000	31.47	7,329	32.10	6,575	754	32.73	5,994	1,335	33.36	5,526	1,803
5,000	39.34	9,162	40.13	8,221	941	40.91	7,492	1,670	41.70	6,908	2,254
6,000	47.21	10,996	48.15	9,863	1,133	49.10	8,993	2,003	50.04	8,290	2,706
7,000	55.07	12,825	56.17	11,505	1,320	57.27	10,487	2,338	58.37	9,668	3,157
8,000	62.94	14,658	64.20	13,151	1,507	65.46	11,988	2,670	66.72	11,053	3,605
9,000	70.81	16,492	72.23	14,796	1,696	73.64	13,486	3,006	75.06	12,434	4,058
10,000	78.68	18,325	80.25	16,439	1,886	81.83	14,987	3,338	83.40	13,816	4,509
11,000	86.54	20,154	88.27	18,081	2,073	90.00	16,481	3,673	91.73	15,195	4,959
12,000	94.41	21,988	96.30	19,726	2,262	98.19	17,982	4,006	100.07	16,576	5,412
13,000	102.28	23,821	104.33	21,372	2,449	106.37	19,480	4,341	108.42	17,961	5,860
14,000	110.14	25,650	112.34	23,011	2,639	114.55	20,978	4,672	116.75	19,340	6,310
15,000	118.01	27,484	120.37	24,656	2,828	122.73	22,475	5,009	125.09	20,721	6,763
16,000	125.88	29,317	128.40	26,302	3,015	130.92	23,976	5,341	133.43	22,103	7,214
17,000	133.74	31,146	136.41	27,941	3,205	139.09	25,471	5,675	141.76	23,482	7,664
18,000	141.61	32,980	144.44	29,586	3,394	147.27	26,969	6,011	150.11	24,866	8,114
19,000	149.48	34,813	152.47	31,232	3,581	155.46	28,469	6,344	158.45	26,248	8,565
20,000	157.35	36,646	160.50	32,877	3,769	163.64	29,967	6,679	166.79	27,629	9,017
21,000	165.21	38,476	168.51	34,516	3,960	171.82	31,465	7,011	175.12	29,008	9,468
22,000	173.08	40,309	176.54	36,161	4,148	180.00	32,963	7,346	183.46	30,390	9,919
23,000	180.95	42,142	184.57	37,807	4,335	188.19	34,463	7,679	191.81	31,774	10,368
24,000	188.81	43,972	192.59	39,449	4,523	196.36	35,958	8,014	200.14	33,153	10,819
25,000	196.68	45,805	200.61	41,091	4,714	204.55	37,459	8,346	208.48	34,534	11,271
26,000	204.55	47,638	208.64	42,737	4,901	212.73	38,957	8,681	216.82	35,916	11,722
27,000	212.41	49,468	216.66	44,379	5,089	220.91	40,454	9,014	225.15	37,295	12,173
28,000	220.28	51,301	224.69	46,025	5,276	229.09	41,952	9,349	233.50	38,679	12,622
29,000	228.15	53,134	232.71	47,667	5,467	237.28	43,453	9,681	241.84	40,061	13,073
30,000	236.02	54,967	240.74	49,312	5,655	245.46	44,951	10,016	250.18	41,442	13,525
32,500	255.68	59,545	260.79	53,418	6,127	265.91	48,695	10,850	271.02	44,894	14,651
35,000	275.35	64,126	280.86	57,530	6,596	286.36	52,439	11,687	291.87	48,348	15,778
40,000	314.69	73,288	320.98	65,748	7,540	327.28	59,934	13,354	333.57	55,256	18,032
45,000	354.02	82,447	361.10	73,965	8,482	368.18	67,423	15,024	375.26	62,161	20,286
50,000	393.36	91,610	401.23	82,186	9,424	409.09	74,915	16,695	416.96	69,069	22,541
55,000	432.69	100,768	441.34	90,400	10,368	450.00	82,407	18,361	458.65	75,974	24,794
60,000	472.03	109,931	481.47	98,621	11,310	490.91	89,898	20,033	500.35	82,882	27,049
65,000	511.36	119,090	521.59	106,839	12,251	531.81	97,387	21,703	542.04	89,787	29,303
70,000	550.70	128,252	561.71	115,056	13,196	572.73	104,882	23,370	583.74	96,695	31,557
75,000	590.03	137,411	601.83	123,274	14,137	613.63	112,371	25,040	625.43	103,600	33,811
80,000	629.37	146,573	641.96	131,495	15,078	654.54	119,862	26,711	667.13	110,508	36,065
85,000	668.70	155,732	682.07	139,709	16,023	695.45	127,354	28,378	708.82	117,413	38,319
90,000	708.04	164,894	722.20	147,930	16,964	736.36	134,846	30,048	750.52	124,321	40,573
95,000	747.37	174,053	762.32	156,148	17,905	777.26	142,335	31,718	792.21	131,227	42,826
100,000	786.71	183,216	802.44	164,365	18,851	818.18	149,830	33,386	833.91	138,135	45,081
105,000	826.04	192,374	842.56	172,583	19,791	859.08	157,318	35,056	875.60	145,040	47,334
110,000	865.38	201,537	882.69	180,804	20,733	900.00	164,813	36,724	917.30	151,948	49,589
115,000	904.71	210,696	922.80	189,018	21,678	940.90	172,302	38,394	958.99	158,853	51,843
120,000	944.05	219,858	962.93	197,239	22,619	981.81	179,794	40,064	1,000.69	165,761	54,097
125,000	983.38	229,017	1,003.05	205,457	23,560	1,022.72	187,286	41,731	1,042.38	172,666	56,351
130,000	1,022.72	238,179	1,043.17	213,674	24,505	1,063.63	194,777	43,402	1,084.08	179,574	58,605
135,000	1,062.05	247,338	1,083.29	221,892	25,446	1,104.53	202,266	45,072	1,125.77	186,479	60,859
140,000	1,101.39	256,500	1,123.42	230,113	26,387	1,145.45	209,761	46,739	1,167.47	193,387	63,113
145,000	1,140.72	265,659	1,163.53	238,327	27,332	1,186.35	217,250	48,409	1,209.16	200,293	65,366
150,000	1,180.06	274,822	1,203.66	246,548	28,274	1,227.26	224,741	50,081	1,250.86	207,201	67,621
155,000	1,219.39	283,980	1,243.78	254,762	29,214	1,268.17	232,233	51,747	1,292.55	214,106	69,874
160,000	1,258.73	293,143	1,283.90	262,983	30,160	1,309.08	239,725	53,418	1,334.25	221,014	72,129
165,000	1,298.06	302,302	1,324.02	271,201	31,101	1,349.98	247,214	55,088	1,375.94	227,919	74,383
170,000	1,337.40	311,464	1,364.15	279,422	32,042	1,390.90	254,709	56,755	1,417.64	234,827	76,637
175,000	1,376.73	320,623	1,404.26	287,636	32,987	1,431.80	262,197	58,426	1,459.33	241,732	78,891
180,000	1,416.07	329,785	1,444.39	295,857	33,928	1,472.71	269,689	60,096	1,501.03	248,640	81,145
185,000	1,455.40	338,944	1,484.51	304,075	34,869	1,513.62	277,181	61,763	1,542.72	255,545	83,399
190,000	1,494.74	348,106	1,524.63	312,294	35,814	1,554.53	284,673	63,433	1,584.42	262,453	85,653
195,000	1,534.07	357,265	1,564.75	320,510	36,755	1,595.43	292,161	65,104	1,626.11	269,358	87,907
200,000	1,573.41	366,428	1,604.88	328,731	37,697	1,636.35	299,656	66,772	1,667.81	276,266	90,162

AMOUNT OF LOAN	30 YEARS		8% PMT INCREASE 268.872 PAYMENTS			10% PMT INCREASE 254.502 PAYMENTS			12% PMT INCREASE 241.935 PAYMENTS		
	MONTHLY PAYMENT	TOTAL INTRST	MONTHLY PAYMENT	TOTAL INTRST	INTRST SAVED	MONTHLY PAYMENT	TOTAL INTRST	INTRST SAVED	MONTHLY PAYMENT	TOTAL INTRST	INTRST SAVED
$ 50	0.40	94	0.43	66	28	0.44	62	32	0.45	59	35
100	0.79	184	0.85	129	55	0.87	121	63	0.88	113	71
200	1.58	369	1.71	260	109	1.74	243	126	1.77	228	141
300	2.37	553	2.56	388	165	2.61	364	189	2.65	341	212
400	3.15	734	3.40	514	220	3.47	483	251	3.53	454	280
500	3.94	918	4.26	645	273	4.33	602	316	4.41	567	351
600	4.73	1,103	5.11	774	329	5.20	723	380	5.30	682	421
700	5.51	1,284	5.95	900	384	6.06	842	442	6.17	793	491
800	6.30	1,468	6.80	1,028	440	6.93	964	504	7.06	908	560
900	7.09	1,652	7.66	1,160	492	7.80	1,085	567	7.94	1,021	631
1,000	7.87	1,833	8.50	1,285	548	8.66	1,204	629	8.81	1,131	702
2,000	15.74	3,666	17.00	2,571	1,095	17.31	2,405	1,261	17.63	2,265	1,401
3,000	23.61	5,500	25.50	3,856	1,644	25.97	3,609	1,891	26.44	3,397	2,103
4,000	31.47	7,329	33.99	5,139	2,190	34.62	4,811	2,518	35.25	4,528	2,801
5,000	39.34	9,162	42.49	6,424	2,738	43.27	6,012	3,150	44.06	5,660	3,502
6,000	47.21	10,996	50.99	7,710	3,286	51.93	7,216	3,780	52.88	6,794	4,202
7,000	55.07	12,825	59.48	8,993	3,832	60.58	8,418	4,407	61.68	7,923	4,902
8,000	62.94	14,658	67.98	10,278	4,380	69.23	9,619	5,039	70.49	9,054	5,604
9,000	70.81	16,492	76.47	11,561	4,931	77.89	10,823	5,669	79.31	10,188	6,304
10,000	78.68	18,325	84.97	12,846	5,479	86.55	12,027	6,298	88.12	11,319	7,006
11,000	86.54	20,154	93.46	14,129	6,025	95.19	13,226	6,928	96.92	12,448	7,706
12,000	94.41	21,988	101.96	15,414	6,574	103.85	14,430	7,558	105.74	13,582	8,406
13,000	102.28	23,821	110.46	16,700	7,121	112.51	15,634	8,187	114.55	14,714	9,107
14,000	110.14	25,650	118.95	17,982	7,668	121.15	16,833	8,817	123.36	15,845	9,805
15,000	118.01	27,484	127.45	19,268	8,216	129.81	18,037	9,447	132.17	16,977	10,507
16,000	125.88	29,317	135.95	20,553	8,764	138.47	19,241	10,076	140.99	18,110	11,207
17,000	133.74	31,146	144.44	21,836	9,310	147.11	20,440	10,706	149.79	19,239	11,907
18,000	141.61	32,980	152.94	23,121	9,859	155.77	21,644	11,336	158.60	20,371	12,609
19,000	149.48	34,813	161.44	24,407	10,406	164.43	22,848	11,965	167.42	21,505	13,308
20,000	157.35	36,646	169.94	25,692	10,954	173.09	24,052	12,594	176.23	22,636	14,010
21,000	165.21	38,476	178.43	26,975	11,501	181.73	25,251	13,225	185.04	23,768	14,708
22,000	173.08	40,309	186.93	28,260	12,049	190.39	26,455	13,854	193.85	24,899	15,410
23,000	180.95	42,142	195.43	29,546	12,596	199.05	27,659	14,483	202.66	26,031	16,111
24,000	188.81	43,972	203.91	30,826	13,146	207.69	28,858	15,114	211.47	27,162	16,810
25,000	196.68	45,805	212.41	32,111	13,694	216.35	30,062	15,743	220.28	28,293	17,512
26,000	204.55	47,638	220.91	33,397	14,241	225.01	31,265	16,373	229.10	29,427	18,211
27,000	212.41	49,468	229.40	34,679	14,789	233.65	32,464	17,004	237.90	30,556	18,912
28,000	220.28	51,301	237.90	35,965	15,336	242.31	33,668	17,633	246.71	31,688	19,613
29,000	228.15	53,134	246.40	37,250	15,884	250.97	34,872	18,262	255.53	32,822	20,312
30,000	236.02	54,967	254.90	38,535	16,432	259.62	36,074	18,893	264.34	33,953	21,014
32,500	255.68	59,545	276.13	41,744	17,801	281.25	39,079	20,466	286.36	36,781	22,764
35,000	275.35	64,126	297.38	44,957	19,169	302.89	42,086	22,040	308.39	39,610	24,516
40,000	314.69	73,288	339.87	51,382	21,906	346.16	48,098	25,190	352.45	45,270	28,018
45,000	354.02	82,447	382.34	57,801	24,646	389.42	54,108	28,339	396.50	50,927	31,520
50,000	393.36	91,610	424.83	64,225	27,385	432.70	60,123	31,487	440.56	56,587	35,023
55,000	432.69	100,768	467.31	70,647	30,121	475.96	66,133	34,635	484.61	62,244	38,524
60,000	472.03	109,931	509.79	77,068	32,863	519.23	72,145	37,786	528.67	67,904	42,027
65,000	511.36	119,090	552.27	83,490	35,600	562.50	78,157	40,933	572.72	73,561	45,529
70,000	550.70	128,252	594.76	89,914	38,338	605.77	84,170	44,082	616.78	79,221	49,031
75,000	590.03	137,411	637.23	96,333	41,078	649.03	90,179	47,232	660.83	84,878	52,533
80,000	629.37	146,573	679.72	102,758	43,815	692.31	96,194	50,379	704.89	90,538	56,035
85,000	668.70	155,732	722.20	109,179	46,553	735.57	102,204	53,528	748.94	96,195	59,537
90,000	708.04	164,894	764.68	115,601	49,293	778.84	108,216	56,678	793.00	101,854	63,040
95,000	747.37	174,053	807.16	122,023	52,030	822.11	114,229	59,824	837.05	107,512	66,541
100,000	786.71	183,216	849.65	128,447	54,769	865.38	120,241	62,975	881.12	113,174	70,042
105,000	826.04	192,374	892.12	134,866	57,508	908.64	126,251	66,123	925.16	118,829	73,545
110,000	865.38	201,537	934.61	141,290	60,247	951.92	132,266	69,271	969.23	124,491	77,046
115,000	904.71	210,696	977.09	147,712	62,984	995.18	138,275	72,421	1,013.28	130,148	80,548
120,000	944.05	219,858	1,019.57	154,134	65,724	1,038.46	144,290	75,568	1,057.34	135,808	84,050
125,000	983.38	229,017	1,062.05	160,556	68,461	1,081.72	150,300	78,717	1,101.39	141,465	87,552
130,000	1,022.72	238,179	1,104.54	166,980	71,199	1,124.99	156,312	81,867	1,145.45	147,124	91,055
135,000	1,062.05	247,338	1,147.01	173,399	73,939	1,168.26	162,325	85,013	1,189.50	152,782	94,556
140,000	1,101.39	256,500	1,189.50	179,823	76,677	1,211.53	168,337	88,163	1,233.56	158,441	98,059
145,000	1,140.72	265,659	1,231.98	186,245	79,414	1,254.79	174,347	91,312	1,277.61	164,099	101,560
150,000	1,180.06	274,822	1,274.46	192,667	82,155	1,298.07	180,361	94,461	1,321.67	169,758	105,064
155,000	1,219.39	283,980	1,316.94	199,088	84,892	1,341.33	186,371	97,609	1,365.72	175,415	108,565
160,000	1,258.73	293,143	1,359.43	205,513	87,630	1,384.60	192,383	100,760	1,409.78	181,075	112,068
165,000	1,298.06	302,302	1,401.90	211,932	90,370	1,427.87	198,396	103,906	1,453.83	186,732	115,570
170,000	1,337.40	311,464	1,444.39	218,356	93,108	1,471.14	204,408	107,056	1,497.89	192,392	119,072
175,000	1,376.73	320,623	1,486.87	224,778	95,845	1,514.40	210,418	110,205	1,541.94	198,049	122,574
180,000	1,416.07	329,785	1,529.36	231,202	98,583	1,557.68	216,433	113,352	1,586.00	203,709	126,076
185,000	1,455.40	338,944	1,571.83	237,621	101,323	1,600.94	222,442	116,502	1,630.05	209,366	129,578
190,000	1,494.74	348,106	1,614.32	244,045	104,061	1,644.21	228,453	119,651	1,674.11	215,026	133,080
195,000	1,534.07	357,265	1,656.80	250,467	106,798	1,687.48	234,467	122,798	1,718.16	220,683	136,582
200,000	1,573.41	366,428	1,699.28	256,889	109,539	1,730.75	240,479	125,949	1,762.22	226,343	140,085

AUGMENTED PAYMENT MORTGAGES

AMOUNT OF LOAN	30 YEARS		2% PMT INCREASE 328.094 PAYMENTS			4% PMT INCREASE 303.252 PAYMENTS			6% PMT INCREASE 283.041 PAYMENTS		
	MONTHLY PAYMENT	TOTAL INTRST	MONTHLY PAYMENT	TOTAL INTRST	INTRST SAVED	MONTHLY PAYMENT	TOTAL INTRST	INTRST SAVED	MONTHLY PAYMENT	TOTAL INTRST	INTRST SAVED
$ 50	0.41	98	0.42	88	10	0.43	80	18	0.43	72	26
100	0.81	192	0.83	172	20	0.84	155	37	0.86	143	49
200	1.61	380	1.64	338	42	1.67	306	74	1.71	284	96
300	2.42	571	2.47	510	61	2.52	464	107	2.57	427	144
400	3.22	759	3.28	676	83	3.35	616	143	3.41	565	194
500	4.03	951	4.11	848	103	4.19	771	180	4.27	709	242
600	4.83	1,139	4.93	1,018	121	5.02	922	217	5.12	849	290
700	5.64	1,330	5.75	1,187	143	5.87	1,080	250	5.98	993	337
800	6.44	1,518	6.57	1,356	162	6.70	1,232	286	6.83	1,133	385
900	7.25	1,710	7.40	1,528	182	7.54	1,387	323	7.69	1,277	433
1,000	8.05	1,898	8.21	1,694	204	8.37	1,538	360	8.53	1,414	484
2,000	16.10	3,796	16.42	3,387	409	16.74	3,076	720	17.07	2,832	964
3,000	24.14	5,690	24.62	5,078	612	25.11	4,615	1,075	25.59	4,243	1,447
4,000	32.19	7,588	32.83	6,771	817	33.48	6,153	1,435	34.12	5,657	1,931
5,000	40.24	9,486	41.04	8,465	1,021	41.85	7,691	1,795	42.65	7,072	2,414
6,000	48.28	11,381	49.25	10,159	1,222	50.21	9,226	2,155	51.18	8,486	2,895
7,000	56.33	13,279	57.46	11,852	1,427	58.58	10,765	2,514	59.71	9,900	3,379
8,000	64.37	15,173	65.66	13,543	1,630	66.94	12,300	2,873	68.23	11,312	3,861
9,000	72.42	17,071	73.87	15,236	1,835	75.32	13,841	3,230	76.77	12,729	4,342
10,000	80.47	18,969	82.08	16,930	2,039	83.69	15,379	3,590	85.30	14,143	4,826
11,000	88.51	20,864	90.28	18,620	2,244	92.05	16,914	3,950	93.82	15,555	5,309
12,000	96.56	22,762	98.49	20,314	2,448	100.42	18,453	4,309	102.35	16,969	5,793
13,000	104.61	24,660	106.70	22,008	2,652	108.79	19,991	4,669	110.89	18,386	6,274
14,000	112.65	26,554	114.90	23,698	2,856	117.16	21,529	5,025	119.41	19,798	6,756
15,000	120.70	28,452	123.11	25,392	3,060	125.53	23,067	5,385	127.94	21,212	7,240
16,000	128.74	30,346	131.31	27,082	3,264	133.89	24,602	5,744	136.46	22,624	7,722
17,000	136.79	32,244	139.53	28,779	3,465	142.26	26,141	6,103	145.00	24,041	8,203
18,000	144.84	34,142	147.74	30,473	3,669	150.63	27,679	6,463	153.53	25,455	8,687
19,000	152.88	36,037	155.94	32,163	3,874	159.00	29,217	6,820	162.05	26,867	9,170
20,000	160.93	37,935	164.15	33,857	4,078	167.37	30,755	7,180	170.59	28,284	9,651
21,000	168.98	39,833	172.36	35,550	4,283	175.74	32,294	7,539	179.12	29,698	10,135
22,000	177.02	41,727	180.56	37,241	4,486	184.10	33,829	7,898	187.64	31,110	10,617
23,000	185.07	43,625	188.77	38,934	4,691	192.47	35,367	8,258	196.17	32,524	11,101
24,000	193.11	45,520	196.97	40,625	4,895	200.83	36,902	8,618	204.70	33,938	11,582
25,000	201.16	47,418	205.18	42,318	5,100	209.21	38,443	8,975	213.23	35,353	12,065
26,000	209.21	49,316	213.39	44,012	5,304	217.58	39,982	9,334	221.76	36,767	12,549
27,000	217.25	51,210	221.60	45,706	5,504	225.94	41,517	9,693	230.29	38,182	13,028
28,000	225.30	53,108	229.81	47,399	5,709	234.31	43,055	10,053	238.82	39,596	13,512
29,000	233.35	55,006	238.02	49,093	5,913	242.68	44,593	10,413	247.35	41,010	13,996
30,000	241.39	56,900	246.22	50,783	6,117	251.05	46,131	10,769	255.87	42,422	14,478
32,500	261.51	61,644	266.74	55,016	6,628	271.97	49,975	11,669	277.20	45,959	15,685
35,000	281.62	66,383	287.25	59,245	7,138	292.88	53,816	12,567	298.52	49,493	16,890
40,000	321.85	75,866	328.29	67,710	8,156	334.72	61,505	14,361	341.16	56,562	19,304
45,000	362.09	85,352	369.33	76,175	9,177	376.57	69,196	16,156	383.82	63,637	21,715
50,000	402.32	94,835	410.37	84,640	10,195	418.41	76,884	17,951	426.46	70,706	24,129
55,000	442.55	104,318	451.40	93,102	11,216	460.25	84,572	19,746	469.10	77,775	26,543
60,000	482.78	113,801	492.44	101,567	12,234	502.09	92,260	21,541	511.75	84,846	28,955
65,000	523.01	123,284	533.47	110,028	13,256	543.93	99,948	23,336	554.39	91,915	31,369
70,000	563.24	132,766	574.50	118,490	14,276	585.77	107,636	25,130	597.03	98,984	33,782
75,000	603.47	142,249	615.54	126,955	15,294	627.61	115,324	26,925	639.68	106,056	36,193
80,000	643.70	151,732	656.57	135,417	16,315	669.45	123,012	28,720	682.32	113,125	38,607
85,000	683.93	161,215	697.61	143,882	17,333	711.29	130,700	30,515	724.97	120,196	41,019
90,000	724.17	170,701	738.65	152,347	18,354	753.14	138,391	32,310	767.62	127,268	43,433
95,000	764.40	180,184	779.69	160,812	19,372	794.98	146,079	34,105	810.26	134,337	45,847
100,000	804.63	189,667	820.72	169,273	20,394	836.82	153,767	35,900	852.91	141,408	48,259
105,000	844.86	199,150	861.76	177,738	21,412	878.65	161,452	37,698	895.55	148,477	50,673
110,000	885.09	208,632	902.79	186,200	22,432	920.49	169,140	39,492	938.20	155,549	53,083
115,000	925.32	218,115	943.83	194,665	23,450	962.33	176,828	41,287	980.84	162,618	55,497
120,000	965.55	227,598	984.86	203,127	24,471	1,004.17	184,517	43,081	1,023.48	169,687	57,911
125,000	1,005.78	237,081	1,025.90	211,592	25,489	1,046.01	192,205	44,876	1,066.13	176,759	60,322
130,000	1,046.01	246,564	1,066.93	220,053	26,511	1,087.85	199,893	46,671	1,108.77	183,827	62,737
135,000	1,086.25	256,050	1,107.98	228,522	27,528	1,129.70	207,584	48,466	1,151.43	190,902	65,148
140,000	1,126.48	265,533	1,149.01	236,983	28,550	1,171.54	215,272	50,261	1,194.07	197,971	67,562
145,000	1,166.71	275,016	1,190.04	245,445	29,571	1,213.38	222,960	52,056	1,236.71	205,040	69,976
150,000	1,206.94	284,498	1,231.08	253,910	30,588	1,255.22	230,648	53,850	1,279.36	212,111	72,387
155,000	1,247.17	293,981	1,272.11	262,372	31,609	1,297.06	238,336	55,645	1,322.00	219,180	74,801
160,000	1,287.40	303,464	1,313.15	270,837	32,627	1,338.90	246,024	57,440	1,364.64	226,249	77,215
165,000	1,327.63	312,947	1,354.18	279,298	33,649	1,380.74	253,712	59,235	1,407.29	233,321	79,626
170,000	1,367.86	322,430	1,395.22	287,763	34,667	1,422.57	261,397	61,033	1,449.93	240,390	82,040
175,000	1,408.09	331,912	1,436.25	296,225	35,687	1,464.41	269,085	62,827	1,492.58	247,461	84,451
180,000	1,448.33	341,399	1,477.30	304,693	36,706	1,506.26	276,776	64,623	1,535.23	254,533	86,866
185,000	1,488.56	350,882	1,518.33	313,155	37,727	1,548.10	284,464	66,418	1,577.87	261,602	89,280
190,000	1,528.79	360,365	1,559.37	321,620	38,744	1,589.94	292,152	68,212	1,620.52	268,674	91,690
195,000	1,569.02	369,847	1,600.40	330,082	39,765	1,631.78	299,841	70,006	1,663.16	275,742	94,105
200,000	1,609.25	379,330	1,641.44	338,547	40,783	1,673.62	307,529	71,801	1,705.81	282,814	96,516

AUGMENTED PAYMENT MORTGAGES 9.00%

AMOUNT OF LOAN	30 YEARS		8% PMT INCREASE 266.096 PAYMENTS			10% PMT INCREASE 251.577 PAYMENTS			12% PMT INCREASE 238.925 PAYMENTS		
	MONTHLY PAYMENT	TOTAL INTRST	MONTHLY PAYMENT	TOTAL INTRST	INTRST SAVED	MONTHLY PAYMENT	TOTAL INTRST	INTRST SAVED	MONTHLY PAYMENT	TOTAL INTRST	INTRST SAVED
$ 50	0.41	98	0.44	67	31	0.45	63	35	0.46	60	38
100	0.81	192	0.87	132	60	0.89	124	68	0.91	117	75
200	1.61	380	1.74	263	117	1.77	245	135	1.80	230	150
300	2.42	571	2.61	395	176	2.66	369	202	2.71	347	224
400	3.22	759	3.48	526	233	3.54	491	268	3.61	463	296
500	4.03	951	4.35	658	293	4.43	614	337	4.51	578	373
600	4.83	1,139	5.22	789	350	5.31	736	403	5.41	693	446
700	5.64	1,330	6.09	921	409	6.20	860	470	6.32	810	520
800	6.44	1,518	6.96	1,052	466	7.08	981	537	7.21	923	595
900	7.25	1,710	7.83	1,184	526	7.98	1,108	602	8.12	1,040	670
1,000	8.05	1,898	8.69	1,312	586	8.86	1,229	669	9.02	1,155	743
2,000	16.10	3,796	17.39	2,627	1,169	17.71	2,455	1,341	18.03	2,308	1,488
3,000	24.14	5,690	26.07	3,937	1,753	26.55	3,679	2,011	27.04	3,461	2,229
4,000	32.19	7,588	34.77	5,252	2,336	35.41	4,908	2,680	36.05	4,613	2,975
5,000	40.24	9,486	43.46	6,565	2,921	44.26	6,135	3,351	45.07	5,768	3,718
6,000	48.28	11,381	52.14	7,874	3,507	53.11	7,361	4,020	54.07	6,919	4,462
7,000	56.33	13,279	60.84	9,189	4,090	61.96	8,588	4,691	63.09	8,074	5,205
8,000	64.37	15,173	69.52	10,499	4,674	70.81	9,814	5,359	72.09	9,224	5,949
9,000	72.42	17,071	78.21	11,811	5,260	79.66	11,041	6,030	81.11	10,379	6,692
10,000	80.47	18,969	86.91	13,126	5,843	88.52	12,270	6,699	90.13	11,534	7,435
11,000	88.51	20,864	95.59	14,436	6,428	97.36	13,494	7,370	99.13	12,685	8,179
12,000	96.56	22,762	104.28	15,748	7,014	106.22	14,723	8,039	108.15	13,840	8,922
13,000	104.61	24,660	112.98	17,064	7,596	115.07	15,949	8,711	117.16	14,992	9,668
14,000	112.65	26,554	121.66	18,373	8,181	123.92	17,175	9,379	126.17	16,145	10,409
15,000	120.70	28,452	130.36	19,688	8,764	132.77	18,402	10,050	135.18	17,298	11,154
16,000	128.74	30,346	139.04	20,998	9,348	141.61	19,626	10,720	144.19	18,451	11,895
17,000	136.79	32,244	147.73	22,310	9,934	150.47	20,855	11,389	153.20	19,603	12,641
18,000	144.84	34,142	156.43	23,625	10,517	159.32	22,081	12,061	162.22	20,758	13,384
19,000	152.88	36,037	165.11	24,935	11,102	168.17	23,308	12,729	171.23	21,911	14,126
20,000	160.93	37,935	173.80	26,247	11,688	177.02	24,534	13,401	180.24	23,064	14,871
21,000	168.98	39,833	182.50	27,563	12,270	185.88	25,763	14,070	189.26	24,219	15,614
22,000	177.02	41,727	191.18	28,872	12,855	194.72	26,987	14,740	198.26	25,369	16,358
23,000	185.07	43,625	199.88	30,187	13,438	203.58	28,216	15,409	207.28	26,524	17,101
24,000	193.11	45,520	208.56	31,497	14,023	212.42	29,440	16,080	216.28	27,675	17,845
25,000	201.16	47,418	217.25	32,809	14,609	221.28	30,669	16,749	225.30	28,830	18,588
26,000	209.21	49,316	225.95	34,124	15,192	230.13	31,895	17,421	234.32	29,985	19,331
27,000	217.25	51,210	234.63	35,434	15,776	238.98	33,122	18,088	243.32	31,135	20,075
28,000	225.30	53,108	243.32	36,746	16,362	247.83	34,348	18,760	252.34	32,290	20,818
29,000	233.35	55,006	252.02	38,062	16,944	256.69	35,577	19,429	261.35	33,443	21,563
30,000	241.39	56,900	260.70	39,371	17,529	265.53	36,801	20,099	270.36	34,596	22,304
32,500	261.51	61,644	282.43	42,653	18,991	287.66	39,869	21,775	292.89	37,479	24,165
35,000	281.62	66,383	304.15	45,933	20,450	309.78	42,934	23,449	315.41	40,359	26,024
40,000	321.85	75,866	347.60	52,495	23,371	354.04	49,068	26,798	360.47	46,125	29,741
45,000	362.09	85,352	391.06	59,060	26,292	398.30	55,203	30,149	405.54	51,894	33,458
50,000	402.32	94,835	434.51	65,621	29,214	442.55	61,335	33,500	450.60	57,660	37,175
55,000	442.55	104,318	477.95	72,181	32,137	486.81	67,470	36,848	495.66	63,426	40,892
60,000	482.78	113,801	521.40	78,742	35,059	531.06	73,602	40,199	540.71	69,189	44,612
65,000	523.01	123,284	564.85	85,304	37,980	575.31	79,735	43,549	585.77	74,955	48,329
70,000	563.24	132,766	608.30	91,866	40,900	619.56	85,867	46,899	630.83	80,721	52,045
75,000	603.47	142,249	651.75	98,428	43,821	663.82	92,000	50,247	675.89	86,487	55,762
80,000	643.70	151,732	695.20	104,990	46,742	708.07	98,134	53,598	720.94	92,251	59,481
85,000	683.93	161,215	738.64	111,549	49,666	752.32	104,266	56,949	766.00	98,017	63,198
90,000	724.17	170,701	782.10	118,114	52,587	796.59	110,404	60,297	811.07	103,785	66,916
95,000	764.40	180,184	825.55	124,676	55,508	840.84	116,536	63,648	856.13	109,551	70,633
100,000	804.63	189,667	869.00	131,237	58,430	885.09	122,668	66,999	901.19	115,317	74,350
105,000	844.86	199,150	912.45	137,799	61,351	929.35	128,803	70,347	946.24	121,080	78,070
110,000	885.09	208,632	955.90	144,361	64,271	973.60	134,935	73,697	991.30	126,846	81,786
115,000	925.32	218,115	999.35	150,923	67,192	1,017.85	141,068	77,047	1,036.36	132,612	85,503
120,000	965.55	227,598	1,042.79	157,482	70,116	1,062.11	147,202	80,396	1,081.42	138,378	89,220
125,000	1,005.78	237,081	1,086.24	164,044	73,037	1,106.36	153,335	83,746	1,126.47	144,142	92,939
130,000	1,046.01	246,564	1,129.69	170,606	75,958	1,150.61	159,467	87,097	1,171.53	149,908	96,656
135,000	1,086.25	256,050	1,173.15	177,171	78,879	1,194.88	165,604	90,446	1,216.60	155,676	100,374
140,000	1,126.48	265,533	1,216.60	183,732	81,801	1,239.13	171,737	93,796	1,261.66	161,442	104,091
145,000	1,166.71	275,016	1,260.05	190,294	84,722	1,283.38	177,869	97,147	1,306.72	167,208	107,808
150,000	1,206.94	284,498	1,303.50	196,856	87,642	1,327.63	184,001	100,497	1,351.77	172,972	111,526
155,000	1,247.17	293,981	1,346.94	203,415	90,566	1,371.89	190,136	103,845	1,396.83	178,738	115,243
160,000	1,287.40	303,464	1,390.39	209,977	93,487	1,416.14	196,268	107,196	1,441.89	184,504	118,960
165,000	1,327.63	312,947	1,433.84	216,539	96,408	1,460.39	202,401	110,546	1,486.95	190,270	122,677
170,000	1,367.86	322,430	1,477.29	223,101	99,329	1,504.65	208,535	113,895	1,532.00	196,033	126,397
175,000	1,408.09	331,912	1,520.74	229,663	102,249	1,548.90	214,668	117,244	1,577.06	201,799	130,113
180,000	1,448.33	341,399	1,564.20	236,228	105,172	1,593.16	220,802	120,597	1,622.13	207,567	133,832
185,000	1,488.56	350,882	1,607.64	242,787	108,095	1,637.42	226,937	123,945	1,667.19	213,333	137,549
190,000	1,528.79	360,364	1,651.09	249,348	111,016	1,681.67	233,069	127,295	1,712.24	219,097	141,267
195,000	1,569.02	369,847	1,694.54	255,910	113,937	1,725.92	239,202	130,645	1,757.30	224,863	144,984
200,000	1,609.25	379,330	1,737.99	262,472	116,858	1,770.18	245,337	133,993	1,802.36	230,629	148,701

211

9.25% AUGMENTED PAYMENT MORTGAGES

AMOUNT OF LOAN	30 YEARS		2% PMT INCREASE 326.683 PAYMENTS			4% PMT INCREASE 301.101 PAYMENTS			6% PMT INCREASE 280.476 PAYMENTS		
	MONTHLY PAYMENT	TOTAL INTRST	MONTHLY PAYMENT	TOTAL INTRST	INTRST SAVED	MONTHLY PAYMENT	TOTAL INTRST	INTRST SAVED	MONTHLY PAYMENT	TOTAL INTRST	INTRST SAVED
$ 50	0.42	101	0.43	90	11	0.44	82	19	0.45	76	25
100	0.83	199	0.85	178	21	0.86	159	40	0.88	147	52
200	1.65	394	1.68	349	45	1.72	318	76	1.75	291	103
300	2.47	589	2.52	523	66	2.57	474	115	2.62	435	154
400	3.30	788	3.37	701	87	3.43	633	155	3.50	582	206
500	4.12	983	4.20	872	111	4.28	789	194	4.37	726	257
600	4.94	1,178	5.04	1,046	132	5.14	948	230	5.24	870	308
700	5.76	1,374	5.88	1,221	153	5.99	1,104	270	6.11	1,014	360
800	6.59	1,572	6.72	1,395	177	6.85	1,263	309	6.99	1,161	411
900	7.41	1,768	7.56	1,570	198	7.71	1,421	347	7.85	1,302	466
1,000	8.23	1,963	8.39	1,741	222	8.56	1,577	386	8.72	1,446	517
2,000	16.46	3,926	16.79	3,485	441	17.12	3,155	771	17.45	2,894	1,032
3,000	24.69	5,888	25.18	5,226	662	25.68	4,732	1,156	26.17	4,340	1,548
4,000	32.91	7,848	33.57	6,967	881	34.23	6,307	1,541	34.88	5,783	2,065
5,000	41.14	9,810	41.96	8,708	1,102	42.79	7,884	1,926	43.61	7,232	2,578
6,000	49.37	11,773	50.36	10,452	1,321	51.34	9,459	2,314	52.33	8,677	3,096
7,000	57.59	13,732	58.74	12,189	1,543	59.89	11,033	2,699	61.05	10,123	3,609
8,000	65.82	15,695	67.14	13,933	1,762	68.45	12,610	3,085	69.77	11,569	4,126
9,000	74.05	17,658	75.53	15,674	1,984	77.01	14,188	3,470	78.49	13,015	4,643
10,000	82.27	19,617	83.92	17,415	2,202	85.56	15,762	3,855	87.21	14,460	5,157
11,000	90.50	21,580	92.31	19,156	2,424	94.12	17,340	4,240	95.93	15,906	5,674
12,000	98.73	23,543	100.70	20,897	2,646	102.68	18,917	4,626	104.65	17,352	6,191
13,000	106.95	25,502	109.09	22,638	2,864	111.23	20,491	5,011	113.37	18,798	6,704
14,000	115.18	27,465	117.48	24,379	3,086	119.79	22,069	5,396	122.09	20,243	7,222
15,000	123.41	29,428	125.88	26,123	3,305	128.35	23,646	5,782	130.81	21,689	7,739
16,000	131.63	31,387	134.26	27,860	3,527	136.90	25,221	6,166	139.53	23,135	8,252
17,000	139.86	33,350	142.66	29,605	3,745	145.45	26,795	6,555	148.25	24,581	8,769
18,000	148.09	35,312	151.05	31,345	3,967	154.01	28,373	6,939	156.98	26,029	9,283
19,000	156.31	37,272	159.44	33,086	4,186	162.56	29,947	7,325	165.69	27,472	9,800
20,000	164.54	39,234	167.83	34,827	4,407	171.12	31,524	7,710	174.41	28,918	10,316
21,000	172.77	41,197	176.23	36,571	4,626	179.68	33,102	8,095	183.14	30,366	10,831
22,000	180.99	43,156	184.61	38,309	4,847	188.23	34,676	8,480	191.85	31,809	11,347
23,000	189.22	45,119	193.00	40,050	5,069	196.79	36,254	8,865	200.57	33,255	11,864
24,000	197.45	47,082	201.40	41,794	5,288	205.35	37,831	9,251	209.30	34,704	12,378
25,000	205.67	49,041	209.78	43,532	5,509	213.90	39,406	9,635	218.01	36,147	12,894
26,000	213.90	51,004	218.18	45,276	5,728	222.46	40,983	10,021	226.73	37,592	13,412
27,000	222.13	52,967	226.57	47,017	5,950	231.02	42,560	10,407	235.46	39,041	13,926
28,000	230.35	54,926	234.96	48,757	6,169	239.56	44,132	10,794	244.17	40,484	14,442
29,000	238.58	56,889	243.35	50,498	6,391	248.12	45,709	11,180	252.89	41,930	14,959
30,000	246.81	58,852	251.75	52,242	6,610	256.68	47,287	11,565	261.62	43,378	15,474
32,500	267.37	63,753	272.72	56,593	7,160	278.06	51,224	12,529	283.41	46,990	16,763
35,000	287.94	68,658	293.70	60,947	7,711	299.46	55,168	13,490	305.22	50,607	18,051
40,000	329.08	78,469	335.66	69,654	8,815	342.24	63,049	15,420	348.82	57,836	20,633
45,000	370.21	88,276	377.61	78,359	9,917	385.02	70,930	17,346	392.42	65,064	23,212
50,000	411.34	98,082	419.57	87,066	11,016	427.79	78,808	19,274	436.02	72,293	25,789
55,000	452.48	107,893	461.53	95,774	12,119	470.58	86,692	21,201	479.63	79,525	28,368
60,000	493.61	117,700	503.49	104,478	13,222	513.35	94,570	23,130	523.23	86,753	30,947
65,000	534.74	127,506	545.43	113,183	14,323	556.13	102,451	25,055	566.82	93,979	33,527
70,000	575.88	137,317	587.40	121,894	15,423	598.92	110,335	26,982	610.43	101,211	36,106
75,000	617.01	147,124	629.35	130,598	16,526	641.69	118,214	28,910	654.03	108,440	38,684
80,000	658.15	156,934	671.31	139,306	17,628	684.48	126,098	30,836	697.64	115,671	41,263
85,000	699.28	166,741	713.27	148,013	18,728	727.25	133,976	32,765	741.24	122,900	43,841
90,000	740.41	176,548	755.22	156,718	19,830	770.03	141,857	34,691	784.83	130,126	46,422
95,000	781.55	186,358	797.18	165,425	20,933	812.81	149,738	36,620	828.44	137,358	49,000
100,000	822.68	196,165	839.13	174,130	22,035	855.59	157,619	38,546	872.04	144,586	51,579
105,000	863.81	205,972	881.09	182,837	23,135	898.36	165,497	40,475	915.64	151,815	54,157
110,000	904.95	215,782	923.05	191,545	24,237	941.15	173,381	42,401	959.25	159,047	56,735
115,000	946.08	225,589	965.00	200,249	25,340	983.92	181,249	44,330	1,002.84	166,273	59,316
120,000	987.22	235,399	1,006.96	208,957	26,442	1,026.71	189,143	46,256	1,046.45	173,504	61,895
125,000	1,028.35	245,206	1,048.92	217,664	27,542	1,069.48	197,021	48,185	1,090.05	180,733	64,473
130,000	1,069.48	255,013	1,090.87	226,369	28,644	1,112.26	204,903	50,110	1,133.65	187,962	67,051
135,000	1,110.62	264,823	1,132.83	235,076	29,747	1,155.04	212,784	52,039	1,177.26	195,193	69,630
140,000	1,151.75	274,630	1,174.79	243,784	30,846	1,197.82	220,665	53,965	1,220.86	202,422	72,208
145,000	1,192.88	284,437	1,216.74	252,488	31,949	1,240.60	228,546	55,891	1,264.45	209,648	74,789
150,000	1,234.02	294,247	1,258.70	261,196	33,051	1,283.38	236,427	57,820	1,308.06	216,879	77,368
155,000	1,275.15	304,054	1,300.65	269,900	34,154	1,326.16	244,306	59,748	1,351.66	224,108	79,946
160,000	1,316.29	313,864	1,342.62	278,611	35,253	1,368.94	252,189	61,675	1,395.27	231,340	82,524
165,000	1,357.42	323,671	1,384.57	287,315	36,356	1,411.72	260,070	63,601	1,438.87	238,569	85,102
170,000	1,398.55	333,478	1,426.52	296,020	37,458	1,454.49	267,948	65,530	1,482.46	245,794	87,684
175,000	1,439.69	343,288	1,468.48	304,727	38,561	1,497.28	275,833	67,455	1,526.07	253,026	90,262
180,000	1,480.82	353,095	1,510.44	313,435	39,660	1,540.05	283,751	69,384	1,569.67	260,255	92,840
185,000	1,521.95	362,902	1,552.39	322,139	40,763	1,582.83	291,592	71,310	1,613.27	267,484	95,418
190,000	1,563.09	372,712	1,594.35	330,847	41,865	1,625.61	299,473	73,239	1,656.88	274,715	97,997
195,000	1,604.22	382,519	1,636.30	339,551	42,968	1,668.39	307,354	75,165	1,700.47	281,941	100,578
200,000	1,645.36	392,330	1,678.27	348,262	44,068	1,711.17	315,235	77,095	1,744.08	289,173	103,157

AUGMENTED PAYMENT MORTGAGES 9.25%

AMOUNT OF LOAN	30 YEARS MONTHLY PAYMENT	30 YEARS TOTAL INTRST	8% PMT INCREASE 263.292 PAYMENTS MONTHLY PAYMENT	TOTAL INTRST	INTRST SAVED	10% PMT INCREASE 248.636 PAYMENTS MONTHLY PAYMENT	TOTAL INTRST	INTRST SAVED	12% PMT INCREASE 235.911 PAYMENTS MONTHLY PAYMENT	TOTAL INTRST	INTRST SAVED
$ 50	0.42	101	0.45	68	33	0.46	64	37	0.47	61	40
100	0.83	199	0.90	137	62	0.91	126	73	0.93	119	80
200	1.65	394	1.78	269	125	1.82	253	141	1.85	236	158
300	2.47	589	2.67	403	186	2.72	376	213	2.77	353	236
400	3.30	788	3.56	537	251	3.63	503	285	3.70	473	315
500	4.12	983	4.45	672	311	4.53	626	357	4.61	588	395
600	4.94	1,178	5.34	806	372	5.43	750	428	5.53	705	473
700	5.76	1,374	6.22	938	436	6.34	876	498	6.45	822	552
800	6.59	1,572	7.12	1,075	497	7.25	1,003	569	7.38	941	631
900	7.41	1,768	8.00	1,206	562	8.15	1,126	642	8.30	1,058	710
1,000	8.23	1,963	8.89	1,341	622	9.05	1,250	713	9.22	1,175	788
2,000	16.46	3,926	17.78	2,681	1,245	18.11	2,503	1,423	18.44	2,350	1,576
3,000	24.69	5,888	26.67	4,022	1,866	27.16	3,753	2,135	27.65	3,523	2,365
4,000	32.91	7,848	35.54	5,357	2,491	36.20	5,001	2,847	36.86	4,696	3,152
5,000	41.14	9,810	44.43	6,698	3,112	45.25	6,251	3,559	46.08	5,871	3,939
6,000	49.37	11,773	53.32	8,039	3,734	54.31	7,503	4,270	55.29	7,044	4,729
7,000	57.59	13,732	62.20	9,377	4,355	63.35	8,751	4,981	64.50	8,216	5,516
8,000	65.82	15,695	71.09	10,717	4,978	72.40	10,001	5,694	73.72	9,391	6,304
9,000	74.05	17,658	79.97	12,055	5,603	81.46	11,254	6,404	82.94	10,566	7,092
10,000	82.27	19,617	88.85	13,393	6,224	90.50	12,502	7,115	92.14	11,737	7,880
11,000	90.50	21,580	97.74	14,734	6,846	99.55	13,752	7,828	101.36	12,912	8,668
12,000	98.73	23,543	106.63	16,075	7,468	108.60	15,002	8,541	110.58	14,087	9,456
13,000	106.95	25,502	115.51	17,413	8,089	117.65	16,252	9,250	119.78	15,257	10,245
14,000	115.18	27,465	124.39	18,751	8,714	126.70	17,502	9,963	129.00	16,433	11,032
15,000	123.41	29,428	133.28	20,092	9,336	135.75	18,752	10,676	138.22	17,608	11,820
16,000	131.63	31,387	142.16	21,430	9,957	144.79	20,000	11,387	147.43	18,780	12,607
17,000	139.86	33,350	151.05	22,770	10,580	153.85	21,253	12,097	156.64	19,953	13,397
18,000	148.09	35,312	159.94	24,111	11,201	162.90	22,503	12,809	165.86	21,128	14,184
19,000	156.31	37,272	168.81	25,446	11,826	171.94	23,750	13,522	175.07	22,301	14,971
20,000	164.54	39,234	177.70	26,787	12,447	180.99	25,001	14,233	184.28	23,474	15,760
21,000	172.77	41,197	186.59	28,128	13,069	190.05	26,253	14,944	193.50	24,649	16,548
22,000	180.99	43,156	195.47	29,466	13,690	199.09	27,501	15,655	202.71	25,822	17,334
23,000	189.22	45,119	204.36	30,806	14,313	208.14	28,751	16,368	211.93	26,997	18,122
24,000	197.45	47,082	213.25	32,147	14,935	217.20	30,004	17,078	221.14	28,169	18,913
25,000	205.67	49,041	222.12	33,482	15,559	226.24	31,251	17,790	230.35	29,342	19,699
26,000	213.90	51,004	231.01	34,823	16,181	235.29	32,502	18,502	239.57	30,517	20,487
27,000	222.13	52,967	239.90	36,164	16,803	244.34	33,752	19,215	248.79	31,692	21,275
28,000	230.35	54,926	248.78	37,502	17,424	253.39	35,002	19,924	257.99	32,863	22,063
29,000	238.58	56,889	257.67	38,842	18,047	262.44	36,252	20,637	267.21	34,038	22,851
30,000	246.81	58,852	266.55	40,180	18,672	271.49	37,502	21,350	276.43	35,213	23,639
32,500	267.37	63,753	288.76	43,528	20,225	294.11	40,626	23,127	299.45	38,144	25,609
35,000	287.94	68,658	310.98	46,879	21,779	316.73	43,750	24,908	322.49	41,079	27,579
40,000	329.08	78,469	355.41	53,577	24,892	361.99	50,004	28,465	368.57	46,950	31,519
45,000	370.21	88,276	399.83	60,272	28,004	407.23	56,252	32,024	414.64	52,818	35,458
50,000	411.34	98,082	444.25	66,967	31,115	452.47	62,500	35,582	460.70	58,684	39,398
55,000	452.48	107,893	488.68	73,666	34,227	497.73	68,754	39,139	506.78	64,555	43,338
60,000	493.61	117,700	533.10	80,361	37,339	542.97	75,002	42,698	552.84	70,421	47,279
65,000	534.74	127,506	577.52	87,056	40,450	588.21	81,250	46,256	598.91	76,289	51,217
70,000	575.88	137,317	621.95	93,754	43,563	633.47	87,503	49,814	644.99	82,160	55,157
75,000	617.01	147,124	666.37	100,450	46,674	678.71	93,752	53,372	691.05	88,026	59,098
80,000	658.15	156,934	710.80	107,148	49,786	723.97	100,005	56,929	737.13	93,897	63,037
85,000	699.28	166,741	755.22	113,843	52,898	769.21	106,253	60,488	783.19	99,763	66,978
90,000	740.41	176,548	799.64	120,539	56,009	814.45	112,502	64,046	829.26	105,632	70,916
95,000	781.55	186,358	844.07	127,237	59,121	859.71	118,755	67,603	875.34	111,502	74,856
100,000	822.68	196,165	888.49	133,932	62,233	904.95	125,003	71,162	921.40	117,368	78,797
105,000	863.81	205,972	932.91	140,628	65,344	950.19	131,251	74,721	967.47	123,237	82,735
110,000	904.95	215,782	977.35	147,328	68,454	995.45	137,505	78,277	1,013.54	129,105	86,677
115,000	946.08	225,589	1,021.77	154,024	71,565	1,040.69	143,753	81,836	1,059.61	134,974	90,615
120,000	987.22	235,399	1,066.20	160,722	74,677	1,085.94	150,004	85,395	1,105.69	140,844	94,555
125,000	1,028.35	245,206	1,110.62	167,417	77,789	1,131.19	156,255	88,951	1,151.75	146,710	98,496
130,000	1,069.48	255,013	1,155.04	174,113	80,900	1,176.43	162,503	92,510	1,197.82	152,579	102,434
135,000	1,110.62	264,823	1,199.47	180,811	84,012	1,221.68	168,756	96,069	1,243.89	158,447	106,376
140,000	1,151.75	274,630	1,243.89	187,506	87,124	1,266.93	175,004	99,626	1,289.96	164,316	110,314
145,000	1,192.88	284,437	1,288.31	194,202	90,235	1,312.17	181,253	10,184	336.03	70,184	114,253
150,000	1,234.02	294,247	1,332.74	200,900	93,347	1,357.42	187,503	106,744	1,382.10	176,053	118,194
155,000	1,275.15	304,054	1,377.16	207,595	96,459	1,402.67	193,754	110,300	1,428.17	181,921	122,133
160,000	1,316.29	313,864	1,421.59	214,293	99,571	1,447.92	200,005	113,859	1,474.24	187,789	126,075
165,000	1,357.42	323,671	1,466.01	220,989	102,682	1,493.16	206,253	117,418	1,520.31	193,658	130,013
170,000	1,398.55	333,478	1,510.43	227,684	105,794	1,538.41	212,504	120,974	1,566.38	199,526	133,952
175,000	1,439.69	343,288	1,554.87	234,385	108,903	1,583.66	218,755	124,533	1,612.45	205,395	137,893
180,000	1,480.82	353,095	1,599.29	241,080	112,015	1,628.90	225,003	128,092	1,658.52	211,263	141,832
185,000	1,521.95	362,902	1,643.71	247,776	115,126	1,674.15	231,254	131,648	1,704.58	217,129	145,773
190,000	1,563.09	372,712	1,688.14	254,474	118,238	1,719.40	237,505	135,207	1,750.66	223,000	149,712
195,000	1,604.22	382,519	1,732.56	261,169	121,350	1,764.64	243,753	138,766	1,796.73	228,868	153,651
200,000	1,645.36	392,330	1,776.99	267,867	124,463	1,809.90	250,006	142,324	1,842.80	234,737	157,593

AMOUNT OF LOAN	30 YEARS		2% PMT INCREASE 325.218 PAYMENTS			4% PMT INCREASE 298.897 PAYMENTS			6% PMT INCREASE 277.870 PAYMENTS		
	MONTHLY PAYMENT	TOTAL INTRST	MONTHLY PAYMENT	TOTAL INTRST	INTRST SAVED	MONTHLY PAYMENT	TOTAL INTRST	INTRST SAVED	MONTHLY PAYMENT	TOTAL INTRST	INTRST SAVED
$ 50	0.43	105	0.44	93	12	0.45	85	20	0.46	78	27
100	0.85	206	0.87	183	23	0.88	163	43	0.90	150	56
200	1.69	408	1.72	359	49	1.76	326	82	1.79	297	111
300	2.53	611	2.58	539	72	2.63	486	125	2.68	445	166
400	3.37	813	3.44	719	94	3.50	646	167	3.57	592	221
500	4.21	1,016	4.29	895	121	4.38	809	207	4.46	739	277
600	5.05	1,218	5.15	1,075	143	5.25	969	249	5.35	887	331
700	5.89	1,420	6.01	1,255	165	6.13	1,132	288	6.24	1,034	386
800	6.73	1,623	6.86	1,431	192	7.00	1,292	331	7.13	1,181	442
900	7.57	1,825	7.72	1,611	214	7.87	1,452	373	8.02	1,329	496
1,000	8.41	2,028	8.58	1,790	238	8.75	1,615	413	8.91	1,476	552
2,000	16.82	4,055	17.16	3,581	474	17.49	3,228	827	17.83	2,954	1,101
3,000	25.23	6,083	25.73	5,368	715	26.24	4,843	1,240	26.74	4,430	1,653
4,000	33.64	8,110	34.31	7,158	952	34.99	6,458	1,652	35.66	5,909	2,201
5,000	42.05	10,138	42.89	8,949	1,189	43.73	8,071	2,067	44.57	7,385	2,753
6,000	50.46	12,166	51.47	10,739	1,427	52.48	9,686	2,480	53.49	8,863	3,303
7,000	58.86	14,190	60.04	12,526	1,664	61.2 i	11,295	2,895	62.39	10,336	3,854
8,000	67.27	16,217	68.62	14,316	1,901	69.96	12,911	3,306	71.31	11,815	4,402
9,000	75.68	18,245	77.19	16,104	2,141	78.71	14,526	3,719	80.22	13,291	4,954
10,000	84.09	20,272	85.77	17,894	2,378	87.45	16,139	4,133	89.14	14,769	5,503
11,000	92.50	22,300	94.35	19,684	2,616	96.20	17,754	4,546	98.05	16,245	6,055
12,000	100.91	24,328	102.93	21,475	2,853	104.95	19,369	4,959	106.96	17,721	6,607
13,000	109.32	26,355	111.51	23,265	3,090	113.69	20,982	5,373	115.88	19,200	7,155
14,000	117.72	28,379	120.07	25,049	3,330	122.43	22,594	5,785	124.78	20,673	7,706
15,000	126.13	30,407	128.65	26,839	3,568	131.18	24,209	6,198	133.70	22,151	8,256
16,000	134.54	32,434	137.23	28,630	3,804	139.92	25,822	6,612	142.61	23,627	8,807
17,000	142.95	34,462	145.81	30,420	4,042	148.67	27,437	7,025	151.53	25,106	9,356
18,000	151.36	36,490	154.39	32,210	4,280	157.41	29,049	7,441	160.44	26,581	9,909
19,000	159.77	38,517	162.97	34,001	4,516	166.16	30,665	7,852	169.36	28,060	10,457
20,000	168.18	40,545	171.54	35,788	4,757	174.91	32,280	8,265	178.27	29,536	11,009
21,000	176.58	42,569	180.11	37,575	4,994	183.64	33,889	8,680	187.17	31,009	11,560
22,000	184.99	44,596	188.69	39,365	5,231	192.39	35,505	9,091	196.09	32,488	12,108
23,000	193.40	46,624	197.27	41,156	5,468	201.14	37,120	9,504	205.00	33,963	12,661
24,000	201.81	48,651	205.85	42,946	5,706	209.88	38,733	9,919	213.92	35,442	13,210
25,000	210.22	50,679	214.42	44,733	5,946	218.63	40,348	10,331	222.83	36,918	13,761
26,000	218.63	52,707	223.00	46,524	6,183	227.38	41,963	10,744	231.75	38,396	14,311
27,000	227.04	54,734	231.58	48,314	6,420	236.12	43,576	11,158	240.66	39,872	14,862
28,000	235.44	56,758	240.16	50,101	6,657	244.86	45,188	11,570	249.57	41,348	15,410
29,000	243.85	58,786	248.73	51,891	6,895	253.60	46,800	11,986	258.48	42,824	15,962
30,000	252.26	60,814	257.31	53,682	7,132	262.35	48,416	12,398	267.40	44,302	16,512
32,500	273.28	65,881	278.75	58,155	7,726	284.21	52,450	13,431	289.68	47,993	17,888
35,000	294.30	70,948	300.19	62,627	8,321	306.07	56,483	14,465	311.96	51,684	19,264
40,000	336.35	81,086	343.08	71,576	9,510	349.80	64,554	16,532	356.53	59,069	22,017
45,000	378.39	91,220	385.96	80,521	10,699	393.53	72,625	18,595	401.09	66,451	24,769
50,000	420.43	101,355	428.84	89,466	11,889	437.25	80,693	20,662	445.66	73,836	27,519
55,000	462.47	111,489	471.72	98,412	13,077	480.97	88,760	22,729	490.22	81,217	30,272
60,000	504.52	121,627	514.61	107,360	14,267	524.70	96,831	24,796	534.79	88,602	33,025
65,000	546.56	131,762	557.49	116,306	15,456	568.42	104,899	26,863	579.35	95,984	35,778
70,000	588.60	141,896	600.37	125,251	16,645	612.14	112,967	28,929	623.92	103,369	38,527
75,000	630.65	152,034	643.26	134,200	17,834	655.88	121,041	30,993	668.49	110,753	41,281
80,000	672.69	162,168	686.14	143,145	19,023	699.60	129,108	33,060	713.05	118,135	44,033
85,000	714.73	172,303	729.02	152,090	20,213	743.32	137,176	35,127	757.61	125,517	46,786
90,000	756.77	182,437	771.91	161,039	21,398	787.04	145,244	37,193	802.18	132,902	49,535
95,000	798.82	192,575	814.80	169,988	22,587	830.77	153,315	39,260	846.75	140,286	52,289
100,000	840.86	202,710	857.68	178,933	23,777	874.49	161,382	41,328	891.31	147,668	55,042
105,000	882.90	212,844	900.56	187,878	24,966	918.22	169,453	43,391	935.87	155,050	57,794
110,000	924.94	222,978	943.44	196,824	26,154	961.94	177,521	45,457	980.44	162,435	60,543
115,000	966.99	233,116	986.33	205,772	27,344	1,005.67	185,592	47,524	1,025.01	169,820	63,296
120,000	1,009.03	243,251	1,029.21	214,718	28,533	1,049.39	193,660	49,591	1,069.57	177,201	66,050
125,000	1,051.07	253,385	1,072.09	223,663	29,722	1,093.11	201,727	51,658	1,114.13	184,583	68,802
130,000	1,093.12	263,523	1,114.98	232,612	30,911	1,136.84	209,798	53,725	1,158.71	191,971	71,552
135,000	1,135.16	273,658	1,157.86	241,557	32,101	1,180.57	217,869	55,789	1,203.27	199,353	74,305
140,000	1,177.20	283,792	1,200.74	250,502	33,290	1,224.29	225,937	57,855	1,247.83	206,735	77,057
145,000	1,219.24	293,926	1,243.62	259,448	34,478	1,268.01	234,004	59,922	1,292.39	214,117	79,810
150,000	1,261.29	304,061	1,286.52	268,399	35,665	1,311.74	242,075	61,989	1,336.97	221,504	82,560
155,000	1,303.33	314,199	1,329.40	277,345	36,854	1,355.46	250,143	64,056	1,381.53	228,886	85,313
160,000	1,345.37	324,333	1,372.28	286,290	38,043	1,399.18	258,211	66,122	1,426.09	236,268	88,065
165,000	1,387.41	334,468	1,415.16	295,236	39,232	1,442.91	266,281	68,187	1,470.65	243,650	90,818
170,000	1,429.46	344,606	1,458.05	304,184	40,422	1,486.64	274,352	70,254	1,515.23	251,037	93,569
175,000	1,471.50	354,740	1,500.93	313,129	41,611	1,530.36	282,420	72,320	1,559.79	258,419	96,321
180,000	1,513.54	364,874	1,543.81	322,075	42,799	1,574.08	290,488	74,386	1,604.35	265,801	99,073
185,000	1,555.59	375,012	1,586.70	331,023	43,989	1,617.81	298,559	76,453	1,648.93	273,188	101,824
190,000	1,597.63	385,147	1,629.58	339,969	45,178	1,661.54	306,629	78,518	1,693.49	280,570	104,577
195,000	1,639.67	395,281	1,672.46	348,914	46,367	1,705.26	314,697	80,584	1,738.05	287,952	107,329
200,000	1,681.71	405,416	1,715.34	357,859	47,557	1,748.98	322,765	82,651	1,782.61	295,334	110,082

AMOUNT OF LOAN	30 YEARS		8% PMT INCREASE 260.462 PAYMENTS			10% PMT INCREASE 245.684 PAYMENTS			12% PMT INCREASE 232.898 PAYMENTS		
	MONTHLY PAYMENT	TOTAL INTRST	MONTHLY PAYMENT	TOTAL INTRST	INTRST SAVED	MONTHLY PAYMENT	TOTAL INTRST	INTRST SAVED	MONTHLY PAYMENT	TOTAL INTRST	INTRST SAVED
$ 50	0.43	105	0.46	70	35	0.47	65	40	0.48	62	43
100	0.85	206	0.92	140	66	0.94	131	75	0.95	121	85
200	1.69	408	1.83	277	131	1.86	257	151	1.89	240	168
300	2.53	611	2.73	411	200	2.78	383	228	2.83	359	252
400	3.37	813	3.64	548	265	3.71	511	302	3.77	478	335
500	4.21	1,016	4.55	685	331	4.63	638	378	4.72	599	417
600	5.05	1,218	5.45	820	398	5.56	766	452	5.66	718	500
700	5.89	1,420	6.36	957	463	6.48	892	528	6.60	837	583
800	6.73	1,623	7.27	1,094	529	7.40	1,018	605	7.54	956	667
900	7.57	1,825	8.18	1,231	594	8.33	1,147	678	8.48	1,075	750
1,000	8.41	2,028	9.08	1,365	663	9.25	1,273	755	9.42	1,194	834
2,000	16.82	4,055	18.17	2,733	1,322	18.50	2,545	1,510	18.84	2,388	1,667
3,000	25.23	6,083	27.25	4,098	1,985	27.75	3,818	2,265	28.26	3,582	2,501
4,000	33.64	8,110	36.33	5,463	2,647	37.00	5,090	3,020	37.68	4,776	3,334
5,000	42.05	10,138	45.41	6,828	3,310	46.26	6,365	3,773	47.10	5,969	4,169
6,000	50.46	12,166	54.50	8,195	3,971	55.51	7,638	4,528	56.52	7,163	5,003
7,000	58.86	14,190	63.57	9,558	4,632	64.75	8,908	5,282	65.92	8,353	5,837
8,000	67.27	16,217	72.65	10,923	5,294	74.00	10,181	6,036	75.34	9,547	6,670
9,000	75.68	18,245	81.73	12,288	5,957	83.25	11,453	6,792	84.76	10,740	7,505
10,000	84.09	20,272	90.82	13,655	6,617	92.50	12,726	7,546	94.18	11,934	8,338
11,000	92.50	22,300	99.90	15,020	7,280	101.75	13,998	8,302	103.60	13,128	9,172
12,000	100.91	24,328	108.98	16,385	7,943	111.00	15,271	9,057	113.02	14,322	10,006
13,000	109.32	26,355	118.07	17,753	8,602	120.25	16,544	9,811	122.44	15,516	10,839
14,000	117.72	28,379	127.14	19,115	9,264	129.49	17,814	10,565	131.85	16,708	11,671
15,000	126.13	30,407	136.22	20,480	9,927	138.74	19,086	11,321	141.27	17,902	12,505
16,000	134.54	32,434	145.30	21,845	10,589	147.99	20,359	12,075	150.68	19,093	13,341
17,000	142.95	34,462	154.39	23,213	11,249	157.25	21,634	12,828	160.10	20,287	14,175
18,000	151.36	36,490	163.47	24,578	11,912	166.50	22,906	13,584	169.52	21,481	15,009
19,000	159.77	38,517	172.55	25,943	12,574	175.75	24,179	14,338	178.94	22,675	15,842
20,000	168.18	40,545	181.63	27,308	13,237	185.00	25,452	15,093	188.36	23,869	16,676
21,000	176.58	42,569	190.71	28,673	13,896	194.24	26,722	15,847	197.77	25,060	17,509
22,000	184.99	44,596	199.79	30,038	14,558	203.49	27,994	16,602	207.19	26,254	18,342
23,000	193.40	46,624	208.87	31,403	15,221	212.74	29,267	17,357	216.61	27,448	19,176
24,000	201.81	48,652	217.95	32,768	15,884	221.99	30,539	18,113	226.03	28,642	20,010
25,000	210.22	50,679	227.04	34,135	16,544	231.24	31,812	18,867	235.45	29,836	20,843
26,000	218.63	52,707	236.12	35,500	17,207	240.49	33,085	19,622	244.86	31,030	21,677
27,000	227.04	54,734	245.20	36,865	17,869	249.74	34,357	20,377	254.28	32,221	22,513
28,000	235.44	56,758	254.28	38,230	18,528	258.98	35,627	21,131	263.69	33,413	23,345
29,000	243.85	58,786	263.36	39,595	19,191	268.24	36,902	21,884	273.11	34,607	24,179
30,000	252.26	60,814	272.44	40,960	19,854	277.49	38,175	22,639	282.53	35,801	25,013
32,500	273.28	65,881	295.14	44,373	21,508	300.61	41,355	24,526	306.07	38,783	27,098
35,000	294.30	70,948	317.84	47,785	23,163	323.73	44,535	26,413	329.62	41,768	29,180
40,000	336.35	81,086	363.26	54,615	26,471	369.99	50,901	30,185	376.71	47,735	33,351
45,000	378.39	91,220	408.66	61,440	29,780	416.23	57,261	33,959	423.80	53,702	37,518
50,000	420.43	101,355	454.06	68,265	33,090	462.47	63,621	37,734	470.88	59,667	41,688
55,000	462.47	111,489	499.47	75,093	36,396	508.72	69,984	41,505	517.97	65,634	45,855
60,000	504.52	121,627	544.88	81,921	39,706	554.97	76,347	45,280	565.06	71,601	50,026
65,000	546.56	131,762	590.28	88,746	43,016	601.22	82,710	49,052	612.15	77,569	54,193
70,000	588.60	141,896	635.69	95,573	46,323	647.46	89,071	52,825	659.23	83,533	58,363
75,000	630.65	152,034	681.10	102,401	49,633	693.72	95,436	56,598	706.33	89,503	62,531
80,000	672.69	162,168	726.51	109,228	52,940	739.96	101,796	60,372	753.41	95,468	66,700
85,000	714.73	172,303	771.91	116,053	56,250	786.20	108,157	64,146	800.50	101,435	70,868
90,000	756.77	182,437	817.31	122,878	59,559	832.45	114,520	67,917	847.58	107,400	75,037
95,000	798.82	192,575	862.73	129,708	62,867	878.70	120,883	71,692	894.68	113,369	79,206
100,000	840.86	202,710	908.13	136,533	66,177	924.95	127,245	75,465	941.76	119,334	83,376
105,000	882.90	212,844	953.53	143,358	69,486	971.19	133,606	79,238	988.85	125,301	87,543
110,000	924.94	222,978	998.94	150,186	72,792	1,017.43	139,966	83,012	1,035.93	131,266	91,712
115,000	966.99	233,116	1,044.35	157,013	76,103	1,063.69	146,332	86,784	1,083.03	137,236	95,880
120,000	1,009.03	243,251	1,089.75	163,838	79,413	1,109.93	152,692	90,559	1,130.11	143,200	100,051
125,000	1,051.07	253,385	1,135.16	170,666	82,719	1,156.18	159,055	94,330	1,177.20	149,168	104,217
130,000	1,093.12	263,523	1,180.57	177,494	86,029	1,202.43	165,415	98,105	1,224.28	155,135	108,388
135,000	1,135.16	273,658	1,225.97	184,319	89,339	1,248.68	171,781	101,877	1,271.38	161,102	112,556
140,000	1,177.20	283,792	1,271.38	191,146	92,646	1,294.92	178,141	105,651	1,318.46	167,067	116,725
145,000	1,219.24	293,926	1,316.78	197,971	95,955	1,341.16	184,502	109,424	1,365.55	173,034	120,892
150,000	1,261.29	304,064	1,362.19	204,799	99,265	1,387.42	190,867	113,197	1,412.64	179,001	125,063
155,000	1,303.33	314,199	1,407.60	211,626	102,573	1,433.66	197,227	116,972	1,459.73	184,968	129,231
160,000	1,345.37	324,333	1,453.00	218,451	105,882	1,479.91	203,590	120,743	1,506.81	190,933	133,400
165,000	1,387.41	334,468	1,498.40	225,276	109,192	1,526.15	209,951	124,517	1,553.90	196,900	137,568
170,000	1,429.46	344,606	1,543.82	232,106	112,500	1,572.41	216,290	128,316	1,601.00	202,870	141,736
175,000	1,471.50	354,740	1,589.22	238,931	115,809	1,618.65	222,676	132,064	1,648.08	208,835	145,905
180,000	1,513.54	364,874	1,634.62	245,756	119,118	1,664.89	229,037	135,837	1,695.16	214,799	150,075
185,000	1,555.59	375,012	1,680.04	252,587	122,425	1,711.15	235,400	139,610	1,742.26	220,769	154,243
190,000	1,597.63	385,147	1,725.44	259,412	125,735	1,757.39	241,763	143,384	1,789.35	226,736	158,411
195,000	1,639.67	395,281	1,770.84	266,237	129,044	1,803.64	248,125	147,156	1,836.43	232,701	162,580
200,000	1,681.71	405,416	1,816.25	273,064	132,352	1,849.88	254,486	150,930	1,883.52	238,668	166,748

AUGMENTED PAYMENT MORTGAGES

AMOUNT OF LOAN	30 YEARS		2% PMT INCREASE 323.698 PAYMENTS			4% PMT INCREASE 296.642 PAYMENTS			6% PMT INCREASE 275.227 PAYMENTS		
	MONTHLY PAYMENT	TOTAL INTRST	MONTHLY PAYMENT	TOTAL INTRST	INTRST SAVED	MONTHLY PAYMENT	TOTAL INTRST	INTRST SAVED	MONTHLY PAYMENT	TOTAL INTRST	INTRST SAVED
$ 50	0.43	105	0.44	92	13	0.45	83	22	0.46	77	28
100	0.86	210	0.88	185	25	0.89	164	46	0.91	150	60
200	1.72	419	1.75	366	53	1.79	331	88	1.82	301	118
300	2.58	629	2.63	551	78	2.68	495	134	2.73	451	178
400	3.44	838	3.51	736	102	3.58	662	176	3.65	605	233
500	4.30	1,048	4.39	921	127	4.47	826	222	4.56	755	293
600	5.16	1,258	5.26	1,103	155	5.37	993	265	5.47	905	353
700	6.02	1,467	6.14	1,288	179	6.26	1,157	310	6.38	1,056	411
800	6.88	1,677	7.02	1,472	205	7.16	1,324	353	7.29	1,206	471
900	7.74	1,886	7.89	1,654	232	8.05	1,488	398	8.20	1,357	529
1,000	8.60	2,096	8.77	1,839	257	8.94	1,652	444	9.12	1,510	586
2,000	17.19	4,188	17.53	3,674	514	17.88	3,304	884	18.22	3,015	1,173
3,000	25.78	6,281	26.30	5,513	768	26.81	4,953	1,328	27.33	4,522	1,759
4,000	34.37	8,373	35.06	7,349	1,024	35.74	6,602	1,771	36.43	6,027	2,346
5,000	42.96	10,466	43.82	9,184	1,282	44.68	8,254	2,212	45.54	7,534	2,932
6,000	51.55	12,558	52.58	11,020	1,538	53.61	9,903	2,655	54.64	9,038	3,520
7,000	60.15	14,654	61.35	12,859	1,795	62.56	11,558	3,096	63.76	10,548	4,106
8,000	68.74	16,746	70.11	14,694	2,052	71.49	13,207	3,539	72.86	12,053	4,693
9,000	77.33	18,839	78.88	16,533	2,306	80.42	14,856	3,983	81.97	13,560	5,279
10,000	85.92	20,931	87.64	18,369	2,562	89.36	16,508	4,423	91.08	15,068	5,863
11,000	94.51	23,024	96.40	20,204	2,820	98.29	18,157	4,867	100.18	16,572	6,452
12,000	103.10	25,116	105.16	22,040	3,076	107.22	19,806	5,310	109.29	18,080	7,036
13,000	111.70	27,212	113.93	23,879	3,333	116.17	21,461	5,751	118.40	19,587	7,625
14,000	120.29	29,304	122.70	25,718	3,586	125.10	23,110	6,194	127.51	21,094	8,210
15,000	128.88	31,397	131.46	27,553	3,844	134.04	24,762	6,635	136.61	22,599	8,798
16,000	137.47	33,489	140.22	29,389	4,100	142.97	26,411	7,078	145.72	24,106	9,383
17,000	146.06	35,582	148.98	31,225	4,357	151.90	28,060	7,522	154.82	25,611	9,971
18,000	154.65	37,674	157.74	33,060	4,614	160.84	29,712	7,962	163.93	27,118	10,556
19,000	163.24	39,766	166.50	34,896	4,870	169.77	31,361	8,405	173.03	28,623	11,143
20,000	171.84	41,862	175.28	36,738	5,124	178.71	33,013	8,849	182.15	30,133	11,729
21,000	180.43	43,955	184.04	38,573	5,382	187.65	34,665	9,290	191.26	31,640	12,315
22,000	189.02	46,047	192.80	40,409	5,638	196.58	36,314	9,733	200.36	33,144	12,903
23,000	197.61	48,140	201.56	42,245	5,895	205.51	37,963	10,177	209.47	34,652	13,488
24,000	206.20	50,232	210.32	44,080	6,152	214.45	39,615	10,617	218.57	36,156	14,076
25,000	214.79	52,324	219.09	45,919	6,405	223.38	41,264	11,060	227.68	37,664	14,660
26,000	223.39	54,420	227.86	47,758	6,662	232.33	42,919	11,501	236.79	39,171	15,249
27,000	231.98	56,513	236.62	49,593	6,920	241.26	44,568	11,945	245.90	40,678	15,835
28,000	240.57	58,605	245.38	51,429	7,176	250.19	46,217	12,388	255.00	42,183	16,422
29,000	249.16	60,698	254.14	53,265	7,433	259.13	47,869	12,829	264.11	43,690	17,008
30,000	257.75	62,790	262.91	55,103	7,687	268.06	49,518	13,272	273.22	45,198	17,592
32,500	279.23	68,023	284.81	59,692	8,331	290.40	53,645	14,378	295.98	48,962	19,061
35,000	300.71	73,256	306.72	64,285	8,971	312.74	57,772	15,484	318.75	52,729	20,527
40,000	343.67	83,721	350.54	73,469	10,252	357.42	66,026	17,695	364.29	60,262	23,459
45,000	386.62	94,183	394.35	82,650	11,533	402.08	74,274	19,909	409.82	67,794	26,389
50,000	429.58	104,649	438.17	91,835	12,814	446.76	82,528	22,121	455.35	75,325	29,324
55,000	472.54	115,114	481.99	101,019	14,095	491.44	90,782	24,332	500.89	82,858	32,256
60,000	515.50	125,580	525.81	110,204	15,376	536.12	99,036	26,544	546.43	90,392	35,188
65,000	558.46	136,046	569.63	119,388	16,658	580.80	107,290	28,756	591.97	97,926	38,120
70,000	601.41	146,508	613.44	128,569	17,939	625.47	115,541	30,967	637.49	105,454	41,054
75,000	644.37	156,973	657.26	137,754	19,219	670.14	123,792	33,181	683.03	112,988	43,985
80,000	687.33	167,439	701.08	146,938	20,501	714.82	132,046	35,393	728.57	120,522	46,917
85,000	730.29	177,904	744.90	156,123	21,781	759.50	140,300	37,604	774.11	128,056	49,848
90,000	773.24	188,366	788.70	165,301	23,065	804.17	148,551	39,815	819.63	135,584	52,782
95,000	816.20	198,832	832.52	174,485	24,347	848.85	156,805	42,027	865.17	143,118	55,714
100,000	859.16	209,298	876.34	183,670	25,628	893.53	165,059	44,239	910.71	150,652	58,646
105,000	902.12	219,763	920.16	192,854	26,909	938.20	173,310	46,453	956.25	158,186	61,577
110,000	945.07	230,225	963.97	202,035	28,190	982.87	181,561	48,664	1,001.77	165,714	64,511
115,000	988.03	240,691	1,007.79	211,220	29,471	1,027.55	189,814	50,877	1,047.31	173,248	67,443
120,000	1,030.99	251,156	1,051.61	220,404	30,752	1,072.23	198,068	53,088	1,092.85	180,782	70,374
125,000	1,073.95	261,622	1,095.43	229,589	32,033	1,116.91	206,322	55,300	1,138.39	188,316	73,306
130,000	1,116.91	272,088	1,139.25	238,773	33,315	1,161.59	214,576	57,512	1,183.92	195,847	76,241
135,000	1,159.86	282,550	1,183.06	247,954	34,596	1,206.25	222,824	59,726	1,229.45	203,378	79,172
140,000	1,202.82	293,015	1,226.88	257,139	35,876	1,250.93	231,078	61,937	1,274.99	210,912	82,103
145,000	1,245.78	303,481	1,270.70	266,323	37,158	1,295.61	239,332	64,149	1,320.53	218,446	85,035
150,000	1,288.74	313,946	1,314.51	275,504	38,442	1,340.29	247,586	66,360	1,366.06	225,977	87,969
155,000	1,331.69	324,408	1,358.32	284,685	39,723	1,384.96	255,837	68,571	1,411.59	233,508	90,900
160,000	1,374.65	334,874	1,402.14	293,870	41,004	1,429.64	264,091	70,783	1,457.13	241,042	93,832
165,000	1,417.61	345,340	1,445.96	303,054	42,286	1,474.31	272,342	72,998	1,502.67	248,575	96,765
170,000	1,460.57	355,805	1,489.78	312,239	43,566	1,518.99	280,596	75,209	1,548.20	256,106	99,699
175,000	1,503.53	366,271	1,533.60	321,423	44,848	1,563.67	288,850	77,421	1,593.74	263,640	102,631
180,000	1,546.48	376,733	1,577.41	330,604	46,129	1,608.34	297,101	79,632	1,639.27	271,171	105,562
185,000	1,589.44	387,198	1,621.23	339,789	47,409	1,653.02	305,355	81,843	1,684.81	278,705	108,493
190,000	1,632.40	397,664	1,665.05	348,973	48,691	1,697.70	313,609	84,055	1,730.34	286,236	111,428
195,000	1,675.36	408,130	1,708.87	358,158	49,972	1,742.37	321,860	86,270	1,775.88	293,770	114,360
200,000	1,718.31	418,592	1,752.68	367,339	51,253	1,787.04	330,111	88,481	1,821.41	301,301	117,291

AUGMENTED PAYMENT MORTGAGES 9.75%

AMOUNT OF LOAN	30 YEARS		8% PMT INCREASE 257.610 PAYMENTS			10% PMT INCREASE 242.723 PAYMENTS			12% PMT INCREASE 229.888 PAYMENTS		
	MONTHLY PAYMENT	TOTAL INTRST	MONTHLY PAYMENT	TOTAL INTRST	INTRST SAVED	MONTHLY PAYMENT	TOTAL INTRST	INTRST SAVED	MONTHLY PAYMENT	TOTAL INTRST	INTRST SAVED
$ 50	0.43	105	0.46	69	36	0.47	64	41	0.48	60	45
100	0.86	210	0.93	140	70	0.95	131	79	0.96	121	89
200	1.72	419	1.86	279	140	1.89	259	160	1.93	244	175
300	2.58	629	2.79	419	210	2.84	389	240	2.89	364	265
400	3.44	838	3.72	558	280	3.78	517	321	3.85	485	353
500	4.30	1,048	4.64	695	353	4.73	648	400	4.82	608	440
600	5.16	1,258	5.57	835	423	5.68	779	479	5.78	729	529
700	6.02	1,467	6.50	974	493	6.62	907	560	6.74	849	618
800	6.88	1,677	7.43	1,114	563	7.57	1,037	640	7.71	972	705
900	7.74	1,886	8.36	1,254	632	8.51	1,166	720	8.67	1,093	793
1,000	8.60	2,096	9.29	1,393	703	9.46	1,296	800	9.63	1,214	882
2,000	17.19	4,188	18.57	2,784	1,404	18.91	2,590	1,598	19.25	2,425	1,763
3,000	25.78	6,281	27.84	4,172	2,109	28.36	3,884	2,397	28.87	3,637	2,644
4,000	34.37	8,373	37.12	5,562	2,811	37.81	5,177	3,196	38.49	4,848	3,525
5,000	42.96	10,466	46.40	6,953	3,513	47.26	6,471	3,995	48.12	6,062	4,404
6,000	51.55	12,558	55.67	8,341	4,217	56.71	7,765	4,793	57.74	7,274	5,284
7,000	60.15	14,654	64.96	9,734	4,920	66.17	9,061	5,593	67.37	8,488	6,166
8,000	68.74	16,746	74.24	11,125	5,621	75.61	10,352	6,394	76.99	9,699	7,047
9,000	77.33	18,839	83.52	12,516	6,323	85.06	11,646	7,193	86.61	10,911	7,928
10,000	85.92	20,931	92.79	13,904	7,027	94.51	12,940	7,991	96.23	12,122	8,809
11,000	94.51	23,024	102.07	15,294	7,730	103.96	14,233	8,791	105.85	13,334	9,690
12,000	103.10	25,116	111.35	16,685	8,431	113.41	15,527	9,589	115.47	14,545	10,571
13,000	111.70	27,212	120.64	18,078	9,134	122.87	16,823	10,389	125.10	15,759	11,453
14,000	120.29	29,304	129.91	19,466	9,838	132.32	18,117	11,187	134.72	16,971	12,333
15,000	128.88	31,397	139.19	20,857	10,540	141.77	19,411	11,986	144.35	18,184	13,213
16,000	137.47	33,489	148.47	22,247	11,242	151.22	20,705	12,784	153.97	19,396	14,093
17,000	146.06	35,582	157.74	23,635	11,947	160.67	21,998	13,584	163.59	20,607	14,975
18,000	154.65	37,674	167.02	25,026	12,648	170.12	23,292	14,382	173.21	21,819	15,855
19,000	163.24	39,766	176.30	26,417	13,349	179.56	24,583	15,183	182.83	23,030	16,736
20,000	171.84	41,862	185.59	27,810	14,052	189.02	25,880	15,982	192.46	24,244	17,618
21,000	180.43	43,955	194.86	29,198	14,757	198.47	27,173	16,782	202.08	25,456	18,499
22,000	189.02	46,047	204.14	30,589	15,458	207.92	28,467	17,580	211.70	26,667	19,380
23,000	197.61	48,140	213.42	31,979	16,161	217.37	29,761	18,379	221.32	27,879	20,261
24,000	206.20	50,232	222.70	33,370	16,862	226.82	31,054	19,178	230.94	29,090	21,142
25,000	214.79	52,324	231.97	34,758	17,566	236.27	32,348	19,976	240.56	30,302	22,022
26,000	223.39	54,420	241.26	36,151	18,269	245.73	33,644	20,776	250.20	31,518	22,902
27,000	231.98	56,513	250.54	37,542	18,971	255.18	34,938	21,575	259.82	32,730	23,783
28,000	240.57	58,605	259.82	38,932	19,673	264.63	36,232	22,373	269.44	33,941	24,664
29,000	249.16	60,698	269.09	40,320	20,378	274.08	37,526	23,172	279.06	35,153	25,545
30,000	257.75	62,790	278.37	41,711	21,079	283.53	38,819	23,971	288.68	36,364	26,426
32,500	279.23	68,023	301.57	45,187	22,836	307.15	42,052	25,971	312.74	39,395	28,628
35,000	300.71	73,256	324.77	48,664	24,592	330.78	45,288	27,968	336.80	42,426	30,830
40,000	343.67	83,721	371.16	55,615	28,106	378.04	51,759	31,962	384.91	48,486	35,235
45,000	386.62	94,183	417.55	62,565	31,618	425.28	58,225	35,958	433.01	54,544	39,639
50,000	429.58	104,649	463.95	69,518	35,131	472.54	64,696	39,953	481.13	60,606	44,043
55,000	472.54	115,114	510.34	76,469	38,645	519.79	71,165	43,949	529.24	66,666	48,448
60,000	515.50	125,580	556.74	83,422	42,158	567.05	77,636	47,944	577.36	72,728	52,852
65,000	558.46	136,046	603.14	90,375	45,671	614.31	84,107	51,939	625.48	78,790	57,256
70,000	601.41	146,508	649.52	97,323	49,185	661.55	90,573	55,935	673.58	84,848	61,660
75,000	644.37	156,973	695.92	104,276	52,697	708.81	97,044	59,929	721.69	90,908	66,065
80,000	687.33	167,439	742.32	111,229	56,210	756.06	103,513	63,926	769.81	96,970	70,469
85,000	730.29	177,904	788.71	118,180	59,724	803.32	109,984	67,920	817.92	103,030	74,874
90,000	773.24	188,366	835.10	125,130	63,236	850.56	116,450	71,916	866.03	109,090	79,276
95,000	816.20	198,832	881.50	132,083	66,749	897.82	122,922	75,910	914.14	115,150	83,682
100,000	859.16	209,298	927.89	139,034	70,264	945.08	129,393	79,905	962.26	121,212	88,086
105,000	902.12	219,763	974.29	145,987	73,776	992.33	135,861	83,902	1,010.37	127,272	92,491
110,000	945.07	230,225	1,020.68	152,937	77,288	1,039.58	142,330	87,895	1,058.48	133,332	96,893
115,000	988.03	240,691	1,067.07	159,888	80,803	1,086.83	148,799	91,892	1,106.59	139,392	101,299
120,000	1,030.99	251,156	1,113.47	166,841	84,315	1,134.09	155,270	95,886	1,154.71	145,454	105,702
125,000	1,073.95	261,622	1,159.87	173,794	87,828	1,181.35	161,741	99,881	1,202.82	151,514	110,108
130,000	1,116.91	272,088	1,206.26	180,745	91,343	1,228.60	168,209	103,879	1,250.94	157,576	114,512
135,000	1,159.86	282,550	1,252.65	187,695	94,855	1,275.85	174,678	107,872	1,299.04	163,634	118,916
140,000	1,202.82	293,015	1,299.05	194,648	98,367	1,323.10	181,147	111,868	1,347.16	169,696	123,319
145,000	1,245.78	303,481	1,345.44	201,599	101,882	1,370.36	187,618	115,863	1,395.27	175,756	127,725
150,000	1,288.74	313,946	1,391.84	208,552	105,394	1,417.61	194,087	119,859	1,443.39	181,818	132,128
155,000	1,331.69	324,408	1,438.23	215,502	108,906	1,464.86	200,555	123,853	1,491.49	187,876	136,532
160,000	1,374.65	334,874	1,484.62	222,453	112,421	1,512.12	207,026	127,848	1,539.61	193,938	140,936
165,000	1,417.61	345,340	1,531.02	229,406	115,934	1,559.37	213,495	131,845	1,587.72	199,998	145,342
170,000	1,460.57	355,805	1,577.42	236,359	119,446	1,606.63	219,966	135,839	1,635.84	206,060	149,745
175,000	1,503.53	366,271	1,623.81	243,310	122,961	1,653.88	226,435	139,836	1,683.95	212,120	154,151
180,000	1,546.48	376,733	1,670.20	250,260	126,473	1,701.13	232,903	143,830	1,732.06	218,180	158,553
185,000	1,589.44	387,198	1,716.60	257,212	129,986	1,748.38	239,372	147,826	1,780.17	224,240	162,958
190,000	1,632.40	397,664	1,762.99	264,164	133,500	1,795.64	245,843	151,821	1,828.29	230,302	167,362
195,000	1,675.36	408,130	1,809.39	271,117	137,013	1,842.90	252,314	155,816	1,876.40	236,362	171,768
200,000	1,718.31	418,592	1,855.77	278,065	140,527	1,890.14	258,780	159,812	1,924.51	242,422	176,170

AUGMENTED PAYMENT MORTGAGES

AMOUNT OF LOAN	30 YEARS		2% PMT INCREASE 322.122 PAYMENTS			4% PMT INCREASE 294.335 PAYMENTS			6% PMT INCREASE 272.549 PAYMENTS		
	MONTHLY PAYMENT	TOTAL INTRST	MONTHLY PAYMENT	TOTAL INTRST	INTRST SAVED	MONTHLY PAYMENT	TOTAL INTRST	INTRST SAVED	MONTHLY PAYMENT	TOTAL INTRST	INTRST SAVED
$ 50	0.44	108	0.45	95	13	0.46	85	23	0.47	78	30
100	0.88	217	0.90	190	27	0.92	171	46	0.93	153	64
200	1.76	434	1.80	380	54	1.83	339	95	1.87	310	124
300	2.64	650	2.69	567	83	2.75	509	141	2.80	463	187
400	3.52	867	3.59	756	111	3.66	677	190	3.73	617	250
500	4.39	1,080	4.48	943	137	4.57	845	235	4.65	767	313
600	5.27	1,297	5.38	1,133	164	5.48	1,013	284	5.59	924	373
700	6.15	1,514	6.27	1,320	194	6.40	1,184	330	6.52	1,077	437
800	7.03	1,731	7.17	1,510	221	7.31	1,352	379	7.45	1,230	501
900	7.90	1,944	8.06	1,696	248	8.22	1,519	425	8.37	1,381	563
1,000	8.78	2,161	8.96	1,886	275	9.13	1,687	474	9.31	1,537	624
2,000	17.56	4,322	17.91	3,769	553	18.26	3,375	947	18.61	3,072	1,250
3,000	26.33	6,479	26.86	5,652	827	27.38	5,059	1,420	27.91	4,607	1,872
4,000	35.11	8,640	35.81	7,535	1,105	36.51	6,746	1,894	37.22	6,144	2,496
5,000	43.88	10,797	44.76	9,418	1,379	45.64	8,433	2,364	46.51	7,676	3,121
6,000	52.66	12,958	53.71	11,301	1,657	54.77	10,121	2,837	55.82	9,214	3,744
7,000	61.44	15,118	62.67	13,187	1,931	63.90	11,808	3,310	65.13	10,751	4,367
8,000	70.21	17,276	71.61	15,067	2,209	73.02	13,492	3,784	74.42	12,283	4,993
9,000	78.99	19,436	80.57	16,953	2,483	82.15	15,180	4,256	83.73	13,821	5,615
10,000	87.76	21,594	89.52	18,836	2,758	91.27	16,864	4,730	93.03	15,355	6,239
11,000	96.54	23,754	98.47	20,719	3,035	100.40	18,551	5,203	102.33	16,890	6,864
12,000	105.31	25,912	107.42	22,602	3,310	109.52	20,236	5,676	111.63	18,425	7,487
13,000	114.09	28,072	116.37	24,485	3,587	118.65	21,923	6,149	120.94	19,962	8,110
14,000	122.87	30,233	125.33	26,372	3,861	127.78	23,610	6,623	130.24	21,497	8,736
15,000	131.64	32,390	134.27	28,251	4,139	136.91	25,297	7,093	139.54	23,031	9,359
16,000	140.42	34,551	143.23	30,138	4,413	146.04	26,985	7,566	148.85	24,569	9,982
17,000	149.19	36,708	152.17	32,017	4,691	155.16	28,669	8,039	158.14	26,101	10,607
18,000	157.97	38,869	161.13	33,904	4,965	164.29	30,356	8,513	167.45	27,638	11,231
19,000	166.74	41,026	170.07	35,783	5,243	173.41	32,041	8,985	176.74	29,170	11,856
20,000	175.52	43,187	179.03	37,670	5,517	182.54	33,728	9,459	186.05	30,708	12,479
21,000	184.30	45,348	187.99	39,556	5,792	191.67	35,415	9,933	195.36	32,245	13,103
22,000	193.07	47,505	196.93	41,435	6,070	200.79	37,100	10,405	204.65	33,777	13,728
23,000	201.85	49,666	205.89	43,322	6,344	209.92	38,787	10,879	213.96	35,315	14,351
24,000	210.62	51,823	214.83	45,201	6,622	219.04	40,471	11,352	223.26	36,849	14,974
25,000	219.40	53,984	223.79	47,088	6,896	228.18	42,161	11,823	232.56	38,384	15,600
26,000	228.17	56,141	232.73	48,967	7,174	237.30	43,846	12,295	241.86	39,919	16,222
27,000	236.95	58,302	241.69	50,854	7,448	246.43	45,533	12,769	251.17	41,456	16,846
28,000	245.73	60,463	250.64	52,737	7,726	255.56	47,220	13,243	260.47	42,991	17,472
29,000	254.50	62,620	259.59	54,620	8,000	264.68	48,905	13,715	269.77	44,526	18,094
30,000	263.28	64,781	268.55	56,506	8,275	273.81	50,592	14,189	279.08	46,063	18,718
32,500	285.22	70,179	290.92	61,212	8,967	296.63	54,809	15,370	302.33	49,900	20,279
35,000	307.16	75,578	313.30	65,921	9,657	319.45	59,025	16,553	325.59	53,739	21,839
40,000	351.03	86,371	358.05	75,336	11,035	365.07	67,453	18,918	372.09	61,413	24,958
45,000	394.91	97,168	402.81	84,754	12,414	410.71	75,886	21,282	418.60	69,089	28,079
50,000	438.79	107,964	447.57	94,172	13,792	456.34	84,317	23,647	465.12	76,768	31,196
55,000	482.67	118,761	492.32	103,587	15,174	501.98	92,750	26,011	511.63	84,444	34,317
60,000	526.55	129,558	537.08	113,005	16,553	547.61	101,181	28,377	558.14	92,120	37,438
65,000	570.43	140,355	581.84	122,423	17,932	593.25	109,614	30,741	604.66	99,799	40,556
70,000	614.31	151,152	626.60	131,842	19,310	638.88	118,045	33,107	651.17	107,476	43,676
75,000	658.18	161,945	671.34	141,253	20,692	684.51	126,475	35,470	697.67	115,149	46,796
80,000	702.06	172,742	716.10	150,672	22,070	730.14	134,906	37,836	744.18	122,826	49,916
85,000	745.94	183,538	760.86	160,090	23,448	775.78	143,339	40,199	790.70	130,504	53,034
90,000	789.82	194,335	805.62	169,508	24,827	821.41	151,770	42,565	837.21	138,181	56,154
95,000	833.70	205,132	850.37	178,923	26,209	867.05	160,203	44,929	883.72	145,857	59,275
100,000	877.58	215,929	895.13	188,341	27,588	912.68	168,634	47,295	930.23	153,533	62,396
105,000	921.46	226,726	939.89	197,759	28,967	958.32	177,067	49,659	976.75	161,212	65,514
110,000	965.33	237,519	984.64	207,174	30,345	1,003.94	185,495	52,024	1,023.25	168,886	68,633
115,000	1,009.21	248,316	1,029.39	216,589	31,727	1,049.58	193,928	54,388	1,069.76	176,562	71,754
120,000	1,053.09	259,112	1,074.15	226,007	33,105	1,095.21	202,359	56,753	1,116.28	184,241	74,871
125,000	1,096.97	269,909	1,118.91	235,426	34,483	1,140.85	210,792	59,117	1,162.79	191,917	77,992
130,000	1,140.85	280,706	1,163.67	244,844	35,862	1,186.48	219,223	61,483	1,209.30	199,594	81,112
135,000	1,184.73	291,503	1,208.42	254,259	37,244	1,232.12	227,656	63,847	1,255.81	207,270	84,233
140,000	1,228.61	302,300	1,253.18	263,677	38,623	1,277.75	236,087	66,213	1,302.33	214,949	87,351
145,000	1,272.48	313,093	1,297.93	273,092	40,001	1,323.38	244,517	68,576	1,348.83	222,622	90,471
150,000	1,316.36	323,890	1,342.69	282,510	41,380	1,369.01	252,948	70,942	1,395.34	230,299	93,591
155,000	1,360.24	334,686	1,387.44	291,925	42,761	1,414.65	261,381	73,305	1,441.85	237,975	96,711
160,000	1,404.12	345,483	1,432.20	301,343	44,140	1,460.28	269,812	75,671	1,488.37	245,654	99,829
165,000	1,448.00	356,280	1,476.96	310,761	45,519	1,505.92	278,245	78,035	1,534.88	253,330	102,950
170,000	1,491.88	367,077	1,521.72	320,179	46,898	1,551.56	286,678	80,399	1,581.39	261,006	106,071
175,000	1,535.76	377,874	1,566.48	329,598	48,276	1,597.19	295,109	82,765	1,627.91	268,685	109,189
180,000	1,579.63	388,667	1,611.22	339,009	49,658	1,642.82	303,539	85,128	1,674.41	276,359	112,308
185,000	1,623.51	399,464	1,655.98	348,428	51,036	1,688.45	311,970	87,494	1,720.92	284,035	115,429
190,000	1,667.39	410,260	1,700.74	357,846	52,414	1,734.09	320,403	89,857	1,767.43	291,711	118,549
195,000	1,711.27	421,057	1,745.50	367,264	53,793	1,779.72	328,834	92,223	1,813.95	299,390	121,667
200,000	1,755.15	431,854	1,790.25	376,679	55,175	1,825.36	337,267	94,587	1,860.46	307,067	124,787

AUGMENTED PAYMENT MORTGAGES 10.00%

AMOUNT OF LOAN	30 YEARS		8% PMT INCREASE 254.740 PAYMENTS			10% PMT INCREASE 239.758 PAYMENTS			12% PMT INCREASE 226.886 PAYMENTS		
	MONTHLY PAYMENT	TOTAL INTRST	MONTHLY PAYMENT	TOTAL INTRST	INTRST SAVED	MONTHLY PAYMENT	TOTAL INTRST	INTRST SAVED	MONTHLY PAYMENT	TOTAL INTRST	INTRST SAVED
$ 50	0.44	108	0.48	72	36	0.48	65	43	0.49	61	47
100	0.88	217	0.95	142	75	0.97	133	84	0.99	125	92
200	1.76	434	1.90	284	150	1.94	265	169	1.97	247	187
300	2.64	650	2.85	426	224	2.90	395	255	2.96	372	278
400	3.52	867	3.80	568	299	3.87	528	339	3.94	494	373
500	4.39	1,080	4.74	707	373	4.83	658	422	4.92	616	464
600	5.27	1,297	5.69	849	448	5.80	791	506	5.90	739	558
700	6.15	1,514	6.64	991	523	6.77	923	591	6.89	863	651
800	7.03	1,731	7.59	1,133	598	7.73	1,053	678	7.87	986	745
900	7.90	1,944	8.53	1,273	671	8.69	1,183	761	8.85	1,108	836
1,000	8.78	2,161	9.48	1,415	746	9.66	1,316	845	9.83	1,230	931
2,000	17.56	4,322	18.96	2,830	1,492	19.32	2,632	1,690	19.67	2,463	1,859
3,000	26.33	6,479	28.44	4,245	2,234	28.96	3,943	2,536	29.49	3,691	2,788
4,000	35.11	8,640	37.92	5,660	2,980	38.62	5,259	3,381	39.32	4,921	3,719
5,000	43.88	10,797	47.39	7,072	3,725	48.27	6,573	4,224	49.15	6,151	4,646
6,000	52.66	12,958	56.87	8,487	4,471	57.93	7,889	5,069	58.98	7,382	5,576
7,000	61.44	15,118	66.36	9,905	5,213	67.58	9,203	5,915	68.81	8,612	6,506
8,000	70.21	17,276	75.83	11,317	5,959	77.23	10,517	6,759	78.64	9,842	7,434
9,000	78.99	19,436	85.31	12,732	6,704	86.89	11,833	7,603	88.47	11,073	8,363
10,000	87.76	21,594	94.78	14,144	7,450	96.54	13,146	8,448	98.29	12,301	9,293
11,000	96.54	23,754	104.26	15,559	8,195	106.19	14,460	9,294	108.12	13,531	10,223
12,000	105.31	25,912	113.73	16,972	8,940	115.84	15,774	10,138	117.95	14,761	11,151
13,000	114.09	28,072	123.22	18,389	9,683	125.50	17,090	10,982	127.78	15,991	12,081
14,000	122.87	30,233	132.70	19,804	10,429	135.16	18,406	11,827	137.61	17,222	13,011
15,000	131.64	32,390	142.17	21,216	11,174	144.80	19,717	12,673	147.44	18,452	13,938
16,000	140.42	34,551	151.65	22,631	11,920	154.46	21,033	13,518	157.27	19,682	14,869
17,000	149.19	36,708	161.13	24,046	12,662	164.11	22,347	14,361	167.09	20,910	15,798
18,000	157.97	38,869	170.61	25,461	13,408	173.77	23,663	15,206	176.93	22,143	16,726
19,000	166.74	41,026	180.08	26,874	14,152	183.41	24,974	16,052	186.75	23,371	17,655
20,000	175.52	43,187	189.56	28,289	14,898	193.07	26,290	16,897	196.58	24,601	18,586
21,000	184.30	45,348	199.04	29,703	15,645	202.73	27,606	17,742	206.42	25,834	19,514
22,000	193.07	47,505	208.52	31,118	16,387	212.38	28,920	18,585	216.24	27,062	20,443
23,000	201.85	49,666	218.00	32,533	17,133	222.04	30,236	19,430	226.07	28,292	21,374
24,000	210.62	51,823	227.47	33,946	17,877	231.68	31,547	20,276	235.89	29,520	22,303
25,000	219.40	53,984	236.95	35,361	18,623	241.34	32,863	21,121	245.73	30,753	23,231
26,000	228.17	56,141	246.42	36,773	19,368	250.99	34,177	21,964	255.55	31,981	24,160
27,000	236.95	58,302	255.91	38,191	20,111	260.65	35,493	22,809	265.38	33,211	25,091
28,000	245.73	60,463	265.39	39,605	20,858	270.30	36,807	23,656	275.22	34,444	26,019
29,000	254.50	62,620	274.86	41,018	21,602	279.95	38,120	24,500	285.04	35,672	26,948
30,000	263.28	64,781	284.34	42,433	22,348	289.61	39,436	25,345	294.87	36,902	27,879
32,500	285.22	70,179	308.04	45,970	24,209	313.74	42,722	27,457	319.45	39,979	30,200
35,000	307.16	75,578	331.73	49,505	26,073	337.88	46,009	29,569	344.02	43,053	32,525
40,000	351.03	86,371	379.11	56,574	29,797	386.13	52,578	33,793	393.15	49,200	37,171
45,000	394.91	97,168	426.50	63,647	33,521	434.40	59,151	38,017	442.30	55,352	41,816
50,000	438.79	107,964	473.89	70,719	37,245	482.67	65,724	42,240	491.44	61,501	46,463
55,000	482.67	118,761	521.28	77,791	40,970	530.94	72,297	46,464	540.59	67,652	51,109
60,000	526.55	129,558	568.67	84,863	44,695	579.21	78,870	50,688	589.74	73,804	55,754
65,000	570.43	140,355	616.06	91,935	48,420	627.47	85,441	54,914	638.88	79,953	60,402
70,000	614.31	151,152	663.45	99,007	52,145	675.74	92,014	59,138	688.03	86,104	65,048
75,000	658.18	161,945	710.83	106,077	55,868	724.00	98,585	63,360	737.16	92,251	69,694
80,000	702.06	172,742	758.22	113,149	59,593	772.27	105,158	67,584	786.31	98,403	74,339
85,000	745.94	183,538	805.62	120,224	63,314	820.53	111,729	71,809	835.45	104,552	78,986
90,000	789.82	194,335	853.01	127,296	67,039	868.80	118,302	76,033	884.60	110,703	83,632
95,000	833.70	205,132	900.40	134,368	70,764	917.07	124,875	80,257	933.74	116,853	88,279
100,000	877.58	215,929	947.79	141,440	74,489	965.34	131,448	84,481	982.89	123,004	92,925
105,000	921.46	226,726	995.18	148,512	78,214	1,013.61	138,021	88,705	1,032.04	129,155	97,571
110,000	965.33	237,519	1,042.56	155,582	81,937	1,061.86	144,589	92,930	1,081.17	135,302	102,217
115,000	1,009.21	248,316	1,089.95	162,654	85,662	1,110.13	151,163	97,153	1,130.32	141,454	106,862
120,000	1,053.09	259,112	1,137.34	169,726	89,386	1,158.40	157,733	101,379	1,179.46	147,603	111,509
125,000	1,096.97	269,909	1,184.73	176,798	93,111	1,206.67	164,309	105,600	1,228.61	153,754	116,155
130,000	1,140.85	280,706	1,232.12	183,870	96,836	1,254.94	170,882	109,824	1,277.75	159,904	120,802
135,000	1,184.73	291,503	1,279.51	190,942	100,561	1,303.20	177,453	114,050	1,326.90	166,055	125,448
140,000	1,228.61	302,300	1,326.90	198,015	104,285	1,351.47	184,026	118,274	1,376.04	172,204	130,096
145,000	1,272.48	313,093	1,374.28	205,084	108,009	1,399.73	190,596	122,497	1,425.18	178,353	134,740
150,000	1,316.36	323,890	1,421.67	212,156	111,734	1,448.00	197,170	126,720	1,474.32	184,503	139,387
155,000	1,360.24	334,686	1,469.06	219,228	115,458	1,496.26	203,740	130,946	1,523.47	190,654	144,032
160,000	1,404.12	345,483	1,516.45	226,300	119,183	1,544.53	210,313	135,170	1,572.61	196,803	148,680
165,000	1,448.00	356,280	1,563.84	233,373	122,907	1,592.80	216,887	139,393	1,621.76	202,955	153,325
170,000	1,491.88	367,077	1,611.23	240,445	126,632	1,641.07	223,460	143,617	1,670.91	209,106	157,971
175,000	1,535.76	377,874	1,658.62	247,517	130,357	1,689.34	230,033	147,841	1,720.05	215,255	162,619
180,000	1,579.63	388,667	1,706.00	254,586	134,081	1,737.59	236,601	152,066	1,769.19	221,404	167,263
185,000	1,623.51	399,464	1,753.39	261,659	137,805	1,785.86	243,174	156,290	1,818.33	227,554	171,910
190,000	1,667.39	410,260	1,800.78	268,731	141,529	1,834.13	249,747	160,513	1,867.48	233,705	176,555
195,000	1,711.27	421,057	1,848.17	275,803	145,254	1,882.40	256,320	164,737	1,916.62	239,854	181,203
200,000	1,755.15	431,854	1,895.56	282,875	148,979	1,930.67	262,894	168,960	1,965.77	246,006	185,848

AUGMENTED PAYMENT MORTGAGES

AMOUNT OF LOAN	30 YEARS		2% PMT INCREASE 320.492 PAYMENTS			4% PMT INCREASE 291.980 PAYMENTS			6% PMT INCREASE 269.841 PAYMENTS		
	MONTHLY PAYMENT	TOTAL INTRST	MONTHLY PAYMENT	TOTAL INTRST	INTRST SAVED	MONTHLY PAYMENT	TOTAL INTRST	INTRST SAVED	MONTHLY PAYMENT	TOTAL INTRST	INTRST SAVED
$ 50	0.45	112	0.46	97	15	0.47	87	25	0.48	80	32
100	0.90	224	0.92	195	29	0.94	174	50	0.95	156	68
200	1.80	448	1.84	390	58	1.87	346	102	1.91	315	133
300	2.69	668	2.74	578	90	2.80	518	150	2.85	469	199
400	3.59	892	3.66	773	119	3.73	689	203	3.81	628	264
500	4.49	1,116	4.58	968	148	4.67	864	252	4.76	784	332
600	5.38	1,337	5.49	1,160	177	5.60	1,035	302	5.70	938	399
700	6.28	1,561	6.41	1,354	207	6.53	1,207	354	6.66	1,097	464
800	7.17	1,781	7.31	1,543	238	7.46	1,378	403	7.60	1,251	530
900	8.07	2,005	8.23	1,738	267	8.39	1,550	455	8.55	1,407	598
1,000	8.97	2,229	9.15	1,933	296	9.33	1,724	505	9.51	1,566	663
2,000	17.93	4,455	18.29	3,862	593	18.65	3,445	1,010	19.01	3,130	1,325
3,000	26.89	6,680	27.43	5,791	889	27.97	5,167	1,513	28.50	4,690	1,990
4,000	35.85	8,906	36.57	7,720	1,186	37.28	6,885	2,021	38.00	6,254	2,652
5,000	44.81	11,132	45.71	9,650	1,482	46.60	8,606	2,526	47.50	7,817	3,315
6,000	53.77	13,357	54.85	11,579	1,778	55.92	10,328	3,029	57.00	9,381	3,976
7,000	62.73	15,583	63.98	13,505	2,078	65.24	12,049	3,534	66.49	10,942	4,641
8,000	71.69	17,808	73.12	15,434	2,374	74.56	13,770	4,038	75.99	12,505	5,303
9,000	80.65	20,034	82.26	17,364	2,670	83.88	15,491	4,543	85.49	14,069	5,965
10,000	89.62	22,263	91.41	19,296	2,967	93.20	17,213	5,050	95.00	15,635	6,628
11,000	98.58	24,489	100.55	21,225	3,264	102.52	18,934	5,555	104.49	17,196	7,293
12,000	107.54	26,714	109.69	23,155	3,559	111.84	20,655	6,059	113.99	18,759	7,955
13,000	116.50	28,940	118.83	25,084	3,856	121.16	22,376	6,564	123.49	20,323	8,617
14,000	125.46	31,166	127.97	27,013	4,153	130.48	24,098	7,068	132.99	21,886	9,280
15,000	134.42	33,391	137.11	28,943	4,448	139.80	25,819	7,572	142.49	23,450	9,941
16,000	143.38	35,617	146.25	30,872	4,745	149.12	27,540	8,077	151.98	25,010	10,607
17,000	152.34	37,842	155.39	32,801	5,041	158.43	29,258	8,584	161.48	26,574	11,268
18,000	161.30	40,068	164.53	34,731	5,337	167.75	30,980	9,088	170.98	28,137	11,931
19,000	170.26	42,294	173.67	36,660	5,634	177.07	32,701	9,593	180.48	29,701	12,593
20,000	179.23	44,523	182.81	38,589	5,934	186.40	34,425	10,098	189.98	31,264	13,259
21,000	188.19	46,748	191.95	40,518	6,230	195.72	36,146	10,602	199.48	32,828	13,920
22,000	197.15	48,974	201.09	42,448	6,526	205.04	37,868	11,106	208.98	34,391	14,583
23,000	206.11	51,200	210.23	44,377	6,823	214.35	39,586	11,614	218.48	35,955	15,245
24,000	215.07	53,425	219.37	46,306	7,119	223.67	41,307	12,118	227.97	37,516	15,909
25,000	224.03	55,651	228.51	48,236	7,415	232.99	43,028	12,623	237.47	39,079	16,572
26,000	232.99	57,876	237.65	50,165	7,711	242.31	44,750	13,126	246.97	40,643	17,233
27,000	241.95	60,102	246.79	52,094	8,008	251.63	46,471	13,631	256.47	42,206	17,896
28,000	250.91	62,328	255.93	54,024	8,304	260.95	48,192	14,136	265.96	43,767	18,561
29,000	259.87	64,553	265.07	55,953	8,600	270.26	49,911	14,642	275.46	45,330	19,223
30,000	268.84	66,782	274.22	57,885	8,897	279.59	51,635	15,147	284.97	46,897	19,885
32,500	291.24	72,346	297.06	62,705	9,641	302.89	55,938	16,408	308.71	50,803	21,543
35,000	313.64	77,910	319.91	67,529	10,381	326.19	60,241	17,669	332.46	54,711	23,199
40,000	358.45	89,042	365.62	77,174	11,868	372.79	68,847	20,195	379.96	62,529	26,513
45,000	403.25	100,170	411.32	86,825	13,345	419.38	77,451	22,719	427.45	70,344	29,826
50,000	448.06	111,302	457.02	96,471	14,831	465.98	86,057	25,245	474.94	78,158	33,144
55,000	492.86	122,430	502.72	106,118	16,312	512.57	94,660	27,770	522.43	85,973	36,457
60,000	537.67	133,561	548.42	115,764	17,797	559.18	103,269	30,292	569.93	93,790	39,771
65,000	582.47	144,689	594.12	125,411	19,278	605.77	111,873	32,816	617.42	101,605	43,084
70,000	627.28	155,821	639.83	135,060	20,761	652.37	120,479	35,342	664.92	109,423	46,398
75,000	672.08	166,949	685.52	144,704	22,245	698.96	129,082	37,867	712.40	117,235	49,714
80,000	716.89	178,080	731.23	154,353	23,727	745.57	137,692	40,388	759.90	125,052	53,028
85,000	761.69	189,208	776.92	163,997	25,211	792.16	146,295	42,913	807.39	132,867	56,341
90,000	806.50	200,340	822.63	173,646	26,694	838.76	154,901	45,439	854.89	140,684	59,656
95,000	851.30	211,468	868.33	183,293	28,175	885.35	163,504	47,964	902.38	148,499	62,969
100,000	896.11	222,600	914.03	192,939	29,661	931.95	172,111	50,489	949.88	156,317	66,283
105,000	940.91	233,728	959.73	202,586	31,142	978.55	180,717	53,011	997.36	164,129	69,599
110,000	985.72	244,859	1,005.43	212,232	32,627	1,025.15	189,323	55,536	1,044.86	171,946	72,913
115,000	1,030.52	255,987	1,051.13	221,879	34,108	1,071.74	197,927	58,060	1,092.35	179,761	76,226
120,000	1,075.33	267,119	1,096.84	231,528	35,591	1,118.34	206,533	60,586	1,139.85	187,578	79,541
125,000	1,120.13	278,247	1,142.53	241,172	37,075	1,164.92	215,139	63,108	1,187.34	195,393	82,854
130,000	1,164.94	289,378	1,188.24	250,821	38,557	1,211.54	223,745	65,633	1,234.84	203,210	86,168
135,000	1,209.74	300,506	1,233.93	260,469	40,041	1,258.13	232,349	68,157	1,282.32	211,023	89,483
140,000	1,254.55	311,638	1,279.64	270,114	41,524	1,304.73	240,955	70,683	1,329.82	218,840	92,798
145,000	1,299.35	322,766	1,325.34	279,761	43,005	1,351.32	249,566	73,200	1,377.31	226,655	96,111
150,000	1,344.16	333,898	1,371.04	289,407	44,491	1,397.93	258,168	75,730	1,424.81	234,472	99,426
155,000	1,388.96	345,026	1,416.74	299,054	45,972	1,444.52	266,771	78,255	1,472.30	242,287	102,739
160,000	1,433.77	356,157	1,462.45	308,704	47,453	1,491.12	275,377	80,780	1,519.80	250,104	106,053
165,000	1,478.57	367,285	1,508.14	318,347	48,938	1,537.71	283,981	83,304	1,567.28	257,916	109,369
170,000	1,523.38	378,417	1,553.85	327,996	50,421	1,584.32	292,590	85,827	1,614.78	265,734	112,683
175,000	1,568.18	389,545	1,599.54	337,640	51,905	1,630.91	301,193	88,352	1,662.27	273,549	115,996
180,000	1,612.99	400,676	1,645.25	347,289	53,387	1,677.51	309,799	90,877	1,709.77	281,366	119,310
185,000	1,657.79	411,804	1,690.95	356,936	54,868	1,724.10	318,403	93,401	1,757.26	289,181	122,623
190,000	1,702.60	422,936	1,736.65	366,582	56,354	1,770.70	327,009	95,927	1,804.75	296,998	125,938
195,000	1,747.40	434,064	1,782.35	376,229	57,835	1,817.30	335,615	98,449	1,852.24	304,810	129,254
200,000	1,792.21	445,196	1,828.05	385,875	59,321	1,863.90	344,222	100,974	1,899.74	312,628	132,568

AMOUNT OF LOAN	30 YEARS		8% PMT INCREASE 251.856 PAYMENTS			10% PMT INCREASE 236.794 PAYMENTS			12% PMT INCREASE 223.895 PAYMENTS		
	MONTHLY PAYMENT	TOTAL INTRST	MONTHLY PAYMENT	TOTAL INTRST	INTRST SAVED	MONTHLY PAYMENT	TOTAL INTRST	INTRST SAVED	MONTHLY PAYMENT	TOTAL INTRST	INTRST SAVED
$ 50	0.45	112	0.49	73	39	0.50	68	44	0.50	62	50
100	0.90	224	0.97	144	80	0.99	134	90	1.01	126	98
200	1.80	448	1.94	289	159	1.98	269	179	2.02	252	196
300	2.69	668	2.91	433	235	2.96	401	267	3.01	374	294
400	3.59	892	3.88	577	315	3.95	535	357	4.02	500	392
500	4.49	1,116	4.85	722	394	4.94	670	446	5.03	626	490
600	5.38	1,337	5.81	863	474	5.92	802	535	6.03	750	587
700	6.28	1,561	6.78	1,008	553	6.91	936	625	7.03	874	687
800	7.17	1,781	7.74	1,149	632	7.89	1,068	713	8.03	998	783
900	8.07	2,005	8.72	1,296	709	8.88	1,203	802	9.04	1,124	881
1,000	8.97	2,229	9.69	1,440	789	9.87	1,337	892	10.05	1,250	979
2,000	17.93	4,455	19.36	2,876	1,579	19.72	2,670	1,785	20.08	2,496	1,959
3,000	26.89	6,680	29.04	4,314	2,366	29.58	4,004	2,676	30.12	3,744	2,936
4,000	35.85	8,906	38.72	5,752	3,154	39.44	5,339	3,567	40.15	4,989	3,917
5,000	44.81	11,132	48.39	7,187	3,945	49.29	6,672	4,460	50.19	6,237	4,895
6,000	53.77	13,357	58.07	8,625	4,732	59.15	8,006	5,351	60.22	7,483	5,874
7,000	62.73	15,583	67.75	10,063	5,520	69.00	9,339	6,244	70.26	8,731	6,852
8,000	71.69	17,808	77.43	11,501	6,307	78.86	10,674	7,134	80.29	9,977	7,831
9,000	80.65	20,034	87.10	12,937	7,097	88.72	12,008	8,026	90.33	11,224	8,810
10,000	89.62	22,263	96.79	14,377	7,886	98.58	13,343	8,920	100.37	12,472	9,791
11,000	98.58	24,489	106.47	15,815	8,674	108.44	14,678	9,811	110.41	13,720	10,769
12,000	107.54	26,714	116.14	17,251	9,463	118.29	16,010	10,704	120.44	14,966	11,748
13,000	116.50	28,940	125.82	18,689	10,251	128.15	17,345	11,595	130.48	16,214	12,726
14,000	125.46	31,166	135.50	20,126	11,040	138.01	18,680	12,486	140.52	17,462	13,704
15,000	134.42	33,391	145.17	21,562	11,829	147.86	20,012	13,379	150.55	18,707	14,684
16,000	143.38	35,617	154.85	23,000	12,617	157.72	21,347	14,270	160.59	19,955	15,662
17,000	152.34	37,842	164.53	24,438	13,404	167.57	22,680	15,162	170.62	21,201	16,641
18,000	161.30	40,068	174.20	25,873	14,195	177.43	24,014	16,054	180.66	22,449	17,619
19,000	170.26	42,294	183.88	27,311	14,983	187.29	25,349	16,945	190.69	23,695	18,599
20,000	179.23	44,523	193.57	28,752	15,771	197.15	26,684	17,839	200.74	24,945	19,578
21,000	188.19	46,748	203.25	30,190	16,558	207.01	28,019	18,729	210.77	26,190	20,558
22,000	197.15	48,974	212.92	31,625	17,349	216.87	29,354	19,620	220.81	27,438	21,536
23,000	206.11	51,200	222.60	33,063	18,137	226.72	30,686	20,514	230.84	28,684	22,516
24,000	215.07	53,425	232.28	34,501	18,924	236.58	32,021	21,404	240.88	29,932	23,493
25,000	224.03	55,651	241.95	35,937	19,714	246.43	33,353	22,298	250.91	31,177	24,474
26,000	232.99	57,876	251.63	37,375	20,501	256.29	34,688	23,188	260.95	32,425	25,451
27,000	241.95	60,102	261.31	38,812	21,290	266.15	36,023	24,079	270.98	33,671	26,431
28,000	250.91	62,328	270.98	40,248	22,080	276.00	37,355	24,973	281.02	34,919	27,409
29,000	259.87	64,553	280.66	41,686	22,867	285.86	38,690	25,863	291.05	36,165	28,388
30,000	268.84	66,782	290.35	43,126	23,656	295.72	40,025	26,757	301.10	37,415	29,367
32,500	291.24	72,346	314.54	46,719	25,627	320.36	43,359	28,987	326.19	40,532	31,814
35,000	313.64	77,910	338.73	50,311	27,599	345.00	46,694	31,216	351.28	43,650	34,260
40,000	358.45	89,042	387.13	57,501	31,541	394.30	53,368	35,674	401.46	49,885	39,157
45,000	403.25	100,170	435.51	64,686	35,484	443.58	60,037	40,133	451.64	56,120	44,050
50,000	448.06	111,302	483.90	71,873	39,429	492.87	66,709	44,593	501.83	62,357	48,945
55,000	492.86	122,430	532.29	79,060	43,370	542.15	73,378	49,052	552.00	68,590	53,840
60,000	537.67	133,561	580.68	86,248	47,313	591.44	80,049	53,512	602.19	74,827	58,734
65,000	582.47	144,689	629.07	93,435	51,254	640.72	86,719	57,970	652.37	81,062	63,627
70,000	627.28	155,821	677.46	100,624	55,199	690.01	93,390	62,431	702.55	87,297	68,524
75,000	672.08	166,949	725.85	107,810	59,139	739.29	100,059	66,890	752.73	93,532	73,417
80,000	716.89	178,080	774.24	114,997	63,083	788.58	106,731	71,349	802.92	99,770	78,310
85,000	761.69	189,208	822.63	122,184	67,024	837.86	113,400	75,808	853.09	106,003	83,205
90,000	806.50	200,340	871.02	129,372	70,968	887.15	120,072	80,268	903.28	112,240	88,100
95,000	851.30	211,468	919.40	136,556	74,912	936.43	126,741	84,727	953.46	118,475	92,993
100,000	896.11	222,600	967.80	143,746	78,854	985.72	133,413	89,187	1,003.64	124,710	97,890
105,000	940.91	233,728	1,016.18	150,931	82,797	1,035.00	140,082	93,646	1,053.82	130,945	102,783
110,000	985.72	244,859	1,064.58	158,121	86,738	1,084.29	146,749	98,110	1,104.01	137,182	107,677
115,000	1,030.52	255,987	1,112.96	165,306	90,681	1,133.57	153,423	102,564	1,154.18	143,415	112,572
120,000	1,075.33	267,119	1,161.36	172,495	94,624	1,182.86	160,094	107,025	1,204.37	149,652	117,467
125,000	1,120.13	278,247	1,209.74	179,680	98,567	1,232.14	166,763	111,484	1,254.55	155,887	122,360
130,000	1,164.94	289,378	1,258.14	186,870	102,508	1,281.43	173,435	115,943	1,304.73	162,123	127,255
135,000	1,209.74	300,506	1,306.52	194,055	106,451	1,330.71	180,104	120,402	1,354.91	168,358	132,148
140,000	1,254.55	311,638	1,354.91	201,242	110,396	1,380.01	186,778	124,860	1,405.10	174,595	137,043
145,000	1,299.35	322,766	1,403.30	208,430	114,336	1,429.29	193,447	129,319	1,455.27	180,828	141,938
150,000	1,344.16	333,898	1,451.69	215,617	118,281	1,478.58	200,119	133,779	1,505.46	187,065	146,833
155,000	1,388.96	345,026	1,500.08	222,804	122,222	1,527.86	206,788	138,238	1,555.64	193,300	151,726
160,000	1,433.77	356,157	1,548.47	229,991	126,166	1,577.15	213,460	142,697	1,605.82	199,535	156,622
165,000	1,478.57	367,285	1,596.86	237,179	130,106	1,626.43	220,129	147,156	1,656.00	205,770	161,515
170,000	1,523.38	378,417	1,645.25	244,366	134,051	1,675.72	226,800	151,617	1,706.19	212,007	166,410
175,000	1,568.18	389,545	1,693.63	251,551	137,994	1,725.00	233,470	156,075	1,756.36	218,240	171,305
180,000	1,612.99	400,676	1,742.03	258,741	141,935	1,774.29	240,141	160,535	1,806.55	224,478	176,198
185,000	1,657.79	411,804	1,790.41	265,926	145,878	1,823.57	246,810	164,994	1,856.72	230,710	181,094
190,000	1,702.60	422,936	1,838.81	273,115	149,821	1,872.86	253,482	169,454	1,906.91	236,948	185,988
195,000	1,747.40	434,064	1,887.19	280,300	153,764	1,922.14	260,151	173,913	1,957.09	243,183	190,881
200,000	1,792.21	445,196	1,935.59	287,490	157,706	1,971.43	266,823	178,373	2,007.28	249,420	195,776

10.50% AUGMENTED PAYMENT MORTGAGES

AMOUNT OF LOAN	30 YEARS		2% PMT INCREASE 318.806 PAYMENTS			4% PMT INCREASE 289.582 PAYMENTS			6% PMT INCREASE 267.105 PAYMENTS		
	MONTHLY PAYMENT	TOTAL INTRST	MONTHLY PAYMENT	TOTAL INTRST	INTRST SAVED	MONTHLY PAYMENT	TOTAL INTRST	INTRST SAVED	MONTHLY PAYMENT	TOTAL INTRST	INTRST SAVED
$ 50	0.46	116	0.47	100	16	0.48	89	27	0.49	81	35
100	0.92	231	0.94	200	31	0.96	178	53	0.98	162	69
200	1.83	459	1.87	396	63	1.90	350	109	1.94	318	141
300	2.75	690	2.81	596	94	2.86	528	162	2.92	480	210
400	3.66	918	3.73	789	129	3.81	703	215	3.88	636	282
500	4.58	1,149	4.67	989	160	4.76	878	271	4.85	795	354
600	5.49	1,376	5.60	1,185	191	5.71	1,054	322	5.82	955	421
700	6.41	1,608	6.54	1,385	223	6.67	1,232	376	6.79	1,114	494
800	7.32	1,835	7.47	1,581	254	7.61	1,404	431	7.76	1,273	562
900	8.24	2,066	8.40	1,778	288	8.57	1,582	484	8.73	1,432	634
1,000	9.15	2,294	9.33	1,974	320	9.52	1,757	537	9.70	1,591	703
2,000	18.30	4,588	18.67	3,952	636	19.03	3,511	1,077	19.40	3,182	1,406
3,000	27.45	6,882	28.00	5,927	955	28.55	5,268	1,614	29.10	4,773	2,109
4,000	36.59	9,172	37.32	7,898	1,274	38.05	7,019	2,153	38.79	6,361	2,811
5,000	45.74	11,466	46.65	9,872	1,594	47.57	8,775	2,691	48.48	7,949	3,517
6,000	54.89	13,760	55.99	11,850	1,910	57.09	10,532	3,228	58.18	9,540	4,220
7,000	64.04	16,054	65.32	13,824	2,230	66.60	12,286	3,768	67.88	11,131	4,923
8,000	73.18	18,345	74.64	15,796	2,549	76.11	14,040	4,305	77.57	12,719	5,626
9,000	82.33	20,639	83.98	17,773	2,866	85.62	15,794	4,845	87.27	14,310	6,329
10,000	91.48	22,935	93.31	19,748	3,185	95.14	17,551	5,382	96.97	15,901	7,032
11,000	100.63	25,227	102.64	21,722	3,505	104.66	19,308	5,919	106.67	17,492	7,735
12,000	109.77	27,517	111.97	23,697	3,820	114.16	21,059	6,458	116.36	19,080	8,437
13,000	118.92	29,811	121.30	25,671	4,140	123.68	22,816	6,995	126.06	20,671	9,140
14,000	128.07	32,105	130.63	27,646	4,459	133.19	24,569	7,536	135.75	22,260	9,845
15,000	137.22	34,399	139.96	29,620	4,779	142.71	26,326	8,073	145.45	23,850	10,549
16,000	146.36	36,690	149.29	31,595	5,095	152.21	28,077	8,613	155.14	25,439	11,251
17,000	155.51	38,984	158.62	33,569	5,415	161.73	29,834	9,150	164.84	27,030	11,954
18,000	164.66	41,278	167.95	35,543	5,735	171.25	31,591	9,687	174.54	28,621	12,657
19,000	173.81	43,572	177.29	37,521	6,051	180.76	33,345	10,227	184.24	30,211	13,361
20,000	182.95	45,862	186.61	39,492	6,370	190.27	35,099	10,763	193.93	31,800	14,062
21,000	192.10	48,156	195.94	41,467	6,689	199.78	36,853	11,303	203.63	33,391	14,765
22,000	201.25	50,450	205.28	43,444	7,006	209.30	38,610	11,840	213.33	34,982	15,468
23,000	210.40	52,744	214.61	45,419	7,325	218.82	40,366	12,378	223.02	36,570	16,174
24,000	219.54	55,034	223.93	47,390	7,644	228.32	42,117	12,917	232.71	38,158	16,876
25,000	228.69	57,328	233.26	49,365	7,963	237.84	43,874	13,454	242.41	39,749	17,579
26,000	237.84	59,622	242.60	51,342	8,280	247.35	45,628	13,994	252.11	41,340	18,282
27,000	246.98	61,913	251.92	53,314	8,599	256.86	47,382	14,531	261.80	42,928	18,985
28,000	256.13	64,207	261.25	55,288	8,919	266.38	49,139	15,068	271.50	44,519	19,688
29,000	265.28	66,501	270.59	57,266	9,235	275.89	50,893	15,608	281.20	46,110	20,391
30,000	274.43	68,795	279.92	59,240	9,555	285.41	52,650	16,145	290.90	47,701	21,094
32,500	297.30	74,528	303.25	64,178	10,350	309.19	57,036	17,492	315.14	51,675	22,853
35,000	320.16	80,258	326.56	69,104	11,149	332.97	61,422	18,836	339.37	55,647	24,611
40,000	365.90	91,724	373.22	78,985	12,739	380.54	70,198	21,526	387.85	63,597	28,127
45,000	411.64	103,190	419.87	88,857	14,333	428.11	78,973	24,217	436.34	71,549	31,641
50,000	457.37	114,653	466.52	98,729	15,924	475.66	87,743	26,910	484.81	79,495	35,158
55,000	503.11	126,120	513.17	108,602	17,518	523.23	96,518	29,602	533.30	87,447	38,673
60,000	548.85	137,586	559.83	118,477	19,109	570.80	105,293	32,293	581.78	95,396	42,190
65,000	594.59	149,052	606.48	128,349	20,703	618.37	114,069	34,983	630.27	103,348	45,704
70,000	640.32	160,515	653.13	138,222	22,293	665.93	122,841	37,674	678.74	111,295	49,220
75,000	686.06	171,982	699.78	148,094	23,888	713.50	131,617	40,365	727.22	119,244	52,738
80,000	731.80	183,448	746.44	157,970	25,478	761.07	140,392	43,056	775.71	127,196	56,252
85,000	777.53	194,911	793.08	167,839	27,072	808.63	149,165	45,746	824.18	135,143	59,768
90,000	823.27	206,377	839.74	177,714	28,663	856.20	157,940	48,437	872.67	143,095	63,282
95,000	869.01	217,844	886.39	187,586	30,258	903.77	166,716	51,128	921.15	151,044	66,800
100,000	914.74	229,306	933.03	197,456	31,850	951.33	175,488	53,818	969.62	158,990	70,316
105,000	960.48	240,773	979.69	207,331	33,442	998.90	184,263	56,510	1,018.11	166,942	73,831
110,000	1,006.22	252,239	1,026.34	217,203	35,036	1,046.47	193,039	59,200	1,066.59	174,892	77,347
115,000	1,051.96	263,706	1,073.00	227,079	36,627	1,094.04	201,814	61,892	1,115.08	182,843	80,863
120,000	1,097.69	275,168	1,119.64	236,948	38,220	1,141.60	210,587	64,581	1,163.55	190,790	84,378
125,000	1,143.43	286,635	1,166.30	246,823	39,812	1,189.17	219,362	67,273	1,212.04	198,742	87,893
130,000	1,189.17	298,101	1,212.95	256,696	41,405	1,236.74	228,138	69,963	1,260.52	206,691	91,410
135,000	1,234.90	309,564	1,259.60	266,568	42,996	1,284.30	236,910	*72,654	1,308.99	214,638	94,926
140,000	1,280.64	321,030	1,306.25	276,440	44,590	1,331.87	245,686	75,344	1,357.48	222,590	98,440
145,000	1,326.38	332,497	1,352.91	286,316	46,181	1,379.44	254,461	78,036	1,405.96	230,539	101,958
150,000	1,372.11	343,960	1,399.55	296,185	47,775	1,426.99	263,231	80,729	1,454.44	238,488	105,472
155,000	1,417.85	355,426	1,446.21	306,060	49,366	1,474.56	272,006	83,420	1,502.92	246,437	108,989
160,000	1,463.59	366,892	1,492.86	315,933	50,959	1,522.13	280,781	86,111	1,551.41	254,389	112,503
165,000	1,509.32	378,355	1,539.51	325,805	52,550	1,569.69	289,554	88,801	1,599.88	262,336	116,019
170,000	1,555.06	389,822	1,586.16	335,677	54,145	1,617.26	298,329	91,493	1,648.36	270,285	119,537
175,000	1,600.80	401,288	1,632.82	345,553	55,735	1,664.83	307,105	94,183	1,696.85	278,237	123,051
180,000	1,646.54	412,754	1,679.47	355,425	57,329	1,712.40	315,880	96,874	1,745.33	286,186	126,568
185,000	1,692.27	424,217	1,726.12	365,297	58,920	1,759.96	324,653	99,564	1,793.81	294,136	130,081
190,000	1,738.01	435,684	1,772.77	375,170	60,514	1,807.53	333,428	102,256	1,842.29	302,085	133,599
195,000	1,783.75	447,150	1,819.43	385,045	62,105	1,855.10	342,204	104,946	1,890.78	310,037	137,113
200,000	1,829.48	458,613	1,866.07	394,914	63,699	1,902.66	350,976	107,637	1,939.25	317,983	140,630

AUGMENTED PAYMENT MORTGAGES 10.50%

AMOUNT OF LOAN	30 YEARS		8% PMT INCREASE 248.961 PAYMENTS			10% PMT INCREASE 233.832 PAYMENTS			12% PMT INCREASE 220.918 PAYMENTS		
	MONTHLY PAYMENT	TOTAL INTRST	MONTHLY PAYMENT	TOTAL INTRST	INTRST SAVED	MONTHLY PAYMENT	TOTAL INTRST	INTRST SAVED	MONTHLY PAYMENT	TOTAL INTRST	INTRST SAVED
$ 50	0.46	116	0.50	74	42	0.51	69	47	0.52	65	51
100	0.92	231	0.99	146	85	1.01	136	95	1.03	128	103
200	1.83	459	1.98	293	166	2.01	270	189	2.05	253	206
300	2.75	690	2.97	439	251	3.03	409	281	3.08	380	310
400	3.66	918	3.95	583	335	4.03	542	376	4.10	506	412
500	4.58	1,149	4.95	732	417	5.04	679	470	5.13	633	516
600	5.49	1,376	5.93	876	500	6.04	812	564	6.15	759	617
700	6.41	1,608	6.92	1,023	585	7.05	949	659	7.18	886	722
800	7.32	1,835	7.91	1,169	666	8.05	1,082	753	8.20	1,012	823
900	8.24	2,066	8.90	1,316	750	9.06	1,219	847	9.23	1,139	927
1,000	9.15	2,294	9.88	1,460	834	10.07	1,355	939	10.25	1,264	1,030
2,000	18.30	4,588	19.76	2,919	1,669	20.13	2,707	1,881	20.50	2,529	2,059
3,000	27.45	6,882	29.65	4,382	2,500	30.20	4,062	2,820	30.74	3,791	3,091
4,000	36.59	9,172	39.52	5,839	3,333	40.25	5,412	3,760	40.98	5,053	4,119
5,000	45.74	11,466	49.40	7,299	4,167	50.31	6,764	4,702	51.23	6,318	5,148
6,000	54.89	13,760	59.28	8,758	5,002	60.38	8,119	5,641	61.48	7,582	6,178
7,000	64.04	16,054	69.16	10,218	5,836	70.44	9,471	6,583	71.72	8,844	7,210
8,000	73.18	18,345	79.03	11,675	6,670	80.50	10,823	7,522	81.96	10,106	8,239
9,000	82.33	20,639	88.92	13,138	7,501	90.56	12,176	8,463	92.21	11,371	9,268
10,000	91.48	22,933	98.80	14,597	8,336	100.63	13,531	9,402	102.46	12,635	10,298
11,000	100.63	25,227	108.68	16,057	9,170	110.69	14,883	10,344	112.71	13,900	11,327
12,000	109.77	27,517	118.55	17,514	10,003	120.75	16,235	11,282	122.94	15,160	12,357
13,000	118.92	29,811	128.43	18,974	10,837	130.81	17,588	12,223	133.19	16,424	13,387
14,000	128.07	32,105	138.32	20,436	11,669	140.88	18,942	13,163	143.44	17,688	14,417
15,000	137.22	34,399	148.20	21,896	12,503	150.94	20,295	14,104	153.69	18,953	15,446
16,000	146.36	36,690	158.07	23,353	13,337	161.00	21,647	15,043	163.92	20,213	16,477
17,000	155.51	38,984	167.95	24,813	14,171	171.06	22,999	15,985	174.17	21,477	17,507
18,000	164.66	41,278	177.83	26,273	15,005	181.13	24,354	16,924	184.42	22,742	18,536
19,000	173.81	43,572	187.71	27,732	15,840	191.19	25,706	17,866	194.67	24,006	19,566
20,000	182.95	45,862	197.59	29,192	16,670	201.25	27,059	18,803	204.90	25,266	20,596
21,000	192.10	48,156	207.47	30,652	17,504	211.31	28,411	19,745	215.15	26,531	21,625
22,000	201.25	50,450	217.35	32,112	18,338	221.38	29,766	20,684	225.40	27,795	22,655
23,000	210.40	52,744	227.23	33,571	19,173	231.44	31,118	21,626	235.65	29,059	23,685
24,000	219.54	55,034	237.10	35,029	20,005	241.49	32,468	22,566	245.88	30,319	24,715
25,000	228.69	57,328	246.99	36,491	20,837	251.56	33,823	23,505	256.13	31,584	25,744
26,000	237.84	59,622	256.87	37,951	21,671	261.62	35,175	24,447	266.38	32,848	26,774
27,000	246.98	61,913	266.74	39,408	22,505	271.68	36,527	25,386	276.62	34,110	27,803
28,000	256.13	64,207	276.62	40,868	23,339	281.74	37,880	26,327	286.87	35,375	28,832
29,000	265.28	66,501	286.50	42,327	24,174	291.81	39,235	27,266	297.11	36,637	29,864
30,000	274.43	68,795	296.38	43,787	25,008	301.87	40,587	28,208	307.36	37,901	30,894
32,500	297.30	74,528	321.08	47,436	27,092	327.03	43,970	30,558	332.98	41,061	33,467
35,000	320.16	80,258	345.77	51,083	29,175	352.18	47,351	32,907	358.58	44,217	36,041
40,000	365.90	91,724	395.17	58,382	33,342	402.50	54,115	37,609	409.81	50,534	41,190
45,000	411.64	103,190	444.57	65,681	37,509	452.80	60,879	42,311	461.04	56,852	46,338
50,000	457.37	114,653	493.96	72,977	41,676	503.11	67,643	47,010	512.25	63,165	51,488
55,000	503.11	126,120	543.36	80,275	45,845	553.42	74,407	51,713	563.48	69,483	56,637
60,000	548.85	137,586	592.76	87,574	50,012	603.74	81,174	56,412	614.71	75,801	61,785
65,000	594.59	149,052	642.16	94,873	54,179	654.05	87,938	61,114	665.94	82,118	66,934
70,000	640.32	160,515	691.55	102,169	58,346	704.35	94,700	65,815	717.16	88,434	72,081
75,000	686.06	171,982	740.94	109,465	62,517	754.67	101,466	70,516	768.39	94,751	77,231
80,000	731.80	183,448	790.34	116,764	66,684	804.98	108,230	75,218	819.62	101,069	82,379
85,000	777.53	194,911	839.73	124,060	70,851	855.28	114,992	79,919	870.83	107,382	87,529
90,000	823.27	206,377	889.13	131,359	75,018	905.60	121,758	84,619	922.06	113,700	92,677
95,000	869.01	217,844	938.53	138,657	79,187	955.91	128,522	89,322	973.29	120,017	97,827
100,000	914.74	229,306	987.92	145,954	83,352	1,006.21	135,284	94,022	1,024.51	126,333	102,973
105,000	960.48	240,773	1,037.32	153,252	87,521	1,056.53	142,051	98,722	1,075.74	132,650	108,123
110,000	1,006.22	252,239	1,086.72	160,551	91,688	1,106.84	148,815	103,424	1,126.97	138,968	113,271
115,000	1,051.96	263,706	1,136.12	167,850	95,856	1,157.16	155,581	108,125	1,178.20	145,286	118,420
120,000	1,097.69	275,168	1,185.51	175,146	100,022	1,207.46	162,343	112,825	1,229.41	151,599	123,569
125,000	1,143.43	286,635	1,234.90	182,442	104,193	1,257.77	169,107	117,528	1,280.64	157,916	128,719
130,000	1,189.17	298,101	1,284.30	189,741	108,360	1,308.09	175,873	122,228	1,331.87	164,234	133,867
135,000	1,234.90	309,564	1,333.69	197,037	112,527	1,358.39	182,635	126,929	1,383.09	170,549	139,015
140,000	1,280.64	321,030	1,383.09	204,335	116,695	1,408.70	189,399	131,631	1,434.32	176,867	144,163
145,000	1,326.38	332,497	1,432.49	211,634	120,863	1,459.02	196,166	136,331	1,485.55	183,185	149,312
150,000	1,372.11	343,960	1,481.88	218,930	125,030	1,509.32	202,927	141,033	1,536.76	189,498	154,462
155,000	1,417.85	355,426	1,531.28	226,229	129,197	1,559.64	209,694	145,732	1,587.99	195,816	159,610
160,000	1,463.59	366,892	1,580.68	233,528	133,364	1,609.95	216,458	150,434	1,639.22	202,133	164,759
165,000	1,509.32	378,355	1,630.07	240,824	137,531	1,660.25	223,220	155,133	1,690.44	208,449	169,906
170,000	1,555.06	389,822	1,679.46	248,120	141,702	1,710.57	229,986	159,836	1,741.67	214,766	175,056
175,000	1,600.80	401,288	1,728.86	255,419	145,869	1,760.88	236,750	164,538	1,792.90	221,084	180,204
180,000	1,646.54	412,754	1,778.26	262,717	150,037	1,811.19	243,514	169,240	1,844.12	227,399	185,355
185,000	1,692.27	424,217	1,827.65	270,014	154,203	1,861.50	250,278	173,939	1,895.34	233,715	190,502
190,000	1,738.01	435,684	1,877.05	277,312	158,372	1,911.81	257,042	178,642	1,946.57	240,032	195,652
195,000	1,783.75	447,150	1,926.45	284,611	162,539	1,962.13	263,809	183,341	1,997.80	246,350	200,800
200,000	1,829.48	458,613	1,975.84	291,907	166,706	2,012.43	270,571	188,042	2,049.02	252,665	205,948

223

AMOUNT OF LOAN	30 YEARS MONTHLY PAYMENT	30 YEARS TOTAL INTRST	2% PMT INCREASE 317.064 PAYMENTS MONTHLY PAYMENT	TOTAL INTRST	INTRST SAVED	4% PMT INCREASE 287.138 PAYMENTS MONTHLY PAYMENT	TOTAL INTRST	INTRST SAVED	6% PMT INCREASE 264.347 PAYMENTS MONTHLY PAYMENT	TOTAL INTRST	INTRST SAVED
$ 50	0.47	119	0.48	102	17	0.49	91	28	0.50	82	37
100	0.94	238	0.96	204	34	0.98	181	57	1.00	164	74
200	1.87	473	1.91	406	67	1.94	357	116	1.98	323	150
300	2.81	712	2.87	610	102	2.92	538	174	2.98	488	224
400	3.74	946	3.81	808	138	3.89	717	229	3.96	647	299
500	4.67	1,181	4.76	1,009	172	4.86	895	286	4.95	809	372
600	5.61	1,420	5.72	1,214	206	5.83	1,074	346	5.95	973	447
700	6.54	1,654	6.67	1,415	239	6.80	1,253	401	6.93	1,132	522
800	7.47	1,889	7.62	1,616	273	7.77	1,431	458	7.92	1,294	595
900	8.41	2,128	8.58	1,820	308	8.75	1,612	516	8.91	1,455	673
1,000	9.34	2,362	9.53	2,022	340	9.71	1,788	574	9.90	1,617	745
2,000	18.67	4,721	19.04	4,037	684	19.42	3,576	1,145	19.79	3,231	1,490
3,000	28.01	7,084	28.57	6,059	1,025	29.13	5,364	1,720	29.69	4,848	2,236
4,000	37.34	9,442	38.09	8,077	1,365	38.83	7,150	2,292	39.58	6,463	2,979
5,000	46.68	11,805	47.61	10,095	1,710	48.55	8,941	2,864	49.48	8,080	3,725
6,000	56.01	14,164	57.13	12,114	2,050	58.25	10,726	3,438	59.37	9,694	4,470
7,000	65.35	16,526	66.66	14,135	2,391	67.96	12,514	4,012	69.27	11,311	5,215
8,000	74.68	18,885	76.17	16,151	2,734	77.67	14,302	4,583	79.16	12,926	5,959
9,000	84.02	21,247	85.70	18,172	3,075	87.38	16,090	5,157	89.06	14,543	6,704
10,000	93.35	23,606	95.22	20,191	3,415	97.08	17,875	5,731	98.95	16,157	7,449
11,000	102.69	25,968	104.74	22,209	3,759	106.80	19,666	6,302	108.85	17,774	8,194
12,000	112.02	28,327	114.26	24,228	4,099	116.50	21,452	6,875	118.74	19,389	8,938
13,000	121.36	30,690	123.79	26,249	4,441	126.21	23,240	7,450	128.64	21,006	9,684
14,000	130.69	33,048	133.30	28,265	4,783	135.92	25,028	8,020	138.53	22,620	10,428
15,000	140.03	35,411	142.83	30,286	5,125	145.63	26,816	8,595	148.43	24,237	11,174
16,000	149.36	37,770	152.35	32,305	5,465	155.33	28,601	9,169	158.32	25,851	11,919
17,000	158.70	40,132	161.87	34,323	5,809	165.05	30,392	9,740	168.22	27,468	12,664
18,000	168.03	42,491	171.39	36,342	6,149	174.75	32,177	10,314	178.11	29,083	13,408
19,000	177.37	44,853	180.92	38,363	6,490	184.46	33,965	10,888	188.01	30,700	14,153
20,000	186.70	47,212	190.43	40,378	6,834	194.17	35,754	11,458	197.90	32,314	14,898
21,000	196.04	49,574	199.96	42,400	7,174	203.88	37,542	12,032	207.80	33,931	15,643
22,000	205.37	51,933	209.48	44,419	7,514	213.58	39,327	12,606	217.69	35,546	16,387
23,000	214.71	54,296	219.00	46,437	7,859	223.30	41,118	13,178	227.59	37,163	17,133
24,000	224.04	56,654	228.52	48,455	8,199	233.00	42,903	13,751	237.48	38,777	17,877
25,000	233.38	59,017	238.05	50,477	8,540	242.72	44,694	14,323	247.38	40,394	18,623
26,000	242.71	61,376	247.56	52,492	8,884	252.42	46,479	14,897	257.27	42,009	19,367
27,000	252.04	63,734	257.08	54,511	9,223	262.12	48,265	15,469	267.16	43,623	20,111
28,000	261.38	66,097	266.61	56,532	9,565	271.84	50,056	16,041	277.06	45,240	20,857
29,000	270.71	68,456	276.12	58,548	9,908	281.54	51,841	16,615	286.95	46,854	21,602
30,000	280.05	70,818	285.65	60,569	10,249	291.25	53,629	17,189	296.85	48,471	22,347
32,500	303.39	76,720	309.46	65,619	11,101	315.53	58,101	18,619	321.59	52,511	24,209
35,000	326.72	82,619	333.25	70,662	11,957	339.79	62,567	20,052	346.32	56,549	26,070
40,000	373.40	94,424	380.87	80,760	13,664	388.34	71,507	22,917	395.80	64,629	29,795
45,000	420.07	106,225	428.47	90,852	15,373	436.87	80,442	25,783	445.27	72,706	33,519
50,000	466.75	118,030	476.09	100,951	17,079	485.42	89,383	28,647	494.76	80,788	37,242
55,000	513.42	129,831	523.69	111,043	18,788	533.96	98,320	31,511	544.23	88,866	40,965
60,000	560.09	141,632	571.29	121,135	20,497	582.49	107,255	34,377	593.70	96,943	44,689
65,000	606.77	153,437	618.91	131,234	22,203	631.04	116,196	37,241	643.18	105,023	48,414
70,000	653.44	165,238	666.51	141,326	23,912	679.58	125,133	40,105	692.65	113,100	52,138
75,000	700.12	177,043	714.12	151,422	25,621	728.12	134,071	42,972	742.13	121,180	55,863
80,000	746.79	188,844	761.73	161,517	27,327	776.66	143,009	45,835	791.60	129,257	59,587
85,000	793.46	200,646	809.33	171,609	29,037	825.20	151,946	48,700	841.07	137,334	63,312
90,000	840.14	212,450	856.94	181,705	30,745	873.75	160,887	51,563	890.55	145,414	67,036
95,000	886.81	224,252	904.55	191,800	32,452	922.28	169,822	54,430	940.02	153,491	70,761
100,000	933.49	236,056	952.16	201,896	34,160	970.83	178,762	57,294	989.50	161,571	74,485
105,000	980.16	247,858	999.76	211,988	35,870	1,019.37	187,700	60,158	1,038.97	169,649	78,209
110,000	1,026.83	259,659	1,047.37	222,083	37,576	1,067.90	196,635	63,024	1,088.44	177,726	81,933
115,000	1,073.51	271,464	1,094.98	232,179	39,285	1,116.45	205,575	65,889	1,137.92	185,806	85,658
120,000	1,120.18	283,265	1,142.58	242,271	40,994	1,164.99	214,513	68,752	1,187.39	193,883	89,382
125,000	1,166.86	295,070	1,190.20	252,370	42,700	1,213.53	223,451	71,619	1,236.87	201,963	93,107
130,000	1,213.53	306,871	1,237.80	262,462	44,409	1,262.07	232,388	74,483	1,286.34	210,040	96,831
135,000	1,260.20	318,672	1,285.40	272,554	46,118	1,310.61	241,326	77,346	1,335.81	218,117	100,555
140,000	1,306.88	330,477	1,333.02	282,653	47,824	1,359.16	250,266	80,211	1,385.29	226,197	104,280
145,000	1,353.55	342,278	1,380.62	292,745	49,533	1,407.69	259,201	83,077	1,434.76	234,275	108,003
150,000	1,400.23	354,083	1,428.23	302,840	51,243	1,456.24	268,142	85,941	1,484.24	242,354	111,729
155,000	1,446.90	365,884	1,475.84	312,936	52,948	1,504.78	277,080	88,804	1,533.71	250,432	115,452
160,000	1,493.58	377,689	1,523.45	323,031	54,658	1,553.32	286,017	91,672	1,583.19	258,512	119,177
165,000	1,540.25	389,490	1,571.06	333,127	56,363	1,601.86	294,955	94,535	1,632.67	266,591	122,899
170,000	1,586.92	401,291	1,618.66	343,219	58,072	1,650.40	303,893	97,398	1,682.14	274,669	126,622
175,000	1,633.60	413,096	1,666.27	353,314	59,782	1,698.94	312,830	100,266	1,731.62	282,749	130,347
180,000	1,680.27	424,897	1,713.88	363,410	61,487	1,747.48	321,768	103,129	1,781.09	290,826	134,071
185,000	1,726.95	436,702	1,761.49	373,505	63,197	1,796.03	330,708	105,994	1,830.57	298,906	137,796
190,000	1,773.62	448,503	1,809.09	383,597	64,906	1,844.56	339,643	108,860	1,880.04	306,983	141,520
195,000	1,820.29	460,304	1,856.70	393,693	66,611	1,893.10	348,581	111,723	1,929.51	315,060	145,244
200,000	1,866.97	472,109	1,904.31	403,788	68,321	1,941.65	357,521	114,588	1,978.99	323,140	148,969

AUGMENTED PAYMENT MORTGAGES 10.75%

AMOUNT OF LOAN	30 YEARS		8% PMT INCREASE 246.060 PAYMENTS			10% PMT INCREASE 230.877 PAYMENTS			12% PMT INCREASE 217.958 PAYMENTS		
	MONTHLY PAYMENT	TOTAL INTRST	MONTHLY PAYMENT	TOTAL INTRST	INTRST SAVED	MONTHLY PAYMENT	TOTAL INTRST	INTRST SAVED	MONTHLY PAYMENT	TOTAL INTRST	INTRST SAVED
$ 50	0.47	119	0.51	75	44	0.52	70	49	0.53	66	53
100	0.94	238	1.02	151	87	1.03	138	100	1.05	129	109
200	1.87	473	2.02	297	176	2.06	276	197	2.09	256	217
300	2.81	712	3.03	446	266	3.09	413	299	3.15	387	325
400	3.74	946	4.04	594	352	4.11	549	397	4.19	513	433
500	4.67	1,181	5.04	740	441	5.14	687	494	5.23	640	541
600	5.61	1,420	6.06	891	529	6.17	825	595	6.28	769	651
700	6.54	1,654	7.06	1,037	617	7.19	960	694	7.32	895	759
800	7.47	1,889	8.07	1,186	703	8.22	1,098	791	8.37	1,024	865
900	8.41	2,128	9.08	1,334	794	9.25	1,236	892	9.42	1,153	975
1,000	9.34	2,362	10.09	1,483	879	10.27	1,371	991	10.46	1,280	1,082
2,000	18.67	4,721	20.16	2,961	1,760	20.54	2,742	1,979	20.91	2,558	2,163
3,000	28.01	7,084	30.25	4,443	2,641	30.81	4,113	2,971	31.37	3,837	3,247
4,000	37.34	9,442	40.33	5,924	3,518	41.07	5,482	3,960	41.82	5,115	4,327
5,000	46.68	11,805	50.41	7,404	4,401	51.35	6,856	4,949	52.28	6,395	5,410
6,000	56.01	14,164	60.49	8,884	5,280	61.61	8,224	5,940	62.73	7,673	6,491
7,000	65.35	16,526	70.58	10,367	6,159	71.89	9,598	6,928	73.19	8,952	7,574
8,000	74.68	18,885	80.65	11,845	7,040	82.15	10,967	7,918	83.64	10,230	8,655
9,000	84.02	21,247	90.74	13,327	7,920	92.42	12,338	8,909	94.10	11,510	9,737
10,000	93.35	23,606	100.82	14,808	8,798	102.69	13,709	9,897	104.55	12,788	10,818
11,000	102.69	25,968	110.91	16,291	9,677	112.96	15,080	10,888	115.01	14,067	11,901
12,000	112.02	28,327	120.98	17,768	10,559	123.22	16,449	11,878	125.46	15,345	12,982
13,000	121.36	30,690	131.07	19,251	11,439	133.50	17,822	12,868	135.92	16,625	14,065
14,000	130.69	33,048	141.15	20,731	12,317	143.76	19,191	13,857	146.37	17,903	15,145
15,000	140.03	35,411	151.23	22,212	13,199	154.03	20,562	14,849	156.83	19,182	16,229
16,000	149.36	37,770	161.31	23,692	14,078	164.30	21,933	15,837	167.28	20,460	17,310
17,000	158.70	40,132	171.40	25,175	14,957	174.57	23,304	16,828	177.74	21,740	18,392
18,000	168.03	42,491	181.47	26,653	15,838	184.83	24,675	17,818	188.19	23,018	19,473
19,000	177.37	44,853	191.56	28,135	16,718	195.11	26,046	18,807	198.65	24,297	20,556
20,000	186.70	47,212	201.64	29,616	17,596	205.37	27,415	19,797	209.10	25,575	21,637
21,000	196.04	49,574	211.72	31,096	18,478	215.64	28,786	20,788	219.56	26,855	22,719
22,000	205.37	51,933	221.80	32,576	19,357	225.91	30,157	21,776	230.01	28,133	23,800
23,000	214.71	54,296	231.89	34,059	20,237	236.18	31,529	22,767	240.48	29,415	24,881
24,000	224.04	56,654	241.96	35,537	21,117	246.44	32,897	23,757	250.92	30,690	25,964
25,000	233.38	59,017	252.05	37,019	21,998	256.72	34,271	24,746	261.39	31,972	27,045
26,000	242.71	61,376	262.13	38,500	22,876	266.98	35,640	25,736	271.84	33,250	28,126
27,000	252.04	63,734	272.20	39,978	23,756	277.24	37,008	26,726	282.28	34,525	29,209
28,000	261.38	66,097	282.29	41,461	24,637	287.52	38,382	27,715	292.75	35,807	30,290
29,000	270.71	68,456	292.37	42,941	25,515	297.78	39,751	28,705	303.20	37,085	31,371
30,000	280.05	70,818	302.45	44,421	26,397	308.06	41,124	29,694	313.66	38,365	32,453
32,500	303.39	76,720	327.66	48,124	28,596	333.73	44,551	32,169	339.80	41,562	35,158
35,000	326.72	82,619	352.86	51,825	30,794	359.39	47,975	34,644	365.93	44,757	37,862
40,000	373.40	94,424	403.27	59,229	35,195	410.74	54,830	39,594	418.21	51,152	43,272
45,000	420.07	106,225	453.68	66,633	39,592	462.08	61,684	44,541	470.48	57,545	48,680
50,000	466.75	118,030	504.09	74,036	43,994	513.43	68,539	49,491	522.76	63,940	54,090
55,000	513.42	129,831	554.49	81,438	48,393	564.76	75,390	54,441	575.03	70,332	59,499
60,000	560.09	141,632	604.90	88,842	52,790	616.10	82,243	59,389	627.30	76,725	64,907
65,000	606.77	153,437	655.31	96,246	57,191	667.45	89,099	64,338	679.58	83,120	70,317
70,000	653.44	165,238	705.72	103,649	61,589	718.78	95,950	69,288	731.85	89,513	75,725
75,000	700.12	177,043	756.13	111,053	65,990	770.13	102,805	74,238	784.13	95,907	81,136
80,000	746.79	188,844	806.53	118,455	70,389	821.47	109,659	79,185	836.40	102,300	86,544
85,000	793.46	200,646	856.94	125,859	74,787	872.81	116,512	84,134	888.68	108,695	91,951
90,000	840.14	212,450	907.35	133,263	79,187	924.15	123,365	89,085	940.96	115,090	97,360
95,000	886.81	224,252	957.75	140,664	83,588	975.49	130,218	94,034	993.23	121,482	102,770
100,000	933.49	236,056	1,008.17	148,070	87,986	1,026.84	137,074	98,982	1,045.51	127,877	108,179
105,000	980.16	247,858	1,058.57	155,472	92,386	1,078.18	143,927	103,931	1,097.78	134,270	113,588
110,000	1,026.83	259,659	1,108.98	162,876	96,783	1,129.51	150,780	108,879	1,150.05	140,663	118,996
115,000	1,073.51	271,464	1,159.39	170,280	101,184	1,180.86	157,633	113,831	1,202.33	147,057	124,407
120,000	1,120.18	283,265	1,209.79	177,681	105,584	1,232.20	164,487	118,778	1,254.60	153,450	129,815
125,000	1,166.86	295,070	1,260.21	185,087	109,983	1,283.55	171,342	123,728	1,306.88	159,845	135,225
130,000	1,213.53	306,871	1,310.61	192,489	114,382	1,334.88	178,193	128,678	1,359.15	166,238	140,633
135,000	1,260.20	318,672	1,361.02	199,893	118,779	1,386.22	185,046	133,626	1,411.42	172,630	146,042
140,000	1,306.88	330,477	1,411.43	207,299	123,181	1,437.57	191,902	138,575	1,463.71	179,027	151,450
145,000	1,353.55	342,277	1,461.83	214,698	127,580	1,488.91	198,755	143,523	1,515.98	185,420	156,858
150,000	1,400.23	354,083	1,512.25	222,104	131,979	1,540.25	205,608	148,475	1,568.26	191,815	162,268
155,000	1,446.90	365,884	1,562.65	229,506	136,378	1,591.59	212,462	153,422	1,620.53	198,207	167,677
160,000	1,493.58	377,689	1,613.07	236,912	140,777	1,642.94	219,317	158,372	1,672.81	204,602	173,087
165,000	1,540.25	389,490	1,663.47	244,313	145,177	1,694.28	226,170	163,320	1,725.08	210,995	178,495
170,000	1,586.92	401,291	1,713.87	251,715	149,576	1,745.61	233,021	168,270	1,777.35	217,388	183,903
175,000	1,633.60	413,096	1,764.29	259,121	153,975	1,796.96	239,877	173,219	1,829.63	223,782	189,314
180,000	1,680.27	424,897	1,814.69	266,523	158,374	1,848.30	246,730	178,167	1,881.90	230,175	194,722
185,000	1,726.95	436,702	1,865.11	273,929	162,773	1,899.65	253,585	183,117	1,934.18	236,570	200,132
190,000	1,773.62	448,503	1,915.51	281,330	167,173	1,950.98	260,436	188,067	1,986.45	242,963	205,540
195,000	1,820.29	460,304	1,965.91	288,732	171,572	2,002.32	267,290	193,014	2,038.72	249,355	210,949
200,000	1,866.97	472,109	2,016.33	296,138	175,971	2,053.67	274,145	197,964	2,091.01	255,752	216,357

AUGMENTED PAYMENT MORTGAGES

AMOUNT OF LOAN	30 YEARS		2% PMT INCREASE 315.268 PAYMENTS			4% PMT INCREASE 284.656 PAYMENTS			6% PMT INCREASE 261.567 PAYMENTS		
	MONTHLY PAYMENT	TOTAL INTRST	MONTHLY PAYMENT	TOTAL INTRST	INTRST SAVED	MONTHLY PAYMENT	TOTAL INTRST	INTRST SAVED	MONTHLY PAYMENT	TOTAL INTRST	INTRST SAVED
$ 50	0.48	123	0.49	104	19	0.50	92	31	0.51	83	40
100	0.96	246	0.98	209	37	1.00	185	61	1.02	167	79
200	1.91	488	1.95	415	73	1.99	366	122	2.02	328	160
300	2.86	730	2.92	621	109	2.97	545	185	3.03	493	237
400	3.81	972	3.89	826	146	3.96	727	245	4.04	657	315
500	4.77	1,217	4.87	1,035	182	4.96	912	305	5.06	824	393
600	5.72	1,459	5.83	1,238	221	5.95	1,094	365	6.06	985	474
700	6.67	1,701	6.80	1,444	257	6.94	1,276	425	7.07	1,149	552
800	7.62	1,943	7.77	1,650	293	7.92	1,454	489	8.08	1,313	630
900	8.58	2,189	8.75	1,859	330	8.92	1,639	550	9.09	1,478	711
1,000	9.53	2,431	9.72	2,064	367	9.91	1,821	610	10.10	1,642	789
2,000	19.05	4,858	19.43	4,126	732	19.81	3,639	1,219	20.19	3,281	1,577
3,000	28.57	7,285	29.14	6,187	1,098	29.71	5,457	1,828	30.28	4,920	2,365
4,000	38.10	9,716	38.86	8,251	1,465	39.62	7,278	2,438	40.39	6,565	3,151
5,000	47.62	12,143	48.57	10,313	1,830	49.52	9,096	3,047	50.48	8,204	3,939
6,000	57.14	14,570	58.28	12,374	2,196	59.43	10,917	3,653	60.57	9,843	4,727
7,000	66.67	17,001	68.00	14,438	2,563	69.34	12,738	4,263	70.67	11,485	5,516
8,000	76.19	19,428	77.71	16,499	2,929	79.24	14,556	4,872	80.76	13,124	6,304
9,000	85.71	21,856	87.42	18,561	3,295	89.14	16,374	5,482	90.85	14,763	7,093
10,000	95.24	24,286	97.14	20,625	3,661	99.05	18,195	6,091	100.95	16,405	7,881
11,000	104.76	26,714	106.86	22,690	4,024	108.95	20,013	6,701	111.05	18,047	8,667
12,000	114.28	29,141	116.57	24,751	4,390	118.85	21,831	7,310	121.14	19,686	9,455
13,000	123.81	31,572	126.29	26,815	4,757	128.76	23,652	7,920	131.24	21,328	10,244
14,000	133.33	33,999	136.00	28,876	5,123	138.66	25,470	8,529	141.33	22,967	11,032
15,000	142.85	36,426	145.71	30,938	5,488	148.56	27,288	9,138	151.42	24,606	11,820
16,000	152.38	38,857	155.43	33,002	5,855	158.48	29,112	9,745	161.52	26,248	12,609
17,000	161.90	41,284	165.14	35,063	6,221	168.38	30,930	10,354	171.61	27,888	13,396
18,000	171.42	43,711	174.85	37,125	6,586	178.28	32,749	10,963	181.71	29,529	14,182
19,000	180.95	46,142	184.57	39,189	6,953	188.19	34,569	11,573	191.81	31,171	14,971
20,000	190.47	48,569	194.28	41,250	7,319	198.09	36,388	12,181	201.90	32,810	15,759
21,000	199.99	50,996	203.99	43,312	7,684	207.99	38,206	12,790	211.99	34,450	16,546
22,000	209.52	53,427	213.71	45,376	8,051	217.90	40,027	13,400	222.09	36,091	17,336
23,000	219.04	55,854	223.42	47,437	8,417	227.80	41,845	14,009	232.18	37,731	18,123
24,000	228.56	58,282	233.13	49,498	8,784	237.70	43,663	14,619	242.27	39,370	18,912
25,000	238.09	60,712	242.85	51,563	9,149	247.61	45,484	15,228	252.38	41,014	19,698
26,000	247.61	63,140	252.56	53,624	9,516	257.51	47,302	15,838	262.47	42,653	20,487
27,000	257.13	65,567	262.27	55,685	9,882	267.42	49,123	16,444	272.56	44,293	21,274
28,000	266.66	67,998	271.99	57,750	10,248	277.33	50,944	17,054	282.66	45,935	22,063
29,000	276.18	70,425	281.70	59,811	10,614	287.23	52,762	17,663	292.75	47,574	22,851
30,000	285.70	72,852	291.41	61,872	10,980	297.13	54,580	18,272	302.84	49,213	23,639
32,500	309.51	78,924	315.70	67,030	11,894	321.89	59,128	19,796	328.08	53,315	25,609
35,000	333.32	84,995	339.99	72,188	12,807	346.65	63,676	21,319	353.32	57,417	27,578
40,000	380.93	97,135	388.55	82,497	14,638	396.17	72,772	24,363	403.79	65,618	31,517
45,000	428.55	109,273	437.12	92,810	16,468	445.69	81,868	27,410	454.26	73,819	35,459
50,000	476.17	121,421	485.69	103,123	18,298	495.22	90,967	30,454	504.74	82,023	39,398
55,000	523.78	133,561	534.26	113,435	20,126	544.73	100,061	33,500	555.21	90,225	43,336
60,000	571.40	145,704	582.83	123,748	21,956	594.26	109,160	36,544	605.68	98,426	47,278
65,000	619.02	157,847	631.40	134,060	23,787	643.78	118,256	39,591	656.16	106,630	51,217
70,000	666.63	169,987	679.96	144,370	25,617	693.30	127,352	42,635	706.63	114,831	55,156
75,000	714.25	182,130	728.54	154,685	27,445	742.82	136,448	45,682	757.11	123,035	59,095
80,000	761.86	194,270	777.10	164,995	29,275	792.33	145,541	48,729	807.57	131,234	63,036
85,000	809.48	206,413	825.67	175,307	31,106	841.86	154,641	51,772	858.05	139,438	66,975
90,000	857.10	218,556	874.24	185,620	32,936	891.38	163,737	54,819	908.53	147,641	70,915
95,000	904.71	230,696	922.80	195,929	34,767	940.90	172,833	57,863	958.99	155,840	74,856
100,000	952.33	242,839	971.38	206,245	36,594	990.42	181,929	60,910	1,009.47	164,044	78,795
105,000	999.94	254,978	1,019.94	216,554	38,424	1,039.94	191,025	63,953	1,059.94	172,245	82,733
110,000	1,047.56	267,122	1,068.51	226,867	40,255	1,089.46	200,121	67,001	1,110.41	180,447	86,675
115,000	1,095.18	279,265	1,117.08	237,180	42,085	1,138.99	209,220	70,045	1,160.89	188,651	90,614
120,000	1,142.79	291,404	1,165.65	247,492	43,912	1,188.50	218,314	73,090	1,211.36	196,852	94,552
125,000	1,190.41	303,548	1,214.22	257,805	45,743	1,238.03	227,413	76,135	1,261.83	205,053	98,495
130,000	1,238.03	315,691	1,262.79	268,117	47,574	1,287.55	236,509	79,182	1,312.31	213,257	102,434
135,000	1,285.64	327,830	1,311.35	278,427	49,403	1,337.07	245,605	82,225	1,362.78	221,458	106,372
140,000	1,333.26	339,974	1,359.93	288,742	51,232	1,386.59	254,701	85,273	1,413.26	229,662	110,312
145,000	1,380.87	352,113	1,408.49	299,052	53,061	1,436.10	263,794	88,319	1,463.72	237,861	114,252
150,000	1,428.49	364,256	1,457.06	309,364	54,892	1,485.63	272,893	91,363	1,514.20	246,065	118,191
155,000	1,476.11	376,400	1,505.63	319,677	56,723	1,535.15	281,990	94,410	1,564.68	254,269	122,131
160,000	1,523.72	388,539	1,554.19	329,986	58,553	1,584.67	291,086	97,453	1,615.14	262,467	126,072
165,000	1,571.34	400,682	1,602.77	340,302	60,380	1,634.19	300,182	100,500	1,665.62	270,671	130,011
170,000	1,618.95	412,822	1,651.33	350,612	62,210	1,683.71	309,278	103,544	1,716.09	278,873	133,949
175,000	1,666.57	424,965	1,699.90	360,924	64,041	1,733.23	318,374	106,591	1,766.56	287,074	137,891
180,000	1,714.19	437,108	1,748.47	371,237	65,871	1,782.76	327,473	109,635	1,817.04	295,278	141,830
185,000	1,761.80	449,248	1,797.04	381,549	67,699	1,832.27	336,567	112,681	1,867.51	303,479	145,769
190,000	1,809.42	461,391	1,845.61	391,862	69,529	1,881.80	345,666	115,725	1,917.99	311,683	149,708
195,000	1,857.04	473,534	1,894.18	402,174	71,360	1,931.32	354,762	118,772	1,968.46	319,884	153,650
200,000	1,904.65	485,674	1,942.74	412,484	73,190	1,980.84	363,858	121,816	2,018.93	328,085	157,589

AMOUNT OF LOAN	30 YEARS		8% PMT INCREASE 243.156 PAYMENTS			10% PMT INCREASE 227.933 PAYMENTS			12% PMT INCREASE 215.019 PAYMENTS		
	MONTHLY PAYMENT	TOTAL INTRST	MONTHLY PAYMENT	TOTAL INTRST	INTRST SAVED	MONTHLY PAYMENT	TOTAL INTRST	INTRST SAVED	MONTHLY PAYMENT	TOTAL INTRST	INTRST SAVED
$ 50	0.48	123	0.52	76	47	0.53	71	52	0.54	66	57
100	0.96	246	1.04	153	93	1.06	142	104	1.08	132	114
200	1.91	488	2.06	301	187	2.10	279	209	2.14	260	228
300	2.86	730	3.09	451	279	3.15	418	312	3.20	388	342
400	3.81	972	4.11	599	373	4.19	555	417	4.27	518	454
500	4.77	1,217	5.15	752	465	5.25	697	520	5.34	648	569
600	5.72	1,459	6.18	903	556	6.29	834	625	6.41	778	681
700	6.67	1,701	7.20	1,051	650	7.34	973	728	7.47	906	795
800	7.62	1,943	8.23	1,201	742	8.38	1,110	833	8.53	1,034	909
900	8.58	2,189	9.27	1,354	835	9.44	1,252	937	9.61	1,166	1,023
1,000	9.53	2,431	10.29	1,502	929	10.48	1,389	1,042	10.67	1,294	1,137
2,000	19.05	4,858	20.57	3,002	1,856	20.96	2,777	2,081	21.34	2,589	2,269
3,000	28.57	7,285	30.86	4,504	2,781	31.43	4,164	3,121	32.00	3,881	3,404
4,000	38.10	9,716	41.15	6,006	3,710	41.91	5,553	4,163	42.67	5,175	4,541
5,000	47.62	12,143	51.43	7,506	4,637	52.38	6,939	5,204	53.33	6,467	5,676
6,000	57.14	14,570	61.71	9,005	5,565	62.85	8,326	6,244	64.00	7,761	6,809
7,000	66.67	17,001	72.00	10,507	6,494	73.34	9,717	7,284	74.67	9,055	7,946
8,000	76.19	19,428	82.29	12,009	7,419	83.81	11,103	8,325	85.33	10,348	9,080
9,000	85.71	21,856	92.57	13,509	8,347	94.28	12,490	9,366	96.00	11,642	10,214
10,000	95.24	24,286	102.86	15,011	9,275	104.76	13,878	10,408	106.67	12,936	11,350
11,000	104.76	26,714	113.14	16,511	10,203	115.24	15,267	11,447	117.33	14,228	12,486
12,000	114.28	29,141	123.42	18,010	11,131	125.71	16,653	12,488	127.99	15,520	13,621
13,000	123.81	31,572	133.71	19,512	12,060	136.19	18,042	13,530	138.67	16,817	14,755
14,000	133.33	33,999	144.00	21,014	12,985	146.66	19,429	14,570	149.33	18,109	15,890
15,000	142.85	36,426	154.28	22,514	13,912	157.14	20,817	15,609	159.99	19,401	17,025
16,000	152.38	38,857	164.57	24,016	14,841	167.62	22,206	16,651	170.67	20,697	18,160
17,000	161.90	41,284	174.85	25,516	15,768	178.09	23,593	17,691	181.33	21,989	19,295
18,000	171.42	43,711	185.13	27,015	16,696	188.56	24,979	18,732	191.99	23,281	20,430
19,000	180.95	46,142	195.43	28,520	17,622	199.05	26,370	19,772	202.66	24,576	21,566
20,000	190.47	48,569	205.71	30,020	18,549	209.52	27,757	20,812	213.33	25,870	22,699
21,000	199.99	50,996	215.99	31,519	19,477	219.99	29,143	21,853	223.99	27,162	23,834
22,000	209.52	53,427	226.28	33,021	20,406	230.47	30,532	22,895	234.66	28,456	24,971
23,000	219.04	55,854	236.56	34,521	21,333	240.94	31,918	23,936	245.32	29,748	26,106
24,000	228.56	58,282	246.84	36,021	22,261	251.42	33,307	24,975	255.99	31,043	27,239
25,000	238.09	60,712	257.14	37,525	23,187	261.90	34,696	26,016	266.66	32,337	28,375
26,000	247.61	63,140	267.42	39,025	24,115	272.37	36,082	27,058	277.32	33,629	29,511
27,000	257.13	65,567	277.70	40,524	25,043	282.84	37,469	28,098	287.99	34,923	30,644
28,000	266.66	67,998	287.99	42,026	25,972	293.33	38,860	29,138	298.66	36,218	31,780
29,000	276.18	70,425	298.27	43,526	26,899	303.80	40,246	30,179	309.32	37,510	32,915
30,000	285.70	72,852	308.56	45,028	27,824	314.27	41,633	31,219	319.98	38,802	34,050
32,500	309.51	78,924	334.27	48,780	30,144	340.46	45,102	33,822	346.65	42,036	36,888
35,000	333.32	84,995	359.99	52,534	32,461	366.65	48,572	36,423	373.32	45,271	39,724
40,000	380.93	97,135	411.40	60,034	37,101	419.02	55,508	41,627	426.64	51,736	45,399
45,000	428.55	109,278	462.83	67,540	41,738	471.41	62,450	46,828	479.98	58,205	51,073
50,000	476.17	121,421	514.26	75,045	46,376	523.79	69,389	52,032	533.31	64,672	56,749
55,000	523.78	133,561	565.68	82,548	51,013	576.16	76,326	57,235	586.63	71,137	62,424
60,000	571.40	145,704	617.11	90,051	55,650	628.54	83,265	62,439	639.97	77,606	68,098
65,000	619.02	157,847	668.54	97,560	60,287	680.92	90,204	67,643	693.30	84,073	73,774
70,000	666.63	169,987	719.96	105,063	64,924	733.29	97,141	72,846	746.63	90,540	79,447
75,000	714.25	182,130	771.39	112,568	69,562	785.68	104,082	78,048	799.96	97,007	85,123
80,000	761.86	194,270	822.81	120,071	74,199	838.05	111,019	83,251	853.28	103,471	90,799
85,000	809.48	206,413	874.24	127,577	78,836	890.43	117,958	88,455	906.62	109,941	96,472
90,000	857.10	218,556	925.67	135,082	83,474	942.81	124,898	93,658	959.95	116,407	102,149
95,000	904.71	230,696	977.09	142,585	88,111	995.18	131,834	98,862	1,013.28	122,874	107,822
100,000	952.33	242,839	1,028.52	150,091	92,748	1,047.56	138,773	104,066	1,066.61	129,341	113,498
105,000	999.94	254,978	1,079.94	157,594	97,384	1,099.93	145,710	109,268	1,119.93	135,806	119,172
110,000	1,047.56	267,122	1,131.36	165,097	102,025	1,152.32	152,652	114,470	1,173.27	142,275	124,847
115,000	1,095.18	279,265	1,182.79	172,602	106,663	1,204.70	159,591	119,674	1,226.60	148,742	130,523
120,000	1,142.79	291,404	1,234.21	180,106	111,298	1,257.07	166,528	124,876	1,279.92	155,207	136,197
125,000	1,190.41	303,548	1,285.64	187,611	115,937	1,309.45	173,467	130,081	1,333.26	161,676	141,872
130,000	1,238.03	315,691	1,337.07	195,117	120,574	1,361.83	180,406	135,285	1,386.59	168,143	147,548
135,000	1,285.64	327,830	1,388.49	202,620	125,210	1,414.20	187,343	140,487	1,439.92	174,610	153,220
140,000	1,333.26	339,974	1,439.92	210,125	129,849	1,466.59	194,284	145,690	1,493.25	181,077	158,897
145,000	1,380.87	352,113	1,491.34	217,628	134,485	1,518.96	201,221	150,892	1,546.57	187,542	164,571
150,000	1,428.49	364,256	1,542.77	225,134	139,122	1,571.34	208,160	156,096	1,599.91	194,011	170,245
155,000	1,476.11	376,400	1,594.20	232,639	143,761	1,623.72	215,099	161,301	1,653.24	200,478	175,922
160,000	1,523.72	388,539	1,645.62	240,142	148,397	1,676.09	222,036	166,503	1,706.57	206,945	181,594
165,000	1,571.34	400,682	1,697.05	247,648	153,034	1,728.47	228,975	171,707	1,759.90	213,412	187,270
170,000	1,618.95	412,820	1,748.47	255,151	157,671	1,780.85	235,914	176,908	1,813.22	219,877	192,945
175,000	1,666.57	424,965	1,799.90	262,656	162,309	1,833.23	242,854	182,111	1,866.56	226,346	198,619
180,000	1,714.19	437,108	1,851.33	270,162	166,946	1,885.61	249,793	187,315	1,919.89	232,813	204,295
185,000	1,761.80	449,248	1,902.74	277,663	171,585	1,937.98	256,730	192,518	1,973.22	239,280	209,968
190,000	1,809.42	461,391	1,954.17	285,168	176,223	1,990.36	263,669	197,722	2,026.55	245,747	215,644
195,000	1,857.04	473,534	2,005.60	292,674	180,860	2,042.74	270,608	202,926	2,079.88	252,214	221,320
200,000	1,904.65	485,674	2,057.02	300,177	185,497	2,095.12	277,547	208,127	2,133.21	258,681	226,993

AMOUNT OF LOAN	30 YEARS		2% PMT INCREASE 313.418 PAYMENTS			4% PMT INCREASE 282.135 PAYMENTS			6% PMT INCREASE 258.771 PAYMENTS		
	MONTHLY PAYMENT	TOTAL INTRST	MONTHLY PAYMENT	TOTAL INTRST	INTRST SAVED	MONTHLY PAYMENT	TOTAL INTRST	INTRST SAVED	MONTHLY PAYMENT	TOTAL INTRST	INTRST SAVED
$ 50	0.49	126	0.50	107	19	0.51	94	32	0.52	85	41
100	0.98	253	1.00	213	40	1.02	188	65	1.04	169	84
200	1.95	502	1.99	424	78	2.03	373	129	2.07	336	166
300	2.92	751	2.98	634	117	3.04	558	193	3.10	502	249
400	3.89	1,000	3.97	844	156	4.05	743	257	4.12	666	334
500	4.86	1,250	4.96	1,055	195	5.05	925	325	5.15	833	417
600	5.83	1,499	5.95	1,265	234	6.06	1,110	389	6.18	999	500
700	6.80	1,748	6.94	1,475	273	7.07	1,295	453	7.21	1,166	582
800	7.78	2,001	7.94	1,689	312	8.09	1,482	519	8.25	1,335	666
900	8.75	2,250	8.93	1,899	351	9.10	1,667	583	9.28	1,501	749
1,000	9.72	2,499	9.91	2,106	393	10.11	1,852	647	10.30	1,665	834
2,000	19.43	4,995	19.82	4,212	783	20.21	3,702	1,293	20.60	3,331	1,664
3,000	29.14	7,490	29.72	6,315	1,175	30.31	5,552	1,938	30.89	4,993	2,497
4,000	38.86	9,990	39.64	8,424	1,566	40.41	7,401	2,589	41.19	6,659	3,331
5,000	48.57	12,485	49.54	10,527	1,958	50.51	9,251	3,234	51.48	8,322	4,163
6,000	58.28	14,981	59.45	12,633	2,348	60.61	11,100	3,881	61.78	9,987	4,994
7,000	67.99	17,476	69.35	14,736	2,740	70.71	12,950	4,526	72.07	11,650	5,826
8,000	77.71	19,976	79.26	16,842	3,134	80.82	14,802	5,174	82.37	13,315	6,661
9,000	87.42	22,471	89.17	18,947	3,524	90.92	16,652	5,819	92.67	14,980	7,491
10,000	97.13	24,967	99.07	21,050	3,917	101.02	18,501	6,466	102.96	16,643	8,324
11,000	106.84	27,462	108.98	23,156	4,306	111.11	20,348	7,114	113.25	18,306	9,156
12,000	116.56	29,962	118.89	25,262	4,700	121.22	22,200	7,762	123.55	19,971	9,991
13,000	126.27	32,457	128.80	27,368	5,089	131.32	24,050	8,407	133.85	21,636	10,821
14,000	135.98	34,953	138.70	29,471	5,482	141.42	25,900	9,053	144.14	23,299	11,654
15,000	145.69	37,448	148.60	31,574	5,874	151.52	27,749	9,699	154.43	24,962	12,486
16,000	155.41	39,948	158.52	33,683	6,265	161.63	29,601	10,347	164.73	26,627	13,321
17,000	165.12	42,443	168.42	35,786	6,657	171.72	31,448	10,995	175.03	28,293	14,150
18,000	174.83	44,939	178.33	37,892	7,047	181.82	33,298	11,641	185.32	29,955	14,984
19,000	184.54	47,434	188.23	39,995	7,439	191.92	35,147	12,287	195.61	31,618	15,816
20,000	194.26	49,934	198.15	42,104	7,830	202.03	37,000	12,934	205.92	33,286	16,648
21,000	203.97	52,429	208.05	44,207	8,222	212.13	38,849	13,580	216.21	34,949	17,480
22,000	213.68	54,925	217.95	46,309	8,616	222.23	40,699	14,226	226.50	36,612	18,313
23,000	223.40	57,424	227.87	48,419	9,005	232.34	42,551	14,873	236.80	38,277	19,147
24,000	233.11	59,920	237.77	50,521	9,399	242.43	44,398	15,522	247.10	39,942	19,978
25,000	242.82	62,415	247.68	52,627	9,788	252.53	46,248	16,167	257.39	41,605	20,810
26,000	252.53	64,911	257.58	54,730	10,181	262.63	48,097	16,814	267.68	43,268	21,643
27,000	262.25	67,410	267.50	56,839	10,571	272.74	49,949	17,461	277.99	44,936	22,474
28,000	271.96	69,906	277.40	58,942	10,964	282.84	51,799	18,107	288.28	46,599	23,307
29,000	281.67	72,401	287.30	61,045	11,356	292.94	53,649	18,752	298.57	48,261	24,140
30,000	291.38	74,897	297.21	63,151	11,746	303.04	55,498	19,399	308.86	49,924	24,973
32,500	315.66	81,138	321.97	68,411	12,727	328.29	60,122	21,016	334.60	54,085	27,053
35,000	339.95	87,382	346.75	73,678	13,704	353.55	64,749	22,633	360.35	58,248	29,134
40,000	388.51	99,864	396.28	84,201	15,663	404.05	73,997	25,867	411.82	66,567	33,297
45,000	437.07	112,345	445.81	94,725	17,620	454.55	83,244	29,101	463.29	74,886	37,459
50,000	485.64	124,830	495.35	105,252	19,578	505.07	92,498	32,332	514.78	83,210	41,620
55,000	534.20	137,312	544.88	115,775	21,537	555.57	101,746	35,566	566.25	91,529	45,783
60,000	582.76	149,794	594.42	126,302	23,492	606.07	110,994	38,800	617.73	99,851	49,943
65,000	631.32	162,275	643.95	136,826	25,449	656.57	120,241	42,034	669.20	108,170	54,105
70,000	679.89	174,760	693.49	147,352	27,408	707.09	129,495	45,265	720.68	116,491	58,269
75,000	728.45	187,242	743.02	157,876	29,366	757.59	138,743	48,499	772.16	124,813	62,429
80,000	777.01	199,724	792.55	168,399	31,325	808.09	147,990	51,734	823.63	133,132	66,592
85,000	825.58	212,209	842.09	178,926	33,283	858.60	157,241	54,968	875.11	141,453	70,756
90,000	874.14	224,690	891.62	189,450	35,240	909.11	166,492	58,198	926.59	149,775	74,915
95,000	922.70	237,172	941.15	199,973	37,199	959.61	175,740	61,432	978.06	158,094	79,078
100,000	971.27	249,657	990.70	210,503	39,154	1,010.12	184,990	64,667	1,029.55	166,418	83,239
105,000	1,019.83	262,139	1,040.23	221,027	41,112	1,060.62	194,238	67,901	1,081.02	174,737	87,402
110,000	1,068.39	274,620	1,089.76	231,550	43,070	1,111.13	203,489	71,131	1,132.49	183,056	91,564
115,000	1,116.96	287,106	1,139.30	242,077	45,029	1,161.64	212,739	74,367	1,183.98	191,380	95,726
120,000	1,165.52	299,587	1,188.83	252,601	46,986	1,212.14	221,987	77,600	1,235.45	199,699	99,888
125,000	1,214.08	312,069	1,238.36	263,124	48,945	1,262.64	231,235	80,834	1,286.92	208,018	104,051
130,000	1,262.64	324,550	1,287.89	273,648	50,902	1,313.15	240,486	84,064	1,338.40	216,339	108,211
135,000	1,311.21	337,036	1,337.43	284,175	52,861	1,363.66	249,736	87,300	1,389.88	224,661	112,375
140,000	1,359.77	349,517	1,386.97	294,701	54,816	1,414.16	258,984	90,533	1,441.36	232,982	116,535
145,000	1,408.33	361,999	1,436.50	305,225	56,774	1,464.66	268,232	93,767	1,492.83	241,301	120,698
150,000	1,456.90	374,484	1,486.04	315,752	58,732	1,515.18	277,485	96,999	1,544.31	249,623	124,861
155,000	1,505.46	386,966	1,535.57	326,275	60,691	1,565.68	286,733	100,233	1,595.79	257,944	129,022
160,000	1,554.02	399,447	1,585.10	336,799	62,648	1,616.18	295,981	103,466	1,647.26	266,263	133,184
165,000	1,602.59	411,932	1,634.64	347,326	64,606	1,666.69	305,232	106,700	1,698.75	274,587	137,345
170,000	1,651.15	424,414	1,684.17	357,849	66,565	1,717.20	314,482	109,932	1,750.22	282,906	141,508
175,000	1,699.71	436,896	1,733.70	368,373	68,523	1,767.70	323,730	113,166	1,801.69	291,225	145,671
180,000	1,748.28	449,381	1,783.25	378,903	70,478	1,818.21	332,981	116,400	1,853.18	299,549	149,832
185,000	1,796.84	461,862	1,832.78	389,426	72,436	1,868.71	342,228	119,634	1,904.65	307,868	153,994
190,000	1,845.40	474,344	1,882.31	399,950	74,394	1,919.22	351,479	122,865	1,956.12	316,187	158,157
195,000	1,893.96	486,826	1,931.84	410,473	76,353	1,969.72	360,727	126,099	2,007.60	324,509	162,317
200,000	1,942.53	499,311	1,981.38	421,000	78,311	2,020.23	369,978	129,333	2,059.08	332,830	166,481

AUGMENTED PAYMENT MORTGAGES 11.25%

AMOUNT OF LOAN	30 YEARS		8% PMT INCREASE 240.253 PAYMENTS			10% PMT INCREASE 225.002 PAYMENTS			12% PMT INCREASE 212.104 PAYMENTS		
	MONTHLY PAYMENT	TOTAL INTRST	MONTHLY PAYMENT	TOTAL INTRST	INTRST SAVED	MONTHLY PAYMENT	TOTAL INTRST	INTRST SAVED	MONTHLY PAYMENT	TOTAL INTRST	INTRST SAVED
$ 50	0.49	126	0.53	77	49	0.54	72	54	0.55	67	59
100	0.98	253	1.06	155	98	1.08	143	110	1.10	133	120
200	1.95	502	2.11	307	195	2.15	284	218	2.18	262	240
300	2.92	751	3.15	457	294	3.21	422	329	3.27	394	357
400	3.89	1,000	4.20	609	391	4.28	563	437	4.36	525	475
500	4.86	1,250	5.25	761	489	5.35	704	546	5.44	654	596
600	5.83	1,499	6.30	914	585	6.41	842	657	6.53	785	714
700	6.80	1,748	7.34	1,063	685	7.48	983	765	7.62	916	832
800	7.78	2,001	8.40	1,218	783	8.56	1,126	875	8.71	1,047	954
900	8.75	2,250	9.45	1,370	880	9.63	1,267	983	9.80	1,179	1,071
1,000	9.72	2,499	10.50	1,523	976	10.69	1,405	1,094	10.89	1,310	1,189
2,000	19.43	4,995	20.98	3,041	1,954	21.37	2,808	2,187	21.76	2,615	2,380
3,000	29.14	7,490	31.47	4,561	2,929	32.05	4,211	3,279	32.64	3,923	3,567
4,000	38.86	9,990	41.97	6,083	3,907	42.75	5,619	4,371	43.52	5,231	4,759
5,000	48.57	12,485	52.46	7,604	4,881	53.43	7,022	5,463	54.40	6,538	5,947
6,000	58.28	14,981	62.94	9,122	5,859	64.11	8,425	6,556	65.27	7,844	7,137
7,000	67.99	17,476	73.43	10,642	6,834	74.79	9,828	7,648	76.15	9,152	8,324
8,000	77.71	19,976	83.93	12,164	7,812	85.48	11,233	8,743	87.04	10,462	9,514
9,000	87.42	22,471	94.41	13,682	8,789	96.16	12,636	9,835	97.91	11,767	10,704
10,000	97.13	24,967	104.90	15,203	9,764	106.84	14,039	10,928	108.79	13,075	11,892
11,000	106.84	27,462	115.39	16,723	10,739	117.52	15,442	12,020	119.66	14,380	13,082
12,000	116.56	29,962	125.88	18,243	11,719	128.22	16,850	13,112	130.55	15,690	14,272
13,000	126.27	32,457	136.37	19,763	12,694	138.90	18,253	14,204	141.42	16,996	15,461
14,000	135.98	34,953	146.86	21,284	13,669	149.58	19,656	15,297	152.30	18,303	16,650
15,000	145.69	37,448	157.35	22,804	14,644	160.26	21,059	16,389	163.17	19,609	17,839
16,000	155.41	39,948	167.84	24,324	15,624	170.95	22,464	17,484	174.06	20,919	19,029
17,000	165.12	42,443	178.33	25,844	16,599	181.63	23,867	18,576	184.93	22,224	20,219
18,000	174.83	44,939	188.82	27,365	17,574	192.31	25,270	19,669	195.81	23,532	21,407
19,000	184.54	47,434	199.30	28,882	18,552	202.99	26,673	20,761	206.68	24,838	22,596
20,000	194.26	49,934	209.80	30,405	19,529	213.69	28,081	21,853	217.57	26,147	23,787
21,000	203.97	52,429	220.29	31,925	20,504	224.37	29,484	22,945	228.45	27,455	24,974
22,000	213.68	54,925	230.77	33,443	21,482	235.05	30,887	24,038	239.32	28,761	26,164
23,000	223.40	57,424	241.27	34,966	22,458	245.74	32,292	25,132	250.21	30,071	27,353
24,000	233.11	59,920	251.76	36,486	23,434	256.42	33,695	26,225	261.08	31,376	28,544
25,000	242.82	62,415	262.25	38,006	24,409	267.10	35,098	27,317	271.96	32,684	29,731
26,000	252.53	64,911	272.73	39,524	25,387	277.78	36,501	28,410	282.83	33,989	30,922
27,000	262.25	67,410	283.23	41,047	26,363	288.48	37,909	29,501	293.72	35,299	32,111
28,000	271.96	69,906	293.72	42,567	27,339	299.16	39,312	30,594	304.60	36,607	33,299
29,000	281.67	72,401	304.20	44,085	28,316	309.84	40,715	31,686	315.47	37,912	34,489
30,000	291.38	74,897	314.69	45,605	29,292	320.52	42,118	32,779	326.35	39,220	35,677
32,500	315.66	81,138	340.91	49,405	31,733	347.23	45,627	35,511	353.54	42,487	38,651
35,000	339.95	87,382	367.15	53,209	34,173	373.95	49,139	38,243	380.74	45,756	41,626
40,000	388.51	99,864	419.59	60,808	39,056	427.36	56,157	43,707	435.13	52,293	47,571
45,000	437.07	112,345	472.04	68,409	43,936	480.78	63,176	49,169	489.52	58,829	53,516
50,000	485.64	124,830	524.49	76,010	48,820	534.20	70,196	54,634	543.92	65,368	59,462
55,000	534.20	137,312	576.94	83,612	53,700	587.62	77,216	60,096	598.30	71,902	65,410
60,000	582.76	149,794	629.38	91,210	58,584	641.04	84,235	65,559	652.69	78,438	71,356
65,000	631.32	162,275	681.83	98,812	63,463	694.45	91,253	71,022	707.08	84,974	77,301
70,000	679.89	174,760	734.28	106,413	68,347	747.88	98,274	76,486	761.48	91,513	83,247
75,000	728.45	187,242	786.73	114,014	73,228	801.30	105,294	81,948	815.86	98,047	89,195
80,000	777.01	199,724	839.17	121,613	78,111	854.71	112,311	87,413	870.25	104,584	95,140
85,000	825.58	212,209	891.63	129,217	82,992	908.13	119,333	92,876	924.65	111,122	101,087
90,000	874.14	224,690	944.07	136,816	87,874	961.55	126,351	98,339	979.04	117,658	107,032
95,000	922.70	237,172	996.52	144,417	92,755	1,014.97	133,370	103,802	1,033.42	124,193	112,979
100,000	971.27	249,657	1,048.97	152,018	97,639	1,068.40	140,392	109,265	1,087.82	130,731	118,926
105,000	1,019.83	262,139	1,101.42	159,619	102,520	1,121.81	147,409	114,730	1,142.21	137,267	124,872
110,000	1,068.39	274,620	1,153.86	167,218	107,402	1,175.23	154,429	120,191	1,196.60	143,804	130,816
115,000	1,116.96	287,106	1,206.32	174,822	112,284	1,228.66	161,451	125,655	1,251.00	150,342	136,764
120,000	1,165.52	299,587	1,258.76	182,421	117,166	1,282.07	168,468	131,119	1,305.38	156,876	142,711
125,000	1,214.08	312,069	1,311.21	190,022	122,047	1,335.49	175,488	136,581	1,359.77	163,413	148,656
130,000	1,262.64	324,550	1,363.65	197,621	126,929	1,388.90	182,505	142,045	1,414.16	169,949	154,601
135,000	1,311.21	337,036	1,416.11	205,225	131,811	1,442.33	189,527	147,509	1,468.56	176,487	160,549
140,000	1,359.77	349,517	1,468.55	212,824	136,693	1,495.75	196,547	152,970	1,522.94	183,022	166,495
145,000	1,408.33	361,999	1,521.00	220,425	141,574	1,549.16	203,564	158,435	1,577.33	189,558	172,441
150,000	1,456.90	374,484	1,573.45	228,026	146,458	1,602.59	210,586	163,898	1,631.73	196,096	178,388
155,000	1,505.46	386,966	1,625.90	235,627	151,339	1,656.01	217,606	169,360	1,686.12	202,633	184,333
160,000	1,554.02	399,447	1,678.34	243,226	156,221	1,709.42	224,623	174,824	1,740.50	209,167	190,280
165,000	1,602.59	411,932	1,730.80	250,830	161,102	1,762.85	231,645	180,287	1,794.90	215,705	196,227
170,000	1,651.15	424,414	1,783.24	258,430	165,985	1,816.27	238,664	185,751	1,849.29	222,242	202,172
175,000	1,699.71	436,896	1,835.69	266,030	170,866	1,869.68	245,682	191,214	1,903.68	228,778	208,118
180,000	1,748.28	449,381	1,888.14	273,631	175,750	1,923.11	252,704	196,677	1,958.07	235,314	214,067
185,000	1,796.84	461,862	1,940.59	281,233	180,629	1,976.52	259,721	202,141	2,012.46	241,851	220,011
190,000	1,845.40	474,344	1,993.03	288,831	185,513	2,029.94	266,741	207,603	2,066.85	248,387	225,957
195,000	1,893.96	486,826	2,045.48	296,433	190,393	2,083.36	273,760	213,066	2,121.24	254,923	231,903
200,000	1,942.53	499,311	2,097.93	304,034	195,277	2,136.78	280,780	218,531	2,175.63	261,460	237,851

AUGMENTED PAYMENT MORTGAGES

AMOUNT OF LOAN	30 YEARS		2% PMT INCREASE 311.513 PAYMENTS			4% PMT INCREASE 279.581 PAYMENTS			6% PMT INCREASE 255.962 PAYMENTS		
	MONTHLY PAYMENT	TOTAL INTRST	MONTHLY PAYMENT	TOTAL INTRST	INTRST SAVED	MONTHLY PAYMENT	TOTAL INTRST	INTRST SAVED	MONTHLY PAYMENT	TOTAL INTRST	INTRST SAVED
$ 50	0.50	130	0.51	109	21	0.52	95	35	0.53	86	44
100	1.00	260	1.02	218	42	1.04	191	69	1.06	171	89
200	1.99	516	2.03	432	84	2.07	379	137	2.11	340	176
300	2.98	773	3.04	647	126	3.10	567	206	3.16	509	264
400	3.97	1,029	4.05	862	167	4.13	755	274	4.21	678	351
500	4.96	1,286	5.06	1,076	210	5.16	943	343	5.26	846	440
600	5.95	1,542	6.07	1,291	251	6.19	1,131	411	6.31	1,015	527
700	6.94	1,798	7.08	1,506	292	7.22	1,319	479	7.36	1,184	614
800	7.93	2,055	8.09	1,720	335	8.25	1,507	548	8.41	1,353	702
900	8.92	2,311	9.10	1,935	376	9.28	1,695	616	9.46	1,521	790
1,000	9.91	2,568	10.11	2,149	419	10.31	1,882	686	10.50	1,688	880
2,000	19.81	5,132	20.21	4,296	836	20.60	3,759	1,373	21.00	3,375	1,757
3,000	29.71	7,696	30.30	6,439	1,257	30.90	5,639	2,057	31.49	5,060	2,636
4,000	39.62	10,263	40.41	8,588	1,675	41.20	7,519	2,744	42.00	6,750	3,513
5,000	49.52	12,827	50.51	10,735	2,092	51.50	9,398	3,429	52.49	8,435	4,392
6,000	59.42	15,391	60.61	12,881	2,510	61.80	11,278	4,113	62.99	10,123	5,268
7,000	69.33	17,959	70.72	15,030	2,929	72.10	13,158	4,801	73.49	11,811	6,148
8,000	79.23	20,523	80.81	17,173	3,350	82.40	15,037	5,486	83.98	13,496	7,027
9,000	89.13	23,087	90.91	19,320	3,767	92.70	16,917	6,170	94.48	15,183	7,904
10,000	99.03	25,651	101.01	21,466	4,185	102.99	18,794	6,857	104.97	16,868	8,783
11,000	108.94	28,218	111.12	23,615	4,603	113.30	20,677	7,541	115.48	18,558	9,660
12,000	118.84	30,782	121.22	25,762	5,020	123.59	22,553	8,229	125.97	20,244	10,538
13,000	128.74	33,346	131.31	27,905	5,441	133.89	24,433	8,913	136.46	21,929	11,417
14,000	138.65	35,914	141.42	30,054	5,860	144.20	26,316	9,598	146.97	23,619	12,295
15,000	148.55	38,478	151.52	32,200	6,278	154.49	28,192	10,286	157.46	25,304	13,174
16,000	158.45	41,042	161.62	34,347	6,695	164.79	30,072	10,970	167.96	26,991	14,051
17,000	168.35	43,606	171.72	36,493	7,113	175.08	31,949	11,657	178.45	28,676	14,930
18,000	178.26	46,174	181.83	38,642	7,532	185.39	33,832	12,342	188.96	30,367	15,807
19,000	188.16	48,738	191.92	40,786	7,952	195.69	35,711	13,027	199.45	32,052	16,686
20,000	198.06	51,302	202.02	42,932	8,370	205.98	37,588	13,714	209.94	33,737	17,565
21,000	207.97	53,869	212.13	45,081	8,788	216.29	39,471	14,398	220.45	35,427	18,442
22,000	217.87	56,433	222.23	47,228	9,205	226.58	41,347	15,086	230.94	37,112	19,321
23,000	227.77	58,997	232.33	49,374	9,623	236.88	43,227	15,770	241.44	38,799	20,198
24,000	237.67	61,561	242.42	51,517	10,044	248.18	45,107	16,454	251.93	40,485	21,076
25,000	247.58	64,129	252.53	53,666	10,463	257.48	46,987	17,142	262.43	42,172	21,957
26,000	257.48	66,693	262.63	55,813	10,880	267.78	48,866	17,827	272.93	43,860	22,833
27,000	267.38	69,257	272.73	57,959	11,298	278.08	50,746	18,511	283.42	45,545	23,712
28,000	277.29	71,824	282.84	60,108	11,716	288.38	52,626	19,198	293.93	47,235	24,589
29,000	287.19	74,388	292.93	62,252	12,136	298.68	54,505	19,883	304.42	48,920	25,468
30,000	297.09	76,952	303.03	64,398	12,554	308.97	56,382	20,570	314.92	50,608	26,344
32,500	321.85	83,366	328.29	69,767	13,599	334.72	61,081	22,285	341.16	54,824	28,542
35,000	346.61	89,780	353.54	75,132	14,648	360.47	65,781	23,999	367.41	59,043	30,737
40,000	396.12	102,603	404.04	85,864	16,739	411.96	75,176	27,427	419.89	67,476	35,127
45,000	445.64	115,430	454.55	96,598	18,832	463.47	84,577	30,853	472.38	75,911	39,519
50,000	495.15	128,254	505.05	107,330	20,924	514.96	93,973	34,281	524.86	84,344	43,910
55,000	544.67	141,081	555.56	118,064	23,017	566.46	103,371	37,710	577.35	92,780	48,301
60,000	594.18	153,905	606.06	128,796	25,109	617.95	112,767	41,138	629.83	101,213	52,692
65,000	643.69	166,728	656.56	139,527	27,201	669.44	122,163	44,565	682.31	109,645	57,083
70,000	693.21	179,556	707.07	150,261	29,295	720.94	131,561	47,995	734.80	118,081	61,475
75,000	742.72	192,379	757.57	160,993	31,386	772.43	140,957	51,422	787.28	126,514	65,865
80,000	792.24	205,206	808.08	171,727	33,479	823.93	150,355	54,851	839.77	134,949	70,257
85,000	841.75	218,030	858.59	182,462	35,568	875.42	159,751	58,279	892.26	143,385	74,645
90,000	891.27	230,857	909.10	193,196	37,661	926.92	169,149	61,708	944.75	151,820	79,037
95,000	940.78	243,681	959.60	203,928	39,753	978.41	178,545	65,136	997.23	160,253	83,428
100,000	990.30	256,508	1,010.11	214,662	41,846	1,029.91	187,943	68,565	1,049.72	168,688	87,820
105,000	1,039.81	269,332	1,060.61	225,394	43,938	1,081.40	197,339	71,993	1,102.20	177,121	92,211
110,000	1,089.33	282,159	1,111.12	236,128	46,031	1,132.90	206,737	75,422	1,154.69	185,557	96,602
115,000	1,138.84	294,982	1,161.62	246,860	48,122	1,184.39	216,133	78,849	1,207.17	193,990	100,992
120,000	1,188.35	307,806	1,212.12	257,591	50,215	1,235.88	225,529	82,277	1,259.65	202,423	105,383
125,000	1,237.87	320,633	1,262.63	268,326	52,307	1,287.38	234,927	85,706	1,312.14	210,858	109,775
130,000	1,287.38	333,457	1,313.13	279,057	54,400	1,338.88	244,325	89,132	1,364.62	219,291	114,166
135,000	1,336.90	346,284	1,363.64	289,792	56,492	1,390.38	253,724	92,560	1,417.11	227,726	118,558
140,000	1,386.41	359,108	1,414.14	300,523	58,585	1,441.87	263,119	95,989	1,469.59	236,159	122,949
145,000	1,435.93	371,935	1,464.65	311,258	60,677	1,493.37	272,518	99,417	1,522.09	244,597	127,338
150,000	1,485.44	384,758	1,515.15	321,989	62,769	1,544.86	281,914	102,844	1,574.57	253,030	131,728
155,000	1,534.96	397,586	1,565.66	332,723	64,863	1,596.36	291,312	106,274	1,627.06	261,466	136,120
160,000	1,584.47	410,409	1,616.16	343,455	66,954	1,647.85	300,708	109,701	1,679.54	269,898	140,511
165,000	1,633.99	423,236	1,666.67	354,189	69,047	1,699.35	310,106	113,130	1,732.03	278,334	144,902
170,000	1,683.50	436,060	1,717.17	364,921	71,139	1,750.84	319,502	116,558	1,784.51	286,767	149,293
175,000	1,733.02	448,887	1,767.68	375,655	73,232	1,802.34	328,900	119,987	1,837.00	295,202	153,685
180,000	1,782.53	461,711	1,818.18	386,387	75,324	1,853.83	338,296	123,415	1,889.48	303,635	158,076
185,000	1,832.04	474,534	1,868.68	397,118	77,416	1,905.32	347,691	126,843	1,941.96	312,068	162,466
190,000	1,881.56	487,362	1,919.19	407,853	79,509	1,956.82	357,090	130,272	1,994.45	320,503	166,859
195,000	1,931.07	500,185	1,969.69	418,584	81,601	2,008.31	366,485	133,700	2,046.93	328,936	171,249
200,000	1,980.59	513,012	2,020.20	429,319	83,693	2,059.81	375,884	137,128	2,099.43	337,374	175,638

AUGMENTED PAYMENT MORTGAGES 11.50%

AMOUNT OF LOAN	30 YEARS		8% PMT INCREASE 237.353 PAYMENTS			10% PMT INCREASE 222.088 PAYMENTS			12% PMT INCREASE 209.215 PAYMENTS		
	MONTHLY PAYMENT	TOTAL INTRST	MONTHLY PAYMENT	TOTAL INTRST	INTRST SAVED	MONTHLY PAYMENT	TOTAL INTRST	INTRST SAVED	MONTHLY PAYMENT	TOTAL INTRST	INTRST SAVED
$ 50	0.50	130	0.54	78	52	0.55	72	58	0.56	67	63
100	1.00	260	1.08	156	104	1.10	144	116	1.12	134	126
200	1.99	516	2.15	310	206	2.19	286	230	2.23	267	249
300	2.98	773	3.22	464	309	3.28	428	345	3.34	399	374
400	3.97	1,029	4.29	618	411	4.37	571	458	4.45	531	498
500	4.96	1,286	5.36	772	514	5.46	713	573	5.56	663	623
600	5.95	1,542	6.43	926	616	6.55	855	687	6.66	793	749
700	6.94	1,798	7.50	1,080	718	7.63	995	803	7.77	926	872
800	7.93	2,055	8.56	1,232	823	8.72	1,137	918	8.88	1,058	997
900	8.92	2,311	9.63	1,386	925	9.81	1,279	1,032	9.99	1,190	1,121
1,000	9.91	2,568	10.70	1,540	1,028	10.90	1,421	1,147	11.10	1,322	1,246
2,000	19.81	5,132	21.39	3,077	2,055	21.79	2,839	2,293	22.19	2,642	2,490
3,000	29.71	7,696	32.09	4,617	3,079	32.68	4,258	3,438	33.28	3,963	3,733
4,000	39.62	10,263	42.79	6,156	4,107	43.58	5,679	4,584	44.37	5,283	4,980
5,000	49.52	12,827	53.48	7,694	5,133	54.47	7,097	5,730	55.46	6,603	6,224
6,000	59.42	15,391	64.17	9,231	6,160	65.36	8,516	6,875	66.55	7,923	7,468
7,000	69.33	17,959	74.88	10,773	7,186	76.26	9,936	8,023	77.65	9,246	8,713
8,000	79.23	20,523	85.57	12,310	8,213	87.15	11,355	9,168	88.74	10,566	9,957
9,000	89.13	23,087	96.26	13,848	9,239	98.04	12,774	10,313	99.83	11,886	11,201
10,000	99.03	25,651	106.95	15,385	10,266	108.93	14,192	11,459	110.91	13,204	12,447
11,000	108.94	28,218	117.66	16,927	11,291	119.83	15,613	12,605	122.01	14,526	13,692
12,000	118.84	30,782	128.35	18,464	12,318	130.72	17,031	13,751	133.10	15,847	14,935
13,000	128.74	33,346	139.04	20,002	13,344	141.61	18,450	14,896	144.19	17,167	16,179
14,000	138.65	35,914	149.74	21,541	14,373	152.52	19,873	16,041	155.29	18,489	17,425
15,000	148.55	38,478	160.43	23,079	15,399	163.41	21,291	17,187	166.38	19,809	18,669
16,000	158.45	41,042	171.13	24,618	16,424	174.30	22,710	18,332	177.46	21,127	19,915
17,000	168.35	43,606	181.82	26,156	17,450	185.19	24,128	19,478	188.55	22,447	21,159
18,000	178.26	46,174	192.52	27,695	18,479	196.09	25,549	20,625	199.65	23,770	22,404
19,000	188.16	48,738	203.21	29,233	19,505	206.98	26,968	21,770	210.74	25,090	23,648
20,000	198.06	51,302	213.90	30,770	20,532	217.87	28,386	22,916	221.83	26,410	24,892
21,000	207.97	53,869	224.61	32,312	21,557	228.77	29,807	24,062	232.93	27,732	26,137
22,000	217.87	56,433	235.30	33,849	22,584	239.66	31,226	25,207	244.01	29,051	27,382
23,000	227.77	58,997	245.99	35,386	23,611	250.55	32,644	26,353	255.10	30,371	28,626
24,000	237.67	61,561	256.68	36,924	24,637	261.44	34,063	27,498	266.19	31,691	29,870
25,000	247.58	64,129	267.39	38,466	25,663	272.34	35,483	28,646	277.29	33,013	31,116
26,000	257.48	66,693	278.08	40,003	26,690	283.23	36,902	29,791	288.38	34,333	32,360
27,000	267.38	69,257	288.77	41,540	27,717	294.12	38,321	30,936	299.47	35,654	33,603
28,000	277.29	71,824	299.47	43,080	28,744	305.02	39,741	32,083	310.56	36,974	34,850
29,000	287.19	74,388	310.17	44,620	29,768	315.91	41,160	33,228	321.65	38,294	36,094
30,000	297.09	76,952	320.86	46,157	30,795	326.80	42,578	34,374	332.74	39,614	37,338
32,500	321.85	83,366	347.60	50,004	33,362	354.04	46,128	37,238	360.47	42,916	40,450
35,000	346.61	89,780	374.34	53,851	35,929	381.27	49,675	40,105	388.20	46,217	43,563
40,000	396.12	102,603	427.81	61,542	41,061	435.73	56,770	45,833	443.65	52,818	49,785
45,000	445.64	115,430	481.29	69,236	46,194	490.20	63,868	51,562	499.12	59,423	56,007
50,000	495.15	128,254	534.76	76,927	51,327	544.67	70,965	57,289	554.57	66,024	62,230
55,000	544.67	141,081	588.24	84,621	56,460	599.14	78,062	63,019	610.03	72,627	68,454
60,000	594.18	153,905	641.71	92,312	61,593	653.60	85,157	68,748	665.48	79,228	74,677
65,000	643.69	166,728	695.19	100,005	66,723	708.06	92,252	74,476	720.93	85,829	80,899
70,000	693.21	179,556	748.67	107,699	71,857	762.53	99,349	80,207	776.40	92,435	87,121
75,000	742.72	192,379	802.14	115,390	76,989	816.99	106,444	85,935	831.85	99,035	93,344
80,000	792.24	205,206	855.62	123,084	82,122	871.46	113,541	91,665	887.31	105,639	99,567
85,000	841.75	218,030	909.09	130,775	87,255	925.93	120,638	97,392	942.76	112,240	105,790
90,000	891.27	230,857	962.57	138,469	92,388	980.40	127,735	103,122	998.22	118,843	112,014
95,000	940.78	243,681	1,016.04	146,160	97,521	1,034.86	134,830	108,851	1,053.67	125,444	118,237
100,000	990.30	256,508	1,069.52	153,854	102,654	1,089.33	141,927	114,581	1,109.14	132,049	124,459
105,000	1,039.81	269,332	1,122.99	161,545	107,787	1,143.79	149,022	120,310	1,164.59	138,650	130,682
110,000	1,089.33	282,159	1,176.48	169,241	112,918	1,198.26	156,119	126,040	1,220.05	145,253	136,906
115,000	1,138.84	294,982	1,229.95	176,932	118,050	1,252.72	163,214	131,768	1,275.50	151,854	143,128
120,000	1,188.35	307,806	1,283.42	184,624	123,182	1,307.19	170,311	137,495	1,330.95	158,455	149,351
125,000	1,237.87	320,633	1,336.90	192,317	128,316	1,361.66	177,408	143,225	1,386.41	165,058	155,575
130,000	1,287.38	333,457	1,390.37	200,008	133,449	1,416.12	184,503	148,954	1,441.87	171,661	161,796
135,000	1,336.90	346,284	1,443.85	207,702	138,582	1,470.59	191,600	154,684	1,497.33	178,264	168,020
140,000	1,386.41	359,108	1,497.32	215,393	143,715	1,525.05	198,695	160,413	1,552.78	184,865	174,243
145,000	1,435.93	371,935	1,550.80	223,087	148,848	1,579.52	205,792	166,143	1,608.24	191,468	180,467
150,000	1,485.44	384,758	1,604.28	230,781	153,977	1,633.98	212,887	171,871	1,663.69	198,069	186,689
155,000	1,534.96	397,586	1,657.76	238,474	159,112	1,688.46	219,987	177,599	1,719.16	204,674	192,912
160,000	1,584.47	410,409	1,711.23	246,166	164,243	1,742.92	227,082	183,327	1,774.61	211,275	199,134
165,000	1,633.99	423,236	1,764.71	253,859	169,377	1,797.39	234,179	189,057	1,830.07	217,878	205,358
170,000	1,683.50	436,060	1,818.18	261,550	174,510	1,851.85	241,274	194,786	1,885.52	224,479	211,581
175,000	1,733.02	448,887	1,871.66	269,244	179,643	1,906.32	248,371	200,516	1,940.98	231,082	217,805
180,000	1,782.53	461,711	1,925.13	276,935	184,776	1,960.78	255,466	206,245	1,996.43	237,683	224,028
185,000	1,832.04	474,534	1,978.60	284,627	189,907	2,015.24	262,561	211,973	2,051.88	244,284	230,250
190,000	1,881.56	487,362	2,032.08	292,320	195,042	2,069.72	269,660	217,702	2,107.35	250,889	236,473
195,000	1,931.07	500,185	2,085.56	300,014	200,171	2,124.18	276,755	223,430	2,162.80	257,490	242,695
200,000	1,980.59	513,012	2,139.04	307,708	205,304	2,178.65	283,852	229,160	2,218.26	264,093	248,919

231

AMOUNT OF LOAN	30 YEARS		2% PMT INCREASE 309.556 PAYMENTS			4% PMT INCREASE 276.994 PAYMENTS			6% PMT INCREASE 253.145 PAYMENTS		
	MONTHLY PAYMENT	TOTAL INTRST	MONTHLY PAYMENT	TOTAL INTRST	INTRST SAVED	MONTHLY PAYMENT	TOTAL INTRST	INTRST SAVED	MONTHLY PAYMENT	TOTAL INTRST	INTRST SAVED
$ 50	0.51	134	0.52	111	23	0.53	97	37	0.54	87	47
100	1.01	264	1.03	219	45	1.05	191	73	1.07	171	93
200	2.02	527	2.06	438	89	2.10	382	145	2.14	342	185
300	3.03	791	3.09	657	134	3.15	573	218	3.21	513	278
400	4.04	1,054	4.12	875	179	4.20	763	291	4.28	683	371
500	5.05	1,318	5.15	1,094	224	5.25	954	364	5.35	854	464
600	6.06	1,582	6.18	1,313	269	6.30	1,145	437	6.42	1,025	557
700	7.07	1,845	7.21	1,532	313	7.35	1,336	509	7.49	1,196	649
800	8.08	2,109	8.24	1,751	358	8.40	1,527	582	8.56	1,367	742
900	9.09	2,372	9.27	1,970	402	9.45	1,718	654	9.64	1,540	832
1,000	10.10	2,636	10.30	2,188	448	10.50	1,908	728	10.71	1,711	925
2,000	20.19	5,268	20.59	4,374	894	21.00	3,817	1,451	21.40	3,417	1,851
3,000	30.29	7,904	30.90	6,565	1,339	31.50	5,725	2,179	32.11	5,128	2,776
4,000	40.38	10,537	41.19	8,751	1,786	42.00	7,634	2,903	42.80	6,835	3,702
5,000	50.48	13,173	51.49	10,939	2,234	52.50	9,542	3,631	53.51	8,546	4,627
6,000	60.57	15,805	61.78	13,124	2,681	62.99	11,448	4,357	64.20	10,252	5,553
7,000	70.66	18,438	72.07	15,310	3,128	73.49	13,356	5,082	74.90	11,961	6,477
8,000	80.76	21,074	82.38	17,501	3,573	83.99	15,265	5,809	85.61	13,672	7,402
9,000	90.85	23,706	92.67	19,687	4,019	94.48	17,170	6,536	96.30	15,378	8,328
10,000	100.95	26,342	102.97	21,875	4,467	104.99	19,082	7,260	107.01	17,089	9,253
11,000	111.04	28,974	113.26	24,060	4,914	115.48	20,987	7,987	117.70	18,795	10,179
12,000	121.13	31,607	123.55	26,246	5,361	125.98	22,896	8,711	128.40	20,504	11,103
13,000	131.23	34,243	133.85	28,434	5,809	136.48	24,804	9,439	139.10	22,212	12,031
14,000	141.32	36,875	144.15	30,622	6,253	146.97	26,710	10,165	149.80	23,921	12,354
15,000	151.42	39,511	154.45	32,811	6,700	157.48	28,621	10,890	160.51	25,632	13,879
16,000	161.51	42,144	164.74	34,996	7,148	167.97	30,527	11,617	171.20	27,338	14,806
17,000	171.60	44,776	175.03	37,182	7,594	178.46	32,432	12,344	181.90	29,047	15,729
18,000	181.70	47,412	185.33	39,370	8,042	188.97	34,344	13,068	192.60	30,756	16,656
19,000	191.79	50,044	195.63	41,558	8,486	199.46	36,249	13,795	203.30	32,464	17,580
20,000	201.89	52,680	205.93	43,747	8,933	209.97	38,160	14,520	214.00	34,173	18,507
21,000	211.98	55,313	216.22	45,932	9,381	220.46	40,066	15,247	224.70	35,882	19,431
22,000	222.08	57,949	226.52	48,121	9,828	230.96	41,975	15,974	235.40	37,590	20,359
23,000	232.17	60,581	236.81	50,306	10,275	241.46	43,883	16,698	246.10	39,299	21,282
24,000	242.26	63,214	247.11	52,494	10,720	251.95	45,789	17,425	256.80	41,008	22,206
25,000	252.36	65,850	257.41	54,683	11,167	262.45	47,697	18,153	267.50	42,716	23,134
26,000	262.45	68,482	267.70	56,868	11,614	272.95	49,604	18,876	278.20	44,425	24,057
27,000	272.55	71,118	278.00	59,057	12,061	283.45	51,514	19,604	288.90	46,134	24,984
28,000	282.64	73,750	288.29	61,242	12,508	293.95	53,420	20,328	299.60	47,842	25,908
29,000	292.73	76,383	298.58	63,427	12,956	304.44	55,328	21,055	310.29	49,548	26,835
30,000	302.83	79,019	308.89	65,619	13,400	314.94	57,236	21,783	321.00	51,260	27,759
32,500	328.06	85,602	334.62	71,084	14,518	341.18	62,005	23,597	347.74	55,529	30,073
35,000	353.30	92,188	360.37	76,555	15,633	367.43	66,776	25,412	374.50	59,803	32,385
40,000	403.77	105,357	411.85	87,491	17,866	419.92	76,315	29,042	428.00	68,346	37,011
45,000	454.24	118,526	463.32	98,423	20,103	472.41	85,855	32,671	481.49	76,887	41,639
50,000	504.71	131,696	514.80	109,359	22,337	524.90	95,394	36,302	534.99	85,430	46,266
55,000	555.18	144,865	566.28	120,295	24,570	577.39	104,934	39,931	588.49	93,973	50,892
60,000	605.65	158,034	617.76	131,231	26,803	629.88	114,473	43,561	641.99	102,517	55,517
65,000	656.12	171,203	669.24	142,167	29,036	682.36	124,010	47,193	695.49	111,060	60,143
70,000	706.59	184,372	720.72	153,103	31,269	734.85	133,549	50,823	748.99	119,603	64,769
75,000	757.06	197,542	772.20	164,039	33,503	787.34	143,088	54,454	802.48	128,144	69,398
80,000	807.53	210,711	823.68	174,975	35,736	839.83	152,628	58,083	855.98	136,687	74,024
85,000	858.00	223,880	875.16	185,911	37,969	892.32	162,167	61,713	909.48	145,230	78,650
90,000	908.47	237,049	926.64	196,847	40,202	944.81	171,707	65,342	962.98	153,774	83,275
95,000	958.94	250,218	978.12	207,783	42,435	997.30	181,246	68,972	1,016.48	162,317	87,901
100,000	1,009.41	263,388	1,029.60	218,719	44,669	1,049.79	190,786	72,602	1,069.97	170,858	92,530
105,000	1,059.89	276,560	1,081.09	229,658	46,902	1,102.29	200,328	76,232	1,123.48	179,403	97,157
110,000	1,110.36	289,730	1,132.57	240,594	49,136	1,154.77	209,864	79,866	1,176.98	187,947	101,783
115,000	1,160.83	302,899	1,184.05	251,530	51,369	1,207.26	219,404	83,495	1,230.48	196,490	106,409
120,000	1,211.30	316,068	1,235.53	262,466	53,602	1,259.75	228,943	87,125	1,283.98	205,033	111,035
125,000	1,261.77	329,237	1,287.01	273,402	55,835	1,312.24	238,483	90,754	1,337.48	213,576	115,661
130,000	1,312.24	342,406	1,338.48	284,335	58,071	1,364.73	248,022	94,384	1,390.97	222,117	120,289
135,000	1,362.71	355,576	1,389.96	295,274	60,306	1,417.22	257,561	98,015	1,444.47	230,660	124,916
140,000	1,413.18	368,745	1,441.44	306,206	62,539	1,469.71	267,101	101,644	1,497.97	239,204	129,541
145,000	1,463.65	381,914	1,492.92	317,142	64,772	1,522.20	276,640	105,274	1,551.47	247,747	134,167
150,000	1,514.12	395,083	1,544.40	328,078	67,005	1,574.68	286,177	108,906	1,604.97	256,290	138,793
155,000	1,564.59	408,252	1,595.88	339,014	69,238	1,627.17	295,716	112,536	1,658.47	264,833	143,419
160,000	1,615.06	421,422	1,647.36	349,950	71,472	1,679.66	305,256	116,166	1,711.96	273,374	148,048
165,000	1,665.53	434,591	1,698.84	360,886	73,705	1,732.15	314,795	119,796	1,765.46	281,917	152,674
170,000	1,716.00	447,760	1,750.32	371,822	75,938	1,784.64	324,335	123,425	1,818.96	290,461	157,299
175,000	1,766.47	460,929	1,801.80	382,758	78,171	1,837.13	333,874	127,055	1,872.46	299,004	161,925
180,000	1,816.94	474,098	1,853.28	393,694	80,404	1,889.62	343,413	130,685	1,925.96	307,547	166,551
185,000	1,867.41	487,268	1,904.76	404,630	82,638	1,942.11	352,953	134,315	1,979.46	316,088	171,180
190,000	1,917.88	500,437	1,956.24	415,566	84,871	1,994.60	362,492	137,945	2,032.95	324,631	175,806
195,000	1,968.35	513,606	2,007.72	426,502	87,104	2,047.08	372,029	141,577	2,086.45	333,174	180,432
200,000	2,018.82	526,775	2,059.20	437,438	89,337	2,099.57	381,568	145,207	2,139.95	341,718	185,057

AUGMENTED PAYMENT MORTGAGES 11.75%

AMOUNT OF LOAN	30 YEARS		8% PMT INCREASE 234.461 PAYMENTS			10% PMT INCREASE 219.194 PAYMENTS			12% PMT INCREASE 206.354 PAYMENTS		
	MONTHLY PAYMENT	TOTAL INTRST	MONTHLY PAYMENT	TOTAL INTRST	INTRST SAVED	MONTHLY PAYMENT	TOTAL INTRST	INTRST SAVED	MONTHLY PAYMENT	TOTAL INTRST	INTRST SAVED
$ 50	0.51	134	0.55	79	55	0.56	73	61	0.57	68	66
100	1.01	264	1.09	156	108	1.11	143	121	1.13	133	131
200	2.02	527	2.18	311	216	2.22	287	240	2.26	266	261
300	3.03	791	3.27	467	324	3.33	430	361	3.39	400	391
400	4.04	1,054	4.36	622	432	4.44	573	481	4.52	533	521
500	5.05	1,318	5.45	778	540	5.56	719	599	5.66	668	650
600	6.06	1,582	6.54	933	649	6.67	862	720	6.79	801	781
700	7.07	1,845	7.64	1,091	754	7.78	1,005	840	7.92	934	911
800	8.08	2,109	8.73	1,247	862	8.89	1,149	960	9.05	1,068	1,041
900	9.09	2,372	9.82	1,402	970	10.00	1,292	1,080	10.18	1,201	1,171
1,000	10.10	2,636	10.91	1,558	1,078	11.11	1,435	1,201	11.31	1,334	1,302
2,000	20.19	5,268	21.81	3,114	2,154	22.21	2,868	2,400	22.61	2,666	2,602
3,000	30.29	7,904	32.71	4,669	3,235	33.32	4,304	3,600	33.92	4,000	3,904
4,000	40.38	10,537	43.61	6,225	4,312	44.42	5,737	4,800	45.23	5,333	5,204
5,000	50.48	13,173	54.52	7,783	5,390	55.53	7,172	6,001	56.54	6,667	6,506
6,000	60.57	15,805	65.42	9,338	6,467	66.63	8,605	7,200	67.84	7,999	7,806
7,000	70.66	18,438	76.31	10,892	7,546	77.73	10,038	8,400	79.14	9,331	9,107
8,000	80.76	21,074	87.22	12,450	8,624	88.84	11,473	9,601	90.45	10,665	10,409
9,000	90.85	23,706	98.12	14,005	9,701	99.94	12,906	10,800	101.75	11,997	11,709
10,000	100.95	26,342	109.03	15,563	10,779	111.05	14,341	12,001	113.06	13,330	13,012
11,000	111.04	28,974	119.92	17,117	11,857	122.14	15,772	13,202	124.36	14,662	14,312
12,000	121.13	31,607	130.82	18,672	12,935	133.24	17,205	14,402	135.67	15,996	15,611
13,000	131.23	34,243	141.73	20,230	14,013	144.35	18,641	15,602	146.98	17,330	16,913
14,000	141.32	36,875	152.63	21,786	15,089	155.45	20,074	16,801	158.28	18,662	18,213
15,000	151.42	39,511	163.53	23,341	16,170	166.56	21,509	18,002	169.59	19,996	19,515
16,000	161.51	42,144	174.43	24,897	17,247	177.66	22,942	19,202	180.89	21,327	20,817
17,000	171.60	44,776	185.33	26,453	18,323	188.76	24,375	20,401	192.19	22,659	22,117
18,000	181.70	47,412	196.24	28,011	19,401	199.87	25,810	21,602	203.50	23,993	23,419
19,000	191.79	50,044	207.13	29,564	20,480	210.97	27,243	22,801	214.80	25,325	24,719
20,000	201.89	52,680	218.04	31,122	21,558	222.08	28,679	24,001	226.12	26,661	26,019
21,000	211.98	55,313	228.94	32,678	22,635	233.18	30,112	25,201	237.42	27,993	27,320
22,000	222.08	57,949	239.85	34,235	23,714	244.29	31,547	26,402	248.73	29,326	28,623
23,000	232.17	60,581	250.74	35,789	24,792	255.39	32,980	27,601	259.03	30,658	29,923
24,000	242.26	63,214	261.64	37,344	25,870	266.49	34,413	28,801	271.33	31,990	31,224
25,000	252.36	65,850	272.55	38,902	26,948	277.60	35,848	30,002	282.64	33,324	32,526
26,000	262.45	68,482	283.45	40,458	28,024	288.70	37,281	31,201	293.94	34,656	33,826
27,000	272.55	71,118	294.35	42,014	29,104	299.81	38,717	32,401	305.26	35,992	35,126
28,000	282.64	73,750	305.25	43,569	30,181	310.90	40,147	33,603	316.56	37,323	36,427
29,000	292.73	76,383	316.15	45,125	31,258	322.00	41,580	34,803	327.86	38,655	37,728
30,000	302.83	79,019	327.06	46,683	32,336	333.11	43,016	36,003	339.17	39,989	39,030
32,500	328.06	85,602	354.30	50,570	35,032	360.87	46,601	39,001	367.43	43,321	42,281
35,000	353.30	92,188	381.56	54,461	37,727	388.63	50,185	42,003	395.70	46,654	45,534
40,000	403.77	105,357	436.07	62,241	43,116	444.15	57,355	48,002	452.22	53,317	52,040
45,000	454.24	118,526	490.58	70,022	48,504	499.66	64,522	54,004	508.75	59,983	58,543
50,000	504.71	131,696	545.09	77,802	53,894	555.18	71,692	60,004	565.28	66,648	65,048
55,000	555.18	144,865	599.59	85,580	59,285	610.70	78,862	66,003	621.80	73,311	71,554
60,000	605.65	158,034	654.10	93,361	64,673	666.22	86,031	72,003	678.33	79,976	78,058
65,000	656.12	171,203	708.61	101,141	70,062	721.73	93,199	78,004	734.85	86,639	84,564
70,000	706.59	184,372	763.12	108,921	75,450	777.25	100,369	84,003	791.38	93,304	91,068
75,000	757.06	197,542	817.62	116,700	80,842	832.77	107,538	90,004	847.91	99,970	97,572
80,000	807.53	210,711	872.13	124,480	86,231	888.28	114,706	96,005	904.43	106,633	104,078
85,000	858.00	223,880	926.64	132,261	91,619	943.80	121,875	102,005	960.96	113,298	110,582
90,000	908.47	237,049	981.15	140,041	97,008	999.32	129,045	108,004	1,017.49	119,963	117,086
95,000	958.94	250,218	1,035.66	147,822	102,396	1,054.83	136,212	114,006	1,074.01	126,626	123,592
100,000	1,009.41	263,388	1,090.16	155,600	107,788	1,110.35	143,382	120,006	1,130.54	133,291	130,097
105,000	1,059.89	276,560	1,144.68	163,383	113,177	1,165.88	150,554	126,006	1,187.08	139,959	136,601
110,000	1,110.36	289,730	1,199.19	171,163	118,567	1,221.40	157,724	132,006	1,243.60	146,622	143,108
115,000	1,160.83	302,899	1,253.70	178,944	123,955	1,276.91	164,891	138,008	1,300.13	153,287	149,612
120,000	1,211.30	316,068	1,308.20	186,722	129,346	1,332.43	172,061	144,007	1,356.66	159,952	156,116
125,000	1,261.77	329,237	1,362.71	194,502	134,735	1,387.95	179,230	150,007	1,413.18	166,615	162,622
130,000	1,312.24	342,406	1,417.22	202,283	140,123	1,443.46	186,398	156,008	1,469.71	173,281	169,125
135,000	1,362.71	355,576	1,471.73	210,063	145,513	1,498.98	193,567	162,009	1,526.24	179,946	175,630
140,000	1,413.18	368,745	1,526.23	217,841	150,904	1,554.50	200,737	168,008	1,582.76	186,609	182,136
145,000	1,463.65	381,914	1,580.74	225,622	156,292	1,610.02	207,907	174,007	1,639.29	193,274	188,640
150,000	1,514.12	395,083	1,635.25	233,402	161,681	1,665.53	215,074	180,009	1,695.81	199,937	195,146
155,000	1,564.59	408,252	1,689.76	241,183	167,069	1,721.05	222,244	186,009	1,752.34	206,602	201,650
160,000	1,615.06	421,422	1,744.26	248,961	172,461	1,776.57	229,413	192,009	1,808.87	213,268	208,154
165,000	1,665.53	434,591	1,798.77	256,741	177,850	1,832.08	236,581	198,010	1,865.39	219,931	214,660
170,000	1,716.00	447,760	1,853.28	264,522	183,238	1,887.60	243,751	204,009	1,921.92	226,596	221,164
175,000	1,766.47	460,929	1,907.79	272,302	188,627	1,943.12	250,920	210,009	1,978.45	233,261	227,668
180,000	1,816.94	474,098	1,962.30	280,083	194,015	1,998.63	258,088	216,010	2,034.97	239,924	234,174
185,000	1,867.41	487,268	2,016.80	287,861	199,407	2,054.15	265,257	222,011	2,091.50	246,589	240,679
190,000	1,917.88	500,437	2,071.31	295,641	204,796	2,109.67	272,427	228,010	2,148.03	253,255	247,182
195,000	1,968.35	513,606	2,125.82	303,422	210,184	2,165.19	279,597	234,009	2,204.55	259,918	253,688
200,000	2,018.82	526,775	2,180.33	311,202	215,573	2,220.70	286,764	240,011	2,261.08	266,583	260,192

233

AUGMENTED PAYMENT MORTGAGES

AMOUNT OF LOAN	30 YEARS		2% PMT INCREASE 307.547 PAYMENTS			4% PMT INCREASE 274.381 PAYMENTS			6% PMT INCREASE 250.322 PAYMENTS		
	MONTHLY PAYMENT	TOTAL INTRST	MONTHLY PAYMENT	TOTAL INTRST	INTRST SAVED	MONTHLY PAYMENT	TOTAL INTRST	INTRST SAVED	MONTHLY PAYMENT	TOTAL INTRST	INTRST SAVED
$ 50	0.52	137	0.53	113	24	0.54	98	39	0.55	88	49
100	1.03	271	1.05	223	48	1.07	194	77	1.09	173	98
200	2.06	542	2.10	446	96	2.14	387	155	2.18	346	196
300	3.09	812	3.15	669	143	3.21	581	231	3.28	521	291
400	4.12	1,083	4.20	892	191	4.28	774	309	4.37	694	389
500	5.15	1,354	5.25	1,115	239	5.36	971	383	5.46	867	487
600	6.18	1,625	6.30	1,338	287	6.43	1,164	461	6.55	1,040	585
700	7.21	1,896	7.35	1,560	336	7.50	1,358	538	7.64	1,212	684
800	8.23	2,163	8.39	1,780	383	8.56	1,549	614	8.72	1,383	780
900	9.26	2,434	9.45	2,006	428	9.63	1,742	692	9.82	1,558	876
1,000	10.29	2,704	10.50	2,229	475	10.70	1,936	768	10.91	1,731	973
2,000	20.58	5,409	20.99	4,455	954	21.40	3,872	1,537	21.81	3,460	1,949
3,000	30.86	8,110	31.48	6,682	1,428	32.09	5,805	2,305	32.71	5,188	2,922
4,000	41.15	10,814	41.97	8,908	1,906	42.80	7,744	3,070	43.62	6,919	3,895
5,000	51.44	13,518	52.47	11,137	2,381	53.50	9,679	3,839	54.53	8,650	4,868
6,000	61.72	16,219	62.95	13,360	2,859	64.19	11,613	4,606	65.42	10,376	5,843
7,000	72.01	18,924	73.45	15,589	3,335	74.89	13,548	5,376	76.33	12,107	6,817
8,000	82.29	21,624	83.94	17,815	3,809	85.58	15,482	6,142	87.23	13,836	7,788
9,000	92.58	24,329	94.43	20,042	4,287	96.28	17,417	6,912	98.13	15,564	8,765
10,000	102.87	27,033	104.93	22,271	4,762	106.98	19,353	7,680	109.04	17,295	9,738
11,000	113.15	29,734	115.41	24,494	5,240	117.68	21,289	8,445	119.94	19,024	10,710
12,000	123.44	32,438	125.91	26,723	5,715	128.38	23,225	9,213	130.85	20,755	11,683
13,000	133.72	35,139	136.39	28,946	6,193	139.07	25,158	9,981	141.74	22,481	12,658
14,000	144.01	37,844	146.89	31,176	6,668	149.77	27,094	10,750	152.65	24,212	13,632
15,000	154.30	40,548	157.39	33,405	7,143	160.47	29,030	11,518	163.56	25,943	14,605
16,000	164.58	43,249	167.87	35,628	7,621	171.16	30,963	12,286	174.45	27,669	15,580
17,000	174.87	45,953	178.37	37,857	8,096	181.86	32,899	13,054	185.36	29,400	16,553
18,000	185.16	48,658	188.86	40,083	8,575	192.57	34,838	13,820	196.27	31,131	17,527
19,000	195.44	51,358	199.35	42,309	9,049	203.26	36,771	14,587	207.17	32,859	18,499
20,000	205.73	54,063	209.84	44,536	9,527	213.96	38,707	15,356	218.07	34,588	19,475
21,000	216.01	56,764	220.33	46,762	10,002	224.65	40,640	16,124	228.97	36,316	20,448
22,000	226.30	59,468	230.83	48,991	10,477	235.35	42,576	16,892	239.88	38,047	21,421
23,000	236.59	62,172	241.32	51,217	10,955	246.05	44,511	17,661	250.79	39,778	22,394
24,000	246.87	64,873	251.81	53,443	11,430	256.74	46,445	18,428	261.68	41,504	23,369
25,000	257.16	67,578	262.30	55,670	11,908	267.45	48,383	19,195	272.59	43,235	24,343
26,000	267.44	70,278	272.79	57,896	12,382	278.14	50,316	19,962	283.49	44,964	25,314
27,000	277.73	72,983	283.28	60,112	12,861	288.84	52,252	20,731	294.39	46,692	26,291
28,000	288.02	75,687	293.78	62,351	13,336	299.54	54,188	21,499	305.30	48,423	27,264
29,000	298.30	78,388	304.27	64,577	13,811	310.23	56,121	22,267	316.20	50,152	28,236
30,000	308.59	81,092	314.76	66,803	14,289	320.93	58,057	23,035	327.11	51,883	29,209
32,500	334.30	87,848	340.99	72,370	15,478	347.67	62,894	24,954	354.36	56,204	31,644
35,000	360.02	94,607	367.22	77,937	16,670	374.42	67,734	26,873	381.62	60,528	34,079
40,000	411.45	108,122	419.68	89,071	19,051	427.91	77,410	30,712	436.14	69,175	38,947
45,000	462.88	121,637	472.14	100,205	21,432	481.40	87,087	34,550	490.65	77,820	43,817
50,000	514.31	135,152	524.60	111,339	23,813	534.88	96,761	38,391	545.17	86,468	48,684
55,000	565.74	148,666	577.05	122,470	26,196	588.37	106,438	42,228	599.68	95,113	53,553
60,000	617.17	162,181	629.51	133,604	28,577	641.86	116,114	46,067	654.20	103,761	58,420
65,000	668.60	175,696	681.97	144,738	30,958	695.34	125,788	49,908	708.72	112,408	63,288
70,000	720.03	189,211	734.43	155,872	33,339	748.83	135,465	53,746	763.23	121,053	68,158
75,000	771.46	202,726	786.89	167,006	35,720	802.32	145,141	57,585	817.75	129,701	73,025
80,000	822.90	216,244	839.36	178,143	38,101	855.82	154,821	61,423	872.27	138,348	77,896
85,000	874.33	229,759	891.82	189,277	40,482	909.30	164,495	65,264	926.79	146,996	82,763
90,000	925.76	243,274	944.28	200,410	42,864	962.79	174,171	69,103	981.31	155,643	87,631
95,000	977.19	256,788	996.73	211,541	45,247	1,016.28	183,848	72,940	1,035.82	164,289	92,499
100,000	1,028.62	270,303	1,049.19	222,675	47,628	1,069.76	193,522	76,781	1,090.34	172,936	97,367
105,000	1,080.05	283,818	1,101.65	233,809	50,009	1,123.25	203,198	80,620	1,144.85	181,581	102,237
110,000	1,131.48	297,333	1,154.11	244,943	52,390	1,176.74	212,875	84,458	1,199.37	190,229	107,104
115,000	1,182.91	310,848	1,206.57	256,077	54,771	1,230.23	222,552	88,296	1,253.88	198,874	111,973
120,000	1,234.34	324,362	1,259.03	267,211	57,151	1,283.71	232,226	92,136	1,308.40	207,521	116,841
125,000	1,285.77	337,877	1,311.49	278,345	59,532	1,337.20	241,902	95,975	1,362.92	216,169	121,708
130,000	1,337.20	351,392	1,363.94	289,476	61,916	1,390.69	251,579	99,813	1,417.43	224,814	126,578
135,000	1,388.63	364,907	1,416.40	300,610	64,297	1,444.18	261,256	103,651	1,471.95	233,461	131,446
140,000	1,440.06	378,422	1,468.86	311,743	66,679	1,497.66	270,929	107,493	1,526.46	242,107	136,315
145,000	1,491.49	391,936	1,521.32	322,877	69,059	1,551.15	280,606	111,330	1,580.98	250,754	141,182
150,000	1,542.92	405,451	1,573.78	334,011	71,440	1,604.64	290,283	115,168	1,635.50	259,400	146,049
155,000	1,594.35	418,966	1,626.24	345,145	73,821	1,658.12	299,957	119,009	1,690.01	268,047	150,919
160,000	1,645.79	432,484	1,678.71	356,282	76,202	1,711.62	309,636	122,848	1,744.54	276,697	155,787
165,000	1,697.22	445,999	1,731.16	367,413	78,586	1,765.11	319,313	126,686	1,799.05	285,342	160,657
170,000	1,748.65	459,514	1,783.62	378,547	80,967	1,818.60	328,989	130,525	1,853.57	293,989	165,525
175,000	1,800.08	473,029	1,836.08	389,681	83,348	1,872.08	338,663	134,366	1,908.08	302,634	170,395
180,000	1,851.51	486,544	1,888.54	400,815	85,729	1,925.57	348,340	138,204	1,962.60	311,282	175,262
185,000	1,902.94	500,058	1,941.00	411,949	88,109	1,979.06	358,016	142,042	2,017.12	319,930	180,128
190,000	1,954.37	513,573	1,993.46	423,083	90,490	2,032.54	367,690	145,883	2,071.63	328,575	184,998
195,000	2,005.80	527,088	2,045.92	434,217	92,871	2,086.03	377,367	149,721	2,126.15	337,222	189,866
200,000	2,057.23	540,603	2,098.37	445,347	95,256	2,139.52	387,044	153,559	2,180.66	345,867	194,736

AMOUNT OF LOAN	30 YEARS		8% PMT INCREASE 231.580 PAYMENTS			10% PMT INCREASE 216.322 PAYMENTS			12% PMT INCREASE 203.523 PAYMENTS		
	MONTHLY PAYMENT	TOTAL INTRST	MONTHLY PAYMENT	TOTAL INTRST	INTRST SAVED	MONTHLY PAYMENT	TOTAL INTRST	INTRST SAVED	MONTHLY PAYMENT	TOTAL INTRST	INTRST SAVED
$ 50	0.52	137	0.56	80	57	0.57	73	64	0.58	68	69
100	1.03	271	1.11	157	114	1.13	144	127	1.15	134	137
200	2.06	542	2.22	314	228	2.27	291	251	2.31	270	272
300	3.09	812	3.34	473	339	3.40	435	377	3.46	404	408
400	4.12	1,083	4.45	631	452	4.53	580	503	4.61	538	545
500	5.15	1,354	5.56	788	566	5.67	727	627	5.77	674	680
600	6.18	1,625	6.67	945	680	6.80	871	754	6.92	808	817
700	7.21	1,896	7.79	1,104	792	7.93	1,015	881	8.08	944	952
800	8.23	2,163	8.89	1,259	904	9.05	1,158	1,005	9.22	1,076	1,087
900	9.26	2,434	10.00	1,416	1,018	10.19	1,304	1,130	10.37	1,211	1,223
1,000	10.29	2,704	11.11	1,573	1,131	11.32	1,449	1,255	11.52	1,345	1,359
2,000	20.58	5,409	22.23	3,148	2,261	22.64	2,898	2,511	23.05	2,691	2,718
3,000	30.86	8,110	33.33	4,719	3,391	33.95	4,344	3,766	34.56	4,034	4,076
4,000	41.15	10,814	44.44	6,291	4,523	45.27	5,793	5,021	46.09	5,380	5,434
5,000	51.44	13,518	55.56	7,867	5,651	56.58	7,239	6,279	57.61	6,725	6,793
6,000	61.72	16,219	66.66	9,437	6,782	67.89	8,686	7,533	69.13	8,070	8,149
7,000	72.01	18,924	77.77	11,010	7,914	79.21	10,135	8,789	80.65	9,414	9,510
8,000	82.29	21,624	88.87	12,581	9,043	90.52	11,581	10,043	92.16	10,757	10,867
9,000	92.58	24,329	99.99	14,156	10,173	101.84	13,030	11,299	103.69	12,103	12,226
10,000	102.87	27,033	111.10	15,729	11,304	113.16	14,479	12,554	115.21	13,448	13,585
11,000	113.15	29,734	122.20	17,299	12,435	124.47	15,926	13,808	126.73	14,792	14,942
12,000	123.44	32,438	133.32	18,874	13,564	135.78	17,372	15,066	138.25	16,137	16,301
13,000	133.72	35,139	144.42	20,445	14,694	147.09	18,819	16,320	149.77	17,482	17,657
14,000	144.01	37,844	155.53	22,018	15,826	158.41	20,268	17,576	161.29	18,826	19,018
15,000	154.30	40,548	166.64	23,590	16,958	169.73	21,716	18,832	172.82	20,173	20,375
16,000	164.58	43,249	177.75	25,163	18,086	181.04	23,163	20,086	184.33	21,515	21,734
17,000	174.87	45,953	188.86	26,736	19,217	192.36	24,612	21,341	195.85	22,860	23,093
18,000	185.16	48,658	199.97	28,309	20,349	203.68	26,060	22,598	207.38	24,207	24,451
19,000	195.44	51,358	211.08	29,882	21,476	214.98	27,505	23,853	218.89	25,549	25,809
20,000	205.73	54,063	222.19	31,455	22,608	226.30	28,954	25,109	230.42	26,896	27,167
21,000	216.01	56,764	233.29	33,025	23,739	237.61	30,400	26,364	241.93	28,238	28,526
22,000	226.30	59,468	244.40	34,598	24,870	248.93	31,849	27,619	253.46	29,585	29,883
23,000	236.59	62,172	255.52	36,173	25,999	260.25	33,298	28,874	264.98	30,930	31,242
24,000	246.87	64,873	266.62	37,744	27,129	271.56	34,744	30,129	276.49	32,272	32,601
25,000	257.16	67,578	277.73	39,317	28,261	282.88	36,193	31,385	288.02	33,619	33,959
26,000	267.44	70,278	288.84	40,890	29,388	294.18	37,638	32,640	299.53	34,961	35,317
27,000	277.73	72,983	299.95	42,462	30,521	305.50	39,086	33,897	311.06	36,308	36,675
28,000	288.02	75,687	311.06	44,035	31,652	316.82	40,535	35,152	322.58	37,652	38,035
29,000	298.30	78,388	322.16	45,606	32,782	328.13	41,982	36,406	334.10	38,997	39,391
30,000	308.59	81,092	333.28	47,181	33,911	339.45	43,431	37,661	345.62	40,342	40,750
32,500	334.30	87,848	361.04	51,110	36,738	367.73	47,048	40,800	374.42	43,703	44,145
35,000	360.02	94,607	388.82	55,043	39,564	396.02	50,668	43,939	403.22	47,065	47,542
40,000	411.45	108,122	444.37	62,907	45,215	452.60	57,907	50,215	460.82	53,787	54,335
45,000	462.88	121,637	499.91	70,769	50,868	509.17	65,146	56,492	518.43	60,512	61,125
50,000	514.31	135,152	555.45	78,631	56,521	565.74	72,382	62,770	576.03	67,235	67,917
55,000	565.74	148,666	611.00	86,495	62,171	622.31	79,619	69,047	633.63	73,958	74,708
60,000	617.17	162,181	666.54	94,357	67,824	678.89	86,859	75,322	691.23	80,681	81,500
65,000	668.60	175,696	722.09	102,222	73,474	735.46	94,096	81,600	748.83	87,404	88,292
70,000	720.03	189,211	777.63	110,084	79,127	792.03	101,334	87,877	806.43	94,127	95,084
75,000	771.46	202,726	833.18	117,948	84,778	848.61	108,573	94,153	864.04	100,852	101,874
80,000	822.90	216,244	888.73	125,812	90,432	905.19	115,813	100,431	921.65	107,577	108,667
85,000	874.33	229,759	944.28	133,676	96,083	961.76	123,050	106,709	979.25	114,300	115,459
90,000	925.76	243,274	999.82	141,538	101,736	1,018.34	130,289	112,985	1,036.85	121,023	122,251
95,000	977.19	256,788	1,055.37	149,403	107,385	1,074.91	137,527	119,261	1,094.45	127,746	129,042
100,000	1,028.62	270,303	1,110.91	157,265	113,038	1,131.48	144,764	125,539	1,152.05	134,469	135,834
105,000	1,080.05	283,818	1,166.45	165,126	118,692	1,188.06	152,004	131,814	1,209.66	141,194	142,624
110,000	1,131.48	297,333	1,222.00	172,991	124,342	1,244.63	159,241	138,092	1,267.26	147,917	149,416
115,000	1,182.91	310,848	1,277.54	180,853	129,995	1,301.20	166,478	144,370	1,324.86	154,639	156,209
120,000	1,234.34	324,362	1,333.09	188,717	135,645	1,357.77	173,716	150,646	1,382.46	161,362	163,000
125,000	1,285.77	337,877	1,388.63	196,579	141,298	1,414.35	180,955	156,922	1,440.06	168,085	169,792
130,000	1,337.20	351,392	1,444.18	204,443	146,949	1,470.92	188,192	163,200	1,497.66	174,808	176,584
135,000	1,388.63	364,907	1,499.72	212,305	152,602	1,527.49	195,430	169,477	1,555.27	181,533	183,374
140,000	1,440.06	378,422	1,555.26	220,167	158,255	1,584.07	202,669	175,753	1,612.87	188,256	190,166
145,000	1,491.49	391,936	1,610.81	228,031	163,905	1,640.64	209,907	182,029	1,670.47	194,979	196,957
150,000	1,542.92	405,451	1,666.35	235,893	169,558	1,697.21	217,144	188,307	1,728.07	201,702	203,749
155,000	1,594.35	418,966	1,721.90	243,758	175,208	1,753.79	224,383	194,583	1,785.67	208,425	210,541
160,000	1,645.79	432,484	1,777.45	251,622	180,862	1,810.37	231,623	200,861	1,843.28	215,150	217,334
165,000	1,697.22	445,999	1,833.00	259,486	186,513	1,866.94	238,860	207,139	1,900.88	221,875	224,124
170,000	1,748.65	459,514	1,888.54	267,348	192,166	1,923.52	246,100	213,414	1,958.49	228,598	230,916
175,000	1,800.08	473,029	1,944.09	275,212	197,817	1,980.09	253,337	219,692	2,016.09	235,321	237,708
180,000	1,851.51	486,544	1,999.63	283,074	203,470	2,036.66	260,574	225,970	2,073.69	242,044	244,500
185,000	1,902.94	500,058	2,055.18	290,939	209,119	2,093.23	267,812	232,246	2,131.29	248,767	251,291
190,000	1,954.37	513,573	2,110.72	298,801	214,772	2,149.81	275,051	238,522	2,188.89	255,489	258,084
195,000	2,005.80	527,088	2,166.26	306,662	220,426	2,206.38	282,289	244,799	2,246.50	262,214	264,874
200,000	2,057.23	540,603	2,221.81	314,527	226,076	2,262.95	289,526	251,077	2,304.10	268,937	271,666

AMOUNT OF LOAN	30 YEARS		2% PMT INCREASE 305.488 PAYMENTS			4% PMT INCREASE 271.742 PAYMENTS			6% PMT INCREASE 247.496 PAYMENTS		
	MONTHLY PAYMENT	TOTAL INTRST	MONTHLY PAYMENT	TOTAL INTRST	INTRST SAVED	MONTHLY PAYMENT	TOTAL INTRST	INTRST SAVED	MONTHLY PAYMENT	TOTAL INTRST	INTRST SAVED
$ 50	0.53	141	0.54	115	26	0.55	99	42	0.56	89	52
100	1.05	278	1.07	227	51	1.09	196	82	1.11	175	103
200	2.10	556	2.14	454	102	2.18	392	164	2.23	352	204
300	3.15	834	3.21	681	153	3.28	591	243	3.34	527	307
400	4.20	1,112	4.28	907	205	4.37	788	324	4.45	701	411
500	5.24	1,386	5.34	1,131	255	5.45	981	405	5.55	874	512
600	6.29	1,664	6.42	1,361	303	6.54	1,177	487	6.67	1,051	613
700	7.34	1,942	7.49	1,588	354	7.63	1,373	569	7.78	1,226	716
800	8.39	2,220	8.56	1,815	405	8.73	1,572	648	8.89	1,400	820
900	9.44	2,498	9.63	2,042	456	9.82	1,769	729	10.01	1,577	921
1,000	10.48	2,773	10.69	2,266	507	10.90	1,962	811	11.11	1,750	1,023
2,000	20.96	5,546	21.38	4,531	1,015	21.80	3,924	1,622	22.22	3,499	2,047
3,000	31.44	8,318	32.07	6,797	1,521	32.70	5,886	2,432	33.33	5,249	3,069
4,000	41.92	11,091	42.76	9,063	2,028	43.60	7,848	3,243	44.44	6,999	4,092
5,000	52.40	13,864	53.45	11,328	2,536	54.50	9,810	4,054	55.54	8,746	5,118
6,000	62.88	16,637	64.14	13,594	3,043	65.40	11,772	4,865	66.65	10,496	6,141
7,000	73.36	19,410	74.83	15,860	3,550	76.29	13,731	5,679	77.76	12,245	7,165
8,000	83.84	22,182	85.52	18,125	4,057	87.19	15,693	6,489	88.87	13,995	8,187
9,000	94.32	24,955	96.21	20,391	4,564	98.09	17,655	7,300	99.98	15,745	9,210
10,000	104.79	27,724	106.89	22,654	5,070	108.98	19,614	8,110	111.08	17,492	10,232
11,000	115.27	30,497	117.58	24,919	5,578	119.88	21,576	8,921	122.19	19,242	11,255
12,000	125.75	33,270	128.27	27,185	6,085	130.78	23,538	9,732	133.30	20,991	12,279
13,000	136.23	36,043	138.95	29,448	6,595	141.68	25,500	10,543	144.40	22,738	13,305
14,000	146.71	38,816	149.64	31,713	7,103	152.58	27,462	11,354	155.51	24,488	14,328
15,000	157.19	41,588	160.33	33,979	7,609	163.48	29,424	12,164	166.62	26,238	15,350
16,000	167.67	44,361	171.02	36,245	8,116	174.38	31,386	12,975	177.73	27,987	16,374
17,000	178.15	47,134	181.71	38,510	8,624	185.28	33,348	13,786	188.84	29,737	17,397
18,000	188.63	49,907	192.40	40,776	9,131	196.18	35,310	14,597	199.95	31,487	18,420
19,000	199.11	52,680	203.09	43,042	9,638	207.07	37,270	15,410	211.06	33,237	19,443
20,000	209.58	55,449	213.77	45,304	10,145	217.96	39,229	16,220	222.15	34,981	20,468
21,000	220.06	58,222	224.46	47,570	10,652	228.86	41,191	17,031	233.26	36,731	21,491
22,000	230.54	60,994	235.15	49,836	11,158	239.76	43,153	17,841	244.37	38,481	22,513
23,000	241.02	63,767	245.84	52,101	11,666	250.66	45,115	18,652	255.48	40,230	23,537
24,000	251.50	66,540	256.53	54,367	12,173	261.56	47,077	19,463	266.59	41,980	24,560
25,000	261.98	69,313	267.22	56,633	12,680	272.46	49,039	20,274	277.70	43,730	25,583
26,000	272.46	72,086	277.91	58,898	13,188	283.36	51,001	21,085	288.81	45,479	26,607
27,000	282.94	74,858	288.60	61,164	13,694	294.26	52,963	21,895	299.92	47,229	27,629
28,000	293.42	77,631	299.29	63,430	14,201	305.16	54,925	22,706	311.03	48,979	28,652
29,000	303.89	80,400	309.97	65,692	14,708	316.05	56,884	23,516	322.12	50,723	29,677
30,000	314.37	83,173	320.66	67,958	15,215	326.94	58,843	24,330	333.23	52,473	30,700
32,500	340.57	90,105	347.38	73,620	16,485	354.19	63,748	26,357	361.00	56,846	33,259
35,000	366.77	97,037	374.11	79,286	17,751	381.44	68,653	28,384	388.78	61,221	35,816
40,000	419.16	110,898	427.54	90,608	20,290	435.93	78,460	32,438	444.31	69,965	40,933
45,000	471.56	124,762	480.99	101,937	22,825	490.42	88,268	36,494	499.85	78,711	46,051
50,000	523.95	138,622	534.43	113,262	25,360	544.91	98,075	40,547	555.39	87,457	51,165
55,000	576.35	152,486	587.88	124,590	27,896	599.40	107,882	44,604	610.93	96,203	56,283
60,000	628.74	166,346	641.31	135,913	30,433	653.89	117,689	48,657	666.46	104,946	61,400
65,000	681.14	180,210	694.76	147,241	32,969	708.39	127,499	52,711	722.01	113,695	66,515
70,000	733.53	194,071	748.20	158,565	35,505	762.87	137,304	56,767	777.54	122,438	71,632
75,000	785.93	207,935	801.65	169,894	38,041	817.37	147,114	60,821	833.09	131,186	76,749
80,000	838.32	221,795	855.09	181,220	40,575	871.85	156,918	64,877	888.62	139,930	81,865
85,000	890.72	235,659	908.53	192,545	43,114	926.35	166,728	68,931	944.16	148,676	86,983
90,000	943.11	249,520	961.97	203,870	45,650	980.83	176,533	72,987	999.70	157,422	92,098
95,000	995.51	263,384	1,015.42	215,199	48,185	1,035.33	186,343	77,041	1,055.24	166,168	97,216
100,000	1,047.90	277,244	1,068.86	226,524	50,720	1,089.82	196,150	81,094	1,110.77	174,911	102,333
105,000	1,100.30	291,108	1,122.31	237,852	53,256	1,144.31	205,957	85,151	1,166.32	183,660	107,448
110,000	1,152.69	304,968	1,175.74	249,174	55,794	1,198.80	215,764	89,204	1,221.85	192,403	112,565
115,000	1,205.09	318,832	1,229.19	260,503	58,329	1,253.29	225,572	93,260	1,277.40	201,151	117,681
120,000	1,257.48	332,693	1,282.63	271,828	60,865	1,307.78	235,379	97,314	1,332.93	209,895	122,798
125,000	1,309.88	346,557	1,336.08	283,156	63,401	1,362.28	245,189	101,368	1,388.47	218,641	127,916
130,000	1,362.27	360,417	1,389.52	294,482	65,935	1,416.76	254,993	105,424	1,444.01	227,387	133,030
135,000	1,414.67	374,281	1,442.96	305,807	68,474	1,471.26	264,803	109,478	1,499.55	236,133	138,148
140,000	1,467.06	388,142	1,496.40	317,132	71,010	1,525.74	274,608	113,534	1,555.08	244,876	143,266
145,000	1,519.45	402,002	1,549.84	328,458	73,544	1,580.23	284,415	117,587	1,610.62	253,622	148,380
150,000	1,571.85	415,866	1,603.29	339,786	76,080	1,634.72	294,222	121,644	1,666.16	262,368	153,498
155,000	1,624.24	429,726	1,656.72	351,108	78,618	1,689.21	304,029	125,697	1,721.69	271,111	158,615
160,000	1,676.64	443,590	1,710.17	362,436	81,154	1,743.71	313,839	129,751	1,777.24	279,860	163,730
165,000	1,729.03	457,451	1,763.61	373,762	83,689	1,798.19	323,644	133,807	1,832.77	288,603	168,848
170,000	1,781.43	471,315	1,817.06	385,090	86,225	1,852.69	333,454	137,861	1,888.32	297,352	173,963
175,000	1,833.82	485,175	1,870.50	396,415	88,760	1,907.17	343,258	141,917	1,943.85	306,095	179,080
180,000	1,886.22	499,039	1,923.94	407,741	91,298	1,961.67	353,068	145,971	1,999.39	314,841	184,198
185,000	1,938.61	512,900	1,977.38	419,066	93,834	2,016.15	362,873	150,027	2,054.93	323,587	189,313
190,000	1,991.01	526,764	2,030.83	430,394	96,370	2,070.65	372,683	154,081	2,110.47	332,333	194,431
195,000	2,043.40	540,624	2,084.27	441,719	98,905	2,125.14	382,490	158,134	2,166.00	341,076	199,548
200,000	2,095.80	554,488	2,137.72	453,048	101,440	2,179.63	392,297	162,191	2,221.55	349,825	204,663

AMOUNT OF LOAN	30 YEARS		8% PMT INCREASE 228.712 PAYMENTS			10% PMT INCREASE 213.475 PAYMENTS			12% PMT INCREASE 200.725 PAYMENTS		
	MONTHLY PAYMENT	TOTAL INTRST	MONTHLY PAYMENT	TOTAL INTRST	INTRST SAVED	MONTHLY PAYMENT	TOTAL INTRST	INTRST SAVED	MONTHLY PAYMENT	TOTAL INTRST	INTRST SAVED
$ 50	0.53	141	0.57	80	61	0.58	74	67	0.59	68	73
100	1.05	278	1.13	158	120	1.16	148	130	1.18	137	141
200	2.10	556	2.27	319	237	2.31	293	263	2.35	272	284
300	3.15	834	3.40	478	356	3.47	441	393	3.53	409	425
400	4.20	1,112	4.54	638	474	4.62	586	526	4.70	543	569
500	5.24	1,386	5.66	795	591	5.76	730	656	5.87	678	708
600	6.29	1,664	6.79	953	711	6.92	877	787	7.04	813	851
700	7.34	1,942	7.93	1,114	828	8.07	1,023	919	8.22	950	992
800	8.39	2,220	9.06	1,272	948	9.23	1,170	1,050	9.40	1,087	1,133
900	9.44	2,498	10.20	1,433	1,065	10.38	1,316	1,182	10.57	1,222	1,276
1,000	10.48	2,773	11.32	1,589	1,184	11.53	1,461	1,312	11.74	1,357	1,416
2,000	20.96	5,546	22.64	3,178	2,368	23.06	2,923	2,623	23.48	2,713	2,833
3,000	31.44	8,318	33.96	4,767	3,551	34.58	4,382	3,936	35.21	4,068	4,250
4,000	41.92	11,091	45.27	6,354	4,737	46.11	5,843	5,248	46.95	5,424	5,667
5,000	52.40	13,864	56.59	7,943	5,921	57.64	7,305	6,559	58.69	6,781	7,083
6,000	62.88	16,637	67.91	9,532	7,105	69.17	8,766	7,871	70.43	8,137	8,500
7,000	73.36	19,410	79.23	11,121	8,289	80.70	10,227	9,183	82.16	9,492	9,918
8,000	83.84	22,182	90.55	12,710	9,472	92.22	11,687	10,495	93.90	10,848	11,334
9,000	94.32	24,955	101.87	14,299	10,656	103.75	13,148	11,807	105.64	12,205	12,750
10,000	104.79	27,724	113.17	15,883	11,841	115.27	14,607	13,117	117.36	13,557	14,167
11,000	115.27	30,497	124.49	17,472	13,025	126.80	16,069	14,428	129.10	14,914	15,583
12,000	125.75	33,270	135.81	19,061	14,209	138.33	17,530	15,740	140.84	16,270	17,000
13,000	136.23	36,043	147.13	20,650	15,393	149.85	18,989	17,054	152.58	17,627	18,416
14,000	146.71	38,816	158.45	22,239	16,577	161.38	20,451	18,365	164.32	18,983	19,833
15,000	157.19	41,588	169.77	23,828	17,760	172.91	21,912	19,676	176.05	20,338	21,250
16,000	167.67	44,361	181.08	25,415	18,946	184.44	23,373	20,988	187.79	21,694	22,667
17,000	178.15	47,134	192.40	27,004	20,130	195.97	24,835	22,299	199.53	23,051	24,083
18,000	188.63	49,907	203.72	28,593	21,314	207.49	26,294	23,613	211.27	24,407	25,500
19,000	199.11	52,680	215.04	30,182	22,498	219.02	27,755	24,925	223.00	25,762	26,918
20,000	209.58	55,449	226.35	31,769	23,680	230.54	29,215	26,234	234.73	27,116	28,333
21,000	220.06	58,222	237.66	33,356	24,866	242.07	30,676	27,546	246.47	28,473	29,749
22,000	230.54	60,994	248.98	34,945	26,049	253.59	32,135	28,859	258.20	29,827	31,167
23,000	241.02	63,767	260.30	36,534	27,233	265.12	33,596	30,171	269.94	31,184	32,583
24,000	251.50	66,540	271.62	38,123	28,417	276.65	35,058	31,482	281.68	32,540	34,000
25,000	261.98	69,313	282.94	39,712	29,601	288.18	36,519	32,794	293.42	33,897	35,416
26,000	272.46	72,086	294.26	41,301	30,785	299.71	37,981	34,105	305.16	35,253	36,833
27,000	282.94	74,858	305.58	42,890	31,968	311.23	39,440	35,418	316.89	36,608	38,250
28,000	293.42	77,631	316.89	44,477	33,154	322.76	40,901	36,730	328.63	37,964	39,667
29,000	303.89	80,400	328.20	46,063	34,337	334.28	42,360	38,040	340.36	39,319	41,081
30,000	314.37	83,173	339.52	47,652	35,521	345.81	43,822	39,351	352.09	40,673	42,500
32,500	340.57	90,105	367.82	51,625	38,480	374.63	47,474	42,631	381.44	44,065	46,040
35,000	366.77	97,037	396.11	55,595	41,442	403.45	51,124	45,911	410.78	47,454	49,583
40,000	419.16	110,898	452.69	63,536	47,362	461.08	58,429	52,469	469.46	54,232	56,666
45,000	471.56	124,762	509.28	71,478	53,284	518.72	65,734	59,028	528.15	61,013	63,749
50,000	523.95	138,622	565.87	79,421	59,201	576.35	73,036	65,586	586.82	67,789	70,833
55,000	576.35	152,486	622.46	87,364	65,122	633.99	80,341	72,145	645.51	74,570	77,916
60,000	628.74	166,346	679.04	95,305	71,041	691.61	87,641	78,705	704.19	81,349	84,997
65,000	681.14	180,210	735.63	103,247	76,963	749.25	94,946	85,264	762.88	88,129	92,081
70,000	733.53	194,071	792.21	111,188	82,883	806.88	102,249	91,822	821.55	94,906	99,165
75,000	785.93	207,935	848.80	119,131	88,804	864.52	109,553	98,382	880.24	101,686	106,249
80,000	838.32	221,795	905.39	127,074	94,721	922.15	116,856	104,939	938.92	108,465	113,330
85,000	890.72	235,659	961.98	135,016	100,643	979.79	124,161	111,498	997.61	115,245	120,414
90,000	943.11	249,520	1,018.56	142,957	106,563	1,037.42	131,463	118,057	1,056.28	122,022	127,498
95,000	995.51	263,384	1,075.15	150,900	112,484	1,095.06	138,767	124,616	1,114.97	128,802	134,582
100,000	1,047.90	277,244	1,131.73	158,840	118,404	1,152.69	146,070	131,174	1,173.65	135,581	141,663
105,000	1,100.30	291,108	1,188.32	166,783	124,325	1,210.33	153,375	137,733	1,232.34	142,361	148,747
110,000	1,152.69	304,968	1,244.91	174,726	130,242	1,267.96	160,678	144,290	1,291.01	149,138	155,830
115,000	1,205.09	318,832	1,301.50	182,669	136,163	1,325.60	167,982	150,850	1,349.70	155,919	162,913
120,000	1,257.48	332,693	1,358.08	190,609	142,084	1,383.23	175,285	157,408	1,408.38	162,697	169,996
125,000	1,309.88	346,557	1,414.67	198,552	148,005	1,440.87	182,590	163,967	1,467.07	169,478	177,079
130,000	1,362.27	360,417	1,471.25	206,493	153,924	1,498.50	189,892	170,525	1,525.74	176,254	184,163
135,000	1,414.67	374,281	1,527.84	214,435	159,846	1,556.14	197,197	177,084	1,584.43	183,035	191,246
140,000	1,467.06	388,142	1,584.42	222,376	165,766	1,613.77	204,500	183,642	1,643.11	189,813	198,329
145,000	1,519.45	402,002	1,641.01	230,317	171,683	1,671.40	211,802	190,200	1,701.78	196,590	205,412
150,000	1,571.85	415,866	1,697.60	238,261	177,605	1,729.04	219,107	196,759	1,760.47	203,370	212,496
155,000	1,624.24	429,726	1,754.18	246,202	183,524	1,786.66	226,407	203,319	1,819.15	210,149	219,577
160,000	1,676.64	443,590	1,810.77	254,145	189,445	1,844.30	233,712	209,878	1,877.84	216,929	226,661
165,000	1,729.03	457,451	1,867.35	262,085	195,366	1,901.93	241,015	216,436	1,936.51	223,706	233,745
170,000	1,781.43	471,315	1,923.94	270,028	201,287	1,959.57	248,319	222,996	1,995.20	230,487	240,828
175,000	1,833.82	485,175	1,980.53	277,971	207,204	2,017.20	255,622	229,553	2,053.88	237,265	247,910
180,000	1,886.22	499,039	2,037.12	285,914	213,125	2,074.84	262,926	236,113	2,112.57	244,046	254,993
185,000	1,938.61	512,900	2,093.70	293,854	219,046	2,132.47	270,229	242,671	2,171.24	250,822	262,078
190,000	1,991.01	526,764	2,150.29	301,797	224,967	2,190.11	277,534	249,230	2,229.93	257,603	269,161
195,000	2,043.40	540,624	2,206.87	309,738	230,886	2,247.74	284,836	255,788	2,288.61	264,381	276,243
200,000	2,095.80	554,488	2,263.46	317,680	236,808	2,305.38	292,141	262,347	2,347.30	271,162	283,326

12.50% AUGMENTED PAYMENT MORTGAGES

AMOUNT OF LOAN	30 YEARS		2% PMT INCREASE 303.381 PAYMENTS			4% PMT INCREASE 269.082 PAYMENTS			6% PMT INCREASE 244.671 PAYMENTS		
	MONTHLY PAYMENT	TOTAL INTRST	MONTHLY PAYMENT	TOTAL INTRST	INTRST SAVED	MONTHLY PAYMENT	TOTAL INTRST	INTRST SAVED	MONTHLY PAYMENT	TOTAL INTRST	INTRST SAVED
$ 50	0.54	144	0.55	117	27	0.56	101	43	0.57	89	55
100	1.07	285	1.09	231	54	1.11	199	86	1.13	176	109
200	2.14	570	2.18	461	109	2.23	400	170	2.27	355	215
300	3.21	856	3.27	692	164	3.34	599	257	3.40	532	324
400	4.27	1,137	4.36	923	214	4.44	795	342	4.53	708	429
500	5.34	1,422	5.45	1,153	269	5.55	993	429	5.66	885	537
600	6.41	1,708	6.54	1,384	324	6.67	1,195	513	6.79	1,061	647
700	7.48	1,993	7.63	1,615	378	7.78	1,393	600	7.93	1,240	753
800	8.54	2,274	8.71	1,842	432	8.88	1,589	685	9.05	1,414	860
900	9.61	2,560	9.80	2,073	487	9.99	1,788	772	10.19	1,593	967
1,000	10.68	2,845	10.89	2,304	541	11.11	1,990	855	11.32	1,770	1,075
2,000	21.35	5,686	21.78	4,608	1,078	22.20	3,974	1,712	22.63	3,537	2,149
3,000	32.02	8,527	32.66	6,908	1,619	33.30	5,960	2,567	33.94	5,304	3,223
4,000	42.70	11,372	43.55	9,212	2,160	44.41	7,950	3,422	45.26	7,074	4,298
5,000	53.37	14,213	54.44	11,516	2,697	55.50	9,934	4,279	56.57	8,841	5,372
6,000	64.04	17,054	65.32	13,817	3,237	66.60	11,921	5,133	67.88	10,608	6,446
7,000	74.71	19,896	76.20	16,118	3,778	77.70	13,908	5,988	79.19	12,375	7,521
8,000	85.39	22,740	87.10	18,424	4,316	88.81	15,897	6,843	90.51	14,145	8,595
9,000	96.06	25,582	97.98	20,725	4,857	99.90	17,881	7,701	101.82	15,912	9,670
10,000	106.73	28,423	108.86	23,026	5,397	111.00	19,868	8,555	113.13	17,680	10,743
11,000	117.40	31,264	119.75	25,330	5,934	122.10	21,855	9,409	124.44	19,447	11,817
12,000	128.08	34,109	130.64	27,634	6,475	133.20	23,842	10,267	135.76	21,217	12,892
13,000	138.75	36,950	141.53	29,938	7,012	144.30	25,829	11,121	147.08	22,986	13,964
14,000	149.42	39,791	152.41	32,238	7,553	155.40	27,815	11,976	158.39	24,753	15,038
15,000	160.09	42,632	163.29	34,539	8,093	166.49	29,799	12,833	169.70	26,521	16,111
16,000	170.77	45,477	174.19	36,846	8,631	177.60	31,789	13,688	181.02	28,290	17,187
17,000	181.44	48,318	185.07	39,147	9,171	188.70	33,776	14,542	192.33	30,058	18,260
18,000	192.11	51,160	195.95	41,448	9,712	199.79	35,760	15,400	203.64	31,825	19,335
19,000	202.78	54,001	206.84	43,751	10,250	210.89	37,747	16,254	214.95	33,592	20,409
20,000	213.46	56,846	217.73	46,055	10,791	222.00	39,736	17,110	226.27	35,362	21,484
21,000	224.13	59,687	228.61	48,356	11,331	233.10	41,723	17,964	237.58	37,129	22,558
22,000	234.80	62,528	239.50	50,660	11,868	244.19	43,707	18,821	248.89	38,896	23,632
23,000	245.47	65,369	250.38	52,961	12,408	255.29	45,694	19,675	260.20	40,663	24,706
24,000	256.15	68,214	261.27	55,264	12,950	266.40	47,683	20,531	271.52	42,433	25,781
25,000	266.82	71,055	272.16	57,568	13,487	277.49	49,668	21,387	282.83	44,200	26,855
26,000	277.49	73,896	283.04	59,869	14,027	288.59	51,654	22,242	294.14	45,968	27,928
27,000	288.16	76,738	293.92	62,170	14,568	299.69	53,641	23,097	305.45	47,735	29,003
28,000	298.84	79,582	304.82	64,477	15,105	310.79	55,628	23,954	316.77	49,504	30,078
29,000	309.51	82,424	315.70	66,777	15,647	321.89	57,615	24,809	328.08	51,272	31,152
30,000	320.18	85,265	326.58	69,078	16,187	332.99	59,602	25,663	339.39	53,039	32,226
32,500	346.86	92,370	353.80	74,836	17,534	360.73	64,566	27,804	367.67	57,458	34,912
35,000	373.55	99,478	381.02	80,594	18,884	388.49	69,536	29,942	395.96	61,880	37,598
40,000	426.91	113,688	435.45	92,107	21,581	443.99	79,470	34,218	452.52	70,719	42,969
45,000	480.27	127,897	489.88	103,620	24,277	499.48	89,401	38,496	509.09	79,560	48,337
50,000	533.63	142,107	544.30	115,130	26,977	554.98	99,335	42,772	565.65	88,398	53,709
55,000	587.00	156,320	598.74	126,646	29,674	610.48	109,269	47,051	622.22	97,239	59,081
60,000	640.36	170,530	653.17	138,159	32,371	665.97	119,201	51,329	678.78	106,078	64,452
65,000	693.72	184,739	707.59	149,669	35,070	721.47	129,135	55,604	735.34	114,916	69,823
70,000	747.09	198,952	762.03	161,185	37,767	776.97	139,069	59,883	791.92	123,760	75,192
75,000	800.45	213,162	816.46	172,698	40,464	832.47	149,003	64,159	848.48	132,598	80,564
80,000	853.81	227,372	870.89	184,211	43,161	887.96	158,934	68,438	905.04	141,437	85,935
85,000	907.17	241,581	925.31	195,721	45,860	943.46	168,868	72,713	961.60	150,276	91,305
90,000	960.54	255,794	979.75	207,238	48,556	998.96	178,802	76,992	1,018.17	159,117	96,677
95,000	1,013.90	270,004	1,034.18	218,751	51,253	1,054.46	188,736	81,268	1,074.73	167,955	102,049
100,000	1,067.26	284,214	1,088.61	230,264	53,950	1,109.95	198,668	85,546	1,131.30	176,796	107,418
105,000	1,120.63	298,427	1,143.04	241,777	56,650	1,165.46	208,604	89,823	1,187.87	185,637	112,790
110,000	1,173.99	312,636	1,197.47	253,290	59,346	1,220.95	218,536	94,100	1,244.43	194,476	118,160
115,000	1,227.35	326,846	1,251.90	264,803	62,043	1,276.44	228,467	98,379	1,300.99	203,315	123,531
120,000	1,280.71	341,056	1,306.32	276,313	64,743	1,331.94	238,401	102,655	1,357.55	212,153	128,903
125,000	1,334.08	355,269	1,360.76	287,829	67,440	1,387.44	248,335	106,934	1,414.12	220,994	134,275
130,000	1,387.44	369,478	1,415.19	299,342	70,136	1,442.94	258,269	111,209	1,470.69	229,835	139,643
135,000	1,440.80	383,688	1,469.62	310,855	72,833	1,498.43	268,201	115,487	1,527.25	238,674	145,014
140,000	1,494.17	397,901	1,524.05	322,368	75,533	1,553.94	278,137	119,764	1,583.82	247,515	150,386
145,000	1,547.53	412,111	1,578.48	333,881	78,230	1,609.43	288,069	124,042	1,640.38	256,353	155,758
150,000	1,600.89	426,320	1,632.91	345,394	80,926	1,664.93	298,003	128,317	1,696.94	265,192	161,128
155,000	1,654.25	440,530	1,687.34	356,907	83,623	1,720.42	307,934	132,596	1,753.51	274,033	166,497
160,000	1,707.62	454,744	1,741.77	368,420	86,323	1,775.92	317,868	136,875	1,810.08	282,874	171,869
165,000	1,760.98	468,953	1,796.20	379,933	89,020	1,831.41	327,802	141,151	1,866.64	291,713	177,240
170,000	1,814.34	483,162	1,850.63	391,446	91,716	1,886.91	337,734	145,428	1,923.20	300,551	182,611
175,000	1,867.71	497,376	1,905.06	402,959	94,417	1,942.42	347,670	149,706	1,979.77	309,392	187,984
180,000	1,921.07	511,585	1,959.49	414,472	97,113	1,997.91	357,602	153,983	2,036.33	318,231	193,354
185,000	1,974.43	525,795	2,013.92	425,985	99,810	2,053.41	367,536	158,259	2,092.90	327,072	198,723
190,000	2,027.79	540,004	2,068.35	437,498	102,506	2,108.90	377,467	162,537	2,149.46	335,911	204,093
195,000	2,081.16	554,218	2,122.78	449,011	105,207	2,164.41	387,404	166,814	2,206.03	344,752	209,466
200,000	2,134.52	568,427	2,177.21	460,524	107,903	2,219.90	397,335	171,092	2,262.59	353,590	214,837

AUGMENTED PAYMENT MORTGAGES 12.50%

AMOUNT OF LOAN	30 YEARS		8% PMT INCREASE 225.860 PAYMENTS			10% PMT INCREASE 210.655 PAYMENTS			12% PMT INCREASE 197.961 PAYMENTS		
	MONTHLY PAYMENT	TOTAL INTRST	MONTHLY PAYMENT	TOTAL INTRST	INTRST SAVED	MONTHLY PAYMENT	TOTAL INTRST	INTRST SAVED	MONTHLY PAYMENT	TOTAL INTRST	INTRST SAVED
$ 50	0.54	144	0.58	81	63	0.59	74	70	0.60	69	75
100	1.07	285	1.16	162	123	1.18	149	136	1.20	138	147
200	2.14	570	2.31	322	248	2.35	295	275	2.40	275	295
300	3.21	856	3.47	484	372	3.53	444	412	3.60	413	443
400	4.27	1,137	4.61	641	496	4.70	590	547	4.78	546	591
500	5.34	1,422	5.77	803	619	5.87	737	685	5.98	684	738
600	6.41	1,708	6.92	963	745	7.05	885	823	7.18	821	887
700	7.48	1,993	8.08	1,125	868	8.23	1,034	959	8.38	959	1,034
800	8.54	2,274	9.22	1,282	992	9.39	1,178	1,096	9.56	1,093	1,181
900	9.61	2,560	10.38	1,444	1,116	10.57	1,327	1,233	10.76	1,230	1,330
1,000	10.68	2,845	11.53	1,604	1,241	11.75	1,475	1,370	11.96	1,368	1,477
2,000	21.35	5,686	23.06	3,208	2,478	23.49	2,948	2,738	23.91	2,733	2,953
3,000	32.02	8,527	34.58	4,810	3,717	35.22	4,419	4,108	35.86	4,099	4,428
4,000	42.70	11,372	46.12	6,417	4,955	46.97	5,894	5,478	47.82	5,466	5,906
5,000	53.37	14,213	57.64	8,019	6,194	58.71	7,368	6,845	59.77	6,832	7,381
6,000	64.04	17,054	69.16	9,620	7,434	70.44	8,839	8,215	71.72	8,198	8,856
7,000	74.71	19,896	80.69	11,225	8,671	82.18	10,312	9,584	83.68	9,565	10,331
8,000	85.39	22,740	92.22	12,829	9,911	93.93	11,787	10,953	95.64	10,933	11,807
9,000	96.06	25,582	103.74	14,431	11,151	105.67	13,260	12,322	107.59	12,299	13,283
10,000	106.73	28,423	115.27	16,035	12,388	117.40	14,731	13,692	119.54	13,664	14,759
11,000	117.40	31,264	126.79	17,637	13,627	129.14	16,204	15,060	131.49	15,030	16,234
12,000	128.08	34,109	138.33	19,243	14,866	140.89	17,679	16,430	143.45	16,398	17,711
13,000	138.75	36,950	149.85	20,845	16,105	152.63	19,152	17,798	155.40	17,763	19,187
14,000	149.42	39,791	161.37	22,447	17,344	164.36	20,623	19,168	167.35	19,129	20,662
15,000	160.09	42,632	172.90	24,051	18,581	176.10	22,096	20,536	179.30	20,494	22,138
16,000	170.77	45,477	184.43	25,655	19,822	187.85	23,572	21,905	191.26	21,862	23,615
17,000	181.44	48,318	195.96	27,260	21,058	199.58	25,043	23,275	203.21	23,228	25,090
18,000	192.11	51,160	207.48	28,861	22,299	211.32	26,516	24,644	215.16	24,593	26,567
19,000	202.78	54,001	219.00	30,463	23,538	223.06	27,989	26,012	227.11	25,959	28,042
20,000	213.46	56,846	230.54	32,070	24,776	234.81	29,464	27,382	239.08	27,329	29,517
21,000	224.13	59,687	242.06	33,672	26,015	246.54	30,935	28,752	251.03	28,694	30,993
22,000	234.80	62,528	253.58	35,274	27,254	258.28	32,408	30,120	262.98	30,060	32,468
23,000	245.47	65,369	265.11	36,878	28,491	270.02	33,881	31,488	274.93	31,425	33,944
24,000	256.15	68,214	276.64	38,482	29,732	281.77	35,356	32,858	286.89	32,793	35,421
25,000	266.82	71,055	288.17	40,086	30,969	293.50	36,827	34,228	298.84	34,159	36,896
26,000	277.49	73,896	299.69	41,688	32,208	305.24	38,300	35,596	310.79	35,524	38,372
27,000	288.16	76,738	311.21	43,290	33,448	316.98	39,773	36,965	322.74	36,890	39,848
28,000	298.84	79,582	322.75	44,896	34,686	328.72	41,247	38,335	334.70	38,258	41,324
29,000	309.51	82,424	334.27	46,498	35,926	340.46	42,720	39,704	346.65	39,623	42,801
30,000	320.18	85,265	345.79	48,100	37,165	352.20	44,193	41,072	358.60	40,989	44,276
32,500	346.86	92,370	374.61	52,109	40,261	381.55	47,875	44,495	388.48	44,404	47,966
35,000	373.55	99,478	403.43	56,119	43,359	410.91	51,560	47,918	418.38	47,823	51,655
40,000	426.91	113,688	461.06	64,136	49,553	469.60	58,924	54,764	478.14	54,653	59,035
45,000	480.27	127,897	518.69	72,151	55,746	528.30	66,289	61,608	537.90	61,483	66,414
50,000	533.63	142,107	576.32	80,168	61,939	586.99	73,652	68,455	597.67	68,315	73,792
55,000	587.00	156,320	633.96	88,186	68,134	645.70	81,020	75,300	657.44	75,147	81,173
60,000	640.36	170,530	691.59	96,203	74,327	704.40	88,385	82,145	717.20	81,978	88,552
65,000	693.72	184,739	749.22	104,219	80,520	763.09	95,749	88,990	776.97	88,810	95,929
70,000	747.09	198,952	806.86	112,237	86,715	821.80	103,116	95,836	836.74	95,642	103,310
75,000	800.45	213,162	864.49	120,254	92,908	880.50	110,482	102,680	896.50	102,472	110,690
80,000	853.81	227,372	922.11	128,268	99,104	939.19	117,845	109,527	956.27	109,304	118,068
85,000	907.17	241,581	979.74	136,284	105,297	997.89	125,211	116,370	1,016.03	116,134	125,447
90,000	960.54	255,794	1,037.38	144,303	111,491	1,056.59	132,576	123,218	1,075.80	122,966	132,828
95,000	1,013.90	270,004	1,095.01	152,319	117,685	1,115.29	139,941	130,063	1,135.57	129,799	140,205
100,000	1,067.26	284,214	1,152.64	160,335	123,879	1,173.99	147,307	136,907	1,195.33	136,629	147,585
105,000	1,120.63	298,427	1,210.28	168,354	130,073	1,232.69	154,672	143,755	1,255.11	143,463	154,964
110,000	1,173.99	312,636	1,267.91	176,370	136,266	1,291.39	162,038	150,598	1,314.87	150,293	162,343
115,000	1,227.35	326,846	1,325.54	184,386	142,460	1,350.09	169,403	157,443	1,374.63	157,123	169,723
120,000	1,280.71	341,056	1,383.17	192,403	148,653	1,408.78	176,767	164,289	1,434.40	163,955	177,101
125,000	1,334.08	355,269	1,440.81	200,421	154,848	1,467.49	184,134	171,135	1,494.17	170,787	184,482
130,000	1,387.44	369,478	1,498.44	208,438	161,040	1,526.18	191,497	177,981	1,553.93	177,618	191,860
135,000	1,440.80	383,688	1,556.06	216,452	167,236	1,584.88	198,863	184,825	1,613.70	184,450	199,238
140,000	1,494.17	397,901	1,613.70	224,470	173,431	1,643.59	206,230	191,671	1,673.47	191,282	206,619
145,000	1,547.53	412,111	1,671.33	232,487	179,624	1,702.28	213,594	198,517	1,733.23	198,112	213,999
150,000	1,600.89	426,320	1,728.96	240,503	185,817	1,760.98	220,959	205,361	1,793.00	204,944	221,376
155,000	1,654.25	440,530	1,786.59	248,519	192,011	1,819.68	228,325	212,205	1,852.76	211,774	228,756
160,000	1,707.62	454,743	1,844.23	256,539	198,205	1,878.38	235,690	219,053	1,912.53	218,606	236,137
165,000	1,760.98	468,953	1,901.86	264,554	204,399	1,937.08	243,056	225,897	1,972.30	225,438	243,515
170,000	1,814.34	483,162	1,959.49	272,570	210,592	1,995.77	250,419	232,743	2,032.06	232,269	250,893
175,000	1,867.71	497,376	2,017.13	280,589	216,787	2,054.48	257,786	239,590	2,091.84	239,103	258,273
180,000	1,921.07	511,585	2,074.76	288,605	222,980	2,113.18	265,152	246,433	2,151.60	245,933	265,652
185,000	1,974.43	525,795	2,132.38	296,619	229,176	2,171.87	272,515	253,280	2,211.36	252,763	273,032
190,000	2,027.79	540,004	2,190.01	304,636	235,368	2,230.57	279,881	260,123	2,271.12	259,593	280,411
195,000	2,081.16	554,218	2,247.65	312,654	241,564	2,289.28	287,248	266,970	2,330.90	266,427	287,791
200,000	2,134.52	568,427	2,305.28	320,671	247,756	2,347.97	294,612	273,815	2,390.66	273,257	295,170

239

AUGMENTED PAYMENT MORTGAGES

AMOUNT OF LOAN	30 YEARS		2% PMT INCREASE 301.227 PAYMENTS			4% PMT INCREASE 266.405 PAYMENTS			6% PMT INCREASE 241.851 PAYMENTS		
	MONTHLY PAYMENT	TOTAL INTRST	MONTHLY PAYMENT	TOTAL INTRST	INTRST SAVED	MONTHLY PAYMENT	TOTAL INTRST	INTRST SAVED	MONTHLY PAYMENT	TOTAL INTRST	INTRST SAVED
$ 50	0.55	148	0.56	119	29	0.57	102	46	0.58	90	58
100	1.09	292	1.11	234	58	1.13	201	91	1.16	181	111
200	2.18	585	2.22	469	116	2.27	405	180	2.31	359	226
300	3.27	877	3.34	706	171	3.40	606	271	3.47	539	338
400	4.35	1,166	4.44	937	229	4.52	804	362	4.61	715	451
500	5.44	1,458	5.55	1,172	286	5.66	1,008	450	5.77	895	563
600	6.53	1,751	6.66	1,406	345	6.79	1,209	542	6.92	1,074	677
700	7.61	2,040	7.76	1,638	402	7.91	1,407	633	8.07	1,252	788
800	8.70	2,332	8.87	1,872	460	9.05	1,611	721	9.22	1,430	902
900	9.79	2,624	9.99	2,109	515	10.18	1,812	812	10.38	1,610	1,014
1,000	10.87	2,913	11.09	2,341	572	11.30	2,010	903	11.52	1,786	1,127
2,000	21.74	5,826	22.17	4,678	1,148	22.61	4,023	1,803	23.04	3,572	2,254
3,000	32.61	8,740	33.26	7,019	1,721	33.91	6,034	2,706	34.57	5,361	3,379
4,000	43.47	11,649	44.34	9,356	2,293	45.21	8,044	3,605	46.08	7,144	4,505
5,000	54.34	14,562	55.43	11,697	2,865	56.51	10,055	4,507	57.60	8,931	5,631
6,000	65.21	17,476	66.51	14,035	3,441	67.82	12,068	5,408	69.12	10,717	6,759
7,000	76.07	20,385	77.59	16,372	4,013	79.11	14,075	6,310	80.63	12,500	7,885
8,000	86.94	23,298	88.68	18,713	4,585	90.42	16,088	7,210	92.16	14,289	9,009
9,000	97.81	26,212	99.77	21,053	5,159	101.72	18,099	8,113	103.68	16,075	10,137
10,000	108.67	29,121	110.84	23,388	5,733	113.02	20,109	9,012	115.19	17,859	11,262
11,000	119.54	32,034	121.93	25,729	6,305	124.32	22,119	9,915	126.71	19,645	12,389
12,000	130.41	34,948	133.02	28,069	6,879	135.63	24,133	10,815	138.23	21,431	13,517
13,000	141.28	37,861	144.11	30,410	7,451	146.93	26,143	11,718	149.76	23,220	14,641
14,000	152.14	40,770	155.18	32,744	8,026	158.23	28,153	12,617	161.27	25,003	15,767
15,000	163.01	43,684	166.27	35,085	8,599	169.53	30,164	13,520	172.79	26,789	16,895
16,000	173.88	46,597	177.36	37,426	9,171	180.84	32,177	14,420	184.31	28,576	18,021
17,000	184.74	49,506	188.43	39,760	9,746	192.13	34,184	15,322	195.82	30,359	19,147
18,000	195.61	52,420	199.52	42,101	10,319	203.43	36,195	16,225	207.35	32,148	20,272
19,000	206.48	55,333	210.61	44,441	10,892	214.74	38,208	17,125	218.87	33,934	21,399
20,000	217.34	58,242	221.69	46,779	11,463	226.03	40,216	18,026	230.38	35,718	22,524
21,000	228.21	61,156	232.77	49,117	12,039	237.34	42,229	18,927	241.90	37,504	23,652
22,000	239.08	64,069	243.86	51,457	12,612	248.64	44,239	19,830	253.42	39,290	24,779
23,000	249.94	66,978	254.94	53,795	13,183	259.94	46,249	20,729	264.94	41,076	25,902
24,000	260.81	69,892	266.03	56,135	13,757	271.24	48,260	21,632	276.46	42,862	27,030
25,000	271.68	72,805	277.11	58,473	14,332	282.55	50,273	22,532	287.98	44,648	28,157
26,000	282.55	75,718	288.20	60,814	14,904	293.85	52,283	23,435	299.50	46,434	29,284
27,000	293.41	78,628	299.28	63,151	15,477	305.15	54,293	24,335	311.01	48,218	30,410
28,000	304.28	81,541	310.37	65,492	16,049	316.45	56,304	25,237	322.54	50,007	31,534
29,000	315.15	84,454	321.45	67,829	16,625	327.76	58,317	26,137	334.06	51,793	32,661
30,000	326.01	87,364	332.53	70,167	17,197	339.05	60,325	27,039	345.57	53,576	33,788
32,500	353.18	94,645	360.24	76,014	18,631	367.31	65,353	29,292	374.37	58,042	36,603
35,000	380.35	101,926	387.96	81,864	20,062	395.56	70,379	31,547	403.17	62,507	39,419
40,000	434.68	116,485	443.37	93,555	22,930	452.07	80,434	36,051	460.76	71,435	45,050
45,000	489.02	131,047	498.80	105,252	25,795	508.58	90,488	40,559	518.36	80,366	50,681
50,000	543.35	145,606	554.22	116,946	28,660	565.08	100,540	45,066	575.95	89,294	56,312
55,000	597.69	160,168	609.64	128,640	31,528	621.60	110,597	49,571	633.55	98,225	61,943
60,000	652.02	174,727	665.06	140,334	34,393	678.10	120,649	54,078	691.14	107,153	67,574
65,000	706.36	189,290	720.49	152,031	37,259	734.61	130,704	58,586	748.74	116,084	73,206
70,000	760.69	203,848	775.90	163,722	40,126	791.12	140,758	63,090	806.33	125,012	78,836
75,000	815.02	218,407	831.32	175,416	42,991	847.62	150,810	67,597	863.92	133,940	84,467
80,000	869.36	232,970	886.75	187,113	45,857	904.13	160,865	72,105	921.52	142,871	90,099
85,000	923.69	247,528	942.16	198,804	48,724	960.64	170,919	76,609	979.11	151,799	95,729
90,000	978.03	262,091	997.59	210,501	51,590	1,017.15	180,974	81,117	1,036.71	160,729	101,362
95,000	1,032.36	276,650	1,053.01	222,195	54,455	1,073.65	191,026	85,624	1,094.30	169,658	106,992
100,000	1,086.70	291,212	1,108.43	233,889	57,323	1,130.17	201,083	90,129	1,151.90	178,588	112,624
105,000	1,141.03	305,771	1,163.85	245,583	60,188	1,186.67	211,135	94,636	1,209.49	187,516	118,255
110,000	1,195.37	320,333	1,219.28	257,280	63,053	1,243.18	221,189	99,144	1,267.09	196,447	123,886
115,000	1,249.70	334,892	1,274.69	268,971	65,921	1,299.69	231,244	103,648	1,324.68	205,375	129,517
120,000	1,304.04	349,454	1,330.12	280,668	68,786	1,356.20	241,298	108,156	1,382.28	214,306	135,148
125,000	1,358.37	364,013	1,385.54	292,362	71,651	1,412.70	251,350	112,663	1,439.87	223,234	140,779
130,000	1,412.71	378,576	1,440.96	304,056	74,520	1,469.22	261,408	117,168	1,497.47	232,165	146,411
135,000	1,467.04	393,134	1,496.38	315,750	77,384	1,525.72	271,459	121,675	1,555.06	241,093	152,041
140,000	1,521.38	407,697	1,551.81	327,447	80,250	1,582.24	281,517	126,180	1,612.66	250,023	157,674
145,000	1,575.71	422,256	1,607.22	339,138	83,118	1,638.74	291,569	130,687	1,670.25	258,952	163,304
150,000	1,630.04	436,814	1,662.64	350,832	85,982	1,695.24	301,620	135,194	1,727.84	267,880	168,934
155,000	1,684.38	451,377	1,718.07	362,529	88,848	1,751.76	311,678	139,699	1,785.44	276,810	174,567
160,000	1,738.71	465,936	1,773.48	374,220	91,716	1,808.26	321,730	144,206	1,843.03	285,739	180,197
165,000	1,793.05	480,498	1,828.91	385,917	94,581	1,864.77	331,784	148,714	1,900.63	294,669	185,829
170,000	1,847.38	495,057	1,884.33	397,611	97,446	1,921.28	341,839	153,218	1,958.22	303,597	191,460
175,000	1,901.72	509,619	1,939.75	409,305	100,314	1,977.79	351,893	157,726	2,015.82	312,528	197,091
180,000	1,956.05	524,178	1,995.17	420,999	103,179	2,034.29	361,945	162,233	2,073.41	321,456	202,722
185,000	2,010.39	538,740	2,050.60	432,696	106,044	2,090.81	372,002	166,738	2,131.01	330,387	208,353
190,000	2,064.72	553,299	2,106.01	444,387	108,912	2,147.31	382,054	171,245	2,188.60	339,315	213,984
195,000	2,119.06	567,862	2,161.44	456,084	111,778	2,203.82	392,109	175,753	2,246.20	348,246	219,616
200,000	2,173.39	582,420	2,216.86	467,778	114,642	2,260.33	402,163	180,257	2,303.79	357,174	225,246

AUGMENTED PAYMENT MORTGAGES 12.75%

AMOUNT OF LOAN	30 YEARS MONTHLY PAYMENT	30 YEARS TOTAL INTRST	8% PMT INCREASE 223.028 PAYMENTS MONTHLY PAYMENT	8% TOTAL INTRST	8% INTRST SAVED	10% PMT INCREASE 207.863 PAYMENTS MONTHLY PAYMENT	10% TOTAL INTRST	10% INTRST SAVED	12% PMT INCREASE 195.234 PAYMENTS MONTHLY PAYMENT	12% TOTAL INTRST	12% INTRST SAVED
$ 50	0.55	148	0.59	82	66	0.61	77	71	0.62	71	77
100	1.09	292	1.18	163	129	1.20	149	143	1.22	138	154
200	2.18	585	2.35	324	261	2.40	299	286	2.44	276	309
300	3.27	877	3.53	487	390	3.60	448	429	3.66	415	462
400	4.35	1,166	4.70	648	518	4.79	596	570	4.87	551	615
500	5.44	1,458	5.88	811	647	5.98	743	715	6.09	689	769
600	6.53	1,751	7.05	972	779	7.18	892	859	7.31	827	924
700	7.61	2,040	8.22	1,133	907	8.37	1,040	1,000	8.52	963	1,077
800	8.70	2,332	9.40	1,296	1,036	9.57	1,189	1,143	9.74	1,102	1,230
900	9.79	2,624	10.57	1,457	1,167	10.77	1,339	1,285	10.96	1,240	1,384
1,000	10.87	2,913	11.74	1,618	1,295	11.96	1,486	1,427	12.17	1,376	1,537
2,000	21.74	5,826	23.48	3,237	2,589	23.91	2,970	2,856	24.35	2,754	3,072
3,000	32.61	8,740	35.22	4,855	3,885	35.87	4,456	4,284	36.52	4,130	4,610
4,000	43.47	11,649	46.95	6,471	5,178	47.82	5,940	5,709	48.69	5,506	6,143
5,000	54.34	14,562	58.69	8,090	6,472	59.77	7,424	7,138	60.86	6,882	7,680
6,000	65.21	17,476	70.43	9,708	7,768	71.73	8,910	8,566	73.04	8,260	9,216
7,000	76.07	20,385	82.16	11,324	9,061	83.68	10,394	9,991	85.20	9,634	10,751
8,000	86.94	23,298	93.90	12,942	10,356	95.63	11,878	11,420	97.37	11,010	12,288
9,000	97.81	26,212	105.63	14,558	11,654	107.59	13,364	12,848	109.55	12,388	13,824
10,000	108.67	29,121	117.36	16,175	12,946	119.54	14,848	14,273	121.71	13,762	15,359
11,000	119.54	32,034	129.10	17,793	14,241	131.49	16,332	15,702	133.88	15,138	16,896
12,000	130.41	34,948	140.84	19,411	15,537	143.45	17,818	17,130	146.06	16,516	18,432
13,000	141.28	37,861	152.58	21,030	16,831	155.41	19,304	18,557	158.23	17,892	19,969
14,000	152.14	40,770	164.31	22,646	18,124	167.35	20,786	19,984	170.40	19,268	21,502
15,000	163.01	43,684	176.05	24,264	19,420	179.31	22,272	21,412	182.57	20,644	23,040
16,000	173.88	46,597	187.79	25,882	20,715	191.27	23,758	22,839	194.75	22,022	24,575
17,000	184.74	49,506	199.52	27,499	22,007	203.21	25,240	24,266	206.91	23,396	26,110
18,000	195.61	52,420	211.26	29,117	23,303	215.17	26,726	25,694	219.08	24,772	27,648
19,000	206.48	55,333	223.00	30,735	24,598	227.13	28,212	27,121	231.26	26,150	29,183
20,000	217.34	58,242	234.73	32,351	25,891	239.07	29,694	28,548	243.42	27,524	30,718
21,000	228.21	61,156	246.47	33,970	27,186	251.03	31,180	29,976	255.60	28,902	32,254
22,000	239.08	64,069	258.21	35,588	28,481	262.99	32,666	31,403	267.77	30,278	33,791
23,000	249.94	66,978	269.94	37,204	29,774	274.93	34,148	32,830	279.93	31,652	35,326
24,000	260.81	69,892	281.67	38,820	31,072	286.89	35,634	34,258	292.11	33,030	36,862
25,000	271.68	72,805	293.41	40,439	32,366	298.85	37,120	35,685	304.28	34,406	38,399
26,000	282.55	75,718	305.15	42,057	33,661	310.81	38,606	37,112	316.46	35,784	39,934
27,000	293.41	78,628	316.88	43,673	34,955	322.75	40,088	38,540	328.62	37,158	41,470
28,000	304.28	81,541	328.62	45,291	36,250	334.71	41,574	39,967	340.79	38,534	43,007
29,000	315.15	84,454	340.36	46,910	37,544	346.67	43,060	41,394	352.97	39,912	44,542
30,000	326.01	87,364	352.09	48,526	38,838	358.61	44,542	42,822	365.13	41,286	46,078
32,500	353.18	94,645	381.43	52,570	42,075	388.50	48,255	46,390	395.56	44,727	49,918
35,000	380.35	101,926	410.78	56,615	45,311	418.39	51,968	49,958	425.99	48,168	53,758
40,000	434.68	116,485	469.45	64,700	51,785	478.15	59,390	57,095	486.84	55,048	61,437
45,000	489.02	131,047	528.14	72,790	58,257	537.92	66,814	64,233	547.70	61,930	69,117
50,000	543.35	145,606	586.82	80,877	64,729	597.69	74,238	71,368	608.55	68,810	76,796
55,000	597.69	160,168	645.51	88,967	71,201	657.46	81,662	78,506	669.41	75,692	84,476
60,000	652.02	174,727	704.18	97,052	77,675	717.22	89,084	85,643	730.26	82,572	92,155
65,000	706.36	189,290	762.87	105,141	84,149	777.00	96,510	92,780	791.12	89,454	99,836
70,000	760.69	203,848	821.55	113,229	90,619	836.76	103,931	99,917	851.97	96,334	107,514
75,000	815.02	218,407	880.22	121,314	97,093	896.52	111,353	107,054	912.82	103,213	115,194
80,000	869.36	232,970	938.91	129,403	103,567	956.30	118,779	114,191	973.68	110,095	122,875
85,000	923.69	247,528	997.59	137,491	110,037	1,016.06	126,201	121,327	1,034.53	116,975	130,553
90,000	978.03	262,091	1,056.27	145,578	116,513	1,075.83	133,625	128,466	1,095.39	123,857	138,234
95,000	1,032.36	276,650	1,114.95	153,665	122,985	1,135.60	141,049	135,603	1,156.24	130,737	145,913
100,000	1,086.70	291,212	1,173.64	161,755	129,457	1,195.37	148,473	142,739	1,217.10	137,619	153,593
105,000	1,141.03	305,771	1,232.31	169,840	135,931	1,255.13	155,895	149,876	1,277.95	144,499	161,272
110,000	1,195.37	320,333	1,291.00	177,929	142,404	1,314.91	163,321	157,012	1,338.81	151,381	168,952
115,000	1,249.70	334,892	1,349.68	186,016	148,876	1,374.67	170,743	164,149	1,399.66	158,261	176,631
120,000	1,304.04	349,454	1,408.36	194,104	155,350	1,434.45	178,167	171,287	1,460.52	165,143	184,311
125,000	1,358.37	364,013	1,467.04	202,191	161,822	1,494.21	185,591	178,422	1,521.37	172,023	191,990
130,000	1,412.71	378,576	1,525.73	210,281	168,295	1,553.98	193,015	185,561	1,582.24	178,907	199,669
135,000	1,467.04	393,134	1,584.40	218,366	174,768	1,613.74	200,437	192,697	1,643.08	185,785	207,349
140,000	1,521.38	407,697	1,643.09	226,455	181,242	1,673.52	207,863	199,834	1,703.95	192,669	215,028
145,000	1,575.71	422,256	1,701.77	234,542	187,714	1,733.28	215,285	206,971	1,764.80	199,549	222,707
150,000	1,630.04	436,814	1,760.44	242,627	194,187	1,793.04	222,707	214,107	1,825.64	206,427	230,387
155,000	1,684.38	451,377	1,819.13	250,717	200,660	1,852.82	230,133	221,244	1,886.51	213,311	238,066
160,000	1,738.71	465,936	1,877.81	258,804	207,132	1,912.58	237,555	228,381	1,947.36	220,191	245,745
165,000	1,793.05	480,498	1,936.49	266,891	213,607	1,972.36	244,981	235,517	2,008.22	227,073	253,425
170,000	1,847.38	495,057	1,995.17	274,979	220,078	2,032.12	252,403	242,654	2,069.07	233,953	261,104
175,000	1,901.72	509,619	2,053.86	283,068	226,551	2,091.89	259,827	249,792	2,129.93	240,835	268,784
180,000	1,956.05	524,178	2,112.53	291,153	233,025	2,151.66	267,251	256,927	2,190.78	247,715	276,463
185,000	2,010.39	538,740	2,171.22	299,243	239,497	2,211.43	274,674	264,066	2,251.64	254,597	284,143
190,000	2,064.72	553,299	2,229.90	307,330	245,969	2,271.19	282,096	271,202	2,312.49	261,477	291,822
195,000	2,119.06	567,862	2,288.58	315,417	252,445	2,330.97	289,522	278,340	2,373.35	268,359	299,503
200,000	2,173.39	582,420	2,347.26	323,505	258,915	2,390.73	296,944	285,476	2,434.20	275,239	307,181

AMOUNT OF LOAN	30 YEARS		2% PMT INCREASE 299.028 PAYMENTS			4% PMT INCREASE 263.713 PAYMENTS			6% PMT INCREASE 239.038 PAYMENTS		
	MONTHLY PAYMENT	TOTAL INTRST	MONTHLY PAYMENT	TOTAL INTRST	INTRST SAVED	MONTHLY PAYMENT	TOTAL INTRST	INTRST SAVED	MONTHLY PAYMENT	TOTAL INTRST	INTRST SAVED
$ 50	0.56	152	0.57	120	32	0.58	103	49	0.59	91	61
100	1.11	300	1.13	238	62	1.15	203	97	1.18	182	118
200	2.22	599	2.26	476	123	2.31	409	190	2.35	362	237
300	3.32	895	3.39	714	181	3.45	610	285	3.52	541	354
400	4.43	1,195	4.52	952	243	4.61	816	379	4.70	723	472
500	5.54	1,494	5.65	1,190	304	5.76	1,019	475	5.87	903	591
600	6.64	1,790	6.77	1,424	366	6.91	1,222	568	7.04	1,083	707
700	7.75	2,090	7.91	1,665	425	8.06	1,426	664	8.22	1,265	825
800	8.85	2,386	9.03	1,900	486	9.20	1,626	760	9.38	1,442	944
900	9.96	2,686	10.16	2,138	548	10.36	1,832	854	10.56	1,624	1,062
1,000	11.07	2,985	11.29	2,376	609	11.51	2,035	950	11.73	1,804	1,181
2,000	22.13	5,967	22.57	4,749	1,218	23.02	4,071	1,896	23.46	3,608	2,359
3,000	33.19	8,948	33.85	7,122	1,826	34.52	6,103	2,845	35.18	5,409	3,539
4,000	44.25	11,930	45.14	9,498	2,432	46.02	8,136	3,794	46.91	7,213	4,717
5,000	55.31	14,912	56.42	11,871	3,041	57.52	10,169	4,743	58.63	9,015	5,897
6,000	66.38	17,897	67.71	14,247	3,650	69.04	12,207	5,690	70.36	10,819	7,078
7,000	77.44	20,878	78.99	16,620	4,258	80.54	14,239	6,639	82.09	12,623	8,255
8,000	88.50	23,860	90.27	18,993	4,867	92.04	16,272	7,588	93.81	14,424	9,436
9,000	99.56	26,842	101.55	21,366	5,476	103.54	18,305	8,537	105.53	16,226	10,616
10,000	110.62	29,823	112.83	23,739	6,084	115.04	20,338	9,485	117.26	18,030	11,793
11,000	121.69	32,808	124.12	26,115	6,693	126.56	22,376	10,432	128.99	19,834	12,974
12,000	132.75	35,790	135.41	28,491	7,299	138.06	24,408	11,382	140.72	21,637	14,153
13,000	143.81	38,772	146.69	30,864	7,908	149.56	26,441	12,331	152.44	23,439	15,333
14,000	154.87	41,753	157.97	33,237	8,516	161.06	28,474	13,279	164.16	25,240	16,513
15,000	165.93	44,735	169.25	35,610	9,125	172.57	30,509	14,226	175.89	27,044	17,691
16,000	177.00	47,720	180.54	37,987	9,733	184.08	32,544	15,176	187.62	28,848	18,872
17,000	188.06	50,702	191.82	40,360	10,342	195.58	34,577	16,125	199.34	30,650	20,052
18,000	199.12	53,683	203.10	42,733	10,950	207.08	36,610	17,073	211.07	32,454	21,229
19,000	210.18	56,665	214.38	45,106	11,559	218.59	38,645	18,020	222.79	34,255	22,410
20,000	221.24	59,646	225.66	47,479	12,167	230.09	40,678	18,968	234.51	36,057	23,589
21,000	232.31	62,632	236.96	49,858	12,774	241.60	42,713	19,919	246.25	37,863	24,769
22,000	243.37	65,613	248.24	52,231	13,382	253.10	44,746	20,867	257.97	39,665	25,948
23,000	254.43	68,595	259.52	54,604	13,991	264.61	46,781	21,814	269.70	41,469	27,126
24,000	265.49	71,576	270.80	56,977	14,599	276.11	48,814	22,762	281.42	43,270	28,306
25,000	276.55	74,558	282.08	59,350	15,208	287.61	50,846	23,712	293.14	45,072	29,486
26,000	287.62	77,543	293.37	61,726	15,817	299.12	52,882	24,661	304.88	46,878	30,665
27,000	298.68	80,525	304.65	64,099	16,426	310.63	54,917	25,608	316.60	48,679	31,846
28,000	309.74	83,506	315.93	66,472	17,034	322.13	56,950	26,556	328.32	50,481	33,025
29,000	320.80	86,488	327.22	68,848	17,640	333.63	58,983	27,505	340.05	52,285	34,203
30,000	331.86	89,470	338.50	71,221	18,249	345.13	61,015	28,455	351.77	54,086	35,384
32,500	359.52	96,927	366.71	77,157	19,770	373.90	66,102	30,825	381.09	58,595	38,332
35,000	387.17	104,381	394.91	83,089	21,292	402.66	71,187	33,194	410.40	63,101	41,280
40,000	442.48	119,293	451.33	94,960	24,333	460.18	81,355	37,938	469.03	72,116	47,177
45,000	497.79	134,204	507.75	106,831	27,373	517.70	91,524	42,680	527.66	81,131	53,073
50,000	553.10	149,116	564.16	118,700	30,416	575.22	101,693	47,423	586.29	90,146	58,970
55,000	608.41	164,028	620.58	130,571	33,457	632.75	111,864	52,164	644.91	99,158	64,870
60,000	663.72	178,939	676.99	142,439	36,500	690.27	122,033	56,906	703.54	108,173	70,766
65,000	719.03	193,851	733.41	154,310	39,541	747.79	132,202	61,649	762.17	117,188	76,663
70,000	774.34	208,762	789.83	166,181	42,581	805.31	142,371	66,391	820.80	126,202	82,560
75,000	829.65	223,674	846.24	178,049	45,625	862.84	152,542	71,132	879.43	135,217	88,457
80,000	884.96	238,586	902.66	189,921	48,665	920.36	162,711	75,875	938.06	144,232	94,354
85,000	940.27	253,497	959.08	201,792	51,705	977.88	172,880	80,617	996.69	153,247	100,250
90,000	995.58	268,409	1,015.49	213,660	54,749	1,035.40	183,048	85,361	1,055.31	162,259	106,150
95,000	1,050.89	283,320	1,071.91	225,531	57,789	1,092.93	193,220	90,100	1,113.94	171,274	112,046
100,000	1,106.20	298,232	1,128.32	237,399	60,833	1,150.45	203,389	94,843	1,172.57	180,289	117,943
105,000	1,161.51	313,144	1,184.74	249,270	63,874	1,207.97	213,557	99,587	1,231.20	189,304	123,840
110,000	1,216.82	328,055	1,241.16	261,142	66,913	1,265.49	223,726	104,329	1,289.83	198,318	129,737
115,000	1,272.13	342,967	1,297.57	273,010	69,957	1,323.02	233,898	109,069	1,348.46	207,333	135,634
120,000	1,327.44	357,878	1,353.99	284,881	72,997	1,380.54	244,066	113,812	1,407.09	216,348	141,530
125,000	1,382.75	372,790	1,410.41	296,752	76,038	1,438.06	254,235	118,555	1,465.72	225,363	147,427
130,000	1,438.06	387,702	1,466.82	308,620	79,082	1,495.58	264,404	123,298	1,524.34	234,375	153,327
135,000	1,493.37	402,613	1,523.24	320,491	82,122	1,553.10	274,573	128,040	1,582.97	243,390	159,223
140,000	1,548.68	417,525	1,579.65	332,360	85,165	1,610.63	284,744	132,781	1,641.60	252,405	165,120
145,000	1,603.99	432,436	1,636.07	344,231	88,205	1,668.15	294,913	137,523	1,700.23	261,420	171,016
150,000	1,659.30	447,348	1,692.49	356,102	91,246	1,725.67	305,082	142,266	1,758.86	270,434	176,914
155,000	1,714.61	462,260	1,748.90	367,970	94,290	1,783.19	315,250	147,010	1,817.49	279,449	182,811
160,000	1,769.92	477,171	1,805.32	379,841	97,330	1,840.72	325,422	151,749	1,876.12	288,464	188,707
165,000	1,825.23	492,083	1,861.73	391,709	100,374	1,898.24	335,591	156,492	1,934.74	297,476	194,607
170,000	1,880.54	506,995	1,918.15	403,581	103,413	1,955.76	345,759	161,235	1,993.37	306,491	200,503
175,000	1,935.85	521,906	1,974.57	415,452	106,454	2,013.28	355,928	165,978	2,052.00	315,506	206,400
180,000	1,991.16	536,818	2,030.98	427,320	109,498	2,070.81	366,100	170,718	2,110.63	324,521	212,297
185,000	2,046.47	551,729	2,087.40	439,191	112,538	2,128.33	376,268	175,461	2,169.26	333,536	218,193
190,000	2,101.78	566,641	2,143.82	451,062	115,579	2,185.85	386,437	180,204	2,227.89	342,550	224,091
195,000	2,157.09	581,552	2,200.23	462,930	118,622	2,243.37	396,606	184,946	2,286.52	351,565	229,987
200,000	2,212.40	596,464	2,256.65	474,802	121,662	2,300.90	406,777	189,687	2,345.14	360,578	235,886

AMOUNT OF LOAN	30 YEARS		8% PMT INCREASE 220.218 PAYMENTS			10% PMT INCREASE 205.103 PAYMENTS			12% PMT INCREASE 192.544 PAYMENTS		
	MONTHLY PAYMENT	TOTAL INTRST	MONTHLY PAYMENT	TOTAL INTRST	INTRST SAVED	MONTHLY PAYMENT	TOTAL INTRST	INTRST SAVED	MONTHLY PAYMENT	TOTAL INTRST	INTRST SAVED
$ 50	0.56	152	0.60	82	70	0.62	77	75	0.63	71	81
100	1.11	300	1.20	164	136	1.22	150	150	1.24	139	161
200	2.22	599	2.40	329	270	2.44	300	299	2.49	279	320
300	3.32	895	3.59	491	404	3.65	449	446	3.72	416	479
400	4.43	1,195	4.78	653	542	4.87	599	596	4.96	555	640
500	5.54	1,494	5.98	817	677	6.09	749	745	6.20	694	800
600	6.64	1,790	7.17	979	811	7.30	897	893	7.44	833	957
700	7.75	2,090	8.37	1,143	947	8.53	1,050	1,040	8.68	971	1,119
800	8.85	2,386	9.56	1,305	1,081	9.74	1,198	1,188	9.91	1,108	1,278
900	9.96	2,686	10.76	1,470	1,216	10.96	1,348	1,338	11.16	1,249	1,437
1,000	11.07	2,985	11.96	1,634	1,351	12.18	1,498	1,487	12.40	1,388	1,597
2,000	22.13	5,967	23.90	3,263	2,704	24.34	2,992	2,975	24.79	2,773	3,194
3,000	33.19	8,948	35.85	4,895	4,053	36.51	4,488	4,460	37.17	4,157	4,791
4,000	44.25	11,930	47.79	6,524	5,406	48.68	5,984	5,946	49.56	5,542	6,388
5,000	55.31	14,912	59.73	8,154	6,758	60.84	7,478	7,434	61.95	6,928	7,984
6,000	66.38	17,897	71.69	9,787	8,110	73.02	8,977	8,920	74.35	8,316	9,581
7,000	77.44	20,878	83.64	11,419	9,459	85.18	10,471	10,407	86.73	9,699	11,179
8,000	88.50	23,860	95.58	13,048	10,812	97.35	11,967	11,893	99.12	11,085	12,775
9,000	99.56	26,842	107.52	14,678	12,164	109.52	13,463	13,379	111.51	12,471	14,371
10,000	110.62	29,823	119.47	16,309	13,514	121.68	14,957	14,866	123.89	13,854	15,969
11,000	121.69	32,808	131.43	17,943	14,865	133.86	16,455	16,353	136.29	15,242	17,566
12,000	132.75	35,790	143.37	19,573	16,217	146.03	17,951	17,839	148.68	16,627	19,163
13,000	143.81	38,772	155.31	21,202	17,570	158.19	19,445	19,327	161.07	18,013	20,759
14,000	154.87	41,753	167.26	22,834	18,919	170.36	20,941	20,812	173.45	19,397	22,356
15,000	165.93	44,735	179.20	24,463	20,272	182.52	22,435	22,300	185.84	20,782	23,953
16,000	177.00	47,720	191.16	26,097	21,623	194.70	23,934	23,786	198.24	22,170	25,550
17,000	188.06	50,702	203.10	27,726	22,976	206.87	25,430	25,272	210.63	23,556	27,146
18,000	199.12	53,683	215.05	29,358	24,325	219.03	26,924	26,759	223.01	24,939	28,744
19,000	210.18	56,665	226.99	30,987	25,678	231.20	28,420	28,245	235.40	26,325	30,340
20,000	221.24	59,646	238.94	32,619	27,027	243.36	29,914	29,732	247.79	27,710	31,936
21,000	232.31	62,632	250.89	34,250	28,382	255.54	31,412	31,220	260.19	29,098	33,534
22,000	243.37	65,613	262.84	35,882	29,731	267.71	32,908	32,705	272.57	30,482	35,131
23,000	254.43	68,595	274.78	37,512	31,083	279.87	34,402	34,193	284.96	31,867	36,728
24,000	265.49	71,576	286.73	39,143	32,433	292.04	35,898	35,678	297.35	33,253	38,323
25,000	276.55	74,558	298.67	40,773	33,785	304.21	37,394	37,164	309.74	34,639	39,919
26,000	287.62	77,543	310.63	42,406	35,137	316.38	38,890	38,653	322.13	36,024	41,519
27,000	298.68	80,525	322.57	44,036	36,489	328.55	40,387	40,138	334.52	37,410	43,115
28,000	309.74	83,506	334.52	45,667	37,839	340.71	41,881	41,625	346.91	38,795	44,711
29,000	320.80	86,488	346.46	47,297	39,191	352.88	43,377	43,111	359.30	40,181	46,307
30,000	331.86	89,470	358.41	48,928	40,542	365.05	44,873	44,597	371.68	41,565	47,905
32,500	359.52	96,927	388.28	53,006	43,921	395.47	48,612	48,315	402.66	45,030	51,897
35,000	387.17	104,381	418.14	57,082	47,299	425.89	52,351	52,030	433.64	48,493	55,888
40,000	442.48	119,293	477.88	65,238	54,055	486.73	59,830	59,463	495.58	55,421	63,872
45,000	497.79	134,204	537.61	73,391	60,813	547.57	67,308	66,896	557.52	62,347	71,857
50,000	553.10	149,116	597.35	81,547	67,569	608.41	74,787	74,329	619.47	69,275	79,841
55,000	608.41	164,028	657.08	89,701	74,327	669.25	82,265	81,763	681.42	76,203	87,825
60,000	663.72	178,939	716.82	97,857	81,082	730.09	89,744	89,195	743.37	83,131	95,808
65,000	719.03	193,851	776.55	106,010	87,841	790.93	97,222	96,629	805.31	90,058	103,793
70,000	774.34	208,762	836.29	114,166	94,596	851.77	104,701	104,061	867.26	96,986	111,776
75,000	829.65	223,674	896.02	122,320	101,354	912.62	112,181	111,493	929.21	103,914	119,760
80,000	884.96	238,586	955.76	130,476	108,110	973.46	119,660	118,926	991.16	110,842	127,744
85,000	940.27	253,497	1,015.49	138,629	114,868	1,034.30	127,138	126,359	1,053.10	117,768	135,729
90,000	995.58	268,409	1,075.23	146,785	121,624	1,095.14	134,616	133,793	1,115.05	124,696	143,713
95,000	1,050.89	283,320	1,134.96	154,939	128,381	1,155.98	142,095	141,225	1,177.00	131,624	151,696
100,000	1,106.20	298,232	1,194.70	163,094	135,138	1,216.82	149,573	148,659	1,238.94	138,550	159,682
105,000	1,161.51	313,144	1,254.43	171,248	141,896	1,277.66	157,052	156,092	1,300.89	145,479	167,665
110,000	1,216.82	328,055	1,314.17	179,404	148,651	1,338.50	164,530	163,525	1,362.84	152,407	175,648
115,000	1,272.13	342,967	1,373.90	187,558	155,409	1,399.34	172,009	170,958	1,424.79	159,335	183,632
120,000	1,327.44	357,878	1,433.64	195,713	162,165	1,460.18	179,487	178,391	1,486.73	166,261	191,617
125,000	1,382.75	372,790	1,493.37	203,867	168,923	1,521.03	186,968	185,822	1,548.68	173,189	199,601
130,000	1,438.06	387,702	1,553.10	212,021	175,681	1,581.87	194,446	193,256	1,610.63	180,117	207,585
135,000	1,493.37	402,613	1,612.84	220,176	182,437	1,642.71	201,925	200,688	1,672.57	187,043	215,570
140,000	1,548.68	417,525	1,672.57	228,330	189,195	1,703.55	209,403	208,122	1,734.52	193,971	223,554
145,000	1,603.99	432,436	1,732.31	236,486	195,950	1,764.39	216,882	215,554	1,796.47	200,900	231,536
150,000	1,659.30	447,348	1,792.04	244,639	202,709	1,825.23	224,360	222,988	1,858.42	207,828	239,520
155,000	1,714.61	462,260	1,851.78	252,795	209,465	1,886.07	231,839	230,421	1,920.36	214,754	247,506
160,000	1,769.92	477,171	1,911.51	260,949	216,221	1,946.91	239,317	237,854	1,982.31	221,682	255,489
165,000	1,825.23	492,083	1,971.25	269,105	222,978	2,007.75	246,796	245,287	2,044.26	228,610	263,473
170,000	1,880.54	506,994	2,030.98	277,258	229,736	2,068.59	254,274	252,720	2,106.20	235,536	271,458
175,000	1,935.85	521,906	2,090.72	285,414	236,492	2,129.44	261,755	260,151	2,168.15	242,464	279,442
180,000	1,991.16	536,818	2,150.45	293,568	243,250	2,190.28	269,233	267,585	2,230.10	249,392	287,426
185,000	2,046.47	551,729	2,210.19	301,724	250,005	2,251.12	276,711	275,018	2,292.05	256,320	295,409
190,000	2,101.78	566,641	2,269.92	309,877	256,764	2,311.96	284,190	282,451	2,353.99	263,247	303,394
195,000	2,157.09	581,552	2,329.66	318,033	263,519	2,372.80	291,668	289,884	2,415.94	270,175	311,377
200,000	2,212.40	596,464	2,389.39	326,187	270,277	2,433.64	299,147	297,317	2,477.89	277,103	319,361

AUGMENTED PAYMENT MORTGAGES

AMOUNT OF LOAN	30 YEARS		2% PMT INCREASE 296.788 PAYMENTS			4% PMT INCREASE 261.009 PAYMENTS			6% PMT INCREASE 236.236 PAYMENTS		
	MONTHLY PAYMENT	TOTAL INTRST	MONTHLY PAYMENT	TOTAL INTRST	INTRST SAVED	MONTHLY PAYMENT	TOTAL INTRST	INTRST SAVED	MONTHLY PAYMENT	TOTAL INTRST	INTRST SAVED
$ 50	0.57	155	0.58	122	33	0.59	104	51	0.60	92	63
100	1.13	307	1.15	241	66	1.18	208	99	1.20	183	124
200	2.26	614	2.31	486	128	2.35	413	201	2.40	367	247
300	3.38	917	3.45	724	193	3.52	619	298	3.58	546	371
400	4.51	1,224	4.60	965	259	4.69	824	400	4.78	729	495
500	5.63	1,527	5.74	1,204	323	5.86	1,030	497	5.97	910	617
600	6.76	1,834	6.90	1,448	386	7.03	1,235	599	7.17	1,094	740
700	7.89	2,140	8.05	1,689	451	8.21	1,443	697	8.36	1,275	865
800	9.01	2,444	9.19	1,927	517	9.37	1,646	798	9.55	1,456	988
900	10.14	2,750	10.34	2,169	581	10.55	1,854	896	10.75	1,640	1,110
1,000	11.26	3,054	11.49	2,410	644	11.71	2,056	998	11.94	1,821	1,233
2,000	22.52	6,107	22.97	4,817	1,290	23.42	4,113	1,994	23.87	3,639	2,468
3,000	33.78	9,161	34.46	7,227	1,934	35.13	6,169	2,992	35.81	5,460	3,701
4,000	45.04	12,214	45.94	9,634	2,580	46.84	8,226	3,988	47.74	7,278	4,936
5,000	56.29	15,264	57.42	12,042	3,222	58.54	10,279	4,985	59.67	9,096	6,168
6,000	67.55	18,318	68.90	14,449	3,869	70.25	12,336	5,982	71.60	10,914	7,404
7,000	78.81	21,372	80.39	16,859	4,513	81.96	14,392	6,980	83.54	12,735	8,637
8,000	90.07	24,425	91.87	19,266	5,159	93.67	16,449	7,976	95.47	14,553	9,872
9,000	101.32	27,475	103.35	21,673	5,802	105.37	18,503	8,972	107.40	16,372	11,103
10,000	112.58	30,529	114.83	24,080	6,449	117.08	20,559	9,970	119.33	18,190	12,339
11,000	123.84	33,582	126.32	26,490	7,092	128.79	22,615	10,967	131.27	20,011	13,571
12,000	135.10	36,636	137.80	28,897	7,739	140.50	24,672	11,964	143.21	21,831	14,805
13,000	146.36	39,690	149.29	31,307	8,383	152.21	26,728	12,962	155.14	23,650	16,040
14,000	157.61	42,740	160.76	33,712	9,028	163.91	28,782	13,958	167.07	25,468	17,272
15,000	168.87	45,793	172.25	36,122	9,671	175.62	30,838	14,955	179.00	27,286	18,507
16,000	180.13	48,847	183.73	38,529	10,318	187.34	32,897	15,950	190.94	29,107	19,740
17,000	191.39	51,900	195.22	40,939	10,961	199.05	34,954	16,946	202.87	30,925	20,975
18,000	202.64	54,950	206.69	43,343	11,607	210.75	37,008	17,942	214.80	32,743	22,207
19,000	213.90	58,004	218.18	45,753	12,251	222.46	39,064	18,940	226.73	34,562	23,442
20,000	225.16	61,058	229.66	48,160	12,898	234.17	41,120	19,938	238.67	36,382	24,676
21,000	236.42	64,111	241.15	50,570	13,541	245.88	43,177	20,934	250.61	38,203	25,908
22,000	247.68	67,165	252.63	52,978	14,187	257.59	45,233	21,932	262.54	40,021	27,144
23,000	258.93	70,215	264.11	55,385	14,830	269.29	47,287	22,928	274.47	41,840	28,375
24,000	270.19	73,268	275.59	57,792	15,476	281.00	49,344	23,924	286.40	43,658	29,610
25,000	281.45	76,322	287.08	60,202	16,120	292.71	51,400	24,922	298.34	45,479	30,843
26,000	292.71	79,376	298.56	62,609	16,767	304.42	53,456	25,920	310.27	47,297	32,079
27,000	303.96	82,426	310.04	65,016	17,410	316.12	55,510	26,916	322.20	49,115	33,311
28,000	315.22	85,479	321.52	67,423	18,056	327.83	57,567	27,912	334.13	50,934	34,545
29,000	326.48	88,533	333.01	69,833	18,700	339.54	59,623	28,910	346.07	52,754	35,779
30,000	337.74	91,586	344.49	72,240	19,346	351.25	61,679	29,907	358.00	54,572	37,014
32,500	365.88	99,217	373.20	78,261	20,956	380.52	66,819	32,398	387.83	59,119	40,098
35,000	394.03	106,851	401.91	84,282	22,569	409.79	71,959	34,892	417.67	63,669	43,182
40,000	450.31	122,112	459.32	96,321	25,791	468.32	82,236	39,876	477.33	72,763	49,349
45,000	506.60	137,376	516.73	108,393	29,017	526.86	92,515	44,861	537.00	81,859	55,517
50,000	562.89	152,640	574.15	120,401	32,239	585.41	102,797	49,843	596.66	90,953	61,687
55,000	619.18	167,905	631.56	132,439	35,466	643.95	113,077	54,828	656.33	100,049	67,856
60,000	675.47	183,169	688.98	144,481	38,688	702.49	123,356	59,813	716.00	109,145	74,024
65,000	731.76	198,434	746.40	156,523	41,911	761.03	133,636	64,798	775.67	118,241	80,193
70,000	788.05	213,698	803.81	168,561	45,137	819.57	143,915	69,783	835.33	127,335	86,363
75,000	844.34	228,962	861.23	180,603	48,359	878.11	154,195	74,767	895.00	136,431	92,531
80,000	900.62	244,223	918.63	192,638	51,585	936.64	164,471	79,752	954.66	145,525	98,698
85,000	956.91	259,488	976.05	204,680	54,808	995.19	174,754	84,734	1,014.32	154,619	104,869
90,000	1,013.20	274,752	1,033.46	216,719	58,033	1,053.73	185,033	89,719	1,073.99	163,715	111,037
95,000	1,069.49	290,016	1,090.88	228,760	61,256	1,112.27	195,312	94,704	1,133.66	172,811	117,205
100,000	1,125.78	305,281	1,148.30	240,802	64,479	1,170.81	205,592	99,689	1,193.33	181,908	123,373
105,000	1,182.07	320,545	1,205.71	252,840	67,705	1,229.35	215,871	104,674	1,252.99	191,001	129,544
110,000	1,238.36	335,810	1,263.13	264,882	70,928	1,287.89	226,151	109,659	1,312.66	200,098	135,712
115,000	1,294.64	351,070	1,320.53	276,917	74,153	1,346.43	236,430	114,640	1,372.32	209,191	141,879
120,000	1,350.93	366,335	1,377.95	288,959	77,376	1,404.97	246,710	119,625	1,431.99	218,288	148,047
125,000	1,407.22	381,599	1,435.36	300,998	80,601	1,463.51	256,989	124,610	1,491.65	227,381	154,218
130,000	1,463.51	396,864	1,492.78	313,039	83,825	1,522.05	267,269	129,595	1,551.32	236,478	160,386
135,000	1,519.80	412,128	1,550.20	325,081	87,047	1,580.59	277,548	134,580	1,610.99	245,574	166,554
140,000	1,576.09	427,392	1,607.61	337,119	90,273	1,639.13	287,828	139,564	1,670.66	254,670	172,722
145,000	1,632.38	442,657	1,665.03	349,161	93,496	1,697.68	298,110	144,547	1,730.32	263,764	178,893
150,000	1,688.67	457,921	1,722.44	361,200	96,721	1,756.22	308,389	149,532	1,789.99	272,860	185,061
155,000	1,744.95	473,182	1,779.85	373,238	99,944	1,814.75	318,666	154,516	1,849.65	281,954	191,228
160,000	1,801.24	488,446	1,837.26	385,277	103,169	1,873.29	328,946	159,500	1,909.31	291,048	197,398
165,000	1,857.53	503,711	1,894.68	397,318	106,393	1,931.83	339,225	164,486	1,968.98	300,144	203,567
170,000	1,913.82	518,975	1,952.10	409,360	109,615	1,990.37	349,504	169,471	2,028.65	309,240	209,735
175,000	1,970.11	534,240	2,009.51	421,398	112,842	2,048.91	359,784	174,456	2,088.32	318,336	215,904
180,000	2,026.40	549,504	2,066.93	433,440	116,064	2,107.46	370,066	179,438	2,147.98	327,430	222,074
185,000	2,082.69	564,768	2,124.34	445,479	119,289	2,166.00	380,345	184,423	2,207.65	336,526	228,242
190,000	2,138.97	580,029	2,181.75	457,517	122,512	2,224.53	390,622	189,407	2,267.31	345,620	234,409
195,000	2,195.26	595,294	2,239.17	469,559	125,735	2,283.07	400,902	194,392	2,326.98	354,716	240,578
200,000	2,251.55	610,558	2,296.58	481,597	128,961	2,341.61	411,181	199,377	2,386.64	363,810	246,748

AUGMENTED PAYMENT MORTGAGES 13.25%

AMOUNT OF LOAN	30 YEARS		8% PMT INCREASE 217.433 PAYMENTS			10% PMT INCREASE 202.377 PAYMENTS			12% PMT INCREASE 189.892 PAYMENTS		
	MONTHLY PAYMENT	TOTAL INTRST	MONTHLY PAYMENT	TOTAL INTRST	INTRST SAVED	MONTHLY PAYMENT	TOTAL INTRST	INTRST SAVED	MONTHLY PAYMENT	TOTAL INTRST	INTRST SAVED
$ 50	0.57	155	0.62	85	70	0.63	77	78	0.64	72	83
100	1.13	307	1.22	165	142	1.24	151	156	1.27	141	166
200	2.26	614	2.44	331	283	2.49	304	310	2.53	280	334
300	3.38	917	3.65	494	423	3.72	453	464	3.79	420	497
400	4.51	1,224	4.87	659	565	4.96	604	620	5.05	559	665
500	5.63	1,527	6.08	822	705	6.19	753	774	6.31	698	829
600	6.76	1,834	7.30	987	847	7.44	906	928	7.57	837	997
700	7.89	2,140	8.52	1,153	987	8.68	1,057	1,083	8.84	979	1,161
800	9.01	2,444	9.73	1,316	1,128	9.91	1,206	1,238	10.09	1,116	1,328
900	10.14	2,750	10.95	1,481	1,269	11.15	1,357	1,393	11.36	1,257	1,493
1,000	11.26	3,054	12.16	1,644	1,410	12.39	1,507	1,547	12.61	1,395	1,659
2,000	22.52	6,107	24.32	3,288	2,819	24.77	3,013	3,094	25.22	2,789	3,318
3,000	33.78	9,161	36.48	4,932	4,229	37.16	4,520	4,641	37.83	4,184	4,977
4,000	45.04	12,214	48.64	6,576	5,638	49.54	6,026	6,188	50.44	5,578	6,636
5,000	56.29	15,264	60.79	8,218	7,046	61.92	7,531	7,733	63.04	6,971	8,293
6,000	67.55	18,318	72.95	9,862	8,456	74.31	9,039	9,279	75.66	8,367	9,951
7,000	78.81	21,372	85.11	11,506	9,866	86.69	10,544	10,828	88.27	9,762	11,610
8,000	90.07	24,425	97.28	13,152	11,273	99.08	12,052	12,373	100.88	11,156	13,269
9,000	101.32	27,475	109.43	14,794	12,681	111.45	13,555	13,920	113.48	12,549	14,926
10,000	112.58	30,529	121.59	16,438	14,091	123.84	15,062	15,467	126.09	13,943	16,586
11,000	123.84	33,582	133.75	18,082	15,500	136.22	16,568	17,014	138.70	15,338	18,244
12,000	135.10	36,636	145.91	19,728	16,910	148.61	18,075	18,561	151.31	16,733	19,903
13,000	146.36	39,690	158.07	21,370	18,320	161.00	19,583	20,107	163.92	18,127	21,563
14,000	157.61	42,740	170.22	23,011	19,729	173.37	21,086	21,654	176.52	19,520	23,220
15,000	168.87	45,793	182.38	24,655	21,138	185.76	22,594	23,199	189.13	20,914	24,879
16,000	180.13	48,847	194.54	26,299	22,548	198.14	24,099	24,748	201.75	22,311	26,536
17,000	191.39	51,900	206.70	27,943	23,957	210.53	25,606	26,294	214.36	23,705	28,195
18,000	202.64	54,950	218.85	29,585	25,365	222.90	27,110	27,840	226.96	25,098	29,852
19,000	213.90	58,004	231.01	31,229	26,775	235.29	28,617	29,387	239.57	26,492	31,512
20,000	225.16	61,058	243.17	32,873	28,185	247.68	30,125	30,933	252.18	27,887	33,171
21,000	236.42	64,111	255.33	34,517	29,594	260.06	31,630	32,481	264.79	29,282	34,829
22,000	247.68	67,165	267.49	36,161	31,004	272.45	33,138	34,027	277.40	30,676	36,489
23,000	258.93	70,215	279.64	37,803	32,412	284.82	34,641	35,574	290.00	32,069	38,146
24,000	270.19	73,268	291.81	39,449	33,819	297.21	36,148	37,120	302.61	33,463	39,805
25,000	281.45	76,322	303.97	41,093	35,229	309.60	37,656	38,666	315.22	34,858	41,464
26,000	292.71	79,376	316.13	42,737	36,639	321.98	39,161	40,215	327.84	36,254	43,122
27,000	303.96	82,426	328.28	44,379	38,047	334.36	40,667	41,759	340.44	37,647	44,779
28,000	315.22	85,479	340.44	46,023	39,456	346.74	42,172	43,307	353.05	39,041	46,438
29,000	326.48	88,533	352.60	47,667	40,866	359.13	43,680	44,853	365.66	40,436	48,097
30,000	337.74	91,586	364.76	49,311	42,275	371.51	45,185	46,401	378.27	41,830	49,756
32,500	365.88	99,217	395.15	53,419	45,798	402.47	48,951	50,266	409.79	45,316	53,901
35,000	394.03	106,851	425.55	57,529	49,322	433.43	52,716	54,135	441.31	48,801	58,050
40,000	450.31	122,112	486.33	65,744	56,368	495.34	60,245	61,867	504.35	55,772	66,340
45,000	506.60	137,376	547.13	73,964	63,412	557.26	67,777	69,599	567.39	62,743	74,633
50,000	562.89	152,640	607.92	82,182	70,458	619.18	75,308	77,332	630.44	69,716	82,924
55,000	619.18	167,905	668.71	90,400	77,505	681.10	82,839	85,066	693.48	76,686	91,219
60,000	675.47	183,169	729.51	98,620	84,549	743.02	90,370	92,799	756.53	83,659	99,510
65,000	731.76	198,434	790.30	106,837	91,597	804.94	97,901	100,533	819.57	90,630	107,804
70,000	788.05	213,698	851.09	115,055	98,643	866.86	105,433	108,265	882.62	97,602	116,096
75,000	844.34	228,962	911.89	123,275	105,687	928.77	112,962	116,000	945.66	104,573	124,389
80,000	900.62	244,223	972.67	131,491	112,732	990.68	120,491	123,732	1,008.69	111,542	132,681
85,000	956.91	259,488	1,033.46	139,708	119,780	1,052.60	128,022	131,466	1,071.74	118,515	140,973
90,000	1,013.20	274,752	1,094.26	147,928	126,824	1,114.52	135,553	139,199	1,134.78	125,486	149,266
95,000	1,069.49	290,016	1,155.05	156,146	133,870	1,176.44	143,084	146,932	1,197.83	132,458	157,558
100,000	1,125.78	305,281	1,215.84	164,364	140,917	1,238.36	150,616	154,665	1,260.87	139,429	165,852
105,000	1,182.07	320,545	1,276.64	172,584	147,961	1,300.28	158,147	162,398	1,323.92	146,402	174,143
110,000	1,238.36	335,810	1,337.43	180,801	155,009	1,362.20	165,678	170,132	1,386.96	153,373	182,437
115,000	1,294.64	351,070	1,398.21	189,017	162,053	1,424.10	173,205	177,865	1,450.00	160,343	190,727
120,000	1,350.93	366,335	1,459.00	197,235	169,100	1,486.02	180,736	185,599	1,513.04	167,314	199,021
125,000	1,407.22	381,599	1,519.80	205,455	176,144	1,547.94	188,267	193,332	1,576.09	174,287	207,312
130,000	1,463.51	396,864	1,580.59	213,672	183,192	1,609.86	195,799	201,065	1,639.13	181,258	215,606
135,000	1,519.80	412,128	1,641.38	221,890	190,238	1,671.78	203,330	208,798	1,702.18	188,230	223,898
140,000	1,576.09	427,392	1,702.18	230,110	197,282	1,733.70	210,861	216,531	1,765.22	195,201	232,191
145,000	1,632.38	442,657	1,762.97	238,328	204,329	1,795.62	218,392	224,265	1,828.27	202,174	240,483
150,000	1,688.67	457,921	1,823.76	246,546	211,375	1,857.54	225,923	231,998	1,891.31	209,145	248,776
155,000	1,744.95	473,182	1,884.55	254,763	218,419	1,919.45	233,453	239,729	1,954.34	216,114	257,068
160,000	1,801.24	488,446	1,945.34	262,981	225,465	1,981.36	240,982	247,464	2,017.39	223,086	265,360
165,000	1,857.53	503,711	2,006.13	271,199	232,512	2,043.28	248,513	255,198	2,080.43	230,057	273,654
170,000	1,913.82	518,975	2,066.93	279,419	239,556	2,105.20	256,044	262,931	2,143.48	237,030	281,945
175,000	1,970.11	534,240	2,127.72	287,637	246,603	2,167.12	263,575	270,665	2,206.52	244,000	290,240
180,000	2,026.40	549,504	2,188.51	295,854	253,650	2,229.04	271,106	278,398	2,269.57	250,973	298,531
185,000	2,082.69	564,768	2,249.31	304,074	260,694	2,290.96	278,638	286,130	2,332.61	257,944	306,824
190,000	2,138.97	580,029	2,310.09	312,290	267,739	2,352.87	286,167	293,862	2,395.65	264,915	315,114
195,000	2,195.26	595,294	2,370.88	320,508	274,786	2,414.79	293,698	301,596	2,458.69	271,886	323,408
200,000	2,251.55	610,558	2,431.67	328,725	281,833	2,476.71	301,229	309,329	2,521.74	278,858	331,700

13.50% AUGMENTED PAYMENT MORTGAGES

AMOUNT OF LOAN	30 YEARS MONTHLY PAYMENT	30 YEARS TOTAL INTRST	2% PMT INCREASE 294.508 PAYMENTS MONTHLY PAYMENT	TOTAL INTRST	INTRST SAVED	4% PMT INCREASE 258.299 PAYMENTS MONTHLY PAYMENT	TOTAL INTRST	INTRST SAVED	6% PMT INCREASE 233.448 PAYMENTS MONTHLY PAYMENT	TOTAL INTRST	INTRST SAVED
$ 50	0.58	159	0.59	124	35	0.60	105	54	0.61	92	67
100	1.15	314	1.17	245	69	1.20	210	104	1.22	185	129
200	2.30	628	2.35	492	136	2.39	417	211	2.44	370	258
300	3.44	938	3.51	734	204	3.58	625	313	3.65	552	386
400	4.59	1,252	4.68	978	274	4.77	832	420	4.87	737	515
500	5.73	1,563	5.84	1,220	343	5.96	1,039	524	6.07	917	646
600	6.88	1,877	7.02	1,467	410	7.16	1,249	628	7.29	1,102	775
700	8.02	2,187	8.18	1,709	478	8.34	1,454	733	8.50	1,284	903
800	9.17	2,501	9.35	1,954	547	9.54	1,664	837	9.72	1,469	1,032
900	10.31	2,812	10.52	2,198	614	10.72	1,869	943	10.93	1,652	1,160
1,000	11.46	3,126	11.69	2,443	683	11.92	2,079	1,047	12.15	1,836	1,290
2,000	22.91	6,248	23.37	4,883	1,365	23.83	4,155	2,093	24.28	3,668	2,580
3,000	34.37	9,373	35.06	7,325	2,048	35.74	6,232	3,141	36.43	5,505	3,868
4,000	45.82	12,495	46.74	9,765	2,730	47.65	8,308	4,187	48.57	7,339	5,156
5,000	57.28	15,621	58.43	12,208	3,413	59.57	10,387	5,234	60.72	9,175	6,446
6,000	68.73	18,743	70.10	14,645	4,098	71.48	12,463	6,280	72.85	11,007	7,736
7,000	80.18	21,865	81.78	17,085	4,780	83.39	14,540	7,325	84.99	12,841	9,024
8,000	91.64	24,990	93.47	19,528	5,462	95.31	16,618	8,372	97.14	14,677	10,313
9,000	103.09	28,112	105.15	21,968	6,144	107.21	18,692	9,420	109.28	16,511	11,601
10,000	114.55	31,238	116.84	24,410	6,828	119.13	20,771	10,467	121.42	18,345	12,893
11,000	126.00	34,360	128.52	26,850	7,510	131.04	22,848	11,512	133.56	20,179	14,181
12,000	137.45	37,482	140.20	29,290	8,192	142.95	24,924	12,558	145.70	22,013	15,469
13,000	148.91	40,608	151.89	31,733	8,875	154.87	27,003	13,605	157.84	23,847	16,761
14,000	160.36	43,730	163.57	34,173	9,557	166.77	29,077	14,653	169.98	25,681	18,049
15,000	171.82	46,855	175.26	36,615	10,240	178.69	31,155	15,700	182.13	27,518	19,337
16,000	183.27	49,977	186.94	39,055	10,922	190.60	33,232	16,745	194.27	29,352	20,625
17,000	194.73	53,103	198.62	41,495	11,608	202.52	35,311	17,792	206.41	31,186	21,917
18,000	206.18	56,225	210.30	43,935	12,290	214.43	37,387	18,838	218.55	33,020	23,205
19,000	217.63	59,347	221.98	46,375	12,972	226.34	39,463	19,884	230.69	34,854	24,493
20,000	229.09	62,472	233.67	48,818	13,654	238.25	41,540	20,932	242.84	36,691	25,781
21,000	240.54	65,594	245.35	51,258	14,336	250.16	43,616	21,978	254.97	38,522	27,072
22,000	252.00	68,720	257.04	53,700	15,020	262.08	45,695	23,025	267.12	40,359	28,361
23,000	263.45	71,842	268.72	56,140	15,702	273.99	47,771	24,071	279.26	42,193	29,649
24,000	274.90	74,964	280.40	58,580	16,384	285.90	49,848	25,116	291.39	44,024	30,940
25,000	286.36	78,090	292.09	61,023	17,067	297.81	51,924	26,166	303.54	45,861	32,229
26,000	297.81	81,212	303.77	63,463	17,749	309.72	54,000	27,212	315.68	47,695	33,517
27,000	309.27	84,337	315.46	65,905	18,432	321.64	56,079	28,258	327.83	49,531	34,806
28,000	320.72	87,459	327.13	68,342	19,117	333.55	58,156	29,303	339.96	51,363	36,096
29,000	332.17	90,581	338.81	70,782	19,799	345.46	60,232	30,349	352.10	53,197	37,384
30,000	343.63	93,707	350.50	73,225	20,482	357.38	62,311	31,396	364.25	55,033	38,674
32,500	372.26	101,514	379.71	79,328	22,186	387.15	67,500	34,014	394.60	59,619	41,895
35,000	400.90	109,324	408.92	85,430	23,894	416.94	72,695	36,629	424.95	64,204	45,120
40,000	458.17	124,941	467.33	97,632	27,309	476.50	83,079	41,862	485.66	73,376	51,565
45,000	515.44	140,558	525.75	109,838	30,720	536.06	93,464	47,094	546.37	82,549	58,009
50,000	572.71	156,176	584.16	122,040	34,136	595.62	103,848	52,328	607.07	91,719	64,457
55,000	629.98	171,793	642.58	134,245	37,548	655.18	114,232	57,561	667.78	100,892	70,901
60,000	687.25	187,410	701.00	146,450	40,960	714.74	124,617	62,793	728.49	110,065	77,345
65,000	744.52	203,027	759.41	158,652	44,375	774.30	135,001	68,026	789.19	119,235	83,792
70,000	801.79	218,644	817.83	170,857	47,787	833.86	145,385	73,259	849.90	128,407	90,237
75,000	859.06	234,262	876.24	183,060	51,202	893.42	155,769	78,493	910.60	137,578	96,684
80,000	916.33	249,879	934.66	195,265	54,614	952.98	166,154	83,725	971.31	146,750	103,129
85,000	973.61	265,500	993.08	207,470	58,030	1,012.55	176,541	88,959	1,032.03	155,925	109,575
90,000	1,030.88	281,117	1,051.50	219,675	61,442	1,072.12	186,928	94,189	1,092.73	165,096	116,021
95,000	1,088.15	296,734	1,109.91	231,877	64,857	1,131.68	197,312	99,422	1,153.44	174,268	122,466
100,000	1,145.42	312,351	1,168.33	244,083	68,268	1,191.24	207,696	104,655	1,214.15	183,441	128,910
105,000	1,202.69	327,968	1,226.74	256,285	71,683	1,250.80	218,080	109,888	1,274.85	192,611	135,357
110,000	1,259.96	343,586	1,285.16	268,490	75,096	1,310.36	228,465	115,121	1,335.56	201,784	141,802
115,000	1,317.23	359,203	1,343.57	280,692	78,511	1,369.92	238,849	120,354	1,396.26	210,954	148,249
120,000	1,374.50	374,820	1,401.99	292,897	81,923	1,429.48	249,233	125,587	1,456.97	220,127	154,693
125,000	1,431.77	390,437	1,460.41	305,102	85,335	1,489.04	259,618	130,819	1,517.68	229,299	161,138
130,000	1,489.04	406,054	1,518.82	317,305	88,749	1,548.60	270,002	136,052	1,578.38	238,470	167,584
135,000	1,546.31	421,672	1,577.24	329,510	92,162	1,608.16	280,386	141,286	1,639.09	247,642	174,030
140,000	1,603.58	437,289	1,635.65	341,712	95,577	1,667.72	290,770	146,519	1,699.79	256,813	180,476
145,000	1,660.85	452,906	1,694.07	353,917	98,989	1,727.28	301,155	151,751	1,760.50	265,985	186,921
150,000	1,718.12	468,523	1,752.48	366,119	102,404	1,786.84	311,539	156,984	1,821.21	275,158	193,365
155,000	1,775.39	484,140	1,810.90	378,325	105,815	1,846.41	321,926	162,214	1,881.91	284,328	199,812
160,000	1,832.66	499,758	1,869.31	390,527	109,231	1,905.97	332,310	167,448	1,942.62	293,501	206,257
165,000	1,889.94	515,378	1,927.74	402,735	112,643	1,965.54	342,697	172,681	2,003.34	302,676	212,702
170,000	1,947.21	530,996	1,986.15	414,937	116,059	2,025.10	353,081	177,915	2,064.04	311,846	219,150
175,000	2,004.48	546,613	2,044.57	427,142	119,471	2,084.66	363,466	183,147	2,124.75	321,019	225,594
180,000	2,061.75	562,230	2,102.99	439,344	122,883	2,144.22	373,850	188,380	2,185.46	330,191	232,039
185,000	2,119.02	577,847	2,161.40	451,550	126,297	2,203.78	384,234	193,613	2,246.16	339,362	238,485
190,000	2,176.29	593,464	2,219.82	463,751	129,709	2,263.34	394,618	198,846	2,306.87	348,534	244,930
195,000	2,233.56	609,082	2,278.23	475,957	133,125	2,322.90	405,003	204,079	2,367.57	357,704	251,378
200,000	2,290.83	624,699	2,336.65	488,162	136,537	2,382.46	415,387	209,312	2,428.28	366,877	257,822

246

AUGMENTED PAYMENT MORTGAGES 13.50%

AMOUNT OF LOAN	30 YEARS MONTHLY PAYMENT	30 YEARS TOTAL INTRST	8% PMT INCREASE 214.673 PAYMENTS MONTHLY PAYMENT	TOTAL INTRST	INTRST SAVED	10% PMT INCREASE 199.685 PAYMENTS MONTHLY PAYMENT	TOTAL INTRST	INTRST SAVED	12% PMT INCREASE 187.280 PAYMENTS MONTHLY PAYMENT	TOTAL INTRST	INTRST SAVED
$ 50	0.58	159	0.63	85	74	0.64	78	81	0.65	72	87
100	1.15	314	1.24	166	148	1.27	154	160	1.29	142	172
200	2.30	628	2.48	332	296	2.53	305	323	2.58	283	345
300	3.44	938	3.72	499	439	3.78	455	483	3.85	421	517
400	4.59	1,252	4.96	665	587	5.05	608	644	5.14	563	689
500	5.73	1,563	6.19	829	734	6.30	758	805	6.42	702	861
600	6.88	1,877	7.43	995	882	7.57	912	965	7.71	844	1,033
700	8.02	2,187	8.66	1,159	1,028	8.82	1,061	1,126	8.98	982	1,205
800	9.17	2,501	9.90	1,325	1,176	10.09	1,215	1,286	10.27	1,123	1,378
900	10.31	2,812	11.13	1,489	1,323	11.34	1,364	1,448	11.55	1,263	1,549
1,000	11.46	3,126	12.38	1,658	1,468	12.61	1,518	1,608	12.84	1,405	1,721
2,000	22.91	6,248	24.74	3,311	2,937	25.20	3,032	3,216	25.66	2,806	3,442
3,000	34.37	9,373	37.12	4,969	4,404	37.81	4,550	4,823	38.49	4,208	5,165
4,000	45.82	12,495	49.49	6,624	5,871	50.40	6,064	6,431	51.32	5,611	6,884
5,000	57.28	15,621	61.86	8,280	7,341	63.01	7,582	8,039	64.15	7,014	8,607
6,000	68.73	18,743	74.23	9,935	8,808	75.60	9,096	9,647	76.98	8,417	10,326
7,000	80.18	21,865	86.59	11,589	10,276	88.20	10,612	11,253	89.80	9,818	12,047
8,000	91.64	24,990	98.97	13,246	11,744	100.80	12,128	12,862	102.64	11,222	13,768
9,000	103.09	28,112	111.34	14,902	13,210	113.40	13,644	14,468	115.46	12,623	15,489
10,000	114.55	31,238	123.71	16,557	14,681	126.01	15,162	16,076	128.30	14,028	17,210
11,000	126.00	34,360	136.08	18,213	16,147	138.60	16,676	17,684	141.12	15,429	18,931
12,000	137.45	37,482	148.45	19,868	17,614	151.20	18,192	19,290	153.94	16,830	20,652
13,000	148.91	40,608	160.82	21,524	19,084	163.80	19,708	20,900	166.78	18,235	22,373
14,000	160.36	43,730	173.19	23,179	20,551	176.40	21,224	22,506	179.60	19,635	24,095
15,000	171.82	46,855	185.57	24,837	22,018	189.00	22,740	24,115	192.44	21,040	25,815
16,000	183.27	49,977	197.93	26,490	23,487	201.60	24,256	25,721	205.26	22,441	27,536
17,000	194.73	53,103	210.31	28,148	24,955	214.20	25,773	27,330	218.10	23,846	29,257
18,000	206.18	56,225	222.67	29,801	26,424	226.80	27,289	28,936	230.92	25,247	30,978
19,000	217.63	59,347	235.04	31,457	27,890	239.39	28,803	30,544	243.75	26,650	32,697
20,000	229.09	62,472	247.42	33,114	29,358	252.00	30,321	32,151	256.58	28,052	34,420
21,000	240.54	65,594	259.78	34,768	30,826	264.59	31,835	33,759	269.40	29,453	36,141
22,000	252.00	68,720	272.16	36,425	32,295	277.20	33,353	35,367	282.24	30,858	37,862
23,000	263.45	71,842	284.53	38,081	33,761	289.80	34,869	36,973	295.06	32,259	39,583
24,000	274.90	74,964	296.89	39,734	35,230	302.39	36,383	38,581	307.89	33,662	41,302
25,000	286.36	78,090	309.27	41,392	36,698	315.00	37,901	40,189	320.72	35,064	43,026
26,000	297.81	81,212	321.63	43,045	38,167	327.59	39,415	41,797	333.55	36,467	44,745
27,000	309.27	84,337	334.01	44,703	39,634	340.20	40,933	43,404	346.38	37,870	46,467
28,000	320.72	87,459	346.38	46,358	41,101	352.79	42,447	45,012	359.21	39,273	48,186
29,000	332.17	90,581	358.74	48,012	42,569	365.39	43,963	46,618	372.03	40,674	49,907
30,000	343.63	93,707	371.12	49,669	44,038	377.99	45,479	48,228	384.87	42,078	51,629
32,500	372.26	101,514	402.04	53,807	47,707	409.49	49,269	52,245	416.93	45,583	55,931
35,000	400.90	109,324	432.97	57,947	51,377	440.99	53,059	56,265	449.01	49,091	60,233
40,000	458.17	124,941	494.82	66,224	58,717	503.99	60,639	64,302	513.15	56,103	68,838
45,000	515.44	140,558	556.68	74,504	66,054	566.98	68,217	72,341	577.29	63,115	77,443
50,000	572.71	156,176	618.53	82,782	73,394	629.98	75,798	80,378	641.44	70,129	86,047
55,000	629.98	171,793	680.38	91,059	80,734	692.98	83,378	88,415	705.58	77,141	94,652
60,000	687.25	187,410	742.23	99,337	88,073	755.98	90,958	96,452	769.72	84,153	103,257
65,000	744.52	203,027	804.08	107,614	95,413	818.97	98,536	104,491	833.86	91,165	111,862
70,000	801.79	218,644	865.93	115,892	102,752	881.97	106,116	112,528	898.00	98,177	120,467
75,000	859.06	234,262	927.78	124,169	110,093	944.97	113,696	120,566	962.15	105,191	129,071
80,000	916.33	249,879	989.64	132,449	117,430	1,007.96	121,274	128,605	1,026.29	112,204	137,675
85,000	973.61	265,500	1,051.50	140,729	124,771	1,070.97	128,857	136,643	1,090.44	119,218	146,282
90,000	1,030.88	281,117	1,113.35	149,006	132,111	1,133.97	136,437	144,680	1,154.59	126,232	154,885
95,000	1,088.15	296,734	1,175.20	157,284	139,450	1,196.97	144,017	152,717	1,218.73	133,244	163,490
100,000	1,145.42	312,351	1,237.05	165,561	146,790	1,259.96	151,595	160,756	1,282.87	140,256	172,095
105,000	1,202.69	327,968	1,298.91	173,841	154,127	1,322.96	159,175	168,793	1,347.01	147,268	180,700
110,000	1,259.96	343,586	1,360.76	182,118	161,468	1,385.96	166,755	176,831	1,411.16	154,282	189,304
115,000	1,317.23	359,203	1,422.61	190,396	168,807	1,448.95	174,334	184,869	1,475.30	161,294	197,909
120,000	1,374.50	374,820	1,484.46	198,673	176,147	1,511.95	181,914	192,906	1,539.44	168,306	206,514
125,000	1,431.77	390,437	1,546.31	206,951	183,486	1,574.95	189,494	200,943	1,603.58	175,318	215,119
130,000	1,489.04	406,054	1,608.16	215,229	190,825	1,637.94	197,072	208,982	1,667.72	182,331	223,723
135,000	1,546.31	421,672	1,670.01	223,506	198,166	1,700.94	204,652	217,020	1,731.87	189,345	232,327
140,000	1,603.58	437,289	1,731.87	231,786	205,503	1,763.94	212,232	225,057	1,796.01	196,357	240,932
145,000	1,660.85	452,906	1,793.72	240,063	212,843	1,826.94	219,813	233,093	1,860.15	203,369	249,537
150,000	1,718.12	468,523	1,855.57	248,341	220,182	1,889.93	227,391	241,132	1,924.29	210,381	258,142
155,000	1,775.39	484,140	1,917.42	256,618	227,522	1,952.93	234,971	249,169	1,988.44	217,395	266,745
160,000	1,832.66	499,758	1,979.27	264,896	234,862	2,015.93	242,551	257,207	2,052.58	224,407	275,351
165,000	1,889.94	515,378	2,041.14	273,178	242,200	2,078.93	250,131	265,247	2,116.73	231,421	283,957
170,000	1,947.21	530,996	2,102.99	281,455	249,541	2,141.93	257,711	273,285	2,180.88	238,435	292,561
175,000	2,004.48	546,613	2,164.84	289,733	256,880	2,204.93	265,291	281,322	2,245.02	245,447	301,166
180,000	2,061.75	562,230	2,226.69	298,010	264,220	2,267.93	272,871	289,358	2,309.16	252,459	309,771
185,000	2,119.02	577,847	2,288.54	306,288	271,559	2,330.92	280,450	297,397	2,373.30	259,472	318,375
190,000	2,176.29	593,464	2,350.39	314,565	278,899	2,393.92	288,030	305,434	2,437.44	266,484	326,980
195,000	2,233.56	609,082	2,412.24	322,843	286,239	2,456.92	295,610	313,472	2,501.59	273,498	335,584
200,000	2,290.83	624,699	2,474.10	331,122	293,577	2,519.91	303,188	321,511	2,565.73	280,510	344,189

247

13.75% AUGMENTED PAYMENT MORTGAGES

AMOUNT OF LOAN	30 YEARS		2% PMT INCREASE 292.189 PAYMENTS			4% PMT INCREASE 255.584 PAYMENTS			6% PMT INCREASE 230.676 PAYMENTS		
	MONTHLY PAYMENT	TOTAL INTRST	MONTHLY PAYMENT	TOTAL INTRST	INTRST SAVED	MONTHLY PAYMENT	TOTAL INTRST	INTRST SAVED	MONTHLY PAYMENT	TOTAL INTRST	INTRST SAVED
$ 50	0.59	162	0.60	125	37	0.61	106	56	0.63	95	67
100	1.17	321	1.19	248	73	1.22	212	109	1.24	186	135
200	2.34	642	2.39	498	144	2.43	421	221	2.48	372	270
300	3.50	960	3.57	743	217	3.64	630	330	3.71	556	404
400	4.67	1,281	4.76	991	290	4.86	842	439	4.95	742	539
500	5.83	1,599	5.95	1,239	360	6.06	1,049	550	6.18	926	673
600	7.00	1,920	7.14	1,486	434	7.28	1,261	659	7.42	1,112	808
700	8.16	2,238	8.32	1,731	507	8.49	1,470	768	8.65	1,295	943
800	9.33	2,559	9.52	1,982	577	9.70	1,679	880	9.89	1,481	1,078
900	10.49	2,876	10.70	2,226	650	10.91	1,888	988	11.12	1,665	1,211
1,000	11.66	3,198	11.89	2,474	724	12.13	2,100	1,098	12.36	1,851	1,347
2,000	23.31	6,392	23.78	4,948	1,444	24.24	4,195	2,197	24.71	3,700	2,692
3,000	34.96	9,586	35.66	7,419	2,167	36.36	6,293	3,293	37.06	5,549	4,037
4,000	46.61	12,780	47.54	9,891	2,889	48.47	8,388	4,392	49.41	7,398	5,382
5,000	58.26	15,974	59.43	12,365	3,609	60.59	10,486	5,488	61.76	9,247	6,727
6,000	69.91	19,168	71.31	14,836	4,332	72.71	12,584	6,584	74.10	11,093	8,075
7,000	81.56	22,362	83.19	17,307	5,055	84.82	14,679	7,683	86.45	12,942	9,420
8,000	93.21	25,556	95.07	19,778	5,778	96.94	16,776	8,780	98.80	14,791	10,765
9,000	104.87	28,753	106.97	22,255	6,498	109.06	18,874	9,879	111.16	16,642	12,111
10,000	116.52	31,947	118.85	24,727	7,220	121.18	20,972	10,975	123.51	18,491	13,456
11,000	128.17	35,141	130.73	27,198	7,943	133.30	23,069	12,072	135.86	20,340	14,801
12,000	139.82	38,335	142.62	29,672	8,663	145.41	25,164	13,171	148.21	22,188	16,147
13,000	151.47	41,529	154.50	32,143	9,386	157.53	27,262	14,267	160.56	24,037	17,492
14,000	163.12	44,723	166.38	34,614	10,109	169.64	29,357	15,366	172.91	25,886	18,837
15,000	174.77	47,917	178.27	37,089	10,828	181.76	31,455	16,462	185.26	27,735	20,182
16,000	186.42	51,111	190.15	39,560	11,551	193.88	33,553	17,558	197.61	29,584	21,527
17,000	198.07	54,305	202.03	42,031	12,274	205.99	35,649	18,657	209.95	31,430	22,875
18,000	209.73	57,503	213.92	44,505	12,998	218.12	37,748	19,755	222.31	33,282	24,221
19,000	221.38	60,697	225.81	46,979	13,718	230.24	39,846	20,851	234.66	35,130	25,567
20,000	233.03	63,891	237.69	49,450	14,441	242.35	41,941	21,950	247.01	36,979	26,912
21,000	244.68	67,085	249.57	51,922	15,163	254.47	44,038	23,047	259.36	38,828	28,257
22,000	256.33	70,279	261.46	54,396	15,883	266.58	46,134	24,145	271.71	40,677	29,602
23,000	267.98	73,473	273.34	56,867	16,606	278.70	48,231	25,242	284.06	42,526	30,947
24,000	279.63	76,667	285.22	59,338	17,329	290.82	50,329	26,338	296.41	44,375	32,292
25,000	291.28	79,861	297.11	61,812	18,049	302.93	52,424	27,437	308.76	46,224	33,637
26,000	302.93	83,055	308.99	64,283	18,772	315.05	54,522	28,533	321.11	48,072	34,983
27,000	314.59	86,252	320.88	66,758	19,494	327.17	56,619	29,633	333.47	49,924	36,328
28,000	326.24	89,446	332.76	69,229	20,217	339.29	58,717	30,729	345.81	51,770	37,676
29,000	337.89	92,640	344.65	71,703	20,937	351.41	60,815	31,825	358.16	53,619	39,021
30,000	349.54	95,834	356.53	74,174	21,660	363.52	62,910	32,924	370.51	55,468	40,366
32,500	378.67	103,821	386.24	80,355	23,466	393.82	68,154	35,667	401.39	60,091	43,730
35,000	407.79	111,804	415.95	86,536	25,268	424.10	73,393	38,411	432.26	64,712	47,092
40,000	466.05	127,778	475.37	98,898	28,880	484.69	83,879	43,899	494.01	73,956	53,822
45,000	524.31	143,752	534.80	111,263	32,489	545.28	94,365	49,387	555.77	83,203	60,549
50,000	582.56	159,722	594.21	123,622	36,100	605.86	104,848	54,874	617.51	92,445	67,277
55,000	640.82	175,695	653.64	135,986	39,709	666.45	115,334	60,361	679.27	101,691	74,004
60,000	699.07	191,665	713.05	148,345	43,320	727.03	125,817	65,848	741.01	110,933	80,732
65,000	757.33	207,639	772.48	160,710	46,929	787.62	136,303	71,336	802.77	120,180	87,459
70,000	815.58	223,609	831.89	173,069	50,540	848.20	146,786	76,823	864.51	129,422	94,187
75,000	873.84	239,582	891.32	185,434	54,148	908.79	157,272	82,310	926.27	138,668	100,914
80,000	932.10	255,556	950.74	197,796	57,760	969.38	167,758	87,798	988.05	147,915	107,641
85,000	990.35	271,526	1,010.16	210,158	61,368	1,029.96	178,241	93,285	1,049.77	157,157	114,369
90,000	1,048.61	287,500	1,069.58	222,520	64,980	1,090.55	188,727	98,773	1,111.53	166,403	121,097
95,000	1,106.86	303,470	1,129.00	234,881	68,589	1,151.13	199,210	104,260	1,173.27	175,645	127,825
100,000	1,165.12	319,443	1,188.42	247,243	72,200	1,211.72	209,696	109,747	1,235.03	184,892	134,551
105,000	1,223.37	335,413	1,247.84	259,605	75,808	1,272.30	220,180	115,233	1,296.77	194,134	141,279
110,000	1,281.63	351,387	1,307.26	271,967	79,420	1,332.90	230,668	120,719	1,358.53	203,380	148,007
115,000	1,339.88	367,357	1,366.68	284,329	83,028	1,393.48	241,151	126,206	1,420.27	212,622	154,735
120,000	1,398.14	383,330	1,426.10	296,691	86,639	1,454.07	251,637	131,693	1,482.03	221,869	161,461
125,000	1,456.40	399,304	1,485.53	309,056	90,248	1,514.66	262,123	137,181	1,543.78	231,113	168,191
130,000	1,514.65	415,274	1,544.94	321,414	93,860	1,575.24	272,606	142,668	1,605.53	240,357	174,917
135,000	1,572.91	431,248	1,604.37	333,779	97,469	1,635.83	283,092	148,156	1,667.28	249,601	181,647
140,000	1,631.16	447,218	1,663.78	346,138	101,080	1,696.41	293,575	153,643	1,729.03	258,846	188,372
145,000	1,689.42	463,191	1,723.21	358,503	104,688	1,757.00	304,061	159,130	1,790.79	268,092	195,099
150,000	1,747.67	479,161	1,782.62	370,862	108,299	1,817.58	314,544	164,617	1,852.53	277,334	201,827
155,000	1,805.93	495,135	1,842.05	383,227	111,908	1,878.17	325,030	170,105	1,914.29	286,581	208,554
160,000	1,864.19	511,108	1,901.47	395,589	115,519	1,938.76	335,516	175,592	1,976.04	295,825	215,283
165,000	1,922.44	527,078	1,960.89	407,950	119,128	1,999.34	345,999	181,079	2,037.79	305,069	222,009
170,000	1,980.70	543,052	2,020.31	420,312	122,740	2,059.93	356,485	186,567	2,099.55	314,313	228,739
175,000	2,038.95	559,022	2,079.73	432,674	126,348	2,120.51	366,968	192,054	2,161.29	323,558	235,464
180,000	2,097.21	574,996	2,139.15	445,036	129,960	2,181.10	377,454	197,542	2,223.04	332,802	242,194
185,000	2,155.46	590,966	2,198.57	457,398	133,568	2,241.68	387,938	203,028	2,284.79	342,046	248,920
190,000	2,213.72	606,939	2,257.99	469,760	137,179	2,302.27	398,423	208,516	2,346.54	351,290	255,649
195,000	2,271.97	622,909	2,317.41	482,122	140,787	2,362.85	408,907	214,002	2,408.29	360,535	262,374
200,000	2,330.23	638,883	2,376.83	494,484	144,399	2,423.44	419,392	219,491	2,470.04	369,779	269,104

248

AUGMENTED PAYMENT MORTGAGES 13.75%

AMOUNT OF LOAN	30 YEARS		8% PMT INCREASE 211.942 PAYMENTS			10% PMT INCREASE 197.028 PAYMENTS			12% PMT INCREASE 184.709 PAYMENTS		
	MONTHLY PAYMENT	TOTAL INTRST	MONTHLY PAYMENT	TOTAL INTRST	INTRST SAVED	MONTHLY PAYMENT	TOTAL INTRST	INTRST SAVED	MONTHLY PAYMENT	TOTAL INTRST	INTRST SAVED
$ 50	0.59	162	0.64	86	76	0.65	78	84	0.66	72	90
100	1.17	321	1.26	167	154	1.29	154	167	1.31	142	179
200	2.34	642	2.53	336	306	2.57	306	336	2.62	284	358
300	3.50	960	3.78	501	459	3.85	459	501	3.92	424	536
400	4.67	1,281	5.04	668	613	5.14	613	668	5.23	566	715
500	5.83	1,599	6.30	835	764	6.41	763	836	6.53	706	893
600	7.00	1,920	7.56	1,002	918	7.70	917	1,003	7.84	848	1,072
700	8.16	2,238	8.81	1,167	1,071	8.98	1,069	1,169	9.14	988	1,250
800	9.33	2,559	10.08	1,336	1,223	10.26	1,222	1,337	10.45	1,130	1,429
900	10.49	2,876	11.33	1,501	1,375	11.54	1,374	1,502	11.75	1,270	1,606
1,000	11.66	3,198	12.59	1,668	1,530	12.83	1,528	1,670	13.06	1,412	1,786
2,000	23.31	6,392	25.17	3,335	3,057	25.64	3,052	3,340	26.11	2,823	3,569
3,000	34.96	9,586	37.76	5,003	4,583	38.46	4,578	5,008	39.16	4,233	5,353
4,000	46.61	12,780	50.34	6,669	6,111	51.27	6,102	6,678	52.20	5,642	7,138
5,000	58.26	15,974	62.92	8,335	7,639	64.09	7,628	8,346	65.25	7,052	8,922
6,000	69.91	19,168	75.50	10,002	9,166	76.90	9,151	10,017	78.30	8,463	10,705
7,000	81.56	22,362	88.08	11,668	10,694	89.72	10,677	11,685	91.35	9,873	12,489
8,000	93.21	25,556	100.67	13,336	12,220	102.53	12,201	13,355	104.40	11,284	14,272
9,000	104.87	28,753	113.26	15,005	13,748	115.36	13,729	15,024	117.45	12,694	16,059
10,000	116.52	31,947	125.84	16,671	15,276	128.17	15,253	16,694	130.50	14,105	17,842
11,000	128.17	35,141	138.42	18,337	16,804	140.99	16,779	18,362	143.55	15,515	19,626
12,000	139.82	38,335	151.01	20,005	18,330	153.80	18,303	20,032	156.60	16,925	21,410
13,000	151.47	41,529	163.59	21,672	19,857	166.62	19,829	21,700	169.65	18,336	23,193
14,000	163.12	44,723	176.17	23,338	21,385	179.43	21,353	23,370	182.69	19,744	24,979
15,000	174.77	47,917	188.75	25,004	22,913	192.25	22,879	25,038	195.74	21,155	26,762
16,000	186.42	51,111	201.33	26,670	24,441	205.06	24,403	26,708	208.79	22,565	28,546
17,000	198.07	54,305	213.92	28,339	25,966	217.88	25,928	28,377	221.84	23,976	30,329
18,000	209.73	57,503	226.50	30,007	27,496	230.70	27,454	30,049	234.90	25,388	32,115
19,000	221.38	60,697	239.09	31,673	29,024	243.52	28,980	31,717	247.95	26,799	33,898
20,000	233.03	63,891	251.67	33,339	30,552	256.33	30,504	33,387	260.99	28,207	35,684
21,000	244.68	67,085	264.25	35,006	32,079	269.15	32,030	35,055	274.04	29,618	37,467
22,000	256.33	70,279	276.84	36,674	33,605	281.96	33,554	36,725	287.09	31,028	39,251
23,000	267.98	73,473	289.42	38,340	35,133	294.78	35,080	38,393	300.14	32,439	41,034
24,000	279.63	76,667	302.00	40,006	36,661	307.59	36,604	40,063	313.19	33,849	42,818
25,000	291.28	79,861	314.58	41,673	38,188	320.41	38,130	41,731	326.23	35,258	44,603
26,000	302.93	83,055	327.16	43,339	39,716	333.22	39,654	43,401	339.28	36,668	46,387
27,000	314.59	86,252	339.76	45,009	41,243	346.05	41,182	45,070	352.34	38,080	48,172
28,000	326.24	89,446	352.34	46,676	42,770	358.86	42,705	46,741	365.39	39,491	49,955
29,000	337.89	92,640	364.92	48,342	44,298	371.68	44,231	48,409	378.44	40,901	51,739
30,000	349.54	95,834	377.50	50,008	45,826	384.49	45,755	50,079	391.48	42,310	53,524
32,500	378.67	103,821	408.96	54,176	49,645	416.54	49,570	54,251	424.11	45,837	57,984
35,000	407.79	111,804	440.41	58,341	53,463	448.57	53,381	58,423	456.72	49,360	62,444
40,000	466.05	127,778	503.33	66,677	61,101	512.66	61,008	66,770	521.98	56,414	71,364
45,000	524.31	143,752	566.25	75,012	68,740	576.74	68,634	75,118	587.23	63,467	80,285
50,000	582.56	159,722	629.16	83,345	76,377	640.82	76,259	83,463	652.47	70,517	89,205
55,000	640.82	175,695	692.09	91,683	84,012	704.90	83,885	91,810	717.72	77,569	98,126
60,000	699.07	191,665	755.00	100,016	91,649	768.98	91,511	100,154	782.96	84,620	107,045
65,000	757.33	207,639	817.92	108,352	99,287	833.06	99,136	108,503	848.21	91,672	115,967
70,000	815.58	223,609	880.83	116,685	106,924	897.14	106,762	116,847	913.45	98,722	124,887
75,000	873.84	239,582	943.75	125,020	114,562	961.22	114,387	125,195	978.70	105,775	133,807
80,000	932.10	255,556	1,006.67	133,356	122,200	1,025.31	122,015	133,541	1,043.95	112,827	142,729
85,000	990.35	271,526	1,069.58	141,689	129,837	1,089.39	129,640	141,886	1,109.19	119,877	151,649
90,000	1,048.61	287,500	1,132.50	150,024	137,476	1,153.47	137,266	150,234	1,174.44	126,930	160,570
95,000	1,106.86	303,470	1,195.41	158,358	145,112	1,217.55	144,891	158,579	1,239.68	133,980	169,490
100,000	1,165.12	319,443	1,258.33	166,693	152,750	1,281.63	152,517	166,926	1,304.93	141,032	178,411
105,000	1,223.37	335,413	1,321.24	175,026	160,387	1,345.71	160,143	175,270	1,370.17	148,083	187,330
110,000	1,281.63	351,387	1,384.16	183,362	168,025	1,409.79	167,768	183,619	1,435.43	155,137	196,250
115,000	1,339.88	367,357	1,447.07	191,695	175,662	1,473.87	175,394	191,963	1,500.67	162,187	205,170
120,000	1,398.14	383,330	1,509.99	200,030	183,300	1,537.95	183,019	200,311	1,565.92	169,240	214,090
125,000	1,456.40	399,304	1,572.91	208,366	190,938	1,602.04	190,647	208,657	1,631.17	176,292	223,012
130,000	1,514.65	415,274	1,635.82	216,699	198,575	1,666.12	198,272	217,002	1,696.41	183,342	231,932
135,000	1,572.91	431,248	1,698.74	225,034	206,214	1,730.20	205,898	225,350	1,761.66	190,394	240,854
140,000	1,631.16	447,218	1,761.65	233,368	213,850	1,794.28	213,523	233,695	1,826.90	197,445	249,773
145,000	1,689.42	463,191	1,824.57	241,703	221,488	1,858.36	221,149	242,042	1,892.15	204,497	258,694
150,000	1,747.67	479,161	1,887.48	250,036	229,125	1,922.44	228,775	250,386	1,957.39	211,548	267,613
155,000	1,805.93	495,135	1,950.40	258,372	236,763	1,986.52	236,400	258,735	2,022.64	218,600	276,535
160,000	1,864.19	511,108	2,013.33	266,709	244,399	2,050.61	244,027	267,080	2,087.89	225,652	285,456
165,000	1,922.44	527,078	2,076.24	275,042	252,036	2,114.68	251,651	275,427	2,153.13	232,702	294,376
170,000	1,980.70	543,052	2,139.16	283,378	259,674	2,178.77	259,279	283,773	2,218.38	239,755	303,297
175,000	2,038.95	559,022	2,202.07	291,711	267,311	2,242.85	266,904	292,118	2,283.62	246,805	312,217
180,000	2,097.21	574,996	2,264.99	300,047	274,949	2,306.93	274,530	300,466	2,348.88	253,859	321,137
185,000	2,155.46	590,966	2,327.90	308,380	282,586	2,371.01	282,155	308,811	2,414.12	260,910	330,056
190,000	2,213.72	606,939	2,390.82	316,715	290,224	2,435.09	289,781	317,158	2,479.37	267,962	338,977
195,000	2,271.97	622,909	2,453.73	325,048	297,861	2,499.17	297,406	325,503	2,544.61	275,012	347,897
200,000	2,330.23	638,883	2,516.65	333,384	305,499	2,563.25	305,032	333,851	2,609.86	282,065	356,818

AUGMENTED PAYMENT MORTGAGES

AMOUNT OF LOAN	30 YEARS		2% PMT INCREASE 289.837 PAYMENTS			4% PMT INCREASE 252.867 PAYMENTS			6% PMT INCREASE 227.921 PAYMENTS		
	MONTHLY PAYMENT	TOTAL INTRST	MONTHLY PAYMENT	TOTAL INTRST	INTRST SAVED	MONTHLY PAYMENT	TOTAL INTRST	INTRST SAVED	MONTHLY PAYMENT	TOTAL INTRST	INTRST SAVED
$ 50	0.60	166	0.61	127	39	0.62	107	59	0.64	96	70
100	1.19	328	1.21	251	77	1.24	214	114	1.26	187	141
200	2.37	653	2.42	501	152	2.46	422	231	2.51	372	281
300	3.56	982	3.63	752	230	3.70	636	346	3.77	559	423
400	4.74	1,306	4.83	1,000	306	4.93	847	459	5.02	744	562
500	5.93	1,635	6.05	1,254	381	6.17	1,060	575	6.29	934	701
600	7.11	1,960	7.25	1,501	459	7.39	1,269	691	7.54	1,119	841
700	8.30	2,288	8.47	1,755	533	8.63	1,482	806	8.80	1,306	982
800	9.48	2,613	9.67	2,003	610	9.86	1,693	920	10.05	1,491	1,122
900	10.67	2,941	10.88	2,253	688	11.10	1,907	1,034	11.31	1,678	1,263
1,000	11.85	3,266	12.09	2,504	762	12.32	2,115	1,151	12.56	1,863	1,403
2,000	23.70	6,532	24.17	5,005	1,527	24.65	4,233	2,299	25.12	3,725	2,807
3,000	35.55	9,798	36.26	7,509	2,289	36.97	6,348	3,450	37.68	5,588	4,210
4,000	47.40	13,064	48.35	10,014	3,050	49.30	8,466	4,598	50.24	7,451	5,613
5,000	59.25	16,330	60.44	12,518	3,812	61.62	10,582	5,748	62.81	9,316	7,014
6,000	71.10	19,596	72.52	15,019	4,577	73.94	12,697	6,899	75.37	11,178	8,418
7,000	82.95	22,862	84.61	17,523	5,339	86.27	14,815	8,047	87.93	13,041	9,821
8,000	94.79	26,124	96.69	20,024	6,100	98.58	16,928	9,196	100.48	14,902	11,222
9,000	106.64	29,390	108.77	22,526	6,864	110.91	19,045	10,345	113.04	16,764	12,626
10,000	118.49	32,656	120.86	25,030	7,626	123.23	21,161	11,495	125.60	18,627	14,029
11,000	130.34	35,922	132.95	27,534	8,388	135.55	23,276	12,646	138.16	20,490	15,432
12,000	142.19	39,188	145.03	30,035	9,153	147.88	25,394	13,794	150.72	22,352	16,836
13,000	154.04	42,454	157.12	32,539	9,915	160.20	27,509	14,945	163.28	24,215	18,239
14,000	165.89	45,720	169.21	35,043	10,677	172.53	29,627	16,093	175.84	26,078	19,642
15,000	177.74	48,986	181.29	37,545	11,441	184.85	31,742	17,244	188.40	27,940	21,046
16,000	189.58	52,249	193.37	40,046	12,203	197.16	33,855	18,394	200.95	29,801	22,448
17,000	201.43	55,515	205.46	42,550	12,965	209.49	35,973	19,542	213.52	31,666	23,849
18,000	213.28	58,781	217.55	45,054	13,727	221.81	38,088	20,693	226.08	33,528	25,253
19,000	225.13	62,047	229.63	47,555	14,492	234.14	40,206	21,841	238.64	35,391	26,656
20,000	236.98	65,313	241.72	50,059	15,254	246.46	42,322	22,991	251.20	37,254	28,059
21,000	248.83	68,579	253.81	52,564	16,015	258.78	44,437	24,142	263.76	39,116	29,463
22,000	260.68	71,845	265.89	55,065	16,780	271.11	46,555	25,290	276.32	40,979	30,866
23,000	272.53	75,111	277.98	57,569	17,542	283.43	48,670	26,441	288.88	42,842	32,269
24,000	284.37	78,373	290.06	60,070	18,303	295.74	50,783	27,590	301.43	44,702	33,671
25,000	296.22	81,639	302.14	62,571	19,068	308.07	52,901	28,738	313.99	46,565	35,074
26,000	308.07	84,905	314.23	65,075	19,830	320.39	55,016	29,889	326.55	48,428	36,477
27,000	319.92	88,171	326.32	67,580	20,591	332.72	57,134	31,037	339.12	50,293	37,878
28,000	331.77	91,437	338.41	70,084	21,353	345.04	59,249	32,188	351.68	52,155	39,282
29,000	343.62	94,703	350.49	72,585	22,118	357.36	61,365	33,338	364.24	54,018	40,685
30,000	355.47	97,969	362.58	75,089	22,880	369.69	63,482	34,487	376.80	55,881	42,088
32,500	385.09	106,132	392.79	81,345	24,787	400.49	68,771	37,361	408.20	60,537	45,595
35,000	414.71	114,296	423.00	87,601	26,695	431.30	74,062	40,234	439.59	65,192	49,104
40,000	473.95	130,622	483.43	100,116	30,506	492.91	84,641	45,981	502.39	74,505	56,117
45,000	533.20	146,952	543.86	112,631	34,321	554.53	95,222	51,730	565.19	83,819	63,133
50,000	592.44	163,278	604.29	125,146	38,132	616.14	105,801	57,477	627.99	93,132	70,146
55,000	651.68	179,605	664.71	137,658	41,947	677.75	116,381	63,224	690.78	102,443	77,162
60,000	710.93	195,935	725.15	150,175	45,760	739.37	126,962	68,973	753.59	111,759	84,176
65,000	770.17	212,261	785.57	162,687	49,574	800.98	137,541	74,720	816.38	121,070	91,191
70,000	829.42	228,591	846.01	175,205	53,386	862.60	148,123	80,468	879.19	130,386	98,205
75,000	888.66	244,918	906.43	187,717	57,201	924.21	158,702	86,216	941.98	139,697	105,221
80,000	947.90	261,244	966.86	200,232	61,012	985.82	169,281	91,963	1,004.77	149,008	112,236
85,000	1,007.15	277,574	1,027.29	212,747	64,827	1,047.44	179,863	97,711	1,067.58	158,324	119,250
90,000	1,066.39	293,900	1,087.72	225,262	68,638	1,109.05	190,442	103,458	1,130.37	167,635	126,265
95,000	1,125.63	310,227	1,148.14	237,773	72,454	1,170.66	201,021	109,206	1,193.17	176,948	133,279
100,000	1,184.88	326,557	1,208.58	250,291	76,266	1,232.28	211,603	114,954	1,255.97	186,262	140,295
105,000	1,244.12	342,883	1,269.00	262,803	80,080	1,293.88	222,180	120,703	1,318.77	195,575	147,308
110,000	1,303.36	359,210	1,329.43	275,318	83,892	1,355.49	232,759	126,451	1,381.56	204,887	154,323
115,000	1,362.61	375,540	1,389.86	287,833	87,707	1,417.11	243,340	132,200	1,444.37	214,202	161,338
120,000	1,421.85	391,866	1,450.29	300,348	91,518	1,478.72	253,919	137,947	1,507.16	223,513	168,353
125,000	1,481.09	408,192	1,510.71	312,860	95,332	1,540.33	264,499	143,693	1,569.96	232,827	175,365
130,000	1,540.34	424,522	1,571.15	325,377	99,145	1,601.95	275,080	149,442	1,632.76	242,140	182,382
135,000	1,599.58	440,849	1,631.57	337,889	102,960	1,663.56	285,659	155,190	1,695.55	251,451	189,398
140,000	1,658.83	457,179	1,692.01	350,407	106,772	1,725.18	296,241	160,938	1,758.36	260,767	196,412
145,000	1,718.07	473,505	1,752.43	362,919	110,585	1,786.79	306,820	166,685	1,821.15	270,078	203,427
150,000	1,777.31	489,832	1,812.86	375,434	114,398	1,848.40	317,399	172,433	1,883.95	279,392	210,440
155,000	1,836.56	506,162	1,873.29	387,949	118,213	1,910.02	327,981	178,181	1,946.75	288,705	217,457
160,000	1,895.80	522,488	1,933.72	400,464	122,024	1,971.63	338,560	183,928	2,009.55	298,019	224,469
165,000	1,955.04	538,814	1,994.14	412,976	125,838	2,033.24	349,139	189,675	2,072.34	307,330	231,484
170,000	2,014.29	555,144	2,054.58	425,493	129,651	2,094.86	359,721	195,423	2,135.15	316,646	238,498
175,000	2,073.53	571,471	2,115.00	438,005	133,466	2,156.47	370,300	201,171	2,197.94	325,957	245,514
180,000	2,132.77	587,797	2,175.43	450,520	137,277	2,218.08	380,879	206,918	2,260.74	335,270	252,527
185,000	2,192.02	604,127	2,235.86	463,035	141,092	2,279.70	391,461	212,666	2,323.54	344,584	259,543
190,000	2,251.26	620,454	2,296.29	475,550	144,904	2,341.31	402,040	218,414	2,386.34	353,897	266,557
195,000	2,310.50	636,780	2,356.71	488,062	148,718	2,402.92	412,619	224,161	2,449.13	363,208	273,572
200,000	2,369.75	653,110	2,417.15	500,580	152,530	2,464.54	423,201	229,909	2,511.94	372,524	280,586

AUGMENTED PAYMENT MORTGAGES 14.00%

AMOUNT OF LOAN	30 YEARS		8% PMT INCREASE 209.242 PAYMENTS			10% PMT INCREASE 194.410 PAYMENTS			12% PMT INCREASE 182.179 PAYMENTS		
	MONTHLY PAYMENT	TOTAL INTRST	MONTHLY PAYMENT	TOTAL INTRST	INTRST SAVED	MONTHLY PAYMENT	TOTAL INTRST	INTRST SAVED	MONTHLY PAYMENT	TOTAL INTRST	INTRST SAVED
$ 50	0.60	166	0.65	86	80	0.66	78	88	0.67	72	94
100	1.19	328	1.29	170	158	1.31	155	173	1.33	142	186
200	2.37	653	2.56	336	317	2.61	307	346	2.65	283	370
300	3.56	982	3.84	503	479	3.92	462	520	3.99	427	555
400	4.74	1,306	5.12	671	635	5.21	613	693	5.31	567	739
500	5.93	1,635	6.40	839	796	6.52	768	867	6.64	710	925
600	7.11	1,960	7.68	1,007	953	7.82	920	1,040	7.96	850	1,110
700	8.30	2,288	8.96	1,175	1,113	9.13	1,075	1,213	9.30	994	1,294
800	9.48	2,613	10.24	1,343	1,270	10.43	1,228	1,385	10.62	1,135	1,478
900	10.67	2,941	11.52	1,510	1,431	11.74	1,382	1,559	11.95	1,277	1,664
1,000	11.85	3,266	12.80	1,678	1,588	13.04	1,535	1,731	13.27	1,418	1,848
2,000	23.70	6,532	25.60	3,357	3,175	26.07	3,068	3,464	26.54	2,835	3,697
3,000	35.55	9,798	38.39	5,033	4,765	39.11	4,603	5,195	39.82	4,254	5,544
4,000	47.40	13,064	51.19	6,711	6,353	52.14	6,137	6,927	53.09	5,672	7,392
5,000	59.25	16,330	63.99	8,389	7,941	65.18	7,672	8,658	66.36	7,089	9,241
6,000	71.10	19,596	76.79	10,068	9,528	78.21	9,205	10,391	79.63	8,507	11,089
7,000	82.95	22,862	89.59	11,746	11,116	91.25	10,740	12,122	92.90	9,924	12,938
8,000	94.79	26,124	102.37	13,420	12,704	104.27	12,271	13,853	106.16	11,340	14,784
9,000	106.64	29,390	115.17	15,098	14,292	117.30	13,804	15,586	119.44	12,759	16,631
10,000	118.49	32,656	127.97	16,777	15,879	130.34	15,339	17,317	132.71	14,177	18,479
11,000	130.34	35,922	140.77	18,455	17,467	143.37	16,873	19,049	145.98	15,594	20,328
12,000	142.19	39,188	153.57	20,133	19,055	156.41	18,408	20,780	159.25	17,012	22,176
13,000	154.04	42,454	166.36	21,809	20,645	169.44	19,941	22,513	172.52	18,430	24,024
14,000	165.89	45,720	179.16	23,488	22,232	182.48	21,476	24,244	185.80	19,849	25,871
15,000	177.74	48,986	191.96	25,166	23,820	195.51	23,009	25,977	199.07	21,266	27,720
16,000	189.58	52,249	204.75	26,842	25,407	208.54	24,542	27,707	212.33	22,682	29,567
17,000	201.43	55,515	217.54	28,519	26,996	221.57	26,075	29,440	225.60	24,100	31,415
18,000	213.28	58,781	230.34	30,197	28,584	234.61	27,611	31,170	238.87	25,517	33,264
19,000	225.13	62,047	243.14	31,875	30,172	247.64	29,144	32,903	252.15	26,936	35,111
20,000	236.98	65,313	255.94	33,553	31,760	260.68	30,679	34,634	265.42	28,354	36,959
21,000	248.83	68,579	268.74	35,232	33,347	273.71	32,212	36,367	278.69	29,771	38,808
22,000	260.68	71,845	281.53	36,908	34,937	286.75	33,747	38,098	291.96	31,189	40,656
23,000	272.53	75,111	294.33	38,586	36,525	299.78	35,280	39,831	305.23	32,606	42,505
24,000	284.37	78,373	307.12	40,262	38,111	312.81	36,813	41,560	318.49	34,022	44,351
25,000	296.22	81,639	319.92	41,941	39,698	325.84	38,347	43,292	331.77	35,442	46,197
26,000	308.07	84,905	332.72	43,619	41,286	338.88	39,882	45,023	345.04	36,859	48,046
27,000	319.92	88,171	345.51	45,295	42,876	351.91	41,415	46,756	358.31	38,277	49,894
28,000	331.77	91,437	358.31	46,974	44,463	364.95	42,950	48,487	371.58	39,694	51,743
29,000	343.62	94,703	371.11	48,652	46,051	377.98	44,483	50,220	384.85	41,112	53,591
30,000	355.47	97,969	383.91	50,330	47,639	391.02	46,018	51,951	398.13	42,531	55,438
32,500	385.09	106,132	415.90	54,524	51,608	423.60	49,852	56,280	431.30	46,074	60,058
35,000	414.71	114,296	447.89	58,717	55,579	456.18	53,686	60,610	464.48	49,619	64,677
40,000	473.95	130,622	511.87	67,105	63,517	521.35	61,356	69,266	530.82	56,704	73,918
45,000	533.20	146,952	575.86	75,494	71,458	586.52	69,025	77,927	597.18	63,794	83,158
50,000	592.44	163,278	639.84	83,881	79,397	651.68	76,693	86,585	663.53	70,881	92,397
55,000	651.68	179,605	703.81	92,267	87,338	716.85	84,363	95,242	729.88	77,969	101,636
60,000	710.93	195,935	767.80	100,656	95,279	782.02	92,033	103,902	796.24	85,058	110,877
65,000	770.17	212,261	831.78	109,043	103,218	847.19	99,702	112,559	862.59	92,146	120,115
70,000	829.42	228,591	895.77	117,433	111,158	912.36	107,372	121,219	928.95	99,235	129,356
75,000	888.66	244,918	959.75	125,820	119,098	977.53	115,042	129,876	995.30	106,323	138,595
80,000	947.90	261,244	1,023.73	134,207	127,037	1,042.69	122,709	138,535	1,061.65	113,410	147,834
85,000	1,007.15	277,574	1,087.72	142,597	134,977	1,107.87	130,381	147,193	1,128.01	120,500	157,074
90,000	1,066.39	293,900	1,151.70	150,984	142,916	1,173.03	138,049	155,851	1,194.36	127,587	166,313
95,000	1,125.63	310,227	1,215.68	159,371	150,856	1,238.19	145,717	164,510	1,260.71	134,675	175,552
100,000	1,184.88	326,557	1,279.67	167,761	158,796	1,303.37	153,388	173,169	1,327.07	141,764	184,793
105,000	1,244.12	342,883	1,343.65	176,148	166,735	1,368.53	161,056	181,827	1,393.41	148,850	194,033
110,000	1,303.36	359,210	1,407.63	184,535	174,675	1,433.70	168,726	190,484	1,459.76	155,938	203,272
115,000	1,362.61	375,540	1,471.62	192,925	182,615	1,498.87	176,395	199,145	1,526.12	163,027	212,513
120,000	1,421.85	391,866	1,535.60	201,312	190,554	1,564.04	184,065	207,801	1,592.47	170,115	221,751
125,000	1,481.09	408,192	1,599.58	209,699	198,493	1,629.20	191,733	216,459	1,658.82	177,202	230,990
130,000	1,540.34	424,522	1,663.57	218,089	206,433	1,694.37	199,402	225,120	1,725.18	184,292	240,230
135,000	1,599.58	440,849	1,727.55	226,476	214,373	1,759.54	207,072	233,777	1,791.53	191,379	249,470
140,000	1,658.83	457,179	1,791.54	234,865	222,314	1,824.71	214,742	242,437	1,857.89	198,469	258,710
145,000	1,718.07	473,505	1,855.52	243,253	230,252	1,889.88	222,412	251,093	1,924.24	205,556	267,949
150,000	1,777.31	489,832	1,919.49	251,638	238,194	1,955.04	230,079	259,753	1,990.59	212,644	277,188
155,000	1,836.56	506,162	1,983.48	260,027	246,135	2,020.22	237,751	268,411	2,056.95	219,733	286,429
160,000	1,895.80	522,488	2,047.46	268,415	254,073	2,085.38	245,419	277,069	2,123.30	226,821	295,667
165,000	1,955.04	538,814	2,111.44	276,802	262,012	2,150.54	253,086	285,728	2,189.64	233,906	304,908
170,000	2,014.29	555,144	2,175.43	285,191	269,953	2,215.72	260,758	294,386	2,256.00	240,996	314,148
175,000	2,073.53	571,471	2,239.41	293,579	277,892	2,280.88	268,426	303,045	2,322.35	248,083	323,388
180,000	2,132.77	587,797	2,303.39	301,966	285,831	2,346.05	276,096	311,701	2,388.70	255,171	332,626
185,000	2,192.02	604,127	2,367.38	310,355	293,772	2,411.22	283,765	320,362	2,455.06	262,260	341,867
190,000	2,251.26	620,454	2,431.36	318,743	301,711	2,476.39	291,435	329,019	2,521.41	269,348	351,106
195,000	2,310.50	636,780	2,495.34	327,130	309,650	2,541.55	299,103	337,677	2,587.76	276,436	360,344
200,000	2,369.75	653,110	2,559.33	335,519	317,591	2,606.73	306,774	346,336	2,654.12	283,525	369,585

251

14.25% AUGMENTED PAYMENT MORTGAGES

AMOUNT OF LOAN	30 YEARS		2% PMT INCREASE 287.453 PAYMENTS			4% PMT INCREASE 250.153 PAYMENTS			6% PMT INCREASE 225.189 PAYMENTS		
	MONTHLY PAYMENT	TOTAL INTRST	MONTHLY PAYMENT	TOTAL INTRST	INTRST SAVED	MONTHLY PAYMENT	TOTAL INTRST	INTRST SAVED	MONTHLY PAYMENT	TOTAL INTRST	INTRST SAVED
$ 50	0.61	170	0.62	128	42	0.63	108	62	0.65	96	74
100	1.21	336	1.23	254	82	1.26	215	121	1.28	188	148
200	2.41	668	2.46	507	161	2.51	428	240	2.55	374	294
300	3.62	1,003	3.69	761	242	3.76	641	362	3.84	565	438
400	4.82	1,335	4.92	1,014	321	5.01	853	482	5.11	751	584
500	6.03	1,671	6.15	1,268	403	6.27	1,068	603	6.39	939	732
600	7.23	2,003	7.37	1,519	484	7.52	1,281	722	7.66	1,125	878
700	8.44	2,338	8.61	1,775	563	8.78	1,496	842	8.95	1,315	1,023
800	9.64	2,670	9.83	2,026	644	10.03	1,709	961	10.22	1,501	1,169
900	10.85	3,006	11.07	2,282	724	11.28	1,922	1,084	11.50	1,690	1,316
1,000	12.05	3,338	12.29	2,533	805	12.53	2,134	1,204	12.77	1,876	1,462
2,000	24.10	6,676	24.58	5,066	1,610	25.06	4,269	2,407	25.53	3,754	2,922
3,000	36.15	10,014	36.87	7,598	2,416	37.60	6,406	3,608	38.32	5,629	4,385
4,000	48.19	13,348	49.15	10,128	3,220	50.12	8,538	4,810	51.08	7,503	5,845
5,000	60.24	16,686	61.44	12,661	4,025	62.65	10,672	6,014	63.85	9,378	7,308
6,000	72.29	20,024	73.74	15,197	4,827	75.18	12,807	7,217	76.63	11,256	8,768
7,000	84.33	23,359	86.02	17,727	5,632	87.70	14,938	8,421	89.39	13,130	10,229
8,000	96.38	26,697	98.31	20,260	6,437	100.24	17,075	9,622	102.16	15,005	11,692
9,000	108.43	30,035	110.60	22,792	7,243	112.77	19,210	10,825	114.94	16,883	13,152
10,000	120.47	33,369	122.88	25,322	8,047	125.29	21,342	12,027	127.70	18,757	14,612
11,000	132.52	36,707	135.17	27,855	8,852	137.82	23,476	13,231	140.47	20,632	16,075
12,000	144.57	40,045	147.46	30,388	9,657	150.35	25,611	14,434	153.24	22,508	17,537
13,000	156.61	43,380	159.74	32,918	10,462	162.87	27,742	15,638	166.01	24,384	18,996
14,000	168.66	46,718	172.03	35,451	11,267	175.41	29,879	16,839	178.78	26,259	20,459
15,000	180.71	50,056	184.32	37,983	12,073	187.94	32,014	18,042	191.55	28,135	21,921
16,000	192.75	53,390	196.61	40,516	12,874	200.46	34,146	19,244	204.32	30,011	23,379
17,000	204.80	56,728	208.90	43,049	13,679	212.99	36,280	20,448	217.09	31,886	24,842
18,000	216.85	60,066	221.19	45,582	14,484	225.52	38,415	21,651	229.86	33,762	26,304
19,000	228.90	63,404	233.48	48,115	15,289	238.06	40,551	22,853	242.63	35,638	27,766
20,000	240.94	66,738	245.76	50,644	16,094	250.58	42,683	24,055	255.40	37,513	29,225
21,000	252.99	70,076	258.05	53,177	16,899	263.11	44,818	25,258	268.17	39,389	30,687
22,000	265.04	73,414	270.34	55,710	17,704	275.64	46,952	26,462	280.94	41,265	32,149
23,000	277.08	76,749	282.62	58,240	18,509	288.16	49,084	27,665	293.70	43,138	33,611
24,000	289.13	80,087	294.91	60,773	19,314	300.70	51,221	28,866	306.48	45,016	35,071
25,000	301.18	83,425	307.20	63,306	20,119	313.23	53,355	30,070	319.25	46,892	36,533
26,000	313.22	86,759	319.48	65,835	20,924	325.75	55,487	31,272	332.01	48,765	37,994
27,000	325.27	90,097	331.78	68,371	21,726	338.28	57,622	32,475	344.79	50,643	39,454
28,000	337.32	93,435	344.07	70,904	22,531	350.81	59,756	33,679	357.56	52,519	40,916
29,000	349.36	96,770	356.35	73,434	23,336	363.33	61,888	34,882	370.32	54,392	42,378
30,000	361.41	100,108	368.64	75,967	24,141	375.87	64,025	36,083	383.09	56,268	43,840
32,500	391.53	108,451	399.36	82,297	26,154	407.19	69,360	39,091	415.02	60,958	47,493
35,000	421.65	116,794	430.08	88,648	28,166	438.52	74,697	42,097	446.95	65,648	51,146
40,000	481.88	133,477	491.52	101,289	32,188	501.16	85,367	48,110	510.79	75,024	58,453
45,000	542.11	150,160	552.95	113,947	36,213	563.79	96,034	54,126	574.64	84,403	65,757
50,000	602.35	166,846	614.40	126,611	40,235	626.44	106,706	60,140	638.49	93,781	73,065
55,000	662.58	183,529	675.83	139,269	44,260	689.08	117,375	66,154	702.33	103,157	80,372
60,000	722.82	200,215	737.28	151,933	48,282	751.73	128,048	72,167	766.19	112,538	87,677
65,000	783.05	216,898	798.71	164,592	52,306	814.37	138,717	78,181	830.03	121,914	94,984
70,000	843.29	233,584	860.16	177,256	56,328	877.02	149,389	84,195	893.89	131,294	102,290
75,000	903.52	250,267	921.59	189,914	60,353	939.66	160,059	90,208	957.73	140,670	109,597
80,000	963.75	266,950	983.03	202,575	64,375	1,002.30	170,728	96,222	1,021.58	150,049	116,901
85,000	1,023.99	283,636	1,044.47	215,236	68,400	1,064.95	181,400	102,236	1,085.43	159,427	124,209
90,000	1,084.22	300,319	1,105.90	227,894	72,425	1,127.59	192,070	108,249	1,149.27	168,803	131,516
95,000	1,144.46	317,006	1,167.35	240,553	76,448	1,190.24	202,742	114,264	1,213.13	178,184	138,822
100,000	1,204.69	333,688	1,228.78	253,216	80,472	1,252.88	213,412	120,276	1,276.97	187,560	146,128
105,000	1,264.93	350,375	1,290.23	265,880	84,495	1,315.53	224,084	126,291	1,340.83	196,940	153,435
110,000	1,325.16	367,058	1,351.66	278,539	88,519	1,378.17	234,753	132,305	1,404.67	206,316	160,742
115,000	1,385.40	383,744	1,413.11	291,203	92,541	1,440.82	245,425	138,319	1,468.52	215,695	168,049
120,000	1,445.63	400,427	1,474.54	303,861	96,566	1,503.46	256,096	144,332	1,532.37	225,073	175,354
125,000	1,505.86	417,110	1,535.98	316,522	100,588	1,566.09	266,762	150,348	1,596.21	234,449	182,661
130,000	1,566.10	433,796	1,597.42	329,183	104,613	1,628.74	277,434	156,362	1,660.07	243,830	189,966
135,000	1,626.33	450,479	1,658.86	341,844	108,635	1,691.38	288,104	162,375	1,723.91	253,206	197,273
140,000	1,686.57	467,165	1,720.30	354,505	112,660	1,754.03	298,776	168,389	1,787.76	262,584	204,581
145,000	1,746.80	483,848	1,781.74	367,167	116,681	1,816.67	309,445	174,402	1,851.61	271,962	211,886
150,000	1,807.04	500,534	1,843.18	379,828	120,706	1,879.32	320,118	180,416	1,915.46	281,341	219,193
155,000	1,867.27	517,217	1,904.62	392,489	124,728	1,941.96	330,787	186,430	1,979.31	290,719	226,498
160,000	1,927.50	533,900	1,966.05	405,147	128,753	2,004.60	341,457	192,443	2,043.15	300,095	233,805
165,000	1,987.74	550,586	2,027.49	417,808	132,778	2,067.25	352,129	198,457	2,107.00	309,473	241,113
170,000	2,047.97	567,269	2,088.93	430,469	136,800	2,129.89	362,798	204,471	2,170.85	318,852	248,417
175,000	2,108.21	583,955	2,150.37	443,130	140,826	2,192.54	373,470	210,486	2,234.70	328,230	255,726
180,000	2,168.44	600,638	2,211.81	455,791	144,847	2,255.18	384,140	216,498	2,298.55	337,608	263,030
185,000	2,228.68	617,325	2,273.25	468,453	148,872	2,317.83	394,812	222,513	2,362.40	346,986	270,339
190,000	2,288.91	634,008	2,334.69	481,114	152,894	2,380.47	405,482	228,526	2,426.24	356,363	277,645
195,000	2,349.14	650,690	2,396.12	493,772	156,918	2,443.11	416,151	234,539	2,490.09	365,741	284,949
200,000	2,409.38	667,377	2,457.57	506,436	160,941	2,505.76	426,823	240,554	2,553.94	375,119	292,258

AUGMENTED PAYMENT MORTGAGES 14.25%

AMOUNT OF LOAN	30 YEARS		8% PMT INCREASE 206.573 PAYMENTS			10% PMT INCREASE 191.828 PAYMENTS			12% PMT INCREASE 179.692 PAYMENTS		
	MONTHLY PAYMENT	TOTAL INTRST	MONTHLY PAYMENT	TOTAL INTRST	INTRST SAVED	MONTHLY PAYMENT	TOTAL INTRST	INTRST SAVED	MONTHLY PAYMENT	TOTAL INTRST	INTRST SAVED
$ 50	0.61	170	0.66	86	84	0.67	79	91	0.68	72	98
100	1.21	336	1.31	171	165	1.33	155	181	1.36	144	192
200	2.41	668	2.60	337	331	2.65	308	360	2.70	285	383
300	3.62	1,003	3.91	508	495	3.98	463	540	4.05	428	575
400	4.82	1,335	5.21	676	659	5.30	617	718	5.40	570	765
500	6.03	1,671	6.51	845	826	6.63	772	899	6.75	713	958
600	7.23	2,003	7.81	1,013	990	7.95	925	1,078	8.10	856	1,147
700	8.44	2,338	9.12	1,184	1,154	9.28	1,080	1,258	9.45	998	1,340
800	9.64	2,670	10.41	1,350	1,320	10.60	1,233	1,437	10.80	1,141	1,529
900	10.85	3,006	11.72	1,521	1,485	11.94	1,390	1,616	12.15	1,283	1,723
1,000	12.05	3,338	13.01	1,688	1,650	13.26	1,544	1,794	13.50	1,426	1,912
2,000	24.10	6,676	26.03	3,377	3,299	26.51	3,085	3,591	26.99	2,850	3,826
3,000	36.15	10,014	39.04	5,065	4,949	39.77	4,629	5,385	40.49	4,276	5,738
4,000	48.19	13,348	52.05	6,752	6,596	53.01	6,169	7,179	53.97	5,698	7,650
5,000	60.24	16,686	65.06	8,440	8,246	66.26	7,711	8,975	67.47	7,124	9,562
6,000	72.29	20,024	78.07	10,127	9,897	79.52	9,254	10,770	80.96	8,548	11,476
7,000	84.33	23,359	91.08	11,815	11,544	92.76	10,794	12,565	94.45	9,972	13,387
8,000	96.38	26,697	104.09	13,502	13,195	106.02	12,338	14,359	107.95	11,398	15,299
9,000	108.43	30,035	117.10	15,190	14,845	119.27	13,879	16,156	121.44	12,822	17,213
10,000	120.47	33,369	130.11	16,877	16,492	132.52	15,421	17,948	134.93	14,246	19,123
11,000	132.52	36,707	143.12	18,565	18,142	145.77	16,963	19,744	148.42	15,670	21,037
12,000	144.57	40,045	156.14	20,254	19,791	159.03	18,506	21,539	161.92	17,096	22,949
13,000	156.61	43,380	169.14	21,940	21,440	172.27	20,046	23,334	175.40	18,518	24,862
14,000	168.66	46,718	182.15	23,627	23,091	185.53	21,590	25,128	188.90	19,944	26,774
15,000	180.71	50,056	195.17	25,317	24,739	198.78	23,132	26,924	202.40	21,370	28,686
16,000	192.75	53,390	208.17	27,002	26,388	212.03	24,673	28,717	215.88	22,792	30,598
17,000	204.80	56,728	221.18	28,690	28,038	225.28	26,215	30,513	229.38	24,218	32,510
18,000	216.85	60,066	234.20	30,379	29,687	238.54	27,759	32,307	242.87	25,642	34,424
19,000	228.90	63,404	247.21	32,067	31,337	251.79	29,300	34,104	256.37	27,068	36,336
20,000	240.94	66,738	260.22	33,754	32,984	265.03	30,840	35,898	269.85	28,490	38,248
21,000	252.99	70,076	273.23	35,442	34,634	278.29	32,384	37,692	283.35	29,916	40,160
22,000	265.04	73,414	286.24	37,129	36,285	291.54	33,926	39,488	296.84	31,340	42,074
23,000	277.08	76,749	299.25	38,817	37,932	304.79	35,467	41,282	310.33	32,764	43,985
24,000	289.13	80,087	312.26	40,504	39,583	318.04	37,009	43,078	323.83	34,190	45,897
25,000	301.18	83,425	325.27	42,192	41,233	331.30	38,553	44,872	337.32	35,614	47,811
26,000	313.22	86,759	338.28	43,880	42,879	344.54	40,092	46,667	350.81	37,038	49,721
27,000	325.27	90,097	351.29	45,567	44,530	357.80	41,636	48,461	364.30	38,462	51,635
28,000	337.32	93,435	364.31	47,257	46,178	371.05	43,178	50,257	377.80	39,888	53,547
29,000	349.36	96,770	377.31	48,942	47,828	384.30	44,720	52,050	391.28	41,310	55,460
30,000	361.41	100,108	390.32	50,630	49,478	397.55	46,261	53,847	404.78	42,736	57,372
32,500	391.53	108,451	422.85	54,849	53,602	430.68	50,116	58,335	438.51	46,297	62,154
35,000	421.65	116,794	455.38	59,069	57,725	463.82	53,974	62,820	472.25	49,860	66,934
40,000	481.88	133,477	520.43	67,507	65,970	530.07	61,682	71,795	539.71	56,982	76,495
45,000	542.11	150,160	585.48	75,944	74,216	596.32	69,391	80,769	607.16	64,102	86,058
50,000	602.35	166,846	650.54	84,384	82,462	662.59	77,103	89,743	674.63	71,226	95,620
55,000	662.58	183,529	715.59	92,822	90,707	728.84	84,812	98,717	742.09	78,348	105,181
60,000	722.82	200,215	780.65	101,261	98,954	795.10	92,522	107,693	809.56	85,471	114,744
65,000	783.05	216,898	845.69	109,697	107,201	861.36	100,233	116,665	877.02	92,593	124,305
70,000	843.29	233,584	910.75	118,136	115,448	927.62	107,943	125,641	944.48	99,716	133,868
75,000	903.52	250,267	975.80	126,574	123,693	993.87	115,652	134,615	1,011.94	106,838	143,429
80,000	963.75	266,950	1,040.85	135,012	131,938	1,060.13	123,363	143,587	1,079.40	113,960	152,990
85,000	1,023.99	283,636	1,105.91	143,451	140,185	1,126.39	131,073	152,563	1,146.87	121,083	162,553
90,000	1,084.22	300,319	1,170.96	151,889	148,430	1,192.64	138,782	161,537	1,214.33	128,205	172,114
95,000	1,144.46	317,006	1,236.02	160,328	156,678	1,258.91	146,494	170,512	1,281.80	135,329	181,677
100,000	1,204.69	333,688	1,301.07	168,766	164,922	1,325.16	154,203	179,485	1,349.25	142,449	191,239
105,000	1,264.93	350,375	1,366.12	177,204	173,171	1,391.42	161,913	188,462	1,416.72	149,573	200,802
110,000	1,325.16	367,058	1,431.17	185,641	181,417	1,457.68	169,624	197,434	1,484.18	156,695	210,363
115,000	1,385.40	383,744	1,496.23	194,081	189,663	1,523.94	177,334	206,410	1,551.65	163,819	219,925
120,000	1,445.63	400,427	1,561.28	202,518	197,909	1,590.19	185,043	215,384	1,619.11	170,941	229,486
125,000	1,505.86	417,110	1,626.33	210,956	206,154	1,656.45	192,753	224,357	1,686.56	178,061	239,049
130,000	1,566.10	433,796	1,691.39	219,396	214,400	1,722.71	200,464	233,332	1,754.03	185,185	248,611
135,000	1,626.33	450,479	1,756.44	227,833	222,646	1,788.96	208,173	242,306	1,821.49	192,307	258,172
140,000	1,686.57	467,165	1,821.50	236,273	230,892	1,855.23	215,885	251,280	1,888.96	199,431	267,734
145,000	1,746.80	483,848	1,886.54	244,708	239,140	1,921.48	223,594	260,253	1,956.42	206,555	277,295
150,000	1,807.04	500,534	1,951.60	253,148	247,386	1,987.74	231,304	269,230	2,023.88	213,675	286,859
155,000	1,867.27	517,217	2,016.65	261,585	255,632	2,054.00	239,015	278,202	2,091.34	220,797	296,420
160,000	1,927.50	533,900	2,081.70	270,023	263,877	2,120.25	246,723	287,177	2,158.80	227,919	305,981
165,000	1,987.74	550,586	2,146.76	278,463	272,123	2,186.51	254,434	296,152	2,226.27	235,043	315,543
170,000	2,047.97	567,269	2,211.81	286,900	280,369	2,252.77	262,144	305,125	2,293.73	242,165	325,104
175,000	2,108.21	583,956	2,276.87	295,340	288,616	2,319.03	269,855	314,101	2,361.20	249,289	334,667
180,000	2,168.44	600,638	2,341.92	303,777	296,861	2,385.28	277,563	323,075	2,428.65	256,409	344,229
185,000	2,228.68	617,325	2,406.97	312,215	305,110	2,451.55	285,276	332,049	2,496.12	263,533	353,792
190,000	2,288.91	634,008	2,472.02	320,653	313,355	2,517.80	292,985	341,023	2,563.58	270,655	363,353
195,000	2,349.14	650,690	2,537.07	329,090	321,600	2,584.05	300,693	349,997	2,631.04	277,777	372,913
200,000	2,409.38	667,377	2,602.13	337,530	329,847	2,650.32	308,406	358,971	2,698.51	284,901	382,476

253

AMOUNT OF LOAN	30 YEARS		2% PMT INCREASE 285.039 PAYMENTS			4% PMT INCREASE 247.445 PAYMENTS			6% PMT INCREASE 222.481 PAYMENTS		
	MONTHLY PAYMENT	TOTAL INTRST	MONTHLY PAYMENT	TOTAL INTRST	INTRST SAVED	MONTHLY PAYMENT	TOTAL INTRST	INTRST SAVED	MONTHLY PAYMENT	TOTAL INTRST	INTRST SAVED
$ 50	0.62	173	0.63	130	43	0.64	108	65	0.66	97	76
100	1.23	343	1.25	256	87	1.28	217	126	1.30	189	154
200	2.45	682	2.50	513	169	2.55	431	251	2.60	378	304
300	3.68	1,025	3.75	769	256	3.83	648	377	3.90	568	457
400	4.90	1,364	5.00	1,025	339	5.10	862	502	5.19	755	609
500	6.13	1,707	6.25	1,281	426	6.38	1,079	628	6.50	946	761
600	7.35	2,046	7.50	1,538	508	7.64	1,290	756	7.79	1,133	913
700	8.58	2,389	8.75	1,794	595	8.92	1,507	882	9.09	1,322	1,067
800	9.80	2,728	10.00	2,050	678	10.19	1,721	1,007	10.39	1,512	1,216
900	11.03	3,071	11.25	2,307	764	11.47	1,938	1,133	11.69	1,701	1,370
1,000	12.25	3,410	12.50	2,563	847	12.74	2,152	1,258	12.99	1,890	1,520
2,000	24.50	6,820	24.99	5,123	1,697	25.48	4,305	2,515	25.97	3,778	3,042
3,000	36.74	10,226	37.47	7,680	2,546	38.21	6,455	3,771	38.94	5,663	4,563
4,000	48.99	13,636	49.97	10,243	3,393	50.95	8,607	5,029	51.93	7,553	6,083
5,000	61.23	17,043	62.45	12,801	4,242	63.68	10,757	6,286	64.90	9,439	7,604
6,000	73.48	20,453	74.95	15,364	5,089	76.42	12,910	7,543	77.89	11,329	9,124
7,000	85.72	23,859	87.43	17,921	5,938	89.15	15,060	8,799	90.86	13,215	10,644
8,000	97.97	27,269	99.93	20,484	6,785	101.89	17,212	10,057	103.85	15,105	12,164
9,000	110.22	30,679	112.42	23,044	7,635	114.63	19,366	11,314	116.83	16,992	13,687
10,000	122.46	34,086	124.91	25,604	8,482	127.36	21,515	12,571	129.81	18,880	15,206
11,000	134.71	37,496	137.40	28,164	9,332	140.10	23,667	13,829	142.79	20,768	16,728
12,000	146.95	40,902	149.89	30,724	10,178	152.83	25,817	15,085	155.77	22,656	18,246
13,000	159.20	44,312	162.38	33,285	11,027	165.57	27,969	16,343	168.75	24,544	19,768
14,000	171.44	47,718	174.87	35,845	11,873	178.30	30,119	17,599	181.73	26,431	21,287
15,000	183.69	51,128	187.36	38,405	12,723	191.04	32,272	18,856	194.71	28,319	22,809
16,000	195.93	54,535	199.85	40,965	13,570	203.77	34,422	20,113	207.69	30,207	24,328
17,000	208.18	57,945	212.34	43,525	14,420	216.51	36,574	21,371	220.67	32,095	25,850
18,000	220.43	61,355	224.84	46,088	15,267	229.25	38,727	22,628	233.66	33,985	27,370
19,000	232.67	64,761	237.32	48,645	16,116	241.98	40,877	23,884	246.63	35,870	28,891
20,000	244.92	68,171	249.82	51,208	16,963	254.72	43,029	25,142	259.62	37,761	30,410
21,000	257.16	71,578	262.30	53,766	17,812	267.45	45,179	26,399	272.59	39,646	31,932
22,000	269.41	74,988	274.80	56,329	18,659	280.19	47,332	27,656	285.57	41,534	33,454
23,000	281.65	78,394	287.28	58,886	19,508	292.92	49,482	28,912	298.55	43,422	34,972
24,000	293.90	81,804	299.78	61,449	20,355	305.66	51,634	30,170	311.53	45,310	36,494
25,000	306.14	85,210	312.26	64,006	21,204	318.39	53,784	31,426	324.51	47,197	38,013
26,000	318.39	88,620	324.76	66,569	22,051	331.13	55,936	32,684	337.49	49,085	39,535
27,000	330.64	92,030	337.25	69,129	22,901	343.87	58,089	33,941	350.48	50,975	41,055
28,000	342.88	95,437	349.74	71,690	23,747	356.60	60,239	35,198	363.45	52,861	42,576
29,000	355.13	98,847	362.23	74,250	24,597	369.34	62,391	36,456	376.44	54,751	44,096
30,000	367.37	102,253	374.72	76,810	25,443	382.06	64,539	37,714	389.41	56,636	45,617
32,500	397.99	110,776	405.95	83,212	27,564	413.91	69,920	40,856	421.87	61,358	49,418
35,000	428.60	119,296	437.17	89,610	29,686	445.74	75,296	44,000	454.32	66,078	53,218
40,000	489.83	136,339	499.63	102,414	33,925	509.42	86,053	50,286	519.22	75,517	60,822
45,000	551.06	153,382	562.08	115,215	38,167	573.10	96,811	56,571	584.12	84,956	68,426
50,000	612.28	170,421	624.53	128,015	42,406	636.77	107,566	62,855	649.02	94,395	76,026
55,000	673.51	187,464	686.98	140,816	46,648	700.45	118,323	69,141	713.92	103,834	83,630
60,000	734.74	204,506	749.43	153,617	50,889	764.13	129,080	75,426	778.82	113,273	91,233
65,000	795.97	221,549	811.89	166,420	55,129	827.81	139,837	81,712	843.73	122,714	98,835
70,000	857.19	238,588	874.33	179,218	59,370	891.48	150,592	87,996	908.62	132,151	106,437
75,000	918.42	255,631	936.79	192,022	63,609	955.16	161,350	94,281	973.53	141,592	114,039
80,000	979.65	272,674	999.24	204,822	67,852	1,018.84	172,107	100,567	1,038.43	151,031	121,643
85,000	1,040.88	289,717	1,061.70	217,626	72,091	1,082.52	182,864	106,853	1,103.33	160,470	129,247
90,000	1,102.11	306,760	1,124.15	230,427	76,333	1,146.19	193,619	113,141	1,168.24	169,911	136,849
95,000	1,163.33	323,799	1,186.60	243,227	80,572	1,209.86	204,374	119,425	1,233.13	179,348	144,451
100,000	1,224.56	340,842	1,249.05	256,028	84,814	1,273.54	215,131	125,711	1,298.03	188,787	152,055
105,000	1,285.79	357,884	1,311.51	268,831	89,053	1,337.22	225,888	131,996	1,362.94	198,228	159,656
110,000	1,347.02	374,927	1,373.96	281,632	93,295	1,400.90	236,646	138,281	1,427.84	207,667	167,260
115,000	1,408.24	391,966	1,436.40	294,430	97,536	1,464.57	247,401	144,565	1,492.73	217,104	174,862
120,000	1,469.47	409,009	1,498.86	307,234	101,775	1,528.25	258,158	150,851	1,557.64	226,545	182,464
125,000	1,530.70	426,052	1,561.31	320,034	106,018	1,591.93	268,915	157,137	1,622.54	235,984	190,068
130,000	1,591.93	443,095	1,623.77	332,838	110,257	1,655.61	279,672	163,423	1,687.45	245,426	197,669
135,000	1,653.16	460,138	1,686.22	345,638	114,500	1,719.29	290,430	169,708	1,752.35	254,865	205,273
140,000	1,714.38	477,177	1,748.67	358,439	118,738	1,782.96	301,185	175,992	1,817.24	264,301	212,876
145,000	1,775.61	494,220	1,811.12	371,240	122,980	1,846.63	311,939	182,281	1,882.15	273,743	220,477
150,000	1,836.84	511,262	1,873.58	384,043	127,219	1,910.31	322,697	188,565	1,947.05	283,182	228,080
155,000	1,898.07	528,305	1,936.03	396,844	131,461	1,973.99	333,454	194,851	2,011.95	292,621	235,684
160,000	1,959.29	545,344	1,998.48	409,645	135,699	2,037.66	344,209	201,135	2,076.85	302,060	243,284
165,000	2,020.52	562,387	2,060.93	422,445	139,942	2,101.34	354,966	207,421	2,141.75	311,499	250,888
170,000	2,081.75	579,430	2,123.39	435,249	144,181	2,165.02	365,723	213,707	2,206.66	320,940	258,490
175,000	2,142.98	596,473	2,185.84	448,050	148,423	2,228.70	376,481	219,992	2,271.56	330,379	266,094
180,000	2,204.21	613,516	2,248.29	460,850	152,666	2,292.38	387,238	226,278	2,336.46	339,818	273,698
185,000	2,265.43	630,555	2,310.74	473,651	156,904	2,356.05	397,993	232,562	2,401.36	349,257	281,298
190,000	2,326.66	647,598	2,373.19	486,452	161,146	2,419.73	408,750	238,848	2,466.26	358,696	288,902
195,000	2,387.89	664,640	2,435.65	499,255	165,385	2,483.41	419,507	245,133	2,531.16	368,135	296,505
200,000	2,449.12	681,683	2,498.10	512,056	169,627	2,547.08	430,262	251,421	2,596.07	377,576	304,107

AUGMENTED PAYMENT MORTGAGES 14.50%

AMOUNT OF LOAN	30 YEARS		8% PMT INCREASE 203.936 PAYMENTS			10% PMT INCREASE 189.286 PAYMENTS			12% PMT INCREASE 177.246 PAYMENTS		
	MONTHLY PAYMENT	TOTAL INTRST	MONTHLY PAYMENT	TOTAL INTRST	INTRST SAVED	MONTHLY PAYMENT	TOTAL INTRST	INTRST SAVED	MONTHLY PAYMENT	TOTAL INTRST	INTRST SAVED
$ 50	0.62	173	0.67	87	86	0.68	79	94	0.69	72	101
100	1.23	343	1.33	171	172	1.35	156	187	1.38	145	198
200	2.45	682	2.65	340	342	2.70	311	371	2.74	286	396
300	3.68	1,025	3.97	510	515	4.05	467	558	4.12	430	595
400	4.90	1,364	5.29	679	685	5.39	620	744	5.49	573	791
500	6.13	1,707	6.62	850	857	6.74	776	931	6.87	718	989
600	7.35	2,046	7.94	1,019	1,027	8.09	931	1,115	8.23	859	1,187
700	8.58	2,389	9.27	1,190	1,199	9.44	1,087	1,302	9.61	1,003	1,386
800	9.80	2,728	10.58	1,358	1,370	10.78	1,241	1,487	10.98	1,146	1,582
900	11.03	3,071	11.91	1,529	1,542	12.13	1,396	1,675	12.35	1,289	1,782
1,000	12.25	3,410	13.23	1,698	1,712	13.48	1,552	1,858	13.72	1,432	1,978
2,000	24.50	6,820	26.46	3,396	3,424	26.95	3,101	3,719	27.44	2,864	3,956
3,000	36.74	10,226	39.68	5,092	5,134	40.41	4,649	5,577	41.15	4,294	5,932
4,000	48.99	13,636	52.91	6,790	6,846	53.89	6,201	7,435	54.87	5,725	7,911
5,000	61.23	17,043	66.13	8,486	8,557	67.35	7,748	9,295	68.58	7,156	9,887
6,000	73.48	20,453	79.36	10,184	10,269	80.83	9,300	11,153	82.30	8,587	11,866
7,000	85.72	23,859	92.58	11,880	11,979	94.29	10,848	13,011	96.01	10,017	13,842
8,000	97.97	27,269	105.81	13,578	13,691	107.77	12,399	14,870	109.73	11,449	15,820
9,000	110.22	30,679	119.04	15,277	15,402	121.24	13,949	16,730	123.45	12,881	17,798
10,000	122.46	34,086	132.26	16,973	17,113	134.71	15,499	18,587	137.16	14,311	19,775
11,000	134.71	37,496	145.49	18,671	18,825	148.18	17,048	20,448	150.88	15,743	21,753
12,000	146.95	40,902	158.71	20,367	20,535	161.65	18,598	22,304	164.58	17,171	23,731
13,000	159.20	44,312	171.94	22,065	22,247	175.12	20,148	24,164	178.30	18,603	25,709
14,000	171.44	47,718	185.16	23,761	23,957	188.58	21,696	26,022	192.01	20,033	27,685
15,000	183.69	51,128	198.39	25,459	25,669	202.06	23,247	27,881	205.73	21,465	29,663
16,000	195.93	54,535	211.60	27,153	27,382	215.52	24,795	29,740	219.44	22,895	31,640
17,000	208.18	57,945	224.83	28,851	29,094	229.00	26,346	31,599	233.16	24,327	33,618
18,000	220.43	61,359	238.06	30,549	30,806	242.47	27,896	33,459	246.88	25,758	35,597
19,000	232.67	64,761	251.28	32,245	32,516	255.94	29,446	35,315	260.59	27,189	37,572
20,000	244.92	68,171	264.51	33,943	34,228	269.41	30,996	37,175	274.31	28,620	39,551
21,000	257.16	71,578	277.73	35,639	35,939	282.88	32,545	39,033	288.02	30,050	41,528
22,000	269.41	74,988	290.96	37,337	37,651	296.35	34,095	40,893	301.74	31,482	43,506
23,000	281.65	78,394	304.18	39,033	39,361	309.82	35,645	42,749	315.45	32,912	45,482
24,000	293.90	81,804	317.41	40,731	41,073	323.29	37,194	44,610	329.17	34,344	47,460
25,000	306.14	85,210	330.63	42,427	42,783	336.75	38,742	46,468	342.88	35,774	49,436
26,000	318.39	88,620	343.86	44,125	44,495	350.23	40,294	48,326	356.60	37,206	51,414
27,000	330.64	92,030	357.09	45,824	46,206	363.70	41,843	50,187	370.32	38,638	53,392
28,000	342.88	95,437	370.31	47,520	47,917	377.17	43,393	52,044	384.03	40,068	55,369
29,000	355.13	98,847	383.54	49,218	49,629	390.64	44,943	53,904	397.75	41,500	57,347
30,000	367.37	102,253	396.76	50,914	51,339	404.11	46,492	55,761	411.45	42,928	59,325
32,500	397.99	110,776	429.83	55,158	55,618	437.79	50,368	60,408	445.75	46,507	64,269
35,000	428.60	119,296	462.89	59,400	59,896	471.46	54,241	65,055	480.03	50,083	69,213
40,000	489.83	136,339	529.02	67,886	68,453	538.81	61,989	74,350	548.61	57,239	79,100
45,000	551.06	153,382	595.14	76,370	77,012	606.17	69,739	83,643	617.19	64,394	88,988
50,000	612.28	170,421	661.26	84,855	85,566	673.51	77,486	92,935	685.75	71,546	98,875
55,000	673.51	187,464	727.39	93,341	94,123	740.86	85,234	102,230	754.33	78,702	108,762
60,000	734.74	204,506	793.52	101,827	102,679	808.21	92,983	111,523	822.91	85,858	118,648
65,000	795.97	221,549	859.65	110,314	111,235	875.57	100,733	120,816	891.49	93,013	128,536
70,000	857.19	238,588	925.77	118,798	119,790	942.91	108,480	130,108	960.05	100,165	138,423
75,000	918.42	255,631	991.89	127,282	128,349	1,010.26	116,228	139,403	1,028.63	107,321	148,310
80,000	979.65	272,674	1,058.02	135,768	136,906	1,077.62	123,978	148,696	1,097.21	114,476	158,198
85,000	1,040.88	289,717	1,124.15	144,255	145,462	1,144.97	131,727	157,990	1,165.79	121,632	168,085
90,000	1,102.11	306,760	1,190.28	152,741	154,019	1,212.32	139,475	167,285	1,234.36	128,785	177,975
95,000	1,163.33	323,799	1,256.40	161,225	162,574	1,279.66	147,222	176,577	1,302.93	135,939	187,860
100,000	1,224.56	340,842	1,322.52	169,709	171,133	1,347.02	154,972	185,870	1,371.51	143,095	197,747
105,000	1,285.79	357,884	1,388.65	178,196	179,688	1,414.37	162,720	195,164	1,440.08	150,248	207,636
110,000	1,347.02	374,927	1,454.78	186,682	188,245	1,481.72	170,469	204,458	1,508.66	157,404	217,523
115,000	1,408.24	391,968	1,520.90	195,166	196,800	1,549.06	178,215	213,751	1,577.23	164,558	227,408
120,000	1,469.47	409,009	1,587.03	203,653	205,356	1,616.42	185,966	223,043	1,645.81	171,713	237,296
125,000	1,530.70	426,052	1,653.16	212,139	213,913	1,683.77	193,714	232,338	1,714.38	178,867	247,185
130,000	1,591.93	443,095	1,719.28	220,623	222,472	1,751.12	201,463	241,632	1,782.96	186,023	257,072
135,000	1,653.16	460,138	1,785.41	229,109	231,029	1,818.48	209,213	250,925	1,851.54	193,178	266,960
140,000	1,714.38	477,177	1,851.53	237,594	239,583	1,885.82	216,959	260,218	1,920.11	200,332	276,845
145,000	1,775.61	494,220	1,917.66	246,080	248,140	1,953.17	224,708	269,512	1,988.68	207,486	286,734
150,000	1,836.84	511,262	1,983.79	254,566	256,696	2,020.52	232,456	278,806	2,057.26	214,641	296,621
155,000	1,898.07	528,305	2,049.92	263,052	265,253	2,087.88	240,206	288,099	2,125.84	221,797	306,508
160,000	1,959.29	545,344	2,116.03	271,535	273,809	2,155.22	247,953	297,391	2,194.40	228,949	316,395
165,000	2,020.52	562,387	2,182.16	280,021	282,366	2,222.57	255,701	306,686	2,262.98	236,104	326,283
170,000	2,081.75	579,430	2,248.29	288,507	290,923	2,289.93	263,452	315,978	2,331.56	243,259	336,170
175,000	2,142.98	596,473	2,314.42	296,994	299,479	2,357.28	271,200	325,273	2,400.14	250,415	346,058
180,000	2,204.21	613,516	2,380.55	305,480	308,036	2,424.63	278,949	334,567	2,468.72	257,571	355,945
185,000	2,265.43	630,555	2,446.66	313,962	316,593	2,491.97	286,695	343,860	2,537.28	264,723	365,832
190,000	2,326.66	647,598	2,512.79	322,448	325,150	2,559.33	294,445	353,153	2,605.86	271,878	375,720
195,000	2,387.89	664,640	2,578.92	330,935	333,705	2,626.68	302,194	362,446	2,674.44	279,034	385,606
200,000	2,449.12	681,683	2,645.05	339,421	342,262	2,694.03	309,942	371,741	2,743.01	286,188	395,495

255

AUGMENTED PAYMENT MORTGAGES

AMOUNT OF LOAN	30 YEARS		2% PMT INCREASE 282.601 PAYMENTS			4% PMT INCREASE 244.743 PAYMENTS			6% PMT INCREASE 219.796 PAYMENTS		
	MONTHLY PAYMENT	TOTAL INTRST	MONTHLY PAYMENT	TOTAL INTRST	INTRST SAVED	MONTHLY PAYMENT	TOTAL INTRST	INTRST SAVED	MONTHLY PAYMENT	TOTAL INTRST	INTRST SAVED
$ 50	0.63	177	0.64	131	46	0.66	112	65	0.67	97	80
100	1.25	350	1.28	262	88	1.30	218	132	1.33	192	158
200	2.49	696	2.54	518	178	2.59	434	262	2.64	380	316
300	3.74	1,046	3.81	777	269	3.89	652	394	3.96	570	476
400	4.98	1,393	5.08	1,036	357	5.18	868	525	5.28	761	632
500	6.23	1,743	6.35	1,295	448	6.48	1,086	657	6.60	951	792
600	7.47	2,089	7.62	1,553	536	7.77	1,302	787	7.92	1,141	948
700	8.72	2,439	8.89	1,812	627	9.07	1,520	919	9.24	1,331	1,108
800	9.96	2,786	10.16	2,071	715	10.36	1,736	1,050	10.56	1,521	1,265
900	11.21	3,136	11.43	2,330	806	11.66	1,954	1,182	11.88	1,711	1,425
1,000	12.45	3,482	12.70	2,589	893	12.95	2,169	1,313	13.20	1,901	1,581
2,000	24.89	6,960	25.39	5,175	1,785	25.89	4,336	2,624	26.38	3,798	3,162
3,000	37.34	10,442	38.09	7,764	2,678	38.83	6,503	3,939	39.58	5,700	4,742
4,000	49.78	13,921	50.78	10,350	3,571	51.77	8,670	5,251	52.77	7,599	6,322
5,000	62.23	17,403	63.47	12,937	4,466	64.72	10,840	6,563	65.96	9,498	7,905
6,000	74.67	20,881	76.16	15,523	5,358	77.66	13,007	7,874	79.15	11,397	9,484
7,000	87.12	24,363	88.86	18,112	6,251	90.60	15,174	9,189	92.35	13,298	11,065
8,000	99.56	27,842	101.55	20,698	7,144	103.54	17,341	10,501	105.53	15,195	12,647
9,000	112.01	31,324	114.25	23,287	8,037	116.49	19,510	11,814	118.73	17,096	14,228
10,000	124.45	34,802	126.94	25,873	8,929	129.43	21,677	13,125	131.92	18,995	15,807
11,000	136.90	38,284	139.64	28,462	9,822	142.38	23,847	14,437	145.11	20,895	17,389
12,000	149.34	41,762	152.33	31,049	10,713	155.31	26,011	15,751	158.30	22,794	18,968
13,000	161.79	45,244	165.03	33,638	11,606	168.26	28,180	17,064	171.50	24,695	20,549
14,000	174.23	48,723	177.71	36,221	12,502	181.20	30,347	18,376	184.68	26,592	22,131
15,000	186.68	52,205	190.41	38,810	13,395	194.15	32,517	19,688	197.88	28,493	23,712
16,000	199.12	55,683	203.10	41,396	14,287	207.08	34,681	21,002	211.07	30,392	25,291
17,000	211.57	59,165	215.80	43,985	15,180	220.03	36,851	22,314	224.26	32,291	26,874
18,000	224.01	62,644	228.49	46,572	16,072	232.97	39,018	23,626	237.45	34,191	28,453
19,000	236.46	66,126	241.19	49,161	16,965	245.92	41,187	24,939	250.65	36,092	30,034
20,000	248.90	69,604	253.88	51,747	17,857	258.86	43,354	26,250	263.83	37,989	31,615
21,000	261.34	73,082	266.57	54,333	18,749	271.79	45,519	27,563	277.02	39,888	33,194
22,000	273.79	76,564	279.27	56,922	19,642	284.74	47,688	28,876	290.22	41,789	34,775
23,000	286.23	80,043	291.95	59,505	20,538	297.68	49,855	30,188	303.40	43,686	36,357
24,000	298.68	83,525	304.65	62,094	21,431	310.63	52,025	31,500	316.60	45,587	37,938
25,000	311.12	87,003	317.34	64,681	22,322	323.56	54,189	32,814	329.79	47,487	39,516
26,000	323.57	90,485	330.04	67,270	23,215	336.51	56,358	34,127	342.98	49,386	41,099
27,000	336.01	93,964	342.73	69,856	24,108	349.45	58,525	35,439	356.17	51,285	42,679
28,000	348.46	97,446	355.43	72,445	25,001	362.40	60,695	36,751	369.37	53,186	44,260
29,000	360.90	100,924	368.12	75,031	25,893	375.34	62,862	38,062	382.55	55,083	45,841
30,000	373.35	104,406	380.82	77,620	26,786	388.28	65,029	39,377	395.75	56,984	47,422
32,500	404.46	113,106	412.55	84,087	29,019	420.64	70,464	42,657	428.73	61,733	51,373
35,000	435.57	121,805	444.28	90,554	31,251	452.99	75,866	45,939	461.70	66,480	55,325
40,000	497.80	139,208	507.76	103,493	35,715	517.71	86,706	52,502	527.67	75,980	63,228
45,000	560.02	156,607	571.22	116,427	40,180	582.42	97,543	59,064	593.62	85,475	71,132
50,000	622.24	174,006	634.68	129,361	44,645	647.13	108,381	65,625	659.57	94,971	79,035
55,000	684.47	191,409	698.16	142,301	49,108	711.85	119,220	72,189	725.54	104,471	86,938
60,000	746.69	208,808	761.62	155,235	53,573	776.56	130,058	78,750	791.49	113,966	94,842
65,000	808.91	226,208	825.09	168,171	58,037	841.27	140,895	85,313	857.44	123,462	102,746
70,000	871.14	243,610	888.56	181,108	62,502	905.99	151,735	91,875	923.41	132,962	110,648
75,000	933.36	261,010	952.03	194,045	66,965	970.69	162,570	98,440	989.36	142,457	118,553
80,000	995.59	278,412	1,015.50	206,981	71,431	1,035.41	173,409	105,003	1,055.33	151,957	126,455
85,000	1,057.81	295,812	1,078.97	219,918	75,894	1,100.12	184,247	111,565	1,121.28	161,453	134,359
90,000	1,120.03	313,211	1,142.43	232,852	80,359	1,164.83	195,084	118,127	1,187.23	170,948	142,263
95,000	1,182.26	330,614	1,205.91	245,791	84,823	1,229.55	206,324	124,690	1,253.20	180,448	150,166
100,000	1,244.48	348,013	1,269.37	258,725	89,288	1,294.26	216,761	131,252	1,319.15	189,944	158,069
105,000	1,306.70	365,412	1,332.83	271,659	93,753	1,358.97	227,598	137,814	1,385.10	199,439	165,973
110,000	1,368.93	382,815	1,396.31	284,599	98,216	1,423.69	238,438	144,377	1,451.07	208,939	173,876
115,000	1,431.15	400,214	1,459.77	297,532	102,682	1,488.40	249,275	150,939	1,517.02	218,435	181,779
120,000	1,493.38	417,617	1,523.25	310,472	107,145	1,553.12	260,115	157,502	1,582.98	227,933	189,684
125,000	1,555.60	435,016	1,586.71	323,406	111,610	1,617.82	270,950	164,066	1,648.94	237,430	197,586
130,000	1,617.82	452,415	1,650.18	336,343	116,072	1,682.53	281,787	170,628	1,714.89	246,926	205,489
135,000	1,680.05	469,818	1,713.65	349,279	120,539	1,747.25	292,627	177,191	1,780.85	256,424	213,394
140,000	1,742.27	487,217	1,777.12	362,216	125,001	1,811.96	303,465	183,752	1,846.81	265,921	221,296
145,000	1,804.49	504,616	1,840.58	375,150	129,466	1,876.67	314,302	190,314	1,912.76	275,417	229,199
150,000	1,866.72	522,019	1,904.05	388,086	133,933	1,941.39	325,142	196,877	1,978.72	284,915	237,104
155,000	1,928.94	539,418	1,967.52	401,023	138,395	2,006.10	335,979	203,439	2,044.68	294,412	245,006
160,000	1,991.17	556,821	2,030.99	413,960	142,861	2,070.82	346,819	210,002	2,110.64	303,910	252,911
165,000	2,053.39	574,220	2,094.46	426,896	147,324	2,135.53	357,656	216,564	2,176.59	313,406	260,814
170,000	2,115.61	591,620	2,157.92	439,830	151,790	2,200.23	368,491	223,129	2,242.55	322,904	268,716
175,000	2,177.84	609,022	2,221.40	452,770	156,252	2,264.95	379,331	229,691	2,308.51	332,401	276,621
180,000	2,240.06	626,422	2,284.86	465,704	160,718	2,329.66	390,168	236,254	2,374.46	341,897	284,525
185,000	2,302.29	643,824	2,348.34	478,643	165,181	2,394.38	401,008	242,816	2,440.43	351,397	292,427
190,000	2,364.51	661,224	2,411.80	491,577	169,647	2,459.09	411,845	249,379	2,506.38	360,892	300,332
195,000	2,426.73	678,623	2,475.26	504,511	174,112	2,523.80	422,682	255,941	2,572.33	370,388	308,235
200,000	2,488.96	696,026	2,538.74	517,450	178,576	2,588.52	433,522	262,504	2,638.30	379,888	316,138

AUGMENTED PAYMENT MORTGAGES 14.75%

AMOUNT OF LOAN	30 YEARS MONTHLY PAYMENT	30 YEARS TOTAL INTRST	8% PMT INCREASE 201.336 PAYMENTS MONTHLY PAYMENT	TOTAL INTRST	INTRST SAVED	10% PMT INCREASE 186.784 PAYMENTS MONTHLY PAYMENT	TOTAL INTRST	INTRST SAVED	12% PMT INCREASE 174.843 PAYMENTS MONTHLY PAYMENT	TOTAL INTRST	INTRST SAVED
$ 50	0.63	177	0.68	87	90	0.69	79	98	0.71	74	103
100	1.25	350	1.35	172	178	1.38	158	192	1.40	145	205
200	2.49	696	2.69	342	354	2.74	312	384	2.79	288	408
300	3.74	1,046	4.04	513	533	4.11	468	578	4.19	433	613
400	4.98	1,393	5.38	683	710	5.48	624	769	5.58	576	817
500	6.23	1,743	6.73	855	888	6.85	779	964	6.98	720	1,023
600	7.47	2,089	8.07	1,025	1,064	8.22	935	1,154	8.37	863	1,226
700	8.72	2,439	9.42	1,197	1,242	9.59	1,091	1,348	9.77	1,008	1,431
800	9.96	2,786	10.76	1,366	1,420	10.96	1,247	1,539	11.16	1,151	1,635
900	11.21	3,136	12.11	1,538	1,598	12.33	1,403	1,733	12.56	1,296	1,840
1,000	12.45	3,482	13.45	1,708	1,774	13.70	1,559	1,923	13.94	1,437	2,045
2,000	24.89	6,960	26.88	3,412	3,548	27.38	3,114	3,846	27.88	2,875	4,085
3,000	37.34	10,442	40.33	5,120	5,322	41.07	4,671	5,771	41.82	4,312	6,130
4,000	49.78	13,921	53.76	6,824	7,097	54.76	6,228	7,693	55.75	5,747	8,174
5,000	62.23	17,403	67.21	8,532	8,871	68.45	7,785	9,618	69.70	7,187	10,216
6,000	74.67	20,881	80.64	10,236	10,645	82.14	9,342	11,539	83.63	8,622	12,259
7,000	87.12	24,363	94.09	11,944	12,419	95.83	10,900	13,463	97.57	10,059	14,304
8,000	99.56	27,842	107.52	13,648	14,194	109.52	12,457	15,385	111.51	11,497	16,345
9,000	112.01	31,324	120.97	15,356	15,968	123.21	14,014	17,310	125.45	12,934	18,390
10,000	124.45	34,802	134.41	17,062	17,740	136.90	15,571	19,231	139.38	14,370	20,432
11,000	136.90	38,284	147.85	18,768	19,516	150.59	17,128	21,156	153.33	15,809	22,475
12,000	149.34	41,762	161.29	20,473	21,289	164.27	18,683	23,079	167.26	17,244	24,518
13,000	161.79	45,244	174.73	22,179	23,065	177.97	20,242	25,002	181.20	18,682	26,562
14,000	174.23	48,723	188.17	23,885	24,838	191.65	21,797	26,926	195.14	20,119	28,604
15,000	186.68	52,205	201.61	25,591	26,614	205.35	23,356	28,849	209.08	21,556	30,649
16,000	199.12	55,683	215.05	27,297	28,386	219.03	24,911	30,772	223.01	22,992	32,691
17,000	211.57	59,165	228.50	29,005	30,160	232.73	26,470	32,695	236.96	24,431	34,734
18,000	224.01	62,644	241.93	30,709	31,935	246.41	28,025	34,619	250.89	25,866	36,778
19,000	236.46	66,126	255.38	32,417	33,709	260.11	29,584	36,542	264.84	27,305	38,821
20,000	248.90	69,604	268.81	34,121	35,483	273.79	31,140	38,464	278.77	28,741	40,863
21,000	261.34	73,082	282.25	35,827	37,255	287.47	32,695	40,387	292.70	30,177	42,905
22,000	273.79	76,564	295.69	37,533	39,031	301.17	34,254	42,310	306.64	31,614	44,950
23,000	286.23	80,043	309.13	39,239	40,804	314.85	35,809	44,234	320.58	33,051	46,992
24,000	298.68	83,525	322.57	40,945	42,580	328.55	37,368	46,157	334.52	34,488	49,037
25,000	311.12	87,003	336.01	42,651	44,352	342.23	38,923	48,080	348.45	35,924	51,079
26,000	323.57	90,485	349.46	44,359	46,126	355.93	40,482	50,003	362.40	37,363	53,122
27,000	336.01	93,964	362.89	46,063	47,901	369.61	42,037	51,927	376.33	38,799	55,165
28,000	348.46	97,446	376.34	47,771	49,675	383.31	43,596	53,850	390.28	40,238	57,208
29,000	360.90	100,924	389.77	49,475	51,449	396.99	45,151	55,773	404.21	41,673	59,251
30,000	373.35	104,406	403.22	51,183	53,223	410.69	46,710	57,696	418.15	43,111	61,295
32,500	404.46	113,106	436.82	55,448	57,658	444.91	50,602	62,504	453.00	46,704	66,402
35,000	435.57	121,805	470.42	59,712	62,093	479.13	54,494	67,311	487.84	50,295	71,510
40,000	497.80	139,208	537.62	68,242	70,966	547.58	62,279	76,929	557.54	57,482	81,726
45,000	560.02	156,607	604.82	76,772	79,835	616.02	70,063	86,544	627.22	64,665	91,942
50,000	622.24	174,006	672.02	85,302	88,704	684.46	77,846	96,160	696.91	71,850	102,156
55,000	684.47	191,409	739.23	93,834	97,575	752.92	85,633	105,776	766.61	79,036	112,373
60,000	746.69	208,808	806.43	102,363	106,445	821.36	93,417	115,391	836.29	86,219	122,589
65,000	808.91	226,208	873.62	110,891	115,317	889.80	101,200	125,008	905.98	93,404	132,804
70,000	871.14	243,610	940.83	119,423	124,187	958.25	108,986	134,624	975.68	100,591	143,019
75,000	933.36	261,010	1,008.03	127,953	133,057	1,026.70	116,771	144,239	1,045.36	107,774	153,236
80,000	995.59	278,412	1,075.24	136,485	141,927	1,095.15	124,556	153,856	1,115.06	114,960	163,452
85,000	1,057.81	295,812	1,142.43	145,012	150,800	1,163.59	132,340	163,472	1,184.75	122,145	173,667
90,000	1,120.03	313,211	1,209.63	153,542	159,669	1,232.03	140,123	173,088	1,254.43	129,328	183,883
95,000	1,182.26	330,614	1,276.84	162,074	168,540	1,300.49	147,911	182,703	1,324.13	136,515	194,099
100,000	1,244.48	348,013	1,344.04	170,604	177,409	1,368.93	155,694	192,319	1,393.82	143,700	204,313
105,000	1,306.70	365,412	1,411.24	179,133	186,279	1,437.37	163,478	201,934	1,463.50	150,883	214,529
110,000	1,368.93	382,815	1,478.44	187,663	195,152	1,505.82	171,263	211,552	1,533.20	158,069	224,746
115,000	1,431.15	400,214	1,545.64	196,193	204,021	1,574.27	179,048	221,166	1,602.89	165,254	234,960
120,000	1,493.38	417,617	1,612.85	204,725	212,892	1,642.72	186,834	230,783	1,672.59	172,441	245,176
125,000	1,555.60	435,016	1,680.05	213,255	221,761	1,711.16	194,617	240,399	1,742.27	179,624	255,392
130,000	1,617.82	452,415	1,747.25	221,784	230,631	1,779.60	202,401	250,014	1,811.96	186,809	265,606
135,000	1,680.05	469,818	1,814.45	230,314	239,504	1,848.06	210,188	259,630	1,881.66	193,995	275,823
140,000	1,742.27	487,217	1,881.65	238,844	248,373	1,916.50	217,972	269,245	1,951.34	201,178	286,039
145,000	1,804.49	504,616	1,948.85	247,374	257,242	1,984.94	225,755	278,861	2,021.03	208,363	296,253
150,000	1,866.72	522,019	2,016.06	255,905	266,114	2,053.39	233,540	288,479	2,090.73	215,550	306,469
155,000	1,928.94	539,418	2,083.26	264,435	274,983	2,121.83	241,324	298,094	2,160.41	222,733	316,685
160,000	1,991.17	556,821	2,150.46	272,965	283,856	2,190.29	249,111	307,710	2,230.11	229,919	326,902
165,000	2,053.39	574,220	2,217.66	281,495	292,725	2,258.73	256,895	317,325	2,299.80	237,104	337,116
170,000	2,115.61	591,620	2,284.86	290,025	301,595	2,327.17	264,678	326,942	2,369.48	244,287	347,333
175,000	2,177.84	609,022	2,352.07	298,556	310,466	2,395.62	272,463	336,559	2,439.18	251,474	357,548
180,000	2,240.06	626,422	2,419.26	307,084	319,338	2,464.07	280,249	346,173	2,508.87	258,658	367,764
185,000	2,302.29	643,824	2,486.47	315,616	328,208	2,532.52	288,034	355,790	2,578.56	265,843	377,981
190,000	2,364.51	661,224	2,553.67	324,146	337,078	2,600.96	295,818	365,406	2,648.25	273,028	388,196
195,000	2,426.73	678,623	2,620.87	332,675	345,948	2,669.40	303,601	375,022	2,717.94	280,213	398,410
200,000	2,488.96	696,026	2,688.08	341,207	354,819	2,737.86	311,388	384,638	2,787.64	287,399	408,627

257

AUGMENTED PAYMENT MORTGAGES

AMOUNT OF LOAN	30 YEARS		2% PMT INCREASE 280.138 PAYMENTS			4% PMT INCREASE 242.052 PAYMENTS			6% PMT INCREASE 217.139 PAYMENTS		
	MONTHLY PAYMENT	TOTAL INTRST	MONTHLY PAYMENT	TOTAL INTRST	INTRST SAVED	MONTHLY PAYMENT	TOTAL INTRST	INTRST SAVED	MONTHLY PAYMENT	TOTAL INTRST	INTRST SAVED
$ 50	0.64	180	0.65	132	48	0.67	112	68	0.68	98	82
100	1.27	357	1.30	264	93	1.32	220	137	1.35	193	164
200	2.53	711	2.58	523	188	2.63	437	274	2.68	382	329
300	3.80	1,068	3.88	787	281	3.95	656	412	4.03	575	493
400	5.06	1,422	5.16	1,046	376	5.26	873	549	5.36	764	658
500	6.33	1,779	6.46	1,310	469	6.58	1,093	686	6.71	957	822
600	7.59	2,132	7.74	1,568	564	7.89	1,310	822	8.05	1,148	984
700	8.86	2,490	9.04	1,832	658	9.21	1,529	961	9.39	1,339	1,151
800	10.12	2,843	10.32	2,091	752	10.52	1,746	1,097	10.73	1,530	1,313
900	11.38	3,197	11.61	2,352	845	11.84	1,966	1,231	12.06	1,719	1,478
1,000	12.65	3,554	12.90	2,614	940	13.16	2,185	1,369	13.41	1,912	1,642
2,000	25.29	7,104	25.80	5,228	1,876	26.30	4,366	2,738	26.81	3,821	3,283
3,000	37.94	10,658	38.70	7,841	2,817	39.46	6,551	4,107	40.22	5,733	4,925
4,000	50.58	14,209	51.59	10,452	3,757	52.60	8,732	5,477	53.61	7,641	6,568
5,000	63.23	17,763	64.49	13,066	4,697	65.76	10,917	6,846	67.02	9,553	8,210
6,000	75.87	21,313	77.39	15,680	5,633	78.90	13,098	8,215	80.42	11,462	9,851
7,000	88.52	24,867	90.29	18,294	6,573	92.06	15,283	9,584	93.83	13,374	11,493
8,000	101.16	28,418	103.18	20,905	7,513	105.21	17,466	10,952	107.23	15,284	13,134
9,000	113.80	31,968	116.08	23,518	8,450	118.35	19,647	12,321	120.63	17,193	14,775
10,000	126.45	35,522	128.98	26,132	9,390	131.51	21,832	13,690	134.04	19,105	16,417
11,000	139.09	39,072	141.87	28,743	10,329	144.65	24,013	15,059	147.44	21,015	18,057
12,000	151.74	42,626	154.77	31,357	11,269	157.81	26,198	16,428	160.84	22,925	19,701
13,000	164.38	46,177	167.67	33,971	12,206	170.96	28,381	17,796	174.24	24,834	21,343
14,000	177.03	49,731	180.57	36,585	13,146	184.11	30,564	19,167	187.65	26,746	22,985
15,000	189.67	53,281	193.46	39,195	14,086	197.26	32,747	20,534	201.05	28,656	24,625
16,000	202.32	56,835	206.37	41,812	15,023	210.41	34,930	21,905	214.46	30,568	26,267
17,000	214.96	60,386	219.26	44,423	15,963	223.56	37,113	23,273	227.86	32,477	27,909
18,000	227.60	63,936	232.15	47,034	16,902	236.70	39,294	24,642	241.26	34,387	29,549
19,000	240.25	67,490	245.06	49,651	17,839	249.86	41,479	26,011	254.67	36,299	31,191
20,000	252.89	71,040	257.95	52,262	18,778	263.01	43,662	27,378	268.06	38,206	32,834
21,000	265.54	74,594	270.85	54,875	19,719	276.16	45,845	28,749	281.47	40,118	34,476
22,000	278.18	78,145	283.74	57,486	20,659	289.31	48,028	30,117	294.87	42,028	36,117
23,000	290.83	81,699	296.65	60,103	21,596	302.46	50,211	31,488	308.28	43,940	37,759
24,000	303.47	85,249	309.54	62,714	22,535	315.61	52,394	32,855	321.68	45,849	39,400
25,000	316.12	88,803	322.44	65,328	23,475	328.76	54,577	34,226	335.09	47,761	41,042
26,000	328.76	92,354	335.34	67,941	24,413	341.91	56,760	35,594	348.49	49,671	42,683
27,000	341.40	95,904	348.23	70,552	25,352	355.06	58,943	36,961	361.88	51,578	44,326
28,000	354.05	99,458	361.13	73,166	26,292	368.21	61,126	38,332	375.29	53,490	45,968
29,000	366.69	103,008	374.02	75,777	27,231	381.36	63,309	39,699	388.69	55,400	47,608
30,000	379.34	106,562	386.93	78,394	28,168	394.51	65,492	41,070	402.10	57,312	49,250
32,500	410.95	115,442	419.17	84,925	30,517	427.39	70,951	44,491	435.61	62,088	53,354
35,000	442.56	124,322	451.41	91,447	32,865	460.26	76,407	47,915	469.11	66,862	57,460
40,000	505.78	142,081	515.90	104,523	37,558	526.01	87,322	54,759	536.13	76,415	65,666
45,000	569.00	159,840	580.38	117,586	42,254	591.76	98,237	61,603	603.14	85,965	73,875
50,000	632.23	177,603	644.87	130,653	46,950	657.52	109,154	68,449	670.16	95,518	82,085
55,000	695.45	195,362	709.36	143,719	51,643	723.27	120,069	75,293	737.18	105,071	90,291
60,000	758.67	213,121	773.84	156,782	56,339	789.02	130,984	82,137	804.19	114,621	98,500
65,000	821.89	230,880	838.33	169,848	61,032	854.77	141,899	88,981	871.20	124,171	106,709
70,000	885.12	248,643	902.82	182,914	65,729	920.52	152,814	95,829	938.23	133,726	114,917
75,000	948.34	266,402	967.31	195,980	70,422	986.27	163,729	102,673	1,005.24	143,277	123,125
80,000	1,011.56	284,162	1,031.79	209,044	75,118	1,052.02	174,644	109,518	1,072.25	152,827	131,335
85,000	1,074.78	301,921	1,096.28	222,110	79,811	1,117.77	185,558	116,363	1,139.27	162,380	139,541
90,000	1,138.00	319,680	1,160.76	235,173	84,507	1,183.52	196,473	123,207	1,206.28	171,930	147,750
95,000	1,201.23	337,443	1,225.25	248,239	89,204	1,249.28	207,391	130,052	1,273.30	181,483	155,960
100,000	1,264.45	355,202	1,289.74	261,305	93,897	1,315.03	218,306	136,896	1,340.32	191,036	164,166
105,000	1,327.67	372,961	1,354.22	274,368	98,593	1,380.78	229,221	143,740	1,407.33	200,586	172,375
110,000	1,390.89	390,720	1,418.71	287,435	103,285	1,446.53	240,135	150,585	1,474.34	210,137	180,583
115,000	1,454.12	408,483	1,483.20	300,501	107,982	1,512.28	251,050	157,433	1,541.37	219,692	188,791
120,000	1,517.34	426,242	1,547.69	313,567	112,675	1,578.03	261,965	164,277	1,608.38	229,242	197,000
125,000	1,580.56	444,002	1,612.17	326,630	117,372	1,643.78	272,880	171,122	1,675.39	238,793	205,209
130,000	1,643.78	461,761	1,676.66	339,696	122,065	1,709.53	283,795	177,966	1,742.41	248,345	213,416
135,000	1,707.00	479,520	1,741.14	352,759	126,761	1,775.28	294,710	184,810	1,809.42	257,896	221,624
140,000	1,770.23	497,283	1,805.63	365,826	131,457	1,841.04	305,627	191,656	1,876.44	267,448	229,835
145,000	1,833.45	515,042	1,870.12	378,892	136,150	1,906.79	316,542	198,500	1,943.46	277,001	238,041
150,000	1,896.67	532,801	1,934.60	391,955	140,846	1,972.54	327,457	205,344	2,010.47	286,551	246,250
155,000	1,959.89	550,560	1,999.09	405,021	145,539	2,038.29	338,372	212,188	2,077.48	296,102	254,458
160,000	2,023.12	568,323	2,063.58	418,087	150,236	2,104.04	349,287	219,036	2,144.51	305,657	262,666
165,000	2,086.34	586,082	2,128.07	431,153	154,929	2,169.79	360,202	225,880	2,211.52	315,207	270,875
170,000	2,149.56	603,842	2,192.55	444,217	159,625	2,235.54	371,117	232,725	2,278.53	324,758	279,084
175,000	2,212.78	621,601	2,257.04	457,283	164,318	2,301.29	382,032	239,569	2,345.55	334,310	287,291
180,000	2,276.00	639,360	2,321.52	470,346	169,014	2,367.04	392,947	246,413	2,412.56	343,861	295,499
185,000	2,339.23	657,123	2,386.01	483,412	173,711	2,432.80	403,864	253,259	2,479.58	353,414	303,709
190,000	2,402.45	674,882	2,450.50	496,478	178,404	2,498.55	414,779	260,103	2,546.60	362,966	311,916
195,000	2,465.67	692,641	2,514.98	509,541	183,100	2,564.30	425,694	266,947	2,613.61	372,517	320,124
200,000	2,528.89	710,400	2,579.47	522,608	187,792	2,630.05	436,609	273,791	2,680.62	382,067	328,333

AUGMENTED PAYMENT MORTGAGES 15.00%

AMOUNT OF LOAN	30 YEARS		8% PMT INCREASE 198.770 PAYMENTS			10% PMT INCREASE 184.322 PAYMENTS			12% PMT INCREASE 172.484 PAYMENTS		
	MONTHLY PAYMENT	TOTAL INTRST	MONTHLY PAYMENT	TOTAL INTRST	INTRST SAVED	MONTHLY PAYMENT	TOTAL INTRST	INTRST SAVED	MONTHLY PAYMENT	TOTAL INTRST	INTRST SAVED
$ 50	0.64	180	0.69	87	93	0.70	79	101	0.72	74	106
100	1.27	357	1.37	172	185	1.40	158	199	1.42	145	212
200	2.53	711	2.73	343	368	2.78	312	399	2.83	288	423
300	3.80	1,068	4.10	515	553	4.18	470	598	4.26	435	633
400	5.06	1,422	5.46	685	737	5.57	627	795	5.67	578	844
500	6.33	1,779	6.84	860	919	6.96	783	996	7.09	723	1,056
600	7.59	2,132	8.20	1,030	1,102	8.35	939	1,193	8.50	866	1,266
700	8.86	2,490	9.57	1,202	1,288	9.75	1,097	1,393	9.92	1,011	1,479
800	10.12	2,843	10.93	1,373	1,470	11.13	1,252	1,591	11.33	1,154	1,689
900	11.38	3,197	12.29	1,543	1,654	12.52	1,408	1,789	12.75	1,299	1,898
1,000	12.65	3,554	13.66	1,715	1,839	13.92	1,566	1,988	14.17	1,444	2,110
2,000	25.29	7,104	27.31	3,428	3,676	27.82	3,128	3,976	28.32	2,885	4,219
3,000	37.94	10,658	40.98	5,146	5,512	41.73	4,692	5,966	42.49	4,329	6,329
4,000	50.58	14,209	54.63	6,859	7,350	55.64	6,256	7,953	56.65	5,771	8,438
5,000	63.23	17,763	68.29	8,574	9,189	69.55	7,820	9,943	70.82	7,215	10,548
6,000	75.87	21,313	81.94	10,287	11,026	83.46	9,384	11,929	84.97	8,656	12,657
7,000	88.52	24,867	95.60	12,002	12,865	97.37	10,947	13,920	99.14	10,100	14,767
8,000	101.16	28,418	109.25	13,716	14,702	111.28	12,511	15,907	113.30	11,542	16,876
9,000	113.80	31,968	122.90	15,429	16,539	125.18	14,073	17,895	127.46	12,985	18,983
10,000	126.45	35,522	136.57	17,146	18,376	139.10	15,639	19,883	141.62	14,427	21,095
11,000	139.09	39,072	150.22	18,859	20,213	153.00	17,201	21,871	155.78	15,870	23,202
12,000	151.74	42,626	163.88	20,574	22,052	166.91	18,765	23,861	169.95	17,314	25,312
13,000	164.38	46,177	177.53	22,288	23,889	180.82	20,329	25,848	184.11	18,756	27,421
14,000	177.03	49,731	191.19	24,003	25,728	194.73	21,893	27,838	198.27	20,198	29,533
15,000	189.67	53,281	204.84	25,716	27,565	208.64	23,457	29,824	212.43	21,641	31,640
16,000	202.32	56,835	218.51	27,433	29,402	222.55	25,021	31,814	226.60	23,085	33,750
17,000	214.96	60,386	232.16	29,146	31,240	236.46	26,585	33,801	240.76	24,527	35,859
18,000	227.60	63,936	245.81	30,860	33,076	250.36	28,147	35,789	254.91	25,968	37,968
19,000	240.25	67,490	259.47	32,575	34,915	264.28	29,713	37,777	269.08	27,412	40,078
20,000	252.89	71,040	273.12	34,288	36,752	278.18	31,275	39,765	283.24	28,854	42,186
21,000	265.54	74,594	286.78	36,003	38,591	292.09	32,839	41,755	297.40	30,297	44,297
22,000	278.18	78,145	300.43	37,716	40,429	306.00	34,403	43,742	311.56	31,739	46,406
23,000	290.83	81,699	314.10	39,434	42,265	319.91	35,966	45,733	325.73	33,183	48,516
24,000	303.47	85,249	327.75	41,147	44,102	333.82	37,530	47,719	339.89	34,626	50,623
25,000	316.12	88,803	341.41	42,862	45,941	347.73	39,094	49,709	354.05	36,068	52,735
26,000	328.76	92,354	355.06	44,575	47,779	361.64	40,658	51,696	368.21	37,510	54,844
27,000	341.40	95,904	368.71	46,288	49,616	375.54	42,220	53,684	382.37	38,953	56,951
28,000	354.05	99,458	382.37	48,004	51,454	389.46	43,786	55,672	396.54	40,397	59,061
29,000	366.69	103,008	396.03	49,719	53,289	403.36	45,348	57,660	410.69	41,837	61,171
30,000	379.34	106,562	409.69	51,434	55,128	417.27	46,912	59,650	424.86	43,282	63,280
32,500	410.95	115,442	443.83	55,720	59,722	452.05	50,823	64,619	460.26	46,887	68,555
35,000	442.56	124,322	477.96	60,004	64,318	486.82	54,732	69,590	495.67	50,495	73,827
40,000	505.78	142,081	546.24	68,576	73,505	556.36	62,549	79,532	566.47	57,707	84,374
45,000	569.00	159,840	614.52	77,148	82,692	625.90	70,367	89,473	637.28	64,921	94,919
50,000	632.23	177,603	682.81	85,722	91,881	695.45	78,187	99,416	708.10	72,136	105,467
55,000	695.45	195,362	751.09	94,294	101,068	765.00	86,006	109,356	778.90	79,348	116,014
60,000	758.67	213,121	819.36	102,864	110,257	834.54	93,824	119,297	849.71	86,561	126,560
65,000	821.89	230,880	887.64	111,436	119,444	904.08	101,642	129,238	920.52	93,775	137,105
70,000	885.12	248,643	955.93	120,010	128,633	973.63	109,461	139,182	991.33	100,989	147,654
75,000	948.34	266,402	1,024.21	128,582	137,820	1,043.17	117,279	149,123	1,062.14	108,202	158,200
80,000	1,011.56	284,162	1,092.48	137,152	147,010	1,112.72	125,099	159,063	1,132.95	115,416	168,746
85,000	1,074.78	301,921	1,160.76	145,724	156,197	1,182.26	132,917	169,004	1,203.75	122,628	179,293
90,000	1,138.00	319,680	1,229.04	154,296	165,384	1,251.80	140,734	178,946	1,274.56	129,841	189,839
95,000	1,201.23	337,443	1,297.33	162,870	174,573	1,321.35	148,554	188,889	1,345.38	137,057	200,386
100,000	1,264.45	355,202	1,365.61	171,442	183,760	1,390.90	156,373	198,829	1,416.18	144,268	210,934
105,000	1,327.67	372,961	1,433.88	180,012	192,949	1,460.44	164,191	208,770	1,486.99	151,482	221,479
110,000	1,390.89	390,720	1,502.16	188,584	202,136	1,529.98	172,009	218,711	1,557.80	158,696	232,024
115,000	1,454.12	408,483	1,570.45	197,158	211,325	1,599.53	179,829	228,654	1,628.61	165,909	242,573
120,000	1,517.34	426,242	1,638.73	205,730	220,512	1,669.07	187,646	238,596	1,699.42	173,123	253,119
125,000	1,580.56	444,002	1,707.00	214,300	229,702	1,738.62	195,466	248,536	1,770.23	180,336	263,666
130,000	1,643.78	461,761	1,775.28	222,872	238,889	1,808.16	203,284	258,477	1,841.03	187,548	274,213
135,000	1,707.00	479,520	1,843.56	231,444	248,076	1,877.70	211,101	268,419	1,911.84	194,762	284,758
140,000	1,770.23	497,283	1,911.85	240,018	257,265	1,947.25	218,921	278,362	1,982.66	201,977	295,306
145,000	1,833.45	515,042	1,980.13	248,590	266,452	2,016.80	226,741	288,301	2,053.46	209,189	305,853
150,000	1,896.67	532,801	2,048.40	257,160	275,641	2,086.34	234,558	298,243	2,124.27	216,403	316,398
155,000	1,959.89	550,560	2,116.68	265,732	284,828	2,155.88	242,376	308,184	2,195.08	223,616	326,944
160,000	2,023.12	568,323	2,184.97	274,306	294,017	2,225.43	250,196	318,127	2,265.89	230,830	337,493
165,000	2,086.34	586,082	2,253.25	282,879	303,203	2,294.97	258,013	328,069	2,336.70	238,043	348,039
170,000	2,149.56	603,842	2,321.52	291,449	312,393	2,364.52	265,833	338,009	2,407.51	245,257	358,585
175,000	2,212.78	621,601	2,389.80	300,021	321,580	2,434.06	273,651	347,950	2,478.31	252,469	369,132
180,000	2,276.00	639,360	2,458.08	308,593	330,767	2,503.60	281,469	357,891	2,549.12	259,682	379,678
185,000	2,339.23	657,123	2,526.37	317,167	339,956	2,573.15	289,288	367,835	2,619.94	266,898	390,225
190,000	2,402.45	674,882	2,594.65	325,739	349,143	2,642.70	297,108	377,774	2,690.74	274,110	400,772
195,000	2,465.67	692,641	2,662.92	334,309	358,332	2,712.24	304,926	387,715	2,761.55	281,323	411,318
200,000	2,528.89	710,400	2,731.20	342,881	367,519	2,781.78	312,743	397,657	2,832.36	288,537	421,863

259

AUGMENTED PAYMENT MORTGAGES

AMOUNT OF LOAN	30 YEARS		2% PMT INCREASE 277.657 PAYMENTS			4% PMT INCREASE 239.375 PAYMENTS			6% PMT INCREASE 214.511 PAYMENTS		
	MONTHLY PAYMENT	TOTAL INTRST	MONTHLY PAYMENT	TOTAL INTRST	INTRST SAVED	MONTHLY PAYMENT	TOTAL INTRST	INTRST SAVED	MONTHLY PAYMENT	TOTAL INTRST	INTRST SAVED
$ 50	0.65	184	0.66	133	51	0.68	113	71	0.69	98	86
100	1.29	364	1.32	267	97	1.34	221	143	1.37	194	170
200	2.57	725	2.62	527	198	2.67	439	286	2.72	383	342
300	3.86	1,090	3.94	794	296	4.01	660	430	4.09	577	513
400	5.14	1,450	5.24	1,055	395	5.35	881	569	5.45	769	681
500	6.43	1,815	6.56	1,321	494	6.69	1,101	714	6.82	963	852
600	7.71	2,176	7.86	1,582	594	8.02	1,320	856	8.17	1,153	1,023
700	9.00	2,540	9.18	1,849	691	9.36	1,541	999	9.54	1,346	1,194
800	10.28	2,901	10.49	2,113	788	10.69	1,759	1,142	10.90	1,538	1,363
900	11.57	3,265	11.80	2,376	889	12.03	1,980	1,285	12.26	1,730	1,535
1,000	12.85	3,626	13.11	2,640	986	13.36	2,198	1,428	13.62	1,922	1,704
2,000	25.69	7,248	26.20	5,275	1,973	26.72	4,396	2,852	27.23	3,841	3,407
3,000	38.54	10,874	39.31	7,915	2,959	40.08	6,594	4,280	40.85	5,763	5,111
4,000	51.38	14,497	52.41	10,552	3,945	53.44	8,792	5,705	54.46	7,682	6,815
5,000	64.23	18,123	65.51	13,189	4,934	66.80	10,990	7,133	68.08	9,604	8,519
6,000	77.07	21,745	78.61	15,827	5,918	80.15	13,186	8,559	81.69	11,523	10,222
7,000	89.92	25,371	91.72	18,467	6,904	93.52	15,386	9,985	95.32	13,447	11,924
8,000	102.76	28,994	104.82	21,104	7,890	106.87	17,582	11,412	108.93	15,367	13,627
9,000	115.61	32,620	117.92	23,741	8,879	120.23	19,780	12,840	122.55	17,288	15,332
10,000	128.45	36,242	131.02	26,379	9,863	133.59	21,978	14,264	136.16	19,208	17,034
11,000	141.30	39,868	144.13	29,019	10,849	146.95	24,176	15,692	149.78	21,129	18,739
12,000	154.14	43,490	157.22	31,653	11,837	160.31	26,374	17,116	163.39	23,049	20,441
13,000	166.98	47,113	170.32	34,291	12,822	173.66	28,570	18,543	177.00	24,968	22,145
14,000	179.83	50,739	183.43	36,931	13,808	187.02	30,768	19,971	190.62	26,890	23,849
15,000	192.67	54,361	196.52	39,565	14,796	200.38	32,966	21,395	204.23	28,810	25,551
16,000	205.52	57,987	209.63	42,205	15,782	213.74	35,164	22,823	217.85	30,731	27,256
17,000	218.36	61,610	222.73	44,843	16,767	227.09	37,360	24,250	231.46	32,651	28,959
18,000	231.21	65,236	235.83	47,480	17,756	240.46	39,560	25,676	245.08	34,572	30,664
19,000	244.05	68,858	248.93	50,117	18,741	253.81	41,756	27,102	258.69	36,492	32,366
20,000	256.90	72,484	262.04	52,757	19,727	267.18	43,956	28,528	272.31	38,413	34,071
21,000	269.74	76,106	275.13	55,392	20,714	280.53	46,152	29,954	285.92	40,333	35,773
22,000	282.59	79,732	288.24	58,032	21,700	293.89	48,350	31,382	299.55	42,257	37,475
23,000	295.43	83,355	301.34	60,669	22,686	307.25	50,548	32,807	313.16	44,176	39,179
24,000	308.28	86,981	314.45	63,309	23,672	320.61	52,744	34,235	326.78	46,098	40,883
25,000	321.12	90,603	327.54	65,944	24,659	333.96	54,942	35,661	340.39	48,017	42,586
26,000	333.96	94,226	340.64	68,581	25,645	347.32	57,140	37,086	354.00	49,937	44,289
27,000	346.81	97,852	353.75	71,221	26,631	360.68	59,338	38,514	367.62	51,859	45,993
28,000	359.65	101,474	366.84	73,856	27,618	374.04	61,536	39,938	381.23	53,778	47,696
29,000	372.50	105,100	379.95	76,496	28,604	387.40	63,734	41,366	394.85	55,700	49,400
30,000	385.34	108,722	393.05	79,133	29,589	400.75	65,930	42,792	408.46	57,619	51,103
32,500	417.45	117,782	425.80	85,726	32,056	434.15	71,425	46,357	442.50	62,421	55,361
35,000	449.57	126,845	458.56	92,322	34,523	467.55	76,920	49,925	476.54	67,223	59,622
40,000	513.79	144,964	524.07	105,512	39,452	534.34	87,908	57,056	544.62	76,827	68,137
45,000	578.01	163,084	589.57	118,698	44,386	601.13	98,895	64,189	612.69	86,429	76,655
50,000	642.23	181,203	655.07	131,885	49,318	667.92	109,883	71,320	680.76	96,031	85,172
55,000	706.46	199,326	720.59	145,077	54,249	734.72	120,874	78,452	748.85	105,637	93,689
60,000	770.68	217,445	786.09	158,263	59,182	801.51	131,861	85,584	816.92	115,238	102,207
65,000	834.90	235,564	851.60	171,453	64,111	868.30	142,849	92,715	884.99	124,840	110,724
70,000	899.13	253,687	917.11	184,642	69,045	935.10	153,840	99,847	953.08	134,446	119,241
75,000	963.35	271,806	982.62	197,831	73,975	1,001.88	164,825	106,981	1,021.15	144,048	127,758
80,000	1,027.57	289,925	1,048.12	211,018	78,907	1,068.67	175,813	114,112	1,089.22	153,650	136,275
85,000	1,091.79	308,044	1,113.63	224,207	83,837	1,135.46	186,801	121,243	1,157.30	163,254	144,790
90,000	1,156.02	326,167	1,179.14	237,396	88,771	1,202.26	197,791	128,376	1,225.38	172,857	153,310
95,000	1,220.24	344,286	1,244.64	250,583	93,703	1,269.05	208,779	135,507	1,293.45	182,459	161,827
100,000	1,284.46	362,406	1,310.15	263,772	98,634	1,335.84	219,767	142,639	1,361.53	192,063	170,343
105,000	1,348.69	380,528	1,375.66	276,962	103,566	1,402.64	230,757	149,771	1,429.61	201,667	178,861
110,000	1,412.91	398,648	1,441.17	290,151	108,497	1,469.43	241,745	156,903	1,497.68	211,269	187,379
115,000	1,477.13	416,767	1,506.67	303,337	113,430	1,536.22	252,733	164,034	1,565.76	220,873	195,894
120,000	1,541.36	434,890	1,572.19	316,530	118,360	1,603.01	263,721	171,169	1,633.84	230,477	204,413
125,000	1,605.58	453,009	1,637.69	329,716	123,293	1,669.80	274,708	178,301	1,701.91	240,078	212,931
130,000	1,669.80	471,128	1,703.20	342,905	128,223	1,736.59	285,696	185,432	1,769.99	249,682	221,446
135,000	1,734.02	489,247	1,768.70	356,092	133,155	1,803.38	296,684	192,563	1,838.06	259,284	229,963
140,000	1,798.25	507,370	1,834.22	369,284	138,086	1,870.18	307,674	199,696	1,906.15	268,890	238,480
145,000	1,862.47	525,489	1,899.72	382,471	143,018	1,936.97	318,662	206,827	1,974.22	278,492	246,997
150,000	1,926.69	543,608	1,965.22	395,657	147,951	2,003.76	329,650	213,958	2,042.29	288,094	255,514
155,000	1,990.92	561,731	2,030.74	408,849	152,882	2,070.56	340,640	221,091	2,110.38	297,700	264,031
160,000	2,055.14	579,850	2,096.24	422,036	157,814	2,137.35	351,628	228,222	2,178.45	307,301	272,549
165,000	2,119.36	597,970	2,161.75	435,225	162,745	2,204.13	362,614	235,356	2,246.52	316,903	281,067
170,000	2,183.58	616,089	2,227.25	448,412	167,677	2,270.92	373,601	242,488	2,314.59	326,505	289,584
175,000	2,247.81	634,212	2,292.77	461,604	172,608	2,337.72	384,592	249,620	2,382.68	336,111	298,101
180,000	2,312.03	652,331	2,358.27	474,790	177,541	2,404.51	395,580	256,751	2,450.75	345,713	306,618
185,000	2,376.25	670,450	2,423.78	487,979	182,471	2,471.30	406,567	263,883	2,518.83	355,317	315,133
190,000	2,440.48	688,573	2,489.29	501,169	187,404	2,538.10	417,558	271,015	2,586.91	364,921	323,652
195,000	2,504.70	706,692	2,554.79	514,355	192,337	2,604.89	428,546	278,146	2,654.98	374,522	332,170
200,000	2,568.92	724,811	2,620.30	527,545	197,266	2,671.68	439,533	285,278	2,723.06	384,126	340,685

AUGMENTED PAYMENT MORTGAGES 15.25%

AMOUNT OF LOAN	30 YEARS		8% PMT INCREASE 196.242 PAYMENTS			10% PMT INCREASE 181.900 PAYMENTS			12% PMT INCREASE 170.166 PAYMENTS		
	MONTHLY PAYMENT	TOTAL INTRST	MONTHLY PAYMENT	TOTAL INTRST	INTRST SAVED	MONTHLY PAYMENT	TOTAL INTRST	INTRST SAVED	MONTHLY PAYMENT	TOTAL INTRST	INTRST SAVED
$ 50	0.65	184	0.70	87	97	0.72	81	103	0.73	74	110
100	1.29	364	1.39	173	191	1.42	158	206	1.44	145	219
200	2.57	725	2.78	346	379	2.83	315	410	2.88	290	435
300	3.86	1,090	4.17	518	572	4.25	473	617	4.32	435	655
400	5.14	1,450	5.55	689	761	5.65	628	822	5.76	580	870
500	6.43	1,815	6.94	862	953	7.07	786	1,029	7.20	725	1,090
600	7.71	2,176	8.33	1,035	1,141	8.48	943	1,233	8.64	870	1,306
700	9.00	2,540	9.72	1,207	1,333	9.90	1,101	1,439	10.08	1,015	1,525
800	10.28	2,901	11.10	1,378	1,523	11.31	1,257	1,644	11.51	1,159	1,742
900	11.57	3,265	12.50	1,553	1,712	12.73	1,416	1,849	12.96	1,305	1,960
1,000	12.85	3,626	13.88	1,724	1,902	14.14	1,572	2,054	14.39	1,449	2,177
2,000	25.69	7,248	27.75	3,446	3,802	28.26	3,140	4,108	28.77	2,896	4,352
3,000	38.54	10,874	41.62	5,168	5,706	42.39	4,711	6,163	43.16	4,344	6,530
4,000	51.38	14,497	55.49	6,889	7,608	56.52	6,281	8,216	57.55	5,793	8,704
5,000	64.23	18,123	69.37	8,613	9,510	70.65	7,851	10,272	71.94	7,242	10,881
6,000	77.07	21,745	83.24	10,335	11,410	84.78	9,421	12,324	86.32	8,689	13,056
7,000	89.92	25,371	97.11	12,057	13,314	98.91	10,992	14,379	100.71	10,137	15,234
8,000	102.76	28,994	110.98	13,779	15,215	113.04	12,562	16,432	115.09	11,584	17,410
9,000	115.61	32,620	124.86	15,503	17,117	127.17	14,132	18,488	129.48	13,033	19,587
10,000	128.45	36,242	138.73	17,225	19,017	141.30	15,702	20,540	143.86	14,480	21,762
11,000	141.30	39,868	152.60	18,947	20,921	155.43	17,273	22,595	158.26	15,930	23,938
12,000	154.14	43,490	166.47	20,668	22,822	169.55	18,841	24,649	172.64	17,377	26,113
13,000	166.98	47,113	180.34	22,390	24,723	183.68	20,411	26,702	187.02	18,824	28,289
14,000	179.83	50,739	194.22	24,114	26,625	197.81	21,982	28,757	201.41	20,273	30,466
15,000	192.67	54,361	208.08	25,834	28,527	211.94	23,552	30,809	215.79	21,720	32,641
16,000	205.52	57,987	221.96	27,558	30,429	226.07	25,122	32,865	230.18	23,169	34,818
17,000	218.36	61,610	235.83	29,280	32,330	240.20	26,692	34,918	244.56	24,616	36,994
18,000	231.21	65,236	249.71	31,004	34,232	254.33	28,263	36,973	258.96	26,066	39,170
19,000	244.05	68,858	263.57	32,724	36,134	268.46	29,833	39,025	273.34	27,513	41,345
20,000	256.90	72,484	277.45	34,447	38,037	282.59	31,403	41,081	287.73	28,962	43,522
21,000	269.74	76,106	291.32	36,169	39,937	296.71	32,972	43,134	302.11	30,409	45,697
22,000	282.59	79,732	305.20	37,893	41,839	310.85	34,544	45,188	316.50	31,858	47,874
23,000	295.43	83,355	319.06	39,613	43,742	324.97	36,112	47,243	330.88	33,305	50,050
24,000	308.28	86,981	332.94	41,337	45,644	339.11	37,684	49,297	345.27	34,753	52,228
25,000	321.12	90,603	346.81	43,059	47,544	353.23	39,253	51,350	359.65	36,200	54,403
26,000	333.96	94,226	360.68	44,781	49,445	367.36	40,823	53,403	374.04	37,649	56,577
27,000	346.81	97,852	374.55	46,502	51,350	381.49	42,393	55,459	388.43	39,098	58,754
28,000	359.65	101,474	388.42	48,224	53,250	395.62	43,963	57,511	402.81	40,545	60,929
29,000	372.50	105,100	402.30	49,948	55,152	409.75	45,534	59,566	417.20	41,993	63,107
30,000	385.34	108,722	416.17	51,670	57,052	423.87	47,102	61,620	431.58	43,440	65,282
32,500	417.45	117,782	450.85	55,976	61,806	459.20	51,028	66,754	467.54	47,059	70,723
35,000	449.57	126,845	485.54	60,283	66,562	494.53	54,955	71,890	503.50	50,682	76,163
40,000	513.79	144,964	554.89	68,893	76,071	565.17	62,804	82,160	575.44	57,920	87,044
45,000	578.01	163,084	624.25	77,504	85,580	635.81	70,654	92,430	647.37	65,160	97,924
50,000	642.23	181,203	693.61	86,115	95,088	706.45	78,503	102,700	719.30	72,400	108,803
55,000	706.46	199,326	762.98	94,729	104,597	777.11	86,354	112,970	791.24	79,642	119,684
60,000	770.68	217,445	832.33	103,338	114,107	847.75	94,206	123,239	863.18	86,880	130,565
65,000	834.90	235,564	901.69	111,949	123,615	918.39	102,055	133,509	935.09	94,121	141,443
70,000	899.13	253,687	971.06	120,563	133,124	989.04	109,906	143,781	1,007.03	101,362	152,325
75,000	963.35	271,806	1,040.42	129,174	142,632	1,059.69	117,758	154,048	1,078.95	108,601	163,205
80,000	1,027.57	289,925	1,109.78	137,785	152,140	1,130.33	125,607	164,318	1,150.88	115,841	174,084
85,000	1,091.79	308,044	1,179.13	146,395	161,649	1,200.97	133,456	174,588	1,222.80	123,079	184,965
90,000	1,156.02	326,167	1,248.50	155,008	171,159	1,271.62	141,308	184,859	1,294.74	130,321	195,846
95,000	1,220.24	344,286	1,317.86	163,619	180,667	1,342.26	149,157	195,129	1,366.67	137,561	206,725
100,000	1,284.46	362,406	1,387.22	172,231	190,175	1,412.91	157,008	205,398	1,438.60	144,801	217,605
105,000	1,348.69	380,528	1,456.59	180,844	199,684	1,483.56	164,860	215,668	1,510.53	152,041	228,487
110,000	1,412.91	398,648	1,525.94	189,454	209,194	1,554.20	172,709	225,939	1,582.46	159,281	239,367
115,000	1,477.13	416,767	1,595.30	198,065	218,702	1,624.84	180,558	236,209	1,654.39	166,521	250,246
120,000	1,541.36	434,890	1,664.67	206,678	228,212	1,695.50	188,411	246,479	1,726.32	173,761	261,129
125,000	1,605.58	453,009	1,734.03	215,290	237,719	1,766.14	196,261	256,748	1,798.25	181,001	272,008
130,000	1,669.80	471,128	1,803.38	223,899	247,229	1,836.78	204,110	267,018	1,870.18	188,241	282,887
135,000	1,734.02	489,247	1,872.74	232,510	256,737	1,907.42	211,960	277,287	1,942.10	195,479	293,768
140,000	1,798.25	507,370	1,942.11	241,124	266,246	1,978.08	219,813	287,557	2,014.04	202,721	304,649
145,000	1,862.47	525,489	2,011.47	249,735	275,754	2,048.72	227,662	297,827	2,085.97	209,961	315,528
150,000	1,926.69	543,608	2,080.83	258,346	285,262	2,119.36	235,512	308,096	2,157.89	217,200	326,408
155,000	1,990.92	561,731	2,150.19	266,958	294,773	2,190.01	243,363	318,368	2,229.83	224,441	337,290
160,000	2,055.14	579,850	2,219.55	275,569	304,281	2,260.65	251,212	328,638	2,301.76	231,681	348,169
165,000	2,119.36	597,970	2,288.91	284,180	313,790	2,331.30	259,063	338,907	2,373.68	238,920	359,050
170,000	2,183.58	616,089	2,358.27	292,792	323,297	2,401.94	266,913	349,176	2,445.61	246,160	369,929
175,000	2,247.81	634,212	2,427.63	301,403	332,809	2,472.59	274,764	359,448	2,517.55	253,401	380,811
180,000	2,312.03	652,331	2,496.99	310,014	342,317	2,543.23	282,614	369,717	2,589.47	260,640	391,691
185,000	2,376.25	670,450	2,566.35	318,626	351,824	2,613.88	290,465	379,985	2,661.40	267,880	402,570
190,000	2,440.48	688,573	2,635.72	327,239	361,334	2,684.53	298,316	390,257	2,733.34	275,122	413,451
195,000	2,504.70	706,692	2,705.08	335,850	370,842	2,755.17	306,165	400,527	2,805.26	282,360	424,332
200,000	2,568.92	724,811	2,774.43	344,460	380,351	2,825.81	314,015	410,796	2,877.19	289,600	435,211

15.50% AUGMENTED PAYMENT MORTGAGES

AMOUNT OF LOAN	30 YEARS		2% PMT INCREASE 275.158 PAYMENTS			4% PMT INCREASE 236.713 PAYMENTS			6% PMT INCREASE 211.912 PAYMENTS		
	MONTHLY PAYMENT	TOTAL INTRST	MONTHLY PAYMENT	TOTAL INTRST	INTRST SAVED	MONTHLY PAYMENT	TOTAL INTRST	INTRST SAVED	MONTHLY PAYMENT	TOTAL INTRST	INTRST SAVED
$ 50	0.66	188	0.67	134	54	0.69	113	75	0.70	98	90
100	1.31	372	1.34	269	103	1.36	222	150	1.39	195	177
200	2.61	740	2.66	532	208	2.71	441	299	2.77	387	353
300	3.92	1,111	4.00	801	310	4.08	666	445	4.16	582	529
400	5.22	1,479	5.32	1,064	415	5.43	885	594	5.53	772	707
500	6.53	1,851	6.66	1,333	518	6.79	1,107	744	6.92	966	885
600	7.83	2,219	7.99	1,599	620	8.14	1,327	892	8.30	1,159	1,060
700	9.14	2,590	9.32	1,864	726	9.51	1,551	1,039	9.69	1,353	1,237
800	10.44	2,958	10.65	2,130	828	10.86	1,771	1,187	11.07	1,546	1,412
900	11.75	3,330	11.99	2,399	931	12.22	1,993	1,337	12.46	1,740	1,590
1,000	13.05	3,698	13.31	2,662	1,036	13.57	2,212	1,486	13.83	1,931	1,767
2,000	26.10	7,396	26.62	5,325	2,071	27.14	4,424	2,972	27.67	3,864	3,532
3,000	39.14	11,090	39.92	7,984	3,106	40.71	6,637	4,453	41.49	5,792	5,298
4,000	52.19	14,788	53.23	10,647	4,141	54.28	8,849	5,939	55.32	7,723	7,065
5,000	65.23	18,483	66.53	13,306	5,177	67.84	11,059	7,424	69.14	9,652	8,831
6,000	78.28	22,181	79.85	15,971	6,210	81.41	13,271	8,910	82.98	11,584	10,597
7,000	91.32	25,875	93.15	18,631	7,244	94.97	15,481	10,394	96.80	13,513	12,362
8,000	104.37	29,573	106.46	21,293	8,280	108.54	17,693	11,880	110.63	15,444	14,129
9,000	117.41	33,268	119.76	23,953	9,315	122.11	19,905	13,363	124.45	17,372	15,896
10,000	130.46	36,966	133.07	26,615	10,351	135.68	22,117	14,849	138.29	19,305	17,661
11,000	143.50	40,660	146.37	29,275	11,385	149.24	24,327	16,333	152.11	21,234	19,426
12,000	156.55	44,358	159.68	31,937	12,421	162.81	26,539	17,819	165.94	23,165	21,193
13,000	169.59	48,052	172.98	34,597	13,455	176.37	28,749	19,303	179.77	25,095	22,957
14,000	182.64	51,750	186.29	37,259	14,491	189.95	30,964	20,786	193.60	27,026	24,724
15,000	195.68	55,445	199.59	39,919	15,526	203.51	33,173	22,272	207.42	28,955	26,490
16,000	208.73	59,143	212.90	42,581	16,562	217.08	35,386	23,757	221.25	30,886	28,257
17,000	221.77	62,837	226.21	45,243	17,594	230.64	37,595	25,242	235.08	32,816	30,021
18,000	234.82	66,535	239.52	47,906	18,629	244.21	39,808	26,727	248.91	34,747	31,788
19,000	247.86	70,230	252.82	50,565	19,665	257.77	42,018	28,212	262.73	36,676	33,554
20,000	260.91	73,928	266.13	53,228	20,700	271.35	44,232	29,696	276.56	38,606	35,322
21,000	273.95	77,622	279.43	55,887	21,735	284.91	46,442	31,180	290.39	40,537	37,085
22,000	287.00	81,320	292.74	58,550	22,770	298.48	48,654	32,666	304.22	42,468	38,852
23,000	300.04	85,014	306.04	61,209	23,805	312.04	50,864	34,150	318.04	44,396	40,618
24,000	313.09	88,712	319.35	63,872	24,840	325.61	53,076	35,636	331.88	46,329	42,383
25,000	326.13	92,407	332.65	66,531	25,876	339.18	55,288	37,119	345.70	48,258	44,149
26,000	339.18	96,105	345.96	69,194	26,911	352.75	57,501	38,604	359.53	50,189	45,916
27,000	352.22	99,799	359.26	71,853	27,946	366.31	59,710	40,089	373.35	52,117	47,682
28,000	365.27	103,497	372.58	74,518	28,979	379.88	61,923	41,574	387.19	54,050	49,447
29,000	378.31	107,192	385.88	77,178	30,014	393.44	64,132	43,060	401.01	55,979	51,213
30,000	391.36	110,890	399.19	79,840	31,050	407.01	66,345	44,545	414.84	57,910	52,980
32,500	423.97	120,129	432.45	86,492	33,637	440.93	71,874	48,255	449.41	62,735	57,394
35,000	456.59	129,372	465.72	93,147	36,225	474.85	77,403	51,969	483.99	67,563	61,809
40,000	521.81	147,852	532.25	106,453	41,399	542.68	88,459	59,393	553.12	77,213	70,639
45,000	587.04	166,334	598.78	119,759	46,575	610.52	99,518	66,816	622.26	86,864	79,470
50,000	652.26	184,814	665.31	133,065	51,749	678.35	110,574	74,240	691.40	96,516	88,298
55,000	717.49	203,296	731.84	146,372	56,924	746.19	121,633	81,663	760.54	106,168	97,128
60,000	782.72	221,779	798.37	159,678	62,101	814.03	132,691	89,088	829.68	115,819	105,960
65,000	847.94	240,258	864.90	172,984	67,274	881.86	143,748	96,510	898.82	125,471	114,787
70,000	913.17	258,741	931.43	186,290	72,451	949.70	154,806	103,935	967.96	135,122	123,619
75,000	978.39	277,220	997.96	199,597	77,623	1,017.53	165,863	111,357	1,037.09	144,772	132,448
80,000	1,043.62	295,703	1,064.49	212,903	82,800	1,085.36	176,919	118,784	1,106.24	154,426	141,277
85,000	1,108.84	314,182	1,131.02	226,209	87,973	1,153.19	187,975	126,207	1,175.37	164,075	150,107
90,000	1,174.07	332,665	1,197.55	239,515	93,150	1,221.03	199,034	133,631	1,244.51	173,727	158,938
95,000	1,239.30	351,148	1,264.09	252,824	98,324	1,288.87	210,092	141,056	1,313.66	183,380	167,768
100,000	1,304.52	369,627	1,330.61	266,128	103,499	1,356.70	221,149	148,478	1,382.79	193,030	176,597
105,000	1,369.75	388,110	1,397.15	279,437	108,673	1,424.54	232,207	155,903	1,451.94	202,684	185,426
110,000	1,434.97	406,589	1,463.67	292,741	113,848	1,492.37	243,263	163,326	1,521.07	212,333	194,256
115,000	1,500.20	425,072	1,530.20	306,047	119,025	1,560.21	254,322	170,750	1,590.21	221,985	203,087
120,000	1,565.43	443,555	1,596.74	319,356	124,199	1,628.05	265,381	178,174	1,659.36	231,638	211,917
125,000	1,630.65	462,034	1,663.26	332,659	129,375	1,695.88	276,437	185,597	1,728.49	241,288	220,746
130,000	1,695.88	480,517	1,729.80	345,968	134,549	1,763.72	287,495	193,022	1,797.63	250,939	229,578
135,000	1,761.10	498,996	1,796.32	359,272	139,724	1,831.54	298,549	200,447	1,866.77	260,587	238,405
140,000	1,826.33	517,479	1,862.86	372,581	144,898	1,899.38	309,608	207,871	1,935.91	270,243	247,236
145,000	1,891.55	535,958	1,929.38	385,884	150,074	1,967.21	320,664	215,294	2,005.04	279,892	256,066
150,000	1,956.78	554,441	1,995.92	399,193	155,248	2,035.05	331,723	222,718	2,074.19	289,546	264,895
155,000	2,022.01	572,924	2,062.45	412,500	160,424	2,102.89	342,781	230,143	2,143.33	299,197	273,727
160,000	2,087.23	591,403	2,128.97	425,803	165,600	2,170.72	353,838	237,565	2,212.46	308,847	282,556
165,000	2,152.46	609,886	2,195.51	439,112	170,774	2,238.56	364,896	244,990	2,281.61	318,501	291,385
170,000	2,217.68	628,365	2,262.03	452,416	175,949	2,306.39	375,952	252,413	2,350.74	328,150	300,215
175,000	2,282.91	646,848	2,328.57	465,725	181,123	2,374.23	387,011	259,837	2,419.88	337,802	309,046
180,000	2,348.14	665,330	2,395.10	479,031	186,299	2,442.07	398,070	267,260	2,489.03	347,455	317,875
185,000	2,413.36	683,810	2,461.63	492,337	191,473	2,509.89	409,124	274,686	2,558.16	357,105	326,705
190,000	2,478.59	702,292	2,528.16	505,643	196,649	2,577.73	420,182	282,110	2,627.31	366,759	335,533
195,000	2,543.81	720,772	2,594.69	518,950	201,822	2,645.56	431,238	289,534	2,696.44	376,408	344,364
200,000	2,609.04	739,254	2,661.22	532,256	206,998	2,713.40	442,297	296,957	2,765.58	386,060	353,194

262

AUGMENTED PAYMENT MORTGAGES 15.50%

AMOUNT OF LOAN	30 YEARS MONTHLY PAYMENT	30 YEARS TOTAL INTRST	8% PMT INCREASE 193.750 PAYMENTS MONTHLY PAYMENT	TOTAL INTRST	INTRST SAVED	10% PMT INCREASE 179.521 PAYMENTS MONTHLY PAYMENT	TOTAL INTRST	INTRST SAVED	12% PMT INCREASE 167.891 PAYMENTS MONTHLY PAYMENT	TOTAL INTRST	INTRST SAVED
$ 50	0.66	188	0.71	88	100	0.73	81	107	0.74	74	114
100	1.31	372	1.41	173	199	1.44	159	213	1.47	147	225
200	2.61	740	2.82	346	394	2.87	315	425	2.92	290	450
300	3.92	1,111	4.23	520	591	4.31	474	637	4.39	437	674
400	5.22	1,479	5.64	693	786	5.74	630	849	5.85	582	897
500	6.53	1,851	7.05	866	985	7.18	789	1,062	7.31	727	1,124
600	7.83	2,219	8.46	1,039	1,180	8.61	946	1,273	8.77	872	1,347
700	9.14	2,590	9.87	1,212	1,378	10.05	1,104	1,486	10.24	1,019	1,571
800	10.44	2,958	11.28	1,386	1,572	11.48	1,261	1,697	11.69	1,163	1,795
900	11.75	3,330	12.69	1,559	1,771	12.93	1,421	1,909	13.16	1,309	2,021
1,000	13.05	3,698	14.09	1,730	1,968	14.36	1,578	2,120	14.62	1,455	2,243
2,000	26.10	7,396	28.19	3,462	3,934	28.71	3,154	4,242	29.23	2,907	4,489
3,000	39.14	11,090	42.27	5,190	5,900	43.05	4,728	6,362	43.84	4,360	6,730
4,000	52.19	14,788	56.37	6,922	7,866	57.41	6,306	8,482	58.45	5,813	8,975
5,000	65.23	18,483	70.45	8,650	9,833	71.75	7,881	10,602	73.06	7,266	11,217
6,000	78.28	22,181	84.54	10,380	11,801	86.11	9,459	12,722	87.67	8,719	13,462
7,000	91.32	25,875	98.63	12,110	13,765	100.45	11,033	14,842	102.28	10,172	15,703
8,000	104.37	29,573	112.72	13,840	15,733	114.81	12,611	16,962	116.89	11,625	17,948
9,000	117.41	33,268	126.80	15,568	17,700	129.15	14,185	19,083	131.50	13,078	20,190
10,000	130.46	36,966	140.90	17,299	19,667	143.51	15,763	21,203	146.12	14,532	22,434
11,000	143.50	40,660	154.98	19,027	21,633	157.85	17,337	23,323	160.72	15,983	24,677
12,000	156.55	44,358	169.07	20,757	23,601	172.21	18,915	25,443	175.34	17,438	26,920
13,000	169.59	48,052	183.16	22,487	25,565	186.55	20,490	27,562	189.94	18,889	29,163
14,000	182.64	51,750	197.25	24,217	27,533	200.90	22,066	29,684	204.56	20,344	31,406
15,000	195.68	55,445	211.33	25,945	29,500	215.25	23,642	31,803	219.16	21,795	33,650
16,000	208.73	59,143	225.43	27,677	31,466	229.60	25,218	33,925	233.78	23,250	35,893
17,000	221.77	62,837	239.51	29,405	33,432	243.95	26,794	36,043	248.38	24,701	38,136
18,000	234.82	66,535	253.61	31,137	35,398	258.30	28,370	38,165	263.00	26,155	40,380
19,000	247.86	70,230	267.69	32,865	37,365	272.65	29,946	40,284	277.60	27,607	42,623
20,000	260.91	73,928	281.78	34,595	39,333	287.00	31,523	42,405	292.22	29,061	44,867
21,000	273.95	77,622	295.87	36,325	41,297	301.35	33,099	44,523	306.82	30,512	47,110
22,000	287.00	81,320	309.96	38,055	43,265	315.70	34,675	46,645	321.44	31,967	49,353
23,000	300.04	85,014	324.04	39,783	45,231	330.04	36,249	48,765	336.04	33,418	51,596
24,000	313.09	88,712	338.14	41,515	47,197	344.40	37,827	50,885	350.66	34,873	53,839
25,000	326.13	92,407	352.22	43,243	49,164	358.74	39,401	53,006	365.27	36,326	56,081
26,000	339.18	96,105	366.31	44,973	51,132	373.10	40,979	55,126	379.88	37,778	58,327
27,000	352.22	99,799	380.40	46,703	53,096	387.44	42,554	57,245	394.49	39,231	60,568
28,000	365.27	103,497	394.49	48,432	55,065	401.80	44,132	59,365	409.10	40,684	62,813
29,000	378.31	107,192	408.57	50,160	57,032	416.14	45,706	61,486	423.71	42,137	65,055
30,000	391.36	110,890	422.67	51,892	58,998	430.50	47,284	63,606	438.32	43,590	67,300
32,500	423.97	120,129	457.89	56,216	63,913	466.37	51,223	68,906	474.85	47,223	72,906
35,000	456.59	129,372	493.12	60,542	68,830	502.25	55,164	74,208	511.38	50,856	78,516
40,000	521.81	147,852	563.55	69,188	78,664	573.99	63,043	84,809	584.43	58,121	89,731
45,000	587.04	166,334	634.00	77,838	88,496	645.74	70,924	95,410	657.48	65,385	100,949
50,000	652.26	184,814	704.44	86,485	98,329	717.49	78,805	106,009	730.53	72,649	112,165
55,000	717.49	203,296	774.89	95,135	108,161	789.24	86,685	116,611	803.59	79,916	123,380
60,000	782.72	221,779	845.34	103,785	117,994	860.99	94,566	127,213	876.65	87,182	134,597
65,000	847.94	240,258	915.78	112,432	127,826	932.73	102,445	137,813	949.69	94,444	145,814
70,000	913.17	258,741	986.22	121,080	137,661	1,004.49	110,327	148,414	1,022.75	101,711	157,030
75,000	978.39	277,220	1,056.66	129,728	147,492	1,076.23	118,206	159,014	1,095.80	108,975	168,245
80,000	1,043.62	295,703	1,127.11	138,378	157,325	1,147.98	126,087	169,616	1,168.85	116,239	179,464
85,000	1,108.84	314,182	1,197.55	147,025	167,157	1,219.72	133,965	180,217	1,241.90	123,504	190,678
90,000	1,174.07	332,665	1,268.00	155,675	176,990	1,291.48	141,848	190,817	1,314.96	130,770	201,895
95,000	1,239.30	351,148	1,338.44	164,323	186,825	1,363.23	149,728	201,420	1,388.02	138,036	213,112
100,000	1,304.52	369,627	1,408.88	172,971	196,656	1,434.97	157,607	212,020	1,461.06	145,299	224,328
105,000	1,369.75	388,110	1,479.33	181,620	206,490	1,506.73	165,490	222,620	1,534.12	152,565	235,545
110,000	1,434.97	406,589	1,549.77	190,268	216,321	1,578.47	173,369	233,220	1,607.17	159,829	246,760
115,000	1,500.20	425,072	1,620.22	198,918	226,154	1,650.22	181,249	243,823	1,680.22	167,094	257,978
120,000	1,565.43	443,555	1,690.66	207,565	235,990	1,721.97	189,130	254,425	1,753.28	174,360	269,195
125,000	1,630.65	462,034	1,761.10	216,213	245,821	1,793.72	197,010	265,024	1,826.33	181,624	280,410
130,000	1,695.88	480,517	1,831.55	224,863	255,654	1,865.47	204,891	275,626	1,899.39	188,890	291,627
135,000	1,761.10	498,996	1,901.99	233,511	265,485	1,937.21	212,770	286,226	1,972.43	196,153	302,843
140,000	1,826.33	517,479	1,972.44	242,160	275,319	2,008.96	220,651	296,828	2,045.46	203,419	314,060
145,000	1,891.55	535,958	2,042.87	250,806	285,152	2,080.71	228,531	307,427	2,118.54	210,684	325,274
150,000	1,956.78	554,441	2,113.32	259,456	294,985	2,152.46	236,412	318,029	2,191.59	217,948	336,493
155,000	2,022.01	572,924	2,183.77	268,105	304,819	2,224.21	244,292	328,632	2,264.65	225,214	347,710
160,000	2,087.23	591,403	2,254.21	276,753	314,650	2,295.95	252,171	339,232	2,337.70	232,479	358,924
165,000	2,152.46	609,886	2,324.66	285,403	324,483	2,367.71	260,054	349,832	2,410.76	239,745	370,141
170,000	2,217.68	628,365	2,395.09	294,049	334,314	2,439.45	267,933	360,432	2,483.80	247,008	381,357
175,000	2,282.91	646,848	2,465.54	302,698	344,150	2,511.20	275,813	371,035	2,556.86	254,274	392,574
180,000	2,348.14	665,330	2,535.99	311,348	353,982	2,582.95	283,694	381,636	2,629.92	261,540	403,790
185,000	2,413.36	683,810	2,606.43	319,996	363,814	2,654.70	291,574	392,236	2,702.96	268,803	415,007
190,000	2,478.59	702,292	2,676.88	328,646	373,646	2,726.45	299,455	402,837	2,776.02	276,069	426,223
195,000	2,543.81	720,772	2,747.31	337,291	383,481	2,798.19	307,334	413,438	2,849.07	283,333	437,439
200,000	2,609.04	739,254	2,817.76	345,941	393,313	2,869.94	315,214	424,040	2,922.12	290,598	448,656

263

AMOUNT OF LOAN	30 YEARS		2% PMT INCREASE 272.646 PAYMENTS			4% PMT INCREASE 234.068 PAYMENTS			6% PMT INCREASE 209.347 PAYMENTS		
	MONTHLY PAYMENT	TOTAL INTRST	MONTHLY PAYMENT	TOTAL INTRST	INTRST SAVED	MONTHLY PAYMENT	TOTAL INTRST	INTRST SAVED	MONTHLY PAYMENT	TOTAL INTRST	INTRST SAVED
$ 50	0.67	191	0.68	135	56	0.70	114	77	0.71	99	92
100	1.33	379	1.36	271	108	1.38	223	156	1.41	195	184
200	2.65	754	2.70	536	218	2.76	446	308	2.81	388	366
300	3.98	1,133	4.06	807	326	4.14	669	464	4.22	583	550
400	5.30	1,508	5.41	1,075	433	5.51	890	618	5.62	777	731
500	6.63	1,887	6.76	1,343	544	6.90	1,115	772	7.03	972	915
600	7.95	2,262	8.11	1,611	651	8.27	1,336	926	8.43	1,165	1,097
700	9.28	2,641	9.47	1,882	759	9.65	1,559	1,082	9.84	1,360	1,281
800	10.60	3,016	10.81	2,147	869	11.02	1,779	1,237	11.24	1,553	1,463
900	11.93	3,395	12.17	2,418	977	12.41	2,005	1,390	12.65	1,748	1,647
1,000	13.25	3,770	13.52	2,686	1,084	13.78	2,225	1,545	14.05	1,941	1,829
2,000	26.50	7,540	27.03	5,370	2,170	27.56	4,451	3,089	28.09	3,881	3,659
3,000	39.74	11,306	40.53	8,050	3,256	41.33	6,674	4,632	42.12	5,818	5,488
4,000	52.99	15,076	54.05	10,737	4,339	55.11	8,899	6,177	56.17	7,759	7,317
5,000	66.24	18,846	67.56	13,420	5,426	68.89	11,125	7,721	70.21	9,698	9,148
6,000	79.48	22,613	81.07	16,103	6,510	82.66	13,348	9,265	84.25	11,637	10,976
7,000	92.73	26,383	94.58	18,787	7,596	96.44	15,574	10,809	98.29	13,577	12,806
8,000	105.97	30,149	108.09	21,470	8,679	110.21	17,797	12,352	112.33	15,516	14,633
9,000	119.22	33,919	121.60	24,154	9,765	123.99	20,022	13,897	126.37	17,455	16,464
10,000	132.47	37,689	135.12	26,840	10,849	137.77	22,248	15,441	140.42	19,397	18,292
11,000	145.71	41,456	148.62	29,521	11,935	151.54	24,471	16,985	154.45	21,334	20,122
12,000	158.96	45,226	162.14	32,207	13,019	165.32	26,696	18,530	168.50	23,275	21,951
13,000	172.21	48,996	175.65	34,890	14,106	179.10	28,922	20,074	182.54	25,214	23,782
14,000	185.45	52,762	189.16	37,574	15,188	192.87	31,145	21,617	196.58	27,153	25,609
15,000	198.70	56,532	202.67	40,257	16,275	206.65	33,370	23,162	210.62	29,093	27,439
16,000	211.94	60,298	216.18	42,941	17,357	220.42	35,593	24,705	224.66	31,032	29,266
17,000	225.19	64,068	229.69	45,624	18,444	234.20	37,819	26,249	238.70	32,971	31,097
18,000	238.44	67,838	243.21	48,310	19,528	247.98	40,044	27,794	252.75	34,912	32,926
19,000	251.68	71,605	256.71	50,991	20,614	261.75	42,267	29,338	266.78	36,850	34,755
20,000	264.93	75,375	270.23	53,677	21,698	275.53	44,493	30,882	280.83	38,791	36,584
21,000	278.17	79,141	283.73	56,358	22,783	289.30	46,716	32,425	294.86	40,728	38,413
22,000	291.42	82,911	297.25	59,044	23,867	303.08	48,941	33,970	308.91	42,669	40,242
23,000	304.67	86,681	310.76	61,727	24,954	316.86	51,167	35,514	322.95	44,609	42,072
24,000	317.91	90,448	324.27	64,411	26,037	330.63	53,390	37,058	336.98	46,546	43,902
25,000	331.16	94,218	337.78	67,094	27,124	344.41	55,615	38,603	351.03	48,487	45,731
26,000	344.41	97,988	351.30	69,781	28,207	358.19	57,841	40,147	365.07	50,426	47,562
27,000	357.65	101,754	364.80	72,461	29,293	371.96	60,064	41,690	379.11	52,366	49,388
28,000	370.90	105,524	378.32	75,147	30,377	385.74	62,289	43,235	393.15	54,305	51,219
29,000	384.14	109,290	391.82	77,828	31,462	399.51	64,513	44,777	407.19	56,244	53,046
30,000	397.39	113,060	405.34	80,514	32,546	413.29	66,738	46,322	421.23	58,183	54,877
32,500	430.51	122,484	439.12	87,224	35,260	447.73	72,299	50,185	456.34	63,033	59,451
35,000	463.62	131,903	472.89	93,932	37,971	482.16	77,858	54,045	491.44	67,881	64,022
40,000	529.85	150,746	540.45	107,352	43,394	551.04	88,981	61,765	561.64	77,578	73,168
45,000	596.08	169,589	608.00	120,769	48,820	619.92	100,103	69,486	631.84	87,274	82,315
50,000	662.31	188,432	675.56	134,189	54,243	688.80	111,226	77,206	702.05	96,972	91,460
55,000	728.54	207,274	743.11	147,606	59,668	757.68	122,349	84,925	772.25	106,668	100,606
60,000	794.77	226,121	810.68	161,029	65,092	826.57	133,474	92,647	842.47	116,369	109,752
65,000	861.01	244,964	878.23	174,446	70,518	895.45	144,596	100,368	912.67	126,065	118,899
70,000	927.24	263,806	945.78	187,863	75,943	964.33	155,719	108,087	982.87	135,761	128,045
75,000	993.47	282,649	1,013.34	201,283	81,366	1,033.21	166,841	115,808	1,053.08	145,459	137,190
80,000	1,059.70	301,492	1,080.89	214,700	86,792	1,102.09	177,964	123,528	1,123.28	155,155	146,337
85,000	1,125.93	320,335	1,148.45	228,120	92,215	1,170.97	189,087	131,248	1,193.49	164,854	155,481
90,000	1,192.16	339,178	1,216.00	241,538	97,640	1,239.85	200,209	138,969	1,263.69	174,550	164,628
95,000	1,258.39	358,020	1,283.56	254,957	103,063	1,308.73	211,332	146,688	1,333.89	184,246	173,774
100,000	1,324.62	376,863	1,351.11	268,375	108,488	1,377.60	222,452	154,411	1,404.10	193,944	182,919
105,000	1,390.85	395,706	1,418.67	281,795	113,911	1,446.48	233,575	162,131	1,474.30	203,640	192,066
110,000	1,457.08	414,549	1,486.22	295,212	119,337	1,515.36	244,697	169,852	1,544.50	213,336	201,213
115,000	1,523.31	433,392	1,553.78	308,632	124,760	1,584.24	255,820	177,572	1,614.71	223,035	210,357
120,000	1,589.55	452,238	1,621.34	322,052	130,186	1,653.13	266,945	185,293	1,684.92	232,733	219,505
125,000	1,655.78	471,081	1,688.90	335,472	135,609	1,722.01	278,067	193,014	1,755.13	242,431	228,650
130,000	1,722.01	489,924	1,756.45	348,889	141,035	1,790.89	289,190	200,734	1,825.33	252,127	237,797
135,000	1,788.24	508,766	1,824.00	362,306	146,460	1,859.77	300,313	208,453	1,895.53	261,824	246,942
140,000	1,854.47	527,609	1,891.56	375,726	151,883	1,928.65	311,435	216,174	1,965.74	271,522	256,087
145,000	1,920.70	546,452	1,959.11	389,144	157,308	1,997.53	322,558	223,894	2,035.94	281,218	265,234
150,000	1,986.93	565,295	2,026.67	402,563	162,732	2,066.41	333,680	231,615	2,106.15	290,916	274,379
155,000	2,053.16	584,138	2,094.22	415,981	168,157	2,135.29	344,803	239,335	2,176.35	300,612	283,526
160,000	2,119.39	602,980	2,161.78	429,401	173,579	2,204.17	355,926	247,054	2,246.55	310,309	292,671
165,000	2,185.62	621,823	2,229.33	442,818	179,005	2,273.04	367,046	254,777	2,316.76	320,007	301,816
170,000	2,251.85	640,666	2,296.89	456,238	184,428	2,341.92	378,169	262,497	2,386.96	329,703	310,963
175,000	2,318.08	659,509	2,364.44	469,655	189,854	2,410.80	389,291	270,218	2,457.16	339,399	320,110
180,000	2,384.32	678,355	2,432.01	483,078	195,277	2,479.69	400,416	277,939	2,527.38	349,099	329,256
185,000	2,450.55	697,198	2,499.56	496,495	200,703	2,548.57	411,539	285,659	2,597.58	358,796	338,402
190,000	2,516.78	716,041	2,567.12	509,915	206,126	2,617.45	422,661	293,380	2,667.79	368,494	347,547
195,000	2,583.01	734,884	2,634.67	523,332	211,552	2,686.33	433,784	301,100	2,737.99	378,190	356,694
200,000	2,649.24	753,726	2,702.22	536,749	216,977	2,755.21	444,906	308,820	2,808.19	387,886	365,840

264

AUGMENTED PAYMENT MORTGAGES 15.75%

AMOUNT OF LOAN	30 YEARS MONTHLY PAYMENT	30 YEARS TOTAL INTRST	8% PMT INCREASE 191.297 PAYMENTS MONTHLY PAYMENT	TOTAL INTRST	INTRST SAVED	10% PMT INCREASE 177.181 PAYMENTS MONTHLY PAYMENT	TOTAL INTRST	INTRST SAVED	12% PMT INCREASE 165.660 PAYMENTS MONTHLY PAYMENT	TOTAL INTRST	INTRST SAVED
$ 50	0.67	191	0.72	88	103	0.74	81	110	0.75	74	117
100	1.33	379	1.44	175	204	1.46	159	220	1.49	147	232
200	2.65	754	2.86	347	407	2.92	317	437	2.97	292	462
300	3.98	1,133	4.30	523	610	4.38	476	657	4.46	439	694
400	5.30	1,508	5.72	694	814	5.83	633	875	5.94	584	924
500	6.63	1,887	7.16	870	1,017	7.29	792	1,095	7.43	731	1,156
600	7.95	2,262	8.59	1,043	1,219	8.75	950	1,312	8.90	874	1,388
700	9.28	2,641	10.02	1,217	1,424	10.21	1,109	1,532	10.39	1,021	1,620
800	10.60	3,016	11.45	1,390	1,626	11.66	1,266	1,750	11.87	1,166	1,850
900	11.93	3,395	12.88	1,564	1,831	13.12	1,425	1,970	13.36	1,313	2,082
1,000	13.25	3,770	14.31	1,737	2,033	14.58	1,583	2,187	14.84	1,458	2,312
2,000	26.50	7,540	28.62	3,475	4,065	29.15	3,165	4,375	29.68	2,917	4,623
3,000	39.74	11,306	42.92	5,210	6,096	43.71	4,745	6,561	44.51	4,374	6,932
4,000	52.99	15,076	57.23	6,948	8,128	58.29	6,328	8,748	59.35	5,832	9,244
5,000	66.24	18,846	71.54	8,685	10,161	72.86	7,909	10,937	74.19	7,290	11,556
6,000	79.48	22,613	85.84	10,421	12,192	87.43	9,491	13,122	89.02	8,747	13,866
7,000	92.73	26,383	100.15	12,158	14,225	102.00	11,072	15,311	103.86	10,205	16,178
8,000	105.97	30,149	114.45	13,894	16,255	116.57	12,654	17,495	118.69	11,662	18,487
9,000	119.22	33,919	128.76	15,631	18,288	131.14	14,236	19,683	133.53	13,121	20,798
10,000	132.47	37,689	143.07	17,369	20,320	145.72	15,819	21,870	148.37	14,579	23,110
11,000	145.71	41,456	157.37	19,104	22,352	160.28	17,399	24,057	163.20	16,036	25,420
12,000	158.96	45,226	171.68	20,842	24,384	174.86	18,982	26,244	178.04	17,494	27,732
13,000	172.21	48,996	185.99	22,579	26,417	189.43	20,563	28,433	192.88	18,953	30,043
14,000	185.45	52,762	200.29	24,315	28,447	204.00	22,145	30,617	207.70	20,408	32,354
15,000	198.70	56,532	214.60	26,052	30,480	218.57	23,726	32,806	222.54	21,866	34,666
16,000	211.94	60,298	228.90	27,788	32,510	233.13	25,306	34,992	237.37	23,323	36,975
17,000	225.19	64,068	243.21	29,525	34,543	247.71	26,890	37,178	252.21	24,781	39,287
18,000	238.44	67,838	257.52	31,263	36,575	262.28	28,471	39,367	267.05	26,240	41,598
19,000	251.68	71,605	271.81	32,996	38,609	276.85	30,053	41,552	281.88	27,696	43,909
20,000	264.93	75,375	286.12	34,734	40,641	291.42	31,634	43,741	296.72	29,155	46,220
21,000	278.17	79,141	300.42	36,469	42,672	305.99	33,216	45,925	311.55	30,611	48,530
22,000	291.42	82,911	314.73	38,207	44,704	320.56	34,797	48,114	326.39	32,070	50,841
23,000	304.67	86,681	329.04	39,944	46,737	335.14	36,380	50,301	341.23	33,528	53,153
24,000	317.91	90,448	343.34	41,680	48,768	349.70	37,960	52,488	356.06	34,985	55,463
25,000	331.16	94,218	357.65	43,417	50,801	364.28	39,543	54,675	370.90	36,443	57,775
26,000	344.41	97,988	371.96	45,155	52,833	378.85	41,125	56,863	385.74	37,902	60,086
27,000	357.65	101,754	386.26	46,890	54,864	393.42	42,707	59,047	400.57	39,358	62,396
28,000	370.90	105,524	400.57	48,628	56,896	407.99	44,288	61,236	415.41	40,817	64,707
29,000	384.14	109,290	414.87	50,363	58,927	422.55	45,868	63,422	430.24	42,274	67,016
30,000	397.39	113,060	429.18	52,101	60,959	437.13	47,451	65,609	445.08	43,732	69,328
32,500	430.51	122,484	464.95	56,444	66,040	473.56	51,406	71,078	482.17	47,376	75,108
35,000	463.62	131,903	500.71	60,784	71,119	509.98	55,359	76,544	519.25	51,019	80,884
40,000	529.85	150,746	572.24	69,468	81,278	582.84	63,268	87,478	593.43	58,308	92,438
45,000	596.08	169,589	643.77	78,151	91,438	655.69	71,176	98,413	667.61	65,596	103,993
50,000	662.31	188,432	715.29	86,833	101,599	728.54	79,083	109,349	741.79	72,885	115,547
55,000	728.54	207,274	786.82	95,516	111,758	801.39	86,991	120,283	815.96	80,172	127,102
60,000	794.78	226,121	858.36	104,202	121,919	874.26	94,902	131,219	890.15	87,462	138,659
65,000	861.01	244,964	929.89	112,885	132,079	947.11	102,810	142,154	964.33	94,751	150,213
70,000	927.24	263,806	1,001.42	121,569	142,237	1,019.96	110,718	153,088	1,038.51	102,040	161,766
75,000	993.47	282,649	1,072.95	130,252	152,397	1,092.82	118,627	164,022	1,112.69	109,328	173,321
80,000	1,059.70	301,492	1,144.48	138,936	162,556	1,165.67	126,535	174,957	1,186.86	116,615	184,877
85,000	1,125.93	320,335	1,216.00	147,617	172,718	1,238.52	134,442	185,893	1,261.04	123,904	196,431
90,000	1,192.16	339,178	1,287.53	156,301	182,877	1,311.38	142,352	196,826	1,335.22	131,193	207,985
95,000	1,258.39	358,020	1,359.06	164,984	193,036	1,384.23	150,259	207,761	1,409.40	138,481	219,539
100,000	1,324.62	376,863	1,430.59	173,668	203,195	1,457.08	158,167	218,696	1,483.57	145,768	231,095
105,000	1,390.85	395,706	1,502.12	182,351	213,355	1,529.94	166,076	229,630	1,557.75	153,057	242,649
110,000	1,457.08	414,549	1,573.65	191,035	223,514	1,602.79	173,984	240,565	1,631.93	160,346	254,203
115,000	1,523.31	433,392	1,645.17	199,716	233,676	1,675.64	181,892	251,500	1,706.11	167,634	265,758
120,000	1,589.55	452,238	1,716.71	208,401	243,837	1,748.51	189,803	262,435	1,780.30	174,924	277,314
125,000	1,655.78	471,081	1,788.24	217,085	253,996	1,821.36	197,710	273,371	1,854.47	182,212	288,869
130,000	1,722.01	489,924	1,859.77	225,768	264,156	1,894.21	205,618	284,306	1,928.65	189,500	300,424
135,000	1,788.24	508,766	1,931.30	234,452	274,314	1,967.06	213,526	295,240	2,002.83	196,789	311,977
140,000	1,854.47	527,609	2,002.83	243,135	284,474	2,039.92	221,435	306,174	2,077.01	204,077	323,532
145,000	1,920.70	546,452	2,074.36	251,819	294,633	2,112.77	229,343	317,109	2,151.18	211,364	335,088
150,000	1,986.93	565,295	2,145.88	260,500	304,795	2,185.62	237,250	328,045	2,225.36	218,653	346,642
155,000	2,053.16	584,138	2,217.41	269,184	314,954	2,258.48	245,160	338,978	2,299.54	225,942	358,196
160,000	2,119.39	602,980	2,288.94	277,867	325,113	2,331.33	253,067	349,913	2,373.72	233,230	369,750
165,000	2,185.62	621,823	2,360.47	286,551	335,272	2,404.18	260,975	360,848	2,447.89	240,517	381,306
170,000	2,251.85	640,666	2,432.00	295,234	345,432	2,477.04	268,884	371,782	2,522.07	247,806	392,860
175,000	2,318.08	659,509	2,503.53	303,918	355,591	2,549.89	276,792	382,717	2,596.25	255,095	404,414
180,000	2,384.32	678,355	2,575.07	312,603	365,752	2,622.75	284,701	393,654	2,670.44	262,385	415,970
185,000	2,450.55	697,198	2,646.59	321,285	375,913	2,695.61	292,611	404,587	2,744.62	269,674	427,524
190,000	2,516.78	716,041	2,718.12	329,968	386,073	2,768.46	300,519	415,521	2,818.79	276,961	439,080
195,000	2,583.01	734,884	2,789.65	338,652	396,232	2,841.31	308,426	426,458	2,892.97	284,249	450,635
200,000	2,649.24	753,726	2,861.18	347,335	406,391	2,914.16	316,334	437,392	2,967.15	291,538	462,188

265

AUGMENTED PAYMENT MORTGAGES

AMOUNT OF LOAN	30 YEARS		2% PMT INCREASE 270.123 PAYMENTS			4% PMT INCREASE 231.445 PAYMENTS			6% PMT INCREASE 206.812 PAYMENTS		
	MONTHLY PAYMENT	TOTAL INTRST	MONTHLY PAYMENT	TOTAL INTRST	INTRST SAVED	MONTHLY PAYMENT	TOTAL INTRST	INTRST SAVED	MONTHLY PAYMENT	TOTAL INTRST	INTRST SAVED
$ 50	0.68	195	0.69	136	59	0.71	114	81	0.72	99	96
100	1.35	386	1.38	273	113	1.40	224	162	1.43	196	190
200	2.69	768	2.74	540	228	2.80	448	320	2.85	389	379
300	4.04	1,154	4.12	813	341	4.20	672	482	4.28	585	569
400	5.38	1,537	5.49	1,083	454	5.60	896	641	5.70	779	758
500	6.73	1,923	6.86	1,353	570	7.00	1,120	803	7.13	975	948
600	8.07	2,305	8.23	1,623	682	8.39	1,342	963	8.55	1,168	1,137
700	9.42	2,691	9.61	1,896	795	9.80	1,568	1,123	9.99	1,366	1,325
800	10.76	3,074	10.98	2,166	908	11.19	1,790	1,284	11.41	1,560	1,514
900	12.11	3,460	12.35	2,436	1,024	12.59	2,014	1,446	12.84	1,755	1,705
1,000	13.45	3,842	13.72	2,706	1,136	13.99	2,238	1,604	14.26	1,949	1,893
2,000	26.90	7,684	27.44	5,412	2,272	27.98	4,476	3,208	28.51	3,896	3,788
3,000	40.35	11,526	41.16	8,118	3,408	41.96	6,711	4,815	42.77	5,845	5,681
4,000	53.80	15,368	54.88	10,824	4,544	55.95	8,949	6,419	57.03	7,794	7,574
5,000	67.24	19,206	68.58	13,525	5,681	69.93	11,185	8,021	71.27	9,739	9,467
6,000	80.69	23,048	82.30	16,231	6,817	83.92	13,423	9,625	85.53	11,689	11,359
7,000	94.14	26,890	96.02	18,937	7,953	97.91	15,661	11,229	99.79	13,638	13,252
8,000	107.59	30,732	109.74	21,643	9,089	111.89	17,896	12,836	114.05	15,587	15,145
9,000	121.03	34,571	123.45	24,347	10,224	125.87	20,132	14,439	128.29	17,532	17,039
10,000	134.48	38,413	137.17	27,053	11,360	139.86	22,370	16,043	142.55	19,481	18,932
11,000	147.93	42,255	150.89	29,759	12,496	153.85	24,608	17,647	156.81	21,430	20,825
12,000	161.38	46,097	164.61	32,465	13,632	167.84	26,846	19,251	171.06	23,377	22,720
13,000	174.82	49,935	178.32	35,168	14,767	181.81	29,079	20,856	185.31	25,324	24,611
14,000	188.27	53,777	192.04	37,874	15,903	195.80	31,317	22,460	199.57	27,273	26,504
15,000	201.72	57,619	205.75	40,578	17,041	209.79	33,555	24,064	213.82	29,221	28,398
16,000	215.17	61,461	219.47	43,284	18,177	223.78	35,793	25,668	228.08	31,170	30,291
17,000	228.61	65,300	233.18	45,987	19,313	237.75	38,026	27,274	242.33	33,117	32,183
18,000	242.06	69,142	246.90	48,693	20,449	251.74	40,264	28,878	256.58	35,064	34,078
19,000	255.51	72,984	260.62	51,399	21,585	265.73	42,502	30,482	270.84	37,013	35,971
20,000	268.96	76,826	274.34	54,106	22,720	279.72	44,740	32,086	285.10	38,962	37,864
21,000	282.40	80,664	288.05	56,809	23,855	293.70	46,975	33,689	299.34	40,907	39,757
22,000	295.85	84,506	301.77	59,515	24,991	307.68	49,211	35,295	313.60	42,856	41,650
23,000	309.30	88,348	315.49	62,221	26,127	321.67	51,449	36,899	327.86	44,805	43,543
24,000	322.75	92,190	329.21	64,927	27,263	335.66	53,687	38,503	342.12	46,755	45,435
25,000	336.19	96,028	342.91	67,628	28,400	349.64	55,922	40,106	356.36	48,700	47,328
26,000	349.64	99,870	356.63	70,334	29,536	363.63	58,160	41,710	370.62	50,649	49,221
27,000	363.09	103,712	370.35	73,040	30,672	377.61	60,396	43,316	384.88	52,598	51,114
28,000	376.54	107,554	384.07	75,746	31,808	391.60	62,634	44,920	399.13	54,545	53,009
29,000	389.98	111,393	397.78	78,450	32,943	405.58	64,869	46,524	413.38	56,492	54,901
30,000	403.43	115,235	411.50	81,156	34,079	419.57	67,107	48,128	427.64	58,441	56,794
32,500	437.05	124,838	445.79	87,918	36,920	454.53	72,699	52,139	463.27	63,310	61,528
35,000	470.67	134,441	480.08	94,681	39,760	489.50	78,292	56,149	498.91	68,181	66,260
40,000	537.91	153,648	548.67	108,208	45,440	559.43	89,477	64,171	570.18	77,920	75,728
45,000	605.15	172,854	617.25	121,733	51,121	629.36	100,662	72,192	641.46	87,662	85,192
50,000	672.38	192,057	685.83	135,258	56,799	699.28	111,845	80,212	712.72	97,399	94,658
55,000	739.62	211,263	754.41	148,783	62,480	769.20	123,027	88,236	784.00	107,141	104,122
60,000	806.86	230,470	823.00	162,311	68,159	839.13	134,212	96,258	855.27	116,880	113,590
65,000	874.10	249,676	891.58	175,836	73,840	909.06	145,397	104,279	926.55	126,622	123,054
70,000	941.33	268,879	960.16	189,361	79,518	978.98	156,580	112,299	997.81	136,359	132,520
75,000	1,008.57	288,085	1,028.74	202,886	85,199	1,048.91	167,765	120,320	1,069.08	146,099	141,986
80,000	1,075.81	307,292	1,097.33	216,414	90,878	1,118.84	178,950	128,342	1,140.36	155,840	151,452
85,000	1,143.05	326,498	1,165.91	229,939	96,559	1,188.77	190,135	136,363	1,211.63	165,580	160,918
90,000	1,210.29	345,704	1,234.50	243,467	102,237	1,258.70	201,320	144,384	1,282.91	175,321	170,383
95,000	1,277.52	364,907	1,303.07	256,989	107,918	1,328.62	212,502	152,405	1,354.17	185,059	179,848
100,000	1,344.76	384,114	1,371.66	270,517	113,597	1,398.55	223,687	160,427	1,425.45	194,800	189,314
105,000	1,412.00	403,320	1,440.24	284,042	119,278	1,468.48	234,872	168,448	1,496.72	204,540	198,780
110,000	1,479.24	422,526	1,508.82	297,567	124,959	1,538.41	246,057	176,469	1,567.99	214,279	208,247
115,000	1,546.48	441,733	1,577.41	311,095	130,638	1,608.34	257,242	184,491	1,639.27	224,021	217,712
120,000	1,613.71	460,936	1,645.98	324,617	136,319	1,678.26	268,425	192,511	1,710.53	233,758	227,178
125,000	1,680.95	480,142	1,714.57	338,145	141,997	1,748.19	279,610	200,532	1,781.81	243,500	236,642
130,000	1,748.19	499,348	1,783.15	351,670	147,678	1,818.12	290,795	208,553	1,853.08	253,239	246,109
135,000	1,815.43	518,555	1,851.74	365,198	153,357	1,888.05	301,980	216,575	1,924.36	262,981	255,574
140,000	1,882.66	537,758	1,920.31	378,720	159,038	1,957.97	313,162	224,596	1,995.62	272,718	265,040
145,000	1,949.90	556,964	1,988.90	392,248	164,716	2,027.90	324,347	232,617	2,066.89	282,458	274,505
150,000	2,017.14	576,170	2,057.48	405,773	170,397	2,097.83	335,532	240,638	2,138.17	292,199	283,971
155,000	2,084.38	595,377	2,126.07	419,300	176,077	2,167.76	346,717	248,660	2,209.44	301,939	293,438
160,000	2,151.62	614,583	2,194.65	432,825	181,758	2,237.68	357,900	256,683	2,280.72	311,680	302,903
165,000	2,218.85	633,786	2,263.23	446,350	187,436	2,307.60	369,082	264,704	2,351.98	321,418	312,368
170,000	2,286.09	652,992	2,331.81	459,876	193,116	2,377.53	380,267	272,725	2,423.26	331,159	321,833
175,000	2,353.33	672,199	2,400.40	473,403	198,796	2,447.46	391,452	280,747	2,494.53	340,899	331,300
180,000	2,420.57	691,405	2,468.98	486,928	204,477	2,517.39	402,637	288,768	2,565.80	350,638	340,767
185,000	2,487.81	710,612	2,537.57	500,456	210,156	2,587.32	413,822	296,790	2,637.08	360,380	350,232
190,000	2,555.04	729,814	2,606.14	513,978	215,836	2,657.24	425,005	304,809	2,708.34	370,117	359,697
195,000	2,622.28	749,021	2,674.73	527,506	221,515	2,727.17	436,190	312,831	2,779.62	379,859	369,162
200,000	2,689.52	768,227	2,743.31	541,031	227,196	2,797.10	447,375	320,852	2,850.89	389,598	378,629

AUGMENTED PAYMENT MORTGAGES 16.00%

AMOUNT OF LOAN	30 YEARS		8% PMT INCREASE 188.882 PAYMENTS			10% PMT INCREASE 174.883 PAYMENTS			12% PMT INCREASE 163.471 PAYMENTS		
	MONTHLY PAYMENT	TOTAL INTRST	MONTHLY PAYMENT	TOTAL INTRST	INTRST SAVED	MONTHLY PAYMENT	TOTAL INTRST	INTRST SAVED	MONTHLY PAYMENT	TOTAL INTRST	INTRST SAVED
$ 50	0.68	195	0.73	88	107	0.75	81	114	0.76	74	121
100	1.35	386	1.46	176	210	1.49	161	225	1.51	147	239
200	2.69	768	2.91	350	418	2.96	318	450	3.01	292	476
300	4.04	1,154	4.36	524	630	4.44	476	678	4.52	439	715
400	5.38	1,537	5.81	697	840	5.92	635	902	6.03	586	951
500	6.73	1,923	7.27	873	1,050	7.40	794	1,129	7.54	733	1,190
600	8.07	2,305	8.72	1,047	1,258	8.88	953	1,352	9.04	878	1,427
700	9.42	2,691	10.17	1,221	1,470	10.36	1,112	1,579	10.55	1,025	1,666
800	10.76	3,074	11.62	1,395	1,679	11.84	1,271	1,803	12.05	1,170	1,904
900	12.11	3,460	13.08	1,571	1,889	13.32	1,429	2,031	13.56	1,317	2,143
1,000	13.45	3,842	14.53	1,744	2,098	14.80	1,588	2,254	15.06	1,462	2,380
2,000	26.90	7,684	29.05	3,487	4,197	29.59	3,175	4,509	30.13	2,925	4,759
3,000	40.35	11,526	43.58	5,231	6,295	44.39	4,763	6,763	45.19	4,387	7,139
4,000	53.80	15,368	58.10	6,974	8,394	59.18	6,350	9,018	60.26	5,851	9,517
5,000	67.24	19,206	72.62	8,717	10,489	73.96	7,934	11,272	75.31	7,311	11,895
6,000	80.69	23,048	87.15	10,461	12,587	88.76	9,523	13,525	90.37	8,773	14,275
7,000	94.14	26,890	101.67	12,204	14,686	103.55	11,109	15,781	105.44	10,236	16,654
8,000	107.59	30,732	116.20	13,948	16,784	118.35	12,697	18,035	120.50	11,698	19,034
9,000	121.03	34,571	130.71	15,689	18,882	133.13	14,282	20,289	135.55	13,158	21,413
10,000	134.48	38,413	145.24	17,433	20,980	147.93	15,870	22,543	150.62	14,622	23,791
11,000	147.93	42,255	159.76	19,176	23,079	162.72	17,457	24,798	165.68	16,084	26,171
12,000	161.38	46,097	174.29	20,920	25,177	177.52	19,045	27,052	180.75	17,547	28,550
13,000	174.82	49,935	188.81	22,663	27,272	192.30	20,630	29,305	195.80	19,008	30,927
14,000	188.27	53,777	203.33	24,405	29,372	207.10	22,218	31,559	210.86	20,469	33,308
15,000	201.72	57,619	217.86	26,150	31,469	221.89	23,805	33,814	225.93	21,933	35,686
16,000	215.17	61,461	232.38	27,892	33,569	236.69	25,393	36,068	240.99	23,395	38,066
17,000	228.61	65,300	246.90	29,635	35,665	251.47	26,978	38,322	256.04	24,855	40,445
18,000	242.06	69,142	261.42	31,378	37,764	266.27	28,566	40,576	271.11	26,319	42,823
19,000	255.51	72,984	275.95	33,122	39,862	281.06	30,153	42,831	286.17	27,780	45,204
20,000	268.96	76,826	290.48	34,866	41,960	295.86	31,741	45,085	301.24	29,244	47,582
21,000	282.40	80,664	304.99	36,607	44,057	310.64	33,326	47,338	316.29	30,704	49,960
22,000	295.85	84,506	319.52	38,352	46,154	325.44	34,914	49,592	331.35	32,166	52,340
23,000	309.30	88,348	334.04	40,094	48,254	340.23	36,500	51,848	346.42	33,630	54,718
24,000	322.75	92,190	348.57	41,839	50,351	355.03	38,089	54,101	361.48	35,091	57,099
25,000	336.19	96,028	363.09	43,581	52,447	369.81	39,673	56,355	376.53	36,552	59,476
26,000	349.64	99,870	377.61	45,324	54,546	384.60	41,260	58,610	391.60	38,015	61,855
27,000	363.09	103,712	392.14	47,068	56,644	399.40	42,848	60,864	406.66	39,477	64,235
28,000	376.54	107,554	406.66	48,811	58,743	414.19	44,435	63,119	421.72	40,939	66,615
29,000	389.98	111,393	421.18	50,553	60,840	428.98	46,021	65,372	436.78	42,401	68,992
30,000	403.43	115,235	435.70	52,296	62,939	443.77	47,608	67,627	451.84	43,863	71,372
32,500	437.05	124,838	472.01	56,654	68,184	480.76	51,577	73,261	489.50	47,519	77,319
35,000	470.67	134,441	508.32	61,012	73,429	517.74	55,544	78,897	527.15	51,174	83,267
40,000	537.91	153,648	580.94	69,729	83,919	591.70	63,478	90,170	602.46	58,485	95,163
45,000	605.15	172,854	653.56	78,446	94,408	665.67	71,414	101,440	677.77	65,796	107,058
50,000	672.38	192,057	726.17	87,160	104,897	739.62	79,347	112,710	753.07	73,105	118,952
55,000	739.62	211,263	798.79	95,877	115,386	813.58	87,281	123,982	828.37	80,414	130,849
60,000	806.86	230,470	871.41	104,594	125,876	887.55	95,217	135,253	903.68	87,725	142,745
65,000	874.10	249,676	944.03	113,310	136,366	961.51	103,152	146,524	978.99	95,036	154,640
70,000	941.33	268,879	1,016.64	122,025	146,854	1,035.46	111,084	157,795	1,054.29	102,346	166,533
75,000	1,008.57	288,085	1,089.26	130,742	157,343	1,109.43	119,020	169,065	1,129.60	109,657	178,428
80,000	1,075.81	307,292	1,161.87	139,456	167,836	1,183.39	126,955	180,337	1,204.91	116,968	190,324
85,000	1,143.05	326,498	1,234.49	148,173	178,325	1,257.36	134,891	191,607	1,280.22	124,279	202,219
90,000	1,210.29	345,704	1,307.11	156,890	188,814	1,331.32	142,825	202,879	1,355.52	131,588	214,116
95,000	1,277.52	364,907	1,379.72	165,604	199,303	1,405.27	150,758	214,149	1,430.82	138,898	226,009
100,000	1,344.76	384,114	1,452.34	174,321	209,793	1,479.24	158,694	225,420	1,506.13	146,209	237,905
105,000	1,412.00	403,320	1,524.96	183,037	220,283	1,553.20	166,628	236,692	1,581.44	153,520	249,800
110,000	1,479.24	422,526	1,597.58	191,754	230,772	1,627.16	174,563	247,963	1,656.75	160,831	261,695
115,000	1,546.48	441,733	1,670.20	200,471	241,262	1,701.13	182,499	259,234	1,732.06	168,142	273,591
120,000	1,613.71	460,936	1,742.81	209,185	251,751	1,775.08	190,431	270,505	1,807.36	175,451	285,485
125,000	1,680.95	480,142	1,815.43	217,902	262,240	1,849.05	198,367	281,775	1,882.66	182,760	297,382
130,000	1,748.19	499,348	1,888.05	226,619	272,729	1,923.01	206,302	293,046	1,957.97	190,071	309,277
135,000	1,815.43	518,555	1,960.66	235,333	283,222	1,996.97	214,236	304,319	2,033.28	197,382	321,173
140,000	1,882.66	537,758	2,033.27	244,048	293,710	2,070.93	222,170	315,588	2,108.58	204,692	333,066
145,000	1,949.90	556,964	2,105.89	252,765	304,199	2,144.89	230,105	326,859	2,183.89	212,003	344,961
150,000	2,017.14	576,170	2,178.51	261,481	314,689	2,218.85	238,039	338,131	2,259.20	219,314	356,856
155,000	2,084.38	595,377	2,251.13	270,198	325,179	2,292.82	245,975	349,402	2,334.51	226,625	368,752
160,000	2,151.62	614,583	2,323.75	278,915	335,668	2,366.78	253,910	360,673	2,409.81	233,934	380,649
165,000	2,218.85	633,786	2,396.36	287,629	346,157	2,440.74	261,844	371,942	2,485.11	241,243	392,543
170,000	2,286.09	652,992	2,468.98	296,346	356,646	2,514.70	269,778	383,214	2,560.42	248,554	404,438
175,000	2,353.33	672,199	2,541.60	305,062	367,137	2,588.66	277,713	394,486	2,635.73	255,865	416,334
180,000	2,420.57	691,405	2,614.22	313,779	377,626	2,662.63	285,649	405,756	2,711.04	263,176	428,229
185,000	2,487.81	710,612	2,686.83	322,494	388,118	2,736.59	293,583	417,029	2,786.35	270,487	440,125
190,000	2,555.04	729,814	2,759.44	331,209	398,605	2,810.54	301,516	428,298	2,861.64	277,795	452,019
195,000	2,622.28	749,021	2,832.06	339,925	409,096	2,884.51	309,452	439,569	2,936.95	285,106	463,915
200,000	2,689.52	768,227	2,904.68	348,642	419,585	2,958.47	317,386	450,841	3,012.26	292,417	475,810

267

AMOUNT OF LOAN	30 YEARS		2% PMT INCREASE 267.594 PAYMENTS			4% PMT INCREASE 228.842 PAYMENTS			6% PMT INCREASE 204.313 PAYMENTS		
	MONTHLY PAYMENT	TOTAL INTRST	MONTHLY PAYMENT	TOTAL INTRST	INTRST SAVED	MONTHLY PAYMENT	TOTAL INTRST	INTRST SAVED	MONTHLY PAYMENT	TOTAL INTRST	INTRST SAVED
$ 50	0.69	198	0.70	137	61	0.72	115	83	0.73	99	99
100	1.37	393	1.40	275	118	1.42	225	168	1.45	196	197
200	2.73	783	2.78	544	239	2.84	450	333	2.89	390	393
300	4.10	1,176	4.18	819	357	4.26	675	501	4.35	589	587
400	5.46	1,566	5.57	1,090	476	5.68	900	666	5.79	783	783
500	6.83	1,959	6.97	1,365	594	7.10	1,125	834	7.24	979	980
600	8.19	2,348	8.35	1,634	714	8.52	1,350	998	8.68	1,173	1,175
700	9.56	2,742	9.75	1,909	833	9.94	1,575	1,167	10.13	1,370	1,372
800	10.92	3,131	11.14	2,181	950	11.36	1,800	1,331	11.58	1,566	1,565
900	12.29	3,524	12.54	2,456	1,068	12.78	2,025	1,499	13.03	1,762	1,762
1,000	13.65	3,914	13.92	2,725	1,189	14.20	2,250	1,664	14.47	1,956	1,958
2,000	27.30	7,828	27.85	5,452	2,376	28.39	4,497	3,331	28.94	3,913	3,915
3,000	40.95	11,742	41.77	8,177	3,565	42.59	6,746	4,996	43.41	5,869	5,873
4,000	54.60	15,656	55.69	10,902	4,754	56.78	8,994	6,662	57.88	7,826	7,830
5,000	68.25	19,570	69.62	13,630	5,940	70.98	11,243	8,327	72.35	9,782	9,788
6,000	81.90	23,484	83.54	16,355	7,129	85.18	13,493	9,991	86.81	11,736	11,748
7,000	95.55	27,398	97.46	19,080	8,318	99.37	15,740	11,658	101.28	13,693	13,705
8,000	109.20	31,312	111.38	21,805	9,507	113.57	17,990	13,322	115.75	15,649	15,663
9,000	122.85	35,226	125.31	24,532	10,694	127.76	20,237	14,989	130.22	17,606	17,620
10,000	136.50	39,140	139.23	27,257	11,883	141.96	22,486	16,654	144.69	19,562	19,578
11,000	150.15	43,054	153.15	29,982	13,072	156.16	24,736	18,318	159.16	21,518	21,536
12,000	163.80	46,968	167.08	32,710	14,258	170.35	26,983	19,985	173.63	23,475	23,493
13,000	177.45	50,882	181.00	35,435	15,447	184.55	29,233	21,649	188.10	25,431	25,451
14,000	191.10	54,796	194.92	38,159	16,637	198.74	31,480	23,316	202.57	27,388	27,408
15,000	204.75	58,710	208.85	40,887	17,823	212.94	33,730	24,980	217.04	29,344	29,366
16,000	218.39	62,620	222.76	43,609	19,011	227.13	35,977	26,643	231.49	31,296	31,324
17,000	232.04	66,534	236.68	46,334	20,200	241.32	38,224	28,310	245.96	33,253	33,281
18,000	245.69	70,448	250.60	49,059	21,389	255.52	40,474	29,974	260.43	35,209	35,239
19,000	259.34	74,362	264.53	51,787	22,575	269.71	42,721	31,641	274.90	37,166	37,196
20,000	272.99	78,276	278.45	54,512	23,764	283.91	44,971	33,305	289.37	39,122	39,154
21,000	286.64	82,190	292.37	57,236	24,954	298.11	47,220	34,970	303.84	41,078	41,112
22,000	300.29	86,104	306.30	59,964	26,140	312.30	49,467	36,637	318.31	43,035	43,069
23,000	313.94	90,018	320.22	62,689	27,329	326.50	51,717	38,301	332.78	44,991	45,027
24,000	327.59	93,932	334.14	65,414	28,518	340.69	53,964	39,968	347.25	46,948	46,984
25,000	341.24	97,846	348.06	68,139	29,707	354.89	56,214	41,632	361.71	48,902	48,944
26,000	354.89	101,760	361.99	70,866	30,894	369.09	58,463	43,297	376.18	50,858	50,902
27,000	368.54	105,674	375.91	73,591	32,083	383.28	60,711	44,963	390.65	52,815	52,859
28,000	382.19	109,588	389.83	76,316	33,272	397.48	62,960	46,628	405.12	54,771	54,817
29,000	395.84	113,502	403.76	79,044	34,458	411.67	65,207	48,295	419.59	56,728	56,774
30,000	409.49	117,416	417.68	81,769	35,647	425.87	67,457	49,959	434.06	58,684	58,732
32,500	443.61	127,200	452.48	88,581	38,619	461.35	73,076	54,124	470.23	63,574	63,626
35,000	477.73	136,983	487.28	95,393	41,590	496.84	78,698	58,285	506.39	68,462	68,521
40,000	545.98	156,553	556.90	109,023	47,530	567.82	89,941	66,612	578.74	78,244	78,309
45,000	614.23	176,123	626.51	122,650	53,473	638.80	101,184	74,939	651.08	88,024	88,099
50,000	682.47	195,689	696.12	136,278	59,411	709.77	112,425	83,264	723.42	97,804	97,885
55,000	750.72	215,259	765.73	149,905	65,354	780.75	123,668	91,591	795.76	107,584	107,675
60,000	818.97	234,829	835.35	163,535	71,294	851.72	134,912	99,917	868.11	117,366	117,463
65,000	887.21	254,396	904.95	177,159	77,237	922.70	146,153	108,243	940.44	127,144	127,252
70,000	955.46	273,966	974.57	190,789	83,177	993.68	157,396	116,570	1,012.79	136,926	137,040
75,000	1,023.71	293,536	1,044.18	204,416	89,120	1,064.66	168,639	124,897	1,085.13	146,706	146,830
80,000	1,091.95	313,102	1,113.79	218,044	95,058	1,135.63	179,880	133,222	1,157.47	156,486	156,616
85,000	1,160.20	332,672	1,183.40	231,671	101,001	1,206.61	191,123	141,549	1,229.81	166,266	166,406
90,000	1,228.45	352,242	1,253.02	245,301	106,941	1,277.59	202,366	149,876	1,302.16	176,048	176,194
95,000	1,296.69	371,808	1,322.62	258,925	112,883	1,348.56	213,607	158,201	1,374.49	185,826	185,982
100,000	1,364.94	391,378	1,392.24	272,555	118,823	1,419.54	224,850	166,528	1,446.84	195,608	195,770
105,000	1,433.19	410,948	1,461.85	286,182	124,766	1,490.52	236,094	174,854	1,519.18	205,388	205,560
110,000	1,501.43	430,515	1,531.46	299,809	130,705	1,561.49	247,334	183,181	1,591.52	215,168	215,347
115,000	1,569.68	450,085	1,601.07	313,437	136,648	1,632.47	258,578	191,507	1,663.86	224,948	225,137
120,000	1,637.93	469,655	1,670.69	327,067	142,588	1,703.45	269,821	199,834	1,736.21	234,730	234,925
125,000	1,706.17	489,221	1,740.29	340,691	148,530	1,774.42	281,062	208,159	1,808.54	244,508	244,713
130,000	1,774.42	508,791	1,809.91	354,321	154,470	1,845.40	292,305	216,486	1,880.89	254,290	254,501
135,000	1,842.67	528,361	1,879.52	367,948	160,413	1,916.38	303,548	224,813	1,953.23	264,070	264,291
140,000	1,910.91	547,928	1,949.13	381,575	166,353	1,987.35	314,789	233,139	2,025.56	273,848	274,080
145,000	1,979.16	567,498	2,018.74	395,203	172,295	2,058.33	326,032	241,466	2,097.91	283,630	283,868
150,000	2,047.41	587,068	2,088.36	408,833	178,235	2,129.31	337,276	249,792	2,170.25	293,410	293,658
155,000	2,115.65	606,634	2,157.96	422,457	184,177	2,200.28	348,516	258,118	2,242.59	303,190	303,444
160,000	2,183.90	626,204	2,227.58	436,087	190,117	2,271.26	359,760	266,444	2,314.93	312,970	313,234
165,000	2,252.15	645,774	2,297.19	449,714	196,060	2,342.24	371,003	274,771	2,387.28	322,752	323,022
170,000	2,320.39	665,340	2,366.80	463,341	201,999	2,413.21	382,244	283,096	2,459.61	332,530	332,810
175,000	2,388.64	684,910	2,436.41	476,969	207,941	2,484.19	393,487	291,423	2,531.96	342,312	342,598
180,000	2,456.89	704,480	2,506.03	490,599	213,881	2,555.17	404,730	299,750	2,604.30	352,092	352,388
185,000	2,525.13	724,047	2,575.63	504,223	219,824	2,626.14	415,971	308,076	2,676.64	361,872	362,175
190,000	2,593.38	743,617	2,645.25	517,853	225,764	2,697.12	427,214	316,403	2,748.98	371,652	371,965
195,000	2,661.63	763,187	2,714.86	531,480	231,707	2,768.10	438,458	324,729	2,821.33	381,434	381,753
200,000	2,729.87	782,753	2,784.47	545,107	237,646	2,839.06	449,696	333,057	2,893.66	391,212	391,541

AMOUNT OF LOAN	30 YEARS		8% PMT INCREASE 186.507 PAYMENTS			10% PMT INCREASE 172.628 PAYMENTS			12% PMT INCREASE 161.324 PAYMENTS		
	MONTHLY PAYMENT	TOTAL INTRST	MONTHLY PAYMENT	TOTAL INTRST	INTRST SAVED	MONTHLY PAYMENT	TOTAL INTRST	INTRST SAVED	MONTHLY PAYMENT	TOTAL INTRST	INTRST SAVED
$ 50	0.69	198	0.75	90	108	0.76	81	117	0.77	74	124
100	1.37	393	1.48	176	217	1.51	161	232	1.53	147	246
200	2.73	783	2.95	350	433	3.00	318	465	3.06	294	489
300	4.10	1,176	4.43	526	650	4.51	479	697	4.59	440	736
400	5.46	1,566	5.90	700	866	6.01	637	929	6.12	587	979
500	6.83	1,959	7.38	876	1,083	7.51	796	1,163	7.65	734	1,225
600	8.19	2,348	8.85	1,051	1,297	9.01	955	1,393	9.17	879	1,469
700	9.56	2,742	10.32	1,225	1,517	10.52	1,116	1,626	10.71	1,028	1,714
800	10.92	3,131	11.79	1,399	1,732	12.01	1,273	1,858	12.23	1,173	1,958
900	12.29	3,524	13.27	1,575	1,949	13.52	1,434	2,090	13.76	1,320	2,204
1,000	13.65	3,914	14.74	1,749	2,165	15.02	1,593	2,321	15.29	1,467	2,447
2,000	27.30	7,828	29.48	3,498	4,330	30.03	3,184	4,644	30.58	2,933	4,895
3,000	40.95	11,742	44.23	5,249	6,493	45.05	4,777	6,965	45.86	4,398	7,344
4,000	54.60	15,656	58.97	6,998	8,658	60.06	6,368	9,288	61.15	5,865	9,791
5,000	68.25	19,570	73.71	8,747	10,823	75.08	7,961	11,609	76.44	7,332	12,238
6,000	81.90	23,484	88.45	10,497	12,987	90.09	9,552	13,932	91.73	8,798	14,686
7,000	95.55	27,398	103.19	12,246	15,152	105.11	11,145	16,253	107.02	10,265	17,133
8,000	109.20	31,312	117.94	13,997	17,315	120.12	12,736	18,576	122.30	11,730	19,582
9,000	122.85	35,226	132.68	15,746	19,480	135.14	14,329	20,897	137.59	13,197	22,029
10,000	136.50	39,140	147.42	17,495	21,645	150.15	15,920	23,220	152.88	14,663	24,477
11,000	150.15	43,054	162.16	19,244	23,810	165.17	17,513	25,541	168.17	16,130	26,924
12,000	163.80	46,968	176.90	20,993	25,975	180.18	19,104	27,864	183.46	17,597	29,371
13,000	177.45	50,882	191.65	22,744	28,138	195.20	20,697	30,185	198.74	19,062	31,820
14,000	191.10	54,796	206.39	24,493	30,303	210.21	22,288	32,508	214.03	20,528	34,268
15,000	204.75	58,710	221.13	26,242	32,468	225.23	23,881	34,829	229.32	21,995	36,715
16,000	218.39	62,620	235.86	27,990	34,630	240.23	25,470	37,150	244.60	23,460	39,160
17,000	232.04	66,534	250.60	29,739	36,795	255.24	27,062	39,472	259.88	24,925	41,609
18,000	245.69	70,448	265.35	31,490	38,958	270.26	28,654	41,794	275.17	26,392	44,056
19,000	259.34	74,362	280.09	33,239	41,123	285.27	30,246	44,116	290.46	27,858	46,504
20,000	272.99	78,276	294.83	34,988	43,288	300.29	31,838	46,438	305.75	29,325	48,951
21,000	286.64	82,190	309.57	36,737	45,453	315.30	33,430	48,760	321.04	30,791	51,399
22,000	300.29	86,104	324.31	38,486	47,618	330.32	35,022	51,082	336.32	32,256	53,848
23,000	313.94	90,018	339.06	40,237	49,781	345.33	36,614	53,404	351.61	33,723	56,295
24,000	327.59	93,932	353.80	41,986	51,946	360.35	38,206	55,726	366.90	35,190	58,742
25,000	341.24	97,846	368.54	43,735	54,111	375.36	39,798	58,048	382.19	36,656	61,190
26,000	354.89	101,760	383.28	45,484	56,276	390.38	41,391	60,369	397.48	38,123	63,637
27,000	368.54	105,674	398.02	47,234	58,440	405.39	42,982	62,692	412.76	39,588	66,086
28,000	382.19	109,588	412.77	48,984	60,604	420.41	44,575	65,013	428.05	41,055	68,533
29,000	395.84	113,502	427.51	50,734	62,768	435.42	46,166	67,336	443.34	42,521	70,980
30,000	409.49	117,416	442.25	52,483	64,933	450.44	47,759	69,657	458.63	43,988	73,428
32,500	443.61	127,200	479.10	56,856	70,344	487.97	51,737	75,463	496.84	47,652	79,548
35,000	477.73	136,983	515.95	61,228	75,755	525.50	55,716	81,267	535.06	51,318	85,665
40,000	545.98	156,553	589.66	69,976	86,577	600.58	63,677	92,876	611.50	58,650	97,903
45,000	614.23	176,123	663.37	78,723	97,400	675.65	71,636	104,487	687.94	65,981	110,142
50,000	682.47	195,689	737.07	87,469	108,220	750.72	79,595	116,094	764.37	73,311	122,378
55,000	750.72	215,259	810.78	96,216	119,043	825.79	87,554	127,705	840.81	80,643	134,616
60,000	818.97	234,829	884.49	104,964	129,865	900.87	95,515	139,314	917.25	87,974	146,855
65,000	887.21	254,396	958.19	113,709	140,687	975.93	103,473	150,923	993.68	95,304	159,092
70,000	955.46	273,966	1,031.90	122,457	151,509	1,051.01	111,434	162,532	1,070.12	102,636	171,330
75,000	1,023.71	293,536	1,105.61	131,204	162,332	1,126.08	119,393	174,143	1,146.56	109,968	183,568
80,000	1,091.95	313,102	1,179.31	139,950	173,152	1,201.15	127,352	185,750	1,222.98	117,296	195,806
85,000	1,160.20	332,672	1,253.02	148,697	183,975	1,276.22	135,311	197,361	1,299.42	124,628	208,044
90,000	1,228.45	352,242	1,326.73	157,444	194,798	1,351.30	143,272	208,970	1,375.86	131,959	220,283
95,000	1,296.69	371,808	1,400.43	166,190	205,618	1,426.36	151,230	220,578	1,452.29	139,289	232,519
100,000	1,364.94	391,378	1,474.14	174,937	216,441	1,501.43	159,189	232,189	1,528.73	146,621	244,757
105,000	1,433.19	410,948	1,547.85	183,685	227,263	1,576.51	167,150	243,798	1,605.17	153,952	256,996
110,000	1,501.43	430,515	1,621.54	192,429	238,086	1,651.57	175,107	255,408	1,681.60	161,282	269,233
115,000	1,569.68	450,085	1,695.25	201,176	248,909	1,726.65	183,068	267,017	1,758.04	168,614	281,471
120,000	1,637.93	469,655	1,768.96	209,923	259,732	1,801.72	191,027	278,628	1,834.48	175,946	293,709
125,000	1,706.17	489,221	1,842.66	218,669	270,552	1,876.79	198,987	290,234	1,910.91	183,276	305,945
130,000	1,774.42	508,791	1,916.37	227,416	281,375	1,951.86	206,946	301,845	1,987.35	190,607	318,184
135,000	1,842.67	528,361	1,990.08	236,164	292,197	2,026.94	214,907	313,454	2,063.79	197,939	330,422
140,000	1,910.91	547,928	2,063.78	244,909	303,019	2,102.00	222,864	325,064	2,140.22	205,269	342,659
145,000	1,979.16	567,498	2,137.49	253,657	313,841	2,177.08	230,825	336,673	2,216.66	212,600	354,898
150,000	2,047.41	587,068	2,211.20	262,404	324,664	2,252.15	238,784	348,284	2,293.10	219,932	367,136
155,000	2,115.65	606,634	2,284.90	271,150	335,484	2,327.22	246,743	359,891	2,369.53	227,262	379,372
160,000	2,183.90	626,204	2,358.61	279,897	346,307	2,402.29	254,703	371,501	2,445.97	234,594	391,610
165,000	2,252.15	645,774	2,432.32	288,645	357,129	2,477.37	262,663	383,111	2,522.41	241,925	403,849
170,000	2,320.39	665,340	2,506.02	297,390	367,950	2,552.43	270,621	394,719	2,598.84	249,255	416,085
175,000	2,388.64	684,910	2,579.73	306,138	378,772	2,627.50	278,580	406,330	2,675.28	256,587	428,323
180,000	2,456.89	704,480	2,653.44	314,885	389,595	2,702.58	286,541	417,939	2,751.72	263,918	440,562
185,000	2,525.13	724,047	2,727.14	323,631	400,416	2,777.64	294,498	429,549	2,828.15	271,248	452,799
190,000	2,593.38	743,617	2,800.85	332,378	411,239	2,852.72	302,459	441,158	2,904.59	278,580	465,037
195,000	2,661.63	763,187	2,874.56	341,126	422,061	2,927.79	310,419	452,768	2,981.03	285,912	477,275
200,000	2,729.87	782,753	2,948.26	349,871	432,882	3,002.86	318,378	464,375	3,057.45	293,240	489,513

AUGMENTED PAYMENT MORTGAGES

AMOUNT OF LOAN	30 YEARS		2% PMT INCREASE 265.057 PAYMENTS			4% PMT INCREASE 226.263 PAYMENTS			6% PMT INCREASE 201.847 PAYMENTS		
	MONTHLY PAYMENT	TOTAL INTRST	MONTHLY PAYMENT	TOTAL INTRST	INTRST SAVED	MONTHLY PAYMENT	TOTAL INTRST	INTRST SAVED	MONTHLY PAYMENT	TOTAL INTRST	INTRST SAVED
$ 50	0.70	202	0.71	138	64	0.73	115	87	0.74	99	103
100	1.39	400	1.42	276	124	1.45	228	172	1.47	197	203
200	2.78	801	2.84	553	248	2.89	454	347	2.95	395	406
300	4.16	1,198	4.24	824	374	4.33	680	518	4.41	590	608
400	5.55	1,598	5.66	1,100	498	5.77	906	692	5.88	787	811
500	6.93	1,995	7.07	1,374	621	7.21	1,131	864	7.35	984	1,011
600	8.32	2,395	8.49	1,650	745	8.65	1,357	1,038	8.82	1,180	1,215
700	9.70	2,792	9.89	1,921	871	10.09	1,583	1,209	10.28	1,375	1,417
800	11.09	3,192	11.31	2,198	994	11.53	1,809	1,383	11.76	1,574	1,618
900	12.47	3,589	12.72	2,472	1,117	12.97	2,035	1,554	13.22	1,768	1,821
1,000	13.86	3,990	14.14	2,748	1,242	14.41	2,260	1,730	14.69	1,965	2,025
2,000	27.71	7,976	28.26	5,491	2,485	28.82	4,521	3,455	29.37	3,928	4,048
3,000	41.56	11,962	42.39	8,236	3,726	43.22	6,779	5,183	44.05	5,891	6,071
4,000	55.41	15,948	56.52	10,981	4,967	57.63	9,040	6,908	58.73	7,854	8,094
5,000	69.26	19,934	70.65	13,726	6,208	72.03	11,298	8,636	73.42	9,820	10,114
6,000	83.11	23,920	84.77	16,469	7,451	86.43	13,556	10,364	88.10	11,783	12,137
7,000	96.97	27,909	98.91	19,217	8,692	100.85	15,819	12,090	102.79	13,748	14,161
8,000	110.82	31,895	113.04	21,962	9,933	115.25	18,077	13,818	117.47	15,711	16,184
9,000	124.67	35,881	127.16	24,705	11,176	129.66	20,337	15,544	132.15	17,674	18,207
10,000	138.52	39,867	141.29	27,450	12,417	144.06	22,595	17,272	146.83	19,637	20,230
11,000	152.37	43,853	155.42	30,195	13,658	158.46	24,854	18,999	161.51	21,600	22,253
12,000	166.22	47,839	169.54	32,938	14,901	172.87	27,114	20,725	176.19	23,563	24,276
13,000	180.07	51,825	183.67	35,683	16,142	187.27	29,373	22,453	190.87	25,527	26,298
14,000	193.93	55,815	197.81	38,431	17,384	201.69	31,635	24,180	205.57	27,494	28,321
15,000	207.78	59,801	211.94	41,176	18,625	216.09	33,893	25,908	220.25	29,457	30,344
16,000	221.63	63,787	226.06	43,919	19,868	230.50	36,154	27,633	234.93	31,420	32,367
17,000	235.48	67,773	240.19	46,664	21,109	244.90	38,412	29,361	249.61	33,383	34,390
18,000	249.33	71,759	254.32	49,409	22,350	259.30	40,670	31,089	264.29	35,346	36,413
19,000	263.18	75,745	268.44	52,152	23,593	273.71	42,930	32,815	278.97	37,309	38,436
20,000	277.03	79,731	282.57	54,897	24,834	288.11	45,189	34,542	293.65	39,272	40,459
21,000	290.89	83,720	296.71	57,645	26,075	302.53	47,451	36,269	308.34	41,238	42,482
22,000	304.74	87,706	310.83	60,388	27,318	316.93	49,710	37,996	323.02	43,201	44,505
23,000	318.59	91,692	324.96	63,133	28,559	331.33	51,968	39,724	337.71	45,166	46,526
24,000	332.44	95,678	339.09	65,878	29,800	345.74	54,228	41,450	352.39	47,129	48,549
25,000	346.29	99,664	353.22	68,623	31,041	360.14	56,486	43,178	367.07	49,092	50,572
26,000	360.14	103,650	367.34	71,366	32,284	374.55	58,747	44,903	381.75	51,055	52,595
27,000	373.99	107,636	381.47	74,111	33,525	388.95	61,005	46,631	396.43	53,018	54,618
28,000	387.85	111,626	395.61	76,859	34,767	403.36	63,265	48,361	411.12	54,983	56,643
29,000	401.70	115,612	409.73	79,602	36,010	417.77	65,524	50,086	425.80	56,946	58,666
30,000	415.55	119,598	423.86	82,347	37,251	432.17	67,784	51,814	440.48	58,910	60,688
32,500	450.18	129,565	459.18	89,209	40,356	468.19	73,434	56,131	477.19	63,819	65,746
35,000	484.81	139,532	494.51	96,073	43,459	504.20	79,082	60,450	513.90	68,729	70,803
40,000	554.06	159,462	565.14	109,794	49,668	576.22	90,377	69,085	587.30	78,545	80,917
45,000	623.32	179,395	635.79	123,521	55,874	648.25	101,675	77,720	660.72	88,364	91,031
50,000	692.58	199,329	706.43	137,244	62,085	720.28	112,973	86,356	734.13	98,182	101,147
55,000	761.84	219,262	777.08	150,970	68,292	792.31	124,270	94,992	807.55	108,002	111,260
60,000	831.09	239,192	847.71	164,691	74,501	864.33	135,566	103,626	880.96	117,819	121,373
65,000	900.35	259,126	918.36	178,418	80,708	936.36	146,864	112,262	954.37	127,637	131,489
70,000	969.61	279,060	989.00	192,146	86,914	1,008.39	158,161	120,899	1,027.79	137,456	141,604
75,000	1,038.87	298,993	1,059.65	205,868	93,125	1,080.42	169,459	129,534	1,101.20	147,274	151,719
80,000	1,108.12	318,923	1,130.28	219,589	99,334	1,152.44	180,755	138,168	1,174.61	157,092	161,831
85,000	1,177.38	338,857	1,200.93	233,315	105,542	1,224.48	192,055	146,802	1,248.02	166,909	171,948
90,000	1,246.64	358,790	1,271.57	247,039	111,751	1,296.51	203,352	155,438	1,321.44	176,729	182,061
95,000	1,315.90	378,724	1,342.22	260,765	117,959	1,368.54	214,650	164,074	1,394.85	186,546	192,178
100,000	1,385.15	398,654	1,412.85	274,486	124,168	1,440.56	225,945	172,709	1,468.26	196,364	202,290
105,000	1,454.41	418,588	1,483.50	288,212	130,376	1,512.59	237,243	181,345	1,541.67	206,181	212,407
110,000	1,523.67	438,521	1,554.14	301,936	136,585	1,584.62	248,541	189,980	1,615.09	216,001	222,520
115,000	1,592.93	458,455	1,624.79	315,662	142,793	1,656.65	259,839	198,616	1,688.51	225,821	232,634
120,000	1,662.18	478,385	1,695.42	329,383	149,002	1,728.67	271,134	207,251	1,761.91	235,636	242,749
125,000	1,731.44	498,318	1,766.07	343,109	155,209	1,800.70	282,432	215,886	1,835.33	245,456	252,862
130,000	1,800.70	518,252	1,836.71	356,833	161,419	1,872.73	293,730	224,522	1,908.74	255,273	262,979
135,000	1,869.95	538,182	1,907.35	370,556	167,626	1,944.75	305,025	233,157	1,982.15	265,091	273,091
140,000	1,939.21	558,116	1,977.99	384,280	173,836	2,016.78	316,323	241,793	2,055.56	274,909	283,207
145,000	2,008.47	578,049	2,048.64	398,006	180,043	2,088.81	327,620	250,429	2,128.98	284,728	293,321
150,000	2,077.73	597,983	2,119.28	411,730	186,253	2,160.84	338,918	259,065	2,202.39	294,546	303,437
155,000	2,146.98	617,913	2,189.92	425,454	192,459	2,232.86	350,214	267,699	2,275.80	304,363	313,550
160,000	2,216.24	637,846	2,260.56	439,177	198,669	2,304.89	361,511	276,335	2,349.21	314,181	323,665
165,000	2,285.50	657,780	2,331.21	452,904	204,876	2,376.92	372,809	284,971	2,422.63	324,001	333,779
170,000	2,354.76	677,714	2,401.86	466,630	211,084	2,448.95	384,107	293,607	2,496.05	333,820	343,894
175,000	2,424.01	697,644	2,472.49	480,351	217,293	2,520.97	395,402	302,242	2,569.45	343,636	354,008
180,000	2,493.27	717,577	2,543.14	494,077	223,500	2,593.00	406,700	310,877	2,642.87	353,455	364,122
185,000	2,562.53	737,511	2,613.78	507,801	229,710	2,665.03	417,998	319,513	2,716.28	363,273	374,238
190,000	2,631.79	757,444	2,684.43	521,527	235,917	2,737.06	429,295	328,149	2,789.70	373,093	384,351
195,000	2,701.04	777,374	2,755.06	535,248	242,126	2,809.08	440,591	336,783	2,863.10	382,908	394,466
200,000	2,770.30	797,308	2,825.71	548,974	248,334	2,881.11	451,889	345,419	2,936.52	392,728	404,580

AMOUNT OF LOAN	30 YEARS		8% PMT INCREASE 184.169 PAYMENTS			10% PMT INCREASE 170.413 PAYMENTS			12% PMT INCREASE 159.219 PAYMENTS		
	MONTHLY PAYMENT	TOTAL INTRST	MONTHLY PAYMENT	TOTAL INTRST	INTRST SAVED	MONTHLY PAYMENT	TOTAL INTRST	INTRST SAVED	MONTHLY PAYMENT	TOTAL INTRST	INTRST SAVED
$ 50	0.70	202	0.76	90	112	0.77	81	121	0.78	74	128
100	1.39	400	1.50	176	224	1.53	161	239	1.56	148	252
200	2.78	801	3.00	353	448	3.06	321	480	3.11	295	506
300	4.16	1,198	4.49	527	671	4.58	480	718	4.66	442	756
400	5.55	1,598	5.99	703	895	6.11	641	957	6.22	590	1,008
500	6.93	1,995	7.48	878	1,117	7.62	799	1,196	7.76	736	1,259
600	8.32	2,395	8.99	1,056	1,339	9.15	959	1,436	9.32	884	1,511
700	9.70	2,792	10.48	1,230	1,562	10.67	1,118	1,674	10.86	1,029	1,763
800	11.09	3,192	11.98	1,406	1,786	12.20	1,279	1,913	12.42	1,177	2,015
900	12.47	3,589	13.47	1,581	2,008	13.72	1,438	2,151	13.97	1,324	2,265
1,000	13.86	3,990	14.97	1,757	2,233	15.25	1,599	2,391	15.52	1,471	2,519
2,000	27.71	7,976	29.93	3,512	4,464	30.48	3,194	4,782	31.04	2,942	5,034
3,000	41.56	11,962	44.88	5,266	6,696	45.72	4,791	7,171	46.55	4,412	7,550
4,000	55.41	15,948	59.84	7,021	8,927	60.95	6,387	9,561	62.06	5,881	10,067
5,000	69.26	19,934	74.80	8,776	11,158	76.19	7,984	11,950	77.57	7,351	12,583
6,000	83.11	23,920	89.76	10,531	13,389	91.42	9,579	14,341	93.08	8,820	15,100
7,000	96.97	27,909	104.73	12,288	15,621	106.67	11,178	16,731	108.61	10,293	17,616
8,000	110.82	31,895	119.69	14,043	17,852	121.90	12,773	19,122	124.12	11,762	20,133
9,000	124.67	35,881	134.64	15,797	20,084	137.14	14,370	21,511	139.63	13,232	22,649
10,000	138.52	39,867	149.60	17,552	22,315	152.37	15,966	23,901	155.14	14,701	25,166
11,000	152.37	43,853	164.56	19,307	24,546	167.61	17,563	26,290	170.65	16,171	27,682
12,000	166.22	47,839	179.52	21,062	26,777	182.84	19,158	28,681	186.17	17,642	30,197
13,000	180.07	51,825	194.48	22,817	29,008	198.08	20,755	31,070	201.68	19,111	32,714
14,000	193.93	55,815	209.44	24,572	31,243	213.32	22,353	33,462	217.20	20,582	35,233
15,000	207.78	59,801	224.40	26,328	33,473	228.56	23,950	35,851	232.71	22,052	37,749
16,000	221.63	63,787	239.36	28,083	35,704	243.79	25,545	38,242	248.23	23,523	40,264
17,000	235.48	67,773	254.32	29,838	37,935	259.03	27,142	40,631	263.74	24,992	42,781
18,000	249.33	71,759	269.28	31,593	40,166	274.26	28,737	43,022	279.25	26,462	45,297
19,000	263.18	75,745	284.23	33,346	42,399	289.50	30,335	45,410	294.76	27,931	47,814
20,000	277.03	79,731	299.19	35,102	44,629	304.73	31,930	47,801	310.27	29,401	50,330
21,000	290.89	83,720	314.16	36,859	46,861	319.98	33,529	50,191	325.80	30,874	52,846
22,000	304.74	87,706	329.12	38,614	49,092	335.21	35,124	52,582	341.31	32,343	55,363
23,000	318.59	91,692	344.08	40,369	51,323	350.45	36,721	54,971	356.82	33,813	57,879
24,000	332.44	95,678	359.04	42,124	53,554	365.68	38,317	57,361	372.33	35,282	60,396
25,000	346.29	99,664	373.99	43,877	55,787	380.92	39,914	59,750	387.84	36,751	62,913
26,000	360.14	103,650	388.95	45,633	58,017	396.15	41,509	62,141	403.36	38,223	65,427
27,000	373.99	107,636	403.91	47,388	60,248	411.39	43,106	64,530	418.87	39,692	67,944
28,000	387.85	111,626	418.88	49,145	62,481	426.64	44,705	66,921	434.39	41,163	70,463
29,000	401.70	115,612	433.84	50,900	64,712	441.87	46,300	69,312	449.90	42,633	72,979
30,000	415.55	119,598	448.79	52,653	66,945	457.11	47,897	71,701	465.42	44,104	75,494
32,500	450.18	129,565	486.19	57,041	72,524	495.20	51,889	77,676	504.20	47,778	81,787
35,000	484.81	139,532	523.59	61,429	78,103	533.29	55,880	83,652	542.99	51,454	88,078
40,000	554.06	159,462	598.38	70,203	89,259	609.47	63,862	95,600	620.55	58,803	100,659
45,000	623.32	179,395	673.19	78,981	100,414	685.65	71,844	107,551	698.12	66,154	113,241
50,000	692.58	199,329	747.99	87,757	111,572	761.84	79,827	119,502	775.69	73,505	125,824
55,000	761.84	219,262	822.79	96,532	122,730	838.02	87,810	131,452	853.26	80,855	138,407
60,000	831.09	239,192	897.58	105,306	133,886	914.20	95,792	143,400	930.82	88,204	150,988
65,000	900.35	259,126	972.38	114,082	145,044	990.39	103,775	155,351	1,008.39	95,555	163,571
70,000	969.61	279,060	1,047.18	122,858	156,202	1,066.57	111,757	167,303	1,085.96	102,905	176,155
75,000	1,038.87	298,993	1,121.98	131,634	167,359	1,142.76	119,741	179,252	1,163.53	110,256	188,737
80,000	1,108.12	318,923	1,196.77	140,408	178,515	1,218.93	127,722	191,201	1,241.09	117,605	201,318
85,000	1,177.38	338,857	1,271.57	149,184	189,673	1,295.12	135,705	203,152	1,318.67	124,957	213,900
90,000	1,246.64	358,790	1,346.37	157,960	200,830	1,371.30	143,687	215,103	1,396.24	132,308	226,482
95,000	1,315.90	378,724	1,421.17	166,735	211,989	1,447.49	151,671	227,053	1,473.81	139,659	239,065
100,000	1,385.15	398,654	1,495.96	175,509	223,145	1,523.67	159,653	239,001	1,551.37	147,008	251,646
105,000	1,454.41	418,588	1,570.76	184,285	234,303	1,599.85	167,635	250,953	1,628.94	154,358	264,230
110,000	1,523.67	438,521	1,645.56	193,061	245,460	1,676.04	175,619	262,902	1,706.51	161,709	276,812
115,000	1,592.93	458,455	1,720.36	201,837	256,618	1,752.22	183,601	274,854	1,784.08	169,059	289,396
120,000	1,662.18	478,385	1,795.15	210,611	267,774	1,828.40	191,583	286,802	1,861.64	176,408	301,977
125,000	1,731.44	498,318	1,869.96	219,389	278,929	1,904.58	199,567	298,751	1,939.21	183,759	314,559
130,000	1,800.70	518,252	1,944.76	228,165	290,087	1,980.77	207,549	310,703	2,016.78	191,110	327,142
135,000	1,869.95	538,182	2,019.55	236,939	301,243	2,056.95	215,531	322,651	2,094.34	198,459	339,723
140,000	1,939.21	558,116	2,094.35	245,714	312,402	2,133.13	223,513	334,603	2,171.92	205,811	352,305
145,000	2,008.47	578,049	2,169.15	254,490	323,559	2,209.32	231,497	346,552	2,249.49	213,162	364,887
150,000	2,077.73	597,983	2,243.95	263,266	334,717	2,285.50	239,479	358,504	2,327.06	220,512	377,471
155,000	2,146.98	617,913	2,318.74	272,040	345,873	2,361.68	247,461	370,452	2,404.62	227,861	390,052
160,000	2,216.24	637,846	2,393.54	280,816	357,030	2,437.86	255,443	382,403	2,482.19	235,212	402,634
165,000	2,285.50	657,780	2,468.34	289,592	368,188	2,514.05	263,427	394,353	2,559.76	242,562	415,218
170,000	2,354.76	677,714	2,543.14	298,368	379,346	2,590.24	271,411	406,303	2,637.33	249,913	427,801
175,000	2,424.01	697,644	2,617.93	307,142	390,502	2,666.41	279,391	418,253	2,714.89	257,262	440,382
180,000	2,493.27	717,577	2,692.73	315,917	401,660	2,742.60	287,375	430,202	2,792.46	264,613	452,964
185,000	2,562.53	737,511	2,767.53	324,693	412,818	2,818.78	295,357	442,154	2,870.03	271,963	465,548
190,000	2,631.79	757,444	2,842.33	333,469	423,975	2,894.97	303,341	454,103	2,947.60	279,314	478,130
195,000	2,701.04	777,374	2,917.12	342,243	435,131	2,971.14	311,321	466,053	3,025.16	286,663	490,711
200,000	2,770.30	797,308	2,991.92	351,019	446,289	3,047.33	319,305	478,003	3,102.74	294,015	503,293

AUGMENTED PAYMENT MORTGAGES

AMOUNT OF LOAN	30 YEARS		2% PMT INCREASE 262.522 PAYMENTS			4% PMT INCREASE 223.710 PAYMENTS			6% PMT INCREASE 199.417 PAYMENTS		
	MONTHLY PAYMENT	TOTAL INTRST	MONTHLY PAYMENT	TOTAL INTRST	INTRST SAVED	MONTHLY PAYMENT	TOTAL INTRST	INTRST SAVED	MONTHLY PAYMENT	TOTAL INTRST	INTRST SAVED
$ 50	0.71	206	0.72	139	67	0.74	116	90	0.75	100	106
100	1.41	408	1.44	278	130	1.47	229	179	1.49	197	211
200	2.82	815	2.88	556	259	2.93	455	360	2.99	396	419
300	4.22	1,219	4.30	829	390	4.39	682	537	4.47	591	628
400	5.63	1,627	5.74	1,107	520	5.86	911	716	5.97	791	836
500	7.03	2,031	7.17	1,382	649	7.31	1,135	896	7.45	986	1,045
600	8.44	2,438	8.61	1,660	778	8.78	1,364	1,074	8.95	1,185	1,253
700	9.84	2,842	10.04	1,936	906	10.23	1,589	1,253	10.43	1,380	1,462
800	11.25	3,250	11.48	2,214	1,036	11.70	1,817	1,433	11.93	1,579	1,671
900	12.65	3,654	12.90	2,487	1,167	13.16	2,044	1,610	13.41	1,774	1,880
1,000	14.06	4,062	14.34	2,765	1,297	14.62	2,271	1,791	14.90	1,971	2,091
2,000	28.11	8,120	28.67	5,527	2,593	29.23	4,539	3,581	29.80	3,943	4,177
3,000	42.17	12,181	43.01	8,291	3,890	43.86	6,812	5,369	44.70	5,914	6,267
4,000	56.22	16,239	57.34	11,053	5,186	58.47	9,080	7,159	59.59	7,883	8,356
5,000	70.27	20,297	71.68	13,818	6,479	73.08	11,349	8,948	74.49	9,855	10,442
6,000	84.33	24,359	86.02	16,582	7,777	87.70	13,619	10,740	89.39	11,826	12,533
7,000	98.38	28,417	100.35	19,344	9,073	102.32	15,890	12,527	104.28	13,795	14,622
8,000	112.44	32,478	114.69	22,109	10,369	116.94	18,161	14,317	119.19	15,769	16,709
9,000	126.49	36,536	129.02	24,871	11,665	131.55	20,429	16,107	134.08	17,738	18,798
10,000	140.54	40,594	143.35	27,633	12,961	146.16	22,697	17,897	148.97	19,707	20,887
11,000	154.60	44,656	157.69	30,397	14,259	160.78	24,968	19,688	163.88	21,680	22,976
12,000	168.65	48,714	172.02	33,159	15,555	175.40	27,239	21,475	178.77	23,650	25,064
13,000	182.71	52,776	186.36	35,924	16,852	190.02	29,509	23,267	193.67	25,621	27,155
14,000	196.76	56,834	200.70	38,688	18,146	204.63	31,778	25,056	208.57	27,592	29,242
15,000	210.81	60,892	215.03	41,450	19,442	219.24	34,046	26,846	223.46	29,562	31,330
16,000	224.87	64,953	229.37	44,215	20,738	233.86	36,317	28,636	238.36	31,533	33,420
17,000	238.92	69,011	243.70	46,977	22,034	248.48	38,587	30,424	253.26	33,504	35,507
18,000	252.98	73,073	258.04	49,741	23,332	263.10	40,858	32,215	268.16	35,476	37,597
19,000	267.03	77,131	272.37	52,503	24,628	277.71	43,127	34,004	283.05	37,445	39,686
20,000	281.08	81,189	286.70	55,265	25,924	292.32	45,395	35,794	297.94	39,414	41,775
21,000	295.14	85,250	301.04	58,030	27,220	306.95	47,668	37,582	312.85	41,388	43,862
22,000	309.19	89,308	315.37	60,792	28,516	321.56	49,936	39,372	327.74	43,357	45,951
23,000	323.25	93,370	329.72	63,559	29,811	336.18	52,207	41,163	342.65	45,330	48,040
24,000	337.30	97,428	344.05	66,321	31,107	350.79	54,475	42,953	357.54	47,300	50,128
25,000	351.35	101,486	358.38	69,083	32,403	365.40	56,744	44,742	372.43	49,269	52,217
26,000	365.41	105,548	372.72	71,847	33,701	380.03	59,017	46,531	387.33	51,240	54,308
27,000	379.46	109,606	387.05	74,609	34,997	394.64	61,285	48,321	402.23	53,211	56,395
28,000	393.52	113,667	401.39	77,374	36,293	409.26	63,556	50,111	417.13	55,183	58,484
29,000	407.57	117,725	415.72	80,136	37,589	423.87	65,824	51,901	432.02	57,152	60,573
30,000	421.62	121,783	430.05	82,898	38,885	438.48	68,092	53,691	446.92	59,123	62,660
32,500	456.76	131,934	465.90	89,809	42,125	475.03	73,769	58,165	484.17	64,052	67,882
35,000	491.89	142,080	501.73	96,715	45,365	511.57	79,443	62,637	521.40	68,976	73,104
40,000	562.16	162,378	573.40	110,530	51,848	584.65	90,792	71,586	595.89	78,831	83,547
45,000	632.43	182,675	645.08	124,348	58,327	657.73	102,141	80,534	670.38	88,685	93,990
50,000	702.70	202,972	716.75	138,163	64,809	730.81	113,490	89,482	744.86	98,538	104,434
55,000	772.97	223,269	788.43	151,980	71,289	803.89	124,838	98,431	819.35	108,392	114,877
60,000	843.24	243,566	860.10	165,795	77,771	876.97	136,187	107,379	893.83	118,245	125,321
65,000	913.51	263,864	931.78	179,613	84,251	950.05	147,536	116,328	968.32	128,099	135,765
70,000	983.78	284,161	1,003.46	193,430	90,731	1,023.13	158,884	125,277	1,042.81	137,954	146,209
75,000	1,054.05	304,458	1,075.13	207,245	97,213	1,096.21	170,233	134,225	1,117.29	147,807	156,651
80,000	1,124.32	324,755	1,146.81	221,063	103,692	1,169.29	181,582	143,173	1,191.78	157,661	167,094
85,000	1,194.59	345,052	1,218.48	234,878	110,174	1,242.37	192,931	152,121	1,266.27	167,516	177,536
90,000	1,264.86	365,350	1,290.16	248,695	116,655	1,315.45	204,279	161,071	1,340.75	177,368	187,982
95,000	1,335.13	385,647	1,361.83	262,510	123,137	1,388.54	215,630	170,017	1,415.24	187,223	198,424
100,000	1,405.40	405,944	1,433.51	276,328	129,616	1,461.62	226,979	178,965	1,489.72	197,075	208,869
105,000	1,475.67	426,241	1,505.18	290,143	136,098	1,534.70	238,328	187,913	1,564.21	206,930	219,311
110,000	1,545.94	446,538	1,576.86	303,960	142,578	1,607.78	249,676	196,862	1,638.70	216,785	229,753
115,000	1,616.21	466,836	1,648.53	317,775	149,061	1,680.86	261,025	205,811	1,713.18	226,637	240,199
120,000	1,686.48	487,133	1,720.21	331,593	155,540	1,753.94	272,374	214,759	1,787.67	236,492	250,641
125,000	1,756.75	507,430	1,791.89	345,411	162,019	1,827.02	283,723	223,707	1,862.16	246,346	261,084
130,000	1,827.02	527,727	1,863.56	359,225	168,502	1,900.10	295,071	232,656	1,936.64	256,199	271,528
135,000	1,897.29	548,024	1,935.24	373,043	174,981	1,973.18	306,420	241,604	2,011.13	266,054	281,970
140,000	1,967.56	568,322	2,006.91	386,858	181,464	2,046.26	317,769	250,553	2,085.61	275,906	292,416
145,000	2,037.83	588,619	2,078.59	400,676	187,943	2,119.34	329,118	259,501	2,160.10	285,761	302,858
150,000	2,108.10	608,916	2,150.26	414,491	194,425	2,192.42	340,466	268,450	2,234.59	295,615	313,301
155,000	2,178.37	629,213	2,221.94	428,308	200,905	2,265.50	351,815	277,398	2,309.07	305,468	323,745
160,000	2,248.64	649,510	2,293.61	442,123	207,387	2,338.59	363,166	286,344	2,383.56	315,322	334,188
165,000	2,318.91	669,808	2,365.29	455,941	213,867	2,411.67	374,515	295,293	2,458.04	325,175	344,633
170,000	2,389.18	690,105	2,436.96	469,756	220,349	2,484.75	385,863	304,242	2,532.53	335,030	355,075
175,000	2,459.45	710,402	2,508.64	483,573	226,829	2,557.83	397,212	313,190	2,607.02	344,884	365,518
180,000	2,529.72	730,699	2,580.31	497,388	233,311	2,630.91	408,561	322,138	2,681.50	354,737	375,962
185,000	2,599.99	750,996	2,651.99	511,206	239,790	2,703.99	419,910	331,086	2,755.99	364,591	386,405
190,000	2,670.26	771,294	2,723.67	525,023	246,271	2,777.07	431,258	340,036	2,830.48	374,446	396,848
195,000	2,740.53	791,591	2,795.34	538,838	252,753	2,850.15	442,607	348,984	2,904.96	384,298	407,293
200,000	2,810.80	811,888	2,867.02	552,656	259,232	2,923.23	453,956	357,932	2,979.45	394,153	417,735

AMOUNT OF LOAN	30 YEARS MONTHLY PAYMENT	30 YEARS TOTAL INTRST	8% PMT INCREASE 181.872 PAYMENTS MONTHLY PAYMENT	TOTAL INTRST	INTRST SAVED	10% PMT INCREASE 168.238 PAYMENTS MONTHLY PAYMENT	TOTAL INTRST	INTRST SAVED	12% PMT INCREASE 157.155 PAYMENTS MONTHLY PAYMENT	TOTAL INTRST	INTRST SAVED
$ 50	0.71	206	0.77	90	116	0.78	81	125	0.80	76	130
100	1.41	408	1.52	176	232	1.55	161	247	1.58	148	260
200	2.82	815	3.05	355	460	3.10	322	493	3.16	297	518
300	4.22	1,219	4.56	529	690	4.64	481	738	4.73	443	776
400	5.63	1,627	6.08	706	921	6.19	641	986	6.31	592	1,035
500	7.03	2,031	7.59	880	1,151	7.73	800	1,231	7.87	737	1,294
600	8.44	2,438	9.12	1,059	1,379	9.28	961	1,477	9.45	885	1,553
700	9.84	2,842	10.63	1,233	1,609	10.82	1,120	1,722	11.02	1,032	1,810
800	11.25	3,250	12.15	1,410	1,840	12.38	1,283	1,967	12.60	1,180	2,070
900	12.65	3,654	13.66	1,584	2,070	13.92	1,442	2,212	14.17	1,327	2,327
1,000	14.06	4,062	15.18	1,761	2,301	15.47	1,603	2,459	15.75	1,475	2,587
2,000	28.11	8,120	30.36	3,522	4,598	30.92	3,202	4,918	31.48	2,947	5,173
3,000	42.17	12,181	45.54	5,282	6,899	46.39	4,805	7,376	47.23	4,422	7,759
4,000	56.22	16,239	60.72	7,043	9,196	61.84	6,404	9,835	62.97	5,896	10,343
5,000	70.27	20,297	75.89	8,802	11,495	77.30	8,005	12,292	78.70	7,368	12,929
6,000	84.33	24,359	91.08	10,565	13,794	92.76	9,606	14,753	94.45	8,843	15,516
7,000	98.38	28,417	106.25	12,324	16,093	108.22	11,207	17,210	110.19	10,317	18,100
8,000	112.44	32,478	121.44	14,087	18,391	123.68	12,808	19,670	125.93	11,791	20,687
9,000	126.49	36,536	136.61	15,846	20,690	139.14	14,409	22,127	141.67	13,264	23,272
10,000	140.54	40,594	151.78	17,605	22,989	154.59	16,008	24,586	157.40	14,736	25,858
11,000	154.60	44,656	166.97	19,367	25,289	170.06	17,611	27,045	173.15	16,211	28,445
12,000	168.65	48,714	182.14	21,126	27,588	185.52	19,212	29,502	188.89	17,685	31,029
13,000	182.71	52,776	197.33	22,889	29,887	200.98	20,812	31,964	204.64	19,160	33,616
14,000	196.76	56,834	212.50	24,648	32,186	216.44	22,413	34,421	220.37	20,632	36,202
15,000	210.81	60,892	227.67	26,407	34,485	231.89	24,013	36,879	236.11	22,106	38,786
16,000	224.87	64,953	242.86	28,169	36,784	247.36	25,615	39,338	251.85	23,579	41,374
17,000	238.92	69,011	258.03	29,928	39,083	262.81	27,215	41,796	267.59	25,053	43,958
18,000	252.98	73,073	273.22	31,691	41,382	278.28	28,817	44,256	283.34	26,528	46,545
19,000	267.03	77,131	288.39	33,450	43,681	293.73	30,417	46,714	299.07	28,000	49,131
20,000	281.08	81,189	303.57	35,211	45,978	309.19	32,018	49,171	314.81	29,474	51,715
21,000	295.14	85,250	318.75	36,972	48,278	324.65	33,618	51,632	330.56	30,949	54,301
22,000	309.19	89,308	333.93	38,733	50,575	340.11	35,219	54,089	346.29	32,421	56,887
23,000	323.25	93,370	349.11	40,493	52,877	355.58	36,822	56,548	362.04	33,896	59,474
24,000	337.30	97,428	364.28	42,252	55,176	371.03	38,421	59,007	377.78	35,370	62,058
25,000	351.35	101,486	379.46	44,013	57,473	386.49	40,022	61,464	393.51	36,842	64,644
26,000	365.41	105,548	394.64	45,774	59,774	401.95	41,623	63,925	409.26	38,317	67,231
27,000	379.46	109,606	409.82	47,535	62,071	417.41	43,224	66,382	425.00	39,791	69,815
28,000	393.52	113,667	425.00	49,296	64,371	432.87	44,825	68,842	440.74	41,264	72,403
29,000	407.57	117,725	440.18	51,056	66,669	448.33	46,426	71,299	456.48	42,738	74,987
30,000	421.62	121,783	455.35	52,815	68,968	463.78	48,025	73,758	472.21	44,210	77,573
32,500	456.76	131,934	493.30	57,217	74,717	502.44	52,030	79,904	511.57	47,896	84,038
35,000	491.89	142,080	531.24	61,618	80,462	541.08	56,030	86,050	550.92	51,580	90,500
40,000	562.16	162,378	607.13	70,420	91,958	618.38	64,035	98,343	629.62	58,948	103,430
45,000	632.43	182,675	683.02	79,222	103,453	695.67	72,038	110,637	708.32	66,316	116,359
50,000	702.70	202,972	758.92	88,026	114,946	772.97	80,043	122,929	787.02	73,684	129,288
55,000	772.97	223,269	834.81	96,829	126,440	850.27	88,048	135,221	865.73	81,054	142,215
60,000	843.24	243,566	910.70	105,631	137,935	927.56	96,051	147,515	944.02	88,422	155,144
65,000	913.51	263,864	986.59	114,433	149,431	1,004.86	104,056	159,808	1,023.13	95,790	168,074
70,000	983.78	284,161	1,062.48	123,235	160,926	1,082.16	112,060	172,101	1,101.83	103,158	181,003
75,000	1,054.05	304,458	1,138.37	132,038	172,420	1,159.46	120,065	184,393	1,180.54	110,528	193,930
80,000	1,124.32	324,755	1,214.27	140,842	183,913	1,236.75	128,068	196,687	1,259.24	117,896	206,859
85,000	1,194.59	345,052	1,290.16	149,644	195,408	1,314.05	136,073	208,979	1,337.94	125,264	219,788
90,000	1,264.86	365,350	1,366.05	158,446	206,904	1,391.35	144,078	221,272	1,416.64	132,632	232,718
95,000	1,335.13	385,647	1,441.94	167,249	218,398	1,468.64	152,081	233,566	1,495.35	140,002	245,645
100,000	1,405.40	405,944	1,517.83	176,051	229,893	1,545.94	160,086	245,858	1,574.05	147,370	258,574
105,000	1,475.67	426,241	1,593.72	184,853	241,388	1,623.24	168,091	258,150	1,652.75	154,738	271,503
110,000	1,545.94	446,538	1,669.62	193,657	252,881	1,700.53	176,094	270,444	1,731.45	162,106	284,432
115,000	1,616.21	466,836	1,745.51	202,459	264,377	1,777.83	184,099	282,737	1,810.16	169,476	297,360
120,000	1,686.48	487,133	1,821.40	211,262	275,871	1,855.13	192,103	295,030	1,888.86	176,844	310,289
125,000	1,756.75	507,430	1,897.29	220,064	287,366	1,932.43	200,108	307,322	1,967.56	184,212	323,218
130,000	1,827.02	527,727	1,973.18	228,866	298,861	2,009.72	208,111	319,616	2,046.26	191,580	336,147
135,000	1,897.29	548,024	2,049.07	237,668	310,356	2,087.02	216,116	331,908	2,124.96	198,948	349,076
140,000	1,967.56	568,322	2,124.96	246,471	321,851	2,164.32	224,121	344,201	2,203.67	206,318	362,004
145,000	2,037.83	588,619	2,200.86	255,275	333,344	2,241.61	232,124	356,495	2,282.37	213,686	374,933
150,000	2,108.10	608,916	2,276.75	264,077	344,839	2,318.91	240,129	368,787	2,361.07	221,054	387,862
155,000	2,178.37	629,213	2,352.64	272,879	356,334	2,396.21	248,134	381,079	2,439.77	228,422	400,791
160,000	2,248.64	649,510	2,428.53	281,682	367,828	2,473.50	256,137	393,373	2,518.48	235,792	413,718
165,000	2,318.91	669,808	2,504.42	290,484	379,324	2,550.80	264,141	405,667	2,597.18	243,160	426,648
170,000	2,389.18	690,105	2,580.31	299,286	390,819	2,628.10	272,146	417,959	2,675.88	250,528	439,577
175,000	2,459.45	710,402	2,656.21	308,090	402,312	2,705.40	280,151	430,251	2,754.58	257,896	452,506
180,000	2,529.72	730,699	2,732.10	316,892	413,807	2,782.69	288,154	442,545	2,833.29	265,266	465,433
185,000	2,599.99	750,996	2,807.99	325,695	425,301	2,859.99	296,159	454,837	2,911.99	272,634	478,362
190,000	2,670.26	771,294	2,883.88	334,497	436,797	2,937.29	304,164	467,130	2,990.69	280,002	491,292
195,000	2,740.53	791,591	2,959.77	343,299	448,292	3,014.58	312,167	479,424	3,069.39	287,370	504,221
200,000	2,810.80	811,888	3,035.66	352,102	459,786	3,091.88	320,172	491,716	3,148.10	294,740	517,148

AUGMENTED PAYMENT MORTGAGES

AMOUNT OF LOAN	30 YEARS		2% PMT INCREASE 259.985 PAYMENTS			4% PMT INCREASE 221.183 PAYMENTS			6% PMT INCREASE 197.021 PAYMENTS		
	MONTHLY PAYMENT	TOTAL INTRST	MONTHLY PAYMENT	TOTAL INTRST	INTRST SAVED	MONTHLY PAYMENT	TOTAL INTRST	INTRST SAVED	MONTHLY PAYMENT	TOTAL INTRST	INTRST SAVED
$ 50	0.72	209	0.73	140	69	0.75	116	93	0.76	100	109
100	1.43	415	1.46	280	135	1.49	230	185	1.52	199	216
200	2.86	830	2.92	559	271	2.97	457	373	3.03	397	433
300	4.28	1,241	4.37	836	405	4.45	684	557	4.54	594	647
400	5.71	1,656	5.82	1,113	543	5.94	914	742	6.05	792	864
500	7.13	2,067	7.27	1,390	677	7.42	1,141	926	7.56	989	1,078
600	8.56	2,482	8.73	1,670	812	8.90	1,369	1,113	9.07	1,187	1,295
700	9.98	2,893	10.18	1,947	946	10.38	1,596	1,297	10.58	1,384	1,509
800	11.41	3,308	11.64	2,226	1,082	11.87	1,825	1,483	12.09	1,582	1,726
900	12.84	3,722	13.10	2,506	1,216	13.35	2,053	1,669	13.61	1,781	1,941
1,000	14.26	4,134	14.55	2,783	1,351	14.83	2,280	1,854	15.12	1,979	2,155
2,000	28.52	8,267	29.09	5,563	2,704	29.66	4,560	3,707	30.23	3,956	4,311
3,000	42.78	12,401	43.64	8,346	4,055	44.49	6,840	5,561	45.35	5,935	6,466
4,000	57.03	16,531	58.17	11,123	5,408	59.31	9,118	7,413	60.45	7,910	8,621
5,000	71.29	20,664	72.72	13,906	6,758	74.14	11,399	9,265	75.57	9,889	10,775
6,000	85.55	24,798	87.26	16,686	8,112	88.97	13,679	11,119	90.68	11,866	12,932
7,000	99.80	28,928	101.80	19,466	9,462	103.79	15,957	12,971	105.79	13,843	15,085
8,000	114.06	33,062	116.34	22,247	10,815	118.62	18,237	14,825	120.90	15,820	17,242
9,000	128.32	37,195	130.89	25,029	12,166	133.45	20,517	16,678	136.02	17,799	19,396
10,000	142.57	41,325	145.42	27,807	13,518	148.27	22,795	18,530	151.12	19,774	21,551
11,000	156.83	45,459	159.97	30,590	14,869	163.10	25,075	20,384	166.24	21,753	23,706
12,000	171.09	49,592	174.51	33,370	16,222	177.93	27,355	22,237	181.36	23,732	25,860
13,000	185.34	53,722	189.05	36,150	17,572	192.75	29,633	24,089	196.46	25,707	28,015
14,000	199.60	57,856	203.59	38,930	18,926	207.58	31,913	25,943	211.58	27,686	30,170
15,000	213.86	61,990	218.14	41,713	20,277	222.41	34,193	27,797	226.69	29,663	32,327
16,000	228.11	66,120	232.67	44,491	21,629	237.23	36,471	29,649	241.80	31,640	34,480
17,000	242.37	70,253	247.22	47,273	22,980	252.06	38,751	31,502	256.91	33,617	36,636
18,000	256.63	74,387	261.76	50,054	24,333	266.90	41,034	33,353	272.03	35,596	38,791
19,000	270.88	78,517	276.30	52,834	25,683	281.72	43,312	35,205	287.13	37,571	40,946
20,0u0	285.14	82,650	290.84	55,614	27,036	296.55	45,592	37,058	302.25	39,550	43,100
21,000	299.40	86,784	305.39	58,397	28,387	311.38	47,872	38,912	317.36	41,527	45,257
22,000	313.65	90,914	319.92	61,174	29,740	326.20	50,150	40,764	332.47	43,504	47,410
23,000	327.91	95,048	334.47	63,957	31,091	341.03	52,430	42,618	347.58	45,481	49,567
24,000	342.17	99,181	349.01	66,737	32,444	355.86	54,710	44,471	362.70	47,460	51,721
25,000	356.42	103,311	363.55	69,518	33,793	370.68	56,988	46,323	377.81	49,437	53,874
26,000	370.68	107,445	378.09	72,298	35,147	385.51	59,268	48,177	392.92	51,413	56,032
27,000	384.94	111,578	392.64	75,081	36,497	400.34	61,548	50,030	408.04	53,392	58,186
28,000	399.19	115,708	407.17	77,858	37,850	415.16	63,826	51,882	423.14	55,367	60,341
29,000	413.45	119,842	421.72	80,641	39,201	429.99	66,106	53,736	438.26	57,346	62,496
30,000	427.71	123,976	436.26	83,421	40,555	444.82	68,387	55,589	453.37	59,323	64,653
32,500	463.35	134,306	472.62	90,374	43,932	481.88	74,084	60,222	491.15	64,267	70,039
35,000	498.99	144,636	508.97	97,325	47,311	518.95	79,783	64,853	528.93	69,210	75,426
40,000	570.28	165,301	581.69	111,231	54,070	593.09	91,181	74,120	604.50	79,099	86,202
45,000	641.56	185,962	654.39	125,132	60,830	667.22	102,578	83,384	680.05	88,984	96,978
50,000	712.84	206,622	727.10	139,035	67,587	741.35	113,974	92,648	755.61	98,871	107,751
55,000	784.13	227,287	799.81	152,939	74,348	815.50	125,375	101,912	831.18	108,760	118,527
60,000	855.41	247,948	872.52	166,842	81,106	889.63	136,771	111,177	906.73	118,645	129,303
65,000	926.69	268,608	945.22	180,743	87,865	963.76	148,167	120,441	982.29	128,532	140,076
70,000	997.98	289,273	1,017.94	194,649	94,624	1,037.90	159,566	129,707	1,057.86	138,421	150,852
75,000	1,069.26	309,934	1,090.65	208,553	101,381	1,112.03	170,962	138,972	1,133.42	148,308	161,626
80,000	1,140.55	330,598	1,163.36	222,456	108,142	1,186.17	182,361	148,237	1,208.98	158,194	172,404
85,000	1,211.83	351,259	1,236.07	236,360	114,899	1,260.30	193,757	157,502	1,284.54	168,081	183,178
90,000	1,283.11	371,920	1,308.77	250,261	121,659	1,334.43	205,153	166,767	1,360.10	177,968	193,952
95,000	1,354.40	392,584	1,381.49	264,167	128,417	1,408.58	216,554	176,030	1,435.66	187,855	204,729
100,000	1,425.68	413,245	1,454.19	278,068	135,177	1,482.71	227,950	185,295	1,511.22	197,742	215,503
105,000	1,496.96	433,906	1,526.90	291,971	141,935	1,556.84	239,347	194,559	1,586.78	207,629	226,277
110,000	1,568.25	454,570	1,599.62	305,877	148,693	1,630.98	250,745	203,825	1,662.35	217,518	237,052
115,000	1,639.53	475,231	1,672.32	319,778	155,453	1,705.11	262,141	213,090	1,737.90	227,403	247,828
120,000	1,710.82	495,895	1,745.04	333,684	162,211	1,779.25	273,540	222,355	1,813.47	237,292	258,603
125,000	1,782.10	516,556	1,817.74	347,585	168,971	1,853.38	284,936	231,620	1,889.03	247,179	269,377
130,000	1,853.38	537,217	1,890.45	361,489	175,728	1,927.52	296,335	240,882	1,964.58	257,064	280,153
135,000	1,924.67	557,881	1,963.16	375,392	182,489	2,001.66	307,733	250,148	2,040.15	266,952	290,929
140,000	1,995.95	578,542	2,035.87	389,296	189,246	2,075.79	319,129	259,413	2,115.71	276,839	301,703
145,000	2,067.23	599,203	2,108.57	403,197	196,006	2,149.92	330,526	268,677	2,191.26	286,724	312,479
150,000	2,138.52	619,867	2,181.29	417,103	202,764	2,224.06	341,924	277,943	2,266.83	296,613	323,254
155,000	2,209.80	640,528	2,254.00	431,006	209,522	2,298.19	353,321	287,207	2,342.39	306,500	334,028
160,000	2,281.09	661,192	2,326.71	444,910	216,282	2,372.33	364,719	296,473	2,417.96	316,389	344,803
165,000	2,352.37	681,853	2,399.42	458,813	223,040	2,446.46	376,115	305,738	2,493.51	326,274	355,579
170,000	2,423.65	702,514	2,472.12	472,714	229,800	2,520.60	387,514	315,000	2,569.07	336,161	366,353
175,000	2,494.94	723,178	2,544.84	486,620	236,558	2,594.74	398,912	324,266	2,644.64	346,050	377,128
180,000	2,566.22	743,839	2,617.54	500,521	243,318	2,668.87	410,309	333,530	2,720.19	355,935	387,904
185,000	2,637.50	764,500	2,690.25	514,425	250,075	2,743.00	421,705	342,795	2,795.75	365,821	398,679
190,000	2,708.79	785,164	2,762.97	528,331	256,833	2,817.14	433,103	352,061	2,871.32	375,710	409,454
195,000	2,780.07	805,825	2,835.67	542,232	263,593	2,891.27	444,500	361,325	2,946.87	385,595	420,230
200,000	2,851.36	826,490	2,908.39	556,138	270,352	2,965.41	455,898	370,592	3,022.44	395,484	431,006

AMOUNT OF LOAN	30 YEARS		8% PMT INCREASE 179.615 PAYMENTS			10% PMT INCREASE 166.104 PAYMENTS			12% PMT INCREASE 155.132 PAYMENTS		
	MONTHLY PAYMENT	TOTAL INTRST	MONTHLY PAYMENT	TOTAL INTRST	INTRST SAVED	MONTHLY PAYMENT	TOTAL INTRST	INTRST SAVED	MONTHLY PAYMENT	TOTAL INTRST	INTRST SAVED
$ 50	0.72	209	0.78	90	119	0.79	81	128	0.81	76	133
100	1.43	415	1.54	177	238	1.57	161	254	1.60	148	267
200	2.86	830	3.09	355	475	3.15	323	507	3.20	296	534
300	4.28	1,241	4.62	530	711	4.71	482	759	4.79	443	798
400	5.71	1,656	6.17	708	948	6.28	643	1,013	6.40	593	1,063
500	7.13	2,067	7.70	883	1,184	7.84	802	1,265	7.99	740	1,327
600	8.56	2,482	9.24	1,060	1,422	9.42	965	1,517	9.59	888	1,594
700	9.98	2,893	10.78	1,236	1,657	10.98	1,124	1,769	11.18	1,034	1,859
800	11.41	3,308	12.32	1,413	1,895	12.55	1,285	2,023	12.78	1,183	2,125
900	12.84	3,722	13.87	1,591	2,131	14.12	1,445	2,277	14.38	1,331	2,391
1,000	14.26	4,134	15.40	1,766	2,368	15.69	1,606	2,528	15.97	1,477	2,657
2,000	28.52	8,267	30.80	3,532	4,735	31.37	3,211	5,056	31.94	2,955	5,312
3,000	42.78	12,401	46.20	5,298	7,103	47.06	4,817	7,584	47.91	4,432	7,969
4,000	57.03	16,531	61.59	7,062	9,469	62.73	6,420	10,111	63.87	5,908	10,623
5,000	71.29	20,664	76.99	8,829	11,835	78.42	8,026	12,638	79.84	7,386	13,278
6,000	85.55	24,798	92.39	10,595	14,203	94.11	9,632	15,166	95.82	8,865	15,933
7,000	99.80	28,928	107.78	12,359	16,569	109.78	11,235	17,693	111.78	10,341	18,587
8,000	114.06	33,062	123.18	14,125	18,937	125.47	12,841	20,221	127.75	11,818	21,244
9,000	128.32	37,195	138.59	15,893	21,302	141.15	14,446	22,749	143.72	13,296	23,899
10,000	142.57	41,325	153.98	17,657	23,668	156.83	16,050	25,275	159.68	14,771	26,554
11,000	156.83	45,459	169.38	19,423	26,036	172.51	17,655	27,804	175.65	16,249	29,210
12,000	171.09	49,592	184.78	21,189	28,403	188.20	19,261	30,331	191.62	17,726	31,866
13,000	185.34	53,722	200.17	22,954	30,768	203.87	20,864	32,858	207.58	19,202	34,520
14,000	199.60	57,856	215.57	24,720	33,136	219.56	22,470	35,386	223.55	20,680	37,176
15,000	213.86	61,990	230.97	26,486	35,504	235.25	24,076	37,914	239.52	22,157	39,833
16,000	228.11	66,120	246.36	28,250	37,870	250.92	25,679	40,441	255.48	23,633	42,487
17,000	242.37	70,253	261.76	30,016	40,237	266.61	27,285	42,968	271.45	25,111	45,142
18,000	256.63	74,387	277.16	31,782	42,605	282.29	28,889	45,498	287.43	26,590	47,797
19,000	270.88	78,517	292.55	33,546	44,971	297.97	30,494	48,023	303.39	28,065	50,452
20,000	285.14	82,650	307.95	35,312	47,338	313.65	32,099	50,551	319.36	29,543	53,107
21,000	299.40	86,784	323.35	37,079	49,705	329.34	33,705	53,079	335.33	31,020	55,764
22,000	313.65	90,914	338.74	38,843	52,071	345.02	35,309	55,605	351.29	32,496	58,418
23,000	327.91	95,048	354.14	40,609	54,439	360.70	36,914	58,134	367.26	33,974	61,074
24,000	342.17	99,181	369.54	42,375	56,806	376.39	38,520	60,661	383.23	35,451	63,730
25,000	356.42	103,311	384.93	44,139	59,172	392.06	40,121	63,188	399.19	36,927	66,384
26,000	370.68	107,445	400.33	45,905	61,540	407.75	41,729	65,716	415.16	38,405	69,040
27,000	384.94	111,578	415.74	47,673	63,905	423.43	43,333	68,245	431.13	39,882	71,696
28,000	399.19	115,708	431.13	49,437	66,271	439.11	44,938	70,770	447.09	41,358	74,350
29,000	413.45	119,842	446.53	51,203	68,639	454.80	46,544	73,298	463.06	42,835	77,007
30,000	427.71	123,976	461.93	52,970	71,006	470.48	48,149	75,827	479.04	44,314	79,662
32,500	463.35	134,306	500.42	57,383	76,923	509.69	52,162	82,144	518.95	48,006	86,300
35,000	498.99	144,636	538.91	61,796	82,840	548.89	56,173	88,463	558.87	51,699	92,937
40,000	570.28	165,301	615.90	70,625	94,676	627.31	64,199	101,102	638.71	59,084	106,217
45,000	641.56	185,962	692.88	79,452	106,510	705.72	72,223	113,739	718.55	66,470	119,492
50,000	712.84	206,622	769.87	88,280	118,342	784.12	80,245	126,377	798.38	73,854	132,768
55,000	784.13	227,287	846.86	97,109	130,178	862.54	88,271	139,016	878.23	81,242	146,045
60,000	855.41	247,948	923.84	105,936	142,012	940.95	96,296	151,652	958.06	88,626	159,322
65,000	926.69	268,608	1,000.83	114,764	153,844	1,019.36	104,320	164,288	1,037.89	96,010	172,598
70,000	997.98	289,273	1,077.82	123,593	165,680	1,097.78	112,346	176,927	1,117.74	103,397	185,876
75,000	1,069.26	309,934	1,154.80	132,419	177,515	1,176.19	120,370	189,564	1,197.57	110,781	199,153
80,000	1,140.55	330,598	1,231.79	141,248	189,350	1,254.61	128,396	202,202	1,277.42	118,169	212,429
85,000	1,211.83	351,259	1,308.78	150,077	201,182	1,333.01	136,418	214,841	1,357.25	125,553	225,706
90,000	1,283.11	371,920	1,385.76	158,903	213,017	1,411.42	144,443	227,477	1,437.08	132,937	238,983
95,000	1,354.40	392,584	1,462.75	167,732	224,852	1,489.84	152,468	240,116	1,516.93	140,324	252,260
100,000	1,425.68	413,245	1,539.73	176,559	236,686	1,568.25	160,493	252,752	1,596.76	147,709	265,536
105,000	1,496.96	433,906	1,616.72	185,387	248,519	1,646.66	168,517	265,389	1,676.60	155,094	278,812
110,000	1,568.25	454,570	1,693.71	194,216	260,354	1,725.08	176,543	278,027	1,756.44	162,480	292,090
115,000	1,639.53	475,231	1,770.69	203,042	272,189	1,803.48	184,565	290,666	1,836.27	169,864	305,367
120,000	1,710.82	495,895	1,847.69	211,873	284,022	1,881.90	192,591	303,304	1,916.12	177,252	318,643
125,000	1,782.10	516,556	1,924.67	220,700	295,856	1,960.31	200,615	315,941	1,995.95	184,636	331,920
130,000	1,853.38	537,217	2,001.65	229,526	307,691	2,038.72	208,640	328,577	2,075.79	192,021	345,196
135,000	1,924.67	557,881	2,078.64	238,355	319,526	2,117.14	216,665	341,216	2,155.63	199,407	358,474
140,000	1,995.95	578,542	2,155.63	247,183	331,359	2,195.55	224,690	353,852	2,235.46	206,791	371,751
145,000	2,067.23	599,203	2,232.61	256,010	343,193	2,273.95	232,712	366,485	2,315.30	214,177	385,026
150,000	2,138.52	619,867	2,309.60	264,839	355,028	2,352.37	240,738	379,129	2,395.14	221,563	398,304
155,000	2,209.80	640,528	2,386.58	273,666	366,862	2,430.78	248,762	391,766	2,474.98	228,949	411,579
160,000	2,281.09	661,192	2,463.58	282,496	378,696	2,509.20	256,788	404,405	2,554.82	236,334	424,858
165,000	2,352.37	681,853	2,540.56	291,323	390,530	2,587.61	264,812	417,041	2,634.65	243,719	438,134
170,000	2,423.65	702,514	2,617.54	300,149	402,365	2,666.02	272,837	429,677	2,714.49	251,104	451,410
175,000	2,494.94	723,178	2,694.54	308,980	414,198	2,744.43	280,861	442,317	2,794.33	258,490	464,688
180,000	2,566.22	743,839	2,771.52	317,807	426,032	2,822.84	288,885	454,954	2,874.17	265,876	477,963
185,000	2,637.50	764,500	2,848.50	326,633	437,867	2,901.25	296,909	467,591	2,954.00	273,260	491,240
190,000	2,708.79	785,164	2,925.49	335,462	449,702	2,979.67	304,935	480,229	3,033.84	280,646	504,518
195,000	2,780.07	805,825	3,002.48	344,290	461,535	3,058.08	312,959	492,866	3,113.68	288,031	517,794
200,000	2,851.36	826,490	3,079.47	353,119	473,371	3,136.50	320,985	505,505	3,193.52	295,417	531,073

17.25% AUGMENTED PAYMENT MORTGAGES

AMOUNT OF LOAN	30 YEARS		2% PMT INCREASE 257.454 PAYMENTS			4% PMT INCREASE 218.685 PAYMENTS			6% PMT INCREASE 194.665 PAYMENTS		
	MONTHLY PAYMENT	TOTAL INTRST	MONTHLY PAYMENT	TOTAL INTRST	INTRST SAVED	MONTHLY PAYMENT	TOTAL INTRST	INTRST SAVED	MONTHLY PAYMENT	TOTAL INTRST	INTRST SAVED
$ 50	0.73	213	0.74	141	72	0.76	116	97	0.77	100	113
100	1.45	422	1.48	281	141	1.51	230	192	1.54	200	222
200	2.90	844	2.96	562	282	3.02	460	384	3.07	398	446
300	4.34	1,262	4.43	841	421	4.51	686	576	4.60	595	667
400	5.79	1,684	5.91	1,122	562	6.02	916	768	6.14	795	889
500	7.23	2,103	7.37	1,397	706	7.52	1,145	958	7.66	991	1,112
600	8.68	2,525	8.85	1,678	847	9.03	1,375	1,150	9.20	1,191	1,334
700	10.13	2,947	10.33	1,959	988	10.54	1,605	1,342	10.74	1,391	1,556
800	11.57	3,365	11.80	2,238	1,127	12.03	1,831	1,534	12.26	1,587	1,778
900	13.02	3,787	13.28	2,519	1,268	13.54	2,061	1,726	13.80	1,786	2,001
1,000	14.46	4,206	14.75	2,797	1,409	15.04	2,289	1,917	15.33	1,984	2,222
2,000	28.92	8,411	29.50	5,595	2,816	30.08	4,578	3,833	30.66	3,968	4,443
3,000	43.38	12,617	44.25	8,392	4,225	45.12	6,867	5,750	45.98	5,951	6,666
4,000	57.84	16,822	59.00	11,190	5,632	60.15	9,154	7,668	61.31	7,935	8,887
5,000	72.30	21,028	73.75	13,987	7,041	75.19	11,443	9,585	76.64	9,919	11,109
6,000	86.76	25,234	88.50	16,785	8,449	90.23	13,732	11,502	91.97	11,903	13,331
7,000	101.22	29,439	103.24	19,580	9,859	105.27	16,021	13,418	107.29	13,886	15,553
8,000	115.68	33,645	117.99	22,377	11,268	120.31	18,310	15,335	122.62	15,870	17,775
9,000	130.14	37,850	132.74	25,174	12,676	135.35	20,599	17,251	137.95	17,854	19,996
10,000	144.60	42,056	147.49	27,972	14,084	150.38	22,886	19,170	153.28	19,838	22,218
11,000	159.06	46,262	162.24	30,769	15,493	165.42	25,175	21,087	168.60	21,821	24,441
12,000	173.52	50,467	176.99	33,567	16,900	180.46	27,464	23,003	183.93	23,805	26,662
13,000	187.98	54,673	191.74	36,364	18,309	195.50	29,753	24,920	199.26	25,789	28,884
14,000	202.44	58,878	206.49	39,162	19,716	210.54	32,042	26,836	214.59	27,773	31,105
15,000	216.90	63,084	221.24	41,959	21,125	225.58	34,331	28,753	229.91	29,755	33,329
16,000	231.36	67,290	235.99	44,757	22,533	240.61	36,618	30,672	245.24	31,740	35,550
17,000	245.82	71,495	250.74	47,554	23,941	255.65	38,907	32,588	260.57	33,724	37,771
18,000	260.28	75,701	265.49	50,351	25,350	270.69	41,196	34,505	275.90	35,708	39,993
19,000	274.74	79,906	280.23	53,146	26,760	285.73	43,485	36,421	291.22	37,690	42,216
20,000	289.20	84,112	294.98	55,944	28,168	300.77	45,774	38,338	306.55	39,675	44,437
21,000	303.66	88,318	309.73	58,741	29,577	315.81	48,063	40,255	321.88	41,659	46,659
22,000	318.12	92,523	324.48	61,539	30,984	330.84	50,350	42,173	337.21	43,643	48,880
23,000	332.58	96,729	339.23	64,336	32,393	345.88	52,639	44,090	352.53	45,625	51,104
24,000	347.04	100,934	353.98	67,134	33,800	360.92	54,928	46,006	367.86	47,609	53,325
25,000	361.50	105,140	368.73	69,931	35,209	375.96	57,217	47,923	383.19	49,594	55,546
26,000	375.96	109,346	383.48	72,728	36,618	391.00	59,506	49,840	398.52	51,578	57,768
27,000	390.42	113,551	398.23	75,526	38,025	406.04	61,795	51,756	413.85	53,562	59,989
28,000	404.88	117,757	412.98	78,323	39,434	421.08	64,084	53,673	429.17	55,544	62,213
29,000	419.34	121,962	427.73	81,121	40,841	436.11	66,371	55,591	444.50	57,529	64,433
30,000	433.80	126,168	442.48	83,918	42,250	451.15	68,660	57,508	459.83	59,513	66,655
32,500	469.95	136,682	479.35	90,911	45,771	488.75	74,382	62,300	498.15	64,472	72,210
35,000	506.10	147,196	516.22	97,903	49,293	526.34	80,103	67,093	536.47	69,432	77,764
40,000	578.40	168,224	589.97	111,890	56,334	601.54	91,548	76,676	613.10	79,349	88,875
45,000	650.70	189,252	663.71	125,875	63,377	676.73	102,991	86,261	689.74	89,268	99,984
50,000	723.00	210,280	737.46	139,862	70,418	751.92	114,434	95,846	766.38	99,187	111,093
55,000	795.30	231,308	811.21	153,849	77,459	827.11	125,877	105,431	843.02	109,106	122,202
60,000	867.60	252,336	884.95	167,834	84,502	902.30	137,319	115,017	919.66	119,026	133,310
65,000	939.90	273,364	958.70	181,821	91,543	977.50	148,765	124,599	996.29	128,943	144,421
70,000	1,012.20	294,392	1,032.44	195,806	98,586	1,052.69	160,208	134,184	1,072.93	138,862	155,530
75,000	1,084.49	315,416	1,106.18	209,790	105,626	1,127.87	171,648	143,768	1,149.56	148,779	166,637
80,000	1,156.79	336,444	1,179.93	223,778	112,666	1,203.06	183,091	153,353	1,226.20	158,698	177,746
85,000	1,229.09	357,472	1,253.67	237,762	119,710	1,278.25	194,534	162,938	1,302.84	168,617	188,855
90,000	1,301.39	378,500	1,327.42	251,750	126,750	1,353.45	205,979	172,521	1,379.47	178,535	199,965
95,000	1,373.69	399,528	1,401.16	265,734	133,794	1,428.64	217,422	182,106	1,456.11	188,454	211,074
100,000	1,445.99	420,556	1,474.91	279,721	140,835	1,503.83	228,865	191,691	1,532.75	198,373	222,183
105,000	1,518.29	441,584	1,548.66	293,709	147,875	1,579.02	240,308	201,276	1,609.39	208,292	233,292
110,000	1,590.59	462,612	1,622.40	307,693	154,919	1,654.21	251,751	210,861	1,686.03	218,211	244,401
115,000	1,662.89	483,640	1,696.15	321,681	161,959	1,729.41	263,196	220,444	1,762.66	228,128	255,512
120,000	1,735.19	504,668	1,769.89	335,665	169,003	1,804.60	274,639	230,029	1,839.30	238,047	266,621
125,000	1,807.49	525,696	1,843.64	349,652	176,044	1,879.79	286,082	239,614	1,915.94	247,966	277,730
130,000	1,879.79	546,724	1,917.39	363,640	183,084	1,954.98	297,525	249,199	1,992.58	257,886	288,838
135,000	1,952.09	567,752	1,991.13	377,624	190,128	2,030.17	308,968	258,784	2,069.22	267,805	299,947
140,000	2,024.39	588,780	2,064.88	391,612	197,168	2,105.37	320,413	268,367	2,145.85	277,722	311,058
145,000	2,096.68	609,805	2,138.61	405,594	204,211	2,180.55	331,854	277,951	2,222.48	287,639	322,166
150,000	2,168.98	630,833	2,212.36	419,581	211,252	2,255.74	343,297	287,536	2,299.12	297,558	333,275
155,000	2,241.28	651,861	2,286.11	433,568	218,293	2,330.93	354,739	297,122	2,375.76	307,477	344,384
160,000	2,313.58	672,889	2,359.85	447,553	225,336	2,406.12	366,182	306,707	2,452.39	317,394	355,495
165,000	2,385.88	693,917	2,433.60	461,540	232,377	2,481.32	377,627	316,290	2,529.03	327,314	366,603
170,000	2,458.18	714,945	2,507.34	475,525	239,420	2,556.51	389,070	325,875	2,605.67	337,233	377,712
175,000	2,530.48	735,973	2,581.09	489,512	246,461	2,631.70	400,513	335,460	2,682.31	347,152	388,821
180,000	2,602.78	757,001	2,654.84	503,499	253,502	2,706.89	411,956	345,045	2,758.95	357,071	399,930
185,000	2,675.08	778,029	2,728.58	517,484	260,545	2,782.08	423,399	354,630	2,835.58	366,988	411,041
190,000	2,747.38	799,057	2,802.33	531,471	267,586	2,857.28	434,844	364,213	2,912.22	376,907	422,150
195,000	2,819.68	820,085	2,876.07	545,456	274,629	2,932.47	446,287	373,798	2,988.86	386,826	433,259
200,000	2,891.98	841,113	2,949.82	559,443	281,670	3,007.66	457,730	383,383	3,065.50	396,746	444,367

AUGMENTED PAYMENT MORTGAGES 17.25%

AMOUNT OF LOAN	30 YEARS		8% PMT INCREASE 177.397 PAYMENTS			10% PMT INCREASE 164.011 PAYMENTS			12% PMT INCREASE 153.150 PAYMENTS		
	MONTHLY PAYMENT	TOTAL INTRST	MONTHLY PAYMENT	TOTAL INTRST	INTRST SAVED	MONTHLY PAYMENT	TOTAL INTRST	INTRST SAVED	MONTHLY PAYMENT	TOTAL INTRST	INTRST SAVED
$ 50	0.73	213	0.79	90	123	0.80	81	132	0.82	76	137
100	1.45	422	1.57	179	243	1.60	162	260	1.62	148	274
200	2.90	844	3.13	355	489	3.19	323	521	3.25	298	546
300	4.34	1,262	4.69	532	730	4.77	482	780	4.86	444	818
400	5.79	1,684	6.25	709	975	6.37	645	1,039	6.48	592	1,092
500	7.23	2,103	7.81	885	1,218	7.95	804	1,299	8.10	741	1,362
600	8.68	2,525	9.37	1,062	1,463	9.55	966	1,559	9.72	889	1,636
700	10.13	2,947	10.94	1,241	1,706	11.14	1,127	1,820	11.35	1,038	1,909
800	11.57	3,365	12.50	1,417	1,948	12.73	1,288	2,077	12.96	1,185	2,180
900	13.02	3,787	14.06	1,594	2,193	14.32	1,449	2,338	14.58	1,333	2,454
1,000	14.46	4,206	15.62	1,771	2,435	15.91	1,609	2,597	16.20	1,481	2,725
2,000	28.92	8,411	31.23	3,540	4,871	31.81	3,217	5,194	32.39	2,961	5,450
3,000	43.38	12,617	46.85	5,311	7,306	47.72	4,827	7,790	48.59	4,442	8,175
4,000	57.84	16,822	62.47	7,082	9,740	63.62	6,434	10,388	64.78	5,921	10,901
5,000	72.30	21,028	78.08	8,851	12,177	79.53	8,044	12,984	80.98	7,402	13,626
6,000	86.76	25,234	93.70	10,622	14,612	95.44	9,653	15,581	97.17	8,882	16,352
7,000	101.22	29,439	109.32	12,393	17,046	111.34	11,261	18,178	113.37	10,363	19,076
8,000	115.68	33,645	124.93	14,162	19,483	127.25	12,870	20,775	129.56	11,842	21,803
9,000	130.14	37,850	140.55	15,933	21,917	143.15	14,478	23,372	145.76	13,323	24,527
10,000	144.60	42,056	156.17	17,704	24,352	159.06	16,088	25,968	161.95	14,803	27,253
11,000	159.06	46,262	171.78	19,473	26,789	174.97	17,697	28,565	178.15	16,284	29,978
12,000	173.52	50,467	187.40	21,244	29,223	190.87	19,305	31,162	194.34	17,763	32,704
13,000	187.98	54,673	203.02	23,015	31,658	206.78	20,914	33,759	210.54	19,244	35,429
14,000	202.44	58,878	218.64	24,786	34,092	222.68	22,522	36,356	226.73	20,724	38,154
15,000	216.90	63,084	234.25	26,555	36,529	238.59	24,131	38,953	242.93	22,205	40,879
16,000	231.36	67,290	249.87	28,326	38,964	254.50	25,741	41,549	259.12	23,684	43,606
17,000	245.82	71,495	265.49	30,097	41,398	270.40	27,349	44,146	275.32	25,165	46,330
18,000	260.28	75,701	281.10	31,866	43,835	286.31	28,958	46,743	291.51	26,645	49,056
19,000	274.74	79,906	296.72	33,637	46,269	302.21	30,566	49,340	307.71	28,126	51,780
20,000	289.20	84,112	312.34	35,408	48,704	318.12	32,175	51,937	323.90	29,605	54,507
21,000	303.66	88,318	327.95	37,177	51,141	334.03	33,785	54,533	340.10	31,086	57,232
22,000	318.12	92,523	343.57	38,948	53,575	349.93	35,392	57,131	356.29	32,566	59,957
23,000	332.58	96,729	359.19	40,719	56,010	365.84	37,002	59,727	372.49	34,047	62,682
24,000	347.04	100,934	374.80	42,488	58,446	381.74	38,610	62,324	388.68	35,526	65,408
25,000	361.50	105,140	390.42	44,259	60,881	397.65	40,219	64,921	404.88	37,007	68,133
26,000	375.96	109,346	406.04	46,030	63,316	413.56	41,828	67,518	421.08	38,488	70,858
27,000	390.42	113,551	421.65	47,799	65,752	429.46	43,436	70,115	437.27	39,968	73,583
28,000	404.88	117,757	437.27	49,570	68,187	445.37	45,046	72,711	453.47	41,449	76,308
29,000	419.34	121,962	452.89	51,341	70,621	461.27	46,653	75,309	469.66	42,928	79,034
30,000	433.80	126,168	468.50	53,110	73,058	477.18	48,263	77,905	485.86	44,409	81,759
32,500	469.95	136,682	507.55	57,538	79,144	516.95	52,285	84,397	526.34	48,109	88,573
35,000	506.10	147,196	546.59	61,963	85,233	556.71	56,307	90,889	566.83	51,810	95,386
40,000	578.40	168,224	624.67	70,815	97,409	636.24	64,350	103,874	647.81	59,212	109,012
45,000	650.70	189,252	702.76	79,668	109,584	715.77	72,394	116,858	728.78	66,613	122,639
50,000	723.00	210,280	780.84	88,519	121,761	795.30	80,438	129,842	809.76	74,015	136,265
55,000	795.30	231,308	858.92	97,370	133,938	874.83	88,482	142,826	890.74	81,417	149,891
60,000	867.60	252,336	937.01	106,223	146,113	954.36	96,526	155,810	971.71	88,817	163,519
65,000	939.90	273,364	1,015.09	115,074	158,290	1,033.89	104,569	168,795	1,052.69	96,219	177,145
70,000	1,012.20	294,392	1,093.18	123,927	170,465	1,113.42	112,613	181,779	1,133.66	103,620	190,772
75,000	1,084.49	315,416	1,171.25	132,776	182,640	1,192.94	120,655	194,761	1,214.63	111,021	204,395
80,000	1,156.79	336,444	1,249.33	141,627	194,817	1,272.47	128,699	207,745	1,295.60	118,421	218,023
85,000	1,229.09	357,472	1,327.42	150,480	206,992	1,352.00	136,743	220,729	1,376.58	125,823	231,649
90,000	1,301.39	378,500	1,405.50	159,331	219,169	1,431.53	144,787	233,713	1,457.56	133,225	245,275
95,000	1,373.69	399,528	1,483.59	168,184	231,344	1,511.06	152,830	246,698	1,538.53	140,626	258,902
100,000	1,445.99	420,556	1,561.67	177,036	243,520	1,590.59	160,874	259,682	1,619.51	148,028	272,528
105,000	1,518.29	441,584	1,639.75	185,887	255,697	1,670.12	168,918	272,666	1,700.48	155,429	286,155
110,000	1,590.59	462,612	1,717.84	194,740	267,872	1,749.65	176,962	285,650	1,781.46	162,831	299,781
115,000	1,662.89	483,640	1,795.92	203,591	280,049	1,829.18	185,006	298,634	1,862.44	170,233	313,407
120,000	1,735.19	504,668	1,874.01	212,444	292,224	1,908.71	193,049	311,619	1,943.41	177,633	327,035
125,000	1,807.49	525,696	1,952.09	221,295	304,401	1,988.24	201,093	324,603	2,024.39	185,035	340,661
130,000	1,879.79	546,724	2,030.17	230,146	316,578	2,067.77	209,137	337,587	2,105.36	192,436	354,288
135,000	1,952.09	567,752	2,108.26	238,999	328,753	2,147.30	217,181	350,571	2,186.34	199,838	367,914
140,000	2,024.39	588,780	2,186.34	247,850	340,930	2,226.83	225,225	363,555	2,267.32	207,240	381,540
145,000	2,096.68	609,805	2,264.41	256,700	353,105	2,306.35	233,267	376,538	2,348.28	214,639	395,166
150,000	2,168.98	630,833	2,342.50	265,552	365,281	2,385.88	241,311	389,522	2,429.26	222,041	408,792
155,000	2,241.28	651,861	2,420.58	274,404	377,457	2,465.41	249,354	402,507	2,510.23	229,442	422,419
160,000	2,313.58	672,889	2,498.67	283,257	389,632	2,544.94	257,398	415,491	2,591.21	236,844	436,045
165,000	2,385.88	693,917	2,576.75	292,108	401,809	2,624.47	265,442	428,475	2,672.19	244,246	449,671
170,000	2,458.18	714,945	2,654.83	300,959	413,986	2,704.00	273,486	441,459	2,753.16	251,646	463,299
175,000	2,530.48	735,973	2,732.92	309,812	426,161	2,783.53	281,530	454,443	2,834.14	259,049	476,924
180,000	2,602.78	757,001	2,811.00	318,663	438,338	2,863.06	289,573	467,428	2,915.11	266,449	490,552
185,000	2,675.08	778,029	2,889.09	327,516	450,513	2,942.59	297,617	480,412	2,996.09	273,851	504,178
190,000	2,747.38	799,057	2,967.17	336,367	462,690	3,022.12	305,661	493,396	3,077.07	281,253	517,804
195,000	2,819.68	820,085	3,045.25	345,218	474,867	3,101.65	313,705	506,380	3,158.04	288,654	531,431
200,000	2,891.98	841,113	3,123.34	354,071	487,042	3,181.18	321,749	519,364	3,239.02	296,056	545,057

277

17.50% AUGMENTED PAYMENT MORTGAGES

AMOUNT OF LOAN	30 YEARS		2% PMT INCREASE 254.927 PAYMENTS			4% PMT INCREASE 216.216 PAYMENTS			6% PMT INCREASE 192.344 PAYMENTS		
	MONTHLY PAYMENT	TOTAL INTRST	MONTHLY PAYMENT	TOTAL INTRST	INTRST SAVED	MONTHLY PAYMENT	TOTAL INTRST	INTRST SAVED	MONTHLY PAYMENT	TOTAL INTRST	INTRST SAVED
$ 50	0.74	216	0.75	141	75	0.77	116	100	0.78	100	116
100	1.47	429	1.50	282	147	1.53	231	198	1.56	200	229
200	2.94	858	3.00	565	293	3.06	462	396	3.12	400	458
300	4.40	1,284	4.49	845	439	4.58	690	594	4.66	596	688
400	5.87	1,713	5.99	1,127	586	6.10	919	794	6.22	796	917
500	7.34	2,142	7.49	1,409	733	7.63	1,150	992	7.78	996	1,146
600	8.80	2,568	8.98	1,689	879	9.15	1,378	1,190	9.33	1,195	1,373
700	10.27	2,997	10.48	1,972	1,025	10.68	1,609	1,388	10.89	1,395	1,602
800	11.74	3,426	11.97	2,251	1,175	12.21	1,840	1,586	12.44	1,593	1,833
900	13.20	3,852	13.46	2,531	1,321	13.73	2,069	1,783	13.99	1,791	2,061
1,000	14.67	4,281	14.96	2,814	1,467	15.26	2,299	1,982	15.55	1,991	2,290
2,000	29.33	8,559	29.92	5,627	2,932	30.50	4,595	3,964	31.09	3,980	4,579
3,000	43.99	12,836	44.87	8,439	4,397	45.75	6,892	5,944	46.63	5,969	6,867
4,000	58.66	17,118	59.83	11,252	5,866	61.01	9,191	7,927	62.18	7,960	9,158
5,000	73.32	21,395	74.79	14,066	7,329	76.25	11,486	9,909	77.72	9,949	11,446
6,000	87.98	25,673	89.74	16,877	8,796	91.50	13,784	11,889	93.26	11,938	13,735
7,000	102.65	29,954	104.70	19,691	10,263	106.76	16,083	13,871	108.81	13,929	16,025
8,000	117.31	34,232	119.66	22,505	11,727	122.00	18,378	15,854	124.35	15,918	18,314
9,000	131.97	38,509	134.61	25,316	13,193	137.25	20,676	17,833	139.89	17,907	20,602
10,000	146.64	42,790	149.57	28,129	14,661	152.51	22,975	19,815	155.44	19,898	22,892
11,000	161.30	47,068	164.53	30,943	16,125	167.75	25,270	21,798	170.98	21,887	25,181
12,000	175.96	51,346	179.48	33,754	17,592	183.00	27,568	23,778	186.52	23,876	27,470
13,000	190.63	55,627	194.44	36,568	19,059	198.26	29,867	25,760	202.07	25,867	29,760
14,000	205.29	59,904	209.40	39,382	20,522	213.50	32,162	27,742	217.61	27,856	32,048
15,000	219.95	64,182	224.35	42,193	21,989	228.75	34,459	29,723	233.15	29,845	34,337
16,000	234.62	68,463	239.31	45,007	23,456	244.00	36,757	31,706	248.70	31,836	36,627
17,000	249.28	72,741	254.27	47,820	24,921	259.25	39,054	33,687	264.24	33,825	38,916
18,000	263.94	77,018	269.22	50,631	26,387	274.50	41,351	35,667	279.78	35,814	41,204
19,000	278.61	81,300	284.18	53,445	27,855	289.75	43,649	37,651	295.33	37,805	43,495
20,000	293.27	85,577	299.14	56,259	29,318	305.00	45,946	39,631	310.87	39,794	45,783
21,000	307.93	89,855	314.09	59,070	30,785	320.25	48,243	41,612	326.41	41,783	48,072
22,000	322.60	94,136	329.05	61,884	32,252	335.50	50,540	43,596	341.96	43,774	50,362
23,000	337.26	98,414	344.01	64,697	33,717	350.75	52,838	45,576	357.50	45,763	52,651
24,000	351.92	102,691	358.96	67,509	35,182	366.00	55,135	47,556	373.04	47,752	54,939
25,000	366.59	106,972	373.92	70,322	36,650	381.25	57,432	49,540	388.59	49,743	57,229
26,000	381.25	111,250	388.88	73,136	38,114	396.50	59,730	51,520	404.13	51,732	59,518
27,000	395.91	115,528	403.83	75,947	39,581	411.75	62,027	53,501	419.66	53,719	61,809
28,000	410.58	119,809	418.79	78,761	41,048	427.00	64,324	55,485	435.21	55,710	64,099
29,000	425.24	124,086	433.74	81,572	42,514	442.25	66,622	57,464	450.75	57,699	66,387
30,000	439.90	128,364	448.70	84,386	43,978	457.50	68,919	59,445	466.29	59,688	68,676
32,500	476.56	139,062	486.09	91,417	47,645	495.62	74,661	64,401	505.15	64,663	74,399
35,000	513.22	149,759	523.48	98,449	51,310	533.75	80,405	69,354	544.01	69,637	80,122
40,000	586.54	171,154	598.27	112,515	58,639	610.00	91,892	79,262	621.73	79,586	91,568
45,000	659.85	192,546	673.05	126,579	65,967	686.24	103,376	89,170	699.44	89,533	103,013
50,000	733.17	213,941	747.83	140,642	73,299	762.50	114,865	99,076	777.16	99,482	114,459
55,000	806.48	235,333	822.61	154,705	80,628	838.74	126,349	108,984	854.87	109,429	125,904
60,000	879.80	256,728	897.40	168,771	87,957	914.99	137,835	118,893	932.59	119,378	137,350
65,000	953.12	278,123	972.18	182,835	95,288	991.24	149,322	128,801	1,010.31	129,327	148,796
70,000	1,026.43	299,515	1,046.96	196,898	102,617	1,067.49	160,808	138,707	1,088.02	139,274	160,241
75,000	1,099.75	320,910	1,121.75	210,964	109,946	1,143.74	172,295	148,615	1,165.74	149,223	171,687
80,000	1,173.07	342,305	1,196.53	225,028	117,277	1,219.99	183,781	158,524	1,243.45	159,170	183,135
85,000	1,246.38	363,697	1,271.31	239,091	124,606	1,296.24	195,268	168,429	1,321.16	169,117	194,580
90,000	1,319.70	385,092	1,346.09	253,155	131,937	1,372.49	206,754	178,338	1,398.88	179,066	206,026
95,000	1,393.01	406,484	1,420.87	267,218	139,266	1,448.73	218,239	188,245	1,476.59	189,013	217,471
100,000	1,466.33	427,879	1,495.66	281,284	146,595	1,524.98	229,725	198,154	1,554.31	198,962	228,917
105,000	1,539.65	449,274	1,570.44	295,348	153,926	1,601.24	241,214	208,060	1,632.03	208,911	240,363
110,000	1,612.96	470,666	1,645.22	309,411	161,255	1,677.48	252,698	217,968	1,709.74	218,858	251,808
115,000	1,686.28	492,061	1,720.01	323,477	168,584	1,753.73	264,184	227,877	1,787.46	228,807	263,254
120,000	1,759.60	513,456	1,794.79	337,540	175,916	1,829.98	275,671	237,785	1,865.18	238,756	274,700
125,000	1,832.91	534,848	1,869.57	351,604	183,244	1,906.23	287,157	247,691	1,942.88	248,701	286,147
130,000	1,906.23	556,243	1,944.35	365,667	190,576	1,982.48	298,644	257,599	2,020.60	258,650	297,593
135,000	1,979.54	577,634	2,019.13	379,731	197,903	2,058.72	310,128	267,506	2,098.31	268,597	309,037
140,000	2,052.86	599,030	2,093.92	393,797	205,233	2,134.97	321,615	277,415	2,176.03	278,546	320,484
145,000	2,126.18	620,425	2,168.70	407,860	212,565	2,211.23	333,103	287,322	2,253.75	288,495	331,930
150,000	2,199.49	641,816	2,243.48	421,924	219,892	2,287.47	344,588	297,228	2,331.46	298,442	343,374
155,000	2,272.81	663,212	2,318.27	435,990	227,222	2,363.72	356,074	307,138	2,409.18	308,391	354,821
160,000	2,346.13	684,607	2,393.05	450,053	234,554	2,439.98	367,563	317,044	2,486.90	318,340	366,267
165,000	2,419.44	705,998	2,467.83	464,116	241,882	2,516.22	379,047	326,951	2,564.61	328,287	377,711
170,000	2,492.76	727,394	2,542.62	478,182	249,212	2,592.47	390,533	336,861	2,642.33	338,236	389,158
175,000	2,566.07	748,785	2,617.39	492,243	256,542	2,668.71	402,018	346,767	2,720.03	348,181	400,604
180,000	2,639.39	770,180	2,692.18	506,309	263,871	2,744.97	413,506	356,674	2,797.75	358,130	412,050
185,000	2,712.71	791,576	2,766.96	520,373	271,203	2,821.22	424,990	366,586	2,875.47	368,079	423,497
190,000	2,786.02	812,967	2,841.74	534,436	278,531	2,897.46	436,477	376,490	2,953.18	378,026	434,941
195,000	2,859.34	834,362	2,916.53	548,502	285,860	2,973.71	447,964	386,398	3,030.90	387,975	446,387
200,000	2,932.66	855,758	2,991.31	562,566	293,192	3,049.97	459,452	396,306	3,108.62	397,924	457,834

278

AMOUNT OF LOAN	30 YEARS		8% PMT INCREASE 175.217 PAYMENTS			10% PMT INCREASE 161.958 PAYMENTS			12% PMT INCREASE 151.208 PAYMENTS		
	MONTHLY PAYMENT	TOTAL INTRST	MONTHLY PAYMENT	TOTAL INTRST	INTRST SAVED	MONTHLY PAYMENT	TOTAL INTRST	INTRST SAVED	MONTHLY PAYMENT	TOTAL INTRST	INTRST SAVED
$ 50	0.74	216	0.80	90	126	0.81	81	135	0.83	76	140
100	1.47	429	1.59	179	250	1.62	162	267	1.65	149	280
200	2.94	858	3.18	357	501	3.23	323	535	3.29	297	561
300	4.40	1,284	4.75	532	752	4.84	484	800	4.93	445	839
400	5.87	1,713	6.34	711	1,002	6.46	646	1,067	6.57	593	1,120
500	7.34	2,142	7.93	889	1,253	8.07	807	1,335	8.22	743	1,399
600	8.80	2,568	9.50	1,065	1,503	9.68	968	1,600	9.86	891	1,677
700	10.27	2,997	11.09	1,243	1,754	11.30	1,130	1,867	11.50	1,039	1,958
800	11.74	3,426	12.68	1,422	2,004	12.91	1,291	2,135	13.15	1,188	2,238
900	13.20	3,852	14.26	1,599	2,253	14.52	1,452	2,400	14.78	1,335	2,517
1,000	14.67	4,281	15.84	1,775	2,506	16.14	1,614	2,667	16.43	1,484	2,797
2,000	29.33	8,559	31.68	3,551	5,008	32.26	3,225	5,334	32.85	2,967	5,592
3,000	43.99	12,836	47.51	5,325	7,511	48.39	4,837	7,999	49.27	4,450	8,386
4,000	58.66	17,118	63.35	7,100	10,018	64.53	6,451	10,667	65.70	5,934	11,184
5,000	73.32	21,395	79.19	8,875	12,520	80.65	8,062	13,333	82.12	7,417	13,978
6,000	87.98	25,673	95.02	10,649	15,024	96.78	9,674	15,999	98.54	8,900	16,773
7,000	102.65	29,954	110.86	12,425	17,529	112.92	11,288	18,666	114.97	10,384	19,570
8,000	117.31	34,232	126.69	14,198	20,034	129.04	12,899	21,333	131.39	11,867	22,365
9,000	131.97	38,509	142.53	15,974	22,535	145.17	14,511	23,998	147.81	13,350	25,159
10,000	146.64	42,790	158.37	17,749	25,041	161.30	16,124	26,666	164.24	14,834	27,956
11,000	161.30	47,068	174.20	19,523	27,545	177.43	17,736	29,332	180.66	16,317	30,751
12,000	175.96	51,346	190.04	21,298	30,048	193.56	19,349	31,997	197.08	17,800	33,546
13,000	190.63	55,627	205.88	23,074	32,553	209.69	20,961	34,666	213.51	19,284	36,343
14,000	205.29	59,904	221.71	24,847	35,057	225.82	22,573	37,331	229.92	20,766	39,138
15,000	219.95	64,182	237.55	26,623	37,559	241.95	24,186	39,996	246.34	22,249	41,933
16,000	234.62	68,463	253.39	29,398	40,065	258.08	25,798	42,665	262.77	23,733	44,730
17,000	249.28	72,741	269.22	30,172	42,569	274.21	27,411	45,330	279.19	25,216	47,525
18,000	263.94	77,018	285.06	31,947	45,071	290.33	29,021	47,997	295.61	26,699	50,319
19,000	278.61	81,300	300.90	33,723	47,577	306.47	30,635	50,665	312.04	28,183	53,117
20,000	293.27	85,577	316.73	35,496	50,081	322.60	32,248	53,333	328.46	29,666	55,911
21,000	307.93	89,855	332.56	37,270	52,585	338.72	33,858	55,997	344.88	31,149	58,706
22,000	322.60	94,136	348.41	39,047	55,089	354.86	35,472	58,664	361.31	32,633	61,503
23,000	337.26	98,414	364.24	40,821	57,593	370.99	37,085	61,329	377.73	34,116	64,298
24,000	351.92	102,691	380.07	42,595	60,096	387.11	38,696	63,995	394.15	35,599	67,092
25,000	366.59	106,972	395.92	44,372	62,600	403.25	40,310	66,662	410.58	37,083	69,889
26,000	381.25	111,250	411.75	46,146	65,104	419.38	41,922	69,328	427.00	38,566	72,684
27,000	395.91	115,528	427.58	47,919	67,609	435.50	43,533	71,995	443.42	40,049	75,479
28,000	410.58	119,809	443.43	49,696	70,113	451.64	45,147	74,662	459.85	41,533	78,276
29,000	425.24	124,086	459.26	51,470	72,616	467.76	46,757	77,329	476.27	43,016	81,070
30,000	439.90	128,364	475.09	53,244	75,120	483.89	48,370	79,994	492.69	44,499	83,865
32,500	476.56	139,062	514.68	57,681	81,381	524.22	52,402	86,660	533.75	48,207	90,855
35,000	513.22	149,759	554.28	62,119	87,640	564.54	56,432	93,327	574.81	51,916	97,843
40,000	586.54	171,154	633.46	70,993	100,161	645.19	64,494	106,660	656.92	59,332	111,822
45,000	659.85	192,500	712.64	79,867	112,679	725.84	72,556	119,990	739.03	66,747	125,799
50,000	733.17	213,941	791.82	88,740	125,201	806.49	80,618	133,323	821.15	74,164	139,777
55,000	806.48	235,333	871.00	97,614	137,719	887.13	88,678	146,655	903.26	81,580	153,753
60,000	879.80	256,728	950.18	106,488	150,240	967.78	96,740	159,988	985.38	88,997	167,731
65,000	953.12	278,123	1,029.37	115,363	162,760	1,048.43	104,802	173,321	1,067.49	96,413	181,710
70,000	1,026.43	299,515	1,108.54	124,235	175,280	1,129.07	112,862	186,653	1,149.60	103,829	195,686
75,000	1,099.75	320,910	1,187.73	133,110	187,800	1,209.73	120,925	199,985	1,231.72	111,246	209,664
80,000	1,173.07	342,305	1,266.92	141,986	200,319	1,290.38	128,987	213,318	1,313.84	118,663	223,642
85,000	1,246.38	363,697	1,346.09	150,858	212,839	1,371.02	137,048	226,649	1,395.95	126,079	237,618
90,000	1,319.70	385,092	1,425.28	159,733	225,359	1,451.67	145,110	239,982	1,478.06	133,494	251,598
95,000	1,393.01	406,484	1,504.45	168,605	237,879	1,532.31	153,170	253,314	1,560.17	140,910	265,574
100,000	1,466.33	427,879	1,583.64	177,481	250,398	1,612.96	161,232	266,647	1,642.29	148,327	279,552
105,000	1,539.65	449,274	1,662.82	186,354	262,920	1,693.62	169,295	279,979	1,724.41	155,745	293,529
110,000	1,612.96	470,666	1,742.00	195,228	275,438	1,774.26	177,356	293,310	1,806.52	163,160	307,506
115,000	1,686.28	492,061	1,821.18	204,102	287,959	1,854.91	185,418	306,643	1,888.63	170,576	321,485
120,000	1,759.60	513,456	1,900.37	212,977	300,479	1,935.56	193,479	319,977	1,970.75	177,993	335,463
125,000	1,832.91	534,848	1,979.54	221,849	312,999	2,016.20	201,540	333,308	2,052.86	185,409	349,439
130,000	1,906.23	556,243	2,058.73	230,724	325,519	2,096.85	209,602	346,641	2,134.98	192,826	363,417
135,000	1,979.54	577,634	2,137.90	239,596	338,038	2,177.49	217,662	359,972	2,217.08	200,240	377,394
140,000	2,052.86	599,030	2,217.09	248,472	350,558	2,258.15	225,725	373,305	2,299.20	207,657	391,373
145,000	2,126.18	620,425	2,296.27	257,346	363,079	2,338.80	233,787	386,638	2,381.32	215,075	405,350
150,000	2,199.49	641,816	2,375.45	266,219	375,597	2,419.44	241,848	399,968	2,463.43	222,490	419,326
155,000	2,272.81	663,212	2,454.63	275,093	388,119	2,500.09	249,910	413,302	2,545.55	229,908	433,304
160,000	2,346.13	684,607	2,533.82	283,968	400,639	2,580.74	257,971	426,636	2,627.67	237,325	447,282
165,000	2,419.44	705,998	2,613.00	292,842	413,156	2,661.38	266,032	439,966	2,709.77	244,739	461,259
170,000	2,492.76	727,394	2,692.18	301,716	425,678	2,742.04	274,095	453,299	2,791.89	252,156	475,238
175,000	2,566.07	748,785	2,771.36	310,589	438,196	2,822.68	282,156	466,629	2,874.00	259,572	489,213
180,000	2,639.39	770,180	2,850.54	319,463	450,717	2,903.33	290,218	479,962	2,956.12	266,989	503,191
185,000	2,712.71	791,576	2,929.73	328,339	463,237	2,983.98	298,279	493,297	3,038.24	274,406	517,170
190,000	2,786.02	812,967	3,008.90	337,210	475,757	3,064.62	306,340	506,627	3,120.34	281,820	531,147
195,000	2,859.34	834,362	3,088.09	346,086	488,276	3,145.27	314,402	519,960	3,202.46	289,238	545,124
200,000	2,932.66	855,758	3,167.27	354,960	500,798	3,225.93	322,465	533,293	3,284.58	296,655	559,103

AUGMENTED PAYMENT MORTGAGES

AMOUNT OF LOAN	30 YEARS		2% PMT INCREASE 252.411 PAYMENTS			4% PMT INCREASE 213.777 PAYMENTS			6% PMT INCREASE 190.058 PAYMENTS		
	MONTHLY PAYMENT	TOTAL INTRST	MONTHLY PAYMENT	TOTAL INTRST	INTRST SAVED	MONTHLY PAYMENT	TOTAL INTRST	INTRST SAVED	MONTHLY PAYMENT	TOTAL INTRST	INTRST SAVED
$ 50	0.75	220	0.77	144	76	0.78	117	103	0.80	102	118
100	1.49	436	1.52	284	152	1.55	231	205	1.58	200	236
200	2.98	873	3.04	567	306	3.10	463	410	3.16	401	472
300	4.47	1,309	4.56	851	458	4.65	694	615	4.74	601	708
400	5.95	1,742	6.07	1,132	610	6.19	923	819	6.31	799	943
500	7.44	2,178	7.59	1,416	762	7.74	1,155	1,023	7.89	1,000	1,178
600	8.93	2,615	9.11	1,699	916	9.29	1,386	1,229	9.47	1,200	1,415
700	10.41	3,048	10.62	1,981	1,067	10.83	1,615	1,433	11.03	1,396	1,652
800	11.90	3,484	12.14	2,264	1,220	12.38	1,847	1,637	12.61	1,597	1,887
900	13.39	3,920	13.66	2,548	1,372	13.93	2,078	1,842	14.19	1,797	2,123
1,000	14.87	4,353	15.17	2,829	1,524	15.46	2,305	2,048	15.76	1,995	2,358
2,000	29.74	8,706	30.33	5,656	3,050	30.93	4,612	4,094	31.52	3,991	4,715
3,000	44.61	13,060	45.50	8,485	4,575	46.39	6,917	6,143	47.29	5,988	7,072
4,000	59.47	17,409	60.66	11,311	6,098	61.85	9,222	8,187	63.04	7,981	9,428
5,000	74.34	21,762	75.83	14,140	7,622	77.31	11,527	10,235	78.80	9,977	11,785
6,000	89.21	26,116	90.99	16,967	9,149	92.78	13,834	12,282	94.56	11,972	14,144
7,000	104.07	30,465	106.15	19,793	10,672	108.23	16,137	14,328	110.31	13,965	16,500
8,000	118.94	34,818	121.32	22,623	12,195	123.70	18,444	16,374	126.08	15,963	18,855
9,000	133.81	39,172	136.49	25,452	13,720	139.16	20,749	18,423	141.84	17,958	21,214
10,000	148.67	43,521	151.64	28,276	15,245	154.62	23,054	20,467	157.59	19,951	23,570
11,000	163.54	47,874	166.81	31,105	16,769	170.08	25,359	22,515	173.35	21,947	25,927
12,000	178.41	52,228	181.98	33,934	18,294	185.55	27,666	24,562	189.11	23,942	28,286
13,000	193.27	56,577	197.14	36,760	19,817	201.00	29,969	26,608	204.87	25,937	30,640
14,000	208.14	60,930	212.30	39,587	21,343	216.47	32,276	28,654	220.63	27,932	32,998
15,000	223.01	65,284	227.47	42,416	22,868	231.93	34,581	30,703	236.39	29,928	35,356
16,000	237.88	69,637	242.64	45,245	24,392	247.40	36,888	32,749	252.15	31,923	37,714
17,000	252.74	73,986	257.79	48,070	25,917	262.85	39,191	34,795	267.90	33,917	40,069
18,000	267.61	78,340	272.96	50,898	27,442	278.31	41,496	36,844	283.67	35,914	42,426
19,000	282.48	82,693	288.13	53,727	28,966	293.78	43,803	38,890	299.43	37,909	44,784
20,000	297.34	87,042	303.29	56,554	30,488	309.23	46,106	40,936	315.18	39,902	47,140
21,000	312.21	91,396	318.45	59,380	32,016	324.70	48,413	42,983	330.94	41,898	49,498
22,000	327.08	95,749	333.62	62,209	33,540	340.16	50,718	45,031	346.70	43,893	51,856
23,000	341.94	100,098	348.78	65,036	35,062	355.62	53,023	47,075	362.46	45,888	54,210
24,000	356.81	104,452	363.95	67,865	36,587	371.08	55,328	49,124	378.22	47,884	56,568
25,000	371.68	108,805	379.11	70,692	38,113	386.55	57,635	51,170	393.98	49,879	58,926
26,000	386.54	113,154	394.27	73,518	39,636	402.00	59,938	53,216	409.73	51,872	61,282
27,000	401.41	117,508	409.44	76,347	41,161	417.47	62,245	55,263	425.49	53,868	63,640
28,000	416.28	121,861	424.61	79,176	42,685	432.93	64,550	57,311	441.26	55,865	65,996
29,000	431.15	126,214	439.77	82,003	44,211	448.40	66,858	59,356	457.02	57,860	68,354
30,000	446.01	130,564	454.93	84,829	45,735	463.85	69,160	61,404	472.77	59,854	70,710
32,500	483.18	141,445	492.84	91,898	49,547	502.51	74,925	66,520	512.17	64,842	76,603
35,000	520.35	152,326	530.76	98,970	53,356	541.16	80,688	71,638	551.57	69,830	82,496
40,000	594.68	174,085	606.57	113,105	60,980	618.47	92,215	81,870	630.36	79,805	94,280
45,000	669.02	195,847	682.40	127,245	68,602	695.78	103,742	92,105	709.16	89,782	106,065
50,000	743.35	217,606	758.22	141,383	76,223	773.08	115,267	102,339	787.95	99,756	117,850
55,000	817.69	239,368	834.04	155,521	83,847	850.40	126,796	112,572	866.75	109,733	129,635
60,000	892.02	261,127	909.86	169,659	91,468	927.70	138,321	122,806	945.54	119,707	141,420
65,000	966.35	282,886	985.68	183,796	99,090	1,005.00	149,846	133,040	1,024.33	129,682	153,204
70,000	1,040.69	304,648	1,061.50	197,934	106,714	1,082.32	161,375	143,273	1,103.13	139,659	164,989
75,000	1,115.02	326,407	1,137.32	212,072	114,335	1,159.62	172,900	153,507	1,181.92	149,633	176,774
80,000	1,189.36	348,170	1,213.15	226,212	121,958	1,236.93	184,427	163,743	1,260.72	159,610	188,560
85,000	1,263.69	369,928	1,288.96	240,348	129,580	1,314.24	195,954	173,974	1,339.51	169,585	200,343
90,000	1,338.03	391,691	1,364.79	254,488	137,203	1,391.55	207,481	184,210	1,418.31	179,561	212,130
95,000	1,412.36	413,450	1,440.61	268,626	144,824	1,468.85	219,006	194,444	1,497.10	189,536	223,914
100,000	1,486.70	435,212	1,516.43	282,764	152,448	1,546.17	230,536	204,676	1,575.90	199,512	235,700
105,000	1,561.03	456,971	1,592.25	296,901	160,070	1,623.47	242,061	214,910	1,654.69	209,487	247,484
110,000	1,635.37	478,733	1,668.08	311,042	167,691	1,700.79	253,588	225,145	1,733.49	219,464	259,269
115,000	1,709.70	500,492	1,743.89	325,177	175,315	1,778.09	265,115	235,377	1,812.28	229,438	271,054
120,000	1,784.04	522,254	1,819.72	339,317	182,937	1,855.40	276,642	245,612	1,891.08	239,415	282,839
125,000	1,858.37	544,013	1,895.54	353,455	190,558	1,932.70	288,167	255,846	1,969.87	249,390	294,623
130,000	1,932.70	565,772	1,971.35	367,590	198,182	2,010.01	299,694	266,078	2,048.66	259,364	306,408
135,000	2,007.04	587,534	2,047.18	381,731	205,803	2,087.32	311,221	276,313	2,127.46	269,341	318,193
140,000	2,081.37	609,293	2,123.00	395,869	213,424	2,164.62	322,746	286,547	2,206.25	279,315	329,978
145,000	2,155.71	631,056	2,198.82	410,006	221,050	2,241.94	334,275	296,781	2,285.05	289,292	341,764
150,000	2,230.04	652,814	2,274.64	424,144	228,670	2,319.24	345,800	307,014	2,363.84	299,267	353,547
155,000	2,304.38	674,577	2,350.47	438,284	236,293	2,396.56	357,329	317,248	2,442.64	309,243	365,334
160,000	2,378.71	696,336	2,426.28	452,420	243,916	2,473.86	368,854	327,482	2,521.43	319,218	377,118
165,000	2,453.05	718,098	2,502.11	466,560	251,538	2,551.17	380,381	337,717	2,600.23	329,195	388,903
170,000	2,527.38	739,857	2,577.93	480,698	259,159	2,628.48	391,909	347,948	2,679.02	339,169	400,688
175,000	2,601.72	761,619	2,653.75	494,836	266,783	2,705.79	403,436	358,183	2,757.82	349,146	412,473
180,000	2,676.05	783,378	2,729.57	508,973	274,405	2,783.09	414,961	368,417	2,836.61	359,120	424,258
185,000	2,750.39	805,140	2,805.40	523,114	282,026	2,860.41	426,490	378,650	2,915.41	369,097	436,043
190,000	2,824.72	826,899	2,881.21	537,249	289,650	2,937.71	438,015	388,884	2,994.20	379,072	447,827
195,000	2,899.05	848,658	2,957.03	551,387	297,271	3,015.01	449,540	399,118	3,072.99	389,046	459,612
200,000	2,973.39	870,420	3,032.86	565,527	304,893	3,092.33	461,046	409,351	3,151.79	399,023	471,397

AUGMENTED PAYMENT MORTGAGES 17.75%

AMOUNT OF LOAN	30 YEARS		8% PMT INCREASE 173.077 PAYMENTS			10% PMT INCREASE 159.945 PAYMENTS			12% PMT INCREASE 149.305 PAYMENTS		
	MONTHLY PAYMENT	TOTAL INTRST	MONTHLY PAYMENT	TOTAL INTRST	INTRST SAVED	MONTHLY PAYMENT	TOTAL INTRST	INTRST SAVED	MONTHLY PAYMENT	TOTAL INTRST	INTRST SAVED
$ 50	0.75	220	0.81	90	130	0.83	83	137	0.84	75	145
100	1.49	436	1.61	179	257	1.64	162	274	1.67	149	287
200	2.98	873	3.22	357	516	3.28	325	548	3.34	299	574
300	4.47	1,309	4.83	536	773	4.92	487	822	5.01	448	861
400	5.95	1,742	6.43	713	1,029	6.55	648	1,094	6.66	594	1,148
500	7.44	2,178	8.04	892	1,286	8.18	808	1,370	8.33	744	1,434
600	8.93	2,615	9.64	1,068	1,547	9.82	971	1,644	10.00	893	1,722
700	10.41	3,048	11.24	1,245	1,803	11.45	1,131	1,917	11.66	1,041	2,007
800	11.90	3,484	12.85	1,424	2,060	13.09	1,294	2,190	13.33	1,190	2,294
900	13.39	3,920	14.46	1,603	2,317	14.73	1,456	2,464	15.00	1,340	2,580
1,000	14.87	4,353	16.06	1,780	2,573	16.36	1,617	2,736	16.65	1,486	2,867
2,000	29.74	8,706	32.12	3,559	5,147	32.71	3,232	5,474	33.31	2,973	5,733
3,000	44.61	13,060	48.18	5,339	7,721	49.07	4,849	8,211	49.96	4,459	8,601
4,000	59.47	17,409	64.23	7,117	10,292	65.42	6,464	10,945	66.61	5,945	11,464
5,000	74.34	21,762	80.29	8,896	12,866	81.77	8,079	13,683	83.26	7,431	14,331
6,000	89.21	26,116	96.35	10,676	15,440	98.13	9,695	16,421	99.92	8,919	17,197
7,000	104.07	30,465	112.40	12,454	18,011	114.48	11,311	19,154	116.56	10,403	20,062
8,000	118.94	34,818	128.46	14,233	20,585	130.83	12,926	21,892	133.21	11,889	22,929
9,000	133.81	39,172	144.51	16,011	23,161	147.19	14,542	24,630	149.87	13,376	25,796
10,000	148.67	43,521	160.56	17,789	25,732	163.54	16,157	27,364	166.51	14,861	28,660
11,000	163.54	47,874	176.62	19,569	28,305	179.89	17,773	30,101	183.16	16,347	31,527
12,000	178.41	52,228	192.68	21,348	30,880	196.25	19,389	32,839	199.82	17,834	34,394
13,000	193.27	56,577	208.73	23,126	33,451	212.60	21,004	35,573	216.46	19,319	37,258
14,000	208.14	60,930	224.79	24,906	36,024	228.95	22,619	38,311	233.12	20,806	40,124
15,000	223.01	65,284	240.85	26,686	38,598	245.31	24,236	41,048	249.77	22,292	42,992
16,000	237.88	69,637	256.91	28,465	41,172	261.67	25,853	43,784	266.43	23,779	45,858
17,000	252.74	73,986	272.96	30,243	43,743	278.01	27,466	46,520	283.07	25,264	48,722
18,000	267.61	78,340	289.02	32,023	46,317	294.37	29,083	49,257	299.72	26,750	51,590
19,000	282.48	82,693	305.08	33,802	48,891	310.73	30,700	51,993	316.38	28,237	54,456
20,000	297.34	87,042	321.13	35,580	51,462	327.07	32,313	54,729	333.02	29,722	57,320
21,000	312.21	91,396	337.19	37,360	54,036	343.43	33,930	57,466	349.68	31,209	60,187
22,000	327.08	95,749	353.25	39,139	56,610	359.79	35,547	60,202	366.33	32,695	63,054
23,000	341.94	100,098	369.30	40,917	59,181	376.13	37,160	62,938	382.97	34,179	65,919
24,000	356.81	104,452	385.35	42,695	61,757	392.49	38,777	65,675	399.63	35,667	68,785
25,000	371.68	108,805	401.41	44,475	64,330	408.85	40,394	68,411	416.28	37,153	71,652
26,000	386.54	113,154	417.46	46,253	66,901	425.19	42,007	71,147	432.92	38,637	74,517
27,000	401.41	117,508	433.52	48,032	69,476	441.55	43,624	73,884	449.58	40,125	77,383
28,000	416.28	121,861	449.58	49,812	72,049	457.91	45,240	76,621	466.23	41,610	80,251
29,000	431.15	126,214	465.64	51,592	74,622	474.27	46,857	79,357	482.89	43,098	83,116
30,000	446.01	130,564	481.69	53,369	77,195	490.61	48,471	82,093	499.53	44,582	85,982
32,500	483.18	141,445	521.83	57,817	83,628	531.50	52,511	88,934	541.16	48,298	93,147
35,000	520.35	152,326	561.98	62,266	90,060	572.39	56,551	95,775	582.79	52,013	100,313
40,000	594.68	174,085	642.25	71,159	102,926	654.15	64,628	109,457	666.04	59,443	114,642
45,000	669.02	195,847	722.54	80,055	115,792	735.92	72,707	123,140	749.30	66,874	128,973
50,000	743.35	217,606	802.82	88,950	128,656	817.69	80,785	136,821	832.55	74,304	143,302
55,000	817.69	239,368	883.11	97,846	141,522	899.46	88,864	150,504	915.81	81,735	157,633
60,000	892.02	261,127	963.38	106,739	154,388	981.22	96,941	164,186	999.06	89,165	171,962
65,000	966.35	282,886	1,043.66	115,634	167,252	1,062.99	105,020	177,866	1,082.31	96,594	186,292
70,000	1,040.69	304,648	1,123.95	124,530	180,118	1,144.76	113,099	191,549	1,165.57	104,025	200,623
75,000	1,115.02	326,407	1,204.22	133,423	192,984	1,226.52	121,176	205,231	1,248.82	111,455	214,952
80,000	1,189.36	348,170	1,284.51	142,319	205,851	1,308.30	129,256	218,914	1,332.08	118,886	229,284
85,000	1,263.69	369,928	1,364.79	151,214	218,714	1,390.06	137,333	232,595	1,415.33	126,316	243,612
90,000	1,338.03	391,691	1,445.07	160,108	231,583	1,471.83	145,412	246,279	1,498.59	133,747	257,944
95,000	1,412.36	413,450	1,525.35	169,003	244,447	1,553.60	153,491	259,959	1,581.84	141,177	272,273
100,000	1,486.70	435,212	1,605.64	177,899	257,313	1,635.37	161,569	273,643	1,665.10	148,608	286,604
105,000	1,561.03	456,971	1,685.91	186,792	270,179	1,717.13	169,646	287,325	1,748.35	156,037	300,934
110,000	1,635.37	478,733	1,766.20	195,689	283,044	1,798.91	177,727	301,006	1,831.61	163,469	315,264
115,000	1,709.70	500,492	1,846.48	204,583	295,909	1,880.67	185,804	314,688	1,914.86	170,898	329,594
120,000	1,784.04	522,254	1,926.76	213,478	308,776	1,962.44	193,882	328,372	1,998.12	178,329	343,925
125,000	1,858.37	544,013	2,007.04	222,372	321,641	2,044.21	201,961	342,052	2,081.37	185,759	358,254
130,000	1,932.70	565,772	2,087.32	231,267	334,505	2,125.97	210,038	355,734	2,164.62	193,189	372,583
135,000	2,007.04	587,534	2,167.60	240,162	347,372	2,207.74	218,117	369,417	2,247.88	200,620	386,914
140,000	2,081.37	609,293	2,247.88	249,056	360,237	2,289.51	226,196	383,097	2,331.13	208,049	401,244
145,000	2,155.71	631,056	2,328.17	257,953	373,103	2,371.28	234,274	396,782	2,414.40	215,482	415,574
150,000	2,230.04	652,814	2,408.44	266,846	385,968	2,453.04	242,351	410,463	2,497.64	222,910	429,904
155,000	2,304.38	674,577	2,488.73	275,742	398,835	2,534.82	250,432	424,145	2,580.91	230,343	444,234
160,000	2,378.71	696,336	2,569.01	284,637	411,699	2,616.58	258,509	437,827	2,664.16	237,772	458,564
165,000	2,453.05	718,098	2,649.29	293,531	424,567	2,698.36	266,589	451,509	2,747.42	245,204	472,894
170,000	2,527.38	739,857	2,729.57	302,426	437,431	2,780.12	274,666	465,191	2,830.67	252,633	487,224
175,000	2,601.72	761,619	2,809.86	311,322	450,297	2,861.89	282,745	478,874	2,913.93	260,064	501,555
180,000	2,676.05	783,378	2,890.13	320,215	463,163	2,943.66	290,824	492,554	2,997.18	267,494	515,883
185,000	2,750.39	805,140	2,970.42	329,111	476,029	3,025.43	298,902	506,238	3,080.44	274,925	530,215
190,000	2,824.72	826,899	3,050.70	338,006	488,893	3,107.19	306,980	519,919	3,163.69	282,355	544,544
195,000	2,899.05	848,658	3,130.97	346,899	501,759	3,188.96	315,058	533,600	3,246.94	289,784	558,874
200,000	2,973.39	870,420	3,211.26	355,795	514,625	3,270.73	323,137	547,283	3,330.20	297,216	573,204

281

AMOUNT OF LOAN	30 YEARS		2% PMT INCREASE 249.903 PAYMENTS			4% PMT INCREASE 211.369 PAYMENTS			6% PMT INCREASE 187.812 PAYMENTS		
	MONTHLY PAYMENT	TOTAL INTRST	MONTHLY PAYMENT	TOTAL INTRST	INTRST SAVED	MONTHLY PAYMENT	TOTAL INTRST	INTRST SAVED	MONTHLY PAYMENT	TOTAL INTRST	INTRST SAVED
$ 50	0.76	224	0.78	145	79	0.79	117	107	0.81	102	122
100	1.51	444	1.54	285	159	1.57	232	212	1.60	200	244
200	3.02	887	3.08	570	317	3.14	464	423	3.20	401	486
300	4.53	1,331	4.62	855	476	4.71	696	635	4.80	601	730
400	6.03	1,771	6.15	1,137	634	6.27	925	846	6.39	800	971
500	7.54	2,214	7.69	1,422	792	7.84	1,157	1,057	7.99	1,001	1,213
600	9.05	2,658	9.23	1,707	951	9.41	1,389	1,263	9.59	1,201	1,457
700	10.55	3,098	10.76	1,989	1,109	10.97	1,619	1,479	11.18	1,400	1,698
800	12.06	3,542	12.30	2,274	1,268	12.54	1,851	1,691	12.78	1,600	1,942
900	13.57	3,985	13.84	2,559	1,426	14.11	2,082	1,903	14.38	1,801	2,184
1,000	15.08	4,429	15.38	2,844	1,585	15.68	2,314	2,115	15.98	2,001	2,428
2,000	30.15	8,854	30.75	5,685	3,169	31.36	4,629	4,225	31.96	4,002	4,852
3,000	45.22	13,279	46.12	8,526	4,753	47.03	6,941	6,338	47.93	6,002	7,277
4,000	60.29	17,704	61.50	11,369	6,335	62.70	9,253	8,451	63.91	8,003	9,701
5,000	75.36	22,130	76.87	14,210	7,920	78.37	11,565	10,565	79.88	10,002	12,128
6,000	90.43	26,555	92.24	17,051	9,504	94.05	13,879	12,676	95.86	12,004	14,551
7,000	105.50	30,980	107.61	19,892	11,088	109.72	16,191	14,789	111.83	14,003	16,977
8,000	120.57	35,405	122.98	22,733	12,672	125.39	18,504	16,901	127.80	16,002	19,403
9,000	135.64	39,830	138.35	25,574	14,256	141.07	20,818	19,012	143.78	18,004	21,826
10,000	150.71	44,256	153.72	28,415	15,841	156.74	23,130	21,126	159.75	20,003	24,253
11,000	165.78	48,681	169.10	31,259	17,422	172.41	25,442	23,239	175.73	22,004	26,677
12,000	180.86	53,110	184.48	34,102	19,008	188.09	27,756	25,354	191.71	24,005	29,105
13,000	195.93	57,535	199.85	36,943	20,592	203.77	30,071	27,464	207.69	26,007	31,528
14,000	211.00	61,960	215.22	39,784	22,176	219.44	32,383	29,577	223.66	28,006	33,954
15,000	226.07	66,385	230.59	42,625	23,760	235.11	34,695	31,690	239.63	30,005	36,380
16,000	241.14	70,810	245.96	45,466	25,344	250.79	37,009	33,801	255.61	32,007	38,803
17,000	256.21	75,236	261.33	48,307	26,929	266.46	39,321	35,915	271.58	34,006	41,230
18,000	271.28	79,661	276.71	51,151	28,510	282.13	41,634	38,027	287.56	36,007	43,654
19,000	286.35	84,086	292.08	53,992	30,094	297.80	43,946	40,140	303.53	38,007	46,079
20,000	301.42	88,511	307.45	56,833	31,678	313.48	46,260	42,251	319.51	40,008	48,503
21,000	316.49	92,936	322.82	59,674	33,262	329.15	48,572	44,364	335.48	42,007	50,929
22,000	331.56	97,362	338.19	62,515	34,847	344.82	50,884	46,478	351.45	44,007	53,355
23,000	346.63	101,787	353.56	65,356	36,431	360.50	53,199	48,588	367.43	46,008	55,779
24,000	361.71	106,216	368.94	68,199	38,017	376.18	55,513	50,703	383.41	48,009	58,207
25,000	376.78	110,641	384.32	71,043	39,598	391.85	57,825	52,816	399.39	50,010	60,631
26,000	391.85	115,066	399.69	73,884	41,182	407.52	60,137	54,929	415.36	52,010	63,056
27,000	406.92	119,491	415.06	76,725	42,766	423.20	62,451	57,040	431.34	54,011	65,480
28,000	421.99	123,916	430.43	79,566	44,350	438.87	64,764	59,152	447.31	56,010	67,906
29,000	437.06	128,342	445.80	82,407	45,935	454.54	67,076	61,266	463.28	58,010	70,332
30,000	452.13	132,767	461.17	85,248	47,519	470.22	69,390	63,377	479.26	60,011	72,756
32,500	489.81	143,832	499.61	92,354	51,478	509.40	75,171	68,661	519.20	65,012	78,820
35,000	527.48	154,893	538.03	99,455	55,438	548.58	80,953	73,940	559.13	70,011	84,882
40,000	602.84	177,022	614.90	113,665	63,357	626.95	92,518	84,504	639.01	80,014	97,008
45,000	678.19	199,148	691.75	127,870	71,278	705.32	104,083	95,065	718.88	90,014	109,134
50,000	753.55	221,278	768.62	142,080	79,198	783.69	115,648	105,630	798.76	100,017	121,261
55,000	828.90	243,404	845.48	156,288	87,116	862.06	127,213	116,191	878.63	110,017	133,387
60,000	904.26	265,534	922.35	170,498	95,036	940.43	138,778	126,756	958.52	120,022	145,512
65,000	979.61	287,660	999.20	184,703	102,957	1,018.79	150,341	137,319	1,038.39	130,022	157,638
70,000	1,054.96	309,786	1,076.06	198,911	110,875	1,097.16	161,906	147,880	1,118.26	140,023	169,763
75,000	1,130.32	331,915	1,152.93	213,121	118,794	1,175.53	173,471	158,444	1,198.14	150,025	181,890
80,000	1,205.67	354,041	1,229.78	227,326	126,715	1,253.90	185,036	169,005	1,278.01	160,026	194,015
85,000	1,281.03	376,171	1,306.65	241,536	134,635	1,332.27	196,601	179,570	1,357.89	170,028	206,143
90,000	1,356.38	398,297	1,383.51	255,743	142,554	1,410.64	208,166	190,131	1,437.76	180,029	218,268
95,000	1,431.74	420,426	1,460.37	269,951	150,475	1,489.01	219,731	200,695	1,517.64	190,031	230,395
100,000	1,507.09	442,552	1,537.23	284,158	158,394	1,567.37	231,293	211,259	1,597.52	200,033	242,519
105,000	1,582.44	464,678	1,614.09	298,366	166,312	1,645.74	242,858	221,820	1,677.39	210,034	254,644
110,000	1,657.80	486,808	1,690.96	312,576	174,232	1,724.11	254,423	232,385	1,757.27	220,036	266,772
115,000	1,733.15	508,934	1,767.81	326,781	182,153	1,802.48	265,988	242,946	1,837.14	230,037	278,897
120,000	1,808.51	531,064	1,844.68	340,991	190,073	1,880.85	277,553	253,511	1,917.02	240,039	291,025
125,000	1,883.86	553,190	1,921.54	355,199	197,991	1,959.21	289,116	264,074	1,996.89	250,040	303,150
130,000	1,959.22	575,319	1,998.40	369,406	205,913	2,037.59	300,683	274,636	2,076.77	260,042	315,277
135,000	2,034.57	597,445	2,075.26	383,614	213,831	2,115.95	312,246	285,199	2,156.64	270,043	327,402
140,000	2,109.92	619,571	2,152.12	397,821	221,750	2,194.32	323,811	295,760	2,236.52	280,045	339,526
145,000	2,185.28	641,701	2,228.99	412,031	229,670	2,272.69	335,376	306,325	2,316.40	290,048	351,653
150,000	2,260.63	663,827	2,305.84	426,236	237,591	2,351.06	346,941	316,886	2,396.27	300,048	363,779
155,000	2,335.99	685,956	2,382.71	440,446	245,510	2,429.43	358,506	327,450	2,476.15	310,051	375,905
160,000	2,411.34	708,082	2,459.57	454,654	253,428	2,507.79	370,069	338,013	2,556.02	320,051	388,031
165,000	2,486.70	730,212	2,536.43	468,861	261,351	2,586.17	381,636	348,576	2,635.90	330,054	400,158
170,000	2,562.05	752,338	2,613.29	483,069	269,269	2,664.53	393,199	359,139	2,715.77	340,054	412,284
175,000	2,637.40	774,464	2,690.15	497,277	277,187	2,742.90	404,764	369,700	2,795.64	350,055	424,409
180,000	2,712.76	796,594	2,767.02	511,487	285,107	2,821.27	416,329	380,265	2,875.53	360,059	436,535
185,000	2,788.11	818,720	2,843.87	525,692	293,028	2,899.63	427,892	390,828	2,955.40	370,060	448,660
190,000	2,863.47	840,849	2,920.74	539,902	300,947	2,978.01	439,459	401,390	3,035.28	380,062	460,787
195,000	2,938.82	862,975	2,997.60	554,109	308,866	3,056.37	451,022	411,953	3,115.15	390,063	472,912
200,000	3,014.18	885,105	3,074.46	568,317	316,788	3,134.75	462,589	422,516	3,195.03	400,065	485,040

AUGMENTED PAYMENT MORTGAGES 18.00%

AMOUNT OF LOAN	30 YEARS MONTHLY PAYMENT	30 YEARS TOTAL INTRST	8% PMT INCREASE 170.975 PAYMENTS MONTHLY PAYMENT	8% TOTAL INTRST	8% INTRST SAVED	10% PMT INCREASE 157.970 PAYMENTS MONTHLY PAYMENT	10% TOTAL INTRST	10% INTRST SAVED	12% PMT INCREASE 147.441 PAYMENTS MONTHLY PAYMENT	12% TOTAL INTRST	12% INTRST SAVED
$ 50	0.76	224	0.82	90	134	0.84	83	141	0.85	75	149
100	1.51	444	1.63	179	265	1.66	162	282	1.69	149	295
200	3.02	887	3.26	357	530	3.32	324	563	3.38	298	589
300	4.53	1,331	4.89	536	795	4.98	487	844	5.07	448	883
400	6.03	1,771	6.51	713	1,058	6.63	647	1,124	6.75	595	1,176
500	7.54	2,214	8.14	892	1,322	8.29	810	1,404	8.44	744	1,470
600	9.05	2,658	9.77	1,070	1,588	9.96	973	1,685	10.14	895	1,763
700	10.55	3,098	11.39	1,247	1,851	11.61	1,134	1,964	11.82	1,043	2,055
800	12.06	3,542	13.02	1,426	2,116	13.27	1,296	2,246	13.51	1,192	2,350
900	13.57	3,985	14.66	1,606	2,379	14.93	1,458	2,527	15.20	1,341	2,644
1,000	15.08	4,429	16.29	1,785	2,644	16.59	1,621	2,808	16.89	1,490	2,939
2,000	30.15	8,854	32.56	3,567	5,287	33.17	3,240	5,614	33.77	2,979	5,875
3,000	45.22	13,279	48.84	5,350	7,929	49.74	4,857	8,422	50.65	4,468	8,811
4,000	60.29	17,704	65.11	7,132	10,572	66.32	6,477	11,227	67.52	5,955	11,749
5,000	75.36	22,130	81.39	8,916	13,214	82.90	8,096	14,034	84.40	7,444	14,686
6,000	90.43	26,555	97.66	10,697	15,858	99.47	9,713	16,842	101.28	8,933	17,622
7,000	105.50	30,980	113.94	12,481	18,499	116.05	11,332	19,648	118.16	10,422	20,558
8,000	120.57	35,405	130.22	14,264	21,141	132.63	12,952	22,453	135.04	11,910	23,495
9,000	135.64	39,830	146.49	16,046	23,784	149.20	14,569	25,261	151.92	13,399	26,431
10,000	150.71	44,256	162.77	17,830	26,426	165.78	16,188	28,068	168.80	14,888	29,368
11,000	165.78	48,681	179.04	19,611	29,070	182.36	17,807	30,874	185.67	16,375	32,306
12,000	180.86	53,110	195.33	21,397	31,713	198.95	19,428	33,682	202.56	17,866	35,244
13,000	195.93	57,535	211.60	23,178	34,357	215.52	21,046	36,489	219.44	19,354	38,181
14,000	211.00	61,960	227.88	24,962	36,998	232.10	22,665	39,295	236.32	20,843	41,117
15,000	226.07	66,385	244.16	26,745	39,640	248.68	24,284	42,101	253.20	22,332	44,053
16,000	241.14	70,810	260.43	28,527	42,283	265.25	25,902	44,908	270.08	23,821	46,989
17,000	256.21	75,236	276.71	30,310	44,926	281.83	27,521	47,715	286.96	25,310	49,926
18,000	271.28	79,661	292.98	32,092	47,569	298.41	29,140	50,521	303.83	26,797	52,864
19,000	286.35	84,086	309.26	33,876	50,210	314.99	30,759	53,327	320.71	28,286	55,800
20,000	301.42	88,511	325.53	35,657	52,854	331.56	32,377	56,134	337.59	29,775	58,736
21,000	316.49	92,936	341.81	37,441	55,495	348.14	33,996	58,940	354.47	31,263	61,673
22,000	331.56	97,362	358.08	39,223	58,139	364.72	35,615	61,747	371.35	32,752	64,610
23,000	346.63	101,787	374.36	41,006	60,781	381.29	37,232	64,555	388.23	34,241	67,546
24,000	361.71	106,216	390.65	42,791	63,425	397.88	38,853	67,363	405.12	35,731	70,485
25,000	376.78	110,641	406.92	44,573	66,068	414.46	40,472	70,169	421.99	37,219	73,422
26,000	391.85	115,066	423.20	46,357	68,709	431.04	42,091	72,975	438.87	38,707	76,359
27,000	406.92	119,491	439.47	48,138	71,353	447.61	43,709	75,782	455.75	40,196	79,295
28,000	421.99	123,916	455.75	49,922	73,994	464.19	45,328	78,588	472.63	41,685	82,231
29,000	437.06	128,342	472.02	51,704	76,638	480.77	46,947	81,395	489.51	43,174	85,168
30,000	452.13	132,767	488.30	53,487	79,280	497.34	48,565	84,202	506.39	44,663	88,104
32,500	489.81	143,832	528.99	57,944	85,888	538.79	52,613	91,219	548.59	48,385	95,447
35,000	527.48	154,893	569.68	62,401	92,492	580.23	56,659	98,234	590.78	52,105	102,788
40,000	602.84	177,022	651.07	71,317	105,705	663.12	64,753	112,269	675.18	59,549	117,473
45,000	678.19	199,148	732.45	80,231	118,917	746.01	72,847	126,301	759.57	66,992	132,156
50,000	753.55	221,278	813.83	89,145	132,133	828.91	80,943	140,335	843.98	74,437	146,841
55,000	828.90	243,404	895.21	98,059	145,345	911.79	89,035	154,369	928.37	81,880	161,524
60,000	904.26	265,534	976.60	106,974	158,560	994.69	97,131	168,403	1,012.77	89,324	176,210
65,000	979.61	287,660	1,057.98	115,888	171,772	1,077.57	105,224	182,436	1,097.16	96,766	190,894
70,000	1,054.96	309,786	1,139.36	124,802	184,984	1,160.46	113,318	196,468	1,181.56	104,210	205,576
75,000	1,130.32	331,915	1,220.75	133,718	198,197	1,243.35	121,412	210,503	1,265.96	111,654	220,261
80,000	1,205.67	354,041	1,302.12	142,630	211,411	1,326.24	129,506	224,535	1,350.35	119,097	234,944
85,000	1,281.03	376,171	1,383.51	151,546	224,625	1,409.13	137,600	238,571	1,434.75	126,541	249,630
90,000	1,356.38	398,297	1,464.89	160,460	237,837	1,492.02	145,694	252,603	1,519.15	133,985	264,312
95,000	1,431.74	420,426	1,546.28	169,375	251,051	1,574.91	153,789	266,637	1,603.55	141,429	278,997
100,000	1,507.09	442,552	1,627.66	178,289	264,263	1,657.80	161,883	280,669	1,687.94	148,872	293,680
105,000	1,582.44	464,678	1,709.04	187,203	277,475	1,740.68	169,975	294,703	1,772.33	156,314	308,364
110,000	1,657.80	486,808	1,790.42	196,117	290,691	1,823.58	178,071	308,737	1,856.74	163,760	323,048
115,000	1,733.15	508,934	1,871.80	205,031	303,903	1,906.47	186,165	322,769	1,941.13	171,202	337,732
120,000	1,808.51	531,064	1,953.19	213,947	317,117	1,989.36	194,259	336,805	2,025.53	178,646	352,418
125,000	1,883.86	553,190	2,034.57	222,861	330,329	2,072.25	202,353	350,837	2,109.92	186,089	367,101
130,000	1,959.22	575,319	2,115.96	231,776	343,543	2,155.14	210,447	364,872	2,194.33	193,534	381,785
135,000	2,034.57	597,445	2,197.34	240,690	356,755	2,238.03	218,542	378,903	2,278.72	200,977	396,468
140,000	2,109.92	619,571	2,278.71	249,602	369,969	2,320.91	226,634	392,937	2,363.11	208,419	411,152
145,000	2,185.28	641,701	2,360.10	258,518	383,183	2,403.81	234,730	406,971	2,447.51	215,863	425,838
150,000	2,260.63	663,827	2,441.48	267,432	396,395	2,486.69	242,822	421,005	2,531.91	223,307	440,520
155,000	2,335.99	685,956	2,522.87	276,348	409,608	2,569.59	250,918	435,038	2,616.31	230,751	455,205
160,000	2,411.34	708,082	2,604.25	285,262	422,820	2,652.47	259,011	449,071	2,700.70	238,194	469,888
165,000	2,486.70	730,212	2,685.64	294,177	436,035	2,735.37	267,106	463,106	2,785.10	245,638	484,574
170,000	2,562.05	752,338	2,767.01	303,090	449,248	2,818.26	275,201	477,137	2,869.50	253,082	499,256
175,000	2,637.40	774,464	2,848.39	312,003	462,461	2,901.14	283,293	491,171	2,953.89	260,524	513,940
180,000	2,712.76	796,594	2,929.78	320,919	475,675	2,984.04	291,389	505,205	3,038.29	267,969	528,625
185,000	2,788.11	818,720	3,011.16	329,833	488,887	3,066.92	299,481	519,239	3,122.68	275,411	543,309
190,000	2,863.47	840,849	3,092.55	338,749	502,100	3,149.82	307,577	533,272	3,207.09	282,857	557,992
195,000	2,938.82	862,975	3,173.93	347,663	515,312	3,232.70	315,670	547,305	3,291.48	290,299	572,676
200,000	3,014.18	885,105	3,255.31	356,577	528,528	3,315.60	323,765	561,340	3,375.88	297,743	587,362